Street by Stre

C000113635

ESSEX

PLUS BISHOP'S STORTFORD, CHESHUNT, FELIXSTOWE, HAVERHILL, IPSWICH, ROMFORD, SUDBURY, WALTHAM ABBEY

Enlarged Areas Basildon, Chelmsford, Clacton-on-Sea, Colchester, Harlow, Harwich, Southend-on-Sea

Ist edition May 2001

© Automobile Association Developments Limited 2001

This product includes map data licensed from Ordnance Survey® with the permission of the Controller of Her Majesty's Stationery Office. © Crown copyright 2000. All rights reserved. Licence No: 399221.

Published by AA Publishing (a trading name of Automobile Association Developments Limited, whose registered office is Norfolk House, Priestley Road, Basingstoke, Hampshire, RG24 9NY. Registered number 1878835).

Mapping produced by the Cartographic Department of The Automobile Association.

A CIP Catalogue record for this book is available from the British Library.

Printed in Italy by Printer Trento srl

The contents of this atlas are believed to be correct at the time of the latest revision. However, the publishers cannot be held responsible for loss occasioned to any person acting or refraining from action as a result of any material in this atlas, nor for any errors, omissions or changes in such material. The publishers would welcome information to correct any errors or omissions and to keep this atlas up to date. Please write to Publishing, The Automobile Association, Fanum House, Basing View, Basingstoke, Hampshire, RG21 4EA.

Ref: MD031

ii

CAMBRIDGE

| 21 | 23 | 25 | 27 | 29 | 31 |

Haverhill

10
9
Royston

| 41 | 45 | 47 | 49 | 51 | 53 | 55 |
43

Sud

A10
A505

| 67 | 69 | 71 | 73 | 75 | 77 | 79 | 81 |

Saffron Walden

| 97 | 99 | 101 | 103 | 105 | 107 | 111 |

A1017

| 133 | 135 | 139 | 141 | 143 | 145 | 147 |

Halstead

M11

| 167 | 169 | 171 | 173 | 175 | 177 | 179 |

Stansted   **Braintree**

Bishop's
Stortford
| 199 | A120 | 205 | 207 | 208 | 211 |
8   201   203

A130

| 231 | 233 | 235 | 237 | 241 | 243 |

A10   Witham

| 263 | 265 | 267 | 269 | 271 | 273 | 275 |

Hertford

Harlow

| 292 | 297 | 299 | 301 | 303 | 305 | 307 |
12 13
295   A12

7   **CHELMSFORD**

| 319 | 321 | 325 | 327 | 329 | 331 | 333 | 335 |
323   A414   14 15

Waltham
Cheshunt   Abbey | 347 | 353 | 355 | 357 | 359 | 361 | A414 |
351   363
A12

24   25 375 26 377 27/6 383 | 385 | 387 | 389 | 391 |
M25   379   M25

M25   5   379 381   Billericay   A130

| 403 | 405 | 407 | 409 | 411 | 413 | 415 | 417 |
28
A406   **Brentwood**

4   A12 | 431 | 433 | 435 | 437 | 439 | 441 |
29   16 17 **Basildon**
Camden Ilford | 453 | 455 | 457 | 459 | 461 |
Town   Romford
Hackney   451

| 469 | 471 | 475 | 477 |
30
City   31 Grays 485 | 487 |
481   483   Tilbury A13
1A
A205   1B   489
2   Gravesend
Bromley   A20

MAIDSTONE

Enlarged scale pages   **1:17,500**   3.6 inches to 1 mile

| 0 | 1/2 | miles | 1 |

| 0 | 1/2 | 1 | kilometres | 1 1/2 |

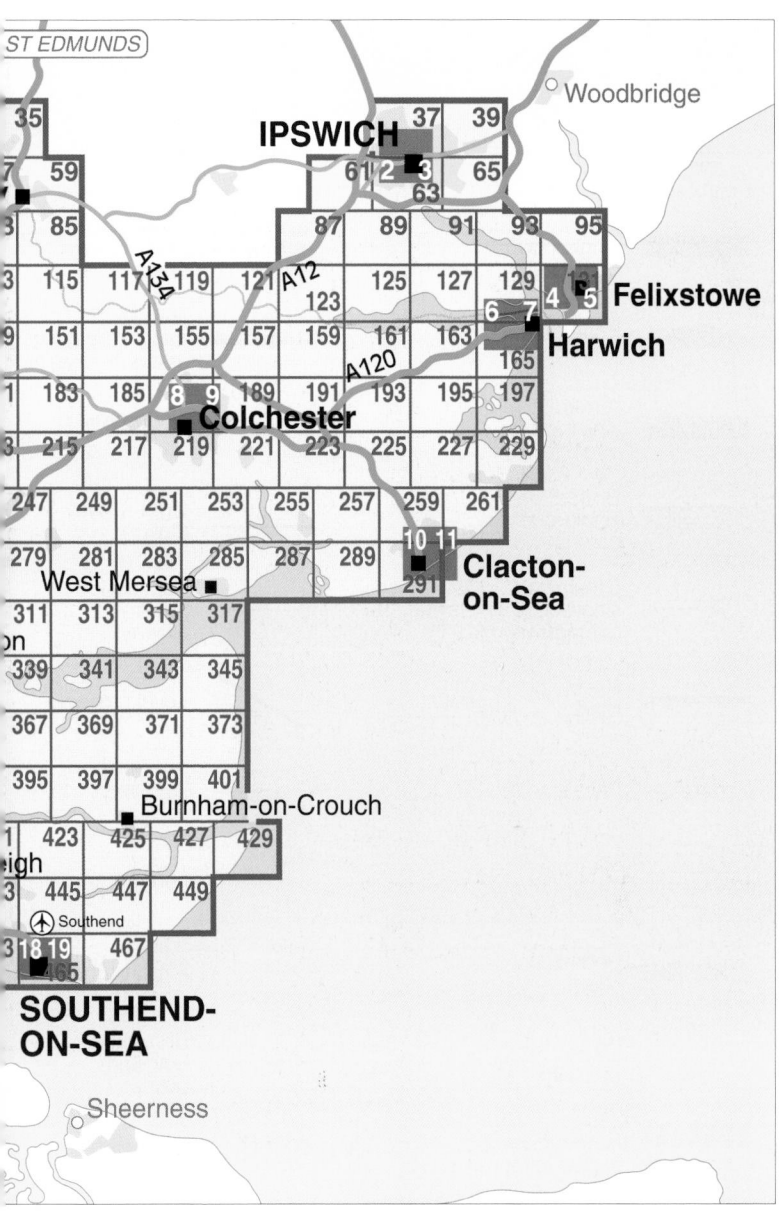

ST EDMUNDS

Woodbridge

35		37	39	
IPSWICH				
7	59	61	2	3	65	
			63		
3	85	87	89	91	93	95
3	115	117	119	121	123	125	127	129	4	Felixstowe
9	151	153	155	157	159	161	163	6	7	Harwich
							165	
1	183	185	8	9	189	191	193	195	197
3	215	217	219	221	223	225	227	229	Colchester
247	249	251	253	255	257	259	261
279	281	283	285	287	289	10	11	Clacton-on-Sea
West Mersea					291	
311	313	315	317
on	339	341	343	345
367	369	371	373
395	397	399	401
Burnham-on-Crouch	
1	423	425	427	429
igh	3	445	447	449
Southend	
3	18	19	467
465	

A134
A12
A120

SOUTHEND-
ON-SEA

Sheerness

2.5 inches to 1 mile   **Scale of main map pages** 1:25,000

| 0 | 1/2 | miles | 1 | 1 1/2 |

| 0 | 1/2 | 1 | kilometres | 1 1/2 | 2 |

iv

Junction 9	Motorway & junction
Services	Motorway service area
	Primary road single/dual carriageway
Services	Primary road service area
	A road single/dual carriageway
	B road single/dual carriageway
	Other road single/dual carriageway
	Restricted road
	Private road
← ←	One way street
	Pedestrian street
---------	Track/ footpath
	Road under construction
]− − − −[	Road tunnel
P	Parking

P+	Park & Ride
	Bus/coach station
	Railway & main railway station
	Railway & minor railway station
⊖	Underground station
⊖	Light railway & station
+++++++++	Preserved private railway
LC	Level crossing
●—●—●	Tramway
----------	Ferry route
....	Airport runway
— · — · — ·	Boundaries- borough/ district
▼▼▼▼▼▼▼	Mounds
93	Page continuation 1:25,000
7	Page continuation to enlarged scale 1:17,500

	River/canal lake, pier		Toilet with disabled facilities
	Aqueduct lock, weir		Petrol station
465 ▲ Winter Hill	Peak (with height in metres)	PH	Public house
	Beach	PO	Post Office
	Coniferous woodland		Public library
	Broadleaved woodland	_i_	Tourist Information Centre
	Mixed woodland		Castle
	Park		Historic house/ building
	Cemetery	Wakehurst Place NT	National Trust property
	Built-up area	M	Museum/ art gallery
	Featured building	†	Church/chapel
⊓⊔⊓⊔⊓	City wall		Country park
A&E	Accident & Emergency hospital		Theatre/ performing arts
	Toilet		Cinema

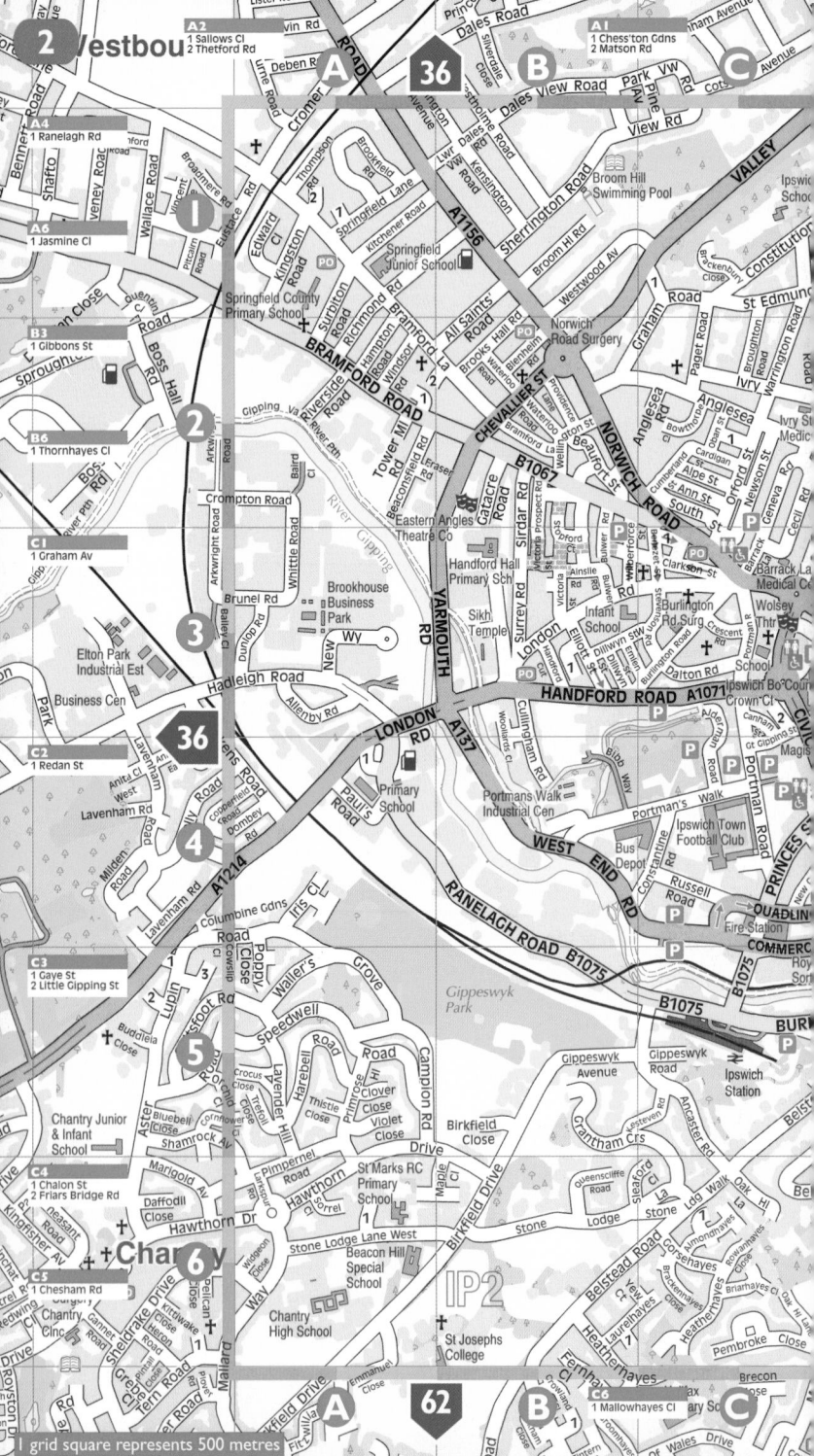

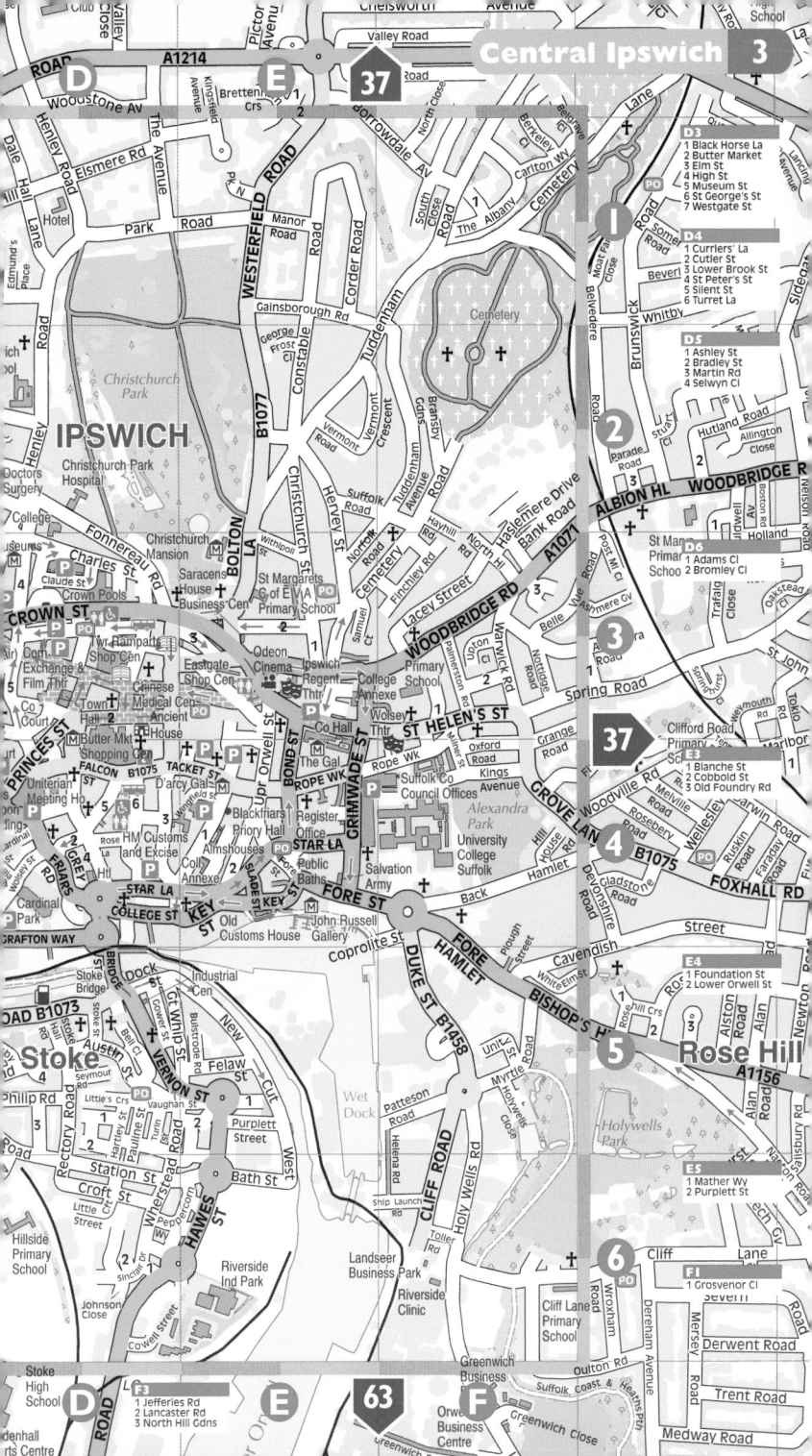

A

94

B

C

Trimley St Mary

Trimley Station

1

2

3

130

4

5

6

Keeper's

Cordy's Lane

Searson's Farm

Clickett Hill

Chatsworth

Suffolk Coast & Heaths Path

Oysterbed Road

Blofield Rd

Nicholas Road

Blofield Rd

Avenue

Parker

Anzani Av.

A14(T)

PORT OF FE

Branc
Euston
Navlar
Lane

Fagbury Road

TRINITY AVENUE A154

Hodgkinson Road

Ferry

Dooley Road

Trinity Av

Byron Avenue

WALTON AVENUE

Cold Store Road

Harwich Harbour

The Port of Felixstowe

A

130

B

C

I grid square represents 500 metres

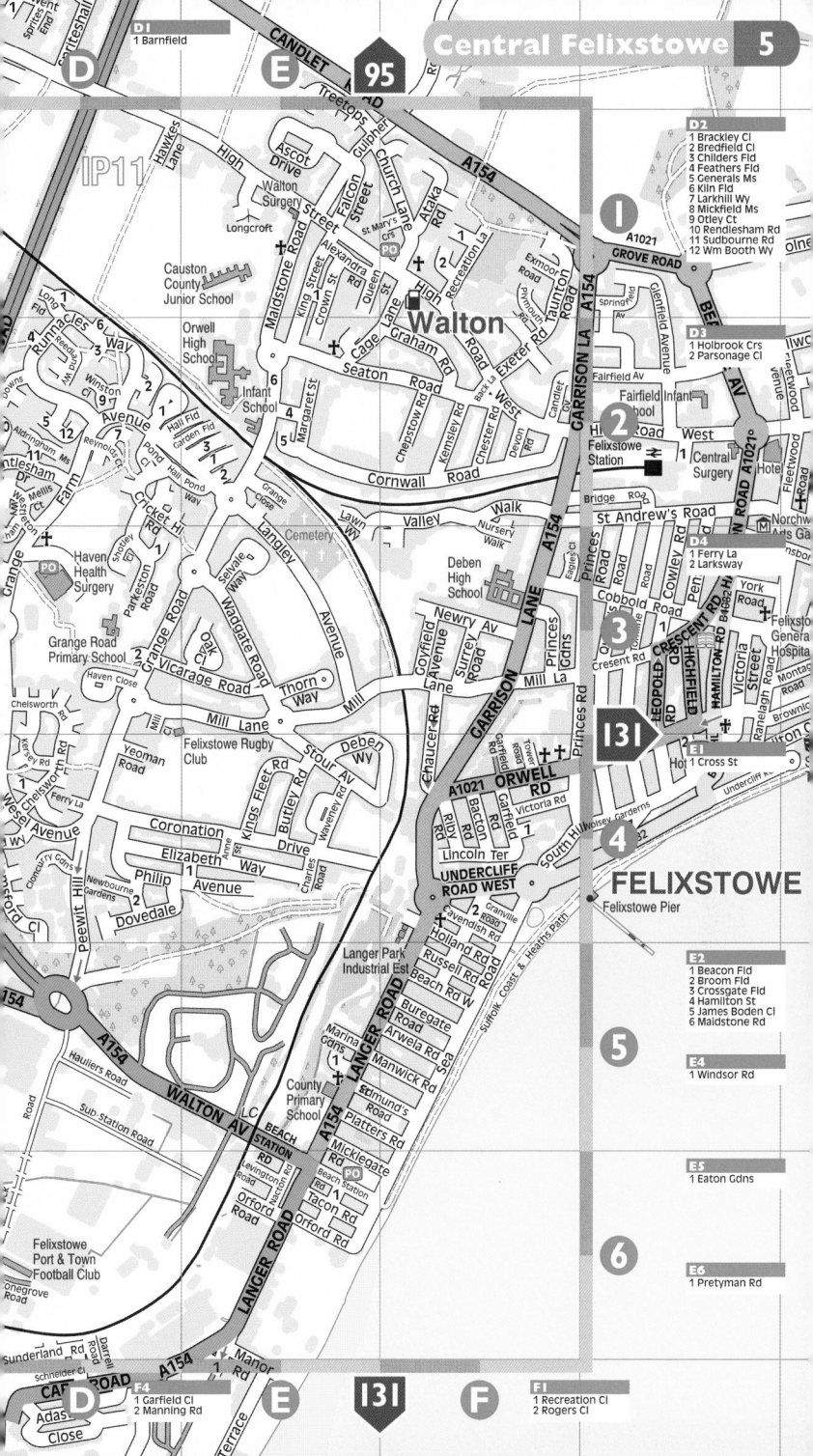

Walton

FELIXSTOWE

Felixstowe Pier

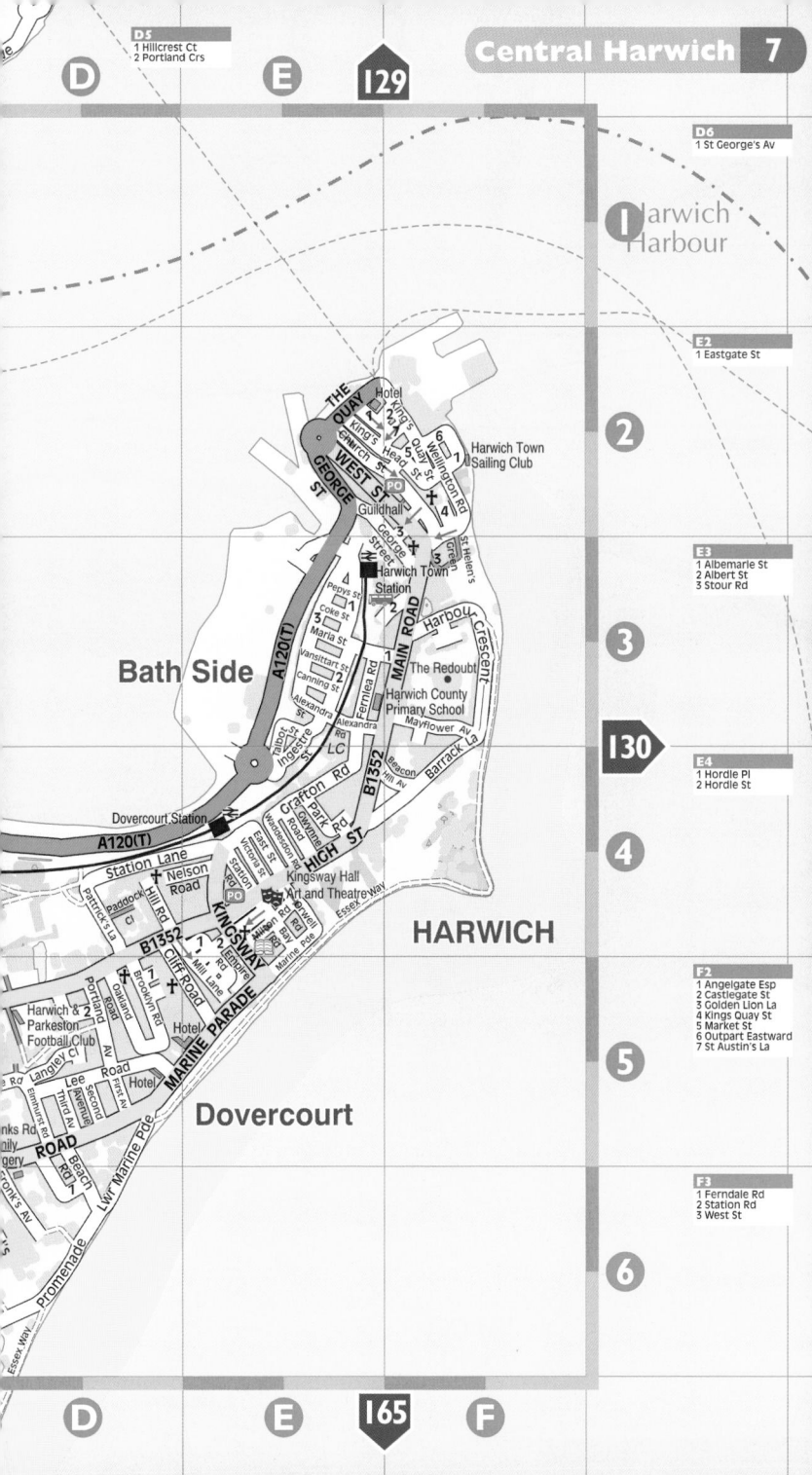

D5
1 Hillcrest Ct
2 Portland Crs

129

D6
1 St George's Av

Harwich Harbour

E2
1 Eastgate St

2

THE QUAY
Hotel
King's Head
King's Quay St
Harwich St
WEST ST
GEORGE ST
PO
Guildhall
George Street
St Helen's Green
Wellington Rd
Harwich Town Sailing Club

E3
1 Albemarle St
2 Albert St
3 Stour Rd

Pepys St
Coke St
Maria St
Vansittart St
Canning St
Alexandra St
Talbot Rd
Ingestre St
Harwich Town Station
Fernlea Rd
MAIN ROAD
Harbour Crescent
The Redoubt
Harwich County Primary School
Mayflower Av
Beacon Hill Av
Barrack La

3

130

E4
1 Hordle Pl
2 Hordle St

Bath Side

A120(T)

LC

Crofton Rd
Park Rd
East St
Victoria Road
Vanneck Rd
Cloyne Road
B1352
HIGH ST

Dovercourt Station
A120(T)
Station Lane
Nelson Road
PO
Kingsway Hall Art and Theatre Way
Essex Way
HARWICH

4

Patrick's La
Paddock Cl
Hill Rd
B1352
CLIFF ROAD
Brooklyn Rd
Oakland Rd
Kingsway
Mill La
Milton Rd
Marine Pde

F2
1 Angelgate Esp
2 Castlegate St
3 Golden Lion La
4 Kings Quay St
5 Market St
6 Outpart Eastward
7 St Austin's La

Harwich & Parkeston Football Club
Portland Av
Langley Av
Lee Road
Second Av
First Av
Marine Av
Third Av
Beach Rd
MARINE PARADE
Hotel
Hotel

5

Dovercourt

nks Rd
ROAD
gery
Monk's Av
Lwr Marine Pde
Promenade
Essex Way

F3
1 Ferndale Rd
2 Station Rd
3 West St

6

D   E   165   F

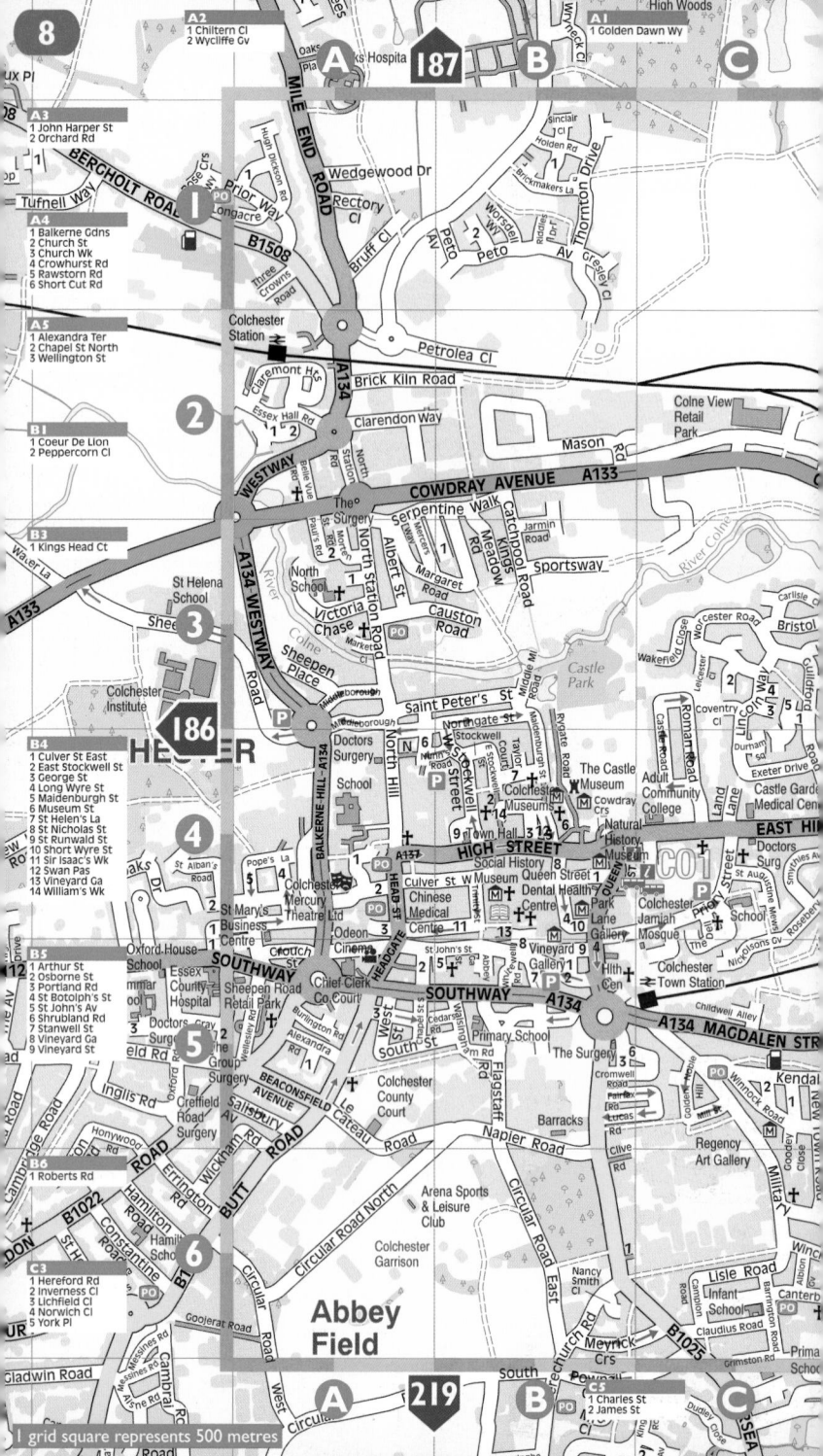

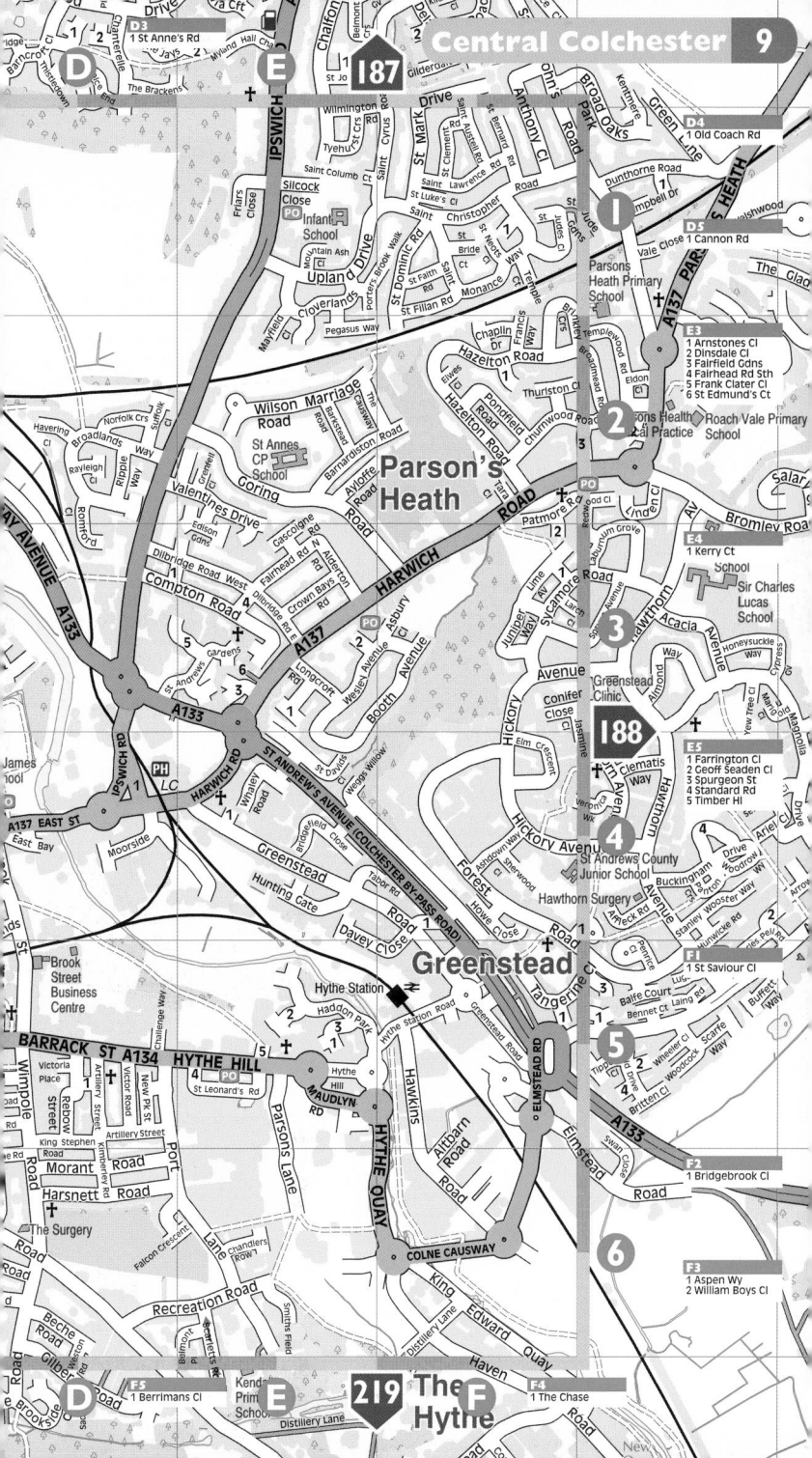

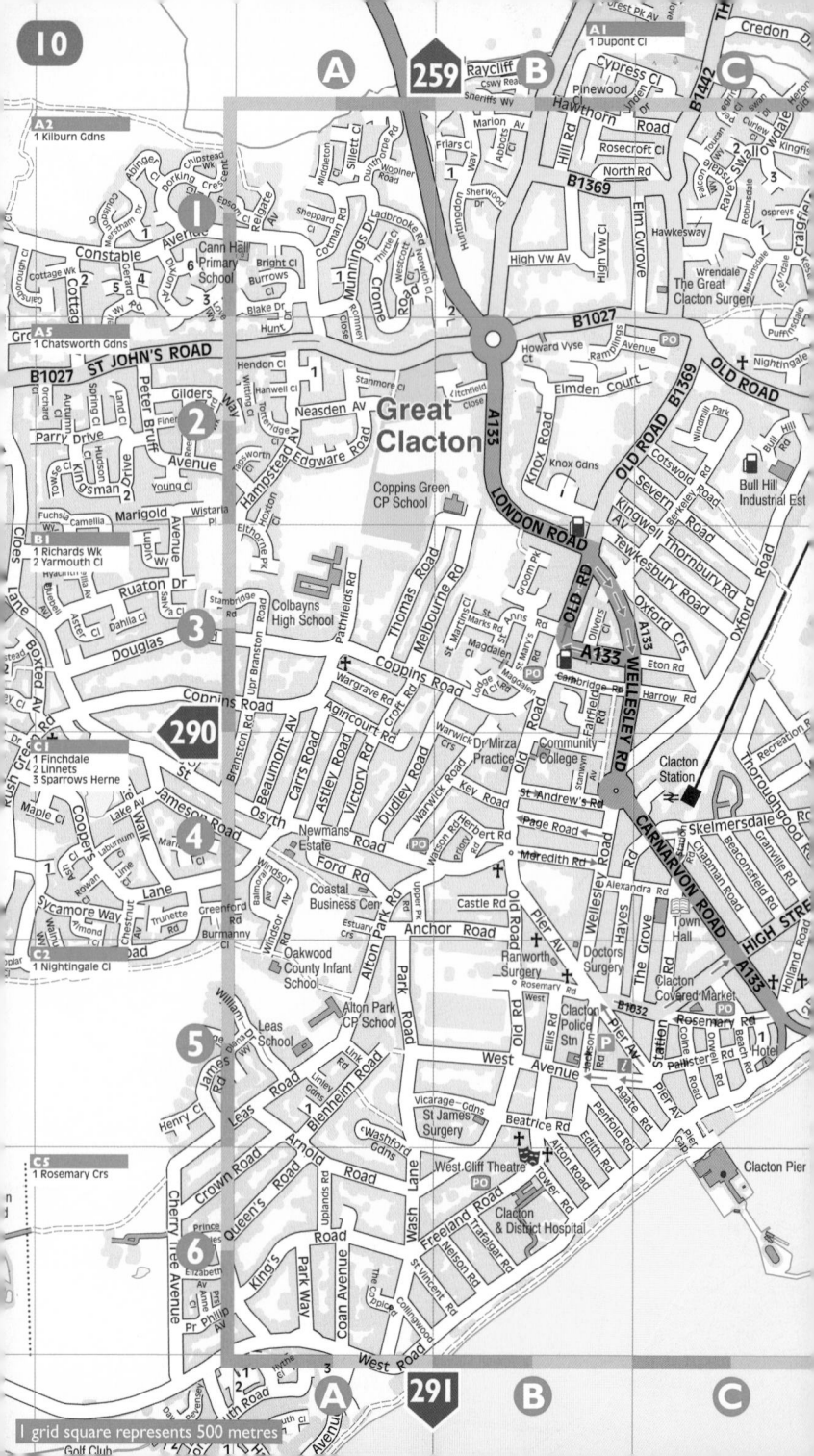

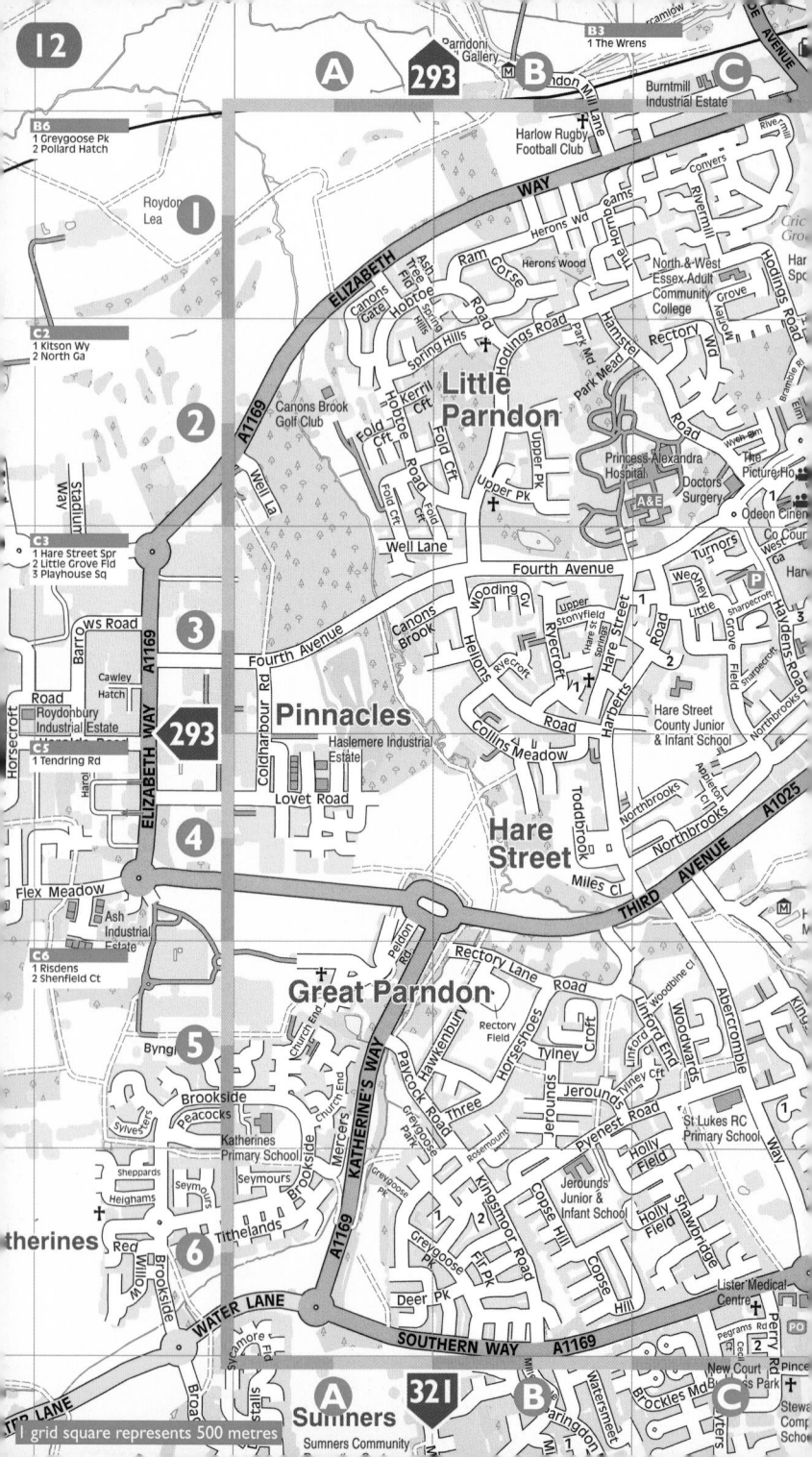

Harlow Town Station

D2
1 Adams House

D E 294

Netteswell

Mark Hall

N D3
1 College Sq

AVENUE ALLENDE AVENUE

Stadium

I

The Stow

Mistley Rd

The Chan

Mandela

Leonard Cft

Mardyke

Mark

Cooks Spinney

Comprehensive School

St Albans RC Primary School

First

Mowbray

Plumtree

A1019

Park Lane

Lane

Avenue

Harlow Urban District Swimming Pool

Mandela School

Oldhouse Croft

The Dashes

Commonfields

The Drive

Netteswell

Halling Hi

IHH Bulleiln

Monkswick

Howard

The Spinney Junior & Infant School

D6
1 Charters Cross

Cooks Spinney

Road

Ch

Blackbush spring

Latton Hall C

Mark

Harefield

Mommples

Fennymead

Road

Ladyshot

Road

VELIZY AVENUE

First

The Hides

Maddox

Broadfield Road

Lavender Close

Pittma's Fld

Broadfield Sch

Rael's Cl

Road

Arkwrights

Way

Vicarage Wd

Turnmeade

Quarry Spring

E2
1 Freshwaters

East Ga

Park Cft

Amberry Cft

School

Harlow College

The Dashes

Whitewaits

Arkwrights

Arkwrights

Crown Ga

Greenhills

The Downs

Parsonage Leys

Maddox

Home Cl

Long

Road

Long Ley

Howard Way

3

Town Hall

Harlow District Co

King Rd

HARLOW

School

Marston Rd

A1025 SECOND AVENUE

294

E6
1 The Briars

THIRD AVENUE

St Marks RC Comprehensive School

Westfield

Tripton Road

Waternoose Moor

Road

Tilwicks

St Brays

Highfield

Sadler's Md

Purford Grn

Tumbler Road

4

Stony Wd

Westfield

Tendring

Church

Ltl Brays

Great Leylands

Purford Green School

Tilbury TMd

Nic

Mar Hat Cl

Brays Grove

Little Brays

Stile Cft

Tilbury Mead

Willowfield

Passmores Comprehensive School

Tye Green

The Mead School

Bushey Cft

Rushes Mead

The Fortunes

Hook Field

Church Leys

Brays Md

PO

Stile Cft

Stile

Longfield

5

Primary School

Tilbury Mead

Sciencers

Travel

Old Orch

Partridge Court

Barn Mead

Upper Hook

Yorkes

Doctors Surgery

The Fairway

A1169 SOUTHE

Pear Tree Md

F5
1 Fountain Farm
2 Oak End

Abbotsweld Primary School

Partridge

Abbotsweld

Road

Barn Md

Five Acres

Bishopsfield Road

Tawneys Road

Primrose Field

Community Clinic

Pinchons

Tilegate Road

Regency Cl

Wharley

6

Upr Mealines

cover

Passmores

SOUTHERN WAY

Woodhill

Aylmers Field

Clarkhill

Latton Bush Business Centre
Sakins Cft

Tysea Road

The Reading

Tysea Rd

Commonside Road

Rundells

Radburn Cl

Latton Bush

Long

Tye

Parnall

Barley Cft

Maunds

Woolmill

Latton Bush Recreation Centre

Latton Green

D

F6
1 Sunny Cft
2 Tye Green Village

E

F4
Street names for this grid square are listed at the back of the index

F

CM1

Infant

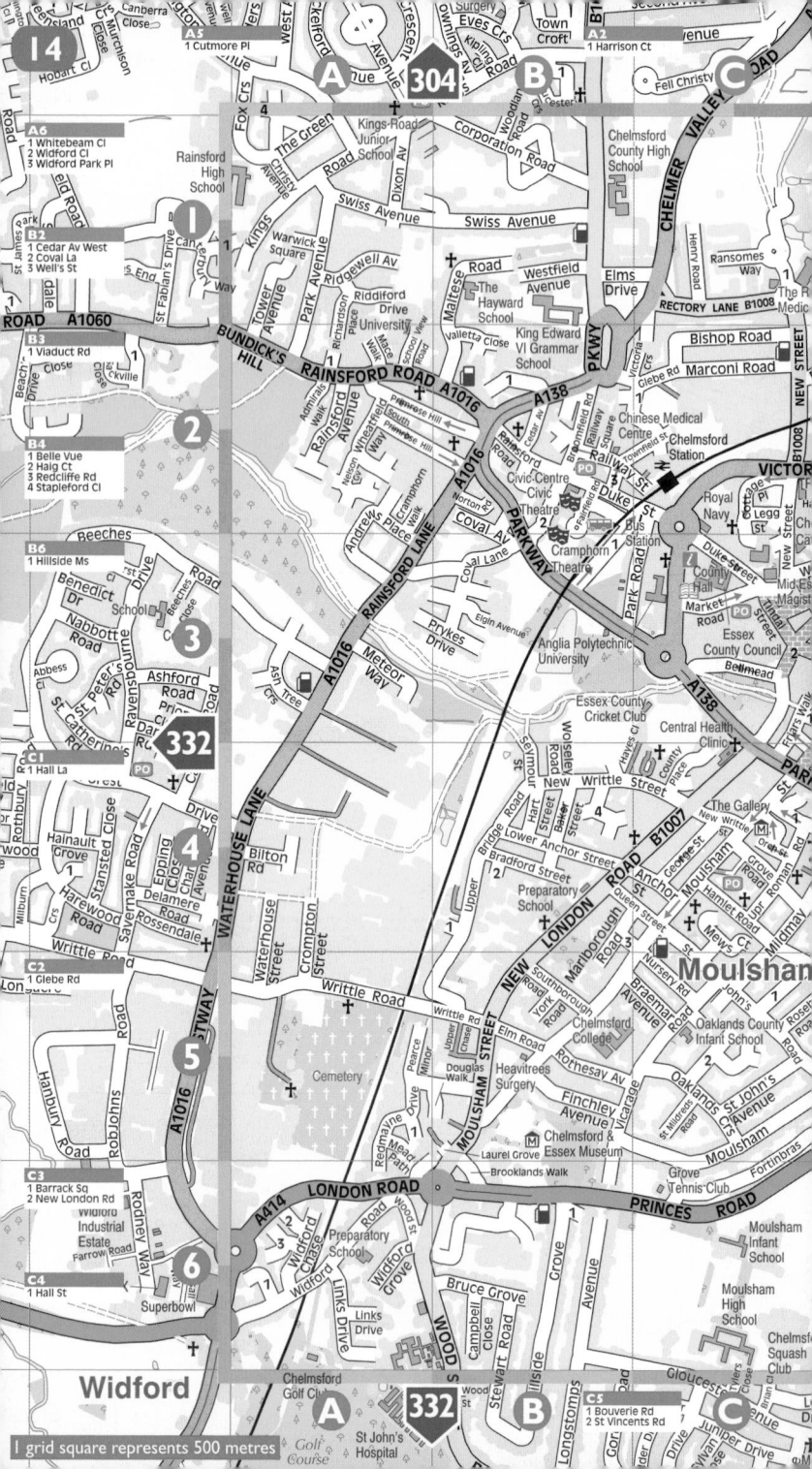

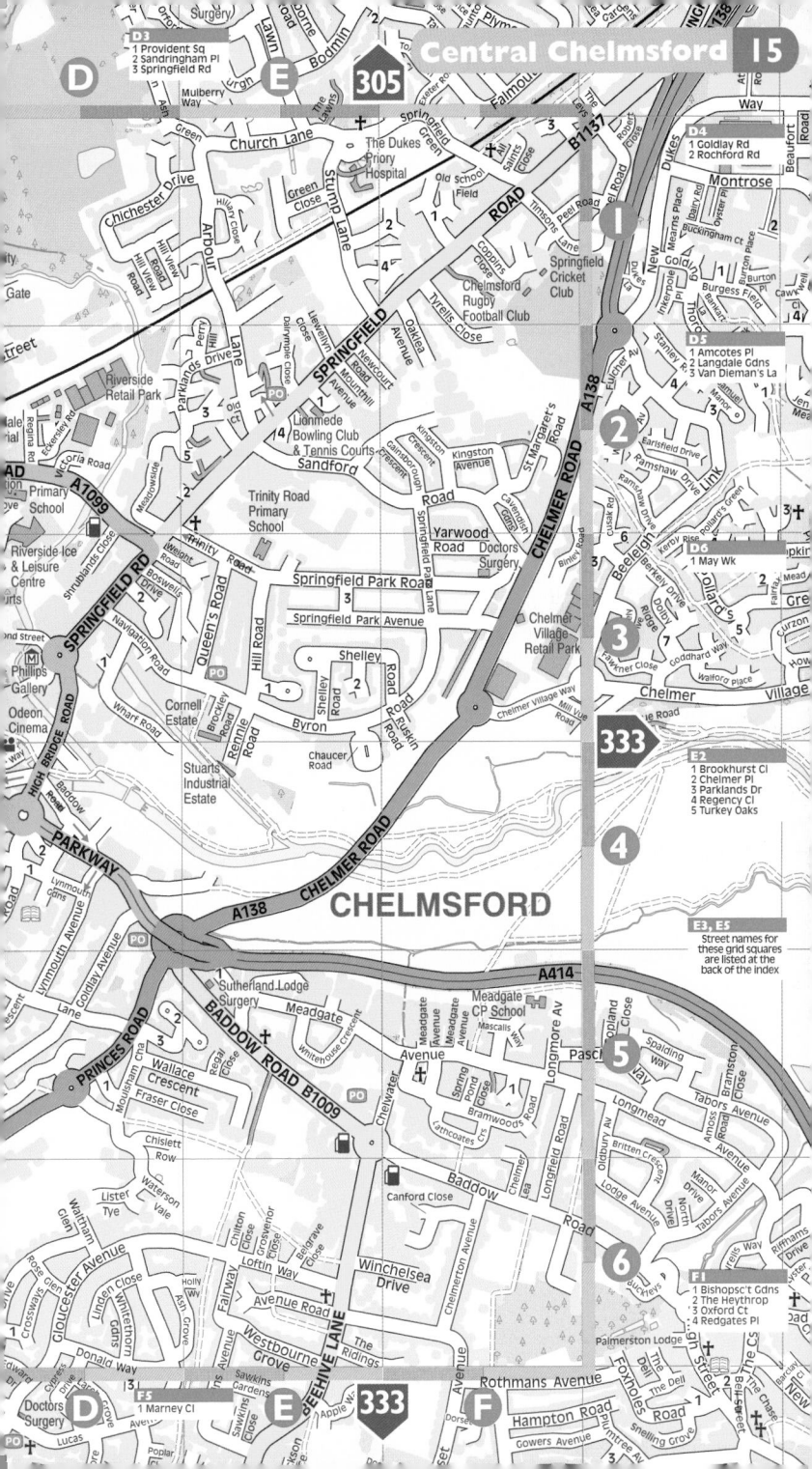

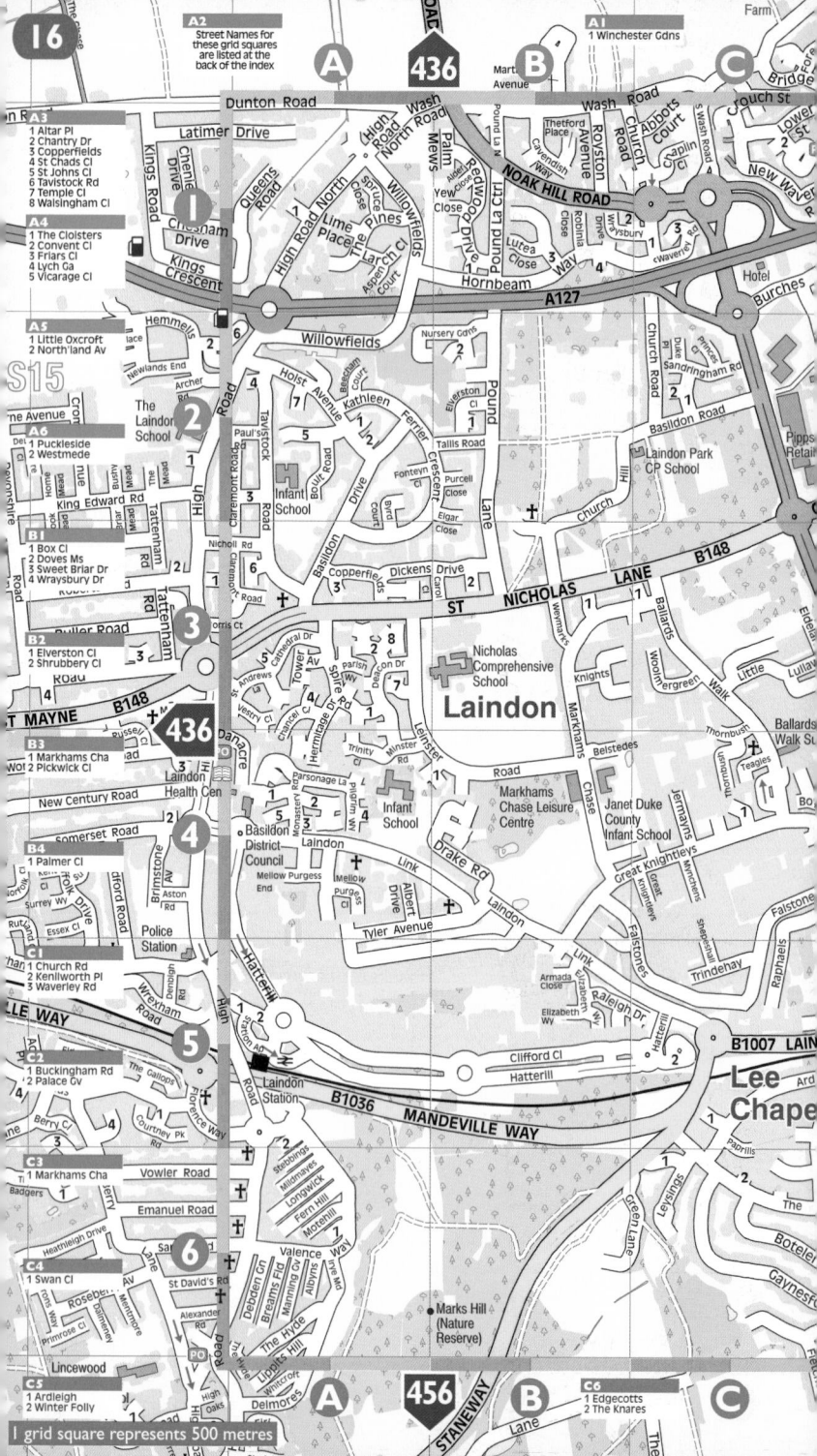

436

Street Names for these grid squares are listed at the back of the index

A2

A1
1 Winchester Gdns

A3
1 Altar Pl
2 Chantry Dr
3 Copperfields
4 St Chads Cl
5 St Johns Cl
6 Tavistock Rd
7 Temple Cl
8 Walsingham Cl

A4
1 The Cloisters
2 Convent Cl
3 Friars Cl
4 Lych Ga
5 Vicarage Cl

A5
1 Little Oxcroft
2 North'land Av

S15

A6
1 Puckleside
2 Westmede

B1
1 Box Cl
2 Doves Ms
3 Sweet Briar Dr
4 Wraysbury Dr

B2
1 Elverston Cl
2 Shrubbery Cl

B3
1 Markhams Cha
2 Pickwick Cl

B4
1 Palmer Rd

C1
1 Church Rd
2 Kenilworth Pl
3 Waverley Rd

C2
1 Buckingham Rd
2 Palace Gv

C3
1 Markhams Cha

C4
1 Swan Cl

C5
1 Ardleigh
2 Winter Folly

C6
1 Edgecotts
2 The Knares

Dunton Road

Latimer Drive

Wash Road

Laindon

436

Laindon Health Cen

New Century Road

Somerset Road

Police Station

LE WAY

5

MANDEVILLE WAY B1036

Lee Chape

B1007 LAIN

Vowler Road

Emanuel Road

Lincewood

456
STANEWAY

Marks Hill (Nature Reserve)

I grid square represents 500 metres

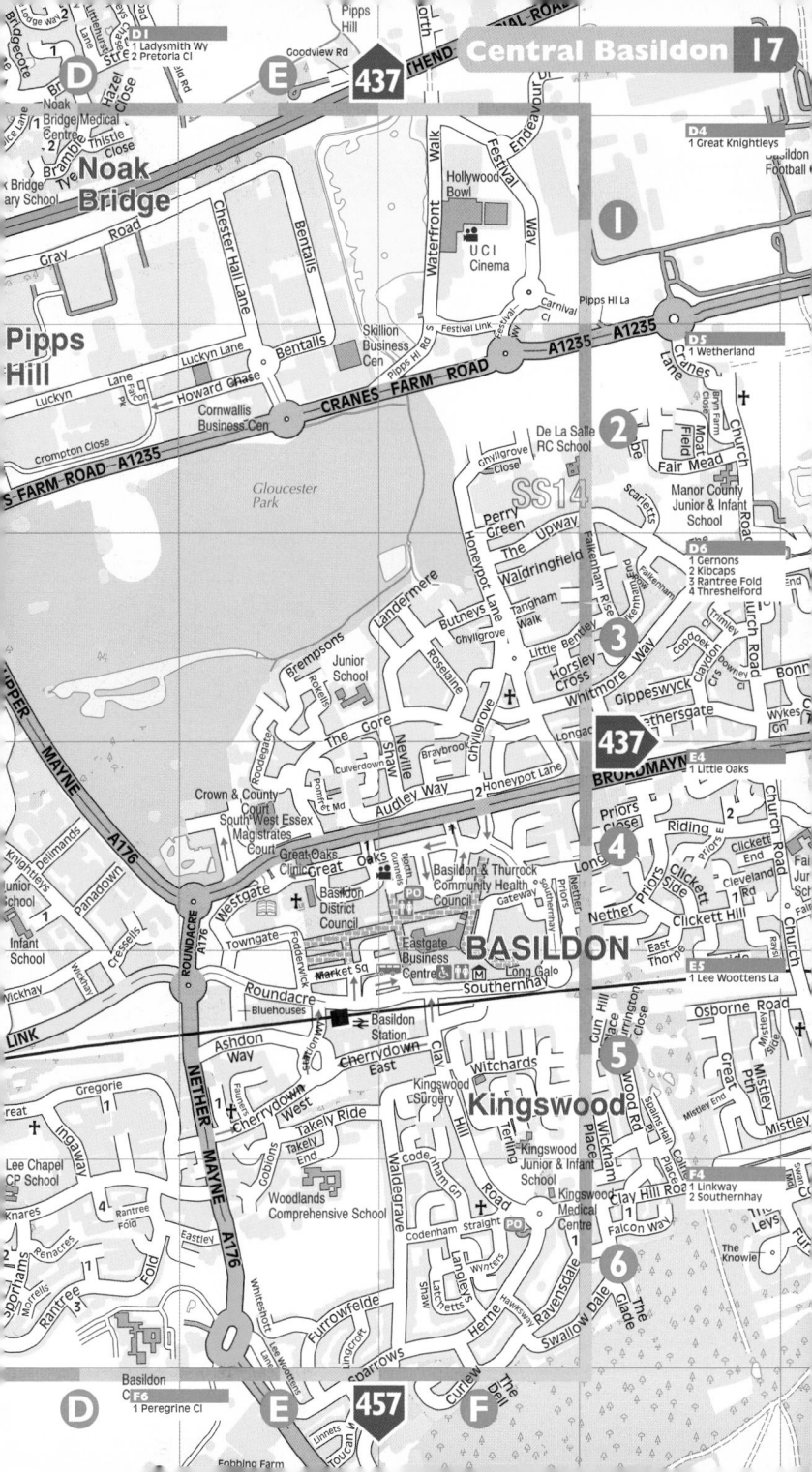

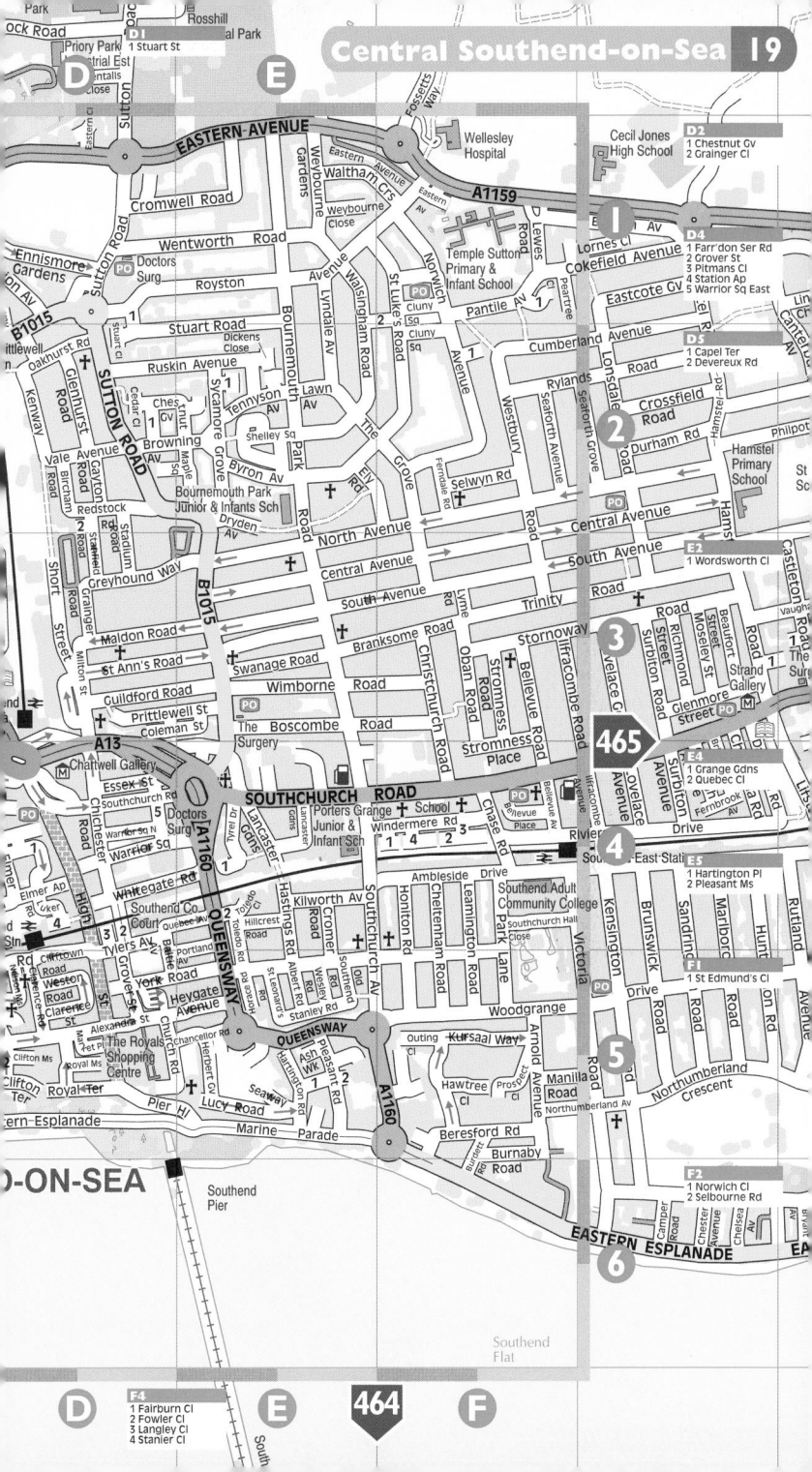

D1 1 Stuart St

D2 1 Chestnut Gv 2 Grainger Cl

D4 1 Farr'don Ser Rd 2 Grover St 3 Pitmans Cl 4 Station Ap 5 Warrior Sq East

D5 1 Capel Ter 2 Devereux Rd

E2 1 Wordsworth Cl

E4 1 Grange Gdns 2 Quebec Cl

E5 1 Hartington Pl 2 Pleasant Ms

F1 1 St Edmund's Cl

F2 1 Norwich Cl 2 Selbourne Rd

F4 1 Fairburn Cl 2 Fowler Cl 3 Langley Cl 4 Stanier Cl

465

464

Pampisford

20

A **B** **C** **D** **E**

Brewery Road

Hammond Close

Town Lane

Church Lane

Beech Lane

CAUSEWAY A505

A505

London Road
Industrial Estate

A1301

Duxford
Chapel

n Road
ast

1

2

3

4

5

6

7

8

Hinxton Grange

Hinxton

A1301

North End Road

LC

Duxford Road

Mill Lane

High Street

Hunts Lane

Church Green

PH

New Road

Ickleton Road

LC

Cemetery

Frogshampton Street

Field Farm

A1301

A11

Stump Cross

Dell's Farm

Duxford Road

Butcher's Hill

Church Street

Mill Lane

River Cam or Granta

Abbey Farm

Street

A **B** ▼**43** **C** **D** **E**

B1383

B1383

B184

1 grid square represents 500 metres

Hildersham

Little Chilfords

Little Linton

CAMBRIDGE ROAD A1307

Linton Village College

Linton C of E (Graded) Infant School

HIGH STREET

CAMBRIDGE ROAD

B1052

Long Lane

THE GRIP

HADSTOCK ROAD

Linton Zoological Gardens

B1052 LINTON ROAD

Cambridgeshire County

Essex County

Icknield Way Path

Pen Farm

WALDEN ROAD

Hadstock

B1052

Hadstock Common

Icknield Way Path

21

45

I grid square represents 500 metres

F3
1 Clover Ct
2 Dolphin Cl
3 Rhugarve Gdns

G3
1 Pembroke La

F G H J K

Horseheath Lodge

ROAD B1052

Linton

BALSAM

Linton Heights
Junior School

Horseheath Road

The Bridgeway

A1307 A1307

Barham Hall

Cambridgeshire County
Essex County

River Bourn

24

Dean Road

Bartlow

PO

Camps Road

Bartlow Road

Hills Farm

River Bourn

F G H 46 J K

F   G   H   J   K

Hare Wood

orseheath

Horseheath Park

Silver Street

Silver Street Farm

1

2

A1307

Cardinal's Green

A1307 PARK HILL

Horseheath Green

3

Cambridgeshire County
Suffolk County

4

26

Shardelow's Farm

5

Barsey Farm

Mill Green

6

Road

New

Main Street

Capel Hill

Park Lane

Shudy Camps Park

7

udy mps

Blacksmiths Lane

Church Road

8

Road

Haverhill

Nosterfield End

F   G   H   J   K

Barlow Road

48

Claydon Close

Street

E4
1 Cambridge Wy
2 Hawthorn Rd
3 Meadowsweet Cl

D4
1 Bramble Cl
2 Reynold's Cl
3 Ruskin Cl
4 Stubbs Cl

C4
1 Horsham Cl
2 Shardlow Cl

A   B   C   D   E

1

E5
1 Castle Wk

2

E6
1 The Causeway
2 Greenwood Cl
3 Horseshoe La
4 Yerril Gdn

3

E7
1 Buckingham Rd
2 Norton Rd

4

25

5

6

7

8

Withersfield

Rose Hill

Withersfield Rd

Horseheath Road

Silver Street

Silver Street Farm

Hollow Hill

Church Street

Turnpike Hill

Queens Street

Hall Farm

Howe Wood

A1307

Hawthorn Road

WITHERSFIELD

Meadowsweet

Hanchet End

Barley Close

Park Road

Horsham Cl

Munnings

Hempstead

Henderson Close

Atterton Road

Constable

Poplar Close

Honeysuckle Cl

Langham Way

Haycocks Rd

Grybaz

Wood Cl

Mellis Close

Notley Drive

Chimswell Way

Chimswell Wy

Hanchet Hall

Horton Rise

Chimswell Way

Parkway Middle School

Castle Man Upper Scho

HAVERHILL

Downton Dr

Princess Wy

Queensway

Clover Field

Raine Avenue

Castle Middle School

School Lane

Castle Av

Haz Clo

Bramley Road

Clivers Road

St Felix RC Primary School

Hazel Stub

Victoria Close

Cherry Fields

Burton End CP School

York Rd

York Rd

Connaught Rd

Leiston

Burton End

Old Rode Wk

Headland Av

Bowen Way

Clivers Road

Green Leas

Gloucester Grove

Doctors Surgery

Homer

A1017

A1017

Barsey Farm

Road

Nosterfield End

Haverhill Hall

A   B   C   D   E

49

Little
Wratting

CB9

B1061

SCHOOL ROAD

The

River Stour

Stour

A8
1 Hicks Wy

A   B   C   A143   D   E

I

Taylor

Old   Haverhill   Road

Little
Wratting

A145

B1061

Stour Valley Path

2

Stour Valley Path

3

Stonebridge
Farm

Dash End Lane

Dash
End

Barton Road

Westward

Hundon

Stourmead Close

Kedington
Primary
School

Deals

Kedington

Mill Road

School Road

Dane Close

Silver St

Westerd Lane

Barton Rise / Bayton Gr

Directory Road

PO

Great Wilsey
Farm

4

B1061 HAVERHILL DANE COMMON ROAD

White Horse Road

King's
Meadow

King's
Arms
Lane

King's Hill

27

River Stour

5

STURMER ROAD B1061

Baythorne
Lodge

Forties
Refuge

Bailey
Close

Orkney Close

Mall
Ostley Close

6

Calford
Green

Woodland
Green

School

Chapman Way

Firthman Road

Amhurst
Victoria

Minerva
Close

B1061

7

Coupals Road

Haverhill
Golf
Club Ltd

Stour Valley Path

ROWLEY
HILL

Adderbury Road

8

Church
Croft

Rowley
Court
Court

WATER LANE

HILL

ROWLEY   A1017

Church

A   Sturmer   B   51   C   D   E

Water Hall
Farm

Linnetts Lane

River Stour

Boost

Hundon

F G H J K

Mount
Pleasant

I

Clock
Hall

Green Lane

Bunfry Lane

**Brockley
Green**

Parsonage
Farm

2

PH

3

Sim's Lane

4

Fords
Wood

30

5

Crooks
Hall

Bank Lane

Will

6

California Farm

Stonard's Farm

7

Cain's Hill

Farmer's Farm

8

Boyton
End

our Valley Path

F G H 52 J K

Blacksmiths Hill

A1092

30

A B C D E

**Mount
Pleasant**

1

Cura Road

B1063

FOLLY ROAD

2

B1063

3

Maple Hill

**Chilton
Street**

4

29

Leys Farm

*Upper
Common*

5

Canham's Farm

Bench Barn
Farm

6

California Farm

7

A1092

Lutus Cl

STOKE

Farmer's Farm

Suffolk County
Essex County

River Stour

8

Mill Farm

Ashen Road

Moor
Hall

A A1092 B **53** C D E

Stour Valley Path

Hollow Road

Blacksmith

1 grid square represents 500 metres

H2
1 Holdsworth Cl

Brook
Street

New Street

Lane

Glemsford

The Surgery

Glemsford
CP School

Kings

BELLS LANE

B1065

Third
Av

First
Av

Kings Road

Park Lane

CHURCHGATE

TYE GREEN

Golding
Way

Drapery

HUNTS HILL

Weavers
Drive

Angel Lane

B1065

EGREMONT ST

New
Cut

George La

SKATE'S HILL

Fox

Lane

Saunders

Long

Lodge Farm

Stour Valley Walk

Stour Valley Walk

Butt Lane

Park Lane

Hobbs

Lane

Lodge
Farm
Road

Grove
Farm

Cavendish Lane

Stour Valley Walk

Lumpit
Wood

I

2

3

AD A1092

LOWER

ROAD

Stour

Suffolk County
Essex County

4

34▶

5

Liston
Garden

Pentlow
Street

THE STREET

PENTLOW HILL

Hoe

Lane

Weston
Hall

6

B1064

Road

Bunting's
Farm

THE STREET

Foxearth

The
Chase

Primary
School

SCHOOL STREET

Claypit Lane

Road

Mill

7

B1064

8

Huntsman's Farm

Bradfield's
Farm

Claypit
Hall

Brook Hall

F **G** **H** **56**▼ **J** **K**

F **G** **H** **J** **K**

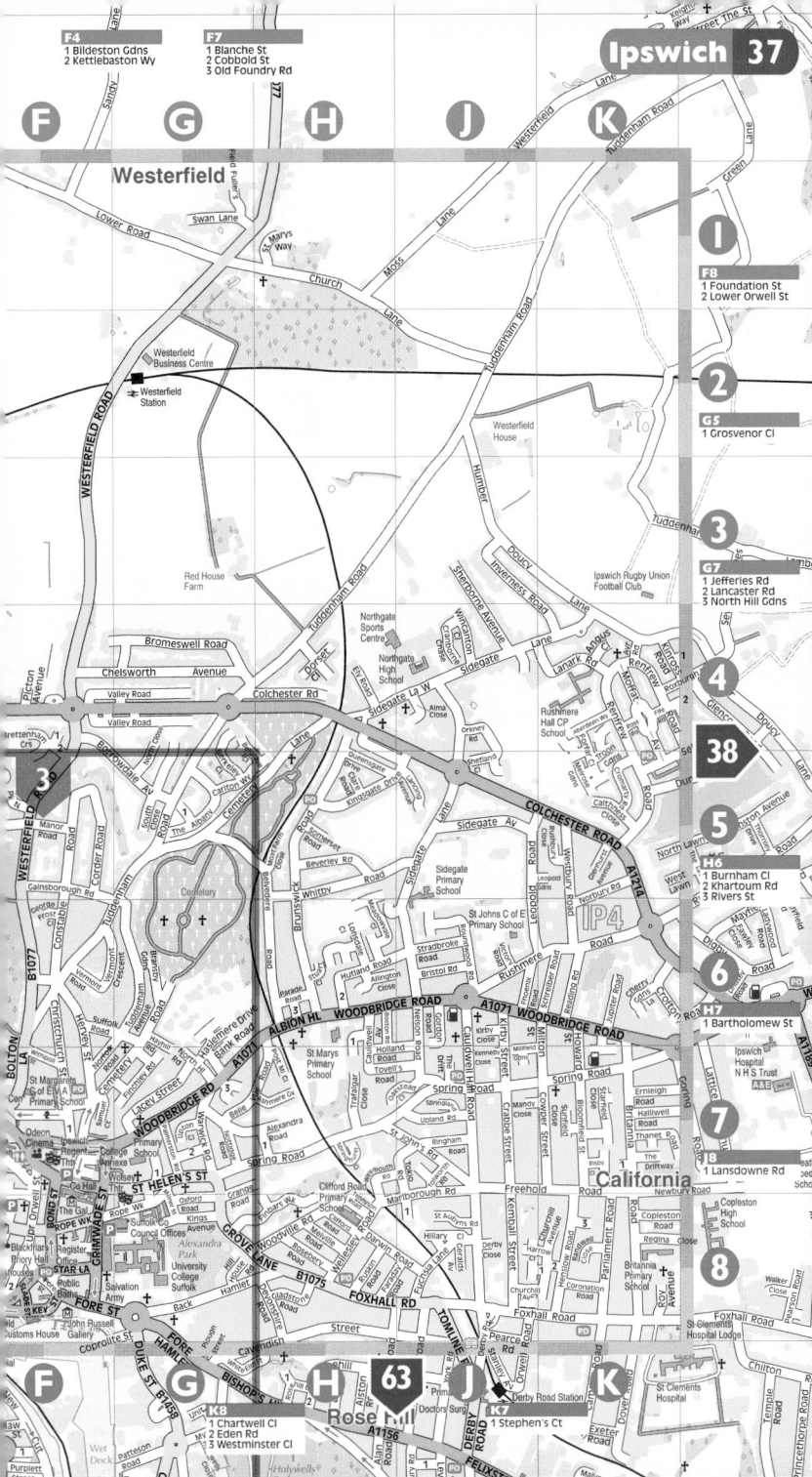

38

Tuddenham

B8
1 Claverton Wy
2 St Andrews Cl

B7
1 Canberra Cl

B6
1 Playford Rd

A4
1 Aberfoyle Cl
2 Renfrew Rd

(A) (B) (C) (D) (E)

1

C4
1 Birchwood Dr
2 Laburnum Gdns

2

C8
1 Sapling Pl

3

D6
1 Histon Cl
2 Malvern Cl
3 Pinetree Cl

4

37

5

D7
1 Fellbrigg Av
2 Haughley Dr
3 Maginley Crs
4 Newquay Cl
5 Wimpole Cl

6

D8
1 Fordham Pl
2 Hintesham Cl
3 Holkham Cl
4 Houghton Pl
5 Mannington Cl

7

E5
1 Grantchester Pl

8

Rushmere Street

Rushmere St Andrew

New Buildings

Hill Farm

St Albans RC High School

Ipswich Hospital N H S Trust

Rushmere Golf Club

Heathside Special School

Copleston High School

St Clements Hospital Lodge

Broke Hall CP School

Football Stadium

St Clements Hospital

64

(A) (B) (C) (D) (E)

E6
1 Alberta Cl

E7
1 Bude Cl
2 St Michael's Cl
3 Truro Crs

1 grid square represents 500 metres

Little Bealings

Beacon Hill

Kesgrave

Martlesham Heath

Playford Heath

IP5

Kesgrave Hall

Kesgrave High School

MAIN ROAD

A1214

Foxhall Heath

Foxhall Road

Foxhall Hall

Pole Hill

Street names for this grid square are listed at the back of the index

F **G** **H** **65** **J** **K**

A B C D E

I

2

int Cross

3

4

5

6

7

8

A B C D E

Dottrell House

A505

Fowlmere Road

Chrishall Road

A505

LANE ROAD

B1368

A505

Heydon Grange

Heydon Grange Golf Club

Icknield Way Path

New Buildings Farm

Icknield Way Path

Heydon

Fowlmere Close

High Road

Heydon Lane

Hardsflow Way

New Road

I grid square represents 500 metres

F G H J K

1
2
3
4
42
5
6
7
8

Duxford Grange House

Grange Road

Chrishall Grange

Ickleton Granges

Grange Road

Redlands

Royston Lane

Cambridgeshire County
Essex County

Hertford Lane

Mill Causeway

Crawley End

Crawley End

Icknield Way Path

Pinkneys

Elmondbury

F G H **67** J K

Crawley End

Elmdon

Heydon Lane

Ickleton

Elm Court

Horseshoe Close

Road

Hollow

Chrishall

A B C D E

1
2
3
4
41
5
6
7
8

Abbey
Farm

Rectory
Farm

ckleton
Granges

Grange Road

Royston Lane

Cambridgeshire County
Essex County

Valance
Farm

Lodge
Farm

The
Poplars

New Jersey
Farm

Quicksel Road

Elmondbury

Elmdon

Ickleton

Road

Elm Court

Horse Close

Hollow

Road

68

thall

Icknield Way

Lutford Road

M11

1 grid square represents 500 metres

F2
1 Icknield Cl

J2
1 Wakefield

Cemetery

Brockhampton Street

Mill Lane

F   **G**   **H**   **20**   **J**   **K**

Stump Cross

Park

Butcher's Hill

Church Street

River Cam or Granta

I

K3
1 Bartholomew Cl

Ickleton

The Stackyard

M11

B1383

NEWMARKET ROAD

B184

WALDEN ROAD

Cow Lane

Icknield Way Path

2

Carmel St

Hyll Close

Jackson's Lane

3

Frogge St

Ickleton ROAD

LC

Church Street

Primary School

School Street

South Street

High Street

Rose Lane

Manor Lane

Great Chesterford

LONDON ROAD

B1383

Great Chesterford Station

Junction 9

Icknield Way Path

River Cam or Granta

4

Rector Farm

44

Bordeaux Farms

High Street

5

Little Chesterford

WALDEN ROAD

M11

6

7

8

F   **G**   **H**   **69**   **J**   **K**

Strethall Road

Strethall Road

Howe Wood

Catmere End

CAMBRIDGE ROAD

Roman Way

Walden Road

High

Littlebury

A   B   21   C   D   E

1

2

3

4

43

5

6

7

8

A   B   70   C   D   E

Park Road

Cow Lane

Crave Hall Farm

Dell's Farm

Burtonwood Farm

Ickfield Way Path

WALDEN ROAD

Cow Lane

Ickfield Way Path

Stapletow Road

High Street

Lane

Great Chesterford

Rectory Farm

Chesterford

River

B1383

Bordeaux Farms

High   Street

WALDEN ROAD

Little Chesterford

Emanuel Wood

B184

Springwell

B1383

SPRINGWELL ROAD

Rowley Hill Farm

Westley Farm

Westley   Lane

Roman Way

Walden

Northend

1 grid square represents 500 metres

F G H 22 J K

I

2

3

4

46

5

6

7

8

B1052

Hadsto Comm

Monk's Hall

Bowsers Lane

Bowsers

Park Farm

B1052

Bowsers Lane

Ravenstock Green Farm

Mitchells

Petts Lane

Little Walden

B1052

Sadlers Farm

THE SLADE

LITTLE WALDEN ROAD

Harcamlow Way

Butlers Farm

Butlers Lane

Ashdon Road

Byrds Farm

Harcamlow Way

Redgate Farm

F G H 71 J K

46

A B 23 C D E

1

2 Bowsers Lane Bowsers

3

Newnham
Hall Farm

4

Ashdon
CP School

45 Rectory Lane

Ashdon

5 Fallowden Lane
Fallowden Lane
Church Hill
Harcamlow Way

6 Church
End
Guildhall Way
Walden Road

7 Little
Hales
Wood

Water
End

8 Hales
Wood
Butlers Lane
Ashdon Road
Ivytodd
Sprigg's Farm

A B 72 C D E

River Bourn

Crown Lane

Radwinter Road

1 grid square represents 500 metres

F   G   H   **24**   J   K

I

Camps Hall

2

Whitensmere Farm

3

Waltons

Lingley Wood

4

Car End

Steventon End

Over Hall Lane

48

5

Sandons

Browning's Farm

e's Lane

Winsey Farm

6

Cambridgeshire

Essex Co.

Goldstones

7

Great Bendysh Wood

Bourne Farm

8

F   G   H   **73**   J   K

Radwinter End

Ashdon Road

House Lane

Littlebendysh Wood

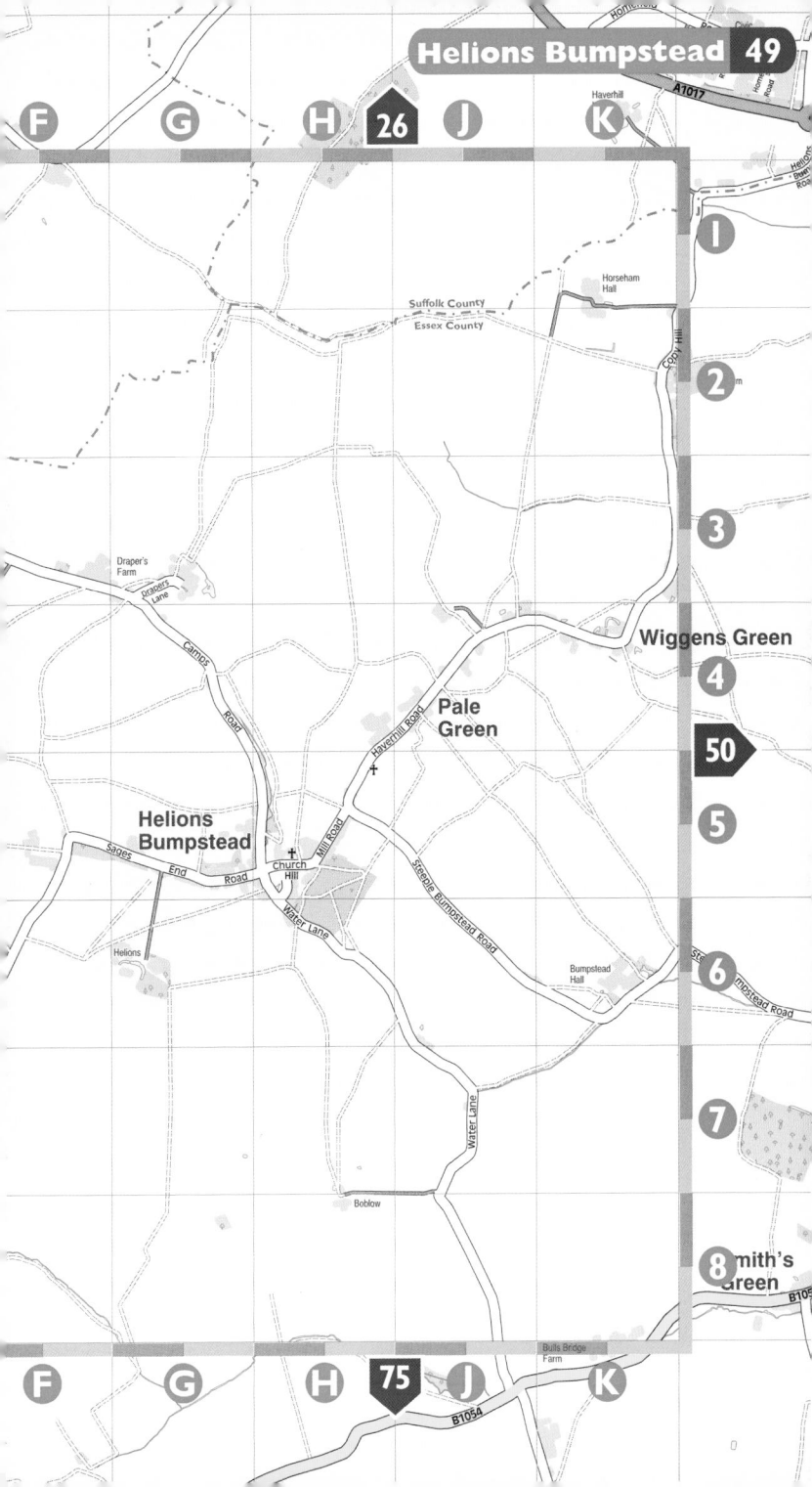

F G H 26 J K

Haverhill

I

Horseham
Hall

Suffolk County

Essex County

Draper's
Farm

Drapers
Lane

2

3

Wiggens Green

4

50

Pale
Green

Camps Road

Haverhill Road

Helions
Bumpstead

Sages
End
Road

Church
Hill

Mill Road

Steeple Bumpstead Road

Water Lane

Helions

Bumpstead
Hall

5

6

7

Water Lane

Boblow

8 mith's
Green

B105

F G H 75 J K

Bulls Bridge
Farm

B1054

A1017

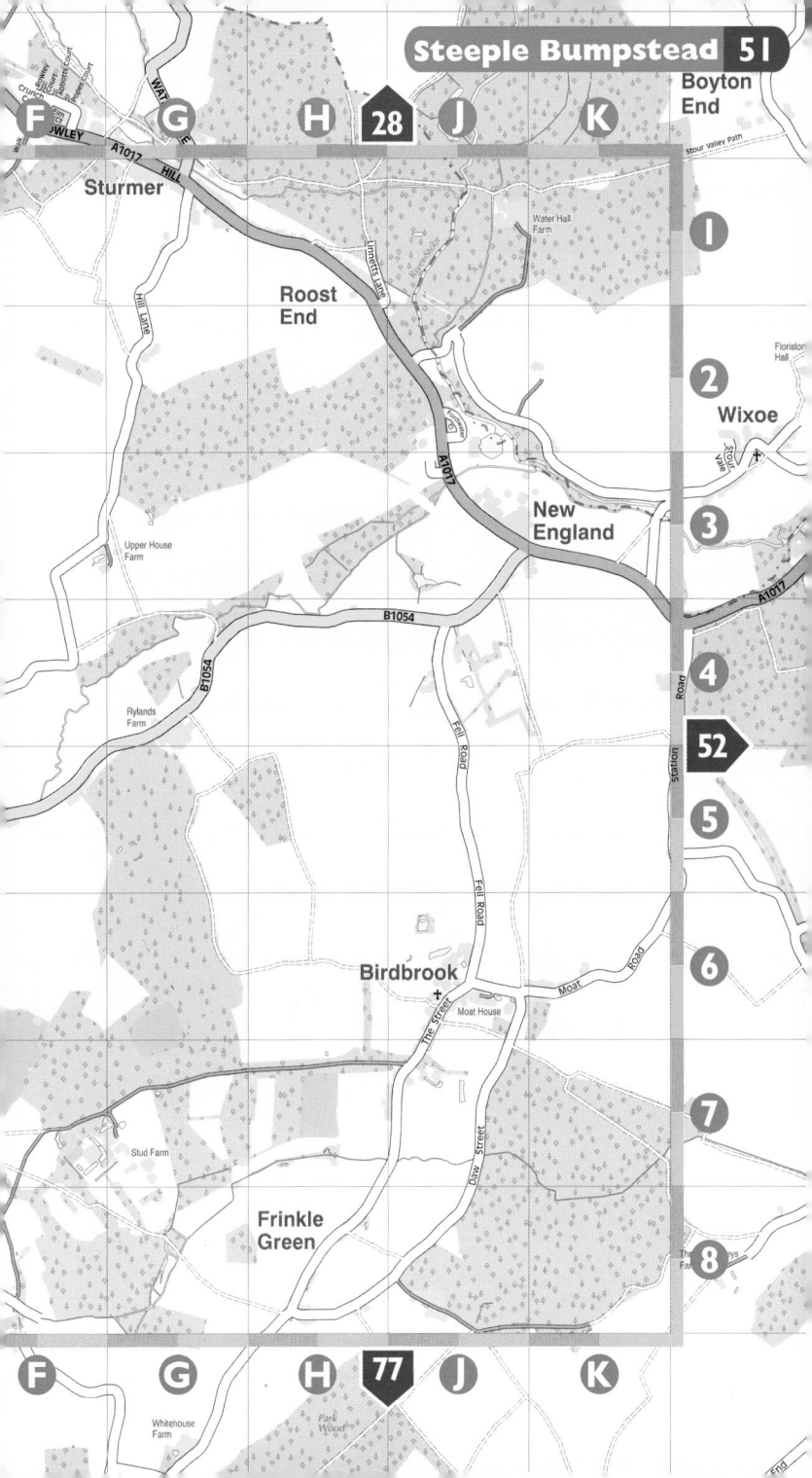

Boyton End

F JWLEY G H 28 J K

Stour Valley Path

A1017

Sturmer

HILL

Water Hall Farm

I

Hill Lane

Roost End

Linnetts Lane

Floriston Hall

2

Wixoe

A1017

New England

3

Stour Valley

Upper House Farm

B1054

B1054

Rylands Farm

Station Road

4

52

5

Fell Road

6

Birdbrook

Moat Road

Moat House

7

The Street

Daw Street

Stud Farm

Frinkle Green

8

F G H 77 J K

Whitehouse Farm

Park Wood

F G H 30 J K

Suffolk County
Essex County
River Stour

Mill Farm

Ashen

Claret
Hall
Stour Valley Path

Bradley hill
Farm

I

A1092

Moor
Hall

Stour Valley Path

PO

Church Park
Cemetery

**Stoke by
Clare**

Stours

2

Stour Valley Path

Ashen
Lane

Doctors Lane

Ashen
House

Ashen Hill

Ashen
Hall

Hollow Road

Ovington
Hall

✝

3

**Pannel's
Ash**

54

The
Street

✝

Ashen

Foxes Road

Foxes
Lane

Ashen

Road

Ovi

4

Silver
End

5

Ridgewell
Road

Upper
Farm

Upper Farm Road

lbury

Road

6

Park
Farm

**Tilbury
Green**

7

Belcha

8

✝

**Tilbury
Juxta Cla**

eadowend

Tilbury Hall

bury Court

F G H 79 J K

A1017

54
Mill Farm
Ashen Road

A B 31 C D E

Claret
Hall
Bradley hill
Farm
Stour Valley Path

1

Ovington
Hall

2

3
Butler's
Farm

Ovington

Belchar
St Paul

4
Road
Ashen

53

Silver
End

Gage's
House

5

Wakeshall Lane

Gage's Road

Knowl
Green

Wakeshall
Farm

6
Park
Farm

Maltby Lane

Twelve Acre
Wood

7

Belchamp Road

Maltby Road

8

Tilbury
Juxta Claire

Tilbury Hall

Tilbury Court

A B 80 C D E
Road
Red
House

+ Little Yeldham

1 grid square represents 500 metres

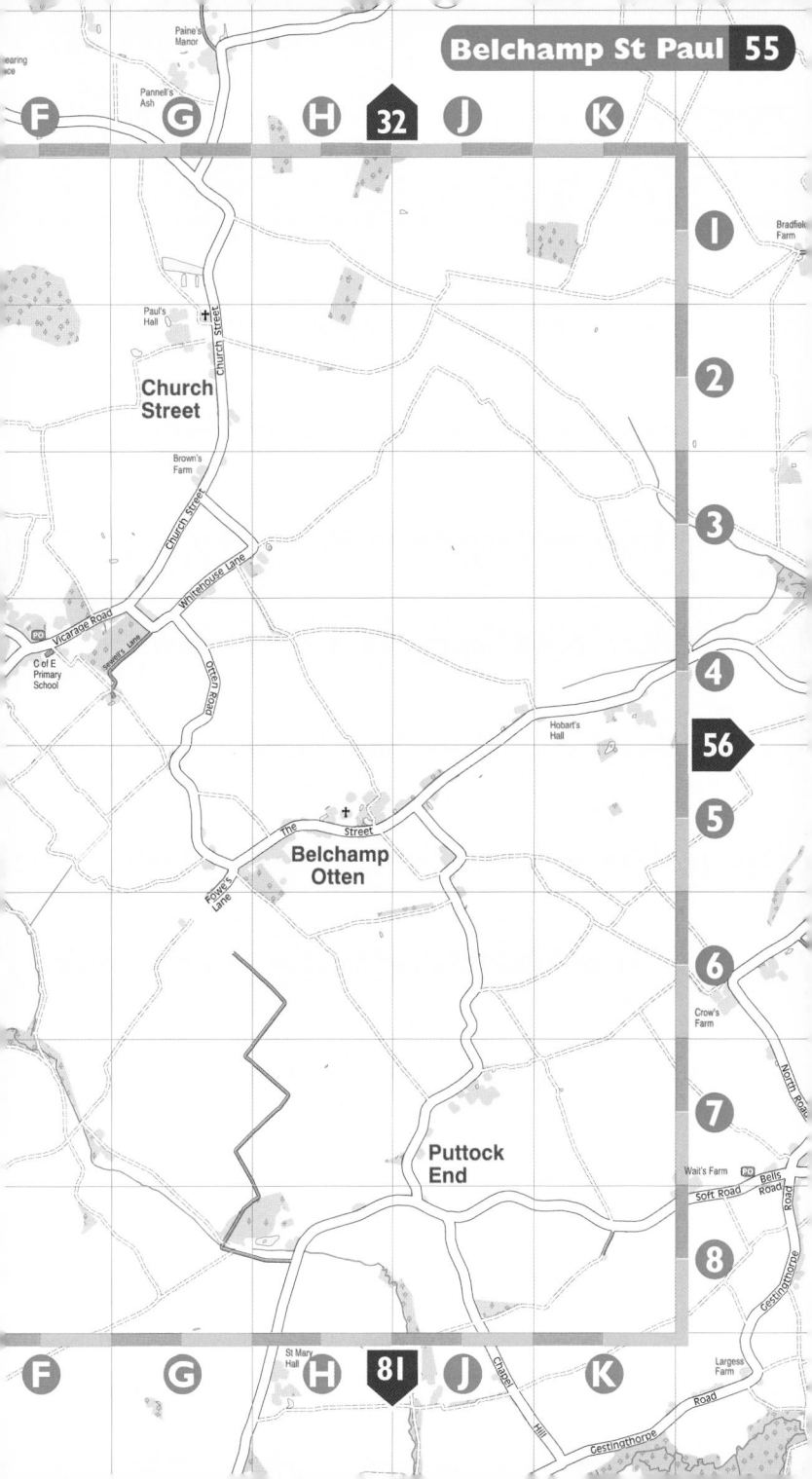

F G H **32** J K

1
2
3
4
56
5
6
7
8

Bradfield Farm

Paine's Manor

Pannell's Ash

Paul's Hall

Church Street

Church Street

Brown's Farm

Whitehouse Lane

Church Street

Vicarage Road

PO

C of E Primary School

Scarlet's Lane

Otten Lane

The Street

Belchamp Otten

Foxe's Lane

Hobart's Hall

Crow's Farm

North Road

Puttock End

Wail's Farm PO Bells Road

Soft Road

Gestingthorpe Road

St Mary Hall

Largess Farm

F G H **81** J K

Chapel Hill

Gestingthorpe Road

F G H 34 J K

I

2

3

4

58

5

6

7

8

F G H 83 J K

Rodbridge House
Rodbridge Lane
BORLEY ROAD
Rodbridge Corner
Ropers Lane
B1064
Mills Lane
B1064 SUDBURY ROAD
Brook Hall
Lower Road
Stour Valley Walk
CO10
+ Borley
Hall Road
Borley Hall
River Stour
Pentlow Cres
Canterbury
Grosvenor
Chaucer Road
Gloucester
Walk
Worcester Way
St Bartholomew
Corner
MELFORD
A131
Brundon La
The Valley Walk
Brundon
St Josephs Primary
Stour valley Walk
SUDBURY
Walnut Tree Hospital
Hotel
he Rookery
Smeetham Hall
Finch Hill
Essex County
Suffolk County
Smeetham Hall Lane
Bulmer Road Industrial Est
Brundon Lane
Bulmer Road Industrial Estate
Kitchen Hill
Bulmer Road Industrial Est
Cross St
Church St
CROSS ST
CHURCH ST
STREET
PO
Ballingdon Trading
7
Ballingdon
Bush Grove
Bulmer
Sudbury Road
Sandy Lane
BALLINGDON
Ballingdon Hill Industrial Estate
Ballingdon Road
Meadow View Road
Middleton
Elizabeth Ave
Bulmer
Church Road
Vicars Orch
BALLINGDON HILL
Hall Road
stour
Sandy Lane
Street
A131
8
stour valley path
Auberies
Armsey Farm

58

A · B · **35** · C · D · E

Rodbridge House
Lane
Mills

Acton Lane

Newman's
Green

Rodbridge Corner 1

A134

B5
1 Humphry Rd
2 Newman's Rd
3 Queens Cl
4 St Gregory's Ct

2

A134

3

C3
1 Rosemary Gdns

River Stour

Woodhall
Business Park

Woodhall
Business Park Drury Drive

Mountbatten
Close

All Saints
VC Middle
School

Primary
School

Hillside Special
School

Sudbury Upper School

4 **Brundon**

River Stour

MELFORD ROAD A131

BRUNDON ROAD

Woodhall Road

Sudbury
Tudor Voluntary
Controlled School

Sudbury
Uplands
Middle School

Chilton
Industrial
Estate

Chilton
Industrial
Estate

NORTHERN ROAD

SPRINGLANDS WAY

WALDINGFIELD ROAD

Sudbury
Bow

57

Chilton
Industrial
Estate

5

C5
1 Minden Rd
2 Prince Charles Cl

St Josephs RC Va
Primary School

Sudbury Health
Cen

Harpcote Rd

Chilton Industrial Est

A134

GIRLING ST A131

Walnut Tree
Hosp

St Leonards
Hospital

South
Suffolk
Hospital

Warner Industrial
Warner
Business Centre

Windham Road

Bulmer Road
Industrial Est

SUDBURY

La
Dabergh
District
Centre

Sudbury Business
Centre

Unity Health
Centre

NEWTON A131 ROAD

Hillside Rd

Yellow Dot
Sports Club

Elm Road

Poplar Road

Hawthorn
Rd

6

Bulmer Road
Industrial Est

STOUR ST

CROSS ST

FRIARS STREET

Station
Rd

Station

Doctors Surg

CORNARD ROAD

B1508

Sudbury
Station

Kings
Meadow

KINGS HILL

Pot Kiln
County
Primary
School

Cemetery

Butt

7 **Ballingdon**

D4
1 Trafalgar Rd

BALLINGDON STREET

CHURCH

Priory
Walk

Nonsuch
Meadow

Sudbury Town
Football Club

The Quay
Theatre

Stour Valley Walk

Ballingdon
Grove

BURES ROAD B1508

Vicarage
Field

8

BALLINGDON HILL

MEADOW
Road

Middleton

Suffolk County
Essex County

River

RADIATOR RD

Recreation
Ground

B6, C6
Street names for
these grid squares
are listed at the
back of the index

A · B · **84** · C · **D6**
1 Chilton Ct
2 Chilton Lodge Rd · D · **D8**
1 Singleton Ct · E

Middleton

Great Cor
Upper Sch

Rugby Union
Football Club

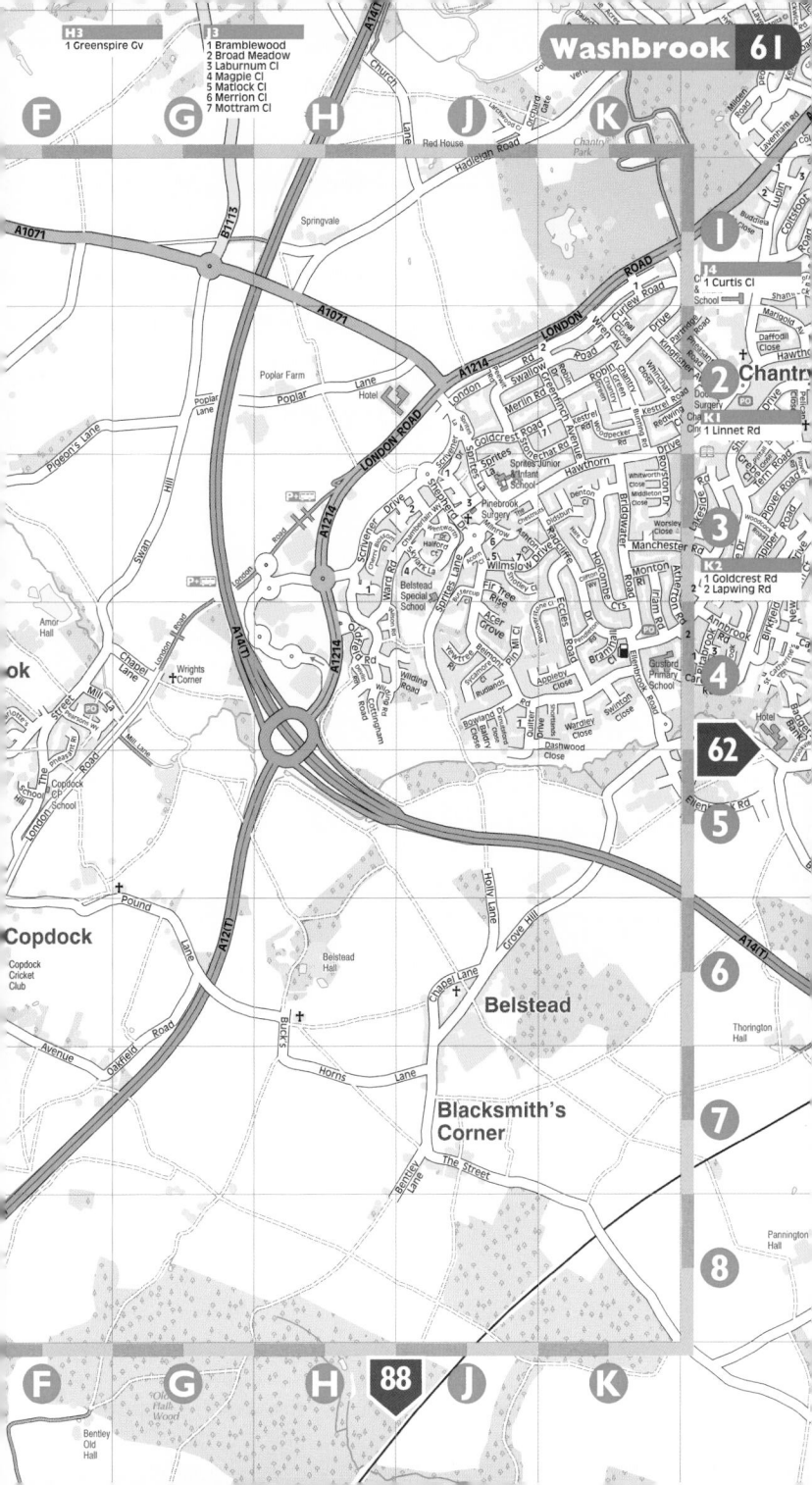

H3
1 Greenspire Gv

J3
1 Bramblewood
2 Broad Meadow
3 Laburnum Cl
4 Magpie Cl
5 Matlock Cl
6 Merrion Cl
7 Mottram Cl

F G H J K

I

J4
1 Curtis Cl
& School

2 Chantry

K1
1 Linnet Rd

3

K2
1 Goldcrest Rd
2 Lapwing Rd

4

62

5

6

7

8

Copdock

Copdock
Cricket
Club

Belstead

Blacksmith's
Corner

F G H **88** J K

64

B5
1 Bluestem Rd

B1
1 Bodiam Cl
2 Claverton Wy

A4
1 Halton Crs
2 Uxbridge Crs

A **HEATH ROAD** **B** **38** **C** **D** **E**

Copleston Road
Newbury Road
Copleston High School
Regina Close
Britannia Primary School
Coronation Road

1

C1
1 Claverton Wy
2 Melplash Cl

St Clements Hospital Lodge
St Clements Hospital
Exeter Road
Camden Road
Cannon Road

Walker Close
Foxhall
PO
Chilton Road
Clovelle
Temple Road
Princethorpe Road
Penshurst Rd
Broke Hall Gdns
Wimborne Avenue
Foxhall Road
Chasworth Drive
Bixley Drive

2

C3
1 Laburnum Cl

Ramsgate Dr
Badsham
Marjate Dr

Bridport Av
Augustine Rd
Pye Close
Winfrith Road
Wareham Av
Helsinki
Melplash Way
Bodiam Rd
Buckfield
Highlands Park

Broke Hall

Queen's Way
Coniston Close

3

Nacton Road
IP3
Ashdown
Dorchester Rd
Poodle Close
Lulworth AV
Lewes Close
Golf Course
Ipswich Golf Club

Ipswich Transport Museum

C4
1 Blackthorn Cl

Clarence Road
Winterton Cl
Hollywells High School
Infant School

Bucklesham Road
Warren Heath Road
Woodrush Rd
Woodrush Rd
Purdis Farm Lane
Purdis Avenue
Bucklesham Road

4

Hilton
Campbell
The Drive

Priory Heath
Clove Crs
Murrills
Warren Heath

63

Leslie Road
Nacton Road
Felixstowe Road
A1156
Ransomes Way
Felixstowe Road

Suffolk
Show

5

D1
1 Eastern Cl

Gainsborough
Ipswich Airport

Front Rd
West Road
Ransomes Industrial Estate
Post Office
Yale Business Park
Foxtail Rd
Bluestem Road
Nacton Heath

6

D4
1 Porter Rd
2 Routh Av
3 Whitethorn Rd

The Havens
Hotel
A14(T)
Square Covert

7

8

Bridge Wood
Goldsmith's Covert
Park Farm

A **B** **91** **C** **Park Farm** **D** **E**

River Orwell

66

40

Heydon

A   B   C   D   E

Flowdene Right Road

Heydon Lane

Harcamlow Way

I

New Road

2

Woodgreen Animal Shelter

Chishill Road

Road

Reeves Pightle

The Pudgell

Great Chishill

BARLEY   ROAD

Chishill Wind

3

Heydon

B1039

HALL LANE

May Street Lane

Maltings Lane

Waller's Close

B1039

The Hall

4

5

Little Chishill

ftenhoe

6

Little Chishill

Building End

Common Lane

Building End Road

7

Cross Leys

Chrishall Common

8

Cambridgeshire County

Essex County

Park Lane

A   B   C   D   E

96

River Stort

I grid square represents 500 metres

Mill Causeway
Hertford Lane
Crawley End
Crawley End
Pinkeneys
Engleric
Palmers Lane
Chrishall
Chrishall C of E Primary School
Icknield Way
Icknield Way Path
Hertford Lane
Heydon Lane
Elmdon
Ickleton
Essex Hill
Freewood
Lofts Hall
Park Wood
Harcamlow Way
High Street
Church Road
Chalky Lane
Hollow Road
Bury Lane
B1039
B1039
Hope Farm
Chiswick Hall
Pond Street
Cemetery
School Lane
Coolmore
Knox Lane
Bridge Gree
High Wood
Harcamlow Way
Brooksies
Duddenhoe End
Rockells Farm
Cooper's End
Beard's Lane
Duddenhoe Grange
Beard's Lane

F G H **4I** J K

I 2 3 4 **68** 5 6 7 8

F G H **97** J K

A   B   42   C   D   E

New Jersey
Farm

Elmondbury

Elmdon

Strethall
Icknield Way

1

Hollow Road
Elm Court
Horseshoe Close

Lane
Freewood
Freewood Farm

2

way

Lofts Hall

3

4

Essex Hill

67

B1039

5

B1039

Coopmore
Cemetery
School

6

New Farm
B1039

Bridge Green

Knox Lane

7

Duddenhoe
End
Rockells
Farm

Long Lane

8

Cooper's
End
Bragg's Lane
Duster Gn

A   B   98   C   D   E

Newland
End

I grid square represents 500 metres

K2
1 Goodwins Cl

F G H 43 J K

Strethall Road
Strethall Road

Holve Wood

tmere
d

Littlebury

AMBRIDGE ROAD
Roman Way
Walden Road
HIGH ST
Mill Lane
PH
2

Littlebury Green Road

I

2

B1383

LONDON ROAD

Howe Hall

3

Littlebury
Green

Chestnut Avenue

4

70

Chestnut Av

5

B1383

6

LONDON ROAD

7

Walde

Nth Lane
B1039 STATION ROAD
Church Street
PH
Bearwalden
Business
Park
8
End Station

MUTLOW HILL

ROYSTON ROAD

B1039

B1039

M11

Duck Street

Chestnut Lane

Wendens
Ambo

Clanverend
Farm

F G H 99 J K

ery Lane

LC

Saffron Walden

SAFFRON WALDEN

F2
1 Aspin Ms
2 Buckenhoe Rd
3 Byrd's Farm La
4 Chalklands
5 Cornwallis Pl
6 Doddenhill Cl
7 Fair Leas

F3
1 Cornwallis Pl
2 Marking's Fld

F4
1 Longhedges
2 Newcroft
3 Victoria Gdns

F5
1 Corn Mill Ct
2 Northfield Rd
3 Pennystone Rd

F6
1 Ansgar Rd
2 Church Fld
3 Mannings Cl
4 Ozier Ct
5 Reddings Cl
6 Well-green Cl

F7
1 Plantation Cl
2 Ross Cl

G3
1 Bradley Ms
2 Dawson Cl
3 Hamilton Ms
4 Nightingale Ms
5 Whiteshot Wy

G5
1 Burnsall Cl
2 Stanleys Farm Rd

H3
1 Ferguson Cl

G6
1 Peal Rd**

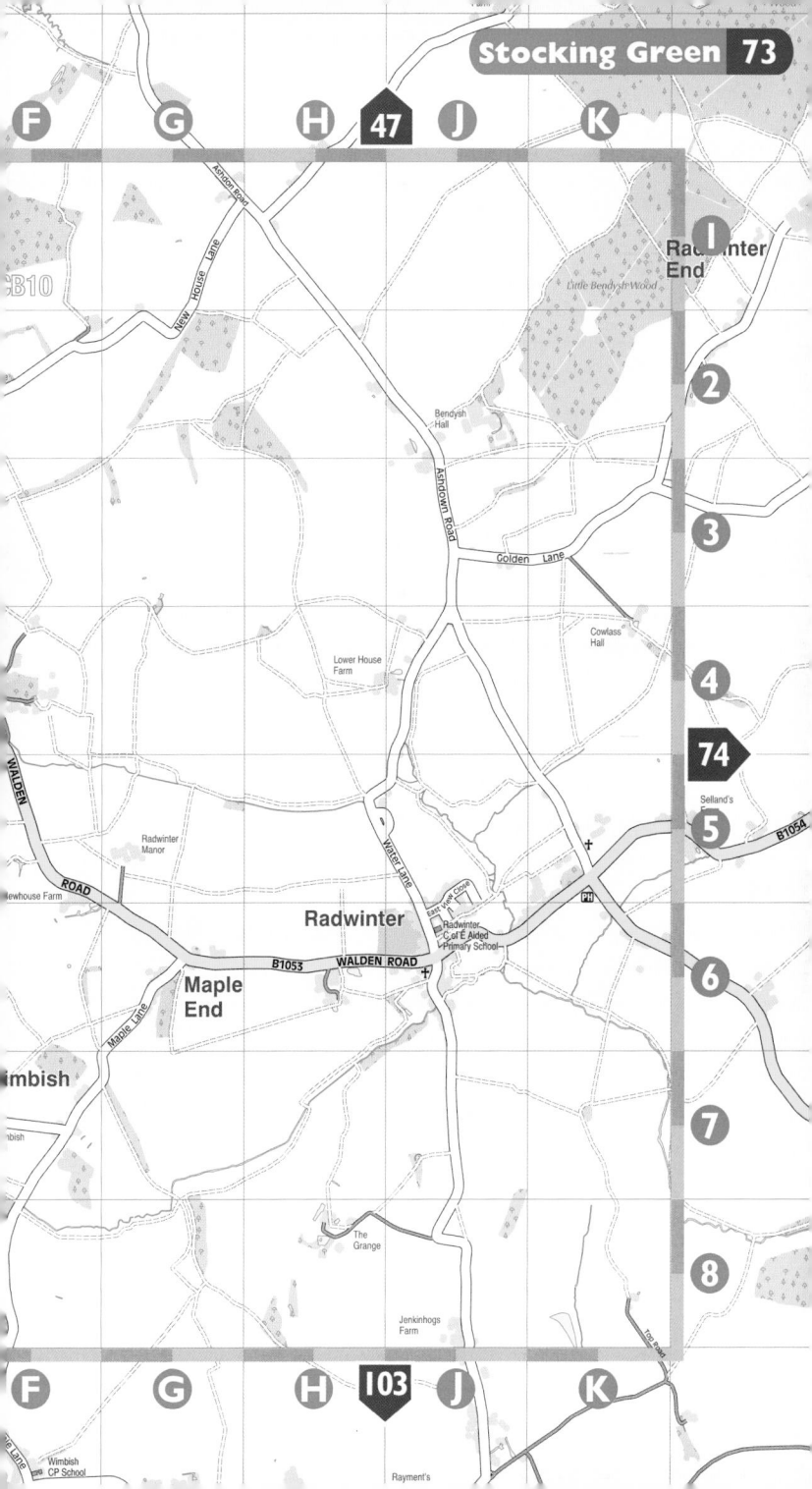

F G H 47 J K

1
Radwinter
End

2

3

4

74

Selland's

5 B1054

6

7

8

Little Bendysh Wood

Bendysh
Hall

Golden Lane

Cowlass
Hall

Lower House
Farm

WALDEN

ROAD

Newhouse Farm

Radwinter
Manor

B1053 WALDEN ROAD

Radwinter

Maple
End

Water Lane

East View Close

Radwinter
C. of E Aided
Primary School

PH

New House Lane

Ashdown Road

Maple Lane

mbish

mbish

The
Grange

Jenkinhogs
Farm

Fox Den

B10

imbish

F G H 103 J K

Wimbish
CP School

Rayment's

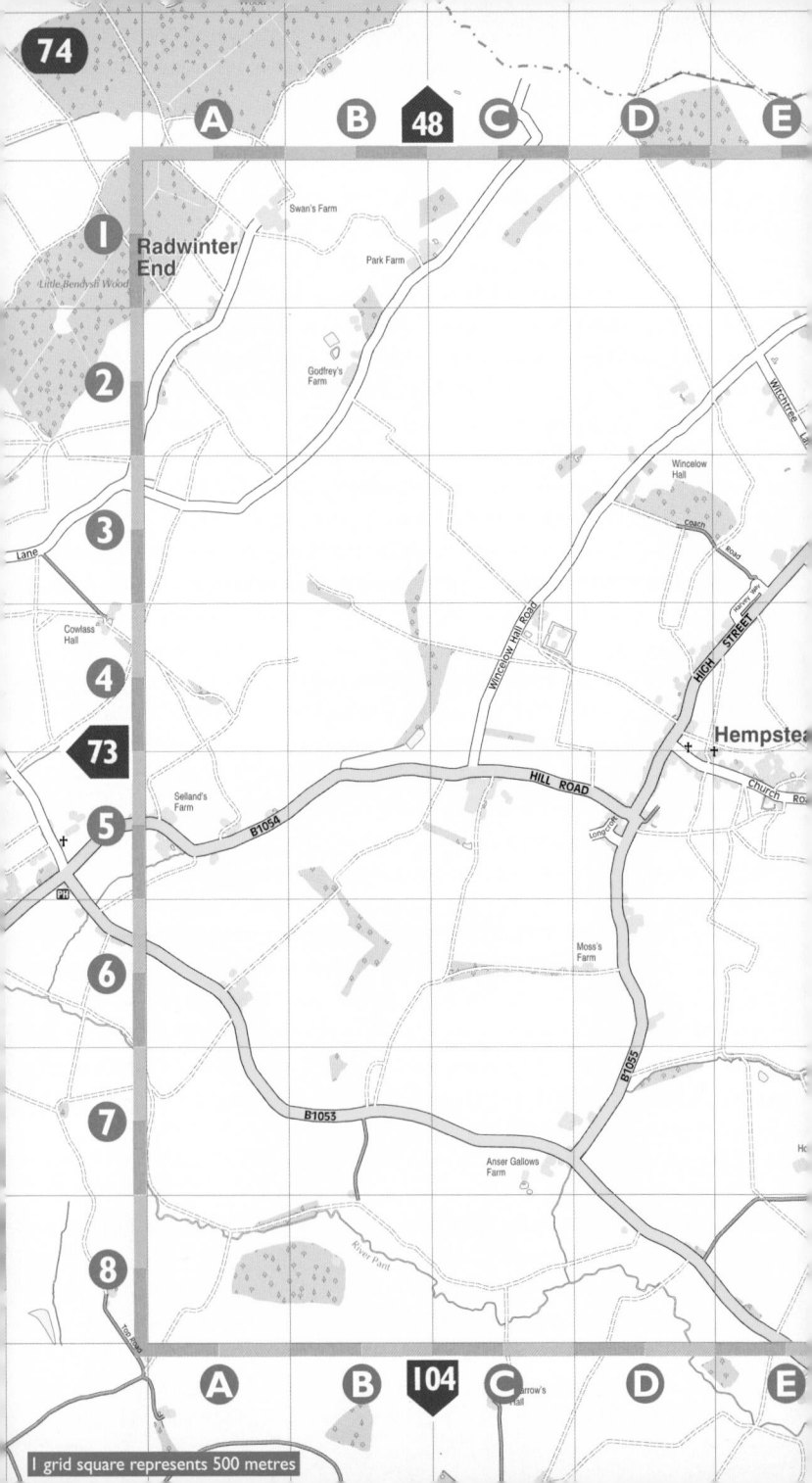

Boblow

Smith's
Green
B1051

F G H 49 J K

Bulls Bridge
Farm

B1054

1

Hillside Farm

2

Hempstead
Hall

3

Hempstead
Wood

4

Hophouse
Farm

76

ards Cross

Lakehouse
Farm

5

Field's
Farm

6

Calthorpes Farm

Spain's End
Farm

7

Free Roberts

Parsonage
Farm

Tinkers
Green

8

Lowerhouse

F G H 105 J K

Great
Sampford

Old House
Farm

Parsonage Farm Lane

Hawkes

Frinkle
Green

Three Chimneys
Farm

F **G** **H** **51** **J** **K**

I

Whitehouse
Farm

Park
Wood

Hill

Wesley End

2

Birdbrook Road

Chapel End Way Mill Road

Stambourne

Church Road

3

Stambourne
Green

Cornish Hall End Road

Revels Farm

4

ld Road

Tagley

78

Nortons

5

Craig's
End

6

Levitt's
Farm

Finchingfield Road

7

Gooseley's
Farm

Thurston
Farm

Robinhood
End

8

Le Hurs

Hole
Farm

F **G** **H** **107** **J** **K**

Jekyll's
Farm

Tilbury
Juxta Cla

J3
1 Duncan Ri

K3
1 Armstrong Wy
2 Carlton Cl
3 The Croft
4 Goodchild Wy
5 Little Hyde Cl

F
e wend

G

H

53

J

Tilbury Ha

K

Tilbury Court

I

K4
1 Bridge St

2

A1017 RIDGEWELL

Stambourne Road

ROAD

Man's Cross

Spencers

Mill Lane

Tilbury

The
Hyc
Far

3

Little

ce's Farm

A1017

Primary
School

Man's Cross

Church Road

CHURCH ROAD

North Road

**Great
Yeldham**

Highfields

Lane

The Croft

Doctors Leather
Surgery

Butlers Wy

4

rets
School

sfield

Numn
Walk

Meadow Dr

Market CV

A1017 HIGH STREET

80

Road

Cherry Lane

5

Great Yeldham Road

Scotneys

Toppesfield

PH

Toppesfield
Hall

POOLE

6

ham Road

Oliver's
Farm

River Colne

7

A1017

F

G

H

109

J

K

8

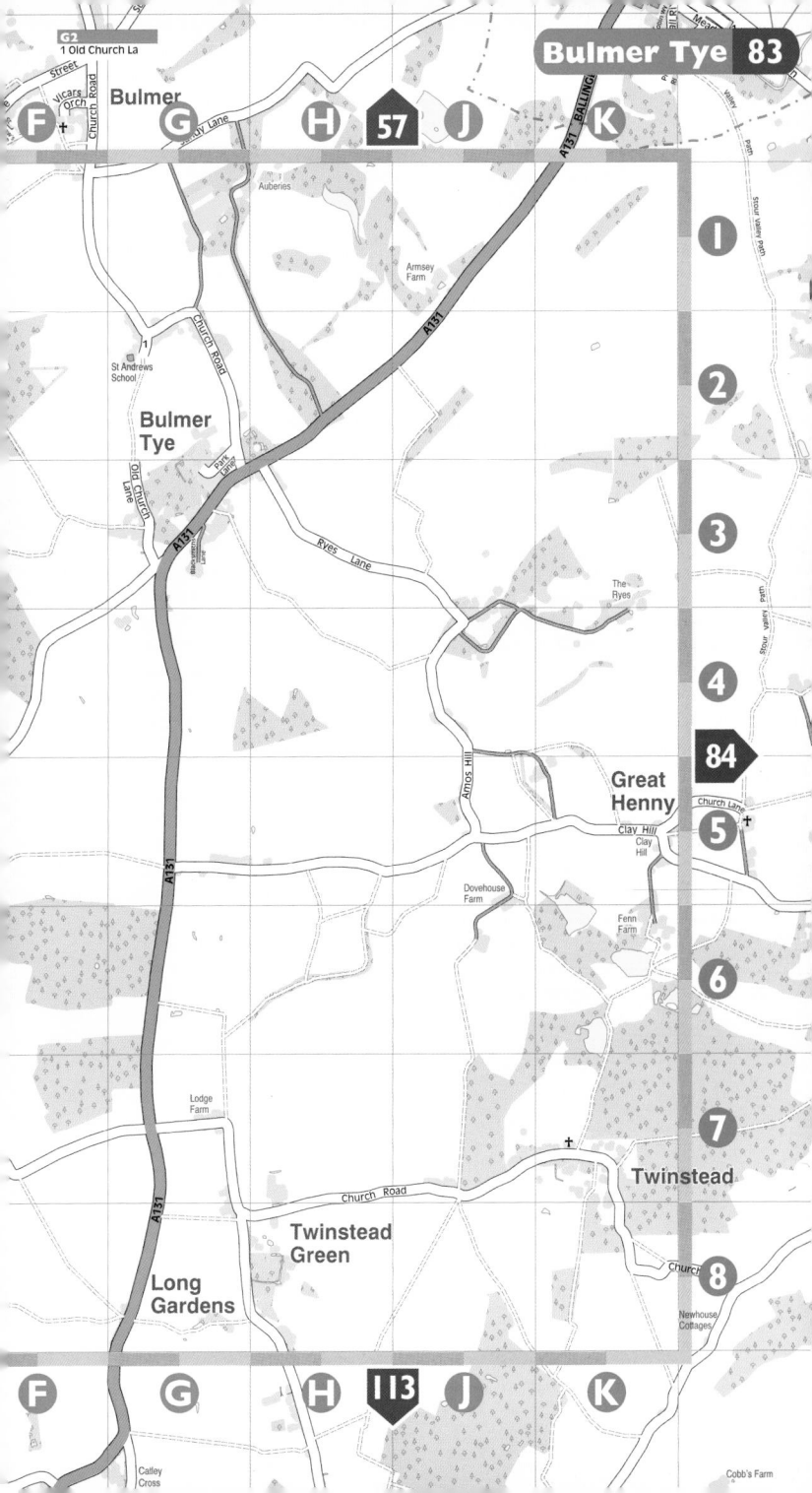

G2
1 Old Church La

Bulmer
Bulmer
Tye

Long
Gardens

Twinstead
Green

Great
Henny

Twinstead

Church Road

A131

Church Road

Old Church Lane

Park Lane

Ryes Lane

Amos Hill

A131 BALLING

Stour valley path

Auberies

Armsey
Farm

St Andrews
School

The
Ryes

Clay Hill
Clay
Hill

Dovehouse
Farm

Fenn
Farm

Lodge
Farm

Church Lane

Newhouse
Cottages

Catley
Cross

Cobb's Farm

Street
Vicars
Orch
Church Road

Kirby Lane

F G H 57 J K

I

2

3

4

84

5

6

7

8

F G H 113 J K

Great Cornard

De Greys Close
Kendon
Turkentine Close
Brands
Chapel

Hall Road
Lane

Corriehall
Prospect Hill

Sackers Green

Rotten Row

Great Greys

Kingswoc House

Kersey Road

Goulding's Farm

Holly Lodge

Little Cornard

Hill

Chapel Lane

Costens Hall

Lord's Wood

Mumford's Wood

Pond Farm

Upper Road

Wyatts Lane

Workhouse Green

Upper Road

BURES ROAD

Spout Lane

Sawyer's

ST EDMUND'S HILL

B1508

B1508

Corn Hall

High Pale Farm

Lamarsh

The Woodlands

E4
1 Aisthorpe

Wen
Thic

Parkhouse

Notley
Enterprise
Park

Grove Farm

Little
Wenham

Jermyns
Farm

Gipsy
Row

Brook   Lane

Days   Road

Dawes
Close

Churchford
Hall

Windmill
Hill

Mill Hill

Days Green

C

Acacia
Farm

Great
Wenham

The Street

Lane

Wenham
Place

Pound

Lane

Wenham
Hill

Old

Lone

Manor
House

Holton St Mary

Oaks Farm

Chaplain's
Farm

A12

Lattinford Hill

Four
Sisters

Cutlers Lane

Cutlers Lane

IPSWICH ROAD

Woodgates
Farm

Woodgates Road

Barn
Business Centre

Rookery
Farm

122

East
Bergholt

East Bergholt
High School

F4
1 Dodmans
2 School Cl

G3
1 Farthings Went
2 Jermyns Cl
3 The Queech
4 Roundridge Rd

F   G   H   60   J   K

Redhouse
Farm

Brockley
Wood

Bentl
Old
Hall

Folly Lane

Lane
Farm

A12(T)

Clay
Hall

Bentley
Long
Wood

Old Hall Lane

London Road

Pond
Hall

Bentley
Park

The Pightle

Little
Tufts

Mary

The Street

Carrots

London Rd

London
Lane

A12(T)

Church Road

88

Potash
Lane

Grove
Farm

Falstaff
Manor

Potash

Church Rd

Bluegate
Lane

Tawneys
Farm

Primary
School

Case
Lane

Bentley

Highfields

The
Link

West Mill
Garden

Station Road

Grove Road

Link Lane

Coppey
Farm

Dodnash
Wood

Martins
Glen

Dodr
Prior
Farm

F   G   H   123   J   K

Levington Heath

A14(T)

F

G

H

J

K

Law's Drift

Law's Drift

I

Croft Farm

Walk Farm

ne

2

Croft House

Drift

3

Stratton Hall

Morston Hall

Morston Hall Rd

LC

4

Suffolk Coast & Heaths Path

94

Suffolk Coast & Heaths Pth

LC

5

Thorpe Lane

Thorpe Common

Grimston Lane

6

Trimley Lower Street

7

Gri

River

8

Orwell

Crane's Hill

F

G

H

129

J

Trimley Marsh

K

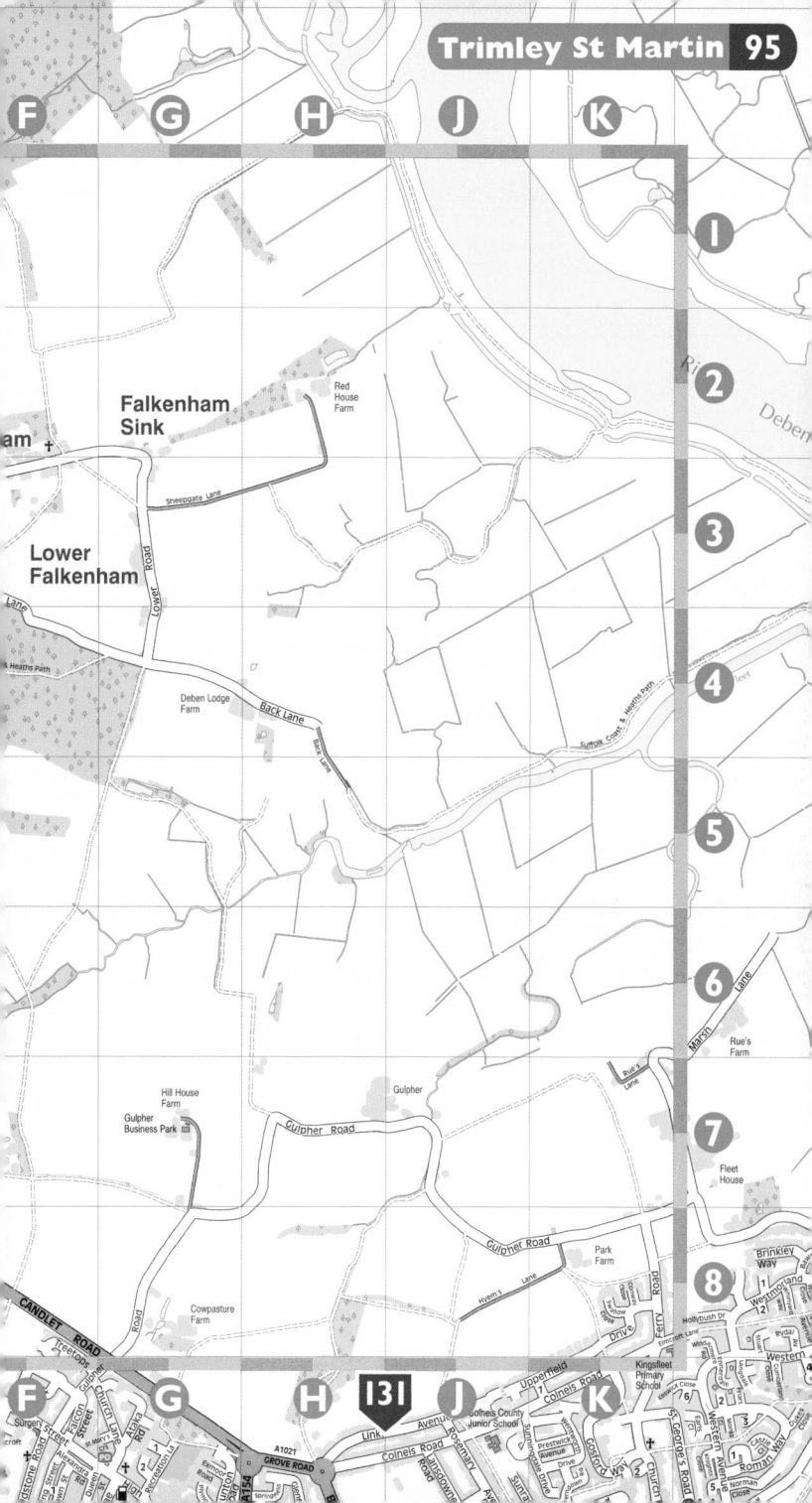

96

A   B   66   C   D   E

1

Cross Leys

Cambridgeshire C
Essex County

Park Lane

River Stort

Morrice Green Farm

2

Hertfordshire Way

3

Park Farm Lane

Hertfordshire Way

Stocking Lane

Park Lane

4

Lowe
Gree

Waterwick Hill

New Farm

5

Scales Park

River Stort

Essex C
Hertfordsh

neapsid 6

Lower Green

7

Wood Lane

Mill Lane

8

Col

Meesden

Anstey
Bury

A   B   132   C   D   E

I grid square represents 500 metres

Pullock's End

F
Clanverend
Farm

G

ROYSTON ROAD

B1039

H

69

J

Duxhall Lane

K
dens
Ambo

B1039 STATION ROAD

Park

Audley End Station

ROW HILL

Rookery

Lane

LC

I

LONDON ROAD

2

M11

Whiteditch
Farm

Harcamlow Way

Wh.. Lane

3

Bury Water Lane

Bury Water Lane

CB11

4

School Lane

Thatchers Green

I00

The Surgery

ROAD

B

Cherry Gard..

5

Harcamlow Way

Frambury Lane

Frambury La..

Newport
CP School

B1038

Wicken
Bonhunt

Wicken
Hall

Bonhunt

6

M11

B1038

Rickling Road

7

Coldhams
Farm

8

F

G

H

I35

J

Harcamlow Way

K

Newport

Rickling

6
1 The Causeway
2 The Close
3 Highfields

F G H **71** J K

Cole End Lane

THAXTED ROAD B184

Thaxted Road

1

The Rees

Deverel's Wood

Pamphillions

Abbots

New House Farm

2

Debden Common

Howe Wood

Debden Road

Newhouse Farm

Airfield

Carver Barracks

3

Debden Manor

Water Lane

4

Brick House Farm

102

Harcamlow Way

Debden Hall Farm

Ivy Todd Hill

Mill Road

Deynes Farm

Harcamlow Way

5

Harcamlow Way

Church Lane

The Causeway
1
High Street
2

Derwent Road

3

Thaxted Road

Debden

Harcamlow Way

6

Smith's Green Farm

Brocton's Farm

Rook End Lane

7

Slough Farm

8

Rook End

F G H **137** J K

The Hall

Swayne's Hall

Cole End Lane

A   **B**   72   **C**   **D**   **E**

THAXTED ROAD

1

New House
Farm

Abbots

Parsonage
Farm

2

Airfield

THAXTED ROAD   B184

Wimbish Wk   Mill Road

THAXTED ROAD

3

Carver
Barracks

Rowney
Close   Howlett
End

Broad Oaks
Close

4

Elder
Street

Pepples
Lane

101

Pepples
Farm

5

eynes
arm

Harcamlow Way

Rowney
Wood

6
ebden

Harcamlow Way

Harcamlow Way

Barnard's
Farm

Smith's Green
Farm

Tendring's
Farm

7
Road

Harcamlow Way

Slough
Farm

Debden
Green

8

PO

A   **B**   Monk's
arm   138   **C**   Roother's
Farm   **D**   **E**

Hempstead Road

1 grid square represents 500 metres

F
G
H
73
J
K

The Grange

ünhogs

1

Dve Lane
Road

Wimbish
CP School

Top Road

Rayment's
Farm

Brockholds

**Tye
Green**

Maypole
Farm

Top Road

2

**Wimbish
Green**

Lower House
Farm

3

Ellis
Green

**Tindon
d**
4

Cemetery

Elms
Farm

Market
Farm

104
5

THAXTED ROAD

Higham's
Farm

Friar's
Farm

Causeway
End Farm

B184

6

Hall Lane

7

Yardley

River Chelmer

Goddard's
Farm

Yardley
Hall

**Boyton
End**
8

dhams

Harcamlow Way

WALDEN ROAD

F
G
H
139
J
K

Millhill
Farm

Harcamlow Way

B1053

Hotel

104

A **B** **74** **C** **D** **E**

1

Brockholds

2

3

Tindon End Road

The Dovehouse

Bush Road

Burr Lane

Byeballs Farm

Sparrow's Hall

Hole Farm

Tindon End

4

Market Farm

103

5

Friar's Farm

Road Farm

Little Clark's

6

Flemings Farm

7

Spriggs

Great Clark's Farm

Goddard's Farm

Millhay Farm

Boyton End

Terrier's Farm

8

Highgates

B1051

A **B** **140** **C** **D** **E**

I grid square represents 500 metres

F G H 75 J K

Parsonage Farm

Old House Farm

Lowerhouse

Great Sampford

I

Parsonage Farm Lane

Skittlewood Lane South

Hawkes Farm

Gt Sampford nty Primary School

Homeridge

B1053

B1051

Maynards

2

Hill Farm

3

Mount Hall

4

106

Park Pale

Tewes Farm

Little Sampford

Hawkin's Hill

5

River Pant

6

Garland's Farm

Gamber's Hall

7

Pitley Farm

Hill Hall

Hawkspur Green

8

F G H 141 J K Cook's Lane

The Hydes

Robinhood
End

La Hurs

F G H **77** J K

I

2

3

4

I08

5

6

7

8

Hole
Farm

Jekyll's
Farm

Mill Lane Mill Farm

Yeldhams

ilbourne's
arm

**Howe
Street**

Howe
Hall

Park Farm

Boyton Hall

Sculpin's
Farm

Chanute Avenue Langley Av

Shaw Drive

053

Mitchell Circle Avenue

Cotton's
Farm Scott Cannon Circle

Tilekiln

Daw Street

F G H **I43** J K

Daw
Street

Nortofts

Gray's
Farm

Pol
Park

A   Le Hurst   B   78   C   D   E

A7
1 Vandenbury Clr

A6
1 Kessler Av

1

Gainsford
End

Mallows   Lane

2

Gainsford
Hall

3

Park Farm

4

107

Flower's
Hall

5

Wethersfield
Airfield

Sculpin's
Farm

6

Chanute Avenue
Drive   Langley Av
Shaw

Whitehall
Farm

7

Kimbell Circle
Scott   Avenue
Cannon Circle

Fairy
Farm

8

Poor
Park

Gray's
Farm

A   B   144   C   D   E

Brickkiln
Green

F G H **79** J K

I

Delvin End

Bloom's Farm

Kentish Farm

Barr Hall

Grave's Hall

Blois Hall

Highstreet Green

Birdgreen Farm

Carter's Farm

Redhouse Farm

Burnt House Farm

110

Hill

Tattersall's Farm

Cuckoos Farm

Morris Green

Deek's Farm

Sugar Lane

School Road

Wright's Farm

Forr Gree

Pevor's Farm

F G H **145** J K

81

112

147

F G H J K

I
2
3
4
5
6
7
8

Pannells Ash Farm

Sudbury Road

Odewells

Byham Hall

Chelmshoe House Farm

Monks Lodge

Hosden's Farm

St Giles C of E Primary School

St Giles Close

Great Maplestead

Church Street

Monks Lodge Road

Lucking Street

Purlshill

Barrett's Hall

Mill Farm

Dyne's Hall Road

Hull's Mill Farm

Wallace's Farm

Bennett's Farm

River Colne

HALSTEAD ROAD

Hepworth Hall

Fitz John's Farm

Doe's Corner

HEDINGHAM ROAD

A1124

A1124

Brook Street Farm

Howe The Howe

River Colne

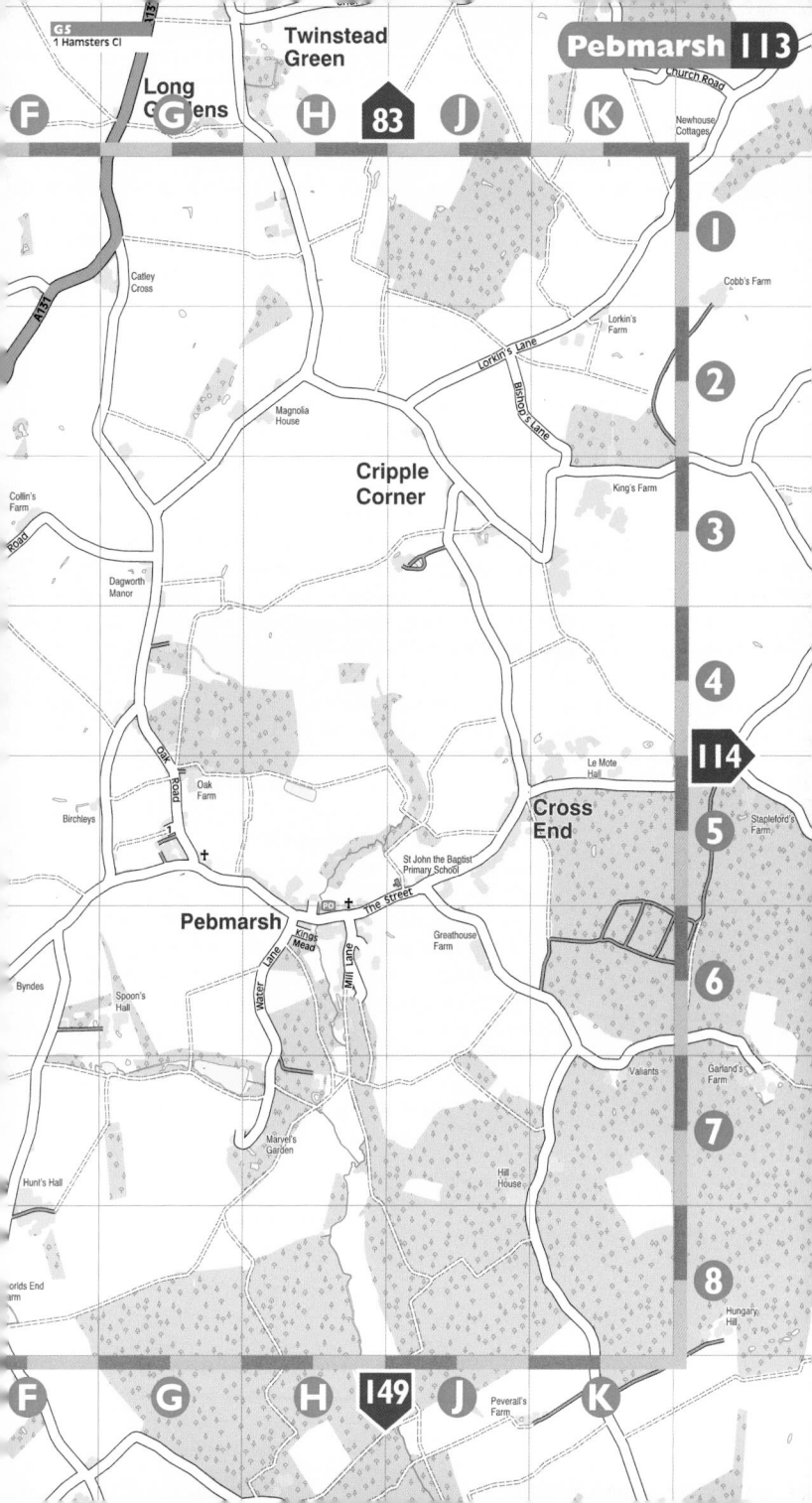

F G H **89** J K

I
PRIMROSE
B1080

Hyams Lane

Argent
Manor Farm

Alton Water
(Reservoir)

Alton
Water Sports
Centre

2
Ward
Infirm

Royal Hospital
School

Bentley Lane

Woodfield Lane

Alton Hall Lane

Carters

Larkspur Rd

Church Rd

MANNINGTREE ROAD

PO
Findley
Close

Stutton
Primary
School

HOLBROOK ROAD   B1080

3

The Drift

Stutton

Creeping

Church Road

Hyams Drive

Manor Lane

Lane

Stutton Cl

Lower   Street

**Lower
Street**

Crowe Hall Lane

Suffolk Coast &

Stutton Gn

Wash Path

4

pper
reet

Crepping
Hall

Crowe
Hall

Stutton
House

126

5 Holbrook
Bay

6

7

8

F G H **161** Jacques
Bay J K

Essex Way

Remembrance
Wood

Wall Lane

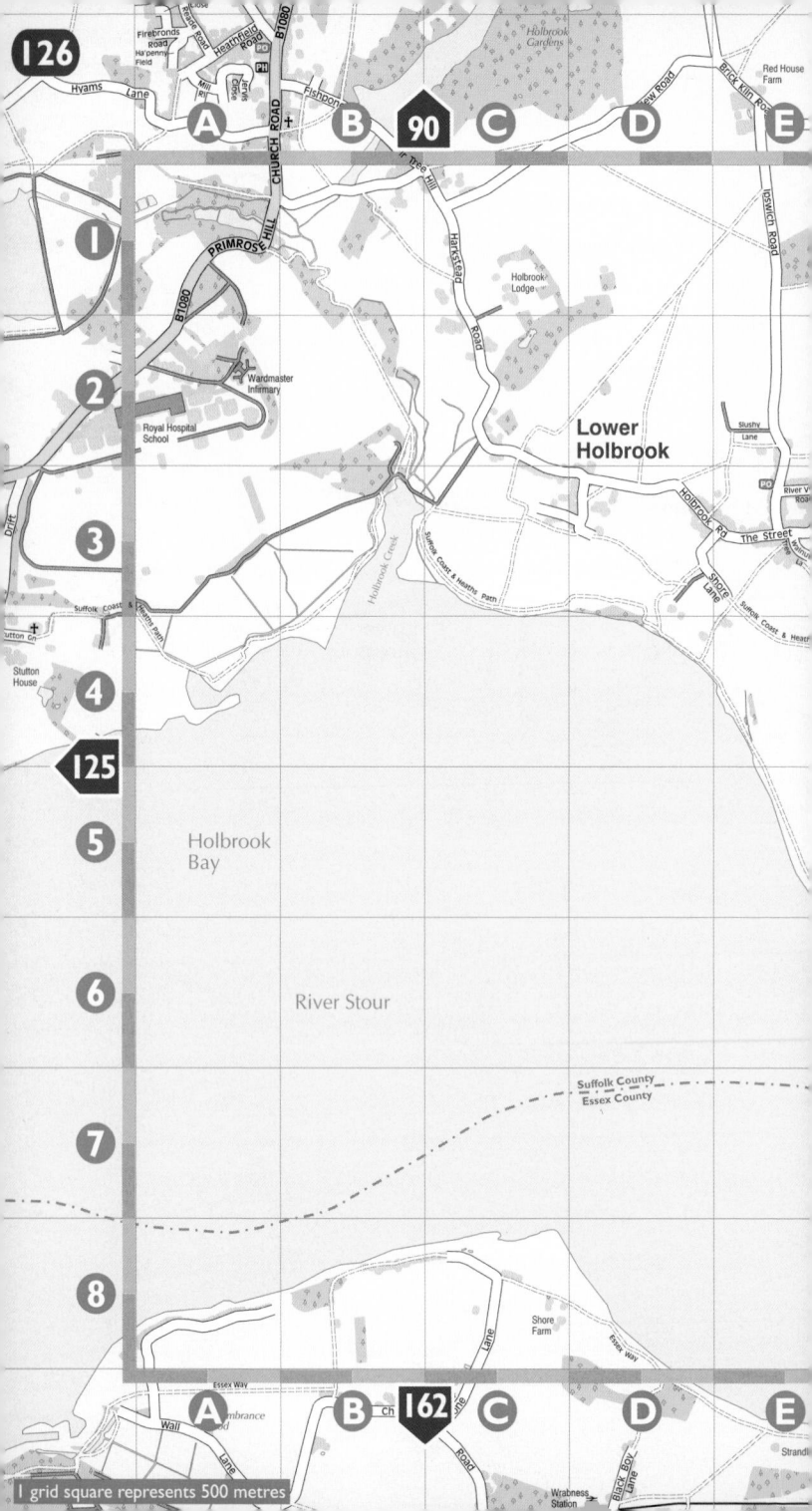

F G H 91 J K

I
2
3
4
128
5
6
7
8

The St

Erwarton

PH

Ness Road

Suffolk County
Essex County

River

Rence Park
Farm

Harkstead
Hall Farm

Lower

Houses

Road

Lovers Lane

Grove
Lane

Ling's Lane

Old
Church School

Rectory Road

Fox Pond Lane

Lane

ead

Nether
Hall

Knights Farm

Pat Hill

Hill House
Farm

**Shop
Corner**

Beaumont
Hall

Suffolk Coast & Heaths Path

Essex Way

F G H 93 J K

I 2 3 4 I30 5 6 7 8

Crane's Hill

Nell

Trimley Marshes

Over Hall

B1456

Shotley Marshes

Shotley Marshes

Shotley Gate

Marina

Ganges Museum

Great Harlings

Tudor Cl

Harlings

Bristol Hill

Caledonia Rd

King Edward VII Drive

Shotley Sailing Club

Battery Rd

6 7

Harwich Harbour

Bath Side

THE QUAY

Hotel

King's

WEST ST

GEORGE ST

Guildhall

PO

Harwich Town Sailing Club

Harwich Town Station

HARBOUR CRESCENT

MAIN ROAD

A120(T)

The Redoubt

Harwich County Primary School

Mayflower

B1352

BARRACK LN

F G H I65 J K

A120(T)

A120(T)

Dover

Rawden Close

Nelson Road

Station Lane

KINGS

HIGH ST

Kingsway Hall Art and Theatre Hall

Primary School

B1352

HARWICH

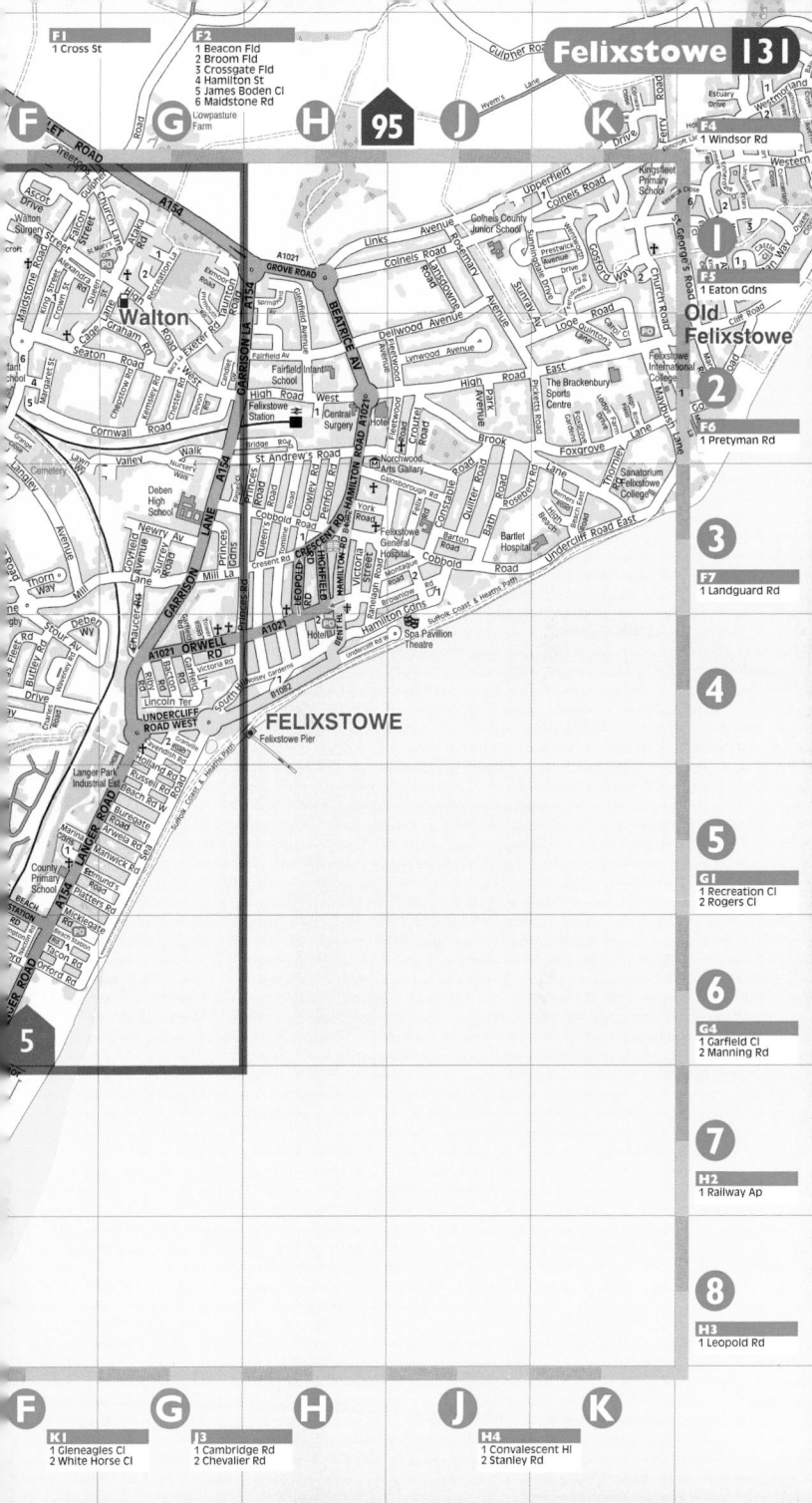

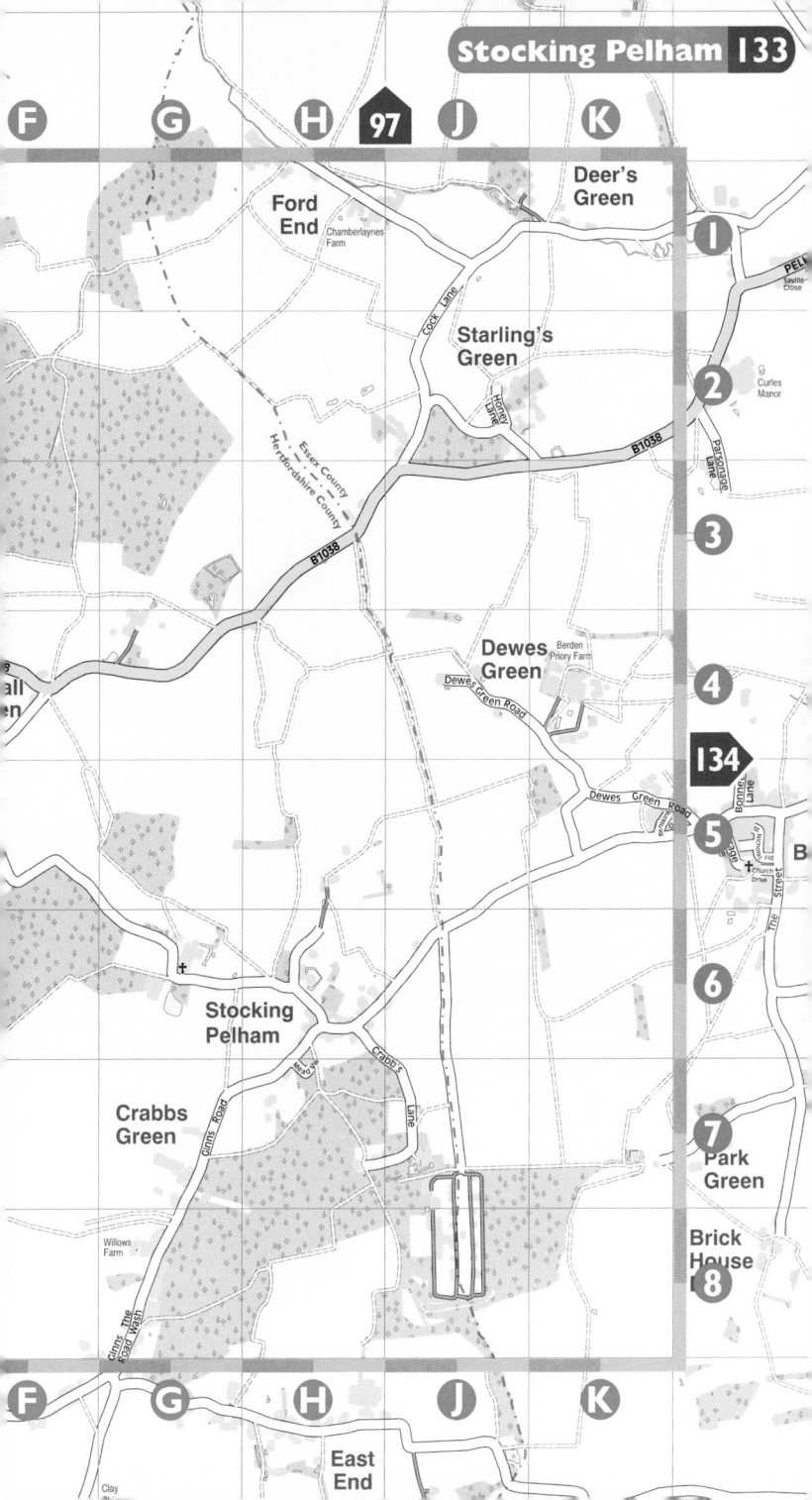

Newport

1

2

Rickling

Harcamlow Way

Harcamlow Way

3 endon

Brick

Kiln

Lane

B1383

4

Rickling Green

136

Rickling & C of E
Primary School

Wood

Brick Kiln

Cripps Hollow

5

Harcamlow Way

Rickling Green
Road

Rickling
Green

Brixton Lane

Fitcham's

Lane

Broom
Wood

6

B1383

Harcamlow Way

7

Ugley

Parsonage Farm

Vicarage
Lane

Parkmore
Fields

8

Brixton Lane

Wade's
Hall

Bollington
Hall

B1383

Quaremead

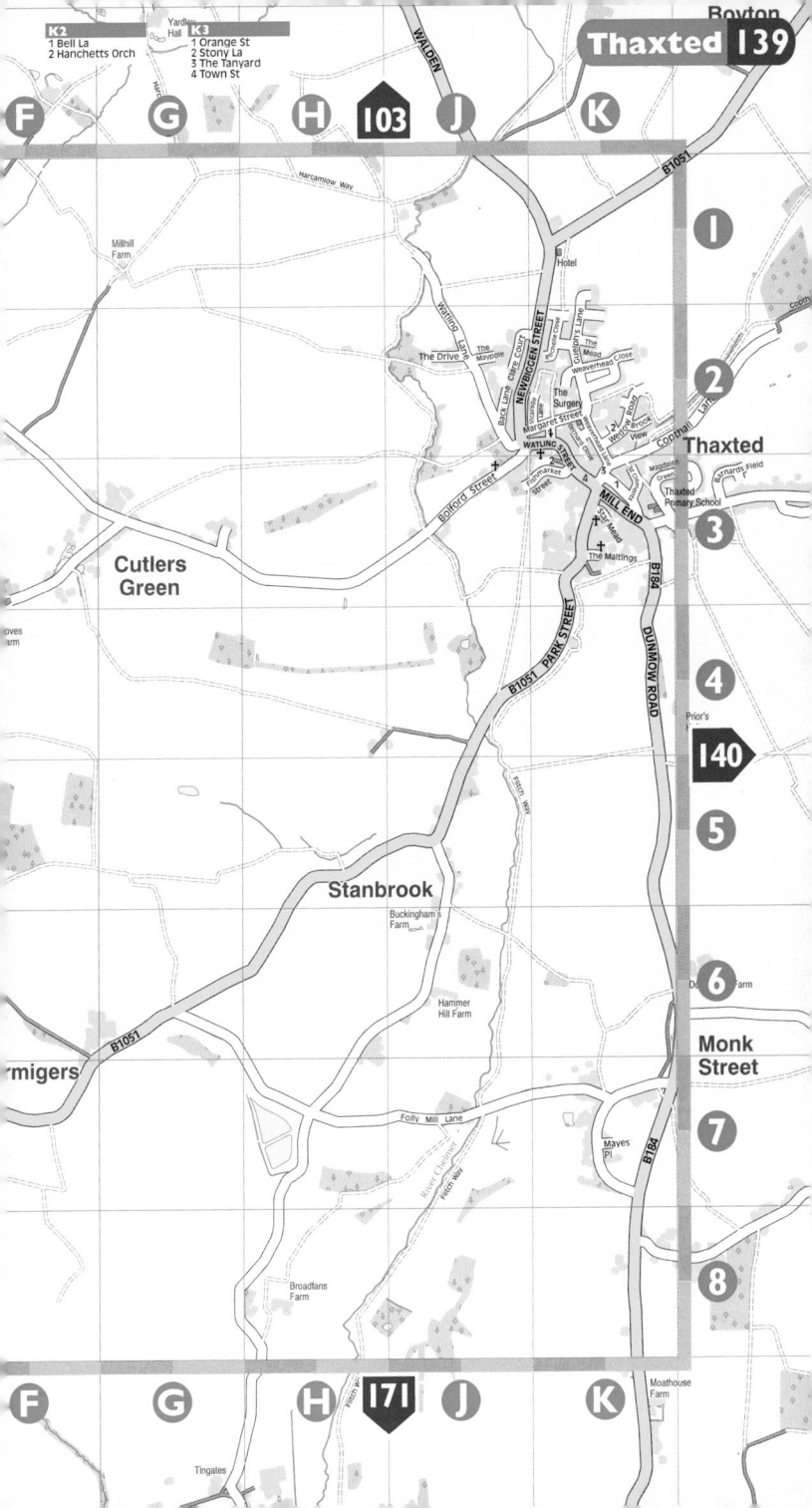

140

Boyton End

A   B   104   C   D   E

B1051

1

Hotel

The Mead
Weaverhead Close
2
The Surgery
Weaverhead Lane
Wenden Brook View

Coptal Lane

Thaxted

Magdalen Green

Thaxted Primary School

Bethards Field

MILL END
3
The Maltings

PARK STREET

B184

DUNMOW ROAD

4
Prior's Hall

139

5

6
Dovehouse Farm

Monk Street

7
May Pl

B184

8

Moathouse Farm

A   B   172   C   D   E

Coptall   Lane

Blunt's Farm

Bardfield End Green

Bardfield Road

The Lodge

Richmond's Green

Holder's Green

Sibley's Green

Cowels Arm Lane

Cowels Farm

Highg

1 grid square represents 500 metres

F G H 105 J Hawkspur Green K

Hill Hall

Cook's Lane

1

The Hydes

Moor Hall

2

Lane

Styles

3

Paul's Farm

✝

Little Bardfield

Stones

4

142

Markswood Farm

5 DUNMOW ROAD B1057

Charity Farm

6

The Grove

Oxen End

7

uck End Farm

Bustard Green

B1057

Coft Hall

8

Dalsvley Road

Porridge Hall

Brazenhead Farm

F G H 173 J K

B1057

K2
1 Dog Cha
2 Saffron Cl

F G H **107** J K

I

B1053

Daw Street

Petches

Norfolts

Tilekiln

Pods Park

Gray'el Farm

Hill

Hudson's

2

Saffron Walk

Saffron Gardens

Hereward W.

High Street

SILVER ST

Dunkirk

Wethersfield Primary School

West Dr

B1053

Wethersfield

Manor House

3

BRAINTREE

ROAD

Golden's Farm

River Pant

Hawkin's Harvest

ham's ss

The Cross Farm

Ashwell Hall

4

144

Mandalay Farm

Redfants Manor Farm

5

6 Shalford

Great Lodge

Hunt's Farm

7

Park Hall

8

F G H **175** J K

Hubbard's Farm

Lane

Dynes Farm

144

I

108

A Gray's Farm
B
C
D
E

Poor Park

Brickkiln Green

Gray's Lane

Hudson's Hill

School Green

Pouches Hall

Widlevbrook Lane

Manor House

Blackmo End

2
Gardens
Hereward
High Street
1053
othershield rimary School
St Dt

3
BRAINTREE ROAD

Golden's Farm

Danes Vale Farm

Hyde Farm

4
B1053

Boydell's Farm

Oak Hill

High Lane

143

Valley Farm

5
Redfants Manor Farm

WETHERSFIELD ROAD

6
Cliff Crescent
Clifffield
BRAINTREE

Rotten End

Shalford

Hall Lane

7
Water Lane

Iron Bridge Farm

8
BRAINTREE

Church End

PD

Nichol's Farm

ROAD

A Hubbard's Farm
B
176
C
D
E

Abbot's Hall

1 grid square represents 500 metres

F
G
H
109
J
K

I

Littlebury Gr

Hawkwoods

Patten's
Farm

2
Little
Hall
Farm

Baker's
Farm

Bounce's
Farm

3

Shinborough

4

146

5

Parkhall Road

Parkhall
Farm

6

Parkhall Road

Beazley End

Parkhall
Wood

7

Harmas
Farm

Bovingdon
Wood

8

F
G
H
177
J
K

Fennes   Road

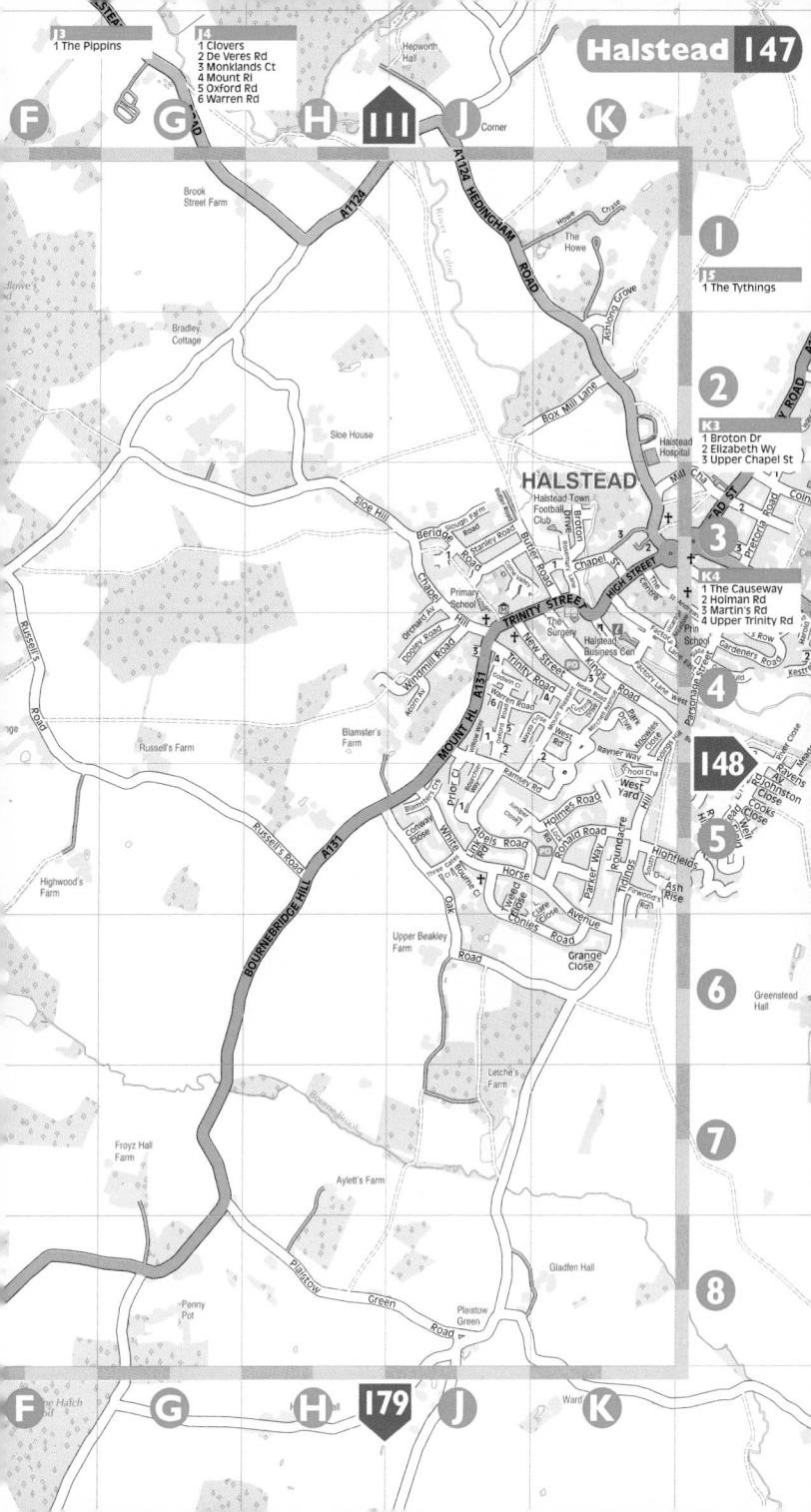

J3
1 The Pippins

J4
1 Clovers
2 De Veres Rd
3 Monklands Ct
4 Mount Ri
5 Oxford Rd
6 Warren Rd

I5
1 The Tythings

K3
1 Broton Dr
2 Elizabeth Wy
3 Upper Chapel St

K4
1 The Causeway
2 Holman Rd
3 Martin's Rd
4 Upper Trinity Rd

HALSTEAD

148

179

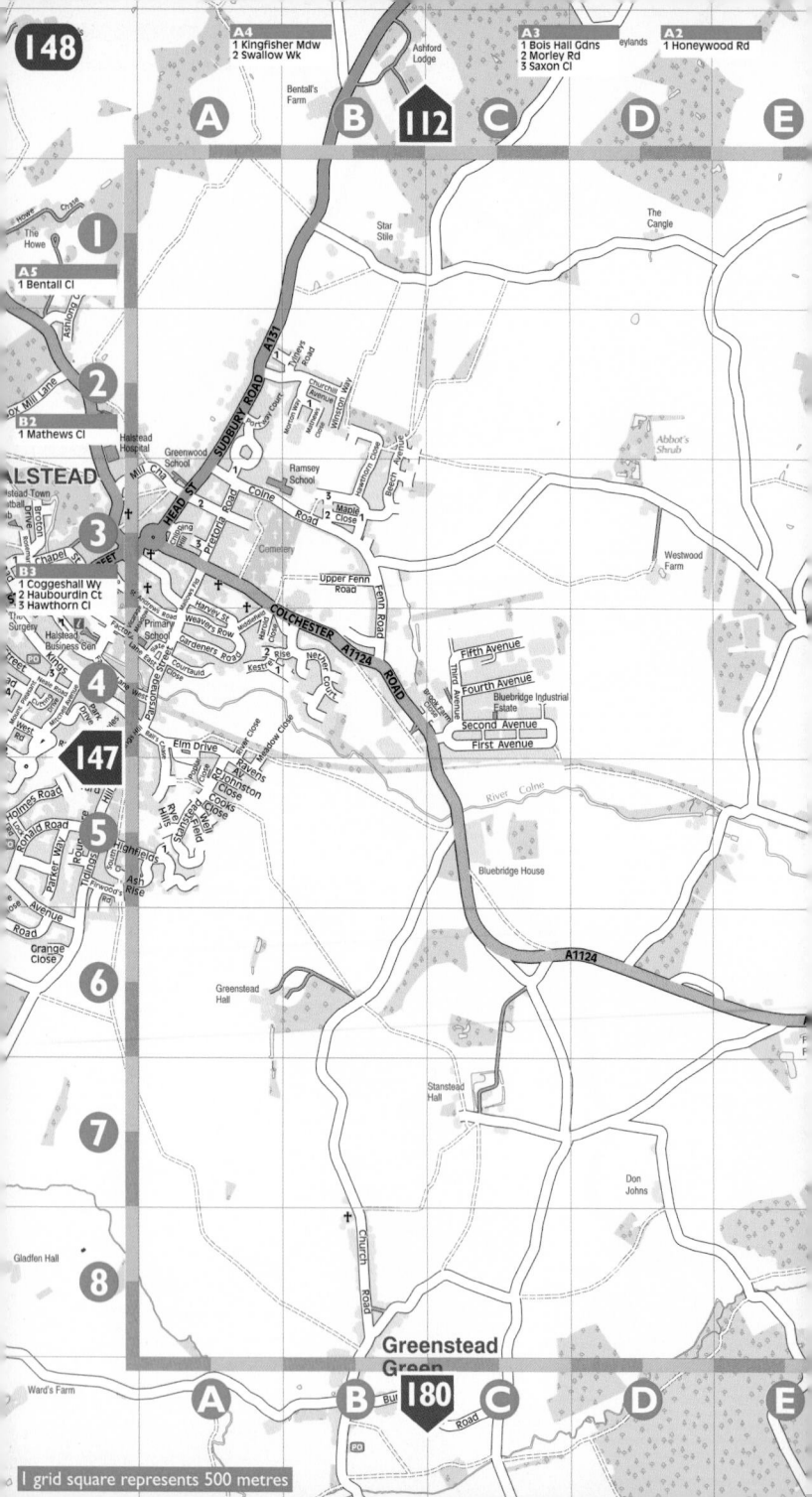

A4
1 Kingfisher Mdw
2 Swallow Wk

Ashford
Lodge

A3
1 Bois Hall Gdns
2 Morley Rd
3 Saxon Cl

eylands

A2
1 Honeywood Rd

Bentall's
Farm

A **B** **112** **C** **D** **E**

The Howe
Crist

The
Howe

1

The
Cangle

Star
Stile

A5
1 Bentall Cl

2

B2
1 Mathews Cl

Halstead
Hospital

Abbot's
Shrub

Greenwood
School

Ramsey
School

Westwood
Farm

3

ALSTEAD

Cemetery

Maple
Close

B3
1 Coggeshall Wy
2 Haubourdin Ct
3 Hawthorn Cl

Upper Fenn
Road

Colne
Road

Fifth Avenue

COLCHESTER A1124 ROAD

Fourth Avenue

Bluebridge Industrial
Estate

147

Elm Drive

Second Avenue

First Avenue

4

River Colne

5

Bluebridge House

Holmes Road

Grange
Close

6

Greenstead
Hall

A1124

7

Stanstead
Hall

Don
Johns

8

Gladfen Hall

Church
Road

Ward's Farm

A **B** **180** **C** **D** **E**

Greenstead
Green

1 grid square represents 500 metres

A **B** 122 **C** **D** **E**

East House
East Lane
astle House

Essex Way

I

**Dedham
Heath**

Long Road East

Gull's Lane

2

Great
Hickle House

3

Stour House
Jupes Hill
Hill Farm

Long Road East

Essex Way

Mill Hill

Dedham Road

WIGNALL STR

A137 HARWICH ROAD Harwich Road

Bargate Lane

Foxash Close

Tile Barn Lane

A137
HARWICH ROAD

4

157

Home Farm Lane

5

Badliss
Hall

Home
Farm

**Foxash
Estate**

Lower Farm

Hungerdown Lane

Glanfields

Wood Barn Lane

Hungerdowns

Hungerdown Lane

Grange Road

Gra

6

Little Bromley Road

Bounds
Farm

Badley
Hall

Barn

Grange Road

7

Morrow Lane

Beck Road

Waterhouse La

Old Shields
Farm

Waterhouse
Farm

Norman's
Farm

Ardleigh Road

8

Chancery
Farm

ROAD Burnt Heath Cottages

**Burnt
Heath**

Mill

Bri

Frantons Road

A **B** 190 **C** **D** **E**

Bromley Cros

Liley's Lane

AR

G1
1 Barker Cl
2 Constable Cl
3 Keating Cl
4 Stubbs Cl

H1
1 Harvey Cl
2 The Rookery

123

I1
1 Falklands Dr
2 Hilton Cl
3 North St
4 Parsons Yd
5 Regent St
6 St Michaels Ct

F G H **123** J K

MANNINGTREE

160

Little
Bromley

F Church G H **191** J K

B1352 THE WALLS
Stour Sailing
Club
Quay
North Ho Gallery
Craft Gallery
HIGH ST
Manningtree
The
Silver Tree
Riverside
Health
Centre
Riverside Av
Jubilee
ROAD

Mistley
Towers

HIGH STREET

A37
COX'S HILL

Lawford

Dale
Hall

Manningtree
Sports Centre

Primary
School

High
School

Lawford C of E
GM Primary School

Claude
Oliver
Close

Lawford
House

B1352 LONG ROAD

Dead Lane

Aldhams

Stacie's
Farm

Lawfordhouse Farm

Hollylodge
Farm

Rose
Farm

Chequers Road

igh Road

Dairy
House

Mistley
Hall

Ford
Farm

Dickley Hall

New
Hall

Braham
Hall

Mutley's
Farm

Church

Bentley Road

Spratts

Essex Way

B1035

Chequers Road

Bromley Road

Milton Road

Colchester Road

New ROAD

Trinity Rd

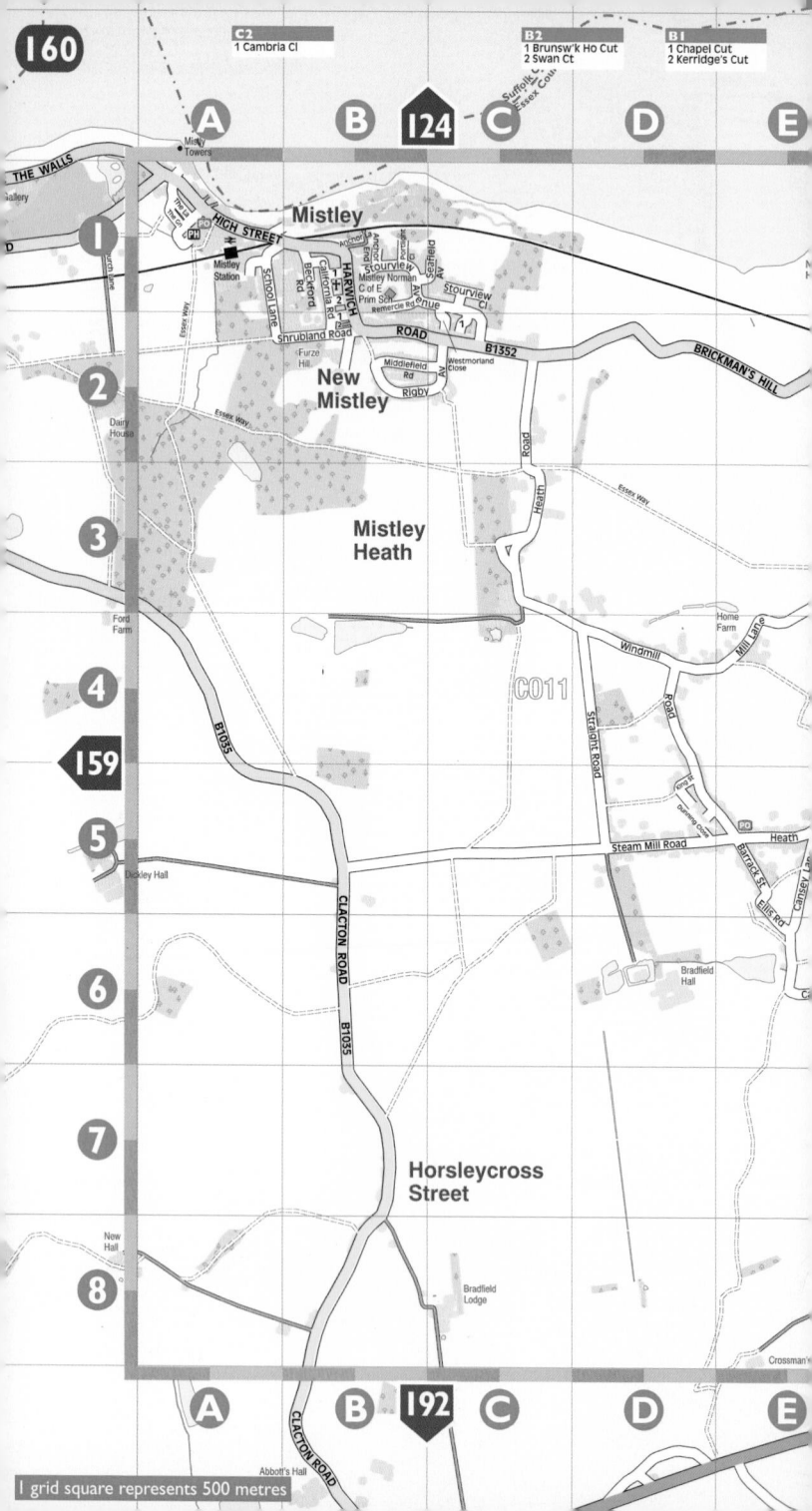

F G H **125** J K

Jacques
Bay

1

Essex Way

Remembrance
Wood

Wheattnear
Close

2

Wheattnear Lane

Stour
Lodge

Shore Lane

ROAD

Essex Way

Ragmarsh
Farm

School

Jacques
Hall

3

HARWICH ROAD

Bradfield

B1352

Station Road

The

Lonbarn

LONBARN HILL

SPINNEL'S HILL

HARWICH ROAD

Spinnel's
Farm

4

162

Barn
Farm

Bluehouse
Farm

5

Willow Hall

Wix
Road

Pond
Hall

Carbonells

6

Dairyhouse Lane

Dairy
House

Bradfield Road

Wix Abbey

Spinnel's

Spinnel's Lane

7

Bradfield Road

Dairyhouse Lane

BY-PASS

WIX

Harwich

Quarry

Cansey Lane

Wix
Lodge

Wix CP
School

PO

Clare Close Road

Wix

Dairy Park Avenue

Clare
Close

Clacton Road

Clayhall

8

F **A120(T)** G H **193** J K

Cansey Lane

Spring
Farm

F1
1 Easterling Cl

F2
1 Newton Rd

F   **G**   **H**   Bathside **129**   **J**   **K**

A120(T)

Dovercourt Station
A120(T)
Station Lane

Rawden Close

Primary School

HARWICH

MAIN   **ROAD**

Harwich & District Hospital

Harwich & Parkeston Football Club

Dovercourt

Old Vicarage Rd

Fronks Rd Family Surgery

B1414

St Josephs RC Primary School

FRONK'S   **ROAD**

The Harwich School

Hudson Close

Dovercourt Swimming Pool

Wick

W End La

7

I

F3
1 Washington Rd

2

F4
1 Acorn Cl
2 Newport Cl
3 St Edmunds Cl

3

G1
1 Lynton Cl

4

5

G2
1 Douglas Rd

6

H2
1 Hillcrest Ct
2 Portland Crs

7

H3
1 St George's Av

8

F   **G**   **H**   **197**   **J**   **K**

J1
1 Hordle Pl
2 Hordle St

Brick
House
End

A   B   134   C   D   E

1

Maggots
End

2

Mount
Pleasant

Butt   Lane

Stewarts Way

Andersc
Close

**Mallows
Green**

Manudeli

Manu

Mallows Green Road

3

Doxber La

Mallows Green Ro

Uppend

4

Watery
Lane

Parsonage Farm

5

Harcamlow Way

**Farnham
Green**

**Chatter
End**

6

Harcamlow Way

Waterside
(School)

Bourne Brook

Farnham
School

Rectory Lane

Globe
Crescent

Farnham

†

7

Level's
Green

P

Mill Hill

8

A   B   198   C   D   E

Essex County
County

1 grid square represents 500 metres

K5
1 Birchalls
2 The Campions
3 Highmead
4 Mary Mcarthur Pl
5 Poulteney Rd
6 The Rookery
7 White Bear

K6
1 Clarence Rd
2 Meadowcroft
3 St John's La

K7
1 Millfields
2 Spencer Cl
3 Station Rd
4 Waterside
5 Woodfield Cl
6 Woodfield Ter

Wade's Hall

Bollington Hall

B1383

Orford House

Alsa Lodge

Alsa Street

Norman House

Business Park

High Lane

B1351

Harcamlow Way

Harcamlow Way

The Hall

School

River Stort

Bentfield Bury

Bentfield Green

Pennington Lane

Hole Farm

Rainford Road

Cambridge Road

Croasdaile

Gibbs Cl's

Five Acres

Primary School

Cotsfield

Norman's Wy

The Surgery

Chapel Lane

STANSTED MOUNTFITCHET

Therfield

Bentfield End Causeway

Cawkell Cl

Bentfield Road

Cambridge Rd

Stansted Clinic

St John's Rd

Brewery Lane

Burnells Wy

Lower St

Grove Hill

Castle Walk Clinic

Primary School

Chapel Hill

B1351

Recreation Grd

Silver Street

Mill Side

Sunnyside

Water Lane

Stansted Mountfitchet Sta

Park Road

Brook

Cross St

Limekiln Lane

Old Bell Cl

The Spinney

Maitland Rd

Mount Dr

Mountfitchet Rd

Manor Road

Riverside Business Park

Stoney Common Rd

Stoney Common

Hazel End

Hazel End Road

Pines Hill

B1383

CM24

Church Rd

Foresthall Rd

The Mountfitchet School

Essex County
Hertfordshire County

Gipsy Lane

Mill Road

Forest Hall

Parsonage Lane

Parsonage Farm

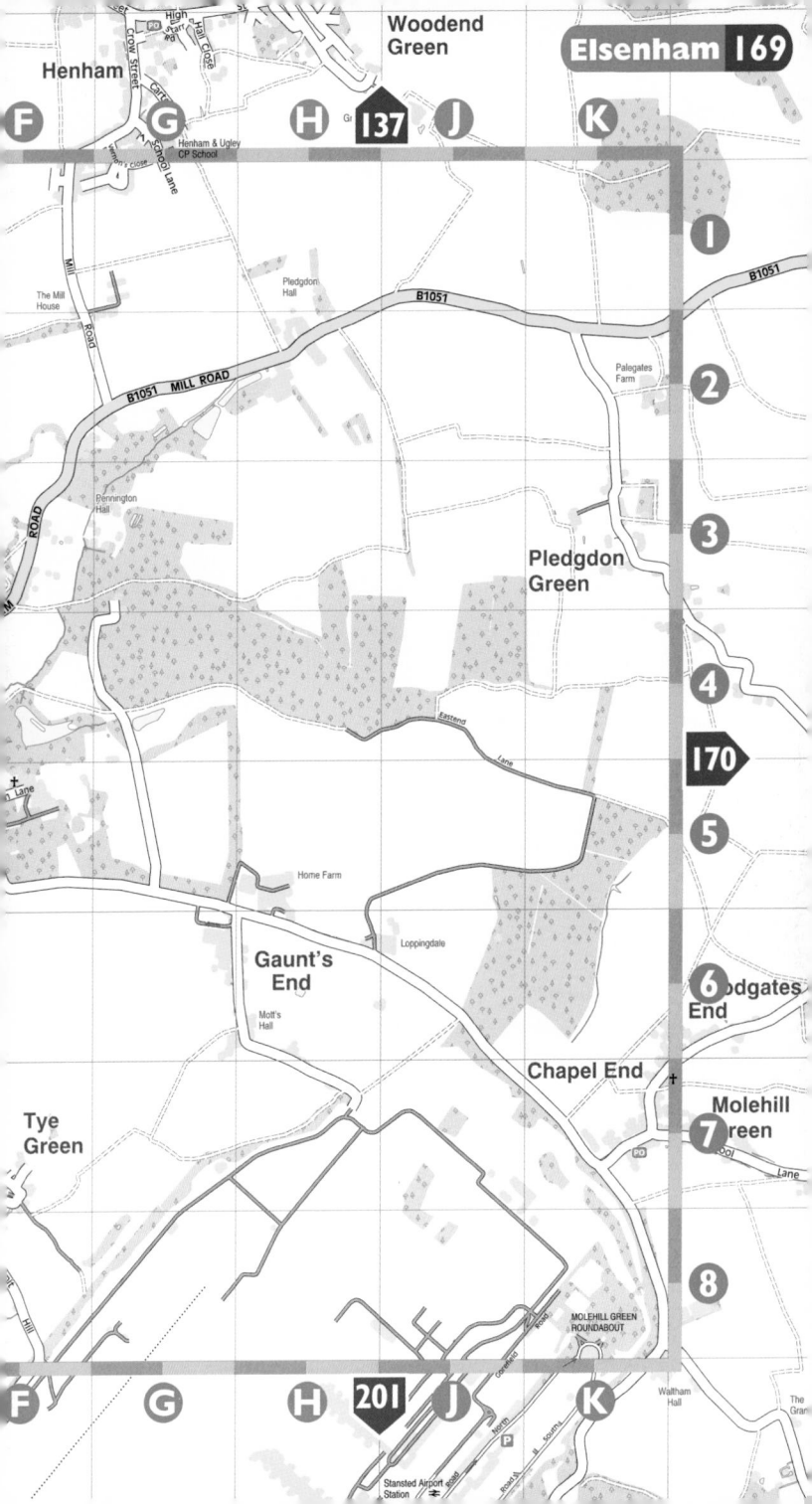

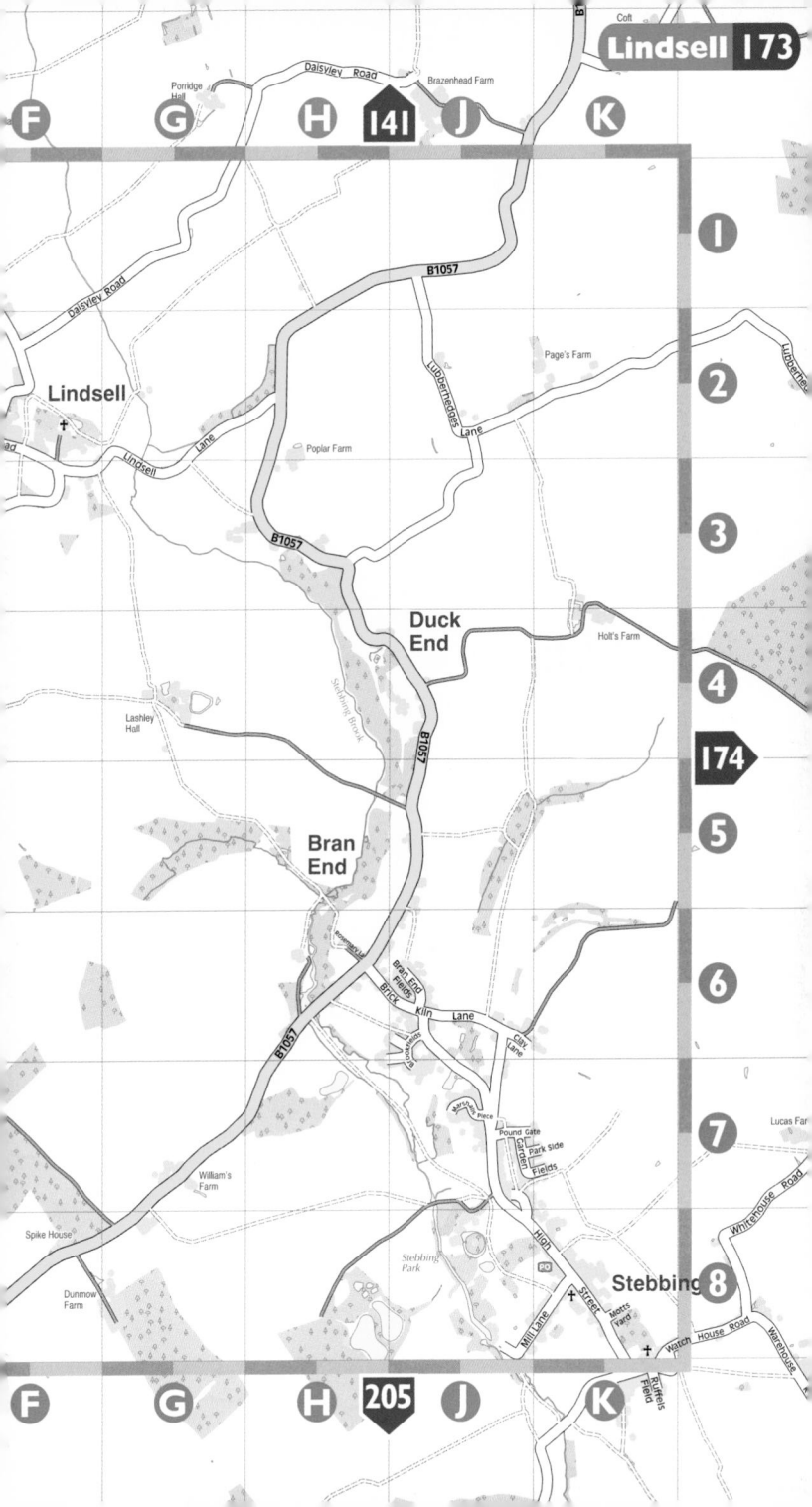

174

Colt Hall

Bushett Farm

A   B   142   C   D   E

Little Lodge

1

...age's Farm

2

Lubberhedges Lane

New Gre... Far...

Tollesburys Farm

3

Long Green Lane

Holt's Farm

Lubberhedges Lane

Bardfield Saling

4

173

5

Whitehouse Farm

6

Badcocks Farm

Lucas Farm

Gatehouse Farm

Andrewsfield (Saling) Aerodr...

7

...side ...ds

Whitehouse Road

St...bing

Morts Yard

8

Street

Watch House Road

Warehouse Road

Ruffels Field

Newpasture Lane

Yew Tree Farm

Bacons Farm

A   B   206   C   D   E

I grid square represents 500 metres

F G H 143 J K

143

Hubbard's Farm

I

Dynes Farm

Parsonage Fa

2

Shalfor Green

Bartlett's Far

3

Jasper's Green

4

176

Pudneys Farm

5

PO

Crow's Green

Great Saling

Piccotts Farm

6

Vicarage Lane

Piccotts Lane

Saling Grove

Mount's Farm

7

's Farm

Onchor's Farm

8

d all

Shalford F

Church End

BRAINTREE

D6
1 Bell La

Nichol's Farm

A

B

144

C

D

E

ROAD

1

Hubbard's Farm

Abbot's Hall

Dynes Farm

B1053

Parsonage Farm

Goldsticks Farm

2

alford Green

Bartlett's Farm

Killhogs Farm

Water Lane

3

Jasper's Green

Sheering Hall

Lowlands Farm

4

Pudneys Farm

Great Priory Farm

175

Cold Hall Farm

Ivy Hall

5

Kynaston

Road

Ketleys View

St. Mary's C

6

Mount's Farm

Meadow Close

Panfield

Hall Road

Hall Road

Lightwaters Farm

7

Perry Childs Farm

8

Old Hall

Pods Brook

A

Shalford Road

B

208

C

D

E

F G H 147 J K

Gladfen Hall

Plaistow

Penny t

Highbam Hall

Ward's Farm

I

2

3

Church Farm

Folly Green

Brookes's Farm

4

180

5

Madgements Road

Gower's Farm

Numey's Lane

Back Lane

Rectory Road

6

Woodhouse Farm

Kings Lane

7

& District

Stisted

The Street

8

Old Road

Pattiswick Hall

Doghouse Road

Church Road

Pattiswick

F G H 211 J K

Water Lane

River Blackwater

COLCHESTER ROAD
Vernons Road
Rose Green
F5
1 Holliland Cft
Chapp 2 Tambour Cl
(Contd) Primary School
Penlan Hall
River Colne
Chapel Hill
SWAN CLOSE

F G H **151** J K

Pope's Hall
Pope's Road

I

A1124 HALSTEAD ROAD
Penlan Hall Lane
Wash Farm

Broom House

Swan Street

Essex Way

2

Bacon's Farm Way
Bacon's Lane
Essex Cl
Farm
Essex Way

3

New

Wick Farm

Belt's Farm

4

New Road
Bo...
H

Essex Way
Tey Road

at Tey
many School
Moor Road
Moor Farm

Great Tey

184
Hardings
Church
Chase

5

Hines Cl

Aldham

Pond Road
Hoe Farm
Rectory Road
Brook Road

6

Rectory Road

Church House Farm

LC

Aldh

7

Brook Road

Little Hey House

8

Roman River

Marks Tey Station
Avn Lane

F G H **215** J K

e Tey
Great Tey Road
Mots ...
Church Lane
Station Rd
A12(T)
A12(T)
LONDON RD
A12(T)
Doctors Surgery

186

B8
1 Magazine Fm Wy

A8
1 Christine Cha

A7
1 Browning Cl

A

B

154

C

D

E

Manor Farm

Healthlands Primary School

1

C8
1 Rembrandt Wy

West

2

D3
1 Anemone Ct
2 Celandine Ct
3 Gentian Ct
4 Lavender Wy

3

E1
1 Old Rose Gdns

4

185

5

E3
1 Warwick Bailey Cl

6

E6
1 Manor Rd
2 Papilion Rd

7

E7
1 Hospital La
2 Hospital Rd
3 Keble Cl
4 Silvanus Cl

8

COLCHESTER ROAD B1508

Armoury Road

Armoury Farm

A1211

BRAISWICK

Braiswick

B1508

BERGHOLT RO

Tufnell Wy

Lexden Lodge

Westhouse Farm

The Chase Way

A133

A12(T)

Lexden

CYMBELINE WAY (COLCHESTER BY-PASS)

Colchester Institute

COLCHE

CYMBELINE WAY (COLCHESTER BY-PASS)

Kingswode Hoe Special School

LEXDEN

LEXDEN ROAD

A1124

Colchester County High School for Girls

Council Offices

St Benedicts College

The Philip Morrant School

MALDON

DRURY ROAD

B1022

A

B

218

C

D

E

J5, K5
Street names for these grid squares are listed at the back of the index

Shrub End

1 grid square represents 500 metres

Colchester 187

F2
1 Greenacres

F3
1 Golden Dawn Wy

F4
1 Chiltern Cl
2 Wycliffe Gv

F5
1 John Harper St
2 Orchard Rd

G5
1 Kings Head Ct

H1
1 Ridgeway Va Vw

H7
1 Charles St
2 James St

J2
1 Briarwood End
2 Harebell Cl
3 West View Cl

J6
1 Old Coach Rd

K1
1 Bilsdale Cl
2 Cotswold Ct
3 Gazelle Ct
4 Hallcroft Cha

K2
1 St Bart Cl
2 Spring Cl

K6
1 Kerry Ct

K7
1 Farrington Cl
2 Geoff Seaden Cl
3 Spurgeon St
4 Standard Rd
5 Timber Hl

G7, G8, H5, I1
Street names for
these grid squares
are listed at the
back of the index

F6, F7, G3, G6
Street names for
these grid squares
are listed at the
back of the index

Mile End

Abbey Field

The Hythe

155

188

219

A4
1 Bridgebrook Cl

A3
1 St Saviour Cl

A2
1 Glentress Cl
2 Rockingham Cl

A

B

156

C

D

E

Ardleigh Reservoir

A5
1 Aspen Wy
2 William Boys Cl

1

Fen Farm

Fox Street

Moze Hall

A6
1 The Chase

2

A7
1 Berrimans Cl

Shaw's Farm

9

3

B3
1 St Thomas Cl

Parsons Heath Primary School

Roach Vale Primary School

Welshwood Park

Crockleford Hill

Wilson Road

4

Parson's Heath

Parsons Heath Medical Practice

Roach Vale Primary School

187

Bromley Road

Hazelmere Junior School

Sir Charles Lucas School

Chun Wood

5

B4
1 Paul Spendl've Ct
2 Royal Ct
3 Woodside Cl

Greenstead Clinic

6

B6
1 Chase Ct
2 Cyril Child Cl
3 Tamarisk Wy
4 Willingham Wy

St Andrews County Junior School

Hawthorn Surgery

University of Essex

Greenstead

Hythe Station

7

THE HILL

B7
1 Alf Eounder Cl
2 Purcell Cl
3 Rochdale Wy
4 Sullivan Cl

8

C5
1 Peregrine Ct
2 Turnstone End
3 Woodpecker Cl

Kendall Primary School

Colne Causeway

A133 SAINT ANDREW'S AVENUE

COLCHESTER RD B1027

The Hythe

A

B

220

C

University

D

D5
1 Fulmar Cl
2 Nightingale Cl

D6
1 Cardinal Cl

E

F G H **157** J K

I7
1 Oatlands

Martells
Industrial
Estate

Slough Lane

**Burnt
Heath**

Chancery
Farm

ROAD

B1029

Mill Lane

Briar

ARDLEIGH ROAD

Park Road

Park
Farm

Hull
Farm

Slough
Farm

Ardleigh
Park

Road

Colchester

2

Jubilee

Lane

A120

Bromley Road

Colchester

Back Road

Collierswood
Farm

3

ckleford
th

Road

Wivenhoe

4

A120

190

†

Elmstead

5

Allen's
Farm

Parsonage
Farm

Church Road

6

Lodge
Farm

Tye

Road

Hollytree

Elmcroft

Church Road

**El stead
Market**

7

The Chase

Blossomwood
Farm

Way
Hornsey
Hawthorn
Flatt
Close
Wheatlands
Meadow

Close

Lucerne Road

Johnson's Cl

School Road

Jupe's Close

Bromley

Elmstead

Road

Clacton

ROAD

Tye
Farm

Fen
Farm

Chapel Lane

COLCHESTER ROAD

A133

Elmstead
Market
Surgery

Beth
Chatto
Garden

Clacton

8

Park
Farm

Market
Field
School

School Road

F G H **221** J K

C6
Street names for
this grid square are
listed at the back of
the index

B1027

Grove
Farm

F G H **159** J K

I

2

3

4

192

5

6

7

8

F G H **223** J K

Braham Hall

Mulley's Farm

Spratts Lane

Church Road

Spratts Lane

Bentley Road

Payne's Lane

Hilliards Road

Welham's Farm

Bentley Road

Red House Farm

A120(T)

A120(T)

Byes Farm

Stone Road

Park Farm

The Chase

Little Bromley Road

The Oaks

Chase Road East

Park Road

Kirkham Road

Rectory Road

Church

Mary Lane North

A120(T)

A120(T)

Clip Hedge Farm

Harwich Road

Fairfield

Chase Road West

Mary Lane South

East

A133

are reen

Raven's Green

Chapel Lane

Furze Lane

Balls Green

Paynes Farm

Rowherns Lane

COLCHESTER ROAD

Warren's

Harwich

F **G** **H** 161 **J** **K**

Wix
Lodge

Carnsey Lane

A120(T)

Colchester

Clayhall

Clayhall

Claton Road

I

Spring
Farm

Green

Honeypot Lane

Dengewell
Hall

2

Colchester Road

Frith's Farm

Tendring Road

Colchester Road

Block Farm

Brocketts
Hall

3

Stones

Stones

Stonehall Lane

Stonehall Farm

Clacton Road

4

Wolves Hall Lane

Stonehall Lane

Higher
Barn Farm

194

Skighaugh

Tendring Green

Wolves
Hall Farm

5

Tendring
Lodge

6

**Goose
Green**

Church Farm

Lodge Lane

Lucas's Lane

Tendring
CP School

7

B1035

Swan Road

Pond Farm

School Road

8

THE STREET

Hollyview Close

Hannam's
Hall

Tendring

THORPE   ROAD   B1035

New
Hall

The
Mill

F **G** **H** 225 **J** **K**

Manor House

Crow Lane

TENDRING

Mitchell Lane

Bradley Hall

F G H 163 J K

Great Oakley

I
2
3
4
196
5
6
7
8

Sparrow's Farm
The
Great Oakley
B1414
CLAC
B1414
HIGH HARWICH RD B1414
Partridge Cl
olt Farm
Back Lane
Farm Road
Mosses Farm
Lane
BEAUMONT ROAD
CROSS HILL
Moze Cross
Old Moze Hall
New Moze Hall
B1414
lland
Dock Lane
pper's Island

F G H 227 J K

White Home

F   G   H   **165**   J   K

1

2

3

Pennyhole
Bay

4

5

Stone
Marsh

6

7

• Nature
Reserve

8   The
Naze

F   G   H   **229**   J   K

Hedge-end
Island

Walton Channel

Walton
Hall

Hazel End
F6
1 Fuller Ct
2 The Old Maltings

F7
1 Great Eastern Cl
2 Station Rd

Bishop's Stortford **199**

F
G
H
167
J
K

I

F8
1 Kimberley Cl

Essex County
Hertfordshire County

Gipsy Lane
Hazelend Road
Foresthall Road
Forest Hall
Church
CM2
Foresthall Rd
The Mountfitc School

A120
STANSTED ROAD

Parsonage Farm Industrial Estate

2

G4
1 Gatwick Cl

MICHAELS ROAD
RED WHITE AND BLUE ROAD
The Aspens
B1004

Stort Valley Industrial Estate
Oaklands Pk
Aynsley Av
Ashby Rise
Cavell Avenue
Heath Row
Hillmead JMI School
Heath
Birchwood Wood Lane
Birchanger Lane

Birchanger

Hall Farm

3

H5
1 The Copse

Cannons Mill Lane
Millcroft
Mill
B1383
Cannons Rd
Cannons Cl
Orchard Road
Heath
Prestwick Drive
Rochford Road
Manston Dr
Blackbushe
Cannell Court
Fullers Row
Woodlands
High View
Birchwood High School
A120

Duck End

Blacklands

4
200
M11

5
A120

STANSTED ROAD
Stortford Rd
Dolphin Way
Legions Way
Kings Court
Foxley Cl
Parsonage Lane
Middle & Infant School
Rise Hall
Raw Hatch
Play Ho
Play Ho
Raynham Rd Ind Est
Summercroft Junior & Infant School
A1250
Mayes Cl
Maze Green
Woodlands
DUNMOW ROAD
Cecil Cl
Birchanger Green Service Area
A120
Junction 8
6
Junction 8

Manor Road
Hockerill Anglo European School
Stortford Hall Industrial Park
Elm Rd
Links Business Centre
Norton
Manor
Golf Course

7
M11

A1184
LONDON RD
Bishop's Stortford Station
DUNMOW RD
A1250
Urban Rd
Church Manor
Warwick
Grange Road
Hertfordshire Road
Havercroft
Hertfordshire & Essex High School
Hertfordshire & Essex General Hospital
Leggs Lane
Hertfordshire County
Essex County

Hockerill
Avenue Rd
Prinfield
Thorn Gv
Thorn Grove Primary School
Highfield Av
Fairway
Rosebery Av
Greenway
Belgrave
Beldams Lane

B1383
Dimsdale Cr
Beldams Ln
Hockerill Sports Club
Rhodes Museum & Commonwealth Centre
A1060
Jenkins La

F
Twyford Business Centre
G
Jenkins Lane
HALLINGBURY
H
232
J
Great Hallingbury
K

Twyford Cl
Haslemere
B1383

K5
1 Beech Cl

K6
1 Elm Close Ext
2 Prior's Wood Rd

F G H **169** J K

I

2

3

202

4

5

6

7

8

F G H **234** J K

Waltham
Hall

Stansted Airport
Station
London Stansted
Airport

Montessori
School

High House

COOPERS END
ROUNDABOUT

Coopers End Rd

Bassingbourn Rd

Thremhall Avenue

Long Border Rd

BASSINGBOURN
ROUNDABOUT

Thirtieth
St

Pinkly Road

Old House
Farm

Parsonage Way

Harcamlow Way

Harcamlow Way

Warish Hall
Farm

Takeley

**Brewer's
End**

Garnetts

North Rd

South Rd

Roseacres

Takeley
GM Primary
School

Elm Cl

St
Valery

Longcroft

Jack's

Warren
Cl

**Smith's
Green**

Church Lane

Chestnut Ww

Millers

CM22

A120

A120

**Takeley
Street**

Flitch Way

DUNMOW ROAD

A120

Hatfield
Park

Hatcamlow Way

STATION ROAD

B183

Three Forests Way

Great
Canfield
Park

Great Canfield

Takeley Business
Centre

Sycamore Cl

Canfield Hart

202

MOLEHILL GREEN ROUNDABOUT

Ⓐ Ⓑ 170 Ⓒ Ⓓ Ⓔ

Wittham Hall
The Grange

1

River Roding

Coopers Lane

2

Bamber's Green

3

Sheering Hall

Fanns

4

Harcamlow Way

Warish Hall Farm

Frogs Hall Farm

201

Little Canfield Hall

5

Takeley GM Primary School

Roseacres

North Rd
South Rd

Jack's Lane

Warren Cl

Clarendon Rd

Warwick Road

Hamilton Road

Thornton Road

PH

6

Smith's Green

Chestnut W
Elm Cl
Sycamore Cl

Broadfield Road

DUNMOW ROAD   A120

Fitch Way

Fitch Way

A120

Church Lane

Ca
End

DUN. ROAD
A120

St Johns Industrial Estate

Takeley Business Centre

Great Canfield Park

7

Great Canfield Road

STATION ROAD

B185

8

Bullocks

Hope End Green

Puttock's End

Ⓐ   **235**   Ⓒ   Ⓓ   Ⓔ
Ⓑ

Cow Common

Coldha
Farm

Canfield Hart

1 grid square represents 500 metres

F G H 171 J K

I

2

3

4

204

5

6

7

8

Maysland

Street

Park Road

Limbridge

Park Road

†

Ravens Farm

Newton Hall

Easto Lodge

Little Ea

Glebe Lane

Butcher's Pasture

Woodside Way

Larch Way

Park Drive

New

XTFORD ROAD

Folly Farm

Stone Hall

High Wood

Strood Hall

ROAD A120

Fitch Way

Burrows Lane

Fitch Way

Hale's Farm

East

Lane

Cross

High

Lane

Langthorns

Minchins

Newlands

Great Oddyns

Tanners

Bedfords

Pharisee House

Pharisee Green

B184

F G H 236 J K

Baconend

E6
1 Timbers Cl

C4
1 Symmons Cl

C3
1 Blyth's Wy
2 Makemores
3 Philips Cl

A

B

176

C

D

E

I

E7
1 Cuckoo Wy
2 Elsham Dr
3 Highclere Rd
4 Penshurst Pl

2

E8
1 Elder Fld
2 Great Notley Av
3 Stanstrete Fld

3

Old Hall

Moor's Farm

Moors Lane

Pound Farmhouse

Duckend Green

Shalford Road

Pods La

Rayne CP School

Capel
Brunwin Road
Elm Walk

Fyside

Rayne

Shalford Road

The Maltings

Rayne Road

Broadfields Farm

The Street

Station Rd

Hance Lane

Gore Lane

Gore Rd

Flitch Way

4

Dunmow Road

Enterprise Trading Estate

Kidder Rd
Warner Close
The Ruskins

New Leyfields

Hall La

New Road

Queenborough Lane

Naylinghurst

A120

207

Fenton's Farm

Draper's Chase

School Road

Long Lane

Great Notley

A131

5

Draper's Farm

6

Bartholomew Green

A131

7

Blackley's Farm

Milch Lane

8

Molehill Green

Road

A

Welwyn Road

B

Main

241

C

Willows Green

D

E

Blackley Lane

Young's End

1 grid square represents 500 metres

Braintree 209

F3
1 Birch Cl
2 Fresian Cl

F6
1 Clevedon Cl
2 Colville Cl
3 Framlingham Wy
4 Harnham Dr
5 Langdale

F7
1 Crummock Cl
2 Grasmere Cl

F8
1 Great Notley Av

G6
1 Springmead
2 Thirlmere Cl

H2
1 Ash Bungalows
2 Bunyan Rd
3 Oak Bungalows

H3
1 Chestnut Gv
2 The Kentings

I2
1 Hills Cl
2 St Peter's Cl

J3
1 Bernside
2 Clairmont Cl
3 Collins Cl
4 New St
5 Strudwick Cl

J4
1 Driberry Wy

J5
1 Newton Cl
2 Tennyson Cl

K1
1 Bawn Cl
2 Rutland Gdns

K2
1 John Ray St
2 Maltings Vw

K3
1 Groomside
2 Jacquard Wy
3 Rose Gdns
4 Skitts Hl

K6
1 Galsworthy Cl
2 Johnson Cl
3 Marlowe Cl

K4, K5
Street names for
these grid squares
are listed at the
back of the index

H1, H5, J2, J4
Street names for
these grid squares
are listed at the
back of the index

Bocking

Braintree

Row
Green

Black

212

Old Road

Coll Road

A **B** **180** **C** **D** **E**

Pattiswick Hall

Boathouse Road

Church Road

Pattiswick

Hovells Farm

1

2

Holfield Grange

COGGESHALL ROAD A120

Coggeshall Road

Whiteshill Farm

Watery Lane

3

Church Road

River Blackwater

Grigg's Farm

Eves Ct

4

Bradwell Hall

Essex Way

211

Essex Way

Essex Way

Curd Hall Farm

5

Gosling's Farm

Herons Farm

Cuthedge Lane

6

Haywards

7

Woodhouse Farm

Sheepcotes Farm

Allshot's Farm

Sheepcotes Lane

8

SILVER END

Daniel Way

Storey's Wood

A **B** **245** **C** **D** **E**

1 grid square represents 500 metres

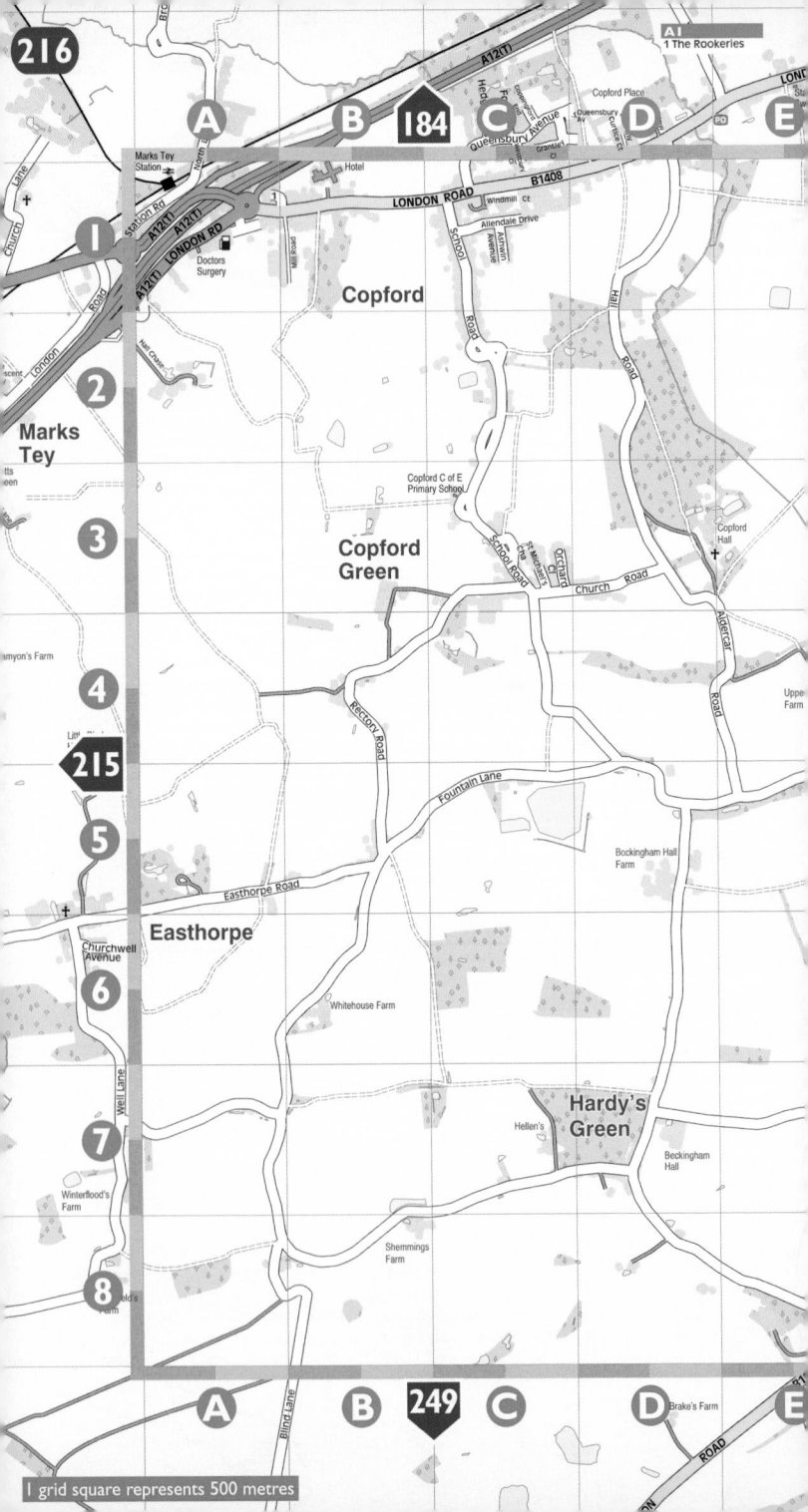

H1
1 Harwood Cl
2 Maple Wy
3 Sandringham Dr
4 Tedder Cl

H2
1 Crosstree Wk
2 Silverthorne Cl
3 Snowberry Gv

187

F bey Field

G

H

J

K

The Hythe

I

H3
1 Armidale Wk
2 Tamworth Cha

2

H4
1 Bathurst Cl
2 Beeleigh Cl
3 Canberra Cl
4 Inworth Wk
5 Middlewick Cl
6 Stansted Rd

3

H5
1 Blenheim Dr
2 Friday Wood Gn
3 Hetherington Cl
4 Lethe Gv

4

220

5

H6
1 Maraschino Crs
2 Merton Ct
3 Prunus Ct

6

J1
1 Brittany Wy
2 Tarragona Ms
3 Tortosa Cl
4 Wetzlar Cl

7

J2
1 Sargeant Cl
2 Waterville Ms

8

J3
1 Mackay Ct

Old Heath

Berechurch

Blackheath

F

G

H

252

J

K

K2
1 Pembroke Cl
2 Swallowdale

J6
1 Garrod Ct
2 Marasca End

J4
1 Fremantle Rd

220

THE QUAY

188

D3
1 Buddleia Ct
2 Rossetta Cl
3 Saran Ct
4 Tolliday Cl

SAINT

ANDRE

C5
1 Ashurst Cl

AVE

A3
1 Fingr'hoe Rd

COLCHESTER RD B1027

A   **B**   **C**   **D**   **E**

COLNE CAUSEWAY

The Hythe

University of Essex

New Quay

Kendall Primary School

I

Distillery Lane

Old Ho

D5
1 Darkhouse La

Haven Road

Commerce Way

Wivenhoe Lodge

Boundary Road

Abbot's Road

Old th **2**

O'Arcy Road

Grange Way Business Park

Grange Park Industrial Estate

Whitehall Industrial Estate

Broomgrove County Infant & Junior Scho

Grove

D6
1 Stephen Cranfield Cl

Primary School

Cottage Drive

Chaney Road

Broom

Heath

3

Speedwell Road

Rowhedge Road

Foxglove Road

Spring Chase

Rosabelle Ave

E3
1 Broome Gv
2 Cracknell Cl
3 Grasby Cl
4 Sonell Ct

Cleavelands

Parkwood Avenue

Fingringhoe Road

Donyland Lodge

4

Road

Battleswick Farm

Woodlands Way

219

Rowhedge

Marsh

Wivenhoe Station

Sharon Ce Complemen Health Ce

5

Hill View Close

Rowhedge Surgery Head Street

Cogne Rise

Church Street

Rowhedge Ferry

STATION

E5
1 Alma St
2 Bath St
3 Blythe La
4 Chapel Rd
5 Falcon Yd
6 Malting Yd
7 Rebow Rd

Road

Primary School

Church

Paget Road

Church Street

Roman River

Ferry

6

Cemetery

E6
1 Anchor Hl
2 Quay St
3 Rose La

Weir Lane

East Donyland Hall

7

Wetch Brook

Holmw Farm

8

Fingringhoe C of E School

Abberton Road

Fingringhoe

West House Farm

Furneaux La

Haye Farm

A   **B**   **C**   **D**   **E**

253

Plane Hall Farm

Jaggers

I grid square represents 500 metres

A6
1 De Staunton Cl

A5
1 Ash Rd
2 Bramley Cl
3 Chestnut Rd

A **B** 190 **C** **D** **E**

Morehams
Hall

1
Troys
Farm

Bottles
Hall

CLACTON
ROAD
A133

Park
Farm

2

FRATING HILL A133
MAIN

Frating
Lodge

3

Church Road

Blue
Gates

Frating

4
Cockaynes Lane

221

Rectory Road

Hockley
Farm

Hockley
Place

Cockaynes

5

B1027
High Road
Cooper's Road
Drews Road
Cox Road

Alresford
Business
Centre

Tenpenny
Farm

Alresford
Alresford Station

Laxton Road
Masons Road

Crestlands

Poplar

Tenpenny Brook

B1027 SAINT OSYTH ROAD

Wivenhoe Road
Furze Cr

6
Church Road
St Andrews

Alresford
Primary
School

Brook
Farm

7

Ford Lane

Sixpenny Brook

Alresford
Hall

TENPENNY HILL

B1027

8
Alresford
Lodge

Tenpenny
Heath

Brick Kiln Lane

The
Ford

A **B** 255 **C** **D** **E**

Plumpton's
Farm

Thors
Farm

B1029

F8
1 Honeysuckle Wy

J4
1 Wren Cl

Raven's Green

F Balls Green

G

H 191

J

K

I

K5
1 Laburnum Cl
2 New Cut
3 Sycamore Pl

2

3

4

224

5

6

7

8

Chapel Lane
e Lane

Paynes Farm

Rowherns Lane

COLCHESTER ROAD   A133   COLCHESTER ROAD

Toxley Road
Franc

A133

Crabtree
Farm

Frating
Green

Mannings

The Cedars
Farm

Ivy
Lodge

The
Grange

Admiral's Fa

Heckfords Road

BT029

Slough House
Farm

Brook Farm

Sturrick Farm

Moors Close

LANE

Great

Bentley

Road

Bentley Brook

Sturrick Lane

Finch
Clo
Larkfie
Linn
Close
Robin
Cher Wood
The Farm

Rd

Doctors Surgery

Thorrington   Road

**Great
Bentley**

Plough   Road

Avenue
Cedar Wk

Birch

Lufkins
Farm

Great   Bentley   Road

PO
Maltin

Great Bentley
CP School

Station Road

Great Bentley
LC Station

Kleine
Court

LC

Frating Abbey

Frating   Abbey   Farm   Road

Plough   Road

Whitehouse
Farm

Thorrington

Church   Road

Court   Drive
and

CLACTON ROAD

Weeley Rd

Colles Brook Road

Aingers Green

Road

Colles Brook Road

F

G

H 256

J

K

B1027   CLACTON

The
Lodge

A | B | 192 | C | D | E

Bentley Hall

1

Gurnhams

Church Rd

Warren's Farm

Bentley Lane

Crown Lane

Brett's Hall

LCHESTER ROAD

2

A133

COLCHESTER ROAD

The Grange

3

Heckfords Road

Fisher's Farm

Admiral's Farm

CO

A133

4

Moors Cl

Shair Lane

223

Swallow's Row

Doctors Surgery

5

Avenue

Cedar Wd

Birch

Weeley Road

Risby's Farm

A133

Plough Road

Station Road

Great Bentley Station LC

Kenton Court

6

St Mary's Farm

The Tye Road

Lover's Lane

7

Tye Homestead

Coppice Farm

Aingers Green

8

Weeley Rd

Colles Brook Road

Plough Road

Aingers

Green

Moynes Farm

Road

Wick

Road

Bentley Road

Road

College Farm

A | B | 257 | C | D | E

The Lodge

St Osyth Wick Farm

I grid square represents 500 metres

Walton-on-the-Naze 229

F5
1 Ockendon Wy
2 Pulpitfield Cl

F6
1 Little Bakers
2 Rochford Wy

197

The Naze

G5
1 Brian Bishop Cl
2 Cartbridge Cl
3 The Ridge
4 Warde Cha

G6
1 Hervilly Wy

H4
1 North St

H6
1 Southcliff

I3
1 Hamford Cl
2 High Tree La
3 Tudor Cl

D6, E6, H5
Street names for these grid squares are listed at the back of the index

K3
1 Spendells Cl

J5
1 Kino Rd
2 The Parade
3 Stratford Pl

F1
1 Armourers Cl

G1
1 The Carpenters
2 Chandlers Cl
3 Drovers Wy
4 Ostler Cl
5 Shepherds Cl
6 Wheelwrights Cl

198

H1
1 Irving Cl

H2
1 Mayfield Pk
2 The Paddock

I1
1 Elmbrook Dr
2 Wheat Cft

232

K2
1 The Green

Haselmere Industrial Estate

Twyford Business Centre

Doctors Surgery

Richard Whittington JMI School

Havers Infant School

The Bishop's Stortford High School

Grace Gdns

Hayley Bell Gdns

Pamela Gdns

Bishop's Avenue

Thorley Street

Highland Road

Hawthorn Rise

Hertfordshire Way

Thorley

Moor Hall

Church Lane

St James Way

Thorley Wash

Brookside Business Centre

Dell Lane

Spellbrook

Spellbrook Lane East

Spellbrook JMI School

Bursteads

Newhouse Farm

Trims Green

Shingle Hall

Tednambury Farm

Tharbies

Parsonage Farm

Clarklands Industrial Estate

Cemetery

263

Northfield Rd

Walnut Tree Avenue

LONDON ROAD

A1184 ST JAMES WAY

199

A B C D E

B5
1 The Beadles

A1
1 Mitre Gdns

Jenkins La

Great
Hallingbury

Twyford
Business
Centre

Jenkins
Lane

The Bishop's
High School

Grace Gdns

Hayley Bell
Gdns
Pamela
Gdns

Thorley Lane
Way

Highland
Road

Hawthorn
Rise

Thorley
Wash

Brookside

231

Spellbrook
Lane East

Spellbrook
CP School

Cemetery

LONDON ROAD

HALLINGBURY ROAD

Haselmere
Industrial
Estate

Bishop's
Park

Lane

Hall
Farm

Church Road

Anvil
Cross

Howe Green
House
School

Howe Gr

Latchmore
Bank

Port Lane

LATCHMORE BANK

Normandale
Farm

New Barn Lane

New Barn Lane

Hallingbury
Close

Spradles

Dell Lane

Dell Lane

Little Hallingbury
C. of E
Primary School

Wright's
Green

Little
Hallingbury

Goose Lane

Sutton
Acres

Gaston
House

Gaston
Green

Tednambury
Farm

Old Mill Lane

Little
Bursteads

Grinstead
Lane

Sawbridgeworth Road

Sawbridgeworth Road

LOWER ROAD A1060

Wright's
Green

Mott's
Green

Three Forests Way

M11

Little
Hallingbury Hall

South House

A B C D E

264

Three Forests Way

Stor
Hall

Great Hyde

1 grid square represents 500 metres

Hatfield
Forest NT

Bedlar's
Green

Beggar's Hall

F　**G**　**H**　**200**　**J**　**K**

Three Forests Way

I

Hallingbury
Street

Forest
Lodge

Collins
Coppice

2

Little Barrington
Hall Farm

Three Forests Way

Forest Way

Lädywell

Lodge
Farm

3

Wall
Wood

4

The
Woods

odside
n

Three Forests Way

234

Forest
Hall

Forest
Farm

5

Monk's
Wood

ose Lane

6

The
Marsh

Three Forests Way

Lane

Forest Way

Ryes

7

ury

FEATHERS HILL

OLD STREET HILL

8

Town
Farm

Corringales

F　**G**　**H**　**265**　**J**　**K**

Camp
Farm

B183

Bullocks

Hope End Green

Puttock's End

F G H 202 J K

Copt Hall

High Cross Lane

Coldharbour Farm

Cow Common

I

Canfield Road

Great

Cuckoo Lane

Green Street

Deal Tree Farm

Ashfield Farm

Ashfield Club House

Bury Farm

2

3

Hellman's Cross

Black Hall

Grange Farm

Canfield Cricket Club

4

Whiteheads

Boxley Lane

236

Great Canfield

5

Marsh Farm

Woolard's Ash

6

Broomshawbury

7

High Rodingbury Farm

8

New Hall

F G H 267 J K

Poplars Farm

F   G   H   204   J   K

Trutons
Clapton Hall

Broadgroves

Puttocks

Barnston   I

Coopers
Mountains Road

Martels

High Easter Road   2

Mountains Farm

Wellstye Green   3

Rofley

Sallets Green

Garnetts Wood   4

238

Bishops Green

Garnetts   5

Mudwall

6

County Farm

Barnfield

Poplar   7

Peakins

Maidens

Chimballs   Bushbarns

8

F   G   H   269   J   K

Greens Farm

Upper Harveys

H6
1 Bohun Cl
2 Bolingbroke Cl
3 Helen How
4 Rich Cl

J6
1 Fortune Cl

F **G** **H** **208** **J** **K**

Willows
Green

Young's
End

Great Siamseys

I

Friar
Farm

Dannets Lane

Lynderswood F

2

Evelyn Road

Main Road

Blackley Lane

LONDON ROAD

Bushy
Wood

3

Gate
Farm

Moulsham Hall Lane

Dunmey Lane

Moulsham
Hall

Moulsham Hall Lane

Essex
Agricultural
Showground

Varren Park
Farm

4

Banters

242

Breams
Farm

Dunmey Lane

A1131 ROAD

Gubbion's
Hall

Gu bion's
Green

5

Rectory Lane

School Lane

Great
Leighs

Mill Lane

6

A131 ROAD

Aragon Road

Woodview
Drive

Great Leighs
CP School

MAIN ROAD

Boreham Road

Rochester
Farm

Castle Close

Boreham Road

Bishop's
Hall
Farm

7

Whites Lane

Church Lane

Catherines

Hill Lane

Poulk

Little
Leighs

Essex Way

Braintree Rd

8

THE CRESCENT

STRAWBROOK HILL

Goodmans

Essex Way

Liberty
Farm La

White Feath

A131

Lowley's
Farm

Lyons
Hall

Cole

River

F **G** **H** **273** **J** **K**

Hawbush
Green

A
B
C
D
E

Bloomfield

Weaverdale

Francis Court

Runnacles St

SIL
EN

Manors Way

Silver Street

Broadway Court

France Way

Police Stn

Daniel Wks

Abraham Dr

PO

Doctors Surgery

Valentine Way

School Road

Bowes Rd

Primary School

Essex Way

B1018

Pettit Lane

Church Road

Polecat Crescent Close

Essex Way

WITHAM ROAD

Temple Lane

Magdalene Crescent

2

White Notley Station

Fambridge Hall

Fambridge Cha

Station Rd

LC

Cressing Temple

Essex Way

Temple Lane

WITHAM ROAD

3

Primary School

Church Rd

Vicarage

4

243

Essex Way

Hungry Hall

Whitehead's Farm

5

Maltings Farm

Church Hill

nk Lane

Oak Farm

Hole Farm

CRESSING ROAD B1018

6

Faulkbourne

River Brain

7

†

8

Troys Farm

Home Farm

Warren Farm

Ebenezer Close

A
B

C
D
E

WITHAM

Honeysuckle

Corner Close

Byrony Close

Flora

Bramble Road

F G H **216** J K

Lower Road
Birch

Brake's Farm

Birch C of E
School

I

B1022

MALDON ROAD

Cadter Lane

School Lane

2

Luard Way

Mill Lane

Birch Street

Straight Way

3

Palmer's Farm

Blind Lane

B1022

Roundbush Farm

Smythe's Green

Roundbush Road

Duke's Farm

Winter's Road

Winter's Road

4

Lower

250

Road

5

Layer Marney Tower

Layer Marney

Wick Farm

Stockhouse Road

6

7

Layer Brook

8

Rockingham's Farm

Long Wood

Haye

Abberton Reservoir

Peldon

Peldon Lodge

Harvey's Farm

Moulsham's Farm

Copthall Grove

Sampson's

218

252

283

A   B   **219**   C   D   E

Abberton Road

Laver Road

1

Laver Road

Abberton Manor

Oxley Hill

Rectory La

Abberton

Oxley Hill

2

Laver Road

Fingringhoe Road

Edward

MERSEA

3

Peldon Road

Meadow Way

Bracken Way

Maze Drive

Pertwee Way

Doctor Close

Langenhoe Park

Langenhoe

Langenhoe CP School

Glebe House

4

Pete Tye Common

Crouch House Farm

251

Peldon Road

Pantile Farm

ROAD

5

Peldon Lodge

Peldon Road

Haxells Farm

Langenhoe Hall Lane

Langenhoe Hall

Lodge Lane

6

Peldon Road

Maling Road

Pete Hall

COLCHESTER

Peld**7**

St Ives Road

Church

ROAD

Lower

Road

8

Newpots Close

NEWPOTS

Mersea Road

Kemps Farm

Moor Farm

B1025

THE

A   B   **284**   C   D   E

Mersea Road

Fingringhoe
C of E
School

West
House
Farm

Abberton Road

Fingringhoe

F G H **220** J K

I

2

3

4

254

5

6

7

8

Plane Hall
Farm

Dudley
Road

South Green Road

South Green

Jaggers

South House
Farm

Lane

Fingringhoe
Marsh

Fingringhoe
Ranges

Wick Marsh

Wick

Langenhoe
Marsh

Langenhoehall
Marsh

Pyefleet Channel

Reeveshall
Marsh

Broad Fleet

Maydays
Marsh

F G H **285** J K

A B **221** C D E

I

Jaggers

Nature Reserve

Wick Lane

2

Aldboro
Point

3

Geedon
Saltings

River Colne

4
Marsh

◀ **253**

5

Geedon Creek

6
Langenhoe
Marsh

Rat
Island

7

Pewit
Island

Pyefleet Channel

8
Reeveshall
Marsh

Broad Fleet

A B **286** C D E

1 grid square represents 500 metres

1 grid square represents 500 metres

F G H 224 J K

1

2

3

4

5

6

7

8

F G H 289 J K

St Osyth

Collier Brook Rd

Angers

Green

Road

Wick

Road

Moynes Farm

Bentley Road

Highbirch Road

College Farm

St Osyth
Wick Farm

High
Birch

Maldon
Wood

Straight Road

South Heath Road

Wick Lane

Ampers Wick

Milton Wood

Highbirch Road

St Fanny's La.

Welches

Frowick Lane

Frowick Hall
Farm

Riddles
Wood

Heath Road

St Osyth
Heath

258

High
Grove

Clay Lane

HILL

Wellwick
Farm

COLCHESTER ROAD

Park Farm

Earls Hall

Lamb
Farm

Cemetery

B1027

Newton

GOLDING
WAY

Swinnick
Walk

Deeping
Way

Broadstrood

St Clair's
Dr

St Clair's Road

D'Arcy Road

Longfields

Clacton

Norman Ct

Johnson Road

Chapel La.

Mill
Street

The Bury

Church La.

St Osyth C of E

BYPASS ROAD

Pim Chase

Park Chase

Orchard Gdns

PUMP HILL

B1027

Mill Farm Lane

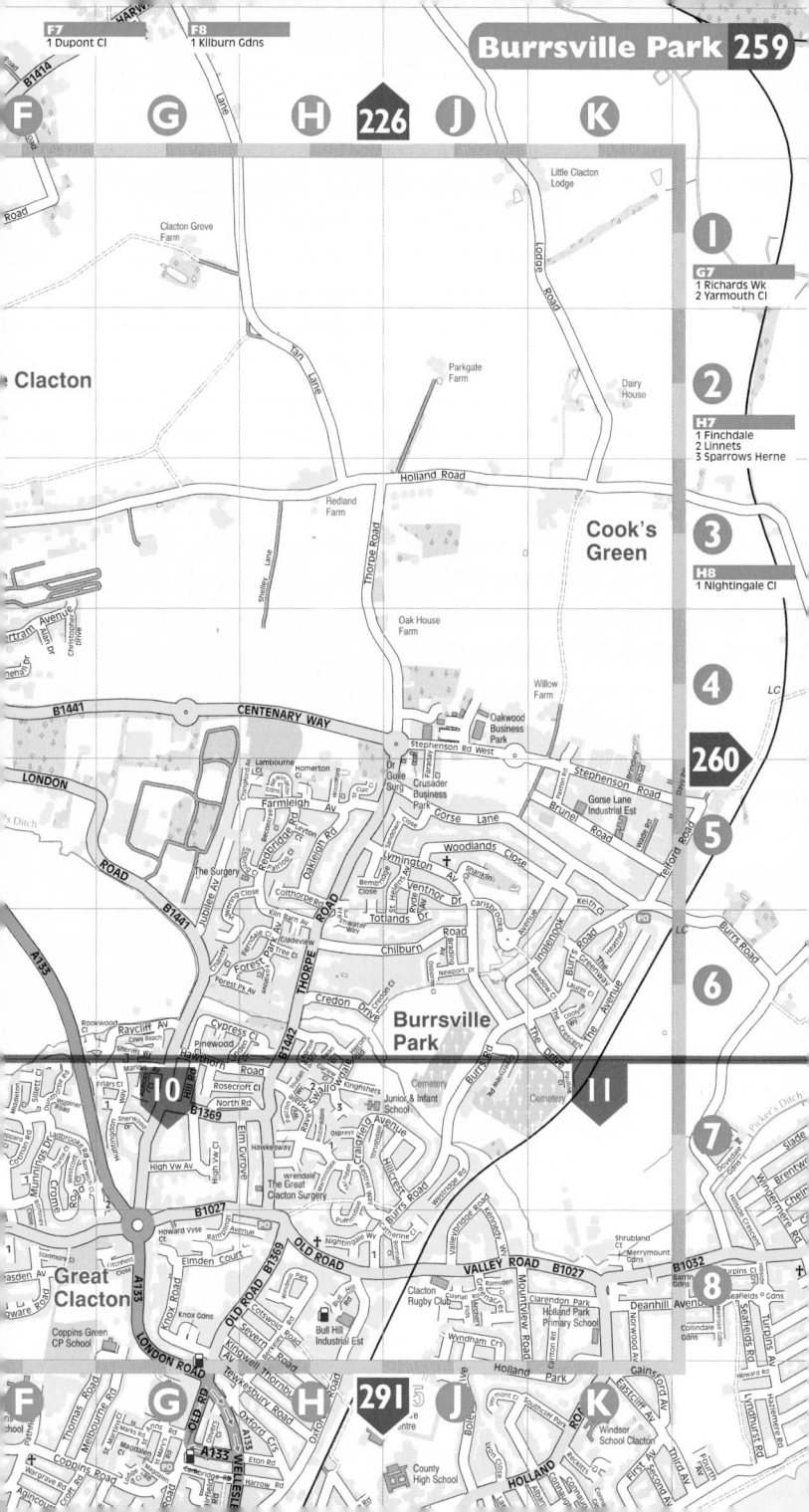

260

227

259

C8
1 Hereford Ct
2 Johnston Cl
3 Salisbury Rd

C7
1 Dorset Cl

C6
1 Devon Wy
2 Fleetwood Cl
3 Hucklesbury Av

I
D7
1 Bournemouth Rd
2 Hall Cl
3 Quilters Cl
4 Southview Dr
5 Sundale Cl

Little Clacton
Lodge

Great Holland

Holland Brook

Clacton   Road

Great Holland Common Road

Holland Brook

Co... s
Green

Willow
Farm

LC

Sladbury's Old
House

Pond
House

Gorse Lane
Industrial Est

Sladburys Lane

Burrs Road

LC

Pickers Way

Fleetwood   Avenue

Kent's Av

Norfolk

Briarwood   Drive

Aylesbury   Drive

Doctors
Surg

Primary
School

Haven Av

The
Esplanade

FRINTON ROAD

Weavers Ditch

Slade

Brentwood

Cheimsford

Colchester

The
Surgery

Frinton Road
Medical Cen

Grove Lodge
Surgery

Hereford

The
Parade

FRINTON ROAD

Shrubland
Ct

Merrymount
Gdns

B1032

Barrington
Gdns

Turpins Cl

Seafields Gdns

Collindale
Gdns

Preston

Bedford

Salisbury

Dulwich Rd

Madeira Rd

Canterbury   Road

Cliff Road

Kings

Holland-
on-Sea

B1027

Clarendon Park
Holland Park
Primary School

Park

Gainsford Av

Norwood Av

Deanhill Av

Avenue

Seafields Rd

Turpins Av

Kings

Madeira

Dulwich   Road

PO

Howard Rd

Windsor
School Clacton

1 grid square represents 500 metres

228

FRINTON-ON-SEA

Green End

Frinton On Sea CP School

Branscombe

Fifth Avenue

The Crescent

Upper Fourth Avenue

Glebe Way

Frinton Summer Thtr

Queen's Road

Hillside

Ashlyn's Rd

First Avenue

First

Second

Third

Fourth

Old Road

The Greensward

CROSS

CONNAUGHT

AVENUE

Harold Road

Harold Road

Cherry Tree Surg

Esplanade

Frinton On Sea Lawn Tennis Club

Holland

Avenue

Avenue

Hotel

Esplanade

Frinton Golf Club

Golf Course

Holland Gap

Sandy Point

Chevaux de frise Point

Holland Haven

Long Lane

Lane

ch Lane

F G H J K

I 2 3 4 5 6 7 8

F4
1 Blacksmiths Wy

G4
1 Durham Cl

Industrial Estate

Cemetery

F   G   H   231   J   K

The Leventhorpe School

CM21

Northfield Rd

Walnut Tree Avenue

Crofters End

West Road

Claylane Farm

Cutforth Road

West Road

SAWBRIDGEWORTH

Nursery Fields

CAMBRIDGE ROAD

LONDON ROAD

New Rd

The Gowan

Gallery Rowan Walk

Eversley College

Hoestock Road

Brook End

East Herts District Council

Sawbridge Health Clinic

Sheering

Sappers Close

Beechfield

Fairwat

The Thomas Rivers Medical Centre

High Wych

Newports

Wisemans Gardens

BONKS MILL ROAD

Hill Tree Close

Vantorts Close

Springhall Rd

Cedar Close

East Drive

Southbrook

HARLOW ROAD

Farnham Close

Mechford Drive

Hand

Rowney

Three Forests Way

Springhall Lane

Rowney Gardens

Pishiobury Park

Rowney Farm

Chaseways

Beech Lane

Oak Drive

Pishiobury Drive

Thomas Rivers Medical Centre

Redricks Lane

Rowneybury

Hertfordshire County

Essex County

CAMBRIDGE ROAD

A1184

Hart Road

Cibbard Garden

Aylmers Farm

Sarbir Industrial Park

Harlow Mill Station

Roman Vale

Priory Avenue

Harlowbury

Old Harlow

EDINBURGH WAY

Jocelyns

Old Field

St. John's

School

295

Watlington Road

Millhurst Mews

Sheering

F   G   H   295   J   K

G4
1 Buttersweet Ri
2 Merefield
3 Yewlands

Old Harlow Health Centre

Mulberry Green

Churchgate

Side panel (right)

I
G8
1 Edinburgh Wy

Sawbridgeworth Station

2
H2
1 Stoneleigh

The Maltings Industrial Estate

3
H3
1 Highgate Gv
2 Wimborne Cl

Lower Sheering

4

264
Newhouse

5
H4
1 Dale Ct
2 High Wych Rd

6
H7
1 Wheatfields

Durrington Hall

7
J2
1 The Mews
2 Riverfield La
3 Walnut Tree Crs

8
Campions

F G H **233** J K

OLD STREE

Town
Farm

I

Camp
Farm

Mill Lane

Home Pastures
Heath
Broomfields

Broomfields

Ongars

Lea
Hall

2

B183

ROAD

B1060

The Surgery
West Haven
Shaw

Clipped
Hedge

Hatfield Heath
CP School
Beehive Ct

**Hatfield
Heath**

Lancasters

CHELMSFORD   ROAD

3

Pond Lane

Park Drive

A1060

Barn
Copse   Hill
Farm

Matching Road

Friars Lane

**Ardley
End**

Friars

4

Friars Lane
Gibsons

266

Forest Way

Matching Road

Stort Valley Way

Forest Way

5

Sparrow's Lane

Parvilles

6

Hotel

Downhall Road

Forest Way

7

**Newman's
End**

Stort Valley Way

Stone
Hall
Farm

Kingstons
Farm

Manw
Gree

8

Collin's
Cross

F   G   H **297** J   K

Brick

Span

266

Town
Farm

STR

Primary
School
Cage End cr.
The
Surgery
Medlars Rd.
Cannons
Cage End
Elfield

Hatfield
d Oak

Needham
Green

Stanways

Anthonys

Philpotts

A   **B**   **C**   **D**   **E**

Pierce
Williams

Row
Wood

Three Forests Way

Lancasters

The
Paddocks

A1060

Barley
Close
Hill
Farm

Hatfield
Grange

265

Forest Way

St Martins
Close

rvilles

Sparrow's Lane

Kingstons

Manwood
Green

Waterloo
Farmhouse

Snows
Farm

Kingstons
Farm

Sparrow's
Lane

Anchor Lane

A   **B**   **C**   **D**   **E**

298

I grid square represents 500 metres

F G H **237** J K

Maidens

Yewtree

I

Chimballs

Bushbarns

Upper Harve

Greens Farm

2

Hopkins

Acrelane Green

The Street

Stagden Cross

3

Crabbs Close

Haydens

High Easter

Raylands

4

Lower House

Essex Way

270

Lowerhouse Farm

5

Harvoon's Lane

Elbows

Kingston

6

Bedfords

Clatterford End

Armours

7

Amadyes

Essex Way

Tye Green

Gurtons Farm

8

School Road

Mill Road

Good Easter

Souther Cross Road

Wares Road

F G H **301** J K

Wares

Little Newarks

Yewtree

Blunts

I

Upper
Harveys

2

Essex Way

Pleshey
Grange

Acreland
Green

Stag n
Cros 3

The Street

Grange Road

Raylands

Essex Way

4

Plesheybury

269

Linsteads

5

Baileys

Elbows

Ducker's Lane

6

Bedfords

Armours

Fridays

Bards
Hall

7

Barrack Road

Smallshoes

8

Gatehouse

Wares Road

Wares

A   B   302   †   C   D   E

Little
Newarks

Mashbury

I grid square represents 500 metres

F G H J K

Ringtail
Green

239

I

2

Mill Ho

3

Fitzandrew's
Farm

4

272

5

6

7

8

Rolphy
Green

Pleshey Road

Park
Farm

Croft Lane

Oak
Hall

Waltham
Bury

Essex Way

Fitzjohn's
Farm

High
Houses

Great
Waltham

Barrack Lane

Brook Me

School

Cherry Garden Road

Glebe

Queries

shbury Road

Israel's Farm

South

Humphrey's Farm Lane

Humphrey's
Farm

Breeds

Hoe Lane

Bro
Gree

Fanner's
Green

F G H J K

Beadle's
Hall

303

Wa
Fa

Partridgegreen

Dyers
Hall

F
G
H
241
J
K

Leighs

Essex Way

I

Lyons' Hall

River Ter

2

3

White House Farm

4

274

Noake' Farm

5

6
Drakes Lane
Drakes Lane Industrial Estate
Lawns Farm

7

8

F
G
H
305
J
K

Boreham Airfield

Lowley's Farm

Liberty Hall

atham een

Daisleys Lane

Lyonshall Wood

Wakering's Farm

Long's Farm

Great Storage Farm

Sheepcotes Farm

Alstead's Farm

Drake's Farm

Power's Farm

Wheeler's Hill

Peverel's Farm

A131 STRAWBROOK HILL
YE CRESCENT
Goodmans Lane
Essex Way
Cole Hill
Boreham Road
Leighs Road
Dunmer Lane
Drakes Lane
A130 ESSEX REGIMENT WAY
Pratts Farm Lane
Whiteheads Farm Lane
Brainтree

274

A   B   242   C   Road   D   E

Braintree Road

Essex Way

**Fuller
Street**

Lyons
Hall

River Ter

Boreham Road

Essex Way

Sandy
Wood

Three
Ashes
Farm

Ridley
Hall

Essex Way

2

3

White
House
Farm

Leyland's
Farm

Sparrow's
Farm

**Gamble's
Green**

Oakfield
Lane

Boreham Road

Pickering's
Farm

4

273

Noake's
Farm

Roll's
Farm

Waltham Road

Terling Hall Road

5

6

Lane

Drakes Lane
Industrial
Estate

Bird's
Farm

Lawn's
Farm

Boreham Road

Russell
Green

Ringer's
Farm

Drake's
Farm

7

Brent
Hall

8

Holts
Farm

A   B   306   C   D   E

Boreham
Airfield

Spence's Lane

Waltham

I grid square represents 500 metres

F G H 243 J K

Home Farm

I

2

Terlin

3

Dancing

4

276
Dancing Dicks

5

6

7

8

F G Berwick Place H 307 J K

Toppinghoe Hall

Great Loyes

Ivy Woo

Essex Way

Sandypits Farm

e Road

Terling

Terling C of E Primary School

Owl's Hill

man Hill

River

The Dismals

The Street

New Road

Crow Pond Road

Hatfield Road

Church Road

ack's een

Terling Place

Fairstead Road

Farding's Farm

Witham Road

Taylor's Farm

Witham Road

Hatfield Road

River Ter

Whitelands

Terling Hall Road

Terling Hall

Termitt's Farm

Termitt's Chase

Lost Wood

Terling Hall Road

Hatfield Wick

Terling Road

Hatfield Peverel Station

The Pines

Woodland

Marina Road

Ash Close

Station Road

BT137

BURTL

THE

STREET

St Andrew's

B12(T)

F1
1 Chippingdell
2 Southcote Rd
3 Taverners Wk
4 Templars Cl

F2
1 Chipping Hi
2 Earismead
3 Templemead
4 White Horse La

F3
1 Coach House Wy
2 Guithavon Ri
3 Nicholas Ct

F4
1 Orchards

F5
1 Denholm Ct
2 Maltings Ct

F6
1 Juvina Cl
2 Kinloch Cha

G1
1 Forest Rd
2 Laburnum Wy
3 Manor Rd
4 Spruce Cl

G3
1 Boone Pl
2 Du Cane Pl
3 Horner Pl
4 Lockram La
5 Mayland Rd

G4
1 Barley Flds
2 Blackman Wy

G5
1 Edinburgh Cl

G6
1 Gay Bowers Wy
2 Hodges Holt
3 Lichfield Cl
4 Sparkey Cl

H1
1 Acacia Gdns
2 Elderberry Gdns
3 Mulberry Gdns

E5, H3
Street names for these grid squares are listed at the back of the index

Little Braxted

Wickham Bishops

245

278

309

F G H J K

F
G
H
247
J
K

New Plantation

Grange Road

Ransom
Harrington Close

Rosemary Crs
Anthon
Pennsylvania Lane
B1022

MAL

Inworth Grange

I

Station
Saffron Wy 3
Corianc
Brook Mdws
Fr Cl
Spring Cl
Surrey Lane
Bull Lane

Tiptree Heath

Tiptree Heath CP School

BIRKIN Close

Parkers Close

2

West End Road

Simpsons Lane

Hall Road

Tiptree Hill

Priory Road

Stone Lane

Tiptree Lane

3

Tiptree Hill

Tiptree Priory

Braxted Road

B1022

xted

MALDON ROAD

Grove Farm Road

Loamy Hill Road

4

280

Grove Farm

5

Primrose Hill Farm

Daymens Hill Farm

Back House Road

6

Brickery Lane

Great Totham

Twitty Fee
Brickspring Lane
Spring Hill
Elm Way
Elton Way

7

Mount Pleasant

ROAD
Chapel Road

Mount Lodge Chase

Totham Hill Green

Plains Road

Totham Plains

Witham Road

7

Road

Totham Hill

Office Lane

The Street

8

Office Farm

Field View
Sawyer's

F
G
H
311
J
K

Chelmer
Priory Cls
Cross
Green Lane

Little Totham

Vine Farm

F   G   H   249   J   K

I

2

3

4

282

5

6

7

8

Rockingham's Farm

Long's Wood

Park Farm

noster

Park Lane

Barnhall Road

Gobolt's Farm

Barn Hall Farm

Barnhall Road

Rectory Road

Honeypot Lane

Blind Lane

High Hall

Hotel

Abbot's Wick Farm

Abbot

B1026

The

Salco -Virle

WHITEHOUSE HILL

B1026

Spital Farm

Bridge Farm

STATION ROAD

B1026

Colchester Road

KELVEDON ROAD

D'Arcy Gate

Limesbrook

Frame Farm

Tolleshunt D'Arcy

313

Salter's Meadow

NORTH STREET

Chapel Road

CHURCH ST

Festival Gdns

Tolleshunt Darcy C of E Primary School

B1023

TOL

Hill Farm

Beckingham Road

Cemetery

Guisnes Court

F   G   H   J   K

F G H 251 J K

I

Harvey's Farm

Newpots Close

Newpots Lane

Moulsham's Farm

Peldon Road

+

Lane

Copthall Grove

Sampson's Farm

Samps

2

gh

Chestnuts Farm

Little Wigborough

Peldon Road

Copt Hall Lane

New Hall

arm

3

Copt Hall Lane

4

284

Copt Hall

5

Abbots Hall Saltings

Copthall Saltings

Feldy Marshes

6

Quince's Corner

Salcott Channel

Little Ditch

7

Old Hall Marshes

8

Joyce's Head

Pennyhole Fleet

F G H 315 J K

E8
1 Kingsland Cl

E6
1 Langwood
2 Trinity Ms

Moor
Farm

D6
1 Cypress Ms

Kemps
Farm

A   B   252   C   D   E

Mersea   Road

Lane   THE

Mersea   New   Road

Newports   Close

Road

Newports
Close

1

Copthall
Grove

Sampson's
Farm

Sampson's   Lane   Newpots

STR

2

Bonner's
Saltings

3

Ray Island
Nature Reserve

Strood Channel

4

283

Sampson's
Creek

5

Feldy
Marshes

Dabchicks
Sailing
Club

Carriers Cl
The Lane

Brickhouse

Whittaker Wy

Woodfield
Drive

Colchester

Spruce

Cemetery

Mersea

Road

Lime
Grove

Upland

6

Little Ditch

Thorn
Fleet

Mersea
Fleet

Stonehill
Way

City Road

Firs Chase

St Peter's Road

Firs

Mersea Avenue

High Street North

7

Victory   Road

New
Captains
Road

Church Road

B1025   HIGH

Melrose Road

BARFI

Coast

WEST
MERSEA

Road

Mersies Community
& Sports Centre

Yorick

Pharos Lane

Grove Av

West Mersea
Museum

Meadow
Lane

8

Besom Fleet

Cobmarsh
Island

A   B   316   C   D   E

Mersea
Quarte.

Quarters
Spit

F6
1 Carrington Ct
2 Oakwood Gdns

F7
1 Birch Wood Cl
2 Goings La
3 Qu Anne Gdns
4 Richmond Rd
5 Thornwood Cl

G7
1 Queenbury Cl

253

286

317

286

254

A B C D E

1

Pyefleet Channel

Reeveshall Marsh

Broad Fleet

Reeves Hall

2

3

C05

285

East Road

Meeting Lane

PO

East Road

Fen Farm

East Road

Shop Lane

Broman's

East Mersea

Church Lane

4

Rewsalls Farm

5

6

Mersea Flats

7

8

A B C D E

I grid square represents 500 metres

F G H 255 J K

Westman Point

St Osyth Stone Point

East Essex Aviation Society & Museum

House

Nature Reserve

Mersea Stone

Grove Park

Brightlingsea Reach

Cindery Island

Brightlingsea Creek

Oyster Tank Sailing Club

Yacht Club

Colne Club

Promenade

Colne

New Way

Mersea

Oakm

Sandy Point

288

Ray Creek

F G H J K

I 2 3 4 5 6 7 8

Lamb Farm
Cemetery
B1027
Golding Way
Newton
Swinwick Walk
Deeping
Broadstrood
Castle
Longfield
Knicaid
Maysbrook
Rochford Road
Clacton
Doctors Surgery
Darcy Road
Carr's Road
Enfield Gdns
PUMP HILL
Abbots Gardens
B1027
Lodge Farm Lane
Earls Hall Farm

I

St Osyth
Mill Street
The Bury
church rd
Norman Cl
Chapel La
Spring Road
Brook Ave
St Osyth C of E Primary School
Daltes Lane
St Osyth Lodge Farm

2

Warren Farm
Brazier's Farm
Dalte Farm
St Church Wer Lane

3

Beach Road

4
Whyers Hall Farm
Cockett Wick Lane
Wigboro Wick Farm
Cockett Wick Farm

5

Osyth Marsh

6

Seawick
PO
Midway
Triumph Av
Starling Av
Osprey Av
Singer Av
Bower Av
Brooklands
Bentley Av
Morris Av
Hillman Av
Austin Av
Gdns
Black Av
Napier Av
Essex Av
Jedrea Av
Triumph Av
Brooklands

7
Ground
Club Parade
Lilac Av
Lilac Av
First Avenue
Third Av
Second Av
Rose Gdns
Promenade

8

257 290

D1
1 Aldeburgh Cl
2 Burstall Cl

C5
1 The Approach

C1
1 Bretten Cl
2 Felixstowe Cl
3 Flixton Cl
4 Linstead Cl
5 Thorndon Cl

Elm

A **B** **258** **C** **D** **E**

B1027

HILL

LOCK RD

Farm Road Drive

1

D2
1 Tanner Cl

St Osyth Farm

Rouses Farm

2

E1
1 Nien-oord

3

E2
1 Raglan Ms

4

289

Rockett Wick Farm

5

E5
1 Little Stone Ct
2 Lulworth Cl
3 Penzance Cl
4 Worthing Ms

6

E7

Promenade

7

8

Jaywick Lane

Rush Green

Rush Green Sports Centre

Clacton Airfield

Clacton On Sea Golf Club

Alton Park Lane

Seymour Road

Frobisher Drive

Miller's Barn Rd

Marlowe Road

Tudor Green

Park Square West

Belfry Way

Aragon Close

Crossways

Jaywick

Gorse Way

Fern Way

Broadway

Brooklands

Midway

Community Care & Health Centre

Frobisher Road Primary School

Tamarisk Way

Beach Way

Meadow Way

Golf Green Road

Crossway Way

Cornflower Way

Ravenscroft School

Saxmundham Way

Tyler Av

St John's Rd

Clare Way

Bockingham Grove

JOHN'S

A **B** **C** **D** **E**

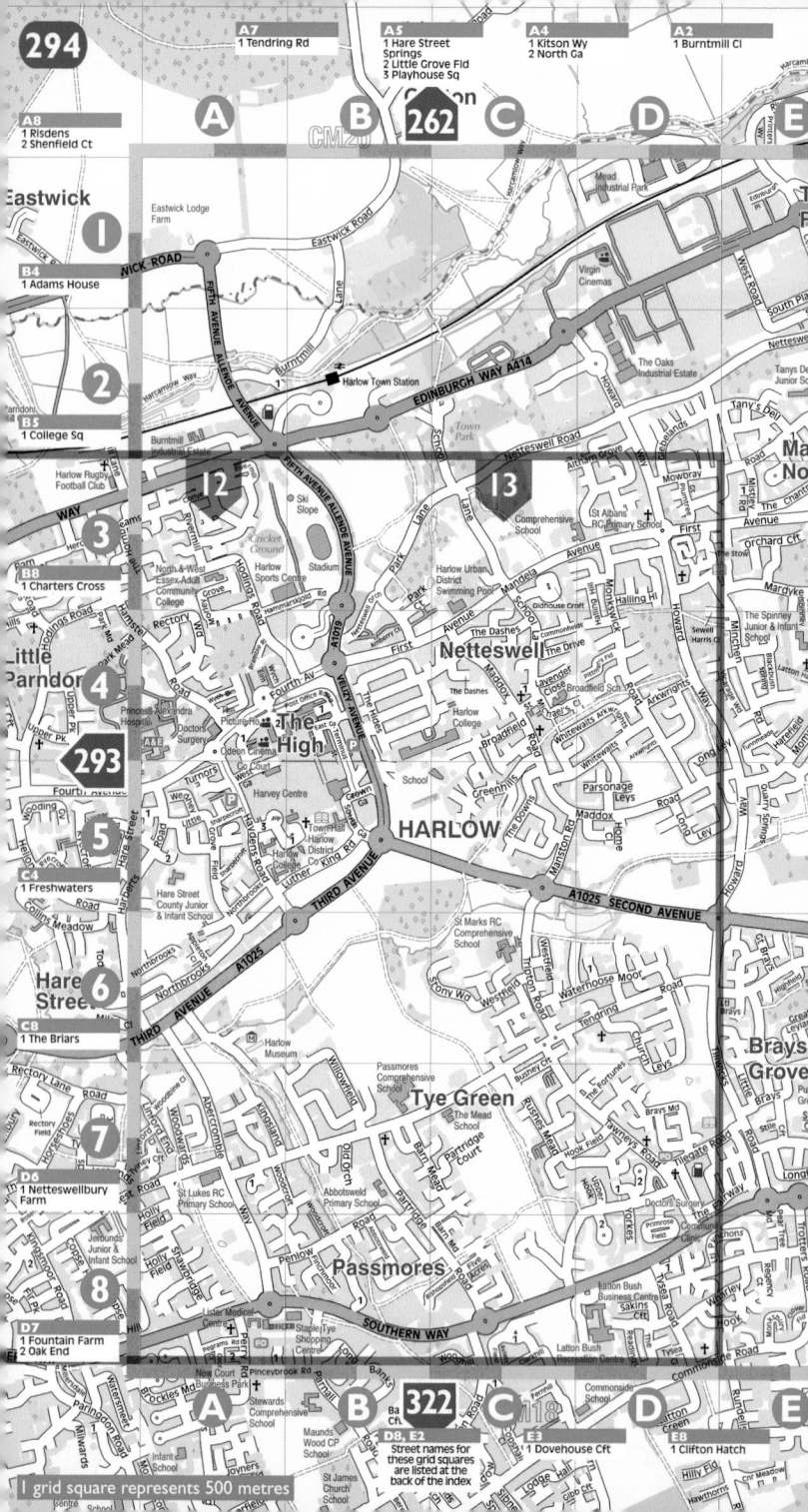

Campi **A** **B** **C** **D** **E**

SHEERING

Wetherly
Close

Moor

1

Hall
Road

Matching
Road

**Churchgate
Street**

Churchgate C of E
Primary School

Feltimores

2

Nicholas
hool

Hobbs Cross Road

Harlow Road

Housham
Hall

Harlow Tye

Rainbow
Road

3

Franklins
Farm

Chalk Lane

Forest Way

**Housham
Tye**

**Carter'
Green**

**Hobbs
Cross**

Forest Way

New Way Lane

4

M11

5

CM17

Roffey
Hall

New Way

New Way

6

Foster
Street

Foster Street

**Threshers
Bush**

New Way La

Green Lane

Tilegate Green

7

School
Lane

Tilegate Road

Hall
Farm

8

Foster Street

Wynter's
Farm

**Magdalen
Laver**

Hastingwood Road

Rolls

Hastingwood

A Wynter's
Grange **B** **C** **D** **E**

Tilegate Road

Humphreys

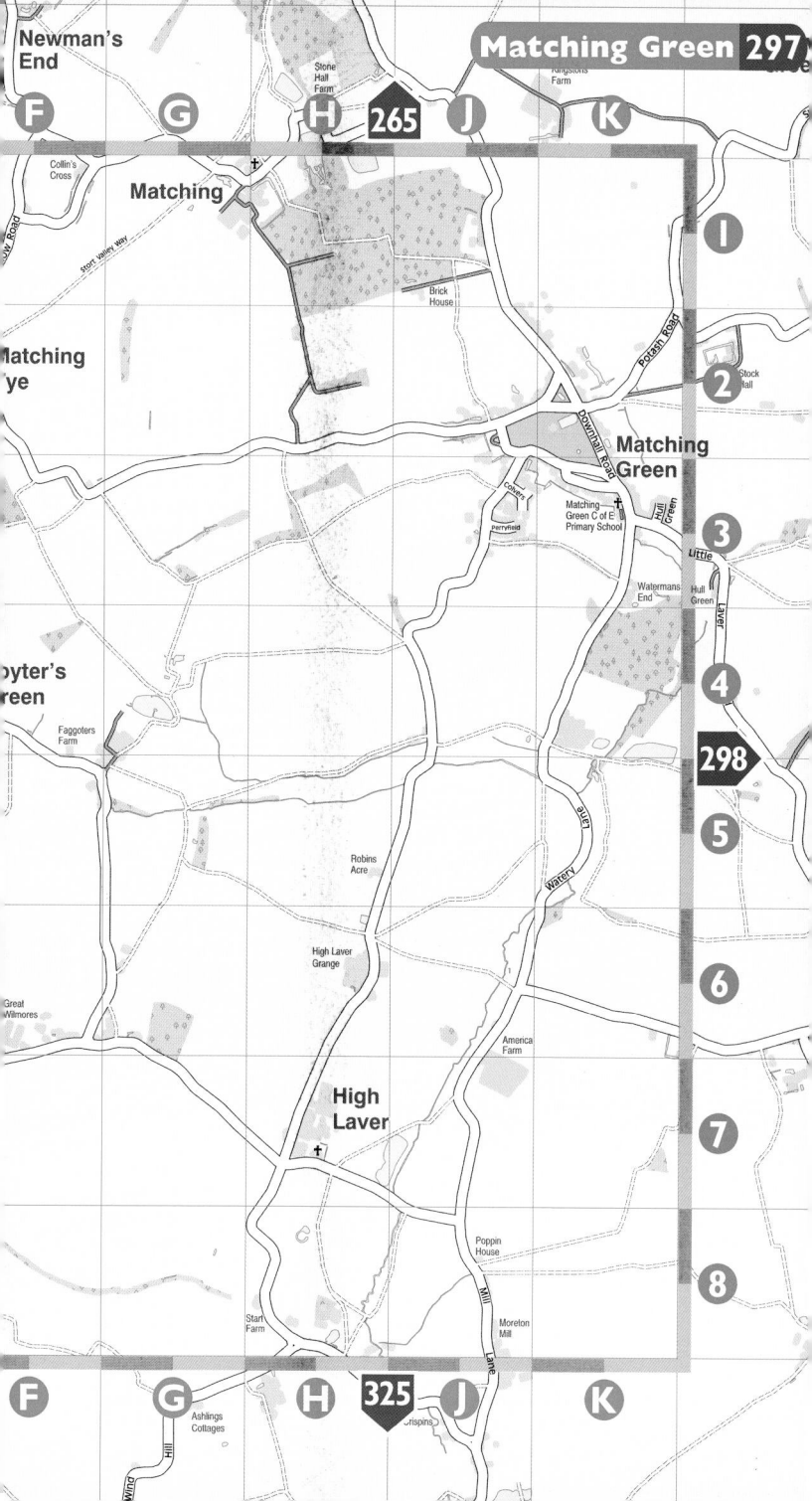

Newman's End

F G H 265 J K

I

Collin's Cross

Stort Valley Way

Matching

Matching Tye

Brick House

Potash Road

Stone Hall Farm

Kingston's Farm

2 Stock Hall

Downhall Road

Matching Green

Hull Green

Corners

Perryfield

Matching Green C of E Primary School

3 Little Hull Green

Watermans End

4

298

5

Poyter's Green

Faggoters Farm

Robins Acre

Watery Lane

High Laver Grange

6

Great Wilmores

America Farm

7

High Laver

Poppin House

8

Start Farm

Moreton Mill

F G H 325 J K

Ashlings Cottages

Wind Hill

Mill Lane

Crispins

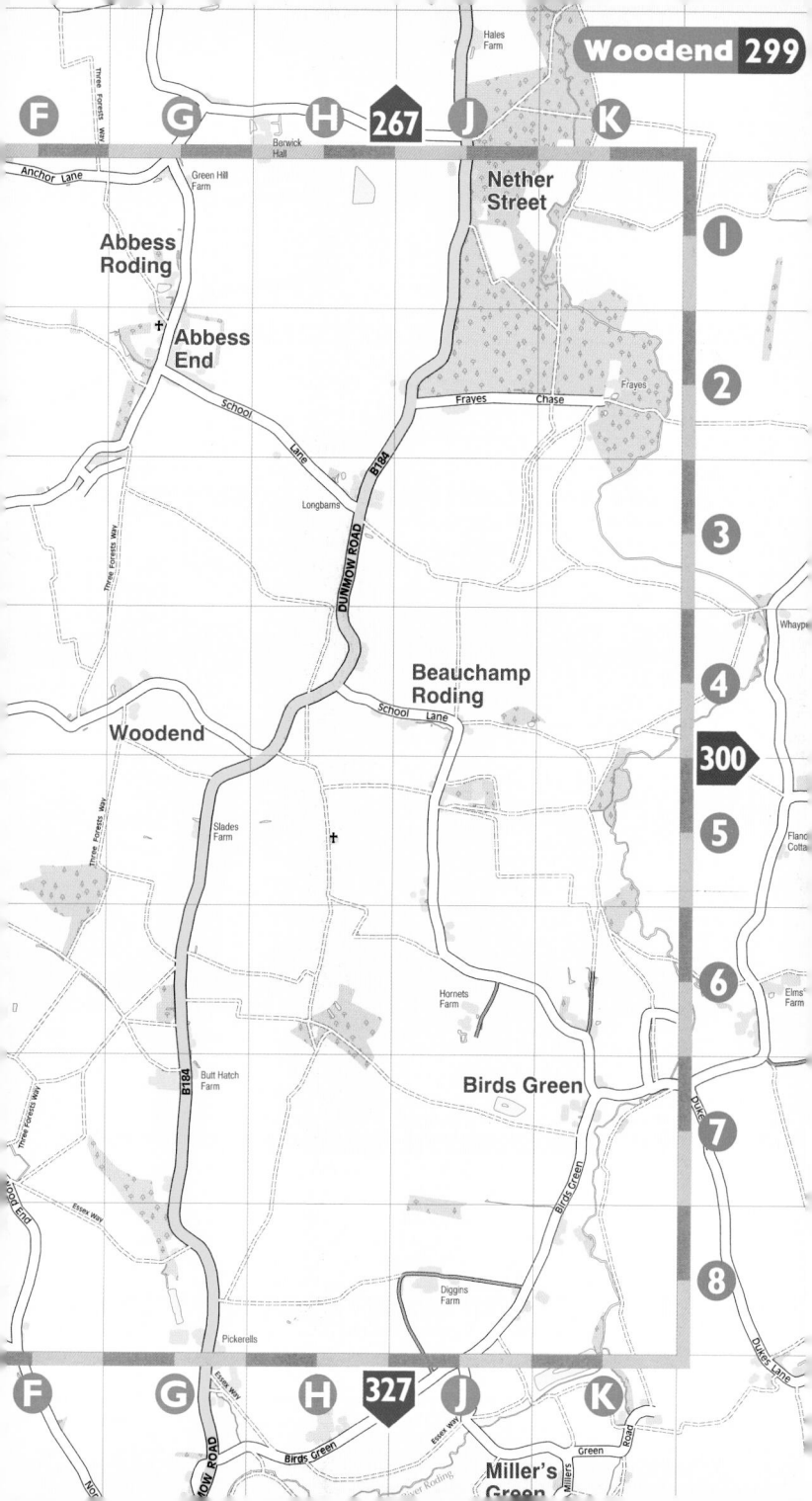

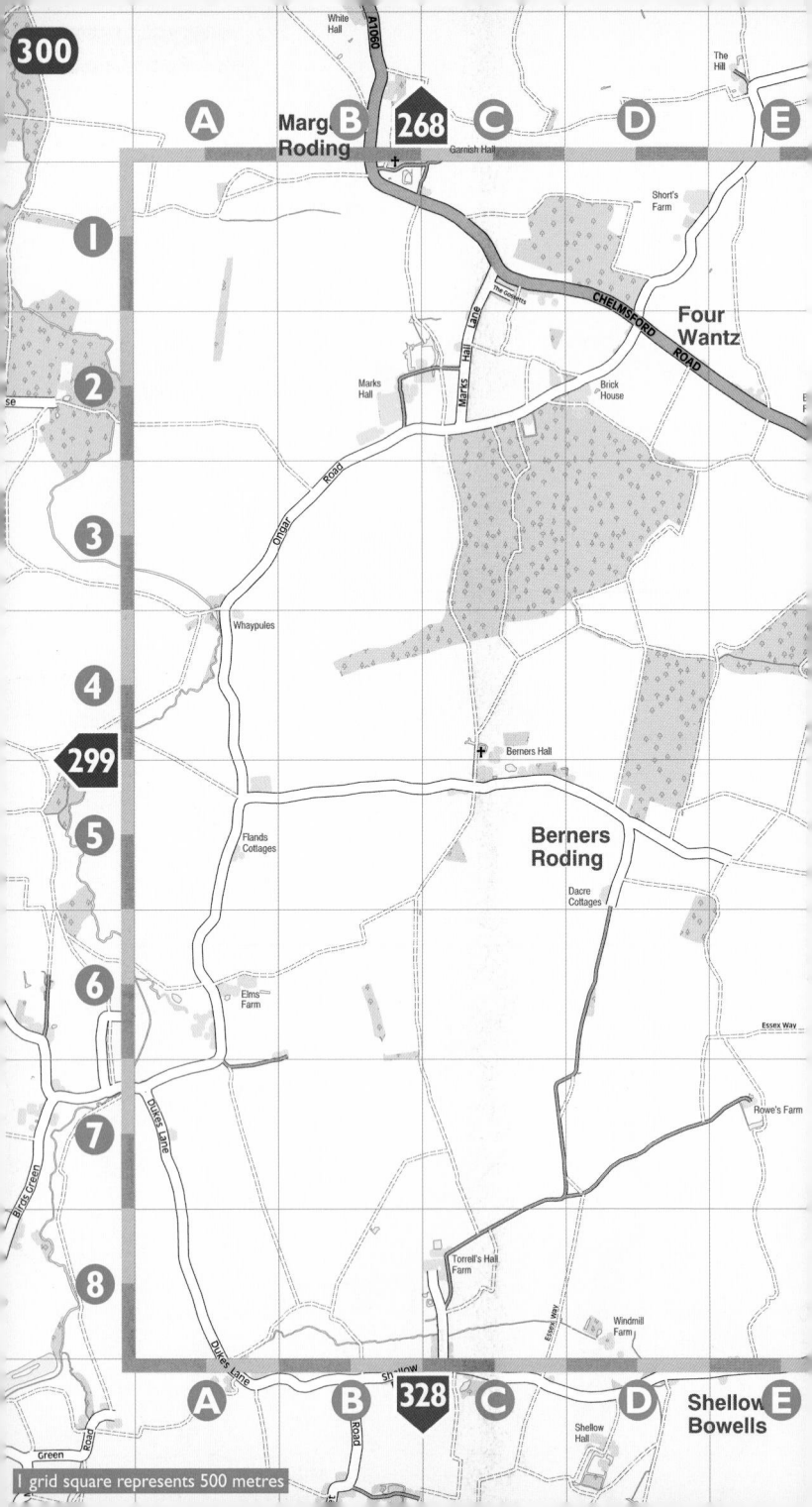

300

A   B 268   C   D   E

Marg   Roding

White
Hall

A1060

Garnish Hall

The
Hill

1

Short's
Farm

CHELMSFORD   ROAD   Four
Wantz

2

Marks
Hall

Marks Hall Lane

Brick
House

3

Ongar Road

Whaypules

4

299

Berners Hall

5

Flands
Cottages

Berners
Roding

Dacre
Cottages

6

Elms
Farm

Essex Way

7

Birds Green

Dukes Lane

Rowe's
Farm

8

Torrell's Hall
Farm

Windmill
Farm

A   B 328   C   D   E

Shellow Road

Essex Way

Shellow
Hall

Shellow
Bowells

Green
Road

1 grid square represents 500 metres

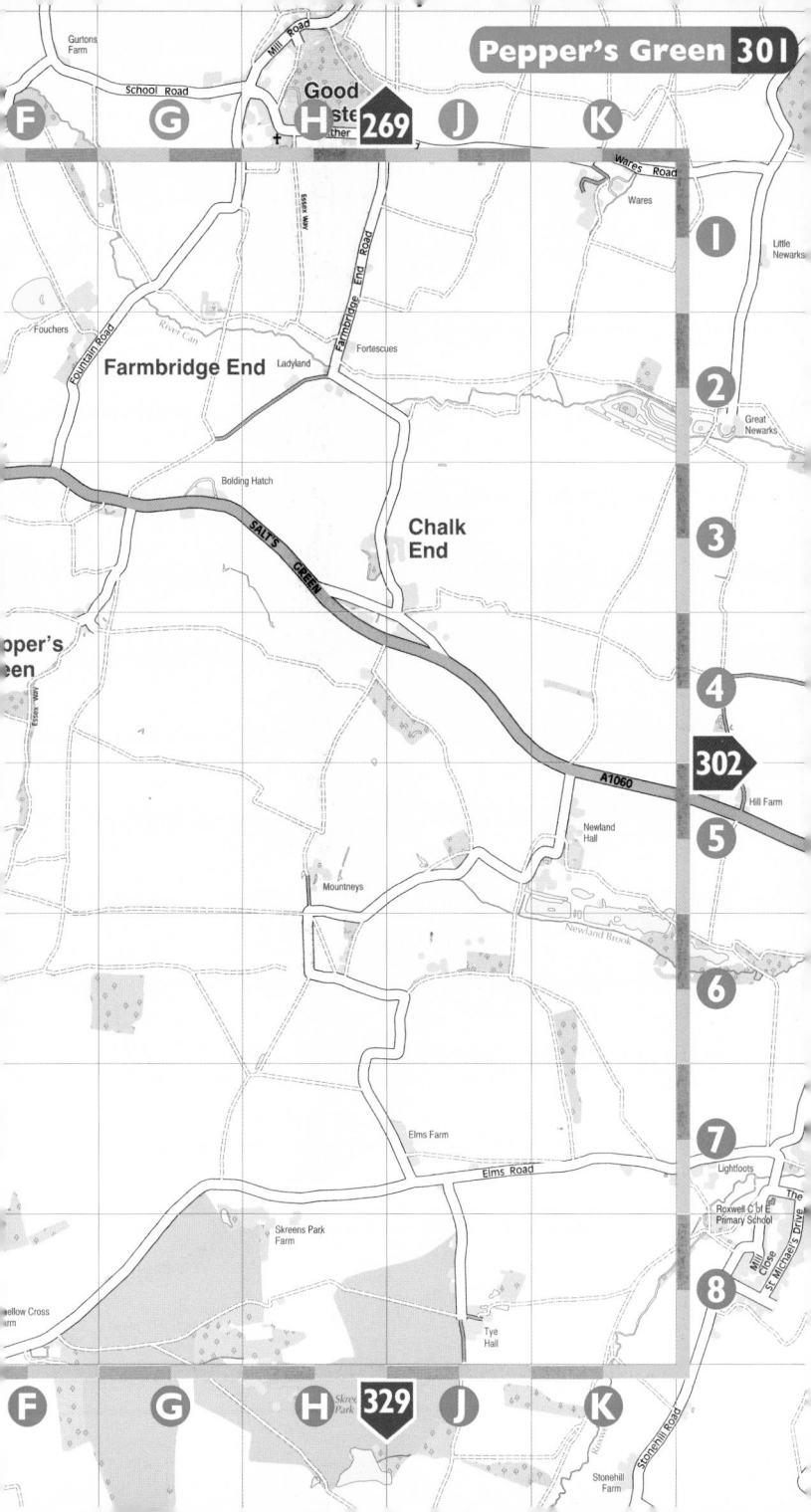

A B 270 C D E

1
Wares Road
Wares
Little Newarks

Mashbury

2
Great Newarks
Langley's Farm

3
Howletts Hall

4
Little Boyton Hall
C H

301
Hill Farm
Boyton Hall

5
Newland Hall

6
Newland Brook

Boyton Cross

7
Dukes
Lightfoots
Roxwell

8
Roxwell C of E Primary School
Mill Close
St Michael's Drive
The Street
Church Green
Green Lane
Galleons Hill
Thatcher's Farm
Vicarage Road
Blackwall Bridge
A1060
ROXI
Stonehill Road
Roxwell Brook
Hoestreet
Street
Hoe

A B 330 C D E

1 grid square represents 500 metres

H1
1 Vicarage Cl

Limesbrook

F
G
H
281
J
K

STATION

ROAD

Chapel Road

Tolleshunt
D'Arcy

Frame
Farm

use JI

Salter's
Meadow

SOUTH STREET

N

D'ARCY Way

Guisnes
Court

I

CHURCH ST

Festival
Gdns

Tolleshunt Darcy
C of E
Primary School

B1023

Hill Farm

Beckingham Road

Cemetery

B1026

Gorwell
Hall

2

Tolleshunts
Farm

TOLLESBURY

ROAD

3

MALDON

ROAD

Brook House
Farm

White
House
Farm

4

314

Hyde Farm

Papes Lane

5

Prentice

Wycke
Farm

6

Joyce's Chase

Joyce's
Farm

Lauriston
Farm

7

Rolf
Far

8

Goldhanger Creek

Gore
Saltings

F
G
H
341
J
K

283

F G H J K

I
2
3
4
316
5
6
7
8

Joyce's Head

Pennyhole Fleet

Old Hall Creek

Tollesbury Fleet

North Channel

Great Cob Island

South Channel

Shinglehead Point

Woodrolfe Creek

Tollesbury Sailing Club

Tollesbury Wick Marshes

Mill Creek

Pewet Island

Brankwell Creek

F G H J K

343

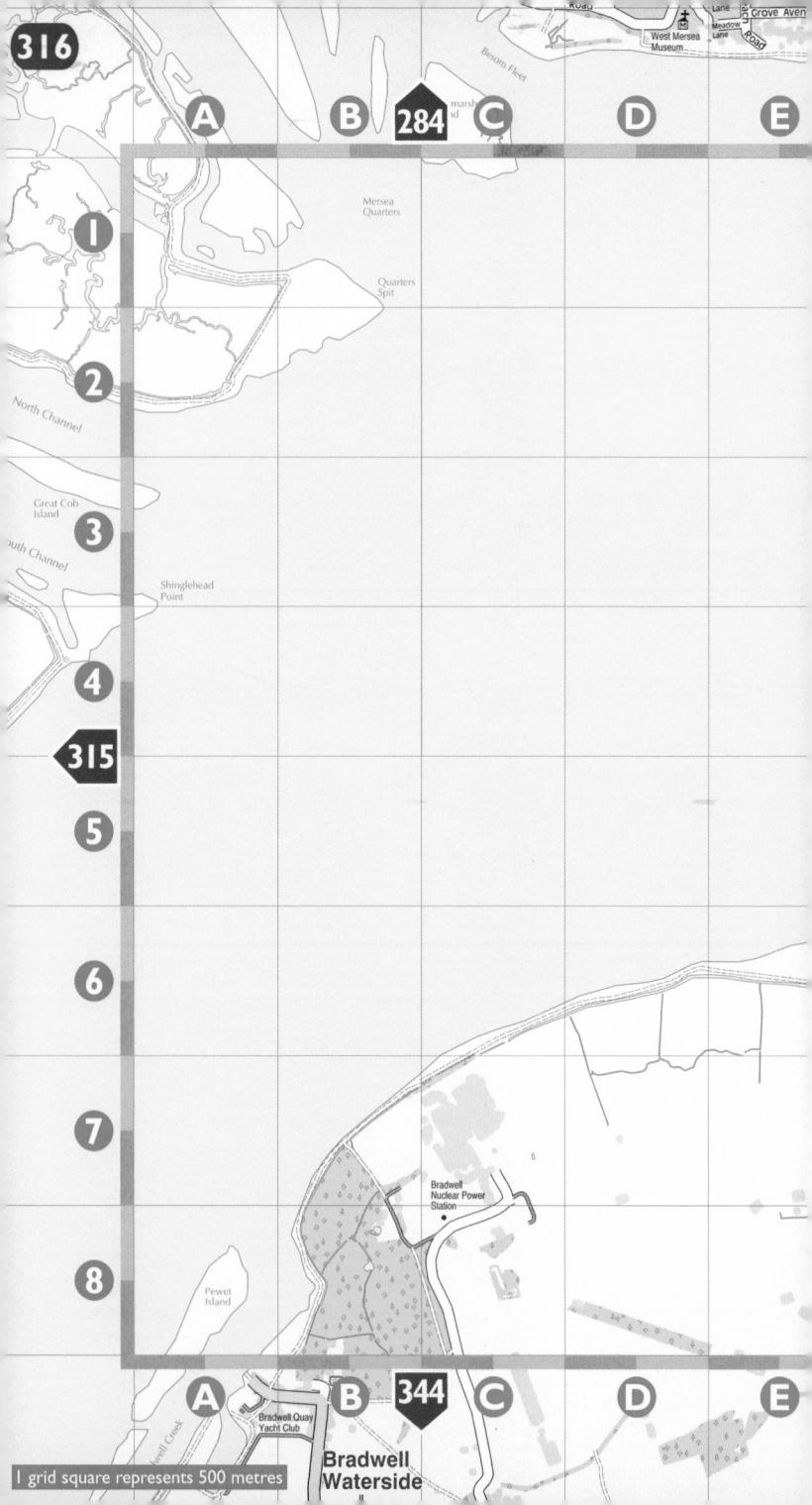

A   B   284   C   D   E

Besom Fleet

West Mersea
Museum

Grove Aven

Mersea
Quarters

1

Quarters
Spit

North Channel

2

Great Cob
Island

3

South Channel

Shinglehead
Point

4

315

5

6

7

Bradwell
Nuclear Power
Station

8

Pewet
Island

A   B   344   C   D   E

Bradwell Quay
Yacht Club

Bradwell Creek

Bradwell
Waterside

1 grid square represents 500 metres

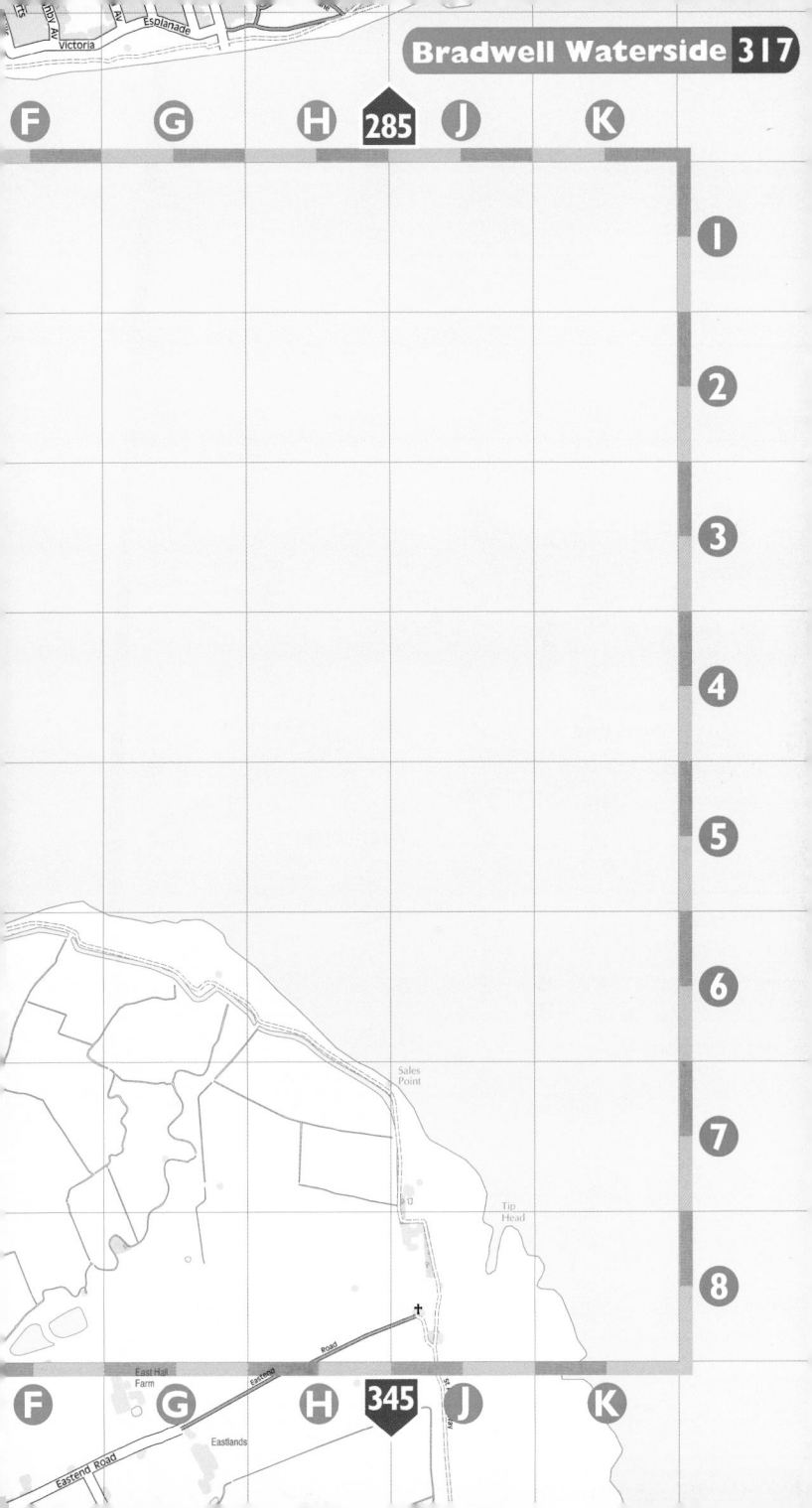

318

A **B** **C** **D** **E** H

E3
1 Ramsay Cl
2 Willoughby Cl

E2
1 Hickman Cl
2 Overlord Cl

D8
1 The Links

E6
1 Priory Cl

E7
1 The Canadas
2 Nunsbury Dr
3 Nursery Rd

E8
1 Brickcroft
2 Perram Cl
3 Robertson Cl

Cock Lane

A10(T)

Alamein Close

Cold Close

Sheriden Walk

Marro Way

Baas Hill

Baas Hill Close

Cold Hall

Baas Manor Farm

Carneles Green

Spring Walk

Pembridge Lane

Wood House Lane

Paradise Wildlife Park

pps Lane

Emanuel Pollards

Wormley West End

West End Road

Holy Cross Hill

Wormleybury

+ Church Lane

EN10

Wormley

Beaumont Road

Thunderfield Grove

Park Lane Paradise

6

Factory Farm

7

A10(T)

Turnford

Canada Lane

Hotel

Broxbourne Borough Council

Broxbourne Business Centre

The Airways

HALFHIDE LANE

A10(T) GREAT CAMBRIDGE ROAD

B156

upr shott

Adamsfield

Cheshunt Park

Fairfields Junior Middle & Infant

Dig Dag Hill

Rags Lane

St Pauls Roman Catholic JMI School

Debenham Rd

A **B** **346** ▽ **C** **D** **E**

Herongate Road

Hillview Gardens

Prescott Rd

Endeavour Road

Spitalbrook

Broxbourne

Keysers Estate

Nazeing Mead

Lower Nazeing

Nazeing Marsh

King's Weir

Langridge

F G H J K

1
F3
1 Ashbourne Rd
2 Royce Cl

2
F4
1 Caldecot Wy
2 Lichfield Wy
3 The Sidings

3
F5
1 Fern Cl
2 The Square
3 Virgil Dr
4 Wormley Lde Cl

4

320

5
F6
1 Orchard Sq
2 Shirley Cl
3 Westlea Cl

6
F7
1 Farmhouse Cl
2 Felton Cl
3 Juniper Cl

7
F8
1 Farriers End
2 Helens Ga
3 Shire Cl

8

1 The Spinney
1 Bassingbourne Cl
2 Monson Rd
3 Richmond Ct
4 St Augustines Cl

F G H **347** J K

K4
1 Nazeingbury Cl

G2
1 Courtfield Cl
2 Stafford Dr

G1
1 Hallmores
2 St Cross Ct
3 Westcroft Ct

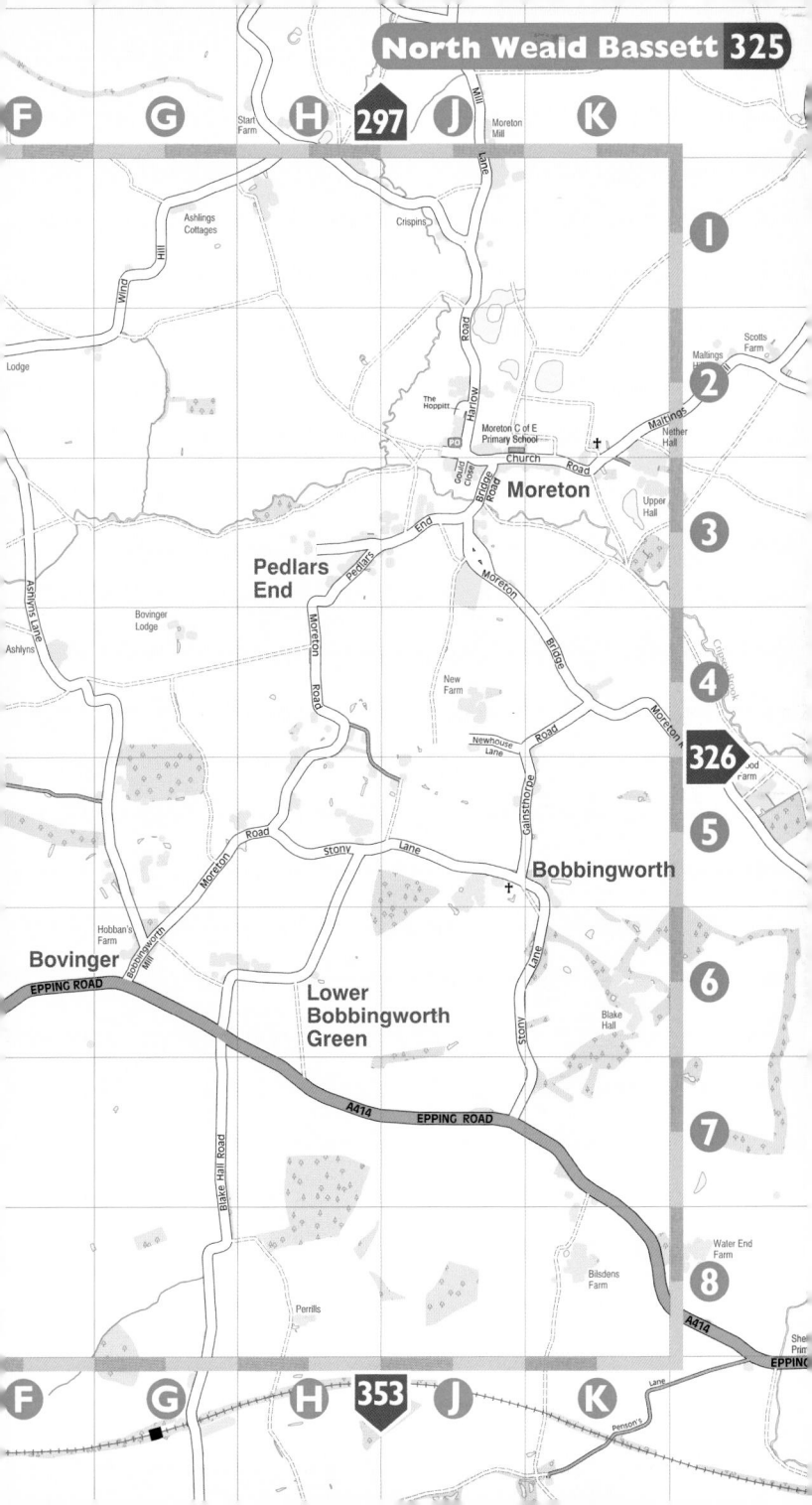

F G H **297** J K

I

2

3

4

326

5

6

7

8

Start Farm

Ashlings Cottages

Crispins

Wind Hill

Lodge

Moreton Mill

Maltings Hill

Scotts Farm

Nether Hall

Church

Maltings Road

Upper Hall

The Hoppitt

Moreton C of E Primary School

Church Road

Moreton

PO

Square Cottage

Bridge Road

Harrow Road

Mill Lane

Pedlars End

Pedlars End

Moreton Road

Bovinger Lodge

Ashlyns Lane

Ashlyns

New Farm

Moreton Bridge

Moreton Road

Newhouse Lane

Stony Lane

Gainsthorpe Lane

Bobbingworth

Hobban's Farm

Bovinger

Bobbingworth Mill

EPPING ROAD

Lower Bobbingworth Green

Stony Lane

Blake Hall

Blake Hall Road

A414 **EPPING ROAD**

Perrills

Bilsdens Farm

Water End Farm

A414

Shell Prim

EPPING

F G H **353** J K

Penson's Lane

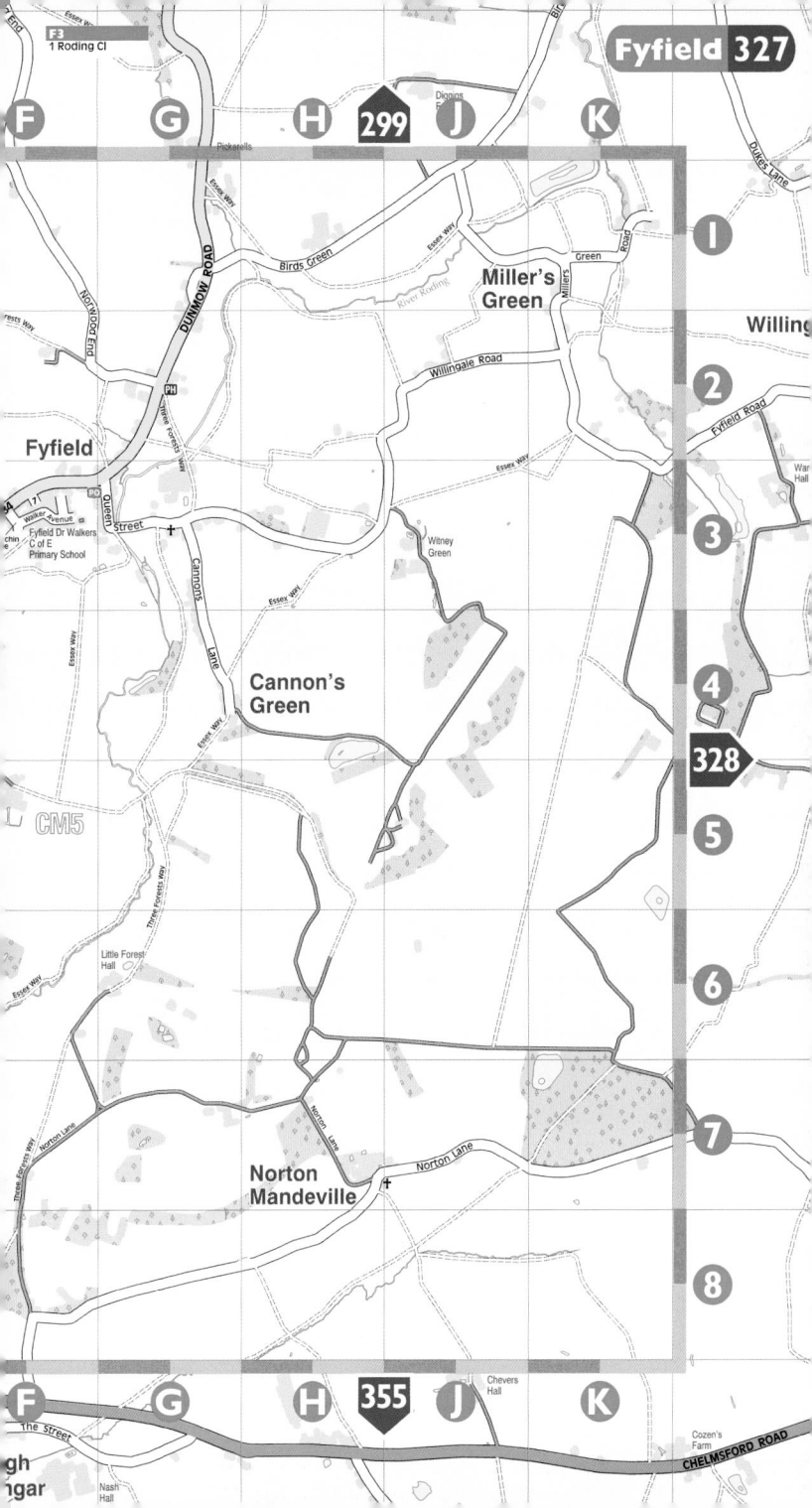

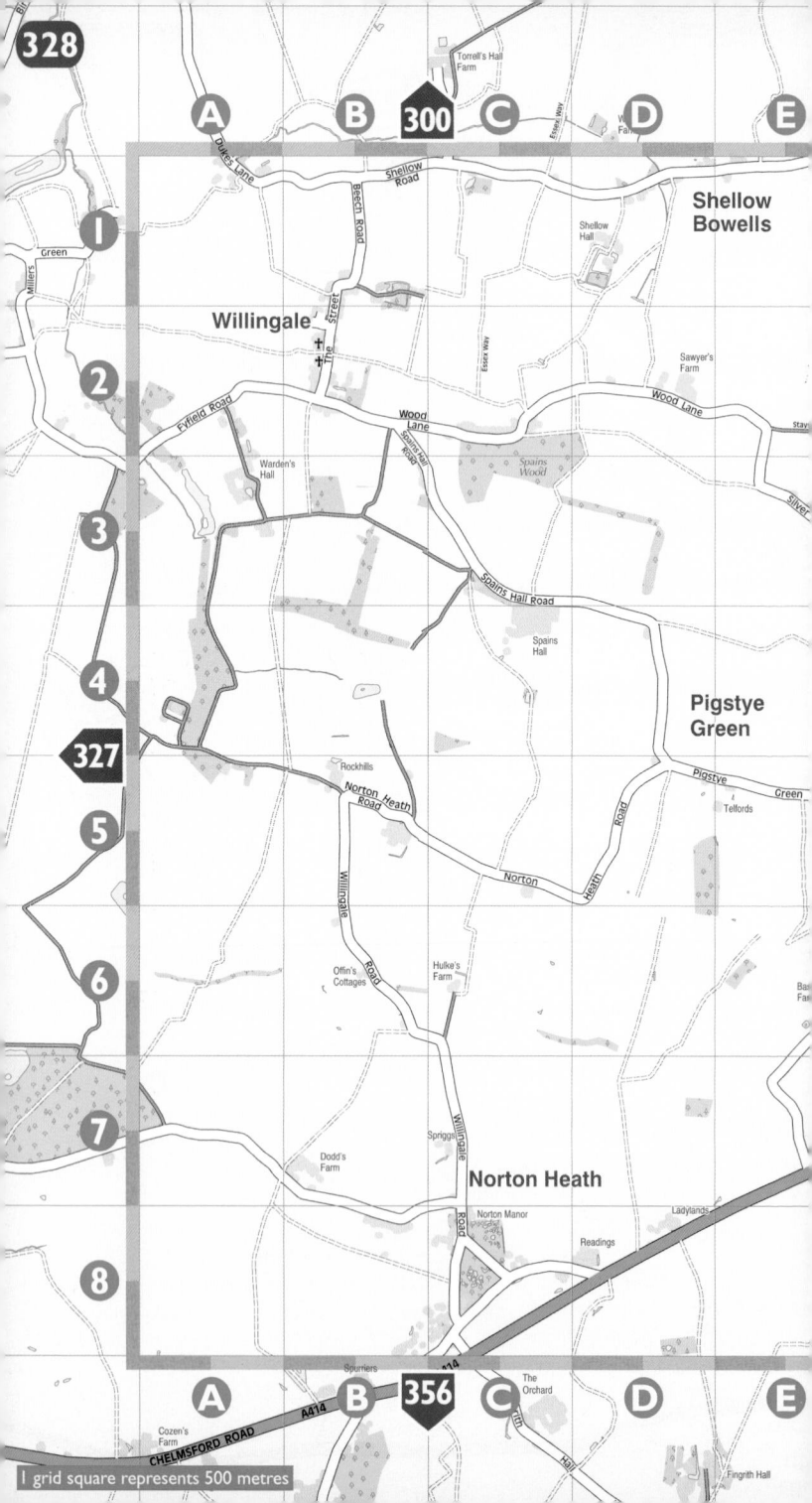

328

300

A B C D E

1

Shellow
Bowells

Shellow
Road

Torrell's Hall
Farm

Dukes Lane

Beech Road

Miller's
Green

Shellow
Hall

Willingale

The Street

2

Eyfield Road

Wood
Lane

Warden's
Hall

Spains Hall Road

Spains
Wood

Wood Lane

Sawyer's
Farm

Essex Way

stay

Silver

3

Spains
Hall

4

327

Pigstye
Green

Rockhills

Norton Heath
Road

Pigstye Green

Telfords

5

Willingale Road

Norton
Heath
Road

6

Offin's
Cottages

Hulke's
Farm

Bas
Far

7

Cozen's
Farm

Dodd's
Farm

Spriggal

Norton Heath

Ladylands

8

Willingale Road

Norton Manor

Readings

A B C D E

356

CHELMSFORD ROAD A414

Spurriers

A414

The
Orchard

Fingrith Hall

Fingrith Hall

I grid square represents 500 metres

F G H 301 J K

I

2

3

4

330

5

6

7

8

F G H 357 J K

Hoxwell C of E
Primary School

Tye
Hall

Skreens Park
Farm

Skreens
Park

Roxwell Brook

Stonehill
Farm

Stonehill Road

Green Lane
Farm

Patience
Bridge

Butt Hatch
Farm

Benedict
Otes

Quires Green

Pooty
Pools

Wall's Green

Blow's Farm

Star House

Chapel Lane

**Cooksmill
Green**

Colleybridge
Farm

Ewson's Brook

Brainwood
Farm

**Radley
Green**

ONGAP ROAD

A414

Ewson's
Farm

Wyse's
Cottage

Wyse's

Hand's
Farm

A414

Wyse's ROAD

smith Park
m

Old Barn Lane

Sparrow's
Lane

**Loves
Gree**

Fithlers Hall
Farm

Ward's
Farm

Highwo...
Pool's Lane

County
Primary
School

Gorrell's
Farm

332

304

B6
1 Whitebeam Cl
2 Widford Cl
3 Widford Park Pl

B5
1 Cutmore Pl

A4
1 Brendon Pl

A5
1 Harrison Ct

A1
1 Lichfield Cl

A2
1 Fitzwalter Pl

C3
1 Viaduct Rd

I4

C6
1 Hillside Ms

C8
1 Osprey Wy

D1
1 Hall La

D2
1 Glebe Rd

D3
1 Barrack Sq
2 New London Rd

D4
1 Hall St

331

D5
1 Bouverie Rd
2 St Vincents Rd

D8
1 Goshawk Dr

E3
1 Provident Sq
2 Sandringham Pl
3 Springfield Rd

E5
1 Amcotes Pl
2 Langdale Gdns
3 Van Dieman's La

C2, C4, E4
Street names for
these grid squares
are listed at the
back of the index

Moulsham

Widford

360

E6
1 May Wk

E7
1 Hawthorn Cl
2 Lilac Cl
3 Yew Tree Gdns

1 grid square represents 500 metres

ROXWELL ROAD A1060

RAINSFORD ROAD A1016

BUNDICK'S HILL

WATERHOUSE LANE

WESTWAY A1016

A414 LONDON ROAD

PRINCES ROAD A414

GALLEYWOOD ROAD

WOOD STREET

NEW LONDON ROAD B1007

PARKWAY A138

CHELMER VALLEY RD

SPRINGFIELD RD A1099

F2
1 Brookhurst Cl
2 Chelmer Pl
3 Parklands Dr
4 Regency Cl
5 Turkey Oaks

F3
1 Hill Crs
2 Morris Rd
3 Spr'field Pk Pde

F **G** **H** **305** **J** **K**

15

The Dukes
Priory
Hospital

Dukes Park
Industrial Estate

Montrose

Richmond
Road

Chelmsford
Rugby
Football Club

Chelmsford
Cricket Club

Springfield

Llanmede
Bowling Club
& Tennis Courts

Sandford
Road

Kingston
Avenue

Yarwood
Road

Doctors
Surgery

Henniker
Gate

Junior
School

Chelmer Village

Springfield Park Road

Springfield Park Avenue

Shelley
Road

Byron
Road

Chaucer
Road

Chelmer
Village
Retail Park

Hopkins

Howard Dr

Chelmer Village

Sandford
Road

Brook End Road

Brook
Lane

Mill
Road

CHELMSFORD

CHELMER ROAD

A414

Meadgate
Avenue

Meadgate
CP School

Longmead

Tabors Avenue

Baddow
Road

Canford Close

Winchelsea
Drive

Avenue Road

BEEHIVE LANE

Rothmans Avenue

Palmerston Lodge

Maldon
Road

Maldon
Road

The Chase

A414   MALDON

Crescent

Baddow

Pirie Close

A1114

Hall

Gilmore
Way

Baddow Hall
Junior &
Infant School

Sandon
School

Sa

Hampton Road

Gowers Avenue

Wood
Dale

Bells Chase

Millers Croft

The
Spires

Church
Street

SOUTHEND ROAD

Reader's Corner

Noakes

Pitt
Chase

Dorset
Avenue

Duffield Road

Great Baddow

Galleywood

Pertwee Dr

Church
Road

Johnson
Road

Hotel

The Grove

CM2

Cemetery

F **G** **H** **361** **J** **K**

F G H **307** J K

H7
1 Highfield Cl

K5
1 Clarks Farm Rd
2 Fairleads

I

K6
1 Belvedere Rd

2

3

4

336

5

6

7

8

Little Baddow

Warren Farm

Tofts

Holybreds Farm

Spring Elms Lane

Spring Elms

Woodham Walter Common

Twitty Fee

Elm Green School

Blake's Wood

New Lodge

CM3

Lingwood Common

Graces Lane

Rifthams

Great Graces Farm

Lingborough Park

Runsell Lane

Bakers Lane

Danbury Park School

Doctors Surgery

Primary School

Runsell Green

A414 BELL HILL MAIN ROAD MALDON ROAD

Danbury Medical Clinic

Woodhill Industrial Estate

DANBURY

Danbury Clinic

MALDON ROAD

Wyncroft Surgery

Mill Lane

Cherry

Danbury Country Park

The Heathcote School

Danbury Palace

Woodhill Road

Horne Row

Woodhill

Paternoster Farm

Danbury Common

Gay Bower

Overshot

F G H **363** J K

G1
1 Saltcote Maltings

G2
1 Maritime Av
2 Spinnaker Dr

F   G   H   311   J   K

Cobb's

Gardener's
Farm

I

B1026

Salcote
Hall

GER ROAD

B1026   GOLDHANGER ROAD

Vaulty
Manor

Basin Road

Wharf Road

Draper's Chase

Heybridge
Basin

Blackwater
Sailing
Club

The Colliery

Chapel Lane

Navigation

2

Mill Reach

Osea Road

Decoy
Point

3

River Blackwater

Collier's
Reach

Hilly
Pool Point

Northey
Island

CM9

4

340

5

Southey
Creek

6

Limbourne Creek

7

Bramble
Hall Farm

Iltney
Farm

Garlands

New Hall Lane

8

Blackwater

F   G   H   367   J   K

White
House
Farm

Brookmead
Farm

Burnham Wash

A5, C6, D1
Street names for
these grid squares
are listed at the
back of the index

F G H 313 J K

Goldhanger Creek

Osea Island

East Point

Stansgate Abbey Farm

342

Ramsey Marsh

Steeple Creek

Steeple Wick

Stansgate Road

Canney Road

and Creek

Canney Road

F G H 369 J K

I 2 3 4 5 6 7 8

Ramsey Island 343

Pewet Island

F G H 315 J K

1

2 Westwick Farm

3

4

344 DON ROAD

5

6 Bradwell Brook

Byhams

7 ROAD Sampsons

Bradwell Brook

Bradwell Hall

Maldon Road

Highfield

Bradwell Wick

Blackbirds

8

East Hyde

Lawrence

St Lawrence Road Brook Road

F G West Hyde H 371 J K

NORTH STREET

St Nicholas Road

Tillingham St Nicholas C of E Primary School

Vicarage Lane

Stowe's Lane Stows

Casey Lane

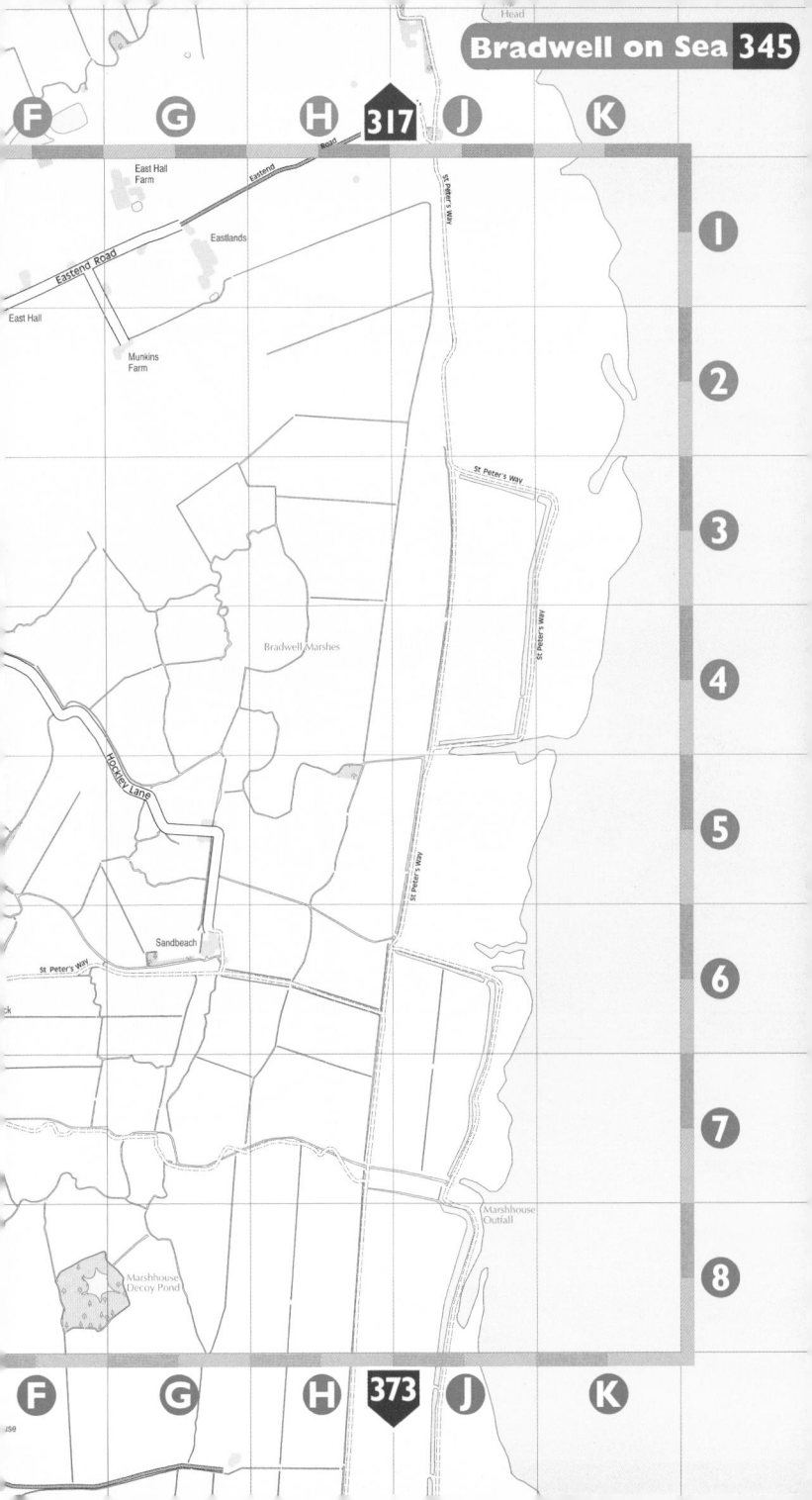

I

2

3

4

5

6

7

8

East Hall
Farm

Eastend

Eastend Road

Eastlands

East Hall

Munkins
Farm

St. Peter's Way

St Peter's Way

St Peter's Way

Bradwell Marshes

Hockley Lane

St Peter's Way

Sandbeach

St Peter's Way

Marshhouse
Outfall

Marshhouse
Decoy Pond

Head

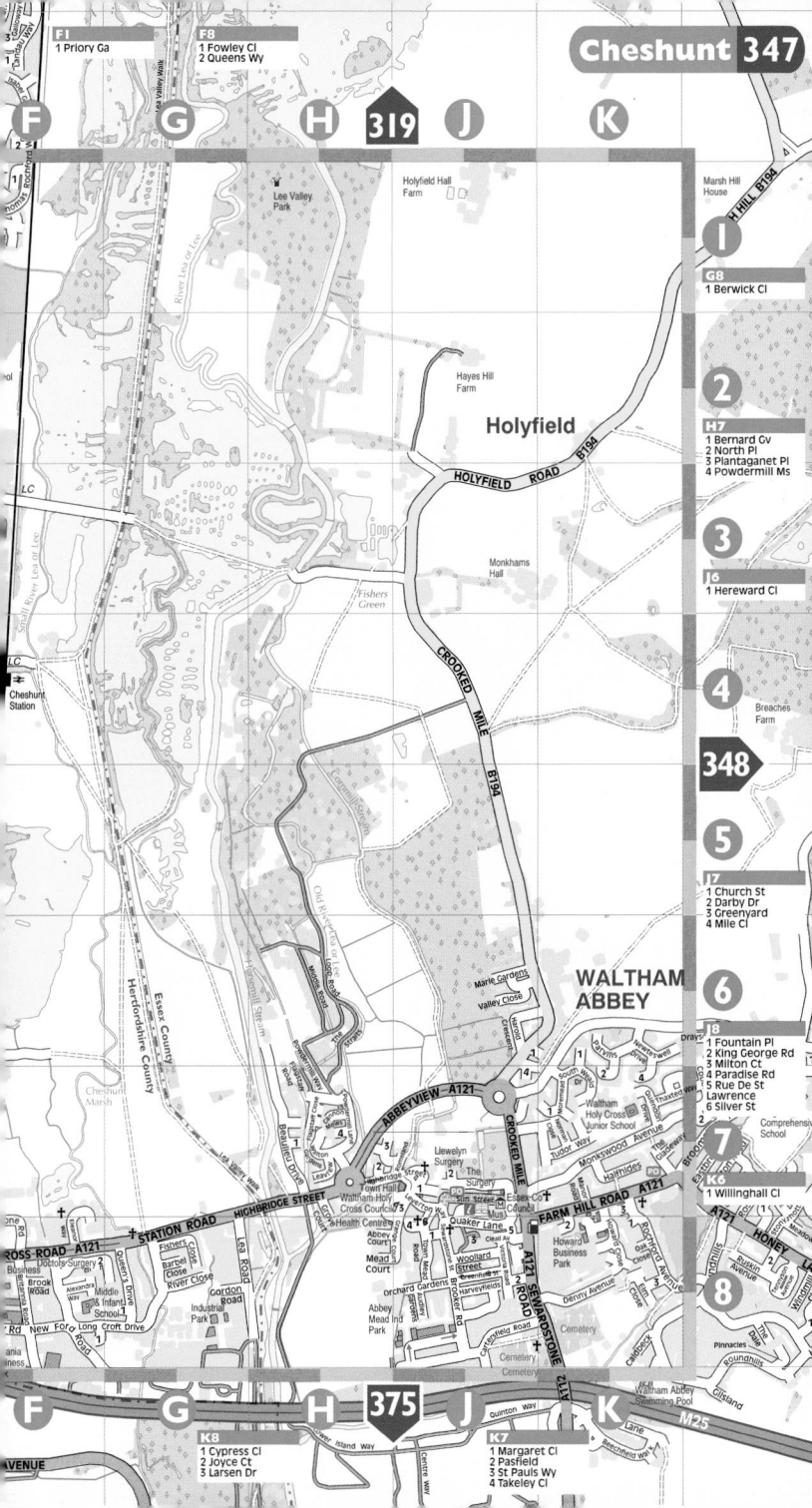

F1
1 Priory Ga

F8
1 Fowley Cl
2 Queens Wy

F   G   H   **319**   J   K

Marsh Hill House

I

G8
1 Berwick Cl

2

H7
1 Bernard Gv
2 North Pl
3 Plantaganet Pl
4 Powdermill Ms

3

J6
1 Hereward Cl

4
Breaches Farm

348

5

I7
1 Church St
2 Darby Dr
3 Greenyard
4 Mile Cl

6

J8
1 Fountain Pl
2 King George Rd
3 Milton Ct
4 Paradise Rd
5 Rue De St Lawrence
6 Silver St

7

K6
1 Willinghall Cl

8

Lee Valley Park

Holyfield Hall Farm

Hayes Hill Farm

Holyfield

HOLYFIELD ROAD B194

Monkhams Hall

Fishers Green

CROOKED MILE

B194

Cheshunt Station

Old River Lee or Lee

WALTHAM ABBEY

Essex County
Hertfordshire County

Cheshunt Marsh

Marie Gardens
Valley Close

ABBEYVIEW A121

CROOKED MILE

FARM HILL ROAD A121

HONEY LA

HIGHBRIDGE STREET

STATION ROAD

ROSS ROAD A121

Quaker Lane

SEWARDSTONE ROAD A112

Howard Business Park

Denny Avenue

Cemetery

Cemetery

A112

Waltham Abbey Swimming Pool

M25

F   G   H   **375**   J   K

AVENUE

Quinton Way

K8
1 Cypress Cl
2 Joyce Ct
3 Larsen Dr

K7
1 Margaret Cl
2 Pasfield
3 St Pauls Wy
4 Takeley Cl

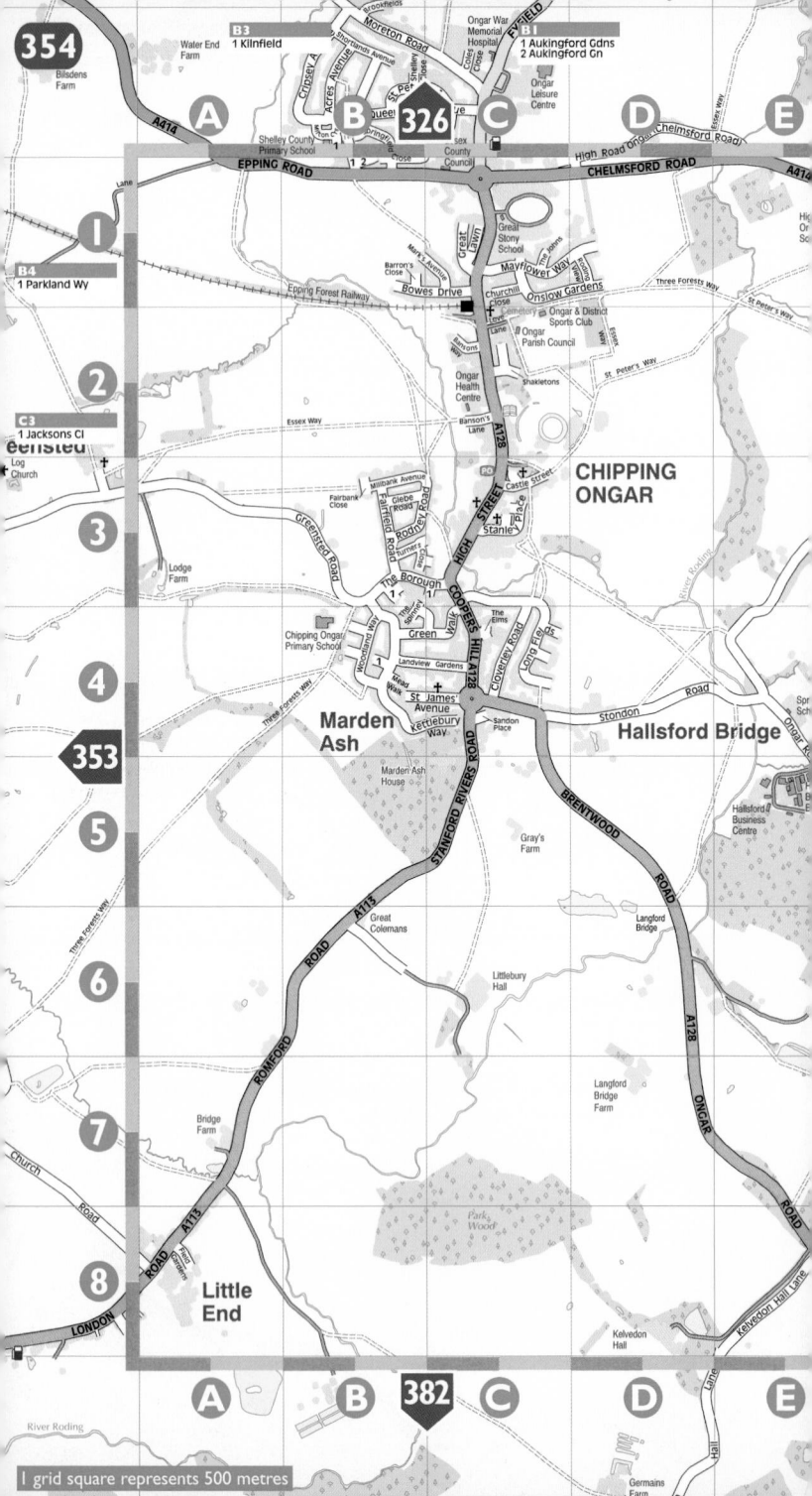

356

328

A B C D E

Norton Manor
D5
1 Blackmore Mead
C5
1 St Lawrence Gdns
Ladylands

Road

I CHELMSFORD ROAD A414 Spurriers The Orchard Fingrith

Cozen's Farm Finghill Hall

King Street

2
King Street

Rookery Road Rookery Farm Fingrith Hall Lane

Saybridge Lodge

Spriggs Lane

3

Nine Ashes Road

Larkins Farm

Nine Ashes

4
Paslow non

355

Well's Farm Redrose Red Rose Farm

Woolard Way

St Peter's Way

Blackmore CP School Jericho Place **Elkins Green**

5
Poplar Close The Green Blackmore Alley

Church Street Orchard

Blackmore Road St Peter's Way Jericho Priory **Blackmore**

6
Copyhold Farm

Ashling's Farm Ingatestone Lane

7
Blackmore Road Wenlocks Lane Wenlock's Farm Blackmore Road

Park Farm Lane

Green Lane

8
First Avenue Second Avenue Nursery Road Hook End Lane

Spring Pond Meadow

Stubbers Farm

Tip's Cross

Hay Green

Blackmore Road Deal Tree Close Hook End Road **384** Hay Lane The Robins Beehive Chase Whitelands Mill Lane

A B C D E

Hook

Field Kiln

I grid square represents 500 metres

F G H **331** J K

I 1

2

3   Lodge Farm

4

360

5   Crondon Hall

6

7

Crondon Park

8

Elm Farm

Hyl... & Park

Southwood Farm

Margaretting Road

Whittle Road

King... Wood

...earman's ...arm

A1016

Centenary Circle

Butts Way

Ricu... Wa...

Whitebridge Lane

Swan Lane

A12(T)

White's Place

Durrant's Farm

Wantz Road

Margaretting

Penny's Lane

...orton Clo...

B1002

Peacocks

...agonsale Lane

Maldon Road

LC

Canterburys

Margaretting Tye

Molehill Common

St Peter's Way

Swan Lane

St Peter's Way

Fristling Hall

F G H **387** J K

St Peter's Way

Crondon...

Tye Green

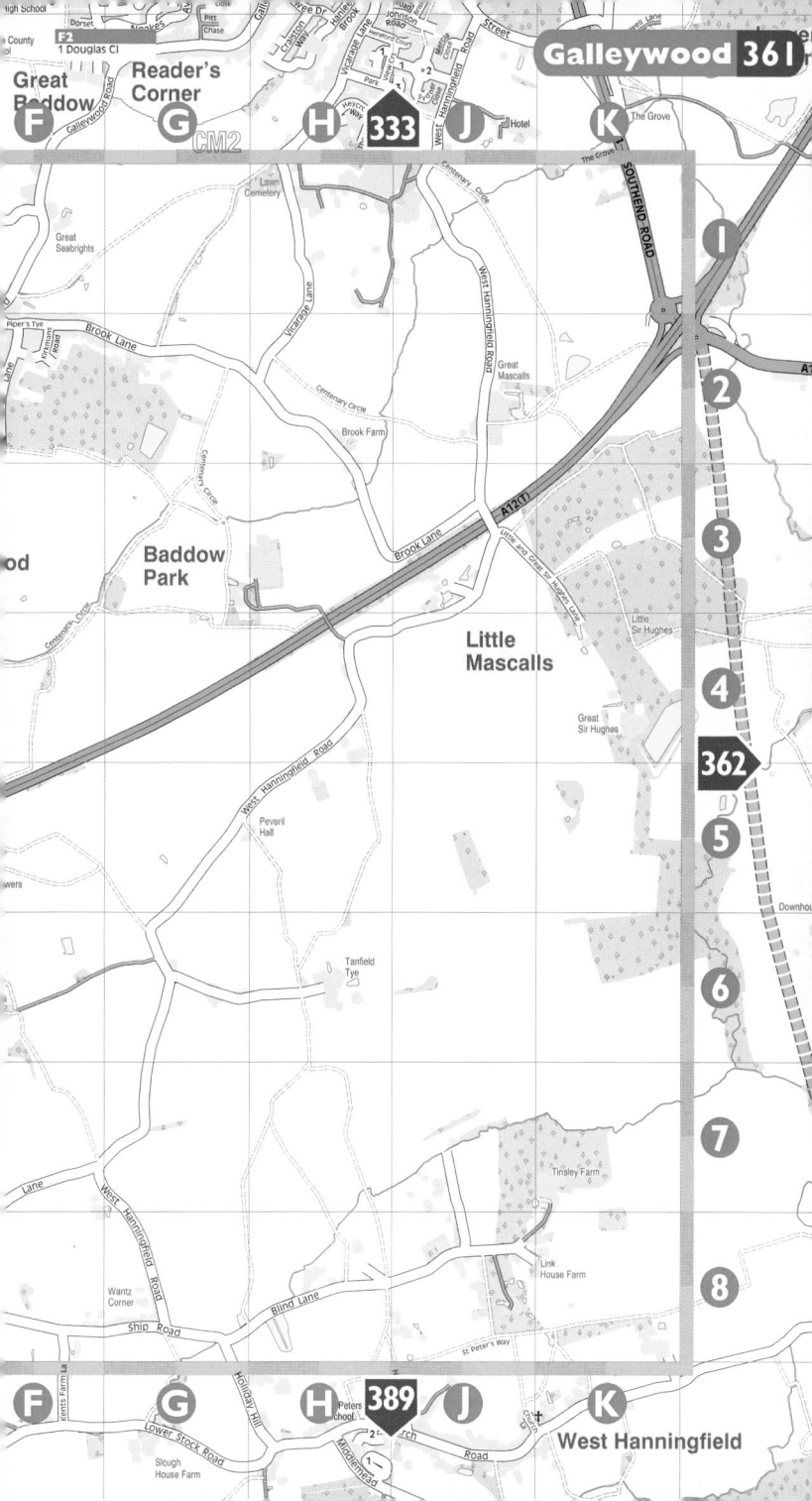

362

Lower Green

Mayes Farm

A **B** 334 **C** **D** **E**

The Grove
A114 SOUTHEND

The Grove

Sandon Hall Farm

Blind Lane

Sporehams Lane

Sporehams

1

Butt's

Green

2
A130

Howe Green

Sandon Hall Bridleway

Butt's Green

East Hanningfield Road

Alexander Mews

Chalklands

Southlands Chase

3

Southlands Farm

Grove Farm

Little Sir Hughes

sughes Lane

SOUTHEND ROAD

4

Great Sir Hughes

Great Claydons

361

Old Southend Road

5

6

Downhouse

Little Claydons Farm

A130 SOUTHEND ROAD

Claydons Farm

Bushy Wood

7

Tinsley Farm

St Peter's Way

Patten's Farm

Hill Farm

8

ink house Farm

A130

Pan Lane

A **B** 390 **C** **D** **E**

West Hanningfield

Barnard's Farm

East Hanningfield Lodge

1 grid square represents 500 metres

A Gay Bowers **B** 336 **C** **D** **E**

Woodham Mortimer

Nursery Farm

Hyde Chase

1

2

3 Bicknacre

4

363

5

6

7 Woodham Lodge

8 Chapel Row

A **B** 392 **C** **D** **E**

Woodham Ferrers

St Marys C of E Aided Primary School

Ormonds Crs

Mill Lane

B1418 SOUTHEND ROAD

Tyndales Lane

Hyde Woods

Hyde Chase

Southwood Chase

HYDE LANE

B1418

Slough Road

White Elm Farm

WHITE ELM ROAD

Jacklett's Farm

Peartree Lane

Bicknacre Road

St Peter's Way

Wickham's Farm

St Peter's Way

Thrift Wood

Woodham Hall

Seven Acre Farm

B1418 MAIN ROAD

Hobclerk's Farm

Crows Lane

Lodge Road

Crows Lane

Brazils

I grid square represents 500 metres

F G H 345 J K

I

2

3

4

5

6

7

8

Marshhouse
Outfall

Marshhouse
Decoy Pond

Tillingham Marshes

Grange Outfall

Round Barn

...am Brook

F G H 401 J K

...se

...e

...ic
...ts Centre

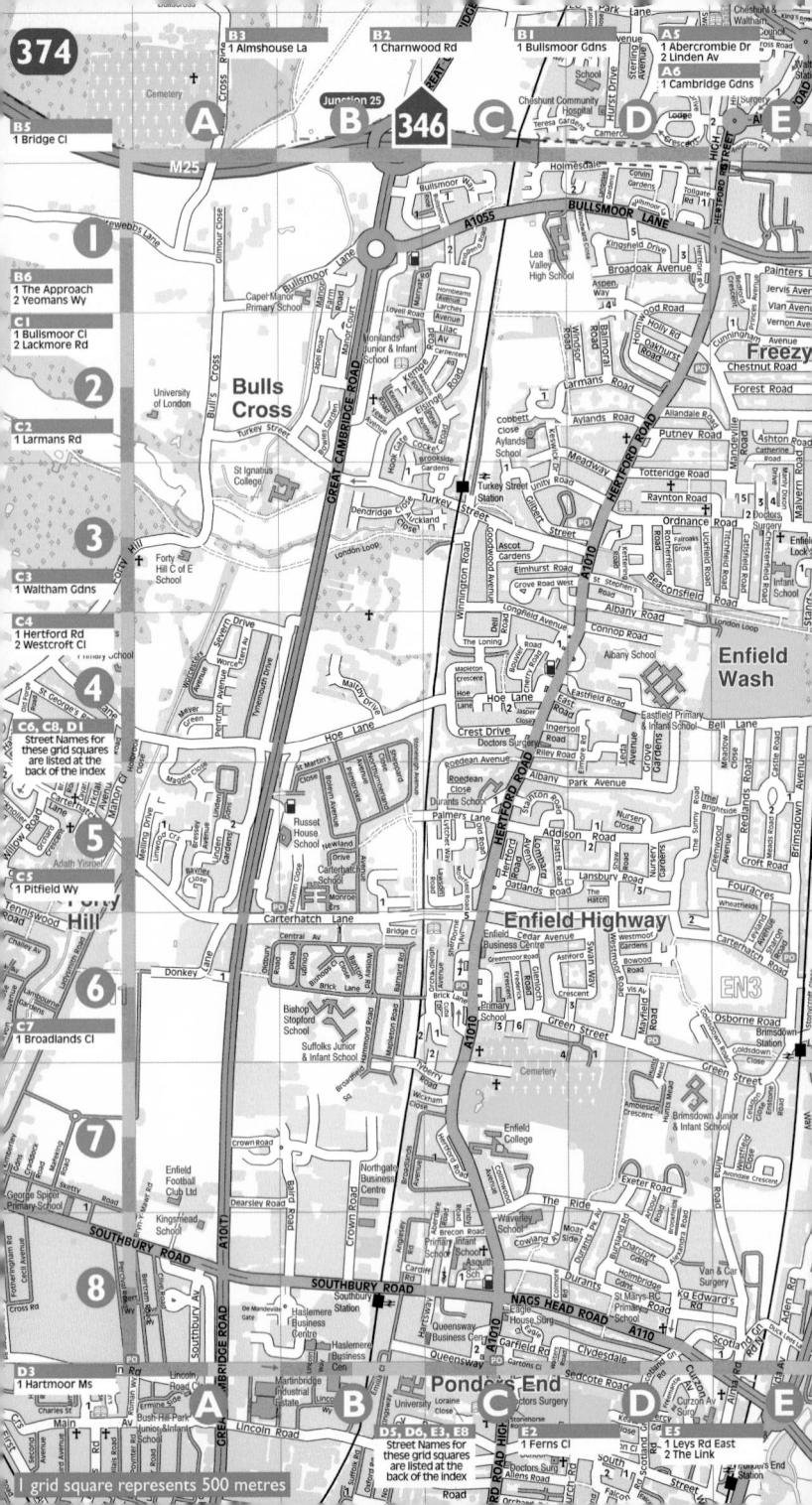

Junction 27/6

F G H 351 J K

I

2

3

4

380

5

6

7

8

F G H 406 J K

Peakes Farm

Garnish Hall

Coopersale Lane

Theydon Garnon

Hobbs Cross

Hobbs Cross Road

M25

Skinners Farm

Brook House

Hydes Farm

Hill Farm

Three Forests Way

Arnolds Farm

ONGAR ROAD

Epping Lane

ONGAR ROAD   A113

Church Lane

Three Forests Way

Doctors Surgery

New Farm Lane

Pancroft

The Mead

Hoe Lane

Knights
Mead
Bay

Alderwood Drive

Abridge

Lambourne

Three Forests Way

Palch Park

Great Wood

The
Poplars

Hoe Lane

Three Forests

Th
Me

Little End

The Old Rectory

LONDON

River Roding

I

Three Forests Way

Murrells Farm

Aspen Wood

2

Traceys Farm

3

BERWICK LANE

Wayletts

Lawns

A113

LONDON ROAD

4

Rose Hall Farm

382

Mitchells Farm

Shonks Mill Road

5

Howletts Hall

Church

6

Mill Lane

Navestock Heath

Sabine's Green

Murthering Lane

Old Road

7

Loft Hall

ering ket

tismill en

M25

8

Horseman Side

Brook Farm

Murthering Lane

Old Road

408

Jenkins Farm

Tyseahill Farm

384

356

411

383

Tip's Cross

A B C D E

B1
1 Glen Hazel

Stubbers Farm

First Avenue
Second Avenue
Nursery Road

HOOK End Lane

Hay Green Lane

Ha
Green

1

**Hook
End**

Hook

End Road

Mill Lane

The Robins

Whitelands

Beehive Chase
Honey Close

Blackmore Road
Deartree Close

Ouring's Cl

2

Church Lane

Widbrook

Barn Mead

Priory Mead

Watts Green Road

Field Kiln

Plover's Mead

Watts Grn La

Whites Lane

Mountnessing Road

All Chru

Adam

Doddinghurst County Infant School

3

Doddinghurst

Doddinghurst C of E Junc

Church Lane

Rectory Chase

Lane

Brook

**Peartree
Green**

Brook La

Middle Green

Parsonage Field

Pettits Lane

**Swallows
Cross**

Wyatt's Green Road

Peartree Lane

Harpers

Dagwood

Lane

Doddinghurst Road

Lime Grove

Apple Tree Crescent

Willow Close

Peartree Close

Park Meadow

Mountnessing Lane

River Wid

4

Davis Lane

Park Farm

383

Park Wood

5

America Farm

CM15

Heard's Farm

6

Wishfields Farm

7

Sumner's Farm

Palmer's Farm

Hall Lane

Heard's Lane

8

**Pilgrims
Hatch**

Lascelles Close

tch Road

Brickhouse Farm

Canterbury Tye Hall

Hall Lane

A12(t)

CHELM

Olive

Rochfor

A B C D E

1 grid square represents 500 metres

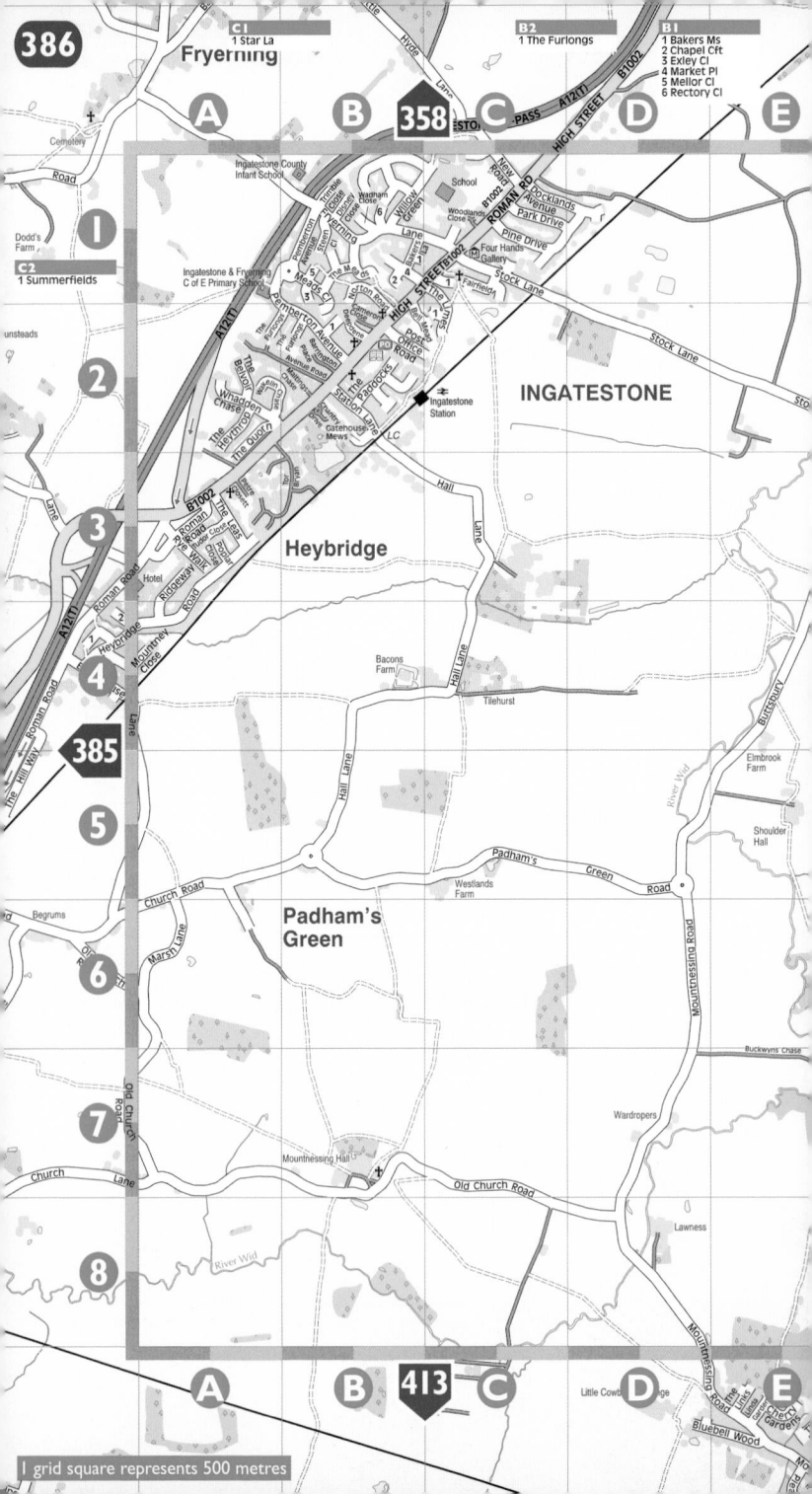

I grid square represents 500 metres

F G H 363 J K

I
2
3
4
392
5
6
7
8

Creephedge

Creephedge
House

Hyde
Hall

Buckhatch
Farm

Bartlett's
Farm

Buckhatch Lane

Mill House

Potter's Lane

Potter's Farm

East Hanningfield Road

Mill La

Coal

Rettendon

Ilgar's
Manor

Willow Grove

Wor

Wickfo

WICKFO

Tabrum's

A132

BURNHAM ROAD

Mark's
Farm

Rettendon
Grange Farm

Rettendon
Hall

Woodham Road

MAIN

County Primary
School

Sonters
Down

ROAD

ROAD

Church
cha

Meadow Road

Rettendon
Lodge

Hayes Chase

F G H 418 J K

Rettendon
Place

Woodham Road

Hayes Chase

Main Road

Creephedge Lane

392

Chapel Row

(A) (B) **364** (C) (D) (E)

Woodham Ferrers

Ormonds Crs
St Marys C of E Aided Primary School

1

2

Edwin's Hall Road

3

Ilgar's Manor

Shaw's Farm

Hamberts Farm

4

Woodville Primary School

BURNHAM ROAD

391

5

Woodham Ferrers Stn

6

Woodham Fenn

The Elmwood CP School

Albert Road

7

Rettendon Grange Farm

Tabrum's Farm

Chetwood CP School

8

Eyott's Farm

Hayes

(A) Hayes Chase (B) **419** (C) (D) (E)

Hayes Farm

Long Reach

I grid square represents 500 metres

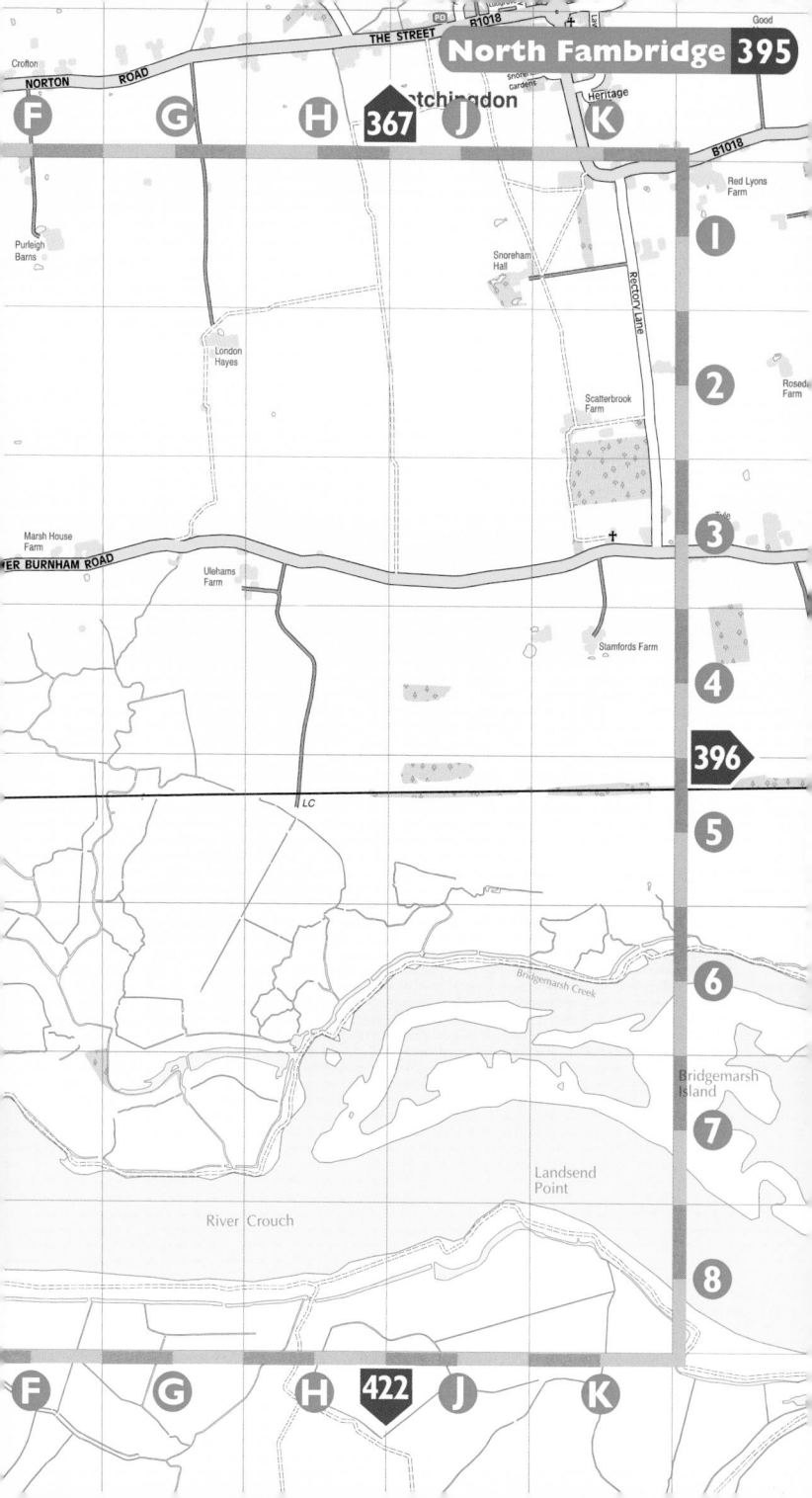

THE STREET

B1018

Good

NORTON ROAD

Crofton

F

G

H

367

J

tchingdon

Heritage

K

B1018

Red Lyons Farm

Purleigh Barns

I

Snoreham Hall

2

Rosed Farm

London Hayes

Scatterbrook Farm

Rectory Lane

Marsh House Farm

ER BURNHAM ROAD

3

Uleharns Farm

Stamfords Farm

4

396

LC

5

Bridgemarsh Creek

6

Bridgemarsh Island

7

Landsend Point

River Crouch

8

F

G

H

422

J

K

F G H **369** J K

SOUTHMINST

Mayland Hall

Bovill Up

Mayland Court

I

Scott's Farm

2

Caidge Far

ROAD BUTTON'S HILL **B1018**

Joyce's Farm

Old Heath Road

Seamer Road

Scarborough Road

Dairy Farm

Dairy Farm Road

The Endway

High House

3

Old Heath Farm

4

The Endway

HAM ROAD

Althorne Lodge

398 Mangapps
ps Farm
ay Museum

5

Andrews Farm

B1010

Stoke's Hall

MALDON ROAD

Elm Farm

Inners Cl

Green Lane

6

Ferry Road

Ostend

Meadow
Way
St Peter's Fld

MALDON ROAD

Creeksea Lane

Welland Road

Creeksea Hall

7

Burnham On Crouch
Golf Club Ltd

Burnham Business Park

Cliff Reach

Springfield Industrial Est

LC

8

Creeksea

Ferry Road

White House

F G H **424** J K

Ferry Road

F G H 371 J K

I
2
3
4
400
5
6
7
8

North Wycke

Wraywick Farm

ncole Farm

ncole

Twizzlefoot Bridge

West Wick
Marsh Road

Redward

F G H 426 J K

400

A   B   372   C   D   E Brook
                                                            Farm

1

2

3   Middle
                                                            Wick

4   Turncole Farm

399

5   Old
           Turncole   Montsale

6
                                                            Deal
                                                            Hall

7   Coney
           Marsh Road   East   Hall
                             Wick

8 Redward   Holliwell Farm

A   B   427   C   D   E

1 grid square represents 500 metres

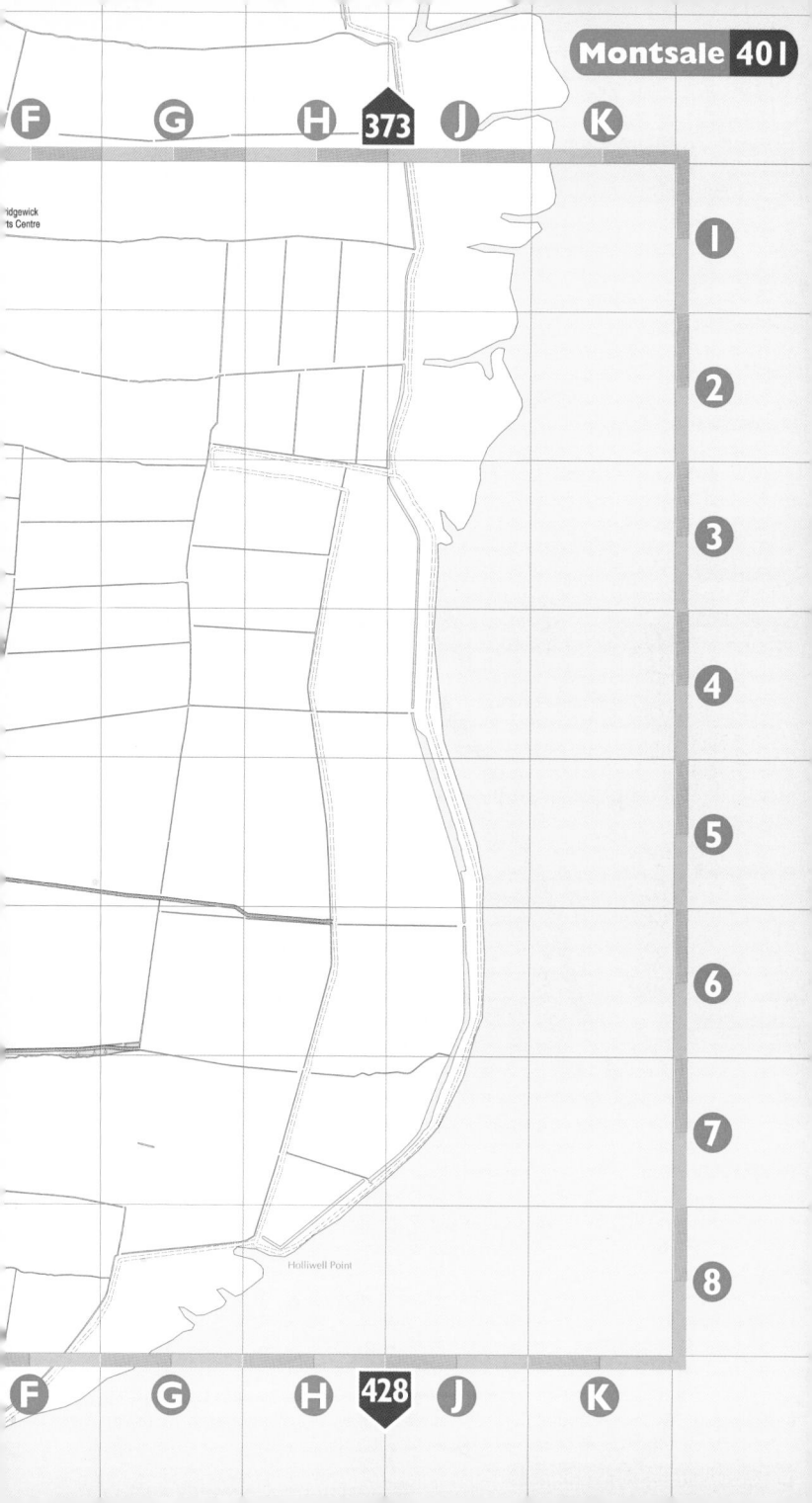

F G H 373 J K

I

2

3

4

5

6

7

8

ridgewick
ts Centre

Holliwell Point

**William
Girling
Reservoir**

I grid square represents 500 metres

F3
1 Connaught Rd

F5
1 Coney Burrows
2 Little Friday Rd

F6
1 Friday Hl
2 Newgate St

376

F
G
H
J
K

Sewardstonebury

EPPING NEW ROAD

HIGH ROAD

1

F7
1 Betoyne Av
2 Brookhouse Gdns
3 Mason Rd
4 Nightingale Cl
5 Waterhall Av

2

G5
1 British Legion Rd
2 Rookwood Gdns

3

G7
1 Hatchwoods
2 The Hollow

4

404

Queen Elizabeth Museum

Chingford Station

Forest

Warren Pond Road

St Johns C of E Primary School

Loyola Preparatory School

Scotland Road

PALMERSTON RD

5

J3
1 Hawsted

Fairfield Clinic

Holly House Private Hospital

Westbury Road

Princes Road

Buckhurst Hill

6

J7
1 Forest Cl

Heathcote School

Whitehall Primary School

WHITEHALL ROAD

A110

Rosslyn Avenue

Whitehall Lane

Bancrofts School

Woodford Wells

Riding Valley Station

Old Bancroftians FC

7

K1
1 Longfield

The Pines

Montrose Close

Woodside Road

Denehurst Gardens

Wells Primary School

Belmont Close

Avon House School

8

gford Hatch

CHINGFORD LANE

A1009

Trinity Catholic Lower School

A1009

Worcester Crescent

Monkham Close

Queen's Ave

Broad Oak

Ray Lodge Junior Infant School

F
G
H
J
K

K7
1 Grangeway

A1009

G4, H8, K8
Street Names for these grid squares are listed at the back of the index

K5
1 Kings Pl

Woodford

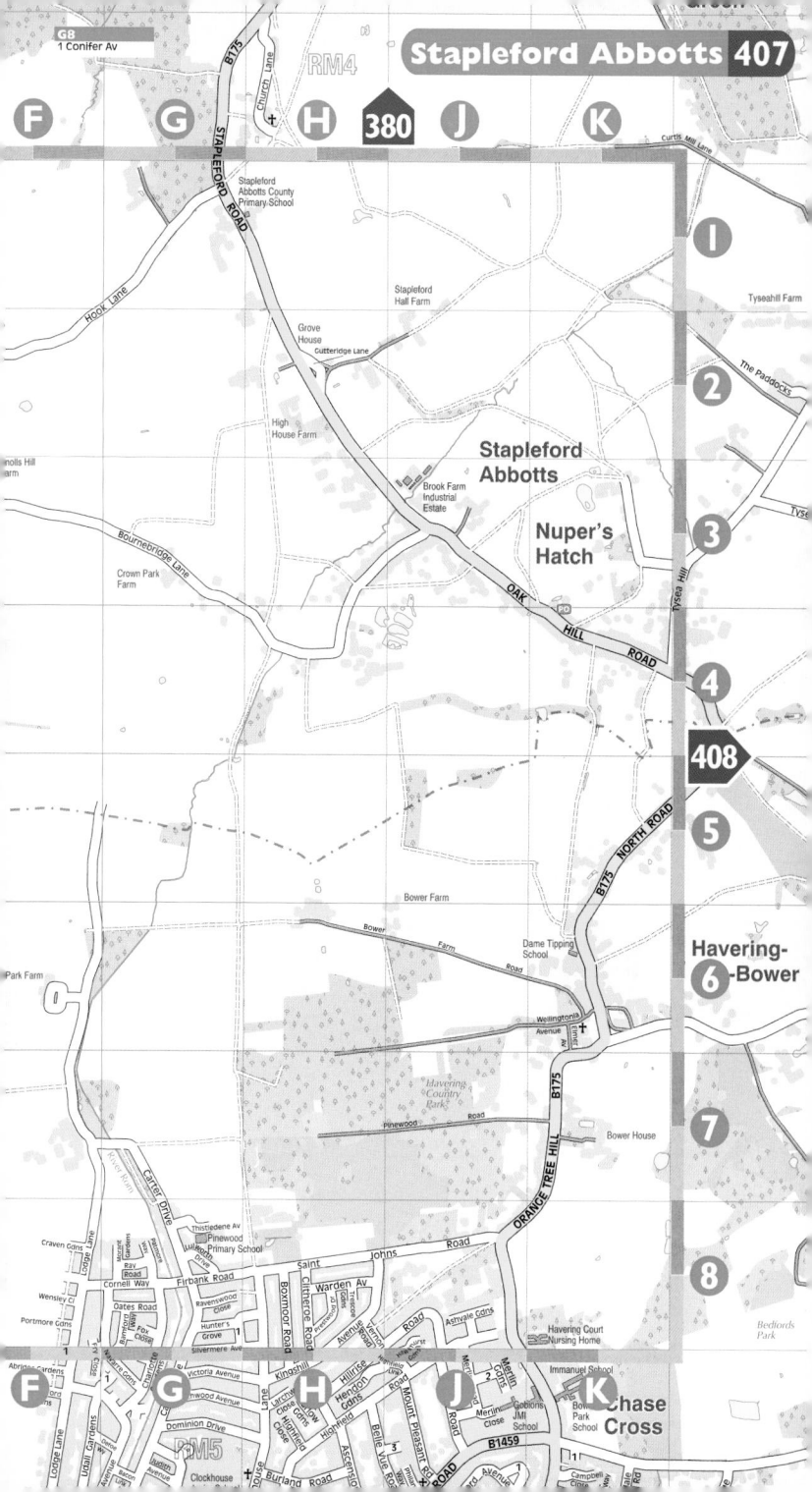

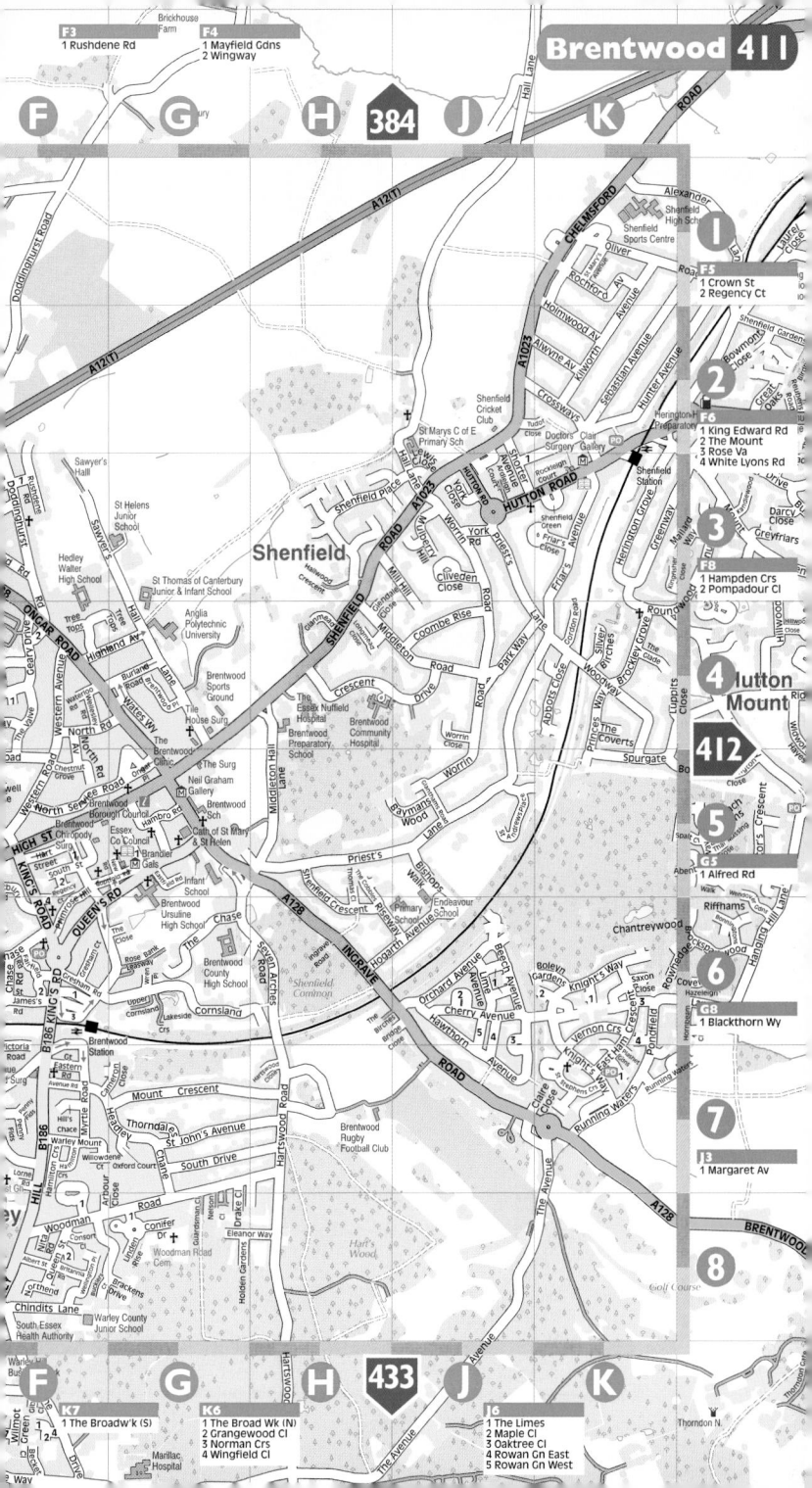

F3
1 Lapwing Rd

F6
1 Bridge House Cl
2 Charlotte Av
3 Farnes Av
4 Laburnum Cl
5 Lavender Wy

F7
1 Park Cl

F5, G5, G7, H4
Street Names for these grid squares are listed at the back of the index

F8
1 Finchingfield Wy
2 Halstead Ct

G3
1 Canewdon Cl

G6
1 South Beech Av
2 Tiptree Gv

G8
1 Campbell Cl
2 Johnson Cl
3 Thackerey Rw

H5
1 Franklins Wy

H6
1 Mendip Cl
2 Nayland Cl

Shotgate

I5
1 Highcliffe Cl
2 St Catherines Cl

I6
1 Hawkins Cl
2 St David's Wy

H7, H8, J8
Street Names for these grid squares are listed at the back of the index

J7
1 Arran Ct
2 Rochford Cl

K7
1 Great Saling
2 Heathercroft Rd
3 Hornchurch Cl
4 Woodberry Rd

K6
1 Bakers Farm Cl
2 Sandown Cl

K5
1 Glencoe Dr

420

E7
1 Beatrice Cl
2 Caernarvon Cl
3 Chatsworth Gdns
4 Gatscombe Cl
5 Hampton Ct
6 Hanover Ms
7 Woodstock Crs

D7
1 Balmoral Gdns
2 Belvedere Av
3 Chevening Gdns
4 Laburnum Cl
5 Lambeth Ms
6 Marlborough Wk
7 St James's Wk
8 Sandringham Av

C7
1 Silvertree Cl

A   B   393   C   D   E

River Crouch

Brandy Hole Yacht Club

Brandy Hole

Clevis Drive

Marsh Farm Country

Marsh Farm

Anchor Reach

Bridge

Walker

Cingle Lock

Brace Walk

Kingsmans Farm Road

I

E8
1 Claybrick Av

Pooles Lane

Lane

Long Lane

Riverside Junior School

2

HULLBRIDGE

Keswick Avenue

Mayfield Avenue
Clinic

Mapledene Avenue

Thorpedene Avenue

Waxwell Road

Oakleigh Av

High Elms Road

South Av

Kendal Close

Coventry Hill

Cherrydene

Beech Rd

Pinewood Close

Cracknell's Farm

3

Brook Rd

Turnham Road

Meadow Rd

Lower Road

Hullbridge

Coventry Close

4

Sheepcotes Farm

Hillcrest Avenue

Central Avenue

Kendal Avenue

First Av

Second Av

Pevensey Gardens

Pevensey Gdns

Doctors Surgery

Rosilian Drive

Lower Hockley

Lower Road

419

5

Blountswood Road

Wadham Park Avenue

Wadham Park Avenue

Merton Road

Church Road

Lower Road

Plumb Mount

6

Wadham Park Farm

Mill Hill

SS5

Murrels Lane

Church Rd

St Peters Road

HOCKLEY

7

Blounts Farm

Folly Chase

Hockley Primary School

Westminster Drive

Folly

Sunnyfield Gdns

Laburnum Grove

Hawthorne Gardens

Marion Road

Spencer Drive

Buckingham Road

Bramerton Road

Betterer Drive

MAIN ROAD

Police Station

Woodlands Cl

The Spinneys

The Hylands

Home Farm

Fountain La

HIGH ROAD

ALDERMAN'S HILL B1013

Hillside Road

Bullwood Approach

Crown Road

Woodside Road

8

Hambro Close

Drake Cl

Hambricks Close

Nelson Road

The Gattens

ROAD

Upr

A   B   442   C   D   E

Bishopsfield Lane

Hockley Woods

Bullwood Hall

422

River Crouch

A8
1 The Bramleys
2 The Laxtons
3 The Russets

A7
1 Copelands

A6
1 Assandune Cl

A   B   395   C   D   E

1

2

3

Pudsey
Hall

4

Scaldhurst
Farm

Pudsey Hall Lane

Larkhill Av

421
on Road

Lark Hill Road

5

Church Road

Rushy Way

Vestry Way

Moon's
Farm

ASHINGDON

6

le Chase

Stanley Road

Clifton Road

York Road

Alexandra Road

Albert

Arnold
Wy

Moons
Close

Ashingdon Road

Mink
Farm

Little
Doggetts

Hyde Wood Lane

7

Rectory Avenue

Hogwood Way

Hogarth Way

Boulton

Moat Crt

Canewdon View Road

Golden Cross Road

Nelson
Road

Harden
Avenue

Lascelles Gardens

Apton Hall Road

Doggetts

Brays

8

Rectory Av

Ashingdon Surgery

Princess Gardens

Central Avenue

Hareweood

The Bramleys

Becket
Close

Brays Lane

King
Edmunds
School

Little
Stambridge Hall

Rectory Road

Oxford Rd

444

Hall

A   B   444   C   D   E

1 grid square represents 500 metres

H1
1 The Quay
2 Riverside Rd
3 Shore Rd

Station

Station Ad

Aldsandra
Mildmay
Industrial Est

Devonshire Road

The Burnham
Surg

Arcadia Road

ON-CROUCH

Winstree
Road

Essex Road

New Road

Sandpit
Lane

B1021

Crouch
Road

Clinic

York
Road

Western Road

Chapel Road

Albert Road

Queen's
Road

HIGH STREET

Orchard Road

Providence

Ramblers
Way

Wick Road

Burnham Wick

Remembrance Av

STATION ROAD

The
Gallery

Normandy Road

Louise Road

Station
Road

Argyle
Road

Crouch
Yacht Club

Museum

PH 3

Royal Burnham
Yacht Club

Old Club House

Belvedere
Road

Royal Corinthian
Yacht Club

River Crouch

Ringwood Bar

Grapnells

0

Wallasea
Island

Paglesham Pool

lesham
tend

Waterside Road

River Roach

Potton
Point

F G H 398 J K

I

2

3

4

426

5

6

7

8

F G H 447 J K

426

A   B   **399**   C   D   E

I   Burnham Wick

2   Ringwood Bar

3   Wallasea Ness

4
425

Brankfleet

5   Wallasea Island

6   The Qua

7

8   Potton Point   River Roach   Quay Reach   Horseshoe Corner

A   B   **448**   C   D   E

Redward

I grid square represents 500 metres

F   G   H   **400**   J   K

Holliwell Farm

1

2

River Crouch   River Crouch

3

Clark's
Hard

4

428

Nase
Wick

5

Monkton
Barn

6

Lodge Farm

PO
Churchend

Foulness Island 7

8 East Wick

Priestwood

Rugwood Farm

F   G   H   **449**   J   K

Holliwell Point

A B **401** C D E

1

2 River Crouch

Great Shell Corner

3 East Newlands

4

427

5 Courtsend

The Chase

6

Lodge Farm New House Farm

7 Foulness Island

Fishermans Head

8 East Wick

A B C D E

Eastwick Head

1 grid square represents 500 metres

F　G　H　J　K

Foulness
Point

I

2

3

4

5

6

7

8

F　G　H　J　K

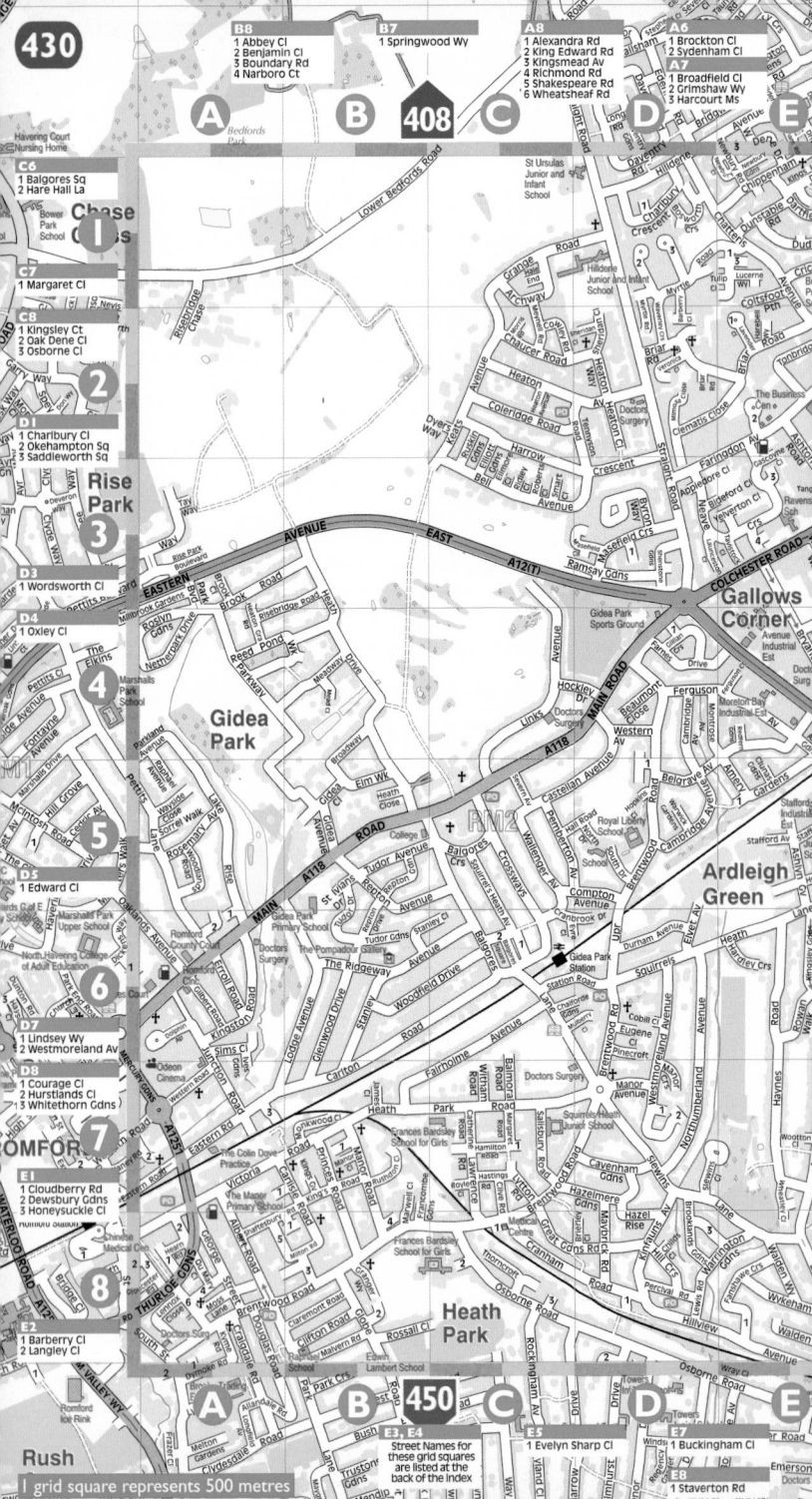

430

408

450

B8
1 Abbey Cl
2 Benjamin Cl
3 Boundary Rd
4 Narboro Ct

B7
1 Springwood Wy

A8
1 Alexandra Rd
2 King Edward Rd
3 Kingsmead Av
4 Richmond Rd
5 Shakespeare Rd
6 Wheatsheaf Rd

A6
1 Brockton Cl
2 Sydenham Cl

A6
1 Broadfield Cl
2 Grimshaw Wy
3 Harcourt Ms

C6
1 Balgores Sq
2 Hare Hall La

C7
1 Margaret Cl

C8
1 Kingsley Ct
2 Oak Dene Cl
3 Osborne Cl

D1
1 Charibury Cl
2 Okehampton Sq
3 Saddleworth Sq

D3
1 Wordsworth Rd

D4
1 Oxley Cl

D5
1 Edward Cl

D7
1 Lindsey Wy
2 Westmoreland Av

D8
1 Courage Cl
2 Hurstlands Cl
3 Whitethorn Gdns

E1
1 Cloudberry Rd
2 Dewsbury Gdns
3 Honeysuckle Cl

E2
1 Barberry Cl
2 Langley Cl

E3, E4
Street Names for these grid squares are listed at the back of the index

E5
1 Evelyn Sharp Cl

E7
1 Buckingham Cl

E8
1 Staverton Rd

Chase Cross

Rise Park

Gidea Park

Gallows Corner

Ardleigh Green

Heath Park

ROMFORD

Rush

1 grid square represents 500 metres

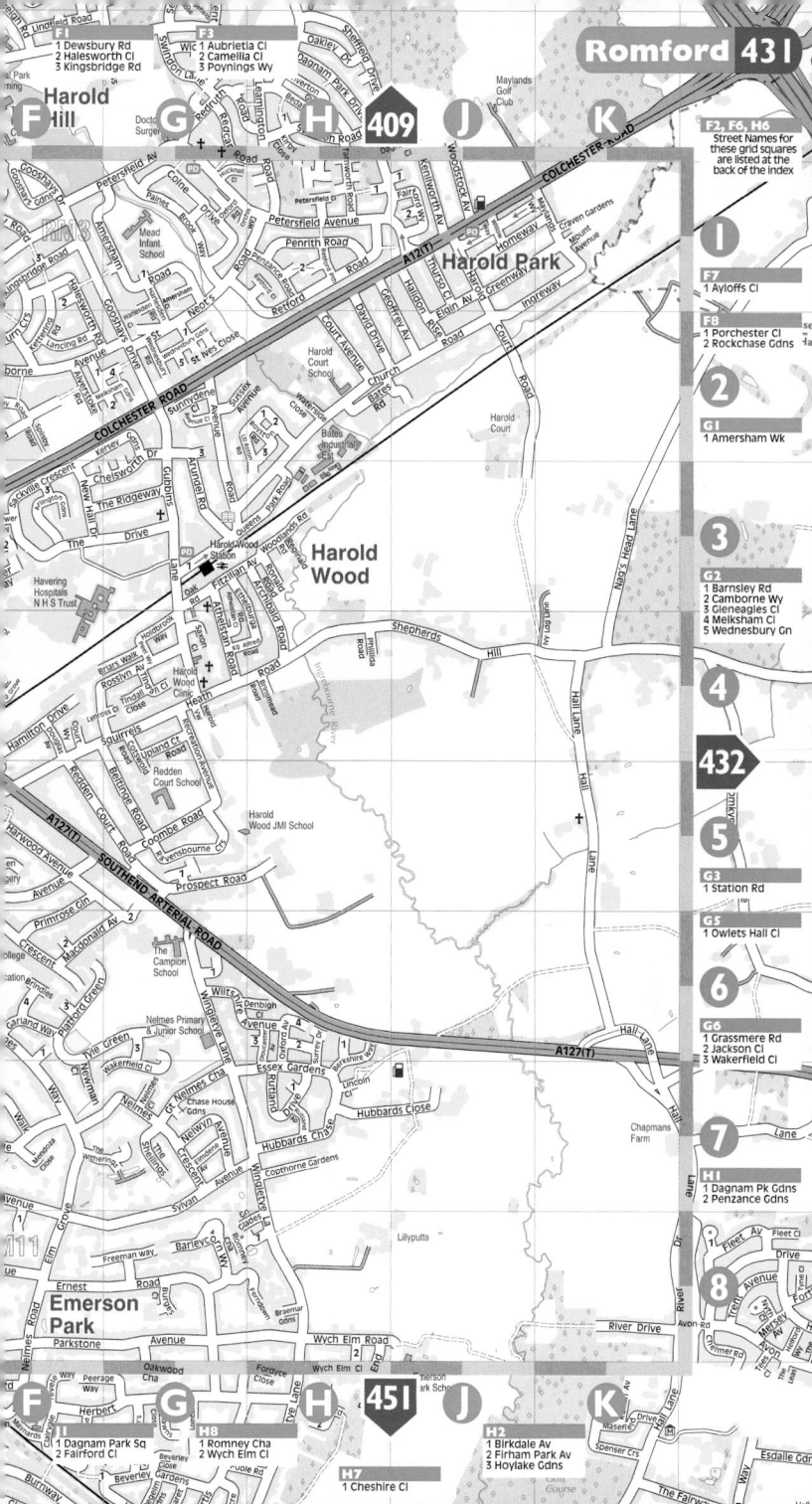

F Harold Hill

G

H 409

J

K

Harold Park

Harold Wood

Emerson Park

F

G

H 451

J

K

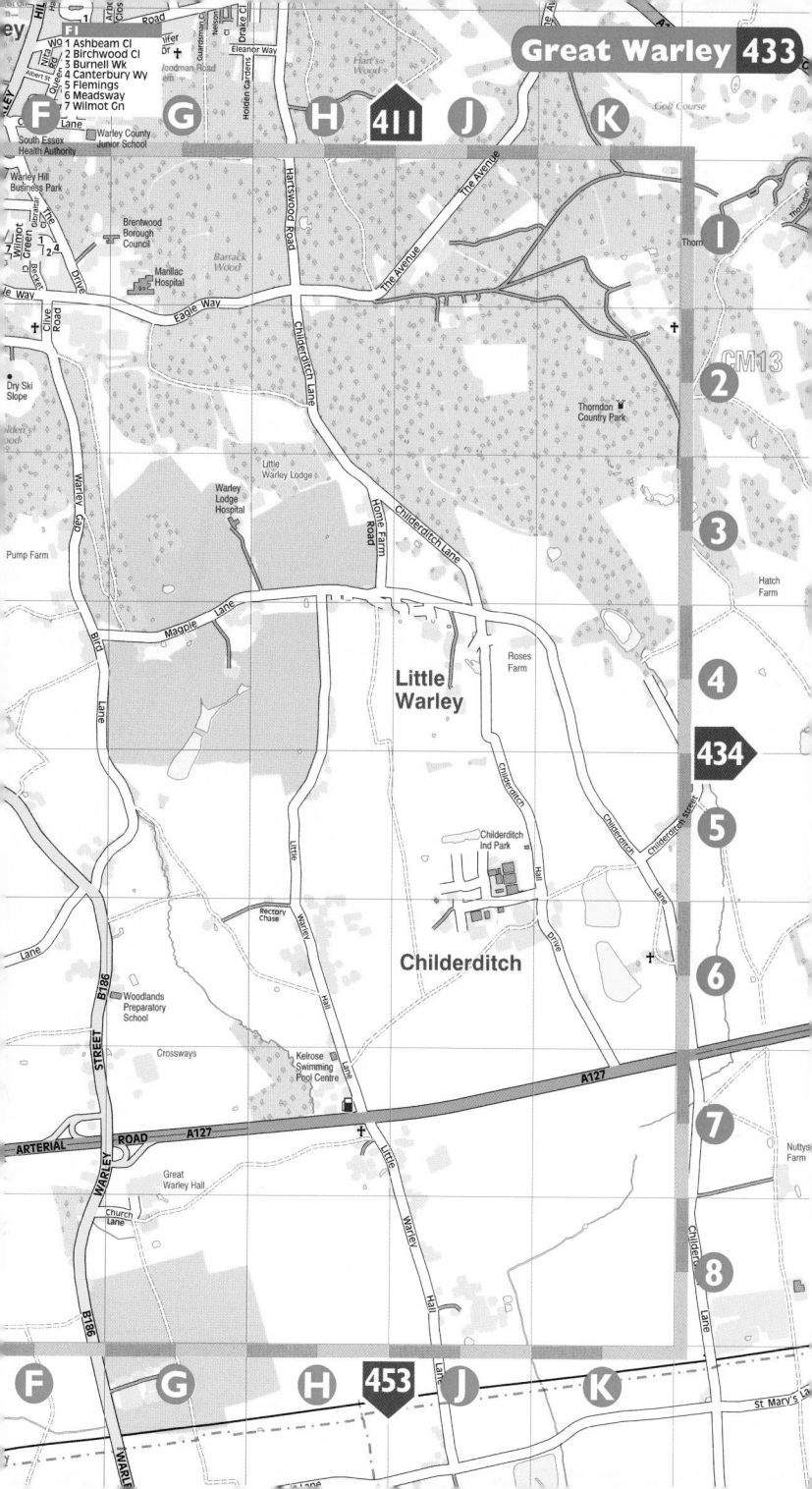

411

F **G** **H** **J** **K** **I**

WY
F1
1 Ashbeam Cl
2 Birchwood Cl
3 Burnell Wk
4 Canterbury Wy
5 Flemings
6 Meadsway
7 Wilmot Gn

South Essex
Health Authority

Warley County
Junior School

Warley Hill
Business Park

Brentwood
Borough
Council

Marillac
Hospital

Barrack Wood

Hart's
Wood

Golf Course

Thorn

CM13

The Avenue

Hartswood Road

Eagle Way

Childerditch Lane

Clive Road

Dry Ski
Slope

Pump Farm

Little
Warley Lodge

Warley
Lodge Hospital

Home Farm Road

Childerditch Lane

Thorndon
Country Park

Hatch
Farm

Magpie Lane

Birch Lane

Bird Lane

Little Warley Hall Lane

**Little
Warley**

Roses
Farm

434

Childerditch

Childerditch Hall Drive

Childerditch Street

Childerditch
Ind Park

Childerditch

Rectory
Chase

Woodlands
Preparatory
School

Crossways

Kelrose
Swimming
Pool Centre

A127

STREET B186

Lane

ARTERIAL ROAD A127

Great
Warley Hall

Church
Lane

WARLEY STREET B186

Little Warley Hall Lane

Nuttys
Farm

Childerditch Lane

F **G** **H** 453 **J** **K**

WARLEY

St Mary's La

A128
BRE**WOOD ROAD**
C2 1 Cricketers Rw
B8 1 Sanderson Cl
B1 1 Meadows Cl

Golf Course

A
Common Road
Monks
Chase
Pittman
Close
Thorndon
Gate
B
412
C
D
E
Ingrave

Heron
Hall

I
The Meadows
Peartrees
Whitty Avenue
Crenan Close
Thorndon N.

C8
1 Burntwood Cl
2 Lombards Cha
3 Witham Gdns

Ingrave
Johnstone
C of E School
Thorndon
Approach
Cricketers Lane
Hernshaw
Donovan's Garden
Billericay Road

CM13

2
Thorridon

D2
1 Glebe Gdns
2 Rectory La
Thorndon
Brentwood Road
Herongate

3
Park House

Hatch Farm
Thorndon S.

4
Brentwood Road
A128

Cockridden
Farm Industrial
Estate

433

5
Childerditch Street
Childerditch Lane

Hotel
Halfway House
A127

6
Ea
Ho

SOUTHEND ARTERIAL ROAD
A127

A127

7
Nuttys Farm
West Horndon CP School
Thorndon Avenue
Tilbury Road

West Horndon
Cadogan Avenue
Station Road

8
Horndon Ind Park
Dunmow Gdns
Pytfield Cl
Freshwell Gdns
Childerditch Lane

West Horndon St

A
St Mary's Lane
B
454
C
D
Tilbury Road
E

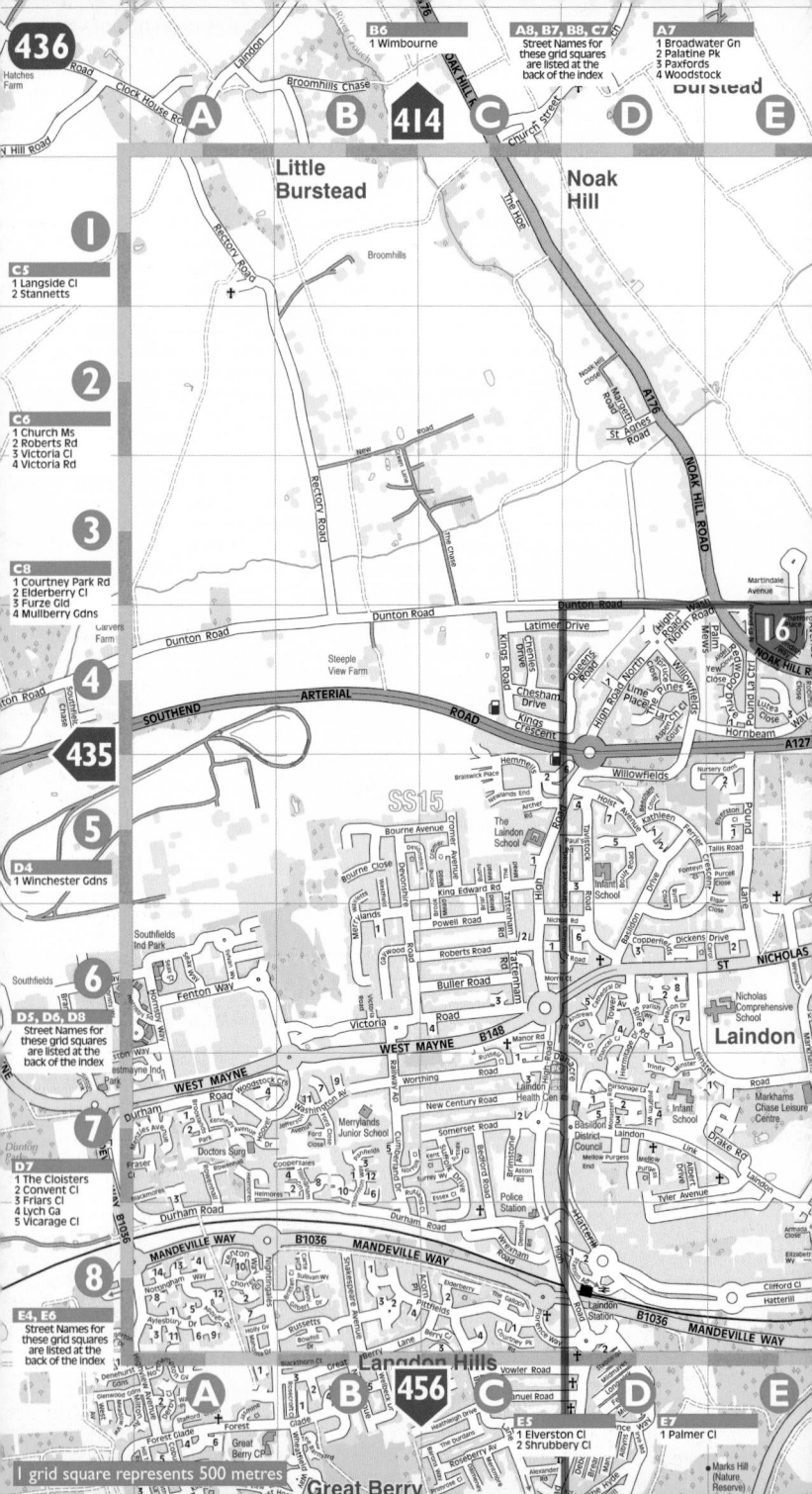

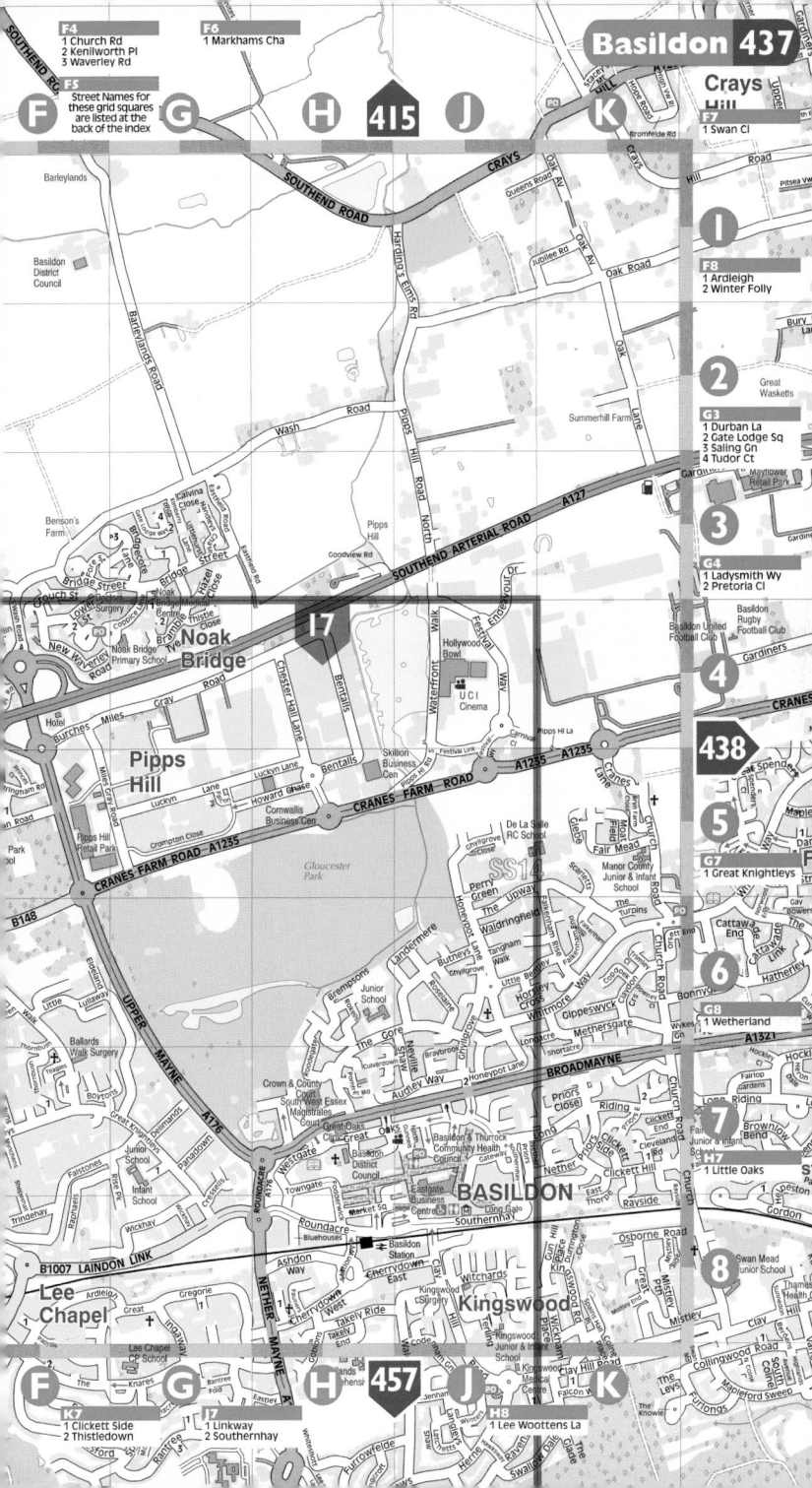

Crays Hill

Barleylands

Basildon District Council

Summerhill Farm

Great Wasketts

Benson's Farm

Pipps Hill

Noak Bridge

Pipps Hill

Gloucester Park

BASILDON

Lee Chapel

Kingswood

WICKFORD
F3
1 Josselin Ct
F4
1 Calvert Dr
2 Charleston Ct
3 Cooks Gn
4 Great Leighs Wy
5 Orlando Dr
6 Wollaston Wy
417
The Robert Frew Medical Centre
F
G
H
J
K
Cranfield Park Road
Elms Business Park
Sappers Farm
Fanton Hall Farm
Lower Park Road
Upper Park Road
Newlands Road
Cranfield
SS12
The Chase
Meadow Way
Fairway Park
Fanton Av
Road
Nevendon
Hovefields Avenue
Hovefields Drive
Cricketers Retail Park
Pantile Farm
Honiley Avenue
A127
SOUTHEND ARTER
Cranfield Pk Av
Hovefields Av
Scimitar Park Industrial Estate
Harrow Road
School Lane
Essex County Council
Josselin Road
Wollaston Way
Watkins Cl
Bradfield's Farm
Burnt Mills Road
Burnt Mills Rd
Lane
Pound
North Benfleet Hall
North Benfleet Hall Road
Elm Road
Barclay Road
Acacia Road
Carlton Road
Upper Avenue
Lower Avenue
Smilers Industrial Estate
Lawrence Road
Grange Road
Windsor Road
Osborne Road
Pound Lane
North Benfleet
Clifton Road
Katherine Road
Thomas Road
Cornwall Road
Cross Road
Clarence Road
Charleston Av
Camelot Gdns
Fairfax
Rushley
Lanhams
Gt Ranton
Havengore
Tyefields
Wilsner
Trenham Avenue
Crown Av
Kenneth Road
SS13
Little Chalvedon Hall
Homestead Road
Page Road
Lee Road
Una Road
Eric Road
Alpha Close
Highlands Crescent
Bowers Court Drive
Kelly Road
Westlake Avenue
William Rd
Canvey Rd
Glenwood School
Eversley CP School
Woodcote Crs
St Mary's
Manor Avenue
Leigh Fells
Crown
Tunstall Cl
Headcorn Cl
Elham Dri
Fairleigh Av
Bearsted Dr
Chilham Close
Eversley Road
Victor Avenue
Ilfracombe Avenue
Bowers Gifford
London Road
B1464
A13
A130
St Margarets School
Old Church Road
Church Road
Sadlers Hall Farm
Ivy Road
Albert Road
Clare Road
Romsey Dr
Romsey Rd
Malwood Road
Bouldrewood Road
Saxonville
Homefields Av
High Rd
Elmhurst Avenue
Primary School
Chestnut Grove
Limetree Avenue
Wavertree Road
HIGH ROAD
Cemetery
459
Bowers Hall
Church Road
1
F5
1 Brecon Cl
2 Meadgate
3 Pembroke Ms
4 Riffams Ct
5 Scaldhurst
2
F7
1 Biddenden Ct
3
F8
1 Bradbourne Wy
2 Challock Lees
4
440
5
G3
1 Rowhedge Cl
Stansfield Road
Woodcote Way
Eversley
6
H1
1 Cheyne Ct
Rushbottom Lane
7
K7
1 Wycombe Av
8

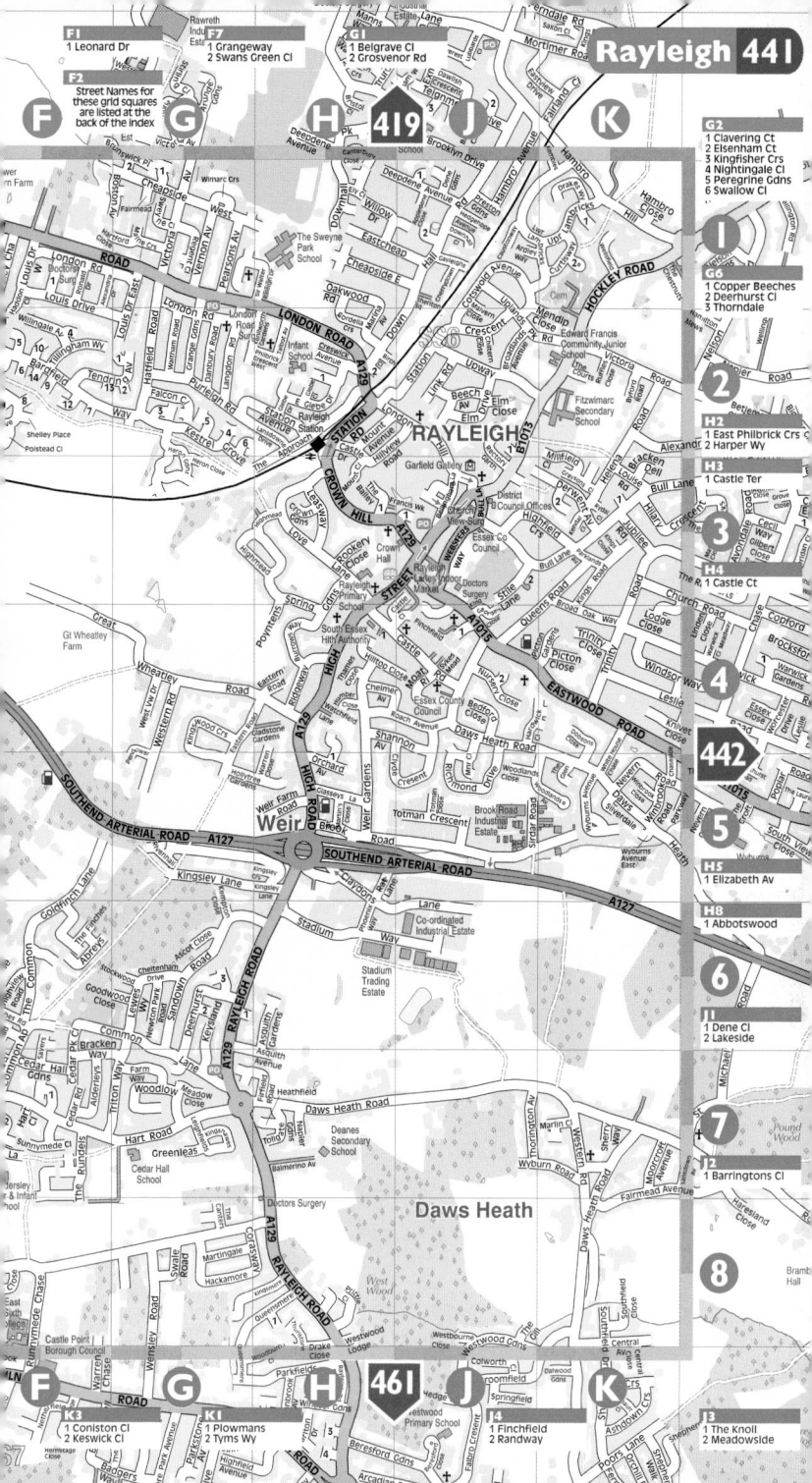

I grid square represents 500 metres

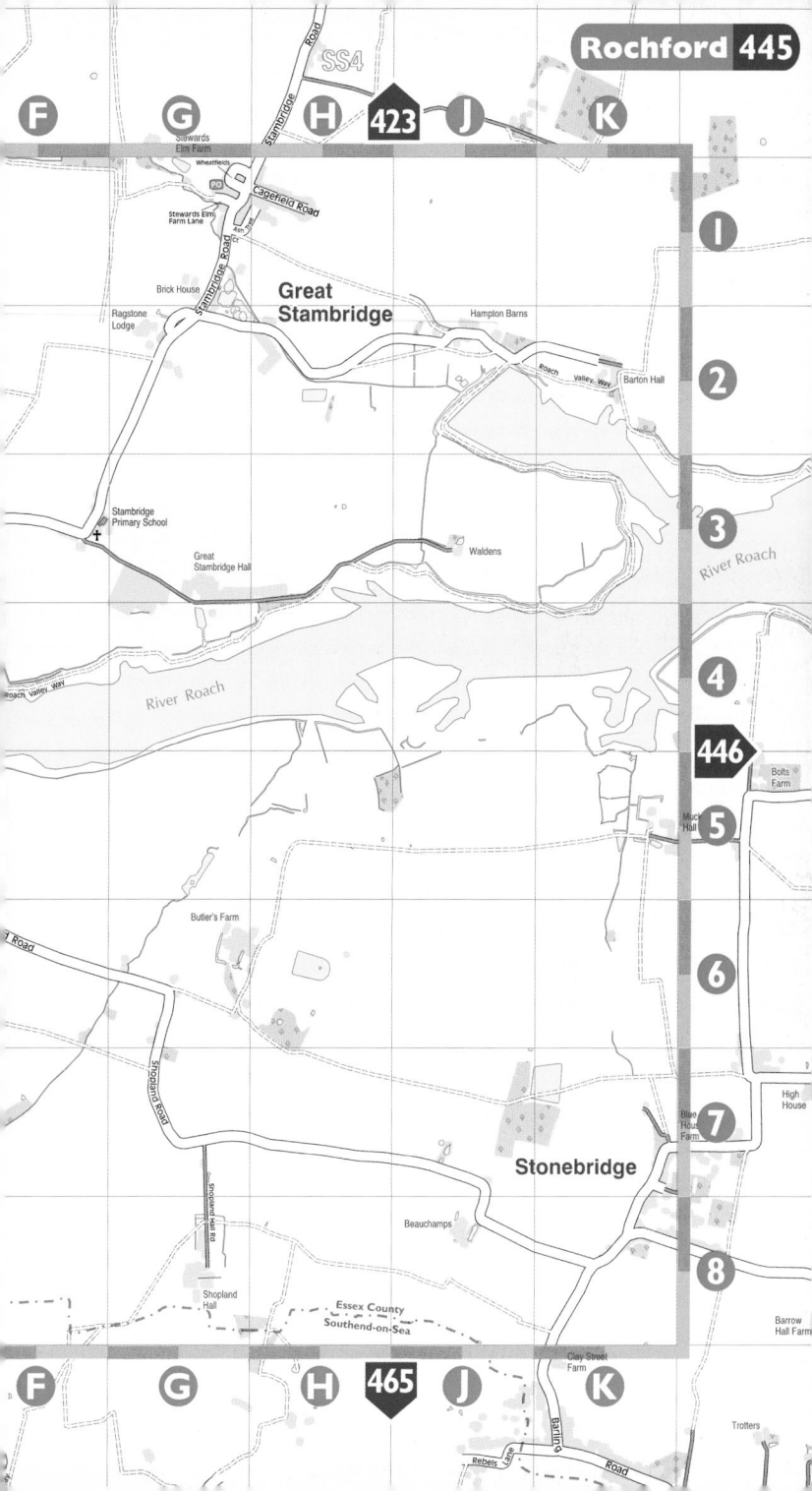

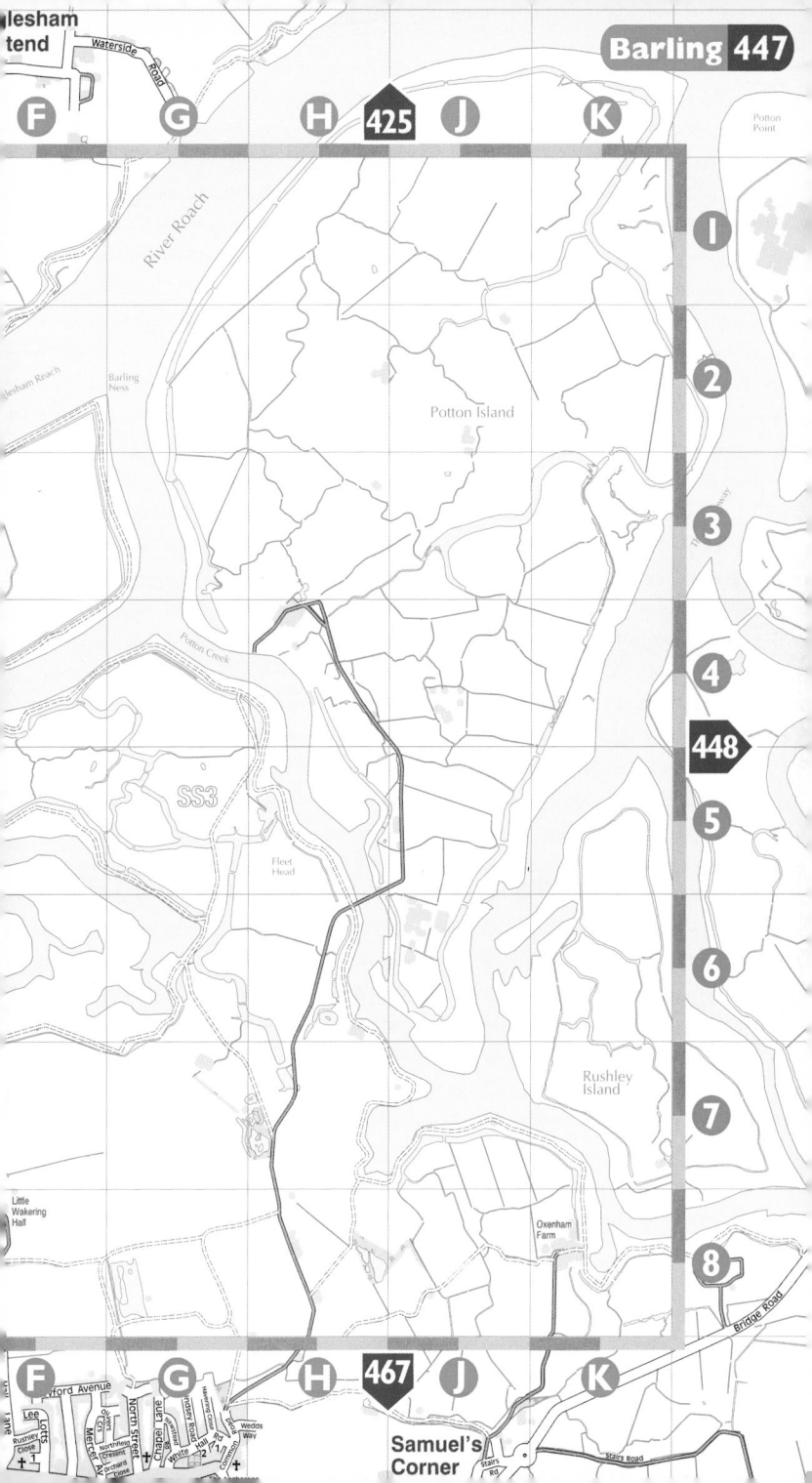

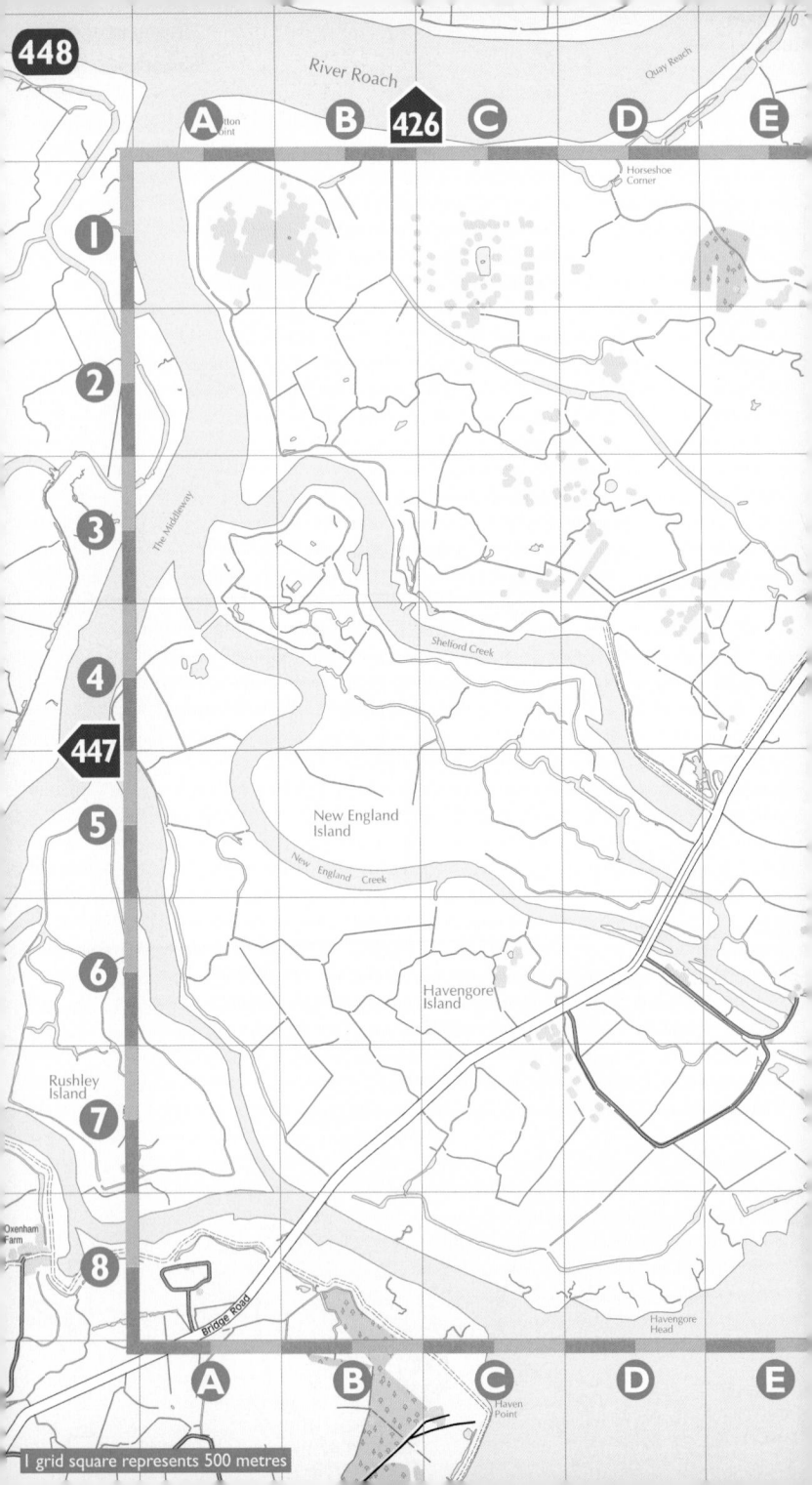

River Roach

Quay Reach

ilton
oint

Horseshoe
Corner

1

2

3

The Middleway

Shelford Creek

4

5

New England
Island

New England Creek

6

Havengore
Island

Rushley
Island

7

Oxenham
Farm

8

Bridge Road

Havengore
Head

A

B

C

Haven
Point

D

E

1 grid square represents 500 metres

F G Ωstwood H 427 J K East Wick

Rugwood Farm

1

2

Great
Burwood Farm

Rug... Head

3

4

Asplins
Head

5

Shelford
Head

6

7

8

F G H J K

Rush

Elm Park

430

I grid square represents 500 metres

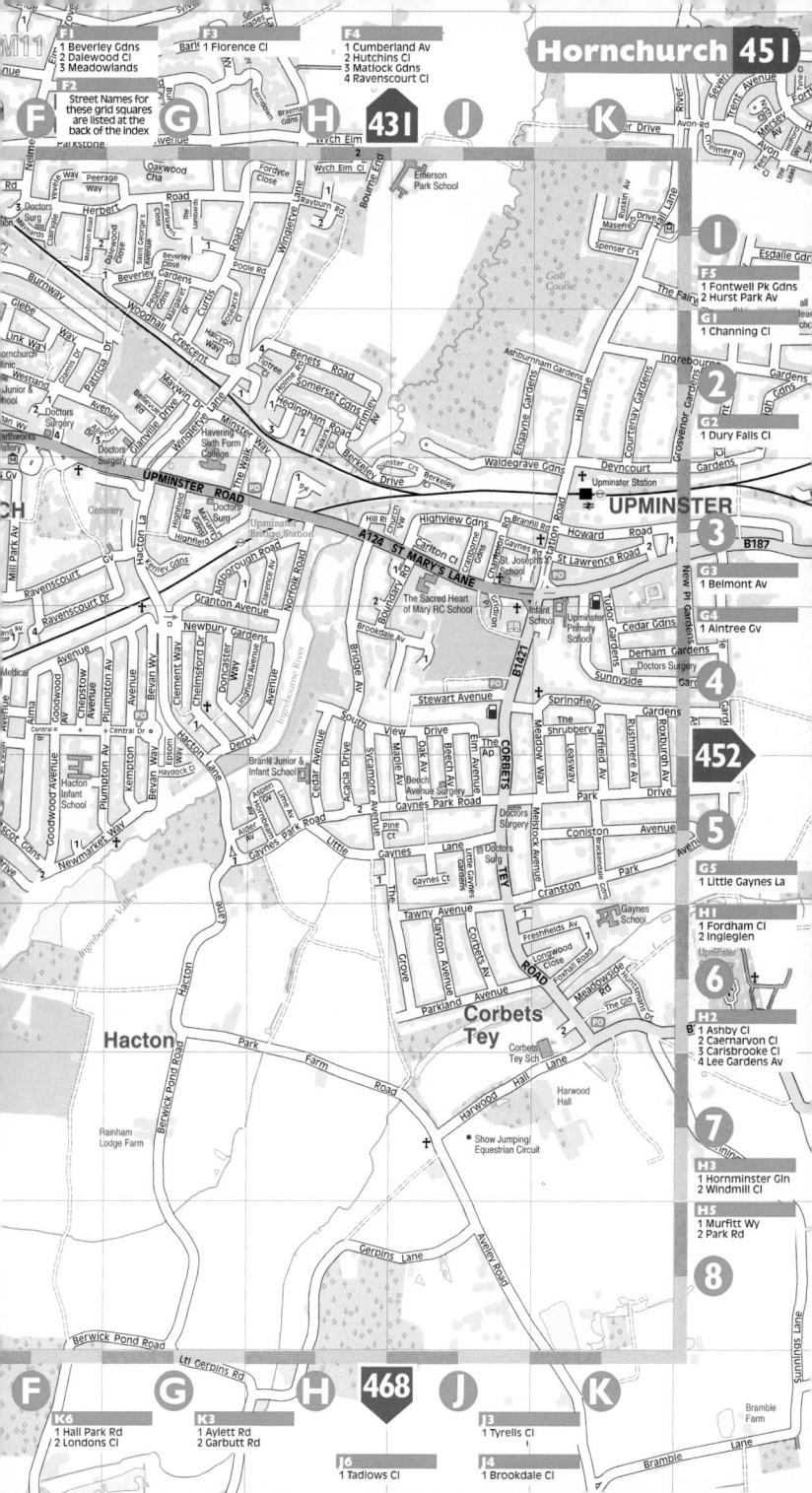

F G H **433** J K

I

2

3

4

454

5

6

7

8

F G H **470** J K

Warley Hall

Church Lane

B186

WARLEY STREET

St Mary's Lane

Monks Farm

Old Englands Farm

Puddle Dock

B186

CLAY TYE

Bury Farm

Clay Tye Farm

ROAD

B186

RM14

White Post Farm

Fen Lane

Corner Farm

Home Farm

OCKENDON ROAD

Havering Thurrock

Fen Farm

NORTH ROAD

St Mary's

Dunnings Lane

Thurrock Havering

Mar Dyke

Fen Lane

Warley Hall Lane

St Mary's Lane

atch Lane

454

West
Horndon

Cadogan Avenue

Station Road

TILBURY ROAD

Childerditch Lane

434

Dunmow Gdns

Dunmow Gdns

West
Horndon Station

Horndon Ind
Park

St Mary's Lane

Brentwood Road A128

454

A   B   C   D   E

1

2
Field House

Tillingham
Hall

3

Dunnings Lane

Peartree Lane

4

Slose

Bulphan
Primary School

453

Fen Lane

5
Blankets
Farm

Hatch Farm

La Plata

Home Farm

Mar D'Air

6
Corner
Farm

Stone
Hall

The
Elms Farm

Fen Lane

Fen Farm

7

Parker's Farm

8

A   B   471   C   D   E

I grid square represents 500 metres

MANDEVILLE WAY · Reed Pond Wk

Durham Road

Durham Road

Essex Pke

MANDEVILLE WAY

Police Station

B1
1 Dovedale Cl
2 Gt Berry Fm Cha
3 Little Berry La
4 Sherwood Cl
5 Welbeck Rl

A1
1 Berberis Cl
2 Derby Cl
3 Forest Gld
4 High Bank
5 Reeves Cl
6 Sunnyside

Tyler Avenue

Clifford Cl

A   **B**   436   **C**   Laindon Station   **D**   36 MANDEVILLE WAY   **E**

I

Langdon Hills

Great Berry CP School

Forest Glade

Great Berry

Vowler Road

Emanuel Road

Samuel Rd

St David's R

Alexander

Valence

Marks Hill (Nature Reserve)

16

C2
1 Lincefield
2 The Waterfalls

2

Roseberry Av

Lincewood County Junior & Infant School

Corona Road

Ferrmore

Westley Heights Country Park

Westley Heights

STANEWAY

Lane

Chapel

Lee

Homestead Dr

D1
1 Puckleside
2 Westmede

3

Langdon Hall Farm

Dry Street

B1007

Stacey Drive

Stormonts Way

Kingston Hill

Southview

D2
1 Victoria Av

Doesgate Farm

HIGH RD

One Tree Hill Country Park

Northlands Av

Coombe Drive

Essex Cou Thurro

4

Old Church Hill

455

Little Malgraves Industrial Estate

Goldsmiths

Thames view

Grays Avenu

5

Lower Dunton Road

Old

Hill

Avenue

6

Kirkham Road

Kirkham Shaw

Kirkham Av

SOUTH

Meadow Dr

South

Avenue

Sutton Hall Farm

7

Great Malgraves

B1007

HILL

8

Wrens Park Farm

HOPE BY-PASS

North Hill Business Pa

A   **B**   473   **C**   **D**   Sliverdale Clo   **E**

Hornâon on the Hill

NORTH

North Hill

Ardon

on-the-hill

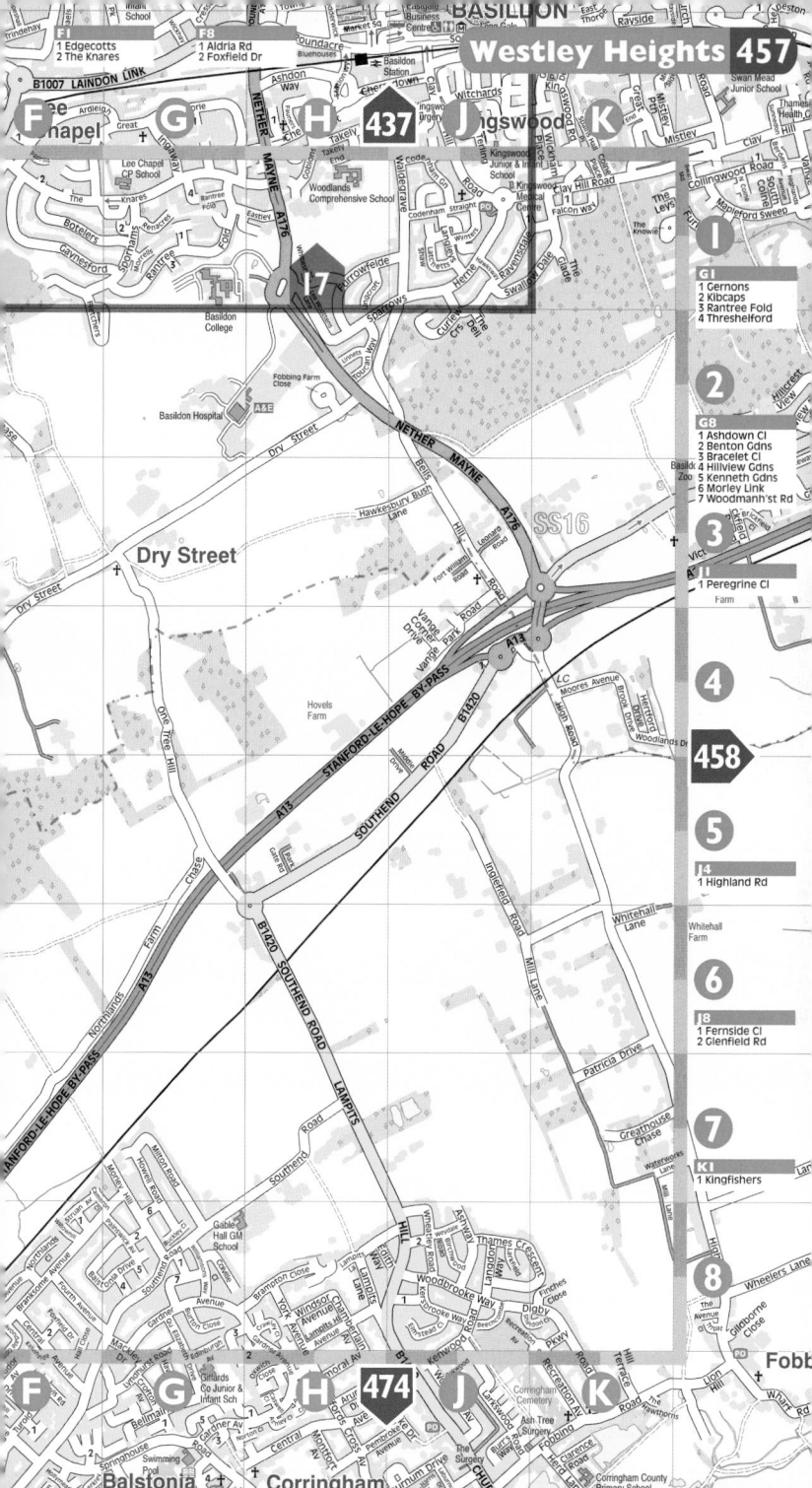

F1
1 Edgecotts
2 The Knares

F8
1 Aldria Rd
2 Foxfield Dr

B1007 LAINDON LINK

F Lee Chapel

G

H 437

J Kingswood

K

BASILDON

Basildon Station

Woodlands Comprehensive School

Basildon College

Basildon Hospital

17

NETHER MAYNE A176

Dry Street

Dry Street

Hawkesbury Bush Lane

SS16

NETHER MAYNE A176

STANFORD-LE-HOPE BY-PASS

SOUTHEND ROAD B1420

Hovels Farm

A13

STANFORD-LE-HOPE BY-PASS

Moores Avenue

Whitehall Lane

Whitehall Farm

Patricia Drive

Greathouse Chase

LAMPITS

SOUTHEND ROAD B1420

HILL

Windsor Avenue

Woodbrooke Way

Gable Hall GM School

F

G Giffards Co Junior & Infant Sch

H 474

J

K

Corringham Cemetery

Fobbing

Balstonia

Corringham

Corringham County Primary School

1

G1
1 Gernons
2 Kibcaps
3 Rantree Fold
4 Threshelford

2

G8
1 Ashdown Cl
2 Benton Gdns
3 Bracelet Cl
4 Hillview Gdns
5 Kenneth Gdns
6 Morley Link
7 Woodmanh'st Rd

3

H1
1 Peregrine Cl

4

458

5

J4
1 Highland Rd

6

J8
1 Fernside Cl
2 Glenfield Rd

7

K1
1 Kingfishers

8

Wheelers Lane

Fobb

I grid square represents 500 metres

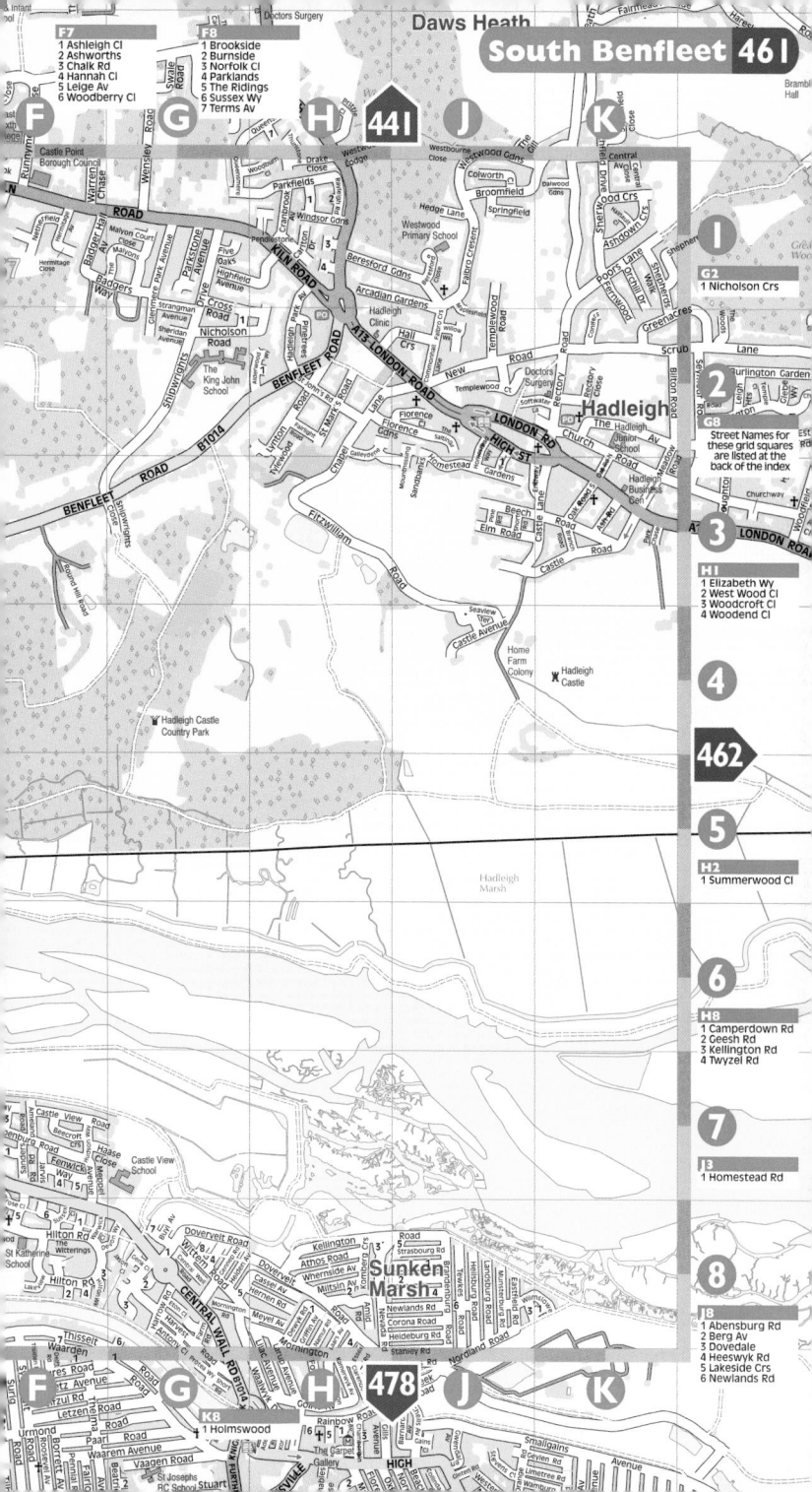

South Benfleet 461

F7
1 Ashleigh Cl
2 Ashworths
3 Chalk Rd
4 Hannah Cl
5 Leige Av
6 Woodberry Cl

F8
1 Brookside
2 Burnside
3 Norfolk Cl
4 Parklands
5 The Ridings
6 Sussex Wy
7 Terms Av

G2
1 Nicholson Crs

G8
Street Names for
these grid squares
are listed at the
back of the index

H1
1 Elizabeth Wy
2 West Wood Cl
3 Woodcroft Cl
4 Woodend Cl

H2
1 Summerwood Cl

H8
1 Camperdown Rd
2 Geesh Rd
3 Kellington Rd
4 Twyzel Rd

J3
1 Homestead Rd

J8
1 Abensburg Rd
2 Berg Av
3 Dovedale
4 Heeswyk Rd
5 Lakeside Crs
6 Newlands Rd

K8
1 Holmswood

Daws Heath

Hadleigh

464

B5
1 Richmond Av
2 Summercourt Rd

B4
1 Avebury Rd
2 Balmoral Rd
3 Claremont Cl
4 Hamlet Court Ms

A3
1 Highfield Cl
2 Highfield Dr

A1
1 Bell Wk

444

B6
1 Lydford Rd
2 Shorefield Gdns
3 Wickford Rd

C3
1 Penhurst Av
2 Wallis Av

C6
1 Cashiobury Ter
2 Milton Pl
3 Prittlewell Sq

D2
1 Stuart St

D3
1 Chestnut Gv
2 Grainger Cl

463

D5
1 Fardon Ser Rd
2 Grover St
3 Pitmans Cl
4 Station Ap
5 Warrior Sq East

D6
1 Capel Ter
2 Devereux Rd

Prittlewell

Westcliff-on-Sea

Clifftown

SOUTHEND-ON-SEA

Southend Pier

E3
1 Wordsworth Cl

E5
1 Grange Gdns
2 Quebec Cl

E6
1 Hartington Pl
2 Pleasant Ms

I grid square represents 500 metres

F2
1 St Edmund's Cl

F3
1 Norwich Cl
2 Selbourne Rd

Beauchamp

F **G** Shopland Hall **H** Essex **445** **J** **K** Barrow Hall Far

Clay Street Farm

I Trotters

F5
1 Fairburn Cl
2 Fowler Cl
3 Langley Cl
4 Stanier Cl

Rebels

Essex County
Southend-on-S

2

G4
1 Droitwich Av

Alleyn Court & Eton House School

Thorpe Hall School

3

Green

H3
1 Eldbert Cl

Wellesley Hospital

Cecil Jones High School

A1159

Temple Sutton Primary & Infant School

Eastern Av

Lloyd Wise Cl

Royal Artillery Way

Cokefield Avenue

Archer Av

Archer Close

Eastcote Gv

Lincoln Chase

A1159

Cumberland Avenue

Newington

Crossfield Road

Durham Rd

Hamlet Primary School

St Nicholas School

SOUTHCHURCH BVD

BOURNES GREEN CHA

Southchurch Boulevard

Avenue

Poynings

Hamstel Road

Wick Chase

Glynde Way

Albert Rd

Shoebury

4

yst Gardens

Burlesco

466

Central Avenue

South Avenue

Trinity Road

Stornoway

Glenmore Street

Strand Gallery

A13

Rectory

The Surgery

Pelham Road

Thorpe Bay School

Forescliffe Chase

The Willows

Burlescomb

Bournes Green Junior

5

Thorpe Bay Stat

Southchurch

Stromness Place

Riviera

Southend-East Station

Southend Adult Community College

Brunswick Road

Sandringham

Kensington

Marlborough Road

Huntingdon Rd

Ruskin

Woodgrange

Chelsworth Cr

Bretenham Road

Watson

Drive

Woodgrange Drive

Rodbridge Drive

Avenue

Acacia Drive

Elm Grove

H4
1 Pavilion Cl

Fermoy Road

Thorpe Bay Surgery

Fermoy

6 Thorpe Bay

Kursaal Way

Hawtree

Beresford Rd

Burnaby Road

Northumberland Crescent

Greenways

Colbert

Avenue

Johnstone Road

The Broadway

St Augustine's Avenue

Saint James

Parkanaur

H5
1 Woodgrange Cl

Southend Flat

Eastern Esplanade

Eastern Esp

Shaftesbury Avenue

Capadocia St

Hotel

B1016

Walton Road

Cliveden

Hotel

Vernon Road

Gloucester

Burges Road

Thorpe

Tyrone

Burges Road

Thorpe

St Augustine's Avenue

Marcus

Dungannon

7

Esplanade

J4
1 Coptfold Cl

8

A   B   446   C   D   E

Clay Street
Farm

Barrow
Hall Farm

Bow Hill

The Crofts

Trotters

Coronation
Close

The Great
Wakering
Health
Centre

I

C5
1 Rackenford

Oldbury
Farm

SOUTHEND ROAD

B1017

Essex County
Southend-on-Sea

Southend Road

2

Star Lane
Industrial
Estate

C6
1 Longsands

1 & Eton
House School

3

D1
1 Townfield Wk

POYNTERS LANE   B1017

1 Churchfields

Bournes
Green

Bournes Green
Chase

1 Keighley
Mews

Ferndale Way

North
Shoebu

Wambrook

Mountdale
Drive

SOUTHCHURCH BVD

BOURNES GREEN CHASE

Bourne Green
Chase

Challacombe

Chertsey
Close

Weydon
Walk

4

Albert Rd

Thorpe Hall Avenue

Broadclyst Gardens

Appledore

North
Shoebury
Surgery

Froghley

The Willows

465

Burlescoombe Road

Pyrmtree

Creston
Barton

Buckland

Doctors
Surgery
Brewsterway

Eagle

Malar

Way

Danes
Close

Ladram
Way

Hayes Barton

Malmesbury

Branscombe
Gardens

Bournes
Green Junior
School

Maplin

Weare Gifford

St Georges
RC School

Ashanti Close

5

The Barnstaple
Surgery

Acacia Drive

Thorpe Bay Station

Bishopsteignton

D3
1 Cookham Ct
2 Lamborni Cl
3 Woodley Wk

Station
Road

Prittlewell

Goldmer Close

Gilman
Drive

Delaware

Road

Elm

6

D4
Street Names for
these grid squares
are listed at the
back of the index

Thorpe
Bay
Surgery

Thorpe
Bay

Fermoy
Road

Blyth
Avenue

Thorpedene
GM Junior
School

Shoeburyness
High School

Wicklow
Walk

Cauifield

Richmond
Avenue Junior
School

The
Eye Clinic

Towerfield
Close

Campfield

Primary
School

D5
1 Chaffinch Cl

THORPE

7

Burges Road

St Augustine's Avenue

Marcus
Chase

Marine
Avenue

Kenway

Burnes
Avenue

Herbert Road

Connaught
Gardens

St Andrews Road

Ness Road

Chapel

The Ter

ESPLANADE

Broadway

Bay
Gardens

Dundonald Drive

Barrowsand

Cambridge Town

Cranley
Gardens

Strolma
Gardens

Tudor
Gardens

Waterford Road

Church
Road

Admirals
Walk

Fremantle
Road

Magazine
Road

Dane's Rd

8

SHOEBURY COMMON RD

Leitrin
Lodwick

Ulster Avenue

Avenue

Ness
Road

Shoebury
Common

I grid square represents 500 metres

Little Wakering Hall

F1 1 Moreland Cl

F2 1 Crouchmans Av

F   G   H   **447**   J   K

Bridge Road

I

F6 1 Southchurch Av

Twyford Avenue

Lee

North Street

Mercer Rd

Northfield (Crescent)

Richmond Av

Lindsey Road

Hall Rd

Weald's Way

The Anchorage

STREET

Fairfield

Great Wakering Primary School

Conway   Avenue

Great Wakering

Samuel's Corner

New   Road

Starrs Rd

Glebe Close

2

G1 1 The Cedars 2 Roding Cl

Shoebury Road

John Rd

Beach Court

Broomways

Mariners Court

Seaview   Drive

Estuary Gardens

Goldsworthy Drive

Victoria Drive

Crouchmans

Cupids Chase

Poynters Lane

Morrin's   Chase

LC

3

H3 1 New England Crs

Cherrytree Chase

LC

4

Black Grounds

Sutton Road

LC

LC

Butts Rd

Brodie Road

Bridport Road

Essex County Southend-on-Sea

Pig's Bay

5

Picasso Way

Wakering

Rubens

Hogarth Drive

Way

Newall Avenue

Castle Cl

Pell Avenue

Blackgate

LC

Road

Rampart Road

Rowcliffe Road

6

Gunners Road

Shoeburyness

7

8

F   G   H   J   K

468

E7
1 St Paul's Cl
2 St Paul's Pl
3 Tyne Gdns

E6
1 Shannon Wy
2 Swale Cl

A3
1 Greenacres Cl

451

A   B   C   D   E

Berwick Pond Road

Ltl Gerpins Rd

I

Berwick
Ponds Farm

E8
1 Alfred Rd
2 Buchanan Cl
3 Hanford Rd
4 The Rowans

Gerpins Lane

Warwick Lane

Berwick Pond Road

Berwick Manor

2

Thorn Lane

Cardinal Way

Stowe Road

Fernview Avenue

Upminster Rd N

Warwick Lane

3

King Edward Av

Doctors Surgery

Cemetery

North

Warwick Lane

4

Launder's Lane

Bretts Farm

Kenningtons

NEW

5

ROAD

Lane

Moor Hall

Doctors Surgery

East Hall Lane

6

A1306

Wennington
Hall Farm
Business Centre

Romford Road

Timber Drive

Shannon Wy

ENNINGTON ROAD B1335

Wennington Gn

7

Wennington

SANDY   LANE B1335

Nethan

Sandy Lane
Farm

A13(1)

Toplands Av

Manor Close

Rowan Grove

Mill

8

Wenning
Marshes

New Road

Lowlands Road

Purfleet

Arnhem Avenue

Cen

Myrtle Grove

Havering
Thurrock

A   B   C   D   E

Kent Way

LONDON ROAD

A13(1)

Hall Rd

View

481

I grid square represents 500 metres

Aveley 469

452
470
482

F8
1 Broome Pl

H6
1 Frances Gdns
2 Fullarton Crs

H7
1 Fusedale Wy
2 Groves Cl

J5
1 Derry Av
2 Deveron Gdns

J6
1 Dale Cl
2 Dent Cl
3 Dunkellin Gv
4 Dunning Cl
5 Faymore Gdns
6 Jack Evans Ct

K4
1 Aire Dr

K5
1 Araglen Av
2 Bovey Wy

K6
1 Avon Gn
2 Bingham Cl
3 Brock Gn
4 Galey Gn

K7
1 Cander Wy
2 Chanlock Pth
3 Clayburn Gdns

F G H J K I 2 3 4 5 6 7 8

SOUTH OCKEN...

Belhus Woods Country Park

Ockendon Station

Belhus Park

Belhus Golf Club & Leisure Centre

Ockendon School

Woodacre School

Dilkes CP School

Loman Path

Fyfield Drive

Knightmead School

Holy Cross RC School

Thurrock Borough Council ...

Health Centre

Infant School

Bonnygate CP School

Aveley School

Aveley Primary School

Doctors Surgery

Thurrock Service Area

Junction 30

STIFFORD ROAD

WEST ROAD

DENNIS ROAD

M25

A13(T)

A126

B186

B1335

B5
1 Paddock Cl
2 The Paddocks

A5
1 St Giles Cl

A4
1 The Spinney

A B C D E

I

D6
1 Beverley Cl

2

3

4

471

5

Baker
Street

RM16

6

7

8

Orsett
Heath

Lorkins
Farm

Black Bush Lane

Robinson Road

CONWAY'S ROAD

B188

Home
Farm

Orsett Road

Cholley
Farm

Orsett Hall

Prince   Charles   Avenue

RECTORY ROAD

Malting Lane

Orsett

Doctors Surgery
Fordhams Rw
South Vw

Lofthall
Farm

A128 BRENTWOOD ROAD

Barrington's
Farm

ROAD

Orsett
Hospital

The Rowley Road

School Lane

Rectory Road

Orsett C of E
Primary School

Mill Lane

HIGH

STANFORD-LE-HOPE BY-PASS

STANFORD

Criton Industrial
Estate

Welling Road

Welling Road

Southfields

STANFORD ROAD A1013

Hornby Lane

Brentwood Road

A13

White
Crofts

Heath
Place

DOCK APPROACH ROAD

Gowers
Lane

Foxes
Cft

Brook Farm

A B C D E

1 grid square represents 500 metres

474

457

487

473

A B C D E

B
1 Bellmaine Av
2 Briceway
3 Nottage Cl
4 St Johns Ms
5 Tasman Cl

A3
1 Cedars
2 Sanctuary Gdn

A1
1 Blythe Rd
2 Rachael Clarke Cl

B2
1 Palmers
2 Pearsons

B3
1 Haskins
2 Semples
3 Whybrews

C1
1 Langland Cl
2 Limeslade Cl

Balstonia

Corringham

Stanford-
le-Hope

Mucking

Mucking
Flats

Mucking
Marshes

SS17

I grid square represents 500 metres

476

A B 459 C D Northwick E

Northwick Roa

1

Holehaven Creek

2 Oozedam

Lower Horse

3 A1014 THE MANORWAY

She Po

4 Oil Refinery

Coryton

475

Shell Haven

Coryton Wharves

5 Thames Haven

6 Thurrock Medway Towns

7

8 Blythe Sands

A B C D E

River Thames

1 grid square represents 500 metres

460

478

G2
1 Arjan Wy
2 Cambria Cl

H1
1 St Andrews Cl
2 St James Cl
3 St Lukes Cl
4 St Peters Rd

H2
1 Palmerstone Rd
2 Village Hall Cl

I1
1 Central Av

J2
1 Beechcroft Rd
2 The Redwoods

Dutch
Village

Northwick Park
Junior & Infant
School

Essex
County
Council

International
Business Park

International
Business
Centre

Charfleet
Industrial
Estate

Kings
Court

CANVEY ISLAND

Hole
Haven

Sea
Reach

River
Thames

Essex County
Medway Towns

Brook Natural
Health Centre

Canvey Village
Surgery

Montague
Place

Infant
School

F G H J K

1 2 3 4 5 6 7 8

Sunken Marsh

HIGH STREET

Leigh Beck

Thorney Bay

Deadman's Point

Thames

1 grid square represents 500 metres

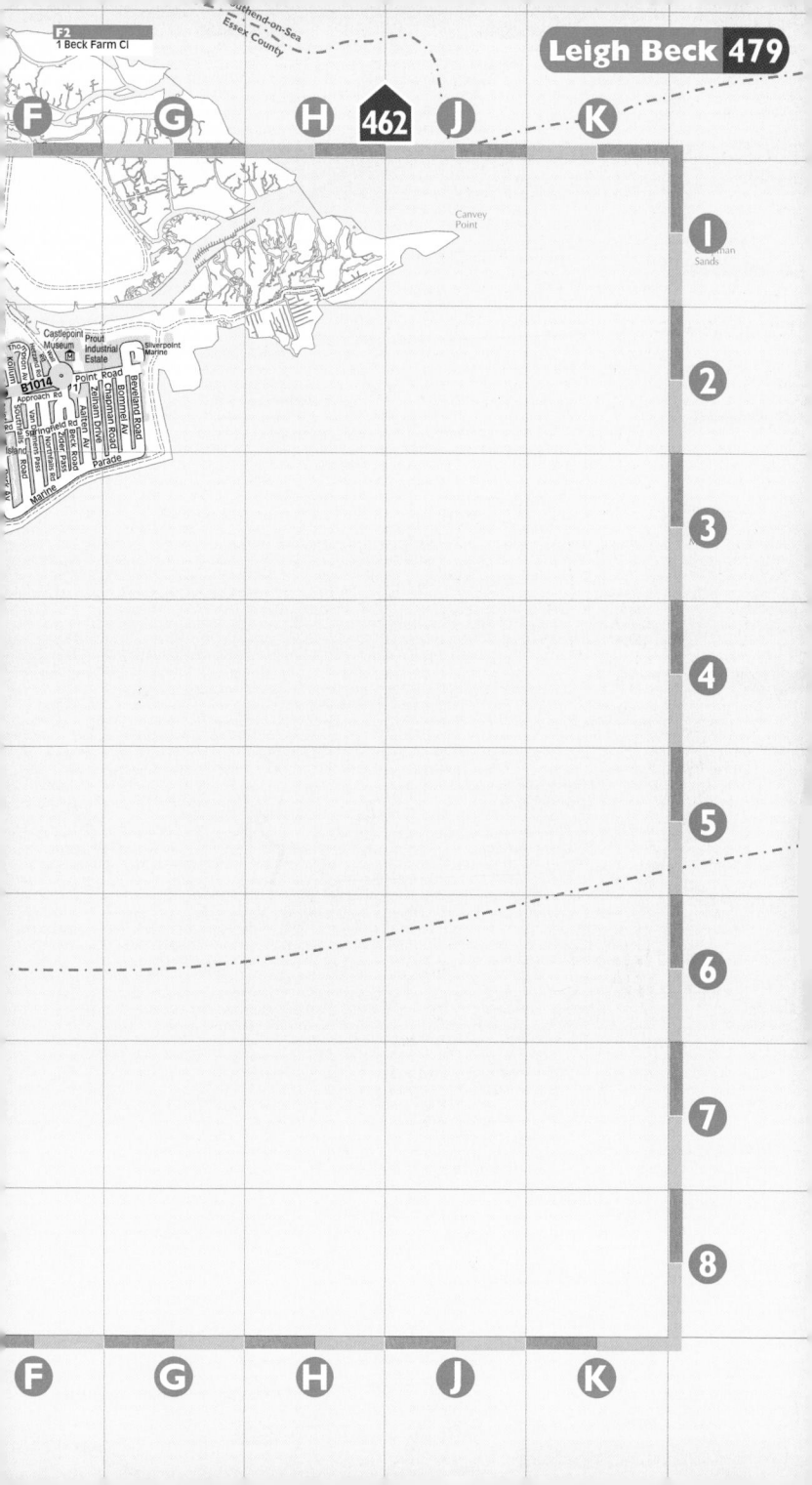

F2
1 Beck Farm Cl

F   G   H   **462**   J   K

Southend-on-Sea
Essex County

Canvey
Point

Chapman
Sands

Castlepoint
Museum

Prout
Industrial
Estate

Silverpoint
Marine

B1014

Point Road

Approach Rd

Springfield Rd

Ashurt Av

Beck Road

Chapman Road

Bommee Av

Sluder Road

Seaview Road

Northlands Pass

Island Rd

Marine

Parade

Penelope Road

F   G   H   J   K

480

A6
1 Fairview

A5
1 Aveley Cl

A4
1 Bexley Rd

A

B

C

D

E

Wennington

I

C6
1 Dabbling Cl
2 Lapwing Cl
3 Moorhen Cl
4 Stevenson Cl
5 Sunset Cl
6 Webber Cl

2

C7
1 Watermeadow Cl

3

Coldharbour

Erith Rands

Crayford
Ness

Havering
Bexley

4

Erith

Erith
Theatre Guild

Erith
Small Business
Centre

Landau Way

Dayton Drive

Manford
Industrial Estate

5

Manor Road

James Watt
Road

Crescent Road

Frobisher Rd

Bilton Road

Canada
Ness Road

Maybold

Wallhouse Road

DA8

Sports
Centre

Reddy Road

Raleigh
Close

Longreach

Turpin

Colyer

6

Thanet
Road

Watermead
Close

Arthur St

The
Nursery

Church
Trading
Estate

School

Alderney

Hilden Dr

Brompton Dr

Hollywood

Darent
Valley Path

7

Health
Centre

Pearswood Road

Colvers Lane

Northend
CP Sch

Slade
Green
Road

Elm Road

Hazel Rd

Hazel Dr

Fern Dr

Leycroft
Gdns

Slade Green
Football Club

Craylord
Marshes

North
End

Scott
Rd

Slade Green
Station

Moat Lane

Slade
Green

8

Eversley Ave

Venners Cl

Chiltern

Cumbrian

Wessex Dr

Whitehall
Lane

Lincoln Road

Dale View

Ely Cl

Lincla

Howbury Rd

NORTHEND ROAD

Kent County
Bexley

Doctors
Surgery

Holmsdale Grove

A2000

A206

A

B

C

Crayside
Industrial Estate

D

E

A206

I grid square represents 500 metres

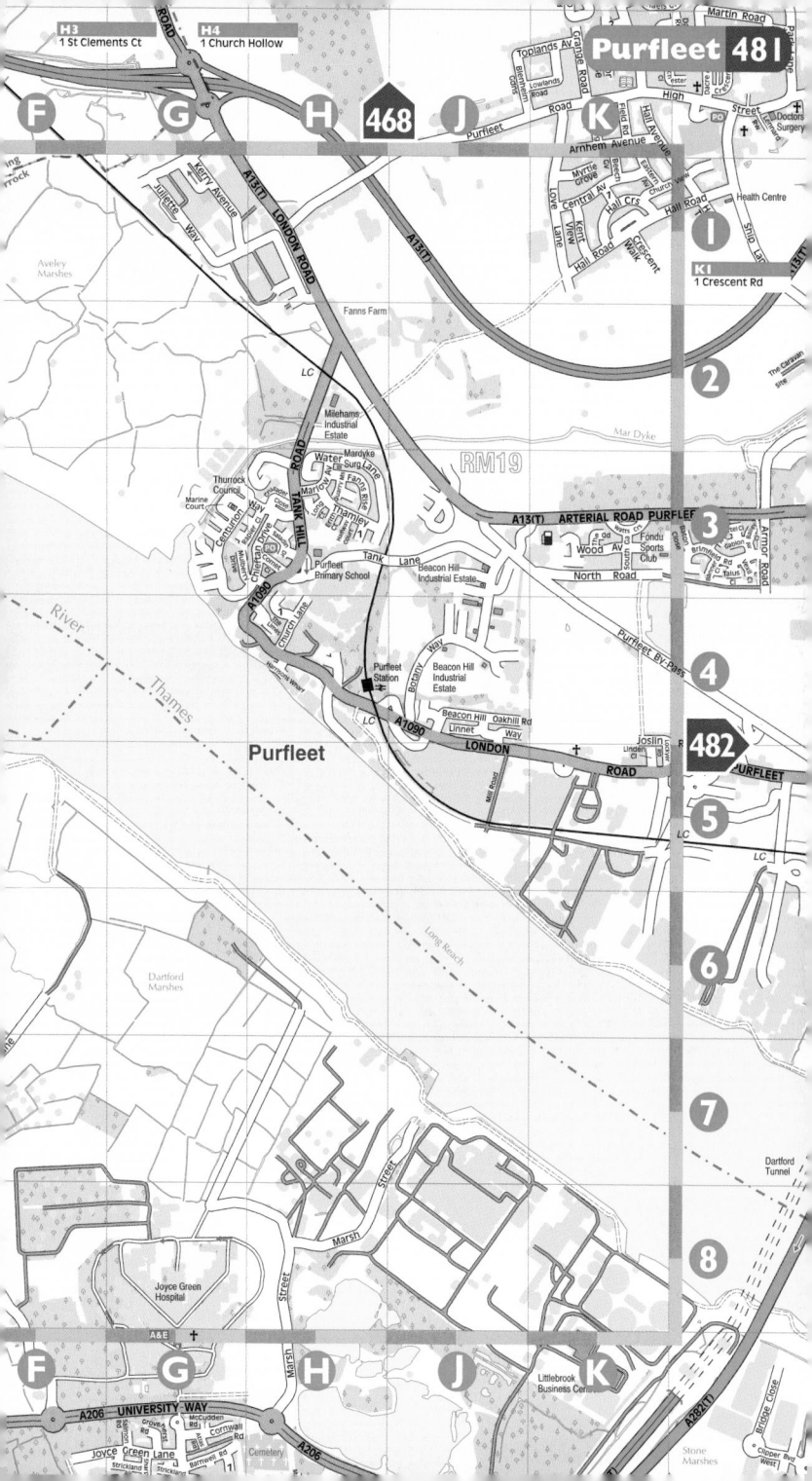

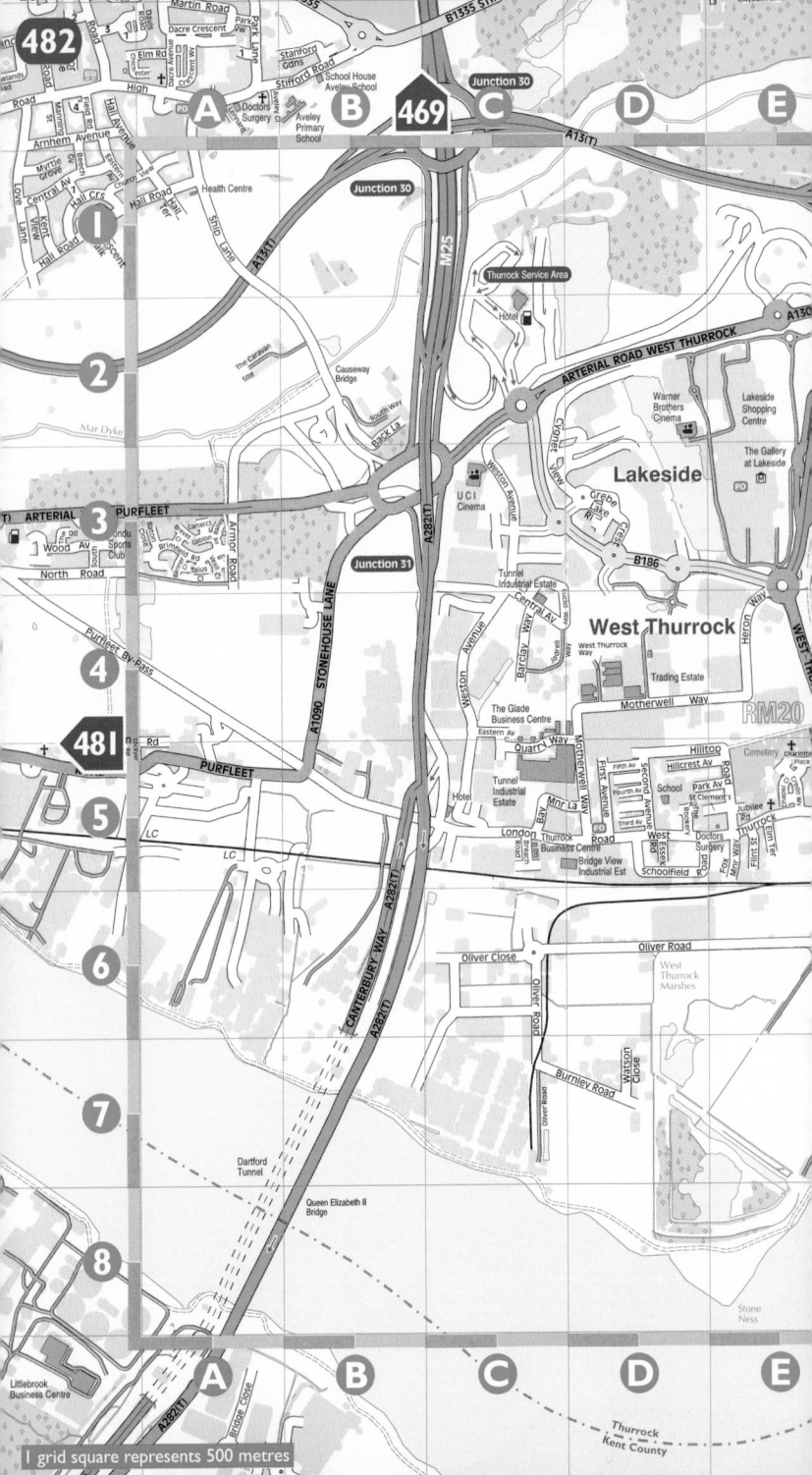

F
G
H **472** Farm
J
K

F1
1 Squirrel's Cha
F2
1 Fanshawe Rd
Heath Place

Greyhound Lane

I
F3
1 Cambridge Gdns
2 Newnham Pl

2
F4
1 Chelmer Rd
Becksland

High House

3
Muckindford Road
F8
1 Canberra Sq

dwell St Mary

Cemetery

Herringham County Infant School
St Patrick's Place

Saint's Walk

Doctors Surgery

Primary School

Atherton Gardens

Mill House

4

Coward Industrial Estate

Linford Road

Turnpike Lane

Rectory Road

West Tilbury

486

Lo.. St...

5
G1
1 Northwood
2 Ravencroft

LC

Biggin Lane

Biggin

Gunhill Farm

Church Road

RM18

6
G2
1 Brockett Rd
2 Errington Cl
3 Nevell Rd

Cooper Shaw Road

Tilbury Manor Infant School

St Chads School

Gainsborough Av

TILBURY

Pageant Cl

Stephenson Avenue
Cowper Avenue

7

Regional Sports Centre

West Tilbury Marshes

8
G8
1 Bown Cl
2 Edinburgh Ms
3 Elizabeth Cl

The Bee..

F
G
H8
1 Austen Cl
2 Bronte Cl
3 Wordsworth Cl
H **489**
J
H1
1 Semper Rd
K

F G H 474 J K

I
2
3
4
5
6
7
8

Thurrock
Medway Towns

Lower
Hope Point

Reed Wall

Saxon Shore Way

Medway Towns
Kent County

F G H J K

488

484

A | B | C | D | E

B4
1 Vicarage Dr

C5
1 Buckingham Rd
2 Hartfield Pl
3 Salem Pl

A4
1 Kingston Ct

A3
1 Fishermen's Hl
2 Ford Rd
3 Hamerton Rd

Medical Centre

Tilbury Town Station

St M RC Co
Primary School

1

Tilbury Ness

C8
1 Ashmore Gdns

2

Northfleet Industrial e

D5
1 Collington Cl

D6
1 Falcon Ms
2 St Thomas Rd

3

Road
Grove
The Creek
College Road
Park Walls
The Shore
The Hill
The Shore

Stonebridge Road

Northfleet

Lawn CP School
Gravesend & Northfleet Football Club

Rosherville

The Shore

Crete Hall Road

Portland Road

Granby

D7
1 Harrowby Gdns
2 Sunninghill

Northfleet Station

Station Road

High Street

Hunter Avenue

The Hill

The Surgery

Church Pth

Rosherville C of E School

4

A226 LONDON   ROAD

Rosherville Vale
Gordon Rd
Burnaby Rd

Fountain Walk

Laburnum Gv
Lime Avenue
St Botolphs C of E Primary School

Thames Way

Beaumont Rd

5

Springhead Rd

B2175

Tooley St
Dudley Road

DOVER   ROAD

St Josephs RC School

Vale Road

DA11

Detling Rd

Dover Road East

Dover Road Primary School

Havelock Rd

D8
1 Everest Cl
2 Tensing Av

6

Gravesham Borough Council

A2260   THAMES WAY

Thames Way

Preston Rd
First Av
Coutton Rd
Park

The Old Guild Theatre

E4
1 Chestnut Cl

Cemetery

Meadow Road

Northfleet Boys School

Cygnet Leisure Centre

Coopers

Newman's Nelson Rd

7

Spring Head

Springhead Road
A2260

Hall Road

Mitchell Avenue
Colyer

Wombwell Gdns

Northfleet School for Girls

New House

E5
1 Cremorne Rd

A2(T)   WATLING   STREET

Viking Rd
Road
Pepper Hill
Dene
Roman Road

Tennyson

Aspdin Road

Johnson Cl
Holm
Rembrandt Dr

Hillary Avenue

Doctors Sg

Infant Sch

E6
1 Lansdown Rd
2 Southfleet Rd

8

Hall Rd

Pepper Hill

Primary School

Landseer   Avenue

Hog La

A2(T)

E7
1 Greenhill Rd

E8
1 Garden Rw
2 St Clements Cl

Hazells

A | B | C | D | E

I grid square represents 500 metres

Abberton ... 252 C2
Abbess End ... 299 G2
Abbess Roding ... 299 F1
Abbey Field ... 8 A6
Abridge ... 379 G7
Acton Place ... 35 J5
Aimes Green ... 348 B2
Aingers Green ... 223 K8
Aldham ... 184 A5
Allen's Green ... 230 D7
Alphamstone ... 114 C2
Alresford ... 221 K5
Althorne ... 396 E3
Ardleigh ... 157 J6
Ardleigh Green ... 430 D5
Ardleigh Heath ... 157 H4
Ardley End ... 265 H4
Arkesden ... 98 D3
Armigers ... 139 F7
Ashdon ... 46 D5
Asheldham ... 371 H6
Ashen ... 53 G4
Ashingdon ... 422 A6
Audley End ... 70 C5
Audley End ... 81 K5
Aveley ... 469 F7
Aythorpe Roding ... 267 K2
Bacon End ... 236 C3
Baconend Green ... 236 C1
Baddow Park ... 361 G3
Baker Street ... 471 K6
Ballards Gore ... 423 J7
Ballingdon ... 58 A7
Balls Green ... 191 F8
Balstonia ... 474 B1
Bamber's Green ... 202 C2
Bannister Green ... 207 G8
Bardfield End Green ... 140 B3
Bardfield Saling ... 174 E4
Barling ... 446 D6
Barnston ... 237 K1
Barstable ... 438 A7
Bartholomew Green ... 208 B6
Bartlow ... 23 J6
Basildon ... 17 F5
Bath Side ... 7 D3
Battlesbridge ... 418 C3
Baythorne End ... 52 B3
Beacon End ... 185 J7
Beacon Hill ... 39 H2
Beacon Hill ... 278 D7
Beauchamp Roding ... 299 J4
Beaumont ... 194 C6
Beazley End ... 145 F7
Bedlar's Green ... 200 B8
Beggar Hill ... 357 J6
Belchamp Otten ... 55 H5
Belchamp St Paul ... 54 E4
Belchamp Walter ... 56 B7
Bell Common ... 350 B6
Belstead ... 61 J6
Bentfield Bury ... 167 G5
Bentfield Green ... 167 H5
Bentley ... 87 K6
Bentley ... 383 G7
Berden ... 134 A5
Berechurch ... 219 F4
Berners Roding ... 300 C5
Bicknacre ... 485 H5
Biggin ... 414 C4
Billericay ... 414 C4
Birch ... 250 A1
Birchanger ... 199 K3
Birch Green ... 250 A3
Birchall Corner ... 157 F3
Birdbrook ... 51 H6
Bird Green ... 97 H5
Birds Green ... 299 J7
Bishops Green ... 237 J5
Bishop's Stortford ... 198 B6
Blackheath ... 219 J5
Blackmore ... 356 D5
Blackmore End ... 144 E3
Black Notley ... 210 A8
Blacksmith's Corner ... 61 J7
Blake End ... 207 H3
Blasford Hill ... 304 D2
Bobbingworth ... 325 K5
Bocking ... 209 J1
Bocking Churchstreet ... 177 K5
Bocking's Elm ... 258 C8
Boreham ... 306 C5
Borley ... 57 G2
Borley Green ... 56 E3
Bournes Green ... 466 A3

Bovinger ... 325 F6
Bowers Gifford ... 439 H8
Boxted ... 119 G6
Boxted ... 155 H1
Boxted Cross ... 119 J8
Boyton Cross ... 302 B6
Boyton End ... 29 F8
Boyton End ... 104 A8
Bradfield ... 161 G3
Bradfield Heath ... 160 E5
Bradwell ... 211 J3
Bradwell on Sea ... 344 D3
Bradwell Waterside ... 344 B1
Braintree ... 177 K8
Braiswick ... 186 C3
Brandy Hole ... 420 B1
Bran End ... 173 H5
Brantham ... 123 J4
Brays Grove ... 294 E6
Breeds ... 271 K7
Brent Pelham ... 132 C3
Brewer's End ... 201 J6
Brick End ... 170 B4
Brick House End ... 134 A8
Brickkiln Green ... 144 D1
Bridge End ... 142 B2
Bridge Green ... 68 A7
Brightlingsea ... 255 H5
Brimsdown ... 374 E6
Broad Green ... 66 E2
Broad Green ... 214 B2
Broadley Common ... 321 F2
Broad's Green ... 272 A8
Broad Street Green ... 310 E5
Brock Hill ... 389 K8
Brockley Green ... 29 G2
Broke Hall ... 64 A2
Bromley Cross ... 190 B1
Brook Street ... 410 B7
Broomfield ... 304 D3
Broxbourne ... 319 G2
Broxted ... 170 C3
Brundon ... 57 K4
Buckhurst Hill ... 403 K6
Building End ... 66 D6
Bulls Cross ... 374 A2
Bulmer ... 57 G8
Bulmer Tye ... 83 G2
Bulphan ... 454 E4
Bumble's Green ... 320 C6
Bures ... 115 J5
Bures Green ... 115 K2
Burnham-on-Crouch ... 398 D8
Burnt Heath ... 158 A8
Burnt Mills ... 439 F3
Burrsville Park ... 259 J6
Burton End ... 200 D1
Burton Green ... 180 C3
Bury Green ... 346 B5
Bush End ... 234 C1
Bustard Green ... 141 G7
Buttsbury ... 386 E3
Butt's Green ... 362 D2
Calford Green ... 28 B6
California ... 37 K7
Cambridge Town ... 466 B7
Campions ... 263 K8
Camps End ... 47 K4
Canewdon ... 423 C3
Canfield End ... 202 E6
Cannon's Green ... 327 H4
Canvey Island ... 477 J3
Capel St Mary ... 86 E4
Cardinal's Green ... 25 F3
Carter's Green ... 296 E3
Castle Camps ... 48 D2
Castle Hedingham ... 110 D1
Castle Hill ... 36 C2
Catmere End ... 69 F1
Cattawade ... 123 J6
Causeway End ... 239 H1
Cavendish ... 32 D3
Chadwell St Mary ... 484 E2
Chalk End ... 301 J3
Chalkwell ... 463 H5
Chalvedon ... 438 D7
Chantry ... 62 A2
Chapel End ... 169 K7
Chapel Row ... 364 A8
Chappel ... 151 F7
Chatham Green ... 273 F2
Chatter End ... 166 A6
Chattisham ... 60 A4
Chelmer Village ... 333 K2
Chelmondiston ... 91 J6

Chelmsford ... 15 E4
Cherry Green ... 138 B5
Cheshunt ... 346 B4
Chickney ... 170 C1
Chignall Smealy ... 303 F2
Chignall St James ... 303 F5
Chigwell ... 404 E5
Chigwell Row ... 406 A5
Childerditch ... 433 J6
Chilton ... 59 F4
Chilton Street ... 30 C3
Chingford ... 402 D5
Chingford Green ... 402 D4
Chingford Hatch ... 403 F7
Chipping Hill ... 276 E2
Chipping Ongar ... 354 D3
Chitts Hills ... 185 J5
Chrishall ... 67 G1
Church End ... 46 C6
Church End ... 92 E8
Church End ... 144 B8
Church End ... 170 D2
Churchend ... 204 D2
Churchend ... 427 H7
Churchgate ... 346 B3
Churchgate Street ... 295 K1
Church Langley ... 295 H5
Church Street ... 55 G2
Clacton-on-Sea ... 11 D5
Clare ... 31 G5
Clatterford End ... 269 F6
Clatterford End ... 326 E3
Clatterford End ... 353 H4
Claverhambury ... 348 D1
Clavering ... 98 B8
Clifftown ... 18 B5
Coalhill ... 390 C6
Cobbs Fenn ... 110 C6
Cobler's Green ... 239 K2
Cock Clarks ... 365 F3
Cock Green ... 240 A1
Coggeshall ... 213 F3
Coggeshall Hamlet ... 213 H5
Colchester ... 186 E6
Coldharbour ... 480 B3
Cold Norton ... 366 A8
Cole End ... 72 A7
Coles Green ... 60 B5
Colliers Hatch ... 352 C4
Colne Engaine ... 149 H4
Cook's Green ... 259 K3
Cooksmill Green ... 329 K4
Coopersale Common ... 351 H3
Coopersale Street ... 351 G5
Cooper's End ... 67 K8
Copdock ... 61 F6
Copford ... 216 B1
Copford Green ... 216 B3
Copthall Green ... 349 F7
Corbets Tey ... 451 J6
Cornard Tye ... 59 H6
Cornish Hall End ... 76 C8
Corringham ... 474 C1
Coryton ... 476 A4
Countess Cross ... 150 A3
Courtsend ... 428 C5
Coxtie Green ... 410 A1
Crabbs Green ... 133 G7
Craig's End ... 77 K6
Cranham ... 452 B1
Crawley End ... 41 G8
Crays Hill ... 416 A8
Creeksea ... 397 J8
Cressing ... 210 E7
Cripple Corner ... 113 H3
Crockleford Heath ... 189 F3
Crockleford Hill ... 188 D4
Cross End ... 113 K5
Crow Green ... 383 J7
Crow's Green ... 175 F5
Cuckoo Tye ... 35 J7
Curling Tye Green ... 337 G2
Curtismill Green ... 381 F7
Cutlers Green ... 139 G3
Danbury ... 335 H6
Danbury Common ... 335 J8
Daws Heath ... 441 J8
Debden ... 101 J6
Debden Green ... 102 C8
Debden Green ... 378 A4
Dedham ... 121 H3
Dedham Heath ... 157 K1
Deer's Green ... 133 K5
Delvin End ... 109 J2
Dengie ... 372 A5

Denton 489 K5
Dewes Green 133 J4
Doddinghurst 383 K3
Dovercourt 7 E5
Downham 416 B1
Dry Street 457 G3
Duck End 106 D6
Duck End 173 J4
Duck End 199 K4
Duckend Green 208 B2
Duddenhoe End 67 K7
Dutch Village 477 H1
Duton Hill 171 H3
Earls Colne 149 K6
East Bergholt 122 B1
East End 123 J3
East End 344 D2
Eastend 293 G4
East Gores 214 D1
East Hanningfield 363 G6
East Horndon 434 E6
Easthorpe 216 A6
East Mersea 286 B4
East Tilbury 486 D6
Eastwick 293 K1
Eastwood 443 F8
Edney Common 330 C8
Eight Ash Green 185 G5
Elder Street 102 B4
Elkins Green 356 D5
Elmdon 67 K1
Elm Park 450 C6
Elmstead 189 K5
Elmstead Heath 221 J2
Elmstead Market 190 A7
Elsenham 168 C3
Emerson Park 431 F8
Enfield Highway 374 C6
Enfield Lock 375 F3
Enfield Wash 374 A4
Epping 350 E4
Epping Green 321 J6
Epping Upland 322 A8
Erith 480 A4
Erwarton 128 A3
Eversley 438 E6
Fairstead 243 F7
Falkenham 94 E2
Falkenham Sink 95 G2
Fanner's Green 271 H8
Farmbridge End 301 G2
Farnham 166 B7
Farnham Green 166 A6
Farther Howegreen 366 A6
Faulkbourne 244 B6
Feering 246 E2
Felixstowe 131 H4
Felmore 438 D5
Felsted 206 C8
Fiddlers Hamlet 351 G6
Finchingfield 106 C7
Fingringhoe 220 D8
Flack's Green 275 F3
Flamstead End 346 B2
Fobbing 475 F1
Ford End 133 H1
Ford End 239 H6
Fordham 152 B7
Fordham Heath 185 F4
Fordstreet 184 B2
Forry's Green 109 K7
Foster Street 295 K6
Four Wantz 300 D2
Foxash Estate 158 B4
Foxearth 33 J7
Fox Hatch 383 H4
Fox Street 188 D1
Frating 222 D4
Frating Green 223 F2
Freezy Water 374 E2
Freston 90 B2
Friday Hill 402 E6
Frinkle Green 51 H8
Frinton-on-Sea 261 H1
Frogs' Green 72 C5
Fryerning 358 A8
Fryerns 438 A5
Fuller's End 168 D5
Fuller Street 274 B1
Furneux Pelham 132 D8
Further Ford End 97 G7
Fyfield 327 F2
Gainsborough 63 K5
Gainsford End 108 B1
Galleyend 360 E2

Galleywood 360 E3
Gallows Corner 430 E3
Gallows Green 172 C2
Gallows Green 184 B4
Gamble's Green 274 D3
Garnetts 237 K5
Gaston Green 232 B6
Gaunt's End 169 H6
Gay Bowers 336 A8
Gestingthorpe 81 K4
Gidea Park 430 A4
Gilston 262 B8
Gilston Park 262 A7
Gilwell Park 375 J7
Gipsy Row 86 C3
Glemsford 33 J1
Goldhanger 312 D6
Good Easter 269 H8
Gooseberry Green 413 K2
Goose Green 192 E2
Goose Green 193 F6
Gore Pit 247 G1
Gosfield 146 D5
Gransmore Green 207 G4
Grass Green 78 E4
Gravesend 489 H4
Grays 483 K6
Great Baddow 333 F6
Great Bardfield 142 D4
Great Bentley 223 J5
Great Berry 456 B1
Great Braxted 278 E4
Great Bromley 190 D4
Great Burstead 414 D8
Great Canfield 236 A5
Great Chesterford 43 K3
Great Chishill 66 B3
Great Clacton 10 A2
Great Claydons 362 E4
Great Cornard 59 G8
Great Dunmow 204 B6
Great Easton 171 J6
Great Hallingbury 232 D1
Great Henny 83 K5
Great Holland 260 D2
Great Horkesley 154 B4
Great Leighs 241 H5
Great Malgraves 456 A1
Great Maplestead 111 H3
Great Notley 208 E6
Great Oakley 195 G1
Great Oxney Green 331 G4
Great Parndon 12 A5
Great Saling 175 H5
Great Sampford 105 F1
Great Stambridge 445 H1
Great Tey 185 F5
Great Totham 279 G6
Great Totham 310 C1
Great Wakering 467 F2
Great Waldingfield 59 J1
Great Waltham 272 A6
Great Warley 432 D3
Great Wenham 86 A4
Great Wigborough 282 E2
Great Yeldham 79 K3
Greenstead 9 F5
Greenstead Green 148 B8
Greensted 353 J2
Greensted Green 353 H2
Green Street 385 H1
The Green 243 G1
Green Tye 230 A4
Greenwich 63 F4
Gubbion's Green 242 A5
Hacton 451 F6
Hadleigh 461 K2
Hadstock 22 E7
Hallingbury Street 233 H1
Hallsford Bridge 354 D4
Halls Green 292 E7
Halstead 147 J3
Hamperden End 138 B3
Hanchet End 26 B4
Handley Green 358 D5
Hardy's Green 216 C7
Hare Green 191 F7
Hare Street 12 B4
Harkstead 126 E3
Harlow 13 D3
Harold Hill 409 F8
Harold Park 431 J1
Harold Wood 431 H3
Hartford End 239 K5
Harwich 7 F4

Hastingwood 323 K1
Hatfield Broad Oak 234 B8
Hatfield Heath 265 H2
Hatfield Peverel 276 B8
Haverhill 26 D5
Havering-atte-Bower 408 A6
Hawbush Green 210 E8
Hawkin's Hill 105 K5
Hawkspur Green 105 J8
Hawkwell 421 H8
Hay Green 356 D8
Hazeleigh 365 F1
Hazel End 167 F7
Hazel Stub 26 C6
Heath Park 430 C8
The Heath 88 C7
Heckfordbridge 217 F6
Helions Bumpstead 49 G5
Hellman's Cross 235 H3
Hemp's Green 152 A7
Hempstead 74 E4
Henham 137 F8
Henny Street 84 C4
Herongate 434 D3
Heybridge 310 D7
Heybridge 386 B3
Heybridge Basin 339 F2
Heydon 40 D8
Higham 120 E1
High Beach 376 D5
High Easter 269 G3
Highfields 247 F6
High Garrett 178 B3
High Houses 271 K6
High Laver 297 H7
High Ongar 355 F1
High Roding 236 C6
Highstreet Green 109 K3
The High 12 C2
High Wych 263 F4
Hill Green 98 D7
Hinxton 20 A5
Hobbs Cross 296 A4
Hobbs Cross 379 H2
Hockerill 199 G7
Hockley 420 D6
Holbrook 90 B7
Holder's Green 140 D7
Holland-on-Sea 260 C8
Holyfield 347 J2
Honey Tye 117 J1
Hook End 384 A1
Hope End Green 202 B8
Hope's Green 460 B3
Hornchurch 450 E3
Horndon on the Hill 473 F1
Horne Row 335 G7
Hornestreet 120 A8
Horseheath 25 F2
Horseman Side 382 A8
Horsley Cross 192 B2
Horsleycross Street 160 B7
Housham Tye 296 D3
Howe Green 232 E3
Howe Green 362 A2
Howegreen 365 J5
Howe Street 107 G4
Howe Street 272 A3
Howlett End 102 D3
Hullbridge 419 K2
Hurst Green 256 A7
Hutton 412 B2
Hutton Mount 412 A4
Hyde Chase 364 D1
The Hythe 220 A1
Ickleton 43 F2
Ingatestone 386 C2
Ingrave 412 C8
Inworth 247 H5
Ipswich 3 D2
Ivy Chimneys 350 C6
Jack's Hatch 321 K3
Janke's Green 151 H5
Jasper's Green 176 A3
Jaywick 290 B5
Katherines 293 G8
Kedington 28 D3
Keelars Tye 221 H2
Keeres Green 268 B4
Kelvedon 247 F4
Kelvedon Hatch 383 F3
Kesgrave 39 G5
Keysers Estate 319 H3
Kings Farm 489 H8
Kingsmoor 322 A2

King Street 355 K2
Kingswood 17 F5
Kirby Cross 228 A6
Kirby-le-Soken 228 B4
Kirton 94 C1
Knowl Green 54 E6
Laindon 16 B3
Lakeside 482 D3
Lamarsh 115 F1
Lamb Corner 157 G1
Lambourne 379 H8
Lambourne End 406 B3
Langdon Hills 456 B1
Langenhoe 252 C3
Langford 309 K6
Langham 156 C1
Langley 97 F3
Langley Green 214 C5
Latchingdon 367 J8
Latchmore Bank 232 A3
Lattinford Hill 86 C7
Latton Bush 322 E1
Lawford 159 F2
Layer Breton 250 B3
Layer de la Haye 218 A8
Layer Marney 249 J5
Leaden Roding 268 B5
Lee Chapel 16 C5
Lee-over-Sands 288 C7
Leigh Beck 478 E2
Leigh-on-Sea 463 F3
Level's Green 166 B8
Levington 92 D2
Lexden 186 B5
Lindsell 486 A1
Linford 23 G2
Linton 376 B6
Lippitts Hill 34 C7
Liston 34 A5
Liston Garden 34 A5
Little Baddow 335 H1
Little Bardfield 141 J3
Little Bealings 39 H1
Little Bentley 192 B5
Little Braxted 277 J3
Little Bromley 159 G7
Little Burstead 436 B1
Littlebury 69 K1
Littlebury Green 69 F4
Little Cambridge 172 A2
Little Chesterford 43 K5
Little Chishill 66 B6
Little Clacton 259 F2
Little Cornard 85 H2
Little Dunmow 205 K6
Little Easton 171 H8
Little End 354 A8
Little Hallingbury 232 C5
Little Henham 136 D4
Little Horkesley 153 K1
Little Laver 298 B5
Little Leighs 241 G7
Little Linton 22 C2
Little London 106 C2
Little London 134 C5
Little Maplestead 112 B4
Little Mascalls 361 J4
Little Oakley 164 B6
Little Oxney Green 330 D5
Little Parndon 12 B2
Little Sampford 105 H5
Little Tey 215 F1
Little Thurrock 484 B3
Little Totham 311 J1
Little Wakering 446 D7
Little Walden 45 G5
Little Waltham 272 E7
Little Warley 433 J4
Little Wenham 86 D2
Little Wigborough 283 H2
Little Wratting 27 K2
Little Yeldham 80 D1
Littley Green 240 B6
Long Gardens 83 G8
Long Melford 35 F6
Loughton 377 H8
Loves Green 330 A8
Lower Bobbingworth Green ... 325 H6
Lower Falkenham 95 F3
Lower Green 96 B6
Lower Green 144 E2
Lower Green 334 A3
Lower Green 360 E4
Lower Holbrook 126 D2
Lower Nazeing 319 K5

Lower Sheering 264 A4
Lower Street 125 J4
Low Street 486 A5
Loyter's Green 297 F4
Lucking Street 111 K3
Mace Green 60 D6
Magdalen Laver 296 D8
Maggots End 166 D1
Maidenhall 62 D3
Maldon 338 D2
Mallows Green 166 B3
Manningtree 159 G1
Manuden 166 E3
Manwood Green 266 A8
Maple End 73 G6
Marden Ash 354 B4
Margaret Roding 268 B8
Margaretting 359 G5
Margaretting Tye 359 H6
Mark Hall North 294 E2
Mark Hall South 294 E3
Marks Tey 215 K2
Martlesham Heath 39 K6
Mashbury 302 C1
Matching 297 G1
Matching Green 297 K2
Matching Tye 297 F2
Mayland 369 G5
Maylandsea 368 C4
Maypole Green 218 E4
Meadowend 53 F8
Meesden 96 C8
Messing 248 A3
Middleton 84 B1
Mile End 187 F1
Millend Green 172 B5
Miller's Green 327 J1
Mill Green 25 G6
Mill Green 357 K6
Mill Hill 420 C6
Milton 272 C6
Minnow End 160 E3
Mistley 160 B3
Mistley Heath 170 A7
Molehill Green 140 A6
Molehill Green 208 A8
Monk Street 140 A6
Montsale 400 D5
Moreton 325 J3
Mott's Green 232 D7
Moulsham 14 C5
Mount Bovers 442 E2
Mount Bures 115 K7
Mount End 351 K6
Mountnessing 385 H5
Mount Pleasant 29 K1
Mowden 307 H4
Mucking 473 K6
Mundon 367 G3
Nacton 65 G8
Navestock Heath 381 J6
Navestock Side 382 E6
Nayland 118 C4
Nazeing 320 D4
Nazeing Gate 320 E7
Nazeing Long Green 320 C7
Nazeing Mead 319 K1
Needham Green 266 C1
Nether Street 299 J1
Netteswell 13 E2
Nevendon 439 F2
New England 51 K3
New House 488 D7
Newman's End 265 F8
Newman's Green 58 D1
New Mistley 160 B2
Newney Green 330 B3
Newport 100 B5
New Thundersley 440 C6
Nine Ashes 356 B4
Noak Bridge 17 D1
Noak Hill 409 F5
Noak Hill 436 D1
North Benfleet 439 J5
North End 80 E2
North End 238 E3
North End 480 A7
Northend 70 B1
Northend 370 D8
North Fambridge 394 D3
Northfleet 488 B3
North Ockendon 452 E6
North Shoebury 466 E4
North Stifford 470 C7
North Weald Bassett 323 K8

Norton Heath 328 C7
Norton Mandeville 327 H7
Norwood End 298 E8
Nosterfield End 25 K8
Nounsley 308 A3
Nuper's Hatch 407 K3
Old Harlow 295 G1
Old Heath 219 K2
Old Mead 168 E1
Olmstead Green 48 D6
Onslow Green 238 C3
Orsett 472 B5
Orsett Heath 484 E1
Ostend 397 J6
Ovington 54 A4
Oxen End 141 K7
Oxley Green 280 E4
Padham's Green 386 B6
Paglesham Churchend 424 C6
Paglesham Eastend 425 F8
Pale Green 49 J4
Panfield 176 D6
Pannel's Ash 53 H4
Parkeston 6 A3
Parkgate 238 E5
Park Green 134 A7
Parney Heath 156 E1
Parrock Farm 489 J8
Parsonage Green 304 C5
Parson's Heath 9 F2
Paslow Wood Common 355 K4
Passingford Bridge 380 D5
Passmores 13 D6
Paternoster Heath 280 E2
Pattiswick 179 K8
Peartree Green 384 B5
Pebmarsh 113 G6
Pedlars End 325 H3
Peldon 251 K7
Pentlow 32 E7
Pentlow Street 33 G5
Pepper's Green 301 F4
Perry Green 211 J4
Perry Street 488 E5
Pharisee Green 203 K8
Philpot End 236 E3
Piercing Hill 378 B1
Pigstye Green 328 D4
Pilgrims Hatch 383 K8
Pinnacles 12 A3
Pipps Hill 17 D2
Pitsea 438 E8
Playford 39 F7
Pledgdon Green 169 K3
Pleshey 270 E3
Point Clear 288 B3
Pond Street 67 J6
The Port of Felixstowe 4 B6
Potash 87 K6
Potter Street 295 H7
Powers Hall End 276 C2
Priory Heath 64 B4
Prittlewell 18 B1
Purfleet 481 H5
Purleigh 366 A4
Puttock End 55 J7
Puttock's End 235 F1
Queen's Park 387 G7
Quendon 136 A3
Racecourse 63 H3
Radley Green 329 G6
Radwinter 73 H6
Radwinter End 73 K1
Ramsden Bellhouse 416 B4
Ramsden Heath 416 A1
Ramsey 163 J3
Ramsey Island 342 B5
Rank's Green 242 B5
Raven's Green 191 H8
Rawreth 418 D6
Rawreth Shot 418 B6
Rayleigh 441 J2
Rayne 208 B3
Reader's Corner 333 G6
Rettendon 391 F4
Richmond's Green 140 C6
Rickling 135 G1
Rickling Green 135 J5
Ridgewell 52 D3
Ringtail Green 239 H8
Rivenhall 245 H4
Rivenhall End 246 A4
Roast Green 97 J7
Robinhood End 77 J3
Rochford 444 D6

oodbridge Corner 57 K1
ook End 101 H8
oost End 51 H1
ose Green 151 H8
ose Hill 63 K1
osherville 488 E3
otten End 144 D6
oundbush 366 C5
oundbush Green 268 A3
ow Green 209 G7
ow Heath 258 C2
owhedge 220 B5
oxwell 302 B7
oydon 292 D4
oydon Hamlet 320 E1
udley Green 365 J2
unsell Green 336 A6
unwell 417 H4
ush Green 290 D2
ushley Green 80 E7
ushmere St Andrew 38 B5
ushmere Street 38 D4
abine's Green 381 K6
ackers Green 85 K1
affron Walden 71 H4
t Lawrence 343 F8
t Osyth 289 G1
t Osyth Heath 258 A4
t Vincent's Hamlet 409 H4
alcott-cum-Virley 282 A5
amuel's Corner 467 J1
andon 334 A7
awbridgeworth 263 F3
chool Green 144 E2
eawick 289 J6
even Star Green 184 E5
ewards End 72 B4
ewardstone 375 K6
ewardstonebury 403 F1
halford 144 A6
halford Green 175 K2
heering 264 D5
helley 326 C6
hellow Bowells 328 D1
henfield 411 H3
hoeburyness 467 F7
hop Corner 127 K4
hotgate 418 A7
hotley 128 D2
hotley Gate 129 G4
hrub End 218 C1
hudy Camps 25 F7
ible Hedingham 110 D3
ibley's Green 140 A8
ilver End 244 E1
kye Green 214 B4
lade Green 480 B8
mith's Green 50 A8
mith's Green 202 A6
mythe's Green 249 G3
outh Benfleet 460 D2
outhchurch 465 H5
outhend-on-Sea 18 C6
outhey Green 110 B8
outh Fambridge 421 J1
outhfields 472 D7
outh Green 253 J2
outh Green 414 E6
outh Hanningfield 390 B5
outh Heath 257 F2
outhminster 398 B1
outh Ockendon 470 A4
outh Stifford 483 G4
outh Weald 410 B5
outh Woodham Ferrers 393 F4
pellbrook 231 J5
pitalbrook 319 G1
pringfield 305 F7
pringwell 44 B6
tafford's Corner 250 E8
tagden Cross 269 K3
tambourne 77 K3
tambourne Green 77 H4
tanbrook 139 H5
tanford-le-Hope 474 B3
tanford Rivers 353 J7
tanstead Abbots 292 A1
tansted Mountfitchet 167 H6
tanway 185 H8
tanway Green 217 J2
tapleford Abbotts 407 J2
tapleford Tawney 380 C2
tarling's Green 133 J2
tart Hill 200 B6

Stebbing 173 K8
Stebbing Green 206 E2
Steeple 369 J2
Steeple Bumpstead 50 C5
Steventon End 47 F3
Stewards 322 C2
Steward's Green 351 F6
Stickling Green 98 C7
Stisted 179 H7
Stock 72 E4
Stocking Pelham 133 G6
Stoke 3 D5
Stoke by Clare 53 F2
Stoke Park 62 B4
Stondon Massey 355 J8
Stonebridge 445 J7
Stones Green 194 A3
Stoneyhills 398 C6
Stow Maries 393 J1
Stratford St Mary 121 F4
Strethall 68 D1
Stroud Green 443 J3
Sturmer 51 F1
Stutton 125 G3
Sucksted Green 138 E7
Sudbury 58 A6
Sunken Marsh 461 H8
Sunnymede 414 E3
Surrex 214 B3
Swallows Cross 384 D3
Swan Street 183 F2
Takeley 201 J5
Takeley Street 201 G6
Tarpots 440 B8
Tattingstone 88 D6
Tattingstone White Horse 88 E4
Taverners Green 234 E5
Temple End 56 C2
Temple Fields 294 E1
Tendring 193 G8
Tendring Green 193 F5
Tendring Heath 192 D4
Terling 275 G2
Thaxted 140 A2
Theydon Bois 378 C8
Theydon Garnon 379 G2
Theydon Mount 380 A2
Thistley Green 240 D1
Thorington Street 119 K2
Thorley 231 G3
Thorley Street 231 J2
Thornwood Common 323 F7
Thorpe Bay 466 A6
Thorpe Common 93 K5
Thorpe Green 226 C1
Thorpe-le-Soken 226 D4
Thorrington 223 G8
Threshers Bush 296 A6
Thundersley 440 D6
Tilbury Juxta Claire 485 F7
Tilbury Green 53 G7
Tilbury Juxta Claire 54 A8
Tilegate Green 296 D7
Tilekiln Green 200 A7
Tilkey 213 G1
Tillingham 372 B1
Tilty 171 G4
Tindon End 104 A4
Tiptree 247 K7
Tiptree Heath 279 K2
Tollesbury 314 C4
Tolleshunt D'Arcy 313 G1
Tolleshunt Knights 280 E3
Tolleshunt Major 312 C1
Toot Hill 353 F4
Toppesfield 78 E6
Totham Hill 279 G8
Totham Plains 279 K8
Trimley Lower Street 93 K7
Trimley St Martin 94 B4
Trimley St Mary 94 C8
Trims Green 231 G6
Turnford 318 D7
Twinstead 83 K7
Twinstead Green 83 H8
Tye Common 414 A6
Tye Green 13 D5
Tye Green 103 F2
Tye Green 169 F7
Tye Green 210 D7
Tye Green 269 J7

Tyler's Green 324 D6
Ugley 136 A7
Ugley Green 168 B2
Ulting Wick 308 C6
Upminster 451 K3
Uppend 166 A4
Upper Dovercourt 164 D2
Upper Green 97 G3
Upper Street 125 F4
Upshire 348 E6
Vange 458 B1
Wakes Colne 150 E7
Wakes Colne Green 151 F4
Waltham Abbey 347 K6
Waltham Cross 346 C7
Waltham's Cross 143 F4
Walton 5 F2
Walton-on-the-Naze 228 D5
Warley 410 E8
Warren Heath 64 D4
Washall Green 132 E4
Washbrook 60 E4
Washbrook Street 60 E3
Watch House Green 207 F6
Water End 46 E7
Waterhales 408 E2
Watton's Green 408 C2
Weeley 225 G4
Weeley Heath 225 G7
Weir 441 H5
Wellstye Green 238 A3
Welshwood Park 188 C4
Wendens Ambo 69 K8
Wennington 468 A7
West Bergholt 185 K2
Westbourne 36 A4
Westcliff-on-Sea 463 K6
West Court 489 K7
Westerfield 37 G1
West Hanningfield 389 K1
West Horndon 434 B8
Westley Heights 456 D3
West Mersea 284 C7
West Thurrock 482 D4
West Tilbury 485 K5
Westwood Park 153 K4
Wethersfield 143 J2
Wherstead 62 D7
Whiteash Green 146 E2
White Colne 150 B7
White House 36 A3
White Notley 243 J4
White Roding or White Roothing ...266 E6
Wicken Bonhunt 99 G5
Wickford 417 J8
Wickham Bishops 277 K8
Wickham St Paul 82 D8
Widdington 136 D1
Widford 332 A7
Wiggens Green 49 K4
Willingale 328 A2
Willows Green 241 G1
Wimbish 73 F7
Wimbish Green 103 H2
Winter Gardens 460 D8
Witham 276 E1
Withersfield 26 D1
Wivenhoe 220 E4
Wix 161 K8
Wixoe 52 A2
Woodend 299 G4
Woodend Green 137 J8
Woodford Wells 403 J6
Woodgates End 170 A6
Wood Green 348 E8
Woodham Ferrers 392 A1
Woodham Mortimer 336 D8
Woodham Walter 336 C3
Woodhill 335 F7
The Woodlands 89 J6
Woodside 323 H8
Woodside Green 233 F4
Woolverstone 90 D4
Workhouse Green 85 H6
Workhouse Hill 155 F1
Wormingford 116 C8
Wormley 318 E6
Wormleybury 318 B5
Wormley West End 318 A4
Wrabness 162 C2
Wright's Green 232 D6
Writtle 331 G5
Young's End 241 J1

USING THE STREET INDEX

Street names are listed alphabetically. Each street name is followed by its postal town or area locality, the Postcode District, the page number, and the reference to the square in which the name is found.

Example: **Abbey Cl** *ROM* RM1......................**430** B8 🔟

Some entries are followed by a number in a blue box. This number indicates the location of the street within the referenced grid square. The full street name is listed at the side of the map page.

GENERAL ABBREVIATIONS

ACC	ACCESS	GA	GATE	PL	PLACE
ALY	ALLEY	GAL	GALLERY	PLN	PLAIN
AP	APPROACH	GDN	GARDEN	PLNS	PLAINS
AR	ARCADE	GDNS	GARDENS	PLZ	PLAZA
ASS	ASSOCIATION	GLD	GLADE	POL	POLICE STATION
AV	AVENUE	GLN	GLEN	PR	PRINCE
BCH	BEACH	GN	GREEN	PREC	PRECINCT
BLDS	BUILDINGS	GND	GROUND	PREP	PREPARATORY
BND	BEND	GRA	GRANGE	PRIM	PRIMARY
BNK	BANK	GRG	GARAGE	PROM	PROMENADE
BR	BRIDGE	GT	GREAT	PRS	PRINCESS
BRK	BROOK	GTWY	GATEWAY	PRT	PORT
BTM	BOTTOM	GV	GROVE	PT	POINT
BUS	BUSINESS	HGR	HIGHER	PTH	PATH
BVD	BOULEVARD	HL	HILL	PZ	PIAZZA
BY	BYPASS	HLS	HILLS	QD	QUADRANT
CATH	CATHEDRAL	HO	HOUSE	QU	QUEEN
CEM	CEMETERY	HOL	HOLLOW	QY	QUAY
CEN	CENTRE	HOSP	HOSPITAL	R	RIVER
CFT	CROFT	HRB	HARBOUR	RBT	ROUNDABOUT
CH	CHURCH	HTH	HEATH	RD	ROAD
CHA	CHASE	HTS	HEIGHTS	RDG	RIDGE
CHYD	CHURCHYARD	HVN	HAVEN	REP	REPUBLIC
CIR	CIRCLE	HWY	HIGHWAY	RES	RESERVOIR
CIRC	CIRCUS	IMP	IMPERIAL	RFC	RUGBY FOOTBALL CLUB
CL	CLOSE	IN	INLET	RI	RISE
CLFS	CLIFFS	IND EST	INDUSTRIAL ESTATE	RP	RAMP
CMP	CAMP	INF	INFIRMARY	RW	ROW
CNR	CORNER	INFO	INFORMATION	S	SOUTH
CO	COUNTY	INT	INTERCHANGE	SCH	SCHOOL
COLL	COLLEGE	IS	ISLAND	SE	SOUTH EAST
COM	COMMON	JCT	JUNCTION	SER	SERVICE AREA
COMM	COMMISSION	JTY	JETTY	SH	SHORE
CON	CONVENT	KG	KING	SHOP	SHOPPING
COT	COTTAGE	KNL	KNOLL	SKWY	SKYWAY
COTS	COTTAGES	L	LAKE	SMT	SUMMIT
CP	CAPE	LA	LANE	SOC	SOCIETY
CPS	COPSE	LDG	LODGE	SP	SPUR
CR	CREEK	LGT	LIGHT	SPR	SPRING
CREM	CREMATORIUM	LK	LOCK	SQ	SQUARE
CRS	CRESCENT	LKS	LAKES	ST	STREET
CSWY	CAUSEWAY	LNDG	LANDING	STN	STATION
CT	COURT	LTL	LITTLE	STR	STREAM
CTRL	CENTRAL	LWR	LOWER	STRD	STRAND
CTS	COURTS	MAG	MAGISTRATE	SW	SOUTH WEST
CTYD	COURTYARD	MAN	MANSIONS	TDG	TRADING
CUTT	CUTTINGS	MD	MEAD	TER	TERRACE
CV	COVE	MDW	MEADOWS	THWY	THROUGHWAY
CYN	CANYON	MEM	MEMORIAL	TNL	TUNNEL
DEPT	DEPARTMENT	MKT	MARKET	TOLL	TOLLWAY
DL	DALE	MKTS	MARKETS	TPK	TURNPIKE
DM	DAM	ML	MALL	TR	TRACK
DR	DRIVE	ML	MILL	TRL	TRAIL
DRO	DROVE	MNR	MANOR	TWR	TOWER
DRY	DRIVEWAY	MS	MEWS	U/P	UNDERPASS
DWGS	DWELLINGS	MSN	MISSION	UNI	UNIVERSITY
E	EAST	MT	MOUNT	UPR	UPPER
EMB	EMBANKMENT	MTN	MOUNTAIN	V	VALE
EMBY	EMBASSY	MTS	MOUNTAINS	VA	VALLEY
ESP	ESPLANADE	MUS	MUSEUM	VIAD	VIADUCT
EST	ESTATE	MWY	MOTORWAY	VIL	VILLA
EX	EXCHANGE	N	NORTH	VIS	VISTA
EXPY	EXPRESSWAY	NE	NORTH EAST	VLG	VILLAGE
EXT	EXTENSION	NW	NORTH WEST	VLS	VILLAS
F/O	FLYOVER	O/P	OVERPASS	VW	VIEW
FC	FOOTBALL CLUB	OFF	OFFICE	W	WEST
FK	FORK	ORCH	ORCHARD	WD	WOOD
FLD	FIELD	OV	OVAL	WHF	WHARF
FLDS	FIELDS	PAL	PALACE	WK	WALK
FLS	FALLS	PAS	PASSAGE	WKS	WALKS
FLS	FLATS	PAV	PAVILION	WLS	WELLS
FM	FARM	PDE	PARADE	WY	WAY
FT	FORT	PH	PUBLIC HOUSE	YD	YARD
FWY	FREEWAY	PK	PARK	YHA	YOUTH HOSTEL
FY	FERRY	PKWY	PARKWAY		

POSTCODE TOWNS AND AREA ABBREVIATIONS

ABR/ST ....Abridge/Stapleford Abbotts
BARK/HLT ....Barkingside/Hainault
BCAYE ....Billericay east
BCAYW ....Billericay west
BKHH ....Buckhurst Hill
BOC ....Burnham-on-Crouch
BROX ....Broxbourne
BRTR ....Braintree
BRW ....Brentwood
BRWN ....Brentwood north
BSDN ....Basildon
BSF ....Bishop's Stortford
BUNT ....Buntingford
BURES ....Bures
BXLYHN ....Bexleyheath north
CBE/LIN ....Cambridge east/Linton
CBS ....Cambridge south
CDH/CHF ....Chadwell St Mary/
Chafford Hundred
CHDH ....Chadwell Heath
CHES/WCR ....Cheshunt/Waltham Cross
CHESW ....Cheshunt west
CHIG ....Chigwell
CHING ....Chingford
CHLM/GWD ....Chelmsford/Galleywood
CHLM/WR ....Chelmsford/Writtle
CHONG ....Chipping Ongar
CHTY ....Chantry
COL ....Colchester
COLN ....Colchester north
COLS ....Colchester south
COLW ....Colchester west
COS ....Clacton-on-Sea
CRW ....Collier Row
CVI ....Canvey Island
DAGE ....Dagenham east
DART ....Dartford
ED ....Edmonton
EMPK ....Emerson Park
EN ....Enfield
ENC/FH ....Enfield Chase/Forty Hill
EPP ....Epping

ERITH ....Erith
FOS ....Frinton-on-Sea
FRAM/WMKT ....Framlingham/
Wickham Market
FX ....Felixstowe
GPK ....Gidea Park
GRAYS ....Grays
GRH ....Greenhithe
GTDUN ....Great Dunmow
GVE ....Gravesend east
GVW ....Gravesend west
HAR ....Harwich
HARH ....Harold Hill
HCH ....Hornchurch
HERT/BAY ....Hertford/Bayford
HLW ....Harlow
HLWE ....Harlow east
HLWS ....Harlow south
HLWW/ROY ....Harlow west/Roydon
HOC/HUL ....Hockley/Hullbridge
HOD ....Hoddesdon
HOO/HM ......Hoo St Werburgh/Higham
HSTD ....Halstead
HVHL ....Haverhill
ING ....Ingatestone
IP ....Ipswich
IPNE ....Ipswich northeast
IPSE ....Ipswich southeast
K/T/MI ......Kelvedon/Tiptree/Mersea Island
KESG ....Kesgrave
KIR/NAC ....Kirton/Nacton
LAIN ....Laindon
LOS ....Leigh-on-Sea
MAL ....Maldon
MEO ....Meopham
MGTR ....Manningtree
MHAD ....Much Hadham
NHMKT ....Needham Market
PEND ....Ponders End
PIT ....Pitsea
PUR ....Purfleet
RAIN ....Rainham (Gt Lon)

RAYL ....Rayleigh
RBRW/HUT ....Rural Brentwood/Hutton
RBSF ....Rural Bishop's Stortford
RCFD ....Rochford
RCHLM ....Rural Chelmsford
RCOLE ....Rural Colchester east
RCOLW ....Rural Colchester west
RCOS ....Rural Clacton-on-Sea
RIPS/CAP ....Rural Ipswich south/
Capel St Mary
RIPW ....Rural Ipswich west
ROM ....Romford
ROMW/RG ....Romford west/Rush Green
ROY ....Royston
SAFWN ....Saffron Walden north
SAFWS ....Saffron Walden south
SBF/HAD ....South Benfleet/Hadleigh
SBN/FI ....Shoeburyness/Foulness Island
SBW ....Sawbridgeworth
SLH/COR ....Stanford-le-Hope/Corringham
SOCK/AV ....South Ockendon/Aveley
SOS ....Southend-on-Sea
SOSN ....Southend-on-Sea north
STSD ....Stansted
SUD ....Sudbury
SWCM ....Swanscombe
TIL ....Tilbury
UED ....Upper Edmonton
UPMR ....Upminster
VGE ....Vange
WAB ....Waltham Abbey
WARE ....Ware
WCHMH ....Winchmore Hill
WDBR ....Woodbridge
WFD ....Woodford
WICKE ....Wickford east
WICKW ....Wickford west
WIT ....Witham
WOS/PRIT ......Westcliff-on-Sea/Prittlewell
WOTN ....Walton-on-the-Naze
WTHK ....West Thurrock

Aal - Agi

Index - streets

A

Aalten Av CVI SS8 .... 479 F2
Abberton Rd COLS CO2 .... 218 C8
K/T/MI CO5 .... 220 D8
Abbess CI CHLM/WR CM1 .... 332 A5 🖫
Abbey CI HOC/HUL SS5 .... 419 J3
ROM KM1 .... 430 B8 🖫
Abbey Ct WAB EN9 .... 347 H8
Abbey Crs RCOS CO16 .... 226 D4
Abbey Dale CI HLWE CM17 .... 295 C6
Abbey Flds RCHLM CM3 .... 363 F6
Abbey Gate St COL CO1 .... 8 B5
Abbey La RCOLW CO6 .... 213 H4
SAFWN CB10 .... 70 C1
Abbey Meadow HSTD CO9 .... 110 C3 🖫
Abbey Rd BAR EN8 .... 346 E5 🖫
BCAYW CM12 .... 414 A4
GVE DA12 .... 489 K6
HOC/HUL SS5 .... 419 J4
SUD CO10 .... 58 B4
Abbey St RCOS CO16 .... 226 D4
SAFWN CB10 .... 43 F1
Abbey Turning MAL CM9 .... 337 K2
Abbeyview WAB EN9 .... 347 H7
Abbotsbury CI CHTY IP2 .... 62 C3
Abbots CI BRWN CM15 .... 411 K4
COS CO15 .... 10 B1
MGTR CO11 .... 161 K8
Abbots Ct LAIN SS15 .... 16 C1
Abbots Gdns RCOS CO16 .... 289 J1
Abbots La COLW CO3 .... 185 F6
Abbotsleigh Rd RCHLM CM3 .... 392 D6
Abbotsmead MAL CM9 .... 310 B8
Abbots Ride BCAYE CM11 .... 414 D3 🖫
Abbot's Rd COLS CO2 .... 219 K2
Abbots Wk SBN/FI SS3 .... 466 B5 🖫
Abbotsweld HLWS CM18 .... 13 C6
Abbots Wick La K/T/MI CO5 .... 282 A2
Abbotswell Rd SBF/HAD SS7 .... 441 H8 🖫
Abbott Rd HAR CO12 .... 6 A6
Abbotts CI BCAYE CM11 .... 443 F8
Abbotts Ct HVHL CB9 .... 28 A8
Abbotts Crs CHING E4 .... 402 E7

Abbotts Dr SLH/COR SS17 .... 474 A3
WAB EN9 .... 348 C8
Abbotts Hall Cha SLH/COR SS17 ..... 474 A3
Abbotts Rd HVHL CB9 .... 27 G4
Abbotts Wy BSF CM23 .... 231 J2
Abbs Cross Gdns HCH RM12 .... 450 D2
Abbs Cross La HCH RM12 .... 450 D4
Abdy Av HAR CO12 .... 164 D3
Abell Wy CHLM/GWD CM2 .... 333 K1
Abels Rd HSTD CO9 .... 147 J5
Abensburg Rd CVI SS8 .... 461 J8 🖫
Abercorn Wy WIT CM8 .... 277 G3
Abercrombie Dr EN EN1 .... 374 A5 🖫
Abercrombie Wy HLWW/ROY CM19 ... 12 C5
Aberdare Rd PEND EN3 .... 374 C8
Aberdeen Gdns LOS SS9 .... 462 B3
Aberdeen Wy IPNE IP4 .... 37 K4
Aberfoyle CI IPNE IP4 .... 38 A4 🖫
Abingdon CI PIT SS13 .... 438 D4 🖫
Abinger CI RCOS CO16 .... 258 E7
Abraham Dr WIT CM8 .... 244 E1
Abram's La ROY SG8 .... 41 F8
Abreys SBF/HAD SS7 .... 441 F6
Abridge CI BAR EN8 .... 374 D1 🖫
Abridge Rd CHIG IG7 .... 405 H2
EPP CM16 .... 378 E3
HCH RM12 .... 450 A3
Acacia Av COLN CO4 .... 188 B5
Acacia CI IPSE IP3 .... 64 C3
Acacia Dr MAL CM9 .... 338 A3
SOS SS1 .... 465 K5
UPMR RM14 .... 451 H5
Acacia Gdns UPMR RM14 .... 452 C1
WIT CM8 .... 277 H1 🖫
Acacia Rd PIT SS13 .... 439 H5
Accommodation Rd RCOLW CO6 ...... 154 E6
Acer Gv RIPW IP8 .... 61 J4
Achilles Wy BRTR CM7 .... 178 A8
Achnacone Dr COLN CO4 .... 186 D2
Acland Av COLW CO3 .... 186 A6
Acorn Av BRTR CM7 .... 209 G3
HSTD CO9 .... 147 J4
Acorn CI CHING E4 .... 402 C8 🖫
HAR CO12 .... 165 F4 🖫
RCOLE CO7 .... 188 A1
RIPW IP8 .... 61 J3
Acorn PI VGE SS16 .... 436 B8

The Acorns HOC/HUL SS5 .... 421 F6
Acres Av CHONG CM5 .... 326 B8
Acres End CHLM/WR CM1 .... 332 A1
The Acres SLH/COR SS17 .... 474 B2
Acton CI BAR EN8 .... 346 E5 🖫
SUD CO10 .... 58 C5
Acton Gn SUD CO10 .... 58 B6
Acton La SUD CO10 .... 58 C1
SUD CO10 .... 58 C5
SUD CO10 .... 58 D3
Adalia Crs LOS SS9 .... 462 C3
Adalia Wy LOS SS9 .... 462 C3
Adams CI CHTY IP2 .... 3 D6 🖫
Adams Ct SAFWS CB11 .... 70 D5
Adams Gld RCFD SS4 .... 422 A7
Adams House HLW CM20 .... 13 D2 🖫
Adams PI KESG IP5 .... 39 G6
Adams Rd SLH/COR SS17 .... 474 A4
Adam Wy WICKE SS11 .... 417 H5
Adastral CI FX IP11 .... 130 E7
Addington Rd FX IP11 .... 94 D8
Addis CI PEND EN3 .... 374 D5 🖫
Addison Gdns GRAYS RM17 .... 484 B3 🖫
Addison Rd FOS CO13 .... 227 K8
PEND EN3 .... 374 C5
SUD CO10 .... 58 D4
Adelaide Dr COLS CO2 .... 219 H4
Adelaide Gdns SBF/HAD SS7 .... 460 C4
Adelaide Rd IPNE IP4 .... 38 B7
TIL RM18 .... 484 E7
Adelaide St HAR CO12 .... 6 A3
Adelphi Crs HCH RM12 .... 450 B3
Adelsburg Rd CVI SS8 .... 478 C1
Aden Rd PEND EN3 .... 374 E8
Admirals Wk CHLM/WR CM1 .... 14 A2
HOD EN11 .... 319 C1
SBN/FI SS3 .... 466 C8
Admiral Ms WOS/PRIT SS0 .... 463 K6
Adnams Wk RAIN RM13 .... 450 B7 🖫
Adstock Wy GRAYS RM17 .... 483 J3
Advice Av CDH/CHF RM16 .... 483 K1
Aetheric Rd BRTR CM7 .... 209 H2
Affleck Rd COLN CO4 .... 188 B6
Afton Dr SOCK/AV RM15 .... 469 K6
Agar Road Ap WOTN CO14 .... 229 H5 🖫
Agate Rd COS CO15 .... 10 B5
Agincourt Rd COS CO15 .... 10 A3
Agister Rd CHIG IG7 .... 405 K8

Agnes Av LOS SS9 .... 462 C3
Ailsa Rd WOS/PRIT SS0 .... 463 K5
Ainger Rd HAR CO12 .... 164 D3
Aingers Green Rd RCOLE CO7 .... 224 A8
Ainslie Rd IP IP1 .... 2 B3
Ainslie Wood Crs CHING E4 .... 402 C8 🔢
Ainslie Wood Gdns CHING E4 .... 402 C7
Ainslie Wood Rd CHING E4 .... 402 B8
Aintree Cl GVE DA12 .... 489 G8
Aintree Gv UPMR RM14 .... 451 G4 🔢
Aire Rd SOCK/AV RM15 .... 469 K4 🔢
Airfield Wy HCH RM12 .... 450 C7
Aisne Rd COLS SS11 .... 218 E1
Aisthorpe RIPS/CAP IP9 .... 86 E4 🔢
Ajax Cl BRTR CM7 .... 178 A8
Akenfield Cl RCHLM CM3 .... 392 E6 🔢
Alamein Cl BROX EN10 .... 318 D2
Alamein Rd BOC CM0 .... 425 H1
  CHLM/WR CM1 .... 304 B7
  COLS SS11 .... 218 D3
Alanbrooke GVE DA12 .... 489 H5
Alanbrooke Rd COLS SS11 .... 220 A3
Alan Cl COS SS19 .... 443 F7
Alan Dr RCOS CO16 .... 259 F4
Alan Gv LOS SS9 .... 443 F7
Alan Rd IPSE IP3 .... 63 H1
  WIT CM8 .... 276 E4
Alan Wy COLW CO3 .... 218 A1
Albany Av WOS/PRIT SS0 .... 18 B3
Albany Cl CHLM/WR CM1 .... 304 A8
  RCOLW CO6 .... 185 K1
Albany Ct EPP CM16 .... 350 D4
Albany Gdns East COS SS15 .... 11 E3
Albany Gdns West COS SS15 .... 11 E3
Albany Park Av PEND EN3 .... 374 C5
Albany Rd BRWN CM15 .... 410 E2
  HCH RM12 .... 450 B2
  PEND EN3 .... 374 D3
  RAYL SS6 .... 442 B4
  RCOLW CO6 .... 186 A1
  TIL RM18 .... 485 F7
  WICKW SS12 .... 417 G7
The Albany IPNE IP4 .... 3 F1
Albany Vw BKHH IG9 .... 403 H4
Albemarle Av BAR EN8 .... 346 C2
Albemarle Cl GRAYS RM17 .... 483 K1
Albemarle Gdns BRTR CM7 .... 178 B8
Albemarle St HAR CO12 .... 7 E3 🔢
Alberta Cl KESG IP5 .... 38 E6 🔢
Albert Av CHING E4 .... 402 B7
Albert Cl CDH/CHF RM16 .... 484 B2
  RAYL SS6 .... 442 A3
  RCFD SS4 .... 421 K6
Albert Crs CHING E4 .... 402 B7 🔢
Albert Dr LAIN SS15 .... 16 A4
Albert Gdns COS SS15 .... 11 D4
  HLWE CM17 .... 295 H6
  RCOLW CO6 .... 213 H5
Albertine Cl COLS SS11 .... 185 H7
Albert Murray Cl GVE DA12 .... 489 H5 🔢
Albert Pl RCOLW CO6 .... 213 H3
Albert Rd BKHH IG9 .... 404 A5
  BOC CM0 .... 425 H1
  BRTR CM7 .... 209 K2
  RAYL SS6 .... 442 A3
  RCFD SS4 .... 421 K7
  RCHLM CM3 .... 392 C6
  RCOLE CO7 .... 256 A7
  ROM RM1 .... 430 A8
  SBF/HAD SS7 .... 440 A7
  SOS SS1 .... 19 E5
  UPMR RM14 .... 454 E5
  WIT CM8 .... 277 G2
Albert St BRW CM14 .... 411 F8
  COL CO1 .... 8 A3
  HAR CO12 .... 7 E3
Albion Gv COLS CO2 .... 8 C6
Albion Hl IPNE IP4 .... 37 H6
  LOU IG10 .... 404 A1
Albion Pk LOU IG10 .... 404 A1
Albion Rd GVE DA12 .... 489 H5
  SBF/HAD SS7 .... 460 B1
  WOS/PRIT SS0 .... 18 B3
Albion Ter GVE DA12 .... 489 H4
Albrighton Cft COLN CO4 .... 187 K1
Albury Grove Rd BAR EN8 .... 346 C4
Albury Ride BAR EN8 .... 346 D5
Albury Wk BAR EN8 .... 346 C4
Albyns GVE SS16 .... 16 A6
Albyns La ABR/ST RM4 .... 380 D6
Alconbury BSF CM23 .... 199 G4
Alcotes BSDN SS14 .... 438 C8
Aldborough Rd UPMR RM14 .... 451 G3 🔢
Aldbrough Cl HVHL CB9 .... 26 E7
  RCOS CO16 .... 290 D1 🔢
Aldeburgh Gdns COLN CO4 .... 187 J1
Aldeburgh Pl WFD IG8 .... 403 H7 🔢
Aldeburgh Wy CHLM/WR CM1 .... 305 F8
Alder Av UPMR RM14 .... 451 G3
Alderbury Lea RCHLM CM3 .... 363 K4 🔢
Alderbury Rd STSD CM24 .... 167 K5 🔢
Aldercar Rd RCOLW CO6 .... 216 E4
Alder Cl BSF CM23 .... 231 H1
  LAIN SS15 .... 16 B1

Aldercroft Cl IP IP1 .... 36 D2
Aldercroft Rd IP IP1 .... 36 D2
Alder Dr CHLM/GWD CM2 .... 332 D7
  SOCK/AV RM15 .... 470 A4
Alderford St HSTD CO9 .... 110 D5
Alderlee CHTY IP2 .... 62 B5
Alderleys SBF/HAD SS7 .... 441 F7
Alderman Rd IP IP1 .... 2 C3
Alderman's Hl HOC/HUL SS5 .... 420 C8
Alderman Wk SLH/COR SS17 .... 457 F8
Alderney Gdns WICKE SS11 .... 417 F3
Alderney Rd ERITH DA8 .... 480 B6
Alde Rd HVHL CB9 .... 27 C5
Alderton Cl BRWN CM15 .... 410 E1
  GTDUN CM6 .... 206 D7
  LOU IG10 .... 377 J8
Alderton Hall La LOU IG10 .... 377 J8
Alderton Hl LOU IG10 .... 404 C1
Alderton Ri LOU IG10 .... 377 J8
Alderton Rd CDH/CHF RM16 .... 472 D6
  COLN CO4 .... 9 E3
Alderton Wy LOU IG10 .... 404 C1
Alderwood Dr ABR/ST RM4 .... 379 F7
Alderwood Wy SBF/HAD SS7 .... 461 H2
Aldham Gdns RAYL SS6 .... 440 E2
Aldingham Gdns HCH RM12 .... 450 B6 🔢
Aldon Cl HAR CO12 .... 164 B4
Aldous Cl RCOLE CO7 .... 122 B2
Aldria Rd SLH/COR SS17 .... 457 F8 🔢
Aldridge Av PEND EN3 .... 375 G4
Aldridge Cl CHLM/GWD CM2 .... 333 J1
Aldrin Cl SLH/COR SS17 .... 474 A3
Aldridge Ms FX IP11 .... 143 H7
Aldrin Wy LOS SS9 .... 443 H7
Aldwych CH HCH RM12 .... 450 B3 🔢
Alexander Dr SUD CO10 .... 59 J2
Alexander La BRWN CM15 .... 411 K1
Alexander Ms CHLM/GWD CM2 ...... 362 B3
Alexander Rd BRTR CM7 .... 209 H1
  VGE SS16 .... 456 C1
Alexandra Cl K/T/MI CO5 .... 285 F7
Alexandra Rd CDH/CHF RM16 .... 485 C1
Alexandra Dr RCOLE CO7 .... 221 F2
Alexandra Rd BOC CM0 .... 398 B8
  COLW CO3 .... 8 A5
  COS SS15 .... 10 A5
  ERITH DA8 .... 480 A5
  FX IP11 .... 5 E1
  GVE DA12 .... 489 K5
  HAR CO12 .... 7 E3
  HSTD CO9 .... 110 C4
  IPNE IP4 .... 3 J2
  LOS SS9 .... 463 F5 🔢
  PEND EN3 .... 374 D8
  RAYL SS6 .... 441 K2
  RCFD SS4 .... 421 K7
  RCOS CO16 .... 225 G5
  ROM RM1 .... 430 A8 🔢
  SBF/HAD SS7 .... 460 C1
  SBN/FI SS3 .... 467 F2
  SOS SS1 .... 18 C5
  SUD CO10 .... 58 D5
  TIL RM18 .... 484 E8 🔢
Alexandra St HAR CO12 .... 7 E3
  SOS SS1 .... 19 D5
Alexandra Ter COLW CO3 .... 8 A5
  TIL RM18 .... 486 C3
Alexandria Dr RAYL SS6 .... 441 F1
Alfells Rd RCOLE CO7 .... 189 J7
Alf Eounder Cl COLN CO4 .... 188 B7 🔢
Alfreda Av HOC/HUL SS5 .... 419 J2
Alfred Gdns WICKE SS11 .... 417 G4
Alfred Pl GVW DA11 .... 404 A5
Alfred Rd BKHH IG9 .... 404 A5
  BRW CM14 .... 411 G5 🔢
  GVW DA11 .... 489 G7
  SOCK/AV RM15 .... 468 A7
Alfred St GRAYS RM17 .... 484 B5
Alfred Ter WOTN CO14 .... 229 H5 🔢
Alfreg Rd WIT CM8 .... 276 D5
Algars Wy RCHLM CM3 .... 392 D5 🔢
Algers Cl LOU IG10 .... 404 A1
Algers Rd LOU IG10 .... 404 B1
Alghers Md LOU IG10 .... 404 A1
Alicia Av WICKE SS11 .... 417 K6
Alicia Cl WICKE SS11 .... 417 K6
Alicia Wk WICKE SS11 .... 417 K6
Alicia Wy WICKE SS11 .... 417 K6
Alienor Av BRTR CM7 .... 142 C4
Allandale SBF/HAD SS7 .... 441 F6
Allandale Rd EMPK RM11 .... 450 A1
  PEND EN3 .... 374 D2
Allard Wy BROX EN10 .... 318 E3
Allectus Wy WFD IG8 .... 276 D5
Allenby Crs GRAYS RM17 .... 484 A4
Allenby Dr EMPK RM11 .... 451 F2
Allenby Rd CHTY IP2 .... 2 A3
Allendale Dr RCOLW CO6 .... 216 C1
Allens Cl RCHLM CM3 .... 306 D4
Allens Rd BCAYE CM11 .... 388 E8 🔢
Allensway SLH/COR SS17 .... 474 B1
Allen Wy RCOS CO16 .... 288 A2
Allerton Cl RCFD SS4 .... 421 K7 🔢

Alley Dock LOS SS9 .... 462 E5
Alleyne Wy COS CO15 .... 290 C5
Alleyn Pl WOS/PRIT SS0 .... 463 K4
Alley Rd KIR/NAC IP10 .... 94 C2
Allfields HAR CO12 .... 6 A6
Allington Cl IPNE IP4 .... 37 H6
Allington Wk HVHL CB9 .... 26 E5
Allison Cl WAB EN9 .... 348 C7
Allistonway SLH/COR SS17 .... 474 B2
Allmains Cl WAB EN9 .... 320 D7
Allnutts Rd EPP CM16 .... 350 E7
All Saints Av COLW CO3 .... 218 B5
All Saints Cl BRWN CM15 .... 383 K2
  BSF CM23 .... 199 F5
  CHIG IG7 .... 406 A6
  CHLM/WR CM1 .... 15 F1
All Saints' Rd GVW DA11 .... 488 E6
  IP IP1 .... 2 B2
Alma Av HCH RM12 .... 451 F4
Alma Cl IPNE IP4 .... 37 J4
  SBF/HAD SS7 .... 462 A3
  WICKW SS12 .... 416 D7
Alma Rd SBF/HAD SS7 .... 462 B3
Almere SBF/HAD SS7 .... 460 C1
Almond Av WICKW SS12 .... 416 E6
Almond Cl CDH/CHF RM16 .... 485 F2
  COS CO15 .... 290 E2
  K/T/MI CO5 .... 248 A7 🔢
  RCOLE CO7 .... 221 F5
Almondhayes CHTY IP2 .... 2 C6
Almonds Av BKHH IG9 .... 403 H5
Almond Wk CVI SS8 .... 477 K1
Almond Wy COLN CO4 .... 188 B5
Almshouse La EN EN1 .... 374 B3 🔢
Alnwick Cl VGE SS16 .... 436 A8 🔢
Alpe St IP IP1 .... 2 C2
Alpha Cl BRTR CM7 .... 209 K3
  PIT SS13 .... 439 J7
Alphamstone Rd BURES CO8 .... 114 E1
Alpha Pl BSF CM23 .... 198 E5 🔢
Alpha Rd BOC CM0 .... 398 C8
  CHING E4 .... 402 B6
  PIT SS13 .... 439 J7
  RCOS CO16 .... 288 B2
Alport Av COLS CO2 .... 218 D1
Alresford Gn WICKW SS12 .... 417 H7
Alresford Rd RCOLE CO7 .... 221 H5
Alsa Gdns RBSF CM22 .... 168 D3
Alsa Leys RBSF CM22 .... 168 D3
Alsa St STSD CM24 .... 168 A4
Alston Rd IPSE IP3 .... 63 H1
Altar Pl LAIN SS15 .... 16 A3
Altbarn Cl COLN CO4 .... 155 K8
Altbarn Rd COLS CO2 .... 9 F6
Altham Gv HLW CM20 .... 13 E1
Althorne Cl PIT SS13 .... 438 E4
Althorne Wy RCFD SS4 .... 423 H3
Althorpe Cl HOC/HUL SS5 .... 420 E1
Alton Dr COLW CO3 .... 186 C5
Alton Gdns SOSN SS2 .... 444 B8
Alton Hall La RIPS/CAP IP9 .... 125 C6
Alton Park La COS CO15 .... 290 C6
Alton Park Rd COS CO15 .... 10 A5
Alton Rd COS CO15 .... 10 B5
Aluric Cl CDH/CHF RM16 .... 485 C2
Alverstoke Rd HARH RM3 .... 431 F2
Alverton Cl BRTR CM7 .... 208 E6
Alverton Wy COLN CO4 .... 187 J2
Alvis Av COS CO15 .... 290 A2
Alwen Gv SOCK/AV RM15 .... 469 K5
Alwyne Av BRWN CM15 .... 411 J2
Alyssum Cl CHLM/WR CM1 .... 305 H7
Amberley Cl RCOLE CO7 .... 221 F4
Amberley Rd BKHH IG9 .... 403 K4
Ambleside EPP CM16 .... 350 E5
  WICKE SS11 .... 418 A6 🔢
Ambleside Av HCH RM12 .... 450 C6
Ambleside Cl COS CO15 .... 11 D4
Ambleside Crs PEND EN3 .... 374 D2
Ambleside Dr SOS SS1 .... 19 F4
Ambleside Gdns HOC/HUL SS5 ...... 419 J8
Ambleside Wk CVI SS8 .... 477 K1
Ambridge Rd RCOLW CO6 .... 213 F5
Ambrose Av COLW CO3 .... 218 A5
Amcotes Pl CHLM/GWD CM2 .... 15 D5
Ameland Rd CVI SS8 .... 461 F4
Amerells Rd RCOS CO16 .... 258 E5
America Rd RCOLW CO6 .... 181 J5
America St MAL CM9 .... 338 C5
Amersham Av VGE SS16 .... 436 A8 🔢
Amersham Cl HARH RM3 .... 431 G1
Amersham Rd HARH RM3 .... 431 G1
Amersham Wk HARH RM3 .... 431 G1 🔢
Amery Gdns GPK RM2 .... 430 E5
Amesbury WAB EN9 .... 348 C6
Amesbury Dr CHING E4 .... 402 C2
Amesbury Rd EPP CM16 .... 350 D7
Amid Rd CVI SS8 .... 461 H6
Amos Hl SUD CO10 .... 338 B5
Amoss Rd CHLM/GWD CM2 .... 333 H1
Ampers End BSDN SS14 .... 438 A7
Amwell Ct WAB EN9 .... 348 A2
Ancaster Rd CHTY IP2 .... 2 C5
The Anchorage SBN/FI SS3 .... 467 G

Anchor Cl *BAR* EN8 .... 346 D2
Anchor End *MGTR* CO11 .... 160 B1
Anchor La *CHONG* CM45 .... 298 D1
   MAL CM9 .... 310 C8
   MGTR CO11 .... 160 B1
   RCFD SS4 .... 425 G4
Anchor Reach *RCHLM* CM3 .... 392 E8
Anchor Rd *COS* CO15 .... 10 A4
   K/T/MI CO5 .... 280 A1
Anchor St *BSF* CM23 .... 199 F7
   CHLM/GWD CM2 .... 14 C4
Anders Fall *LOS* SS9 .... 443 H7
Anderson Av *CHLM/WR* CM1 .... 304 B8
Anderson Cl *BSF* CM23 .... 166 E3
Andersons *SLH/COR* SS17 .... 474 B3
Andrea Av *CDH/CHF* RM16 .... 483 J1
Andrew Cl *BRTR* CM7 .... 177 J8
   SLH/COR SS17 .... 473 K1
Andrews Cl *BKHH* IG9 .... 403 K5
Andrews Farm La *GTDUN* CM6 .... 172 B5
Andrew's La *EBAR* EN7 .... 346 A2
Andrews Pl *CHLM/WR* CM1 .... 14 A3
Andros Cl *IPSE* IP3 .... 63 J5
Andyk Rd *IP* IP1 .... 2 C2
   RCOLE CO7 .... 221 F5
Anemone Ct *COLN* CO4 .... 186 D3
Anerley Rd *WOS/PRIT* SS0 .... 18 A4
Angel Cl *VGE* SS16 .... 458 A2
Angelgate Esp *HAR* CO12 .... 7 F2
Angel La *GTDUN* CM6 .... 204 C5
   SUD CO10 .... 33 H1
Angle Rd *WTHK* RM20 .... 483 C5
Anglesea Pl *GVE* DA12 .... 489 G4
   GVW DA11 .... 489 G4
Anglesea Rd *IP* IP1 .... 2 C1
   RCOLE CO7 .... 221 F5
Anglesey Cl *BSF* CM23 .... 198 C5
Anglesey Gdns *WICKW* SS12 .... 417 J8
Anglesey Rd *PEND* EN3 .... 374 B8
Angle Side *BRTR* CM7 .... 210 A3
Anglia Cl *COLS* CO2 .... 218 C2
Anglia Wy *BRTR* CM7 .... 210 A3
Angus Cl *IPNE* IP4 .... 37 K4
Angus Cl *IPNE* IP4 .... 37 K4
Anita Cl East *CHTY* IP2 .... 36 A8
Anita Cl West *CHTY* IP2 .... 36 A8
Anjou Gn *CHLM/WR* CM1 .... 305 J6
Annabell Av *CDH/CHF* RM16 .... 472 D6
Annalee Gdns *SOCK/AV* RM15 .... 469 K5
Annalee Rd *SOCK/AV* RM15 .... 469 K5
Ann Boleyn Dr *RCFD* SS4 .... 425 F4
Annbrook Rd *CHTY* IP2 .... 62 A4
Ann Coles Cl *HVHL* CB9 .... 50 D7
Anne Cl *RCOLE* CO7 .... 255 K7
Anne St *FX* IP11 .... 5 E4
Ann St *IP* IP1 .... 2 C2
Ann Suckling Rd *HVHL* CB9 .... 27 G3
Ansgar Rd *SAFWS* CB11 .... 71 F6
Anson Cha *SBN/FI* SS3 .... 466 D5
Anson Cl *HAR* CO12 .... 6 B6
   RCHLM CM3 .... 392 E4
Anson Wy *BRTR* CM7 .... 210 B1
Anstey Cl *LOS* SS9 .... 442 E6
Antelope Av *CDH/CHF* RM16 .... 483 K2
Anthony Cl *SLH/COR* SS17 .... 474 A1
Anthony Dr *SLH/COR* SS17 .... 474 A1
Antlers *CVI* SS8 .... 477 K3
Antlers Hi *CHING* E4 .... 402 D1
Antonia Cl *HVHL* CB9 .... 28 A6
Antonius Wy *COLN* CO4 .... 155 J7
Anton Rd *SOCK/AV* RM15 .... 469 K4
Antony Cl *CVI* SS8 .... 461 G8
Antrim Rd *SBN/FI* SS3 .... 466 C5
Anvil Wy *BCAYW* CM12 .... 387 G6
   CHLM/WR CM1 .... 305 C5
Anzani Av *FX* IP11 .... 4 C3
Apeldoorn *SBF/HAD* SS7 .... 440 A6
Aperfield Rd *ERITH* DA8 .... 480 A5
Apollo Cl *HCH* RM12 .... 450 C3
Appleby Cl *RIPW* IP8 .... 61 J4
Appleby Dr *HARH* RM3 .... 408 D3
   VGE SS16 .... 436 M4
Appledene Cl *RAYL* SS6 .... 441 J1
Appledore Cl *SBN/FI* SS3 .... 466 C5
Appledore Ct *HARH* RM3 .... 430 D3
Apple Ga *BRW* CM14 .... 410 C1
Appleperow *LOS* SS9 .... 443 G7
Appleton Cl *HLWW/ROY* CM19 .... 12 C4
Appleton Flds *BSF* CM23 .... 231 J1
Appleton Rd *LOU* IG10 .... 377 K7
   SBF/HAD SS7 .... 460 A2
Appleton Wy *HCH* RM12 .... 450 E2
Appletree Cl *BRTR* CM7 .... 210 B1
   SOSN SS2 .... 465 H2
Apple Tree Crs *BRWN* CM15 .... 384 A4
Apple Tree Wy *WICKE* SS11 .... 417 C5
Apple Wy *CHLM/GWD* CM2 .... 333 F7
Appleyard Av *HOC/HUL* SS5 .... 421 F5
Appold St *ERITH* DA8 .... 480 A5
Approach Rd *BCAYE* CM11 .... 416 A2
   CVI SS8 .... 479 F2
The Approach *COS* CO15 .... 290 C5
   EN EN1 .... 374 B6
   RAYL SS6 .... 441 H3

UPMR RM14 .... 451 J4
Apsley Cl *BSF* CM23 .... 231 J1
Apton Ct *BSF* CM23 .... 198 E6
Apton Flds *BSF* CM23 .... 198 E7
Apton Hall Rd *RCFD* SS4 .... 422 D7
Apton Rd *BSF* CM23 .... 198 E6
Arabia Cl *CHING* E4 .... 402 D3
Aragon Av *SOCK/AV* RM15 .... 469 K5
Aragon Cl *COS* CO15 .... 290 B5
   SOSN SS2 .... 464 B1
Aragon Rd *RCHLM* CM3 .... 241 H6
Arakan Cl *COLS* CO2 .... 218 C4
Arbor Rd *CHING* E4 .... 402 E6
Arbour Cl *BRW* CM14 .... 411 C8
Arbour La *CHLM/WR* CM1 .... 15 E1
   WIT CM8 .... 278 A8
Arbour Rd *PEND* EN3 .... 374 D8
Arbour Wy *COLN* CO4 .... 187 K1
   HCH RM12 .... 450 C6
Arcadian Gdns *SBF/HAD* SS7 .... 461 H1
Arcadia Rd *BOC* CM0 .... 398 C8
   CVI SS8 .... 478 D2
Arcany Rd *SOCK/AV* RM15 .... 469 K4
Archangel Gdns *CHTY* IP2 .... 62 D1
Archates Av *CDH/CHF* RM16 .... 483 K2
Archer Av *SOSN* SS2 .... 465 G3
Archer Rd *SOSN* SS2 .... 465 H2
Archers *EPP* CM16 .... 321 K2
Archers Cl *BCAYW* CM12 .... 414 B5
Archers Dr *PEND* EN3 .... 374 C6
Archers Fields Cl *PIT* SS13 .... 438 E4
Archers Fields Cl *PIT* SS13 .... 438 D4
Archery Flds *COS* CO15 .... 10 D2
Archibald Rd *HARH* RM3 .... 431 H3
Archway *HARH* RM3 .... 430 C1
Arden Cl *COLN* CO4 .... 187 K2
Arderne Cl *HAR* CO12 .... 6 A6
Ardleigh Gdns 412 D2
   RBRW/HUT CM13 .... 412 D2
Ardleigh Green Rd *EMPK* RM11 .... 430 E7
Ardleigh Ct *BRWN* CM15 .... 411 J3
Ardleigh Gdns
   RBRW/HUT CM13 .... 412 D2
Ardleigh Green Rd *EMPK* RM11 .... 430 E7
Ardleigh Rd *MGTR* CO11 .... 158 D3
   RCOLE CO7 .... 157 G2
   RCOLE CO7 .... 190 B1
Ardley Crs *BSF* CM22 .... 265 H3
Ardley Wy *RAYL* SS6 .... 441 J4
Ardmore Cl *BKHH* IG9 .... 403 J4
Ardmore Rd *SOCK/AV* RM15 .... 469 K4
Argents La *COLW* CO5 .... 185 G3
Argent St *GRAYS* RM17 .... 483 K2
   WTHK RM20 .... 483 H5
Argyle Cl *UPMR* RM14 .... 452 A4
Argyle Rd *BOC* CM0 .... 425 J1
   RCOS CO16 .... 226 D3
Argyll Rd *GRAYS* RM17 .... 483 K4
   WOS/PRIT SS0 .... 18 A4
Ariel Cl *COLN* CO4 .... 188 B6
Arisdale Av *SOCK/AV* RM15 .... 469 K3
Arjan Wy *CDH/CHF* RM16 .... 483 K2
Ark Av *CDH/CHF* RM16 .... 483 K2
Ark La *RCFD* SS4 .... 443 H4
Arkle Ct *KESG* IP5 .... 39 H6
   TIL RM18 .... 485 F8
Arkwright Rd *CHTY* IP2 .... 36 A8
   TIL RM18 .... 485 F8
Arkwrights *HLW* CM20 .... 13 F2
Arlington Crs *BAR* EN8 .... 346 E8
Arlington Gdns *HARH* RM3 .... 431 H3
Arlington Rd *RAYL* SS6 .... 441 J4
Arlington Wy *BCAYW* CM12 .... 387 F8
Armada Cl *LAIN* SS15 .... 16 B5
Armadale *CVI* SS8 .... 477 K1
Armagh Rd *SBN/FI* SS3 .... 466 C6
Armath La *VGE* SS16 .... 456 A1
Armidale Wk *COLS* CO2 .... 219 H3
Armiger Wy *WIT* CM8 .... 277 H5
Armitage Rd *SOS* SS1 .... 465 K4
Armonde Cl *RCHLM* CM3 .... 306 C4
Armond Rd *WIT* CM8 .... 276 E2
Armor Rd *PUR* RM19 .... 482 A3
Armourers Cl *BSF* CM23 .... 231 F1
Armoury Dr *GVE* DA12 .... 489 H5
Armoury Rd *RCOLW* CO6 .... 186 A1
Arms La *HVHL* CB9 .... 28 C4
Armstrong Cl *RCHLM* CM3 .... 335 K5
   SLH/COR SS17 .... 474 A3
Armstrong Rd *SBF/HAD* SS7 .... 440 C6
Armstrong Wy *HSTD* CO9 .... 79 K3
Arne Cl *SLH/COR* SS17 .... 473 K2
Arne Ct *LAIN* SS15 .... 16 A2
Arne Ms *LAIN* SS15 .... 16 A2
Arnheim Rd *BOC* CM0 .... 425 H1
Arnhem Av *SOCK/AV* RM15 .... 468 E3
Arnhem Gv *BRTR* CM7 .... 177 H8
Arnhem Rd *CHLM/WR* CM1 .... 304 A7
Arnold Av *SOS* SS1 .... 19 F5
Arnold Av East *PEND* EN3 .... 375 F4
Arnold Cl *IP* IP1 .... 36 B2
Arnold Pl *TIL* RM18 .... 485 H7
Arnold Rd *COS* CO15 .... 10 A5
   GVE DA12 .... 489 H7
Arnolds Av *RBRW/HUT* CM13 .... 412 B1
Arnolds Cl *RBRW/HUT* CM13 .... 412 B1

Arnolds Farm La *RBRW/HUT* CM13 .... 385 J7
Arnolds Wy *RCFD* SS4 .... 421 K6
Arnold Vls *K/T/MI* CO5 .... 248 A7
Arnold Wy *CHLM/GWD* CM2 .... 360 E2
Arnstones Cl *COLN* CO4 .... 9 E3
Arran Ct *WICKW* SS12 .... 417 J7
Arras Rd *COLS* CO2 .... 218 E1
Arrendene Rd *CHIG* CB9 .... 27 F4
Arrow Rd *COLN* CO4 .... 188 C6
Arrowsmith Rd *CHIG* IG7 .... 405 J8
Artemis Cl *GVE* DA12 .... 489 K5
Arterial Road North Stifford
   CDH/CHF RM16 .... 483 H1
Arterial Road Purfleet *PUR* RM19 .... 481 K3
Arterial Road West Thurrock
   WTHK RM20 .... 482 C2
Artesian Cl *ROM* RM1 .... 450 A1
Arthur Ct *CHLM/WR* CM1 .... 304 B8
Arthur St *COL* CO1 .... 9 D5
   ERITH DA8 .... 480 A6
   GRAYS RM17 .... 484 B5
   GVW DA11 .... 489 F5
Arthy Cl *RCHLM* CM3 .... 308 A1
Artillery Rw *GVE* DA12 .... 489 H5
Artillery St *COL* CO1 .... 9 D5
Arun *TIL* RM18 .... 486 D3
Arun Cl *CHLM/WR* CM1 .... 304 E8
Arundel Cl *BAR* EN8 .... 346 E2
Arundel Dr *SLH/COR* SS17 .... 474 C1
Arundel Gdns *RAYL* SS6 .... 419 G8
   WOS/PRIT SS0 .... 463 H2
Arundel Rd *HARH* RM3 .... 431 G2
   SBF/HAD SS7 .... 440 A6
   WICKE SS11 .... 417 F4
Arundel Wy *BCAYW* CM12 .... 387 J7
   IPSE IP5 .... 64 C2
Arwela Rd *FX* IP11 .... 5 F5
Arwen Gv *RCHLM* CM3 .... 392 C7
Asbury Cl *COLN* CO4 .... 9 F3
Asbury Dr *RCOLW* CO6 .... 215 J2
Ascot Cl *BSF* CM23 .... 199 H5
   BSF CM23 .... 441 G6
Ascot Dr *FX* IP11 .... 5 E1
   IPSE IP3 .... 63 K2
Ascot Gdns *HCH* RM12 .... 451 F5
   PEND EN3 .... 374 C3
Ascot Rd *GVW* DA11 .... 489 G8
Ashanti Cl *SBN/FI* SS3 .... 466 E5
Ashbeam Cl *RBRW/HUT* CM13 .... 433 F1
Ashbourne Rd *BROX* EN10 .... 319 F5
   HARH RM3 .... 408 D7
Ash Bungalows *BRTR* CM7 .... 209 H2
Ashburnham Gdns *UPMR* RM14 .... 451 J2
Ashburnham Rd *SOS* SS1 .... 18 C4
Ashby Cl *CDH/CHF* RM16 .... 472 E6
   EMPK RM11 .... 451 H2
Ashby Ri *BSF* CM23 .... 199 G4
Ashby Rd *WIT* CM8 .... 277 G6
Ash Cl *BRWN* CM15 .... 410 C1
   COS CO15 .... 290 E2
   RCHLM CM3 .... 308 A1
   RCOLE CO7 .... 255 J6
Ashcombe *RCFD* SS4 .... 444 A2
Ashcombe Cl *LOS* SS9 .... 442 C7
Ashcombe Wy *RAYL* SS6 .... 442 A3
Ashcroft Rd *IP* IP1 .... 36 B4
Ashdale *BSF* CM23 .... 231 H1
Ashdale Rd *KESG* IP5 .... 39 H5
Ashdene Cl *HOC/HUL* SS5 .... 419 K3
Ashdon Cl *RBRW/HUT* CM13 .... 412 B2
   SOCK/AV RM15 .... 469 K6
Ashdon Rd *SAFWN* CB10 .... 46 A8
   SAFWN CB10 .... 71 F3
   SAFWN CB10 .... 73 G1
Ashdon Wy *VGE* SS16 .... 17 E5
Ashdown Cl *SLH/COR* SS17 .... 457 G8
Ashdown Crs *BAR* EN8 .... 346 E2
   SBF/HAD SS7 .... 461 K1
Ashdown Rd *PEND* EN3 .... 374 D3
   SAFWN CB10 .... 73 J3
Ashdown Wy *COLN* CO4 .... 9 F4
   IPSE IP3 .... 64 B2
Ashen Cl *SUD* CO10 .... 53 G4
Ashen Hi *SUD* CO10 .... 53 F3
Ashen La *SUD* CO10 .... 53 F2
Ashen Rd *HSTD* CO9 .... 52 E5
   SUD CO10 .... 31 F7
   SUD CO10 .... 53 K4
Ashes Cl *FOS* CO13 .... 228 E5
Ashes Rd *BRTR* CM7 .... 210 E6
Ash Fall *WIT* CM8 .... 245 C8
Ashfield *RAYL* SS6 .... 440 E2
Ashfield Farm Rd *MAL* CM9 .... 308 D5
Ashfields *LOU* IG10 .... 377 H6
   PIT SS13 .... 439 F6
Ashford Av *BRW* CM14 .... 410 E6
Ashford Crs *PEND* EN3 .... 374 C6
Ashford Rd *CHLM/WR* CM1 .... 332 A3
Ash Gn *RCFD* SS4 .... 423 C4
   SAFWN CB10 .... 43 J4
Ash Ground Cl *FX* IP11 .... 94 C5
   MGTR CO11 .... 123 J3
Ash Gv *BOC* CM0 .... 398 B7
   CHLM/GWD CM2 .... 15 D6
   COLS CO2 .... 219 H5

GTDUN CM6.............................. 204 C6
HVHL CB9 .... 26 E4
MAL CM9 .... 310 D7
RCOLE CO7 .... 221 F2
RIPS/CAP IP9 .... 87 F4
SUD CO10 .... 58 E8
Ash Groves *SBW* CM21 .... 264 A3
Ashingdale Cl *CVI* SS8 .... 478 C5 🗓
Ashingdon Cl *CHING* E4 .... 402 D6 🗓
Ashingdon Rd *HOC/HUL* SS5 .... 421 J4
Ashlea Cl *HVHL* CB9 .... 27 H7 🗓
Ashlea Rd *HVHL* CB9 .... 27 H7 🗓
Ashleigh Cl *CVI* SS8 .... 461 F7 🗓
Ashleigh Dr *LOS* SS9 .... 463 G5
Ashleigh Gdns *UPMR* RM14 .... 452 A4
Ashley Cl *SLH/COR* SS17 .... 474 C1
   COLW CO3 .... 186 D7
Ashley Gn *RCHLM* CM3 .... 363 F6
Ashley Rd *CHING* E4 .... 402 D6
   HAR CO12 .... 6 B5
   PEND EN3 .... 374 C6 🗓
Ashley St *CHTY* IP2 .... 3 D5 🗓
Ashlong Gv *HSTD* CO9 .... 147 K2
Ashlyn Gv *EMPK* RM11 .... 430 E5
Ashlyns La *CHONG* CM5 .... 325 F3
Ashlyns Rd *EPP* CM16 .... 350 D4 🗓
   FOS CO13 .... 261 J1
Ashmans Rw *RCHLM* CM3 ...... 392 D7 🗓
Ashmere Gv *IPNE* IP4 .... 37 H7
Ashmere Ri *SUD* CO10 .... 58 D5
Ashmole Dr *FOS* CO13 .... 228 E7
Ashmore Gdns *GVW* DA11 .... 488 C8 🗓
Ashpole Rd *BRTR* CM7 .... 178 A4
Ash Ri *HSTD* CO9 .... 147 K5
   RCOLW CO6 .... 189 G6
Ash Rd *CVI* SS8 .... 478 C2
   RCOLE CO7 .... 222 A5 🗓
   SBF/HAD SS7 .... 461 K3
Ashstead Cl *RCOS* CO16 .... 258 D7 🗓
Ashton Cl *CHTY* IP2 .... 61 J3
Ashton Pl *CHLM/GWD* CM2 .... 333 J2
Ashton Rd *HARH* RM3 .... 430 E2
   PEND EN3 .... 374 E2
Ash Tree Ct *RCFD* SS4 .... 445 G1
Ash Tree Crs *CHLM/WR* CM1 .... 14 A3
Ash Tree Fld *HLW* CM20 .... 12 A1
Ashurst Av *SOSN* SS2 .... 465 J3
Ashurst Cl *K/T/MI* CO5 .... 220 C5 🗓
Ashurst Dr *CHLM/WR* CM1 .... 305 F6 🗓
Ashvale Cl *UPMR* RM14 .... 452 B3
Ashvale Gdns *CRW* RM5 .... 407 J8
   UPMR RM14 .... 452 B3
Ash Wk *SOCK/AV* RM15 .... 470 B3
   SOS SS1 .... 19 E5
Ash Wy *COLW* CO3 .... 218 A2
   HOC/HUL SS5 .... 421 F5
Ashway *SLH/COR* SS17 .... 457 J8
Ashwells Rd *BRWN* CM15 ...... 383 H7
Ashwin Av *RCOLW* CO6 .... 216 C1
Ashwood Rd *CHING* E4 .... 402 E6
Ashwood Pl *HLWE* CM17 .... 152 A5
Ashworths *CVI* SS8 .... 461 F7 🗓
   RCFD SS4 .... 421 K7
Askews Farm Rd *GRAYS* RM17 ...... 483 H4
Askins Rd *RCOLE* CO7 .... 122 B2
Aspdin Rd *GVW* DA11 .... 488 C8
Aspen Cl *CVI* SS8 .... 477 J1
   HVHL CB9 .... 26 E4
Aspen Ct *LAIN* SS15 .... 16 A1
Aspen Gv *UPMR* RM14 .... 451 H5
The Aspens *BSF* CM23 .... 199 G3
Aspen Wy *COLN* CO4 .... 9 F3 🗓
   HAR CO12 .... 164 A6
   PEND EN3 .... 374 D1
Aspin Ms *SAFWN* CB10 .... 71 F2 🗓
Asquith Av *SBF/HAD* SS7 ...... 441 H7
Asquith Dr *COLN* CO4 .... 155 K8 🗓
Asquith Gdns *SBF/HAD* SS7 .... 441 H6
Assandune Cf *RCFD* SS4 .... 422 A6 🗓
Aster Cl *BSF* CM23 .... 198 C7
   CHLM/WR CM1 .... 305 H7
   RCOS CO16 .... 200 E1
Aster Rd *CHTY* IP2 .... 62 A1
Astley *GRAYS* RM17 .... 483 J5
Astley Rd *COS* CO15 .... 10 A4
Aston Rd *LAIN* SS15 .... 436 C7
Astra Cl *RAIN* RM13 .... 450 C7 🗓
Ataka Rd *FX* IP11 .... 5 F1
Athelstan Cl *HARH* RM3 .... 431 G3
Athelstan Gdns *WICKE* SS11 .... 417 G4
   WICKE SS11 .... 417 J4
Athelstan Rd *COLW* CO3 .... 186 D8
   HARH RM3 .... 431 G3
Atherstone Cl *CVI* SS8 .... 478 C5 🗓
Atherstone Rd *CVI* SS8 .... 478 C5
Atherton End *SBW* CM21 .... 263 J2
Atherton Gdns *CDH/CHF* RM16 ...... 485 H3
Atherton Rd *CHTY* IP2 .... 61 K3
Athos Rd *CVI* SS8 .... 461 H8
Atlas Ct *RCOLW* CO6 .... 149 H6
Atlas Rd *RCOLW* CO6 .... 149 G6
Atridge Cha *BCAYW* CM12 ...... 414 B1
Atterton Rd *HVHL* CB9 .... 26 D4

Attlee Ct *GRAYS* RM17 .... 483 K2
Attwood Cl *COLN* CO4 .... 155 J8
Attwoods Cl *CHLM/GWD* CM2 ...... 360 D2
Aubrey Cl *CHLM/WR* CM1 ...... 304 D6
Aubrietia Cl *HARH* RM3 .... 431 F3 🗓
Auckland Cl *CHLM/WR* CM1 .... 304 A8 🗓
   EN EN1 .... 374 B3
   TIL RM18 .... 485 F8 🗓
Audley End Rd *SAFWS* CB11 .... 70 B4
Audley Gdns *LOU* IG10 .... 378 B6
   WAB EN9 .... 347 J8
Audley Rd *COLW* CO3 .... 186 D8
   RCHLM CM3 .... 241 H6
   SAFWS CB11 .... 70 E4
Audleys Cl *SOSN* SS2 .... 444 B8 🗓
Audley Wy *BSDN* SS14 .... 17 E4
   CBE/LIN CB1 .... 24 E2
   FOS CO13 .... 229 F7
Audrey Gdns *BSF* CM23 .... 231 K2
Audwick Cl *BAR* EN6 .... 346 D2
Augustine Cl *GVE* DA12 .... 489 H5
Augustine Wy *RCHLM* CM3 .... 363 K3
Augustus Cl *COLN* CO4 .... 155 J7 🗓
   HVHL CB9 .... 27 K7 🗓
Augustus Wy *WIT* CM8 .... 276 E5
Aukingford Gdns *CHONG* CM5 .... 354 B1 🗓
Aukingford Gn *CHONG* CM5 .... 354 B1 🗓
Austen Cl *BRTR* CM7 .... 209 K5 🗓
   LOU IG10 .... 378 B7 🗓
   TIL RM18 .... 485 H8 🗓
Austen Dr *ING* CM4 .... 387 K3 🗓
Austin Av *COS* CO15 .... 290 A7
Austin Rd *GVW* DA11 .... 488 E6
Austin St *CHTY* IP2 .... 3 D5
Austral Dr *EMPK* RM11 .... 450 E1
Austral Wy *RCHLM* CM3 .... 396 E2
Auton Cft *SAFWS* CB11 .... 70 E6 🗓
Autoway *COLN* CO4 .... 187 K1
Autumn Cl *EN* EN1 .... 374 B6
   RCOS CO16 .... 258 E8
Avebury Rd *WOS/PRIT* SS0 .... 18 B3 🗓
Aveley By-pass *SOCK/AV* RM15 .... 468 E7
Aveley Cl *ERITH* DA8 .... 480 A5 🗓
Aveley Rd *UPMR* RM14 .... 451 J8
Aveley Wy *MAL* CM9 .... 338 B5
Aveline Rd *RCOLE* CO7 .... 157 G6
Avenue Cl *HARH* RM3 .... 431 G2
Avenue Rd *BRW* CM14 .... 411 F7
   BSF CM23 .... 199 F5
   CHLM/GWD CM2 .... 15 E6
   EPP CM16 .... 378 B2
   HARH RM3 .... 431 G2
   HOD EN11 .... 319 K1
   ING CM4 .... 386 B2
   LOS SS9 .... 463 F5
   SBF/HAD SS7 .... 460 D2
   WIT CM8 .... 277 G2
   WOS/PRIT SS0 .... 18 B4
Avenue Ter *WOS/PRIT* SS0 .... 18 B4
The Avenue *BCAYW* CM12 ...... 414 B5
   BRTR CM7 .... 209 J2
   COS CO15 .... 259 K6
   CVI SS8 .... 478 B2
   FX IP11 .... 94 C8
   GTDUN CM6 .... 204 D5
   GVW DA11 .... 489 F6
   HAR CO12 .... 194 E2
   HCH RM12 .... 450 E3
   HOC/HUL SS5 .... 419 J2
   HOD EN11 .... 319 F1
   IP IP1 .... 36 E4
   LOU IG10 .... 404 B2
   RBRW/HUT CM13 .... 433 H1
   RCHLM CM3 .... 335 K7
   RCHLM CM3 .... 394 C6
   RCOLW CO6 .... 185 J2
   RIPW IP8 .... 61 F6
   SBF/HAD SS7 .... 461 K2
   SLH/COR SS17 .... 458 A8
   WAB EN9 .... 320 E7
   WIT CM8 .... 277 G2
   WIT CM8 .... 278 C2
Avey La *LOU* IG10 .... 376 B3
Aviation Wy *SOSN* SS2 .... 443 K6
Avignon Cl *COLS* CO2 .... 219 J1
Avila Cha *CHLM/GWD* CM2 .... 360 D4
Avocet Cl *FOS* CO13 .... 228 D7 🗓
   K/T/MI CO5 .... 247 F5
   K/T/MI CO5 .... 285 F6
Avocet Wy *MAL* CM9 .... 310 E8 🗓
Avon Cl *GVE* DA12 .... 489 J7 🗓
   RCFD SS4 .... 421 K8
Avondale Cl *LOU* IG10 .... 404 C3
   RAYL SS6 .... 442 A3
Avondale Crs *PEND* EN3 .... 374 E7
Avondale Dr *LOS* SS9 .... 463 G1
   LOU IG10 .... 404 C2
Avondale Gdns *SLH/COR* SS17 .... 457 F8
Avondale Rd *COS* CO15 .... 11 J4
   IPSE IP3 .... 63 J5
   RAYL SS6 .... 442 A3
   SBF/HAD SS7 .... 460 C2
   VGE SS16 .... 458 D1
Avon Gn *SOCK/AV* RM15 .... 469 K6 🗓

Avon Rd *CHLM/WR* CM1 .... 331 K1
   CVI SS8 .... 478 A2
   UPMR RM14 .... 431 K8
Avontar Rd *SOCK/AV* RM15 .... 469 K4
Avon Wy *COLN* CO4 .... 188 C6
   SBN/FI SS3 .... 466 C7
Avril Wy *CHING* E4 .... 402 D7
Avro Rd *SOSN* SS2 .... 444 A7
Aylands Rd *PEND* EN3 .... 374 D2
Aylesbeare *SBN/FI* SS3 .... 466 C5
Aylesbury Dr *COS* CO15 .... 260 D7
   VGE SS16 .... 436 A6
Aylets Fld *HLWS* CM18 .... 13 E6
Aylett Cl *CVI* SS8 .... 478 C3 🗓
Aylett Rd *UPMR* RM14 .... 451 K5
Ayletts *CHLM/WR* CM1 .... 304 D2
Ayloffe Rd *COLN* CO4 .... 9 E2
Ayloffs Cl *EMPK* RM11 .... 431 F7 🗓
Ayloff's Wk *EMPK* RM11 .... 431 F7
Aylsham La *HARH* RM3 .... 408 D7
Aynsley Gdns *HLWE* CM17 .... 295 G5
Aynsworth Av *BSF* CM23 .... 199 F5
Ayron Rd *SOCK/AV* RM15 ...... 469 K4
Ayr Rd *IPNE* IP4 .... 37 K4
Azalea Av *WICKW* SS12 .... 417 F6

B

Baardwyk Av *CVI* SS8 .... 478 E2
Baas Hl *BROX* EN10 .... 318 D3
Baas Hill Cl *BROX* EN10 .... 318 E3
Baas La *BROX* EN10 .... 318 E3
Babington Rd *HCH* RM12 .... 450 C2
Back Hamlet *IPSE* IP3 .... 3 F6
Back Hl *CBE/LIN* CB1 .... 22 D1
Back La *BRTR* CM7 .... 179 H2
   CDH/CHF RM16 .... 470 A4
   COLW CO3 .... 185 K6
   FX IP11 .... 5 F7
   GTDUN CM6 .... 139 J2
   HAR CO12 .... 195 F2
   ING CM4 .... 358 A6
   ING CM4 .... 387 J3
   KIR/NAC IP10 .... 95 H4
   PUR RM19 .... 482 B3
   RBSF CM22 .... 232 B6
   RBSF CM22 .... 264 C5
   RCFD SS4 .... 444 B5
   RCHLM CM3 .... 239 G5
   RCHLM CM3 .... 270 E8
   RCHLM CM3 .... 272 E8
   RCHLM CM3 .... 362 E6
   RIPS/CAP IP9 .... 88 D3
   RIPW IP8 .... 60 E1
   SAFWN CB10 .... 43 F7
   WAB EN9 .... 320 E6
   WIT CM8 .... 310 B8
Back La East *RCOLE* CO7 .... 191 F5
Back La West *RCOLE* CO7 .... 190 E4
Back Rd *CBE/LIN* CB1 .... 22 D1
   CHLM/WR CM1 .... 331 F6
   KIR/NAC IP10 .... 94 C2
   MAL CM9 .... 314 B4
   RCOLE CO7 .... 158 A4
Back Waterside La *RCOLE* CO7 .... 255 K6
Bacons Cha *BOC* CM0 .... 344 C0
Bacon's La *RCOLW* CO6 .... 185 F7
Bacton Rd *FX* IP11 .... 5 F5
Badburgham Ct *WAB* EN9 ...... 348 B1
Baddow Hall Av *CHLM/GWD* CM2 ...... 333 J4
Baddow Hall Crs *CHLM/GWD* CM2 .... 333 J4
Baddow Place Av
   CHLM/GWD CM2 .... 333 J3
Baden Powell Dr *COLW* CO3 .... 218 B3
Bader Cl *IPSE* IP3 .... 64 A4
Bader Wk *GVW* DA11 .... 488 D0
Bader Wy *RAIN* RM13 .... 450 B3
Badger Gv *BRTR* CM7 .... 210 A2 🗓
Badgers *BSF* CM23 .... 198 D5
Badger Hall Av *SBF/HAD* SS7 .... 461 F5
Badgers Bank *CHTY* IP2 .... 62 A5
Badgers Cl *CHLM/GWD* CM2 .... 360 D3
   WOS/PRIT SS0 .... 463 J1 🗓
Badgers Cft *BROX* EN10 .... 318 E5
Badgers Gn *RCOLW* CO6 .... 215 H4
Badgers Gv *RCOLW* CO6 .... 154 C0
Badgers Keep *BOC* CM0 .... 398 B5 🗓
Badgers Mt *CDH/CHF* RM16 .... 484 E5
   HOC/HUL SS5 .... 420 D7
The Badgers *VGE* SS16 .... 456 B6
Badgers Wy *SBF/HAD* SS7 ...... 461 J8
Badley Hall Rd *RCOLE* CO7 .... 190 E5
Badleys Cl *SUD* CO10 .... 59 J4
Badminton Pl *BROX* EN10 ...... 318 E5
Badminton Rd *COS* CO15 .... 290 C5
Badshah Av *IPSE* IP3 .... 63 J5
Bag La *ING* CM4 .... 385 J2 🗓
Bailey Bridge Rd *BRTR* CM7 .... 177 H5
Bailey Cl *CHTY* IP2 .... 36 A3
   HVHL CB9 .... 27 K1
   PUR RM19 .... 482 A3

Bailey Dl *COLW* C03 ..... 217 H1
Bailey La *SUD* C010 ..... 31 G6
Bailey Rd *LOS* SS9 ..... 462 C3
The Bailey *RAYL* SS6 ..... 441 H8
Bainbridge Dr *K/T/MI* C05 ..... 280 B1
Baines CI *COLW* C03 ..... 186 A8
Baird Rd *EN* EN1 ..... 374 B7
Baker Av *RCHLM* CM3 ..... 308 A2
Baker Rd *RIPS/CAP* IP9 ..... 129 F5 🗓
Bakers CI *RCHLM* CM3 ..... 392 D5 🗓
Baker's Ct *BSDN* SS14 ..... 458 D3
Bakers Farm *WICKE* SS11 ..... 417 K6 🗓
Bakers Fld *ING* CM4 ..... 387 K3
Baker's La *BRTR* CM7 ..... 209 F8
  CBE/LIN CB1 ..... 23 F3
  CHLM/GWD CM2 ..... 360 D6
  COLN C04 ..... 186 C3
  COLW C03 ..... 186 B4
  EPP CM16 ..... 350 D2
  GTDUN CM6 ..... 239 J1
  ING CM4 ..... 386 B1
  MAL CM9 ..... 312 A1
  RCHLM CM3 ..... 335 J3
Bakers Md *RCHLM* CM3 ..... 272 B6 🗓
Bakers Meadow *BRWN* CM15 ..... 384 A3
Bakers Ms *ING* CM4 ..... 386 B1 🗓
Bakers Rd *EBAR* EN7 ..... 346 B4
  SUD C010 ..... 54 E4
Baker St *CDH/CHF* RM16 ..... 471 J8
  CHLM/GWD CM2 ..... 14 B4
Bakery CI *BOC* CM0 ..... 372 A2
  HLWW/ROY CM19 ..... 292 E5
Baldocks Rd *EPP* CM16 ..... 378 C1
Baldry CI *RIPW* IP8 ..... 61 J4
Baldwin's HI *LOU* IG10 ..... 377 H5
Baldwin's La *RCOLW* C06 ..... 182 B5
Bale CI *COLN* C04 ..... 217 K1
Balfe Ct *COLN* C04 ..... 188 B7
Balfour CI *WICKW* SS12 ..... 417 H8 🗓
Balfour Rd *GRAYS* RM17 ..... 484 B3
Balgonie Rd *CHING* E4 ..... 402 E4
Balgores Crs *GPK* RM2 ..... 430 C5
Balgores La *GPK* RM2 ..... 430 C6
Balgores Sq *GPK* RM2 ..... 430 C6 🗓
Balingdon La *CBE/LIN* CB1 ..... 23 F2
Balkerne HI *COLW* C03 ..... 8 A4
Ballards Wk *LAIN* SS15 ..... 16 C3
Ballast Quay Rd *K/T/MI* C05 ..... 220 E7
  RCOLE C07 ..... 221 F5
Ballater CI *IP* IP1 ..... 36 A1
Balliol Av *CHING* E4 ..... 402 E7
Ball La *COLS* C02 ..... 219 H8
Ball's Chace *RCOLW* C06 ..... 151 J3
Ball's Cha *HSTD* C09 ..... 148 A4
Balmerino Av *SBF/HAD* SS7 ..... 441 H7
Balmoral Av *COS* C015 ..... 10 A4
Balmoral CI *BAR* EN8 ..... 346 D8
  BCAYE CM11 ..... 415 F4
  CHTY IP2 ..... 62 B1
Balmoral Gdns *HOC/HUL* SS5 ..... 420 D7 🗓
Balmoral Rd *BRWN* CM15 ..... 410 E2
  GPK RM2 ..... 430 C6
  HCH RM12 ..... 450 E4
  PEND EN3 ..... 374 D2
  WOS/PRIT SS0 ..... 18 B3 🗓
Balsham Rd *CBE/LIN* CB1 ..... 23 F2
Balstonia Dr *SLH/COR* SS17 ..... 457 F8
Baltic Av *SOS* SS1 ..... 19 D4
Balton Wy *HAR* C012 ..... 6 A6
Bamford Wy *CRW* RM5 ..... 407 G8
Bampton Rd *HARH* RM3 ..... 431 F2
Bancrofts Rd *RCHLM* CM3 ..... 392 E5
Bandhills CI *RCHLM* CM3 ..... 392 D5
Banes Down *WAB* EN9 ..... 320 A4
Banham Dr *SUD* C010 ..... 58 C5
Banister Rd *RCOS* C016 ..... 258 E8 🗓
Bankart La *CHLM/GWD* CM2 ..... 333 J1
Bankfoot *GRAYS* RM17 ..... 483 J3
Bank Rd *IPNE* IP4 ..... 3 F3
Banyard CI *KESG* IP5 ..... 39 H6 🗓
Banyards *EMPK* RM11 ..... 431 F6 🗓
Banyardway *RCFD* SS4 ..... 443 K1
Barbara Av *CVI* SS8 ..... 477 K2
Barbara CI *RCFD* SS4 ..... 444 A2
Barbel CI *BAR* EN8 ..... 347 G8

Barbel Rd *COLN* C04 ..... 188 C4
Barberry CI *HARH* RM3 ..... 430 E2 🗓
Barbour Gdns *COLS* C02 ..... 218 A3
Barbrook La *K/T/MI* C05 ..... 248 B7
Barbrook Wy *RCHLM* CM3 ..... 363 J4
Barclay CI *CHLM/GWD* CM2 ..... 333 H7
Barclay Rd *PIT* SS13 ..... 439 H4
Barclay Ov *WFD* IG8 ..... 403 H7
Barclay Wy *WTHK* RM20 ..... 482 C4
Bardell CI *CHLM/WR* CM1 ..... 304 B7
Bardenville Rd *CVI* SS8 ..... 478 E2
Bardeswell CI *BRW* CM14 ..... 411 F5
Bardfield *VGE* SS16 ..... 438 D8
Bardfield Rd *BRTR* CM7 ..... 175 G4
  COLS C02 ..... 219 H4
  GTDUN CM6 ..... 140 E4
Bardfield Wy *FOS* C013 ..... 228 E7 🗓
  RAYL SS6 ..... 441 F2
Barfield Rd *K/T/MI* C05 ..... 284 E7
Barfields *LOU* IG10 ..... 377 J8
Bargate La *RCOLE* C07 ..... 158 A2
Barge Pier Rd *SBN/FI* SS3 ..... 466 D8
Barington Ct *RBRW/HUT* CM13 ..... 412 B2
Bark Burr Rd *CDH/CHF* RM16 ..... 483 J1
Barker CI *HVHL* CB9 ..... 50 C7 🗓
  MGTR C011 ..... 159 G1 🗓
Barker Rd *SUD* C010 ..... 58 B5 🗓
Barkis CI *CHLM/WR* CM1 ..... 303 K6
Barkstead Rd *COLN* C04 ..... 9 E2
Barlee CI *SAFWS* CB11 ..... 134 B2
Barle Gdns *SOCK/AV* RM15 ..... 469 K6
Barley CI *RBSF* CM22 ..... 266 A3
  VGE SS16 ..... 456 B2
Barleycorn Wy *EMPK* RM11 ..... 431 G8
Barley Ct *SAFWS* CB11 ..... 70 E4 🗓
Barley Cft *HLWS* CM18 ..... 322 B1
Barley Fld *BRWN* CM15 ..... 383 H3
Barley Flds *WIT* CM8 ..... 277 G4 🗓
Barley Hills *BSF* CM23 ..... 231 J1
Barleylands Rd *LAIN* SS15 ..... 437 G2
Barley Md *RCHLM* CM3 ..... 336 B9
Barley Wy *CBE/LIN* CB1 ..... 23 F3
  COLW C03 ..... 185 J8
Barling Rd *SBN/FI* SS3 ..... 446 B7
Barlon Rd *MGTR* C011 ..... 190 E1
Barlow's Reach *CHLM/GWD* CM2 ..... 333 J1
Barnaby Rudge *CHLM/WR* CM1 ..... 304 B6
Barnaby Wy *CHIG* IG7 ..... 404 D6
Barnard Acres *WAB* EN9 ..... 320 A5
Barnard CI *SAFWS* CB11 ..... 100 A5 🗓
  VGE SS16 ..... 458 B2
Barnardiston Rd *COLN* C04 ..... 9 E2
Barnardiston Wy *WIT* CM8 ..... 277 F2
Barnard Rd *CHLM/GWD* CM2 ..... 333 J1
  EN EN1 ..... 374 B6
  LOS SS9 ..... 462 C5
  SBW CM21 ..... 263 J2
Barnards Av *CVI* SS8 ..... 478 D1
Barnards Fld *COLN* C04 ..... 140 A3
Barncombe CI *SBF/HAD* SS7 ..... 440 C7
Barncroft CI *COLN* C04 ..... 187 J2
  LOU IG10 ..... 404 D1 🗓
Barncroft Gn *LOU* IG10 ..... 404 D1
Barncroft Rd *LOU* IG10 ..... 404 D1
Barnes Farm Dr *RCHLM* CM3 ..... 396 C5
Barnet Park Rd *WICKE* SS11 ..... 417 J6
Barnett CI *ERITH* DA8 ..... 480 A8
Barnfield *EPP* CM16 ..... 350 E2
  FX IP11 ..... 5 D1 🗓
  GVW DA11 ..... 489 F7 🗓
  K/T/MI C05 ..... 247 F2
  MGTR C011 ..... 159 J1
  RBSF CM22 ..... 234 C8
  RIPS/CAP IP9 ..... 87 G4
Barnfield Ms *CHLM/WR* CM1 ..... 304 C7
Barnfield Rd *RCOLW* C06 ..... 154 D7
Barn Flds *COLW* C03 ..... 185 H7
Barn Gn *CHLM/WR* CM1 ..... 305 C5
Barn Hall Av *COLS* C02 ..... 219 J1
Barnhall Rd *MAL* CM9 ..... 281 F3
Barnham Pl *KESG* IP5 ..... 38 D7
Barn HI *HLWW/ROY* CM19 ..... 320 D1
Barn Md *MGTR* C011 ..... 158 E6
Barnmead Wy *BOC* CM0 ..... 398 B6
Barns Ct *EPP* CM16 ..... 321 K2
Barnsley Rd *HARH* RM3 ..... 431 G2 🗓
Barnstable CI *SOS* SS1 ..... 465 K5
Barnstaple Rd *HARH* RM3 ..... 408 D8
  SOS SS1 ..... 466 A5
Barnston Gn *GTDUN* CM6 ..... 238 A1
Barnston Wy *RBRW/HUT* CM13 ..... 412 B1 🗓
Barn View Rd *RCOLW* C06 ..... 213 H4
Barnwell Dr *HOC/HUL* SS5 ..... 420 E7
The Barnyard *VGE* SS16 ..... 456 B1
Baronia Cft *COLN* C04 ..... 187 K2
Baron Rd *RCHLM* CM3 ..... 392 E6
Baronsdale CI *IP* IP1 ..... 36 D4
Baron's La *RCHLM* CM3 ..... 366 A4
Barons Wy *VGE* SS16 ..... 456 C1
Baronswood Wy *COLS* C02 ..... 218 E5
Barrack La *HAR* C012 ..... 7 F4

IP IP1 ..... 2 C3
  RCHLM CM3 ..... 272 A5
Barrack Rd *CHLM/WR* CM1 ..... 270 A7
Barrack Rw *GVW* DA11 ..... 489 F4 🗓
Barrack Sq *CHLM/GWD* CM2 ..... 14 C5 🗓
Barrack St *COL* C01 ..... 9 D5
  MGTR C011 ..... 160 E5
Barra Gld *WICKW* SS12 ..... 417 J8
Barr CI *RCOLE* C07 ..... 221 F4
Barrel CI *RCOLE* C07 ..... 223 F2
Barrells Down Rd *BSF* CM23 ..... 198 D4
Barrett La *BSF* CM23 ..... 198 E6 🗓
Barrington CI *BSDN* SS14 ..... 438 C2
  CHLM/GWD CM2 ..... 333 J7 🗓
  RCOS C016 ..... 258 E3
  SBN/FI SS3 ..... 466 D4 🗓
Barrington Gdns *BSDN* SS14 ..... 438 C5
  COS C015 ..... 11 F2
Barrington Gn *LOU* IG10 ..... 378 A8
Barrington Pl *ING* CM4 ..... 386 B2
Barrington Rd *COLS* C02 ..... 8 C6
  LOU IG10 ..... 378 A8
Barringtons CI *RAYL* SS6 ..... 441 J2 🗓
Barron's CI *CHONG* CM5 ..... 354 B1
Barrow Hall Rd *SBN/FI* SS3 ..... 446 B8
Barrowsand *SOS* SS1 ..... 466 A7
Barrows Rd *HLWW/ROY* CM19 ..... 293 H5
Barry CI *CDH/CHF* RM16 ..... 485 F2
Barryfields *BRTR* CM7 ..... 144 B6
Barsey CI *HVHL* CB9 ..... 26 C4
Barstable Rd *SLH/COR* SS17 ..... 473 K3
Bartholomew CI *SAFWN* CB10 ..... 43 K3 🗓
Bartholomew Dr *HARH* RM3 ..... 430 E4
Bartholomew Rd *BSF* CM23 ..... 198 E7
Bartholomew St *IPNE* IP4 ..... 37 H7 🗓
Bartlett CI *RCHLM* CM3 ..... 368 D4
Bartlett Rd *GVW* DA11 ..... 489 F6
Bartletts *RAYL* SS6 ..... 442 B5
Bartley CI *SBF/HAD* SS7 ..... 440 A7
Bartley Rd *SBF/HAD* SS7 ..... 440 A7
Bartlow End *PIT* SS13 ..... 438 E5
Bartlow Rd *CBE/LIN* CB1 ..... 23 F3
  CBE/LIN CB1 ..... 48 B1
Bartlow Side *PIT* SS13 ..... 438 E5
Barton CI *CHIG* IG7 ..... 405 F5
  CHTY IP2 ..... 62 A3 🗓
  RCHLM CM3 ..... 392 D4
Barton Dr *HVHL* CB9 ..... 28 D3
Barton Gv *HVHL* CB9 ..... 28 D3
Barton Rd *FX* IP11 ..... 131 J3
  HCH RM12 ..... 450 B2
Bartram Av *BRTR* CM7 ..... 210 B2
Barwell Wy *WIT* CM8 ..... 277 G3
Baryta CI *SLH/COR* SS17 ..... 473 J4 🗓
Basbow La *BSF* CM23 ..... 198 E5
Basildon Dr *LAIN* SS15 ..... 16 A3
Basildon Rd *LAIN* SS15 ..... 16 C2
Basin Rd *MAL* CM9 ..... 339 G1
Bassenthwaite Rd *SBF/HAD* SS7 ..... 440 D7
Bassett Gdns *EPP* CM16 ..... 324 B8
Bassett's La *CHONG* CM5 ..... 329 F5
  MAL CM9 ..... 336 A1
Bassingbourne CI *BROX* EN10 ..... 319 F2 🗓
Bassingbourn La *STSD* CM24 ..... 201 G3
Bassingbourn Rbt *RBSF* CM22 ..... 201 G4
Bata Av *TIL* RM18 ..... 486 C4
Batavia Rd *CVI* SS8 ..... 477 H1
Bate-dudley Dr *BOC* CM0 ..... 344 D2
Bateman Rd *RCOLE* C07 ..... 255 J5
Bateman's La *RCOS* C016 ..... 258 D1
Bates Rd *HARH* RM3 ..... 431 H2
  MAL CM9 ..... 338 C1
Bath Rd *FX* IP11 ..... 131 J3
Bath St *CHTY* IP2 ..... 3 E6
  GVW DA11 ..... 489 G4 🗓
  RCOLE C07 ..... 220 E5 🗓
Bathurst CI *COLS* C02 ..... 219 H4 🗓
Baton CI *PUR* RM19 ..... 482 A5
Battery La *RIPS/CAP* IP9 ..... 129 G5
Battisford Dr *RCOS* C016 ..... 290 C1
Battlesbrook Rd *COLS* C02 ..... 220 A3
Battles La *KESG* IP5 ..... 39 H6
Battleswick *BSDN* SS14 ..... 438 E4
Batt's Rd *BOC* CM0 ..... 369 K4
Bawdsey CI *RCOS* C016 ..... 290 D1
Bawn CI *BRTR* CM7 ..... 209 K1 🗓
Bawtree Crs *CBE/LIN* CB1 ..... 23 G2
Bawtree Wy *COLW* C03 ..... 186 B8
Baxter Av *SOSN* SS2 ..... 18 C3
Baxters *RCHLM* CM3 ..... 336 A6 🗓
Bayard Av *RCOLE* C07 ..... 255 K6
Bay CI *CVI* SS8 ..... 478 B3
Bayleys Md *RBRW/HUT* CM13 ..... 412 B5
Bayley St *HSTD* C09 ..... 110 E1
Bay Manor La *WTHK* RM20 ..... 482 C5
Baymans Wd *BRWN* CM15 ..... 411 H5
Baynards Crs *RCOS* C015 ..... 228 D7
Baynes CI *EN* EN1 ..... 374 A5
Bay Rd *HAR* C012 ..... 7 F4
Bay Vw *BOC* CM0 ..... 342 C5
Bay View Crs *HAR* C012 ..... 164 B5
Baywood Sq *CHIG* IG7 ..... 406 A7
Beach Av *LOS* SS9 ..... 463 H5
Beach Ct *SBN/FI* SS3 ..... 467 H2
Beach Crs *COS* C015 ..... 290 B7

Beachcroft Av FOS CO13 .... 228 C7 🅼
Beaches CI HOC/HUL SS5 .... 421 G7
Beach House Gdns CVI SS8 .... 478 E3
Beach Rd COS CO15 .... 10 C5
  CVI SS8 .... 478 D1
  HAR CO12 .... 7 D5
  K/T/MI CO5 .... 284 E7
  RCOS CO16 .... 288 C8
  SBN/FI SS3 .... 466 E8
Beach Rd East FX IP11 .... 131 K3
Beach Rd West FX IP11 .... 5 F5
Beach's Dr CHLM/WR CM1 .... 331 K2
Beach Station Rd FX IP11 .... 5 E6
Beach Wy COS CO15 .... 290 B7
Beachway CVI SS8 .... 478 B3
Beachy Dr BOC CM0 .... 342 C5
Beacon Fld FX IP11 .... 5 E2 🅼
Beaconfield Av EPP CM16 .... 350 D3
Beaconfield Rd EPP CM16 .... 350 D5
Beaconfield Wy EPP CM16 .... 350 E3 🅼
Beacon Hts RCOS CO16 .... 288 B3
Beacon HI BRW CM14 .... 382 C5
  MAL CM9 .... 338 A3
  PUR RM19 .... 481 J4
  WIT CM8 .... 278 C1
Beacon Hill Av HAR CO12 .... 7 F4
Beacon Hill Rd BRW CM14 .... 382 C3
Beacon La FRAM/WMKT IP13 ..... 39 K2
Beacon Rd ERITH DA8 .... 480 C6
Beaconsfield Av COLW CO15 ...... 8 A5
Beaconsfield Rd COS CO15 .... 10 C4
  IP IP1 .... 2 A2
  PEND EN3 .... 374 E1
  SUD CO10 .... 58 B5
The Beacons LOU IG10 .... 377 J4
Beacon Wy COLW CO3 .... 288 B3 🅼
  RCOS CO16 .... 288 B3
The Beadles RBSF CM22 .... 232 B5 🅼
Beadle Dr BRTR CM7 .... 209 K4
Beadon Dr BRTR CM7 .... 209 K4
Beads Hall La BRWN CM15 .... 383 K8
Beambridge PIT SS13 .... 438 D7
Beamish CI EPP CM16 .... 324 C7
Beams Wy BCAYE CM11 .... 414 D5
Beanfield Rd SBW CM21 .... 262 E1
Beard's La SAFWS CB11 .... 97 K1
Beardsley Dr CHLM/WR CM1 .... 305 G6
Bearing CI CHIG IG7 .... 405 K7
Bearing Wy CHIG IG7 .... 405 K7
Bearsted Dr PIT SS13 .... 439 F8
Bear St RCOLW CO6 .... 118 A4
Beatrice Av CVI SS8 .... 478 B1
  FX IP11 .... 131 H4
Beatrice CI HOC/HUL SS5 .... 420 E7 🅼
  IPSE IP3 .... 63 J2
Beatrice Gdns GVW DA11 .... 488 D7
Beatrice Rd COS CO15 .... 10 B5
  WOTN CO14 .... 229 J3
Beattie Av COS CO15 .... 10 C5 🅼
Beatty Dr BSDN SS14 .... 438 B7
Beatty La BSDN SS14 .... 438 B7
Beatty Ri RCHLM CM3 .... 393 F7
Beatty Rd BAR EN8 .... 347 F8
  IPSE IP3 .... 63 K3
  SUD CO10 .... 58 D4
Beauchamps BOC CM0 .... 398 B5
Beauchamps Dr WICKE SS11 .... 417 K6
Beaufort CI CDH/CHF RM16 ...... 483 J2
  EPP CM16 .... 352 A1 🅼
Beaufort Gdns BRTR CM7 .... 209 K4
Beaufort Rd BCAYW CM12 .... 414 A3
  CHLM/GWD CM2 .... 333 J1
Beaufort St IP IP1 .... 2 B7
  SOSN SS2 .... 465 G4
Beaulieu Bvd CHLM/WR CM1 .... 305 H6
Beaulieu Dr WAB EN9 .... 347 H7
Beaumont Av COS CO15 .... 10 A4
  RCOLE CO7 .... 256 H6
Beaumont CI COLN CO4 .... 187 F1
  FOS CO13 .... 228 E6
  GPK RM2 .... 430 D4
Beaumont Ct HVHL CB9 .... 27 H7
Beaumont Crs RAIN RM13 .... 450 D3 🅼
Beaumont Dr GVW DA11 .... 488 D5
Beaumont Gdns
  RBRW/HUT CM13 .... 412 B2 🅼
Beaumont HI GTDUN CM6 .... 204 C3
Beaumont Pk CHLM CM3 .... 335 G7
Beaumont Park Dr
  HLWW/ROY CM19 .... 292 D5
Beaumont PI BRTR CM7 .... 210 A2
Beaumont Rd GVW DA11 .... 488 D5
  HAR CO12 .... 195 F3
Beaumont V HVHL CB9 .... 27 H7
Beaumont Wy MAL CM9 .... 338 C5
Beaver CI COLW CO3 .... 185 K6
Beazley End WICKW SS12 .... 417 H7 🅼
Bebington CI BCAYW CM12 .... 414 D2
Beccles Ct WICKE SS11 .... 417 G5 🅼
Beche Rd COLS CO2 .... 9 D6
Becker Rd COLW CO3 .... 217 K1
Beckers Green Rd BRTR CM7 .... 210 C3
Becket CI RBRW/HUT CM13 ...... 433 F1
  RCFD SS4 .... 422 A8
Beckett Dr SLH/COR SS17 .... 473 K1 🅼

Becketts LAIN SS15 .... 436 B7 🅼
Becket Wy RCHLM CM3 .... 392 E8
Beck Farm CI CVI SS8 .... 479 F2 🅼
Beckford Rd MGTR CO11 .... 160 B1
Beckingham Rd MAL CM9 .... 278 E8
  MAL CM9 .... 313 G1
Beckingham St MAL CM9 .... 312 A3
Beck Rd CVI SS8 .... 479 F2
  SAFWN CB10 .... 70 E4
Becontree CI COS CO15 .... 259 H5
Bedale Rd HARH RM3 .... 409 H8
Bedells Av BRTR CM7 .... 210 A8
Bedford CI BRTR CM7 .... 210 A1
  K/T/MI CO5 .... 248 B8 🅼
  RAYL SS6 .... 441 J4
Bedford Crs PEND EN3 .... 374 E1
Bedford Gdns HCH RM12 .... 450 D3
Bedford Rd COLN CO4 .... 155 G8
  COS CO15 .... 260 B8
  GRAYS RM17 .... 484 A4 🅼
  GVW DA11 .... 488 C7
  LAIN SS15 .... 436 C7
Bedloes Av WICKE SS11 .... 418 D6 🅼
Bedwell Rd RBSF CM22 .... 168 C2
Beecham Ct LAIN SS15 .... 16 A2
Beech Av BKHH IG9 .... 403 J5
  BRTR CM7 .... 177 J8
  HSTD CO9 .... 148 B3
  RAYL SS6 .... 441 J2
  RBRW/HUT CM13 .... 411 J6
  RCOLE CO7 .... 220 E4
  UPMR RM14 .... 451 J4
Beech CI BOC CM0 .... 398 B7 🅼
  HCH RM12 .... 450 C4
  LOU IG10 .... 377 K7 🅼
  RBSF CM22 .... 201 K5 🅼
Beechcombe SLH/COR SS17 .... 457 J8
Beechcroft Av TIL RM18 .... 486 B3
Beechcroft Rd CVI SS8 .... 477 J2 🅼
  IP IP1 .... 36 B3
Beech Dr SBW CM21 .... 263 G5
Beeches CHLM/WR CM1 .... 332 A3
  SAFWS CB11 .... 70 D6
Beeches Rd CHLM/WR CM1 ...... 332 A3
  MAL CM9 .... 310 B8
  WICKE SS11 .... 418 D3
The Beeches BRW CM14 .... 410 E6
  IPSE IP3 .... 63 H1 🅼
  MGTR CO11 .... 159 H2
  TIL RM18 .... 485 G8
Beechfield SBW CM21 .... 263 K3
Beechfield Wk WAB EN9 .... 375 H1
Beech Gn WIT CM8 .... 278 B8
Beech Gv HAR CO12 .... 164 A6
  HSTD CO9 .... 110 C4
  HVHL CB9 .... 26 E4
  IPSE IP3 .... 63 H2
  SOCK/AV RM15 .... 481 K1
Beech HI COLW CO3 .... 186 B8
Beech Hill Gdns WAB EN9 .... 376 D3
Beechlands BSF CM23 .... 198 A8
Beechmont Gdns SOSN SS2 ..... 464 B5
Beech PI EPP CM16 .... 350 D5
Beech Ri RCHLM CM3 .... 308 A1
Beech Rd BSDN SS14 .... 438 B8
  CHONG CM5 .... 328 B1
  HOC/HUL SS5 .... 439 G6
  KESG IP5 .... 38 D6
  SBF/HAD SS7 .... 461 J3
  SUD CO10 .... 58 E7
  WIT CM8 .... 245 H6
Beech Tree Gld CHING E4 .... 403 G4 🅼
Beech Wy CBE/LIN CB1 .... 22 E5
Beechwood CI COLS CO2 .... 218 E3
Beechwood Dr WFD IG8 .... 403 G8
Beecroft Crs CVI SS8 .... 461 F7
Beedell Av WICKE SS11 .... 417 J7
  WOS/PRIT SS0 .... 18 A2
Beehive Cha BRWN CM15 .... 384 B1
Beehive Ct RBSF CM22 .... 265 G2
Beehive La CHLM/GWD CM2 ..... 360 C7
Beeleigh Av VGE SS16 .... 456 D2
Beeleigh Cha MAL CM9 .... 337 K5
Beeleigh CI COLS CO2 .... 219 H4 🅼
  SOSN SS2 .... 18 B1
Beeleigh Cross BSDN SS14 ...... 438 B6
Beeleigh East BSDN SS14 .... 438 B6
Beeleigh Link CHLM/GWD CM2 .. 333 H3
Beeleigh Rd MAL CM9 .... 338 B2
Beeleigh West BSDN SS14 .... 438 A5
Beeston Dr BAR EN8 .... 346 D1
Beggarhill ING CM4 .... 357 H6
Begonia CI CHLM/WR CM1 .... 305 H7
Beke Hall Cha North RAYL SS6 . 440 D1
Beke Hall Cha South RAYL SS6 . 440 D2
Bekeswell La CHLM/GWD CM2 .. 360 B2
Belchamp Rd HSTD CO9 .... 54 A7
Belchamps Rd WICKE SS11 ...... 417 J3 🅼
Belchamps Wy HOC/HUL SS5 .. 421 F8
Belcham's La SAFWS CB11 ...... 135 K5
Belchers La WAB EN9 .... 320 E6
Beldams Ct RCOS CO16 .... 226 D4 🅼
Beldams La BSF CM23 .... 199 H7
Belfairs CI LOS SS9 .... 462 E3
Belfairs Dr LOS SS9 .... 462 E3

Belfairs Park CI LOS SS9 .... 442 D8
Belfairs Park Dr LOS SS9 .... 442 C8
Belgrave Av GPK RM2 .... 430 D5
Belgrave CI CHLM/GWD CM2 ..... 15 G6
  IPNE IP4 .... 37 G4
  LOS SS9 .... 442 C6
  RAYL SS6 .... 441 G1 🅼
Belgrave Rd BCAYW CM12 .... 414 B1
  LOS SS9 .... 442 C7
Bellamy CI FOS CO15 .... 228 C7
Bellamy Rd BAR EN8 .... 346 E3
Bell Av HARH RM3 .... 430 C3
Bell CI CHTY IP2 .... 3 D5
  COLS CO2 .... 220 A8
Bell Common EPP CM16 .... 350 C6
Bellcroft WIT CM8 .... 277 G2
Belle Staines Pleasaunce
  CHING E4 .... 402 B5 🅼
Belle Vue CHLM/GWD CM2 .... 14 B4 🅼
Bellevue Av SOS SS1 .... 19 F4
Bellevue PI SOS SS1 .... 19 F4
Belle Vue Rd COL CO1 .... 8 A2
  IPNE IP4 .... 3 F9
  RCOLE CO7 .... 220 E5
  SUD CO10 .... 58 C6
Bellevue Rd BCAYW CM12 .... 414 A3
  EMPK RM11 .... 451 G2
  SOSN SS2 .... 19 F3
Bellfield VGE SS16 .... 458 B7 🅼
Bellfield Av RCOLE CO7 .... 255 K5
Bellfield CI RCOLE CO7 .... 256 A6
Bellfield Gdns HLWE CM17 .... 295 G6
Bellfield Rd RCOLE CO7 .... 256 A6
Bell HI BURES CO8 .... 115 F1
  RCHLM CM3 .... 335 G6
Bell Hill CI BCAYW CM12 .... 414 C5
Bellhouse La BRW CM14 .... 410 B1
  LOS SS9 .... 462 E1
Bellhouse Rd LOS SS9 .... 442 E7
Bellingham La RAYL SS6 .... 441 J3
Bell La BROX EN10 .... 318 E3
  BRTR CM7 .... 142 E8
  BRTR CM7 .... 176 D6 🅼
  GTDUN CM6 .... 139 K2 🅼
  KESG IP5 .... 39 F7
  PEND EN3 .... 374 D4
Bellmaine Av SLH/COR SS17 .... 474 B1 🅼
Bellman Av GVE DA12 .... 489 K6
Bellmead CHLM/GWD CM2 .... 14 C5
Bell Mdw ING CM4 .... 386 B2
  SBW CM21 .... 263 J3
Bells Cha CHLM/GWD CM2 ...... 333 G2
Bells CI SAFWS CB11 .... 70 E5
Bells HI BSF CM23 .... 198 D6
  BURES CO8 .... 151 K1
Bells Hill Rd VGE SS16 .... 457 J3
  RCOS CO16 .... 56 A3
Bell St CHLM/GWD CM2 .... 333 H2
  SBW CM21 .... 263 J3
Bell Wk WOS/PRIT SS0 .... 464 A1 🅼
Belmer Rd STSD CM24 .... 200 C5
Belmonde Dr CHLM/WR CM1 .... 305 F6
Belmont Av UPMR RM14 .... 451 G3 🅼
  WICKW SS12 .... 416 D2
Belmont CI CHING E4 .... 402 E8 🅼
  CHLM/WR CM1 .... 305 G6
  WFD IG8 .... 403 J2
  WICKW SS12 .... 416 E8
Belmont Crs COLN CO4 .... 187 K5
Belmont HI SAFWS CB11 .... 100 B4
Belmont PI COL CO1 .... 219 K6
Belmont Rd GRAYS RM17 .... 483 J6
  HCH RM12 .... 450 E4
  RIPW IP8 .... 61 J4
Belsize Av COS CO15 .... 289 K2
Belstead Av CHTY IP2 .... 2 C1
Belstead Rd CHTY IP2 .... 62 B1
Belsteads Farm La
  CHLM/WR CM1 .... 305 F1
Belstedes LAIN SS15 .... 16 B1
Beltinge Rd HARH RM3 .... 431 G2
Beltona Gdns BAR EN8 .... 346 D1
Belton Br LOS SS9 .... 462 E2
Belton Gdns LOS SS9 .... 462 D5
Belton Wy East LOS SS9 .... 462 D5
Belton Wy West LOS SS9 .... 462 C5
Belvamey CI CHLM/WR CM1 ..... 304 A3
Belvedere Av HOC/HUL SS5 ...... 420 D7
Belvedere CI GVE DA12 .... 489 H6
  RCHLM CM3 .... 335 K6
Belvedere PI MAL CM9 .... 338 B7
Belvedere Rd BOC CM0 .... 425 H7
  BRW CM14 .... 410 C6
  IPNE IP4 .... 37 H4
  RCHLM CM3 .... 335 K6
  RCHLM CM3 .... 336 A6
The Belvoir ING CM4 .... 386 A1
Bembridge CI COS CO15 .... 259 H4
Bemerton Gdns FOS CO13 .... 228 B3
Benacre Rd IPSE IP3 .... 63 J2
Benbow Dr RCHLM CM3 .... 392 E4
Bencroft EBAR EN7 .... 318 A4
Benderloch CVI SS8 .... 477 J1
Bendlowes Rd BRTR CM7 .... 142 C1

enedict Dr CHLM/WR CM1 ...... 332 A3
enets Rd EMPK RM11 ...... 451 H2
enezet St IP IP1 ...... 2 C3
enfield Wy BRTR CM7 ...... 210 A3
enfleet Park Rd SBF/HAD SS7 ...... 460 A2
enfleet Rd SBF/HAD SS7 ...... 461 F3
enford Rd HOD EN11 ...... 319 F1
enhooks Av BSF CM23 ...... 198 D8
enhurst Av HCH RM12 ...... 450 C5
enjamin Cl EMPK RM11 ...... 430 B8
ennett Ct COLN CO4 ...... 188 B7
ennett Cl BRTR CM7 ...... 209 K5
   WOTN CO14 ...... 229 F5
ennett's La GTDUN CM6 ...... 390 D2
ennett's La GTDUN CM6 ...... 238 D3
ennett Wy RCHLM CM3 ...... 308 A1
ennions Cl HCH RM12 ...... 450 E7
enison Dr HARH RM3 ...... 430 E4
enskins Cl BSF CM23 ...... 133 K5
enskins La ABR/ST RM4 ...... 408 E4
enson Rd GRAYS RM17 ...... 484 A5
entall Cl HSTD CO9 ...... 148 A5
entalls BSDN SS16 ...... 17 E2
entalls Cl SOSN SS2 ...... 464 D1
entfield Caravan Stwy STSD CM24 ...... 167 J6
entfield Gdns STSD CM24 ...... 167 J6
entfield St STSD CM24 ...... 167 J6
ent La IPNE IP4 ...... 38 C5
entley Av COS CO15 ...... 290 A7
entley Cl BSF CM23 ...... 198 E8
entley Dr HLWE CM17 ...... 295 C6
entley La RIPS/CAP IP9 ...... 124 E1
   RIPW IP8 ...... 61 J8
he Bentleys LOS SS9 ...... 443 G6
entley St GVE DA12 ...... 489 H4
entley Wy WFD IG8 ...... 403 H6
enton Cl BRTR CM7 ...... 210 D7
   WIT CM8 ...... 277 C6
enton Gdns SLH/COR SS17 ...... 457 G8
envenue Av LOS SS9 ...... 443 G6
enyon Pth SOCK/AV RM15 ...... 470 A3
erberis Cl VGE SS16 ...... 456 A1
erbice La GTDUN CM6 ...... 204 B3
erdens VGE SS16 ...... 438 A8
erechurch Hall Rd COLS CO2 ...... 218 D4
erechurch Rd COLS CO2 ...... 218 E4
erecroft HLWS CM18 ...... 322 K3
eredens La RBRW/HUT CM13 ...... 432 C4
erens Cl WICKE SS11 ...... 417 J4
eresford Cl SBF/HAD SS7 ...... 461 J1
eresford Dr WFD IG8 ...... 403 K7
eresford Gdns BCAYW CM12 ...... 387 F8
eresford Gdns SBF/HAD SS7 ...... 461 H1
eresford Rd CHING E4 ...... 403 F4
   GVW DA11 ...... 488 D5
   SOS SS1 ...... 19 F5
ergholt Rd COLN CO4 ...... 186 E3
   MGTR CO11 ...... 123 C6
eridge Rd HSTD CO9 ...... 147 J3
erkeley Cl IPNE IP4 ...... 37 C4
   UPMR RM14 ...... 451 J3
erkeley Dr BCAYW CM12 ...... 387 G8
   EMPK RM11 ...... 451 H2
erkeley Gdns LOS SS9 ...... 462 B4
erkeley La CVI SS8 ...... 478 A3
erkeley Rd COS CO15 ...... 10 C3
erkeley Cl COS CO15 ...... 187 K1
erkeley Hl SLH/COR SS17 ...... 474 B1
erkeley Rd GVE DA12 ...... 489 G4
erkshire Cl LOS SS9 ...... 442 D8
erkshire Wy EMPK RM11 ...... 431 H7
ermuda Rd KIR/NAC IP10 ...... 64 C6
   TIL RM18 ...... 485 F8
ernard Cl FOS CO13 ...... 228 D7
ernard Crs IPSE IP5 ...... 64 C8
ernard Gv WAB EN9 ...... 347 H7
ernard St GVE DA12 ...... 489 G4
erners End EMPK RM11 ...... 259 F4
ernard Rd EN EN1 ...... 374 A8
erners Wy BROX EN10 ...... 319 F5
ernside BRTR CM7 ...... 209 J8
ernwell Rd CHING E4 ...... 403 F6
errimans Cl COLN CO4 ...... 9 F5
erriman CHING E4 ...... 402 D5
rry Cl HCH RM12 ...... 450 E6
   IPSE IP3 ...... 64 D4
   VGE SS16 ...... 436 C8
   WICKW SS12 ...... 416 E7
rry La VGE SS16 ...... 456 C1
rry V RCHLM CM3 ...... 392 E7
ersham La GRAYS RM17 ...... 483 J3
erther Rd EMPK RM11 ...... 451 F1
rtram Av RCOS CO16 ...... 259 F4
rtram Rd EN EN1 ...... 374 A8
rwick Av CHLM/WR CM1 ...... 304 C5
rwick Cl BAR EN8 ...... 347 G8
rwick La CHONG CM5 ...... 352 E7
   CHONG CM5 ...... 381 G2
rwick Pond Rd RAIN RM13 ...... 468 A2

UPMR RM14 ...... 451 G7
Berwood Rd SLH/COR SS17 ...... 474 B2
Beryl Rd HAR CO12 ...... 164 C4
Beslyns Rd BRTR CM7 ...... 142 B2
Bethany St RCOLE CO7 ...... 220 E6
Betjeman Cl BRTR CM7 ...... 209 K5
   EBAR EN7 ...... 346 A2
   RAYL SS6 ...... 442 A2
Betjeman Wy CHONG CM5 ...... 326 B8
Betony Cns BCAYW CM12 ...... 387 F8
Betoyne Av CHING E4 ...... 403 F7
Betoyne Cl BCAYE CM11 ...... 414 E3
Betsham Rd ERITH DA8 ...... 480 A6
Betts Green Rd RCOS CO16 ...... 226 A8
Bett's La HOC/HUL SS5 ...... 420 E7
   WAB EN9 ...... 320 E3
Beulah Rd EPP CM16 ...... 350 E3
   HCH RM12 ...... 450 D4
Bevan Wy HCH RM12 ...... 451 G4
Beveland Rd CVI SS8 ...... 479 G2
Beverley Av CVI SS8 ...... 477 K2
   K/T/MI CO5 ...... 285 F6
Beverley Cl CDH/CHF RM16 ...... 472 D6
   EMPK RM11 ...... 451 G1
Beverley Dr FOS CO13 ...... 228 D6
Beverley Gdns EMPK RM11 ...... 451 F1
   SOSN SS2 ...... 464 B1
Beverley Ri BCAYE CM11 ...... 414 D4
Beverley Rd COLW CO3 ...... 186 E7
   IPNE IP4 ...... 37 H5
Beverly Cl BROX EN10 ...... 318 E3
Bevington Ms WIT CM8 ...... 277 H3
Bewick Ct HSTD CO9 ...... 110 D3
Bewley Ct BAR EN8 ...... 346 D5
Bexhill Cl COS CO15 ...... 290 E5
Bexhill Dr GRAYS RM17 ...... 483 H5
Bexley Av HAR CO12 ...... 164 E4
Bexley Rd ERITH DA8 ...... 480 A4
Bibb Wy IP IP1 ...... 2 B4
Bibby St SLH/COR SS17 ...... 474 C3
Bickenhall St HLWS CM18 ...... 323 J6
Bickerton Point RCHLM CM3 ...... 393 F7
Bicknacre Rd RCHLM CM3 ...... 335 H8
Biddenden Ct PIT SS13 ...... 439 F7
Bideford Cl HARH RM3 ...... 430 D3
   WOS/PRIT SS0 ...... 443 H8
Bideford Rd PEND EN3 ...... 375 F4
Biggin La GRAYS RM17 ...... 485 C5
The Bight RCHLM CM3 ...... 393 F8
Bignalls Cft COLN CO4 ...... 187 K1
Bigods La GTDUN CM6 ...... 172 C8
Bijou Cl K/T/MI CO5 ...... 248 B7
Bilberry End CBE/LIN CB1 ...... 22 E6
Bildeston Gdns IP IP1 ...... 37 H4
Billericay Rd RBRW/HUT CM13 ...... 434 D2
Billet La EMPK RM11 ...... 450 E2
   SLH/COR SS17 ...... 474 A4
Billy's La RCOLE CO7 ...... 121 G3
Bilsdale Cl COLN CO4 ...... 187 K1
Bilton Rd CHLM/WR CM1 ...... 14 A4
   SBF/HAD SS7 ...... 461 K2
Bilton Wy PEND EN3 ...... 375 F5
Bingham St SOCK/AV RM15 ...... 469 K6
Binley Rd CHLM/GWD CM2 ...... 15 F3
Birchalls STSD CM24 ...... 167 K5
Bircham Rd SOSN SS2 ...... 19 D2
Birchanger La BSF CM23 ...... 199 J3
Birch Av HAR CO12 ...... 6 C5
   RCOLE CO7 ...... 223 K5
Birch Cl BKHH IG9 ...... 404 A6
   BRTR CM7 ...... 209 F3
   COS CO15 ...... 290 E2
   CVI SS8 ...... 477 K2
   RAYL SS6 ...... 441 H2
   RCFD SS4 ...... 423 H4
   RCOLE CO7 ...... 255 J7
   SBF/HAD SS7 ...... 440 A6
   SOCK/AV RM15 ...... 470 B4
Birch Crs EMPK RM11 ...... 431 F6
   SOCK/AV RM15 ...... 470 B3
Birchcroft Rd IP IP1 ...... 36 D3
Birchdale HOC/HUL SS5 ...... 419 J2
Birch Dr MGTR CO11 ...... 123 J4
Birche Cl LOS SS9 ...... 463 F1
The Birches EPP CM16 ...... 324 B8
   FOS CO13 ...... 228 D7
   RBRW/HUT CM13 ...... 411 H6
   SBF/HAD SS7 ...... 440 B5
Birches Wk CHLM/GWD CM2 ...... 360 C3
Birch Fall RCOLW CO6 ...... 119 A4
Birchfield Rd BAR EN8 ...... 346 B3
Birch Gn WICKW SS12 ...... 417 G6
Birch La ING CM4 ...... 388 B2
Birch Ri WIT CM8 ...... 278 A7
Birch Rd BOC CM0 ...... 372 A1
   COLS CO2 ...... 217 J8
Birch St COLS CO2 ...... 250 A2
   RCOLW CO6 ...... 118 B4
Birchway COLS CO2 ...... 250 A3
Birchwood BSF CM23 ...... 199 J3
   SBF/HAD SS7 ...... 440 A6
Birchwood Cl K/T/MI CO5 ...... 280 C1
Birch Wood Cl K/T/MI CO5 ...... 285 F7
Birchwood Dr RBRW/HUT CM13 ...... 433 F1
Birchwood Rd KESG CO10 ...... 38 C4

LOS SS9 ...... 463 H3
Birchwood Rd COLN CO4 ...... 156 D1
   RCHLM CM3 ...... 365 F3
   RCOLE CO7 ...... 156 E2
   SLH/COR SS17 ...... 457 J8
Birchwood Wy K/T/MI CO5 ...... 248 D8
Birdbrook Cl RBRW/HUT CM13 ...... 412 A2
Birdbrook Rd HSTD CO9 ...... 77 H2
Birdbush Av SAFWS CB11 ...... 70 E6
Bird La K/T/MI CO5 ...... 280 C1
   RBRW/HUT CM13 ...... 433 F4
   UPMR RM14 ...... 432 A7
Birds Cl SAFWN CB10 ...... 42 E2
Birds Gn CHONG CM5 ...... 327 H1
Birkbeck Rd RBRW/HUT CM13 ...... 412 C2
Birkdale Av HARH RM3 ...... 431 H2
Birkdale Ri RCHLM CM3 ...... 308 B1
Birkfield Cl CHTY IP2 ...... 2 B5
Birkfield Dr CHTY IP2 ...... 62 A4
Birkin Cl K/T/MI CO5 ...... 279 K1
Biros Rd BCAYE CM11 ...... 388 E2
Birs Cl WICKE SS11 ...... 417 C4
Biscay SOSN SS2 ...... 443 H6
Biscay Cl HVHL CB9 ...... 27 J6
Bishop Rd CHLM/WR CM1 ...... 14 C2
   COLS CO2 ...... 218 B2
Bishops Av BRTR CM7 ...... 210 A2
   BSF CM23 ...... 231 K2
Bishops Cl EN EN1 ...... 374 B6
   PIT SS13 ...... 438 D3
Bishopscourt Gdns
   CHLM/WR CM1 ...... 15 F1
Bishops Dr RCOS CO16 ...... 289 H7
Bishopsfield HLWS CM18 ...... 13 D6
Bishop's Hall Rd BRWN CM15 ...... 410 E2
Bishop's Hl IPSE IP3 ...... 3 F5
Bishop's La HSTD CO9 ...... 113 J2
   K/T/MI CO5 ...... 248 A6
Bishops Park Wy BSF CM23 ...... 198 A6
Bishops Rd SLH/COR SS17 ...... 474 B2
   WICKW SS12 ...... 439 G2
Bishopsteignton SBN/FI SS3 ...... 466 B5
Bishops Wk BRWN CM15 ...... 411 J5
Bisley Cl BAR EN8 ...... 346 D7
   RCOS CO16 ...... 258 D7
Bittern Cl CHTY IP2 ...... 62 A2
   K/T/MI CO5 ...... 247 F3
Bixley Dr IPNE IP4 ...... 38 C8
Bixley La IPNE IP4 ...... 38 D8
Bixley Rd IPSE IP3 ...... 64 B2
Blackacre Rd EPP CM16 ...... 378 C3
Black Barns FX IP11 ...... 94 D8
Blackberry Rd COLW CO3 ...... 217 H1
Black Boy La MGTR CO11 ...... 162 D1
Blackbrook Rd RCOLW CO6 ...... 154 D6
Blackbushe BSF CM23 ...... 199 H4
Black Bush La CDH/CHF RM16 ...... 472 C1
Blackbush Spring HLW CM20 ...... 294 E4
Black Chapel La GTDUN CM6 ...... 238 E5
Blackdale EBAR EN7 ...... 346 A1
Black Ditch Rd WAB EN9 ...... 375 J2
Black Ditch Wy WAB EN9 ...... 375 H2
Blackdown Av KESG IP5 ...... 38 D7
Blackfriars SUD CO10 ...... 58 A7
Blackgate Rd SBN/FI SS3 ...... 467 F6
Blackheath COLS CO2 ...... 219 H5
Blackhorse La EPP CM16 ...... 324 D7
Black Horse La IP IP1 ...... 3 D5
Blackhouse La SUD CO10 ...... 84 E2
Blacklands Cl SAFWS CB11 ...... 70 D6
Black La BRTR CM7 ...... 142 A3
Blackley La RCHLM CM3 ...... 241 H2
Black Lion Ct HLWE CM17 ...... 295 C1
Blacklock CHLM/GWD CM2 ...... 333 J2
Blackman Wy WIT CM8 ...... 277 G4
Blackmore Av CVI SS8 ...... 478 B3
Blackmore Cl HVHL CB9 ...... 27 F4
Blackmore Ct WAB EN9 ...... 348 C7
Blackmore Md CHLM/GWD CM2 ...... 356 D5
Blackmore Rd BKHH IG9 ...... 404 B3
   BRWN CM15 ...... 383 K1
   GRAYS RM17 ...... 484 B4
   ING CM4 ...... 356 A7
   ING CM4 ...... 385 J1
Blackmores LAIN SS15 ...... 435 K7
Blacksdale Cl CDH/CHF RM16 ...... 471 G7
Blacksmith Cl BCAYW CM12 ...... 387 H8
   CHLM/WR CM1 ...... 305 C5
Blacksmiths Aly ING CM4 ...... 356 C5
Blacksmiths Cl BSF CM23 ...... 198 A8
Blacksmiths Hl SUD CO10 ...... 52 E1
Blacksmiths La CBE/LIN CB1 ...... 25 C8
   HAR CO12 ...... 6 A5
   SUD CO10 ...... 83 C3
   WIT CM8 ...... 278 A8
Blacksmiths Wy SBW CM21 ...... 263 F4
Blackthorn Av COLN CO4 ...... 188 B5
Blackthorn Cl CHLM/WR CM1 ...... 331 G4
   IPSE IP3 ...... 64 C4
Blackthorn Ct VGE SS16 ...... 456 B1
Blackthorne Rd CHING E4 ...... 402 E7
Blackthorne Rd CVI SS8 ...... 478 C2
Blackthorn Rd CDH/CHF RM16 ...... 471 F8
   HAR CO12 ...... 6 A6
   HOC/HUL SS5 ...... 421 C5

WIT CM8 .... 276 E1
Blackthorn Wy BRW CM14 .... 411 C8 田
MAL CM9 .... 280 E3
Blackwall Br CHLM/WR CM1 .... 302 D8
Blackwater Av COLN CO4 .... 188 B4
Blackwater CI BOC CM0 .... 398 C8 田
CHLM CM1 .... 304 F2
MAL CM9 .... 339 G2
SBN/FI SS3 .... 466 D4 田
Blackwater Dr K/T/MI CO5 .... 284 C7
Blackwater La WIT CM8 .... 277 H5
Blackwater Wy BRTR CM7 .... 209 K1
Blackwood Chine RCHLM CM3 ...... 392 E7
Bladen Dr IPNE IP4 .... 38 D8
Bladon CI BRTR CM7 .... 177 H6
K/T/MI CO5 .... 248 C8
Bladon Wy CHLG CB9 .... 27 H4
Blaine Dr FOS CO13 .... 228 D6
Blair CI BSF CM23 .... 198 B6
IPNE IP4 .... 38 C8
Blake Av RIPS/CAP IP9 .... 129 F4
Blake CI MGTR CO11 .... 159 G1
Blake Dr BRTR CM7 .... 210 B1
RCOS CO16 .... 189 H7
Blake Hall Dr WICKE SS11 .... 417 K7
Blake Hall Rd CHONG CM5 .... 325 G8
Blake Rd IP IP1 .... 36 B2
WIT CM8 .... 245 F8
Blamsters Crs HSTD CO9 .... 147 J5
Blanchard CI FOS CO13 .... 227 K6
Blanche St IPNE IP4 .... 3 E3 田
Blandford Crs CHING E4 .... 402 D3
Blandford Rd IPSE IP3 .... 64 B2
Blatches CI LOS SS9 .... 445 G7
Blenheim Cha LOS SS9 .... 462 E2
Blenheim CI BSF CM23 .... 198 B6
HOC/HUL SS5 .... 421 F5
HVHL CB9 .... 27 H4
MGTR CO11 .... 123 J4
RCHLM CM3 .... 363 K3
SBW CM21 .... 263 F5
UPMR RM14 .... 452 B2 田
Blenheim Ct BSF CM23 .... 198 B6
Blenheim Crs LOS SS9 .... 463 F2
Blenheim Dr COLS CO2 .... 219 H5 田
Blenheim Gdns RBRW CM15 .... 410 D2
COS CO15 .... 10 A5
IP IP1 .... 2 B2
Blenheim Gv GVE DA12 .... 489 H5 田
Blenheim Ms LOS SS9 .... 463 F2
Blenheim Park CI LOS SS9 .... 463 G1
Blenheim Rd BRWN CM15 .... 410 D2
COS CO15 .... 10 A5
Blenheim Wy EPP CM16 .... 352 A1
K/T/MI CO5 .... 248 C8 田
Blickling CI CHTY IP2 .... 62 D3 田
Bligh Rd GVW DA11 .... 489 F4
Blind La BCAYW CM12 .... 413 G4
CHLM/GWD CM2 .... 361 H8
CHLM/GWD CM2 .... 362 C1
K/T/MI CO5 .... 249 F2
MAL CM9 .... 281 F4
MAL CM9 .... 312 A6
MAL CM9 .... 866 D3
Blindman's La BAR EN8 .... 346 C4
Blockhouse Rd GRAYS RM17 .... 484 B5 田
Blofield Rd IP IP11 .... 4 C3
Blois Rd HVHL CB9 .... 50 E5
Bloom CI FOS CO13 .... 228 C7
Bloomfield Av FOS CO13 .... 228 D6 田
Bloomfield St IPNE IP4 .... 37 K7
Blountswood Rd HOC/HUL SS5 ... 420 D8
Blower Rd RAYL SS6 .... 442 A2
Blue Anchor La TIL RM18 .... 485 K3
Blue Barn La FX IP11 .... 94 B5
Bluebell Av RCOS CO16 .... 290 E1
Bluebell CI CHTY IP2 .... 62 A1
WIT CM8 .... 276 E2 田
Bluebell Wd BCAYW CM12 .... 413 J1
Bluegate La RIPS/CAP IP9 .... 87 F2
Bluehouse Av RCOS CO16 .... 290 C1
Blyford Wy FX IP11 .... 4 C3
Blyth Av SBN/FI SS3 .... 466 B6
Blyth CI CHTY IP2 .... 62 C4
Blythe La RCOLE CO7 .... 220 E5 田
Blythe Rd HOC EN11 .... 379 K1
SLH/COR SS17 .... 474 A1 田
Blythe Wy MAL CM9 .... 338 C5
SBF/HAD SS7 .... 440 C1
Blyth's Meadow BRTR CM7 .... 209 J2 田
Blyth's Wy BRTR CM7 .... 208 C3 田
Blythe Wk UPMR RM14 .... 452 B1
Blythwood Gdns STSD CM24 .... 167 J7
Blyton CI WICKW SS12 .... 417 G8
Boadicea Wy COLS CO2 .... 218 D1
Boardman Av CHING E4 .... 402 C1
Boars Tye Rd WIT CM8 .... 211 H7
Bobbing Rd RCFD SS4 .... 444 C3
Bobbingworth MI CHONG CM5 .... 325 G6
Bobbits La RIPS/CAP IP9 .... 62 A5
Bobbits Wy RCOLE CO7 .... 221 F5
Bober Ct COLS CO2 .... 219 J6
Bocking End BRTR CM7 .... 209 J2
Bockingham Gn PIT SS13 .... 438 D5
Bocking's Gv RCOS CO16 .... 258 D8
Bodell CI CDH/CHF CM16 .... 484 A1
Bodiam CI IPSE IP3 .... 64 B1 田
Bodiam Rd IPSE IP3 .... 64 B1
Bodley CI EPP CM16 .... 350 D4
Bodmin CI KESG IP5 .... 38 C7
Bodmin Rd CHLM/WR CM1 .... 305 F8
Bohemia Cha LOS SS9 .... 442 D8
Bohun CI RCHLM CM3 .... 241 H6 田
Bois Hall Gdns HSTD CO9 .... 148 A3 田
Boley Dr COS CO15 .... 11 D3
Boleyn Av EN EN1 .... 374 B5
Boleyn CI BCAYW CM12 .... 387 G8 田
CDH/CHF RM16 .... 483 J2 田
LOS SS9 .... 442 D6
Boleyn Ct BKHH IG9 .... 403 H4
BROX EN10 .... 318 E3
Boleyn Gdns RBRW/HUT CM13 .. 411 K6
Boleyns Av BRTR CM7 .... 177 J7
Boleyn Wy COS CO15 .... 290 B5
HVHL CB9 .... 26 D6
RCHLM CM3 .... 306 D4
Boley Rd RCOLE CO7 .... 150 C6
Bolford St GTDUN CM6 .... 139 J3
Bolingbroke CI RCHLM CM3 .... 241 H6 田
Bolney Dr LOS SS9 .... 442 D6
Bolton La IP IP1 .... 3 E5
Bommel Av CVI SS8 .... 479 G2
Bonchurch Av LOS SS9 .... 462 E3
Bond St CHLM/WR CM1 .... 15 D3
GRAYS RM17 .... 484 B5 田
IPNE IP4 .... 3 E4
Bonham CI COS CO15 .... 11 D2
Bonington Cha CHLM/WR CM1 ... 305 G7
Bonington Rd HCH RM12 .... 450 E6 田
Bonks HI SBW CM21 .... 263 H4
Bonner Wk CDH/CHF RM16 .... 483 J2 田
Bonneting La BSF CM23 .... 134 A5
Bonney Gv EBAR EN7 .... 346 A4
Bonnington Av IPSE IP3 .... 63 H4 田
Bonningtons RBRW/HUT CM13 .. 412 A6
Bonnygate BSDN SS14 .... 437 K6
Boone PI WIT CM8 .... 277 G3 田
Bootham CI BCAYW CM12 .... 414 A4
Booth Av BCAYW CM12 .... 414 A4
Booth Av COLN CO4 .... 9 E3
Booth La KESG IP5 .... 39 J5
Borda CI CHLM/WR CM1 .... 304 C8
Border's La LOU IG10 .... 377 J8
Boreham CI WICKE SS11 .... 418 A8 田
Boreham Rd RCHLM CM3 .... 273 K2
Borley Rd SUD CO10 .... 87 J5
Borman CI LOS SS9 .... 443 H7 田
Borough La SAFWS CB11 .... 70 E5
The Borough CHONG CM5 .... 354 B3
Borradale Ct CVI SS8 .... 479 K5
Borrell CI BROX EN10 .... 318 E2
Borrett Av CVI SS8 .... 478 A1
Borrowdale Av IPNE IP4 .... 37 F4
Borrowdale Rd SBF/HAD SS7 ...... 440 E7
Borrowdale Rd SBF/HAD SS7 ...... 440 C5 田
Borwick La BCAYE CM11 .... 438 B1
WICKW SS12 .... 438 E1
Boscawen Gdns BRTR CM7 .... 210 A1
Boscombe Av COLN CO4 .... 9 E3
Boscombe Rd SOSN SS2 .... 19 E3
Bosgrove CI CHING E4 .... 402 D4
Boss Hall Rd IP IP1 .... 36 A6
Bostock Rd CHTY IP2 .... 62 E4
Boston Av RAYL SS6 .... 441 G1
SOSN SS2 .... 18 C3
Boston Rd IPNE IP4 .... 37 H6
Boswell Av RCFD SS4 .... 422 A8
Bosswells Dr CHLM/GWD CM2 ... 15 D3
Bosworth CI HOC/HUL SS5 .... 443 G1
Bosworth Crs HARH RM3 .... 430 D1
Bosworth Rd LOS SS9 .... 442 D6
Botanical Wy RCOS CO16 .... 289 G2
Botany La RCOS CO16 .... 225 J8
Botany Wy PUR RM19 .... 481 J2
Botelers VGE SS16 .... 16 C6
Boteley Ct CHING E4 .... 402 E5
Botney Hill Rd BCAYW CM12 ...... 435 H1
Boucher Dr GVW DA11 .... 488 E8
Bouchers Md CHLM/WR CM1 ...... 305 H7 田
Bouldrewood Rd SBF/HAD SS7 ... 440 C4
The Boulevard RCFD SS4 .... 444 C2
Boulter Gdns RAIN RM13 .... 450 B7
Boult Rd LAIN SS15 .... 16 A2
Boundary Dr RBRW/HUT CM13 .. 412 D3

Boundary Rd BSF CM23 .... 199 F3
COLN CO4 .... 220 C2
HVHL CB9 .... 27 H1
LOS SS9 .... 442 C5
ROM RM1 .... 430 B8
UPMR RM14 .... 451 H4
Boundary St ERITH DA8 .... 480 A7
Bounderby Gv CHLM/WR CM1 ... 304 A7
Bounstead HI COLS CO2 .... 218 C7
Bounstead Rd COLS CO2 .... 218 B8
Bourchier Avene BRTR CM7 .... 178 C8
Bourchier Wy HSTD CO9 .... 147 J5
Bourne Av LAIN SS15 .... 436 E2
Bournebridge CI
   RBRW/HUT CM13 .... 412 D3
Bournebridge HI HSTD CO9 .... 147 H5
Bournebridge La ABR/ST RM4 ..... 407 G2
Bourne CI BROX EN10 .... 319 F8
   HSTD CO9 .... 147 H5
   LAIN SS15 .... 436 E2
Bourne End EMPK RM11 .... 451 H5
Bourne Gdns CHING E4 .... 402 C2
Bourne HI CHTY IP2 .... 62 B3
Bournemouth Park Rd SOSN SS2 . 19 E4
Bournemouth Rd COS CO15 .... 260 D7
Bourne Rd COLS CO2 .... 219 H5
   HVHL CB9 .... 27 J6
   RCOLW CO6 .... 185 K3
Bournes Green Cha SBN/FI SS3 ... 466 C6
   SOS SS1 .... 466 B7
The Bourne BSF CM23 .... 199 F2
Bouvel Dr BOC CM0 .... 398 B8
Bouverie Rd CHLM/GWD CM2 .... 14 C5
Bouvier Rd PEND EN3 .... 374 C1
Bovey Wy SOCK/AV RM15 .... 469 K5
Bovingdon Rd BRTR CM7 .... 177 J2
Bovinger Wy SOS SS1 .... 465 J3
Bowbank CI SBN/FI SS3 .... 466 D3
Bowden Dr EMPK RM11 .... 451 F2 田
Bowdens La RCOLW CO6 .... 116 B7
Bower Farm Rd ABR/ST RM4 .... 407 F6
Bower Gdns MAL CM9 .... 338 D5
Bower Hall Dr HVHL CB9 .... 50 C6
Bower Hall La K/T/MI CO5 .... 285 J4
Bower HI EPP CM16 .... 350 D3
Bower Rd BSDN SS14 .... 438 A5
Bowerman Rd CDH/CHF RM16 .... 485 H3
Bowers CI WIT CM8 .... 244 D5
Bowers Court Dr PIT SS13 .... 439 J8
Bowers Rd SBF/HAD SS7 .... 440 E7
Bower V EPP CM16 .... 350 D4
Bowes Dr CHONG CM5 .... 354 B3
Bowes Rd RCOLE CO7 .... 221 F1
Bowfell Dr VGE SS16 .... 436 B8
Bowhay RBRW/HUT CM13 .... 412 C4
Bowland Dr RIPW IP9 .... 61 J4 田
Bowles Gn EN EN1 .... 374 B1
Bowling CI BSF CM23 .... 198 E5
Bowman Av LOS SS9 .... 442 B8
Bowmans Pk HSTD CO9 .... 110 D4 田
Bowmont Ct RBRW/HUT CM13 .. 412 B3
Bown CI TIL RM18 .... 485 G8 田
Bowness Wy HCH RM12 .... 450 B6 田
Bowood Rd PEND EN3 .... 374 D1
Bowsers La SAFWN CB10 .... 45 K3 田
Bowthorpe CI IP IP1 .... 2 B2
Box CI LAIN SS15 .... 16 B3 田
Boxford CI RAYL SS6 .... 440 E2 田
Boxford Ct FX IP11 .... 4 C3
Boxhouse La RCOLE CO7 .... 120 D2
Boxley La RBSF CM22 .... 235 F2
Box Mill La HSTD CO9 .... 147 F2
Boxmoor Rd CRW RM5 .... 407 J3
Boxted Av RCOS CO16 .... 290 B3 田
Boxted Church Rd RCOLW CO6 ... 118 A4
Boxted CI BKHH IG9 .... 404 A2
Boxted Rd COLN CO4 .... 154 E4
   RCOLW CO6 .... 154 B1 田
Boxted Straight Rd COLN CO4 ...... 119 G2
Boyce Gn SBF/HAD SS7 .... 460 B4
Boyce Hill CI LOS SS9 .... 442 D8
Boyce Rd SBN/FI SS3 .... 467 F3
   SLH/COR SS17 .... 473 G4 田
Boyce View Dr SBF/HAD SS7 ...... 460 B4
Boyd CI BSF CM23 .... 199 F3
Boyd Ct WICKW SS12 .... 417 J8 田
Boyden CI SOSN SS2 .... 465 J1 田
Boydlands RIPS/CAP IP9 .... 87 F1
Boyles Ct COLS CO2 .... 219 H5
Boyne Dr CHLM/WR CM1 .... 305 G8
Boyton CI HVHL CB9 .... 27 J6
   SBF/HAD SS7 .... 440 D8
Boyton Rd IPSE IP3 .... 63 J4
Boytons LAIN SS15 .... 16 A2
Boytons Acre SAFWS CB11 .... 70 E4
Boyton's La SAFWN CB10 .... 74 C2
Brabant Rd RCHLM CM3 .... 394 C7
Brabner Gdns BCAYE CM11 .... 415 J2
Bracelet CI SLH/COR SS17 .... 457 G1 田
Brace Wk RCHLM CM3 .... 392 E2
Bracken Av KESG IP5 .... 39 H6
Bracken CI LOU IG10 .... 377 G6
Brackendale BCAYE CM11 .... 414 E7
Brackendale Av PIT SS13 .... 459 F1

Brackendale Cl HOC/HUL SS5 ...... 421 F6
Brackendale Gdns UPMR RM14 .... 451 K5
Bracken Dell RAYL SS6 .... 441 K3
Brackenden Dr CHLM/WR CM1 .... 305 F6
Brackenhayes Cl CHTY IP2 .... 2 C6
Brackens Dr BRW CM14 .... 411 G8
The Brackens COLN CO4 .... 187 J2
The Bracken CHING E4 .... 402 D5
Bracken Wy K/T/MI CO5 .... 252 C5
   SBF/HAD SS7 .... 441 F6
Brackley Cl FX IP11 .... 5 D2
Brackley Crs PIT SS13 .... 438 D4
Bracks La RCOLW CO6 .... 214 C2
Bradbourne Av GRAYS RM17 .... 484 A5
Bradbourne Wy PIT SS13 .... 439 F8
Bradd Cl SOCK/AV RM15 .... 470 A3
Bradfield Rd MCTR CO11 .... 161 K8
Bradford Bury LOS SS9 .... 442 D7
Bradford St BRTR CM7 .... 209 K1
   CHLM/CWD CM2 .... 14 B4
Brading Av COS CO15 .... 259 J6
Bradleigh Av GRAYS RM17 .... 484 B3
Bradley Av SBF/HAD SS7 .... 460 C1
Bradley Cl CVI SS8 .... 461 F8
   GTDUN CM6 .... 204 B3
   SBF/HAD SS7 .... 440 E8
Bradley Common BSF CM23 .... 199 G2
Bradley Link SBF/HAD SS7 .... 440 E8
Bradley Ms SAFWN CB10 .... 71 G3
Bradley Rd PEND EN3 .... 374 E4
Bradley St CHTY IP2 .... 3 D5
Bradley Wy RCFD SS4 .... 444 B4
Bradshaw Rd CDH/CHF RM16 .... 470 E8
Bradwell Cl HCH RM12 .... 450 C7
Bradwell Gn BRW/HUT CM13 ..... 412 B2
Bradwell Rd BKHH IG9 .... 404 B4
   BOC CMO 342 E7
   BOC CMO 344 A8
   BOC CMO 370 A2
Brady Av LIG IG10 .... 378 A6
Braemar Av CHLM/CWD CM2 .... 14 B5
Braemar Crs LOS SS9 .... 462 B3
Braemar Gdns EMPK RM11 .... 431 H8
Braemore CVI SS8 .... 460 E8
Brain Cl COLN CO4 .... 188 A2
Brain Rd WIT CM8 .... 276 C2
Braintree Rd BRTR CM7 .... 142 B5
   BRTR CM7 .... 144 B7
   BRTR CM7 .... 210 C6
   GTDUN CM6 .... 204 D5
   HSTD CO9 .... 146 D8
   RCHLM CM3 .... 242 A8
   WIT CM8 .... 277 C2
Brain Valley Av BRTR CM7 .... 210 A7
Brairwood Cl LOS SS9 .... 442 E8
Braiswick COLN CO4 .... 186 C3
Braiswick La COLN CO4 .... 186 F5
Braiswick Pl LAIN SS15 .... 436 C5
Braithwaite Dr SUD CO10 .... 59 J2
Braithwaite Rd PEND EN3 .... 375 F7
   LOS SS9 .... 442 C6
Bramble Crs SBF/HAD SS7 .... 442 B8
Bramble Dr IPSE IP3 .... 64 C4
Bramble La GTDUN CM6 .... 205 K4
   UPMR RM14 .... 468 E1
Bramble Ri HLW CM20 .... 12 C2
Bramble Rd CVI SS8 .... 478 C1
   LOS SS9 .... 442 C6
   SBF/HAD SS7 .... 442 A7
   WIT CM8 .... 276 E1
Brambles WOTN CO14 .... 229 F6
The Brambles BAR EN8 .... 346 D5
   BOC CMO 398 D2
   BSF CM23 .... 198 B7
   COLW CO3 .... 218 A2
Bramble Tye LAIN SS15 .... 17 D1
Bramblewood BSF CM23 .... 199 J5
The Bramblings CHING E4 .... 402 E7
Bramerton Rd HOC/HUL SS5 ...... 420 E7
Bramfield Rd East RAYL SS6 ..... 442 B3
Bramfield Rd West RAYL SS6 .... 442 A3
Bramford La IP IP1 .... 2 B2
Bramhall Cl FX IP11 .... 61 K4
Bramley Cl BRTR CM7 .... 209 K1
   COLW CO3 .... 186 C6
   RCOLE CO7 .... 222 E3
Bramley Gdns LAIN SS15 .... 16 A2
Bramley Rd HVHL CB9 .... 26 C5
Bramleys SLH/COR SS17 .... 473 K2
Bramley Shaw WAB EN9 .... 348 B7
The Bramleys RCFD SS4 .... 422 A8
   RCOLW CO6 .... 213 H2
Bramley Wy RCHLM CM3 .... 368 E4
Brampstead LAIN SS15 .... 436 E2
Brampton Cl EBAR EN7 .... 346 A2
   SLH/COR SS17 .... 457 H8
   WOS/PRIT SS0 .... 463 H1
Bramston Cl CHLM/CWD CM2 .... 333 H5
Bramston Link LAIN SS15 .... 435 K6
Bramston Wy LAIN SS15 .... 435 K7
Bramwoods Rd CHLM/CWD CM2 ... 15 F5
Branch Rd BARK/HLT IG6 .... 406 A8
   SBF/HAD SS7 .... 461 K3
Brancroft Wy PEND EN3 .... 374 E5

Brand Ct BRTR CM7 .... 177 J6
Brand Dr K/T/MI CO5 .... 252 D2
Brandenburg Rd CVI SS8 .... 461 J8
Brandeston Cl SUD CO10 .... 59 H2
Brandon Cl BCAYW CM12 .... 387 G8
Brandon Groves Av
   SOCK/AV RM15 .... 470 A3
Brandon Rd BRTR CM7 .... 209 G3
   FX IP11 .... 4 C3
Brandon St GVW DA11 .... 489 C5
Brands Cl SUD CO10 .... 59 F8
Bran End Flds GTDUN CM6 .... 173 J6
Branfill Rd UPMR RM14 .... 451 J3
Branksome Av HOC/HUL SS5 ..... 421 F5
   SLH/COR SS17 .... 473 K1
   WICKW SS12 .... 416 C6
Branksome Cl SLH/COR SS17 .... 473 J2
Branksome Gdns SS1 .... 19 E5
Bransby Gdns IPNE IP4 .... 3 J3
Branscombe Cl FOS CO13 .... 228 C8
Branscombe Gdns SS1 .... 466 A5
Branscombe Sq SOS SS1 .... 466 A4
Branscombe Wk SOS SS1 .... 466 A4
Branston Rd COS CO15 .... 290 C2
Brantham Hl MGTR CO11 .... 123 H5
Brassingham Crs K/T/MI CO5 ..... 248 C8
Braxted Cl RCFD SS4 .... 443 K1
Braxted La WIT CM8 .... 278 C7
Braxted Rd WIT CM8 .... 278 C7
Braxteds LAIN SS15 .... 436 B7
Braybrooke BSDN SS14 .... 17 F4
Brayers Ms RCFD SS4 .... 444 C4
Brays La RCFD SS4 .... 422 B8
Brays Md HLWS CM18 .... 13 F5
Braziers Cl CHLM/CWD CM2 ...... 360 E2
Braziers Quay BSF CM23 .... 199 F7
Brazier's Wood Rd IPSE IP3 .... 63 K5
Breachfield Rd COLS CO2 .... 218 D3
Breach La GTDUN CM6 .... 172 A3
Breach Rd WTHK RM20 .... 482 C5
Break Egg Hl BCAYE CM11 .... 414 E2
Breams Fld VGE SS16 .... 16 A6
Brecon Cl CHTY IP2 .... 62 D5
   PIT SS13 .... 439 F5
Brecon Rd PEND EN3 .... 374 C8
Bredfield Cl FX IP11 .... 5 D2
Bree Av RCOLW CO6 .... 215 H2
Bree Hl RCHLM CM3 .... 392 C7
Brempsons BSDN SS14 .... 17 E3
Brendans Cl EMPK RM11 .... 451 F2
Brendon Dr KESG IP5 .... 38 D7
Brendon Pl CHLM/WR CM1 .... 332 A4
Brendon Wy WOS/PRIT SS0 .... 443 H8
Brennan Rd TIL RM18 .... 495 G4
Brent Av RCHLM CM3 .... 392 D4
Brent Cl FOS CO13 .... 228 E6
   WIT CM8 .... 276 E3
Brent Hall Rd BRTR CM7 .... 106 C7
Brentwood Pl BRWN CM15 .... 411 G4
Brentwood Rd CDH/CHF RM16 ... 472 C5
   CDH/CHF RM16 .... 472 C8
   CHONG CM5 .... 354 C5
   COS CO15 .... 11 F1
   GPK RM2 .... 430 D7
   RBRW/HUT CM13 .... 412 A8
   RBRW/HUT CM13 .... 434 D5
   RBRW/HUT CM13 .... 454 B2
   ROM RM1 .... 430 A8
   UPMR RM14 .... 455 F4
Bressey Av EN EN1 .... 374 A5
Bressingham Gdns RCHLM CM3 .. 392 C6
Bretten Cl RCOS CO16 .... 290 C3
Brettenham Crs IP IP1 .... 37 F4
Brettenham Dr SOS SS1 .... 465 H5
The Bretts KESG IP5 .... 39 J3
Brevet Cl PUR RM19 .... 482 A3
Brewers Cl BSF CM23 .... 198 B8
Brewery La STSD CM24 .... 167 K6
Brewhouse Yd GVE DA12 .... 489 G4
Brewster Cl CVI SS8 .... 478 A3
Brian Bishop Cl WOTN CO14 ...... 229 G5
Brian Cl CHLM/CWD CM2 .... 332 D7
   HCH RM12 .... 450 C5
Briar Cl BAR EN8 .... 346 C3
   BCAYW CM11 .... 414 F6
   BKHH IG9 .... 404 A5
   HOC/HUL SS5 .... 443 C1
Briardale Av HAR CO12 .... 6 A5
Briarfields FOS CO13 .... 228 B5
Briarhayes Cl CHTY IP2 .... 2 C6
Briarlea Gdns UPMR RM14 .... 452 B1
Briarley Cl BROX EN10 .... 319 F4
Briar Md LAIN SS15 .... 436 C6
Briar Rd HARH RM3 .... 430 D2
   RCOLE CO7 .... 190 A1
The Briars BAR EN8 .... 346 E5
   HLWS CM18 .... 13 E6
Briars Wk HARH RM3 .... 431 F4
Briarswood CHLM/WR CM1 .... 305 F6
   CVI SS8 .... 461 F8
Briar Vw BCAYE CM11 .... 414 E6
Briarwood BRWN CM15 .... 383 H3
Briarwood Av COS CO15 .... 260 C7

Briarwood Dr LOS SS9 .... 442 E8
Briarwood End COLN CO4 .... 187 J2
The Briary WICKW SS12 .... 416 E6
Briceway SLH/COR SS17 .... 474 B1
Brickburn Cl GTDUN CM6 .... 239 J1
Brickcroft BROX EN10 .... 318 E8
Brickfield Cl VGE SS16 .... 458 A3
Brickfield Rd EPP CM16 .... 351 H3
   VGE SS16 .... 458 A3
Brickfields Rd RCHLM CM3 .... 392 E6
Brickfields Wy RCFD SS4 .... 444 D4
Brickhouse Cl K/T/MI CO5 .... 284 D6
Brick House La RCHLM CM3 .... 306 C4
Brick House Rd MAL CM9 .... 279 K5
Brickhouse Rd RCOLW CO6 .... 149 H2
Brick Kiln Cl FX IP11 .... 94 B6
   RCOLW CO6 .... 213 H2
Brick Kiln La GTDUN CM6 .... 173 H6
   RCOLE CO7 .... 222 D8
   SAFWS CB11 .... 135 J5
Brick Kiln Rd CHLM/CWD CM2 ... 334 A6
   COL CO1 .... 8 A2
   RCOLW CO6 .... 154 C7
   RIPS/CAP IP9 .... 90 E8
Brick Kiln Wy BRTR CM7 .... 210 C3
Brick La EN EN1 .... 374 B6
   PEND EN3 .... 374 C6
Brickmakers La COLN CO4 .... 8 B1
Brickman's Hl MGTR CO11 .... 160 D2
Brickspring La MAL CM9 .... 279 F6
Brick St COLW CO3 .... 185 G4
Brickwall Cl BOC CMO 425 G1
Bridewell St SUD CO10 .... 31 G5
Bridge Av UPMR RM14 .... 451 H4
Bridgebrook Cl COLN CO4 .... 9 F2
Bridge Cl EN EN1 .... 374 B5
   RBRW/HUT CM13 .... 411 H6
   SBN/FI SS3 .... 466 D6
Bridgecote La LAIN SS15 .... 437 G3
Bridge Cft RCHLM CM3 .... 272 B3
Bridge End La BRTR CM7 .... 209 F5
Bridgefield Cl COL CO1 .... 9 E4
Bridge Hall Rd BRTR CM7 .... 211 H2
Bridge Hl EPP CM16 .... 350 D7
   RCOLE CO7 .... 152 B6
Bridge House Cl WICKW SS12 .... 417 F6
Bridgemans Gn RCHLM CM3 ...... 367 J7
Bridgemarsh La RCHLM CM3 ..... 396 D6
Bridgend Cl RCHLM CM3 .... 392 E5
Bridgend Rd EN EN1 .... 374 C1
Bridge Rd CHONG CM5 .... 325 J3
   ERITH DA8 .... 480 B7
   FX IP11 .... 131 H2
   GRAYS RM17 .... 484 A5
   KIR/NAC IP10 .... 65 K8
   SBN/FI SS3 .... 448 A8
   WICKE SS11 .... 417 K6
Bridge St BRTR CM7 .... 106 D7
   BSF CM23 .... 198 E6
   BURES CO8 .... 115 J5
   CHLM/WR CM1 .... 331 H4
   HSTD CO9 .... 79 K4
   IP IP1 .... 3 D5
   LAIN SS15 .... 437 F3
   RCOLW CO6 .... 213 G4
   SAFWN CB10 .... 70 D5
   WIT CM8 .... 277 F4
Bridgewick Rd BOC CMO 372 C5
   BOC CMO 400 C1
Bridgwater Dr LOS SS9 .... 443 G8
   WOS/PRIT SS0 .... 463 H1
Bridgwater Rd CHTY IP2 .... 61 K3
   HARH RM3 .... 408 D8
Bridgwater Wk HARH RM3 .... 408 E8
Bridle Cl PEND EN3 .... 375 F3
Bridleway BCAYE CM11 .... 387 K8
Bridon Cl RCHLM CM3 .... 363 F7
Bridport Av IPSE IP3 .... 64 B2
Bridport Rd CHLM/WR CM1 .... 305 F8
Bridport Wy BRTR CM7 .... 178 C8
Brierley Av K/T/MI CO5 .... 285 G6
Brierley Rd EMPK RM11 .... 430 D8
Bright Cl RCOS CO16 .... 10 A1
Brighten Rd WOS/PRIT SS0 .... 18 A2
Brightlingsea Rd RCOLE CO7 ..... 221 F1
   RCOLE CO7 .... 255 H5
Brighton Av SOS SS1 .... 465 G4
Brighton Rd COS CO15 .... 260 D7
Brightside BCAYW CM12 .... 413 K1
   FOS CO13 .... 228 D6
Brightside Cl BCAYW CM12 .... 413 K1
The Brightside PEND EN3 .... 374 D5
Brightwell Av WOS/PRIT SS0 .... 18 A2
Brightwell Cl FX IP11 .... 4 C3
Brimfield Rd PUR RM19 .... 482 A3
Brimsdown Av PEND EN3 .... 374 E5
Brimstone Av LAIN SS15 .... 436 C7
Brimstone Ct BRTR CM7 .... 209 H5
Brindles CVI SS8 .... 477 K1
   EMPK RM11 .... 431 F6
Brindles Cl RBRW/HUT CM13 ..... 412 B5
   TIL RM18 .... 486 B3
Brindley Rd COS CO15 .... 259 K5
Brindwood Rd CHING E4 .... 402 B6
The Bringey CHLM/CWD CM2 ..... 333 J7

Brinkley Crs COLN CO4 ... 9 F1
Brinkley Grove Rd COLN CO4 ... 155 H8
Brinkley La COLN CO4 ... 155 K8
Brinkman Rd CBE/LIN CB1 ... 23 F2
Brinkworth Hl HOC/HUL SS5 ... 421 G7
Brinley Cl BAR EN8 ... 346 D5
Brinsmead Rd HARH RM3 ... 38 B7
Brisbane Rd IPNE IP4 ... 219 H4
Brisbane Wy COLS CO2 ... 219 H4
Briscoe Rd PIT SS13 ... 438 E6
Brise Cl BRTR CM7 ... 209 K4
Bristol Cl RAYL SS6 ... 419 H8
Bristol Ct WIT CM8 ... 244 E2
Bristol Hl RIPS/CAP IP9 ... 129 G5
Bristol Rd COL CO1 ... 8 C3
  GVE DA12 ... 489 J8
  IPNE IP4 ... 37 J6
  SOSN SS2 ... 444 A7
Bristowe Av CHLM/GWD CM2 ... 333 J8
Bristowe Dr CDH/CHF RM16 ... 472 D6
Britannia St HOC/HUL SS5 ... 463 K5
Britannia Gdns WOS/PRIT SS0 ... 465 K5
Britannia Rd RCOLE CO7 ... 220 E4
Britannia St HOC/HUL SS5 ... 463 K5
British Legion Rd CHING E4 ... 403 G5
Brittany Wy COLS CO2 ... 188 B7
Britten Cl COLN CO3 ... 188 B7
  VGE SS16 ... 436 B8
Britten Crs CHLM/GWD CM2 ... 333 H5
Brittons La ING CM4 ... 388 B5
Brixham Cl COS CO15 ... 290 E5
  RAYL SS6 ... 419 J8
Brixton La BSF CM23 ... 135 F8
  RBSF CM22 ... 135 J6
Broad Cl ROM RM1 ... 430 A7
Broadclyst Av LOS SS9 ... 442 E8
Broadclyst Cl SOS SS1 ... 465 K4
Broadclyst Gdns SOS SS1 ... 466 A4
Broadcroft Rd HVHL CB9 ... 26 E5
Broadfield BSF CM23 ... 198 E3
  GTDUN CM6 ... 236 C6
  HLW CM20 ... 13 E2
Broadfield Rd RBSF CM22 ... 135 F8
Broadfields RCOLE CO7 ... 221 F1
  SBW CM21 ... 263 F4
Broadfield Sq EN EN1 ... 374 B7
Broadfield Wy BKHH IG9 ... 403 K6
Broadgate WAB EN9 ... 348 B7
Broadhope Rd SLH/COR SS17 ... 473 J5
Broadlands RCOLW CO6 ... 154 D3
Broadlands Av HOC/HUL SS5 ... 421 G6
  PEND EN3 ... 374 B7
  RAYL SS6 ... 441 J2
Broadlands Cl HOC/HUL SS5 ... 421 G7
Broadlands Wy COLN CO4 ... 9 D8
  IPNE IP4 ... 38 D8
Broad La RCOLW CO6 ... 154 D3
Broadlawn LOS SS9 ... 462 D1
Broadleaf Av BSF CM23 ... 231 C1
Broadley Rd HLWW/ROY CM19 ... 437 K7
Broadmayne BSDN SS14 ... 383 H4
  RIPH IP8
Broadmead Rd COLN CO4 ... 188 B4
Broadmere Cl COS CO15 ... 260 C6
Broadmere Rd IP IP1 ... 36 A5
Broad Oak WFD IG8 ... 403 J8
Broadoak Av PEND EN3 ... 374 D1
Broad Oak Cl CHING E4 ... 402 B8
Broadoaks EPP CM16 ... 350 D6
Broad Oaks WICKW SS12 ... 417 H6
Broad Oaks Cl SAFWN CB10 ... 102 A3
Broadoaks Crs BRTR CM7 ... 210 C3
Broad Oaks Pk COLN CO4 ... 188 B2
Broad Oaks Wy RAYL SS6 ... 441 K3
Broad Pde HOC/HUL SS5 ... 421 G6
Broad Rd BRTR CM7 ... 178 A7
  HSTD CO9 ... 82 C6
Broadstone Rd HCH RM12 ... 450 B3
Broad St HVHL CB9 ... 27 F5
  RBSF CM22 ... 234 B7
Broad Street Green Rd MAL CM9 ... 310 E5
  RCOS CO16 ... 257 G8
Broadview Rd CDH/CHF RM16 ... 484 C1
Broad Wk HOC/HUL SS5 ... 421 G7
The Broad Wk (North)
  RBRW/HUT CM13 ... 411 K6
The Broad Wk (South)
  RBRW/HUT CM13 ... 411 K7
Broadwater Gdns RIPS/CAP IP9 ... 129 F5
Broadwater Gn LAIN SS15 ... 436 A7
Broad Wy HOC/HUL SS5 ... 421 G6
Broadway COS CO15 ... 290 C7
  GPK RM2 ... 430 B5
  GRAYS RM17 ... 484 B5
  LOS SS9 ... 463 F5
  TIL RM18 ... 484 E8
  WIT CM8 ... 211 J8
Broadway Av HLWE CM17 ... 295 F1

Broadway Ct WIT CM8 ... 211 J8
The Broadway GTDUN CM6 ... 204 E1
  HCH RM12 ... 450 C5
  LOU IG10 ... 378 A7
  SOS SS1 ... 465 K7
  WICKW SS12 ... 417 G5
Broadway West LOS SS9 ... 462 D5
Brock Cl WIT CM8 ... 276 E5
Brockenhurst Dr SLH/COR SS17 ... 473 F5
Brockenhurst Wy RCHLM CM3 ... 363 K4
Brocket Cl CHIG IG7 ... 405 J7
Brockett Rd CDH/CHF RM16 ... 485 G2
Brocket Wy CHIG IG7 ... 405 H8
Brock Gn SOCK/AV RM15 ... 469 K6
Brockham Dr RCOS CO16 ... 258 D7
Brock Hl WICKE SS11 ... 389 K8
Brock Hill Dr WICKE SS11 ... 417 F2
Brockles Md HLWW/ROY CM19 ... 322 A1
Brockley Gv RBRW/HUT CM13 ... 411 K4
Brockley Rd CHLM/GWD CM2 ... 442 A4
Brocksford St IPNE IP4 ... 37 J6
Brocks Md GTDUN CM6 ... 171 H6
Brocksparkwood
  RBRW/HUT CM13 ... 412 A6
Brockton Cl ROM RM1 ... 430 A6
Brockwell La K/T/MI CO5 ... 246 E4
Brodie Rd CHING E4 ... 402 D4
  SBN/FI SS3 ... 467 G4
Brodie Wk WICKW SS11 ... 417 J8
Brograve Cl CHLM/GWD CM2 ... 361 F2
Broke Hall Gdns IPSE IP3 ... 64 B1
Broman's La K/T/MI CO5 ... 286 E3
Bromefield Ct WAB EN9 ... 348 C7
Bromeswell Rd IPNE IP4 ... 37 J4
Bromfelde Rd BCAYE CM11 ... 415 K8
Bromfords Cl WICKW SS12 ... 416 E8
Bromfords Dr WICKW SS12 ... 416 E8
Bromleigh Cl BAR EN8 ... 346 C2
Bromley Cl SAFWS CB11 ... 441 F2
Bromley Ms RAYL SS6 ... 188 B4
Bromley Rd COLN CO4 ... 159 G6
  MGTR CO11 ... 100 C4
  RCOLE CO7 ... 190 A8
  RCOLE CO7 ... 223 F1
Brompton Cl BCAYW CM12 ... 387 G8
Brompton Dr ERITH DA8 ... 480 C6
Brompton Gdns MAL CM9 ... 338 A5
Bronte Av WIT CM8 ... 245 F8
Bronte Rd BRTR CM7 ... 209 K5
Bronte Vw GVE DA12 ... 489 H6
Brook Cl BRTR CM7 ... 209 F3
  GPK RM2 ... 430 A3
  K/T/MI CO5 ... 280 C2
  MAL CM9 ... 310 D2
  MAL CM9 ... 336 D3
  RCFD SS4 ... 444 D5
Brook Dr SLH/COR SS17 ... 417 F7
  WICKW SS12 ... 417 F7
Brooke Av SAFWN CB10 ... 71 F2
Brooke Gdns BSF CM23 ... 199 H6
Brook End SBW CM21 ... 263 H3
Brook End Rd CHLM/GWD CM2 ... 333 J1
Brooker Rd GRAYS RM17 ... 483 K4
Brooke Sq MAL CM9 ... 338 C4
Brookfield EPP CM16 ... 323 C2
Brookfield Gdns BAR EN8 ... 346 D1
Brookfield La BAR EN8 ... 346 B2
Brookfield La East BAR EN8 ... 346 D1
Brookfield La West BAR EN8 ... 346 C1
Brookfield Rd IP IP1 ... 326 B8
Brookfields CHONG CM5 ... 173 J7
  GTDUN CM6 ... 442 E8
  LOS SS9 ... 374 B8
  PEND EN3 ... 374 B8
  SBW CM21 ... 263 H3
Brookfields Cl BSF CM23 ... 442 E8
Brook Gdns CHING E4 ... 402 C7
Brook Hall Rd K/T/MI CO5 ... 220 E7
Brookhampton St SAFWN CB10 ... 20 A8
Brook Hl GTDUN CM6 ... 239 F4
  RCHLM CM3 ... 272 D7
Brookhill Wy IPNE IP4 ... 64 D1
Brookhouse Gdns CHING E4 ... 403 F7
Brookhouse Rd RCOLW CO6 ... 182 D5
Brookhurst Cl CHLM/GWD CM2 ... 15 E2
Brookland K/T/MI CO5 ... 280 A1
Brooklands COL CO1 ... 8 C5
  COS CO15 ... 290 A7
  WICKW SS12 ... 416 E6
Brooklands Av LOS SS9 ... 443 F7
Brooklands Gdns COS CO15 ... 290 B7
  EMPK RM11 ... 430 D7
Brooklands Pk LAIN SS15 ... 436 A7
Brooklands Ri MGTR CO11 ... 123 J5
Brooklands Rd MGTR CO11 ... 123 H6

Brooklands Sq CVI SS8 ... 477 J3
Brooklands Wk CHLM/GWD CM2 ... 14 B6
  CHLM/GWD CM2 ... 333 K5
  CHLM/GWD CM2 ... 361 F2
  FX IP11 ... 131 J2
  KIR/NAC IP10 ... 94 E4
  NHMKT IP6 ... 38 E1
  RIPS/CAP IP9 ... 86 D3
  SBW CM21 ... 263 H3
Brooklane Fld HLWS CM18 ... 295 F8
Brooklyn Av LOU IG10 ... 377 G8
Brooklyn Dr RAYL SS6 ... 419 J8
Brooklyn Rd HAR CO12 ... 7 D5
Brookman's Av CDH/CHF RM16 ... 471 G8
Brookmans Ct UPMR RM14 ... 452 B1
Brookmans Rd ING CM4 ... 387 K3
Brook Md LAIN SS15 ... 436 C6
  RCHLM CM3 ... 272 A5
Brook Meadow HSTD CO9 ... 110 C4
  HSTD CO9 ... 110 D4
Brook Mdw K/T/MI CO5 ... 280 A1
Brook Ri CHIG IG7 ... 404 D6
Brook Rd BAR EN8 ... 347 F8
  BKHH IG9 ... 403 H5
  BOC CM0 ... 343 G8
  BRW CM14 ... 410 C6
  EPP CM16 ... 350 E7
  GPK RM2 ... 430 A4
  GVW DA11 ... 488 D6
  K/T/MI CO5 ... 280 D2
  LOU IG10 ... 404 B1
  RAYL SS6 ... 441 H8
  RCOLW CO6 ... 183 F6
  RCOLW CO6 ... 184 A6
  SBF/HAD SS7 ... 460 B4
  SBW CM21 ... 263 H4
  STSD CM24 ... 167 K7
Brook Service Rd HVHL CB9 ... 27 G5
Brooks Hall Rd IP IP1 ... 2 B7
Brookside BCAYE CM11 ... 387 J7
  CVI SS8 ... 461 F8
  EMPK RM11 ... 431 F7
  HLWW/ROY CM19 ... 293 H6
  HOC/HUL SS5 ... 443 G1
  WAB EN9 ... 348 A6
Brookside Av SBN/FI SS3 ... 467 H5
Brookside Cl COLS CO2 ... 219 J3
Brookside Gdns EN EN1 ... 374 B3
Brooksies SAFWS CB11 ... 67 J3
Brook St BRTR CM7 ... 142 C1
  BRW CM14 ... 410 B7
  CHLM/WR CM1 ... 14 C2
  COL CO1 ... 9 D4
  GTDUN CM6 ... 205 J6
  MGTR CO11 ... 159 J7
  RCOLE CO7 ... 121 J4
  RCOLE CO7 ... 190 D7
  RCOLE CO7 ... 220 E1
  RCOLW CO6 ... 149 F6
Brook Ter HSTD CO9 ... 110 D4
Brook V RCOS CO16 ... 289 G7
Brook Vw CHLM/GWD CM2 ... 334 A2
  GTDUN CM6 ... 139 K2
Brookview CHTY IP2 ... 62 A1
Brook Wy CHIG IG7 ... 404 D2
Broom Cl EBAR EN7 ... 346 A3
Broome Gv RCOLE CO7 ... 220 E3
Broome La BCAYE CM11 ... 387 K6
Broome Rd BCAYE CM11 ... 387 K6
Broomer Pl BAR EN8 ... 346 C2
Broom Farm Rd RBSF CM22 ... 168 D1
Broom Fld FX IP11 ... 5 E2
Broomfield HLW CM20 ... 295 F2
  KESG IP5 ... 39 K4
  SBF/HAD SS7 ... 461 J1
  WIT CM8 ... 211 H4
Broomfield Av BROX EN10 ... 318 E5
  LOS SS9 ... 443 G6
  LOU IG10 ... 404 C1
  RAYL SS6 ... 441 F2
Broomfield Crs RCOLE CO7 ... 220 E2
Broomfield Gn CVI SS8 ... 460 E8
Broomfield Rd CHLM/WR CM1 ... 14 B2
Broomfields PIT SS13 ... 438 D2
  RBSF CM22 ... 265 G2
Broomfords Dr WICKW SS12 ... 416 E8
Broomhall Cl CHLM/WR CM1 ... 304 D3
Broomhall Rd CHLM/WR CM1 ... 304 C1
Broomhayes CHTY IP2 ... 62 C1
Broom Hill Rd IP IP1 ... 2 B7
Broomhills Dr BCAYW CM12 ... 414 B8
Broomhills Rd K/T/MI CO5 ... 285 F1
Broom Knoll MGTR CO11 ... 123 H3
Broom Rd HOC/HUL SS5 ... 419 K8
Broomstick Hall Rd WAB EN9 ... 348 A7
Broom St SUD CO10 ... 58 E7
Broom Wy K/T/MI CO5 ... 252 D1
  RIPS/CAP IP9 ... 87 J4
Broomways SBN/FI SS3 ... 467 K4
Broomwood Gdns BRWN CM15 ... 410 B2
Broomwood La ING CM4 ... 388 C2
Broseley Gdns HARH RM3 ... 409 H5
Broseley Rd HARH RM3 ... 409 H5

Brotherton Av FX IP11 .... 94 C7
Broton Dr HSTD CO9 .... 147 K3 🔲
Brougham Cl SBN/FI SS3 .... 467 F1
Brougham Glades COLW CO3 ...... 185 J8
Broughton Cl COLS CO2 .... 218 D2
Broughton Rd IP IP1 .... 2 C2
　RCHLM CM3 .... 392 B7
　SBF/HAD SS7 .... 462 A3
Browne Cl BRW CM14 .... 410 E4
Browning Av SOSN SS2 .... 19 D2
Browning Cl COLW CO3 .... 186 A7 🔲
Browning Rd BRTR CM7 .... 209 K5
　IP IP1 .... 36 B2
　MAL CM9 .... 538 C5
　MGTR CO11 .... 123 H6 🔲
Brownings Av CHLM/WR CM1 ...... 304 C8
Brownlow Bend BSDN SS14 .... 438 A7
Brownlow Rd FX IP11 .... 131 H5
Brownlows Cl GTDUN CM6 .... 268 A6
Brown Rd GVE DA12 .... 489 K7
Browns Av WICKE SS11 .... 417 J3
Brownsea Wy COLW CO3 .... 218 B1
Brown's End Rd GTDUN CM6 ...... 170 C6
Browns Gv KESG IP5 .... 39 H6 🔲
Broxburn Dr SOCK/AV RM15 ...... 470 A7 🔲
Broxhill Rd ABR/ST RM4 .... 408 B6
Broxted Dr WICKW SS12 .... 417 H7
Bruce Av HCH RM12 .... 450 D3
Bruce Gv CHLM/GWD CM2 .... 14 B6
　WICKE SS11 .... 417 K7
Bruce Rd CHLM/WR CM1 .... 331 H4
Bruces Wharf Rd GRAYS RM17 ... 483 K5
Bruce Wy BAR EN8 .... 346 D7
Bruff Cl COLN CO4 .... 8 A1
Bruff Dr FOS CO13 .... 229 F6
Bruges Cl HAR CO12 .... 165 F4
Bruges Rd CVI SS8 .... 478 C3 🔲
Brundells Rd RCOLE CO7 .... 190 E8
Brundish PIT SS13 .... 438 D8
Brundon La SUD CO10 .... 58 A4
Brunel Cl TIL RM18 .... 485 G8
Brunel Ct COLN CO4 .... 155 K7
Brunel Rd BRTR CM7 .... 209 K4
　CHTY IP2 .... 36 A7
　COS CO15 .... 259 K5
　LOS SS9 .... 442 D6
　SBF/HAD SS7 .... 440 C6
　WFD IG8 .... 404 C3
Brunel Wy COLN CO4 .... 155 K7
　RCHLM CM3 .... 392 C6
Brunswick Av UPMR RM14 .... 452 B1
Brunswick House Cut
　MGTR CO11 .... 160 B2 🔲
Brunswick Pl RAYL SS6 .... 419 F8
Brunswick Rd IPNE IP4 .... 37 H6
　SOS SS1 .... 465 G5
　WAB EN9 .... 375 G4
Brunswick Wk GVE DA12 .... 489 J4 🔲
Brunwin Rd BRTR CM7 .... 208 C3
Brunwins Cl WICKE SS11 .... 417 J6
Brussels Cl HAR CO12 .... 165 C4
Brussum Rd CVI SS8 .... 478 D3 🔲
Bruton Av WOS/PRIT SS0 .... 443 H8
Bryan Rd BSF CM23 .... 198 E5
Bryanstone Rd BAR EN8 .... 347 F8
Bryanston Rd TIL RM18 .... 485 H8
Bryant Cl BARH RM3 .... 430 E4
　SOS SS1 .... 465 H7
Bryant's La MAL CM9 .... 336 D6
Brybank Rd HVHL CB9 .... 26 C4
Bryn Farm Cl BSDN SS14 .... 437 K5
Bryn-y-mawr Rd EN EN1 .... 374 A8
Bryony Cl HVHL CB9 .... 26 E4
Buchanan Cl SOCK/AV RM15 ...... 468 E8 🔲
Buchanan Gdns WICKW SS12 ...... 417 H8 🔲
Buchanan Wy RCHLM CM3 .... 367 F8
Buchan Cl BRTR CM7 .... 209 K5 🔲
Buckenhoe Rd SAFWN CB10 .... 71 F2 🔲
Buckeridge Wy BOC CM0 .... 344 D7 🔲
Buckerills PIT SS13 .... 438 D8
Buckfast Av FOS CO13 .... 228 C7
Buckfast Cl CHTY IP2 .... 62 C5 🔲
Buckhatch La RCHLM CM3 .... 363 H8
　RCHLM CM3 .... 391 G3
Buck HI BRTR CM7 .... 209 J7
Buckhurst Wy BKHH IG9 .... 404 A6
Buckingham Cl EMPK RM11 .... 430 E7 🔲
Buckingham Ct COLW/CWD CM2 ... 333 J1
Buckingham Dr COLN CO4 .... 188 B6
Buckingham Hill Rd
　CDH/CHF RM16 .... 473 F8
Buckingham Rd GVW DA11 .... 488 C5 🔲
　HOC/HUL SS5 .... 420 E7
　HVHL CB9 .... 26 E7 🔲
　LAIN SS15 .... 16 C2 🔲
Buckland SBN/FI SS3 .... 466 B4
Buckland Heath RCHLM CM3 ...... 392 D7
Bucklers Cl BROX EN10 .... 319 F4
Bucklers Ct BRW CM14 .... 411 F8
Bucklesham Rd IPSE IP3 .... 64 D4
　KIR/NAC IP10 .... 94 C1
Buckles La SOCK/AV RM15 .... 470 A5
Buckley Cl DART DA1 .... 480 A8
　SLH/COR SS17 .... 457 G8
Buckleys CHLM/GWD CM2 .... 333 H6

Buckleys Cl WIT CM8 .... 278 A8
Buckley's La RCOLW CO6 .... 182 A7
Buckrell Rd CHING E4 .... 402 E5
Bucks Cross Rd GVW DA11 .... 488 E8
Buck's Horns La RIPW IP8 .... 61 H6
Buckwoods Rd BRTR CM7 .... 209 J4
Buckwyns Cha BCAYW CM12 ...... 386 E7
Buckwyns Ct BCAYW CM12 .... 414 A1 🔲
Buddleia Cl CHTY IP2 .... 62 A1
Buddleia Ct RCOLE CO7 .... 220 D3 🔲
Bude Cl KESG IP5 .... 38 E7 🔲
Budna Rd CVI SS8 .... 460 E8
Buffett Wy COLN CO4 .... 188 B7
Buglers Ri CHLM/WR CM1 .... 331 H5
Bugsby Wy KESG IP5 .... 39 J6
Buick Av COS CO15 .... 289 K7
Building End Rd ROY SG8 .... 66 E6
Bulbecks Wk RCHLM CM3 .... 392 D8
Bulford La BRTR CM7 .... 210 B8
Bulford Mill La BRTR CM7 .... 210 B8
Bullace Cl COLN CO4 .... 188 A2
Bull Cl CDH/CHF RM16 .... 483 J1 🔲
　VGE SS16 .... 438 B8
Buller Rd LAIN SS15 .... 436 C6
　RCHLM CM3 .... 394 C4
Bullfields SAFWS CB11 .... 100 B5
　SBW CM21 .... 263 J2
Bullfinch Cl COLN CO4 .... 188 C5
Bull Hill Rd COS CO15 .... 10 C2
Bull La HOC/HUL SS5 .... 420 D7
　K/T/MI CO5 .... 280 A1
　MAL CM9 .... 338 B2
　RAYL SS6 .... 441 J3
　SAFWS CB11 .... 96 E3
　SUD CO10 .... 35 G5
Bullocks La SUD CO10 .... 58 B6
Bullock Wood Cl RCOLE CO7 .... 188 A1
Bull's Cross ENC/FH EN2 .... 374 A2
Bulls Cross Ride EBAR EN7 .... 346 A8
Bullsmoor Cl BAR EN8 .... 374 C1 🔲
Bullsmoor La EN EN1 .... 374 B1
　PEND EN3 .... 374 D1
Bullsmoor Rdge BAR EN8 .... 374 C1
Bullsmoor Wy BAR EN8 .... 374 B1
Bullwell Crs BAR EN8 .... 346 E3
Bullwood Ap HOC/HUL SS5 .... 420 C8
Bullwood Hall La HOC/HUL SS5 ... 442 B1
Bullwood Rd HOC/HUL SS5 .... 420 E8
Bulmer Rd SUD CO10 .... 57 K7
Bulmer St SUD CO10 .... 82 E1
Bulow Av CVI SS8 .... 478 B2 🔲
Bulphan By-pass UPMR RM14 ..... 455 F3
Bulphan Cl WICKW SS12 .... 417 H7
Bulstrode Av CHTY IP2 .... 3 E5
Bulwark Rd SBN/FI SS3 .... 466 D5
Bulwer Rd IP IP1 .... 2 B3
Bumbles Green La WAB EN9 .... 320 D7
Bumfords La RCHLM CM3 .... 308 A6
Bumpstead Rd CHTY IP2 .... 36 C2
　HVHL CB9 .... 50 C1
Bundick's HI CHLM/WR CM1 ...... 332 A2
Bung Rw WIT CM8 .... 278 D4
Bunters Av SBN/FI SS3 .... 466 B7
Bunting Cl CHLM/GWD CM2 .... 332 D8
Bunting La BCAYE CM11 .... 414 D3
Bunting Rd CHTY IP2 .... 61 K2
Buntry La SUD CO10 .... 29 G1
Bunyan Cl IP IP1 .... 36 C2
Bunyan Rd BRTR CM7 .... 209 H2 🔲
Burbage Cl BAR EN8 .... 346 E5
Burches LAIN SS15 .... 16 C1
Burches Md SBF/HAD SS7 .... 441 F6
Burches Rd SBF/HAD SS7 .... 440 F5
Burdett Av WOS/PRIT SS0 .... 18 B4
Burdett Rd ERITH DA8 .... 480 E5
Bure TIL RM18 .... 486 D2
Bure Dr WIT CM8 .... 276 D2
Buregate Rd FX IP11 .... 5 F5
Buren Av CVI SS8 .... 478 E2
Burfield Cl LOS SS9 .... 443 G7
Burfield Rd LOS SS9 .... 443 G7
Burgate Rd RCOS CO16 .... 290 C1
Burges Cl EMPK RM11 .... 431 G8
　SOS SS1 .... 466 B7
Burges Rd SOS SS1 .... 465 K7
Burgess Av SLH/COR SS17 .... 474 A4
Burgess Fld CHLM/GWD CM2 ..... 333 H1
Burges Ter SOS SS1 .... 465 J7
Burghley Av BSF CM23 .... 198 B6
Burghley Cl BRTR CM7 .... 208 E7
　CHTY IP2 .... 62 C3 🔲
Burghley Rd CDH/CHF RM16 ...... 483 F2
Burghstead Cl BCAYW CM12 ...... 414 A4 🔲
Burgundy Gdns PIT SS13 .... 438 E5 🔲
Burke Cl IP IP11 .... 36 B2
Burke Rd IP IP1 .... 36 B2
Burkitts La SUD CO10 .... 58 B6
Burland Rd BRWN CM15 .... 411 G4
Burleigh Cl BCAYW CM12 .... 387 H8
Burleigh Rd BAR EN8 .... 346 E6 🔲
Burleigh Sq SOS SS1 .... 466 A5 🔲
Burlescoombe Cl SOS SS1 .... 465 K5 🔲

Burlescoombe Leas SOS SS1 ...... 466 A4 🔲
Burlescoombe Rd SOS SS1 .... 466 A4
Burley Cl CHING E4 .... 402 B8 🔲
Burley HI HLWE CM17 .... 295 H6
Burley Rd BSF CM23 .... 232 A1
Burlington Ct PIT SS13 .... 438 E5
Burlington Gdns SBF/HAD SS7 ... 462 A2
Burlington Pl WFD IG8 .... 403 H6
Burlington Rd COLW CO3 .... 8 A5
　IP IP1 .... 2 C3
Burmanny Cl COS CO15 .... 290 E2
Burnaby Rd GVW DA11 .... 488 D5
　SOS SS1 .... 19 F5
Burncroft Av PEND EN3 .... 374 D6 🔲
　PEND EN3 .... 374 C6 🔲
Burne Av WICKW SS12 .... 416 E7 🔲
Burnell Ga CHLM/WR CM1 .... 305 J6
Burnells Wy STSD CM24 .... 167 K6
Burnell Wk RBRW/HUT CM13 ... 433 F1 🔲
Burnett Pk HLWW/ROY CM19 ... 321 K2 🔲
Burnett Rd ERITH DA8 .... 480 E5
Burney Dr LOU IG10 .... 378 A7
Burnham Av RCHLM CM3 .... 366 C8
Burnham Cl FX IP11 .... 94 D8
　IPNE IP4 .... 37 H6 🔲
　WOTN CO14 .... 229 G5
Burnham Rd BOC CM0 .... 398 C3
　CHING E4 .... 402 A8
　CHLM/WR CM1 .... 305 F8
　HOC/HUL SS5 .... 419 K3
　LOS SS9 .... 462 D4
　MAL CM9 .... 337 F8
　RCHLM CM3 .... 368 B8
　RCHLM CM3 .... 392 B5
　WICKE SS11 .... 418 D2
Burnham Road (Summerhill)
　RCHLM CM3 .... 396 D1
Burnley Rd WTHK RM20 .... 482 C5
Burnsall Cl SAFWS CB11 .... 71 G5 🔲
Burns Av COLW CO3 .... 186 A8
　PIT SS13 .... 438 E8
Burns Cl ERITH DA8 .... 480 A7
　MAL CM9 .... 538 C4 🔲
Burns Crs CHLM/GWD CM2 .... 14 C5
Burnside CVI SS8 .... 461 F8 🔲
　SBW CM21 .... 263 H3
Burnside Crs CHLM/WR CM1 ...... 304 C8
Burns Pl TIL RM18 .... 485 G7
Burns Rd IP IP1 .... 36 A2
Burns Wy RBRW/HUT CM13 ...... 412 C3
Burnt Dick Hl COLN CO4 .... 118 E6
Burnt Heath Cottages RCOLE CO7 ... 157 K8
Burnthouse La ING CM4 .... 385 K4
Burnt House La KIR/NAC IP10 ...... 94 C1
Burnthouse Rd RCOLW CO6 .... 182 B4
Burntmill Cl HLW CM20 .... 294 A2 🔲
Burntmill La HLW CM20 .... 294 A2
Burnt Mills Rd PIT SS13 .... 438 D5
Burntwood Av EMPK RM11 .... 430 E8
Burntwood Cl BCAYW CM12 ...... 414 A3
　RBRW/HUT CM13 .... 434 C8 🔲
Burnway EMPK RM11 .... 451 F1
Burr Cl HAR CO12 .... 166 B4
　VGE SS16 .... 435 K8
Burrell Rd CHTY IP2 .... 2 C5
Burr Hill Cha WOS/PRIT SS0 .... 18 B1
Burroughs Piece Rd SUD CO10 ... 58 C6 🔲
Burrow Gn CHIG IG7 .... 405 J8
Burrow Rd CHIG IG7 .... 405 K8
Burrows Cl MGTR CO11 .... 159 G1
　RCOS CO16 .... 10 A1
Burrows Rd RCOLW CO6 .... 149 J7
Burrows Wy RAYL SS6 .... 441 H4
Burrs Cl COS CO15 .... 11 D2
Burr's Wy SLH/COR SS17 .... 474 D1
Burrswood Pl MAL CM9 .... 339 F2
Burses Wy RBRW/HUT CM13 ...... 412 A3
Bursland Rd PEND EN3 .... 374 D8
Burstall Cl RCOS CO16 .... 290 D1 🔲
Burstead Dr BCAYE CM11 .... 414 E6
Burton Cl HVHL CB9 .... 26 E6
　SLH/COR SS17 .... 457 G8
Burton End HVHL CB9 .... 26 D6
Burton Pl CHLM/GWD CM2 .... 333 H1
Burton Rd LOU IG10 .... 378 A8
Burton's Green Rd HSTD CO9 ..... 180 B1
Burwell Av CVI SS8 .... 460 E8
Bury Cl COL CO1 .... 8 C3
　RCOLW CO6 .... 215 J2
Bury Farm La BCAYE CM11 .... 438 A2
Bury Fids GTDUN CM6 .... 206 B8
Bury Green Rd EBAR EN7 .... 346 A5
Bury Holme BROX EN10 .... 319 F5
Bury La EPP CM16 .... 350 B4
　RCHLM CM3 .... 271 K5
　RCHLM CM3 .... 275 K8
　ROY SG8 .... 67 G4
Bury Lodge La RBSF CM22 .... 200 D5
　STSD CM24 .... 200 B3
Bury Rd CHING E4 .... 375 K8
　EPP CM16 .... 350 C5
　HLWE CM17 .... 295 C1
The Bury RCOS CO16 .... 289 C1
Bury to Clare Wk SUD CO10 .... 31 G2
Burywoods COLN CO4 .... 186 C3

Bushbarns *EBAR* EN7 .... 346 A3
Bushby Av *BROX* EN10 .... 319 E6
Bushell Wy *FOS* CO13 .... 228 D7
Bush Elms Rd *EMPK* RM11 .... 402 D6
Bushey Cl *CHING* E4 .... 392 E6
   RCHLM CM3 .... 392 E6
   RIPS/CAP IP9 .... 87 F4
Bushey Ct *HLWS* CM18 .... 15 E5
Bushey Ley *BRTR* CM7 .... 210 C2
Bushfields *LOU* IG10 .... 404 D1
Bush Gv *SUD* CO10 .... 57 K7
Bush Hall Rd *BCAYW* CM12 .... 387 H8
Bush La *SAFWN* CB10 .... 104 C3
Bush Rd *BKHH* IG9 .... 404 A7
   SAFWN CB10 .... 104 D3
Bushy Md *LAIN* SS15 .... 436 C5
Butcher Rw *SAFWN* CB11 .... 70 E3
Butcher's Hl *SAFWN* CB10 .... 43 F1
Butchers Dr *RIPS/CAP* IP9 .... 87 G4
   WOTN CO14 .... 229 G6
Butchers Pasture *GTDUN* CM6 .... 171 J8
Butler Cl *SAFWS* CB11 .... 71 F4
Butler Rd *HSTD* CO9 .... 147 J5
Butlers Cl *CHLM/WR* CM1 .... 304 D3
Butlers Dr *CHING* E4 .... 375 J4
Butlers Gv *VGE* SS16 .... 456 C2
Butler's La *MGTR* CO11 .... 162 B4
Butlers CB10 .... 45 K7
Butter Smith Gdns *KESG* IP5 .... 39 G6
Butlers Wy *HSTD* CO9 .... 79 K4
Butley Cl *IP* IP2 .... 62 B5
Butley Rd *FX* IP11 .... 5 E4
Butneys *BSDN* SS14 .... 17 F5
Butterbur Cha *RCHLM* CM3 .... 392 C7
Buttercross La *EPP* CM16 .... 350 E4
Buttercup Cl *BCAYW* CM12 .... 414 B1
   HARH RM3 .... 430 E3
   RIPW IP8 .... 61 J4
Buttercup Wk *WIT* CM8 .... 276 E1
Buttercup Wy *BOC* CM0 .... 398 C2
Butterfield Rd *RCHLM* CM3 .... 306 C5
Butterfly Gdns *IPNE* IP4 .... 38 C8
Butter Market *IP* IP1 .... 3 D5
Buttermere *BRTR* CM7 .... 209 F6
Buttersweet Ri *SBW* CM21 .... 263 J4
Butterworth Gdns *WFD* IG8 .... 403 H8
Butterys *SOS* SS1 .... 166 C3
Butt La *BSF* CM23 .... 166 C3
   MAL CM9 .... 338 C2
Buttleys La *GTDUN* CM6 .... 203 J5
Buttondene Crs *BROX* EN10 .... 319 H4
Button Rd *CDH/CHF* RM16 .... 483 J3
Butt Rd *COLS* CO2 .... 186 E8
   SUD CO10 .... 58 E7
Buttsbury *ING* CM4 .... 386 E4
Butt's Green Rd *CHLM/GWD* CM2 .... 362 D1
   EMPK RM11 .... 430 E8
Butts La *RCHLM* CM3 .... 335 J6
   SLH/COR SS17 .... 473 J6
Butts Paddock *RCFD* SS4 .... 423 G3
Butts Rd *SLH/COR* SS17 .... 473 J4
The Butts *BROX* EN10 .... 318 E6
Butts Wy *CHLM/GWD* CM2 .... 360 A2
Buxey Cl *K/T/MI* CO5 .... 284 C6
Buxton Av *LOS* SS9 .... 462 B2
Buxton Cl *LOS* SS9 .... 462 B2
Buxton Link *LAIN* SS15 .... 435 K7
Buxton Rd *CDH/CHF* RM16 .... 402 E3
   CHING E4 .... 392 E6
   COLS CO2 .... 219 H2
   EPP CM16 .... 378 C2
   RCOLW CO6 .... 213 G2
   WAB EN9 .... 348 C6
Buxton Sq *LOS* SS9 .... 462 B2
Buyl Av *CVI* SS8 .... 461 G8
Byfield Cl *LOS* SS9 .... 443 G6
Byfletts *VGE* SS16 .... 458 C1
Byford Rd *RAYL* SS6 .... 441 K2
   SUD CO10 .... 58 D4
Bylam La *RIPS/CAP* IP9 .... 91 F6
Byland Cl *CHTY* IP2 .... 62 C3
Bylands *BSF* CM23 .... 198 D7
Byng Crs *RCOS* CO16 .... 226 E4
Byng Gdns *BRTR* CM7 .... 210 B1
Bynghams *HLWW/ROY* CM19 .... 293 H7
Bypass Rd *RCOS* CO16 .... 257 H8
By-pass Rd *SLH/COR* SS17 .... 473 G3
Byrd Ct *LAIN* SS15 .... 16 A2
Byrd Md *BRWN* CM15 .... 355 J7
Byrd's Farm La *SAFWN* CB10 .... 71 F2
Byrne Dr *SOSN* SS2 .... 444 B4
Byron Av *COLW* CO3 .... 186 A6
   SOSN SS2 .... 19 E2
Byron Cl *BRTR* CM7 .... 209 K5
   CVI SS8 .... 478 C1
Byron Ct *LAIN* SS15 .... 436 C7
Byron Dr *WIT* CM8 .... 278 A8
Byron Gdns *TIL* RM18 .... 485 H7
Byron Rd *CHLM/GWD* CM2 .... 15 D3
   IP IP1 .... 36 A1
   RBRW/HUT CM13 .... 412 C5
Byron Wy *HARH* RM3 .... 430 D1
Byrony Cl *WIT* CM8 .... 276 D1
Bywater Rd *RCHLM* CM3 .... 392 C7

C

Cabborns Crs *SLH/COR* SS17 .... 473 K5
Cabinet Wy *LOS* SS9 .... 442 D7
Cadenhouse Ms *COLW* CO3 .... 185 K6
Cadmore La *BAR* EN8 .... 346 E2
Cadogan Av *RBRW/HUT* CM15 .... 434 C8
Caernarvon Cl *EMPK* RM11 .... 451 H2
   HOC/HUL SS5 .... 420 E7
Cage End *RBSF* CM22 .... 234 B8
Cage End Cl *RBSF* CM22 .... 234 B8
Cagefield Rd *RCFD* SS4 .... 445 K1
Cage La *COLN* CO4 .... 119 J8
   FX IP11 .... 5 E2
Cairns Rd *COLS* CO2 .... 219 H3
Caister Dr *PIT* SS13 .... 438 E7
Caithness Cl *IPNE* IP4 .... 37 K5
Caladonia La *WICKW* SS12 .... 417 H8
Calamint Rd *WIT* CM8 .... 276 D2
Calbourne Av *HCH* RM12 .... 450 C6
Calcott Cl *BRW* CM14 .... 410 E4
Calcutta Rd *TIL* RM18 .... 484 E8
Caldbeck *WAB* EN9 .... 347 K8
Caldecot Wy *BROX* EN10 .... 319 F4
Caldwell Rd *SLH/COR* SS17 .... 473 H4
Caledonia Rd *RIPS/CAP* IP9 .... 129 C5
California Rd *COLN* CO4 .... 187 J1
California Rd *MGTR* CO11 .... 160 B1
Callan Gv *SOCK/AV* RM15 .... 470 A7
Callis St *SUD* CO10 .... 31 F5
Callowood Cft *RCHLM* CM3 .... 365 K4
Calmore Cl *HCH* RM12 .... 450 D6
Calshot Av *CDH/CHF* RM16 .... 483 J1
Calverley Cl *BSF* CM23 .... 231 J2
Calvert Dr *PIT* SS13 .... 439 F4
Calvina Cl *LAIN* SS15 .... 437 G3
Camberly Rd *IPNE* IP4 .... 38 B6
Camberton Rd *BRTR* CM7 .... 177 H7
Camborne Av *HARH* RM3 .... 431 F2
   KESG IP5 .... 39 F6
Camborne Wy *HARH* RM3 .... 431 G2
Cambrai Av *COLS* CO2 .... 186 E8
Cambria Cl *CVI* SS8 .... 477 G2
   MGTR CO11 .... 160 C2
Cambrian Gv *GVW* DA11 .... 489 F5
Cambridge Av *GPK* RM2 .... 430 D5
   HSTD CO9 .... 110 D5
Cambridge Cl *BAR* EN8 .... 346 C3
   HVHL CB9 .... 26 E4
   ING CM4 .... 387 K3
   VGE SS16 .... 436 A8
Cambridge Dr *CHTY* IP2 .... 62 A4
Cambridge Gdns
   CDH/CHF RM16 .... 485 F3
   EN EN1 .... 374 A6
   RCFD SS4 .... 421 K8
Cambridge Rd *CBE/LIN* CB11 .... 22 D3
   CHING E4 .... 402 E4
   COLW CO3 .... 186 D8
   COS CO15 .... 10 B3
   CVI SS8 .... 477 K2
   FOS CO13 .... 229 F8
   FX IP11 .... 131 J3
   HLW CM20 .... 263 G7
   KESG IP5 .... 38 E5
   SAFWS CB11 .... 70 A1
   SBW CM21 .... 231 J8
   SOS SS1 .... 18 C5
   STSD CM24 .... 167 K5
Cambridge Wy *BURES* CO8 .... 115 J5
   HVHL CB9 .... 26 E4
Camden Cl *CDH/CHF* RM16 .... 485 G3
   GVW DA11 .... 488 B6
Camden Rd *CDH/CHF* RM16 .... 483 H2
   IPSE IP3 .... 63 K1
Camellia Av *RCOS CO16 .... 290 E1
Camellia Cl *CHLM/WR* CM1 .... 305 H7
   HARH RM3 .... 431 F3
Camellia Crs *RCOS* CO16 .... 290 E1
Camelot Cl *CHLM/WR* CM1 .... 304 B8
Camelot Gdns *PIT* SS13 .... 439 F5
Cameron Cl *BRW* CM14 .... 411 F7
   ING CM4 .... 386 B2
   LOS SS9 .... 462 D3
   SLH/COR SS17 .... 457 F7
Cameron Dr *BAR* EN8 .... 346 D8
Cameron Pl *WICKW* SS12 .... 417 H8
Cam Gn *SOCK/AV* RM15 .... 469 G7
Camoise Cl *HSTD* CO9 .... 78 E6
Camomile Dr *WICKE* SS11 .... 417 K5
Camomile Wy *COLN* CO4 .... 186 D3
Campbell Cl *CHLM/GWD* CM2 .... 14 B6
   HLWE CM17 .... 295 F6
   WICKW SS12 .... 417 G8
Campbell Dr *COLN* CO4 .... 188 D3
Campbell Rd *GVW* DA11 .... 488 E6
   IPSE IP3 .... 64 A4
   WIT CM8 .... 245 F8
Camperdown Rd *CVI* SS8 .... 461 H8
Campernell Cl *RCOLE* CO7 .... 255 K5
Camper Rd *SOS* SS1 .... 465 J7
Campfield Rd *SBN/FI* SS3 .... 466 D7

Campine Cl *BAR* EN8 .... 346 D2
Campion Rd *WFD* IG8 .... 403 H8
Campion La *RCOLW* CO6 .... 117 J2
Campion Rd *CHTY* IP2 .... 2 A5
   COLS CO2 .... 8 C6
Campions *LOU* IG10 .... 377 J4
Campions Hl *RCOLW* CO6 .... 117 J4
The Campions *WIT* CM24 .... 167 K5
Campion Wy *WIT* CM8 .... 276 E2
Cample La *SOCK/AV* RM15 .... 469 J7
Camp Rd *RCOLE* CO7 .... 190 E6
Camps Rd *CBE/LIN* CB1 .... 23 K6
   HVHL CB9 .... 27 F6
   HVHL CB9 .... 49 G4
Camulodunum Wy *COLS* CO2 .... 218 D4
Camulus Cl *COLS* CO2 .... 218 B3
Cam Wy *WIT* CM8 .... 276 D3
Camwood Gdns *IPSE* IP3 .... 63 K1
Canada La *BROX* EN10 .... 318 E7
Canada Rd *ERITH* DA8 .... 480 C6
The Canadas *BROX* EN10 .... 318 E7
Canal Basin *GVE* DA12 .... 489 J4
Canal Rd *GVE* DA12 .... 489 J4
Canberra Cl *CHLM/WR* CM1 .... 304 A8
   COLS CO2 .... 219 H4
   HCH RM12 .... 450 D5
   IPNE IP4 .... 38 B7
Canberra Sq *TIL* RM18 .... 485 F8
Can Bridge Wy *CHLM/GWD* CM2 .... 15 D4
Cander Wy *SOCK/AV* RM15 .... 469 K7
The Candlemakers *SOSN* SS2 .... 444 D6
Candlet Gv *FX* IP11 .... 5 F2
Candlet Rd *FX* IP11 .... 95 F8
Candover Rd *HCH* RM12 .... 450 C2
Candyturft Rd *CHLM/WR* CM1 .... 305 H7
Cane Hl *HARH* RM3 .... 430 E6
Canes Cl *HLWE* CM17 .... 323 J2
Canewdon Cl *WICKE* SS11 .... 417 G3
Canewdon Gdns *WICKE* SS11 .... 417 G3
Canewdon Hall Cl *RCFD* SS4 .... 423 G3
Canewdon Rd *RCFD* SS4 .... 421 K5
   WOS/PRIT SS0 .... 18 A4
Canewdon View Rd *RCFD* SS4 .... 422 A7
Canfield *BSF* CM23 .... 198 D5
Canfield Rd *GTDUN* CM6 .... 236 B8
Canford Av *WICKW* SS12 .... 416 C5
Canford Cl *CHLM/GWD* CM2 .... 15 F6
Canhams Rd *SUD* CO10 .... 58 E8
Canham St *IP* IP1 .... 2 C2
Canney Rd *BOC* CM0 .... 341 G8
Canning St *LAIN* CO12 .... 7 F7
Cannon Cir *BRTR* CM7 .... 108 A3
Cannon Leys *CHLM/GWD* CM2 .... 360 C2
Cannon Ms *WAB* EN9 .... 347 H1
Cannons Cl *COL* CO1 .... 9 D5
Cannons Ct *BSF* CM23 .... 199 F7
   COLS CO2 .... 218 E2
Cannons La *CHONG* CM5 .... 327 C3
   RBSF CM22 .... 234 B8
Cannons Md *BRWN* CM15 .... 355 J4
   STSD CM24 .... 167 J2
Cannons Mill La *BSF* CM23 .... 199 F7
Canon Cl *HVHL* CB9 .... 27 F5
   SLH/COR SS17 .... 474 B8
Canonium Ms *K/T/MI* CO5 .... 246 E1
Canons Brook *HLWW/ROY* CM19 .... 12 A4
Canons Cl *RCHLM* CM3 .... 363 J4
Canons Ga *BAR* EN8 .... 319 F7
   HLW CM20 .... 12 A4
Canonsleigh Crs *LOS* SS9 .... 463 F7
Cansey La *MGTR* CO11 .... 160 E6
Canterbury Av *SOSN* SS2 .... 465 H4
   UPMR RM14 .... 452 C6
Canterbury Cl *BSDN* SS14 .... 438 C5
   CHIG IG7 .... 405 J2
   CHTY IP2 .... 62 B4
   RAYL SS6 .... 419 H1
Canterbury Gra *BRTR* CM7 .... 177 J2
Canterbury Rd *COLS* CO2 .... 8 C1
   COS CO15 .... 260 C2
   GVE DA12 .... 489 H7
Canterbury Wy
   RBRW/HUT CM13 .... 433 F1
   WTHK RM20 .... 482 B6
The Canters *SBF/HAD* SS7 .... 441 C6
Canuden Rd *CHLM/WR* CM1 .... 332 A4
Canute Cl *RCFD* SS4 .... 423 H4
Canvey Rd *CVI* SS8 .... 460 E7
   CVI SS8 .... 477 C5
   LOS SS9 .... 462 C5
   PIT SS13 .... 439 F2
Canvey Wk *CHLM/WR* CM1 .... 305 G4
Canvey Wy *CVI* SS8 .... 460 B7
   SBF/HAD SS7 .... 459 K1
Canwick Gv *COLS* CO2 .... 219 J8
Capadocia St *SOS* SS1 .... 465 H4
Capel Cl *COLW* CO3 .... 186 A2
Capel Cl *BRTR* CM7 .... 208 C2
   CHLM/WR CM1 .... 304 C2
   FX IP11 .... 94 C7
   SLH/COR SS17 .... 474 B8
Capel Dr *FX* IP11 .... 94 C7
Capel Hall La *FX* IP11 .... 94 C7
Capel Pk *FOS* CO13 .... 228 D5
Capel Rd *BRTR* CM7 .... 208 C2

COLW CO3 .... 186 D8
EN EN1................................ 374 B2
Capel Ter SOS SS1 .... 19 D5 🇮
Caper La COLS CO2 .... 249 K1
Capon Cl BRW CM14 .... 410 E4
Capons La RCHLM CM3........ 336 A7
Cap Pillar Cl RCOLE CO7 ...... 220 E3
Captains Rd K/T/MI CO5 ...... 284 D7
Captains Wood Rd MAL CM9... 310 C3
The Caravan Site SOCK/AV RM15 .. 482 A3
Caravel Cl CDH/CHF RM16 .... 483 J2
Carbis Cl CHING E4................ 402 E4 🇮
Carbonels SUD CO10 .... 59 H2
Carbury Cl HCH RM12 .... 450 D7
Cardew Drift KESC IP5 .... 39 H5
Cardiff Av CHTY IP2............... 62 D4
Cardiff Rd PEND EN3 .... 374 B8
Cardigan Av WOS/PRIT SS0 .. 463 K2
Cardigan St IP IP1................. 2 C2
Cardinal Cl COLN CO4 .... 188 D6 🇮
Cardinal St IP IP1.................. 3 D4
Cardinal Wy HVHL CB9 .... 27 F4 🇮
Card's Rd CHLM/GWD CM2 .. 334 A7
Carfax Rd HCH RM12 .... 450 A5
Carisbrooke Av COS CO15 .... 259 J5
Carisbrooke Cl EMPK RM11 .. 451 H2 🇮
PIT SS15 .... 438 E7 🇮
Carisbrooke Dr RCHLM CM3 .. 392 C6
SLH/COR SS17 .... 474 C1
Carisbrooke Rd BRWN CM15.. 410 E2
WOS/PRIT SS0...................... 18 B3
Carleton Rd BAR EN8 .... 346 D1
Carlina Gdns WFD IG8........... 403 J8
Carlingford Dr WOS/PRIT SS0.. 463 K2
Carlisle Cl COL CO1............... 8 C3
Carlisle Rd ROM RM1 .... 430 A7
Carlisle Wy PIT SS13............. 438 E7
Carlton Av WOS/PRIT SS0 .... 463 K1
Carlton Cl CDH/CHF RM16 .. 484 E1
COS CO15............................ 11 E3
GPK RM2.............................. 430 B7
KESG IP5.............................. 38 E6
PIT SS15.............................. 439 H5
WICKE SS11.......................... 417 H5
Carlton Wy IPNE IP4.............. 3 F1
Carlyle Cl IP IP1.................... 36 B1
Carlyle Gdns BCAYW CM12.. 387 F8
WICKW SS12......................... 417 H8
Carmania Cl SBN/FI SS3........ 466 E4
Carmarthen Cl CHTY IP2 ...... 62 C4
Carmel St SAFWN CB10......... 43 J1
Carmen St SAFWN CB10........ 43 J2
Carnaby Rd BROX EN10 .... 318 E2
Carnach Gn SOCK/AV RM15.. 469 K7
Carnarvon Rd COS CO15 ...... 10 C3
SOSN SS2............................. 18 C3
Carnation Cl CHLM/WR CM1 .. 305 H8
Carnation Dr SAFWN CB10.... 71 G3
Carnforth Gdns HCH RM12 .. 450 B6
Carnival Cl BSDN SS14 .... 17 F1
Carolbrook Rd CHTY IP2 ...... 62 A4
Carol Cl FX IP11.................... 131 K2
LAIN SS15............................ 16 B3
Carolina Wy K/T/MI CO5 ...... 248 B8 🇮
Caroline Cl RCOLE CO7 .... 221 F2
Caroline's Cl SOSN SS2......... 444 B8 🇮
Caro Rd CVI SS8 .... 478 C2
Carpenter La BCAYW CM12 .. 414 A1
Carpenter Pth
RBRW/HUT CM13................... 412 C1 🇮
Carpenters SBN/FI SS3 .... 446 C7
Carpenters Arms La EPP CM16 .. 323 F2 🇮
Carpenters Rd EN EN1 .... 374 C2
The Carpenters BSF CM23 .... 231 G1 🇮
Carraways WIT CM8 .... 277 H5
Carriage Cl FX IP11 .... 94 D7 🇮
Carriage Dr CHLM/WR CM1 .. 305 G5
Carriers Cl K/T/MI CO5 .... 284 C6
Carrigans BSF CM23 .... 198 D5
Carringtons Rd RCOLE CO7 .. 190 A1
Carringtons Dr BRTR CM7 .... 177 J5
Carroll Hi LOU IG10 .... 377 H7
Carron Md RCHLM CM3 .... 593 F7
Carr Rd FX IP11.................... 130 E7
Carrs Rd COS CO15............... 10 A4
Carruthers Dr WICKE SS11 .. 417 G4
Carsey Cl BCAY CM11 .... 415 K1
Carsey Rd CBE/LIN CB1 .... 25 F7
Carshalton End COLW CO3 .. 218 A1
Carson Rd BCAYE SS4........... 387 K8
Carsons Dr SUD CO10 .... 59 F8
Carswell Rd RBRW/HUT CM13.. 412 C2 🇮
Cartbridge Cl WOTN CO14 .. 229 G5 🇮
Cartel Pl PUR RM19............... 482 A3
Carte Pl VGE SS16 .... 436 B8
Carter Dr CRW RM5............... 407 C7
Carterhatch La EN EN1 .... 374 A6
PEND EN3............................. 374 C6 🇮
Carterhatch Rd PEND EN3 .... 374 E6

Carters Cl RCOS CO16 .... 290 D2
Carters Cft SAFWN CB10 ...... 46 E4
Cartersfield Rd WAB EN9 ...... 347 J8
Carters Hi BSF CM23 .... 167 F4
COLN CO4 .... 119 H7
Carters La EPP CM16 .... 321 K6
RBSF CM22.......................... 137 G8
WIT CM8.............................. 278 B7
Carters Leys BSF CM23 .... 198 C5
Carters Md HLWE CM17 .... 295 F6
Cart La CHING E4 .... 403 F4
Cartlodge Av WICKE SS11 .... 417 H5
Cartwright Rd SBF/HAD SS7 .. 440 C6
Cartwright Wk
CHLM/GWD CM2 .... 333 H3 🇮
Carvers Wd BCAYE CM11 ...... 414 D6 🇮
Cascade Rd BKHH IG9 .... 404 A5
Case La RIPS/CAP IP9 .... 87 J7
Casey La BOC CM0................ 572 A1
Cashiobury Ter SOS SS1 .... 18 C5 🇮
Cashmere Wy VGE SS16 .... 458 A2
Cassandra Ga BAR EN8......... 347 F1
Cassel Av CVI SS8 .... 461 H8
Cassino Rd CHLM/WR CM1 .. 304 A7 🇮
COLS CO2 .... 218 D2
Castellan Av GPK RM2 .... 430 C5
Castell Rd LOU IG10 .... 378 A5
Castle Av HVHL CB9 .... 26 E5
SBF/HAD SS7 .... 461 J4
Castle Cl HARH RM3 .... 408 D2
HSTD CO9 .... 110 E1 🇮
RAYL SS6.............................. 441 J4
RCHLM CM3 .... 241 H7
SBN/FI SS3 .... 467 F5
Castle Cl RAYL SS6 .... 441 H4 🇮
Castle Cross SAFWN CB10 .... 71 F2
Castledon Rd BCAYE CM11 .. 416 C2
Castle Dr LOS SS9 .... 462 C5
RAYL SS6.............................. 441 H2
Castlegate St HAR CO12 .... 7 F2 🇮
Castle Hi RCOLE CO7 .... 157 J1
Castle La HSTD CO9 .... 110 E1
HVHL CB9 .... 26 E5
SBF/HAD SS7 .... 461 K3
Castle Meadow HSTD CO9 ... 110 C3
Castle Rd COL CO1................ 8 C5
COS CO15............................ 10 B4
GRAYS RM17......................... 483 H5
IP IP1.................................. 36 A4
RAYL SS6.............................. 441 H4
SBF/HAD SS7 .... 461 J4
Castle St BSF CM23 .... 198 C5 🇮
CHONG CM5 .... 354 C3
SAFWN CB10 .... 70 E5
Castle Ter RAYL SS6 .... 441 H4 🇮
Castleton Rd SOSN SS2........ 465 H4
Castle Vw BSF CM23 .... 199 F6
Castle Wk CVI SS8 .... 461 F7
Castleward Cl RCOLE CO7 ... 221 F5 🇮
Castle Wy RCOS CO16 .... 289 G1
Caswell Cl SLH/COR SS17 .... 474 C1
Caswell Ms CHLM/GWD CM2 .. 333 H3 🇮
Catalina Av CDH/CHF RM16.. 483 J1
Catchpole La MAL CM9 .... 310 C1
Catchpool Rd COL CO1.......... 8 B2
Caterham Cl RCOS CO16 ...... 258 C2 🇮
Caterham St WAB EN9 .... 348 B8
Cater Wd BCAYW CM12 .... 414 C2
Catesbray RIPS/CAP IP9 .... 86 E4
Catharine Cl CDH/CHF RM16.. 483 J1
Cathedral Dr LAIN SS15........ 16 A3
Catherine Cl BRWN CM15..... 410 D1
COS CO15............................ 10 C2
Catherine Hunt Wy COLS CO2.. 218 C3
Catherine Rd GPK RM2 .... 430 C7
PEND EN3............................. 374 E2
SBF/HAD SS7 .... 460 C1
Catherines Cl RCHLM CM3 ... 241 H7
Catisfield Rd PEND EN3 .... 374 E3
Catkin Cl HVHL CB9 .... 26 D4
Catons La SUD CO10 .... 58 D7
Cat's La SUD CO10 .... 58 D7
Cattawade Cl BSDN SS14 ..... 438 A6
Cattawade Link BSDN SS14 .. 438 A6
Cattawade St MGTR CO11 .... 123 H6
Cattermole Ct RCOS CO16 .... 290 D2
Catts Cl RIPS/CAP IP9 .... 125 C3
Cattsfield RIPS/CAP IP9 .... 125 C3
Cauldwell Av IPNE IP4 .... 37 H7
Cauldwell Hall Rd IPNE IP4 .. 37 J6
Caulfield Rd SBN/FI SS3 .... 466 B6
Causeway RCHLM CM3 .... 240 B4
Causeway Br SOCK/AV RM15.. 482 B2
Causeway End MGTR CO11 .. 123 C6 🇮
Causeway End Rd GTDUN CM6.. 239 J2
Causeway Reach RCOS CO16.. 259 C6
The Causeway BRTR CM7 ..... 106 D7
BRTR CM7............................ 209 J2
BSF CM23............................. 198 E6
BUNT SG9............................. 132 D4
CHLM/GWD CM2.................. 333 H7
CHLM/WR CM1 .... 330 D7
COLN CO4 .... 9 E2

GTDUN CM6......................... 204 C3
HSTD CO9 .... 52 C5
HSTD CO9 .... 78 E7
HSTD CO9 .... 147 K4 🇮
HVHL CB9 .... 26 E6 🇮
MAL CM9.............................. 308 D7
MAL CM9.............................. 338 C1
RCOLW CO6.......................... 154 C4
SAFWS CB11 .... 97 F2
SAFWS CB11 .... 101 J6 🇮
Causton Rd COL CO1............. 8 A3
Caustons Cl SUD CO10 .... 59 F8 🇮
Caustonway RAYL SS6 .... 441 J1
Cavell Rd BCAYE CM11 .... 414 D4
Cavendish Av COLS CO2........ 219 K1
RAIN RM13........................... 450 C7
Cavendish Crs RAIN RM13 .... 450 C7
Cavendish Dr MGTR CO11 .... 159 G2
RCOS CO16........................... 290 C1
Cavendish Gdns BRTR CM7 .. 178 B8
CHLM/GWD CM2.................. 15 F2
WOS/PRIT SS0...................... 463 H3
Cavendish La SUD CO10........ 33 F1
Cavendish Rd FX IP11........... 5 F4
HOC/HUL SS5....................... 421 H4
SUD CO10 .... 31 H6
Cavendish St IPSE IP3........... 3 F5
Cavendish Wy LAIN SS15 ..... 16 B1
SUD CO10 .... 58 C6 🇮
Cavenham Gdns EMPK RM11.. 430 D7
Caversham Av SBN/FI SS3 .... 466 D4
Caversham Park Av RAYL SS6.. 419 H8 🇮
Cawdor Av SOCK/AV RM15... 469 J7
Cawkell Cl STSD CM24 .... 167 J6
Cawkwell Cl CHLM/GWD CM2.. 333 H1
Caxton Ct COLN CO4............. 155 K7
Cecil Av CDH/CHF RM16 ...... 483 J1
EMPK RM11........................... 431 F5
Cecil Cl BSF CM23 .... 199 J6
Cecil Ct HLWS CM18 .... 12 C6
Cecilia St IP IP1.................... 3 D4
Cecil Rd BAR EN8 .... 346 D6
GVW DA11............................ 488 E6
IP IP1.................................. 2 C3
Cecil Wy RAYL SS6 .... 442 A3
Cedar Av BAR EN8................. 346 D7
CHLM/WR CM1 .... 14 B2
K/T/MI CO5.......................... 248 A6
KESG IP5.............................. 38 E7
PEND EN3............................. 374 C6
RCOLE CO7 .... 255 H6
UPMR RM14.......................... 451 H5
WICKW SS12......................... 417 F8
Cedar Av West CHLM/WR CM1.. 14 B2 🇮
Cedar Cha MAL CM9 .... 310 E8
Cedar Cl BKHH IG9 .... 404 A5
FOS CO15............................. 229 F6
MGTR CO11 .... 123 J4
RAYL SS6.............................. 442 A5 🇮
RBRW/HUT CM13................... 412 C5
SBW CM21............................ 263 J4
SOSN SS2............................. 19 D2
Cedar Ct BSF CM23 .... 198 E4
RCOLW CO6.......................... 153 J8
Cedar Crs MGTR CO11.......... 159 H2
Cedarcroft Rd IP IP1.............. 36 B3
Cedar Dr HOC/HUL SS5......... 419 K3
LOU IG10 .... 377 K6
WIT CM8.............................. 245 G8
Cedar Gdns UPMR RM14 ...... 451 K4
Cedar Gv BOC CM0 .... 398 B7
Cedar Hall Gdns SBF/HAD SS7.. 441 F7
Cedar Ms HOC/HUL SS5 .... 420 D7
Cedar Pk BSF CM23 .... 231 H1
Cedar Park Cl SBF/HAD SS7.. 441 F7
Cedar Ri SOCK/AV RM15 ...... 470 B4 🇮
Cedar Rd CDH/CHF RM16..... 485 F2
CVI SS8................................ 477 K1
ERITH DA8............................ 480 B7
HCH RM12............................ 450 D4
RBRW/HUT CM13................... 412 C2 🇮
SBF/HAD SS7 .... 441 F7 🇮
Cedars SLH/COR SS17 .... 474 A3 🇮
Cedars La RIPS/CAP IP9 .... 86 E4
Cedars Rd COLS CO2 .... 8 A5
The Cedars BKHH IG9 .... 403 H4
RCHLM CM3 .... 392 D5 🇮
SBN/FI SS3 .... 467 G1 🇮
Cedar Wk RCFD SS4.............. 423 G4
Cedar Wy RCOLE CO7 .... 223 K5
Celadon Cl PEND EN3 .... 374 E7
Celandine Cl BCAYW CM12 .. 414 A1 🇮
SOCK/AV RM15 .... 470 A4
Celandine Ct COLN CO4 .... 186 D5 🇮
Celeborn St RCHLM CM3 ...... 392 C7
Celedon Cl CDH/CHF RM16 .. 483 H1
Cement Block Cottages
GRAYS RM17......................... 484 B4
Cemetery La RCOLE CO7....... 121 K3
Cemetery Rd BSF CM23 .... 198 E8
IPNE IP4.............................. 3 E3
Centaur Wy MAL CM9........... 338 C5
Century Cl COLW CO3 .... 185 H6
Centenary Cir CHLM/GWD CM2.. 360 D4
RCHLM CM3 .... 305 J4

Centenary Wk EPP CM16 ... 350 A8
  LOU IG10 ... 403 A2
Centenary Av RCOS CO16 ... 259 C4
Central Av BAR EN8 ... 346 E7
  BCAYW CM12 ... 387 J8
  CVI SS8 ... 460 D8
  CVI SS8 ... 477 J1 🗆
  EN EN1 ... 374 B6
  FOS CO13 ... 229 F7
  GVE DA12 ... 489 C7
  HOC/HUL SS5 ... 420 A4
  IPSE IP3 ... 64 B5
  RCFD SS4 ... 422 A8
  SBF/HAD SS7 ... 441 K8
  SLH/COR SS17 ... 457 F8
  SLH/COR SS17 ... 474 C1
  SOCK/AV RM15 ... 481 K1
  SOSN SS2 ... 19 E3
  TIL RM18 ... 485 F7
  WTHK RM20 ... 482 C4
Central Cl SBF/HAD SS7 ... 461 K1
Central Ct RCH RM12 ... 463 J5
Central Rd HLW CM20 ... 294 E1
  SLH/COR SS17 ... 473 K4
Central Wall CVI SS8 ... 461 F7
Central Wall Rd CVI SS8 ... 461 G8
Centre Av EPP CM16 ... 350 D6
Centre Dr EPP CM16 ... 350 D6
Centre Gn EPP CM16 ... 350 D6 🗆
The Centre HSTD CO9 ... 147 K3
Centre Wy WAB EN9 ... 375 J1
Centurion Rd SBN/FI SS3 ... 466 E5
Centurion Wy COLS CO2 ... 218 B3
  PUR RM19 ... 481 C3
Ceylon Rd WOS/PRIT SS0 ... 18 A4
Chadacre Rd SOS SS1 ... 466 A4
Chadburn Rd SUD CO10 ... 35 F5
Chadfields TIL RM18 ... 485 F6
Chadwell Av BAR EN8 ... 346 C2
Chadwell By-pass GRAYS RM17 ... 485 F4
Chadwell Hl CDH/CHF RM16 ... 485 K2
Chadwell Rd GRAYS RM17 ... 484 D3
Chadwick Av CHING E4 ... 402 E7 🗆
Chadwick Cl GVW DA11 ... 488 D7
Chadwick Dr HARH RM3 ... 430 E4 🗆
Chadwick Rd RCHLM CM3 ... 392 E4 🗆
  WOS/PRIT SS0 ...
Chaffinch Cl SBN/FI SS3 ... 466 D5 🗆
Chafford Gdns RBRW/HUT CM13 ... 434 C8
Chafford Wy CDH/CHF RM16 ... 470 E8
Chaingate Av SOSN SS2 ... 465 H3
Chalfont Cl LOS SS9 ... 462 E1
Chalfont Rd COLN CO4 ... 187 K2
Chalfonde Gdns GPK RM2 ... 430 C6
Chalice Cl BSDN SS14 ... 438 B7
Chalk End PIT SS13 ... 438 D6
Chalklands CBE/LIN CB1 ... 22 E2
  CHLM/GWD CM2 ... 362 B3
  SAFWN CB10 ... 71 F2 🗆
Chalk La HLWE CM17 ... 296 A3
Chalkners Cl RIPS/CAP IP9 ... 87 F2
Chalk Rd CVI SS8 ... 461 F7 🗆
Chalks Av SBW CM21 ... 263 H2
Chalks Rd WIT CM8 ... 277 J7
Chalkstone Wy HVHL CB9 ... 390 D5
Chalk St RCHLM CM3 ... 365 K5
Chalkwell Av WOS/PRIT SS0 ... 463 J6
Chalkwell Esp WOS/PRIT SS0 ... 463 J6
Chalkwell Park Dr LOS SS9 ... 463 G3
Chalky La ROY SG8 ... 67 G3
Chalky Rd CBE/LIN CB1 ... 21 H2
Challacombe SBN/FI SS3 ... 466 B4
Challacombe Cl
  RBRW/HUT CM13 ... 412 B4 🗆
Challenge Wy COL CO1 ... 9 D5
Challinor HLWE CM17 ... 295 J5
Challis La BRTR CM7 ... 209 K5
Challock Lees PIT SS13 ... 439 F8 🗆
Chalon St IP IP1 ... 2 C4 🗆
Chalvedon Av PIT SS13 ... 438 E6
Chamberlain Av CVI SS8 ... 478 C1
  SLH/COR SS17 ... 457 H8
  WOTN CO14 ... 229 G6
Chamberlain Cl HLWE CM17 ... 295 G5
Chamberlains Ride RCHLM CM3 ... 392 D7 🗆
Chamberlain Wy RIPW IP8 ... 474 A2
Champion Cl SLH/COR SS17 ... 61 J3
Champion Dr
  WICKW SS12 ... 417 G7 🗆
Champion Rd UPMR RM14 ... 451 J3
Champions Wy RCHLM CM3 ... 392 C5
Champlain Av CVI SS8 ... 460 E8
Chance Cl CDH/CHF RM16 ... 483 J2
  LAIN SS15 ... 16 A4
  SBF/HAD SS7 ... 440 B7
Chancellor Av CHLM/GWD CM2 ... 333 K1
Chancellor Rd SOS SS1 ... 19 D5
Chancery Gv COLS CO2 ... 219 H5
Chancery Pl CHLM/WR CM1 ... 331 H4
Chandler Rd LOU IG10 ... 377 K5
Chandlers BOC CM0 ... 398 A7
Chandlers Cl BSF CM23 ... 231 G1 🗆
  RCOS CO16 ... 290 D2
Chandlers Rw COL CO1 ... 9 E6
Chandlers Wk BRWN CM15 ... 383 G3

Chandlers Wy SOSN SS2 ... 444 C8
Chandos Cl BKHH IG9 ... 403 J5
Chandos Pde SBF/HAD SS7 ... 462 A2
Chaney Rd RCOLE CO7 ... 220 D3
Chanlock Pth SOCK/AV RM15 ... 469 K7 🗆
Channing Cl EMPK RM11 ... 451 G1 🗆
Chanton Cl LOS SS9 ... 442 E6 🗆
Chantry Cl BSF CM23 ... 198 D5
  COS CO15 ... 259 G6
Chantry Crs SLH/COR SS17 ... 473 J4
Chantry Dr ING CM4 ... 386 B2
  LAIN SS15 ... 16 A3 🗆
Chantry Gn CHTY IP2 ... 61 K2
Chantry La RCHLM CM3 ... 306 E2
Chantry Rd BSF CM23 ... 198 D5
The Chantry COLW CO3 ... 294 E2 🗆
  HLW CM20 ...
Chantry Wy BCAYE CM11 ... 107 K6
Chanute Av BRTR CM7 ... 87 F4
Chapel Cl RIPS/CAP IP9 ... 59 H2 🗆
  SUD CO10 ...
  WTHK RM20 ... 482 E5
Chapel Ct BCAYE CM11 ... 414 C3
Chapel Cft ING CM4 ... 386 B1 🗆
  RCOLE CO7 ... 157 H6
Chapel Cut MGTR CO11 ... 160 B1 🗆
Chapel Dr BCAYW CM12 ... 272 D7
Chapel End Wy HSTD CO9 ... 77 J3
Chapelfields FOS CO13 ... 228 D7
Chapel Flds HLWE CM17 ... 295 C2
Chapel Hl BRTR CM7 ... 210 A3
  HSTD CO9 ... 147 J3
  SUD CO10 ... 81 J1
Chapel La BOC CM0 ... 372 A1
  CHIG IG7 ... 405 J6
  CHLM/WR CM1 ... 329 K4
  COLN CO4 ... 155 H2
  FOS CO13 ... 227 K7
  HLWE CM17 ... 295 G7
  MAL CM9 ... 339 G3
  RCHLM CM3 ... 335 F2
  RCHLM CM3 ... 365 K5
  RCOLE CO7 ... 188 E4
  RCOLE CO7 ... 189 K7
  RCOLE CO7 ... 191 F8
  RCOLE CO7 ... 223 F8
  RCOLW CO6 ... 185 K2
  RCOS CO16 ... 193 F5
  RCOS CO16 ... 289 G1
  RIPH IP8 ... 61 G4
  RIPH IP8 ... 61 J6
  SAFWS CB11 ... 100 B5 🗆
  SBF/HAD SS7 ... 461 H3
  SBN/FI SS3 ... 467 C1
  SUD CO10 ... 85 F4
Chapel Rd BOC CM0 ... 425 H1
  COLN CO4 ... 155 H2
  COLW CO3 ... 185 H7
  EPP CM16 ... 350 D4
  HSTD CO9 ... 52 E6
  K/T/MI CO5 ... 280 C1
  MAL CM9 ... 279 F7
  MAL CM9 ... 313 J1
  RCOLE CO7 ... 220 E5 🗆
  RCOLE CO7 ... 256 A6
  RCOLW CO6 ... 185 J2
  RCOS CO16 ... 194 A6
  SBN/FI SS3 ... 466 A6
Chapel St BCAYW CM12 ... 414 B3
  HSTD CO9 ... 52 C2
  HSTD CO9 ... 147 K3
  HVHL CB9 ... 50 D6
  K/T/MI CO5 ... 220 C5
Chapel St North COLS CO2 ... 8 A5 🗆
Chapel St South COLS CO2 ... 8 A5
Chaplaincy Gdns EMPK RM11 ... 451 J3 🗆
Chaplains Cl HVHL CB9 ... 27 F4 🗆
Chaplin Cl CHLM/GWD CM2 ... 360 D5
  LAIN SS15 ... 16 C1 🗆
Chaplin Dr COLN CO4 ... 9 F2
Chaplin Rd RCOLE CO7 ... 122 B3
Chaplins FOS CO13 ... 228 E5 🗆
Chaplin Wk SUD CO10 ... 59 G8
Chapman Rd COS CO15 ... 10 C4
Chapmans Cl LOS SS9 ... 462 C4
Chapmans La K/T/MI CO5 ... 285 H4
Chapmans Wk LOS SS9 ... 462 C4
Chappel Hl RCOLW CO6 ... 151 F8
Chappel Rd RCOLW CO6 ... 151 H2
  RCOLW CO6 ... 152 C6
  RCOLW CO6 ... 183 F3
Chapple Dr HVHL CB9 ... 27 F4 🗆
Charcroft Gdns PEND EN3 ... 374 D8
Charfinch Crs BCAYE CM11 ... 414 D4
Charfleets Cl CVI SS8 ... 477 H2 🗆
Charfleets Rd CVI SS8 ... 477 G2
Charfleets Service Rd CVI SS8 ... 477 G2
Charity Farm Cha BCAYW CM12 ... 414 A2 🗆
Charlbury Cl HARH RM3 ... 430 D1 🗆
Charlbury Crs HARH RM3 ... 430 D1
Charlecote Rd BRTR CM7 ... 209 F6
Charles Cl WOS/PRIT SS0 ... 443 H8

Charles Pell Rd COLN CO4 ... 188 B7
Charles Rd FX IP11 ... 5 E4
  RCOLE CO7 ... 255 K7
Charles St COL CO1 ... 8 C5 🗆
  EPP CM16 ... 350 E6
  GRAYS RM17 ... 484 A5
  IP IP1 ... 3 D3
Charleston Av PIT SS13 ... 439 F4
Charleston Ct PIT SS13 ... 439 F4 🗆
Charlotte Av WICKW SS12 ... 417 F6 🗆
Charlotte Ct RCHLM CM3 ... 392 D7 🗆
Charlotte Dr FOS CO13 ... 228 D7 🗆
Charlotte Pl WTHK RM20 ... 482 E5
Charlotte's RIPW IP8 ... 61 F4 🗆
Charlotte Wy WIT CM8 ... 277 H3 🗆
Charlton Av IP IP1 ... 36 B3
Charlton Cl PIT SS13 ... 439 F6
Charlton St WTHK RM20 ... 483 C5
Charnock Cl FOS CO13 ... 228 E7 🗆
Charnwood Av CHLM/WR CM1 ... 332 A4
Charnwood Rd EN EN1 ... 374 B2 🗆
Charters Cross HLWS CM18 ... 13 D6 🗆
The Charters GTDUN CM6 ... 204 C3
Charter Wy BRTR CM7 ... 210 B4
Chartfield Dr FOS CO13 ... 228 C5
Chartwell Cl BRTR CM7 ... 177 H6
  IPNE IP4 ... 37 K8 🗆
  WAB EN9 ... 348 A7
Chase Cl HVHL CB9 ... 27 G4
  SBF/HAD SS7 ... 440 E8
Chase Ct COLN CO4 ... 188 B6 🗆
Chase Dr RCHLM CM3 ... 392 C5
Chase End RAYL SS6 ... 442 A3
Chase Gdns CHING E4 ... 402 B7
  WOS/PRIT SS0 ... 18 A1
Chase House Gdns EMPK RM11 ... 431 G2
Chase La CHIG IG7 ... 405 K6
  HAR CO12 ... 164 D3
Chase Rd BRW CM14 ... 411 F6
  SLH/COR SS17 ... 474 C2
  SOS SS1 ... 19 F6
Chase Rd East RCOLE CO7 ... 191 H6
Chaseside RAYL SS6 ... 441 K5
Chase Sq GVE DA12 ... 489 G4 🗆
The Chase BCAYE CM11 ... 414 D3 🗆
  BOC CM0 ... 398 D7
  BRTR CM7 ... 177 K6
  BRTR CM7 ... 209 F8
  BRW CM14 ... 410 E2
  BRW CM14 ... 411 G6 🗆
  BSF CM23 ... 198 E3
  CHIG IG7 ... 404 E2
  CHLM/GWD CM2 ... 333 H1
  COL CO1 ... 9 F4 🗆
  COS CO15 ... 260 C8
  DAGE RM10 ... 450 A4
  GTDUN CM6 ... 238 B6
  HVHL CB9 ... 50 C6
  K/T/MI CO5 ... 246 E2
  K/T/MI CO5 ... 284 E1
  LAIN SS15 ... 436 C3
  LOU IG10 ... 403 K1
  MAL CM9 ... 313 F6
  MAL CM9 ... 314 D6
  MAL CM9 ... 340 D5
  MGTR CO11 ... 124 A4
  MGTR CO11 ... 159 J2
  RAYL SS6 ... 442 A4
  RBRW/HUT CM13 ... 412 B6
  RBSF CM22 ... 137 C2
  RCFD SS4 ... 421 K4
  RCHLM CM3 ... 306 C4
  RCHLM CM3 ... 392 C5
  RCOLE CO7 ... 157 K4
  RCOLE CO7 ... 190 A1
  RCOLW CO6 ... 183 F1
  SBF/HAD SS7 ... 440 E8
  SBN/FI SS3 ... 428 C2
  SUD CO10 ... 33 J1
  UPMR RM14 ... 452 B8
  VGE SS16 ... 457 F2
  WICKE SS11 ... 417 K1
  WICKW SS12 ... 416 D8 🗆
  WICKW SS12 ... 439 H1
  WTHK RM20 ... 483 G5
Chaseway VGE SS16 ... 458 C2
Chaseways SBW CM21 ... 263 F7
The Chase Wy COLW CO3 ... 186 D5
The Chaseway ING CM4 ... 388 C2
Chaters Hl SAFWN CB10 ... 272 C2
Chatham Hall La RCHLM CM3 ... 272 C7
Chatley Rd RCHLM CM3 ... 241 H1
Chatsworth SBF/HAD SS7 ... 440 E7 🗆
Chatsworth Av BRTR CM7 ... 208 E2 🗆
Chatsworth Cl BSF CM23 ... 198 B3
Chatsworth Crs CHTY IP2 ... 62 C3
  FX IP11 ... 94 D1 🗆
Chatsworth Dr IPNE IP4 ... 38 C3
Chatsworth Gdns COS CO15 ... 10 A5
  HOC/HUL SS5 ... 420 E7
Chatsworth Rd K/T/MI CO5 ... 284 E7 🗆
Chattisham Rd RIPW IP8 ... 60 B6 🗆
Chatton Cl WICKW SS12 ... 417 H8 🗆
Chaucer Cl COS CO15 ... 290 C4

MAL CM9 .... 338 C5
TIL RM18 .... 485 H8
Chaucer Crs BRTR CM7 .... 209 K5
Chaucer Rd CHLM/GWD CM2 ..... 15 E4
FX IP11 .... 5 F7
GVW DA11 .... 488 C8
HARH RM3 .... 430 C2
IP IP1 .... 36 B2
SUD CO10 .... 58 A3
Chaucer Wk WICKW SS12 .... 417 F8
Chaucer Wy COLW CO3 .... 186 A6
Chauntry Rd HVHL CB9 .... 27 F6
Cheapside East RAYL SS6 .... 441 H1
Cheapside West RAYL SS6 .... 441 G1
Cheddar Av WOS/PRIT SS0 ...... 463 H5
Chedington SBN/FI SS3 .... 466 D4
Cheelson Rd SOCK/AV RM15 .... 470 A2
Cheldon Barton SBN/FI SS3 ..... 466 B5
Chelmer Av RAYL SS6 .... 441 H4
RCHLM CM3 .... 272 D8
Chelmer Ct FOS CO13 .... 228 D6
MAL CM9 .... 311 K1
Chelmer Dr GTDUN CM6 .... 204 D5
RBRW/HUT CM13 .... 412 D2
SOCK/AV RM15 .... 470 A7
Chelmer Lea CHLM/GWD CM2 .... 15 F6
Chelmer Pl CHLM/GWD CM2 ...... 15 E2
CDH/CHF RM16 .... 485 F4
CHLM/GWD CM2 .... 15 E4
HVHL CB9 .... 27 H5
UPMR RM14 .... 432 A8
WIT CM8 .... 276 E3
Chelmer Ter MAL CM9 .... 338 D3
Chelmerton Av CHLM/GWD CM2 ... 15 H5
Chelmer Valley Rd CHLM/WR CM1 ... 14 C1
Chelmer Village Wy
CHLM/GWD CM2 .... 15 F3
Chelmer Wy BOC CM0 .... 398 A7
SBN/FI SS3 .... 466 C6
Chelmsford Av SOSN SS2 .... 18 C3
Chelmsford Dr UPMR RM14 ...... 451 G4
Chelmsford Rd BRWN CM15 ..... 385 C7
BRWN CM15 .... 411 K1
CHLM/WR CM1 .... 331 J4
CHONG CM5 .... 354 D1
COS CO15 .... 11 F1
GTDUN CM6 .... 204 E7
GTDUN CM6 .... 300 D1
ING CM4 .... 356 E4
MAL CM9 .... 336 C6
RBSF CM22 .... 265 H3
RCHLM CM3 .... 272 C6
RCHLM CM3 .... 365 H2
WICKE SS11 .... 418 E8
WICKE SS11 .... 418 D8
Chelsea Av SOS SS1 .... 465 G7
Chelsea Cl IP IP1 .... 36 B4
Chelsea Ct SUD CO10 .... 58 C6
Chelsea Gdns HLWE CM17 .... 295 J6
Chelsea Rd SUD CO10 .... 58 C6
Chelsworth Av IPNE IP4 .... 37 F4
SUD CO10 .... 58 E7
Chelsworth Cl SOS SS1 .... 465 J5
Chelsworth Crs SOS SS1 .... 465 H5
Chelsworth Dr HARH RM3 .... 431 F4
Chelsworth Rd FX IP11 .... 5 D3
Cheltenham Av IP IP1 .... 36 D4
Cheltenham Dr LOS SS9 .... 463 G3
SBF/HAD SS7 .... 441 G6
Cheltenham Gdns LOU IG10 .... 239 J3
Cheltenham Rd HOC/HUL SS5 .. 421 G6
SOS SS1 .... 19 F4
Chelwater CHLM/GWD CM2 .... 15 E5
Chelwood Cl CHIG IG7 .... 402 C2
Chelwood Rd WICKE SS11 .... 418 D4
Chenies Dr LAIN SS15 .... 436 C4
Cheniston Rd BRTR CM7 .... 210 C8
The Cherries CVI SS8 .... 478 A5
Cherry Av RBRW/HUT CM13 ..... 411 J6
Cherry Blossom Cl RIPW IP8 .... 61 H3
Cherry Blossom La RCHLM CM3 ... 366 B8
Cherrybrook SOS SS1 .... 466 B4
Cherry Cha K/T/MI CO5 .... 280 E1
Cherry Cl CBE/LIN CB1 .... 22 D2
CVI SS8 .... 477 J1
HOC/HUL SS5 .... 421 F6
Cherrydene Cl HOC/HUL SS5 ... 419 K3
Cherrydown CDH/CHF RM16 ..... 471 H8
RAYL SS6 .... 441 J1
Cherrydown Av CHING E4 .... 402 A6
Cherrydown Cl CHING E4 .... 402 A6

Cherrydown East VGE SS16 ..... 17 E5
Cherrydown West VGE SS16 .... 17 E5
Cherry Garden La RCHLM CM3 .. 336 A6
SAFWS CB11 .... 100 A5
Cherry Garden Rd MAL CM9 ..... 338 A3
Cherry Gdns BCAYW CM12 .... 413 K1
BSF CM23 .... 199 F5
SBW CM21 .... 263 J1
Cherry Gardens La IPNE IP4 ..... 37 K6
Cherry La HSTD CO9 .... 79 K5
WICKE SS11 .... 417 J6
Cherrymeade SBF/HAD SS7 ..... 461 F5
Cherry Orch BOC CM0 .... 398 E1
Cherry Orchard La RCFD SS4 ... 443 D5
Cherry Orchard Wy RCFD SS4 ... 443 J5
SOSN SS2 .... 443 J6
Cherry Rd PEND EN3 .... 374 C4
Cherry Rw COLW CO3 .... 186 A8
Cherry Tree Av COS CO15 .... 290 E4
Cherrytree Cha SBN/FI SS3 ...... 467 H4
Cherry Tree Cl HAR CO12 .... 164 A6
Cherry Tree Dr SOCK/AV RM15 ... 470 B3
Cherry Tree Ri BKHH IG9 .... 404 A7
Cherrytree Ri WIT CM8 .... 245 C8
Cherrytree Rd SUD CO10 .... 58 E6
Cherry Tree Wk RBRW/HUT CM16 ... 485 F2
Cherrywood Dr COLW CO3 .... 186 A8
Cherrywoods RCOLE CO7 .... 223 J5
Chervil Cl K/T/MI CO5 .... 280 A1
Cherwell Dr CHLM/WR CM1 ...... 303 J3
Cherwell Gv SOCK/AV RM15 .... 469 K7
Chesapeake Cl RIPS/CAP IP9 ... 91 J2
Chesapeake Rd RIPS/CAP IP9 ... 63 J5
Chesfield Cl BSF CM23 .... 198 E8
Chesham Dr LAIN SS15 .... 436 C4
Chesham Rd CHTY IP2 .... 2 C5
Cheshire Cl EMPK RM11 .... 431 H7
Cheshunt Cl RAYL SS6 .... 419 G7
Cheshunts PIT SS13 .... 438 D7
Cheshunt Wash BAR EN8 .... 346 L1
Chessington Gdns IP IP1 .... 2 A1
Chess La WIT CM8 .... 277 G3
Chester Av SOS SS1 .... 465 C7
UPMR RM14 .... 452 B3
Chesterfield Av SBF/HAD SS7 ... 440 C7
Chesterfield Crs LOS SS9 .... 442 E7
Chesterfield Dr IP IP1 .... 36 B3
Chesterford Gdns BSDN SS14 ... 438 C5
Chester Hall La BSDN SS14 ...... 11 F4
Chester Pl CHLM/WR CM1 .... 304 C8
Chester Rd CHIG IG7 .... 404 C6
FX IP11 .... 5 F2
LOU IG10 .... 378 A5
Chesterton Cl CHTY IP2 .... 62 B4
Chestnut Av BCAYW CM12 .... 414 A3
BKHH IG9 .... 404 A6
CDH/CHF RM16 .... 484 A1
COLS CO2 .... 219 H5
COS CO15 .... 290 C3
FOS CO13 .... 228 B7
HCH RM12 .... 450 A3
HSTD CO9 .... 146 D5
MAL CM9 .... 310 E7
RCHLM CM3 .... 308 A2
SAFWS CB11 .... 69 H4
Chestnut Cl BKHH IG9 .... 404 A5
BOC CM0 .... 398 A8
BSF CM23 .... 198 E7
GVW DA11 .... 488 E4
HCH RM12 .... 450 D5
HOC/HUL SS5 .... 421 G7
HVHL CB9 .... 27 F5
KESG IP5 .... 38 C4
SUD CO10 .... 59 H2
Chestnut Gt SAFWS CB11 .... 100 B5
VGE SS16 .... 458 D7
Chestnut Farm Dr RCHLM CM3 .. 396 C3
Chestnut Gln RCHLM CM3 .... 450 A3
Chestnut Gv BRTR CM7 .... 209 H3
BRW CM14 .... 411 F5
SBF/HAD SS7 .... 460 A1
SOSN SS2 .... 19 D2
Chestnut Rd PEND EN3 .... 374 E2
RCOLE CO7 .... 222 A5
VGE SS16 .... 458 D1
Chestnuts RBRW/HUT CM13 .... 412 A4
The Chestnuts CHTY IP2 .... 61 J3
RAYL SS6 .... 441 K1
Chestnut Wk CHLM/WR CM1 .... 304 C8
EPP CM16 .... 321 K6
GTDUN CM6 .... 206 D7
RCHLM CM3 .... 335 J4
Chestnut Wy K/T/MI CO5 .... 248 A7
RBSF CM22 .... 201 K6
RCOLE CO7 .... 255 J6
Chestwood Cl BCAYW CM12 .... 414 C1
Chevalier Rd FX IP11 .... 131 J5
Chevallier St IP IP1 .... 2 B2
Cheveling Rd COLS CO2 .... 220 A3
Chevely Cl EPP CM16 .... 351 H3

Chevening Gdns HOC/HUL SS5 ... 420 D7
Chevers Pawen PIT SS13 .... 438 D8
Chevington Wy HCH RM12 .... 450 E5
Cheviot Dr CHLM/WR CM1 .... 303 K8
Cheviot Rd EMPK RM11 .... 450 B1
Chevy Ct HAR CO12 .... 164 B3
Cheyne Ct SUD CO10 .... 58 B6
WICKW SS12 .... 439 H1
Chichester Cl BSDN SS14 .... 438 C5
CVI SS8 .... 478 A3
SOCK/AV RM15 .... 468 E8
Chichester Dr CHLM/WR CM1 ... 15 D1
Chichester Rd SAFWS CB11 ..... 71 F5
SOS SS1 .... 19 D4
Chichester Wy MAL CM9 .... 338 D5
Chickney Rd RBSF CM22 .... 137 K7
Chieftan Dr PUR RM19 .... 481 H3
Chiffinch Gdns GVW DA11 .... 488 D8
Chigborough Rd MAL CM9 .... 311 H6
Chignall Rd CHLM/WR CM1 ...... 331 K1
The Chignalls LAIN SS15 .... 436 B7
Chigwell La LOU IG10 .... 405 F7
LOU IG10 .... 378 A8
Chigwell Park Dr CHIG IG7 ...... 404 D7
Chigwell Ri CHIG IG7 .... 404 D5
Chilburn Rd COS CO15 .... 259 H6
Childerditch Hall Dr
RBRW/HUT CM13 .... 433 J5
Childerditch La RBRW/HUT CM13 ... 433 K5
Childerditch St RBRW/HUT CM13 ... 433 K5
Childers Cl RIPS/CAP IP9 .... 129 F4
Childers Fld FX IP11 .... 5 D2
The Childers WFD IG8 .... 404 C8
Childs Cl EMPK RM11 .... 430 D8
Childwell Aly COL CO1 .... 8 C5
Chilham Cl PIT SS13 .... 439 F8
Chiltern Cl COL CO1 .... 8 A2
RAYL SS6 .... 441 J2
Chiltern Gdns HCH RM12 .... 450 D4
Chiltern Rd CVW DA11 .... 488 D8
The Chilterns CVI SS8 .... 477 K1
Chiltern Wy WFD IG8 .... 403 H6
Chilton Cl CHLM/GWD CM2 ...... 15 E6
RCOLW CO6 .... 154 C6
Chilton Ct SUD CO10 .... 58 D6
Chilton Lodge Rd SUD CO10 .... 58 D6
Chilton Rd CDH/CHF RM16 ...... 485 F4
IPSE IP3 .... 64 A1
Chilworth Ga BROX EN10 .... 319 F4
The Chimes WFD IG8 .... 460 D1
Chimney Pot La RCHLM CM3 .... 364 E2
Chimswell Wy HVHL CB9 .... 26 D5
China La UPMR RM14 .... 454 C5
Chinchilla Rd SOS SS1 .... 465 G4
Chindit Cl BROX EN10 .... 318 D2
Chindits La RBRW/HUT CM13 ... 411 F8
Chingdale Rd CHING E4 .... 403 F6
Chingford Av CHING E4 .... 402 C6
COS CO15 .... 259 H5
Chingford La WFD IG8 .... 403 F7
Chingford Mount Rd CHING E4 .. 402 B8
Chinnel La SAFWS CB11 .... 69 J8
Chinnery Hl BSF CM23 .... 198 E8
Chinook COLN CO4 .... 187 J1
Chippenham Gdns HARH RM3 ... 408 E8
Chippenham Rd HARH RM3 ...... 430 E1
Chipperfield Cl UPMR RM14 ..... 452 B2
Chippets La COLW CO3 .... 184 B6
Chippingdell WIT CM8 .... 277 F1
Chippingfield HLWE CM17 .... 295 G2
Chipping Hl HSTD CO9 .... 148 A3
WIT CM8 .... 277 F2
Chipstead Wk RCOS CO16 .... 258 E7
Chishill Rd ROY SG8 .... 66 C2
Chisholm Ct WICKW SS12 .... 417 H8
Chislett Rw CHLM/GWD CM2 ... 15 D5
Chittock Cl RCOS CO16 .... 290 D2
Chittock Ga BSDN SS14 .... 438 B7
Chittock Md BSDN SS14 .... 438 B7
Chitts Hl COLW CO3 .... 185 J6
Chivers Rd BRWN CM15 .... 355 H8
BRWN CM15 .... 383 H1
CHING E4 .... 402 C6
HVHL CB9 .... 26 D6
Choats Wd RCOLW CO6 .... 184 E4
Chorley Cl VGE SS16 .... 436 A8
Chrismund Wy RCOLW CO6 ..... 183 F4
Christchurch Av WICKW SS12 ... 416 D5
Christchurch Rd SOSN SS2 ...... 19 F3
TIL RM18 .... 485 F7
Christchurch St IPNE IP4 .... 3 E2
Christie Cl BROX EN10 .... 319 F3
Christina Rd WIT CM8 .... 276 D5
Christine Cha COLW CO3 .... 186 A8
Christmas Fld HSTD CO9 .... 110 C3
Christopher Cl HCH RM12 .... 450 E5
Christopher Dr RCOS CO16 ...... 259 F4
Christopher La SUD CO10 .... 58 B6
Christopher Martin Rd
BSDN SS14 .... 438 B3
Christy Av CHLM/WR CM1 .... 14 A1
Christy Wy LAIN SS15 .... 435 K6
Chudleigh Rd HARH RM3 .... 409 F7
Church Av CHLM/WR CM1 .... 304 C3

Church Cha RCHLM CM3 ..... 391 G8
WIT CM8 ..... 278 B2
Church Cl BRW CM14 ..... 385 F3
BRWN CM15 ..... 385 J5
CVI SS8 ..... 39 F5
KESG IP5 .....
RCOLW CO6 ..... 185 K1
SBN/FI SS3 ..... 466 C7
SLH/COR SS17 ..... 473 F2
SUD CO10 ..... 32 D3
WIT CM8 ..... 277 K8
Church Cnr SBF/HAD SS7 ..... 460 C4
Church Crs BRWN CM15 ..... 385 J5
COS CO15 ..... 10 C5
SOCK/AV RM15 ..... 470 A3
Church Dr BSF CM23 ..... 134 A5
Church End BRTR CM7 ..... 176 E6
GTDUN CM6 ..... 204 C3
HLWW/ROY CM19 ..... 12 A5
Church End Av WICKE SS11 ..... 417 H3
Church End La WICKE SS11 ..... 417 G3
Church Farm Wy COLN CO4 ..... 187 F1
Church Fld EPP CM16 ..... 350 E3
Churchfield HLW CM20 ..... 294 E3
Church Fld SAFWS CB11 ..... 71 F6
Church Field Pth BAR EN8 ..... 346 E3
Church Field Rd SUD CO10 ..... 58 E4
Churchfield Rd RCOLW CO6 ..... 213 H2
WOTN CO14 ..... 229 H5
Church Flds HSTD CO9 ..... 79 J3
Churchfields BROX EN10 ..... 319 G2
K/T/MI CO5 ..... 284 D7
LOU IG10 ..... 377 G8
SBN/FI SS3 ..... 466 D5
STSD CM24 ..... 168 A7
Churchfields Av COLW CO3 ..... 217 H1
Churchfields Dr HVHL CB9 ..... 50 C7
Churchfields La BROX EN10 ..... 319 G2
Church Gdns GTDUN CM6 ..... 204 C3
Churchgate BAR EN8 ..... 346 B4
Churchgate Rd BAR EN8 ..... 346 B3
Church Gn CHLM/WR CM1 ..... 302 B8
HSTD CO9 ..... 80 C1
RCFD SS4 ..... 423 C4
RCOLW CO6 ..... 213 H3
SAFWN CB10 ..... 20 B6
Church Ov RCOLW CO6 ..... 184 A5
Church Hl BRTR CM7 ..... 106 E7
EPP CM16 ..... 350 E3
HAR CO12 ..... 163 K4
HVHL CB9 ..... 49 H5
K/T/MI CO5 ..... 220 C5
LAIN SS15 ..... 16 B3
LOU IG10 ..... 377 H7
MAL CM9 ..... 336 D3
MGTR CO11 ..... 158 E2
RCHLM CM3 ..... 272 E7
RCHLM CM3 ..... 365 K4
RCOLW CO6 ..... 149 K7
SAFWN CB10 ..... 46 D5
SLH/COR SS17 ..... 473 J4
WIT CM8 ..... 243 K5
Church Hollow PUR RM19 ..... 481 H4
Churchill Av HSTD CO9 ..... 78 B2
HVHL CB9 ..... 27 H4
IPNE IP3 ..... 37 K8
Churchill Cl CHONG CM5 ..... 354 C1
RCOLE CO7 ..... 255 K5
Churchill Crs SLH/COR SS17 ..... 474 A1
Churchill Dr SUD CO10 ..... 58 B3
Churchill Ri CHLM/WR CM1 ..... 305 G6
Churchill Rd BRTR CM7 ..... 177 H7
GRAYS RM17 ..... 484 C4
GVW DA11 ..... 488 B4
K/T/MI CO5 ..... 248 D8
Churchill Ter CHING E4 ..... 402 B7
Churchill Wy COLS CO2 ..... 219 J1
Church La ABR/ST RM4 ..... 379 H8
ABR/ST RM4 ..... 380 C3
BAR EN8 ..... 346 C3
BCAYE CM11 ..... 415 J7
BROX EN10 ..... 318 D5
BRTR CM7 ..... 177 J6
BRWN CM15 ..... 231 H3
BSF CM23 ..... 22 E3
CBE/LIN CB1 ..... 48 C2
CBE/LIN CB1 ..... 15 E1
CHLM/WR CM1 ..... 331 H4
CHLM/WR CM1 ..... 305 G6
CHONG CM5 ..... 326 C6
COLW CO3 ..... 186 A7
COLW CO3 ..... 217 F1
EPP CM16 ..... 324 A7
FOS CO13 ..... 261 F2
FX IP11 ..... 5 E1
FX IP11 ..... 94 C6
GTDUN CM6 ..... 202 E6
GTDUN CM6 ..... 266 E6
HSTD CO9 ..... 52 E7
HSTD CO9 ..... 78 E6
HSTD CO9 ..... 110 D1
ING CM4 ..... 358 E7
K/T/MI CO5 ..... 283 F2
K/T/MI CO5 ..... 286 B4

KIR/NAC IP10 ..... 92 D2
KIR/NAC IP10 ..... 94 D2
LOU IG10 ..... 377 H7
MAL CM9 ..... 311 H5
MAL CM9 ..... 311 K3
MGTR CO11 ..... 123 K4
MGTR CO11 ..... 159 K1
NHMKT IP6 ..... 37 H1
NHMKT IP6 ..... 39 F1
PIT SS13 ..... 438 D3
PUR RM19 ..... 481 H4
RBRW/HUT CM13 ..... 412 E4
RBRW/HUT CM13 ..... 433 F8
RBSF CM22 ..... 169 F5
RBSF CM22 ..... 201 J6
RBSF CM22 ..... 264 D5
RCHLM CM3 ..... 239 H7
RCHLM CM3 ..... 240 E5
RCHLM CM3 ..... 389 J1
RCHLM CM3 ..... 390 B5
RCHLM CM3 ..... 393 J2
RCOLW CO6 ..... 118 C4
RCOLW CO6 ..... 215 F2
RCOLW CO6 ..... 215 K1
RCOS CO16 ..... 194 D7
RCOS CO16 ..... 225 H6
RIPS/CAP IP9 ..... 126 E2
RIPS/CAP IP9 ..... 128 B3
RIPW IP8 ..... 60 D5
SAFWS CB11 ..... 101 H6
SUD CO10 ..... 84 A5
UPMR RM14 ..... 452 E6
UPMR RM14 ..... 454 E6
Church Langley Wy HLWE CM17 ..... 295 G5
Church Leys HLWS CM18 ..... 13 F4
Church Md HLWW/ROY CM19 ..... 292 D4
WIT CM8 ..... 243 K4
Church Ms LAIN SS15 ..... 436 C6
Church Pde CVI SS8 ..... 460 D8
Church Pk SUD CO10 ..... 53 F2
Church Park Rd PIT SS13 ..... 438 E8
Church Pth CBE/LIN CB1 ..... 22 D7
GVW DA11 ..... 488 B4
Churchponds HSTD CO9 ..... 110 D1
Church Rd ABR/ST RM4 ..... 381 K5
ABR/ST RM4 ..... 408 E4
BCAYE CM11 ..... 415 K1
BOC CM0 ..... 398 B7
BRTR CM7 ..... 180 A8
BRTR CM7 ..... 209 J3
BRTR CM7 ..... 211 F7
BRTR CM7 ..... 211 J3
BRW CM14 ..... 382 E3
BSDN SS14 ..... 437 K6
BSDN SS14 ..... 438 A7
CBE/LIN CB1 ..... 25 G8
CHLM/GWD CM2 ..... 389 H1
CHONG CM5 ..... 325 J5
CHONG CM5 ..... 353 K7
COLN CO4 ..... 119 H6
COLS CO2 ..... 251 F1
COLS CO15 ..... 10 C5
FX IP11 ..... 131 K1
HARH RM3 ..... 431 H2
HLWE CM17 ..... 295 G8
HOC/HUL SS5 ..... 420 C6
HSTD CO9 ..... 78 A3
HSTD CO9 ..... 79 J3
HSTD CO9 ..... 82 C6
HSTD CO9 ..... 146 C6
HSTD CO9 ..... 148 B8
K/T/MI CO5 ..... 246 E3
K/T/MI CO5 ..... 248 A3
K/T/MI CO5 ..... 251 K8
K/T/MI CO5 ..... 284 D7
KIR/NAC IP10 ..... 92 A1
LAIN SS15 ..... 16 C1
LOU IG10 ..... 376 C2
MAL CM9 ..... 308 C7
MAL CM9 ..... 311 F3
MAL CM9 ..... 312 D3
MGTR CO11 ..... 162 B1
PIT SS13 ..... 439 H8
RAYL SS6 ..... 441 K3
RBRW/HUT CM13 ..... 385 J3
RBRW/HUT CM13 ..... 435 H8
RBSF CM22 ..... 200 B8
RBSF CM22 ..... 232 C3
RCFD SS4 ..... 421 K6
RCHLM CM3 ..... 275 F3
RCHLM CM3 ..... 306 C5
RCHLM CM3 ..... 308 A2
RCHLM CM3 ..... 394 B6
RCOLE CO7 ..... 189 K7
RCOLE CO7 ..... 192 A6
RCOLE CO7 ..... 222 A6
RCOLE CO7 ..... 222 A5
RCOLE CO7 ..... 223 F8
RCOLE CO7 ..... 255 J4
RCOLW CO6 ..... 119 F7
RCOLW CO6 ..... 152 C8
RCOLW CO6 ..... 216 D3
RIPS/CAP IP9 ..... 87 K6
RIPS/CAP IP9 ..... 88 C7

RIPS/CAP IP9 ..... 125 H3
RIPS/CAP IP9 ..... 126 B1
ROY SG8 ..... 67 G2
SAFWN CB10 ..... 74 E5
SBF/HAD SS7 ..... 440 B7
SBF/HAD SS7 ..... 461 K2
SBN/FI SS3 ..... 446 D6
SBN/FI SS3 ..... 466 B7
SLH/COR SS17 ..... 474 D7
SOS SS1 ..... 19 D5
STSD CM24 ..... 168 A8
SUD CO10 ..... 57 F8
SUD CO10 ..... 58 D8
SUD CO10 ..... 83 G2
SUD CO10 ..... 83 H7
TIL RM18 ..... 484 D7
TIL RM18 ..... 485 K5
UPMR RM14 ..... 454 E8
VGE SS16 ..... 459 H1
WICKE SS11 ..... 418 C6
WIT CM8 ..... 245 H6
WIT CM8 ..... 277 K8
WOTN CO14 ..... 229 H5
Church Sq BURES CO8 ..... 115 J4
RCOS CO16 ..... 289 G1
Church St BCAYE CM11 ..... 414 D8
BCAYW CM12 ..... 414 C8
BRTR CM7 ..... 177 K4
BSF CM23 ..... 198 E6
CHLM/GWD CM2 ..... 333 J7
COLN CO4 ..... 119 H6
COLW CO3 ..... 8 A4
GRAYS RM17 ..... 484 B5
GTDUN CM6 ..... 204 C3
GVW DA11 ..... 489 G4
HAR CO12 ..... 7 E2
HSTD CO9 ..... 81 K5
HSTD CO9 ..... 110 C4
HSTD CO9 ..... 111 J4
HVHL CB9 ..... 26 C5
HVHL CB9 ..... 50 C6
ING CM4 ..... 356 C2
K/T/MI CO5 ..... 220 C5
K/T/MI CO5 ..... 246 D3
MAL CM9 ..... 312 C2
MAL CM9 ..... 313 H7
MAL CM9 ..... 314 D4
MAL CM9 ..... 338 D3
RBSF CM22 ..... 137 F1
RCOLW CO6 ..... 149 H6
RCOLW CO6 ..... 213 H2
RIPS/CAP IP9 ..... 91 H6
SAFWN CB10 ..... 43 F7
SAFWN CB10 ..... 43 J2
SAFWN CB10 ..... 70 E8
SAFWS CB11 ..... 69 K6
SAFWS CB11 ..... 100 B6
SAFWS CB11 ..... 136 E1
SBW CM21 ..... 263 J3
SUD CO10 ..... 31 F7
SUD CO10 ..... 55 C2
SUD CO10 ..... 58 A
WAB EN9 ..... 347 J7
WIT CM8 ..... 277 F7
Church Vw BROX EN10 ..... 319 F2
RCOLE CO7 ..... 157 H6
SOCK/AV RM15 ..... 481 K
UPMR RM14 ..... 451 J
Church View Rd SBF/HAD SS7 ..... 440 B7
Church Wk COL CO1 ..... 8 A4
GVE DA12 ..... 489 J
HVHL CB9 ..... 51 F
SAFWS CB11 ..... 70 A
SBW CM21 ..... 263 K
SUD CO10 ..... 35 F
SUD CO10 ..... 58 B6
Churchway SBF/HAD SS7 ..... 462 A1
Churchwell Av K/T/MI CO5 ..... 215 K
Chuzzlewit Dr CHLM/WR CM1 ..... 304 A6
Cimarron Cl RCHLM CM3 ..... 392 D6
Cinque Port Rd RCOLE CO7 ..... 255 K
Circular Rd East COLS CO2 ..... 8 B
Circular Rd North COLS CO2 ..... 8 A
Circular Rd South COLS CO2 ..... 219 F
Circular Rd West COLS CO2 ..... 8 A
City Rd K/T/MI CO5 ..... 284 C
Civic Dr IP IP1 ..... 2 C
Civic Sq TIL RM18 ..... 485 F
Clachar Cl CHLM/GWD CM2 ..... 333 J2
Clacton Rd FOS CO13 ..... 260 E
HAR CO12 ..... 163 K
MGTR CO11 ..... 160 A
RCOLE CO7 ..... 189 F
RCOLE CO7 ..... 190 A
RCOLE CO7 ..... 223 F
RCOS CO16 ..... 225 H
RCOS CO16 ..... 289 F
Claire Cl RBRW/HUT CM13 ..... 411 K
Claire Rd FOS CO13 ..... 228 A
Clairmont Cl BRTR CM7 ..... 209 J3
Clairmont Rd COLW CO3 ..... 185 G
Clairvale EMPK RM11 ..... 451 K
Clapgate Dr RCOS CO16 ..... 258 E
Clapgate La IPSE IP3 ..... 63 J

Clapton Hall La *GTDUN* CM6 .... 204 C8
Clara Reeve Cl *COLW* CO3 .... 218 A1
Clare Av *WICKE* SS11 .... 417 G3
Clare Cl *HSTD* CO9 .... 147 K6
Clare Ct *GTDUN* CM6 .... 139 J2
Clare Ms *CHONG* CM5 .... 326 C8
Claremont Cl *CDH/CHF* RM16 .... 484 B2 🔟
WOS/PRIT SS0 .... 18 B3 🔟
Claremont Dr *VGE* SS16 .... 458 C1
Claremont Gdns *UPMR* RM14 .... 452 A2
Claremont Hts *COL* CO1 .... 8 A2
Claremont Rd *EMPK* RM11 .... 430 B8
LAIN SS15 .... 16 A3
LAIN SS15 .... 436 C6
RCOLE CO7 .... 221 F5
WOS/PRIT SS0 .... 18 A3
Clarence Av *UPMR* RM14 .... 451 H3
Clarence Cl *CHLM/GWD* CM2 .... 333 J1 🔟
SBF/HAD SS7 .... 460 C1
Clarence Pl *BCAYW* CM12 .... 489 G5
Clarence Rd *BRWN* CM15 .... 410 E2
GRAYS RM17 .... 483 K5
IPSE IP3 .... 63 K4
PIT SS13 .... 439 J6
RAYL SS6 .... 442 B4
SBF/HAD SS7 .... 460 C1
SLH/COR SS17 .... 474 E1
SOS SS1 .... 19 D5
STSD CM24 .... 167 K6 🔟
SUD CO10 .... 31 F4
SUD CO10 .... 58 B5
Clarence Rd North *SBF/HAD* SS7 .... 460 C1
Clarence Rw *GVE* DA12 .... 489 G5
Clarence St *SOS* SS1 .... 19 D5
Clarendon Pk *COS* CO15 .... 11 E2
Clarendon Rd *BAR* EN8 .... 346 D3
CVI SS8 .... 478 B3
GVE DA12 .... 478 C1
HVHL CB9 .... 27 F6
PIT SS13 .... 439 F6
RBSF CM22 .... 202 B6
Clarendon Wy *COL* CO1 .... 8 A2
Clare Rd *BRTR* CM7 .... 209 G3
IPNE IP4 .... 37 H5
SBF/HAD SS7 .... 439 K7
SUD CO10 .... 31 F5
Clare Wy *RCOS* CO16 .... 258 C8
Clarkbourne Dr *GRAYS* RM17 .... 484 C5
Clark Cl *ERITH* DA8 .... 480 B7
Clarke Ri *RCHLM* CM3 .... 366 B8
Clarkesmead *K/T/MI* CO5 .... 280 A1 🔟
Clarke's Rd *HAR* CO12 .... 6 A5
Clarkhill *HLWS* CM18 .... 322 C1
Clarks Farm Rd *RCHLM* CM3 .... 335 K5 🔟
Clarks La *EPP* CM16 .... 350 D5 🔟
Clarkson St *IP* IP1 .... 2 C3
Clarks Wood Dr *BRTR* CM7 .... 210 C2 🔟
Clark Wy *CHLM/WR* CM1 .... 304 C4 🔟
Claters Cl *SOSN* SS2 .... 465 J3
Clatterbury La *CBE/LIN* CB11 .... 98 D6
Clatterfield Gdns *WOS/PRIT* SS0 .... 463 H3
Claude Oliver Cl *MGTR* CO11 .... 159 F3
Claude St *IP* IP1 .... 3 D3
Claudian Cl *HVHL* CB9 .... 27 K6
Claudian Rd *CDH/CHF* RM16 .... 485 G2
Claud Ince Av *BRTR* CM7 .... 210 C7
Claudius Rd *COLS* CO2 .... 8 C6
Claudius Wy *WIT* CM8 .... 276 E5
Claughton Wy *RBRW/HUT* CM13 .... 412 C2
Claverhambury Rd *WAB* EN9 .... 348 B3
Clavering Cl *RAYL* SS6 .... 441 G2 🔟
Clavering Gdns *RBRW/HUT* CM13 .... 434 C8
Clavering Rd *BRTR* CM7 .... 177 J7 🔟
Clavering Wy *RBRW/HUT* CM13 .... 412 A2
Claverton *IPNE* IP4 .... 38 B8 🔟
IPNE IP4 .... 64 C1 🔟
Claybrick Av *HOC/HUL* SS5 .... 420 E8 🔟
Clayburn Cir *BSDN* SS14 .... 458 A7
Clayburn Gdns *SOCK/AV* RM15 .... 469 K7 🔟
Claydon Cl *CBE/LIN* CB11 .... 48 D1
Claydon Crs *BSDN* SS14 .... 437 H5
Claydons La *SBF/HAD* SS7 .... 441 H5
Claygate Cl *HCH* RM12 .... 450 B5 🔟
Clayhall Rd *COS* CO15 .... 11 D2
Clay Hl *SUD* CO10 .... 83 K5
Clay Hill Rd *VGE* SS16 .... 17 F5
VGE SS16 .... 438 B3
VGE SS16 .... 458 B1 🔟
Clayhive Dr *HVHL* CB9 .... 27 F6 🔟
Clay La *GTDUN* CM6 .... 173 J6
RCOS CO16 .... 257 J5
Clay Lane Gv *COLN* CO4 .... 188 A1
Claypit Hl *RBSF* CM22 .... 169 F8
WAB EN9 .... 376 E2
Clay Pit Piece *SAFWS* CB11 .... 71 F7
Claypits La *SUD* CO10 .... 115 J5
Claypits Rd *RCHLM* CM3 .... 306 D4
Clay Pits Wy *BRTR* CM7 .... 210 C2 🔟
Clayponds *BSF* CM23 .... 199 F6
Clayshotts Dr *WIT* CM8 .... 277 H5
Clay's La *LOU* IG10 .... 377 J5
Clayspring Cl *HOC/HUL* SS5 .... 420 E6
Clays Rd *WOTN* CO14 .... 229 F5

Clayton Av *UPMR* RM14 .... 451 J6
Clayton Rd *HAR* CO12 .... 164 B3
Clayton Wy *MAL* CM9 .... 338 C5
Clay Tye Rd *UPMR* RM14 .... 453 F4
Claywall Br *HVHL* CB9 .... 50 C6
Cleall Av *WAB* EN9 .... 347 J8
Clearwater *COLS* CO2 .... 219 J1
Cleland Pth *LOU* IG10 .... 377 K5
Clematis Cl *HARH* RM3 .... 430 D2
Clematis Gdns *WFD* IG8 .... 403 H8
Clematis Wy *COLN* CO4 .... 188 B6
Clement Cl *BAR* EN8 .... 346 E1 🔟
Clements Cl *CHLM/GWD* CM2 .... 333 K2
HVHL CB9 .... 27 F6
Clements Dr *HVHL* CB9 .... 27 F6
Clements Gdns *HOC/HUL* SS5 .... 421 H8
Clements Green La *RCHLM* CM3 .... 392 D5
Clements Hall La *HOC/HUL* SS5 .... 421 H8
Clements Hall Wy *HOC/HUL* SS5 .... 443 H1
Clement's La *HVHL* CB9 .... 27 F6
Clements Pl *RCHLM* CM3 .... 392 D5 🔟
Clement Wy *RCH* RM12 .... 451 G4
Clench Rd *RIPS/CAP* IP9 .... 90 A6
Clerks Piece *LOU* IG10 .... 377 H7
Clermont Av *SUD* CO10 .... 58 B3
Clevedon Cl *BRTR* CM7 .... 209 F6 🔟
Cleveland Cl *COLN* CO4 .... 187 K1
Cleveland Dr *WOS/PRIT* SS0 .... 18 A1
Cleveland Rd *BSDN* SS14 .... 437 K7
CVI SS8 .... 478 B3
Cleves Av *BRW* CM14 .... 410 E4
Cleves Ct *RCHLM* CM3 .... 306 C4 🔟
Cleves Rd *HVHL* CB9 .... 26 D6
Clevis Dr *RCHLM* CM3 .... 393 F8
Clicket Hl *BURES* CO8 .... 116 A5
Clickett End *BSDN* SS14 .... 437 K7
Clickett Hl *BSDN* SS14 .... 437 K7
Clickett Side *BSDN* SS14 .... 437 K7 🔟
Clieveden Rd *SOS* SS1 .... 465 J7
Cliff Av *WOS/PRIT* SS0 .... 18 B3
WOS/PRIT SS0 .... 463 H5
Cliff Crs *BRTR* CM7 .... 144 B6
Cliff Gdns *LOS* SS9 .... 463 H5
Cliffield *BRTR* CM7 .... 144 B6
Cliff La *IPSE* IP3 .... 63 H2
Clifford Cl *LAIN* SS15 .... 16 B5
Clifford Rd *CDH/CHF* RM16 .... 483 J1
IPNE IP4 .... 37 H8
Cliff Pde *LOS* SS9 .... 463 F5
WOTN CO14 .... 229 K3
Cliff Rd *COS* CO15 .... 260 C8
HAR CO12 .... 7 D4
IPSE IP3 .... 3 F6
LOS SS9 .... 463 H5
Cliffsea Gv *LOS* SS9 .... 463 G4
Clifftown Pde *SOS* SS1 .... 18 C5
Clifftown Rd *SOS* SS1 .... 19 D5
Cliff Wy *FOS* CO13 .... 229 F8
Clifton Av *SBF/HAD* SS7 .... 460 B1
Clifton Cl *BAR* EN8 .... 346 E3
SBF/HAD SS7 .... 460 C1
Clifton Dr *WOS/PRIT* SS0 .... 18 A5
Clifton Gv *GVW* DA11 .... 489 G5
Clifton Hatch *HLWS* CM18 .... 294 E8 🔟
Clifton Marine Pde *GVW* DA11 .... 488 E4
Clifton Ms *SOS* SS1 .... 19 D5
Clifton Rd *CVI* SS8 .... 478 D5
EMPK RM11 .... 430 B8
GVW DA11 .... 489 F4
LOU IG10 .... 377 J5
PIT SS13 .... 439 J6
RCFD SS4 .... 421 K6
Clifton Ter *SOS* SS1 .... 19 D5
Clifton Wy *CHTY* IP2 .... 61 K3
RBRW/HUT CM13 .... 412 C4
SBF/HAD SS7 .... 460 B1
Clifton Wd *RIPS/CAP* IP9 .... 90 A7
Climmen Rd *CVI* SS8 .... 461 G8 🔟
Clinton Cl *RCHLM* CM3 .... 363 G6 🔟
Clinton Rd *CVI* SS8 .... 477 H2
Clipped Hedge *RBSF* CM22 .... 265 G2
Clitheroe Rd *CRW* RM5 .... 407 H8
Clive Av *IP* IP1 .... 36 D3
Cliveden Cl *BRWN* CM15 .... 411 J3
CHLM/WR CM1 .... 332 A2
Clivedon Rd *CHING* E4 .... 403 F8
Clive Rd *COLS* CO2 .... 8 B6
EN EN1 .... 374 A8
GPK RM2 .... 430 C7
GVW DA11 .... 489 G4
RBRW/HUT CM13 .... 433 F2
Clive Wy *EN* EN1 .... 374 A8
Clockhouse La *CDH/CHF* RM16 .... 470 B8
Clock House Rd *BCAYW* CM12 .... 413 K8
Clockhouse Wy *BRTR* CM7 .... 210 A3
Cloes La *RCOS* CO16 .... 290 D1
Cloisters *SLH/COR* SS17 .... 474 A3
The Cloisters *BRTR* CM7 .... 177 K8
K/T/MI CO5 .... 246 D4
LAIN SS15 .... 16 A4 🔟
Cloncurry Gdns *FX* IP11 .... 5 D4
Clopton Dr *SUD* CO10 .... 34 E7
The Close *BRTR* CM7 .... 210 D7
BRW CM14 .... 411 G6

CDH/CHF RM16 .... 484 A1
COS CO15 .... 290 C6
FOS CO13 .... 228 D8
FOS CO13 .... 260 E2
HAR CO12 .... 6 B5
RBSF CM22 .... 265 G2
RIPS/CAP IP9 .... 88 E6
SAFWS CB11 .... 101 J6 🔟
SUD CO10 .... 58 C5
Cloudberry Rd *HARH* RM3 .... 430 E1 🔟
Clouded Yellow Cl *BRTR* CM7 .... 209 H5 🔟
Cloudesley Rd *ERITH* DA8 .... 480 A7
Clough Rd *COLN* CO4 .... 155 K7
Clova Rd *LOS* SS9 .... 463 G3 🔟
Clovelly Cl *IPNE* IP4 .... 64 D1
Clovelly Gdns *WICKE* SS11 .... 417 F5
Clover Av *BSF* CM23 .... 198 A7
Clover Cl *CHTY* IP2 .... 2 A5
VGE SS16 .... 458 B2 🔟
Clover Ct *CBE/LIN* CB1 .... 23 F3 🔟
SUD CO10 .... 59 F7
Clover Dr *RCOLE* CO7 .... 223 F8
Clover Fld *HLWS* CM18 .... 294 E8
HVHL CB9 .... 26 C5
Cloverlands *COLN* CO4 .... 9 E2
Clover Leas *EPP* CM16 .... 350 D3
Cloverley Rd *CHONG* CM5 .... 354 C4
Clovers *HSTD* CO9 .... 147 J4 🔟
Clover Wy *RCOLE* CO7 .... 156 E8
VGE SS16 .... 458 B2
Cluanie Orch *SUD* CO10 .... 32 E4
Club Pde *RCOS* CO16 .... 289 H7
Clunas Gdns *GPK* RM2 .... 430 E5
Cluny Sq *SOSN* SS2 .... 19 F2
Clyde *TIL* RM18 .... 486 D3
Clyde Crs *CHLM/WR* CM1 .... 331 K1
RAYL SS6 .... 441 H4
UPMR RM14 .... 432 B8
Clyde Rd *HOD* EN11 .... 319 K1
Clydesdale *PEND* EN3 .... 374 D8
Clydesdale Rd *BRTR* CM7 .... 209 H2
EMPK RM11 .... 450 A1
Clyfton Cl *BROX* EN10 .... 319 F5
Coach House Wy *WIT* CM8 .... 277 F3 🔟
Coach La *MAL* CM9 .... 338 B2 🔟
Coachman's Paddock
RIPS/CAP IP9 .... 90 A7
Coach Ms *RCALE* CM11 .... 387 K8
Coach Rd *RCOLE* CO7 .... 222 A6
RCOLW CO6 .... 153 K5
SAFWN CB10 .... 74 D3
Coalport Cl *HLWE* CM17 .... 295 G6
Coan Av *COS* CO15 .... 10 A6
Coast Rd *K/T/MI* CO5 .... 284 C7
Coates Cl *MAL* CM9 .... 338 D1 🔟
Coats Hutton Rd *COLS* CO2 .... 218 C2
Cobbett Cl *PEND* EN3 .... 374 C2
Cobbin's Br *EPP* CM16 .... 350 B1
Cobbins Cha *BOC* CM0 .... 398 B5
Cobbins Cl *BOC* CM0 .... 398 B6
Cobbinsend Rd *WAB* EN9 .... 349 F3
The Cobbins *BOC* CM0 .... 398 B5
WAB EN9 .... 348 A6
Cobbins Wy *HLWE* CM17 .... 295 J1
The Cobbles *BRWN* CM15 .... 411 H5
UPMR RM14 .... 452 C1
Cobbold Rd *FX* IP11 .... 131 H3
Cobbold St *IPNE* IP4 .... 3 E3 🔟
Cobbs La *RBSF* CM22 .... 202 C2
Cobham *CDH/CHF* RM16 .... 484 A1
Cobham Rd *IPSE* IP3 .... 64 A2
WOS/PRIT SS0 .... 463 K6
Cobham St *GVW* DA11 .... 489 F5
Cobill Cl *EMPK* RM11 .... 430 E6
Coburg La *VGE* SS16 .... 456 A1
Coburg Pl *RCHLM* CM3 .... 392 D7
Cock and Bell La *SUD* CO10 .... 34 E5
Cockaynes La *RCOLE* CO7 .... 221 K4
Cockerell Cl *PIT* SS13 .... 438 E4
Cocker Rd *EN* EN1 .... 374 B2
Cockethurst Cl *WOS/PRIT* SS0 .... 463 H1
Cockett Wick La *RCOS* CO16 .... 289 J4
Cock La *BROX* EN10 .... 318 C1
CHLM/WR CM1 .... 357 K3
SAFWS CB11 .... 133 J2
Cockrell's Rd *RCOLW* CO6 .... 153 G1
Cock Rd *HSTD* CO9 .... 112 C4
Codenham Gn *VGE* SS16 .... 17 F6
Codenham Straight *VGE* SS16 .... 17 F6
Codham Hall La *RBRW/HUT* CM13 .... 432 E7
Codham Little Park Dr *BRTR* CM7 .... 144 E7
Cody Rd *IPSE* IP3 .... 64 A4
Coeur De Lion *COLN* CO4 .... 8 B1 🔟
Coggeshall Rd *BRTR* CM7 .... 209 J2
K/T/MI CO5 .... 213 J7
RCOLE CO7 .... 157 J3
RCOLW CO6 .... 181 K1
RCOLW CO6 .... 212 B3
Coggeshall Road (Feering)
K/T/MI CO5 .... 213 J4
Coggeshall Wy *HSTD* CO9 .... 148 B3 🔟
Cogmore *SAFWS* CB11 .... 68 A6
Cohen Cl *BAR* EN8 .... 346 E6
Cohort Dr *COLS* CO2 .... 218 B3
Cokefield Av *SOSN* SS2 .... 19 F1

Coker Rd *CVI* SS8............................... 477 H3
Coke St *HAR* CO12............................... 7 E3
Colam La *RCHLM* CM3............................ 335 C2
Colbert Av *SOS* SS1............................. 465 H6
Colbourne Cl *SLH/COR* SS17..................... 474 B2
Colchester Cl *WOS/PRIT* SS0.................... 18 C2
Colchester Rd *BURES* CO8....................... 115 J6
  CHLM/GWD CM2................................ 305 J7
  COLN CO4..................................... 188 D8
  COS CO15..................................... 11 F2
  HAR CO12..................................... 193 H2
  HARH RM3.................................... 431 F2
  HSTD CO9.................................... 148 A4
  IPNE IP4.................................... 37 G4
  K/T/MI CO5................................. 284 E6
  MAL CM9.................................... 279 F8
  MAL CM9.................................... 282 A7
  MAL CM9.................................... 282 B3
  MAL CM9.................................... 310 D8
  MGTR CO11................................. 159 G2
  RCOLE CO7................................. 121 H8
  RCOLE CO7................................. 157 F7
  RCOLE CO7................................. 189 H7
  RCOLE CO7................................. 220 E1
  RCOLE CO7................................. 223 K2
  RCOLW CO6................................ 150 B6
  RCOLW CO6................................ 213 K3
  RCOS CO16................................ 224 E4
  SOSN SS2................................. 18 C2
  WIT CM8.................................. 277 H2
Cold Hall Cha *RCOLE* CO7...................... 190 D7
Coldham Gv *PEND* EN3......................... 374 E3
Coldharbour Rd *GVW* DA11..................... 488 D7
  HLWW/ROY CM19........................... 12 A4
Coldnailhurst Av *BRTR* CM7................... 177 J8
  BRTR CM7................................. 209 H1
Cold Norton Rd *RCHLM* CM3.................... 367 F8
Cold Store Rd *FX* IP11........................ 4 B5
Cole Av *CDH/CHF* RM16......................... 485 H3
Colebrook Gdns *LOU* IG10..................... 377 K6
Colebrook La *LOU* IG10........................ 377 K6
Cole Hl *RCHLM* CM3............................ 134 B1
Colehills Cl *SAFWS* CB11...................... 464 A1
Colemans Av *WOS/PRIT* SS0................... 335 H6
Colemans La *RCHLM* CM3....................... 319 K8
  WAB EN9.................................. 19 D3
Coleman St *SOSN* SS2........................ 19 D3
Cole Ness Rd *IPSE* IP3........................ 63 J5
Coleridge Rd *HARH* RM3....................... 430 C2
  IP IP1.................................... 36 B2
  MAL CM9................................. 338 C4
  TIL RM18................................ 485 H8
Coleridge Wk *RBRW/HUT* CM13................. 412 B3
Coles Cl *CHONG* CM5.......................... 326 C8
Coles Gn *LOU* IG10........................... 377 K5
Coles La *CBE/LIN* CB1......................... 22 E3
  WOTN CO14............................... 229 F2
Coles Oak La *RCOLE* CO7...................... 121 F7
Colet Rd *RBRW/HUT* CM13..................... 412 D1
College Av *IPSE* IP3.......................... 78 D1
College Cl *GVW* DA11......................... 488 D3
Collingwood Av *IPSE* IP3...................... 63 K2
Collingwood Cl *BRTR* CM7..................... 178 B8
Collingwood Flds *RCOLE* CO7.................. 122 A1
Collingwood Rd *COLW* CO6..................... 185 K7
  COS CO15................................ 10 A6
  RCHLM CM3.............................. 393 F7
  VGE SS16................................ 458 A1
  WIT CM8................................ 277 G3
Collingwood Wk *VGE* SS16..................... 438 A8
Collingwood Wy *SBN/FI* SS3.................. 466 D4
Collins Cl *BRTR* CM7.......................... 209 J3
  SLH/COR SS17........................... 474 A3
Collins Cross *BSF* CM23...................... 199 G4
Collins Meadow *HLWW/ROY* CM19.............. 12 B3
Collins Rd *HSTD* CO9......................... 113 F3
Collins Wy *LOS* SS9.......................... 300 A1
  RBRW/HUT CM13.......................... 412 D1
Collinwood Av *PEND* EN3..................... 374 C7
Colman Cl *SLH/COR* SS17..................... 473 K2
Colmore Rd *PEND* EN3........................ 374 C8

Colne *TIL* RM18.............................. 486 D2
Colne Cha *WIT* CM8.......................... 276 E3
Colne Cl *RCHLM* CM3......................... 392 D6
  SOCK/AV RM15........................... 470 A7
Colne Dr *HARH* RM3.......................... 431 G1
  SBN/FI SS3.............................. 466 D4
Coleford Hl *RCOLW* CO6....................... 150 A7
Colneis Rd *FX* IP11.......................... 131 H1
Colne Park Rd *RCOLW* CO6.................... 150 A5
Colne Pl *VGE* SS16.......................... 437 K8
Colne Ri *K/T/MI* CO5......................... 220 C5
Colne Rd *BURES* CO8......................... 115 H5
  COS CO15............................... 10 C5
  HSTD CO9............................... 110 D5
  HSTD CO9............................... 148 A3
  RCOLE CO7.............................. 255 J7
  RCOLW CO6............................. 181 H6
  RCOLW CO6............................. 213 H2
Colne Springs *HSTD* CO9..................... 52 E6
Colne Va *UPMR* RM14......................... 432 B8
Colne Valley Cl *HSTD* CO9................... 147 J3
Colne Valley Rd *HVHL* CB9.................. 27 G6
Colne Vw *RCOS* CO16........................ 288 A3
Colne Wy *RCOS* CO16........................ 287 K1
Colneys Cl *SUD* CO10........................ 58 A4
The Colonnade *BAR* EN8..................... 346 D2
Colson Pth *LOU* IG10........................ 377 J8
Colson Rd *LOU* IG10......................... 377 K8
Colthorpe Rd *COS* CO15...................... 259 H5
Coltishall Cl *WICKE* SS11................... 418 A7
Coltishall Rd *HCH* RM12..................... 450 D7
Colts Cft *ROY* SG8........................... 66 B3
Coltsfield *STSD* CM24....................... 107 K6
Coltsfoot Cl *COLN* CO4...................... 186 D5
  GRAYS RM17............................ 484 C5
Coltsfoot Pth *HARH* RM3.................... 430 E2
Coltsfoot Rd *CHTY* IP2...................... 62 A1
The Colts *BSF* CM23......................... 231 J2
Columbia Cl *KESG* IP5........................ 38 E6
Columbia Wharf Rd *GRAYS* RM17............. 483 K5
Columbine Gdns *CHTY* IP2.................... 36 A8
  FOS CO13.............................. 229 G6
Columbine Ms *COLW* CO3..................... 185 H6
The Columbines *SUD* CO10................... 32 E3
Columbine Wy *HARH* RM3.................... 431 F3
Colvers *HLWE* CM17.......................... 297 J3
Colville Cl *BRTR* CM7........................ 209 F6
  SLH/COR SS17.......................... 457 C8
Colville Ms *BCAYW* CM12.................... 387 F8
Colvin Cha *CHLM/GWD* CM2................... 360 D4
Colvin Cl *COLW* CO3......................... 186 A7
Colvin Gdns *BAR* EN8........................ 374 D1
  CHING E4.............................. 402 D6
Colwall Gdns *WFD* IG8....................... 403 H8
Colworth Rd *SBF/HAD* SS7................... 461 J1
Colyer Rd *GVW* DA11......................... 488 C7
Colyers Reach *CHLM/CWD* CM2............... 333 J3
Comet Cl *PUR* RM19.......................... 481 H3
Comfrey Ct *GRAYS* RM17..................... 484 C5
Comma Cl *BRTR* CM7......................... 209 H4
Commerce Pk *COLS* CO2...................... 220 A1
Commerce Rd *COLS* CO2...................... 220 A1
  MGTR CO11............................ 123 H8
Commercial Pl *GVE* DA12.................... 489 H4
Commercial Rd *IP* IP1....................... 2 C5
  WOS/PRIT SS0.......................... 18 A1
Common Ap *SBF/HAD* SS7.................... 441 F7
Commonfields *HLW* CM20.................... 13 E2
Commonhall La *SBF/HAD* SS7................. 461 J2
Common Hl *SAFWN* CB10...................... 70 E3
Common La *ING* CM4......................... 388 A3
  MAL CM9............................... 336 B3
  RCHLM CM3............................. 335 J3
  ROY SG8............................... 66 E6
  SBF/HAD SS7........................... 441 F6
Common Rd *ING* CM4......................... 388 A2
  RBRW/HUT CM13........................ 412 B6
  SBN/FI SS3............................ 467 G1
  WAB EN9.............................. 321 C3
Commonside Rd *HLWS* CM18................... 322 D1
The Commons *COLW* CO3...................... 186 B6
Common St *SUD* CO10......................... 31 F5
The Common *RCHLM* CM3...................... 335 J7
  RCHLM CM3............................ 363 F5
  SBF/HAD SS7.......................... 441 F6
Compasses Rd *BRTR* CM7.................... 180 A8
Compton Av *GPK* RM2........................ 430 C5
  RBRW/HUT CM13....................... 412 B4
Compton Ct *CVI* SS8........................ 478 D3
Compton Pl *ERITH* DA8..................... 480 A5
Compton Rd *COLN* CO4....................... 9 D3
Comyns Pl *CHLM/WR* CM1.................... 331 H4
Conan Doyle Cl *BRTR* CM7................. 209 K5
Concord Rd *CVI* SS8......................... 219 K1
Conder Wy *COLS* CO2......................... 336 E7
Conduit La *MAL* CM9......................... 336 C6
Coney Burrows *CHING* E4.................... 403 F5
Coney Gn *SBW* CM23......................... 263 H2
Conference Cl *CHING* E4.................... 402 D5
Congreve Rd *IP* IP1.......................... 36 D3
  WAB EN9.............................. 348 A7
Conies Rd *HSTD* CO9......................... 147 J6
Conifer Av *CRW* RM5......................... 407 G8
Conifer Cl *COLN* CO4........................ 9 F3
  RCOLE CO7............................. 221 J6

Conifer Dr *BRW* CM14........................ 411 G8
Conifers *SBF/HAD* SS7...................... 461 K6
Coniston *LOS* SS9........................... 445 H8
Coniston Av *UPMR* RM14..................... 209 F7
Coniston Cl *BRTR* CM7....................... 177 K5
  RAYL SS6............................. 441 K5
Coniston Rd *CVI* SS8........................ 478 A2
  IPSE IP5............................. 63 K5
  SBF/HAD SS7.......................... 440 D6
Coniston Wy *HCH* RM12...................... 450 B6
Connaught Av *CDH/CHF* RM16................ 484 A5
  CHING E4............................. 402 E3
  FOS CO13............................. 261 K5
  LOU IG10............................. 377 F8
Connaught Cl *COS* CO15..................... 11 E2
Connaught Dr *RCHLM* CM3................... 392 C6
Connaught Gdns *BRTR* CM7.................. 210 A3
  SBN/FI SS3........................... 466 B8
Connaught Gdns East *COS* CO15............. 11 E3
Connaught Gdns West *COS* CO15............. 11 E3
Connaught Hl *LOU* IG10..................... 377 F6
Connaught Rd *CHING* E4..................... 403 F3
  HCH RM12............................. 450 E5
  HVHL CB9............................. 26 E6
  RAYL SS6............................. 442 C5
  RCOS CO16............................ 225 J8
Connaught Wy *BCAYW* CM12................. 387 G5
Connington Crs *CHING* E4.................... 402 E6
Connop Rd *PEND* EN3........................ 374 D7
Conqueror Cl *RCHLM* CM3................... 308 B2
Conrad Cl *CDH/CHF* RM16................... 484 A4
Conrad Gdns *CDH/CHF* RM16................. 483 K6
Conrad Rd *SLH/COR* SS17.................... 474 A4
  WIT CM8.............................. 245 F7
Consort Cl *BRW* CM14....................... 411 F7
Constable Av *RCOS* CO16.................... 258 E5
Constable Cl *COLN* CO4...................... 187 F7
  K/T/MI CO5........................... 285 F1
  MGTR CO11........................... 159 G1
Constable Rd *FX* IP11....................... 131 J2
  GVW DA11............................. 488 D7
  HVHL CB9............................. 26 D5
  IPNE IP4............................. 58 B3
  SUD CO10............................. 58 B8
Constable Wy *SBN/FI* SS3................... 466 E5
Constance Cl *CHLM/WR* CM1................. 304 D2
  WIT CM8............................. 277 G2
Constantine Rd *COLW* CO3.................. 186 E5
  IP IP1............................... 2 C5
  WIT CM8.............................. 276 E5
Constitution Hl *GVE* DA12.................. 489 H4
  IP IP1............................... 2 C5
  SBF/HAD SS7......................... 460 C5
  SUD CO10............................ 58 C5
Convalescent Hl *FX* IP11................... 131 H4
Convent Cl *LAIN* SS15....................... 16 A4
Convent Hl *BRTR* CM7....................... 177 K5
Convent La *BRTR* CM7....................... 177 K5
Convent Rd *CVI* SS8......................... 478 B6
Con Wy *SBF/HAD* SS7........................ 460 C5
Conway Av *SBN/FI* SS3...................... 467 G5
Conway Cl *CHTY* IP2......................... 62 D6
  FX IP11.............................. 95 K4
  HSTD CO9............................. 147 J7
  RAIN RM13........................... 450 B8
  RCOLE CO7........................... 221 F7
Conway Gdns *GRAYS* RM17.................. 484 A4
Conway's Rd *CDH/CHF* RM16................ 472 A4
Conybury Cl *WAB* EN9....................... 348 C5
Conyer Cl *MAL* CM9......................... 338 B8
Conyer Wy *LOU* IG10........................ 377 K4
Conyers Rd *HLW* CM20....................... 12 C6
Conyers Wy *LOU* IG10....................... 377 K4
Cook Cl *HAR* CO12........................... 164 E1
Cookham Ct *SBN/FI* SS3.................... 466 D3
Cook Pl *CHLM/GWD* CM2..................... 333 H4
Cooks Cl *HSTD* CO9......................... 148 A6
  KESG IP5............................. 39 J1
Cooks Gn *PIT* SS13......................... 439 F4
Cook's Hall Rd *RCOLW* CO6................. 185 H4
Cooks Hl *COLN* CO4......................... 119 J4
Cook's La *BRTR* CM7........................ 141 K5
  COLW CO3............................ 185 K4
Cooks Spinney *HLW* CM20................... 294 E3
Coolgardie Av *CHIG* IG7..................... 404 D4
  CHING E4............................ 402 E4
Coolyne Wy *COS* CO15....................... 259 K1
Coombe Dr *VGE* SS16........................ 456 D3
Coombe Ri *BRWN* CM15....................... 411 J7
  CHLM/WR CM1......................... 304 D6
  SLH/COR SS17........................ 474 A4
Coombe Rd *BOC* CM0........................ 398 A7
  GVE DA12............................ 489 H4
  HARH RM3............................ 431 A2
Coombers Cl *BCAYW* CM12................... 414 A4
Coombes Gv *RCFD* SS4....................... 444 A6
Coombewood Dr *SBF/HAD* SS7............... 440 E6
Coopersale Common *EPP* CM16.............. 351 G7
Coopersale La *EPP* CM16.................... 378 K4
Coopersales *LAIN* SS15..................... 436 A6
Coopers Av *MAL* CM9........................ 310 E4
Coopers Cl *BSF* CM23....................... 231 F4
  CHIG IG7............................ 406 A4
Coopers Crs *RCOLW* CO6.................... 186 A5
Coopers Dr *BCAYE* CM11..................... 414 E1

Coopers End Rd *RBSF* CM22 ..... 201 H2
Coopers End Rbt *RBSF* CM22 ..... 201 J2
Cooper Shaw Rd *TIL* RM18 ..... 485 J6
Coopers La *COS* CO15 ..... 290 E2
  RCHLM CM3
  RCOLE CO7 ..... 121 J8
Cooper's Rd *GVW* DA11 ..... 488 D6
Coopers Vls *RBSF* CM22 ..... 201 J3
Coopers Wy *SOSN* SS2 ..... 444 D8
Copdoek *BSDN* SS14 ..... 437 K6
Copelands *RCFD* SS4 ..... 422 A7 🔲
Copellis Cl *HVHL* CB9 ..... 27 G3
Copeman Rd *RBRW/HUT* CM13 ..... 412 C3 🔲
Copford Av *RAYL* SS6 ..... 442 A4
Copford Rd *BCAYE* CM11 ..... 414 D3 🔲
Copland Cl *CHLM/GWD* CM2 ..... 333 H5⁻
  CHLM/WR CM1 ..... 304 C4
Copland Rd *SLH/COR* SS17 ..... 473 K4
Copleston Rd *IPNE* IP4 ..... 37 K8
Coploe Rd *SAFWN* CB10 ..... 43 F2
Coppens Gn *WICKW* SS12 ..... 417 G7
Copperas Rd *RCOLE* CO7 ..... 255 K8 🔲
Copper Beech Cl *GVE* DA12 ..... 489 J5 🔲
Copper Beeches *COLW* CO3 ..... 185 J8
  SBF/HAD SS7 ..... 441 G6 🔲
Copper Beech Rd
  SOCK/AV RM15 ..... 470 A3 🔲
Copperfield *BCAYE* CM11 ..... 414 E7 🔲
Copperfield Gdns *BRW* CM14 ..... 410 E4
Copperfield Rd *CHLM/WR* CM1 ..... 303 K6
  CHTY IP2 ..... 36 A8
Copperfields *LAIN* SS15 ..... 16 A3 🔲
  SAFWS CB11 ..... 70 D5
Copperfields Wy *HARH* RM3 ..... 430 E5
Coppice Cl *GTDUN* CM6 ..... 204 C4
Coppice End *COLN* CO4 ..... 187 J2
Coppice La *GTDUN* CM6 ..... 238 E5
  LAIN SS15 ..... 17 D1
Coppice Pth *CHIG* IG7 ..... 406 A7
Coppice Rd *RCOLE* CO7 ..... 222 A5
Coppice Rw *EPP* CM16 ..... 378 B2
The Coppice *COS* CO15 ..... 10 A6
Coppingford End *RCOLW* CO6 ..... 184 C8
Coppins Cl *CHLM/WR* CM1 ..... 15 F1
Coppins Rd *COS* CO15 ..... 290 E1
Copprolite St *IPSE* IP3 ..... 3 E5
Copse Hl *HLWW/ROY* CM19 ..... 12 B6
The Copse *BCAYW* CM12 ..... 414 B1
  BSF CM23 ..... 199 H5 🔲
  CHING E4 ..... 403 G4
  GTDUN CM6 ..... 207 G2
Copshall Cl *HLWS* CM18 ..... 322 C1
Copswood Cl *KESG* IP5 ..... 39 K6
Coptfold Cl *SOS* SS1 ..... 465 J4 🔲
Coptfold Rd *BRW* CM14 ..... 411 H5
Copthall La *GTDUN* CM6 ..... 139 K2
Copt Hall *K/T/MI* CO5 ..... 283 K2
Copt Hl *RCHLM* CM3 ..... 335 J7
Copthorne Av *BROX* EN10 ..... 319 F2
Copthorne Gdns *EMPK* RM11 ..... 431 H7
Copy Hl *HVHL* CB9 ..... 49 K7
Coral Cl *RCHLM* CM3 ..... 392 C5 🔲
Coralin Wk *COLW* CO3 ..... 185 H7
Coram Gn *RBRW/HUT* CM13 ..... 412 C2
Corans *BRWN* CM15 ..... 410 C8
Coraswary *SBF/HAD* SS7 ..... 441 G8
Corbets Cl *UPMR* RM14 ..... 451 K6
Corbets Tey Rd *UPMR* RM14 ..... 451 J4
Cordelia Crs *RAYL* SS6 ..... 441 H2
The Cordwainers *SOSN* SS2 ..... 444 D8
Cordwinders *RCFD* SS4 ..... 422 A7
Cordy's La *FX* IP11 ..... 4 B1
Corfe Cl *PIT* SS13 ..... 438 E7
Coriander Av *K/T/MI* CO5 ..... 280 A1
Cornec Av *LOS* SS9 ..... 442 C7
Cornec Cha *LOS* SS9 ..... 442 C7
Cornel Cl *WIT* CM8 ..... 276 D1
Cornelius V *CHLM/GWD* CM2 ..... 333 K1
Cornelis La *SAFWS* CB11 ..... 137 F2
Cornell Wy *CRW* RM5 ..... 407 G8
Corner Meadow *HLWS* CM18 ..... 322 C1
Corner Pk *SAFWN* CB10 ..... 71 F2
Corner Rd *BCAYE* CM11 ..... 416 A7
Cornerth Crs *SUD* CO10 ..... 58 E7
Cornfields *RCHLM* CM3 ..... 392 C5
Cornflower Cl *CHTY* IP2 ..... 62 A1
  COLW CO3 ..... 185 H6
Cornflower Dr *CHLM/WR* CM1 ..... 305 H8
Cornflower Gdns *BCAYW* CM12 ..... 387 F8
Cornflower Rd *COS* CO15 ..... 290 C6
Cornflower Wy *HARH* RM3 ..... 431 F3
Cornford Wy *MGTR* CO11 ..... 159 G1
Cornhill Av *HOC/HUL* SS5 ..... 421 F6
Cornhill Dr *PEND* EN3 ..... 374 E3 🔲
Cornish Cl *CBE/LIN* CB1 ..... 24 E2
Cornish Gv *RCHLM* CM3 ..... 392 E7
Cornish Hall End Rd *BRTR* CM7 ..... 76 E6
Cornland *BRW* CM14 ..... 411 G6

Cornwall Cl *BAR* EN8 ..... 346 E7
  EMPK RM11 ..... 431 H6 🔲
  MGTR CO11 ..... 159 G2
Cornwall Crs *CHLM/WR* CM1 ..... 304 C6
Cornwall Gdns *BRTR* CM7 ..... 210 A3
  RCFD SS4 ..... 421 K8
Cornwalls Cl *ERITH* DA8 ..... 480 A5
Cornwalls Dr *RCHLM* CM3 ..... 393 F6
Cornwalls Pl *SAFWN* CB10 ..... 71 F3 🔲
  SAFWN CB10 ..... 71 F2 🔲
Cornwalls Rd *HVHL* CB9 ..... 27 F6
Cornwall Rd *BRWN* CM15 ..... 410 E1
  FX IP11 ..... 5 E2
  PIT SS13 ..... 439 J6
Cornwalls Dr *RCOLW* CO6 ..... 215 J2 🔲
Cornwell Av *GVE* DA12 ..... 489 H8
Cornwell Crs *SLH/COR* SS17 ..... 474 A2
Cornworthy *SBN/FI* SS3 ..... 466 A5
Corona Rd *CVI* SS8 ..... 461 H8
  VGE SS16 ..... 456 C2
Coronation Av *BRTR* CM7 ..... 209 J3
  COLS CO2 ..... 219 H4
  TIL RM18 ..... 486 C3
Coronation Cl *SBN/FI* SS3 ..... 466 E1
Coronation Dr *FX* IP11 ..... 5 D4
  HCH RM12 ..... 450 D4
Coronation Hl *EPP* CM16 ..... 350 D4
Coronation Ri *SUD* CO10 ..... 59 J1
Coronation Rd *BOC* CM0 ..... 425 G1
  BSF CM23 ..... 198 D8
  COS CO15 ..... 290 C2
  IPNE IP4 ..... 37 K8
Corporation Av *CHTY* IP2 ..... 62 C5
Corporation Rd *CHLM/WR* CM1 ..... 14 B1
Corran Wy *SOCK/AV* RM15 ..... 469 K4
Corsel Rd *CVI* SS8 ..... 478 E2 🔲
Cortoncroft Cl *FOS* CO13 ..... 228 E6
Corton Rd *IPSE* IP3 ..... 63 J4
Corve La *SOCK/AV* RM15 ..... 469 K7
Cory Dr *RBRW/HUT* CM13 ..... 412 C3
Cosgrove Av *LOS* SS9 ..... 462 C2
Cossington Rd *WOS/PRIT* SS0 ..... 18 B5
Costead Manor Rd *BRW* CM14 ..... 410 E4
Coteford Cl *LOU* IG10 ..... 377 K6
Cotelands *VGE* SS16 ..... 458 C2
Cotman Av *MGTR* CO11 ..... 123 G8
Cotman Rd *COLW* CO3 ..... 186 B8
  IPSE IP3 ..... 63 J4
  RCOS CO16 ..... 10 A1
Cotswold Av *IP* IP1 ..... 36 D4
  RAYL SS6 ..... 441 J2
Cotswold Cl *COLN* CO4 ..... 187 K1 🔲
Cotswold Crs *CHLM/WR* CM1 ..... 303 K7
Cotswold Dr *SUD* CO10 ..... 34 E7
Cotswold Gdns *RBRW/HUT* CM13 ..... 412 D3
Cotswold Rd *COS* CO15 ..... 10 C2
  GVW DA11 ..... 488 D8
  HARH RM3 ..... 431 G4
  WOS/PRIT SS0 ..... 18 A4
Cottage Dr *COLS* CO2 ..... 219 K2
Cottage Gdns *BAR* EN8 ..... 346 C3
Cottage Gn *RCOS* CO16 ..... 258 E7 🔲
Cottage Gv *RCOS* CO16 ..... 258 E7
Cottage Pl *CHLM/WR* CM1 ..... 14 C2
Cottage Wk *RCOS* CO16 ..... 258 D7
Cottesmore Cl *CVI* SS8 ..... 478 A3
Cottesmore Gdns *LOS* SS9 ..... 462 B4
Cottingham Rd *RIPW* IP8 ..... 61 H4
Cottis Cl *VGE* SS16 ..... 456 B2
Cottonwood Cl *COLS* CO2 ..... 219 K2
Coulde Dennis *RCHLM* CM3 ..... 363 F6 🔲
Coulsdon Cl *RCOS* CO16 ..... 258 E7
Coulton Av *GVW* DA11 ..... 488 D5
Council Av *GVW* DA11 ..... 488 D4
Council Rd *BSF* CM23 ..... 199 G6
Counting House La *GTDUN* CM6 ..... 204 C3
County Pl *CHLM/GWD* CM2 ..... 14 C4
Coupals Cl *HVHL* CB9 ..... 27 J7
Coupals Rd *HVHL* CB9 ..... 27 J7
Courage Cl *EMPK* RM11 ..... 430 D8 🔲
Courtauld Cl *HSTD* CO9 ..... 148 A4
Courtauld Rd *BRTR* CM7 ..... 209 K1
  PIT SS13 ..... 438 E3
Court Av *HARH* RM3 ..... 431 H2
Courtenay Cl *SUD* CO10 ..... 58 A3 🔲
Courtenay Dr *CDH/CHF* RM16 ..... 483 J2 🔲
Courtenay Gdns *UPMR* RM14 ..... 451 K3
Courtfield Cl *BROX* EN10 ..... 319 G2 🔲
Courtland Av *CHING* E4 ..... 403 G5
Courtland Dr *CHIG* IG7 ..... 405 F6
Courtland Ms *MAL* CM9 ..... 338 D5 🔲
Courtland Pl *MAL* CM9 ..... 338 B5
Courtlands *BCAYW* CM12 ..... 413 K3
  CHLM/WR CM1 ..... 304 C7
Courtney Park Rd *VGE* SS16 ..... 436 C8 🔲
Courtney Rd *CDH/CHF* RM16 ..... 485 H1
Court Rd *CHLM/WR* CM1 ..... 304 C2
The Courts *RAYL* SS6 ..... 441 K2
Court St *RCOLW* CO6 ..... 118 B4
Court Vw *ING* CM4 ..... 385 K4 🔲
Court Wy *HARH* RM3 ..... 431 F4
Coval Av *CHLM/WR* CM1 ..... 14 B2
Coval La *CHLM/WR* CM1 ..... 14 B2 🔲
Covenbrook *RBRW/HUT* CM13 ..... 411 K6

Coventry Cl *COL* CO1 ..... 8 C3
  HOC/HUL SS5 ..... 420 A4
Coventry Hill Lower Rd
  HOC/HUL SS5 ..... 419 K4
Coverley Cl *RBRW/HUT* CM13 ..... 433 F1 🔲
Covert Cl *HVHL* CB9 ..... 27 G4
The Coverts *CHLM/WR* CM1 ..... 331 H6
  K/T/MI CO5 ..... 285 F7
  RBRW/HUT CM13 ..... 411 K4
Cowdray Crs *COL* CO1 ..... 8 B4
Cowdray Wy *HCH* RM12 ..... 450 B5
Cowell Av *CHLM/WR* CM1 ..... 304 A8
Cowell St *CHTY* IP2 ..... 3 D6
Cowels Farm La *GTDUN* CM6 ..... 140 D8
Cowland Av *PEND* EN3 ..... 374 C8
Cow La *RCOS* CO16 ..... 288 C2
  SAFWN CB10 ..... 44 A2
Cowley Rd *FX* IP11 ..... 131 H3
  HARH RM3 ..... 430 C2
Cowlins *HLWE* CM17 ..... 295 H1 🔲
Cowpar Ms *BRTR* CM7 ..... 209 K5 🔲
Cowper Av *TIL* RM18 ..... 485 G7
Cowper St *IPNE* IP4 ..... 37 K7
Cowslip Cl *CHTY* IP2 ..... 36 A8
Cowslip St *COLW* CO3 ..... 185 H6
Cow Watering La *CHLM/WR* CM1 ..... 331 F2
Coxbridge Ct *BCAYW* CM12 ..... 414 B3
Coxes Cl *SLH/COR* SS17 ..... 473 K2
Coxes Farm Rd *BCAYE* CM11 ..... 415 F6
Coxhall Rd *RIPS/CAP* IP9 ..... 88 E4
Cox Ley *RBSF* CM22 ..... 265 G2
Cox Rd *RCOLE* CO7 ..... 222 A5
Coxs Cl *RCHLM* CM3 ..... 392 E5
Cox's Hl *MGTR* CO11 ..... 159 F2
Coxtie Green Rd *BRW* CM14 ..... 382 D8
  BRW CM14 ..... 409 H2
Cozens La East *BROX* EN10 ..... 319 F4
Cozens La West *BROX* EN10 ..... 318 E4
Crabbe St *IPNE* IP4 ..... 37 J7
Crabb's Hl *CHLM* CM3 ..... 307 K4
Crabb's La *BUNT* SC9 ..... 133 H6
Crabs Cft *BRTR* CM7 ..... 210 B2
Crabtree *FOS* CO13 ..... 228 B5 🔲
Crabtree Cft *CBE/LIN* CB1 ..... 22 D2
Crabtree La *RCOLW* CO6 ..... 153 H3
Cracknell Cl *RCOLE* CO7 ..... 220 E3 🔲
Craftsmans Sq *SOSN* SS2 ..... 444 D8
Craig Cl *FX* IP11 ..... 94 C5
Craigdale Rd *ROM* RM1 ..... 430 A8
Craigfield Av *COS* CO15 ..... 10 C1
Craig's La *BURES* CO8 ..... 115 H7
Craigs Wk *BAR* EN8 ..... 346 D2
Craiston Wy *CHLM/GWD* CM2 ..... 333 H8
Crammavill St *CDH/CHF* RM16 ..... 470 E8
Cramphorn Wk *CHLM/WR* CM1 ..... 14 A2
Cranborne Cha *IPNE* IP4 ..... 37 J4
Cranborne Gdns *UPMR* RM14 ..... 451 J3
Cranborne Rd *BAR* EN8 ..... 346 C6 🔲
Cranbrook Av *SBF/HAD* SS7 ..... 461 H1 🔲
Cranbrook Dr *GPK* RM2 ..... 430 C6
Cranbrook La *SUD* CO10 ..... 34 B4
Cranes Cl *BSDN* SS14 ..... 438 C4
Cranes Farm Rd *BSDN* SS14 ..... 17 E2
  BSDN SS14 ..... 437 K5
  LAIN SS15 ..... 16 C2
Cranes La *BSDN* SS14 ..... 437 K5
  K/T/MI CO5 ..... 246 B4
Cranfield Park Av *WICKW* SS12 ..... 439 H3
Cranfield Park Rd *WICKW* SS12 ..... 439 H1
Cranford Cl *FOS* CO13 ..... 228 D8
Cranham Gdns *UPMR* RM14 ..... 452 C1
Cranham Rd *EMPK* RM11 ..... 430 C8
  GTDUN CM6 ..... 170 C3
Cranleigh Cl *EBAR* EN7 ..... 346 A2
  RCOS CO16 ..... 258 D7
Cranleigh Dr *LOS* SS9 ..... 463 F3
Cranleigh Gdns *HOC/HUL* SS5 ..... 419 J8 🔲
  LOU IG10 ..... 404 C2 🔲
Cranley Av *WOS/PRIT* SS0 ..... 18 A3
Cranley Gdns *SBN/FI* SS3 ..... 466 B7
Cranley Rd *WOS/PRIT* SS0 ..... 18 A4
Cranmer Cl *BCAYW* CM12 ..... 387 H7
Cranmer's La *RCOLW* CO6 ..... 182 B7
Cranmore Cl *RBSF* CM22 ..... 168 D3 🔲
Cranmoregreen La *SUD* CO10 ..... 34 B2
Cranston Av *WOS/PRIT* SS0 ..... 444 A8
Cranston Park Av *UPMR* RM14 ..... 451 K5
Cranwell Crs *IPSE* IP3 ..... 64 A4
Cranwell Gdns *BSF* CM23 ..... 199 H4
Cranwell Rd *KESG* IP5 ..... 39 G6
Cranworth Crs *CHING* E4 ..... 402 E4 🔲
Craven Av *CVI* SS8 ..... 478 A2
Craven Cl *RCFD* SS4 ..... 422 A8
Craven Dr *COLN* CO4 ..... 187 K2
Craven Gdns *CRW* RM5 ..... 407 F8
  HARH RM3 ..... 431 K1
Crawford Av *CDH/CHF* RM16 ..... 471 F8
Crawford Cha *WICKW* SS12 ..... 417 H8
Crawford Cl *BCAYW* CM12 ..... 387 J8
Crawford La *KESG* IP5 ..... 39 G6 🔲
Crawley Cl *SLH/COR* SS17 ..... 457 H8
Crawley End *ROY* SC8 ..... 67 G1
Craword Compton Cl
  HCH RM12 ..... 450 D7 🔲
Craydene Rd *ERITH* DA8 ..... 480 A7

Crayfields *GTDUN* CM6 .... 204 C4
Crayford Cl *MAL* CM9 .... 338 A5 🔲
Craylands *BSDN* SS14 .... 438 C6
Crays Hi *BCAYE* CM11 .... 437 J1
Crays Hill Rd *BCAYE* CM11 .... 415 K8
Crays Vw *BCAYW* CM12 .... 414 C5
Crealock Gv *WFD* IG8 .... 403 G8
Creasen Butt Cl *MAL* CM9 .... 338 C1 🔲
Creasey Cl *HCH* RM12 .... 450 E3
Credon Cl *COS* CO15 .... 259 H6
Credon Dr *COS* CO15 .... 259 H6
Credo Wy *WTHK* RM20 .... 482 E5
Creekhurst Cl *RCOLE* CO7 .... 256 A7
Creek Rd *CVI* SS8 .... 478 D1
Creeksea Ferry Rd *RCFD* SS4 .... 423 J5
Creeksea La *BOC* CM0 .... 397 K7
The Creek *GVW* DA11 .... 488 A3
Creek Vw *RAYL* SS6 .... 458 B2 🔲
Creek View Av *HOC/HUL* SS5 .... 419 H2
Creekview Rd *RCHLM* CM3 .... 393 F6
Creephedge La *RCHLM* CM3 .... 363 H8
    RCHLM CM3 .... 391 K2
Creffield Rd *COLW* CO3 .... 186 E7
Cremorne Rd *GVW* DA11 .... 488 E5 🔲
Cropping Hall Br *RIPS/CAP* IP9 .... 125 C3
Crescent *BCAYW* CM12 .... 414 A1 🔲
Crescent *BCAYW* CM12 .... 414 A1 🔲
    BRW CM14 .... 410 E7
    BSF CM23 .... 199 F7
    CHING E4 .... 403 F3
    CHLM/GWD CM2 .... 333 J6
    CVI SS8 .... 478 D3
    ERITH DA8 .... 480 A5
    FX IP11 .... 131 H3
    IP IP1 .... 2 C3
    LOS SS9 .... 462 C3
    MAL CM9 .... 310 B8
    MAL CM9 .... 314 E4
    SBF/HAD SS7 .... 460 C3
    SOCK/AV RM15 .... 481 K1 🔲
    WOTN CO14 .... 229 H5 🔲
The Crescent *COLN* CO4 .... 155 K6
    COS CO15 .... 259 K6
    EPP CM16 .... 350 D6
    FOS CO13 .... 228 E8
    GVW DA11 .... 488 E7
    HLWE CM17 .... 263 G7
    LOU IG10 .... 404 A3
    RCHLM CM3 .... 241 G8
    RCOLW CO6 .... 153 J8
    RCOLW CO6 .... 154 C4
    RCOLW CO6 .... 215 K2
    RCOS CO16 .... 226 C3
    SBF/HAD SS7 .... 462 A3
    UPMR RM14 .... 452 B1
Crescent Vw *LOU* IG10 .... 404 A2
Crescent Wk *SOCK/AV* RM15 .... 481 K1
Crescent Wy *SOCK/AV* RM15 .... 469 F8
Cressages Cl *GTDUN* CM6 .... 207 F7
Cress Cft *BRTR* CM7 .... 210 C4 🔲
Cressells *LAIN* SS15 .... 17 D5
Cressing Rd *BRTR* CM7 .... 210 A3
    WIT CM8 .... 244 D5
Crest Av *GRAYS* RM17 .... 484 A6
    PIT SS13 .... 439 F7
Crest Dr *PEND* EN3 .... 374 E4
Cresthill Av *GRAYS* RM17 .... 484 B4
Crestlands *RCOLE* CO7 .... 222 A6
The Crest *STSD* CM24 .... 442 E7
    SBW CM21 .... 263 H3
Creswick Av *RAYL* SS6 .... 441 H2
Crete Hall Rd *GVW* DA11 .... 488 C4
Cricketers Cl *RIPS/CAP* IP9 .... 87 F4
Cricketers La *RBRW/HUT* CM13 .... 434 C2
Cricketers Rw
    RBRW/HUT CM13 .... 434 C2 🔲
Cricketers Vw *PIT* SS13 .... 438 E2
Cricketfield Gv *LOS* SS9 .... 463 G5
Cricketfield La *BSF* CM23 .... 198 C5
Cricket Hill Rd *FX* IP11 .... 5 D2
Crickhollow *RCHLM* CM3 .... 392 C8
Cricklade Av *HARH* RM3 .... 430 E1
Cringle Cnr *RCHLM* CM3 .... 392 E8
Cripplegate *BOC* CM0 .... 370 E8
Cripsey Av *CHONG* CM5 .... 326 B8
Crispin Cl *HVHL* CB9 .... 26 D6
Crittall Cl *WIT* CM8 .... 244 E1 🔲
Crittall Rd *WIT* CM8 .... 277 H2
Croasdaile Rd *STSD* CM24 .... 167 K5
Croasdale Cl *STSD* CM24 .... 167 K5
Crocus Cl *CHTY* IP2 .... 62 A1
Crocus Flds *SAFWN* CB10 .... 71 F2
Crocus Wy *CHLM/WR* CM1 .... 305 G6
Croft Cl *BRTR* CM7 .... 209 K2
    LOS SS9 .... 463 F1
    SBF/HAD SS7 .... 440 B8
Croft Ct *CHLM/WR* CM1 .... 305 C5
    KIR/NAC IP10 .... 94 A2

RCHLM CM3 .... 271 F2
Crofton Av *SLH/COR* SS17 .... 474 B1
Crofton Gv *CHING* E4 .... 402 E7
Crofton Rd *CDH/CHF* RM16 .... 484 D1
    IPNE IP4 .... 37 K6
Croft Rd *COS* CO15 .... 10 A3
    K/T/MI CO5 .... 246 D3 🔲
    PEND EN3 .... 374 E5
    SBF/HAD SS7 .... 440 A8
    SUD CO10 .... 58 A5
The Crofts *SBN/FI* SS3 .... 466 D1
Croft St *CHTY* IP2 .... 3 D6
The Croft *BROX* EN10 .... 318 E3
    BURES CO8 .... 115 J4
    CHING E4 .... 403 F5
    HSTD CO9 .... 79 K3 🔲
    LOU IG10 .... 404 C5
    RAYL SS6 .... 442 A5
    RBSF CM22 .... 168 C4
    RCOLW CO6 .... 149 H7
    SUD CO10 .... 33 H1
Croft Vw *WIT* CM8 .... 277 C2
Cromarty Rd *IPNE* IP4 .... 37 K5
Crome Cl *COLW* CO3 .... 186 B8
Cromer Av *LAIN* SS15 .... 436 C5
Cromer Cl *LAIN* SS15 .... 436 C5
Cromer Rd *RCOS* CO16 .... 10 A1
Cromer Rd *EMPK* RM11 .... 450 E1
    IP IP1 .... 2 A1
    SOS SS1 .... 19 E4
Crompton Rd *CHTY* IP2 .... 36 A6
Crompton St *CHLM/WR* CM1 .... 14 A5
Cromwell Av *BCAYW* CM12 .... 414 B2
    EBAR EN7 .... 346 B4
Cromwell Cl *BSF* CM23 .... 198 A6
Cromwell Hl *CHLM* CM9 .... 338 B2
Cromwell La *MAL* CM9 .... 338 B2
Cromwell Pk *GTDUN* CM6 .... 206 C8
Cromwell Rd *BRW* CM14 .... 410 E7
    COLS CO2 .... 8 B5
    GRAYS RM17 .... 483 K3
    HOC/HUL SS5 .... 421 F7
    SAFWS CB11 .... 71 F6
    SOSN SS2 .... 19 D1
Cromwell Wy *WIT* CM8 .... 276 C3
Crondon Park La *ING* CM4 .... 388 A1
Crooked Park La *GVE* DA12 .... 489 G4
Crooked Mile *WAB* EN9 .... 347 J4
Crooked Wy *WAB* EN9 .... 320 A4
Cropenburg Wk *CVI* SS8 .... 461 G8 🔲
Crosby Rd *WOS/PRIT* SS0 .... 463 J5
Crossbow Rd *CHIG* IG7 .... 405 J8
Crossbrook St *BAR* EN8 .... 346 D4 🔲
Crossby Cl *BRWN* CM15 .... 385 J3
Cross Cl *HVHL* CB9 .... 27 G4
Cross Field Wy *COLN* CO4 .... 119 J8
Crossfell Rd *SBF/HAD* SS7 .... 440 E6
Crossfield Av *SOSN* SS2 .... 465 C3
Crossgate Fld *FX* IP11 .... 5 E2 🔲
Cross Hl *HAR* CO12 .... 195 F4
Crossing Rd *EPP* CM16 .... 350 E6
Cross La *K/T/MI* CO5 .... 285 H6
Cross La East *GVE* DA12 .... 489 C3
Cross La West *GVW* DA11 .... 489 C3
Crossley Av *COS* CO15 .... 290 A6
Cross Rd *BAR* EN8 .... 346 E7 🔲
    GVW DA11 .... 488 C4
    MAL CM9 .... 338 C4
    PIT SS13 .... 439 J6
    SBF/HAD SS7 .... 461 C1
    WIT CM8 .... 277 G1
Cross Roads *LOU* IG10 .... 376 D6
Cross St *FX* IP11 .... 5 E1 🔲
    SAFWN CB10 .... 70 E4 🔲
    SUD CO10 .... 58 A6
Crosstree Wk *COLS* CO2 .... 219 H2 🔲
Cross Wy *K/T/MI* CO5 .... 285 C6
Crossways *BRWN* CM15 .... 411 K2
    CBE/LIN CB1 .... 23 F3
    CHLM/GWD CM2 .... 15 D6
    COS CO15 .... 290 B5
    GPK RM2 .... 430 C5
    RCOLW CO6 .... 149 C4 🔲
The Crossways *WOS/PRIT* SS0 .... 463 H5
Crotchets Cl *RIPS/CAP* IP9 .... 87 F4
Crouch Av *HOC/HUL* SS5 .... 419 K4
Crouch Beck *RCHLM* CM3 .... 392 E6 🔲
Crouch Dr *WICKE* SS11 .... 417 C5
    WIT CM8 .... 276 E3 🔲
Crouchmans Av *SBN/FI* SS3 .... 467 F2 🔲
Crouchman's Farm Rd *MAL* CM9 .... 308 C7
Crouch Meadow *HOC/HUL* SS5 .... 419 K1 🔲
Crouch Rd *BOC* CM0 .... 398 B8
    GRAYS RM17 .... 485 F4
Crouch St *COLW* CO3 .... 8 A5
    LAIN SS15 .... 16 C1
Crouch Va *UPMR* RM14 .... 452 B1
Crouchview Cl *WICKE* SS11 .... 418 A6 🔲
Crouch View Crs *HOC/HUL* SS5 .... 421 C5
Crouch View Gv *HOC/HUL* SS5 .... 419 J2
Croutel La *FX* IP11 .... 131 J2
Crowborough Rd *SOSN* SS2 .... 18 C2

Crowe Hall La *RIPS/CAP* IP9 .... 125 H3
Crow Green La *BRWN* CM15 .... 410 D1
Crow Green Rd *BRWN* CM15 .... 410 C1
Crowhall La *MGTR* CO11 .... 160 E5
Crowhurst Rd *COLW* CO3 .... 8 A4 🔲
Crowland Cl *CHTY* IP2 .... 62 C3
Crowland Rd *HVHL* CB9 .... 27 F5
Crow La *RCOS* CO16 .... 225 C3
Crown Av *PIT* SS13 .... 439 F6
Crown Bays Rd *COLN* CO4 .... 9 E3
Crown Cl *PIT* SS13 .... 439 F7
    RBSF CM22 .... 264 C5
Crownfield *BROX* EN10 .... 319 C3
Crown Gdns *RAYL* SS6 .... 441 H3
Crown Ga *COLN* CO4 .... 156 A7
    HLW CM20 .... 13 D3
Crown Hl *RAYL* SS6 .... 441 H3
    WAB EN9 .... 349 H7
Crown La *RCOS* CO16 .... 224 E2
Crown La North *RCOLE* CO7 .... 156 B6
Crown La South *RCOLE* CO7 .... 188 D1
Crown Meadow *BRTR* CM7 .... 210 C1 🔲
Crown Rd *BCAYE* CM11 .... 414 C3
    BRW CM14 .... 383 F5
    COS CO15 .... 290 E4
    EN EN1 .... 374 A7
    GRAYS RM17 .... 483 K5
    HOC/HUL SS5 .... 420 C8
    RCHLM CM3 .... 366 B7
Crown St *BRTR* CM7 .... 142 C3 🔲
    BRW CM14 .... 411 F5 🔲
    FX IP11 .... 5 E2
    HSTD CO9 .... 110 D1
    IP IP1 .... 3 D3
    RCOLE CO7 .... 121 J7
Crown Ter *BSF* CM23 .... 199 F6
Crown Wy *BOC* CM0 .... 398 C7
Crow Pond Rd *RCHLM* CM3 .... 275 C3
Crowsheath La *BCAYE* CM11 .... 389 C7
Crows La *RCHLM* CM3 .... 364 B7
    RCHLM CM3 .... 393 F2
Crows Rd *EPP* CM16 .... 350 D4
Crowstone Av *WOS/PRIT* SS0 .... 463 K6
Crowstone Cl *WOS/PRIT* SS0 .... 463 K4
Crowstone Rd *CDH/CHF* RM16 .... 484 B1
    WOS/PRIT SS0 .... 463 K5
Crow St *RBSF* CM22 .... 137 C8
Crowswell Ct *FX* IP11 .... 94 C5 🔲
Croxon Wy *BOC* CM0 .... 398 B6
Croxton Cl *KIR/NAC* IP10 .... 94 D2
Crozier Av *BSF* CM23 .... 198 B5
Cruce Wy *RCOS* CO16 .... 287 K2
Cruick Av *SOCK/AV* RM15 .... 470 A6
Crummock Cl *BRTR* CM7 .... 209 F7 🔲
Crunch Cft *HVHL* CB9 .... 28 A8
Crusader Cl *PUR* RM19 .... 481 H3
Crusader Wy *BRTR* CM7 .... 210 C3
Crushes Cl *RBRW/HUT* CM13 .... 412 D2
Crystal Av *HCH* RM12 .... 451 F5
Cuba Dr *PEND* EN3 .... 374 C6
Cuckfield Av *IPSE* IP3 .... 64 C2
Cuckoo Hl *BURES* CO8 .... 115 J4
    HSTD CO9 .... 110 A5
Cuckoo La *CDH/CHF* RM16 .... 470 D8
Cuckoos La *GTDUN* CM6 .... 235 H3
Cuckoo Wy *BRTR* CM7 .... 208 E7 🔲
Culford Rd *CDH/CHF* RM16 .... 484 B1
Cullen Sq *SOCK/AV* RM15 .... 470 A7
Cullingham Rd *IP* IP1 .... 2 B3
Cullings Ct *WAB* EN9 .... 348 B7
Culverdown *BSDN* SS14 .... 17 E4
Culver Ri *RCHLM* CM3 .... 392 E6
Culver St East *COL* CO1 .... 8 B4 🔲
Culver St West *COL* CO1 .... 8 A4
Cumberland Rd *GVE* DA12 .... 489 H5 🔲
    HCH RM12 .... 451 F4 🔲
    MAL CM9 .... 338 A4 🔲
    SBF/HAD SS7 .... 460 B2
    SOSN SS2 .... 19 F2
Cumberland Cl *BRTR* CM7 .... 210 A1 🔲
Cumberland Crs *CHLM/WR* CM1 .... 304 C6
Cumberland Dr *LAIN* SS15 .... 436 B7 🔲
Cumberland St *IP* IP1 .... 2 C2
Cumley Rd *CHONG* CM5 .... 352 E4
Cumming Rd *BCAYE* CM11 .... 416 D3
Cummings Hall La *ABR/ST* RM4 .... 408 D6
Cunningham Av *PEND* EN3 .... 374 E2
Cunningham Cl *SBN/FI* SS3 .... 466 E4
Cunningham Dr *WICKW* SS12 .... 417 H8
Cunningham Ri *EPP* CM16 .... 324 D7 🔲
Cunningham Rd *BAR* EN8 .... 346 E1
Cunnington Rd *BRTR* CM7 .... 210 B2
Cunobelin Wy *COLS* CO2 .... 218 A3
Cupids Cha *SBN/FI* SS3 .... 466 E3
Cuppers Cl *WIT* CM8 .... 276 E4
Curds Rd *RCOLW* CO6 .... 181 H2
Curlew Av *RCHLM* CM3 .... 368 E5
Curlew Cl *COS* CO15 .... 10 C1
    K/T/MI CO5 .... 247 F3
    MAL CM9 .... 310 E8 🔲
Curlew Crs *VGE* SS16 .... 457 J2
Curlew Cl *COLN* CO4 .... 188 C5
Curlew Dr *SBF/HAD* SS7 .... 460 B3
Curlew Rd *CHTY* IP2 .... 61 K2 🔲
The Curlews *GVE* DA12 .... 489 J7

Curling La *GRAYS* RM17 .... 483 J4
Curling Tye *BSDN* SS14 .... 438 A6
Curling Tye La *MAL* CM9 .... 337 F2
Curling Wk *BSDN* SS14 .... 438 A6
Currants Farm Rd *BRTR* CM7 .... 177 H6
Curriers' La *IP* IP1 .... 3 D4 🄸
Curteys *HLWE* CM17 .... 263 H8
Curtis Cl *RCOS* CO16 .... 290 D2
RIPW IP8 .... 61 J4 🄸
Curtis Mill La *ABR/ST* RM4 .... 380 E8
ABR/ST RM4 .... 408 B2
Curtis Rd *EMPK* RM11 .... 451 G2
Curtisway *RAYL* SS6 .... 441 K1
Curzon Dr *GRAYS* RM17 .... 484 B6
Curzon Rd *SUD* CO10 .... 58 E5
Curzon Wy *CHLM/GWD* CM2 .... 333 J5
Cusak Rd *CHLM/GWD* CM2 .... 333 H3
Cussons Cl *EBAR* EN7 .... 346 A3
Cut-a-thwart La *MAL* CM9 .... 337 H2
Cutforth Rd *SBW* CM21 .... 263 J2
Cut Hedge *BRTR* CM7 .... 209 F7
Cuthedge La *RCOLW* CO6 .... 212 C6
Cutlers La *RCOE* CO7 .... 86 C8
Cutlers Rd *RCHLM* CM3 .... 392 E5
Cutler St *IP* IP1 .... 3 D4 🄸
Cutmore Pl *CHLM/GWD* CM2 .... 14 A5 🄸
Cutmore St *GVW* DA11 .... 489 G5
Cuton Hall La *CHLM/GWD* CM2 ...... 305 J8
The Cut *K/T/MI* CO5 .... 248 A8
Cut Throat La *WIT* CM8 .... 277 C2
Cutting Dr *HSTD* CO9 .... 147 K4
Cygnet Ct *BSF* CM23 .... 198 E7
HSTD CO9 .... 110 D4
Cygnet Vw *WTHK* RM20 .... 482 C7
Cymbeline Wy
(Colchester By-Pass) *COLW* CO3 .. 186 A6
Cypress Cl *COS* CO15 .... 259 C6
WAB EN9 .... 347 K8 🄸
Cypress Gdns *SOCK/AV* RM15 .... 469 F8
Cypress Dr *GTDUN* CM6 .... 204 A4
Cypress Dr *CHLM/GWD* CM2 .... 332 E7
Cypress Gv *COLN* CO4 .... 188 B5
Cypress Ms *K/T/MI* CO5 .... 284 D6 🄸
Cypress Rd *WIT* CM8 .... 277 C1
Cyril Child Cl *COLN* CO4 .... 188 B6 🄸

D

Daarle Av *CVI* SS8 .... 478 A2
Dabbling Cl *BRTR* DA8 .... 480 C6 🄸
Dacre Av *SOCK/AV* RM15 .... 469 F8
Dacre Cl *CHIG* IG7 .... 405 F7 🄸
Dacre Crs *SOCK/AV* RM15 .... 469 F8
Dacre Gdns *CHIG* IG7 .... 405 F7
Daen Ingas *RCHLM* CM3 .... 335 G6
Daffodil Av *BRWN* CM15 .... 410 E1
Daffodil Cl *CHTY* IP2 .... 62 A2
Daffodil Wy *CHLM/GWD* CM2 .... 305 G6
Dagnam Park Cl *HARH* RM3 .... 409 H8
Dagnam Park Dr *HARH* RM3 .... 409 F8
Dagnam Park Gdns *HARH* RM3 ...... 431 H1 🄸
Dagnam Park Sq *HARH* RM3 .... 431 J1 🄸
Dagnets La *BRTR* CM7 .... 242 A1
Dagwood La *BRWN* CM15 .... 383 K4
Dahlia Cl *CHLM/WR* CM1 .... 305 H8 🄸
COS CO15 .... 290 E1
Daiglen Dr *SOCK/AV* RM15 .... 469 J7
Daimler Av *COS* CO15 .... 289 K6
Daines Cl *SOCK/AV* RM15 .... 469 J4
SOS SS1 .... 466 A5
Daines Rd *BCAYE* CM11 .... 414 C3
Daines Wy *SOS* SS1 .... 466 A4
Dains Pl *FX* IP11 .... 94 D8
Dairy Farm Rd *RCHLM* CM3 .... 397 H2
Dairyglen Av *BAR* EN8 .... 346 D5
Dairyhouse La *MGTR* CO11 .... 161 F5
Daisleys La *RCHLM* CM3 .... 273 J3
Daisy Green Rd *COLW* CO3 .... 184 C5
Daisyley Rd *GTDUN* CM6 .... 173 F2
Dakyn Dr *INC* CM4 .... 387 K2
Dale Cl *COLW* CO3 .... 185 G6
SOCK/AV RM15 .... 469 J6 🄸
Dale Ct *SBW* CM21 .... 263 H4 🄸
Dale Hall La *IP* IP1 .... 36 D3
Dalen Av *CVI* SS8 .... 478 A2
Dale Rd *LOS* SS9 .... 462 C4
Daleside Gdns *CHIG* IG7 .... 405 F6
Dales Rd *IP* IP1 .... 36 C4
The Dales *HAR* CO12 .... 164 E4
RCFD SS4 .... 444 A2
Dales Vw *RIPW* IP8 .... 60 E5
Dales View Rd *IP* IP1 .... 2 B1
The Dale *RCOE* CO7 .... 221 F5
SBF/HAD SS7 .... 461 F1
WAB EN9 .... 348 A8
Dale Vw *ERITH* DA8 .... 480 B8
Dale View Av *CHING* E4 .... 402 D5
Daleview Av *MGTR* CO11 .... 161 K9
Dale View Crs *CHING* E4 .... 402 D6
Dale View Gdns *CHING* E4 .... 402 E6
Dalewood Cl *EMPK* RM11 .... 451 F1 🄸

Dallwood Wy *BRTR* CM7 .... 210 A2 🄸
Dalmatia Rd *SOS* SS1 .... 465 G4
Dalmeney Rd *VGE* SS16 .... 456 C1
Dalroy Cl *SOCK/AV* RM15 .... 469 J6
Daltes La *RCOS* CO16 .... 289 H2
Dalton Gdns *BSF* CM23 .... 231 J2
Dalton Rd *IP* IP1 .... 2 C3
Daltons Fen *PIT* SS13 .... 439 F5
Dalwood *SBN/FI* SS3 .... 466 C5
Dalwood Gdns *SBF/HAD* SS7 .... 461 K1
Dalys Rd *RCFD* SS4 .... 444 B3
Damant's Farm La *FOS* CO13 .... 227 G5
Damases La *RCHLM* CM3 .... 307 F3
Damask Rd *COLW* CO3 .... 185 H6
Dampier Rd *RCOLW* CO6 .... 213 G2
Danacre *LAIN* SS15 .... 426 C7
Danbury Cl *BRW* CM14 .... 410 C1
LOS SS9 .... 463 G1
Danbury Crs *SOCK/AV* RM15 .... 469 K6
Danbury Down *BSDN* SS14 .... 438 A5
Danbury Rd *LOU* IG10 .... 404 B2
RAYL SS6 .... 441 G2
Danbury V *RCHLM* CM3 .... 336 A7
Dancing Dicks La *WIT* CM8 .... 276 A9
Dandies Cha *LOS* SS9 .... 442 E6
Dandies Cl *LOS* SS9 .... 442 E6
Dandies Dr *LOS* SS9 .... 442 E6
Dane Acres *BSF* CM23 .... 198 C5
Dane Cl *HVHL* CB9 .... 28 C3
Dane Common *HVHL* CB9 .... 28 C3
Dane O'coys Rd *BSF* CM23 .... 198 C5
Dane Pk *BSF* CM23 .... 198 C5
Dane Rd *CHLM/WR* CM1 .... 332 A3
Dane's Av *SBN/FI* SS3 .... 466 E7
Danes Cl *GVW* DA11 .... 488 B8
Danes Ct *SUD* CO10 .... 84 E1
Danescroft Cl *LOS* SS9 .... 462 E1
Danescroft Dr *LOS* SS9 .... 462 E1
Danesfield *SBF/HAD* SS7 .... 460 A5
Danesleigh Gdns *LOS* SS9 .... 462 E1
Dane St *BSF* CM23 .... 199 F7
SBN/FI SS3 .... 467 F7
Danes Wy *BRWN* CM15 .... 410 C1
Daniel Cl *CDH/CHF* RM16 .... 483 H1
CDH/CHF RM16 .... 485 G2
Daniel Cole Rd *COLS* CO2 .... 219 G1
Daniell Cl *RCOS* CO16 .... 258 E7 🄸
Daniell Dr *COLS* CO2 .... 218 C3
Daniel Wy *WIT* CM8 .... 244 E1
Daphne Cl *BRTR* CM7 .... 209 F6
Dapifer Dr *BRTR* CM7 .... 210 C2
Darby Dr *WAB* EN9 .... 347 J7 🄸
D'arcy Av *MAL* CM9 .... 338 D4
D'arcy Av *MAL* CM9 .... 338 D4
Darcy Dr *BAR* EN8 .... 346 E5
BOC CM0 .... 398 C7
FOS CO13 .... 228 E7 🄸
RBRW/HUT CM13 .... 412 A3
D'arcy Hts *COLS* CO2 .... 219 K2
Darcy Ri *RCHLM* CM3 .... 335 J4
D'arcy Rd *COLS* CO2 .... 219 K2
K/T/MI CO5 .... 280 D2
RCOS CO16 .... 257 H8
D'arcy Wy *MAL* CM9 .... 313 J1
RCOE CO7 .... 255 J6 🄸
Darell Wy *BCAYE* CM11 .... 414 E4 🄸
Darenth La *SOCK/AV* RM15 .... 469 J6
Darenth Rd *LOS* SS9 .... 462 C4
Darent Valley Pth *DART* DA1 .... 480 E7
Darkhouse La *K/T/MI* CO5 .... 220 D5 🄸
Dark La *BRW* CM14 .... 432 D2
EBAR EN7 .... 346 A3
SBF/HAD SS7 .... 441 F7
Darlinghurst Gv *LOS* SS9 .... 463 H3
Darlington Ct *BRWN* CM15 .... 410 D2 🄸
Darlington Gdns *HARH* RM3 .... 408 E8
Dariton Cl *DART* DA1 .... 480 A8
Darnel Wy *COLW* CO3 .... 185 G6
Darnet Rd *MAL* CM9 .... 314 E4
Darnley St *GVW* DA11 .... 488 A5 🄸
Darnley St *GVW* DA11 .... 489 F5 🄸
Darrell Cl *CHLM/WR* CM1 .... 304 C1
Darrell Rd *FX* IP11 .... 5 D6
Darsham Cl *UPMR* RM14 .... 432 A8 🄸
Dart Cl *UPMR* RM14 .... 432 A8 🄸
WIT CM8 .... 276 D3
Dartfields *HARH* RM3 .... 430 E1
Dart Gn *SOCK/AV* RM15 .... 469 K6
Dartmouth Cl *RAYL* SS6 .... 419 J8 🄸
Dartmouth Rd *CHLM/WR* CM1 .... 305 G7
Dartview Cl *GRAYS* RM17 .... 484 D3
Darwin Cl *BRTR* CM7 .... 209 J4 🄸
COLS CO2 .... 219 J4
Darwin Rd *IPNE* IP4 .... 37 H5
TIL RM18 .... 484 E7
Dash End *HVHL* CB9 .... 28 D3
Dash End La *HVHL* CB9 .... 28 D3
The Dashes *HLW* CM20 .... 13 E2
Dashwood Cl *RIPW* IP8 .... 61 K4
Dashwood Rd *GVW* DA11 .... 489 F6
Datchet Dr *SBN/FI* SS3 .... 466 D5
Davall Cl *HAR* CO12 .... 164 B4
Davenants *PIT* SS13 .... 438 E5
Davenport *HLWE* CM17 .... 295 J6

Daventry Gdns *HARH* RM3 .... 408 D8
Daventry Rd *HARH* RM3 .... 408 D8
Davey Cl *COL* CO1 .... 9 E4
IPSE IP3 .... 63 H4
David Av *WICKE* SS11 .... 417 G3
David Dr *HARH* RM3 .... 431 H1
Davidson Cl *SUD* CO10 .... 85 F1
Davidson Gdns *WICKW* SS12 .... 417 H8
David's Wk *BCAYE* CM11 .... 414 D3 🄸
Davis Av *GVW* DA11 .... 488 D6
Davison Cl *BAR* EN8 .... 346 D2
Davison Dr *BAR* EN8 .... 346 D2
Davis Rd *CDH/CHF* RM16 .... 483 J2
SOCK/AV RM15 .... 469 F8
Davy Rd *COS* CO15 .... 260 A5
Dawes Av *HCH* RM12 .... 450 E4
Dawes Cl *RIPS/CAP* IP9 .... 86 E4
Dawes La *K/T/MI* CO5 .... 285 G4
Dawley Gn *SOCK/AV* RM15 .... 469 J6
Dawlish Crs *RAYL* SS6 .... 419 J8
Dawlish Dr *LOS* SS9 .... 463 F4
Dawlish Rd *COS* CO15 .... 290 E5
Dawn Cl *MAL* CM9 .... 338 D5
Dawnford Cl *COLW* CO3 .... 185 H6 🄸
Daws Cl *CHLM/WR* CM1 .... 331 F4
Daws Heath Rd *RAYL* SS6 .... 441 J4
SBF/HAD SS7 .... 441 H7
Daws Hl *CHING* E4 .... 375 J7
Dawson Cl *SAFWN* CB10 .... 71 G3 🄸
Dawson Drift *KESG* IP5 .... 39 G6 🄸
Dawson Dr *FX* IP11 .... 94 D7
RAIN RM13 .... 450 C8 🄸
Daw St *BRTR* CM7 .... 143 F1
HSTD CO9 .... 51 J8
Daylop Dr *CHIG* IG7 .... 406 A6
Days Cl *CHLM/WR* CM1 .... 304 D5
Days Gn *RIPS/CAP* IP9 .... 86 E4
Days La *BRWN* CM15 .... 383 J8
Days Rd *RIPS/CAP* IP9 .... 86 E3
Dayton Dr *RITH* DA8 .... 480 E4
Dazeley's La *RCOLE* CO7 .... 122 E5
Deacon Dr *LAIN* SS15 .... 16 A3
Dead La *BURES* CO8 .... 116 D3
MGTR CO11 .... 159 G3
RCOLE CO7 .... 157 F5
RCOS CO16 .... 257 F3
RCOS CO16 .... 258 D4
Deadman's La *CHLM/GWD* CM2 .... 360 E1
Deal Cl *BRTR* CM7 .... 177 H7 🄸
COS CO15 .... 290 E5
Dealtree Cl *BRWN* CM15 .... 383 K1
Deal Wy *RCOLE* CO7 .... 255 J4
Deanery Gdns *BRTR* CM7 .... 177 J6
Deanery Hl *BRTR* CM7 .... 177 H6 🄸
Deane's Cl *HAR* CO12 .... 6 B6
Deanes Ct *HAR* CO12 .... 6 B6
Deanhill Av *COS* CO15 .... 11 E2
Dean Rd *CBE/LIN* CB1 .... 23 K6
Dean Rogers Pl *BRTR* CM7 .... 177 J6 🄸
Deans Cl *HVHL* CB9 .... 27 F4
Deans Rd *BRW* CM14 .... 410 E6
Dean St *RCOLE* CO7 .... 255 J6
Dearsley Rd *EN* EN1 .... 374 A7
Debden Cl *SAFWN* CB10 .... 102 B3
Debden Gn *VGE* SS16 .... 16 A6
Debden La *LOU* IG10 .... 377 K4
Debden Rd *LOU* IG10 .... 377 K4
SAFWS CB11 .... 70 E5
SAFWS CB11 .... 71 F7
SAFWS CB11 .... 100 B5
Debden Wy *BOC* CM0 .... 398 A7 🄸
De Beauvoir Cha *BCAYE* CM11 ...... 416 A2
Deben Av *KESG* IP5 .... 39 K5
Deben Dr *SUD* CO10 .... 58 D5
Debenham Rd *EBAR* EN7 .... 346 B1
Deben Rd *COLN* CO4 .... 188 B4
HVHL CB9 .... 27 H5
IP IP1 .... 36 B4
Deben Valley Dr *KESG* IP5 .... 39 G6
Deben Wk *RCOS* CO16 .... 258 E7 🄸
Deben Wy *FX* IP11 .... 5 E4
De Bohun Ct *SAFWN* CB10 .... 71 F3
De Burgh Pl *SUD* CO10 .... 31 H4
De Burgh Rd *COLW* CO3 .... 185 K7
Dedham Av *RCOS* CO16 .... 290 D1
Dedham Cl *BCAYE* CM11 .... 414 D3
Dedham Meade *RCOLE* CO7 .... 157 J2
Dedham Rd *BCAYE* CM11 .... 414 D3
COLN CO4 .... 119 J7
MGTR CO11 .... 158 D1
RCOLE CO7 .... 121 J4
Dee Cl *UPMR* RM14 .... 432 A8
Deepdale *SBF/HAD* SS7 .... 440 E7
Deepdale Rd *HAR* CO12 .... 6 B4
Deepdene *INC* CM4 .... 386 B2
Deepdene Av *RAYL* SS6 .... 419 H8
Deepdene Pth *LOU* IG10 .... 377 K8
Deepdene Rd *LOU* IG10 .... 377 J8
Deeping Wk *RCOS* CO16 .... 257 H8
Deepwater Rd *CVI* SS8 .... 477 J3
Deerbank Rd *BCAYE* CM11 .... 414 D2
Deere Av *RAIN* RM13 .... 450 B7
Deerhurst *SBF/HAD* SS7 .... 441 G6
Deerhurst Cha *RCHLM* CM3 .... 363 K4
Deerhurst Cl *SBF/HAD* SS7 .... 441 G6 🄸

Deerleap Gv CHING E4 402 C1
Deerleap Wy BRTR CM7 210 C1
Deer Pk HLWW/ROY CM19 12 A6
Defoe Crs COLN CO4 155 F8
Defoe Pde CDH/CHF RM16 485 G2
Defoe Rd IP IP1 36 C1
Deford Rd WIT CM8 276 D5
De Greys Cl SUD CO10 59 F8
Deirdre Av WICKW SS12 416 E6
Deirdre Cl WICKW SS12 416 E6
Delafield Rd GRAYS RM17 484 C4
Delamare Rd BAR EN8 347 F3
Delamere Rd CHLM/WR CM1 332 A4
COLN CO4 188 A2
Delargy Cl CDH/CHF RM16 485 G2
Delaware Crs SBN/FI SS3 466 C6
Delaware Rd SBN/FI SS3 466 B6
Delder Av CVI SS8 478 D3
Delft Rd CVI SS8 478 A1
Delfzul Rd CVI SS8 478 A1
Delgada Rd CVI SS8 478 D2
Delhi Rd PIT SS13 439 F7
Delimands LAIN SS15 17 D4
Dell Cl WFD IG8 403 J6
Dell La BSF CM23 199 F6
RBSF CM22 232 A5
Dellows La RBSF CM22 168 B3
Dell Rd GRAYS RM17 484 A3
PEND EN3 374 C4
Dells Cl CHING E4 402 C3
The Dell BRW CM14 432 E1
CHLM/GWD CM2 333 H6
COL CO1 8 C5
GTDUN CM6 204 D4
VGE SS16 457 J2
WFD IG8 403 J6
WICKE SS11 417 H6
Dellwood Av FX IP11 131 H2
Delmar Gdns WICKE SS11 417 F3
Delmores VGE SS16 456 D2
Delta Rd RBRW/HUT CM13 412 C2
Delview CVI SS8 460 E8
Delvins PIT SS13 438 D5
Delvyn's La HSTD CO9 81 H7
De Mandeville Ga EN EN1 374 A8
De Mandeville Rd RBSF CM22 168 D3
De-marci Ct BRTR CM7 210 C2
Denbigh Cl EMPK RM11 431 G6
Denbigh Rd LAIN SS15 436 C8
Denby Gra HLWE CM17 295 J5
Dencourt Crs BSDN SS14 438 C8
Dendridge Cl EN EN1 374 B3
Dene Cl RAYL SS6 441 J1 1
Dene Ct CHLM/WR CM1 303 K8
Denecroft Gdns GRAYS RM17 484 C2
Dene Gdns RAYL SS6 441 J1
Dene Holm Rd GVW DA11 488 C8
Denehurst Gdns VGE SS16 455 K1
WFD IG8 403 J7
Dene Pth SOCK/AV RM15 469 J6
Dene Rd BKHH IG9 404 B4
Denesmere SBF/HAD SS7 460 B1 1
Deneway VGE SS16 458 A3
Dengayne BSDN SS14 438 A7
Dengie Cl WIT CM8 277 F5
Denham Cl RCOLE CO7 221 F5 2
Denham Rd CVI SS8 478 A1
Denham V RAYL SS6 441 F2 3
Denholm Ct WIT CM8 277 F5 1
Denholme Wk RAIN RM13 450 A7 1
Denmark Gdns RIPS/CAP IP9 90 A7
Denner Rd CHING E4 402 B5
Dennises La UPMR RM14 452 C8
Dennis Rd GVW DA11 489 F8
UPMR RM14 469 J1
Denny Av WAB EN9 347 K8
Denny Ct BSF CM23 199 G3
Denny Ga BAR EN8 347 F1
Dent Cl SOCK/AV RM15 469 J6 2
Denton Ap WOS/PRIT SS0 443 K8 1
Denton Av WOS/PRIT SS0 443 K8
Denton Cl CHTY IP2 61 K3
WOS/PRIT SS0 443 K8
Denton Court Rd GVE DA12 489 K6
Denton St GVE DA12 489 K5
Denver Dr PIT SS13 439 F4
Denys Dr BSDN SS14 438 C4
Derby Av UPMR RM14 451 G4
Derby Cl BCAYE CM11 387 K8
IPNE IP4 37 J8
RCHLM CM3 368 D4
VGE SS16 456 A1 2
Derbydale RCFD SS4 421 K7
Derby Rd HOD EN11 319 K1
IPSE IP3 63 J1
Derby Road Br GRAYS RM17 484 A4
Dereham Av IPSE IP3 63 H2
Dereham Cl COLS CO2 218 D2
Derek Gdns SOSN SS2 444 B8
Derham Gdns UPMR RM14 451 K4
Dering Crs LOS SS9 442 E6
Derry Av SOCK/AV RM15 469 J5 1
Derventer Av CVI SS8 461 F7
Derwent Av RAYL SS6 441 K3
Derwent Gdns COS CO15 11 F1
Derwent Pde SOCK/AV RM15 469 J6
Derwent Rd COLN CO4 155 K8
IPSE IP3 63 H2
Derwent Wy BRTR CM7 209 F7
HCH RM12 450 C6 1
De Staunton Cl RCOLE CO7 222 A6 1
Detling Cl HCH RM12 450 D6 1
Detling Rd GVW DA11 488 C6
Devereaux Cl FOS CO13 228 E5
Devereaux Pl COLN CO4 186 D2
De Vere Av MAL CM9 338 D4
De Vere Cl RCHLM CM3 308 B2
RCOLE CO7 220 E5
De Vere La RCOLE CO7 220 E5
De Vere Rd COLW CO3 186 A8
RCOLW CO6 149 G6
De Veres Rd HSTD CO9 147 J4 2
Devereux Rd CDH/CHF RM16 483 J2
SOS SS1 19 D5 2
Devereux Wy BCAYW CM12 387 F8
De Vere Wy HAR CO12 6 A6 2
Deveron Gdns SOCK/AV RM15 469 J5 2
De Vigier Av SAFWN CB10 71 H3
Devlin Rd RIPW IP8 61 H4
Devoils La BSF CM23 198 E6 2
Devon Cl BKHH IG9 403 J5
Devon Gdns RCFD SS4 421 K8
Devon Rd COLS CO2 218 C2
FX IP11 5 F2
Devonshire Cl LAIN SS15 436 B5
Devonshire Gdns BRTR CM7 210 A1
SLH/COR SS17 486 B2
Devonshire Rd BOC CM0 398 B8
CDH/CHF RM16 483 H3
GVW DA11 489 G6
HCH RM12 450 E3
IPSE IP3 37 H8
LAIN SS15 436 B5
Devon Wy COS CO15 260 C6 1
CVI SS8 461 F8
HAR CO12 164 C3 1
Dewar La KESG IP5 39 G6
Dewes Green Rd BSF CM23 133 J4
Dewgrass Gv BAR EN8 374 D1 2
Dewhurst Rd BAR EN8 346 C3
Dewlands BRTR CM7 210 A8
Dewsbury Gdns HARH RM3 430 E1 2
Dewsbury Rd HARH RM3 431 F1 1
Dewsgreen VGE SS16 458 B1
Dewyk Rd CVI SS8 461 H8
Dexter Cl GRAYS RM17 483 K2
Deyncourt Gdns UPMR RM14 451 K3
Deynes Rd SAFWS CB11 101 J6
Dial Rd RCOLE CO7 256 E2
Diamond Cl CDH/CHF RM16 483 J2
Diana Cl CDH/CHF RM16 483 J2
Diana Wy COS CO15 290 E3
Diban Av HCH RM12 450 C5
Dickens Av TIL RM18 485 G7
Dickens Cl BRTR CM7 209 K5 3
SOSN SS2 19 E2
Dickens Dr LAIN SS15 16 A3
Dickens Pl CHLM/WR CM1 303 K6
Dickens Ri CHIG IG7 404 D6
Dickens Rd CHTY IP2 36 A7
GVE DA12 489 K6
Dickins Cl EBAR EN7 346 A1
Dickinson Ter KESG IP5 39 H6 3
Dicky Moors RCHLM CM3 272 B6
Didsbury Cl CHTY IP2 61 K3
Digby Rd IPNE IP4 38 A6
SLH/COR SS17 457 J8
Dilbridge Rd East COLN CO4 9 E3
Dilbridge Rd West COLN CO4 9 D3
Dillwyn St IP IP1 2 B3
Dillwyn St West IP IP1 2 B3
Dilston RCHLM CM3 336 A7
Dimsdale Crs BSF CM23 199 G8
Dinant Av CVI SS8 460 D8
Dinants Crs RCOLW CO6 215 H2
Dinsdale Cl COLN CO4 9 E3 2
The Dismals RCHLM CM3 275 F3
Disney Cl ING CM4 386 B1
Dison Cl PEND EN3 374 D5 2
Disraeli Rd RAYL SS6 442 C5
Distillery La COLS CO2 220 A1
Ditchingham Gv IPNE IP4 38 C7
Ditton Court Rd WOS/PRIT SS0 18 A4
Dixon Av CHLM/WR CM1 14 A1
RCOS CO16 258 E7
Dixon Cl MGTR CO11 159 G1
Dixon Wy RCOLE CO7 220 D2
Dobbies La RCOLW CO6 215 J2
Dobbs Drift KESG IP5 39 K6
Dobbs La KESG IP5 39 J5
KIR/NAC IP10 39 J8
Dobsons Cl LOS SS9 463 G3
RAYL SS6 441 K4
Dock Approach Rd
CDH/CHF RM16 471 K8
GRAYS RM17 484 D4
Dockfield Av HAR CO12 6 A5
Docklands Av ING CM4 386 C1
Dock La HAR CO12 195 K1
Dock Rd GRAYS RM17 484 C5
RCHLM CM3 369 F4
TIL RM18 484 D7
Dock St CHTY IP2 3 D5
Dockwra La RCHLM CM3 335 K6
Doctor's La SUD CO10 53 G3
Doctor Watson's La KESG IP5 38 E4
Docwra Rd K/T/MI CO5 246 E3
Doddenhill Cl SAFWN CB10 71 F2 6
Doddinghurst Rd BRWN CM15 384 A3
BRWN CM15 411 F3
Dodmans RIPS/CAP IP9 87 F4 1
Dodson V KESG IP5 39 G6
Doesgate La UPMR RM14 455 G4
Doeshill Dr WICKW SS12 417 H6
Dog Cha BRTR CM7 143 K2 1
Dogden La BSF CM23 166 D3
Doggetts Cha RCFD SS4 422 C7
Doggetts Cl RCFD SS4 444 C2
Doggetts La RCOLW CO6 215 J3
Doghouse Rd BRTR CM7 179 K8
Dog Kennel La ING CM4 358 B6
Dogs Head St IPNE IP4 3 D4
Dolby Ri CHLM/GWD CM2 333 H3
Dollant Av CVI SS8 478 A2
Dolphin Ap ROM RM1 430 A6
Dolphin Cl CBE/LIN CB1 23 F3 2
Dolphin Gdns BCAYW CM12 387 F8 3
Dolphins WOS/PRIT SS0 444 A8
Dolphin Wy BSF CM23 199 F5
Dombey Cl CHLM/WR CM1 304 B6
Dombey Rd CHTY IP2 36 A8
Domitian Cl COLN CO4 155 J8
Domsey Bank RCOLW CO6 215 H2
Domsey Cha K/T/MI CO5 214 E5
Domsey La RCHLM CM3 305 G2
Doms La RCHLM CM3 274 E3
Donald Thorn Cl WICKW SS12 417 G7 2
Donald Wy CHLM/GWD CM2 15 D6
Donard Dr RCOLW CO6 185 J1
Doncaster Wy UPMR RM14 451 G4
Don Ct WIT CM8 276 D3
Donkey La EN EN1 374 A6
Donne Dr COS CO15 290 C5
Donovan's Gdn RBRW/HUT CM13 434 D2
Donyland Wy K/T/MI CO5 220 C6
Dooley Rd HSTD CO9 147 J4
Dorchester End COLS CO2 219 J2
Dorchester Gdns CHING E4 402 B7 2
Dorchester Rd BCAYW CM12 387 G8 4
GVE DA12 489 J8
IPSE IP3 64 B2
Dorewards Av BRTR CM7 177 J6
Dorian Rd HCH RM12 450 B2
Doric Av RCFD SS4 422 A8
Dorking Crs RCOS CO16 258 E7
Dorking Ri HARH RM3 408 E7
Dorking Rd HARH RM3 408 E7
Dorking Wk HARH RM3 408 E7
Dorkins Wy UPMR RM14 452 B1
Dorothy Farm Rd RAYL SS6 442 B4 1
Dorothy Gdns SBF/HAD SS7 440 E8
Dorothy Sayers Dr WIT CM8 245 F8
Dorrington Gdns HCH RM12 450 E2
Dorset Av CHLM/GWD CM2 333 F7
Dorset Cl CHLM/GWD CM2 333 G7
COS CO15 260 C7 1
IPNE IP4 37 H4
Dorset Gdns RCFD SS4 421 K8
Dorset Rd BOC CM0 425 H1
MAL CM9 338 B4
Dorset Wy BCAYW CM12 387 G8
Dorvis La SAFWN CB10 46 E4
Doubleday Dr MAL CM9 310 B8
Doubleday Gdns BRTR CM7 178 A8
Doubleday Rd LOU IG10 378 A7
Doublegate La WICKE SS11 418 B8
WICKW SS12 440 A1
Doublet Ms BCAYE CM11 387 K8
Douglas Av HARH RM3 431 F4
Douglas Cl CDH/CHF RM16 483 H2
CHLM/GWD CM2 361 F2 1
Douglas Dr WICKW SS12 417 G8
Douglas Gv WIT CM8 276 D3 2
Douglas Rd CHING E4 403 F3
COS CO15 290 E1
HAR CO12 6 C5 1
ROM RM1 430 A8
SBF/HAD SS7 462 A2
Douglas Wk CHLM/GWD CM2 14 B5
Doug Siddons Ct GRAYS RM17 484 B5 2
Doulton Cl HLWE CM17 295 J6
Doulton Wy RCFD SS4 421 K7
Dove Cl BSF CM23 231 J2
STSD CM24 167 K6
Dovecote SBN/FI SS3 466 D4 3
Dove Crs HAR CO12 164 C3
Dovedale CVI SS8 461 J8 3
FX IP11 5 D4
Dovedale Cl BCAYE CM11 415 K1 1
VGE SS16 456 B1 1
Dovedale Gdns COS CO15 11 F1
Dove Dr SBF/HAD SS7 460 A3
Dovehouse Cft HLW CM20 294 E3 1
Dove House Gdns CHING E4 402 B5 2
Dove House Rd HVHL CB9 27 G5 1

Dove La *CHLM/GWD* CM2 .... 332 C7
Dovercliff Rd *CVI* SS8 .... 478 C2
Dover Cl *BRTR* CM7 .... 177 H7
  COS CO15 .... 291 F5 ◪
Dover Rd *GVW* DA11 .... 488 C5
  IPSE IP3 .... 63 K1
  RCOLE CO7 .... 255 K5
Dover Rd East *SBF/HAD* SS7 ...... 488 D5
Dovervelt Rd *CVI* SS8 .... 461 G8
Dover Wy *PIT* SS13 .... 438 E7
Dovesgate *SBF/HAD* SS7 .... 460 A1 ◪
Doves La *GTDUN* CM6 .... 236 E3
Doves Ms *LAIN* SS15 .... 16 B1 ◪
Dowches Dr *K/T/MI* CO5 .... 246 E2
Dowches Gdns *K/T/MI* CO5 .... 246 E2 ◪
Dow Ct *BOC* CM0 .... 398 C1
Dowding Cl *RAIN* RM13 .... 450 C8
Dowland Cl *SLH/COR* SS17 .... 473 J2 ◪
Dowling Rd *BURES* CO8 .... 151 J2
The Downage *DA11* 489 F7
Downer Rd *SBF/HAD* SS7 .... 460 C1
Downer Rd North *SBF/HAD* SS7 .. 440 D5
Downesway *SBF/HAD* SS7 .... 460 C2
Downey Cl *BSDN* SS14 .... 437 K6
Downfield Rd *BAR* EN8 .... 346 E5
Downhall Cl *RAYL* SS6 .... 441 J1
Downhall Park Wy *RAYL* SS6 ...... 441 H1
Downhall Rd *RAYL* SS6 .... 441 H1
Downhill Rd *RBSF* CM22 .... 265 H7
Downham Rd *BCAYE* CM11 .... 389 F8
  CVI SS8 .... 478 A2
  ING CM4 .... 388 C1
  ING CM4 .... 388 D4
  WICKE SS11 .... 417 F3
Downing Cl *CHTY* IP2 .... 62 B3
Downlands *WAB* EN9 .... 348 A8 ◪
Downleaze *RCHLM* CM3 .... 392 E5
Downs Crs *GTDUN* CM6 .... 204 B4
  HVHL CB9 .... 27 F5
Downs Gv *VGE* SS16 .... 458 B2
Downside Cl *CHTY* IP2 .... 62 B5
Downsland Dr *BRW* CM14 .... 411 F6
Downs Rd *MAL* CM9 .... 338 C2
The Downs *FX* IP11 .... 5 D2
  GTDUN CM6 .... 204 C4
  HLW CM20 .... 13 E3
Downsway *CHLM/WR* CM1 .... 305 F6
Downton Dr *HVHL* CB9 .... 26 E5
Dowsetts La *BCAYE* CM11 .... 388 E8
Dragon Cl *BOC* CM0 .... 398 A8
Dragon's Gn *SAFWN* CB10 .... 72 A1 ◪
Drake Av *IPSE* IP3 .... 63 K3
  RCHLM CM3 .... 368 E5
Drake Cl *BRW* CM14 .... 411 G8
  SBF/HAD SS7 .... 461 H1
Drake Gdns *BRTR* CM7 .... 210 B1 ◪
Drake Ms *RAIN* RM13 .... 450 B8 ◪
Drake Rd *CDH/CHF* RM16 .... 483 H1
  LAIN SS15 .... 16 B4
  SUD CO10 .... 58 D4
  WOS/PRIT SS0 .... 463 K5
Drakes Ap *COS* CO15 .... 290 C4
Drakes Cl *BAR* EN8 .... 346 D2 ◪
Drakes La *RCHLM* CM3 .... 273 H6
Drake Sq North *IPSE* IP3 .... 63 K3
Drake Sq South *IPSE* IP3 .... 63 K3
The Drakes *FIL* SS3 .... 466 D5
Drakes Wy *RAYL* SS6 .... 441 K1
Drapers Ct *BRTR* CM7 .... 208 A4
  MAL CM9 .... 339 F1
Drapers La *HVHL* CB9 .... 49 G5
Drapers Rd *RCHLM* CM3 .... 392 E5 ◪
Drapery Common *SUD* CO10 .... 33 H1
Drayman's Cl *BSF* CM23 .... 198 A8
Drayson Cl *WAB* EN9 .... 347 K6
The Drays *SUD* CO10 .... 34 D8
Drayton Av *LOU* IG10 .... 404 C2
Drayton Cl *MAL* CM9 .... 338 C4 ◪
Drewsteignton *SBN/FI* SS3 .... 466 C5
The Dreys *SAFWN* CB10 .... 72 A1
Driberg Wy *BRTR* CM7 .... 209 K4
The Drift *IPNE* IP4 .... 37 J7
  IPSE IP3 .... 64 A4
  RIPS/CAP IP9 .... 92 B8
  RIPS/CAP IP9 .... 125 K3
  SUD CO10 .... 59 F8
Driftway *VGE* SS16 .... 458 C2
The Driftway *IPNE* IP4 .... 37 K7
The Drive *BKHH* IG9 .... 403 K3
  CHING E4 .... 402 C2
  CHLM/WR CM1 .... 304 C7
  COS CO15 .... 259 K6
  EBAR EN7 .... 346 B2
  GTDUN CM6 .... 139 J2
  HAR CO12 .... 6 C1
  HARH RM3 .... 431 F3
  HLW CM20 .... 13 E4
  HOC/HUL SS5 .... 419 J2
  LOU IG10 .... 377 G7
  RAYL SS6 .... 442 C5
  RBRW/HUT CM13 .... 433 F1
  RCFD SS4 .... 444 D3
  RCHLM CM3 .... 368 D5
  SBW CM21 .... 263 J3

WIT CM8 .... 246 A7
  WOS/PRIT SS0 .... 463 J5
The Driveway *CVI* SS8 .... 478 B3
Droitwich Av *SOSN* SS2 .... 465 J4 ◪
Drood Cl *CHLM/WR* CM1 .... 304 B6
Drover's Ct *FX* IP11 .... 94 C7
Drovers Wy *BSF* CM23 .... 231 G1 ◪
The Druce *SAFWS* CB11 .... 134 C1
Drum Fld *RCOLE* CO7 .... 121 G4
Drummond Pl *WICKW* SS12 .... 417 H8 ◪
The Drummonds *EPP* CM16 .... 350 E4 ◪
Drury La *BRTR* CM7 .... 209 J2 ◪
  GTDUN CM6 .... 267 K3
  HSTD CO9 .... 52 D7
Drury Rd *COLS* CO2 .... 186 D8
Dryden Av *SOSN* SS2 .... 19 G3
Dryden Cl *MAL* CM9 .... 338 C5 ◪
Dryden Pl *TIL* RM18 .... 485 G7
Dryden Rd *IP* IP1 .... 36 C2
Drysdale Av *CHING* E4 .... 402 C2
Dry St *VGE* SS16 .... 456 D3
Drywoods *RCHLM* CM3 .... 392 D8 ◪
Ducker's La *CHLM/WR* CM1 .... 270 C6
Ducketts La *MHAD* SG10 .... 230 B4
Ducketts Md *HLWW/ROY* CM19 .. 292 D4
  RCFD SS4 .... 423 G3
Duck La *EPP* CM16 .... 323 G8
Duck Lees La *PEND* EN3 .... 374 E8
Duckling La *SBW* CM21 .... 263 J5 ◪
Duck St *GTDUN* CM6 .... 171 J8
  SAFWS CB11 .... 69 K8
Dudbrook Rd *BRW* CM14 .... 382 C4
Duddery Hl *HVHL* CB9 .... 27 F6
Duddery Rd *HVHL* CB9 .... 27 G6
Dudely Rd *GVW* DA11 .... 488 D5
Dudley Av *BAR* EN8 .... 346 D6
Dudley Cl *CDH/CHF* RM16 .... 483 H1
  COLS CO2 .... 219 H1
  RCHLM CM3 .... 306 C4
Dudley Rd *COS* CO15 .... 10 A4
  HARH RM3 .... 430 E1
  K/T/MI CO5 .... 253 G2
  RCOLW CO6 .... 149 G6
Duffield Cl *CDH/CHF* RM16 .... 483 J2
Duffield Rd *CHLM/GWD* CM2 ..... 337 F7
Duffries Cl *RCHLM* CM3 .... 272 A6
Dugard Av *COLW* CO3 .... 217 K1
Duggers La *BRTR* CM7 .... 209 K4
Dugmore Av *FOS* CO13 .... 228 B5
Duke Pl *LAIN* SS15 .... 16 C2
Dukes Av *BOC* CM0 .... 398 C2
  CDH/CHF RM16 .... 483 K2
  EPP CM16 .... 378 C1
Dukes Cl *EPP* CM16 .... 352 B1
Dukes Farm Cl *BCAYW* CM12 .... 387 J8
Dukes Farm Rd *BCAYW* CM12 ... 414 C1
Dukes La *CHLM/GWD* CM2 .... 333 H1
  CHONG CM5 .... 300 A7
Dukes Orch *RBSF* CM22 .... 234 B7
Dukes Ride *BSF* CM23 .... 198 B6
Dukes Rd *BCAYE* CM11 .... 414 D1
  BRTR CM7 .... 177 J8 ◪
Duke St *IPSE* IP3 .... 3 F4
  RCOLE CO7 .... 255 J7
Dulverton Av *WOS/PRIT* SS0 ..... 463 H1
Dulverton Cl *WOS/PRIT* SS0 ...... 443 H8
Dumbarton Av *BAR* EN8 .... 346 D8 ◪
Dumbarton Cl *IPNE* IP4 .... 37 K5
Dumney La *RCHLM* CM3 .... 240 D2
Dumont Av *RCOS* CO16 .... 288 B3
Dunbar Pl *WICKW* SS12 .... 417 H8
Duncan Cl *WICKW* SS12 .... 417 J8 ◪
Duncan Ri *HSTD* CO9 .... 79 J3 ◪
Duncan Rd *COLS* CO2 .... 218 C1
Dundee Av *COS* CO15 .... 11 F5
Dundee Ct *BSDN* SS14 .... 438 C5
Dundee Wy *PEND* EN3 .... 374 D7
Dundonald Dr *LOS* SS9 .... 463 G4
Dunfane *BCAYW* CM12 .... 387 J8
Dungannon Cha *SOS* SS1 .... 466 A7
Dungannon Dr *SOS* SS1 .... 466 A7
Dunkellin Gv *SOCK/AV* RM15 ..... 469 J6 ◪
Dunkellin Wy *SOCK/AV* RM15 .... 469 J6
Dunkirk Rd *BOC* CM0 .... 425 H1
Dunlin Cl *MAL* CM9 .... 310 E8 ◪
  RCHLM CM3 .... 392 D4
Dunlin Ct *K/T/MI* CO5 .... 246 E3
Dunlop Cl *CHTY* IP2 .... 62 A3
Dunlop Rd *CHTY* IP2 .... 2 A3
  TIL RM18 .... 484 E7
Dunmore Rd *CHLM/GWD* CM2 ... 333 J2 ◪
Dunmow Cl *LOU* IG10 .... 404 B2
Dunmow Gdns *RBRW/HUT* CM13 . 434 C8
Dunmow Rd *BRTR* CM7 .... 141 J8
  BRTR CM7 .... 207 K4
  BSF CM23 .... 199 D5
  CHONG CM5 .... 299 H4

GTDUN CM6 .... 139 K4
GTDUN CM6 .... 236 D5
  RBSF CM22 .... 200 B6
Dunning Cl *MGTR* CO11 .... 160 D5
  SOCK/AV RM15 .... 469 J6 ◪
Dunningford Cl *HCH* RM12 .... 450 A6 ◪
Dunnings La *RBRW/HUT* CM13 .. 454 A3
Dunnock Wy *COLN* CO4 .... 188 D6
Dunoon Cl *BRTR* CM7 .... 210 C1 ◪
Dunsey Wood Cl *HVHL* CB9 .... 26 D4
Dunstable Rd *HARH* RM3 .... 430 E1
  SLH/COR SS17 .... 473 J2
Dunstalls *HLWW/ROY* CM19 ...... 321 J1
Dunster Av *WOS/PRIT* SS0 .... 443 H8
Dunster Crs *UPMR* RM14 .... 451 H3
Dunster Dr *HVHL* CB9 .... 26 E5
Dunthorne Rd *COLN* CO4 .... 188 E3
Dunthorpe Rd *RCOS* CO16 .... 10 A1
Dunton Rd *RBRW/HUT* CM13 ..... 435 J4
Dupont Cl *RCOS* CO16 .... 10 A1 ◪
Durants Park Av *PEND* EN3 .... 374 D8
Durants Rd *PEND* EN3 .... 374 C8
Durban La *LAIN* SS15 .... 437 G3 ◪
The Durdans *VGE* SS16 .... 456 C1
Durham Av *GPK* RM2 .... 430 D6
  WFD IG8 .... 404 A8
Durham Cl *BRTR* CM7 .... 142 B4
  SBW CM21 .... 263 G4 ◪
Durham Rd *LAIN* SS15 .... 435 K7
  RCFD SS4 .... 421 J8
  SOSN SS2 .... 465 G3
Durham Sq *COL* CO1 .... 8 C4
Durham Wy *RAYL* SS6 .... 419 J8
Durian Wy *ERITH* DA8 .... 480 C6
Durley Av *WICKW* SS12 .... 416 C5
Durley Cl *SBF/HAD* SS7 .... 460 B1
Durnell Wy *LOU* IG10 .... 377 J7
Durrington Cl *VGE* SS16 .... 437 K8
Dury Falls Cl *EMPK* RM11 .... 451 G2 ◪
Duxford *WICKE* SS11 .... 417 K7
Duxford Cl *HCH* RM12 .... 450 C7
Duxford Rd *SAFWN* CB10 .... 20 A6
Dyer's Rd *COLW* CO3 .... 217 H2
  HSTD CO9 .... 78 B4
  MAL CM9 .... 338 C3
Dyers Wy *HARH* RM3 .... 430 B2
Dyke Crs *CVI* SS8 .... 477 H1
Dykes Cha *MAL* CM9 .... 338 A2
Dyke St *IP* IP1 .... 3 D3
Dymoke Rd *ROM* RM1 .... 450 A1
Dyne's Hall Rd *HSTD* CO9 .... 111 H5
Dynevor Gdns *LOS* SS9 .... 462 C4
Dysons Cl *BAR* EN8 .... 346 D7
Dytchleys Rd *BRW* CM14 .... 382 B8

E

Eagle Av *WOTN* CO14 .... 229 J4
Eagle Cl *PEND* EN3 .... 374 C8
  RAIN RM13 .... 450 C7
  WAB EN9 .... 348 C8
Eagle La *BRTR* CM7 .... 177 J8
  BRWN CM15 .... 383 C3
Eagles Cl *FX* IP11 .... 5 F3
Eagle Wy *RBRW/HUT* CM13 ...... 433 F1
  SBN/FI SS3 .... 466 D5
Earlhams Cl *HAR* CO12 .... 6 A6
Earl Mountbatten Dr
  BCAYW CM12 .... 414 A2 ◪
Earl Rd *GVW* DA11 .... 488 D7
Earls Cl *BSF* CM23 .... 198 C7
Earls Colne Rd *RCOLW* CO6 ...... 182 C3
Earlsfield Dr *CHLM/GWD* CM2 ... 333 H2
Earls Hall Av *SOSN* SS2 .... 18 B1
Earls Hall Dr *RCOS* CO16 .... 290 A1
Earls Hall Pde *SOSN* SS2 .... 464 B1
Earlsmead *WIT* CM8 .... 277 F2 ◪
Earl's Pth *LOU* IG10 .... 376 E7
Earlswood *SBF/HAD* SS7 .... 460 C1
Earlswood Wy *COLS* CO2 .... 218 E3
Easedale Dr *HCH* RM12 .... 450 C6
Easington Wy *SOCK/AV* RM15 ... 469 J5
East Bay *COL* CO1 .... 9 D4
Eastbourne Gv *WOS/PRIT* SS0 ... 463 K2
East Bridge Rd *RCHLM* CM3 ...... 392 D5
Eastbrook Rd *WAB* EN9 .... 348 A7
Eastbrooks *PIT* SS13 .... 438 E6
Eastbury Av *RCFD* SS4 .... 444 A1
Eastby Cl *SAFWS* CB11 .... 71 G5
Eastcheap *RAYL* SS6 .... 441 H1
Eastcliff Av *COS* CO15 .... 11 E5
Eastcote Gv *SOSN* SS2 .... 465 G2
East Crs *CVI* SS8 .... 477 K1
East Dene Dr *HARH* RM3 .... 408 E8
East Dock Rd *HAR* CO12 .... 6 A2
East Dr *SBW* CM21 .... 263 J4
Eastend La *RBSF* CM22 .... 169 J4
East End La *RCOLE* CO7 .... 123 H2
Eastend Rd *BOC* CM0 .... 344 D5
East End Rd *RCOLE* CO7 .... 123 F3
Easterford Rd *K/T/MI* CO5 .... 246 E3

Entry	Location	Ref
Easterling Cl HAR	CO12	6 B4
Eastern Av BAR	EN8	347 F7
HVHL	CB9	27 F5
SBF/HAD	SS7	440 B8
SOCK/AV	RM15	481 K1
SOSN	SS2	19 F1
WTHK	RM20	482 C4
Eastern Av East GPK	RM2	430 A3
Eastern Cl IPNE	IP4	64 D1
SOSN	SS2	19 D1
Eastern Crs CHLM/WR	CM1	304 B8
Eastern Esp CVI	SS8	478 D3
SOS	SS1	19 F6
Eastern Rd BOC	CM0	398 C7
GRAYS	RM17	484 C3
RAYL	SS6	441 G5
RCOLE	CO7	255 J7
ROM	RM1	430 A7
Eastern Wy GRAYS	RM17	483 K5
Eastfield Rd BAR	EN8	347 F6
BRW	CM14	411 G5
CVI	SS8	461 J8
LAIN	SS15	437 G3
PEND	EN3	374 D4
East Ga HLW	CM20	13 D2
Easthorpe Rd K/T/MI	CO5	215 J3
K/T/MI	CO5	248 C1
East Kent Av GVW	DA11	488 B4
Eastland Ct FX	IP11	94 E8
East La RCOLE	CO7	171 K8
East Lawn IPNE	IP4	38 A5
Eastleigh Rd SBF/HAD	SS7	460 D5
Eastley VGE	SS16	17 E6
East Mayne BSDN	SS14	438 D3
PIT	SS13	438 C6
East Mersea Rd K/T/MI	CO5	285 F3
East Mill Gn RIPS/CAP	IP9	87 K7
East Milton Rd GVE	DA12	489 J5
Easton End LAIN	SS15	436 B7
Easton Rd WIT	CM8	277 G2
Easton Wy FOS	CO13	229 G7
East Pk HLWE	CM17	295 G2
SBW	CM21	263 J4
East Philbrick Crs RAYL	SS6	441 H2
East Rd BSF	CM23	199 G6
HLW	CM20	295 F1
K/T/MI	CO5	285 F6
PEND	EN3	374 C4
East Side COLN	CO4	155 H1
East Stockwell St COL	CO1	8 B4
East St BRTR	CM7	209 K2
COL	CO1	7 E4
HAR	CO12	7 D4
LOS	SS9	463 F5
MAL	CM9	314 D4
RCFD	SS4	444 C3
RCOLE	CO7	220 E6
RCOLW	CO6	213 H3
SAFWN	CB10	71 F4
SOSN	SS2	18 C2
SUD	CO10	58 B6
WTHK	RM20	483 H5
East Ter GVE	DA12	489 H4
WOTN	CO14	229 J4
East Thorpe BSDN	SS14	437 K8
East Thurrock Rd GRAYS	RM17	484 A5
East Tilbury Rd SLH/COR	SS17	486 B1
East Vw FX	IP11	402 D8
CHLM/WR	CM1	331 F4
East View Cl SAFWN	CB10	119 J8
Eastview Dr RAYL	SS6	419 J8
East Wy WAB	EN9	375 K1
Eastways CVI	SS8	460 E8
WIT	CM8	277 G1
Eastwick Rd HLW	CM20	293 K1
Eastwood Bvd WOS/PRIT	SS0	463 J3
Eastwoodbury La SOSN	SS2	444 A7
Eastwoodbury Crs SOSN	SS2	444 B7
Eastwoodbury La SOSN	SS2	443 J7
Eastwood Dr COLN	CO4	187 J2
Eastwood La South WOS/PRIT	SS0	463 J3
Eastwood Old Rd LOS	SS9	442 D8
SBF/HAD	SS7	442 B6
Eastwood Park Dr LOS	SS9	443 F7
Eastwood Ri LOS	SS9	442 D6
Eastwood Rd LOS	SS9	462 E2
RAYL	SS6	441 K4
Eastwood Rd North LOS	SS9	462 E1
Eaton Cl BCAYW	CM12	97 G8
FX	IP11	5 E5
Eaton Gdns FX	IP11	5 E5
Eaton Ms COLS	CO2	219 J2
Eaton Rd LOS	SS9	462 D3
UPMR	RM14	452 B3
Eatons Md CHING	E4	402 B5
Eaton Wy MAL	CM9	279 F6
Ebenezer Cl WIT	CM8	244 E8
Ebony Cl COLS	CO2	218 E3
Eccles Rd CHTY	IP2	61 K3
Eccleston Gdns BCAYW	CM12	387 G8
Echo Ct GVE	DA12	489 H7
Echo Hts CHING	E4	402 C4
Eckersley Rd CHLM/WR	CM1	15 D2
Eden Cl WIT	CM8	276 E2
Eden Gn SOCK/AV	RM15	469 K5
Edenhall Rd HARH	RM3	408 D8
Eden Pl GVE	DA12	489 G5
Eden Rd HVHL	CB9	27 G6
IPNE	IP4	37 K8
Edens Cl BSF	CM23	199 G6
Edenside FOS	CO13	228 E6
Edgecotts VGE	SS16	16 C6
Edgefield Av MGTR	CO11	159 G2
Edgeworth Rd CHTY	IP2	62 A3
Edgware Rd COS	CO15	10 A2
Edgworth Rd SUD	CO10	58 B6
Edinburgh Av LOS	SS9	462 C3
SLH/COR	SS17	474 B1
Edinburgh Cl RAYL	SS6	419 G8
WIT	CM8	277 G5
Edinburgh Crs BAR	EN8	346 E7
Edinburgh Gdns BRTR	CM7	210 A1
Edinburgh Ms TIL	RM18	485 G8
Edinburgh Pl HLW	CM20	294 E1
Edinburgh Wy HLW	CM20	295 F1
HLWE	CM17	263 G8
PIT	SS13	438 E7
Edington Rd PEND	EN3	374 C6
Edison Av HCH	RM12	450 A2
Edison Cl BRTR	CM7	209 J4
HCH	RM12	450 A2
Edison Gdns COLN	CO4	9 E3
Edison Rd COS	CO15	260 C7
PEND	EN3	375 F6
Edith Cavell Wy HVHL	CB9	50 C7
Edith Rd COS	CO15	10 B5
CVI	SS8	477 J2
FOS	CO13	228 C5
SOSN	SS2	18 C2
Edith Wy SLH/COR	SS17	457 H8
Edmonton Cl HSTD	CO9	38 E6
Edmonton Rd KESG	IP5	38 E5
Edmund Cl HVHL	CB9	27 F5
Edmund Gn HSTD	CO9	146 D5
Edmund Rd CDH/CHF	RM16	483 G5
WIT	CM8	276 E5
Edridge Cl HCH	RM12	450 E6
Edward Av CHING	E4	402 C8
RCOLE	CO7	255 K6
Edward Cl BCAYW	CM12	387 F8
IP	IP1	2 A1
RCFD	SS4	421 K7
RCOS	CO16	226 B8
Edward Dr CHLM/GWD	CM2	15 D6
Edward Gdns WICKE	SS11	417 G5
Edward Marke Dr K/T/MI	CO5	252 D2
Edward Rd RCOS	CO16	226 C6
HAR	CO12	128 D8
Edward St HAR	CO12	7 F4
Edward Wy RBRW/HUT	CM13	412 D2
Edwin Hall Vw RCHLM	CM3	392 C4
Edwin's Hall Rd RCHLM	CM3	392 C2
Edwin St GVE	DA12	489 G5
Egbert Gdns WICKE	SS11	417 G4
Egerton Dr VGE	SS16	435 K8
Egerton Green Rd COLS	CO2	218 B2
Egg Hall EPP	CM16	350 E5
Egglestone Cl CHTY	IP2	77 F2
Eggshell La HSTD	CO9	118 C1
Eglington Rd CHING	E4	402 E3
Egremont St COL	CO1	33 H2
Egremont Wy COLW	CO3	217 H1
Egret Crs COLN	CO4	188 D5
Ehringshausen Wy HVHL	CB9	27 G6
Eight Acre La COLS	CO2	218 D3
Eisenhower Rd LAIN	SS15	436 B7
Elan Rd SOCK/AV	RM15	469 J5
Eldbert Cl SOSN	SS2	465 H3
Eldeland LAIN	SS15	16 C3
Elder Av WICKW	SS12	416 E7
Elderbeck Rd EBAR	EN7	346 A2
Elderberry Cl VGE	SS16	436 C8
Elderberry Gdns WIT	CM8	277 H1
Elder Fld BRTR	CM7	208 E8
Elderstep Av CVI	SS8	478 E2
Elderton Rd WOS/PRIT	SS0	18 A4
Elder Wy WICKW	SS12	417 F7
Eldon Cl COLN	CO4	188 B4
Eldon Rd HOD	EN11	319 K1
Eldon Wy HOC/HUL	SS5	420 E7
Eldred Av COLS	CO2	218 C2
Eldred Dr SUD	CO10	85 F1
Eldred Gdns UPMR	RM14	452 B1
Eleanor Cha WICKW	SS12	417 F6
Eleanor Cl K/T/MI	CO5	248 B2
Eleanor Cross Rd BAR	EN8	346 E8
Eleanor Rd BAR	EN8	346 E7
Eleanor Wy BAR	EN8	411 G8
BRW	CM14	411 G8
Electric Av WOS/PRIT	SS0	463 K5
Eleven Acre Ri LOU	IG10	377 H7
Elgar Cl BKHH	IG9	404 A5
LAIN	SS15	16 B2
SBF/HAD	SS7	440 A2
Elgar Gdns TIL	RM18	485 F7
Elgin Av CHLM/WR	CM1	14 B5
HARH	RM3	431 J2
Elgin Rd BAR	EN8	346 C4
BROX	EN10	319 F6
Elham Dr PIT	SS13	439 F8
Elianore Rd COLW	CO3	186 C6
Eliot Wy MAL	CM9	338 C2
Elizabeth Av RAYL	SS6	441 H5
WIT	CM8	277 G6
Elizabeth Cl COLN	CO4	187 K1
HOC/HUL	SS5	443 F1
SAFWN	CB10	71 G3
TIL	RM18	485 G8
WAB	EN9	319 K5
Elizabeth Dr EPP	CM16	378 C2
WICKW	SS12	416 E8
Elizabeth Rd BRWN	CM15	410 E3
BSF	CM23	198 D6
CDH/CHF	RM16	483 J4
HAR	CO12	6 B5
Elizabeth Wy FX	IP11	5 D4
HLW	CM20	12 A3
HLWW/ROY	CM19	293 H6
HSTD	CO9	147 K5
LAIN	SS15	16 B5
MAL	CM9	310 C8
RCHLM	CM3	308 A1
RCOLE	CO7	221 F2
RCOLE	CO7	255 K5
SAFWN	CB10	71 G3
SBF/HAD	SS7	461 H1
SUD	CO10	57 K6
Ellenborough Cl BSF	CM23	198 C6
Ellenbrook Cl LOS	SS9	463 F1
Ellenbrook Rd CHTY	IP2	61 K6
RIPW	IP8	62 A5
Ellen Wy BRTR	CM7	209 F6
Ellerman Rd TIL	RM18	484 E8
Ellesmere Rd CVI	SS8	477 J2
Elliot Cl RCHLM	CM3	393 F7
Elliots Dr WOTN	CO14	229 G5
Elliott Gdns HARH	RM3	430 C6
Elliott St GVE	DA12	489 J3
IP	IP1	2 B3
Ellis Cl CDH/CHF	RM16	472 D6
Ellis Rd COLN	CO4	155 G1
COS	CO15	10 B5
MGTR	CO11	160 E5
Ellmore Rd HARH	RM3	430 C3
Elm Av MAL	CM9	310 D6
UPMR	RM14	451 J4
Elmbridge HLWE	CM17	295 K2
Elmbrook Dr BSF	CM23	231 J1
Elm Bungalows BRTR	CM7	209 G3
Elm Cl BKHH	IG9	404 A5
CHLM/GWD	CM2	333 G2
EPP	CM16	321 K6
HSTD	CO9	110 C3
HVHL	CB9	27 F5
K/T/MI	CO5	248 A6
MGTR	CO11	123 J4
RAYL	SS6	441 J2
RBSF	CM22	168 D3
RBSF	CM22	201 K6
RCOLE	CO7	222 A3
SBN/FI	SS3	466 D6
WAB	EN9	347 K5
Elm Close Extension RBSF	CM22	201 K6
Elm Ct HVHL	CB9	28 A6
SAFWS	CB11	68 A7
Elm Crs COLN	CO4	189 J2
Elmcroft La FX	IP11	95 K8
Elmcroft Rd IP	IP1	36 C3
Elmdale Dr MGTR	CO11	159 J1
Elmdene Av EMPK	RM11	431 G6
Elmdon Rd SOCK/AV	RM15	469 J8
Elm Dr BAR	EN8	346 E6
HAR	CO12	6 C6
HSTD	CO9	148 A6
RAYL	SS6	441 J2
RCOLE	CO7	255 H6
Elmer Ap SOS	SS1	19 D6
Elmer Av ABR/ST	RM4	407 K6
SOS	SS1	19 D6
Elmer Cl RAIN	RM13	450 B8
Elmer Gdns RAIN	RM13	450 B8
Elmers La KESG	IP5	39 H6
Elmfield Cl COS	CO15	260 C6
CVW	DA11	489 J1
Elmfield Rd CHING	E4	402 D2
Elmgate Rd	RM11	94 D1
Elm Gdns EPP	CM16	324 D2
FX	IP11	94 D1
Elm Gn PIT	SS13	438 C9
Elm Green La RCHLM	CM3	335 G5

Elm Gv *BSF* CM23 .... 199 G6
 COS CO15 .... 10 B1
 EMPK RM11 .... 431 F8
 FOS CO13 .... 228 B7
 HOC/HUL SS5 .... 419 J3
 RCOLE CO7 .... 220 E4
 RCOLW CO6 .... 118 A4
 SAFWN CO10 .... 70 E4 ⑪
 SOS SS1 .... 465 K5
Elmham Dr *KIR/NAC* IP10 .... 65 F5
Elmhurst Av *SBF/HAD* SS7 .... 460 A1
Elmhurst Cl *BSF* CM23 .... 198 D6
 HVHL CB9 .... 27 H6 ⑬
Elmhurst Dr *EMPK* RM11 .... 450 D1
 IPSE IP5 .... 63 H2
Elmhurst Rd *HAR* CO12 .... 7 D5
 PEND EN3 .... 374 C3
Elmhurst Wy *LOU* IG10 .... 404 C3
Elm La *K/T/MI* CO5 .... 214 D4
 RIPS/CAP IP9 .... 87 F1
 RIPW IP8 .... 60 E5
Elmore Rd *PEND* EN3 .... 374 D5
Elmores *LOU* IG10 .... 377 J7
Elm Park Av *HCH* RM12 .... 450 C5
Elm Ri *WTHK* RM20 .... 482 A4
Elm Rd *BSF* CM23 .... 198 D5
 CHLM/GWD CM2 .... 14 B5
 CVI SS8 .... 478 C2
 ERITH DA8 .... 480 B7
 GRAYS RM17 .... 484 D5
 GVE DA12 .... 489 H8
 KESC IP5 .... 58 D6
 LOS SS9 .... 463 F4
 PIT SS13 .... 439 H4
 RCHLM CM3 .... 392 C5
 RCOLE CO7 .... 122 A2
 RCOS CO16 .... 258 E2
 SBF/HAD SS7 .... 461 J3
 SBN/FI SS3 .... 466 D6
 SOCK/AV RM15 .... 469 F8
 SUD CO10 .... 58 D6
 WICKE SS11 .... 417 C5
Elms Dr *CHLM/WR* CM1 .... 14 B1
Elms Farm Rd *HCH* RM12 .... 450 D6
Elms Hall Rd *RCOLW* CO6 .... 148 C5
Elmsleigh Dr *LOS* SS9 .... 463 F2
Elms Rd *CHLM/WR* CM1 .... 301 J7
Elmstead Cl *SLH/COR* SS17 ..... 457 J8
Elmstead Rd *COLS* CO2 .... 9 F5
 RCOLE CO7 .... 221 F2
The Elms *CHONG* CM5 .... 354 C4
 SAFWN CO10 .... 43 K2
Elm St *IP* IP1 .... 3 D3 ⑬
Elm Ter *WTHK* RM20 .... 482 E5
Elmtree Av *BRWN* CM15 .... 383 H3
Elm Tree Av *FOS* CO13 .... 228 E6
Elm Tree Cl *FOS* CO13 .... 228 E7
Elmtree Rd *VGE* SS16 .... 458 C1
Elm View Rd *SBF/HAD* SS7 ...... 460 A2
Elm Wk *BRTR* CM7 .... 208 C3
 GPK RM2 .... 430 B5
Elm Wy *BRW* CM14 .... 410 D6
 RCHLM CM3 .... 306 C4
Elmway *CDH/CHF* RM16 .... 471 C2
Elmwood Av *BRW* CM14 .... 263 K4
Elmwood Av *COLS* CO2 .... 218 C3
 HOC/HUL SS5 .... 443 F1
Elmwood Dr *K/T/MI* CO5 .... 285 F7
Elm Wych *COLS* CO2 .... 219 H3
Elounda Ct *SBF/HAD* SS7 .... 460 C1
Elrington Rd *WFD* IG8 .... 403 H8 ⑬
Elronds Rd *RCHLM* CM3 .... 392 C7
Elsden Cha *BOC* CM0 .... 398 D1 ⑬
Elsenham Cl *RAYL* SS6 .... 441 G2 ⑬
Elsenham Crs *BSDN* SS14 .... 438 C7
Elsham Dr *BRTR* CM7 .... 208 E7 ⑬
Elsinge Rd *EN* EN1 .... 374 A2
Elsinor Av *CVI* SS8 .... 461 F7
Elsmere Rd *IP* IP1 .... 3 D1
Elsmere Pk *COS* CO15 .... 10 A3
Elthorne Pk *COS* CO15 .... 10 A3
Elvaston Gdns *EMPK* RM11 ...... 431 H7
Elver Av *EMPK* RM11 .... 430 D6
Elwes Cl *COLN* CO4 .... 9 F2
Elwick Rd *SOCK/AV* RM15 .... 470 A6 ⑬
Elwin Rd *K/T/MI* CO5 .... 248 B8
Elwood *HLWE* CM17 .... 295 J6
Elwood Rd *CVW* DA11 .... 488 A8
 RAYL SS6 .... 441 G2
Ely Pl *WFD* IG8 .... 404 D8
Ely Rd *IPNE* IP4 .... 39 F2
 SOSN SS2 .... 19 E2
Elysian Gdns *MAL* CM9 .... 314 C4
Emanuel Rd *VGE* SS16 .... 456 C1
Emanuel Ct *CHTY* IP2 .... 62 B3
Emmaus Wy *CHIG* IG7 .... 404 D8
Empire Rd *HAR* CO12 .... 7 E4
Empress Av *K/T/MI* CO5 .... 285 F6
Empress Dr *K/T/MI* CO5 .... 285 F7

Empress Rd *GVE* DA12 .... 489 K5
Emson's Cl *CBE/LIN* CB1 .... 23 F3
Enborne Gn *SOCK/AV* RM15 .... 469 K8
Endean Ct *RCOLE* CO7 .... 220 D3
Endeavour Cl *MAL* CM9 .... 314 D3
Endeavour Dr *BSDN* SS14 .... 17 F1
Endeavour Rd *BAR* EN8 .... 346 D1
Endlebury Rd *CHING* E4 .... 402 D5
Endsleigh Ct *COLW* CO3 .... 186 D6
Endway *SBF/HAD* SS7 .... 461 K3
The Endway *GTDUN* CM6 .... 171 H6
 HVHL CB9 .... 50 D5
 RCHLM CM3 .... 397 C3
Enfield Cl *WICKE* SS11 .... 418 B6
Engayne Gdns *UPMR* RM14 ...... 451 J2
England's La *LOU* IG10 .... 377 J6
Englefield Cl *HOC/HUL* SS5 ..... 443 H1
Englefields *BOC* CM0 .... 372 A2
Engleric *RPO* SG8 .... 67 G1
Enid Wy *COLN* CO4 .... 186 E3
Ennerdale Av *BRTR* CM7 .... 209 F7
 HCH RM12 .... 450 B6
Ennismore Gdns *SOSN* SS2 .... 19 D1
Ensign Cl *LOS* SS9 .... 463 H4 ⑬
Enterprise Ct *BRTR* CM7 .... 210 A3
Enterprise Wy *WICKW* SS12 .... 417 J7
Enville Wy *COLN* CO4 .... 187 J1
Epping Cl *CHLM/WR* CM1 .... 332 A4
 COS CO15 .... 259 H5
 LOS SS9 .... 443 F6 ⑬
Epping Old *CHING* E4 .... 402 D2
Epping La *ABR/ST* RM4 .... 379 F6
Epping New Rd *BKHH* IG9 .... 403 J3
 LOU IG10 .... 377 F4
Epping Rd *CHONG* CM5 .... 325 F6
 EPP CM16 .... 321 K6
 LOU IG10 .... 377 H1
 WAB EN9 .... 321 H2
Epping Wy *CHING* E4 .... 402 C2
 WIT CM8 .... 276 E5
Epsom Cl *RCOS* CO16 .... 258 E2
Epsom Dr *IP* IP1 .... 36 D1
Epsom Wy *HCH* RM12 .... 451 G5
Erbury Pl *SUD* CO10 .... 31 F5
Erick Av *CHLM/WR* CM1 .... 304 D6
Erica Rd *PIT* SS13 .... 439 J7
Eridge Cl *CHLM/WR* CM1 .... 305 F6 ⑬
Eriswell Rd *HVHL* CB9 .... 27 H5
Erith Ct *PUR* RM19 .... 481 H4
Erith High St *ERITH* DA8 .... 480 A5
Erith Haward Rd *RCOLW* CO6 ... 185 K1
Ermine Cl *EBAR* EN7 .... 346 B5 ⑬
Ernan Cl *SOCK/AV* RM15 .... 469 J5
Ernan Rd *SOCK/AV* RM15 .... 469 J5
Ernest Rd *EMPK* RM11 .... 431 F8
 RCOLE CO7 .... 221 F4
Ernleigh Rd *IPNE* IP4 .... 37 K7
Erriff Dr *SOCK/AV* RM15 .... 469 J5
Errington Cl *CDH/CHF* RM16 .... 485 G2 ⑬
Errington Rd *COLW* CO3 .... 186 E8
Erroll Rd *ROM* RM1 .... 430 A6
Erskine Pl *WICKW* SS12 .... 417 H7 ⑬
Erskine Rd *MGTR* CO11 .... 159 J1
Erwarton Wk *RIPS/CAP* IP9 ..... 128 B2
Esdaile Gdns *UPMR* RM14 .... 452 A1
Eskley Gdns *SOCK/AV* RM15 ... 469 J5
Esmond Cl *RAIN* RM13 .... 450 C8 ⑬
Esplanade *FOS* CO13 .... 229 F8
 FOS CO13 .... 261 K2
Esplanade Gdns *WOS/PRIT* SS0 . 463 J5
The Esplanade *COS* CO15 .... 260 E7
 HOC/HUL SS5 .... 419 J5
 RCHLM CM3 .... 368 C4
Essex Av *CHLM/WR* CM1 .... 304 C6
 COS CO15 .... 290 A7
 SUD CO10 .... 58 C3
Essex Cl *CVI* SS8 .... 478 A3
 LAIN SS15 .... 436 C7
 RAYL SS6 .... 442 A4
Essex Gdns *EMPK* RM11 .... 431 H7
 LOS SS9 .... 463 F1
 SLH/COR SS17 .... 486 B1
Essex Hall Rd *COLW* CO3 .... 8 A2
Essex Hl *SAFWS* CB11 .... 67 K2
Essex Regiment Wy *RCHLM* CM3 . 272 C5
Essex Rd *BOC* CM0 .... 398 C8
 BRTR CM7 .... 210 A1 ⑬
 CHING E4 .... 403 F4
 CVI SS8 .... 478 C1
 CVW DA11 .... 489 F6 ⑬
 MAL CM9 .... 338 B4
 WTHK RM20 .... 482 D5
Essex St *SOS* SS1 .... 19 D4
Essex Wy *BRTR* CM7 .... 211 F8
 BRTR CM7 .... 243 K1
 CHONG CM5 .... 301 K4
 CHONG CM5 .... 328 C2
 COLN CO4 .... 120 D5
 EPP CM16 .... 350 E6
 HAR CO12 .... 7 D6
 IPSE IP5 .... 64 C4
 MGTR CO11 .... 160 A1
 RBRW/HUT CM13 .... 433 F1
 RCOLW CO6 .... 118 E8
 RCOLW CO6 .... 183 H2

SBF/HAD SS7 .... 460 D4
 WIT CM8 .... 211 H7
Essex Yeomanry Wy *COLW* CO3 . 185 G6
Estate Rd *SBF/HAD* SS7 .... 462 A2
Estella Md *CHLM/WR* CM1 .... 304 A6
Estuary Cl *COLN* CO4 .... 187 F1
Estuary Crs *COS* CO15 .... 10 A4
 RIPS/CAP IP9 .... 129 C5
Estuary Gdns *SBN/FI* SS3 .... 467 H3
Estuary Ms *MAL* CM9 .... 314 D3 ⑬
Estuary Park Rd *K/T/MI* CO5 .... 285 G7
Estuary Rd *RIPS/CAP* IP9 .... 129 F5
Ethelburga Rd *HARH* RM3 .... 431 G3
Ethelred Gdns *WICKE* SS11 ..... 417 H4
Ethel Rd *RAYL* SS6 .... 442 C5
Etheridge Rd *LOU* IG10 .... 393 A7
Eton Cl *CVI* SS8 .... 461 G8
Eton Rd *COS* CO15 .... 10 C5
 FOS CO13 .... 229 F8
Eton Wk *SBN/FI* SS3 .... 466 D4
Etton Cl *HCH* RM12 .... 451 F3
Euclid Wy *WTHK* RM20 .... 482 C3
Eudo Rd *COLS* CO2 .... 218 D1
Eugene Cl *GPK* RM2 .... 430 D6
Europa Wy *HAR* CO12 .... 6 A4
Eustace Rd *IP* IP1 .... 36 A5
Euston Av *IPNE* IP4 .... 38 D7
Euston Ct *FX* IP11 .... 4 C3
Evabrook Cl *CHTY* IP2 .... 62 A4 ⑬
Evelyn Rd *HOC/HUL* SS5 .... 421 F8
 RCHLM CM3 .... 241 F1
Evelyn Sharp Cl *GPK* RM2 .... 430 E5 ⑬
Evelyn Wood Rd *BRTR* CM7 ..... 210 D7 ⑬
Everard Rd *BSDN* SS14 .... 438 C5
Everest *RAYL* SS6 .... 419 J8
Everest Cl *GVW* DA11 .... 488 D8 ⑬
Everest Ri *BCAYW* CM12 .... 414 A4
Everest Wy *MAL* CM9 .... 310 D8
Evergreen Dr *RCOLE* CO7 .... 188 A1
Everitt Rd *SAFWN* CB10 .... 71 G3
Everitt Wy *HSTD* CO9 .... 110 D3 ⑬
Eversleigh Gdns *UPMR* RM14 ... 452 A2
Eversley Rd *PIT* SS13 .... 439 G8
 SBF/HAD SS7 .... 440 A6
Everton Crs *IP* IP1 .... 36 B4
Eves Cnr *RCHLM* CM3 .... 335 J6
Eves Ct *HAR* CO12 .... 164 C4
Eves Crs *CHLM/WR* CM1 .... 304 C8
Evesham Cl *CHTY* IP2 .... 62 C3
Evesham Rd *GVE* DA12 .... 489 J7 ⑬
Ewan Cl *COLW* CO3 .... 185 H7
 LOS SS9 .... 462 B2 ⑬
Ewanrigg Ter *WFD* IG8 .... 403 K8 ⑬
Ewan Rd *HARH* RM3 .... 430 E4
Ewan Wy *COLW* CO3 .... 185 H7
 SBF/HAD SS7 .... 462 B2
Ewell Hall Cha *K/T/MI* CO5 ..... 246 E4
Exeter Cl *BRTR* CM7 .... 178 A8 ⑬
 BSDN SS14 .... 438 C6
 RCOLW CO6 .... 154 C6
 SBN/FI SS3 .... 466 E4
Exeter Dr *COL* CO1 .... 8 C4
Exeter Rd *CHLM/WR* CM1 .... 305 G8
 FX IP11 .... 5 F2
 GVE DA12 .... 489 J8
 IPSE IP3 .... 63 K1
 PEND EN3 .... 374 D7
Exford Av *WOS/PRIT* SS0 .... 443 H8
Exhibition La *SBN/FI* SS3 .... 466 E1
Exley Cl *ING* CM4 .... 386 B1 ⑬
Exmoor Cl *CHLM/WR* CM1 ...... 331 K4
Exmoor Rd *FX* IP11 .... 5 F1
Exmouth Dr *RAYL* SS6 .... 419 J8
Exmouth Rd *GRAYS* RM17 ...... 484 A5
Eyhurst Av *HCH* RM12 .... 450 B4
Eynesham Wy *PIT* SS13 .... 438 D4 ⑬
Eyre Cl *GPK* RM2 .... 430 C6

F

Fabians Cl *RCOLW* CO6 .... 213 H2
Factory Hl *K/T/MI* CO5 .... 280 C2
Factory La *MGTR* CO11 .... 123 H6
Factory La East *HSTD* CO9 .... 147 K4
Factory La West *HSTD* CO9 ...... 147 K4
Factory Rd *CVW* DA11 .... 488 B4
Fagbury Rd *FX* IP11 .... 4 A3
Faggotters La *HLWE* CM17 ...... 296 E4
Fairbairn Av *KESC* IP5 .... 59 H6
Fairbank Cl *CHONG* CM5 .... 354 B5
Fairburn Cl *SOS* SS1 .... 19 E4 ⑬
Fair Cl *RCOLE* CO7 .... 256 A7
Fairclough Av *RCOS* CO16 .... 290 D2
Fairfax Av *PIT* SS13 .... 439 F5
Fairfax Dr *WOS/PRIT* SS0 .... 463 K3
Fairfax Md *CHLM/GWD* CM2 .... 333 H3
Fairfax Rd *COLS* CO2 .... 8 B5
 GRAYS RM17 .... 484 A4 ⑬
 TIL RM18 .... 484 E7
Fairfield *ING* CM4 .... 386 C1
 SBN/FI SS3 .... 467 F2

Fairfield Av CDH/CHF RM16 ..... **471** G8
  FX IP11 ..... **131** H2
  UPMR RM14 ..... **451** K4
Fairfield Cl HCH RM12 ..... **450** B2
  PEND EN3 ..... **374** E8
Fairfield Crs LOS SS9 ..... **443** G6
Fairfield Dr BROX EN10 ..... **319** F6
Fairfield Gdns COLN CO4 ..... **9** E3
  LOS SS9 ..... **443** F6
Fairfield Ri BCAYW CM12 ..... **414** A3
Fairfield Rd BRTR CM7 ..... **209** J3
  BRW CM14 ..... **411** F6
  CHLM/WR CM1 ..... **14** B2
  CHONG CM5 ..... **354** B3
  COS CO15 ..... **10** B4
  EPP CM16 ..... **351** F3
  IPS3 ..... **63** J3
  LOS SS9 ..... **443** F6
Fairfield Wy CBE/LIN CB1 ..... **23** F7
Fairford Cl HARH RM3 ..... **431** J1
Fairford Wy HARH RM3 ..... **431** J1
Fairham Av SOCK/AV RM15 ..... **469** J7
Fairhaven Av K/T/MI CO5 ..... **285** G6
Fairhead Rd North COLN CO4 ..... **9** E3
Fairhead Rd South COLN CO4 ..... **9** E3
Fairholme Av GPK RM2 ..... **430** B7
Fairholme Rd UPMR RM14 ..... **452** C1
Fairkytes Av EMPK RM11 ..... **450** E2
Fairland Cl RAYL SS6 ..... **419** K8
Fairlands BKHH IG9 ..... **403** H5
Fairlawn Gdns SOSN SS2 ..... **444** B8
Fairlawns Cl EMPK RM11 ..... **451** G1
Fairleads RCHLM CM3 ..... **335** K5
Fair Leas SAFWN CB10 ..... **71** F2
Fairleigh Av PIT SS13 ..... **439** G8
Fairleigh Dr LOS SS9 ..... **462** E4
Fairleigh Rd PIT SS13 ..... **439** G8
Fairley Wy EBAR EN7 ..... **346** B2
Fairlight Av CHING E4 ..... **402** E5
Fairlight Cl CHING E4 ..... **402** E5
  SBF/HAD SS7 ..... **461** K4
Fairlop Av CVI SS8 ..... **478** A1
Fairlop Cl COS CO15 ..... **259** H5
  HCH RM12 ..... **450** C7
Fairlop Gdns BSDN SS14 ..... **438** A7
Fair Md BSDN SS14 ..... **437** K5
Fairmead RAYL SS6 ..... **441** G1
Fairmead Av SBF/HAD SS7 ..... **441** K8
  WOS/PRIT SS0 ..... **463** K3
Fairmead Rd LOU IG10 ..... **376** D8
Fairmeads LOU IG10 ..... **377** K6
Fairoaks Gv PEND EN3 ..... **374** D3
Fairstead Hall Rd RCHLM CM3 ..... **242** E7
Fairstead Rd RCHLM CM3 ..... **243** G7
Fairview BCAYW CM12 ..... **414** B4
  CVI SS8 ..... **460** E8
  ERITH DA8 ..... **480** A6
Fairview Av RBRW/HUT CM13 ..... **412** D3
  SLH/COR SS17 ..... **473** J4
Fairview Cha SBF/HAD SS7 ..... **440** B6
Fairview Cl CHIG IG7 ..... **405** H7
  SBF/HAD SS7 ..... **440** B6
Fairview Crs SBF/HAD SS7 ..... **440** B6
Fairview Dr CHIG IG7 ..... **405** H8
  WOS/PRIT SS0 ..... **463** K1
Fairview Gdns LOS SS9 ..... **462** D3
Fairview Rd BSDN SS14 ..... **438** B7
  CHIG IG7 ..... **405** H7
Fairway BSF CM23 ..... **199** H7
  CDH/CHF RM16 ..... **471** F8
  CHLM/WR CM1 ..... **484** A1
  CHLM/GWD CM2 ..... **15** E6
  SBW CM21 ..... **263** K3
  WFD IG8 ..... **403** K8
  WICKW SS12 ..... **439** H2
Fairway Dr BOC CM0 ..... **398** B3
Fairway Gdns LOS SS9 ..... **442** D8
Fairway Gardens Cl LOS SS9 ..... **442** D8
Fairways BAR EN8 ..... **318** D8
  COLN CO4 ..... **186** C2
The Fairways IPNE IP4 ..... **38** B5
  RCHLM CM3 ..... **366** B8
The Fairway CVW DA11 ..... **489** F7
  HLWS CM18 ..... **13** F6
  LOS SS9 ..... **442** D8
  SBF/HAD SS7 ..... **440** B6
  UPMR RM14 ..... **451** K1
Fairycroft Rd SAFWN CB10 ..... **70** E4
Fairy Hall La BRTR CM7 ..... **208** D3
Falbro Crs SBF/HAD SS7 ..... **461** J2
Falbro Cresent SBF/HAD SS7 ..... **461** J1
Falcon Av GRAYS RM17 ..... **484** A6
Falcon Cl HVHL CB9 ..... **27** J5
  LOS SS9 ..... **443** F8
  RAYL SS6 ..... **441** G2
  SBW CM21 ..... **263** G4
Falcon Crs COL CO1 ..... **9** D6
Falcon Flds MAL CM9 ..... **488** D6
Falcon Ms CVW DA11 ..... **338** B5
  MAL CM9 ..... **488** D6
Falcon Pk BSDN SS14 ..... **17** D2

Falcon Rd BOC CM0 ..... **398** C1
Falcon St FX IP11 ..... **5** E1
  IP IP1 ..... **3** D4
Falcon Wy CHLM/GWD CM2 ..... **332** C7
  COS CO15 ..... **10** C1
  VGE SS16 ..... **457** K1
Falcon Yd RCOLE CO7 ..... **220** E5
Fal Dr WIT CM8 ..... **276** E3
Falkenham End BSDN SS14 ..... **437** K6
Falkenham Ri BSDN SS14 ..... **437** K5
Falkenham Rd KIR/NAC IP10 ..... **94** D2
Falkenham Rw BSDN SS14 ..... **437** K6
Falkirk Cl EMPK RM11 ..... **451** H2
Falkland Cl RCHLM CM3 ..... **306** C5
Falklands Dr MGTR CO11 ..... **159** J1
Falklands Rd BOC CM0 ..... **398** B8
  HVHL CB9 ..... **27** G3
Falkner Cl INC CM4 ..... **388** B2
Fallow Cl CHLM CM1 ..... **405** J8
Fallowden La SAFWN CB10 ..... **46** B5
Fallowfield SBN/FI SS3 ..... **466** C4
Fallowfield Cl HAR CO12 ..... **6** A5
Fallowfield Rd COLS CO2 ..... **218** D3
Fallow Flds LOU IG10 ..... **404** A3
The Fallows CVI SS8 ..... **460** E7
Falmouth Av CHING E4 ..... **402** E8
Falmouth Cl KESG IP5 ..... **39** F7
Falmouth Rd CHLM/WR CM1 ..... **305** G8
Falstones LAIN SS15 ..... **16** B4
Fambridge Cha WIT CM8 ..... **243** K3
Fambridge Cl MAL CM9 ..... **338** C4
Fambridge Dr WICKW SS12 ..... **417** H7
Fambridge Rd MAL CM9 ..... **338** B3
  RCFD SS4 ..... **421** J2
  RCHLM CM3 ..... **394** E1
  RCHLM CM3 ..... **95** E3
Fane Rd SBF/HAD SS7 ..... **440** C5
Fanns Ri PUR RM19 ..... **481** H5
Fanny's La RCOS CO16 ..... **257** K3
Fanshawe Crs EMPK RM11 ..... **430** E8
Fanshawe Rd CDH/CHF RM16 ..... **485** F2
Fanton Av WICKW SS12 ..... **439** J2
Fanton Cha WICKE SS11 ..... **417** K7
Fanton Gdns WICKE SS11 ..... **418** A7
Fanton Wk WICKE SS11 ..... **418** A7
Faraday Cl BRTR CM7 ..... **209** J4
  COS CO15 ..... **259** J5
Faraday Rd IPSE IP3 ..... **37** H8
  LOS SS9 ..... **442** D7
Farford Fld SUD CO10 ..... **59** F7
Faringdon Av HARH RM3 ..... **430** D3
Farlow Cl GVW DA11 ..... **488** E8
Farmadine Gv SAFWS CB11 ..... **71** F4
Farmadine Gv SAFWS CB11 ..... **71** F4
Farmbridge End Rd
  CHLM/WR CM1 ..... **301** H2
Farm Cl BAR EN8 ..... **346** C4
  BKHH IG9 ..... **403** K6
  RBRW/HUT CM13 ..... **412** B5
Farm Crs RCHLM CM3 ..... **418** D1
Farmcroft GVW DA11 ..... **489** F7
Farm End CHING E4 ..... **403** F1
Farmer Ct WAB EN9 ..... **348** C7
Farmers Wy RCOS CO16 ..... **290** D2
Farmfield Rd RCOLW CO6 ..... **182** E4
Farm Hill Rd WAB EN9 ..... **347** K8
Farmhouse Cl BROX EN10 ..... **319** F7
Farm La CDH/CHF RM16 ..... **484** C1
  CVI SS8 ..... **461** G8
  HAR CO12 ..... **195** F1
  TIL RM18 ..... **486** D3
Farm Rd CDH/CHF RM16 ..... **484** C1
  CVI SS8 ..... **461** G8
  HAR CO12 ..... **195** F1
  TIL RM18 ..... **486** D3
Farm Vw RAYL SS6 ..... **419** J6
Farm Wk RCOLE CO7 ..... **255** J5
Farm Wy BKHH IG9 ..... **403** K7
  HCH RM12 ..... **450** C6
  SBF/HAD SS7 ..... **441** G1
Farnes Av WICKW SS12 ..... **417** F6
Farnes Dr GPK RM2 ..... **430** D4
Farnham Cl SBW CM21 ..... **263** G4
Farnham Rd HARH RM3 ..... **408** A3
Farnley Rd CHING E4 ..... **403** F3
Farriers Dr BCAYW CM12 ..... **387** G8
Farriers End BROX EN10 ..... **319** H8
  COLW CO3 ..... **185** J8
Farriers Wy SOSN SS2 ..... **444** C8
Farriers Went FX IP11 ..... **5** F1
Farringdon Service Rd SOS SS1 ..... **19** D4
Farrington Cl COL CO1 ..... **9** E5
Farrow Gdns CDH/CHF RM16 ..... **471** F8
Farthingale La WAB EN9 ..... **348** C8
Farthing Cl BRTR CM7 ..... **210** C1
Farthings Cl CHING E4 ..... **403** F6
Farthings Went RIPS/CAP IP9 ..... **87** G3
Fastnet SOSN SS2 ..... **443** H6
Fastnet Cl HVHL CB9 ..... **27** K5
Faulkbourne Rd WIT CM8 ..... **276** C1
Faulkeners Wy FX IP11 ..... **14** D7
Fauners VGE SS16 ..... **457** F7
Faverolle Gn BAR EN8 ..... **346** D2
Faversham Av CHING E4 ..... **403** F4
Faversham Cl CHLM IG7 ..... **406** A5
Fawkner Cl CHLM/GWD CM2 ..... **333** H5
Fawley Cl IPNE IP4 ..... **38** A6

Fawn Rd CHIG IG7 ..... **405** J8
Fawters Cl RBRW/HUT CM13 ..... **412** C2
Faymore Gdns SOCK/AV RM15 ..... **469** J6
Featherby Wy RCFD SS4 ..... **444** D4
Feathers Fld FX IP11 ..... **5** D2
Feathers HI RBSF CM22 ..... **234** A7
Feeches Rd SOSN SS2 ..... **444** A8
Feedhams Cl RCOLE CO7 ..... **221** F2
Feenan Hwy TIL RM18 ..... **485** G6
Feering Dr BSDN SS14 ..... **438** C6
Feering Gn BSDN SS14 ..... **438** C8
Feering Hl K/T/MI CO5 ..... **247** F2
Feering Rd BCAYE CM11 ..... **414** D3
Feering Rw BSDN SS14 ..... **438** C8
Felaw St CHTY IP2 ..... **3** E5
Felicia Wy CDH/CHF RM16 ..... **485** G3
Felipe Rd CDH/CHF RM16 ..... **483** F8
Felix Cl KESG IP5 ..... **39** F6
Felix Rd FX IP11 ..... **131** J3
  IPSE IP3 ..... **64** A3
Felixstowe Cl RCOS CO16 ..... **290** C1
Felixstowe Rd IPSE IP3 ..... **63** J1
  KIR/NAC IP10 ..... **64** E5
Fellbrigg Av KESG IP5 ..... **38** D7
Fell Christy CHLM/WR CM1 ..... **304** D8
Fell Rd HSTD CO9 ..... **51** J4
Felmongers HLW CM20 ..... **295** F3
Felmores PIT SS13 ..... **438** D5
Felstead Cl COLS CO2 ..... **219** H8
  RBRW/HUT CM13 ..... **412** B2
  SBF/HAD SS7 ..... **460** C7
Felstead Rd BAR EN8 ..... **346** E8
  LOU IG10 ..... **404** B3
  SBF/HAD SS7 ..... **460** C7
Felsted Rd BCAYE CM11 ..... **414** D3
Felton Cl BROX EN10 ..... **319** F7
Fen Br RCOLE CO7 ..... **122** A5
Fenbridge La RCOLE CO7 ..... **122** A3
Fen Cl BRWN CM15 ..... **385** G2
  UPMR RM14 ..... **454** E8
Fengates RCHLM CM3 ..... **392** C5
Fen La CDH/CHF RM16 ..... **471** K4
  RCOLE CO7 ..... **157** G4
  UPMR RM14 ..... **453** G6
Fen Meadow FX IP11 ..... **94** D7
Fenn Cl RCHLM CM3 ..... **392** C5
  RCOLE CO7 ..... **223** F2
Fennell Cl K/T/MI CO5 ..... **248** A8
Fennells CI HVHL CB9 ..... **27** G6
Fenner Cl CDH/CHF RM16 ..... **483** F2
Fenners Wy PIT SS13 ..... **438** D5
Fennes Rd BRTR CM7 ..... **177** J1
Fennfields Rd RCHLM CM3 ..... **392** B5
Fenno Cl COLW CO3 ..... **217** K3
Fenn Rd HSTD CO9 ..... **148** B3
Fen St RCOLW CO6 ..... **118** C4
Fentiman Av EMPK RM11 ..... **451** F2
Fenton Gra HLWE CM17 ..... **295** G6
Fenton Rd HVHL CB9 ..... **27** H5
Fentons Wy KESG IP5 ..... **39** G6
Fenton Wy LAIN SS15 ..... **436** A6
Fen Vw RIPW IP8 ..... **60** E5
Fenwick Wy CVI SS8 ..... **461** F1
Ferguson Av GPK RM2 ..... **430** D6
Ferguson Cl SAFWS CB11 ..... **71** H3
Ferguson Ct GPK RM2 ..... **430** E6
Fermbank BCAYW CM12 ..... **414** A4
  BKHH IG9 ..... **403** J4
Fernbank Av HCH RM12 ..... **450** D5
Fernbrook Av SOS SS1 ..... **465** G3
Fern Cl BCAYW CM12 ..... **414** C4
  BROX EN10 ..... **319** F5
  ERITH DA8 ..... **480** C7
Ferndale Cl COS CO15 ..... **259** H6
  LAIN SS15 ..... **436** C7
Ferndale Crs CVI SS8 ..... **478** B3
Ferndale Rd GVE DA12 ..... **489** G1
  HAR CO12 ..... **7** F3
  PEND EN3 ..... **374** E3
  RAYL SS6 ..... **419** J2
  SOSN SS2 ..... **19** F2
Ferndown EMPK RM11 ..... **431** H6
Ferndown Rd FOS CO13 ..... **228** D8
  FX IP11 ..... **131** K2
Ferndown Wy RCHLM CM3 ..... **308** B9
Fern Gv HVHL CB9 ..... **26** E3
Fernhall La WAB EN9 ..... **349** F7
Fernhayes Cl CHTY IP2 ..... **2** B8
Fernhill HLWS CM18 ..... **322** C7
Fern HI VGE SS16 ..... **16** A7
Fern Hill La HLWS CM18 ..... **322** C7
Fernlea COLN CO4 ..... **186** D3
Fernlea Rd BOC CM0 ..... **398** B6
  HAR CO12 ..... **7** F1
  SBF/HAD SS7 ..... **460** D2
Fernleigh Dr LOS SS9 ..... **463** H4
Ferns Cl PEND EN3 ..... **374** E2
Fernside BKHH IG9 ..... **403** J6
Fernside Cl SLH/COR SS17 ..... **457** J8
Fern Wk VGE SS16 ..... **455** K1
Fern Wy COS CO15 ..... **290** B6
Fernwood SBF/HAD SS7 ..... **441** G6
Fernwood Av COS CO15 ..... **260** D6

errers Rd RCHLM CM3 ... 392 C5
erris Rd RCHLM CM3 ... 366 B8
erry La FX IP11 ... 5 D4
errymead CVI SS8 ... 460 E8
erry Rd BOC CM0 ... 397 J8
  FX IP11 ... 95 K8
  HOC/HUL SS5 ... 419 J3
  K/T/MI CO5 ... 220 E7
  RCHLM CM3 ... 394 C6
  SBF/HAD SS7 ... 460 C5
  TIL RM18 ... 485 F8
eryby Rd CDH/CHF RM16 ... 485 G2
esants Cft HLW CM20 ... 295 F2
estival Cl ERITH DA8 ... 480 A6
estival Gdns MAL CM9 ... 313 H1
estival Link BSDN SS14 ... 17 F2
estival Wy BSDN SS14 ... 17 F1
etherston Rd SLH/COR SS17 ... 473 K3
everills Rd RCOS CO16 ... 258 C1
iat Av COS CO15 ... 289 K7
iddlers Folly RCOLW CO6 ... 184 D4
iddlers Hl COLW CO5 ... 184 D3
iddlers La RCOLE CO7 ... 122 B2
ield Cl ABR/ST RM4 ... 379 F7
  BKHH IG9 ... 403 K6
  CBE/LIN CB1 ... 22 D3
he Fielders CVI SS8 ... 477 K3
ieldfare BCAYW CM12 ... 414 D5
ield Gdns CHONG CM5 ... 354 A8
ield Gate La RBSF CM22 ... 168 B1
ielding Av TIL RM18 ... 485 G7
ieldings Rd BAR EN8 ... 347 F3
ield Kiln BRWN CM15 ... 384 B1
ield Rd SOCK/AV RM15 ... 468 E8
ields Cl RCOS CO16 ... 225 G6
ields Farm Rd COLS CO2 ... 251 H1
ield View Dr MAL CM9 ... 280 A8
ield Wy RCOLE CO7 ... 221 F3
ieldway CDH/CHF RM16 ... 470 E8
  PIT SS13 ... 458 E1
  WICKW SS12 ... 439 G2
ife Rd IPNE IP4 ... 37 K4
ifth Av CHLM/WR CM1 ... 304 D7
  CVI SS8 ... 477 J1
  FOS CO13 ... 228 D8
  HSTD CO9 ... 148 C4
  WICKE SS11 ... 417 K7
  WTHK RM20 ... 482 D5
ifth Avenue Allende Av
  HLW CM20 ... 13 D2
iley Rd ROW CM0 ... 398 A3
ilebrook Av LOS SS9 ... 463 H3
inbars Wk IPNE IP4 ... 37 H8
inborough Ct KESG IP5 ... 38 D7
incham's Cl CBE/LIN CB1 ... 23 F3
inchdale COS CO15 ... 10 C1
inch Dr RCOLE CO7 ... 223 J4
inches Cl SLH/COR SS17 ... 457 K8
he Finches SBF/HAD SS7 ... 441 F6
inchfield RAYL SS6 ... 441 J4
inch Hl SUD CO10 ... 57 H6
inchingfield Rd HSTD CO9 ... 77 J7
  HVHL CB9 ... 50 D7
he Finchingfields BRWN CM15 ... 383 G3
inchingfield Wy COLS CO2 ... 219 H5
  WICKW SS12 ... 417 F8
inchland Vw RCHLM CM5 ... 392 D7
inchley Av CHLM/GWD CM2 ... 14 B5
inchley Rd GRAYS RM17 ... 484 A5
  IPNE IP4 ... 3 F3
inchmoor HLWS CM18 ... 13 D6
inch's WIT CM8 ... 278 B7
indley Cl RIPS/CAP IP9 ... 125 G3
iner Cl RCOS CO16 ... 258 E8
ingringhoe Rd COLS CO2 ... 220 A3
  K/T/MI CO5 ... 252 D2
ingrith Hall La MCM4 ... 356 C1
inham Cl COLN CO4 ... 188 C6
inney's Drift KIR/NAV IP10 ... 65 G3
inucane Gdns RAIN RM13 ... 450 B7
irbank Rd CRW RM5 ... 407 G8
ircroft Rd IP IP1 ... 36 C3
irsgrove Crs BRW CM14 ... 410 C2
irs Cha K/T/MI CO5 ... 284 C7
irs Ed K/T/MI CO5 ... 280 B1
irs Dr CHLM/WR CM1 ... 331 H4
  LOU IG10 ... 377 J5
irs Hamlet K/T/MI CO5 ... 284 C7
irst Av BCAYW CM12 ... 413 K6
  BRWN CM15 ... 356 A8
  CHLM/WR CM1 ... 304 D8
  COS CO15 ... 11 E3
  CVI SS8 ... 477 H2
  FOS CO13 ... 261 J1
  GVW DA11 ... 488 D6
  HAR CO12 ... 7 D5
  HOC/HUL SS5 ... 420 A4
  HSTD CO9 ... 148 C4
  RCOS CO16 ... 225 G4
  RCOS CO16 ... 289 J1
  SLH/COR SS17 ... 473 K2
  SUD CO10 ... 58 D4
  WICKE SS11 ... 417 K7
  WOS/PRIT SS0 ... 463 J5
  WOTN CO14 ... 229 J2
  WTHK RM20 ... 482 D5
First Avenue Mandela Av
  HLW CM20 ... 13 D2
  HLWE CM17 ... 295 F2
The Firs BRWN CM15 ... 410 D2
  CDH/CHF RM16 ... 470 E8
  CVI SS8 ... 460 E8
Firstore Dr COLW CO3 ... 185 K6
Firs Wk WFD IG8 ... 403 H8
Fir Tree Cl COLN CO4 ... 187 J1
Fir Tree Hl RIPS/CAP IP9 ... 90 B8
Fir Tree La RCHLM CM3 ... 335 J4
Fir Tree Ri CHLM/GWD CM2 ... 332 C2
  RIPW IP8 ... 61 J3
Fir Tree Wk ABR/ST RM4 ... 379 F7
Fir Wy COS CO15 ... 290 C7
Firwood's Rd HSTD CO9 ... 147 K5
Fishbane Cl IPSE IP3 ... 63 J3
Fisher Cl HVHL CB9 ... 27 K6
Fishermen's HI GVW DA11 ... 488 A3
Fishers Cl BAR EN8 ... 347 G8
Fisher's La RCOLE CO7 ... 123 H2
Fisher Wy BRTR CM7 ... 210 B1
Fishmarket St GTDUN CM6 ... 139 J3
Fish Pond Hl RIPS/CAP IP9 ... 127 F2
Fishponds Hl RCOLW CO6 ... 117 K8
Fishponds La RIPS/CAP IP9 ... 90 B8
Fish St MAL CM9 ... 312 C7
Fishn Wk COLW CO3 ... 217 K2
Fitches Crs MAL CM9 ... 338 D4
Fitzgerald Cl MGTR CO11 ... 159 G1
Fitzgilbert Rd COLS CO2 ... 218 D1
Fitzilian Av HARH RM3 ... 431 G3
Fitzmaurice Rd IPSE IP3 ... 63 K2
Fitzpiers SAFWN CB10 ... 71 F3
Fitzroy Cl BCAYW CM12 ... 414 B1
Fitzwalter La RCHLM CM3 ... 335 H7
Fitzwalter Pl CHLM/WR CM1 ... 332 A2
Fitzwalter Rd COLW CO3 ... 186 C7
  RCHLM CM3 ... 306 D5
Fitzwarren SBN/FI SS3 ... 466 C4
Fitzwilliam Cl CHTY IP2 ... 62 B3
Fitzwilliam Rd COLW CO3 ... 186 C6
  SBF/HAD SS7 ... 461 H5
Fitzwilliams Ct HLWE CM17 ... 295 J1
Five Acres HLWS CM18 ... 13 E6
  RCHLM CM3 ... 363 K3
  STSD CM24 ... 167 K5
  WOTN CO14 ... 229 G5
Fiveash La BRTR CM7 ... 211 K4
Fiveash Rd GVW DA11 ... 488 E5
Five Oaks SBF/HAD SS7 ... 461 G1
Flag Hl RCOS CO16 ... 257 F4
Flagstaff Cl WAB EN9 ... 347 H7
Flagstaff Rd COLS CO2 ... 8 B5
  WAB EN9 ... 347 H6
Flail Cl RCOLE CO7 ... 189 J2
Flambird's Cha RCHLM CM3 ... 365 F6
Flamboro Cl LOS SS9 ... 442 E7
Flamingo Wk RAIN RM13 ... 450 B8
Flamstead End Rd BAR EN8 ... 346 B2
Flanders Cl BRTR CM7 ... 177 H8
Flanders Fld COLS CO2 ... 219 J2
Flatford Dr RCOS CO16 ... 290 D1
Flatford Rd RCOLE CO7 ... 122 B4
Flavian Cl HVHL CB9 ... 27 K6
Flaxen Cl COLN CO4 ... 402 C6
Flaxen Rd CHING E4 ... 402 C6
Flaxfields CBE/LIN CB1 ... 22 E2
Flax La SUD CO10 ... 33 J1
Fleet Av UPMR RM14 ... 432 A3
Fleet Cl UPMR RM14 ... 432 A8
Fleethall Gv CDH/CHF RM16 ... 470 E8
Fleethall Rd RCFD SS4 ... 444 D5
Fleet Rd GVW DA11 ... 488 B8
  SBF/HAD SS7 ... 460 C3
Fleetwood Av COS CO15 ... 260 C6
  FX IP11 ... 131 H2
  WOS/PRIT SS0 ... 463 K3
Fleetwood Cl COS CO15 ... 260 C6
Fleetwood Rd FX IP11 ... 131 J2
Fleming Cl BRTR CM7 ... 209 J4
  EBAR EN4 ... 318 A2
Fleming Gdns HARH RM3 ... 430 E4
  TIL RM18 ... 485 H7
Fleming Rd CDH/CHF RM16 ... 483 F3
Flemings RBRW/HUT CM15 ... 433 F1
Flemings Farm Rd LOS SS9 ... 442 E5
Flemming Av LOS SS9 ... 462 C2
Flemming Crs LOS SS9 ... 462 E2
Fletcher Dr WICKW SS12 ... 417 G7
Fletcher Rd CHIG IG7 ... 405 J8
  IPSE IP3 ... 63 J5
Fletchers La KESG IP5 ... 16 C6
Fletchers La KESG IP5 ... 39 H5
Fletchers Sq SOSN SS2 ... 444 D8
Flex Meadow HLWW/ROY CM19 ... 293 C6
Flint Cl CHTY IP2 ... 62 D3
  VGE SS16 ... 436 A8
Flint St WTHK RM20 ... 482 E5
Flintwich Mnr CHLM/WR CM1 ... 304 A6
Flitch La GTDUN CM6 ... 204 D6
Flitch Wy BRTR CM7 ... 207 H5
  GTDUN CM6 ... 171 H3
  RBSF CM22 ... 200 E6
  RBSF CM22 ... 202 C6
Flixton Cl RCOS CO16 ... 290 C1
Flora Rd WIT CM8 ... 276 D1
Florence Cl HCH RM12 ... 451 F5
  HLWE CM17 ... 295 G7
  SBF/HAD SS7 ... 461 J2
  WTHK RM20 ... 483 H5
Florence Gdns SBF/HAD SS7 ... 461 H2
Florence Rd CVI SS8 ... 478 C1
  WOTN CO14 ... 229 J3
Florence Wy VGE SS16 ... 436 C8
Florie's Rd RCOLW CO6 ... 182 C5
Flowers Wy COS CO15 ... 290 C6
Flowmere Rd ROY SG8 ... 40 D8
Flux's La EPP CM16 ... 350 E7
Fobbing Farm Cl VGE SS16 ... 457 H2
Fobbing Rd SLH/COR SS17 ... 474 E1
Fodderwick BSDN SS14 ... 17 E4
Foksville Rd CVI SS8 ... 478 C2
Fold Cft HLW CM20 ... 12 A2
Folkards La RCOLE CO7 ... 255 K5
Folkes La UPMR RM14 ... 432 C7
Folly Cha HOC/HUL SS5 ... 420 C7
Folly La HOC/HUL SS5 ... 420 C7
  RIPW IP8 ... 87 J1
Folly Mill La GTDUN CM6 ... 139 J7
Folly Rd SUD CO10 ... 59 J2
The Folly COLS CO2 ... 218 B7
  K/T/MI CO5 ... 280 D3
  RCOLE CO7 ... 220 E6
Fonnereau Rd IP IP1 ... 3 D2
Fontayne Av CHIG IG7 ... 405 F7
Fonteyn Cl LAIN SS15 ... 16 A2
Fontwell Park Gdns HCH RM12 ... 451 F5
Forbes Cl HCH RM12 ... 450 C2
Ford Cl LAIN SS15 ... 436 B7
  RAIN RM13 ... 450 A8
Fordham Cl EMPK RM11 ... 451 H1
Fordham Pl IPNE IP4 ... 38 D8
Fordham Rd RCOLW CO6 ... 151 J3
Fordhams Rw CDH/CHF RM16 ... 472 B5
Ford La COLN CO4 ... 154 D8
  RAIN RM13 ... 450 A8
  RCOLE CO7 ... 222 A8
Ford Rd COS CO15 ... 10 A4
  GVW DA11 ... 488 A3
Fords La COLN CO4 ... 154 E8
Fordson Rd CHLM/GWD CM2 ... 305 K7
Ford St RCOLW CO6 ... 183 K1
Fordstreet Hl RCOLW CO6 ... 184 B3
Fordwater Cl HSTD CO9 ... 51 J2
Fordwich Rd RCOLE CO7 ... 255 J4
Fordyce Cl EMPK RM11 ... 451 H1
Forebury Av SBW CM21 ... 263 K3
The Forebury SBW CM21 ... 263 K3
Fore Fld BRTR CM7 ... 210 C2
Forefield Gn CHLM/WR CM1 ... 305 H6
Fore Hamlet IPSE IP3 ... 3 F4
Foremark Cl BARK/HLT IG6 ... 405 J8
Foresight Rd COLS CO2 ... 220 A3
Forest Ap CHING E4 ... 403 F3
Forest Av CHIG IG7 ... 404 D8
  CHING E4 ... 403 F3
Forest Cl WAB EN9 ... 376 D3
  WFD IG8 ... 403 J7
Forest Ct CHING E4 ... 403 G4
Forest Dr CHLM/WR CM1 ... 332 A4
  EPP CM16 ... 378 C2
Forest Edge BKHH IG9 ... 403 J4
Forest Gld CHING E4 ... 403 F8
  EPP CM16 ... 351 J1
  HVHL CB9 ... 27 F3
  VGE SS16 ... 456 A1
Foresthall Rd STSD CM24 ... 199 J1
Forest La CHIG IG7 ... 404 D8
Forest Park Av COS CO15 ... 259 G6
Fore St HLWE CM17 ... 295 G1
  IPNE IP4 ... 3 E4
  LAIN SS15 ... 437 D5
Forest Rd BAR EN8 ... 346 D3
  COLN CO4 ... 9 F4
  ERITH DA8 ... 480 B7
  LOU IG10 ... 377 F8
  PEND EN3 ... 374 E2
  WFD IG8 ... 403 H6
  WIT CM8 ... 277 G1
Forest Side BKHH IG9 ... 403 J4
  CHING E4 ... 403 G3
  EPP CM16 ... 550 B7
Forest Vw CHING E4 ... 402 E3
Forest View Dr LOS SS9 ... 462 B2
Forest Wy HLWE CM17 ... 296 C3

HLWE CM17	323 F1
LOU IG10	376 E4
WAB EN9	349 G5
WFD IG8	403 J7
Forfar Cl *IPNE* IP4	37 K4
LOS SS9	462 C3
Forge Crs *BRTR* CM7	211 H2
Forge St *RCOLE* CO7	121 J7
Forrest Cl *RCHLM* CM3	392 C6
Forsyth Dr *BRTR* CM7	209 K5
Forsythia Cl *CHLM/WR* CM1	305 G6 🔲
Fortescue Cha *SOS* SS1	465 J4
Forth Rd *UPMR* RM14	432 A8
Forties Cl *HVHL* CB9	27 K5
Fortinbras Wy *CHLM/GWD* CM2	14 D5
Fortin Cl *SOCK/AV* RM15	469 J7
Fortin Wy *SOCK/AV* RM15	469 J7
Fort Rd *TIL* RM18	489 G2
Fortrye Cl *GVW* DA11	488 D7
Fortune Cl *RCHLM* CM3	241 J6 🔲
The Fortunes *HLWS* CM18	13 F5
Fort William Rd *SLH/COR* SS17	457 J3
Fossetts La *RCOLW* CO6	152 C8
Fossetts Wy *SOSN* SS2	19 F1
Fostal Cl *LOS* SS9	463 F2
Foster Cl *BAR* EN8	346 E4
Foster Rd *CVI* SS8	478 C1
HAR CO12	128 D8
MAL CM9	310 C1
Fosters Cl *CHLM/WR* CM1	331 F4
Foster St *HLWE* CM17	295 K7
Foulgar Cl *RCHLM* CM3	392 C5 🔲
Foundation St *IPNE* IP4	3 E4 🔲
Foundry La *BOC* CM0	398 A8
RCOLW CO6	149 J7
RCOLW CO6	184 C8
Fountain Farm *HLWS* CM18	13 F5 🔲
Fountain La *HOC/HUL* SS5	420 C8
K/T/MI CO5	216 C5
Fountain Pl *WAB* EN9	347 J8 🔲
Fountain Rd *CHLM/WR* CM1	301 F2
Fountains Rd *CHTY* IP2	62 B4
Fountain Wk *GVW* DA11	488 D4
Fouracres *PEND* EN3	374 C5
Four Acres *SAFWN* CB10	43 J2
SAFWS CB11	71 F4
The Four Acres *SBW* CM21	264 A3
Four Ash Hl *HSTD* CO9	52 B4
Four Sisters Cl *LOS* SS9	443 G8 🔲
Four Sisters Wy *LOS* SS9	443 G7
Fourth Av *CHLM/WR* CM1	304 C8
COS CO15	11 F3
FOS CO15	261 K1
HLW CM20	12 C2
HLWW/ROY CM19	12 A3
HSTD CO9	148 C4
RCOS CO16	289 H7
SLH/COR SS17	457 F8
WICKE SS11	417 K7
WTHK RM20	482 D5
Fourways *RBSF* CM22	168 D4
The Four Wents *CHIG* IG7	402 E5 🔲
Fowe's La *SUD* CO10	55 G6
Fowler Cl *SOS* SS1	19 F4 🔲
Fowler Rd *BARK/HLT* IG6	406 B8
Fowley Cl *BAR* EN8	347 F8 🔲
Fowlmere Rd *ROY* SG8	40 B1
Foxborough Cha *ING* CM4	360 C8
Fox Burrow Rd *CHIG* IG7	27 F4
Fox Burrows La *CHLM/WR* CM1	331 H3
Fox Cl *CRW* RM5	407 G8
SBF/HAD SS7	440 E7
Fox Crs *CHLM/WR* CM1	14 A1
Foxdells La *BSF* CM23	198 E3
Foxden *WIT* CM8	245 K7
Foxes Cn *CDH/CHF* RM16	485 F1
Foxes Gv *GVW/HUT* CM13	413 G3
Foxes La *RCOLW* CO6	184 C5
SUD CO10	53 G4
Foxes Rd *SUD* CO10	53 G4
Foxfield Cl *HOC/HUL* SS5	421 H7 🔲
Foxfield Dr *SLH/COR* SS17	457 F8 🔲
Foxglove Cl *BSF* CM23	198 B7
COS CO15	259 H6
WIT CM8	276 D2
Foxglove Crs *IPSE* IP3	64 C4
Foxglove Rd *SOCK/AV* RM15	470 A6 🔲
The Foxgloves *BCAYW* CM12	414 A1 🔲
Foxglove Wy *CHLM/WR* CM1	305 H7 🔲
Foxgrove Gdns *FX* IP11	131 K2
Foxgrove La *FX* IP11	131 K2
Foxhall Cl *RCOLE* CO7	122 B1 🔲
Foxhall Flds *RCOLE* CO7	122 B1
Foxhall Rd *BOC* CM0	370 B6
IPNE IP4	64 C1
IPSE IP3	37 J8
UPMR RM14	451 K6
Fox Hatch *BRWN* CM15	383 G4
Foxhatch *WICKW* SS12	417 H7
Foxhills Rd *CDH/CHF* RM16	471 H8 🔲
Foxholes Rd *CHLM/GWD* CM2	333 H7 🔲
Fox Lea *KESC* IP5	39 J5
Foxleigh *BCAYW* CM12	414 B5 🔲
Foxleigh Cl *BCAYW* CM12	414 B5

Foxley Dr *BSF* CM23	199 F5
Fox Manor Wy *WTHK* RM20	482 E5
Foxmead *WIT* CM8	245 K7
Foxmeadows *SBF/HAD* SS7	440 E7 🔲
Foxtail Rd *IPSE* IP3	64 B5
Foxton Rd *WTHK* RM20	482 E5
Foxwood Cl *RCOLE* CO7	158 A3
Foxwood Crs *IPNE* IP4	38 D8
Foxwood Gv *GVW* DA11	488 D6
Foxwood Pl *LOS* SS9	462 E3
Foyle Dr *SOCK/AV* RM15	469 J5
Foys Wk *BCAYE* CM11	414 D6 🔲
Frambury La *SAFWS* CB11	100 A5
Framlingham Wy *BRTR* CM7	209 F6 🔲
Frampton Rd *BSDN* SS14	438 E7
EPP CM16	350 E2
IPS IP3	63 J5
Frances Cl *RCOLE* CO7	220 E3
Frances Gdns *SOCK/AV* RM15	469 H6 🔲
Frances Ga *CHLM/WR* CM1	305 J6 🔲
Francis Cl *HVHL* CB9	27 F5
K/T/MI CO5	280 A1
KESC IP5	39 J5
SLH/COR SS17	473 F2
Francisco Cl *CDH/CHF* RM16	483 F2 🔲
Francis Ct *WIT* CM8	211 H8
Francis Ms *MAL* CM9	338 D5 🔲
Francis Rd *BRTR* CM7	209 G3
SUD CO10	58 B6 🔲
Francis St *RCOLE* CO7	255 K8 🔲
Francis Wk *RAYL* SS6	441 H3
Francis Wy *COLN* CO4	9 F2
WIT CM8	244 C1
Francombe Gdns *ROM* RM1	430 B8
Frank Clater Cl *COLN* CO4	9 E3 🔲
Frankland Cl *WFD* IG8	403 K8 🔲
Frankland Rd *CHING* E4	402 B8
Franklin Av *EBAR* EN7	346 A4
Franklin Rd *HCH* RM12	450 D7 🔲
IPSE IP3	63 K3
RCHLM CM3	394 D5
Franklins Wy *WICKE* SS11	417 H5 🔲
Frank Martin Ct *EBAR* EN7	346 A4
Franmil Rd *EMPK* RM11	450 A1
Fraser Cl *CHLM/GWD* CM2	15 D5
LAIN SS15	435 K7
SBN/FI SS3	466 E4
Fraser Rd *BAR* EN8	346 E2 🔲
IP IP1	2 A2
Frating Abbey Farm Rd
RCOLE CO7	223 H7
Frating Hl *RCOLE* CO7	222 C2
Frating Rd *RCOLE* CO7	157 J8
Frayes Cha *CHONG* CM5	299 J2
Frazer Rd *ROMW/RG* RM7	450 A1
Frederica Rd *CHING* E4	402 E3
Frederick Crs *PEND* EN3	374 C6
Freeborne Gdns *RAIN* RM13	450 B7 🔲
Freebournes Rd *WIT* CM8	277 H4
Freehold Rd *IPNE* IP4	37 J7
Freeland Rd *COS* CO15	10 A6
Freelands *RCOLE* CO7	256 C7
Freeland St *LH/COR* SS17	474 B2
Freeman Cl *SLH/COR* SS17	474 B2
Freeman Rd *GVE* DA12	489 K8
Freeman Wy *EMPK* RM11	431 F6
Freewood La *SAFWS* CB11	67 J2
Fremantle *SBN/FI* SS3	466 C8
Fremantle Cl *RCHLM* CM3	392 D4 🔲
Fremantle Rd *COLS* CO2	219 J4 🔲
The Fremnells *BSDN* SS14	438 A6
French Rd *RCHLM* CM3	394 B4
Frensham Cl *COLW* CO3	185 J6 🔲
Frere Wy *K/T/MI* CO5	220 E7
Frerichs Cl *WICKW* SS12	417 G8
Freshfields *HAR* CO12	164 E4
Freshfields Av *UPMR* RM14	451 J6
Freshwater Crs *MAL* CM9	338 D1
Freshwater Dr *VGE* SS16	458 C2
Freshwaters *HLW* CM20	13 E2 🔲
Freshwater Wy *COS* CO15	259 H5
Freshwell Gdns *RBRW/HUT* CM13	434 C8
Freshwell St *SAFWN* CB10	70 D5 🔲
Fresian Cl *BRTR* CM7	209 F3 🔲
Freston Hl *RIPS/CAP* IP9	90 B1
Freston St *RIPS/CAP* IP9	90 A2
Frettons *BSDN* SS14	438 B9
Friar Cl *HVHL* CB9	27 F5
Friars *RIPS/CAP* IP9	87 G5
Friar's Av *BRWN* CM15	411 K3
Friars Bridge Rd *IP* IP1	2 C4 🔲
Friar's Cl *BRWN* CM15	411 K3
CHING E4	402 D6
COLN CO4	9 E1
HSTD CO9	110 B3
LAIN SS15	16 A4 🔲
RCOLE CO7	221 F5
RCOS CO16	10 B1
Friarscroft *BROX* EN10	319 G2
Friars Gate *WFD* IG8	403 H7
Friars La *BRTR* CM7	209 J1
MAL CM9	338 B3 🔲
RBSF CM22	265 H4
Friars St *SBN/FI* SS3	466 E6

SUD CO10	58 A6
The Friars *CHIG* IG7	405 H1
Friars Wk *CHLM/GWD* CM2	14 C4
Friars Wd *BSF* CM23	199 H5
Friary La *WFD* IG8	403 H7
Friday Hl *CHING* E4	403 F6 🔲
Friday Hl East *CHING* E4	403 F6
Friday Hl West *CHING* E4	403 F6
Friday Wood Gn *COLS* CO2	219 H5 🔲
Friedberg Av *BSF* CM23	198 C6
Friends Av *BAR* EN8	346 D6
Friends Fld *BURES* CO8	115 J4
Friends Wk *KESG* IP5	39 H1
SAFWS CB11	70 E6
Friern Gdns *WICKW* SS12	416 E6
Friern Pl *WICKW* SS12	416 E6
Friern Wk *WICKW* SS12	416 E6
Frietuna Rd *FOS* CO15	228 D7
Frimley Av *EMPK* RM11	451 H1
Frinton Rd *COS* CO15	260 D7
FOS CO15	228 B7
RCOS CO16	226 E6
Frithwood Cl *BCAYW* CM12	414 A6
Frithwood La *BCAYW* CM12	414 A6
Fritton Cl *CHTY* IP2	62 C6
Frobisher Dr *COS* CO15	290 B6
Frobisher Rd *ERITH* DA8	480 B6
HAR CO12	164 E6
IPSE IP3	63 G6
Frobisher Wy *BRTR* CM7	210 B3
SBN/FI SS3	466 D2
Froden Brook *BCAYE* CM11	414 D7
Froden Ct *BCAYE* CM11	414 D7 🔲
Frogge St *SAFWN* CB10	43 G2
Frog Hall Cl *K/T/MI* CO5	220 E7
Frogs Aly *RIPS/CAP* IP9	92 E1
Frog St *BRWN* CM15	383 G9
Frome *TIL* RM18	486 D7
Fronk's Av *HAR* CO12	7 D7
Fronk's Rd *HAR* CO12	6 C7
Front La *UPMR* RM14	452 B3
Front Rd *IPSE* IP3	64 D8
Frowick La *RCOS* CO16	257 H7
Fryatt Av *HAR* CO12	6 B7
Fry Cl *CRW* RM5	407 F1
Fryerning La *ING* CM4	386 B7
Fryth Cl *HVHL* CB9	27 G1
The Fryth *BSDN* SS14	438 B3
Fuchsia La *IPNE* IP4	37 J2
Fuchsia Wy *RCOS* CO16	258 E6
Fulbrook La *SOCK/AV* RM15	469 H1
Fulcher Av *CHLM/GWD* CM2	333 H2
Fulfen Wy *SAFWS* CB11	70 E6
Fulford Dr *LOS* SS9	443 H1
Fullarton Crs *SOCK/AV* RM15	469 H6 🔲
Fullbridge *MAL* CM9	338 C2
Fuller Ct *BSF* CM23	199 F6 🔲
Fuller's Cl *K/T/MI* CO5	246 D3
WAB EN9	348 B1
Fullers Md *HLWE* CM17	295 C6
Fullers Rd *COLS* CO2	220 A3
Fulmar Cl *COLN* CO4	188 D5
Fulmar Rd *RAIN* RM13	450 C1
Fulmar Wy *WICKE* SS11	417 K8
Fulton Crs *BSF* CM23	199 H4
Fulton Rd *SBF/HAD* SS7	440 C6
Furlongs *VGE* SS16	458 A1
The Furlongs *ING* CM4	386 B2 🔲
Furneaux La *K/T/MI* CO5	220 C6
Furness Cl *CDH/CHF* RM16	485 G4
CHTY IP2	62 B5
Furness Wy *HCH* RM12	450 B6
The Furrells *CBE/LIN* CB1	21 H8
Furriers Cl *BSF* CM23	198 E5
Furrow Cl *COLW* CO3	185 K8
Furrowfelde *VGE* SS16	17 E2
Further Meadow *CHLM/WR* CM1	331 C6
Furtherwick Rd *CVI* SS8	478 B3
Furze Crs *RCOLE* CO7	221 K6
Furze Gld *VGE* SS16	436 C8
Furze La *ING* CM4	388 C6
RCOLE CO7	191 F6
Fusedale Wy *SOCK/AV* RM15	469 H7
Fyefields *PIT* SS13	439 F6
Fyfield Av *WICKW* SS12	417 F6
Fyfield Cl *RBRW/HUT* CM13	434 C6
Fyfield Dr *SOCK/AV* RM15	469 H1
Fyfield Rd *CHONG* CM5	326 B2
Fynn Valley Wk *NHMKT* IP6	38 D7

G

Gabion Av *PUR* RM19	482 A3
Gablefields *CHLM/GWD* CM2	334 A1
The Gables *PIT* SS13	438 E8
SBF/HAD SS7	442 B6
Gaces Acre *SAFWS* CB11	100 B4
Gadsden Cl *UPMR* RM14	432 B8
Gadwall Reach *K/T/MI* CO5	247 F3
Gafzelle Dr *CVI* SS8	478 E3
Gager Dr *K/T/MI* CO5	248 C1

Gage's Rd *SUD* CO10 .... 54 D6
Gaiger Cl *CHLM/WR* CM1 .... 305 F6
Gainsborough Av *CVI* SS8 .... 478 E3
TIL RM18 .... 485 F7
Gainsborough Cl *BCAYW* CM12 .... 414 C4
K/T/MI CO5 .... 285 F7
RCOS CO16 .... 258 E7
Gainsborough Crs *CHLM/GWD* CM2.. 15 F2
Gainsborough Dr *GVW* DA11 .... 488 C8
MGTR CO11 .... 159 G1
Gainsborough La *IPSE* IP3 .... 63 H5
Gainsborough Pl
RBRW/HUT CM13 .... 412 C4
Gainsborough Rd *COLW* CO3 .... 186 C8
FX IP11 .... 131 H3
HVHL CB9 .... 26 D4
IPNE IP4 .... 3 E1
Gainsborough St *SUD* CO10 .... 58 B6
Gains Cl *CVI* SS8 .... 478 D1
Gainsford Av *COS* CO15 .... 11 E3
Gainsford End Rd *HSTD* CO9 .... 78 E7
Gainsthorpe Rd *CHONG* CM5 ...... 325 K5
Galadriel *RCHLM* CM3 .... 392 B7
Galahad Cl *BOC* CM0 .... 398 B8
Galey Gn *SOCK/AV* RM15 .... 469 K6
Gall End La *STSD* CM24 .... 168 A6
Galleons Hill Vicarage Rd
CHLM/WR CM1 .... 302 B8
Galleydene *SBF/HAD* SS7 .... 461 H2
Galleyhill Rd *WAB* EN9 .... 348 A6
Galliford Rd *MAL* CM9 .... 338 C1
The Gallops *MAL* CM9 .... 338 C1
Galloway Cl *BROX* EN10 .... 319 F8
BSF CM23 .... 198 E5
Galloway Dr *RCOS* CO16 .... 258 E2
Galloway Rd *BSF* CM23 .... 198 E5
Gallows Green Rd *GTDUN* CM6 .... 172 C2
Gallows Hl *SAFWS* CB11 .... 70 D6
Galsworthy Cl *BRTR* CM7 .... 209 K6
Galsworthy Rd *TIL* RM18 .... 485 H7
Galton Rd *WOS/PRIT* SS0 .... 463 J5
Galway Av *IP* IP1 .... 36 A4
Gambleside *VGE* SS16 .... 458 B2
Gandalf's Ride *RCHLM* CM3 .... 392 C7
Gandish Rd *RCOLE* CO7 .... 122 D3
Ganels Cl *BCAYE* CM11 .... 414 D6
Ganels Rd *BCAYE* CM11 .... 414 C6
Ganges Rd *RIPS/CAP* IP9 .... 129 F5
Gangies Hl *SBW* CM21 .... 262 E2
Gannet Cl *HVHL* CB9 .... 27 J5
Gannet Rd *CHTY* IP2 .... 62 A2
Gant Ct *WAB* EN9 .... 348 D8
Ganwick Cl *HVHL* CB9 .... 27 F5
Gaol La *SUD* CO10 .... 58 B6
The Gap *COS* CO15 .... 260 E7
SAFWS CB11 .... 98 E4
Garbutt Rd *UPMR* RM14 .... 451 K3
Garden Cl *CHING* E4 .... 402 B8
RCHLM CM3 .... 396 D1
RIPS/CAP IP9 .... 128 D2
Garden End CM4 .... 388 B3
Gardeners *CHLM/GWD* CM2 .... 333 F8
Gardeners La *RCFD* SS4 .... 423 H4
Gardeners Rd *HSTD* CO9 .... 148 A4
Garden Farm *K/T/MI* CO5 .... 285 F5
Garden Fld *IP* IP11 .... 5 D2
RCHLM CM3 .... 307 K1
The Gardens *BRWN* CM15 .... 383 K2
Garden Terrace Rd *HLWE* CM17 ... 295 G1
Garden Wy *LOU* IG10 .... 377 J1
Gardiners Cl *BSDN* SS14 .... 438 A4
Gardiners La North *BCAYW* CM11 . 416 A8
Gardiners La South *BSDN* SS14 .... 438 A3
Gardiners Link *BSDN* SS14 .... 438 A3
The Gardiners *HLWE* CM17 .... 295 F6
Gardiners Wy *BSDN* SS14 .... 438 A3
Gardner Av *SLH/COR* SS17 .... 457 G8
SLH/COR SS17 .... 474 B1
Garfield Cl *FX* IP11 .... 5 F4
Garfield Rd *CHING* E4 .... 402 E4
FX IP11 .... 5 F4
PEND EN3 .... 374 C8
Garland Cl *BAR* EN8 .... 346 E5
Garland Rd *HAR* CO12 .... 6 A3
Garland Wy *EMPK* RM11 .... 431 F6
Garner Dr *BROX* EN10 .... 318 E8
Garnetts *RBSF* CM22 .... 201 J5
Garnetts La *GTDUN* CM6 .... 206 D7
Garnon Md *EPP* CM16 .... 351 H2
Garnons Cha *RCOLW* CO6 .... 117 F8
Garrettlands *CHLM/GWD* CM2 .... 334 D7
Garrick St *GVW* DA11 .... 489 G4
Garrick Wy *IP* IP11 .... 36 C2
Garrison La *FX* IP11 .... 5 F4
SUD CO10 .... 59 H2
Garrod Ct *COLS* CO2 .... 219 J6
Garrods *RIPS/CAP* IP9 .... 87 G4
Garron La *SOCK/AV* RM15 .... 469 H6

Garth Rd *SOCK/AV* RM15 .... 470 A4
Garthwood Cl *RCOLW* CO6 .... 185 K1
Gascoigne Cl *COLN* CO4 .... 9 E3
Gascoigne Wy *BCAYE* CM11 .... 414 E3
Gascoyne *HARH* RM3 .... 430 E3
Gaston End *RCOLE* CO7 .... 122 B2
Gaston St *RCOLE* CO7 .... 122 B3
Gatacre Rd *IP* IP1 .... 2 B2
Gate Farm Rd *RIPS/CAP* IP9 ...... 129 C4
Gatefield Cl *FOS* CO15 .... 228 E6
Gatehope Dr *SOCK/AV* RM15 ...... 469 H6
Gatehouse Ms *ING* CM4 .... 386 B2
Gatekeeper Cl *BRTR* CM7 .... 209 J4
Gate Lodge Sq *LAIN* SS15 .... 437 G5
Gate Lodge Wy *LAIN* SS15 .... 437 G5
Gate St *MAL* CM9 .... 338 B2
Gate Street Ms *MAL* CM9 .... 338 B2
Gatscombe Cl *HOC/HUL* SS5 ...... 420 E7
The Gattens *RAYL* SS6 .... 442 A1
Gatwick Cl *BSF* CM23 .... 199 G4
Gatwick Rd *GVE* DA12 .... 489 G7
Gatwick Vw *BCAYW* CM12 .... 414 C5
Gauden Rd *BRTR* CM7 .... 177 J6
Gavenny Pth *SOCK/AV* RM15 ..... 469 H6
Gavin Wy *COLN* CO4 .... 155 J8
Gay Bowers *BSDN* SS14 .... 438 A6
HOC/HUL SS5 .... 420 C7
Gay Bowers La *RCHLM* CM3 ...... 335 K7
Gay Bowers Rd *RCHLM* CM3 ...... 363 J1
Gay Bowers Wy *WIT* CM8 .... 277 G6
Gaye St *IP* IP1 .... 2 C3
Gayfer Av *KESG* IP5 .... 39 K5
Gayleighs *RAYL* SS6 .... 441 J1
Gaylor Rd *TIL* RM18 .... 484 D7
Gaymers La *FX* IP11 .... 94 C7
Gaynes Ct *UPMR* RM14 .... 451 J5
Gaynes Park Rd *UPMR* RM14 ..... 451 J5
Gaynesford *VGE* SS16 .... 16 C6
Gaynes Rd *UPMR* RM14 .... 451 J3
Gays La *RCFD* SS4 .... 423 H5
Gayton Rd *SOSN* SS2 .... 19 D2
Gaywood *LAIN* SS15 .... 436 B6
Gaywood Av *BAR* EN8 .... 346 D4
Gazelle Cl *COLN* CO4 .... 187 K1
Geary Dr *BRW* CM14 .... 411 F4
The Geerings *SLH/COR* SS17 ...... 474 C2
Geesh Rd *CVI* SS8 .... 461 H8
Geisthorp Ct *WAB* EN9 .... 348 C7
Generals Ms *FX* IP11 .... 5 D2
The Generals Wk *PEND* EN3 .... 374 E3
Genesta Cl *MAL* CM9 .... 314 D3
Genesta Rd *WOS/PRIT* SS0 .... 463 K5
Geneva Rd *IP* IP1 .... 2 C2
Genever Cl *CHING* E4 .... 402 B8
Genk Cl *CVI* SS8 .... 461 G8
Gennep Rd *CVI* SS8 .... 461 G8
Gentian Cl *COLN* CO4 .... 186 D3
Gentry Cl *SLH/COR* SS17 .... 473 J5
Geoffrey Av *HARH* RM3 .... 431 H1
Geoff Seaden Cl *COL* CO1 .... 9 E5
George Av *RCOLE* CO7 .... 255 K6
George Avey Cft *EPP* CM16 .... 324 B8
George Cardnell Wy *RCHLM* CM3 . 368 C4
George Cl *COS* CO15 .... 290 E3
CVI SS8 .... 460 E7
George Cut *RCOLE* CO7 .... 255 K7
George Frost Cl *IPNE* IP4 .... 3 E2
George Gent Cl *HVHL* CB9 .... 50 C7
George La *SUD* CO10 .... 33 H2
George Rd *BRTR* CM7 .... 209 G3
Georges Dr *BRWN* CM15 .... 410 C1
George St *CHLM/GWD* CM2 .... 14 C4
COL CO1 .... 8 B4
GRAYS RM17 .... 483 K5
HAR CO12 .... 7 E2
ROM RM1 .... 430 A8
SBN/FI SS3 .... 467 F7
Gepps Cl *CHLM/WR* CM1 .... 269 H3
Gerald Rd *GVE* DA12 .... 489 K5
Geralds Av *IPNE* IP4 .... 37 J8
Gerard Av *BSF* CM23 .... 231 J1
Gerard Rd *RCOS* CO16 .... 258 E7
Gernon Cl *CHLM/WR* CM1 .... 304 D2
Gernon Rd *RCOLE* CO7 .... 157 H6
Gernons *VGE* SS16 .... 17 D6
Gerpins La *UPMR* RM14 .... 468 B2
Gerrard Crs *BRW* CM14 .... 411 F6
Gestingthorpe Rd *SUD* CO10 ...... 56 A8
Gew's Cnr *BAR* EN8 .... 346 D3
Geylen Rd *CVI* SS8 .... 478 D1
Ghyllgrove *BSDN* SS14 .... 17 F4
Ghyllgrove Cl *BSDN* SS14 .... 17 F2
Gibb Cft *HLWS* CM18 .... 322 C1
Gibbons Ct *GTDUN* CM6 .... 204 C4
Gibbons St *IP* IP1 .... 2 B3
Gibbs Cl *BAR* EN8 .... 346 D3
Gibbs Fld *BSF* CM23 .... 198 C8
Gibcracks *BSDN* SS14 .... 438 B7
Gibraltar Cl *RBRW/HUT* CM13 .... 433 F1
Gibson Cl *EPP* CM16 .... 324 C7
GVW DA11 .... 488 E8
SAFWN CB10 .... 70 A4
Gibson Gdns *SAFWN* CB10 .... 70 E4
Gibson Rd *HSTD* CO9 .... 110 C5
Gibson Wy *SAFWN* CB10 .... 70 E4

Gidea Av *GPK* RM2 .... 430 B5
Gidea Cl *GPK* RM2 .... 430 B5
Gideons Wy *SLH/COR* SS17 .... 473 K2
Giffins Cl *BRTR* CM7 .... 209 H4
Gifford Cl *RIPS/CAP* IP9 .... 90 A7
Gifford Gn *PIT* SS13 .... 438 E8
Gifford Rd *SBF/HAD* SS7 .... 440 C8
Giffords Cross Av *SLH/COR* SS17 . 474 C1
Giffords Cross Rd *SLH/COR* SS17 . 474 C1
Giffordside *CDH/CHF* RM16 .... 485 G4
Giffords Pl *IPNE* IP4 .... 38 D7
Gifhorn Rd *CVI* SS8 .... 478 E2
Gilberd Ct *COLN* CO4 .... 155 K7
Gilberd Rd *COLS* CO2 .... 219 J1
Gilbert Cl *RAYL* SS6 .... 442 A3
Gilbert Dr *VGE* SS16 .... 436 B8
Gilbert Rd *CDH/CHF* RM16 .... 485 F2
ROM RM1 .... 430 A6
SUD CO10 .... 31 F4
Gilbert St *PEND* EN3 .... 374 C3
Gilbert Wy *BRTR* CM7 .... 178 B8
Gilbey Av *BSF* CM23 .... 199 G7
Gilbey Crs *STSD* CM24 .... 167 K5
Gilbey Gn *SAFWS* CB11 .... 100 A4
Gilchrist Wy *BRTR* CM7 .... 209 H1
Gildborne Cl *SLH/COR* SS17 ...... 458 A8
Gilden Cl *HLWE* CM17 .... 295 J1
Gilden Wy *HLWE* CM17 .... 295 H2
Gilderdale Cl *COLN* CO4 .... 188 A2
Gilders *SBW* CM21 .... 263 H3
Gilders Wy *RCOS* CO16 .... 258 E8
Gillam Wy *RAIN* RM13 .... 450 B2
Gill Cl *MAL* CM9 .... 310 B7
Gill Crs *GVW* DA11 .... 488 E8
Gillian Crs *GPK* RM2 .... 430 D4
Gills Av *CVI* SS8 .... 478 C1
The Gill *SBF/HAD* SS7 .... 441 J8
Gilman Dr *SBN/FI* SS3 .... 466 B6
Gilmore Wy *CHLM/GWD* CM2 .... 333 K7
Gilmour Cl *ENC/FH* EN2 .... 374 A1
Gilmour Ri *BCAYW* CM12 .... 414 A4
Gilpin Wy *BRTR* CM7 .... 209 F6
Gilroy Cl *RAIN* RM13 .... 450 A7
Gilsland *WAB* EN9 .... 376 A1
Gilwell Cl *CHING* E4 .... 375 H8
Gilwell La *CHING* E4 .... 375 K8
Gilwell Park Cl *COLW* CO3 .... 218 B1
Gimson Cl *WIT* CM8 .... 276 E3
Ginns Rd *BUNT* SG9 .... 133 C7
Gippeswyck *BSDN* SS14 .... 437 K6
Gippeswyck Av *CHTY* IP2 .... 2 B5
Gippeswyck Rd *CHTY* IP2 .... 2 C5
Gipping Cl *HVHL* CB9 .... 26 E7
Gipson Park Cl *LOS* SS9 .... 442 E7
Gipsy La *BSF* CM23 .... 199 H1
GRAYS RM17 .... 484 B5
Girling St *SUD* CO10 .... 58 B5
Girton Cl *BAR* EN8 .... 346 E4
Girton Rd *HVHL* CB9 .... 27 H6
Girton Wy *CHTY* IP2 .... 62 B4
Gladden Ct *HLWS* CM18 .... 322 C1
Gladden Flds *RCHLM* CM3 .... 392 C7
The Glade *COLN* CO4 .... 188 B3
RBRW/HUT CM13 .... 411 K4
UPMR RM14 .... 451 K6
VGE SS16 .... 457 K1
WFD IG8 .... 403 J6
Gladeview *COS* CO15 .... 259 H6
The Gladeway *WAB* EN9 .... 347 K7
Gladiator Wy *COLS* CO2 .... 218 B3
Gladstone Gdns *RAYL* SS6 .... 441 G4
Gladstone Rd *BKHH* IG9 .... 403 K4
COL CO1 .... 8 C6
HOC/HUL SS5 .... 421 F8
IPSE IP3 .... 37 H8
K/T/MI CO5 .... 280 E1
Gladwin Rd *COLS* CO2 .... 218 D1
Glamis Cl *EBAR* EN7 .... 346 A3
Glamis Dr *EMPK* RM11 .... 451 F2
Glamorgan Rd *CHTY* IP2 .... 62 D4
Glanmead *BRWN* CM15 .... 411 H4
Glanmire *BCAYE* CM11 .... 387 K7
Glanthams Rd *BRWN* CM15 ...... 411 J5
Glanville Dr *EMPK* RM11 .... 451 G2
Glanville Pl *KESG* IP5 .... 39 F7
Glasseys La *RAYL* SS6 .... 441 H5
Glastonbury Cha *WOS/PRIT* SS0 .. 443 J8
Glastonbury Cl *CHTY* IP2 .... 62 B4
Glebe *BSDN* SS14 .... 437 K5
Glebe Av *BRTR* CM7 .... 177 H6
Glebe Cl *MGTR* CO11 .... 161 K8
RAYL SS6 .... 441 H2
RCOLE CO7 .... 189 K7
RIPS/CAP IP9 .... 88 D6
SBN/FI SS3 .... 467 J2
SOS SS1 .... 465 H5
Glebe Ct *BSF* CM23 .... 199 G5
Glebe Crs *CBS* CB2 .... 20 B1
CHLM/WR CM1 .... 304 D4
WIT CM8 .... 276 E1
Glebe Dr *RAYL* SS6 .... 441 H2
Glebe End *RBSF* CM22 .... 168 E4
RIPS/CAP IP9 .... 87 G3
Glebefield Rd *RCHLM* CM3 .... 308 B1
Glebe Gdns *K/T/MI* CO5 .... 214 B8

RBRW/HUT CM13 .... 434 D2 🔟
Glebelands CHIG IG7 .... 406 A6
  HLW CM20 .... 294 D2
  RCOLW CO6 .... 154 C4
  SBF/HAD SS7 .... 440 A6
Glebe La BOC CM0 .... 371 K4
  CTDUN CM6 .... 170 J8
  RIPS/CAP IP5 .... 90 D5
Glebe Meadow RCHLM CM3 ..... 272 A6
Glebe Rd BCAYE CM11 .... 416 B5
  CHLM/WR CM1 .... 14 C2 🔟
  CHONG CM5 .... 354 D3
  COLS CO2 .... 218 D3
  GVW DA11 .... 488 E6
  K/T/MI CO5 .... 246 D3
  K/T/MI CO5 .... 248 A8
  MAL CM9 .... 310 E8
  WICKE SS11 .... 417 H6
The Glebe HVHL CB9 .... 27 G4
  RCHLM CM3 .... 365 K4
  SAFWS CB11 .... 71 F6
Glebe Wy BOC CM0 .... 398 B7
  COS CO15 .... 290 C6
  EMPK RM11 .... 451 F1
  FOS CO13 .... 228 E8
  SBF/HAD SS7 .... 462 A2
Glebeway WFD IG8 .... 403 K8
Glemham Dr HPIN 64 D1
Glemsford Cl FX IP11 .... 5 D4
Glen Av COLW CO3 .... 186 C6
Glenavon Rd IPNE IP4 .... 38 B6
Glenbervie Dr LOS SS9 .... 463 C3
Glencoe Dr WICKE SS11 .... 417 K5 🔟
Glencoe Rd IPNE IP4 .... 38 A4
Glencree BCAYE CM11 .... 387 K7
Glen Cft HOC/HUL SS5 .... 421 G8
Glendale RCHLM CM3 .... 392 E4
  CI BRWN CM15 .... 411 H4
Glendale Gdns LOS SS9 .... 462 C4
Glendale Gv COLN CO4 .... 187 K2
Glendale Rd BOC CM0 .... 398 C7
Glendower Rd CHING E4 .... 402 E4 🔟
Gleneagles SBF/HAD SS7 .... 440 A8
Gleneagles CI FX IP11 .... 131 K1 🔟
  HARH RM3 .... 431 G2 🔟
Gleneagles Dr IPNE IP4 .... 38 B8
Gleneagles Rd LOS SS9 .... 442 D8 🔟
Gleneagles Wy RCHLM CM3 ...... 308 B7
Glen Faba Rd HLWW/ROY CM19 .. 292 B7
Glenfield Av FX IP11 .... 131 H1
Glenfield Cl SLH/COR SS17 .... 457 J8 🔟
Glen Hazel BRWN CM15 .... 384 B1 🔟
Glenhurst Av IPNE IP4 .... 37 K5
Glenhurst Rd SOSN SS2 .... 19 D2
Glenloch Ct PEND EN3 .... 374 C6
Glenmere VGE SS16 .... 458 A3
Glenmere Park Av SBF/HAD SS7 .. 461 G2
Glenmore St SOSN SS2 .... 465 C4
Glenridding SBF/HAD SS7 .... 440 C8 🔟
Glen Rd LOS SS9 .... 463 H5
  SBF/HAD SS7 .... 440 D8
Glenside BCAYE CM11 .... 414 E3
  SUD CO10 .... 58 D7
The Glen RAYL SS6 .... 441 K5
  SLH/COR SS17 .... 474 B2
  VGE SS16 .... 458 D1
Glentress Cl COLN CO4 .... 188 A2 🔟
Glen Vw GVE DA12 .... 489 H6
Glenwood BROX EN10 .... 319 F1
Glenwood Av HOC/HUL SS5 ...... 421 G8 🔟
  LOS SS9 .... 442 C6
  WOS/PRIT SS0 .... 18 A2
Glenwood Cl GPK RM2 .... 430 B7
Glenwood Gdns VGE SS16 .... 455 K1
Gleten Rd CVI SS8 .... 478 D1
Glisson Sq COLS CO2 .... 218 C1
Globe Cl K/T/MI CO5 .... 248 B7 🔟
Globe Crs BSF CM23 .... 166 C7
Globe Rd EMPK RM11 .... 430 B8
Gloucester Av BAR EN8 .... 346 E7
  CDH/CHF RM16 .... 484 D1 🔟
  CHLM/GWD CM2 .... 332 D7
  COLS CO2 .... 218 C2 🔟
  EMPK RM11 .... 431 H7
  MAL CM9 .... 338 D5
  RAYL SS6 .... 442 B5
  TIL RM18 .... 436 E6
Gloucester Crs CHLM/WR CM1 ... 304 C8
Gloucester Gdns BRTR CM7 ...... 210 A2
Gloucester Pl BCAYW CM12 .... 387 C8
Gloucester Rd BRWN CM15 .... 410 E1
  HVHL CB9 .... 26 E6
  IPSE IP3 .... 63 J5
Gloucester Ter SOS SS1 .... 465 J7
Glovers Fld BRWN CM15 .... 383 H3
Glovers La HLWE CM17 .... 323 J2
Glynde Wy SOSN SS2 .... 465 J4
Glynn Rd BOC CM0 .... 398 B7
Glyn Pd PEND EN3 .... 374 C8 🔟
Goat Hall La CHLM/GWD CM2 .... 360 B2
Goat House La RCHLM CM3 .... 364 E2
Goat Lodge Rd MAL CM9 .... 278 C8
Goatsmoor La BCAYE CM11 .... 388 A8
Goatswood La ABR/ST RM4 .... 408 C3

Gobions VGE SS16 .... 17 E6
Godbold Cl KESG IP5 .... 39 H6 🔟
Goddard Cl CDH/CHF RM16 ...... 470 E8
Goddard Wy CHLM/GWD CM2 .... 333 H5
  SAFWN CB10 .... 71 F2
Godfrey Wy CTDUN CM6 .... 204 C3
Godlings Wy BRTR CM7 .... 209 H5
Godman Rd CDH/CHF RM16 ...... 485 C2
Godmans La RCOLW CO6 .... 215 H2
Godric Rd WIT CM8 .... 276 E5
Godwin Cl CHING E4 .... 375 J4
  HSTD CO9 .... 147 J4
Goff's La RCOS CO16 .... 194 C5
Goings La K/T/MI CO5 .... 285 F7 🔟
Goirle Av CVI SS8 .... 478 C1
Goldace GRAYS RM17 .... 483 J5 🔟
Goldberry Md RCHLM CM3 .... 392 C7 🔟
Gold Cl BROX EN10 .... 318 E2
  RBSF RM22 .... 168 C2
Goldcrest Cl COLN CO4 .... 188 C5
Goldcrest Dr BCAYE CM11 .... 414 D4
Goldcrest Rd CHTY IP2 .... 61 K2 🔟
Goldenacres CHLM/WR CM1 ...... 305 H5 🔟
Golden Cross Rd RCFD SS4 .... 422 A7
Golden Dawn Wy COLN CO4 ...... 8 A1 🔟
Golden La BROX EN10 .... 226 C2
Golden Lion La HAR CO12 .... 75 J3
Golden Manor Dr SBF/HAD SS7 .. 440 E8
Golden Noble HI COLS CO2 .... 8 C5
Goldfinch Cl COLN CO4 .... 188 C6
Goldfinch La SBF/HAD SS7 .... 441 F6
Goldhanger Cl RAYL SS6 .... 441 F2 🔟
Goldhanger Cross BSDN SS14 .... 438 B6
Goldhanger Rd MAL CM9 .... 338 C1
Golding Crs SLH/COR SS17 ...... 474 A2
Goldingham Av LOU IG10 .... 378 A6
Goldingham Dr BRTR CM7 .... 209 K5
Goldings BSF CM23 .... 199 C5
Goldings Cl HVHL CB9 .... 27 C3
Goldings Crs VGE SS16 .... 458 B2
Golding's HI LOU IG10 .... 377 H4
Goldings Ri LOU IG10 .... 377 J5
Goldings Rd LOU IG10 .... 377 J5
Golding Thoroughfare
  CHLM/GWD CM2 .... 333 H2 🔟
Goldington Crs BCAYW CM12 ..... 387 F8
Golding Wy RCOS CO16 .... 257 C8
  SUD CO10 .... 33 H1
Goldlay Av CHLM/GWD CM2 ...... 15 D5
Goldlay Rd CHLM/GWD CM2 ...... 15 D5 🔟
Goldmer Cl SBN/FI SS3 .... 466 B5
Goldsands Rd BOC CM0 .... 398 E3
Goldsborough Crs CHING E4 ..... 402 D5 🔟
Goldsdown Cl PEND EN3 .... 374 E6
Goldsdown Rd PEND EN3 .... 374 D6
Goldsmith Dr RAYL SS6 .... 419 C6
Goldsmith Rd IP IP1 .... 36 A1
Goldsmiths Av SLH/COR SS17 .... 474 C2
Gold St SAFWN CB10 .... 70 E4
Goldsworthy Dr SBN/FI SS3 ...... 467 H5
Golf Green Rd COS CO15 .... 290 C5
Golf Ride SBF/HAD SS7 .... 460 C2
Goodchild Av LAIN SS15 .... 437 H5
Goodey Cl COLC CO1 .... 8 C6
Goodlake Cl HAR CO12 .... 164 D5
Goodliffe Pk BSF CM23 .... 199 C5
Goodmans La RCHLM CM3 .... 241 C8
Goodview Rd LAIN SS15 .... 437 H5
Goodwin Ct BAR EN8 .... 346 E2 🔟
Goodwins Cl SAFWS CB11 .... 69 K2 🔟
Goodwin Stile BSF CM23 .... 198 C5 🔟
Goodwood Cl IP IP1 .... 36 D1
  PEND EN3 .... 374 C5
  RBRW/HUT CM13 .... 412 E2
Goodwood Ct IP IP1 .... 36 D1
  SBF/HAD SS7 .... 441 F6
Goojerat Rd COS CO2 .... 186 E8
Goose La RBSF CM22 .... 232 D6
Gooshays Dr HARH RM3 .... 431 F1
Gooshays Gdns HARH RM3 .... 431 F1
Gordon Av HCH RM12 .... 450 A4 🔟
Gordon Cl BCAYW CM12 .... 414 A2
  TIL RM18 .... 436 E6
Gordon Dr COLN CO4 .... 155 J8
Gordon Pl GVE DA12 .... 489 H4 🔟
  SOS SS1 .... 18 C4
Gordon Rd BAR EN8 .... 347 C8
  BRWN CM15 .... 411 K4
  BSDN SS14 .... 438 A8
  CDH/CHF RM16 .... 484 D1
  CHING E4 .... 403 F3
  CHLM/GWD CM2 .... 332 C7
  GVW DA11 .... 488 D5
  HAR CO12 .... 6 C6
  IPNE IP4 .... 37 J6
  LOS SS9 .... 462 C3
  SLH/COR SS17 .... 474 B2
  SOS SS1 .... 18 C4
Gordons PIT SS13 .... 438 D8 🔟
Gordon Wy HAR CO12 .... 6 C6
Gorefield Rd RBSF CM22 .... 201 J1
Gore La BRTR CM7 .... 208 C3
Gore Rd BRTR CM7 .... 208 D3

RCFD SS4 .... 423 H7
The Gore BSDN SS14 .... 17 E4
Goring Rd COLN CO4 .... 9 E2
  IPNE IP4 .... 37 K7
Gorsehayes CHTY IP2 .... 2 C6
Gorse La COS CO15 .... 259 J5
  K/T/MI CO5 .... 280 B1
Gorse Rd IPSE IP3 .... 63 K3
Gorse Wy COLW CO3 .... 217 J1
  COS CO15 .... 290 B6
Gosbecks Rd COLS CO2 .... 218 B2
Gosbecks Vw COLS CO2 .... 218 B3
Gosfield Cl RAYL SS6 .... 441 F2 🔟
Gosfield Rd BRTR CM7 .... 178 C2
  COLS CO2 .... 219 H5
Gosford Cl SUD CO10 .... 31 F5
Gosford Wy FX IP11 .... 131 K1
Goshawk Dr CHLM/GWD CM2 .... 332 D8 🔟
The Goslings SBN/FI SS3 .... 467 F6
  WIT CM8 .... 211 H8
Gosport Dr HCH RM12 .... 450 D7 🔟
The Gossetts CTDUN CM6 .... 500 C5
Gostling Pl KESG IP5 .... 39 J5
Gouge Av GVW DA11 .... 488 D6
Gough Rd EN EN1 .... 374 B6
Gould Cl CHONG CM5 .... 325 J3
Gouldings Av WOTN CO14 .... 229 C5
Goulds Rd BURES CO8 .... 114 B4
Coulton Rd CHLM/WR CM1 .... 304 C4
Gourney Gv CDH/CHF RM16 ...... 471 F7
Government Rw PEND EN3 .... 375 C3
Gowan Brae SBF/HAD SS7 .... 440 A8 🔟
Gowan Cl SBF/HAD SS7 .... 440 A8
Gowers Av CHLM/GWD CM2 ...... 333 G7
Gowers Cl KESG IP5 .... 39 J6 🔟
Gowers La CDH/CHF RM16 .... 484 E1
The Gowers HLW CM20 .... 294 E8
Gower St CHTY IP2 .... 3 D5
Goya Ri SBN/FI SS3 .... 467 F5
Goyfield Av FX IP11 .... 5 F3
Grace Gdns BSF CM23 .... 231 K1
Graces Cl WIT CM8 .... 277 C6
Graces La RCHLM CM3 .... 335 F4
Graces Wk FOS CO13 .... 229 F7
  RCHLM CM3 .... 334 D3
Grafton Pl CHLM/GWD CM2 ...... 333 J7
Grafton Rd CVI SS8 .... 478 C3
  HAR CO12 .... 7 E4
Grafton Wy IP IP1 .... 3 D4
Graham Av BROX EN10 .... 318 E2
  IP IP1 .... 2 C1 🔟
Graham Cl BCAYW CM12 .... 387 H8
  HOC/HUL SS5 .... 421 F6
  RBRW/HUT CM13 .... 412 B1
  SLH/COR SS17 .... 473 K1
Graham Rd FX IP11 .... 5 F2
  IP IP1 .... 2 C2
Grailands BSF CM23 .... 198 C5
Grainger Cl SOSN SS2 .... 19 D2 🔟
Grainger Rd SOSN SS2 .... 19 D3
Grammar School Pl SUD CO10 .... 58 B6 🔟
Grampian Gv CHLM/WR CM1 ..... 303 K7
The Granaries WAB EN9 .... 348 A7 🔟
Granary Cl RCHLM CM3 .... 367 K8
The Granary HLWW/ROY CM19 .. 292 D4
  SUD CO10 .... 31 F7
Granby Rd GVW DA11 .... 488 C4
Grand Dr LOS SS9 .... 463 C5
Grand Pde LOS SS9 .... 463 C5
Grandview Rd SBF/HAD SS7 ...... 440 E6
Grange Av LOS SS9 .... 442 B6
  RCHLM CM3 .... 369 F6
  WICKW SS12 .... 416 E7
Grange Cl FOS CO13 .... 229 F6
  FX IP11 .... 5 D4
  HSTD CO9 .... 147 K6
  KESG IP5 .... 39 J5
  LOS SS9 .... 463 F2
  RBRW/HUT CM13 .... 412 B8
Grange Ct WAB EN9 .... 347 J8
Grange Crs CHIG IG7 .... 405 C8
Grange Farm Av FX IP11 .... 5 D3
Grange Gdns RAYL SS6 .... 441 C2
  SOS SS1 .... 19 E4 🔟
Grange HI RCOLW CO6 .... 213 C4
Grange La GTDUN CM6 .... 205 C6
  HLWW/ROY CM19 .... 292 C5
  KESG IP5 .... 39 J5
Grange Pk BSF CM23 .... 198 E4
Grange Park Dr LOS SS9 .... 463 G5
Granger Av MAL CM9 .... 338 B9
Grange Rd BCAYE CM11 .... 414 D6
  BOC CM0 .... 372 B2
  BSF CM23 .... 199 F6
  FX IP11 .... 5 D3
  GRAYS RM17 .... 484 A5
  GVW DA11 .... 489 F6
  HAR CO12 .... 6 B6
  HARH RM3 .... 430 C7
  IPNE IP4 .... 3 F4
  K/T/MI CO5 .... 247 J8
  LOS SS9 .... 462 E4
  MGTR CO11 .... 158 D5
  PIT SS13 .... 439 H5
  RCHLM CM3 .... 270 C6

RCOLW CO6 .... 154 C6
ROY SG8 .... 41 G1
SAFWN CB10 .... 41 K5
SBF/HAD SS7 .... 440 D5
SOCK/AV RM15 .... 468 E8
WICKE SS11 .... 409 K1
WIT CM8 .... 309 K1
Granger Wy *EMPK* RM11 .... 430 B8
Grangeside *BSF* CM23 .... 198 E3
Grange Wk *BSF* CM23 .... 199 F6
Grange Wy *COLS* CO2 .... 220 A1
ERITH DA8 .... 480 C6
Grangeway *SBF/HAD* SS7 ...... 441 F7 🖪
WFD IG8 .... 403 K7 🖪
Grangewood Cl
RBRW/HUT CM13 .... 411 K6 🖪
Granites Cha *BCAYE* CM11 ..... 415 G7
Granta Cl *SAFWN* CB10 .... 43 J4
Granta Leys *CBE/LIN* CB1 .... 22 D2
Granta V *CBE/LIN* CB1 .... 23 F5
Grantchester Pl *KESG* IP5 .... 38 E5 🖪
Grant Cl *WICKW* SS12 .... 417 H8 🖪
Grantham Crs *CHTY* IP2 .... 2 B5
Grantham Rd *RCOLW* CO6 ...... 154 C7
Grantham Wy *CDH/CHF* RM16 .. 470 E7
Grantley Cl *RCOLW* CO6 .... 184 C8
Granton Av *HCH* RM12 .... 451 G3
Granville Cl *BCAYW* CM12 ...... 387 F7 🖪
RCOLW CO6 .... 185 K2
SBF/HAD SS7 .... 460 D1
Granville Rd *COL* CO1 .... 9 D6
COS CO15 .... 10 C4
EPP CM16 .... 351 F3 🖪
FX IP11 .... 5 F4
GVW DA11 .... 488 E5
Granville Wy *RCOLE* CO7 .... 256 A6
Grapnells *VGE* SS16 .... 458 C1
Grasby Cl *RCOLE* CO7 .... 220 E3 🖪
Grasmead Av *HOC/HUL* SS5 ... 419 J2
Grasmere Av *BRTR* CM7 .... 209 F7 🖪
IPSE IP3 .... 63 K4 🖪
LOU IG10 .... 377 H9
Grasmere Gdns *FOS* CO13 ...... 228 E6 🖪
Grasmere Rd *CVI* SS8 .... 477 J2
SBF/HAD SS7 .... 440 D1
Grassfields *FOS* CO13 .... 228 D7 🖪
Grassmere *COLN* CO4 .... 187 J1 🖪
Grassmere Rd *EMPK* RM11 ...... 431 G6 🖪
Gratmore Gn *VGE* SS16 .... 458 B2
Gravel Cl *CHIG* IG7 .... 405 K5
Gravel Hl *RCOLW* CO6 .... 118 B3
Gravel Hill Wy *HAR* CO12 .... 164 C6
Gravel La *CHIG* IG7 .... 405 K2
Gravelly La *CHLM/WR* CM1 ...... 330 D2
Gravelpit La *MGTR* CO11 .... 123 K2
Gravel Pit La *MGTR* CO11 .... 123 K3
Gravel Rd *LOS* SS9 .... 442 C5
The Gravel *RCOLW* CO6 .... 213 G3
Gray Gdns *RAIN* RM13 .... 450 B7
Grayling Cl *BRTR* CM7 .... 209 H4
Grayling Dr *COLN* CO4 .... 188 C2
Gray Rd *COLW* CO3 .... 186 E7
Grays Av *VGE* SS16 .... 456 D4
Grays Cl *K/T/MI* CO5 .... 284 E7
Grays Ct *BSF* CM23 .... 198 D5
Grays End Cl *CDH/CHF* RM16 .. 483 K2
Gray's La *BRTR* CM7 .... 144 B1
Grays Md *HSTD* CO9 .... 110 C3 🖪
Graysons Cl *RAYL* SS6 .... 441 K3
Gray's Orch *KIR/NAC* IP10 .... 94 D2
Grays Wk *RBRW/HUT* CM13 .... 412 C5
Great Bentley Rd *RCOLE* CO7 .. 223 F5
Great Berry Farm Cha *VGE* SS16 456 B1 🖪
Great Berry La *VGE* SS16 .... 456 B1
Great Brays *HLWS* CM18 .... 294 E6
Great Burches Rd *SBF/HAD* SS7 441 F6
Great Cambridge Rd *BAR* EN8 . 346 C8
BROX EN10 .... 318 E8
Great Canfield Rd *RBSF* CM22 . 202 A6
Great Cob *CHLM* CM1 .... 305 G8
Great Eastern Cl *BSF* CM23 ..... 199 F7 🖪
Great Eastern Rd *BRW* CM14 ... 411 F7
HOC/HUL SS5 .... 421 F4
SUD CO10 .... 58 C6
Great Fld FX IP11 .... 94 D7
Great Fox Meadow *BRWN* CM15 383 H9
Great Gardens Rd *EMPK* RM11 . 430 C8
Great Gibcracks Cha *RCHLM* CM3 362 E5
Great Gipping St *IP* IP1 .... 2 C4
Great Godfreys *CHLM/WR* CM1 . 331 F4
Great Gregorie *VGE* SS16 .... 17 D5
Great Gregories La *EPP* CM16 ... 350 C7
Great Hadham Rd *BSF* CM23 .... 198 B3
Great Harlings *RIPS/CAP* IP9 .... 129 F4
Great Harrods *FOS* CO13 .... 229 F6
Great Hays *LOS* SS9 .... 442 D8
Great Holland Common Rd
COS CO15 .... 260 B3
Greathouse Cha *SLH/COR* SS17 457 K7
Great House Farm Rd *COLS* CO2 218 D3
Great Knightleys *LAIN* SS15 .... 16 C4
LAIN SS15 .... 17 D4 🖪
Great Lawn *CHONG* CM5 .... 354 C1
Great Leighs Wy *PIT* SS13 .... 439 F4 🖪
Great Leylands *HLWS* CM18 ...... 294 E6
Great Meadow *BROX* EN10 .... 319 G4
Great Mistley *VGE* SS16 .... 437 K8
Great Nelmes Cha *EMPK* RM11 . 431 G7
Great Notley Av *BRTR* CM7 .... 208 E8 🖪
BRTR CM7 .... 209 F8 🖪
Great Oak Ct *HSTD* CO9 .... 79 K4
Great Oaks *BSDN* SS14 .... 17 E4
CHIG IG7 .... 405 F7
RBRW/HUT CM13 .... 412 A2
Great Owl Rd *CHIG* IG7 .... 404 D6
Great Plumtree *HLW* CM20 .... 13 F1
Great Ranton *PIT* SS13 .... 439 F5
Great Ropers La *BRW* CM14 ..... 432 D1
Great Sq *BRTR* CM7 .... 209 J2 🖪
Great Smials *RCHLM* CM3 .... 392 C7
Great Spenders *BSDN* SS14 ...... 438 A5
Great Tey Rd *RCOLW* CO6 .... 183 F8
Great Totham Rd *WIT* CM8 .... 278 B8
Great Tufts *RIPS/CAP* IP9 .... 87 G4
Great Warley St *RBRW/HUT* CM13 432 D3
Great Wheatley Rd *RAYL* SS6 ... 441 F4
Great Whip St *IPSE* IP3 .... 3 D5
Great Yeldham Rd *HSTD* CO9 .... 78 E7
Grebe Cl *CHTY* IP2 .... 62 A3
RCHLM CM3 .... 368 C5
Grebe Crest *WTHK* RM20 .... 482 D3
Greding Wk *RBRW/HUT* CM13.. 412 A5
Green Acre *SUD* CO10 .... 59 H2
Greenacre La *CHL* CM4 .... 388 A5
Greenacres Ms *LOS* SS9 .... 463 F3
Greenacres *COLN* CO4 .... 187 F2 🖪
COS CO15 .... 11 D2
EPP CM16 .... 350 D2 🖪
RCOLW CO6 .... 213 G4
SBF/HAD SS7 .... 461 K2
Greenacres Cl *RAIN* RM13 .... 468 A3 🖪
Green Acres Rd *COLS* CO2 .... 218 A3
Greenall Cl *BAR* EN8 .... 346 E4
Green Av *CVI* SS8 .... 477 J2
Greenbank *EBAR* EN7 .... 346 B2
Greenbank Cl *CHING* E4 .... 402 D5
HARH RM3 .... 408 E6
Greenbanks *LOS* SS9 .... 463 H3
UPMR RM14 .... 452 B3 🖪
Green Cl *BAR* EN8 .... 346 E6
CHLM/WR CM1 .... 15 E1
EPP CM16 .... 321 K6
RCHLM CM3 .... 308 C2
Greendyke *CVI* SS8 .... 460 E8 🖪
Green End La *FOS* CO13 .... 227 K8
Greene Vw *BRTR* CM7 .... 210 A5
Green Farm Rd *RCOLW* CO6 .... 149 J3
Greenfield *WIT* CM8 .... 277 G4
Greenfield Dr *RCOLW* CO6 .... 182 E4
Greenfields *BCAYW* CM12 .... 414 B5
HSTD CO9 .... 146 D6
LOU IG10 .... 377 J8
STSD CM24 .... 167 K6
Greenfields Cl *BCAYW* CM12 ... 414 A5
Greenfield St *WAB* EN9 .... 347 J8
Greenfields Wy *HVHL* CB9 .... 26 E7
Greenfinch Av *CHTY* IP2 .... 61 K2
Greenfinch End *COLN* CO4 .... 188 C5
Greenford Rd *COS* CO15 .... 290 E2
Green Glades *EMPK* RM11 .... 431 G8
Green Gld *EPP* CM16 .... 378 C3
Green La *BCAYW* CM12 .... 435 H1
BCAYW CM12 .... 436 B2
BOC CM0 .... 397 K6
BROX EN10 .... 319 H5
BRW CM14 .... 383 F5
BRW CM14 .... 410 D4
BRWN CM15 .... 411 F2
CBE/LIN CB1 .... 22 E3
CDH/CHF RM16 .... 471 C5
CHIG IG7 .... 405 H6
CHLM/WR CM1 .... 330 B1
COLN CO4 .... 188 B2
CVI SS8 .... 477 K2
CTDUN CM6 .... 204 B4
HLWE CM17 .... 296 B6
K/T/MI CO5 .... 248 B7
K/T/MI CO5 .... 280 C4
LOS SS9 .... 442 E6
MAL CM9 .... 312 A1
NHMKT IP6 .... 38 A1
RBRW/HUT CM13 .... 432 D2
RCHLM CM3 .... 368 E7
RCOLE CO7 .... 121 F2
RCOLE CO7 .... 157 G7
RCOLE CO7 .... 189 F4
RCOLW CO6 .... 118 E8
RCOLW CO6 .... 154 D7
RCOLW CO6 .... 184 A5
RCOS CO16 .... 225 H8
RIPS/CAP IP9 .... 88 D6
SUD CO10 .... 29 J1
VGE SS16 .... 16 B6
WAB EN9 .... 377 F1
WIT CM8 .... 242 E3
WOTN CO14 .... 229 J3
Greenleas *SBF/HAD* SS7 .... 441 G7
Green Man La *WIT* CM8 .... 278 B7
Green Md *RCHLM* CM3 .... 392 C6
Greenmoor Rd *PEND* EN3 .... 374 C6
Greenoaks *SBF/HAD* SS7 .... 460 D2
Green Ride *LOU* IG10 .... 403 H2
Green Rd *SBF/HAD* SS7 .... 460 C4
The Greens Cl *LOU* IG10 .... 377 J6
Greens Farm La *BCAYE* CM11 .. 414 D4
Greenshaw *BRW* CM14 .... 410 E4
Greensmill *MGTR* CO11 .... 123 G8 🖪
Greenspire Gv *RIPW* IP8 .... 61 H3 🖪
Greenstead Cl
RBRW/HUT CM13 .... 412 D3 🖪
Greenstead Rd *COL* CO1 .... 9 E4
COLS CO2 .... 9 F5
Greensted Cl *BSDN* SS14 .... 438 C8
Greensted Rd *CHONG* CM5 ..... 353 C2
LOU IG10 .... 404 B3
The Greensted *BSDN* SS14 ...... 438 C8
The Greens *IPNE* IP4 .... 64 D1
Green St *GTDUN* CM6 .... 235 G2
ING CM4 .... 357 G7
PEND EN3 .... 374 D7
Greensward La *HOC/HUL* SS5 .. 421 G7
The Green *BAR* EN8 .... 346 C2
BSF CM23 .... 231 K2 🖪
CDH/CHF RM16 .... 472 A5
CHLM/WR CM1 .... 14 A1
CHLM/WR CM1 .... 331 H4
COS CO15 .... 290 D3
EPP CM16 .... 378 C3
ING CM4 .... 356 C5
LOS SS9 .... 443 F6
MGTR CO11 .... 160 A1
SLH/COR SS17 .... 473 K4 🖪
Green Trees *EPP* CM16 .... 350 E5
Green Trees Av *RCHLM* CM3 ... 366 B8
Greenview Pk *COS* CO15 .... 259 J6
Green Wk *CHONG* CM5 .... 354 B4
The Green Wk *CHING* E4 .... 402 E4 🖪
Greenway *BCAYE* CM11 .... 414 E4
BSF CM23 .... 199 H7
FOS CO13 .... 228 E8
HARH RM3 .... 431 J1
HLWW/ROY CM19 .... 293 C5
RBRW/HUT CM13 .... 411 K3
Green Wy *RCOLW* CO6 .... 149 H3
Greenway Gdns *BRTR* CM7 ..... 209 G7
Greenways *CHLM/WR* CM1 ...... 304 D7
CVI SS8 .... 460 E8 🖪
HSTD CO9 .... 146 D6 🖪
K/T/MI CO5 .... 247 F2
MAL CM9 .... 338 B3 🖪
RCFD SS4 .... 444 C3
SAFWS CB11 .... 71 F6
SBF/HAD SS7 .... 460 A3
SOS SS1 .... 465 H6
Greenways Cl *IP* IP1 .... 2 C1
The Greenways *RCOLW* CO6 .... 213 H2
The Greenway *COS* CO15 .... 259 K6
PEND EN3 .... 374 D1 🖪
WICKE SS11 .... 417 F2
Greenwich Cl *IPSE* IP3 .... 63 G3
Greenwich Rd *IPSE* IP3 .... 63 F3
Greenwood Av *EBAR* EN7 .... 346 B5
PEND EN3 .... 374 E5
SBF/HAD SS7 .... 460 C4
Greenwood Cl *EBAR* EN7 .... 346 B5 🖪
HVHL CB9 .... 26 E6 🖪
Greenwood Dr *CHING* E4 .... 402 E8 🖪
Greenwood Gv *COLN* CO4 .... 187 K2
Greenwood Rd *CHIG* IG7 .... 406 A7
Greenyard *WAB* EN9 .... 347 J7 🖪
Gregory Cl *HOC/HUL* SS5 .... 443 G1 🖪
Grendel Wy *COS* CO15 .... 260 D7
Grenfell Av *COS* CO15 .... 260 C6
HCH RM12 .... 450 A2
Grenfell Cl *COLN* CO4 .... 9 E2
Grennan Cl *RBRW/HUT* CM13 .. 434 C1
Grenville Av *BROX* EN10 .... 319 F3
Grenville Cl *BAR* EN8 .... 346 D6
Grenville Rd *BRTR* CM7 .... 209 H2
SUD CO10 .... 58 C3
Gresham Ct *BRW* CM14 .... 411 F6
Gresham Rd *BRW* CM14 .... 411 F6
Gresley Cl *COLN* CO4 .... 8 B1
Greville Cl *WOTN* CO14 .... 229 K3
Greyfriars *RBRW/HUT* CM13 .... 412 A3
Grey Friars Rd *IP* IP1 .... 3 D4
Greygoose Pk *HLWW/ROY* CM19 12 B6 🖪
Greyhound Hl *COLN* CO4 .... 156 B1
Greyhound La *CDH/CHF* RM16 . 485 F1
Greyhound Rd *SUD* CO10 .... 33 H2
Greyhound Wy *SOSN* SS2 .... 19 D3
Grey Ladys *CHLM/GWD* CM2 ... 360 C2
Greys Cl *SUD* CO10 .... 32 C4
Greys Hollow *SAFWS* CB11 ...... 135 J5
Greystones Cl *COLW* CO3 .... 218 B2

Grey Towers Av EMPK RM11 ... 450 E2
Grey Towers Gdns EMPK RM11 ... 450 D1
Gridiron Pl UPMR RM14 ... 451 J3
Grieves Cl CVW CO3 ... 217 H1
Grieves Rd GVW DA11 ... 488 C6
Griffin Av CVI SS8 ... 461 H8
　UPMR RM14 ... 432 B8
The Griffins CDH/CHF RM16 ... 484 A1
Grifon Cl CDH/CHF RM16 ... 485 F2
Grifon Rd CDH/CHF RM16 ... 483 F2
Griggs Gdns HCH RM12 ... 450 D6
Grimshaw Wy ROM RM1 ... 430 A7
Grimston Rd BSDN SS14 ... 438 C4
　COLS CO2 ... 219 H1
Grimston Wy WOTN CO14 ... 229 G6
Grimwade St IPNE IP4 ... 3 E4
Grinstead Cl IPNE IP4 ... 232 C7
The Grip CBE/LIN CB1 ... 22 D4
Groom Pk COLS CO15 ... 319 F8
Groom Rd BROX EN10 ... 319 F8
Gromside BRTR CM7 ... 209 K3
Grooms La WIT CM8 ... 244 E1
Grosvenor Cl BSF CM23 ... 231 H2
　CHLM/GWD CM2 ... 15 E6
　IPNE IP4 ... 3 F1
　K/T/MI CO5 ... 248 D8
　LOU IG10 ... 377 K5
Grosvenor Dr EMPK RM11 ... 450 D2
　LOU IG10 ... 377 K6
Grosvenor Gdns BCAYW CM12 ... 414 B1
　UPMR RM14 ... 452 A3
Grosvenor Ms WOS/PRIT SS0 ... 463 K6
Grosvenor Rd BROX EN10 ... 319 F2
　CDH/CHF RM16 ... 472 D6
　RAYL SS6 ... 441 G1
　SBF/HAD SS7 ... 460 D4
　SUD CO10 ... 58 A3
　WOS/PRIT SS0 ... 463 K6
Grove Av K/T/MI CO5 ... 284 E8
　VGE SS16 ... 456 C2
　WOTN CO14 ... 229 G5
Grove Cl RAYL SS6 ... 442 A3
Grove Ct RAYL SS6 ... 442 B4
　WAB EN9 ... 347 H7
Grove Farm Rd WIT CM8 ... 279 H4
Grove Fld BRTR CM7 ... 178 B3
Grove Gdns PEND EN3 ... 374 D5
The Grove, Henley Rd IP IP1 ... 36 E3
Grove Hl COLN CO4 ... 156 C5
　LOS SS9 ... 442 C6
　RCOLE CO7 ... 157 G1
　RIPW IP8 ... 61 J6
　STSD CM24 ... 167 K6
Grovelands Rd WICKW SS12 ... 417 C7
Grovelands Wy GRAYS RM17 ... 483 J4
Grove La CHIG IG7 ... 405 J6
　EPP CM16 ... 350 E4
　IPNE IP4 ... 3 F4
　RIPS/CAP IP9 ... 91 G8
Grove Orch BRTR CM7 ... 178 B4
Grove Rd BCAYW CM12 ... 414 A3
　CHING E4 ... 402 D6
　CHLM/GWD CM2 ... 14 C4
　CVI SS8 ... 478 C1
　FX IP11 ... 131 H1
　GRAYS RM17 ... 484 B5
　GVW DA11 ... 488 A3
　K/T/MI CO5 ... 248 B8
　MGTR CO11 ... 123 J3
　RAYL SS6 ... 442 A3
　RCOS CO16 ... 226 A8
　RIPS/CAP IP9 ... 87 K7
　SBF/HAD SS7 ... 460 C3
　SLH/COR SS17 ... 473 C5
　WIT CM8 ... 277 G3
Grove Rd West PEND EN3 ... 374 C3
Grover St SOS SS1 ... 19 D4
Groves Cl SOCK/AV RM15 ... 469 H7
Groveside CHING E4 ... 403 F6
The Grove BCAYE CM11 ... 410 C7
　BRW CM14 ... 410 D2
　CBE/LIN CB1 ... 22 D2
　CHLM/GWD CM2 ... 333 K8
　COS CO15 ... 10 C5
　GVE DA12 ... 489 G5
　RBSF CM22 ... 235 F3
　RCHLM CM3 ... 363 K4
　SOSN SS2 ... 19 E2
　UPMR RM14 ... 451 H5
　WIT CM8 ... 277 G3
Grove Wk SBN/FI SS3 ... 466 E5
Grovewood Av LOS SS9 ... 442 C6
Grovewood Cl LOS SS9 ... 442 C6
Gryme's Dyke Wy COLW CO3 ... 217 G3
Guardian Cl HCH RM12 ... 450 C3
Guardsman Cl BRW CM14 ... 411 G8
Gubbins La HARH RM3 ... 431 G3
Guelph's La GTDUN CM6 ... 139 K2
Guernsey Gdns WICKE SS11 ... 417 F4
Guernsey Wy BRTR CM7 ... 209 G3
Guildford Rd COL CO1 ... 431 F1
　HARH RM3 ... 431 F1
　SOSN SS2 ... 19 D3
Guildhall Wy SAFWN CB10 ... 46 D6

Guild Rd ERITH DA8 ... 480 A6
The Guilfords HLWE CM17 ... 263 H8
Guinea Cl BRTR CM7 ... 210 C1
Guinevere Gdns BAR EN8 ... 346 E4
Guithavon Rd WIT CM8 ... 277 F3
Guithavon St WIT CM8 ... 277 F4
Guithavon Rd WIT CM8 ... 277 F3
Guithavon Va WIT CM8 ... 277 F3
Gulls Cft BRTR CM7 ... 210 B2
Gull's La FXLE CO7 ... 157 K2
Gulpher Rd IP11 ... 5 E1
Gumley Rd WTHK RM20 ... 483 C5
Gunfleet Cl GVE DA12 ... 489 K5
　K/T/MI CO5 ... 284 D6
Gun Hl COLN CO4 ... 120 E6
　TIL RM18 ... 485 J5
Gun Hill Pl VGE SS16 ... 437 K8
Gunners Gv CHING E4 ... 402 D6
Gunners Rd SBN/FI SS3 ... 467 F6
Gurdon Rd COLS CO2 ... 219 G2
Curlings Cl HVHL CB9 ... 28 D3
Gurney Benham Cl COLS CO2 ... 218 C1
Gurton Rd RCOLW CO6 ... 213 H2
Gustedhall La HOC/HUL SS5 ... 443 F3
Guston Gdns KIR/NAC IP10 ... 94 D2
Gutteridge Hall La RCOS CO16 ... 225 F6
Gutteridge La ABR/ST RM4 ... 407 H2
Gutters La CHLM/WR CM1 ... 304 D6
Guy Cook Cl SUD CO10 ... 59 F8
Guys Farm Rd RCHLM CM3 ... 392 D6
Gwendalen Av CVI SS8 ... 478 D1
Gwendolen Rd IPNE IP4 ... 64 C1
Gwyn Cl RCHLM CM3 ... 306 C4
Gwynne Rd HAR CO12 ... 7 E4
Gwynns Rd GVW DA11 ... 488 B7
Gypsy La K/T/MI CO5 ... 214 E6

H

Haarlem Rd CVI SS8 ... 477 H1
Haarle Rd CVI SS8 ... 478 D3
Haase Cl CVI SS8 ... 461 F7
Habgood Rd LOU IG10 ... 377 G2
Hackamore St SBF/HAD SS7 ... 441 G8
Hackmans La RCHLM CM3 ... 364 E2
Hacton Dr HCH RM12 ... 451 F5
Hacton La HCH RM12 ... 451 G3
　UPMR RM14 ... 451 G6
Haddestoke Ga BROX EN10 ... 319 F8
Haddon Cl RAYL SS6 ... 441 F2
Haddon Md RCHLM CM3 ... 392 D8
Haddon Pk COL CO1 ... 9 E5
Hadfield Rd SLH/COR SS17 ... 473 K7
Hadham Cl BSF CM23 ... 198 C5
Hadham Gv BSF CM23 ... 198 B5
Hadham Rd BSF CM23 ... 198 C5
Hadleigh Ct BROX EN10 ... 319 F4
Hadleigh Park Av SBF/HAD SS7 ... 461 H2
Hadleigh Rd FOS CO13 ... 229 F8
　LOS SS9 ... 462 D4
　RCOLE CO7 ... 122 A2
　RCOS CO16 ... 258 D8
　RIPW IP8 ... 61 J1
　WOS/PRIT SS0 ... 18 B5
Hadley Cl BRTR CM7 ... 178 A4
Hadley Gra HLWE CM17 ... 295 G6
Hadrian Cl COLN CO4 ... 155 J7
Hadrians Cl WIT CM8 ... 276 E5
Hadrians Wy MAL CM9 ... 310 C3
Haggars La RCOLE CO7 ... 222 E2
Hagg Hl RCHLM CM3 ... 365 J8
Haig Cl CHLM/GWD CM2 ... 14 B4
Haig Gdns GVE DA12 ... 489 H5
Hailes Wd RBSF CM22 ... 168 E3
Hailsham Rd HARH RM3 ... 408 D8
Hailsham Rd HARH RM3 ... 408 D8
Hainault Av RCFD SS4 ... 443 K1
　SBF/HAD SS7 ... 461 K1
　WOS/PRIT SS0 ... 18 A2
Hainault Gdns CVW DA11 ... 488 B6
Hainault Gv CHIG IG7 ... 405 F7
　CHLM/WR CM1 ... 332 A4
Hainault Rd CHIG IG7 ... 405 F7
　CHIG IG7 ... 394 C4
Halcyon Wy EMPK RM11 ... 451 G2
Haldane Gdns CVW DA11 ... 488 B6
Hale Cl CHING E4 ... 402 D6
　CHTY IP2 ... 61 K5
Hale End HARH RM3 ... 430 C1
Halesowen Cl CHTY IP2 ... 62 B5
Halesworth Cl HARH RM3 ... 431 F1
Halesworth Rd HARH RM3 ... 431 F1
Half Acres BSF CM23 ... 198 E5
Halfacres WIT CM8 ... 277 G6
Halfhide La BAR EN8 ... 318 D8
Halfhides WAB EN9 ... 347 K7
Half Moon La EPP CM16 ... 350 D5
Halford Ct RIPW IP8 ... 61 J3
Halfway Ct PUR RM19 ... 481 H3

Halidon Ri HARH RM3 ... 431 J1
Halifax Rd CHTY IP2 ... 62 D3
Hallam Cl BRWN CM15 ... 383 K3
Hallam Ct BCAYW CM12 ... 414 A1
Hall Av SOCK/AV RM15 ... 468 E8
Hall Bridge Ri MAL CM9 ... 338 E2
Hall Cha GTDUN CM6 ... 238 D5
　RCOLW CO6 ... 216 A2
Hall Cl CHLM/GWD CM2 ... 333 J7
　COS CO15 ... 260 D7
　SLH/COR SS17 ... 474 A1
　SOCK/AV RM15 ... 481 K5
Hallcroft Cha COLN CO4 ... 187 K1
Hall Cut RCOLE CO7 ... 255 K7
Hall Dr HSTD CO9 ... 146 C5
Hallet Rd CVI SS8 ... 478 E2
Hall Farm Cl K/T/MI CO5 ... 247 G5
　SBF/HAD SS7 ... 460 C4
Hall Farm Rd SBF/HAD SS7 ... 460 C3
Hall Fld FX IP11 ... 5 D5
Hall Gdns CHING E4 ... 402 A3
Hall Green La RBRW/HUT CM13 ... 412 C5
Hallingbury Cl RBSF CM22 ... 232 B6
Hallingbury Rd BSF CM23 ... 199 G6
　BSF CM23 ... 232 B5
　SBW CM21 ... 264 A1
Halling Hl HLW CM20 ... 13 F2
Halliwell Rd IPNE IP4 ... 57 K2
Hall La BRWN CM15 ... 411 K4
　CHING E4 ... 402 A4
　CHLM/GWD CM2 ... 334 A3
　CHLM/GWD CM2 ... 361 F5
　CHLM/WR CM1 ... 14 C1
　HAR CO12 ... 6 B5
　HARH RM3 ... 431 K2
　HSTD CO9 ... 52 E1
　ING CM4 ... 386 C2
　RCOS CO16 ... 226 D7
　ROY SG8 ... 66 C2
　UPMR RM14 ... 431 K5
　WOTN CO14 ... 229 J3
Hallmores BROX EN10 ... 319 G1
Hallowell Down RCHLM CM3 ... 392 E4
Hall Park Av WOS/PRIT SS0 ... 463 J1
Hall Park Rd UPMR RM14 ... 451 K6
Hall Pond Wy FX IP11 ... 5 D5
Hall Ri SUD CO10 ... 57 K5
Hall Rd BOC CM0 ... 371 H4
　BRTR CM7 ... 178 A4
　BURES CO8 ... 115 H6
　GPK RM2 ... 430 C4
　GVW DA11 ... 488 C6
　HOC/HUL SS5 ... 443 H4
　HVHL CB9 ... 28 D5
　K/T/MI CO5 ... 280 A4
　KESG IP5 ... 39 J1
　KIR/NAC IP10 ... 65 J2
　MAL CM9 ... 310 D2
　MAL CM9 ... 314 D6
　MAL CM9 ... 338 D2
　RBSF CM22 ... 168 E4
　RCFD SS4 ... 444 A4
　RCOLE CO7 ... 190 B6
　RCOLW CO6 ... 152 C1
　RCOLW CO6 ... 153 J3
　RCOLW CO6 ... 216 D6
　SOCK/AV RM15 ... 481 K6
　SUD CO10 ... 57 K5
Hall St CHLM/GWD CM2 ... 14 C4
　SUD CO10 ... 34 E1
Hall Ter SOCK/AV RM15 ... 482 A4
Hall View Rd RCOLE CO7 ... 223 K5
Hallwood Crs BRWN CM15 ... 411 H4
Halstead Cl WICKW SS12 ... 417 F8
Halstead Rd BRTR CM7 ... 178 D3
　COLW CO3 ... 185 G6
　FOS CO13 ... 228 B5
　HSTD CO9 ... 111 F7
　HSTD CO9 ... 146 D4
　RCOLW CO6 ... 149 G6
　RCOLW CO6 ... 183 K4
Halstead Wy RBRW/HUT CM13 ... 412 A4
Halston Pl MAL CM9 ... 338 B5
Halstow Wy PIT SS13 ... 439 F1
Halt Dr TIL RM18 ... 486 B6
Halton Crs IPSE IP5 ... 64 A4
Halton Rd CDH/CHF RM16 ... 485 G2
Haitwhistle Rd RCHLM CM3 ... 392 C3
Halyard Reach RCHLM CM3 ... 392 D2
Hamberts Rd RCHLM CM3 ... 392 D2
Hamble Cl WIT CM8 ... 276 E3
Hamble La SOCK/AV RM15 ... 469 H1
Hamble Wy BOC CM0 ... 398 A7
Hambro Gdns LOS SS9 ... 462 C1
Hambro' Av RAYL SS6 ... 441 F4
Hambro Cl RAYL SS6 ... 441 K4
Hambro Hl RAYL SS6 ... 419 K8
Hambro Rd BRW CM14 ... 411 D1
Hamburgh Ct BAR EN8 ... 346 D2
Hamel Wy SAFWS CB11 ... 136 E3
Hamerton Rd GVW DA11 ... 488 A3
Hamford Cl WOTN CO14 ... 229 J3
Hamford Dr HAR CO12 ... 195 F4
Hamilton Cl LOS SS9 ... 462 B1

Hamilton Crs *BRW* CM14 .... 411 F8
Hamilton Dr *EMPK* RM11 .... 431 F4
Hamilton Gdns *FX* IP11 .... 131 H4
   HOC/HUL SS5 .... 421 F6
Hamilton Ms *RAYL* SS6 .... 442 A2
   SAFWS CB11 .... 71 G3 🔲
Hamilton Rd *COLW* CO3 .... 186 E8
   FOS CO13 .... 227 K8
   FX IP11 .... 131 H3
   GPK RM2 .... 430 C7
   IPSE IP3 .... 38 C6
   RBSF CM22 .... 202 C5
   RCOLE CO7 .... 220 E5
   SUD CO10 .... 58 B6
Hamilton St *FX* IP11 .... 5 E2 🔲
   HAR CO12 .... 6 A3
Hamlet Ct *BURES* CO8 .... 115 H5 🔲
Hamlet Court Ms *WOS/PRIT* SS0 ... 18 B3 🔲
Hamlet Court Rd *WOS/PRIT* SS0 ... 18 A4
Hamlet Dr *COLN* CO4 .... 188 A6
Hamlet Hi *HLWW/ROY* CM19 .... 320 E1
Hamlet Rd *CHLM/GWD* CM2 .... 14 C4
   HVHL CB9 .... 27 G6
   SOS SS1 .... 18 C5
Hamley Cl *SBF/HAD* SS7 .... 440 A7
Hammarskjold Rd *HLW* CM20 .... 12 C2
Hammond Rd *EN* EN1 .... 374 B7
Hammonds La *BCAYE* CM11 .... 414 D6 🔲
   RBRW/HUT CM13 .... 432 E1 🔲
Hammonds Rd *CHLM/GWD* CM2 ... 334 B4
   RBSF CM22 .... 234 C7
Hampden Cl *EPP* CM16 .... 332 A1
Hampden Crs *BRW* CM14 .... 411 F8 🔲
   EBAR EN7 .... 346 B5
Hampden Rd *GRAYS* RM17 .... 484 A4
Hampit Rd *SAFWS* CB11 .... 100 C2
Hampshire Rd *EMPK* RM11 .... 431 H6 🔲
Hampstead Av *COS* CO15 .... 10 A2
Hampstead Gdns *HOC/HUL* SS5 ... 421 G6
Hampton Cl *SOSN* SS2 .... 464 E3
Hampton Ct *HOC/HUL* SS5 .... 420 E7 🔲
Hampton Crs *GVE* DA12 .... 489 K7
Hampton Gdns *SBW* CM21 .... 263 G4
   SOSN SS2 .... 464 B1
Hampton Rd *CHING* E4 .... 402 A8
   CHLM/GWD CM2 .... 333 G7
   IP IP1 .... 2 A2
Hamstel Rd *HLW* CM20 .... 12 B1
   SOSN SS2 .... 465 J3
Hamsters Cl *HSTD* CO9 .... 113 G5 🔲
Hanbury Cl *BAR* EN8 .... 346 D4
Hanbury Gdns *COLN* CO4 .... 155 J8
Hanbury Rd *CHLM/WR* CM1 .... 332 A5
Hance La *BRTR* CM7 .... 208 C3
Hanchetts Orchard *GTDUN* CM6 ... 139 K2 🔲
Handel Crs *TIL* RM18 .... 485 F6
Handel Rd *CVI* SS8 .... 478 D3
Handford Cut *IP* IP1 .... 2 B3
Handford Rd *IP* IP1 .... 2 B3
Hand La *SBW* CM21 .... 263 G4
Handleys Cha *LAIN* SS15 .... 437 G3
Hanford Rd *SOCK/AV* RM15 .... 468 E4
Hanging Hill La *RBRW/HUT* CM13 .. 412 A6
Haning Hill La *RBRW/HUT* CM13 ... 412 B3
Hankin Av *HAR* CO12 .... 164 B4
Hanlee Brook *CHLM/GWD* CM2 ... 333 H8
Hannah Cl *CVI* SS8 .... 461 F7 🔲
Hannards Wy *CHIC* IG7 .... 406 A8
Hanwell Cl *RCOS* CO16 .... 10 A2
Ha'penny Fld *RIPS/CAP* IP9 .... 90 A3
Harberts Rd *HLWW/ROY* CM19 ... 12 B4
Harberts Wy *RAYL* SS6 .... 419 H8
Harborough Hall Rd *K/T/MI* CO5 . 248 B3
Harbour Crs *HAR* CO12 .... 7 F3
Harbour Rd *BARK/HLT* IG6 .... 406 A8
Harcamlow Wy *GTDUN* CM6 .... 139 H1
   GTDUN CM6 .... 171 F6
   RBSF CM22 .... 135 H5
   RBSF CM22 .... 200 D8
   ROY SG8 .... 66 E1
   SAFWN CB10 .... 45 H8
   SAFWS CB11 .... 100 D2
Harcourt Av *HAR* CO12 .... 6 B4
   SOSN SS2 .... 18 C3
Harcourt Ms *ROM* RM1 .... 430 A7 🔲
Harden Rd *GVW* DA11 .... 488 C5
Hardie Rd *SLH/COR* SS17 .... 473 K3
Harding Cl *CDH/CHF* RM16 .... 485 F2
Hardings Cl *RCOLW* CO6 .... 184 A5
Harding's Elms Rd *BCAYE* CM11 ... 437 J1
Harding's La *ING* CM4 .... 357 K6
Hardley Crs *EMPK* RM11 .... 430 E6
Hardwick Cl *IPNE* IP4 .... 38 C1
   RAYL SS6 .... 441 J4
Hardwick Rd *HVHL* CB9 .... 27 H5
Hardy Av *GVW* DA11 .... 488 D7

Hardy Cl *BRTR* CM7 .... 209 K5 🔲
   MGTR CO11 .... 123 H6
Hardy Crs *IP* IP1 .... 36 B1
Hardys Wy *CVI* SS8 .... 461 F7
Harebell Cl *BCAYW* CM12 .... 414 A1
   COLN CO4 .... 187 J2 🔲
Harebell Dr *WIT* CM8 .... 276 E2
Harebell Rd *CHTY* IP2 .... 2 A5
Harebell Wy *HARH* RM3 .... 430 E2
Harefield *MAL* CM20 .... 294 E4
   SUD CO10 .... 35 F3
Harefield Rd *CBE/LIN* CB1 .... 23 G3
Hare Hall La *GPK* RM2 .... 430 C6 🔲
Hares Cha *BCAYW* CM12 .... 414 A2
Haresland Cl *SBF/HAD* SS7 .... 442 A8
Hare St *HLWW/ROY* CM19 .... 12 B3
Hare Street Springs
   HLWW/ROY CM19 .... 12 C3 🔲
Harewood Av *RCFD* SS4 .... 421 K8
Harewood Hi *EPP* CM16 .... 378 C1
Harewood Rd *BRWN* CM15 .... 410 E2
   CHLM/WR CM1 .... 332 A3
Harford Cl *CHING* E4 .... 402 C3
Harford Rd *CHING* E4 .... 402 C3
Harfred Av *MAL* CM9 .... 339 G2
Hargrave Rd *STSD* CM24 .... 167 K5
Hargreaves Av *EBAR* EN7 .... 346 B5
Hargreaves Rd *EBAR* EN7 .... 346 B5 🔲
Harkilees Wy *BRTR* CM7 .... 177 J8
Harkness *HARH* RM3 .... 409 G8
Harkstead La *RIPS/CAP* IP9 .... 90 D4
Harkstead Rd *RIPS/CAP* IP9 .... 126 C1
Harlech Rd *PIT* SS13 .... 438 E8
Harlesden Cl *HARH* RM3 .... 431 G1
Harlesden Rd *HARH* RM3 .... 431 G1
Harley St *LOS* SS9 .... 462 D4
Harlings Gv *CHLM/WR* CM1 .... 14 C2
Harlow Common *HLWE* CM17 .... 295 H8
Harlow Rd *CHONG* CM5 .... 325 J2
   HLWE CM17 .... 264 B6
   HLWW/ROY CM19 .... 292 K1
   SBW CM21 .... 263 G5
Harman Cl *CHING* E4 .... 402 E7 🔲
Harmer St *GVE* DA12 .... 489 H4
Harness Cl *CHLM/WR* CM1 .... 305 G2
Harnham Dr *BRTR* CM7 .... 209 F6 🔲
Harold Cl *HSTD* CO9 .... 148 A4
Harold Court Rd *HARH* RM3 .... 431 J1
Harold Gv *FOS* CO13 .... 261 K1
Harold Gdns *WICKE* SS11 .... 417 G4
Harold Rd *BRTR* CM7 .... 209 H2
   CHING E4 .... 402 D6
   COS CO15 .... 10 C4
   FOS CO13 .... 261 K1
Harolds Rd *HLWW/ROY* CM19 .... 293 H6
Harold Vw *HARH* RM3 .... 431 G4
Harold Wy *FOS* CO13 .... 261 K1
Haron Cl *CVI* SS8 .... 478 B2
Harpclose Rd *SUD* CO10 .... 58 C5
Harper's Hi *RCOLW* CO6 .... 117 K3
Harper's Hill Est *RCOLW* CO6 ... 118 A4
Harpers La *BRWN* CM15 .... 384 B3
Harper Wy *RAYL* SS6 .... 441 H2 🔲
Harpur's Rd *SUD* CO10 .... 33 H1
Harrap Cha *GRAYS* RM17 .... 483 J4
Harridge Cl *LOS* SS9 .... 463 F2
Harridge Rd *LOS* SS9 .... 463 F2
Harrier Cl *RAIN* RM13 .... 450 C7 🔲
Harrier Wy *WAB* EN9 .... 348 C8
Harrierscourt *WAB* EN9 .... 348 C6
Harrington Cl *K/T/MI* CO5 .... 247 K8
Harris Cl *GVW* DA11 .... 488 D8 🔲
   SLH/COR SS17 .... 474 D1
   WICKW SS12 .... 417 J8
Harrison Cl *RBRW/HUT* CM13 ...... 412 C1
Harrison Ct *CHLM/WR* CM1 .... 14 A2 🔲
Harrison Dr *BRTR* CM7 .... 209 K4 🔲
   EPP CM16 .... 324 B8 🔲
Harrison Gdns *HOC/HUL* SS5 .... 419 J3
Harrison Rd *COLS* CO2 .... 219 C2
Harrisons *BSF* CM23 .... 199 J3
Harrison Whf *BAR* EN8 .... 346 A4
Harrods Ct *BCAYE* CM11 .... 415 F5 🔲
Harrogate Dr *HOC/HUL* SS5 .... 421 J5
Harrogate Rd *HOC/HUL* SS5 .... 421 G6
Harrowby Gdns *GVW* DA11 .... 488 D7 🔲
Harrow Cl *HOC/HUL* SS5 .... 421 H8
   IPNE IP4 .... 37 J1
Harrow Crs *HARH* RM3 .... 430 C2
Harrow Dr *EMPK* RM11 .... 450 D1
Harrow Gdns *HOC/HUL* SS5 .... 421 H8
Harrow Hi *HSTD* CO9 .... 78 C7
Harrow Rd *COS* CO15 .... 10 C3
   CVI SS8 .... 461 G8
   HVHL CB9 .... 26 E6
   WICKW SS12 .... 439 K3
Harrow Wy *CHLM/GWD* CM9 .... 333 J7
Harsnett Rd *COL* CO1 .... 9 D6
Harston Dr *PEND* EN3 .... 375 G4
Hart Cl *HVHL* CB9 .... 27 F3
   SBF/HAD SS7 .... 441 F7
Hart Crs *CHIC* IG7 .... 405 J8

Hartest Wy *SUD* CO10 .... 58 E7
Hartfield Pl *GVW* DA11 .... 488 C5 🔲
Hartford Cl *RAYL* SS6 .... 441 F1
Hartford End *PIT* SS13 .... 438 D8
Hartington Pl *SOS* SS1 .... 19 E5 🔲
Hartington Rd *SOS* SS1 .... 19 E5
Hartland Cl *LOS* SS9 .... 442 E6
Hartland Rd *BAR* EN8 .... 346 D4
   EPP CM16 .... 350 E5
   HCH RM12 .... 450 B3
Hartley Cl *CHLM/GWD* CM2 .... 333 J1
Hartley St *CHTY* IP2 .... 3 D6
Hartmoor Ms *PEND* EN3 .... 374 D5 🔲
Hart Rd *HLWE* CM17 .... 263 G8
   SBF/HAD SS7 .... 440 E7
Hart Row *WFD* IG8 .... 403 H8
Hartshill Rd *GVW* DA11 .... 488 E7
Hart's La *RCOLE* CO7 .... 156 C4
Hart St *BRW* CM14 .... 411 F5
   CHLM/GWD CM2 .... 14 B4
Hartsway *PEND* EN3 .... 374 B8
Hartswood Cl *BRW* CM14 .... 411 H7
Hartswood Rd *BRW* CM14 .... 411 H7
Harty Cl *CDH/CHF* RM16 .... 471 F8
Harvard Ct *COLN* CO4 .... 187 J1
Harvest Cl *RCHLM* CM3 .... 392 D6
Harvest Ct *K/T/MI* CO5 .... 247 G1 🔲
Harvest End *COLW* CO3 .... 185 J8
Harvesters Wy *KESG* IP5 .... 39 K7
   RCOLW CO6 .... 182 E5
Harvest La *LOU* IG10 .... 404 A3
Harvest Rd *CVI* SS8 .... 461 G8
Harvest Wy *MAL* CM9 .... 310 B8
   RCOLE CO7 .... 189 J7
Harvey *CDH/CHF* RM16 .... 484 A1
Harvey Cl *MGTR* CO11 .... 159 H1 🔲
Harvey Crs *COLW* CO3 .... 185 H8
Harveyfields *WAB* EN9 .... 347 J8
Harvey Gdns *LOU* IG10 .... 377 K7
Harvey Rd *COLS* CO2 .... 218 C3
   MAL CM9 .... 310 C1
   PIT SS13 .... 438 E3
   RCOLE CO7 .... 220 E4
Harvey St *HSTD* CO9 .... 148 A3
Harvey Wy *SAFWN* CB10 .... 71 G3
   SAFWN CB10 .... 74 E4
Harwater Dr *LOU* IG10 .... 377 H6
Harwich Rd *COLN* CO4 .... 9 F3
   HAR CO12 .... 164 A6
   MGTR CO11 .... 160 B1
   RCOLE CO7 .... 157 J5
   RCOLE CO7 .... 157 H5 🔲
   RCOLE CO7 .... 190 E7
   RCOS CO16 .... 258 E1
Harwood Av *EMPK* RM11 .... 431 F5
Harwood Cl *COLS* CO2 .... 219 H1 🔲
Harwood Hall La *UPMR* RM14 ...... 451 J7
Haselfoot Rd *RCHLM* CM3 .... 306 D5
Haselmere Gdns *FOS* CO13 .... 228 E6 🔲
Haskell Ms *BRTR* CM7 .... 209 K5 🔲
Haskins *SLH/COR* SS17 .... 474 B5 🔲
Haskins Wk *KESG* IP5 .... 39 J6
Haslemere *BSF* CM23 .... 232 A1
Haslemere Rd *IPNE* IP4 .... 3 F3
Haslemere Rd *WICKE* SS11 .... 417 F3
Hasler Rd *MAL* CM9 .... 314 D3
Haslers La *GTDUN* CM6 .... 204 C5
Hassell Rd *CVI* SS8 .... 478 D2
Hassenbrook Rd *SLH/COR* SS17 .. 473 K3
Hastings Av *COS* CO15 .... 291 F5
Hastings Cl *WTHK* RM20 .... 483 H5
Hastings Pl *RCOLE* CO7 .... 255 K5 🔲
Hastings Rd *COLW* CO3 .... 218 B1
   GPK RM2 .... 430 C7
   SOS SS1 .... 19 E4
The Hastings *WICKE* SS11 .... 417 G4
Hastingwood Rd *HLWE* CM17 ...... 323 J2
Hatchcroft Gdns *RCOLE* CO7 ...... 189 K7
Hatches Farm Rd *BCAYW* CM12 ... 413 J6
Hatchfields *RCHLM* CM3 .... 272 B6
Hatch Gn *RBSF* CM22 .... 232 B5
Hatch La *CHING* E4 .... 402 E7
Hatch Rd *BRWN* CM15 .... 410 D1
Hatch Side *CHIC* IG7 .... 404 D8 🔲
The Hatch *PEND* EN3 .... 374 D5
Hatchwoods *WFD* IG8 .... 403 G7 🔲
Hatfield Cl *HCH* RM12 .... 450 E6 🔲
   RBRW/HUT CM13 .... 412 C3 🔲
Hatfield Dr *BCAYE* CM11 .... 414 E3 🔲
Hatfield Gv *CHLM/WR* CM1 .... 331 K4
Hatfield Rd *IPSE* IP3 .... 63 J1
   MAL CM9 .... 309 H6
   RAYL SS6 .... 441 G2
   RCHLM CM3 .... 275 C2
   WIT CM8 .... 276 D7
Hatfields *LOU* IG10 .... 377 K7
Hathaway Rd *GRAYS* RM17 .... 484 A2
Hatherleigh Wy *HARH* RM3 .... 430 E3 🔲
The Hatherley *BSDN* SS14 .... 438 A6
Hatley Gdns *SBF/HAD* SS7 .... 440 B8
Hatterill *LAIN* SS15 .... 16 B5
Hatton Cl *CDH/CHF* RM16 .... 483 G2
   GVW DA11 .... 488 D8
Hatton Rd *BAR* EN8 .... 346 D3
Haubourdin Ct *HSTD* CO9 .... 148 B3 🔲

Haughley Dr *IPNE* IP4 .... 38 D7 ⊡
Havana Ct *RAYL* SS6 .... 419 G7
Havelock Rd *GVW* DA11 .... 488 E6
Haven Av *COS* CO15 .... 260 D7
Haven Cl *CVI* SS8 .... 477 H2
  FX IP11 .... 5 D3
  VGE SS16 .... 458 B2
Havengore *CHLM/WR* CM1 .... 305 G8
  PIT SS13 .... 439 F5
Havengore Av *GVE* DA12 .... 489 K5
Haven Pl *CDH/CHF* CM16 .... 484 B1
Haven Ri *BCAYE* CM11 .... 414 E7
Haven Rd *COLS* CO2 .... 220 A1
  CVI SS8 .... 477 H3
Havenside *SBN/FI* SS3 .... 446 D8
The Havens *KIR/NAC* IP10 .... 64 C6
The Haven *GRAYS* RM17 .... 484 E4 ⊡
  HAR CO12 .... 6 A5
Haverhill Rd *CBE/LIN* CB1 .... 24 E2
  CHING E4 .... 402 D4
  HVHL CB9 .... 27 H3
  HVHL CB9 .... 28 C3
  HVHL CB9 .... 49 H5
  HVHL CB9 .... 50 C4
Havering Gn *COLN* CO4 .... 9 D2
  COS CO15 .... 259 G6
  SBN/FI SS3 .... 467 G1
Havers La *BSF* CM23 .... 198 E8
Havisham Wy *CHLM/WR* CM1 .... 303 K6
Havis Rd *SLH/COR* RM19 .... 474 A1
Hawbridge *RIPS/CAP* IP9 .... 87 F3
Hawes Av *WAB* EN9 .... 375 J4
Hawes St *CHTY* IP2 .... 3 E6
Hawfinch Rd *COLS* CO2 .... 218 B8
Hawkbush Gn *PIT* SS13 .... 438 E4 ⊡
Hawk Cl *WAB* EN9 .... 348 C8 ⊡
Hawkdene *CHING* E4 .... 402 C2
Hawkenbury *HLWW/ROY* CM19 .... 12 A5
Hawkendon Rd *RCOS* CO16 .... 290 C1
Hawke Rd *IPSE* IP3 .... 5 J3
Hawkesbury Bush La *VGE* SS16 .... 457 H3
Hawkesbury Cl *CVI* SS8 .... 477 J3
Hawkesbury Rd *CVI* SS8 .... 477 J2
Hawkes Cl *GRAYS* RM17 .... 484 A5 ⊡
Hawkes Cl *COLS* CO2 .... 9 F5
  RCOLE CO7 .... 222 A5
  SUD CO10 .... 58 D3
Hawkins Av *BRTR* CM7 .... 210 B1
Hawk La *WICKE* SS11 .... 418 C3
Hawkridge *SBN/FI* SS3 .... 466 B5
Hawks Cl *RCHLM* CM3 .... 352 A1
Hawks Hl *EPP* CM16 .... 421 F8
Hawks La *HOC/HUL* SS5 .... 421 G8 ⊡
Hawkshead Cl *PEND* EN3 .... 374 D1 ⊡
Hawksmoor Gn *RBRW/HUT* CM13 .... 412 C1
Hawksmouth *CHING* E4 .... 402 C2
Hawksway *VGE* SS16 .... 17 F6
Hawkswood Rd *BCAYE* CM11 .... 389 H6
Hawkwell Cha *BCAYE* CM11 .... 443 F1
Hawkwell Park Dr *HOC/HUL* SS5 .... 421 G8
Hawkwell Rd *HOC/HUL* SS5 .... 421 F7
Hawkwood Cl *RCHLM* CM3 .... 392 E4
Hawkwood Crs *CHING* E4 .... 402 C2
Hawkwood Rd *HSTD* CO9 .... 110 D5 ⊡
Hawlmark End *RCOLW* CO6 .... 215 H2
Hawsted *BKHH* IG9 .... 403 J3 ⊡
Hawthorn Av *COLN* CO4 .... 188 B5
  RBRW/HUT CM13 .... 411 J6
Hawthorn Cl *CHLM/GWD* CM2 .... 332 E7 ⊡
  HOC/HUL SS5 .... 421 G8 ⊡
  HSTD CO9 .... 148 B3 ⊡
  RBSF CM22 .... 201 K6
Hawthorne Av *CHTY* IP2 .... 2 A6
Hawthorne Av *EBAR* EN7 .... 346 N4
Hawthorne Cl *EBAR* EN7 .... 346 B5
Hawthorne Gdns *HOC/HUL* SS5 .... 420 C8
Hawthorne Rd *SLH/COR* SS17 .... 474 B1
Hawthornes *RCHLM* CM3 .... 365 K4
Hawthorn Ri *BSF* CM23 .... 231 K2
Hawthorn Rd *BKHH* IG9 .... 403 K7
  COS CO15 .... 259 G6
  CVI SS8 .... 478 C2
  HVHL CB9 .... 26 E4 ⊡
  MAL CM9 .... 280 E3
  RCHLM CM3 .... 276 A8
  SUD CO10 .... 58 E6
Hawthorns *HLWS* CM18 .... 322 D1
  HSTD CO9 .... 110 C3 ⊡
  LOS SS9 .... 463 F1
  SBF/HAD SS7 .... 460 B1 ⊡
  WFD IG8 .... 403 H6
The Hawthorns *RCHLM* CM3 .... 336 A6 ⊡
  SLH/COR SS17 .... 474 E1
Hawthorn Wk *RCHLM* CM3 .... 392 E4
Hawthorn Wy *RAYL* SS6 .... 442 A5 ⊡
Hawtree Cl *SOS* SS1 .... 19 F5
Hayburn Wy *HCH* RM12 .... 450 A2

Haycocks La *K/T/MI* CO5 .... 285 H4
Haycocks Rd *HVHL* CB9 .... 26 C4
Haycroft *BSF* CM23 .... 199 H7
Haydens Rd *HLWW/ROY* CM19 .... 12 C3
Haydock Cl *HCH* RM12 .... 451 C5
Haye La *K/T/MI* CO5 .... 252 E1
Hayes Barton *SOS* SS1 .... 466 B5
Hayes Cha *RCHLM* CM3 .... 391 K8
  WICKE SS11 .... 418 E1
Hayes Cl *CHLM/GWD* CM2 .... 14 B4
  WTHK RM20 .... 483 F5
Hayes Dr *RAIN* RM13 .... 450 C8
Hayes La *CVI* SS8 .... 477 K2
Hayes Rd *COS* CO15 .... 10 B5
Hay Gn *RCHLM* CM3 .... 335 K5
Hay Green La *BRWN* CM15 .... 384 B1
  ING CM4 .... 356 D8
Hayhill Rd *IPNE* IP4 .... 3 F2
Hayhouse Rd *RCOLW* CO6 .... 149 H8
Hay La *BRTR* CM7 .... 210 B2
Hayle *TIL* RM18 .... 486 D2
Hayley Bell Gdns *BSF* CM23 .... 231 K2
Haymeads La *BSF* CM23 .... 199 H7
Haynes Green Rd *K/T/MI* CO5 .... 248 E5
Haynes Rd *EMPK* RM11 .... 430 E7
  GVW DA11 .... 488 E8
Hayron's La *CHLM/WR* CM1 .... 269 H5
Haytor Cl *BRTR* CM7 .... 210 B3
The Haywain *COLW* CO3 .... 185 J8 ⊡
Haywards Cl *RBRW/HUT* CM13 .... 412 D2
Haywards Flds *KESG* IP5 .... 39 H5 ⊡
Hayword Ct *WAB* EN9 .... 348 B8
Hazel Cl *HCH* RM12 .... 450 C4 ⊡
  HVHL CB9 .... 26 E6
  LAIN SS15 .... 437 C5
  LOS SS9 .... 462 D4
  RCOLE CO7 .... 223 F8
  SBF/HAD SS7 .... 462 A3
Hazelcroft Rd *IP* IP1 .... 36 D3
Hazeldene *BAR* EN8 .... 346 E6
Hazeldon Cl *RCHLM* CM3 .... 272 E7 ⊡
  IPSE IP3 .... 64 C4
  SOCK/AV RM15 .... 470 A3
Hazeleigh *RBRW/HUT* CM13 .... 412 D2
Hazeleigh Gdns *WFD* IG8 .... 404 B3
Hazeleigh Hall La *MAL* CM9 .... 337 J8
Hazelend Rd *BSF* CM23 .... 199 G2
Hazel Gdns *CDH/CHF* CM16 .... 484 D2
Hazel Gv *BRTR* CM7 .... 209 H4
Hazell Av *COLS* CO2 .... 218 B2
Hazelmere *PIT* SS13 .... 458 D1
Hazelmere Gdns *EMPK* RM11 .... 430 C1
Hazel Ri *EMPK* RM11 .... 430 D8
Hazel Rd *ERITH* DA8 .... 480 B7
Hazelton Rd *COLN* CO4 .... 9 F2
Hazelville Cl *HAR* CO12 .... 164 D4
Hazelwood *HOC/HUL* SS5 .... 443 C1 ⊡
Hazelwood Ct *MAL* CM9 .... 310 D7 ⊡
Hazelwood Crs *RCOS* CO16 .... 258 E4
Hazelwood Gdns *BRWN* CM15 .... 410 D2 ⊡
Hazelwood Gv *LOS* SS9 .... 443 F8
Hazelwood Park Cl *BARK/HLT* IG6 .... 405 H8
Hazlemere Rd *COS* CO15 .... 11 F3
  SBF/HAD SS7 .... 440 C8
Hazlitt Rd *IP* IP1 .... 36 C2
Headcorn Cl *PIT* SS13 .... 439 F8
Headgate *COLS* CO2 .... 8 A5
Headingham Cl *CHTY* IP2 .... 62 C3 ⊡
Headland Av *PURL* RM16 .... 26 E6
Headley Cha *BRW* CM14 .... 411 F7
Headley Rd *BCAYE* CM11 .... 414 D1
Head St *COL* CO1 .... 8 A4
  HSTD CO9 .... 148 A3
  K/T/MI CO5 .... 220 C5
  MAL CM9 .... 312 C7
Heards La *BRTR* CM7 .... 76 D7
  BRTR CM7 .... 76 E8
  BRWN CM15 .... 384 D7
Hearn Rd *ROM* RM1 .... 430 A8
Hearsall Av *CHLM/WR* CM1 .... 304 D6
  SLH/COR SS17 .... 474 A4
Heath Cl *BCAYW* CM12 .... 414 A4
  GPK RM2 .... 430 A8
  RCOLE CO7 .... 122 C2
Heathcote Gdns *HLWE* CM17 .... 295 J5
Heathcote Gv *CHING* E4 .... 402 B6
Heath Ct *CHLM/GWD* CM2 .... 332 D7
  EPP CM16 .... 378 C1
  GPK RM2 .... 430 A8
Heath Dr *CHLM/GWD* CM2 .... 332 D7
Heather Av *IPSE* IP3 .... 64 A2
Heather Bank *BCAYE* CM11 .... 414 D3 ⊡
Heather Cl *BRWN* CM15 .... 410 E1 ⊡
  BSF CM23 .... 198 C1
  COLS CO2 .... 218 A7
  COS CO15 .... 259 K6
  KIR/NAC IP10 .... 64 D7
Heather Ct *CHLM/WR* CM1 .... 305 H7 ⊡
Heathercroft Rd *IP* IP1 .... 36 A2
  WICKE SS11 .... 417 K7 ⊡
Heather Dr *COLW* CO3 .... 186 A8

SBF/HAD SS7 .... 462 A3
Heatherhayes *CHTY* IP2 .... 2 D6
Heathfield *CHING* E4 .... 402 D6
  KESG IP5 .... 39 K7
  SBF/HAD SS7 .... 441 H7
Heathfield Ms *KIR/NAC* IP10 .... 39 K6
Heathfield Rd *CHLM/WR* CM1 .... 304 D5
  RIPS/CAP IP9 .... 90 A6
Heathfields *COLW* CO3 .... 185 G5
  FX IP11 .... 94 B4
Heathgate *WIT* CM8 .... 277 K7
Heathgate Piece *FX* IP11 .... 94 D7 ⊡
Heathlands *RCOLE* CO7 .... 223 F8
Heathlands Pk *IPNE* IP4 .... 64 C1
Heath La *IPNE* IP4 .... 38 A6
Heathleigh Dr *VGE* SS16 .... 456 C1
Heath Park Rd *GPK* RM2 .... 430 B7
Heath Rd *BCAYE* CM11 .... 415 F1
  CDH/CHF RM16 .... 471 K8
  COLW CO3 .... 184 C6
  COLW CO3 .... 186 A8
  COLW CO3 .... 217 J1
  IPNE IP4 .... 38 A6
  K/T/MI CO5 .... 220 C5
  MGTR CO11 .... 160 E5
  RCOLE CO7 .... 122 C2
  RCOLE CO7 .... 220 E3
  RCOLE CO7 .... 222 A5
  RCOLE CO7 .... 192 E4
  RCOS CO16 .... 258 A4
Heath Rw *BSF* CM23 .... 199 G4
Heathside *RCOLW* CO6 .... 185 K1 ⊡
The Heath *COLS* CO2 .... 218 B7
  RCOLE CO7 .... 157 J1
  SUD CO10 .... 59 H1
Heath Vw *KESG* IP5 .... 38 E7
Heath View Gdns *CDH/CHF* RM16 .... 484 B1
Heath View Rd *CDH/CHF* RM16 .... 484 B1
Heath Wy *SUD* CO10 .... 59 H1
Heathway *WFD* IG8 .... 403 K7
Heatley Wy *COLN* CO4 .... 188 C5
Heaton Av *HARH* RM3 .... 430 C2
Heaton Cl *CHING* E4 .... 402 D6
  HARH RM3 .... 430 D2
Heaton Grange Rd *GPK* RM2 .... 430 A3
Heaton Wy *HARH* RM3 .... 430 C2
  K/T/MI CO5 .... 248 E5
Heckford's Rd *RCOLE* CO7 .... 223 K5
Heckworth Cl *COLN* CO4 .... 155 K4
Hedge Dr *COLS* CO2 .... 218 C3
Hedgehope Av *RAYL* SS6 .... 441 J3
Hedgelands *COLW* CO3 .... 184 C8
Hedge La *SBF/HAD* SS7 .... 461 J1
Hedgerows *SBW* CM21 .... 263 K2
The Hedgerows *GVW* DA11 .... 488 D2
Hedingham Rd *EMPK* RM11 .... 451 H1
  HSTD CO9 .... 82 B6
  HSTD CO9 .... 146 D5
  SUD CO10 .... 82 D3
Hedley Av *WTHK* RM20 .... 483 H6
Hedworth Av *BAR* EN8 .... 346 D2
Heeswyk Rd *CVI* SS8 .... 461 J8 ⊡
Heideburg Rd *CVI* SS8 .... 461 H8
Heighams *HLWW/ROY* CM19 .... 295 H6
The Heights *LOU* IG10 .... 377 H6
  RCHLM CM3 .... 335 C2
  WAB EN9 .... 320 D2
Heilsburg Rd *CVI* SS8 .... 461 J8
Helden Av *CVI* SS8 .... 461 K8
Helena Cl *HOC/HUL* SS5 .... 421 G8
Helena Ct *RCHLM* CM3 .... 392 D1
Helena Rd *IPSE* IP3 .... 3 F3
  RAYL SS6 .... 441 K3
Helen How *RCHLM* CM3 .... 241 H6 ⊡
Helen Rd *EMPK* RM11 .... 430 E5
Helens Ga *BAR* EN8 .... 319 F8
Helford Ct *WIT* CM8 .... 276 D3
Helford Wy *UPMR* RM14 .... 432 A1
Helions Bumpstead Rd *HVHL* CB9 .... 27 G1
  HVHL CB9 .... 50 A1
Helions Park Av *HVHL* CB9 .... 27 G1
Helions Park Gdns *HVHL* CB9 .... 27 G1
Helions Park Gv *HVHL* CB9 .... 27 G6 ⊡
Helions Rd *HLWW/ROY* CM19 .... 12 B3
  HVHL CB9 .... 50 B1
Helions Service Rd *HVHL* CB9 .... 27 G6
Helions Wk *HVHL* CB9 .... 27 G6
Helleborine *GRAYS* RM17 .... 483 J1
Hellendoorn Rd *CVI* SS8 .... 460 C6
Helm Cl *RCOLW* CO6 .... 154 D6
Helmons La *CHLM/GWD* CM2 .... 389 J7
Helmores *LAIN* SS15 .... 436 A1
Helmsdale *CVI* SS8 .... 460 E8 ⊡
Helpeston *BSDN* SS14 .... 438 A1
Helston Cl *KESG* IP5 .... 39 F7
Helston Rd *CHLM/WR* CM1 .... 305 G6
Hemingway Rd *WIT* CM8 .... 244 B1
Hemley Rd *CDH/CHF* RM16 .... 472 D6
Hemmells *LAIN* SS15 .... 436 E1
Hemmings Ct *MAL* CM9 .... 338 A5
Hemnall St *EPP* CM16 .... 350 D4
Hempstead Cl *BKHH* IG9 .... 403 H4
Hempstead Rd *HVHL* CB9 .... 26 C1
Henderson Cl *HVHL* CB9 .... 26 C2
Henderson Gdns *WICKW* SS12 .... 417 H1

Hendersons Cl HCH RM12 .... 450 C3
Hendon Cl RCOS CO16 .... 10 A2
  WICKW SS12 .... 417 C7
Hengist Gdns WICKE SS11 .... 417 G4
Hengrave Cl CHTY IP2 .... 62 C3
Henham Cl BCAYE CM11 .... 414 E3
Henham Rd RBSF CM22 .... 169 F4
  SAFWS CB11 .... 138 A3
Henley Av IP IP11 .... 36 D2
Henley Ct COLW CO3 .... 185 K7
Henley Crs WOS/PRIT SS0 .... 464 A1
Henley Rd IP IP11 .... 36 E3
Henney Cl RCHLM CM3 .... 366 B7
Henniker Ga CHLM/GWD CM2 .... 333 J2
Henny Back Rd BURES CO8 .... 114 B1
Henny Rd BURES CO8 .... 84 E7
Henrietta Cl RCOLE CO7 .... 221 F2
Henry Cl COS CO15 .... 290 C5
Henry Dixon Rd WIT CM8 .... 245 K7
Henry Dr LOS SS9 .... 462 C3
Henry Rd CHLM/WR CM1 .... 14 C1
  IPSE IP3 .... 63 K4
Henry St GRAYS RM17 .... 484 B5
Henslow Rd IPNE IP4 .... 37 K8
Henson Av CVI SS8 .... 478 C2
Henstead Gdns IPSE IP3 .... 63 J5
Herald Cl BSF CM23 .... 198 C7
Herbage Park Rd MAL CM9 .... 336 C4
Herbert Gv SOS SS1 .... 19 E5
Herbert Rd COS CO15 .... 10 A3
  CVI SS8 .... 478 C1
  EMPK RM11 .... 451 J1
  KESG IP5 .... 39 J5
  SBN/FI SS3 .... 466 B7
Herd La SLH/COR SS17 .... 474 E1
Hereford Ct CHLM/GWD CM2 .... 333 H8
  COS CO15 .... 260 C8
Hereford Rd COL CO1 .... 8 C3
  COS CO15 .... 260 C7
Hereward Cl RCOLE CO7 .... 221 F2
  WAB EN9 .... 347 J6
Hereward Gdns WICKE SS11 .... 417 G4
Hereward Gn LOU IG10 .... 378 A5
Hereward Wy BRTR CM7 .... 143 K2
Herga Hyll CDH/CHF RM16 .... 472 A5
Herington Gv RBRW/HUT CM13 .. 411 K3
Hermen Rd CVI SS8 .... 461 G8
Hernshaw Rd CHLM/WR CM13 .. 434 C2
Heron Av WICKE SS11 .... 417 J7
Heron Cha RBRW/HUT CM13 ..... 434 C2
Heron Cl BKHH IG9 .... 403 H4
  RAYL SS6 .... 441 G3
  SBW CM21 .... 263 H4
Heron Ct BSF CM23 .... 199 F6
Heron Dl BSDN SS14 .... 438 A7
Heron Flight Av RAIN RM13 .... 450 C8
Heron Gdns RAYL SS6 .... 441 G2
Herongate SBF/HAD SS7 .... 460 A1
  SBN/FI SS3 .... 466 D5
Herongate Rd BAR EN8 .... 346 D1
Heron Gld COS CO15 .... 259 H6
Heron Rd CHTY IP2 .... 62 A2
  K/T/MI CO5 .... 247 F2
Heronsgate FOS CO13 .... 228 E7
Herons La CHONG CM5 .... 326 E4
Herons Wd HLW CM20 .... 12 B1
Heron Wy FOS CO13 .... 228 D6
  MAL CM9 .... 310 A8
  RCHLM CM3 .... 368 E5
  UPMR RM14 .... 452 B2
  WTHK RM20 .... 482 E4
Heronway RBRW/HUT CM13 ...... 412 A4
Herrick Cl COLW CO3 .... 186 B7
Herring's Wy RCOLW CO6 .... 152 C7
Herschell Rd LOS SS9 .... 462 D3
Hervey Cl RIPS/CAP IP9 .... 129 F4
Hervey St IPNE IP4 .... 3 E2
Hervilly Wy WOTN CO14 .... 229 G6
Hesselyn Dr RAIN RM13 .... 450 C8
Hester Pl BOC CM0 .... 398 C4
Hetherington Cl COLS CO2 .... 219 H5
Hetzand Rd CVI SS8 .... 479 F2

Hever Cl HOC/HUL SS5 .... 420 E7
Hewes Cl COLN CO4 .... 188 C6
Hewitt Rd HAR CO12 .... 164 B4
Hexham Cl CHTY IP2 .... 62 C3
Heybridge Ap MAL CM9 .... 310 B8
Heybridge Dr WICKW SS12 .... 417 H6
Heybridge Rd ING CM4 .... 385 K4
Heybridge St MAL CM9 .... 310 C8
Heycroft Dr BRTR CM7 .... 210 C7
Heycroft Rd HOC/HUL SS5 .... 421 G8
  LOS SS9 .... 443 G6
Heycroft Wy CHLM/GWD CM2 ... 333 H8
  K/T/MI CO5 .... 248 B7
  RCOLW CO6 .... 118 A4
Heydon La ROY SG8 .... 40 E8
  SAFWS CB11 .... 67 J1
Heydon Rd ROY SG8 .... 66 B3
Heygate Av SOS SS1 .... 19 D5
The Heythrop CHLM/WR CM1 ..... 15 F1
  ING CM4 .... 386 A2
Heywood Cl CHTY IP2 .... 62 A4
Heywood Cha MAL CM9 .... 310 D7
Heywood La GTDUN CM6 .... 204 C6
Heywood Wy MAL CM9 .... 310 D7
Hickford Hl SUD CO10 .... 31 H7
Hickling Cl LOS SS9 .... 442 C7
Hickman Cl BROX EN10 .... 318 E2
Hickory Av COLN CO4 .... 9 F4
Hickstars La BCAYE CM11 .... 414 D6
Hicks Wy HVHL CB9 .... 28 A8
Hidcote Wy BRTR CM7 .... 208 E6
The Hides HLW CM20 .... 13 D2
Higham Rd RCOLE CO7 .... 120 D2
Highams Cha MAL CM9 .... 312 D5
Highams Rd HOC/HUL SS5 .... 421 F8
High Ash Cl TIL RM18 .... 486 B2
High Bank VGE SS16 .... 456 A1
Highbank Cl LOS SS9 .... 443 G8
High Beach FX IP11 .... 131 K3
High Beeches SBF/HAD SS7 .... 460 A3
High Beech Rd LOU IG10 .... 377 G8
Highbirch Rd RCOS CO16 .... 224 E8
High Bridge Rd CHLM/GWD CM2 . 15 D4
Highbridge St WAB EN9 .... 347 H7
Highbury Wy SUD CO10 .... 58 E7
Highclere Rd BRTR CM7 .... 208 E7
  COLN CO4 .... 127 J1
Highcliff Crs RCFD SS4 .... 421 K6
High Cliff Dr LOS SS9 .... 463 G5
Highcliff Dr WICKW SS12 .... 417 J6
High Cloister BCAYE CM11 .... 414 C3
High Cl ROY SG8 .... 40 D8
Highcross La GTDUN CM6 .... 203 F8
High Cross La BSF CM23 .... 235 K1
High Cross La East GTDUN CM6 .. 203 H8
High Easter Rd GTDUN CM6 ...... 237 K3
  GTDUN CM6 .... 268 C7
High Elms CHIG IG7 .... 405 H7
  UPMR RM14 .... 452 B2
  WFD IG8 .... 403 H8
High Elms Rd HOC/HUL SS5 .... 419 K4
Highfield Ap BCAYE CM11 .... 414 E5
  IP IP11 .... 36 B4
Highfield Av BSF CM23 .... 199 H7
  HAR CO12 .... 6 C5
  SBF/HAD SS7 .... 461 G1
Highfield Cl BRTR CM7 .... 177 K7
  RCHLM CM3 .... 335 H7
  WOS/PRIT SS0 .... 18 A2
Highfield Crs HCH RM12 .... 451 H3
  RAYL SS6 .... 441 H3
  WOS/PRIT SS0 .... 18 A2
Highfield Dr BROX EN10 .... 318 E3
  COLW CO3 .... 186 D3
  WOS/PRIT SS0 .... 18 A2
Highfield Gdns CDH/CHF RM16 .. 484 C5
  WOS/PRIT SS0 .... 18 A1
Highfield Gn EPP CM16 .... 350 C5
Highfield Pl EPP CM16 .... 350 C5
Highfield Ri RCHLM CM3 .... 396 E2
Highfield Rd BCAYE CM11 .... 414 E6
  CHLM/WR CM1 .... 332 A1
  FX IP11 .... 131 H3
  HCH RM12 .... 451 G3
  IP IP11 .... 36 A3
  SUD CO10 .... 58 D4
High Flds GTDUN CM6 .... 204 C5
Highfields HSTD CO9 .... 79 K3
Highfields La K/T/MI CO5 .... 247 F6
Highfields Rd RCHLM CM3 .... 363 F5
Highfields Rd WIT CM8 .... 276 E2
Highfield Stile Rd BRTR CM7 ...... 177 K7

Highfield Wy WOS/PRIT SS0 ...... 18 A1
High Garrett BRTR CM7 .... 178 B4
Highgate Gv SBW CM21 .... 263 H3
High Hall Cl FX IP11 .... 94 B5
High House La CDH/CHF RM16 .. 485 J2
Highland Av BRW CM14 .... 411 F4
  LOU IG10 .... 404 C2
Highland Gv BCAYE CM11 .... 414 C2
Highland Rd BSF CM23 .... 231 K2
  SLH/COR SS17 .... 457 J4
  WAB EN9 .... 320 A4
Highlands HSTD CO9 .... 146 D4
Highlands Av VGE SS16 .... 458 A1
Highlands Bvd LOS SS9 .... 462 B2
Highlands Crs PIT SS13 .... 439 J7
Highlands Dr MAL CM9 .... 338 A3
Highlands Hl RCHLM CM3 .... 369 H7
Highlands Rd PIT SS13 .... 439 J7
  WICKE SS11 .... 419 G3
High La RBSF CM22 .... 264 E7
  STSD CM24 .... 167 K5
High Md CHIG IG7 .... 405 F5
  HOC/HUL SS5 .... 421 F8
Highmead RAYL SS6 .... 441 H3
  STSD CM24 .... 167 K5
High Meadow BCAYE CM11 ...... 414 D3
  GTDUN CM6 .... 204 B5
High Mdw CHIG IG7 .... 405 G8
High Oaks VGE SS16 .... 456 C2
High Pastures RBSF CM22 .... 264 C5
High Rd BKHH IG9 .... 403 J5
  BROX EN10 .... 319 F2
  CDH/CHF RM16 .... 470 C8
  CDH/CHF RM16 .... 471 K5
  CHIG IG7 .... 404 E5
  COLS CO2 .... 218 A8
  EPP CM16 .... 323 F6
  EPP CM16 .... 324 D6
  EPP CM16 .... 350 A7
  EPP CM16 .... 352 B1
  FX IP11 .... 94 C6
  HOC/HUL SS5 .... 420 B8
  LAIN SS15 .... 436 C6
  RAYL SS6 .... 441 H5
  SBF/HAD SS7 .... 440 A8
  SBF/HAD SS7 .... 460 A1
  SLH/COR SS17 .... 457 K4
  SLH/COR SS17 .... 473 F2
  SLH/COR SS17 .... 474 C4
  VGE SS16 .... 456 C4
  VGE SS16 .... 456 D2
  VGE SS16 .... 458 C1
High Road Broxbourne
  BROX EN10 .... 319 F3
High Rd East FX IP11 .... 131 J2
High Rd North LAIN SS15 .... 16 A1
High Road Ongar
  (Chelmsford Road) CHONG CM5 . 354 D1
High Rd Turnford BROX EN10 ... 318 E8
High Rd West FX IP11 .... 5 F1
High Road Woodford Gn WFD IG8 . 403 H8
High Row Fld FX IP11 .... 131 K2
High Silver LOU IG10 .... 377 F8
High Stile GTDUN CM6 .... 204 B5
High St BAR EN8 .... 346 E8
  BCAYW CM12 .... 414 B3
  BOC CM0 .... 344 C2
  BOC CM0 .... 398 D1
  BOC CM0 .... 425 G1
  BROX EN10 .... 318 E7
  BRTR CM7 .... 142 C3
  BRTR CM7 .... 143 K2
  BRTR CM7 .... 209 J2
  BRW CM14 .... 411 F5
  BSF CM23 .... 198 E6
  BURES CO8 .... 115 J4
  CBE/LIN CB1 .... 22 D3
  CBE/LIN CB1 .... 48 D2
  CHLM/GWD CM2 .... 333 H6
  CHLM/WR CM1 .... 14 C3
  CHONG CM5 .... 354 C3
  COL CO1 .... 8 B4
  COLN CO4 .... 156 A1
  COS CO15 .... 10 C5
  CVI SS8 .... 478 C1
  EMPK RM11 .... 450 E2
  EPP CM16 .... 350 D5
  FX IP11 .... 5 E1
  GRAYS RM17 .... 483 K4
  GTDUN CM6 .... 173 J8
  GTDUN CM6 .... 204 C5
  GVE DA12 .... 489 G4
  GVW DA11 .... 489 G4
  HAR CO12 .... 7 F4
  HAR CO12 .... 195 F1
  HLWE CM17 .... 295 G1
  HLWW/ROY CM19 .... 292 D4
  HOD EN11 .... 319 G1
  HSTD CO9 .... 79 K4
  HSTD CO9 .... 147 K3
  HVHL CB9 .... 27 G6
  ING CM4 .... 358 C8
  ING CM4 .... 386 B2
  ING CM4 .... 388 A3

IP IP1 ... 3 D3
K/T/MI CO5 ... 220 D5
K/T/MI CO5 ... 246 E3
K/T/MI CO5 ... 284 D7
LOS SS9 ... 462 D5
MAL CM9 ... 314 C4
MAL CM9 ... 338 B2
MGTR CO11 ... 159 J1
RAYL SS6 ... 441 H4
RBSF CM22 ... 137 C8
RBSF CM22 ... 234 B7
RCFD SS4 ... 423 G3
RCOLE CO7 ... 121 H7
RCOLE CO7 ... 220 E5
RCOLE CO7 ... 255 K7
RCOLW CO6 ... 149 H7
RCOLW CO6 ... 149 H7
RCOS CO16 ... 226 C3
ROY SG8 ... 67 G2
SAFWN CB10 ... 20 A6
SAFWN CB10 ... 43 K3
SAFWN CB10 ... 70 E4
SAFWN CB10 ... 74 D4
SAFWS CB11 ... 70 A1
SAFWS CB11 ... 100 B5
SAFWS CB11 ... 101 J6
SAFWS CB11 ... 134 B1
SAFWS CB11 ... 136 E1
SBF/HAD SS7 ... 460 C4
SBF/HAD SS7 ... 461 J2
SBN/FI SS3 ... 466 E1
SBN/FI SS3 ... 467 F6
SLH/COR SS17 ... 473 K4
SOCK/AV RM15 ... 468 E8
SOS SS1 ... 19 D4
SUD CO10 ... 31 H6
SUD CO10 ... 32 D4
SUD CO10 ... 35 K2
WICKW SS12 ... 417 G6
WOTN CO14... ... 229 H5
High St North K/T/MI CO5 ... 284 E7
High Tree La WOTN CO14 ... 229 H3
Hightrees ING CM4 ... 387 K3
High Vw BOC CM0 ... 342 C5
  BSF CM23 ... 199 H2
High View Av COS CO15 ... 10 B1
  GRAYS RM17 ... 484 B4
Highview Av VGE SS16 ... 455 K1
High View Cl COS CO15 ... 10 B1
  LOU IG10 ... 403 K1
Highview Cl SUD CO10 ... 58 B3
Highview Crs RBRW/HUT CM13 ... 412 B2
High View Gdns GRAYS RM17 ... 484 B4
Highview Gdns UPMR RM14 ... 451 J3
Highview Ri BCAYE CM11 ... 415 H3
Highview Rd SBF/HAD SS7 ... 441 H6
Highwood Cl BRW CM14 ... 410 E3
  LOS SS9 ... 463 C1
Highwood La LOU IG10... ... 404 D2
Highwood La WOS/PRIT SS0 ... 357 K7
Highwoods Ap COLN CO4 ... 187 J1
Highwoods Sq COLN CO4 ... 187 J2
High Wych La SBW CM21 ... 262 E3
High Wych Rd HLW CM20 ... 262 C7
  SBW CM21 ... 263 H4
Hilary Cl HCH RM12 ... 450 E6
  RCFD SS4 ... 422 B8
Hilary Crs RAYL SS6 ... 441 K3
Hilbery Rd CVI SS8 ... 478 C2
Hildabrook Cl CHTY IP2 ... 62 A4
Hildaville Dr WOS/PRIT SS0 ... 463 K3
Hilden Dr ERITH DA8 ... 480 C6
Hillary Av GVW DA11 ... 488 D8
Hillary Cl CHLM/WR CM1 ... 15 E1
  IPNE IP4 ... 37 J8
  MAL CM9 ... 310 D8
Hillary Mt BCAYW CM12 ... 414 A4
Hillborough Rd WOS/PRIT SS0 ... 18 A1
Hill Cl SBF/HAD SS7 ... 460 D1
  SUD CO10 ... 35 F5
Hill Crs CHLM/GWD CM2 ... 15 E3
  EMPK RM11 ... 430 D8
  HVHL CM17 ... 27 G4
Hillcrest COS CO15 ... 10 C1
  FOS CO13 ... 228 C5
  RCHLM CM3 ... 368 E4
Hillcrest Av HOC/HUL SS5 ... 419 K3
  WTHK RM20 ... 482 D5
Hillcrest Cl SLH/COR SS17 ... 473 F1
Hillcrest Ct HAR CO12 ... 7 D5
Hill Crest Rd CHONG CM5 ... 352 E4
Hillcrest Rd EMPK RM11 ... 450 B1
  HOC/HUL SS5 ... 421 F8
  LOU IG10 ... 404 A2
  RCHLM CM3 ... 392 C6
  SLH/COR SS17 ... 472 E2
  SOS SS1 ... 19 E4
  SUD CO10 ... 58 B3
Hillcrest Vw VGE SS16 ... 458 A2
Hillcrest Wy EPP CM16 ... 350 E5
Hillcroft LOU IG10 ... 377 J6
Hilldene Av HARH RM3 ... 430 D1
Hilldene Cl HARH RM3 ... 408 E8
Hill Farm La RIPS/CAP IP9 ... 91 J6

Hill Farm Rd NHMKT IP6 ... 39 F1
Hillhouse WAB EN9 ... 348 B7
Hillhouse Cl BCAYW CM12 ... 414 C1
Hill House Ct RCOLE CO7 ... 256 A6
Hillhouse Dr BCAYW CM12 ... 414 C1
Hillhouse La RCOS CO16 ... 225 J2
Hilliards Rd RCOLE CO7 ... 191 H3
Hillie Bunnies RCOLW CO6 ... 149 J6
Hillingdon Rd GVW DA11 ... 489 G7
Hill La HOC/HUL SS5 ... 421 G8
  HVHL CB9 ... 51 G1
Hillman Av COS CO15 ... 290 A7
Hillman Cl EMPK RM11 ... 430 E5
Hillridge COLN CO4 ... 187 J2
Hill Ri UPMR RM14 ... 451 H3
Hill Rd BRW CM14 ... 410 D6
  CHLM/GWD CM2... ... 15 G3
  COS CO15... ... 10 B1
  EPP CM16 ... 378 C3
  HAR CO12 ... 7 D4
  HAR CO12 ... 163 H5
  HAR CO12 ... 213 J3
  SAFWN CB10 ... 74 C5
  SBF/HAD SS7 ... 460 D2
Hill's Chace BRW CM14 ... 411 F7
Hills Cl BRTR CM7 ... 209 J1
Hills Crs COLW CO3 ... 186 B8
Hillside FOS CO13 ... 261 J1
  GRAYS RM17 ... 484 C3
  HLWE CM17 ... 295 C7
Hillside Av BAR EN8 ... 346 D5
  BSF CM23 ... 199 F6
  GVE DA12 ... 489 J7
  HOC/HUL SS5 ... 403 K8
Hillside Cl BCAYE CM11 ... 414 C4
  WFD IG8 ... 403 K8
Hillside Crs BAR EN8 ... 346 D5
  COS CO15 ... 11 F2
  IPSE IP3 ... 63 K2
  LOS SS9 ... 463 H5
Hillside Dr GVE DA12 ... 489 J7
Hillside Gdns BRTR CM7 ... 209 J4
  IPSE IP3 ... 63 K2
Hillside Gv CHLM/GWD CM2... ... 332 C7
Hillside Ms CHLM/GWD CM2 ... 14 B6
Hillside Rd BCAYW CM12 ... 414 C4
  BOC CM0 ... 398 B8
  BOC CM0 ... 398 C1
  GTDUN CM6... ... 206 A7
  HOC/HUL SS5 ... 420 C8
  LOS SS9 ... 462 D5
  SBF/HAD SS7 ... 460 C4
  SUD CO10 ... 58 D6
Hillside Wk BRW CM14 ... 410 D6
Hill's Rd BSF CM1 ... 403 J4
  HSTD CO9 ... 110 C5
Hill St SAFWN CB10 ... 70 E4
Hill Ter SLH/COR SS17 ... 457 K8
The Hill GVW DA11 ... 488 D8
Hilltop Av HOC/HUL SS5 ... 419 K4
Hill Top Av SBF/HAD SS7 ... 460 E3
Hilltop Cl LOU IG10 ... 377 J7
  RAYL SS6 ... 441 H4
Hilltop Crs RCOS CO16 ... 225 G4
Hill Top La SAFWS CB11 ... 70 E6
Hilltop Ri RCOS CO16 ... 225 F4
Hilltop Rd VGE SS16 ... 445 H7
Hilltop Wy WTHK RM20 ... 482 D5
Hill Tree La SBW CM21 ... 263 H4
Hill Vw RCHLM CM3 ... 363 K4
Hillview Av EMPK RM11 ... 430 D8
Hill View La K/T/MI CO5 ... 220 C5
Hillview Gdns BAR EN8... ... 346 E4
  SLH/COR SS17 ... 457 G8
Hill View Rd CHLM/WR CM1 ... 15 D1
Hillview Rd RAYL SS6 ... 441 H3
Hillway BCAYE CM11 ... 414 E3
  CBE/LIN CB1 ... 22 E3
  WOS/PRIT SS0 ... 463 H5
The Hill Wy BRWN CM15... ... 385 J5
Hillwood Cl RBRW/HUT CM13 ... 412 A4
Hillwood Gv RBRW/HUT CM13 ... 412 A4
  WICKW SS12 ... 417 H6
Hilly Fld HLWS CM18 ... 322 D1
Hillyfields LOU IG10 ... 377 J6
Hilton Cl MGTR CO11 ... 159 J1
Hilton Rd CVI SS8 ... 461 F8
  IPSE IP3 ... 64 A4
Hilton Wk CVI SS8 ... 461 F9
Hilton Wy HSTD CO9 ... 110 D5
Hilversum Wy CVI SS8 ... 461 G8
Hind Cl CHIG IG7 ... 405 J8
Hindles Rd CVI SS8 ... 478 D1
Hines Cl RCOLW CO6 ... 184 A5
Hinguar St SBN/FI SS3 ... 466 E7
Hintesham Cl IPNE IP4 ... 38 D8
Hintlesham Dr FX IP11 ... 5 D2
Hipkins BSF CM23 ... 231 J1
Histon Cl KESG IP5 ... 38 D6
Hitcham Rd RCOLW CO6 ... 213 G2
Hitchcock Pl SUD CO10 ... 58 B4

Hitch Common Rd SAFWS CB11 .. 100 A5
Hitchin Cl HARH RM3 ... 408 D7
Hitchin Ms BRTR CM7 ... 210 A5
Hither Blakers SAFWS CB11 ... 392 D5
Hitherwood Cl HCH RM12 ... 450 E5
Hitherwood Rd COLS CO2 ... 218 D3
Hive La GVW DA11 ... 488 A3
Hobart Cl CHLM/WR CM1 ... 304 A8
Hobart Rd TIL RM18 ... 485 F7
Hobbiton Hl RCHLM CM3 ... 392 C7
Hobbs Cl BAR EN8 ... 346 D3
Hobbs Cross Rd EPP CM16 ... 351 G8
  HLWE CM17 ... 295 K2
Hobbs Dr COLN CO4 ... 119 H8
Hobbs La SUD CO10 ... 33 K2
Hobhouse Rd SLH/COR SS17 ... 473 K1
Hobleythick La WOS/PRIT SS0 ... 18 A1
Hobtoe Rd HLW CM20 ... 12 A2
Hockerill St BSF CM23 ... 199 F6
Hockley Cl BOC CM0 ... 344 E3
  BSDN SS14 ... 438 A7
Hockley Dr GPK RM2 ... 430 C4
Hockley Gn BSDN SS14 ... 438 B7
Hockley La BOC CM0 ... 344 E2
Hockley Ri HOC/HUL SS5 ... 421 F8
Hockley Rd BSDN SS14 ... 438 A7
  RAYL SS6 ... 441 K2
Hockney Gdns IPSE IP3 ... 63 J5
Hodges Holt WIT CM8 ... 277 G6
Hodgson Ct WICKW SS12 ... 417 K8
Hodgson Wy WICKW SS12 ... 417 J7
Hodings Rd HLW CM20 ... 12 B2
Hoecroft WAB EN9 ... 320 B4
Hoe Dr COLW CO3 ... 186 B8
Hoe La ABR/ST RM4 ... 379 F7
  EN EN1 ... 374 B4
  PEND EN3 ... 374 C4
  RCHLM CM3 ... 390 D7
  RCHLM CM3 ... 392 D7
  SUD CO10 ... 33 F5
  WAB EN9 ... 320 B4
Hoe Mill Rd MAL CM9 ... 336 D1
Hoestock Rd SBW CM21 ... 263 H3
Hoe St CHLM/WR CM1 ... 330 C1
The Hoe BCAYW CM12 ... 436 C7
Hogarth Av BRW CM14 ... 411 H6
Hogarth Cl K/T/MI CO5 ... 285 F7
Hogarth Dr SBN/FI SS3 ... 467 F5
Hogarth End FOS CO13 ... 228 D3
Hogarth Reach LOU IG10 ... 404 C1
  IPSE IP3 ... 63 H4
Hogarth Sq IPSE IP3 ... 63 H4
Hogarth Wy RCFD SS4 ... 421 K7
Hoggla La CDH/CHF RM16... ... 483 K2
  GRAYS RM17 ... 483 K3
Hog La MEO DA13 ... 488 C8
Hog's La ROY SG8 ... 67 G2
Hogwell Cha RCHLM CM3 ... 393 H4
Holbech Rd BSDN SS14 ... 438 C5
Holbek Rd CVI SS8 ... 478 E2
Holborough Cl COLN CO4 ... 188 C6
Holbrook Cl BCAYE CM11 ... 414 E3
  RCHLM CM3 ... 392 D6
  RCOS CO16 ... 290 D7
  SUD CO10 ... 59 H7
Holbrook Crs FX IP11 ... 5 D5
Holbrook Rd HVHL CB9 ... 26 E7
  IPSE IP3 ... 63 G6
  RIPS/CAP IP9 ... 125 H3
  RIPS/CAP IP9 ... 126 D3
Holcombe Crs CHTY IP2 ... 61 K3
Holdbrook Wy HARH RM3 ... 431 G4
Holden Gdns BRW CM14 ... 411 G6
  BSDN SS14 ... 438 C4
Holden Rd BSDN SS14 ... 438 B4
  COLN CO4 ... 8 B1
Holden Wy UPMR RM14 ... 452 A2
Holdsworth Cl SUD CO10 ... 33 H2
Holecroft WAB EN9 ... 348 A8
Holford Rd CDH/CHF RM16 ... 485 K2
  TIL RM18 ... 485 J3
Holgate PIT SS13 ... 439 F5
Holkham Av RCHLM CM3 ... 392 D6
Holkham Cl IPNE IP4 ... 38 D8
Holland Av CVI SS8 ... 460 C6
Holland Pk COS CO15 ... 11 D3
Holland Rd COS CO15 ... 10 C5
  FOS CO13 ... 228 A4
  FOS CO13 ... 261 J2
  FX IP11 ... 5 F4
  IPNE IP4 ... 37 H1
  RCOS CO16 ... 259 J3
  WOS/PRIT SS0 ... 18 A1
Hollands Rd HVHL CB9 ... 27 G1
Hollands Wk VGE SS16 ... 458 A1
Holledge Crs FOS CO13 ... 228 D2
Holliday Hl CHLM/GWD CM2 ... 389 G1
Hollies Rd BRTR CM7 ... 211 H2
The Hollies SLH/COR SS17 ... 473 J4
Hollington Cft RCOLW CO6 ... 183 F5
Hollingtons Gv COLS CO2 ... 250 A3
Hollis Lock CHLM/GWD CM2 ... 333 J2
Hollis Pl GRAYS RM17 ... 485 K1
Holliwel Cl COLW CO3 ... 185 J2

Holloway Crs *GTDUN* CM6 .... 268 A6
Holloway Rd *MAL* CM9 .... 310 B7
Hollowfield Av *GRAYS* RM17 .... 484 C3
Hollow HI *HVHL* CB9 .... 26 B1
Hollow La *BURES* CO8 .... 115 J2
  CHLM/WR CM1 .... 303 K6
  RIPS/CAP IP9 .... 91 J6
Hollow Rd *GTDUN* CM6 .... 207 J8
  K/T/M CO5 .... 246 B3
  RIPW IP8 .... 60 D5
  ROY SG8 .... 67 G4
  SAFWS CB11 .... 68 A1
  SAFWS CB11 .... 136 D2
  SUD CO10 .... 53 H3
The Hollow *WFD* IG8 .... 403 G7
Hollybank *WIT* CM8 .... 277 F4
Hollybush HI *RCOLE* CO7 .... 256 E2
Hollybush Rd *GVE* DA12 .... 489 H7
Hollybush Wy *CBE/LIN* CB1 .... 23 G2
  EBAR EN7 .... 346 A2
Holly Cl *BKHH* IG9 .... 404 A6
  BOC CM0 .... 398 B7
  COLS CO2 .... 218 D3
Hollycroft Cl *IP* IP1 .... 36 C2
Holly Dr *CHING* E4 .... 402 C3
  SOCK/AV RM15 .... 470 B4
Holly End *KESG* IP5 .... 39 K7
Holly Fld *HLWW/ROY* CM19 .... 12 C6
Hollyfields *BROX* EN10 .... 318 E8
Hollyford *BCAYE* CM11 .... 387 J8
Holly Gv *VGE* SS16 .... 436 A8
Hollyhock Rd *SAFWN* CB10 .... 71 F3
Holly La *KESG* IP5 .... 38 C3
  RCOLW CO6 .... 154 D1
  RIPS/CAP IP9 .... 125 F2
  RIPW IP8 .... 61 J5
Hollymead *SLH/COR* SS17 .... 474 A1
Hollymead Cl *COLN* CO4 .... 187 G2
Holly Oaks *RCOLW* CO6 .... 152 D1
Holly Rd *COLW* CO3 .... 217 H1
  IP IP1 .... 2 C2
  KESG IP5 .... 38 D6
  PEND EN3 .... 374 D2
Hollytree Ct *COLS* CO2 .... 218 D2
Hollytree Gdns *RAYL* SS6 .... 441 G5
Hollyview Ct *RCOS* CO16 .... 193 G8
Holly Wy *CHLM/GWD* CM2 .... 15 D6
  K/T/M CO5 .... 248 A8
  RCOLE CO7 .... 189 J7
Hollywood Cl *CHLM/GWD* CM2 .. 333 C7
Hollywood Wy *ERITH* DA8 .... 480 C7
Holman Crs *COLW* CO3 .... 218 B1
Holman Rd *HSTD* CO9 .... 147 K4
Holmans *RCHLM* CM3 .... 306 C5
Holmbridge Gdns *PEND* EN3 ...... 374 D8
Holmbrook Wy *FOS* CO13 .... 228 D8
Holme Cl *BAR* EN8 .... 346 E5
Holme Rd *EMPK* RM11 .... 451 J1
Holmes Cl *SLH/COR* SS17 .... 473 F2
Holmesdale *BAR* EN8 .... 374 C1
Holmes Meadow *EPP* CM16 .... 321 K3
Holme Wk *WICKW* SS12 .... 417 J8
Holmsdale Cl *WOS/PRIT* SS0 ...... 463 J2
Holmwood *CVI* SS8 .... 461 K8
Holst Av *LAIN* SS15 .... 16 A2
Holst Cl *SLH/COR* SS17 .... 473 F2
Holt Cl *CHIG* IG7 .... 405 J6
Holt Dr *COLS* CO2 .... 219 H6
  WIT CM8 .... 278 A8
Holt Farm Wy *RCFD* SS4 .... 444 A1
  RAYL SS6 .... 442 B4
Holt's Rd *RCOLW* CO6 .... 153 G2
Holt Wy *CHIG* IG7 .... 405 J8
Holtynge *SBF/HAD* SS7 .... 460 B1
Holybread La *RCHLM* CM3 .... 335 G1
Holy Cross HI *BROX* EN10 .... 318 E8
Holyfield Rd *WAB* EN9 .... 347 J3
Holyoak La *HOC/HUL* SS5 .... 443 F1
Holyrood *HAR* CO12 .... 6 A6
Holyrood Cl *CHTY* IP2 .... 62 B4
Holyrood Dr *WOS/PRIT* SS0 .... 463 J3
Holyrood Gdns *CDH/CHF* RM16 .. 485 H3
Holywells Cl *IPSE* IP3 .... 3 F5
Holy Wells Rd *IPSE* IP3 .... 3 F6
Homebridge Cl *BROX* EN10 .... 319 F6
Home Cl *BROX* EN10 .... 319 F6
  HLW CM20 .... 13 F3
  HVHL CB9 .... 26 E5
Homecroft Gdns *LOU* IG10 .... 377 K8
Home Farm La *RCOLE* CO7 .... 157 K5
Home Farm Rd *RBRW/HUT* CM13 .. 433 H3
Homefield *BOC* CM0 .... 370 E8
  RIPS/CAP IP9 .... 87 G2
  WAB EN9 .... 348 C6
Homefield Cl *BCAYE* CM11 .... 414 E7
  CHLM/WR CM1 .... 303 K8
  EPP CM16 .... 350 E3
Homefield Rd *COLS* CO2 .... 218 D4
  HVHL CB9 .... 26 E8
  WIT CM8 .... 277 G1

Homefields Av *SBF/HAD* SS7 ...... 440 A8
Homefield Wy *BRTR* CM7 .... 210 C6
  RCOLW CO6 .... 149 J6
Homelands Gv *BCAYE* CM11 ...... 415 K1
Homeleigh Ct *BAR* EN8 .... 346 B4
Homelye Cha *CHLM* CM6 .... 205 G4
Home Md *CHLM/GWD* CM2 .... 360 E3
  CHLM/WR CM1 .... 331 G4
  LAIN SS15 .... 436 C5
Home Mead Cl *CVE* DA12 .... 489 G5
Home Mdw *BCAYW* CM12 .... 414 B3
Home Pastures *RBSF* CM22 .... 265 F2
Homer Cl *IP* IP1 .... 36 B1
Homerton Dr *COS* CO15 .... 259 H5
Homestead *CHLM/WR* CM1 .... 304 D6
Homestead Dr *VGE* SS16 .... 456 D3
Homestead Gdns *SBF/HAD* SS7 .. 461 J2
Homestead Rd *BCAYE* CM11 ...... 416 A5
  PIT SS13 .... 439 H6
  SBF/HAD SS7 .... 461 J3
Homestead Wy *SBF/HAD* SS7 .... 461 J3
Homeway *HARH* RM3 .... 431 J1
Homing Rd *RCOS* CO16 .... 258 E1
Honeybourne *BSF* CM23 .... 231 J1
Honey Brook *WAB* EN9 .... 348 A7
Honey Cl *BRWN* CM15 .... 384 B1
  CHLM/GWD CM2 .... 333 F7
Honeycroft *LOU* IG10 .... 377 J8
Honey La *BAR* EN8 .... 347 F8
  RCOLW CO6 .... 117 H1
  SAFWS CB11 .... 133 J2
  WAB EN9 .... 348 B8
Honeymeade *HLW* CM20 .... 263 G6
Honey Pot La *RCHLM* CM3 .... 394 A2
Honeypot La *BRW* CM14 .... 410 D5
  BSDN SS14 .... 17 F4
  ING CM4 .... 387 J4
  MAL CM9 .... 281 F4
  MGTR CO11 .... 193 G1
  RCOS CO16 .... 258 C1
Honeypots *CHLM/GWD* CM2 ...... 332 E7
Honeysuckle Cl *BRWN* CM15 ...... 410 E1
  BSF CM23 .... 198 B7
  HARH RM3 .... 430 E1
  HVHL CB9 .... 26 E4
Honeysuckle Gdns *CHTY* IP2 ...... 62 A1
Honeysuckle Wy *COLN* CO4 .... 188 B5
  RCOLE CO7 .... 223 F8
  WIT CM8 .... 276 D1
Honeywood Av *RCOLW* CO6 .... 213 H2
Honeywood Rd *HSTD* CO9 .... 148 A2
Honiley Av *WICKW* SS12 .... 439 H3
Honington Cl *WICKE* SS11 .... 418 A7
Honiton Rd *SOS* SS1 .... 5 J9
Honorius Dr *COLN* CO4 .... 155 J8
Honywood Cl *RCOLW* CO6 .... 215 H2
Honywood Rd *BSDN* SS14 .... 438 C3
  COLW CO3 .... 186 E7
Honywood Wy *FOS* CO13 .... 228 E6
Hood Cl *WICKW* SS12 .... 417 H7
Hood Gdns *BRTR* CM7 .... 210 B1
Hood Rd *IPSE* IP3 .... 63 G4
Hook End La *BRWN* CM15 .... 356 A8
Hook End Rd *BRWN* CM15 .... 383 K1
Hook Fld *HLWS* CM18 .... 13 E5
Hookfields *BRWN* CM15 .... 411 K1
Hook Ga *EN* EN1 .... 374 B3
Hook La *ABR/ST* RM4 .... 406 F2
Hooley Dr *RAYL* SS6 .... 419 H7
The Hoo *HLWE* CM17 .... 263 G8
Hoover Dr *LAIN* SS15 .... 436 A7
Hope Av *SLH/COR* SS17 .... 457 F8
Hope Cl *BRWN* CM15 .... 385 J5
Hope Rd *BCAYE* CM11 .... 415 K8
  CVI SS8 .... 478 D2
  SBF/HAD SS7 .... 460 B4
Hop Gardens La *MAL* CM9 .... 337 F1
The Hopgrounds *BRTR* CM7 .... 106 E7
Hopkins Cl *CHLM/GWD* CM2 ...... 333 J3
  FOS CO13 .... 228 F7
  GPK RM2 .... 430 D5
Hopkins Md *CHLM/GWD* CM2 .... 333 H3
Hopkirk Cl *RCHLM* CM3 .... 335 K3
Hop Meadow *RCOLE* CO7 .... 122 A3
Hoppett Rd *CHING* E4 .... 403 K3
Hopping Jacks La *RCHLM* CM3 .. 335 K6
Hoppit Md *BRTR* CM7 .... 209 J4
The Hoppitt *CHING* CM5 .... 325 J2
Hopton Ri *HVHL* CB9 .... 26 C5
Horace Rd *BCAYE* CM11 .... 414 C1
  SOS SS1 .... 19 E5
Hordle Pl *HAR* CO12 .... 7 E4
Hordle St *HAR* CO12 .... 7 E4
Horkesley HI *RCOLW* CO6 .... 118 B5
Horkesley Rd *RCOLW* CO6 .... 118 B5
  RCOLW CO6 .... 154 E5
Horkesley Wy *WICKW* SS12 .... 417 H7
Horksley Gdns
  RBRW/HUT CM13 .... 412 B2
Horley Cl *RCOS* CO16 .... 258 E1
Hornbeam Av *UPMR* RM14 .... 451 H5
Hornbeam Cha *SOCK/AV* RM15 .. 470 B3
Hornbeam Cl *CHLM/GWD* CM2 .. 332 C7
  COLS CO2 .... 218 C3
  EPP CM16 .... 378 C3

RBRW/HUT* CM13 .... 412 A6
Hornbeam Gv *CHING* E4 .... 403 F6
Hornbeam Rd *BKHH* IG9 .... 403 F1
  EPP CM16 .... 378 B3
Hornbeams *SBF/HAD* SS7 .... 440 A5
Hornbeams Av *EN* EN1 .... 374 C1
The Hornbeams *HAR* CO12 .... 164 A6
  HLW CM20 .... 12 C1
Hornbeam Wy *LAIN* SS15 .... 16 B1
Hornby La *WOS/PRIT* SS0 .... 443 K8
Hornby Cl *WOS/PRIT* SS0 .... 444 A8
Hornchurch Cl *WICKE* SS11 .... 417 K7
Hornchurch Rd *EMPK* RM11 ...... 450 C2
  HCH RM12 .... 450 B2
Horndon Rd *SLH/COR* SS17 .... 473 G4
Horne Rw *RCHLM* CM3 .... 335 H8
Horner Pl *WIT* CM8 .... 277 C3
Hornet Wy *BOC* CM0 .... 398 B8
Horn La *CBE/LIN* CB1 .... 22 D3
Hornminster Gln *EMPK* RM11 .... 451 H3
Hornsby La *CDH/CHF* RM16 ...... 472 A7
Hornsby Sq *LAIN* SS15 .... 435 K6
Hornsby Wy *LAIN* SS15 .... 436 A6
Hornsland Rd *CVI* SS8 .... 478 E2
Horn Yd *GVE* DA12 .... 489 G4
Horrocks Cl *COLS* CO2 .... 219 H1
Horsecroft Rd *HLWW/ROY* CM19 .. 293 G6
Horseheath Gn *CBE/LIN* CB1 ...... 25 G4
Horseheath Rd *CBE/LIN* CB1 ...... 23 F3
  HVHL CB9 .... 26 A1
Horseman Side *BRW* CM14 .... 408 E2
Horseshoe Cl *BCAYW* CM12 ...... 387 G8
  SAFWS CB11 .... 68 A1
Horseshoe HI *WAB* EN9 .... 348 E7
Horseshoe La *HVHL* CB9 .... 26 E6
Horsey Rd *FOS* CO13 .... 228 B5
Horsham Av *IPSE* IP3 .... 64 B2
Horsham Cl *HVHL* CB9 .... 26 C4
Horsley Cross *BSDN* SS14 .... 17 F3
Horsley Rd *CHING* E4 .... 402 D5
Hospital Ap *CHLM/WR* CM1 .... 304 D2
Hospital La *COLW* CO3 .... 186 E7
Hospital Rd *COLW* CO3 .... 186 E7
  SBN/FI SS3 .... 466 E7
Hossack Rd *IPSE* IP3 .... 63 J5
Houblons HI *EPP* CM16 .... 351 H5
Houchin Dr *CHONG* CM5 .... 327 F3
Houchin's La *RCOLW* CO6 .... 214 B2
Houghton Pl *IPNE* IP4 .... 38 D8
Hove Cl *GRAYS* RM17 .... 483 K5
  RBRW/HUT CM13 .... 412 B5
Hovefields Av *PIT* SS13 .... 439 G3
  WICKW SS12 .... 439 G2
Hovefields Dr *WICKW* SS12 .... 439 G2
Howard Av *HAR* CO12 .... 6 A6
Howard Cl *BSDN* SS14 .... 17 D2
  WAB EN9 .... 347 K8
Howard Crs *PIT* SS13 .... 439 F8
Howard Dr *CHLM/GWD* CM2 ...... 333 J3
Howard Pl *CVI* SS8 .... 478 B3
Howard Rd *CDH/CHF* RM16 ...... 483 F2
  COS CO15 .... 11 F3
  SAFWN CB10 .... 71 F3
  UPMR RM14 .... 451 K3
Howards Cha *WOS/PRIT* SS0 ...... 18 B2
Howards Cl *RCHLM* CM3 .... 306 C5
Howards Cft *COLN* CO4 .... 154 E8
Howard's La *CBE/LIN* CB1 .... 24 E3
Howard St *IPNE* IP4 .... 37 K6
Howards Wy *KESC* IP5 .... 39 J5
Howard Wy *HLW* CM20 .... 13 F1
Howbridge Hall Rd *WIT* CM8 ...... 277 F5
Howbridge Rd *WIT* CM8 .... 277 F5
Howbury La *ERITH* DA8 .... 480 B8
Howbury Rd *DART* DA1 .... 480 B8
Howe Av *IPSE* IP3 .... 64 A2
Howe Cha *HSTD* CO9 .... 147 K1
Howe Cl *COLN* CO4 .... 9 F4
Howe Green Rd *RCHLM* CM3 ...... 366 A4
Howe La *SAFWN* CB10 .... 105 F1
Howell Rd *SLH/COR* SS17 .... 457 G7
Howe Rd *HVHL* CB9 .... 26 E4
Hows Md *EPP* CM16 .... 324 D6
Hoxter Wy *SUD* CO10 .... 58 B3
Hoxton Cl *COS* CO15 .... 10 A3
Hoylake Gdns *HARH* RM3 .... 431 H2
Hoynors *RCHLM* CM3 .... 336 A6
Hubbards Cha *EMPK* RM11 .... 431 H7
  WOTN CO14 .... 229 G4
Hubbards Cl *EMPK* RM11 .... 431 H7
Hubert Rd *BRW* CM14 .... 410 E6
  COLW CO3 .... 186 C5
Hucklesbury Av *COS* CO15 .... 260 C6
Hucknall Cl *HARH* RM3 .... 431 G1
Hudson Cl *HAR* CO12 .... 165 F4
  HVHL CB9 .... 27 J7
  RCOS CO16 .... 258 E8
Hudson Crs *LOS* SS9 .... 443 F7
Hudson Rd *LOS* SS9 .... 442 E7
Hudsons Cl *SLH/COR* SS17 .... 473 K2
Hudson's HI *BRTR* CM7 .... 144 A2

Hudsons La RCOLW CO6 ..... 119 K1
Hudson Wy CVI SS8 ..... 461 F7
Hugh Dickson Rd COLN CO4 ..... 8 A1
Hughes Rd CDH/CHF RM16 ..... 485 F2
  RCOLE CO7 ..... 121 K1
Hugo Gdns RAIN RM13 ..... 450 A7
Hullbridge Rd RAYL SS6 ..... 419 J5
  RCHLM CM3 ..... 392 D7
Hullett's La BRWN CM15 ..... 383 H8
Hull Gn HLWE CM17 ..... 297 K3
Hull Gv HLWW/ROY CM19 ..... 321 J2
Hull La RCHLM CM3 ..... 274 E3
Hull's La CHLM/GWD CM2 ..... 334 C7
Hulton Cl RCHLM CM3 ..... 306 D4
Humber Av COS CO15 ..... 290 A7
  SOCK/AV RM15 ..... 469 H6
Humber Cl RAYL SS6 ..... 441 H4
Humber Doucy La IPNE IP4 ..... 37 J3
Humber Dr UPMR RM14 ..... 432 A8
Humber Rd CHLM/WR CM3 ..... 304 E8
  WIT CM8 ..... 276 D3
Hume Av TIL RM18 ..... 489 G1
Hume Cl TIL RM18 ..... 489 F1
Humphrey's Farm La RCHLM CM3.. 271 J6
Humphry Rd SUD CO10 ..... 58 B5
Hundon Rd HVHL CB9 ..... 28 E3
Hundred La COLN CO4 ..... 155 J1
Hungerdown CHING E4 ..... 402 D4
Hungerdown La MGTR CO11 ..... 158 D3
  RCOLE CO7 ..... 158 B6
Hunnable Rd BRTR CM7 ..... 209 H2
Hunsdon Rd WARE SG12 ..... 292 A1
Hunt Av MAL CM9 ..... 310 D8
Hunt Cl K/T/MI CO5 ..... 247 F1
Hunt Dr RCOS CO16 ..... 10 A2
Hunter Av BRWN CM15 ..... 411 K2
Hunter Dr RCHLM RM12 ..... 450 D5
  MGTR CO11 ..... 159 G2
  WICKW SS12 ..... 417 H8
Hunter Rd BRTR CM7 ..... 210 B3
Hunters Av BCAYW CM12 ..... 414 C6
Hunters Cha RBRW/HUT CM13 ..... 413 H4
  RCOLE CO7 ..... 157 H5
Hunters End FX IP11 ..... 94 D8
Hunter's Gv CRW RM5 ..... 407 G8
Hunters Rdg COLN CO4 ..... 187 J1
Hunters Wy CHLM/WR CM1 ..... 305 H6
  SAFWN CB11 ..... 70 E6
Huntingdon Cl BROX EN10 ..... 318 E6
Huntingdon Rd SOS SS1 ..... 465 G5
Huntingdon Wy COS CO15 ..... 10 B1
Hunting Ga COL CO1 ..... 9 E4
Huntley Av GVW DA11 ..... 488 B3
Hunt Rd GVW DA11 ..... 488 D8
  RCOLW CO7 ..... 149 G7
Hunt's Cl CHLM/WR CM1 ..... 331 H5
Hunt's Dr CHLM/WR CM1 ..... 331 H5
Hunts Farm Cl MAL CM9 ..... 314 D3
Hunts La SAFWN CB10 ..... 20 B6
Huntsmans Dr UPMR RM14 ..... 451 K6
Hunts Md BCAYW CM12 ..... 414 A4
  PEND EN3 ..... 374 D7
Hunt Wy FOS CO13 ..... 228 A7
Hurdcote Rd RCOLN CO4 ..... 188 B7
Hurdle Makers Hl RIPW IP8 ..... 60 D1
Hurlock Rd BCAYE CM11 ..... 414 C5
Hurnard Dr COLW CO3 ..... 186 B5
Hurrell Down COLN CO4 ..... 187 H1
  RCHLM CM3 ..... 306 D4
Hurrells La RCHLM CM3 ..... 334 E2
Hurricane Cl WICKE SS11 ..... 418 A8
Hurricane Wy EPP CM16 ..... 351 K1
  WICKE SS11 ..... 417 K8
Hursley Rd CHIG IG7 ..... 405 J8
Hurst Av CHING E4 ..... 402 B6
Hurst Cl CHING E4 ..... 402 B6
  RCOLE CO7 ..... 256 A7
Hurst Dr BAR EN8 ..... 346 D8
Hurstlands Cl EMPK RM11 ..... 430 D8
Hurst Park Av HCH RM12 ..... 451 F5
Hurst Rd BKHH IG9 .....
Hurst Wy CHLM/GWD CM2 ..... 333 H3
  LOS SS9 ..... 463 G1
Hurstwood Av BRWN CM15 ..... 410 E3
Hutchins Cl HCH RM12 ..... 451 F4
Hutland Rd IPNE IP4 ..... 37 H6
Hutton Dr RBRW/HUT CM13 ..... 412 C3
Hutton Ga RBRW/HUT CM13 ..... 412 A3
Hutton Rd BRWN CM15 ..... 411 J3
Hutton Village RBRW/HUT CM13 ..... 412 D3
Huxtables La COLW CO3 ..... 185 F4
Hyacinth Cl MAL CM9 ..... 314 E4
  RCOS CO16 ..... 290 A4
Hyams La RIPS/CAP IP9 ..... 89 K1
  RIPS/CAP IP9 ..... 125 G4
Hycliffe Gdns CHIG IG7 ..... 405 F7
Hyde Cha MAL CM9 ..... 364 C1
Hyde Gn RCHLM CM3 ..... 336 B6
Hyde La BRTR CM7 ..... 144 E4
Hyde Md WAB EN9 .....
Hyde Rd SUD CO10 ..... 58 B5
Hyder Rd CDH/CHF RM16 ..... 485 H2
The Hyde VGE SS16 .....
Hydeway SBF/HAD SS7 ..... 440 E8

Hyde Wy WICKW SS12 ..... 417 G7
Hyde Wood La RCFD SS4 ..... 422 C6
Hydewood Rd HSTD CO9 ..... 80 A2
Hyem's La FX IP11 ..... 95 J8
Hyland Cl EMPK RM11 ..... 450 A7
Hylands Cl GTDUN CM6 ..... 238 A1
The Hylands HOC/HUL SS5 ..... 420 E8
Hyland Wy EMPK RM11 ..... 450 C1
Hyll Cl SAFWN CB10 ..... 43 J2
Hyntle Cl IPNE IP4 ..... 36 A8
Hythe Cl BRTR CM7 ..... 177 H7
  COS CO15 ..... 291 F5
Hythe Gv RCOLE CO7 ..... 255 J4
Hythe Hl COL CO1 ..... 9 E5
Hythe Station Rd COLS CO2 ..... 9 F5
The Hythe MAL CM9 ..... 338 D3

Ian Rd BCAYW CM12 ..... 414 A1
Ibbetson Pth LOU IG10 ..... 377 K7
I Butts Rd SBN/FI SS3 ..... 467 H1
Iceni Wy COLS CO2 ..... 218 C2
Ickleton Rd SAFWN CB10 ..... 20 A8
  SAFWS CB11 ..... 67 K1
Icknield Cl SAFWN CB10 ..... 43 F2
Icknield Wy ROY SG8 ..... 67 G2
  SAFWS CB11 ..... 67 K1
Icknield Way Pth SAFWN CB10 ..... 43 G5
Ickworth Ct FX IP11 ..... 4 C4
Ickworth Crs IPNE IP4 ..... 38 C1
Ilex Cl COLS CO2 ..... 218 E3
Ilfracombe Av PIT SS13 ..... 439 G8
  SOS SS1 ..... 465 C5
Ilfracombe Crs HCH RM12 ..... 450 D5
Ilfracombe Rd SOSN SS2 ..... 19 F3
Ilgars Rd WICKE SS11 ..... 417 H4
Ilmington Dr PIT SS13 ..... 438 D4
Imogen Cl COLN CO4 ..... 188 C6
Imperial Av RCHLM CM3 ..... 368 C4
  WOS/PRIT SS0 ..... 463 J4
Imphal Cl COLS CO2 ..... 218 D4
Inchbonnie Rd RCHLM CM3... 392 E7
Ingarfield Rd COS CO15 ..... 260 C7
Ingatestone By-pass ING CM4 ..... 358 B8
Ingatestone Rd CHLM/WR CM1 ..... 357 J3
  ING CM4 ..... 356 D6
Ingaway VGE SS16 ..... 387 F4
Ingelrica Av RCHLM CM3 ..... 308 B2
Ingels Md EPP CM16 ..... 350 D3
Ingersoll Rd PEND EN3 ..... 374 C4
Ingestre St HAR CO12 ..... 7 E4
Ingham Rd HVHL CB9 ..... 27 H5
Ingleby Gdns CHIG IG7 ..... 406 A6
Ingleby Rd CDH/CHF RM16 ..... 485 C2
Inglefield Rd SLH/COR SS17 ..... 457 J7
Ingleglen EMPK RM11 ..... 451 H1
Inglenook COS CO15 ..... 259 K6
Ingleside Cl SAFWS CB11 ..... 70 E4
Inglewood Cl HCH RM12 ..... 450 E5
Inglis Rd COLW CO3 ..... 186 E7
Ingoldsby Rd GVE DA12 ..... 489 K6
Ingram Ms BRTR CM7 ..... 210 A5
Ingram Rd GRAYS RM17 ..... 484 B3
Ingram's Well Rd SUD CO10 ..... 58 C6
Ingrave Cl WICKW SS12 ..... 417 H7
Ingrave Rd BRW CM14 ..... 411 H6
Ingrebourne Gdns UPMR RM14 ..... 431 J1
Ingreway HARH RM3 .....
Inkerpole Pl CHLM/GWD CM2 ..... 333 H1
Inks Gn CHING E4 ..... 402 D8
Inmans Rw WFD IG8 ..... 403 H7
Innes Cl COS CO15 ..... 417 G8
Innham Hl HSTD CO9 ..... 110 B7
Inskip Dr EMPK RM11 ..... 451 F2
Institute Rd MAL CM9 ..... 351 H3
Inverness Av WOS/PRIT SS0 ..... 18 A2
Inverness Cl COL CO1 ..... 8 C5
Inverness Rd IPNE IP4 ..... 37 J3
Invicta Ct BCAYW CM12 ..... 413 K1
Inworth La RCOLW CO6 ..... 151 J3
Inworth Rd K/T/MI CO5 ..... 247 G1
Inworth Wk COLS CO2 ..... 219 H4
Iona Wy WICKE SS11 ..... 417 J8
Ipswich Ms VGE SS16 ..... 436 A8
Ipswich Rd COL CO1 ..... 156 C1
  COLN CO4 ..... 120 E7
  COLN CO4 ..... 156 A8
  COS CO15 ..... 260 B7
  KIR/NAC IP10 ..... 64 D7
  MGTR CO11 ..... 123 J4
  RCOLE CO7 ..... 121 H3
  RIPS/CAP IP9 ..... 90 A6
Ireland Rd IPSE IP3 ..... 63 H4
Ireton Pl GRAYS RM17 ..... 483 K3
Ireton Rd COL CO3 ..... 186 E8
Iris Cl BRWN CM15 ..... 410 E1
  CHLM/WR CM1 ..... 305 H8
  CHTY IP2 ..... 2 A4

Irlam Rd CHTY IP2 ..... 61 K3
Iron Latch La COLW CO3... 185 H5
Ironwell La HOC/HUL SS5 ..... 443 C7
  RCFD SS4 ..... 444 A3
Irvine Gdns SOCK/AV RM15 ..... 469 K6
Irvine Pl WICKW SS12 ..... 417 J8
Irvine Rd COLW CO3 ..... 186 D8
Irvine Wy BCAYW CM12 ..... 414 B4
Irving Cl BSF CM23 ..... 231 H1
Irvington Cl LOS SS9 ..... 462 E1
Irvon Hill Rd WICKW SS12 ..... 417 F6
Irye Md VGE SS16 ..... 16 A6
Isabel Ga BAR EN8 ..... 319 F8
Isbourne Rd COLN CO4 ..... 188 C6
Ishams Cha WIT CM8 ..... 277 J6
Isis Dr UPMR RM14 ..... 432 B8
Island La FOS CO13 ..... 228 D4
Island Rd FOS CO13 ..... 228 D2
Ives Gdns ROM RM1 ..... 430 A6
Ivry St IP IP1 ..... 2 C2
Ivy Barns La ING CM4 ..... 358 A4
Ivybridge BROX EN10 ..... 319 G5
Ivy Chimneys Rd EPP CM16 ..... 350 C6
Ivy La K/T/MI CO5 ..... 287 F2
Ivy Lodge La HARH RM3... 431 K4
Ivy Lodge Rd RCOLW CO6 ..... 154 D5
Ivy Rd SBF/HAD SS7 ..... 439 K7
Ivy Todd Hl SAFWS CB11... 101 H5
Ixworth Rd HVHL CB9 ..... 26 E7

Jacaranda Cl CHLM/WR CM1... 305 H7
Jack Andrews Av COLN CO4... 155 J8
Jackdaw Cl BCAYE CM11 ..... 414 D5
  SBN/FI SS3 ..... 466 D5
Jack Evans Ct SOCK/AV RM15.. 469 J6
Jack Hatch Wy RCOLE CO7 ..... 220 D2
Jacks Cl WICKE SS11 ..... 417 J6
Jack's La RBSF CM22 ..... 202 A6
Jackson Cl EMPK RM11 ..... 431 C6
Jackson Pl CHLM/GWD CM2 ..... 333 F7
Jackson Rd COS CO15 ..... 10 B5
Jacksons Cl CHONG CM5 ..... 354 C3
Jacksons Dr EBAR EN7 ..... 346 A2
Jacksons La BCAYE CM11 ..... 414 C2
  SAFWN CB10 ..... 43 J2
Jacksons Ms BCAYE CM11 ..... 414 D3
Jackson's Sq SAFWN CB10 ..... 43 J2
Jack Stevens Cl HLWE CM17 ..... 295 F7
Jacobs Av HARH RM3 ..... 431 F4
Jacquard Wy BRTR CM7 ..... 209 K3
Jacqueline Gdns BCAYW CM12 ..... 414 C1
Jaggards Rd RCOLW CO6 ..... 213 H2
James Boden Cl FX IP11 ..... 5 E2
James Carter Rd COLW CO3 ..... 217 K2
James Cl GPK RM2 ..... 430 B7
  RCOLE CO7 ..... 221 F2
James Cft CHLM/GWD CM2 ..... 360 C3
James Gdns RCOS CO16 ..... 257 H6
Jameson Rd COS CO15 ..... 290 E2
James Rd COS CO15 ..... 290 E8
James St COL CO1 ..... 8 C5
  EPP CM16 ..... 350 D2
James Watt Wy ERITH DA8 ..... 480 A5
Janebrook Rd CHTY IP2 ..... 62 A3
Janette Av CVI SS8 ..... 477 J1
Janmead RBRW/HUT CM13 ..... 412 A3
  WIT CM8 ..... 277 C2
Janus Cl HVHL CB9 ..... 27 K7
Jardine Rd PIT SS13 ..... 439 F5
Jarmin Rd COL CO1 ..... 8 B7
Jarndyce CHLM/WR CM1 ..... 304 B3
Jarvis Fld RCHLM CM3 ..... 307 H6
Jarvis Rd CVI SS8 ..... 461 F7
  SBF/HAD SS7 ..... 480 B1
Jarvis Wy HARH RM3 ..... 431 F4
Jasmin Cl BSF CM23 ..... 198 B7
Jasmine Cl CHTY IP2 ..... 2 A6
  COLN CO4 ..... 9 E5
  FX IP11 ..... 94 C5
  VGE SS16 ..... 456 A7
Jasmine Wy COS CO15 ..... 290 C6
Jason Cl CDH/CHF RM16 ..... 472 E6
  CVI SS8 ..... 461 C8
Jasons Cl BRW CM14 ..... 410 C2
Jasper Cl PEND EN3 ..... 374 C4
Jay Cl HVHL CB9 ..... 27 J1
Jays La RCOLW CO6 ..... 215 J2
The Jays RCOLN CO4 ..... 187 J2
Jaywick La RCOS CO16 ..... 290 C3
Jaywick Rd HVHL CB9 ..... 27 C5
Jeans La BSF CM23 ..... 198 D6
Jefferies Rd IPNE IP4 ..... 3 F1
Jefferson Av LAIN SS15 ..... 436 B7
Jefferson Cl COLW CO3 ..... 185 K5
Jeffery Rd CHLM/GWD CM2 ..... 333 J6
Jeffery's Cl COLW CO3 ..... 186 A6
Jeffrey Cl COLW CO3 ..... 186 A6
Jeffrey's Rd BRTR CM7 ..... 210 C7
  PEND EN3 ..... 375 F2
Jekylls La BRTR CM7 ..... 106 E3

Jellicoe Av *GVE* DA12 .... **489** H8
Jellicoe Wy *BRTR* CM7 .... **210** B1 🔢
Jena Cl *SBN/FI* SS3 .... **466** D6
Jenkins Dr *BRTR* CM22 .... **168** D2
Jenkins La *BSF* CM23 .... **199** H8
Jenner Cl *BRTR* CM7 .... **209** J4 🔢
Jenner Md *CDH/CHF* CM2 .... **333** J2
Jenningham Dr *CDH/CHF* RM16 .... **470** E8
Jenningtree Rd *ERITH* DA8 .... **480** C6
Jericho Pl *INC* CM4 .... **356** C5
Jermayns *LAIN* SS15 .... **16** C4
Jermyns Cl *RIPS/CAP* IP9 .... **87** G3 🔢
Jerounds *HLWW/ROY* CM19 .... **12** B5
Jersey Gdns *SS11* **417** G5
Jersey Rd *MAL* CM9 .... **338** D4
    RAIN RM13 .... **450** B8
Jersey Wy *BRTR* CM7 .... **209** G3
Jervis Av *PEND* EN3 .... **374** E1
Jervis Cl *RIPS/CAP* IP9 .... **90** A8
Jervis Rd *BSF* CM23 .... **198** E7
Jesmond Rd *CDH/CHF* RM16 .... **471** H8
    CVI SS8 .... **478** B3
Jessel Dr *LOU* IG10 .... **378** A6
Jessica Cl *COLN* CO4 .... **188** C6 🔢
Jetty Wk *GRAYS* RM17 .... **483** K5 🔢
Jewell Vw *KESG* IP5 .... **39** H6
Jimmy's La *MCTR* CO11 .... **124** A3
Jocelyns *HLWE* CM17 .... **295** C3
Jodrell Wy *WTHK* RM20 .... **482** C4
Joes Rd *SUD* CO10 .... **59** H6
Johnby Cl *PEND* EN3 .... **374** E3 🔢
John Eliot Cl *WAB* EN9 .... **320** A4
John English Av *BRTR* CM7 .... **209** G1
John Harper St *COL* CO1 .... **8** A3 🔢
John Kent Av *COLS* CO2 .... **218** C3
John Raven Ct *K/T/MI* CO5 .... **247** F2
John Ray St *BRTR* CM7 .... **209** K2 🔢
Johnson Cl *BRTR* CM7 .... **209** K6 🔢
    CHTY IP2 .... **3** D6
    GVW DA11 .... **488** C8
    RCFD SS4 .... **422** A8
    WICKW SS12 .... **417** G8
Johnson Rd *CHLM/GWD* CM2 .... **333** H8
    RCOS CO16 .... **289** H1
Johnson's Dr *RCOLE* CO7 .... **189** H1
Johns Rd *BSF* CM23 .... **199** F4
The Johns *CHONG* CM5 .... **354** C1
Johnston Ct *COS* CO15 .... **260** C8 🔢
    HSTD CO9 .... **148** A5
Johnstone Rd *SOS* SS1 .... **465** K6
Johnston Rd *WFD* IG8 .... **403** H8 🔢
Johnston Wy *MAL* CM9 .... **338** C5 🔢
John St *GRAYS* RM17 .... **484** B5
    RCOLE CO7 .... **255** K7
    SBN/FI SS3 .... **467** F7
John Tibauld Ct *HVHL* CB9 .... **50** C7 🔢
Joiner's Ct *CBE/LIN* CB1 .... **22** D3
Joiner's Rd *CBE/LIN* CB1 .... **22** D3
Jollyboys La North *GTDUN* CM6 .... **206** D7
Jollyboys La South *GTDUN* CM6 .... **239** J1
Jones Cl *SOSN* SS2 .... **18** B1
Jonquil Wy *COLN* CO4 .... **186** C3
Joseph Gdns *WIT* CM8 .... **244** E1 🔢
Joslin La *PUR* RM19 .... **481** K4
Joslyn Cl *PEND* EN3 .... **375** C4
Josselin Cl *RCOLW* CO6 .... **149** J6
Josselin Ct *PIT* SS13 .... **439** F3 🔢
Josselin Rd *PIT* SS13 .... **439** F3
The Josselyns *FX* IP11 .... **94** D7
Jotmans La *SBF/HAD* SS7 .... **459** K2
Journeymans Wy *SOSN* SS2 .... **444** D8
Joyce Ct *WAB* EN9 .... **347** K8 🔢
Joyce Green La *DART* DA1 .... **480** E7
Joyce's Cha *MAL* CM9 .... **312** E5
Joyners Fld *HLWS* CM18 .... **322** A1
Joy Rd *GVE* DA12 .... **489** H6
Jubilee Av *CHLM/WR* CM1 .... **304** D3
    COS CO15 .... **259** G6
Jubilee Cl *FX* IP11 .... **94** D7
    HAR CO12 .... **164** D4
    HOC/HUL SS5 .... **421** F8
Jubilee Ct *GTDUN* CM6 .... **239** J1
    HSTD CO9 .... **110** D5 🔢
Jubilee Dr *GVE* DA12 .... **489** K7
Jubilee Dr *WICKW* SS12 .... **417** G5
Jubilee End *MCTR* CO11 .... **123** H8
Jubilee La *RCOLE* CO7 .... **189** F2
Jubilee Ri *CHLM* CM3 .... **335** K7
Jubilee Rd *BCAYE* CM11 .... **437** J1
    RAYL SS6 .... **441** K3
    SUD CO10 .... **58** C5
    WTHK RM20 .... **482** E5
Jubilee Wy *FOS* CO13 .... **228** E7
Julian Cl *COLN* CO4 .... **155** J7
Julian Cl *CHLM/WR* CM1 .... **304** D4
    HVHL CB9 .... **27** K6
Julien Court Rd *BRTR* CM7 .... **209** K1
Juliers Cl *CVI* SS8 .... **478** D2
Juliers Rd *CVI* SS8 .... **478** D2
Juliette Wy *PUR* RM19 .... **481** G1
Junction Rd *BRW* CM14 .... **411** F7
    RCHLM CM3 .... **366** C7
    ROM RM1 .... **430** A6
    VGE SS16 .... **458** E1
June Av *IP* IP1 .... **36** D3

Juniper Cl *BCAYE* CM11 .... **414** D1
    BROX EN10 .... **319** F7 🔢
    HSTD CO9 .... **147** J5
Juniper Ct *GTDUN* CM6 .... **204** A4 🔢
Juniper Crs *WIT* CM8 .... **277** G1
Juniper Dr *CHLM/GWD* CM2 .... **332** D7
    SOCK/AV RM15 .... **470** C3
Juniper Rd *COLW* CO3 .... **185** H8
    LOS SS9 .... **463** G4
    RCHLM CM3 .... **306** C5
Juniper Wy *COLN* CO4 .... **9** F3
    HARH RM3 .... **431** F3
Jupes Hl *RCOLE* CO7 .... **122** B8
    RCOLW CO6 .... **151** G3
Jupiter Cl *HVHL* CB9 .... **27** J7 🔢
Jupiter Rd *IPNE* IP4 .... **37** K6
Jury St *GVE* DA12 .... **489** G4 🔢
Justinian Cl *HVHL* CB9 .... **27** K6
Jute La *PEND* EN3 .... **374** E6
Juvina Cl *WIT* CM8 .... **277** F6 🔢

K

Kale Cft *COLW* CO3 .... **185** J8
Kale Rd *SBF/HAD* SS7 .... **460** D1
Kamerwyk Av *CVI* SS8 .... **478** C1
Kandlewood *RBRW/HUT* CM13, ... **412** A3
Karen Cl *BRWN* CM15 .... **411** F5
    IP IP1 .... **36** D4
    SBF/HAD SS7 .... **460** C5
    SLH/COR SS17 .... **473** J4 🔢
    WICKW SS12 .... **417** F7
Karina Cl *CHIG* IG7 .... **405** H8
Kate's La *SAFWN* CB10 .... **47** F5
Katherine Cl *RAYL* SS6 .... **442** B4
Katherine Rd *PIT* SS13 .... **439** H6
Kathleen Cl *SLH/COR* SS17 .... **473** K1
Kathleen Dr *LOS* SS9 .... **463** G3
Kathleen Ferrier Crs *LAIN* SS15 .... **16** A2
Katonia Av *RCHLM* CM3 .... **368** D4
Kavanaghs Rd *BRW* CM14 .... **410** D6
Kavanaghs Ter *BRW* CM14 .... **410** E6
Kay Cl *RCHLM* CM3 .... **241** J5
Keable Rd *RCOLW* CO6 .... **215** H2
Keating Cl *MCTR* CO11 .... **159** G1 🔢
Keats Av *BRTR* CM7 .... **209** J5
    HARH RM3 .... **430** C2
Keats Cl *MAL* CM9 .... **338** C5
Keats Crs *IP* IP1 .... **36** B2 🔢
Keats Gdns *TIL* RM18 .... **485** C8
Keats Rd *COLW* CO3 .... **186** A7
Keats Wk *RBRW/HUT* CM13, ... **412** C3
Keats Wy *WICKW* SS12 .... **417** F5
Keble Cl *COLW* CO3 .... **186** E7 🔢
Kecksy's *SBW* CM21 .... **263** K1
Kedington Hl *SUD* CO10 .... **84** E3
Keeble Cl *K/T/MI* CO5 .... **248** C8
Keeble Ct *RCOLE* CO7 .... **223** K6
Keeble Pk *MAL* CM9 .... **338** B5
Keeble Wy *BRTR* CM7 .... **209** K2
Keegan Pl *CVI* SS8 .... **478** C1 🔢
Keelars La *RCOLE* CO7 .... **221** H3
Keelers Wy *RCOLW* CO6 .... **154** C6
Keelings La *BOC* CM8 .... **372** A5
Keelings Rd *BOC* CM8 .... **371** K5
Keene Wy *CHLM/GWD* CM2 .... **360** D2
Keepers Gn *COLN* CO4 .... **186** C2
Keeper's La *FX* IP11 .... **94** B8
Keer Av *CVI* SS8 .... **478** D3
Keighley Ms *SBN/FI* SS3 .... **466** C5
Keith Av *WICKE* SS11 .... **417** G4
Keith Cl *COS* CO15 .... **259** K5
Keith Wy *EMPK* RM11 .... **451** F1
    SOSN SS2 .... **444** B8
Kellington Rd *CVI* SS8 .... **461** H8 🔢
Kelly Rd *CHTY* IP2 .... **36** A8
    PIT SS13 .... **439** H7
Kelman Ct *BAR* EN8 .... **346** D5 🔢
Kelso Rd *RCOLW* CO6 .... **154** D7
Kelvedon Cl *CHLM/WR* CM1 .... **304** D2
    RAYL SS6 .... **441** F2 🔢
    RBRW/HUT CM13, ... **412** D2
Kelvedon Dr *IPNE* IP4 .... **38** D8
Kelvedon Gn *BRWN* CM15 .... **383** H3
Kelvedon Hall La *BRW* CM14 .... **354** E8
    BRW CM14, ... **382** D2
    K/T/MI CO5 .... **247** F8
Kelvedon Rd *BCAYE* CM11 .... **414** D3 🔢
    K/T/MI CO5 .... **247** K6
    MAL CM9 .... **281** G7
    RCOLW CO6 .... **213** H5
    WIT CM8 .... **278** B3
Kelvin Rd *IP* IP1 .... **36** B4
    SBF/HAD SS7 .... **440** C4
    TIL RM18 .... **485** F8
Kelvinside *SLH/COR* SS17 .... **457** F8
Kemball St *IPNE* IP4 .... **37** J8
Kembles *RAYL* SS6 .... **419** K8
Kempe Rd *BRTR* CM7 .... **106** E7
    EN EN1 .... **374** B2
Kempson Dr *SUD* CO10 .... **59** F8

The Kempsters *FX* IP11 .... **94** E8 🔢
Kempton Av *HCH* RM12 .... **451** G5
Kempton Cl *IP* IP1 .... **36** C2
    SBF/HAD SS7 .... **441** G5
Kempton Pk *RCOS* CO16 .... **225** J8
Kempton Rd *IP* IP1 .... **36** C2
Kemsley Rd *FX* IP11 .... **5** F2
    RCOLW CO6 .... **149** H7
Kendal Av *EPP* CM16 .... **350** E4
Kendal Cl *HOC/HUL* SS5 .... **419** K4
    RAYL SS6 .... **441** K3
    WFD IG8 .... **403** G5
Kendal Ct *WICKE* SS11 .... **417** K8
Kendal Cft *HCH* RM12 .... **450** B6
Kendale *CDH/CHF* RM16, ... **485** G2
Kendall Rd *COL* CO1 .... **8** C5
Kendal Wy *LOS* SS9 .... **443** F6
Kenhome *LOS* SS9 .... **463** F1
Kenilworth Av *HARH* RM3 .... **409** J8
Kenilworth Cl *BCAYW* CM12 .... **413** K3 🔢
Kenilworth Gdns *HCH* RM12 .... **450** D4
    LOU IG10 .... **404** C2
    RAYL SS6 .... **441** H2
    WOS/PRIT SS0 .... **463** H2
Kenilworth Gv *RCOS* CO16 .... **226** D3
Kenilworth Pl *LAIN* SS15 .... **16** C1 🔢
Kenilworth Rd *COS* CO15 .... **260** C7
Kenley Cl *WICKE* SS11 .... **417** K7
Kenley Gdns *HCH* RM12 .... **451** G3
Kenmore Cl *CVI* SS8 .... **478** E3 🔢
Kennedy Av *LAIN* SS15 .... **436** A7
Kennedy Cl *BAR* EN8 .... **346** E2
    IPNE IP4 .... **37** J7
    RAYL SS6 .... **442** B5
    SBF/HAD SS7 .... **440** A6
Kennel La *BCAYW* CM12 .... **414** C6
Kennels Rd *KIR/NAC* IP10 .... **65** J3
Kennet Cl *UPMR* RM14 .... **432** B8
Kenneth Gdns *SLH/COR* SS17 .... **457** G8 🔢
Kenneth Rd *PIT* SS13 .... **439** F6
    SBF/HAD SS7 .... **440** D8
Kennington Av *SBF/HAD* SS7 .... **440** B8
Kensington Gdns *BCAYW* CM12 .... **414** B1 🔢
Kensington Rd *BRWN* CM15 .... **410** D2
    IP IP1 .... **2** B1
    SOS SS1 .... **465** G5
Kent Av *CVI* SS8 .... **461** G8 🔢
    LOS SS9 .... **463** G3
Kent Cl *LAIN* SS15, ... **436** C7
    RCOLE CO7 .... **255** K6
Kent Crs *BSF* CM23 .... **231** J1
Kent Dr *HCH* RM12 .... **450** E5
Kent Elms Cl *SOSN* SS2 .... **443** G8
Kentford Rd *FX* IP11 .... **4** C3 🔢
Kent Gdns *BRTR* CM7 .... **210** A1
Kent Green Cl *HOC/HUL* SS5 .... **421** G8
The Kentings *BRTR* CM7 .... **209** H3 🔢
Kentmere Coln CO4 .... **188** B2
Kenton Wy *VGE* SS16 .... **436** A8
Kent Rd *GRAYS* RM17 .... **484** B5
    GVW DA11, ... **489** F6
Kent's Av *COS* CO15 .... **260** C7
Kents Farm La *CHLM/GWD* CM2 .... **389** C1
Kents Grass *MAL* CM9, ... **314** D3
Kents Hill Rd *SBF/HAD* SS7 .... **460** C2
Kents Hill Rd North *SBF/HAD* SS7 .... **440** C8
Kents La *EPP* CM16 .... **324** D3
Kents Yd *SAFWS* CB11 .... **70** A1 🔢
Kent Vw *SOCK/AV* RM15 .... **481** K1
Kent View *LOS* SS9 .... **463** H5
Kent View Rd *VGE* SS16 .... **438** C8
Kent Wy *RAYL* SS6 .... **442** B5
Kentwell Cl *IPNE* IP4 .... **64** D1
Kenway *SOSN* SS2 .... **19** D2
Kenwood Gdns *CBE/LIN* CB1 .... **23** G3
Kenwood Rd *SLH/COR* SS17 .... **474** D1
Kenworthy Rd *BRTR* CM7 .... **209** H3
Kenyon Dr *SUD* CO10 .... **59** J2
Kerby Ri *CHLM/GWD* CM2 .... **333** H3
Kerridge's Cut *MCTR* CO11 .... **160** B1 🔢
Kerril Cft *HLW* CM20 .... **12** A2
Kerry Av *PUR* RM19 .... **481** J4
Kerry Cl *UPMR* RM14 .... **452** C1
Kerry Ct *COL* CO1 .... **9** E4 🔢
Kerry Dr *UPMR* RM14 .... **452** C1
Kerry Rd *CDH/CHF* RM16 .... **471** H8
Kersbrooke Wy *SLH/COR* SS17 .... **457** J8
Kersey Av *SUD* CO10 .... **58** E7
Kersey Dr *RCOS* CO16 .... **258** D8
Kersey Gdns *HARH* RM3 .... **431** F2
Kersey Rd *FX* IP11 .... **5** D4
Kershaw Cl *CDH/CHF* RM16 .... **483** F2
    EMPK RM11, ... **450** E1
Kershaws Cl *WICKW* SS12 .... **417** F8
Kessler Av *BRTR* CM7 .... **108** A6 🔢
Kesteven Rd *CHTY* IP2 .... **2** B5
Kestrel Cl *BARK/HLT* IG6 .... **406** B7 🔢
    RAIN RM13 .... **450** C8 🔢
Kestrel Gdns *BSF* CM23 .... **198** B7
Kestrel Gv *RAYL* SS6 .... **441** G2
Kestrel Ri *HSTD* CO9 .... **148** A7
Kestrel Wy *CHTY* IP2 .... **61** K2
    WAB EN9 .... **348** C8

Kestrel Wy COS C015 ...... 10 C1
Keswick Av COS C015 ...... 11 F1
  EMPK RM11 ...... 450 E2
  HOC/HUL SS5 ...... 419 K3
Keswick Cl FX IP11 ...... 131 K1
  RAYL SS6 ...... 441 K3 🔲
Keswick Dr PEND EN3 ...... 374 C2
Ketleys CHLM/CWD CM2 ...... 560 E2
Ketleys Vw BRTR CM7 ...... 176 D6
Kettering Rd HARH RM3 ...... 374 D3
  PEND EN3 ...... 37 F4
Kettlebaston Wy IP IP11 ...... 37 F4 🔲
Kettlebury Wy CHONG CM5 ...... 354 B4
Kevin Cl BCAYE CM11 ...... 414 E6
Kew La FOS C013 ...... 260 E1
Keyes Cl SBN/FI SS3 ...... 466 D4
Keyes Wy BRTR CM7 ...... 210 B1
Keymer Av COLW C03 ...... 218 A1 🔲
Keynes Wy WFD IG8 ...... 164 E4
Keynsham Av WFD IG8 ...... 403 F7
Key Rd COS C015 ...... 10 B4
Keysers Rd BROX EN10 ...... 319 G4
Keysland SBF/HAD SS7 ...... 441 G6
Key St IPSE IP3 ...... 3 E4
Khartoum Rd IPNE IP4 ...... 37 H6 🔲
Kibcaps VGE SS16 ...... 17 D6 🔲
Kidder Rd BRTR CM7 ...... 208 C4
Kildermorie Cl COLN C04 ...... 188 A2
Kilmaine Rd HAR C012 ...... 164 E4
Kilmartin Wy HCH RM12 ...... 450 C6
Kilmington Cl RBRW/HUT CM13 ...... 412 A5
Kiln Barn Av COS C015 ...... 259 H6
Kiln Dr SUD C010 ...... 58 E7
Kilnfield CHONG CM5 ...... 354 B5 🔲
Kiln Fld FX IP11 ...... 5 D2 🔲
Kiln La HLWE CM17 ...... 295 H6
Kiln Rd EPP CM16 ...... 352 A1
  SBF/HAD SS7 ...... 461 F1 🔲
Kiln Wy GRAYS RM17 ...... 483 J4
Kilnwood Av HOC/HUL SS5 ...... 420 E8
Kilowan Cl VGE SS16 ...... 456 A1
Kilsmore La BAR EN8 ...... 346 D2
Kiltie Rd K/T/MI C05 ...... 248 C8
Kilworth Av BRWN CM15 ...... 411 K2
  SOS SS1 ...... 19 E4
Kimberley Cl BSF CM23 ...... 199 F8 🔲
Kimberley Rd CHING E4 ...... 403 F4
  COL C01 ...... 9 D5
  SBF/HAD SS7 ...... 460 B2
  SBN/FI SS3 ...... 446 D7
Kimberly Cl HAR C012 ...... 9 D5
Kimberly Dr LAIN SS15 ...... 437 G3
Kimpton Av BRWN CM15 ...... 410 E3
Kimpton's Cl CHONG CM5 ...... 326 B8 🔲
Kincaid Rd RCOS C016 ...... 289 G1
Kinfauns Av EMPK RM11 ...... 430 D8
Kingaby Gdns RAIN RM13 ...... 450 B8
King Alfred Rd HARH RM3 ...... 431 G4
King Arthur Ct BAR EN8 ...... 346 E5
King Charles Rd K/T/MI C05 ...... 285 F7
King Coel Rd COLW C03 ...... 185 J6
King Edward Av BOC CM0 ...... 398 B7
King Edward Dr CDH/CHF RM16 ...... 484 D2
  GRAYS RM17 ...... 484 D3
King Edward Quay COLS C02 ...... 9 F6
King Edward Rd BAR EN8 ...... 346 E7
  BRW CM14 ...... 411 F6 🔲
  IPSE IP3 ...... 63 K2
  LAIN SS15 ...... 436 C5
  ROM RM1 ...... 430 A8 🔲
King Edward's Rd PEND EN3 ...... 374 D8
  RCHLM CM3 ...... 392 E5 🔲
  SLH/COR SS17 ...... 473 K5
King Edward Vii Dr RIPS/CAP IP9 ...... 129 C5
King Edward Vi WIT CM8 ...... 276 C5
Kingfisher Av CHTY IP2 ...... 61 K2
Kingfisher Cl COLN C04 ...... 188 C5
  HVHL CB9 ...... 27 J5 🔲
  MAL CM9 ...... 310 E8
  RBRW/HUT CM13 ...... 411 K3
  SBN/FI SS3 ...... 466 D4
Kingfisher Crs RAYL SS6 ...... 441 G2 🔲
Kingfisher Dr SBF/HAD SS7 ...... 460 B3
Kingfisher Ga BRTR CM7 ...... 177 K8 🔲
Kingfisher Mdw UPMR RM14 ...... 452 C2
Kingfishers COS C015 ...... 10 C1
  VGE SS16 ...... 457 K1 🔲
Kingfisher Wy BSF CM23 ...... 199 F6
  K/T/MI C05 ...... 246 E3 🔲
King George Rd COLS C02 ...... 219 H1
  WAB EN9 ...... 347 J8 🔲
King George's Av HAR C012 ...... 6 C3
King George's Cl RAYL SS6 ...... 441 J4
King George's Rd BRWN CM15 ...... 410 E2
King George Vi Av TIL RM18 ...... 486 C3
King Harold Rd COLW C03 ...... 218 B1
King Henry's Dr RCFD SS4 ...... 441 K4
King Henry's Ms PEND EN3 ...... 375 G3 🔲
Kingley Cl WICKW SS12 ...... 416 E6
Kingley Dr WICKW SS12 ...... 416 E6
Kings Acre RCOLW C06 ...... 213 G4
Kings Av COS C015 ...... 11 F2

IPNE IP4 ...... 3 F4
  WFD IG8 ...... 403 K8
Kingsbridge Cl BRTR CM7 ...... 177 J5 🔲
Kingsbridge Rd BSF CM23 ...... 199 F5
  HARH RM3 ...... 431 F1 🔲
Kingsbury Rd FX IP11 ...... 411 F6
King's Cha BRW CM14 ...... 277 C8
  WIT CM8 ...... 477 C2
Kings Cl FX IP11 SS8 ...... 159 H1
  MGTR C011 ...... 441 K3
  RAYL SS6 ...... 289 C2
  RCOS C016 ...... 199 F5
Kings Ct BSF CM23 ...... 436 C4
Kings Crs LAIN SS15 ...... 398 C1
Kings Cft BOC CM0 ...... 295 C6
Kingsdon La HLWE CM17 ...... 439 F7
Kingsdown Ct PIT SS13 ...... 489 C8
Kings Dr GVE DA12 ...... 419 K8
Kings Farm RAYL SS6 ...... 37 F4
Kingsfield Av IP IP1 ...... 374 D1
Kingsfield Dr PEND EN3 ...... 374 D1 🔲
Kingsfield Wy PEND EN3 ...... 5 E4
Kings Fleet Rd FX IP11 ...... 533 K2
Kingsford Dr CHLM/CWD CM2 ...... 452 B1
Kings Gdns UPMR RM14 ...... 57 H5
Kingsgate Dr IPNE IP4 ...... 377 G7 🔲
King's Gn IGLO IG10 ...... 430 B7
Kings Gv ROM RM1 ...... 441 G5
Kingshawes SBF/HAD SS7 ...... 8 B5
Kings Head Ct COL C01 ...... 402 C3
Kings Head Hl CHING E4 ...... 7 E2
King's Head St HAR C012 ...... 28 C4
Kingsland HLWS CM18 ...... 12 C5
  RIPS/CAP IP9 ...... 128 D3
Kingsland Beach K/T/MI C05 ...... 284 E8 🔲
Kingsland Cl K/T/MI C05 ...... 284 E8 🔲
Kingsland Rd K/T/MI C05 ...... 284 E8
  SUD C010 ...... 35 H6
Kingsley Av BAR EN8 ...... 346 B3
Kingsley Cl IP IP1 ...... 36 C2
Kingsley Ct EMPK RM11 ...... 430 C8 🔲
Kingsley Crs SBF/HAD SS7 ...... 441 C5
Kingsley Gdns CHING E4 ...... 402 B8
  EMPK RM11 ...... 430 E6
Kingsley La SBF/HAD SS7 ...... 441 C5
Kingsley Rd LOU IG10 ...... 378 B7
  RBRW/HUT CM13 ...... 412 C3
Kingsley Wk CDH/CHF RM16 ...... 485 F5
Kings Lynn Dr HARH RM3 ...... 430 E1
Kingsman Dr CDH/CHF RM16 ...... 471 F7 🔲
  RCOS C016 ...... 258 E8
Kingsman Rd SLH/COR SS17 ...... 473 H4
Kingsmans Farm Rd HOC/HUL SS5 ...... 420 A1
Kingsmead BAR EN8 ...... 346 D2
Kings Md HSTD C09 ...... 113 H6
Kingsmead SBW CM21 ...... 263 J4
Kingsmead Cl HLWW/ROY CM19 ...... 292 D6
Kingsmead Ct ROM RM1 ...... 430 A8 🔲
Kings Meadow HVHL CB9 ...... 28 C3
  SUD C010 ...... 58 D7
Kings Meadow Rd COL C01 ...... 8 B5
Kingsmere SBF/HAD SS7 ...... 441 H8
Kingsmere K/T/MI C05 ...... 285 F7
Kings Ms RCOLE C07 ...... 221 F1
Kingsmoor Rd HLWW/ROY CM19 ...... 12 B6
Kings Pde COS C015 ...... 260 C8
Kings Pk SBF/HAD SS7 ...... 440 E8
Kings Pl BKHH IG9 ...... 403 K5 🔲
King's Quay St HAR C012 ...... 7 F2
  HAR C012 ...... 7 F2 🔲
King's Rd BOC CM0 ...... 346 E8
  BOC CM0 ...... 398 D2
  BOC CM0 ...... 425 G1
  BRTR CM7 ...... 177 H7 🔲
  BRW CM14 ...... 411 F6
  CHING E4 ...... 402 C3
  CHLM/WR CM1 ...... 14 A1
  COS C015 ...... 10 A6
  CVI SS8 ...... 477 C2
  HAR C012 ...... 6 C5
  HSTD C09 ...... 147 K4
  LAIN SS15 ...... 436 C4
  MAL CM9 ...... 279 H6
  RAYL SS6 ...... 441 K3
  ROM RM1 ...... 430 B7
  SBF/HAD SS7 ...... 460 D3
  WOS/PRIT SS0 ...... 463 J4
Kingsteignton SBN/FI SS3 ...... 466 B4
King Stephen Rd COL C01 ...... 9 D5
Kingston Av CHLM/CWD CM2 ...... 15 F2
  SBN/FI SS3 ...... 466 B3
Kingston Cha MAL CM9 ...... 310 B7
Kingston Crs GVW DA11 ...... 488 A4 🔲
Kingston Crs CHLM/CWD CM2 ...... 15 F2
Kingston Hl VGE SS16 ...... 456 E3
Kingston Rd IP IP1 ...... 2 A1
  ROM RM1 ...... 430 A6
Kingston Wy SBF/HAD SS7 ...... 440 D8
King St BSF CM23 ...... 198 E6
  CHONG CM5 ...... 355 K2
  FX IP11 ...... 5 E2

GVE DA12 ...... 489 G4
HSTD C09 ...... 110 E1 🔲
MAL CM9 ...... 338 C4
MGTR C011 ...... 160 D5
SLH/COR SS17 ...... 473 J4
Kings Wk MAL CM9 ...... 314 E4
Kings Wy BCAYE CM11 ...... 414 E7
  IPSE IP3 ...... 63 K3
  RCHLM CM3 ...... 392 C4
Kingsway HAR C012 ...... 7 E4
  HOC/HUL SS5 ...... 419 J4
  K/T/MI C05 ...... 248 A7
  WOS/PRIT SS0 ...... 465 H3
Kingsway Ms WOS/PRIT SS0 ...... 463 J3 🔲
Kingswood Cha LOS SS9 ...... 462 E2
Kingswood Cl BCAYE CM11 ...... 414 D2
Kingswood Ct BOC CM0 ...... 344 C2
Kingswood Crs RAYL SS6 ...... 441 G4
Kingswood Rd COLN C04 ...... 187 G1
  VGE SS16 ...... 437 K8
Kingwell Av COS C015 ...... 10 B2
Kinlett Cl COLN C04 ...... 187 J1
Kinloch Cha WIT CM8 ...... 277 F6 🔲
Kino Rd WOTN C014 ...... 229 J5 🔲
Kinross Rd IPNE IP4 ...... 37 K4
Kipling Av TIL RM18 ...... 485 G7
Kipling Cl CHLM/WR CM1 ...... 304 C8
Kipling Rd IP IP1 ...... 36 B2
Kipling Wy BRTR CM7 ...... 209 K5
Kirby Cl HARH RM3 ...... 409 H8
  IPNE IP4 ...... 37 J6
  LOU IG10 ...... 404 B3 🔲
Kirby Hall Rd HSTD C09 ...... 80 C8
Kirby Rd BSDN SS14 ...... 438 B7
  FOS C013 ...... 227 K8
  FOS C013 ...... 229 F5
  FOS C013 ...... 260 E1
Kirby St IPNE IP4 ...... 37 J6
Kirkbaye FOS C013 ...... 228 D7
Kirkham Av SLH/COR SS17 ...... 456 A6
Kirkham Cl CHTY IP2 ...... 62 C3
Kirkham Rd SLH/COR SS17 ...... 456 A6
Kirkham Shaw SLH/COR SS17 ...... 456 A5
Kirkhurst Cl RCOLE C07 ...... 256 A7 🔲
Kirkmans Rd CHLM/CWD CM2 ...... 361 F2
Kirk Pl CHLM/CWD CM2 ...... 333 H2 🔲
Kirkton Cl RIPS/CAP IP9 ...... 129 F4
Kirton Cl HCH RM12 ...... 450 D7
Kirton Rd KIR/NAC IP10 ...... 94 C3
Kitchener Rd IP IP1 ...... 2 A1
  RCHLM CM3 ...... 394 C4
Kitchener Wy RIPS/CAP IP9 ...... 129 F5
Kitchen Fld BRTR CM7 ...... 210 C2
Kitchen Hl SUD C010 ...... 57 J7
Kitkatts Rd CVI SS8 ...... 478 A2
Kitson Wy HLW CM20 ...... 12 C2 🔲
Kittiwake Cl CHTY IP2 ...... 62 A2
Kittiwake Dr MAL CM9 ...... 310 E8 🔲
Knapton Cl CHLM/WR CM1 ...... 305 F6
The Knares VGE SS16 ...... 16 C6 🔲
Knightbridge Wk BCAYW CM12 ...... 414 B2
Knighton Cl WFD IG8 ...... 403 F7
Knighton Dr WFD IG8 ...... 403 J7
Knighton La BKHH IG9 ...... 403 J5
Knights LAIN SS15 ...... 16 B3
Knightsbridge Cl COLS C02 ...... 218 D2 🔲
Knights Cl BSF CM23 ...... 198 A5
  K/T/MI C05 ...... 280 D2
  MGTR C011 ...... 159 H1
Knightsdale Rd IP IP1 ...... 36 C4
Knights La KESG IP5 ...... 39 H6
Knights Rd BRTR CM7 ...... 210 B4
  RCOLW C06 ...... 213 G3
Knight St RCHLM CM3 ...... 392 E6
  SBW CM21 ...... 263 J3
Knights Wk ABR/ST RM4 ...... 379 F7
Knights Wy GTDUN CM6 ...... 204 C4
  RBRW/HUT CM13 ...... 411 K7
Knightswick Rd CVI SS8 ...... 478 B9
Knivet Cl RAYL SS6 ...... 441 K4
Knole La SAFWS CB11 ...... 67 K6
Knollcroft SBN/FI SS3 ...... 466 C8
The Knoll AYW CM12 ...... 414 C7 🔲
  RAYL SS6 ...... 441 J3 🔲
Knowles Cl HSTD C09 ...... 147 K4
The Knowle VGE SS16 ...... 457 K1
Knox Cl MAL CM9 ...... 338 C5
Knox Ct WICKW SS12 ...... 417 J8 🔲
Knox Gdns COS C015 ...... 10 B2
Knox Rd COS C015 ...... 10 B2
Knutsford Cl RIPW IP8 ...... 61 J4
Kohima Rd COLS C02 ...... 218 C4
Kolburg Rd CVI SS8 ...... 478 D5 🔲
Kollum Rd CVI SS8 ...... 479 F2
Koln Cl CVI SS8 ...... 477 C2
Komberg Crs CVI SS8 ...... 461 H8
Konnybrook SBF/HAD SS7 ...... 461 F1 🔲
Korndyk Av CVI SS8 ...... 478 C4
Kreswell Gv HAR C012 ...... 6 C6
Kursaal Wy SOS SS1 ...... 19 F5
Kyme Rd ROM RM1 ...... 430 A8
Kynance Cl HARH RM3 ...... 408 D6
Kynaston Pl WIT CM8 ...... 277 H3 🔲
Kynaston Rd BRTR CM7 ...... 176 C5 🔲
Kynoch Ct SLH/COR SS17 ...... 474 A4

L

Laars Av CVI SS8 .... 478 C1
Laburnham CI UPMR RM14 .... 452 D1
Laburnham Gdns UPMR RM14 .... 452 C1
Laburnum RCHLM CM3 .... 308 A2
Laburnum Av HCH RM12 .... 450 B3
　WICKW SS12 .... 417 F7
Laburnum CI BAR EN8 .... 346 C8
　COS CO15 .... 290 E2
　HOC/HUL SS5 .... 420 D7
　IPSE IP3 .... 64 C3
　RCOLE CO7 .... 223 K5
　RIPW IP8 .... 61 J3
　WICKW SS12 .... 417 F6
Laburnum Crs FOS CO13 .... 228 C7
Laburnum Dr CHLM/GWD CM2 .... 332 D3
　SLH/COR SS17 .... 474 C2
Laburnum Gdns KESG IP5 .... 38 C4
Laburnum Gv COLN CO4 .... 188 B5
　CVI SS8 .... 477 C1
　GVW DA11 .... 488 C5
　HOC/HUL SS5 .... 420 C8
　SOCK/AV RM15 .... 470 B4
Laburnum Rd EPP CM16 .... 351 G3
Laburnum Wk HCH RM12 .... 450 D6
Laburnum Wy RAYL SS6 .... 419 G7
　RCOLW CO6 .... 118 A4
　WIT CM8 .... 277 C1
Labworth Rd CVI SS8 .... 478 C3
Lacey St IPNE IP4 .... 3 F3
Lackmore Rd EN EN1 .... 374 C1
Ladbrook Dr COLS CO2 .... 219 H2
Ladbrooke Rd RCOS CO16 .... 10 A1
Ladell CI COLW CO3 .... 217 K2
Ladram CI SOS SS1 .... 466 K5
Ladram Rd SOS SS1 .... 466 A5
Ladram Wy SOS SS1 .... 466 A5
Ladyfields LOU IG10 .... 377 K8
Lady La CHLM/GWD CM2 .... 14 C1
Ladyshot HLWE CM20 .... 294 E4
Ladysmith Av RCOLE CO7 .... 255 J6
Ladysmith Av LAIN SS15 .... 17 D1
Ladywell La CHLM/GWD CM2 .... 333 K8
Ladywell Prospect SBW CM21 .... 263 K4
Ladywood Rd IPNE IP4 .... 38 A6
Laindon Common Rd
　BCAYW CM12 .... 414 A8
Laindon Link LAIN SS15 .... 16 B4
Laindon Rd BCAYW CM12 .... 414 C8
Laindon West LAIN SS15 .... 435 K7
Laing Rd COLN CO4 .... 188 B7
Laird Av CDH/CHF RM16 .... 484 C1
Lake Av BCAYW CM12 .... 414 B2
　COS CO15 .... 290 E2
Lake Dr SBF/HAD SS7 .... 440 C8
Lakeland CI CHIG IG7 .... 406 A7
Lake Ri ROM RM1 .... 430 A5
　WTHK RM20 .... 482 D3
Lake Rd WAB EN9 .... 320 A3
Lakeside CI CHIG IG7 .... 405 J7
Lakeside Crs BRW CM14 .... 411 C6
　CVI SS8 .... 461 J8
Lakeside Rd BAR EN8 .... 346 C2
　CHTY IP2 .... 62 A3
Lakes Meadow RCOLW CO6 .... 213 H4
Lakes Rd BRTR CM7 .... 210 A3
Lakeview CVI SS8 .... 461 F8
Lake Vw VGE SS16 .... 456 A1
Lake Wk COS CO15 .... 290 E2
Lake Wy COS CO15 .... 290 B6
Lakforth SUD CO10 .... 35 F5
Lakin CI CHLM/GWD CM2 .... 333 J2
Lamarsh HI BURES CO8 .... 84 E6
　BURES CO8 .... 115 H4
Lamarsh Rd BURES CO8 .... 114 C3
Lamb CI TIL RM18 .... 485 H8
Lambert Cross SAFWN CB10 .... 71 F2
Lamberts La KESG IP5 .... 38 A3
Lambert's Rd RCOLW CO6 .... 182 C3
Lambeth Ms HOC/HUL SS5 .... 420 D7
Lambeth Rd LOS SS9 .... 443 F7
　SBF/HAD SS7 .... 440 B7
Lamb La HSTD CO9 .... 110 C6
Lambourne CVI SS8 .... 478 A3
Lambourne CI CHIG IG7 .... 406 A6
　COLW CO3 .... 217 J1
　COS CO15 .... 259 H5
Lambourne Crs BSDN SS14 .... 438 C8
　CHIG IG7 .... 406 A5
Lambourne Dr RBRW/HUT CM13 .... 412 D2
Lambourne Gdns CHING E4 .... 402 B5
　HCH RM12 .... 450 E3
Lambourne Gv MAL CM9 .... 338 B5
Lambourne Hall Rd RCFD SS4 .... 423 J4
Lambourne Rd CHIG IG7 .... 405 J7
　IP IP1 .... 36 D1
Lambourni CI SBN/FI SS3 .... 466 D3
Lambton Av BAR EN8 .... 346 D7
Lammasmead BROX EN10 .... 319 F5

Lammas Wy RCOLE CO7 .... 221 F2
Lamont CI WICKW SS12 .... 417 H8
Lamorna Av GVE DA12 .... 489 J8
Lampern Crs BCAYW CM12 .... 387 J7
Lampits HI SLH/COR SS17 .... 457 H7
Lampits Hill Av SLH/COR SS17 .... 457 H8
Lampits La SLH/COR SS17 .... 457 H8
Lamplighters CI WAB EN9 .... 348 C8
Lanark Rd IPNE IP4 .... 37 K4
Lancaster CI BRWN CM15 .... 410 D1
　LOU IG10 .... 404 B2
　VGE SS16 .... 436 A8
Lancaster Gdns RAYL SS6 .... 442 B5
　SOS SS1 .... 19 E4
Lancaster Gdns East COS CO15 .... 11 D3
Lancaster Gdns West COS CO15 .... 11 D4
Lancaster Rd EPP CM16 .... 324 A8
　IPNE IP4 .... 3 F5
　RAYL SS6 .... 442 B4
　SUD CO10 .... 58 A3
Lancaster Wy BRTR CM7 .... 209 H1
　BSF CM23 .... 198 A5
　RCOLW CO6 .... 181 G3
Lancer Wy BCAYW CM12 .... 414 A2
Lanchester Av COS CO15 .... 289 K7
Lancing Av IPNE IP4 .... 37 J5
Lancing Rd HARH RM3 .... 431 F2
Landau Wy BROX EN10 .... 319 F8
　ERITH DA8 .... 480 E4
Land CI RCOS CO16 .... 258 E8
Landermere BSDN SS14 .... 17 E3
Landermere Rd RCOS CO16 .... 226 D4
Lander Rd GRAYS RM17 .... 484 C1
Landguard Rd FX IP11 .... 131 F7
Landisdale RCHLM CM3 .... 336 A6
Land La COL CO1 .... 8 C4
Landmead Rd BAR EN8 .... 346 E3
Landsburg Rd CVI SS8 .... 461 J8
Landscape Vw SAFWS CB11 .... 70 E7
Landsdown Rd SUD CO10 .... 58 A4
Landseer CI HCH RM12 .... 450 C2
　IPSE IP3 .... 63 J4
Landseer Rd COLW CO3 .... 186 C8
　IPSE IP3 .... 63 G3
Landview Gdns CHONG CM5 .... 354 B4
Landwick La BOC CM0 .... 372 B6
Lane End HLWE CM17 .... 295 J6
Lanercost Wy CHTY IP2 .... 62 C4
Lane Rd RCOLW CO6 .... 150 E7
Lanes Av GVW DA11 .... 488 E8
The Lane K/T/MI CO5 .... 284 C5
　MGTR CO11 .... 160 A1
Langdale BRTR CM7 .... 209 F6
Langdale Dr COLN CO4 .... 187 J1
Langdale Gdns CHLM/GWD CM2 .... 15 D5
　HCH RM12 .... 450 B6
　PEND EN3 .... 374 D1
Langdon Br CHONG CM5 .... 354 D6
Langdon Rd RAYL SS6 .... 441 G8
Langdon Wy SLH/COR SS17 .... 457 J8
Langemore Wy BCAYE CM11 .... 414 C3
Langenhoe WICKW SS12 .... 417 H7
Langenhoe Hall La K/T/MI CO5 .... 252 D3
Langenhoe Rd K/T/MI CO5 .... 252 D3
Langer Rd FX IP11 .... 5 E5
Langfield CI WAB EN9 .... 320 A4
Langford Br CHONG CM5 .... 354 D6
Langford Crs SBF/HAD SS7 .... 440 E7
Langford Gn RBRW/HUT CM13 .... 412 B2
Langford Gv PIT SS13 .... 439 F5
Langford Rd MAL CM9 .... 310 B7
　WIT CM8 .... 309 J2
Langfords BKHH IG9 .... 404 A5
Langham CI EMPK RM11 .... 450 E1
Langham Crs BCAYW CM12 .... 414 C5
Langham Dr RAYL SS6 .... 441 F2
　RCOS CO16 .... 290 D1
Langham Gv COLN CO4 .... 155 H5
Langham Rd COLN CO4 .... 155 H5
Langland CI SLH/COR SS17 .... 474 C1
Langley Av BRTR CM7 .... 108 A5
　FX IP11 .... 5 E3
Langley CI HAR CO12 .... 7 D5
　HARH RM3 .... 430 E2
　LOS SS9 .... 442 C6
　SOS SS1 .... 19 F4
Langley Dr BRW CM14 .... 410 D6
Langley Hi BURES CO8 .... 115 F2
Langleys VGE SS16 .... 17 F6
Langport Dr WOS/PRIT SS0 .... 463 H1
Langside CI LAIN SS15 .... 436 C5
Langstons FX IP11 .... 94 E7
Langthorne Crs GRAYS RM17 .... 484 B3
Langton Av CHLM/WK CM1 .... 304 A8
Langton Wy CDH/CHF RM16 .... 485 H3
Langwood K/T/MI CO5 .... 284 E6
Lanham Green Rd BRTR CM7 .... 211 F6
Lanhams PIT SS13 .... 438 E5
Lansbury Rd EN EN1 .... 374 D5
Lansdown Av SBF/HAD SS7 .... 442 A7
Lansdowne Av LOS SS9 .... 460 A8
Lansdowne CI K/T/MI CO5 .... 248 A7
Lansdowne Dr RAYL SS6 .... 441 H2

Lansdowne Rd CHING E4 .... 402 B5
　FX IP11 .... 131 J1
　IPNE IP4 .... 37 J8
Lansdowne Sq GVW DA11 .... 488 E4
Lansdown Rd GVW DA11 .... 488 E6
　TIL RM18 .... 484 E8
Lanvalley Rd COLW CO3 .... 185 K7
La Plata Gv BRW CM14 .... 410 E6
Lappmark Rd CVI SS8 .... 478 D2
Lapwater CI LOS SS9 .... 462 D3
Lapwing CI ERITH DA8 .... 480 C6
Lapwing Dr K/T/MI CO5 .... 247 F3
　MAL CM9 .... 310 E8
Lapwing Rd CHTY IP2 .... 61 K2
　WICKE SS11 .... 417 F3
Larch CI COLN CO4 .... 9 F3
　LAIN SS15 .... 16 A1
Larchcroft CI IP IP1 .... 36 D3
Larchcroft Rd IP IP1 .... 36 C3
Larches Av EN EN1 .... 374 C1
The Larches RCHLM CM3 .... 306 C5
　SBF/HAD SS7 .... 440 A5
Larch Gv CHLM/GWD CM2 .... 332 C7
　RCOLW CO6 .... 118 A4
　WIT CM8 .... 245 C8
Larch Wk MAL CM9 .... 310 E7
Larch Wy GTDUN CM6 .... 203 K4
Larchwood BSF CM23 .... 198 C8
Larchwood CI LOS SS9 .... 442 C7
Larchwood Gdns BRWN CM15 .... 410 D2
Largent Gv KESG IP5 .... 39 J5
Larke Ri WOS/PRIT SS0 .... 464 A1
Larkfield SLH/COR SS17 .... 457 J8
Larkfield CI RCFD SS4 .... 444 A1
Larkfield Rd RCOLE CO7 .... 223 J4
Larkfields GVW DA11 .... 488 D8
Larkhill Av RCFD SS4 .... 422 D3
Lark Hill Rd RCFD SS4 .... 422 C4
Larkhill Wy FX IP11 .... 5 D2
Larkin CI RBRW/HUT CM13 .... 412 B3
Lark Ri SUD CO10 .... 58 A8
Larks CI HVHL CB9 .... 27 J6
Larksfield Crs HAR CO12 .... 6 C4
Larksfield Rd RIPS/CAP IP9 .... 125 H2
Larkshall Crs CHING E4 .... 402 D7
Larkshall Rd CHING E4 .... 402 D8
Lark's La RCHLM CM3 .... 272 B8
Larkspur CI BSF CM23 .... 198 C7
　SOCK/AV RM15 .... 470 A3
　WIT CM8 .... 276 E1
Larkspur Rd CHTY IP2 .... 2 A6
Larksway BSF CM23 .... 198 B7
　FX IP11 .... 5 D4
Larkswood HLWE CM17 .... 295 G7
Larkswood CI ERITH DA8 .... 480 B7
Larkswood Rd CHING E4 .... 402 B7
　SLH/COR SS17 .... 474 D1
Larkway FOS CO13 .... 228 D6
Larmans Rd PEND EN3 .... 374 D2
The Larneys FOS CO13 .... 228 D6
Larsen Dr WAB EN9 .... 347 K8
Larup Av CVI SS8 .... 461 H8
Lascelles CI BRWN CM15 .... 410 C1
Lascelles Gdns RCFD SS4 .... 421 K8
Latchetts Shaw VGE SS16 .... 17 F6
Latchford PI CHIG IG7 .... 406 A7
Latchingdon CI RAYL SS6 .... 441 F2
Latchingdon Rd RCHLM CM3 .... 366 B8
Latchmore Bank RBSF CM22 .... 232 B3
Lathcoates Crs CHLM/GWD CM2 .... 15 F5
Latimer Dr HCH RM12 .... 450 E4
　LAIN SS15 .... 436 C4
Lattice Av IPNE IP4 .... 38 A7
Latton Gn HLWS CM18 .... 322 D1
Latton Hall CI HLW CM20 .... 294 E4
Latton House HLWS CM18 .... 295 F8
Latton St HLW CM20 .... 295 F5
　HLWE CM17 .... 295 G8
Laud's CI FX IP11 .... 94 C7
Launceston CI COLS CO2 .... 219 J4
　HARH RM3 .... 430 D3
Launder's La RAIN RM13 .... 468 A5
Laundry La BRWN CM15 .... 385 H5
　WAB EN9 .... 320 B7
Laurel Av GVE DA12 .... 489 H7
　KESG IP5 .... 38 E6
　WICKW SS12 .... 417 F6
Laurel CI COS CO15 .... 259 K6
　HVHL CB9 .... 26 D4
　LOS SS9 .... 462 E5
　RBRW/HUT CM13 .... 412 A1
Laurel Dr GTDUN CM6 .... 204 A4
　SOCK/AV RM15 .... 470 B4
　SUD CO10 .... 34 E6
Laurel Gdns CHING E4 .... 402 C5
Laurel Gv CHLM/GWD CM2 .... 14 B5
Laurelhayes CHTY IP2 .... 2 B6
The Laurels RAYL SS6 .... 442 A5
　RCHLM CM3 .... 392 D5
Laurence Av WIT CM8 .... 277 G5
Laurence CI RCOLE CO7 .... 189 J7
Laurence Cft CHLM/WK CM1 .... 331 H4
Lavender Av BRWN CM15 .... 410 E1
Lavender CI BSF CM23 .... 198 C7
　HARH RM3 .... 430 E2

HLW CM20 .... 13 E2
K/T/MI CO5 .... 280 A1 🆂
SOCK/AV RM15 .... 470 C4 🆂
WIT CM8 .... 276 E1 🆂
Lavender Ct CHLM/WR CM1 ...... 305 H8 🆂
Lavender Dr BOC CM0 .... 398 C2
Lavender Gv WOS/PRIT SS0 .... 18 A1
Lavender Hl CHTY IP2 .... 2 A5
Lavender Ms WOS/PRIT SS0 ...... 464 A1
Lavender Wk COS CO15 .... 290 C6
Lavender Wy COLN CO4 .... 186 D5 🆂
WICKW SS12 .... 417 F6 🆂
Lavenham Cl RCOS CO16 .... 290 C1
Lavenham Rd CHTY IP2 .... 36 A8
SUD CO10 .... 35 J4
Lawford Cl HCH RM12 .... 450 D5 🆂
Lawling Av MAL CM9 .... 310 E8
Lawlinge Rd RCHLM CM3 .... 367 K8
Lawn Av SOSN SS2 .... 19 E2
Lawn Cha WIT CM8 .... 277 F4
Lawn La CHLM/WR CM1 .... 305 F7 🆂
Lawn Rd COL CO3 .... 488 B4
Lawns Cl K/T/MI CO5 .... 284 E6
Lawnscourt SBF/HAD SS7 .... 440 A6 🆂
Lawns Crs GRAYS RM17 .... 484 C5
The Lawns Dr BROX CM0 .... 319 F6 🆂
The Lawns CHING E4 .... 402 B8 🆂
CHLM/WR CM1 .... 305 F8
IPNE IP4 .... 38 A5
SBF/HAD SS7 .... 440 B6 🆂
Lawn Wy FX IP11 .... 5 E2
Lawrance Gdns BAR EN8 .... 346 D2
Lawrence Av SBW CM21 .... 263 J1
Lawrence Gdns TIL RM18 .... 485 G1
Lawrence Hl CHING E4 .... 402 B5
Lawrence Moorings SBW CM21 .. 263 K4
Lawrence Rd GPK RM2 .... 430 C7
PIT SS13 .... 439 J5
Laws Cl LAINS CB11 .... 70 E6
Law's Drift KIR/NAC IP10 .... 93 K1
Lawshall's HI RCOLW CO6 .... 150 A5
Lawson Rd PEND EN3 .... 374 C5
Lawton Rd LOU IG10 .... 377 K7
Laxton Gv FOS SS3 .... 227 K8
Laxton Rd RCOLE CO7 .... 222 A5
Laxtons SLH/COR SS17 .... 473 K2 🆂
The Laxtons RCFD SS4 .... 422 A8 🆂
Layer Breton Hl COLS CO2 .... 250 A4
Layer Rd COLS CO2 .... 218 C3
HVHL CB9 .... 26 E6
K/T/MI CO5 .... 252 A1
K/T/MI CO5 .... 282 D1
Layzell Cft SUD CO10 .... 85 F1
Leach Cl CHLM/GWD CM2 .... 333 K6
Leadale Av CHING E4 .... 402 B5
Leaden Ct GTDUN CM6 .... 268 A5
Leaforis Rd EBAR EN7 .... 346 A2
Leafy Wy RBRW/HUT CM13 .... 412 C4
Lea Gv BSF SS19 .... 199 G4
MAL CM9 .... 309 F4
Lea La WIT CM8 .... 278 B4
Leam Cl COLN CO4 .... 188 C6 🆂
Leamington Rd HARH RM3 .... 409 H8
HOC/HUL SS5 .... 221 G6
SOS SS1 .... 19 F4
Leapingwell Cl CHLM/GWD CM2 .. 333 J2 🆂
Lea Rd CDH/CHF RM16 .... 485 F4
SBF/HAD SS7 .... 440 B8
WAB EN9 .... 347 G8
Leas Cl WOS/PRIT SS0 .... 463 J5
Leas Gdns WOS/PRIT SS0 .... 463 J5
Lea Side K/T/MI CO5 .... 285 F7
Leaside SLH/COR SS17 .... 487 H1
Leas La COLS CO2 .... 217 H7
Leas Rd COLS CO2 .... 218 D4
COS CO15 .... 290 E3
The Leas BOC CM0 .... 398 C2
FOS SS3 .... 229 G7
ING CM4 .... 386 A3
UPMR RM14 .... 452 B3
WOS/PRIT SS0 .... 463 K6
The Leasway WOS/PRIT SS0 .... 463 J5
Leat Cl SBW CM21 .... 263 K2
Leathart Cl HCH RM12 .... 450 D8 🆂
Leatherbottle Hl ING CM4 .... 388 C2
Leather La EMPK RM11 .... 450 E2
HSTD CO9 .... 79 K4
HVHL CB9 .... 26 E6
Lea Valley Rd CHING E4 .... 402 A2
Lea Valley Wk CHING E4 .... 319 G8
Leaview WAB EN9 .... 347 H7
Lea Wy BCAYW CM12 .... 414 C5
Le Cateau Rd COLS CO2 .... 8 A5
Lechmere Av CHIG IG7 .... 405 F8
Leda Av PEND EN3 .... 374 D5
Lede Rd CVI SS8 .... 478 B1 🆂
Lee Chapel La VGE SS16 .... 456 D2
Leech's La COLN CO4 .... 186 E1

Leecon Wy RCFD SS4 .... 444 A2
Lee Gardens Av EMPK RM11 .... 451 H2 🆂
Lee Gv CHIG IG7 .... 404 C5
Lee Lotts SBN/FI SS3 .... 467 F1
Lee Rd HAR CO12 .... 7 D5
IPSE IP3 .... 63 H2
PIT SS13 .... 439 J7
Leeward Rd RCHLM CM3 .... 392 E8
The Leeway RCHLM CM3 .... 335 K6
Lee Woottens La VGE SS16 .... 17 E5 🆂
Leez La RCHLM CM3 .... 239 K4
Legg St CHLM/WR CM1 .... 14 C2
Legions Wy BSF CM23 .... 199 F5
Leicester Av RAYL SS6 .... 444 C5
Leicester Cl CHTY IP2 .... 62 B4
COL CO1 .... 8 C3
COS CO15 .... 290 A4
Leicester Ct WIT CM8 .... 244 D2 🆂
Leicester Rd TIL RM18 .... 484 E7 🆂
Leige Av CVI SS8 .... 461 F7 🆂
Leigham Court Dr LOS SS9 .... 463 C3
Leighams Rd RCHLM CM3 .... 363 J8
Leigh Beck La CVI SS8 .... 478 E3
Leigh Beck Rd CVI SS8 .... 479 F2
Leigh Cliff Rd LOS SS9 .... 463 G5
Leighcroft Gdns LOS SS9 .... 463 F1
Leigh Dr HARH RM3 .... 408 E7
RBSF CM22 .... 168 D4
WIT CM8 .... 277 K8
Leigh Fells PIT SS13 .... 439 F7
Leighfields SBF/HAD SS7 .... 441 C5
Leighfields Av LOS SS9 .... 442 E7
Leighfields Rd LOS SS9 .... 442 D7
Leigh Gdns LOS SS9 .... 462 D4
Leigh Hall Rd LOS SS9 .... 463 F4
Leigh Hts SBF/HAD SS7 .... 442 A2
Leigh Hl LOS SS9 .... 463 F5
Leigh Hill Cl LOS SS9 .... 463 F5
Leighlands Rd RCHLM CM3 ...... 392 D6
Leigh Park Cl LOS SS9 .... 462 E5
Leigh Park Rd LOS SS9 .... 462 E5
Leigh Rd CVI SS8 .... 478 B3
GVW DA11 .... 489 C7
LOS SS9 .... 463 C4
Leighs Rd RCHLM CM3 .... 273 C7
Leighton Av LOS SS9 .... 463 C3
Leighton Gdns TIL RM18 .... 485 F6
Leighton Rd IPSE IP3 .... 63 J5
SBF/HAD SS7 .... 440 B6
Leighton Sq IPSE IP3 .... 63 J5
Leigh View LOS SS9 .... 463 G1
Leighville Gv LOS SS9 .... 442 E8
Leighwood Av LOS SS9 .... 442 E8
Leinster Rd LAIN SS15 .... 16 A3
Leiston Rd HVHL CB9 .... 26 E6
Leith Park Rd GVW DA11 .... 489 C6
Leitrim Av SBN/FI SS3 .... 466 B7
Lekoe Rd CVI SS8 .... 460 E7 🆂
Lely Rd IPSE IP3 .... 63 H5
Lely Rd IPSE IP3 .... 37 J5
IPNE IP4 .... 37 J5
Les Bois COLS CO2 .... 218 B8
Leslie Cl LOS SS9 .... 442 E7
Leslie Dr LOS SS9 .... 442 E7
Leslie Gdns RAYL SS6 .... 442 A4
Leslie Pk BOC CM0 .... 64 A4
Leslie Rd IPSE IP3 .... 441 K7
RAYL SS6 .... 441 H5
Lesney Gdns RCFD SS4 .... 444 A2
Lethe Gv COLS CO2 .... 219 H5 🆂
Letton Cl RIPS/CAP IP9 .... 87 F4
Lettons Cha RCHLM CM3 .... 392 D7
Letzen Rd CVI SS8 .... 478 D4
Leven Cl BAR EN8 .... 346 D7 🆂
Leven Dr BAR EN8 .... 346 D7
Levens Wy BRTR CM7 .... 209 F7
Lever La RCFD SS4 .... 444 C4 🆂
Lever Sq CDH/CHF RM16 .... 485 F3
Leverton Wy WAB EN9 .... 347 J7
Leveson Rd CDH/CHF RM16 ...... 485 G2
Levett Rd SLH/COR SS17 .... 474 A3
Levington Rd FX IP11 .... 5 E6
IPSE IP3 .... 63 J1
KIR/NAC IP10 .... 92 B3
Lewes Cl GRAYS RM17 .... 483 K5
IPSE IP3 .... 64 C2
Lewes Rd HARH RM3 .... 408 E7
SOSN SS2 .... 19 F1

Lewes Wy SBF/HAD SS7 .... 441 C6
Lewin Pl RCHLM CM3 .... 306 C5
Lewis Cl BRWN CM15 .... 411 J3
Lewis Dr CHLM/GWD CM2 .... 332 D7
Lewis La RIPS/CAP IP9 .... 124 E3
Lewis Rd EMPK RM11 .... 430 D8
Lexden Ct COLW CO3 .... 186 D6
Lexden Gv COLW CO3 .... 186 A7
Lexden Ms COLW CO3 .... 186 A6
Lexden Rd COLW CO3 .... 186 B6
RCOLW CO6 .... 185 J1
Lexington Wy UPMR RM14 ...... 432 B8 🆂
Leybourne Dr CHLM/WR CM1 .. 305 F6
Leyburn Crs HARH RM3 .... 431 F2
Leyburn Rd HARH RM3 .... 431 F2
Leycroft Gdns ERITH DA8 .... 480 C7
Ley Fld RBSF CM22 .... 201 K6
RCOLW CO6 .... 215 H2
Leyfields BRTR CM7 .... 208 C4
Leyland Av PEND EN3 .... 374 E6
Leyland Cl BAR EN8 .... 346 C2 🆂
Leys Dr RCOS CO16 .... 258 E4
Leyside BRTR CM7 .... 208 B3
Leysings VGE SS16 .... 16 C6
Leys Rd RCOLE CO7 .... 221 F2
Leys Rd East PEND EN3 .... 374 E5 🆂
The Leys CHLM/GWD CM2 .... 305 H8
VGE SS16 .... 457 K1
The Ley BRTR CM7 .... 210 C4 🆂
Leyton Ct COS CO15 .... 259 H5
Leywood Cl BRTR CM7 .... 210 B3
Lichfield Cl CHLM/WR CM1 ...... 332 A1 🆂
COL CO1 .... 8 C5 🆂
Lichfield Rd WFD IG8 .... 403 F7
The Lichfields BSDN SS14 .... 438 C6
Lichfield Ter UPMR RM14 .... 452 C5 🆂
UPMR RM14 .... 452 B3 🆂
Lichfield Wy BROX EN10 .... 319 F4 🆂
Lidgate Ct FX IP11 .... 4 C3
Lifchild Cl WIT CM8 .... 277 C6 🆂
Lifstan Wy SOS SS1 .... 465 H5
Lilac Av CVI SS8 .... 461 H8
EN EN1 .... 374 C2
RCOS CO16 .... 289 H7
WICKW SS12 .... 417 F6
Lilac Cl BRWN CM15 .... 410 E1
CHLM/GWD CM2 .... 332 E7 🆂
EBAR EN7 .... 346 B5 🆂
Lilac Rd RCOLE CO7 .... 220 D3
Lilford Rd BCAYE CM11 .... 414 D1
Lilian Crs RBRW/HUT CM13 ...... 412 B5
Lilian Pl RAYL SS6 .... 442 B5
Lilian Rd BOC CM0 .... 398 C5
Lilley Cl BRW CM14 .... 410 C7
Lilley's La RCOLE CO7 .... 190 B1
The Lillies BRTR CM7 .... 178 A4
Lillyville Wk RAYL SS6 .... 442 B4 🆂
Lily Cl CHLM/WR CM1 .... 305 H7
Limbourne Dr MAL CM9 .... 310 E8
Limburg Rd CVI SS8 .... 477 H1
Lime Av COLN CO4 .... 9 F3
GVW DA11 .... 488 C5
HAR CO12 .... 6 C5
LOS SS9 .... 462 D3
RBRW/HUT CM13 .... 411 J6
UPMR RM14 .... 451 H5
Limebrook Wy MAL CM9 .... 338 C6
Lime Cl BKHH IG9 .... 404 A5
COS CO15 .... 290 E2
SOCK/AV RM15 .... 470 A3
WIT CM8 .... 245 G8
Limecroft Cl IP IP1 .... 36 C2 🆂
Limefields SAFWN CB10 .... 70 E1 🆂
Lime Gv BRWN CM15 .... 384 A4
SUD CO10 .... 51 K8
Limekiln La STSD CM24 .... 167 H7 🆂
Lime Pl LAIN SS15 .... 16 A1
Limerick Cl IP IP1 .... 36 A3
Limerick Gdns UPMR RM14 ...... 452 C1
Lime Rd SBF/HAD SS7 .... 460 D1 🆂
Limes Av CHIG IG7 .... 405 F8
Limes Crs BSF CM23 .... 199 F6
Limeslade Cl SLH/COR SS17 ..... 474 C1 🆂
Limes Rd BAR EN8 .... 346 D6
The Limes CHLM/GWD CM2 ..... 360 D5
HSTD CO9 .... 146 D6
ING CM4 .... 386 C1
KESG IP5 .... 38 B2
PUR RM19 .... 481 H4
RAYL SS6 .... 442 B4
RBRW/HUT CM13 .... 411 J6 🆂
RCOLE CO7 .... 157 J6 🆂
SUD CO10 .... 34 E6
Lime St RCOLE CO7 .... 255 K8 🆂
Limetree Av SBF/HAD SS7 .... 460 A1 🆂
Limetree Rd CVI SS8 .... 478 D1 🆂
Lime Wk CHLM/GWD CM2 .... 332 E3 🆂
Lime Wy BOC CM0 .... 398 A4
Lincefield VGE SS16 .... 456 C2 🆂
Lincoln Cl ERITH DA8 .... 480 A4
COS CO15 .... 289 K7
Lincoln Cha SOSN SS2 .... 465 H2
Lincoln Cl BSF CM23 .... 198 C8
EMPK RM11 .... 431 H1
IP IP1 .... 36 D2

Lincoln La *RCOLW* CO6 .... 154 D4
Lincoln Rd *BSDN* SS14.......................... 438 C6
  ERITH DA8 .... 480 A8
  RCFD SS4 .... 421 J7
Lincolns Fld *EPP* CM16 .... 350 D3
Lincolns La *BRW* CM14 .... 409 K2
Lincoln Ter *FX* IP11 .... 5 F4
Lincoln Wy *COL* CO1 .... 8 C4
  CVI SS8 .... 477 J1
  RAYL SS6 .... 419 H8
Linda Gdns *BCAYW* CM12 .... 413 K1
Lindbergh Rd *IPSE* IP3 .... 64 A4
Linden Av *EN* EN1 .... 374 A5 ⬓
Linden Cl *CHLM/GWD* CM2.................... 15 D6
  COLN CO4 .... 188 D4
  EBAR EN7 .... 346 B4 ⬓
  MGTR CO11 .... 159 C2
  PUR RM19 .... 481 K5
  RAYL SS6 .... 442 A4
  SBF/HAD SS7 .... 440 B8
Linden Dr *COS* CO15 .... 10 B1
Linden Gdns *EN* EN1 .... 374 A5
Linden Leas *SBF/HAD* SS7 .... 440 B7 ⬓
Linden Ri *BRW* CM14............................ 411 G8
Linden Rd *SBF/HAD* SS7 .... 440 B7
The Lindens *BRTR* CM7 .... 209 K4 ⬓
  BSF CM23 .... 198 E7
  ING CM4 .... 388 A3
  LOU IG10 .... 404 C1
  VGE SS16 .... 436 B8 ⬓
Linden Wy *CVI* SS8................................ 477 K1
Linde Rd *CVI* SS8.................................. 478 B1
Lindfield Rd *HARH* RM3........................ 409 F8
Lindhill Cl *PEND* EN3 .... 374 D6 ⬓
Lindhurst Dr *BCAYE* CM11 .... 415 K1
Lindisfarne Av *LOS* SS9...................... 463 H3
Lindisfarne Cl *CHTY* IP2 .... 62 C4 ⬓
  GVE DA12 .... 489 K7 ⬓
Lindon Dr *WICKE* SS11 .... 417 F5
Lindsay Pl *EBAR* EN7 .... 346 B4 ⬓
Lindsell Gn *BSDN* SS14 .... 438 B8 ⬓
Lindsell Rd *BSDN* SS14 .... 438 B8 ⬓
  GTDUN CM6.................................... 173 G2
Lindsey Av *SUD* CO10 .... 58 E7
Lindsey Cl *BRW* CM14 .... 410 D7
  BSF CM23 .... 198 E4
  IPNE IP4 .... 38 A6
  SBN/FI SS3 .... 467 G1
Lindsey St *EPP* CM16 .... 350 E3
Lindsey Wy *EMPK* RM11 .... 430 D7 ⬓
Linfold Cl *BRTR* CM7 .... 210 C1
Linford Cl *HLWW/ROY* CM19 .... 12 C5
Linford Dr *BSDN* SS14 .... 438 B8
Linford End *HLWW/ROY* CM19 .... 12 C5
Lingcroft *VGE* SS16 .... 457 H2
Lingfield Av *UPMR* RM14 .... 451 G4
Lingfield Dr *RCFD* SS4 .... 444 D2
Lingfield Rd *GVE* DA12 .... 489 C7
  IP IP1 .... 36 D1
Lingmere Cl *CHIG* IG7 .... 405 F5
Lingside *KESG* IP5 .... 39 F1
Ling's La *RIPS/CAP* IP9 .... 91 H7
Lingwood Cl *RCHLM* CM3.................... 335 J6
Link Cl *COLN* CO4 .... 187 F1
Linkdale *BCAYW* CM12 .... 414 C5
Link La *RIPS/CAP* IP9 .... 87 J2
Link Rd *BSF* CM23 .... 198 E5
  COS CO15...................................... 10 A5
  CVI SS8 .... 477 J1
  HSTD CO9 .... 147 J5
  RAYL SS6 .... 441 J2
  RCOLE CO7 .... 256 A7
  RIPS/CAP IP9.................................. 87 F4
  RIPS/CAP IP9.................................. 129 F4
  SLH/COR SS17 .... 473 K2
Links Av *FX* IP11 .... 131 H1
  GPK RM2 .... 430 C4
Links Dr *CHLM/GWD* CM2.................... 14 A6
Linksfield *KESG* IP5 .... 38 C6
Linksfield Gdns *KESG* IP5 .... 38 C6
Linkside *CHIG* IG7 .... 405 F8
Links Rd *BRTR* CM7 .... 211 H6
  RCOS CO16 .... 289 H7
  WFD IG8 .... 403 H8
The Links *BAR* EN8 .... 318 D8 ⬓
  BCAYW CM12.................................. 413 K1
Linksway *LOS* SS9.............................. 462 D1
Links Wy *SBF/HAD* SS7 .... 462 A2
The Link *PEND* EN3 .... 374 E5 ⬓
  RIPS/CAP IP9.................................. 87 J7
Linkway *BSDN* SS14 .... 17 F4 ⬓
Link Wy *BSF* CM23 .... 198 D7
  EMPK RM11.................................... 451 F2
Linkway Rd *BRW* CM14 .... 410 C6
Linley Cl *TIL* RM18 .... 486 E6
Linley Gdns *COS* CO15 .... 10 A5
Linnet Cl *SBN/FI* SS3 .... 466 D4
Linnet Dr *CHLM/GWD* CM2.................. 332 D2
  SBF/HAD SS7 .... 460 B3
Linnet Rd *CHTY* IP2 .... 61 K1 ⬓
Linnets *COS* CO15 .... 10 C1 ⬓
  VGE SS16 .... 457 H2

Linnett Cl *CHING* E4.............................. 402 D7
Linnetts La *HVHL* CB9 .... 51 H1
Linnet Wy *PUR* RM19 .... 481 J4
  RCOLE CO7 .... 223 J5
Linroping Av *CVI* SS8.......................... 479 F2
Linstead Cl *RCOS* CO16 .... 290 C1 ⬓
Linton Cl *SAFWS* CB11........................ 71 G5
Linton Rd *CBE/LIN* CB1........................ 22 D5
  CBE/LIN CB1.................................... 24 C7
  SBN/FI SS3 .... 466 D7
The Lintons *CHLM/GWD* CM2 .... 334 B7
Linwood *SBW* CM21 .... 263 J3 ⬓
Linwood Crs *EN* EN1............................ 374 A5
Lionel Cl *SUD* CO10 .... 59 F8
Lionel Rd *CVI* SS8................................ 478 A2
Lion Hl *SLH/COR* SS17 .... 475 F1
Lion La *BCAYW* CM12 .... 414 B5
Lion Meadow *RCOLE* CO7.................... 50 C6 ⬓
Liphook Cl *HCH* RM12 .... 450 A5 ⬓
Lippits Hl *VGE* SS16 .... 456 D2
Lippitts Hl *LOU* IG10 .... 376 A6
Lisa Cl *BCAYW* CM12 .... 387 H7
Lisle Pl *GRAYS* RM17 .... 483 K2
Lisle Cl *COLS* CO2 .... 8 C6
Lister Av *HARH* RM3............................ 430 E4
Lister Rd *BRTR* CM7 .... 209 J5
  IP IP1 .... 36 B4
  TIL RM18 .... 485 F8
Lister Tye *CHLM/GWD* CM2 .... 15 D6
Listonhall Cha *HSTD* CO9 .... 110 A8
Liston La *SUD* CO10.............................. 34 D6
Litchborough Pk *RCHLM* CM3............ 335 K5
Litchfield *HAR* CO12 .... 164 D3 ⬓
Litchfield Cl *COS* CO15 .... 10 B2
Litell Tweed *CHLM/GWD* CM2 .... 333 J2
Little & Great Sir Hughes La
  CHLM/GWD CM2.............................. 361 J3
Little Aston Rd *HARH* RM3.................. 431 G2
Little Baddow Rd *SAX* CM9.................. 336 C2
  RCHLM CM3.................................... 335 J6
Little Bakers *FOS* CO13 .... 229 F6 ⬓
Little Belhus *SOCK/AV* RM15 .... 469 J4
Little Bentley *BSDN* SS14 .... 17 F3
Little Bentley Rd *RCOLE* CO7 .... 192 C4
Little Berry La *VGE* SS16 .... 456 B1 ⬓
Little Braxted La *WIT* CM8.................. 277 J2
Little Brays *HLWS* CM18 .... 294 E7
Little Bromley Rd *RCOLE* CO7 .... 157 K6
  RCOLE CO7 .... 190 D2
Littlebrook Gdns *BAR* EN8.................. 346 D4
Little Brook Rd *HLWW/ROY* CM19 ...... 292 E5
Littlebury Ct *BRWN* CM15 .... 383 H3 ⬓
  PIT SS13.. 438 D5
Littlebury Gdns *COLS* CO2 .... 219 K1
Littlebury Gn *PIT* SS13 .... 438 D5
Littlebury Green Rd *SAFWS* CB11........ 69 H2
Little Cattins *HLWW/ROY* CM19 .... 321 H1
Little Chariton *PIT* SS13...................... 439 F7
Little Chittock *BSDN* SS14 .... 438 B7
Little Clacton Rd *FOS* CO13 .... 260 C3
  RCOS CO16.................................... 258 D6
Littlecotes *COLN* CO4 .... 186 E1
Littlecroft *RCHLM* CM3...................... 392 D7
Little Croft St *CHTY* IP2 .... 3 D6
Little Dorrit *CHLM/WR* CM1.................. 304 A6
Little Dragons *LOU* IG10 .... 377 F8
Little Elds *RCHLM* CM3 .... 336 A6
Little Friday Rd *CHING* E4 .... 403 F5 ⬓
Little Garth *PIT* SS13 .... 438 D8
Little Gaynes Gdns *UPMR* RM14........ 451 J5
Little Gaynes La *UPMR* RM14 .... 451 G5 ⬓
Little Gerpins Rd *UPMR* RM14............ 468 B1
Little Gipping St *IP* IP1 .... 2 C3 ⬓
Little Gregories La *EPP* CM16 .... 378 B1
Little Gv *RIPS/CAP* IP9 .... 87 F5
Little Grove Fld
  HLWW/ROY CM19 .... 12 C3 ⬓
Little Gulls *RIPS/CAP* IP9 .... 86 E4
Little Gypps Cl *CVI* SS8 .... 477 K1
Little Gypps Rd *CVI* SS8 .... 477 K2
Little Harrods *FOS* CO15...................... 229 F6
Little Hayes Cha *RCHLM* CM3 .... 393 J4
Little Hays *LOS* SS9 .... 442 C7
Little Heath *RBSF* CM22 .... 265 F2
Little Horkesley Rd *RCOLW* CO6 .... 152 E1
Littlehurst La *LAIN* SS15 .... 437 G3
Little Hyde Cl *HSTD* CO9 .... 79 K3 ⬓
Little Hyde La *ING* CM4 .... 358 B7
Little Hyde Rd *HSTD* CO9 .... 79 K3
Little Larchmount *SAFWS* CB11 .... 70 E5 ⬓
Little Laver Rd *CHONG* CM5................ 326 B2
  HLWE CM17.................................... 298 A3
Little London Hl *BRTR* CM7 .... 106 C5
Little London La *MAL* CM9 .... 308 C8
Little Lullabway *LAIN* SS15 .... 16 C3
Little Meadow *CHLM/WR* CM1 .... 331 C4
Little Mdw *MAL* CM9............................ 336 C7
Little Nell *CHLM/WR* CM1.................... 304 A6
Little Norsey Rd *BCAYW* CM12 .... 414 D1
Little Oaks *BSDN* SS14 .... 17 E4 ⬓
Little Oxcroft *LAIN* SS15 .... 16 A5 ⬓
Little Pluckett's Wy *BKHH* IG9............ 404 A4
Little Pynchons *HLWS* CM18 .... 13 F6
Little Russets *RBRW/HUT* CM13 .... 412 D3 ⬓

Little St Mary's *SUD* CO10 .... 34 E7
Little's Crs *CHTY* IP2 .... 3 D5
Little Searles *PIT* SS13 .... 438 E6
Little Spenders *BSDN* SS14 .... 438 A5
Little Stambridge Hall Rd
  RCFD SS4 .... 444 E3
Little Stile *CHLM/WR* CM1 .... 331 C5
Little Stone Ct *COS* CO15 .... 290 E5 ⬓
Little Tey Rd *K/T/MI* CO5 .... 214 C6
Little Thorpe *SOS* SS1.......................... 465 K4
Littlethorpe *VGE* SS16 .... 458 C1 ⬓
Littleton Av *CHING* E4 .... 403 G4 ⬓
Little Totham Rd *MAL* CM9 .... 312 A4
Little Tufts *RIPS/CAP* IP9 .... 87 C4
Little Wakering Hall La
  SBN/FI SS3..................................... 447 F8
Little Wakering Rd *SBN/FI* SS3 .... 446 D6
Little Walden Rd *SAFWN* CB10 .... 70 E1 ⬓
  SAFWN CB10 .... 70 E3 ⬓
Little Waltham Rd *CHLM/WR* CM1 .. 305 F4
Little Warley Hall La
  RBRW/HUT CM13............................ 433 H7
Little Wheatley Cha *RAYL* SS6 .... 441 F2
Little Wd *FOS* CO13 .... 228 D7
Little Yeldham Rd *HSTD* CO9.............. 80 A3
Llewellyn Cl *CHLM/GWD* CM2 .... 15 E1
Lloyd Rd *RIPS/CAP* IP9 .... 129 F5
The Lloyds *KESG* IP5 .... 39 G6
Lloyd Wise Cl *SOSN* SS2 .... 465 G2
Loamy Hill Rd *WIT* CM8 .... 279 H4
Lobelia Cl *CHLM/WR* CM1.................... 305 H7
Locarno Av *WICKE* SS11 .... 417 H4
Locarno Rd *IPSE* IP3 .... 63 K2
Locke Cl *RAIN* RM13 .... 450 A7 ⬓
  SLH/COR SS17................................ 473 J2
Lockfield Av *PEND* EN3 .... 374 E6
Lockhart Av *COLW* CO3 .... 186 D6
Lockram La *WIT* CM8 .... 277 C3 ⬓
Lock Rd *HSTD* CO9.............................. 147 K5
Locks Hl *RCFD* SS4 .... 444 C4 ⬓
Locksley Cl *SOSN* SS2 .... 465 J5
Lockyer Rd *PUR* RM19 .... 481 K4
Lodge Av *CHLM/GWD* CM2 .... 333 H6
  GPK RM2 .... 430 B7
Lodge Cl *CHIG* IG7 .... 405 K6
  COS CO15...................................... 10 B3
  RAYL SS6 .... 441 K4
  RBRW/HUT CM13 .... 412 D3
  SBF/HAD SS7 .... 441 F8
Lodge Ct *RCOLW* CO6 .... 186 A1
Lodge Crs *BAR* EN8............................ 346 E8 ⬓
  RCHLM CM3.................................... 306 C5
Lodge Farm Cl *LOS* SS9 .... 442 E8 ⬓
Lodge Farm Dr *FX* IP11 .... 131 K2
Lodge Farm La *RCOS* CO16 .... 289 K1
Lodge Farm Rd *SUD* CO10 .... 33 J2
Lodge Hall *HLWS* CM18...................... 322 C1
Lodgelands Cl *RAYL* SS6 .... 442 A4 ⬓
Lodge La *CDH/CHF* RM16.................... 483 K1
  COLN CO4 .... 156 A5
  GRAYS RM17 .... 484 B2
  K/T/MI CO5 .... 251 K5
  K/T/MI CO5 .... 252 E4
  RCHLM CM3.................................... 365 H3
  RCOLE CO7 .... 157 F7
  RCOLE CO7 .... 255 H6
  RCOS CO16.................................... 193 G7
  WAB EN9 .... 375 K1
Lodge Rd *BRTR* CM7 .... 209 J4
  CHLM/WR CM1................................ 331 F5
  EPP CM16 .... 349 J8
  HAR CO12 .... 164 B5
  K/T/MI CO5 .... 248 B2
  MAL CM9 .... 337 H6
  RCHLM CM3.................................... 363 J7
  RCHLM CM3.................................... 365 G1
  RCOLE CO7 .... 255 J5 ⬓
  RCOS CO16.................................... 226 C7
Lodwick *SBN/FI* SS3 .... 466 B8
Loewen Rd *CDH/CHF* RM16 .... 485 F2
Logan Cl *PEND* EN3............................ 374 D5 ⬓
Logan Link *WICKW* SS12 .... 417 J8
Loman Pth *SOCK/AV* RM15 .... 469 H6
Lombard Av *PEND* EN3 .... 374 C5
Lombards Cha
  RBRW/HUT CM13............................ 434 C8 ⬓
The Lombards *EMPK* RM11 .... 451 C1
Lombardy Rd *SUD* CO10 .... 58 A3
Lomond Cl *CHLM/GWD* CM2 .... 360 C3
  RAYL SS6 .... 441 H2
London Hl *ABR/ST* RM4...................... 378 E7
  ABR/ST RM4.................................. 380 C5
  ABR/ST RM4.................................. 381 F4
  BCAYE CM11 .... 416 B7
  BCAYW CM12.................................. 413 K3
  BRTR CM7 .... 209 C5
  BRW CM14...................................... 410 D6
  BSF CM23 .... 199 F8
  CHLM/GWD CM2.............................. 14 A6
  CHONG CM5 .... 353 K8
  CHTY IP2 .... 36 A8
  COLW CO3 .... 185 G7
  COS CO15...................................... 10 B2
  EPP CM16 .... 323 F4

GRAYS RM17 .... 483 H5
GVW DA11 .... 488 C4
HLWE CM17 .... 295 C2
IP IP1 .... 2 B3
K/T/MI CO5 .... 215 F5
MAL CM9 .... 337 H3
PIT SS13 .... 439 Q8
RAYL SS6 .... 441 C1
RCHLM CM3 .... 241 K3
RCOLW CO6 .... 153 K5
RCOLW CO6 .... 215 K2
RCOS CO16 .... 259 F5
RIPS/CAP IP9 .... 87 H2
RIPW IP8 .... 61 G4
SAFWN CB10 .... 43 H3
SAFWS CB11 .... 70 E5
SBF/HAD SS7 .... 439 K8
SBW CM21 .... 263 J3
SLH/COR SS17 .... 475 H4
SOCK/AV RM15 .... 481 H1
SOS SS1 .... 18 C4
TIL RM18 .... 485 Q8
VGE SS16 .... 458 A3
WICKE SS11 .... 418 C8
WOS/PRIT SS0 .... 18 A3
WTHK RM20 .... 483 C5

London Road Purfleet *PUR* RM19 ... 481 J5
London Road West Thurrock
WTHK RM20 .... 482 C5
Londons Cl *UPMR* RM14 .... 451 K6 ▣
Longacre *BSDN* SS14 .... 17 F4
CHLM/WR CM1 .... 331 K5
Long Acre *HLWE* CM17 .... 295 F1
Longacre *BRTR* CM7 .... 210 D7 ▣
Longacres *BRTR* CM7 .... 209 K4 ▣
Long Acres *K/T/MI* CO5 .... 214 C7
Longaford Wy *RBRW/HUT* CM13 .... 412 B4
Long Banks *HLWS* CM18 .... 13 D6
Long Border Rd *RBSF* CM22 ..... 201 F4
Longborough Cl *PIT* SS13 .... 438 D4 ▣
Long Brandocks *CHLM/WR* CM1 ... 331 F4
Long Common *MAL* CM9 .... 310 B8 ▣
Long Ct *PUR* RM19 .... 481 H5
Longcroft *FX* IP11 .... 5 E1
RBSF CM22 .... 201 K6
SAFWN CB10 .... 74 D5
Long Crft *STSD* CM24 .... 167 J5
Long Croft *BAR* EN8 .... 347 F8
Longcroft Ri *LOU* IG10 .... 404 E1 ▣
Longcroft Rd *COLN* CO4 .... 9 E5
Long Deacon Rd *CHING* E4 ...... 403 F4
Longfellow Dr *RBRW/HUT* CM13 .... 412 B3
Longfellow Rd *MAL* CM9 .... 338 C4
Long Fld *FX* IP11 .... 5 D1
Longfield *HLWS* CM18 .... 294 E7
LOU IG10 .... 403 K1 ▣
WIT CM8 .... 244 E8 ▣
Longfield Av *EMPK* RM11 .... 450 A1
PEND EN3 .... 374 C3
Longfield Cl *WICKE* SS11 .... 417 K6
Longfield La *EBAR* EN7 .... 346 B2
Longfield Rd *CHLM/WR* CM2 ..... 15 F6
RCHLM CM3 .... 392 D5
RIPS/CAP IP9 .... 87 F5
WICKE SS11 .... 417 K6
Long Flds *CHONG* CM5 .... 354 C4
Longfields *RCOS* CO16 .... 289 H1
Long Gn *BRTR* CM7 .... 210 D5
CHIG IG7 .... 405 H7
Long Green La *BRTR* CM7 .... 174 D3
Long Gv *HAR* RM3 .... 431 F4
Longhams Dr *RCHLM* CM3 .... 392 D5 ▣
Longhedges *SAFWS* CB11 .... 71 F4 ▣
Longhouse Rd *CDH/CHF* RM16 .... 485 C2
Longlands Cl *BAR* EN8 .... 346 D6 ▣
Long La *BRTR* CM7 .... 208 C5
CBE/LIN CB1 .... 22 E4
CDH/CHF RM16 .... 471 K8
FOS CO13 .... 261 C2
HOC/HUL SS5 .... 420 A1
SAFWS CB11 .... 68 E8
Longleaf Dr *BRTR* CM7 .... 209 J5
Longleat Cl *BRTR* CM7 .... 304 B6
Long Ley *HLW* CM20 .... 7 F3
Longmead Av *CHLM/GWD* CM2 ... 333 H5
Longmead Cl *BRWN* CM15 .... 411 H4
Long Meadow *BRTR* CM7 .... 208 E8
BSF CM23 .... 198 C7
RBRW/HUT CM13 .... 412 B5
Long Meadow Dr *WICKE* SS11 .... 417 H5
Longmeads *WIT* CM8 .... 278 A8
Longmeads Cl *CHLM/WR* CM1 .... 331 F4
Long Moor *BAR* EN8 .... 346 E3
Longmore Av *CHLM/GWD* CM2 .... 15 F5
Long Pastures *SUD* CO10 .... 33 J2
Long Perry *RIPS/CAP* IP9 .... 87 C4
Longreach Rd *ERITH* DA8 .... 480 C6
Longridge *COLN* CO4 .... 188 C5
Long Riding *BSDN* SS14 .... 17 F4
Long Ridings Av *RBRW/HUT* CM13. 412 A1
Longrise *BCAYW* CM12 .... 478 K2
Long Rd *CVI* SS8 .... 477 K2
MGTR CO11 .... 159 H2
Long Rd East *RCOLE* CO7 .... 157 K2

Long Rd West *RCOLE* CO7 .... 157 H2
Longsands *SBN/FI* SS3 .... 466 C6 ▣
Longshaw Rd *CHING* E4 .... 402 E6
Longship Wy *MAL* CM9 .... 338 A5
Longshots Cl *CHLM/WR* CM1 ..... 304 C5
Longs La *RCHLM* CM3 .... 273 H4
Longstomps Av *CHLM/GWD* CM2 . 332 C7
Longstraw Cl *COLW* CO3 .... 185 J7
Long St *WAB* EN9 .... 349 C4
Longtail *BCAYE* CM11 .... 387 J8
Longtown Rd *HARH* RM3 .... 408 D8
Longwick *VGE* SS16 .... 16 A6
Long Wd *HLWS* CM18 .... 322 B2
Longwood Cl *UPMR* RM14 .... 451 K6
Long Wyre St *COL* CO1 .... 8 B4 ▣
The Loning *PEND* EN3 .... 374 C4
Lonsdale Av *RBRW/HUT* CM13 .... 412 C2
Lonsdale Cl *IPNE* IP4 .... 37 H6
Lonsdale Rd *RCOS* CO16 .... 226 D5
SOSN SS2 .... 5 G2
Looe Rd *FX* IP11 .... 5 F1
Loompits Wy *SAFWS* CB11 .... 70 D6
Loop Rd *WAB* EN9 .... 347 H6
Lophams Cl *HVHL* CB9 .... 27 F4
Lord Holland Rd *COLS* CO2 ...... 219 C2
Lord Roberts Av *LOS* SS9 .... 463 C4
Lords Av *BSF* CM23 .... 198 A6
Lordship Cl *RBRW/HUT* CM13 .... 412 C4
Lordship Rd *CHLM/WR* CM1 ..... 331 H3
EBAR EN7 .... 346 B4
Lordsland La *BRTR* CM7 .... 179 H4
Lord St *CVE* DA12 .... 489 C5
Lordswood Rd *COLS* CO2 .... 218 D3
Lordswood Vw *CHLM/GWD* CM6 . 268 B6
Lorien Gdns *RCHLM* CM3 .... 392 C7
Lorkin's La *HSTD* CO9 .... 113 J2
Lorkin Wy *RCOLW* CO6 .... 186 A1
Lorne Rd *BRW* CM14 .... 411 F7
Lornes Cl *SOSN* SS2 .... 5 C2
Lorraine Cl *BCAYE* CM11 .... 414 E7 ▣
Lorrimore Cl *BCAYW* CM12 .... 387 F8 ▣
Lorton Cl *CVE* DA12 .... 489 K7
Loten Rd *SBF/HAD* SS7 .... 460 A3
Lottem Rd *CVI* SS8 .... 478 D3
Lott's Rd *RCOS* CO16 .... 258 D1
Loughton La *EPP* CM16 .... 378 B3
Loughton Wy *BKHH* IG9 .... 404 A4
Louisa Av *SBF/HAD* SS7 .... 440 A7
Louis Dr *RAYL* SS6 .... 441 F1
Louis Dr East *RAYL* SS6 .... 441 C2
Louis Dr West *RAYL* SS6 .... 441 F1
Louise Cl *WOTN* CO14 .... 229 K2
Louise Rd *RAYL* SS6 .... 441 K3
Louse La *RCOLE* CO7 .... 157 K2
Louvaine Av *WICKW* SS12 .... 416 E6
Louvain Rd *HAR* CO12 .... 165 F4
Lovelace Av *SOS* SS1 .... 465 C5
Lovelace Gdns *SOSN* SS2 .... 465 C4
Love La *CHONG* CM5 .... 354 C2
RAYL SS6 .... 441 H3
RCOLE CO7 .... 255 J5
SOCK/AV RM15 .... 481 K1
TIL RM18 .... 486 D1
Lovell Ri *LOS* SS9 .... 443 H7 ▣
Lovell Rd *EN* EN1 .... 374 B1
Lovell Wk *RAIN* RM13 .... 450 B7
Lovens Cl *CVI* SS8 .... 478 C3
Lover's La *RCOLE* CO7 .... 224 B6
RIPS/CAP IP9 .... 127 F1
Loves Wk *CHLM/WR* CM1 .... 331 H5
Lovet Rd *HLWW/ROY* CM19 ...... 12 A4
Love Wy *RCOS* CO16 .... 258 E7
Lowe Cha *WOTN* CO14 .... 229 K4
Lowe Cl *CHIG* IG7 .... 405 K8
Lowefields *RCOLW* CO6 .... 150 A8
Lower Anchor St *CHLM/GWD* CM2 . 14 B4
Lower Av *PIT* SS13 .... 439 H5
Lower Barn Rd *RIPW* IP8 .... 60 A4
Lower Bedfords Rd *ROM* RM1 .... 3 D4 ▣
Lower Brook St *IPNE* IP4 .... 3 C4 ▣
Lower Burnham Rd *RCHLM* CM3 .. 395 F3
Lower Bury La *EPP* CM16 .... 350 C5
Lower Cha *RCHLM* CM3 .... 396 D1
Lower Church Rd *SBF/HAD* SS7 .. 440 A7
Lower Cloister St *BCAYE* CM11 .. 414 C3 ▣
Lower Dales View Rd *IP* IP1 ..... 2 B1
Lower Downs Slade *HVHL* CB9 .... 27 C5
Lower Dunton Rd
RBRW/HUT CM13 .... 435 J7
Lower Farm Rd *COLN* CO4 .... 119 J5
Lower Gn *CHLM/GWD* CM2 .... 360 A4
RCOLW CO6 .... 151 F4
Lower Harlings *RIPS/CAP* IP9 ... 129 F5
Lower Holt St *RCOLW* CO6 .... 149 K7
Lower Houses Rd *RIPS/CAP* IP9 . 127 C2
Lower Island Wy *WAB* EN9 .... 375 H1
Lower King *BRTR* CM7 .... 210 C4
Lower Lambricks *RAYL* SS6 ...... 441 J1
Lower Langley *RCOLW* CO6 .... 183 F4
Lower Marine Pde *HAR* CO12 .... 7 D6
Lower Meadow *BAR* EN8 .... 346 D1
HLWS CM18 .... 322 C1
Lower Ml *GTDUN* CM6 .... 204 D6

Lower Noke Cl *BRW* CM14 .... 409 F5
Lower Orwell St *IPNE* IP24 .... 3 E4 ▣
Lower Park Crs *BSF* CM23 .... 198 E8
Lower Park Rd *LOU* IG10 .... 404 A1
RCOLE CO7 .... 255 J7
WICKW SS12 .... 439 F1
Lower Queen's Rd *BKHH* IG9 .... 404 B5
Lower Range Rd *GVE* DA12 ...... 489 K5
Lower Rd *BRWN* CM15 .... 385 H7
BURES CO8 .... 116 A8
COLS CO2 .... 217 F8
HOC/HUL SS5 .... 419 J4
K/T/MI CO5 .... 249 K4
K/T/MI CO5 .... 251 K8
KIR/NAC IP10 .... 91 H4
LOU IG10 .... 377 J5
RBSF CM22 .... 232 C6
SUD CO10 .... 33 H3
SUD CO10 .... 57 J2
TIL RM18 .... 489 F2
Lower Southend Rd *WICKE* SS11 . 417 C5
Lower Stock Rd *ING* CM4 .... 388 D4
Lower St *LAIN* SS15 .... 16 C1
RCOLE CO7 .... 121 F4
RIPS/CAP IP9 .... 125 H3
STSD CM24 .... 168 A6 ▣
SUD CO10 .... 32 D3
Lower Swaines *EPP* CM16 .... 350 C4
The Lowe *CHIG* IG7 .... 405 K8
Lowfield *SBW* CM21 .... 263 J4
Low Hall Cl *CHING* E4 .... 402 B3
Low Hill Rd *HLWW/ROY* CM19 ... 292 B7
Lowlands Rd *SOC/AV* RM15 ...... 468 E8
Low Rd *HAR* CO12 .... 164 E4
Lowry Cl *HVHL* CB9 .... 26 D4
Lowry Gdns *IPSE* IP3 .... 63 J5 ▣
Low Street La *TIL* RM18 .... 486 A4
Loxford *PIT* SS13 .... 438 D5
Luard Wy *COLS* CO2 .... 250 A2
WIT CM8 .... 277 F4
Lubbards Cl *RAYL* SS6 .... 419 J8
Lubberhedges La *GTDUN* CM6 ... 173 J2
Lucas Av *CHLM/GWD* CM2 .... 332 E7
RCOLW CO6 .... 152 C8
Lucas Rd *COLS* CO2 .... 8 B5
GRAYS RM17 .... 483 K2
SUD CO10 .... 58 C6
Lucas's La *RCOS* CO16 .... 194 A7
Lucerne Dr *WICKE* SS11 .... 417 K6
Lucerne Rd *RCOLE* CO7 .... 189 K7
Lucerne Wk *WICKE* SS11 .... 417 K6
Lucerne Wy *CHLM/WR* CM1 ..... 331 H5 ▣
HARH RM3 .... 430 E1
Luces La *HSTD* CO9 .... 110 E1 ▣
Luck's La *RCHLM* CM3 .... 272 B5
Luckyn La *BSDN* SS14 .... 17 D2
Luctons Av *BKHH* IG9 .... 403 K4
Lucy Cl *COLW* CO3 .... 185 H7
Lucy La North *COLW* CO3 .... 185 C6
Lucy La South *COLW* CO3 .... 185 H6
Lucy Rd *SOS* SS1 .... 19 E5
Ludgores La *RCHLM* CM3 .... 335 H8
Ludgrove *RCHLM* CM3 .... 367 J7
Ludham Hall La *BRTR* CM7 .... 209 C6
Ludlow Cl *IP* IP1 .... 36 D1
Ludlow Pl *GRAYS* RM17 .... 484 A2
Luff Wy *FOS* CO13 .... 228 E6
Lufkin Rd *COLN* CO4 .... 187 C2
Lugar Cl *COLN* CO4 .... 188 B7
Luker Rd *SOS* SS1 .... 19 D4
Lukin Crs *CHING* E4 .... 402 E6
Lukin's Dr *GTDUN* CM6 .... 204 C5
Lulworth Cl *COS* CO15 .... 290 E5 ▣
SLH/COR SS17 .... 473 H5
Lulworth Dr *CRW* RM5 .... 407 C8
HVHL CB9 .... 26 E5
Lumber Leys *FOS* CO13 .... 229 F6
Lummis V *KESG* IP5 .... 39 C6
Luncies Rd *BSDN* SS14 .... 438 B8
Lundy Cl *HVHL* CB9 .... 27 K6
SOSN SS2 .... 443 J6
Lunnish Hl *HAR* CO12 .... 163 J3
Lupin Dr *CHLM/WR* CM1 .... 305 H7
Lupin Rd *CHTY* IP2 .... 62 A1
Lupin Wy *RCOS* CO16 .... 290 E1
Luppits Cl *RBRW/HUT* CM13 ..... 411 K4
Lushes Ct *LOU* IG10 .... 404 E1
Lushes Rd *LOU* IG10 .... 404 E1 ▣
Lushington Av *FOS* CO13 .... 228 C7
Lushington Rd *MGTR* CO11 .... 159 H1
Lutea Cl *LAIN* SS15 .... 16 B1
Luther King Rd *HLW* CM20 .... 12 C3
Luther Rd *CHTY* IP2 .... 2 C5
Luthers Cl *BRWN* CM15 .... 383 C3
Lutus Cl *SUD* CO10 .... 30 E7
Luxborough La *CHIG* IG7 .... 404 C7
Luxford Rd *GRAYS* RM17 .... 263 K4
Lych Ga *LAIN* SS15 .... 16 A4 ▣
Lydford Rd *WOS/PRIT* SS0 .... 18 B5 ▣
Lydgate Cl *MGTR* CO11 .... 159 C1
Lydia Dr *RCOS* CO16 .... 288 A3
Lydia Rd *ERITH* DA8 .... 480 A5
Lyit Rd *CVI* SS8 .... 478 A2 ▣
Lyme Rd *SOSN* SS2 .... 19 F3

Lymington Av COS CO15 .... 259 H5
 LOS SS9 .... 463 F3
Lympstone Cl WOS/PRIT SS0 ...... 443 H8
Lynceley Gra EPP CM16 .... 350 E3
Lyndale BRWN CM15 .... 383 H3 ☐
Lyndale Av SOSN SS2 .... 19 E1
Lyndene SBF/HAD SS7 .... 440 A8
Lyndhurst Av IPNE IP4 .... 38 A7
Lyndhurst Dr EMPK RM11 .... 450 D2
 RCHLM CM3 .... 363 K4
Lyndhurst Ri CHIG IG7 .... 404 D7
Lyndhurst Rd COS CO15 .... 11 F3
 SLH/COR SS17 .... 474 B1
Lyndhurst Wy RBRW/HUT CM13.. 412 B4
Lynfords Av WICKE SS11 .... 417 J2
Lynfords Dr WICKE SS11 .... 417 J2
Lynmouth Av CHLM/GWD CM2 .... 15 D5
Lynmouth Gdns CHLM/GWD CM2.. 15 D4
Lynne Cl FOS CO13 .... 228 C7
Lynn's Hall Cl SUD CO10 .... 59 J2
Lynn View Cl SBF/HAD SS7 .... 440 B8
Lynross Cl HARH RM3 .... 431 F5
Lynstede BSDN SS14 .... 438 D8
Lynton Cl HAR CO12 .... 6 C4 ☐
Lynton Dr CHLM/WR CM1 .... 305 G8
Lynton Rd CHING E4 .... 402 C8
 GVW DA11 .... 489 F6
 SBF/HAD SS7 .... 461 H2
 SOS SS1 .... 465 J7
Lynton Rd South GVW DA11 .... 489 F6
Lynwood Av FX IP11 .... 131 J2
Lynwood Gn RAYL SS6 .... 442 B5
Lyon Cl CHLM/GWD CM2 .... 360 C2
 COS CO15 .... 11 D3
Lyon Rd ROM RM1 .... 450 A1
Lyons Hall Rd BRTR CM7 .... 178 C5
Lyster Av CHLM/GWD CM2 .... 333 J6
Lytchet Wy PEND EN3 .... 174 C5
Lytton Av PEND EN3 .... 374 E4
Lytton Rd CDH/CHF RM16 .... 485 F3
 GPK RM2 .... 430 C7

M

Mabbitt Wy COLN CO4 .... 155 J8 ☐
Maberly Ct SAFWN CB10 .... 70 E3 ☐
Mabey's Wk SBW CM21 .... 263 F4
Macaulay Rd IP IP11 .... 36 C2
 VGE SS16 .... 436 B8 ☐
Macbeth Cl COLN CO4.. .... 188 C6
Macdonald Av EMPK RM11 .... 431 F6
 WOS/PRIT SS0 .... 18 B2
Macdonald Wy EMPK RM11 .... 431 F6 ☐
Macer's La BROX EN10 .... 319 F6
Mace Wk CHLM/WR CM1 .... 14 A2
Macgregor Dr WICKW SS12 .... 417 H8
Macintyres Wk RCFD SS4 .... 421 K7
Mackay Cl COLS CO2 .... 219 J3 ☐
Mackenzie Cl WICKW SS12 .... 417 H7 ☐
Mackenzie Dr KESG IP5 .... 39 F5
Mackley Dr SLH/COR SS17 .... 457 G8
Maclarens WIT CM8 .... 278 C1
Maclaren Wy WICKW SS12 .... 417 H8
Macleod Cl GRAYS RM17 .... 484 C3 ☐
Macmurdo Cl LOS SS9 .... 442 E6
Macmurdo Rd LOS SS9 .... 442 F6
Macon Wy UPMR RM14 .... 432 C8
Maddox Rd HLW CM20 .... 13 E3
Madeira Av LOS SS9 .... 463 F3
Madeira Rd COS CO15 .... 260 B8
Madeline Pl CHLM/WR CM1 .... 304 A7
Madelis EPP CM16 .... 350 D5
Madgements Rd BRTR CM7 .... 179 H5
Madles La ING CM4 .... 388 B4
Madrid Av RAYL SS6 .... 419 F6
Magazine Farm Wy COLW CO3 .... 186 B8 ☐
Magazine Rd SBN/FI SS3 .... 466 D7
Magdalen Cl COS CO15 .... 10 B3
Magdalene Cl CHTY IP2 .... 62 B3
Magdalene Ct WIT CM8 .... 244 D2
Magdalen Gdns
 RBRW/HUT CM13 .... 412 D2 ☐
Magdalen Gn GTDUN CM6 .... 139 K3
Magdalen Rd COS CO15 .... 10 B3
Magdalen St COL CO1 .... 8 C5
Magenta Cl BCAYW CM12 .... 413 K2
Magingley Crs KESG IP5 .... 38 D7 ☐
Magna Md SBN/FI SS3 .... 466 C6
Magnaville Rd BSF CM23 .... 231 J1
Magnet Rd WTKH RM20 .... 483 F5
Magnolia Cl CHLM/GWD CM2 ...... 332 D7
 SOCK/AV RM15 .... 470 C4
 WIT CM8 .... 245 G8 ☐
Magnolia Dr COLN CO4.. .... 188 G5
Magnolia Rd HOC/HUL SS5 .... 421 J8
Magnolias BCAYE CM11 .... 414 D7 ☐
Magnolia Wy BRWN CM15 .... 410 E1
 RCFD SS4 .... 444 E5
Magpie Cl EN EN1 .... 374 A5
 RIPW IP8 .... 61 J3 ☐
Magpie La RBRW/HUT CM13 .... 433 G4

Magpies EPP CM16 .... 321 J6
Magwitch Cl CHLM/WR CM1 .... 304 B6
Mahonia Dr VGE SS16 .... 436 A8
Maida Av CHING E4 .... 402 C3
Maida Wy CHING E4 .... 402 C3
Maidenburgh St COL CO1 .... 8 B4 ☐
Maidenhall Ap CHTY IP2 .... 62 D3
Maidment Crs WIT CM8 .... 277 F5
Maidstone Rd FX IP11 .... 5 E2 ☐
 GRAYS RM17 .... 483 K5
Mailers La BSF CM23 .... 166 C3
Maine Crs RAYL SS6 .... 441 G1
Main Av BOC CM0 .... 342 C5
 CHLM/WR CM1 .... 304 D4
 FOS CO13 .... 260 E2
 GPK RM2 .... 430 D4
 HAR CO12 .... 6 C5
 HOC/HUL SS5 .... 420 E7
 KESG IP5 .... 38 E5
 KIR/NAC IP10 .... 65 K4
 RCHLM CM3 .... 334 C6
 RCHLM CM3 .... 390 E4
 RCHLM CM3 .... 391 F7
 RCHLM CM3 .... 391 G1
 RCHLM CM3 .... 392 B1
 RCOLW CO6 .... 152 C1
 RIPS/CAP IP9 .... 90 D3
 RIPS/CAP IP9 .... 91 H6
 ROM RM1 .... 430 A6
Main St BOC CM0 .... 342 C5
Maitland Dr SBN/FI SS3 .... 466 D4
Maitland Rd STSD CM24 .... 167 K7
 WICKW SS12 .... 417 H8
Maizey Ct BRWN CM15 .... 410 D1
Makemores BRTR CM7 .... 208 C3 ☐
Makins Rd HAR CO12 .... 6 A3
Malan Sq RAIN RM13 .... 450 C7
Maldon Ct SUD CO10 .... 58 E6
Maldon Rd BOC CM0 .... 343 J6
 BOC CM0 .... 397 J5
 COLS CO2 .... 217 F7
 COLW CO3 .... 186 D8
 ING CM4 .... 359 H5
 K/T/MI CO5 .... 246 E4
 K/T/MI CO5 .... 282 D3
 MAL CM9 .... 309 F5
 MAL CM9 .... 310 D1 ☐
 RCHLM CM3 .... 308 B1
 RCHLM CM3 .... 335 J6
 RCHLM CM3 .... 369 G5
 SOSN SS2 .... 19 D1
 WIT CM8 .... 277 F8
Maldon Wy RCOS CO16 .... 290 D1
Malgraves PIT SS13 .... 438 E6
Malgraves Pl PIT SS13 .... 438 E6
Mallard Cl BRTR CM7 .... 209 F8
 COLS CO2 .... 218 B8
 K/T/MI CO5 .... 246 E2 ☐
 MAL CM9 .... 314 D3
 UPMR RM14 .... 452 C1 ☐
Mallard Rd CHLM/GWD CM2 .... 332 C8
 RCHLM CM3 .... 368 E5
 SBN/FI SS3 .... 466 D4
Mallards Ri HLWE CM17 .... 295 G5
Mallard Wy CHTY IP2 .... 62 B3
 RBRW/HUT CM13 .... 411 K3
 SUD CO10 .... 59 F8
Mallinson Cl HCH RM12 .... 450 D6 ☐
Mallion Ct WAB EN9 .... 348 B7
Mallory Wy BCAYW CM12 .... 414 B4 ☐
Mallow Ct GRAYS RM17 .... 484 C5
Mallow Gdns BCAYW CM12 .... 387 F8
Mallowhayes Cl CHTY IP2 .... 2 C6 ☐
Mallows Fld HSTD CO9 .... 148 A4
Mallows Gn RBRW/HUT CM13 .... 411 K3
Mallows Green Rd BSF CM23 .... 166 B3
Mallows La HSTD CO9 .... 108 C2
The Mall HCH RM12 .... 450 C2
Malmesbury Dr CHIG IG7 .... 62 C3
Malmsmead SBN/FI SS3 .... 466 B5
Malpas Rd CDH/CHF RM16 .... 485 H2
Malta Rd TIL RM18 .... 484 E8
Maltby Dr EN EN1 .... 374 B4
Maltese Cl CHLM/WR CM1 .... 14 B1
Malthouse Rd MGTR CO11 .... 159 J1
Malting Farm La RCOLE CO7 .... 157 F3
Malting Green Rd COLS CO2 .... 218 A8
Malting La CDH/CHF RM16 .... 472 A4
 FOS CO13 .... 228 B4
 SUD CO10 .... 31 F6
Malting Rd COLS CO2 .... 218 D4
 K/T/MI CO5 .... 252 A6
Maltings Cha ING CM4 .... 386 B2
Maltings Cl BURES CO8 .... 115 H4
Maltings Ct WIT CM8 .... 277 F5 ☐
Maltings Hl CHONG CM5 .... 325 K2
Maltings La EPP CM16 .... 350 E3 ☐
 ROY SG8 .... 66 B3
 WIT CM8 .... 277 F5
Maltings Rd CHLM/GWD CM2 ...... 333 J8 ☐
 RCOLE CO7 .... 255 J5
 WICKE SS11 .... 418 D3
The Maltings BOC CM0 .... 398 E1
 BRTR CM7 .... 208 D3

 GTDUN CM6 .... 139 K3
 GTDUN CM6 .... 204 C4
 HAR CO12 .... 163 H5
 ROMW/RG RM7 .... 450 A1 ☐
Maltings Vw BRTR CM7 .... 209 K2 ☐
Malting Villas Rd RCFD SS4 .... 444 C3
Malting Yd RCOLE CO7 .... 220 E5 ☐
Maltings Park Rd RCOLW CO6...... 186 A1
Malvern Av CVI SS8 .... 477 H2
Malvern Cl IPSE IP3 .... 63 K1
 KESG IP5 .... 38 D6 ☐
 RAYL SS6 .... 441 J1
Malvern Dr WFD IG8 .... 403 K8
Malvern Gdns LOU IG10 .... 404 C2
Malvern Rd EMPK RM11 .... 430 B8
 GRAYS RM17 .... 484 D3
 HOC/HUL SS5 .... 421 G5
 PEND EN3 .... 374 E3
Malvern Wy RCOLW CO6 .... 154 C6
Malvina Av GVE DA12 .... 489 G7
Malwood Dr SBF/HAD SS7 .... 440 A8
Malwood Rd SBF/HAD SS7 .... 440 A8
Malyon Court Cl SBF/HAD SS7 .... 461 G1
Malyon Rd WIT CM8 .... 277 F5
Malyons PIT SS13 .... 438 E6
Malyons Cl PIT SS13 .... 438 E6
Malyons Gn PIT SS13 .... 438 E6
Malyons La HOC/HUL SS5 .... 419 J3
Malyons Ms PIT SS13 .... 438 E6
Malyons Pl PIT SS13 .... 438 E6
The Malyons SBF/HAD SS7 .... 461 G1
Manchester Dr LOS SS9 .... 462 E3
Manchester Rd CHTY IP2 .... 61 K3
 COS CO15 .... 260 C7
Mandeville Cl BROX EN10 .... 319 F2
Mandeville Rd PEND EN3 .... 374 E3
 RCOLW CO6 .... 215 H2
 SAFWS CB11 .... 70 E5
Mandeville Wy CHLM/WR CM1 .... 304 D2
 FOS CO13 .... 228 E6
 SBF/HAD SS7 .... 440 B6 ☐
 VGE SS16 .... 16 A5
Mandy Cl IPNE IP4 .... 37 J7
Manfield Gdns RCOS CO16 .... 257 H8
Manford Cl CHIG IG7 .... 406 A7
Manford Cross CHIG IG7 .... 405 K8
Manford Wy CHIG IG7 .... 405 K8
Mangapp Cha BOC CM0 .... 398 A5
Manilla Rd SOS SS1 .... 19 F5
Manly Dixon Dr PEND EN3 .... 374 E3
Mannall Wk KESG IP5 .... 39 J5
Mannering Gdns WOS/PRIT SS0 .. 463 J2
Manners Wy SOSN SS2 .... 444 B8
Manning Gv VGE SS16.................... 16 A6
Manning Rd FX IP11 .... 5 F4 ☐
Mannings Cl SAFWS CB11 .... 71 F6 ☐
Mannings La RIPS/CAP IP9 .... 90 D3
Manning St SOCK/AV RM15 .... 468 E8
Mannington Cl IPNE IP4 .... 38 D8 ☐
Manningtree Rd RCOLE CO7 .... 121 K7
 RCOLE CO7 .... 192 A5
 RIPS/CAP IP9 .... 125 F3
Mannock Dr LOU IG10.. .... 378 A6
Manns Wy RAYL SS6 .... 419 H8
Manor Av EMPK RM11 .... 430 D7
 PIT SS13 .... 439 F7
Manor Cl BCAYE CM11 .... 415 K2
 RAYL SS6 .... 441 J5
 RCOLW CO6 .... 154 D6
 ROM RM1 .... 430 B7
 SOCK/AV RM15 .... 468 E8
 SUD CO10 .... 32 C3 ☐
Manor Ct EN EN1 .... 374 B2
Manor Crs EMPK RM11 .... 430 D7
 RCHLM CM3 .... 272 D8
Manor Dr CHLM/GWD CM2 .... 333 H6
Manor Farm Dr CHING E4 .... 403 F6
Manor Farm Rd EN EN1 .... 374 B1
Manor Hatch HLWS CM18 .... 294 E6
Manor Hatch Cl HLWS CM18 .... 295 F6
Manor House Wy RCOLE CO7 ...... 255 J6
Manor La HAR CO12 .... 6 B6
 RIPS/CAP IP9 .... 125 F3
 SAFWN CB10 .... 43 J3
Manor Links BSF CM23 .... 199 H6
Manor Rd ABR/ST RM4 .... 406 C4
 BOC CM0 .... 371 K4
 BSF CM23 .... 199 F6
 CHIG IG7 .... 405 F8
 CHLM/GWD CM2.. .... 14 C5
 COLW CO3 .... 186 E6 ☐
 ERITH DA8 .... 480 A5
 FOS CO13 .... 260 E2
 FX IP11 .... 5 E6
 FX IP11 .... 94 C7
 GRAYS RM17 .... 484 B5
 GTDUN CM6 .... 171 J8
 GVE DA12 .... 489 G4 ☐☐
 HAR CO12 .... 6 B5
 HLWE CM17 .... 263 G8
 HOC/HUL SS5 .... 420 D7
 HVHL CB9 .... 27 H6
 IPNE IP4 .... 3 E1
 LAIN SS15 .... 436 C6
 LOU IG10 .... 376 D5

MAL CM9 .... 308 E8
RCHLM CM3 .... 308 C4
RCHLM CM3 .... 392 C5
RCOLE C07 .... 221 F4
RCOLW C06 .... 153 K8
SBF/HAD SS7 .... 430 B7
ROM RM1 .... 440 B7
SBF/HAD SS7 .... 473 K3
SLH/COR SS17 .... 167 K8
STSD CM24 .... 58 B4
SUD CO10 .... 347 K7
TIL RM18 .... 485 F8
WAB EN9 .... 277 G1
WIT CM8 .... 18 A5
WOS/PRIT SS0 .... 483 F5
WTHK RM20 ....

Manor St *BRTR* CM7 .... 209 J2
Manors Wy *WIT* CM8 .... 244 C5
Manor Ter *FX* IP11 .... 131 F7
Manor Wy *BRW* CM14 .... 410 D6
  CHING E4 .... 402 E2
  COS CO15 .... 260 E7
  GRAYS RM17 .... 484 B6
Manorway *WFD* IG8 .... 403 K8
The Manorway *SLH/COR* SS17 .... 473 J3
Mansard Cl *HCH* RM12 .... 450 B3
Manse Cha *MAL* CM9 .... 338 C4
Mansel Cl *LOS* SS9 .... 443 F7
Mansfield *SBW* CM21 .... 262 E4
Mansfield Av *IP* IP1 .... 36 B5
Mansfield Gdns *HCH* RM12 .... 450 E3
Mansfield Hl *CHING* E4 .... 402 C4
Mansfields *CHLM/WR* CM1 .... 331 F4
Mansted Gdns *RCFD* SS4 .... 422 A8
Manston Dr *BAR* EN8 .... 346 C4
Manston Dr *BSF* CM23 .... 199 G4
Manston Rd *HLW* CM20 .... 13 C3
Manston Wy *HCH* RM12 .... 450 C7
Manwick Rd *FX* IP11 .... 5 E5
Maple Av *BRTR* CM7 .... 209 J2
  BSF CM23 .... 198 C5
  LOS SS9 .... 463 G5
  MAL CM9 .... 310 E7
  UPMR RM14 .... 451 J4
Maple Cl *BARK/HLT* IG6 .... 405 H8
  BKHH IG9 .... 404 A6
  BSF CM23 .... 198 C5
  CBE/LIN CB1 .... 22 D2
  CHTY IP2 .... 2 B6
  HAR CO12 .... 6 C5
  HCH RM12 .... 450 C4
  HSTD CO9 .... 148 B3
  RBRW/HUT CM13 .... 411 J6
Maplecroft La *WAB* EN9 .... 320 A3
Mapledene Av *HOC/HUL* SS5 .... 419 K3
Maple Dr *CHLM/GWD* CM2 .... 332 D7
  FOS CO13 .... 228 C7
  RAYL SS6 .... 419 H6
  SOCK/AV RM15 .... 470 B4
  WIT CM8 .... 245 G8
Mapleford Sweep *VGE* SS16 .... 458 A4
Maple Ga *LOU* IG10 .... 377 J6
Maple Gv *BSF* CM23 .... 198 C5
Maple Hl *SUD* CO10 .... 30 B3
Maple Leaf *K/T/MI* CO5 .... 248 A6
Mapleleaf Cl *HOC/HUL* SS5 .... 421 G6
Mapleleaf Gdns *WICKW* SS12 ...... 416 E7
Maple Md *BCAYW* CM12 .... 414 D5
Maple Rd *GRAYS* RM17 .... 484 B5
  SUD CO10 .... 58 E8
Maplesfield *SBF/HAD* SS7 .... 461 J1
Maple Spring *BSF* CM23 .... 198 B5
Maple Springs *WAB* EN9 .... 348 C7
Maple Sq *SOSN* SS2 .... 19 E2
Maplestead *BSDN* SS14 .... 438 A5
The Maples *HLWW/ROY* CM19 ...... 321 K2
  KESG IP5 .... 38 C5
Mapleton Crs *PEND* EN3 .... 374 C4
Mapleton Rd *CHING* E4 .... 402 D6
  EN EN1 .... 374 B6
Mapletree La *ING* CM4 .... 357 K6
Maple Tree La *VGE* SS16 .... 436 A8
Maplin Cl *SBF/HAD* SS7 .... 440 B6
Maplin Gdns *BSDN* SS14 .... 438 D8
Maplin Wy *SOS* SS1 .... 466 B6
Maplin Wy North *SBN/FI* SS3 .... 466 B5
Marasca End *COLS* CO2 .... 219 J6
Maraschino Crs *COLS* CO2 .... 219 H6
Marchant Cl *HCH* RM12 .... 450 D4
March Pl *SUD* CO10 .... 31 F4
Marconi Rd *CHLM/WR* CM1 .... 14 C2
  GVW DA11 .... 488 C8
Marcos Rd *CVI* SS8 .... 478 D2
Marcus Av *SOS* SS1 .... 466 A7
Marcus Cha *SOS* SS1 .... 466 A6
Marcus Ct *COLN* CO4 .... 155 J7
  HVHL CB9 .... 27 K6
Marcus Gdns *SOS* SS1 .... 466 A6
Marden Ash *LAIN* SS15 .... 436 B7
Mardyke Rd *HLW* CM20 .... 294 E3
Marennes Crs *RCOLE* CO7 .... 255 J2
Mareth Rd *COLS* CO2 .... 218 D3

Margaret Av *BRWN* CM15 .... 411 J3
  CHING E4 .... 402 C2
Margaret Ct *GPK* RM2 .... 430 C7
  RCOLE CO7 .... 255 K7
  WAB EN9 .... 347 K7
Margaret Dr *EMPK* RM11 .... 451 G2
Margaret Rd *COL* CO1 .... 8 A3
  EPP CM16 .... 350 E3
  GPK RM2 .... 430 C7
Margaret St *FX* IP11 .... 5 E5
  GTDUN CM6 .... 139 J2
Margaretting Rd *CHLM/GWD* CM2 .. 360 C3
  CHLM/WR CM1 .... 331 C5
  ING CM4 .... 360 B4
Margarite Wy *WICKW* SS12 .... 416 E5
Margate Rd *BCAYW* CM12 .... 414 C3
Margeth Rd *BCAYW* CM12 .... 414 C3
Margherita Pl *WAB* EN9 .... 348 B8
Margraten Av *CVI* SS8 .... 478 D5
Marguerite Dr *LOS* SS9 .... 463 C4
Marguerite Wy *BSF* CM23 .... 198 B7
Mariam Gdns *HCH* RM12 .... 451 G3
Marian Cl *CDH/CHF* RM16 .... 470 C8
Maria St *HAR* CO12 .... 7 E3
Marigold Av *CHTY* IP2 .... 62 A2
  RCOS CO16 .... 258 E8
Marigold Cl *CHLM/WR* CM1 .... 305 H7
  COLN CO4 .... 188 B5
Marigold La *ING* CM4 .... 388 A5
Marigold Pl *HLWE* CM17 .... 295 F1
Marina Av *RAYL* SS6 .... 441 H2
Marina Cl *SOSN* SS2 .... 464 B1
Marina Dr *GVW* DA11 .... 488 E5
Marina Gdns *BAR* EN8 .... 346 C4
  COS CO15 .... 11 F2
  FX IP11 .... 5 E5
Marina Ms *WOTN* CO14 .... 229 H5
Marina Rd *RCHLM* CM3 .... 308 A1
Marine Ap *CVI* SS8 .... 478 B3
Marine Av *CVI* SS8 .... 478 B3
  LOS SS9 .... 462 E4
  WOS/PRIT SS0 .... 18 B5
Marine Cl *CDH/CHF* RM16 .... 485 C3
Marine Ct *PUR* RM19 .... 481 C3
Marine Pde *CVI* SS8 .... 479 F5
  FX IP11 .... 7 E5
  LOS SS9 .... 462 B4
  RCHLM CM3 .... 368 C4
  SOS SS1 .... 19 E5
Marine Pde East *COS* CO15 .... 11 D4
Mariners Ct *SBN/FI* SS3 .... 467 H2
Mariners Wy *MAL* CM9 .... 338 C5
Marion Av *RCOS* CO16 .... 10 B1
Marion Gv *WFD* IG8 .... 403 F8
Marisco Cl *CDH/CHF* RM16 .... 485 C3
Mariskals *PIT* SS13 .... 438 D8
Maritime Av *MAL* CM9 .... 339 G2
Marjorams Av *LOU* IG10 .... 377 J6
Mark Av *CHING* E4 .... 402 C2
Market Av *WICKW* SS12 .... 417 F5
Market Cl *COLW* CO5 .... 8 A3
Market Gv *HSTD* CO9 .... 148 B1
Market End *RCOLW* CO6 .... 79 J4
Market Gv *HSTD* CO9 .... 148 B1
Market Hl *HVHL* CB9 .... 27 C6
  MAL CM9 .... 338 C2
  RCOLW CO6 .... 213 H3
  SUD CO10 .... 58 B6
Market Pl *BRTR* CM7 .... 209 H7
  GTDUN CM6 .... 204 C3
  ING CM4 .... 386 B1
  SOS SS1 .... 19 D5
Market Rd *CHLM/WR* CM1 .... 14 C3
  WICKW SS12 .... 417 F6
Market Rw *SAFWN* CB10 .... 70 E4
Market Sq *BSDN* SS14 .... 17 E5
  BSF CM23 .... 198 E6
Market St *BSF* CM23 .... 198 E6
  HAR CO12 .... 7 F2
  HLWE CM17 .... 295 C1
  SAFWN CB10 .... 70 E3
Markfield Gdns *CHING* E4 .... 402 C3
Mark Hall Moors *HLW* CM20 .... 295 F2
Markhams *SLH/COR* SS17 .... 474 B2
Markhams Cha *LAIN* SS15 .... 16 B3
  LAIN SS15 .... 16 C3
Markhams Cl *HVHL* CB9 .... 27 F4
Marking's Fld *SAFWN* CB10 .... 71 F5
Markland Dr *MAL* CM9 .... 338 A3
Mark La *GVE* DA12 .... 489 K5
Marklay Dr *RCHLM* CM3 .... 392 C6
Mark Rd *BOC* CM0 .... 344 B7
Mark's Av *CHONG* SM5 .... 354 B1
Marks Cl *BCAYW* CM12 .... 413 K1
  ING CM4 .... 385 K7
Marks Gdns *BRTR* CM7 .... 210 B2
Marks Hall La *GTDUN* CM6 .... 300 C2
Marks Hall Rd *RCOLW* CO6 .... 181 G8
Marks La *RCHLM* CM3 .... 390 D5
Markwells *RBSF* CM22 .... 168 E3
Markwell Wd *EPP* CM16 .... 321 K3
Marlborough Av *BOC* CM0 .... 372 A2
Marlborough Cl *BSF* CM23 .... 198 E8
  CDH/CHF RM16 .... 484 B1

  COS CO15 .... 290 E2
  SBF/HAD SS7 .... 440 C6
  UPMR RM14 .... 452 B2
Marlborough Dr *SUD* CO10 .... 58 C5
Marlborough Gdns *UPMR* RM14 .. 452 B2
Marlborough Rd *BRTR* CM7 .... 209 K1
  BRWN CM15 .... 410 D2
  CHLM/GWD CM2 .... 14 B5
  IPNE IP4 .... 37 H8
  SOS SS1 .... 465 C5
Marlborough Wk *HOC/HUL* SS5 ... 420 D7
Marlborough Wy *BCAYW* CM12 .... 387 G8
Marie Gdns *WAB* EN9 .... 347 J6
Marlescroft Wy *LOU* IG10 .... 404 E1
Marlin Cl *SBF/HAD* SS7 .... 441 K7
Marlow Av *PUR* RM19 .... 481 H3
Marlowe Cl *BCAYW* CM12 .... 387 H8
  BRTR CM7 .... 209 K6
  MAL CM9 .... 338 C5
Marlowe Rd *COS* CO15 .... 290 C4
Marlowe Wy *COLW* CO3 .... 186 A6
Marlpits Rd *MAL* CM9 .... 364 E1
Marlyon Rd *BARK/HLT* IG6 .... 406 A8
Marmion Ap *CHING* E4 .... 402 B7
Marmion Av *CHING* E4 .... 402 A7
Marmion Cl *CHING* E4 .... 402 A7
Marne Rd *COLS* CO2 .... 219 F1
Marney Cl *CHLM/GWD* CM2 .... 15 F5
Marney Dr *BSDN* SS14 .... 438 C8
Marney Wy *FOS* CO13 .... 229 G7
Marquis Cl *BSF* CM23 .... 198 A6
Marram Cl *COLW* CO3 .... 185 G7
Marrilyne Av *PEND* EN3 .... 375 F4
Mar Rd *SOCK/AV* RM15 .... 470 A4
Marryat Rd *EN* EN1 .... 374 B7
Marshall Cl *K/T/MI* CO5 .... 247 F1
  KESG IP5 .... 39 C5
  LOS SS9 .... 462 B2
Marshalls *RCFD* SS4 .... 444 A1
Marshalls Cl *RAYL* SS6 .... 442 A3
Marshalls Piece *GTDUN* CM6 .... 173 J7
Marshalls Rd *BRTR* CM7 .... 209 H4
Marshbarns *BSF* CM23 .... 198 B5
Marsh Cl *BAR* EN8 .... 347 F7
Marsh Crs *K/T/MI* CO5 .... 220 C5
Marshcroft Dr *BAR* EN8 .... 346 E4
Marsh Farm La *RCOLE* CO7 .... 256 D3
Marsh Farm Rd *RCHLM* CM3 .... 392 D8
Marshfoot Rd *GRAYS* RM17 .... 484 E4
Marsh Hl *WAB* EN9 .... 348 A1
Marsh La *HLWE* CM17 .... 263 J8
  RBRW/HUT CM13 .... 386 A6
  SLH/COR SS17 .... 458 A7
Marsh Rd *BOC* CM0 .... 344 C8
  BOC CM0 .... 398 C4
  RCOLW CO6 .... 120 C7
Marsh St *DART* DA1 .... 481 H6
Marsh View *CE* VGE SS16 .... 458 B2
Marsh Wy *RCOLE* CO7 .... 255 J7
Marshy La *SUD* CO10 .... 54 B6
Marston Beck *CHLM/GWD* CM2 .... 333 J3
Martello Rd *WOTN* CO14 .... 229 H5
Martens Meadow *BRTR* CM7 .... 210 C2
Martin Cl *BCAYE* CM11 .... 414 C4
Martin End *COLS* CO2 .... 218 B8
Martindale Av *LAIN* SS15 .... 436 E3
Martingale Cl *SBF/HAD* SS7 .... 441 C8
Martingale Cl *BCAYE* CM11 .... 387 K8
Martingale Dr *CHLM/WR* CM1 .... 305 H6
Martingale Rd *BCAYE* CM11 .... 387 K8
Martin Rd *CHTY* IP2 .... 3 D5
  SOCK/AV RM15 .... 469 F8
Martins Cl *SLH/COR* SS17 .... 473 K2
Martinsdale *COS* CO15 .... 10 C1
Martins Dr *BAR* EN8 .... 346 E2
Martins La *CBE/LIN* CB1 .... 23 C3
Martins Ms *SBF/HAD* SS7 .... 460 B1
Martin's Rd *HSTD* CO9 .... 147 K4
  SUD CO10 .... 58 E4
Martin Wk *HOC/HUL* SS5 .... 445 C1
Martlesham Cl *HCH* RM12 .... 450 D6
Martlesham Rd *FRAM/WMKT* IP13 ... 39 K2
Martock Av *WOS/PRIT* SS0 .... 443 H8
Martyns Gv *WOS/PRIT* SS0 .... 463 J3
Martyns Ri *SUD* CO10 .... 34 E8
Marvens *CHLM/GWD* CM2 .... 361 F2
Marwell Cl *ROM* RM1 .... 430 B8
Maryborough Gv *COLS* CO2 .... 219 J3
Marylands Av *HOC/HUL* SS5 .... 420 C6
Mary La North *RCOLE* CO7 .... 190 E5
Mary La South *RCOLE* CO7 .... 191 C6
Mary Mcarthur Pl *STSD* CM24 ...... 167 K5
Maryon Rd *IPSE* IP3 .... 63 J5
Mary Park Gdns *BSF* CM23 .... 231 K1
Mary Warner Rd *RCOLE* CO7 .... 157 H6
Mascalls Gdns *BRW* CM14 .... 410 C7
Mascalls La *BRW* CM14 .... 410 C7
Mascalls Wy *CHLM/GWD* CM2 ..... 15 F5
Masefield Cl *ERITH* DA8 .... 480 A7
  HARH RM3 .... 430 C8
Masefield Crs *GPK* RM2 .... 430 D3
Masefield Dr *COLW* CO3 .... 186 A1
  UPMR RM14 .... 451 K2
Masefield Rd *BRTR* CM7 .... 209 J3

CDH/CHF RM16 .... 484 D1
GVW DA11 .... 488 C8
MAL CM9 .... 338 C2
Mashay Rd HSTD CO9 .... 80 C1
SUD CO10 .... 54 B7
Mashbury Rd RCHLM CM3 .... 271 F6
Mason Cl COLS CO2 .... 218 C2
Mason Dr HARH RM3 .... 431 F4
Mason Rd COL CO1 .... 8 B2
RCOS CO16 .... 290 D2
WFD IG8 .... 403 F7 🔲
Masons Ct BSF CM23 .... 198 D6
Masons Rd EN EN1 .... 374 B2
Mason Wy WAB EN9 .... 348 A7
Matching Gn BRWN CM15 .... 383 H3 🔲
Matching Gn BSDN SS14 .... 438 A4
Matching La BSF CM23 .... 198 C5
Matching Rd HLWE CM17 ...... 296 B1
RBSF CM22 .... 265 H4
Matfield Cl CHLM/WR CM1 .... 305 F6 🔲
Mathams Dr BSF CM23 .... 198 C8
Mather Wy CHTY IP2 .... 3 E5 🔲
Mathews Cl HSTD CO9 .... 148 B2 🔲
RCOLE CO7 .... 121 F4
Matlock Cl RIPW IP8 .... 61 J3 🔲
Matlock Gdns HCH RM12 ...... 451 F3 🔲
Matlock Rd CVI SS8 .... 477 K2
Matson Rd IP IP1 .... 2 A1 🔲
Maudlyn Rd COL CO1 .... 9 E5
Maugham Cl WICKW SS12 .... 417 G8
Maycroft Av GRAYS RM17 ...... 484 C4
Maycroft Cl IP IP1 .... 36 C1
Maycroft Gdns GRAYS RM17 .. 484 C4
Mayda Cl HSTD CO9 .... 147 J4
Maydells PIT SS13 .... 338 E8
Mayes Cl BSF CM23 .... 199 J5
Mayes La CHLM/GWD CM2 .... 334 C7
HAR CO12 .... 164 A4
RCHLM CM3 .... 335 J7
Mayes Rd GTDUN CM6 .... 139 K7
Mayfair Av PIT SS13 .... 439 F5
Mayfield Av HOC/HUL SS5 .... 419 K3
SOSN SS2 .... 464 B1
Mayfield Cl COLN CO4 .... 9 E2
HLWE CM17 .... 295 K5
Mayfield Gdns BRW CM14 .... 410 E4 🔲
BRW CM14 .... 411 F4 🔲
Mayfield Pk BSF CM23 .... 231 H2 🔲
Mayfield Rd CHING E4 .... 402 E5
CHLM/WR CM1 .... 331 G3
GVW DA11 .... 488 C3
IPNE IP4 .... 38 A6
PEND EN3 .... 374 D6
Mayfields CDH/CHF RM16 .... 484 D1
Mayflower Av HAR CO12 .... 7 F3
Mayflower Cl SOCK/AV RM15 470 A4
SOSN SS2 .... 443 J7
WAB EN9 .... 320 A5
Mayflower Dr MAL CM9 .... 338 C6
Mayflower Gdns BSF CM23 .. 198 A7
Mayflower Rd BCAYE CM11 .. 414 C3 🔲
Mayflowers SBF/HAD SS7 .... 440 A6 🔲
Mayflower Wy CHONG CM5 .. 354 C1
SUD CO10 .... 58 C3
Mayford Wy RCOS CO16 .... 258 D7
Maygreen Crs EMPK RM11 .... 450 B1
Mayhew Cl CHING E4 .... 402 E6
Mayland Av CVI SS8 .... 477 K3
Mayland Cl MAL CM9 .... 339 F1
RCHLM CM3 .... 368 E6
Mayland Gn RCHLM CM3 ...... 369 F5
Mayland Hl RCHLM CM3 ...... 369 F5
Mayland Rd WIT CM8 .... 277 G3 🔲
Maylands Av HCH RM12 .... 450 C5
Maylands Dr BRTR CM7 .... 209 C5
Maylands Wy HARH RM3 ...... 431 K1
Maylins Dr SBW CM21 .... 263 H3
Maynard Cl ERITH DA8 .... 480 A6
GTDUN CM6 .... 204 C4 🔲
Maynards EMPK RM11 .... 451 F1
Mayne Crest CHLM/WR CM1 . 305 G6
Mayo Cl BAR EN8 .... 346 C2
Maypole Cl SAFWS CB11 ...... 70 D6 🔲
Maypole Crs ERITH DA8 .... 480 E5
Maypole Dr CHIG IG7 .... 405 K6
RCOS CO16 .... 289 G1
Maypole Green Rd COLS CO2 218 D5
Maypole Rd K/T/MI CO5 .... 248 A7
MAL CM9 .... 310 B6
WIT CM8 .... 278 B8

The Maypole GTDUN CM6 .... 139 J2
May Rd IPSE IP3 .... 64 A3
Maysent Av BRTR CM7 .... 177 J8
May's La RCOLE CO7 .... 157 H1
May St ROY SG8 .... 66 B3
May Wk CHLM/GWD CM2 ...... 15 D6 🔲
STSD CM24 .... 168 B4
Maywin Dr EMPK RM11 .... 451 G2
Maze Green Hts BSF CM23 .. 198 D5
Maze Green Rd BSF CM23 .... 198 C6
The Maze LOS SS9 .... 442 E6
Mazoe Cl BSF CM23 .... 198 E8
Mazoe Rd BSF CM23 .... 198 E8
Mccalmont Dr RAYL SS6 ...... 419 H6
Mcdivitt Wk LOS SS9 .... 443 H7 🔲
Mc Kenzie Rd BROX EN10 .... 319 G2
Mead Barn EPP CM16 .... 378 C2
Mead Cl CDH/CHF RM16 ...... 484 A1
GPK RM2 .... 430 B4
LOU IG10 .... 377 K6
Mead Crs WAB EN9 .... 347 H8
Mead Crs CHING E4 .... 402 D7
Meade Rd BCAYE CM11 .... 387 K8
Meadgate CHLM/GWD CM2 .... 15 C5
WFD IG8 .... 404 B8
Meadgate Rd HOD EN11 .... 319 K2
Mead Monks RCHLM CM3 .... 363 K3
Meadow Clays SAFWS CB11 .. 70 A1 🔲
Meadow Cl BRTR CM7 .... 176 D6
CHING E4 .... 402 C4 🔲
COS CO15 .... 259 K6
FX IP11 .... 94 C5
HSTD CO9 .... 148 A5
PEND EN3 .... 374 A2
RCOLE CO7 .... 191 F7
SBF/HAD SS7 .... 441 G4
SLH/COR SS17 .... 486 B2
Meadow Ct WICKE SS11 ...... 417 H5
Meadowcroft STSD CM24 .... 167 K6 🔲
Meadowcroft Wy FOS CO13 .. 228 E6
Meadowcross WAB EN9 .... 348 A8
Meadow Dr SOS SS1 .... 465 H5
VGE SS16 .... 456 C5
Meadowford SAFWS CB11 .... 100 A4
Meadowgate ING CM4 .... 388 B2
Meadow Grass Cl COLW CO3 185 G7 🔲
Meadow Rd WICKE SS11 ...... 417 K7
Meadowlands BSF CM23 ...... 199 F4
EMPK RM11 .... 451 F1 🔲
KIR/NAC IP10 .... 94 C2
Meadow La CBE/LIN CB1 ...... 22 C3
K/T/MI CO5 .... 284 E8
SUD CO10 .... 58 B6 🔲
WICKE SS11 .... 417 H2
Meadows Cl RBRW/HUT CM13 434 B1 🔲
RCOLE CO7 .... 189 J7
Meadows Gn RCHLM CM3 .... 336 A7
Meadowside BRTR CM7 .... 177 H8
CHLM/GWD CM2 .... 15 D2
RAYL SS6 .... 441 J3 🔲
Meadowside Gdns IPNE IP4 .. 38 C5
Meadowside Rd UPMR RM14 451 K6
The Meadows BSF CM23 ...... 198 D8
RBRW/HUT CM13 .... 434 B1
SBW CM21 .... 264 A3
Meadowsweet Cl BSF CM23 198 B7 🔲
HVHL CB9 .... 26 E4 🔲
Meadowvale Cl IPNE IP4 .... 37 H6
Meadow Vw EPP CM16 .... 350 E3 🔲
K/T/MI CO5 .... 247 K8 🔲
VGE SS16 .... 455 K1
Meadow View Cl COLW CO3 .. 185 K8
The Meadow Wy BCAYE CM11 414 C3
Mead Pastures MAL CM9 ...... 336 D2
Mead Pth CHLM/GWD CM2 .... 14 A5
Mead Rd GVW DA11 .... 489 C7
Meads Cl ING CM4 .... 386 B1
Meads Rd PEND EN3 .... 374 E5
The Meads ING CM4 .... 386 B1
UPMR RM14 .... 452 B3 🔲
VGE SS16 .... 458 D2

Meadsway RBRW/HUT CM13 433 F1 🔲
The Mead ABR/ST RM4 .... 379 F7
BAR EN8 .... 346 C3
GTDUN CM6 .... 139 K2
GTDUN CM6 .... 204 B3
LAIN SS15 .... 436 C5
SUD CO10 .... 84 E1
Mead Vw BUNT SG9 .... 133 H7
Mead Wk CHONG CM5 .... 354 B4
Meadway CVI SS8 .... 478 C3
GPK RM2 .... 430 B4
GRAYS RM17 .... 484 C3
HOD EN11 .... 319 G1
HSTD CO9 .... 146 D5
MAL CM9 .... 338 D4
MGTR CO11 .... 159 F2
PEND EN3 .... 374 D2
RAYL SS6 .... 442 A4
SBF/HAD SS7 .... 440 B6
WFD IG8 .... 403 K8 🔲
The Meadway BKHH IG9 ...... 404 A4
WOS/PRIT SS0 .... 463 J5
Meakins Cl LOS SS9 .... 443 G7
Mearns Pl CHLM/GWD CM2 .. 333 H1
Medcalf Rd PEND EN3 .... 375 F3
Medebridge Rd CDH/CHF RM16 470 D6
Mede Wy RCOLE CO7 .... 221 F2
Medick Ct GRAYS RM17 .... 484 D5
Medina Rd GRAYS RM17 ...... 484 C4
Medina Rd GRAYS RM17 ...... 484 C4
Medlar Dr SOCK/AV RM15 .... 470 C4 🔲
Medlar Rd GRAYS RM17 ...... 484 C5
Medlars Md RBSF CM22 .... 234 B8
Medley Rd BRTR CM7 .... 208 C3
Medoc Cl PIT SS13 .... 439 F5
Medway Av WIT CM8 .... 76 D3
Medway Cl CHLM/WR CM1 .. 331 K1
Medway Crs LOS SS9 .... 462 C4
Medway Rd IPSE IP3 .... 63 H3
Meekings Rd SUD CO10 .... 58 C5
The Meers FOS CO13 .... 228 D7
Meeson Mdw MAL CM9 .... 338 A5
Meesons La GRAYS RM17 .... 483 J3
Meesons Md RCFD SS4 .... 444 A2
Meeting Fld SUD CO10 .... 34 E6
Meeting La HSTD CO9 .... 52 E6
K/T/MI CO5 .... 286 A3
Meggison Wy SBF/HAD SS7 .. 460 B2
Megs Wy BRTR CM7 .... 210 A4
Melba Ct CHLM/WR CM1 ...... 331 J4
Melba Gdns TIL RM18 .... 485 F6
Melbourne Av CHLM/WR CM1 303 K8
Melbourne Cha COLS CO2 .... 219 J4
Melbourne Rd COS CO15 ...... 10 A3
IPNE IP4 .... 38 B6
TIL RM18 .... 484 D7
Melcombe Rd SBF/HAD SS7 460 B2
Melford Cl IPNE IP4 .... 38 D8
Melford Rd SUD CO10 .... 32 E3
SUD CO10 .... 35 K5
SUD CO10 .... 57 K3
Melford Wy FX IP11 .... 4 C4
Melksham Cl HARH RM3 ...... 431 G2 🔲
Melksham Dr HARH RM3 ...... 431 F2
Melksham Gn HARH RM3 .... 431 F2 🔲
Melling Dr EN EN1 .... 374 A5
Mellis Cl HVHL CB9 .... 26 B4
Mellis Ct FX IP11 .... 5 D2
Mellish Gdns WFD IG8 .... 403 H8
Mellor Cha COLW CO3 .... 185 K6
Mellor Cl ING CM4 .... 386 B1 🔲
Mellow Purgess Cl LAIN SS15 16 A4
Mellow Purgess End LAIN SS15 16 A4
Mell Rd MAL CM9 .... 314 E5
Melplash Cl IPSE IP3 .... 64 C1 🔲
Melplash Rd IPSE IP3 .... 64 C1
Melrose Gdns COS CO15 .... 11 F2
IPNE IP4 .... 37 K5
Melrose Rd K/T/MI CO5 .... 284 D7
Melstock Av UPMR RM14 ...... 451 K5
Melton Cl RCOS CO16 .... 290 C1
Melton Gdns ROM RM1 .... 450 A1
Melville Dr WICKW SS12 ...... 417 G8
Melville Heath RCHLM CM3 .. 392 E7
Melville Rd IPNE IP4 .... 37 H8
Memory Cl MAL CM9 .... 338 C6 🔲
Mendip Cl RAYL SS6 .... 441 J2
WICKE SS11 .... 417 H6 🔲
Mendip Crs WOS/PRIT SS0 .. 443 H8
Mendip Dr KESG IP5 .... 38 D7
Mendip Rd CHLM/WR CM1 .. 303 K7
EMPK RM11 .... 450 B1
LOS SS9 .... 463 H1
Mendlesham Cl RCOS CO16 290 D1
Mendoza Cl EMPK RM11 ...... 431 F7
Menin Rd COLS CO2 .... 218 E1
Mentmore VGE SS16 .... 456 C1
Menzies Av LAIN SS15 .... 436 A7
Meon Cl CHLM/WR CM1 ...... 305 F7
Meppel Av CVI SS8 .... 461 F7
Mercer Av SBN/FI SS3 .... 467 F1
Mercer Rd BCAYE CM11 ...... 387 K8
Mercers Av HLWW/ROY CM19 12 A6
Mercers Av BSF CM23 .... 231 F1
Mercers Wy COL CO1 .... 8 A3
Merchant St RCHLM CM3 .... 392 E6 🔲

Mercia Cl *CHLM/GWD* CM2....333 J8
Mercury Cl *WICKE* SS11....417 J5
Mercury Gdns *ROM* RM1....430 A7
Meredene *BSDN* SS14....438 C8
Meredith Rd *CDH/CHF* RM16....485 F3
  COS CO15....10 B4
  IP IP1....36 A3
Merefield *SBW* CM21....263 J4
Meres Cl *WIT* CM8....276 E4
Meriadoc Dr *RCHLM* CM3....392 D7
Merilies Cl *WOS/PRIT* SS0....463 J2
Merilies Gdns *WOS/PRIT* SS0....463 J2
Merival Ct *MGTR* CO11....159 G2
Merivale Rd *MGTR* CO11....159 G2
Merlin Ct *CVI* SS8....478 B2
Merlin End *COLN* CO4....188 C4
Merlin Pl *CHLM/WR* CM1....304 B8
Merlin Rd *CHTY* IP2....61 J2
Merlin Wy *EPP* CM16....324 A7
  WICKE SS11....417 G4
Mermagen Dr *RAIN* RM13....450 C8
Mermaid Wy *MAL* CM9....338 D5
Merriam Ct *CHLM* E4....402 D8
  MGTR CO11....123 J5
Merricks La *VGE* SS16....458 B3
Merrilees Crs *COS* CO15....260 B7
Merrion Cl *RIPW* IP8....61 J3
Merrivale *SBF/HAD* SS7....460 B3
Merryfield Ap *LOS* SS9....463 F1
Merryfields Rd *HOC/HUL* SS5....420 E6
Merryhill Cl *CHING* E4....402 C3
Merrylands *LAIN* SS15....436 B6
Merrymount Gdns *COS* CO15....11 E2
Mersea Cl *K/T/MI* CO5....284 D7
Mersea Crs *WICKW* SS12....417 J7
Mersea Fleet Wy *BRTR* CM7....210 B3
Mersea Rd *COLS* CO2....219 H4
  K/T/MI CO5....252 A8
Mersea Vw *RCOS* CO16....288 A2
Mersey Av *UPMR* RM14....433 A8
Mersey Rd *IPSE* IP3....63 H2
  WIT CM8....276 E2
Merstham Dr *RCOS* CO16....258 E7
Merton Ct *COLS* CO2....219 H6
Merton Pl *CDH/CHF* RM16....485 F3
  RCHLM CM3....393 F7
Merton Rd *HOC/HUL* SS5....420 B5
  SBF/HAD SS7....460 B1
Messant Cl *GPK* RM2....430 E4
Messines Cl *COLS* CO2....218 E1
Mess Rd *SBN/FI* SS3....466 E8
Meteor Rd *WOS/PRIT* SS0....18 A4
Meteor Wy *CHLM/WR* CM1....14 A3
Methersgate *BSDN* SS14....437 K6
Metsons La *CHLM/WR* CM1....357 H3
Metz Av *CVI* SS8....478 A1
Meux Cl *EBAR* EN7....346 A5
Mews Ct *CHLM/GWD* CM2....14 C4
Mews Pl *WFD* IG8....403 H7
The Mews *HOC/HUL* SS5....420 D7
  SBW CM21....263 J2
Meyel Av *CVI* SS8....461 H8
Meyer Gn *EN* EN1....374 A4
Meynell Av *CVI* SS8....478 C3
Meynell Rd *HARH* RM3....430 C1
Meyrick Crs *COLS* CO2....8 B6
Mey Wk *HOC/HUL* SS5....420 D7
Micawber Wy *CHLM/WR* CM1....303 K6
Michael Gdns *EMPK* RM11....430 E6
Michaelgate Cl *HAR* CO12....164 B3
Michaelstowe Dr *HAR* CO12....164 B3
Michigan Cl *KESC* IP5....39 F6
Mickfield Ms *FX* IP11....5 D2
Micklegate Rd *FX* IP11....5 E5
Middleborough *COLW* CO3....8 A3
Middle Boy *ABR/ST* RM4....379 F7
Middlefield *HSTD* CO9....148 A4
Middlefield Rd *MGTR* CO11....160 B2
Middle Gn *CHLM* CM15....384 A3
  RCOLW CO6....111 F4
Middle King *BRTR* CM7....210 C4
Middlemead *CHLM/GWD* CM2....389 H1
Middle Met *RCFD* SS4....444 C3
Middlemead *RCHLM* CM3....390 A5
Middle Mead Cl
  CHLM/GWD CM2....389 H1
Middle Mill Rd *COL* CO1....8 B3
Middle Rd *RBRW/HUT* CM13....412 B7
  WAB EN9....347 H6
Middle Rw *BSF* CM23....198 E7
Middlesbury *CVI* SS8....460 D8
Middlesex Av *LOS* SS9....463 G3
Middle St *SAFWS* CB11....134 B1
  WAB EN9....320 B5
Middleton Av *CHING* E4....402 A4
Middleton Cl *CHING* E4....402 A6
  CHTY IP2....61 K3
  RCOS CO16....10 A1
Middleton Hall La *BRWN* CM15....411 H5
Middleton Rd *BRWN* CM15....411 H5
Middleton Rw *RCHLM* CM3....392 E7
Middle Wy *SUD* CO10....35 F5
Middlewick Cl *COLS* CO2....219 H4

Midguard Wy *MAL* CM9....338 A5
Midhurst Av *WOS/PRIT* SS0....464 A1
Midhurst Dr *HCH* RM12....450 B5
Midland Cl *COLS* CO2....219 G1
Midsummer Meadow
  SBN/FI SS3....466 D4
Midway *COS* CO15....290 D4
Midway Rd *COLS* CO2....218 D3
Milbanke Cl *SBN/FI* SS3....466 D4
Milburn Crs *CHLM/WR* CM1....331 K4
Milch La *RCHLM* CM3....208 B8
Milden Rd *CHTY* IP2....36 A8
Mildmayes *VGE* SS16....16 A6
Mildmay Rd *BOC* CM0....398 C8
  CHLM/GWD CM2....14 C5
  IPSE IP3....63 J4
Mildmays *RCHLM* CM3....335 C5
Mile Cl *WAB* EN9....347 J7
Mile End Rd *COLN* CO4....187 F2
Miles Cl *COLW* CO3....185 H7
Miles Ct *GTDUN* CM6....12 B4
  HLWW/ROY CM19....
Miles Gray Rd *BSDN* SS14....16 C2
Milford Cl *RCOLE* CO7....221 F4
Milford Rd *CDH/CHF* RM16....471 H8
Millais Pl *TIL* RM18....485 F6
Millars Cl *RCHLM* CM3....392 E5
The Millars *CHLM/WR* CM1....304 C2
Millbank Av *CHONG* CM5....354 B3
Millbridge Rd *WIT* CM8....277 F3
Mill Cha *CHTY* IP2....147 K3
  HVHL CB9....50 D8
Mill Cl *BOC* CM0....572 A1
  BRTR CM7....142 C3
  CHLM/WR CM1....302 A8
  FX IP11....5 D3
  FX IP11....94 B5
  K/T/MI CO5....248 A7
  RBSF CM22....168 D4
  RIPS/CAP IP9....86 D4
Mill Ct *GTDUN* CM6....202 E6
Millcroft *BSF* CM23....199 F4
Mill End *GTDUN* CM6....139 K3
Millennium Wy *BRTR* CM7....210 B4
Miller's Barn Rd *COS* CO15....290 C4
Millers Cl *BRTR* CM7....177 K5
  BSF CM23....198 B8
  CBE/LIN CB1....23 F2
  CHIG IG7....406 A5
  COLW CO3....185 H7
Millers Cft *CHLM/GWD* CM2....333 J7
  GTDUN CM6....204 D4
Millersdale *HLWW/ROY* CM19....321 K1
Millers Green Rd *CHONG* CM5....327 K1
Miller's La *CHIG* IG7....406 A4
  COLW CO3....185 J7
Millers Md *K/T/MI* CO5....247 G1
Millers Rw *BRTR* CM7....76 D7
Millfield *CHONG* CM5....354 E2
Millfield Cl *RAYL* SS6....441 K2
Millfield Dr *GVW* DA11....488 D7
Millfield Gdns *IPNE* IP4....37 J7
Millfields *CHLM/WR* CM1....331 C4
Mill Flds *RCHLM* CM3....336 A7
Millfields *SBW* CM21....263 K2
  STSD CM24....167 K7
Millfields Wy *HVHL* CB9....27 H5
Mill Gra *BOC* CM0....398 B6
Mill Gn *PIT* SS13....438 D7
Mill Green Pl *PIT* SS13....438 D6
Mill Green Rd *ING* CM4....357 K5
Millhead Wy *RCFD* SS4....444 E4
Mill HI *BRTR* CM7....210 A3
  BRWN CM15....411 H3
  BSF CM23....166 D8
  CHLM/GWD CM2....360 B3
  HVHL CB9....27 H6
  MGTR CO11....158 C1
  MGTR CO11....159 H1
  RCHLM CM3....365 J5
  RCOLW CO6....116 D7
  RIPS/CAP IP9....86 D4
  SBF/HAD SS7....460 D4
  STSD CM24....167 J7
Mill Hill Dr *BCAYW* CM12....387 H8
Millhurst Ms *HLWE* CM17....295 J1
Milligans Cha *CHLM/GWD* CM2....360 D4
Milliners Wy *BSF* CM23....231 G1
Mill La *ABR/ST* RM4....381 J6
  BAR EN8....346 A2
  BCAYE CM11....388 D8
  BROX EN10....319 F3
  BRTR CM7....107 G2
  BRTR CM7....208 B5
  BRTR CM7....210 C7
  BRWN CM15....96 D8
  BUNT SG9....
  CBE/LIN CB1....22 E3
  CDH/CHF RM16....472 A6
  CHING E4....375 H7
  CHLM/WR CM1....304 D4

  CHONG CM5....297 J8
  CHONG CM5....352 E3
  CHONG CM5....354 E3
  COLS CO2....218 C8
  COLS CO2....249 K2
  FOS CO13....260 C2
  FX IP11....5 E3
  FX IP11....94 B5
  GTDUN CM6....173 J8
  GTDUN CM6....204 C5
  HAR CO12....7 E5
  HLWE CM17....295 J1
  HSTD CO9....79 K2
  HSTD CO9....111 K5
  HSTD CO9....113 H6
  ING CM4....358 A7
  ING CM4....388 B3
  K/T/MI CO5....214 C3
  MAL CM9....282 B5
  MAL CM9....312 C2
  MAL CM9....338 B2
  MGTR CO11....159 G2
  MGTR CO11....160 E4
  RBSF CM22....265 F1
  RCFD SS4....444 E4
  RCHLM CM3....239 K6
  RCHLM CM3....241 K6
  RCHLM CM3....274 C2
  RCHLM CM3....365 J4
  RCOLE CO7....121 J6
  RCOLE CO7....190 A1
  RCOLW CO6....149 H4
  RCOS CO16....225 C7
  RCOS CO16....226 C4
  RIPW IP8....61 F4
  SAFWN CB10....20 A6
  SAFWN CB10....43 G1
  SAFWN CB10....71 F3
  SAFWS CB11....70 A2
  SBW CM21....263 K2
  SLH/COR SS17....457 J6
  SLH/COR SS17....473 F2
  SUD CO10....32 B5
  SUD CO10....58 A6
  WFD IG8....403 G8
  WIT CM8....277 F3
  WOTN CO14....229 H4
  WTHK RM20....483 G4
Mill Lane Cl *BROX* EN10....319 F3
  RCOS CO16....225 H7
Millmarsh La *PEND* EN3....374 E6
Mill Park Av *HCH* RM12....451 F3
Mill Park Dr *BRTR* CM7....210 A4
Mill Piece *KIR/NAC* IP10....65 F7
Mill Ri *RIPS/CAP* IP9....90 A8
Mill Rd *BCAYE* CM11....414 E7
  BOC CM0....372 A1
  BOC CM0....398 B6
  BRTR CM7....106 E8
  BRTR CM7....142 C3
  CHLM/WR CM1....269 H8
  COLN CO4....155 G1
  COLN CO4....155 H7
  COLN CO4....187 F3
  GTDUN CM6....206 B8
  GTDUN CM6....239 G2
  GVW DA11....488 D5
  HSTD CO9....52 B3
  HSTD CO9....77 K2
  HVHL CB9....27 G6
  HVHL CB9....28 C3
  HVHL CB9....49 H5
  ING CM4....388 A3
  IPSE IP3....64 D4
  K/T/MI CO5....284 E5
  MAL CM9....279 F6
  MAL CM9....338 D4
  PUR RM19....481 J5
  RBSF CM22....169 F1
  RCHLM CM3....322 D7
  RCOLE CO7....122 D2
  RCOLW CO6....184 C1
  SAFWN CB10....102 D3
  SAFWS CB11....101 H5
  SOCK/AV RM15....468 E1
  SUD CO10....31 G6
  SUD CO10....33 J8
Mills Ct *PIT* SS13....439 F4
Mill Side *STSD* CM24....167 J7
Mills La *SUD* CO10....57 K1
Millsmead Wy *LOU* IG10....377 H6
Millson Bank *CHLM/GWD* CM2....333 J1
Mills Rd *SUD* CO10....58 D5
The Mills *IPNE* IP4....37 J7
Mill St *BSF* CM23....199 F8
  COLS CO2....8 C5
  HLWE CM17....295 J8
  RCOLE CO7....256 A7
  RCOLW CO6....118 B4
  RCOS CO16....289 F1
Mills Wy *RBRW/HUT* CM13....412 B4
Mill Tye *SUD* CO10....84 D7
Millview Mdw *RCFD* SS4....444 C4
Mill Vue Rd *CHLM/GWD* CM2....15 F3
Mill Wk *K/T/MI* CO5....248 A7

Millways *MAL* CM9 .... 310 D1
Millwell Crs *CHIG* IG7 .... 405 G8
Millwrights *K/T/MI* CO5 .... 248 A3
Milner Pl *BCAYW* CM12 .... 387 F8
Milner Rd *SUD* CO10 .... 58 E5
Milner St *IPNE* IP4 .... 3 F3
Milnrow *RIPW* IP8 .... 61 J3
Milroy Av *GVW* DA11 .... 488 D7
Milton Av *BRTR* CM7 .... 209 K5
 GVE DA12.. 489 J6
 HCH RM12 .... 450 A3
 VGE SS16 .... 455 K1
 WOS/PRIT SS0 .... 18 B5
Milton Cl *COLW* CO3 .... 186 A7
 RAYL SS6 .... 442 A3
Milton Ct *WAB* EN9 .... 347 J8
Milton Crs *CHONG* CM5 .... 326 B8
Milton Gdns *TIL* RM18 .... 485 G7
Milton Hall Cl *SBN/FI* SS3 .... 466 E2
Milton Hall Rd *GVE* DA12 .... 489 J6
Milton Pl *CHLM/WR* CM1 .... 304 B8
 GVE DA12.. 489 H4
 SOS SS1 .... 18 C5
Milton Rd *BRW* CM14 .... 410 E6
 GRAYS RM17...................................... 484 A3
 GVE DA12.. 489 H4
 HAR CO12 .... 7 F4
 MAL CM9 .... 338 C5
 MGTR CO11 .... 159 C3
 ROM RM1 .... 430 B8
 SLH/COR SS17 .... 457 D7
 WIT CM8 .... 245 F8
 WOS/PRIT SS0 .... 18 B4
Milton St *IPNE* IP4 .... 37 J6
 SOSN SS3 .... 19 D3
Miltsin Av *CVI* SS8 .... 461 H8
Milwards *HLWW/ROY* CM19 .... 321 K1
Mimosa Cl *BRWN* CM15 .... 410 E1
 CHLM/WR CM1 .... 305 J7
 HARH RM3 .... 430 D2
Minchen Rd *HLW* CM20 .... 294 E4
Minden Rd *SUD* CO10 .... 58 C5
Minerva Cl *HAR* CO12 .... 6 A6
 HVHL CB9 .... 27 K7
Minsmere Dr *RCOS* CO16 .... 258 E7
Minsmere Wy *SUD* CO10 .... 59 F7
Minster Rd *HVHL* CB9 .... 27 F4
 LAIN SS15 .... 16 A4
Minster Wy *EMPK* RM11 .... 451 G2
 MAL CM9 .... 338 A5
Minton Hts *RCFD* SS4 .... 421 K7
Minton La *HLWE* CM17 .... 295 C5
Miramar Av *CVI* SS8 .... 477 J2
Miramar Wy *HCH* RM12 .... 450 E6
Mirosa Dr *MAL* CM9 .... 338 C5
Mirosa Reach *MAL* CM9 .... 338 C5
Mission La *RCOLE* CO7 .... 123 G2
Mistley End *VGE* SS16 .... 437 K8
Mistley Pth *VGE* SS16 .... 437 K8
Mistley Rd *HLW* CM20 .... 294 E4
Mistley Side *VGE* SS16 .... 437 K8
Mitchell Av *GVW* DA11 .... 488 C7
 HSTD CO9 .... 147 K4
Mitchell Cir *BRTR* CM7 .... 107 K7
Mitchells Av *CVI* SS8 .... 478 D1
Mitchell Wy *RCHLM* CM3 .... 392 D5
Mitford Cl *IP* IP1 .... 36 C1
Mitre Gdns *BSF* CM23 .... 232 A1
Mitton V *CHLM/GWD* CM2 .... 333 H3
Moat Cl *BCAYE* CM11...................... 415 K2
Moat Edge Gdns *BCAYW* CM12 ... 414 B3
Moat End *SOS* SS1 .... 466 A4
Moat Farm Cha *WIT* CM8 .... 277 F7
Moat Farm Cl *IPNE* IP4 .... 37 H5
Moat Fld *BSDN* SS14 .... 437 K5
Moat Flds *RCOLW* CO6 .... 152 C7
Moat La *BURES* CO8 .... 114 D1
 ERITH DA8 .... 480 B7
Moat Ri *RAYL* SS6 .... 441 J4
Moat Rd *HSTD* CO9 .... 51 K6
 RCOLW CO6 .... 152 C7
Moat Side *PEND* EN3 .... 374 C8
Modlen Rd *WOTN* CO14 .... 229 F6
Moffat Av *IPNE* IP4 .... 37 K4
Mole Hall La *SAFWS* CB11 .... 137 G2
Molehill Green Rbt *RBSF* CM22 ... 169 K8
Mollands *VGE* SS16 .... 458 C1
Mollands St *SOCK/AV* RM15 .... 470 C4
Mollands La *SOCK/AV* RM15 .... 470 A4
Mollison Av *PEND* EN3 .... 374 E7
Molrams La *CHLM/GWD* CM2 ...... 333 K7
Momples Rd *HLW* CM20 .... 294 E4
Monarch Cl *TIL* RM18 .... 485 G8
Monarch Pl *BKHH* IG9 .... 403 K5
Monarch's Wy *BAR* EN8 .... 346 D7
Monastery Rd *LAIN* SS15 .... 16 A4
Moneypiece Cl *HVHL* CB9 .... 27 F4
Monkchester Cl *LOU* IG10 .... 377 J5
Monkdowns Rd *RCOLW* CO6 .... 213 J2
Monkham's Av *WFD* IG8 .... 403 J8
Monkham's Dr *WFD* IG8 .... 403 J8
Monkham's La *WFD* IG8 .... 403 J7
Monklands Ct *HSTD* CO9 .... 147 J4
Monksbury *HLWS* CM18 .... 294 E8
Monks Cha *RBRW/HUT* CM13 .... 412 B8

Monks Cl *BROX* EN10 .... 319 G2
Monks Ct *WIT* CM8 .... 276 E2
Monksford Dr *HOC/HUL* SS5 ...... 419 J4
Monksgrove *LOU* IG10 .... 404 D1
Monks Hvn *SLH/COR* SS17 .... 474 A2
Monks Hl *SAFWS* CB11 .... 71 G5
Monk's La *RCOLE* CO7 .... 157 G1
Monks Lodge Rd *HSTD* CO9 .... 111 J2
Monks Rd *RCOLW* CO6 .... 149 G6
Monks Wk *MAL* CM9 .... 314 E5
Monkswick Rd *HLW* CM20 .... 13 F1
Monkswood Av *WAB* EN9 .... 347 K7
Monkswood Dr *BSF* CM23 .... 198 C7
Monkwick Av *COLS* CO2 .... 219 H4
Monkwood Cl *ROM* RM1 .... 430 B7
Monmouth Cl *CHTY* IP2 .... 62 D4
Monmouth Ms *VGE* SS16 .... 436 A8
Monnow Rd *SOCK/AV* RM15 ...... 468 E7
Monoux Cl *BCAYE* CM11 .... 414 E4
Monroe Crs *EN* EN1 .... 374 B5
Mons Av *BCAYE* CM11 .... 414 E3
Monson Rd *BROX* EN10 .... 319 F2
Mons Rd *COLS* CO2 .... 218 E1
Montague La *LOS* SS9 .... 462 C5
Montague Pl *CVI* SS8 .... 477 J2
Montague Wy *BCAYW* CM12 .... 387 G8
Montalt Rd *WFD* IG8 .... 403 G8
Montana Rd *KESG* IP5 .... 38 E6
Montayne Rd *BAR* EN8 .... 346 D6
Montbretia Cl *COLW* CO3 .... 185 J7
Montefiore Av *RAYL* SS6 .... 419 H5
Montfort Av *SLH/COR* SS17 .... 474 C1
Montgomery Cl *CHLM/WR* CM1 .. 305 C6
 COLS CO2 .... 219 J1
Montgomery Ct *SBN/FI* SS3 ...... 466 D4
Montgomery Crs *HARH* RM3 .... 408 E8
Montgomery Dr *BAR* EN8 .... 346 E2
Montgomery Rd *CHTY* IP2 .... 62 D4
Monton Ri *CHTY* IP2 .... 61 K3
Montpelier Cl *BCAYW* CM12 .... 387 G8
Montreal Rd *TIL* RM18 .... 489 F1
Montrose Cl *WFD* IG8 .... 403 H7
Montrose Cl *CHLM/GWD* CM2 .... 333 H1
Montsale *PIT* SS13 .... 439 F5
Monument Farm Rd *KIR/NAC* IP10 .. 65 G1
Moon Hall La *HVHL* CB9 .... 27 F8
Moons Cl *RCFD* SS4 .... 422 A6
Moorcroft *RCFD* SS4 .... 421 K7
Moorcroft Av *SBF/HAD* SS7 .... 441 K7
Moore Av *TIL* RM18 .... 485 C8
 WTHK RM20 .... 483 H4
Moore Cl *BCAYE* CM11 .... 387 K8
Moore Rd *IP* IP1 .... 36 B2
Moores Av *SLH/COR* SS17 .... 457 K4
Moorescroft *BRWN* CM15 .... 383 J3
Moorfield Cl *KESG* IP5 .... 39 G6
Moorfield Rd *PEND* EN3 .... 374 C5
Moorfields *HLWS* CM18 .... 322 A2
Moor Hall La *RCHLM* CM3 .... 363 J2
Moor Hall Rd *HLW* CM20 .... 295 K1
Moorhen Av *BOC* CM0 .... 342 C5
Moorhen Cl *ERITH* DA8 .... 480 C6
Moorhouse Gn *RCOLE* CO7 .... 157 H5
The Moorings *BSF* CM23 .... 199 F7
Moor La *UPMR* RM14 .... 452 C2
Moor Park Cl *LOS* SS9 .... 442 D8
Moor Park Gdns *LOS* SS9 .... 442 D8
Moor Pasture Wy *HVHL* CB9 .... 27 H1
Moor Rd *COLN* CO4 .... 156 A2
 RCOLW CO6 .... 183 F5
Moors Cl *RCOLE* CO7 .... 223 K4
Moor's Farm Cha *MAL* CM9 .... 311 J2
Moorsfield *SUD* CO10 .... 84 E1
Moorside *COL* CO1 .... 9 D4
Moors La *BRTR* CM7 .... 208 A2
 GTDUN CM6 .... 205 J6
Mope La *WIT* CM8 .... 277 K8
Mopsies Rd *BSDN* SS14 .... 438 E1
Moran Av *CHLM/WR* CM1 .... 304 D6
Morant Gdns *CRW* RM5 .... 407 G8
Morant Rd *CDH/CHF* RM16 .... 485 G2
 COL CO1 .... 9 G5
Morebarn Rd *RCOLE* CO7 .... 190 D3
Morecambe Cl *HCH* RM12 .... 450 A3
Moreland Av *SBF/HAD* SS7 .... 440 B6
Moreland Rd *WICKE* SS11 .... 417 F3
Morelands Av *CDH/CHF* RM16 .... 484 E7
Moreland Wy *CHING* E4 .... 402 C6
Morella Cl *RCOLE* CO7 .... 223 K6
Morello Ct *COLS* CO2 .... 219 H6
Moremead *WAB* EN9 .... 347 J5
Mores La *BRW* CM14 .... 383 F7
Moreton Cl *CHONG* CM5 .... 325 J3
Moreton Cl *EBAR* EN7 .... 346 B1
Moreton Gdns *WFD* IG8 .... 404 B8
Moreton Rd *CHONG* CM5 .... 325 G5
Moretons *CHLM/GWD* CM2 .... 360 D3
Morgan Crs *EPP* CM16 .... 378 C2
Morland Rd *IPSE* IP3 .... 63 H5
Morland Wy *BAR* EN8 .... 346 E2
Morley Gv *HLW* CM20 .... 12 C2

Morley Hl *SLH/COR* SS17 .... 457 G7
Morley Link *SLH/COR* SS17 .... 457 G8
Morley Rd *HSTD* CO9 .... 148 A3
 K/T/MI CO5 .... 280 B1
Morley Sq *CDH/CHF* RM16 .... 485 F3
Morleys Rd *RCOLW* CO6 .... 149 H7
Mornington Av *IP* IP1 .... 36 B4
 RCFD SS4 .... 444 D3
Mornington Crs *CVI* SS8 .... 478 C1
 SBF/HAD SS7 .... 462 A2
Mornington Rd *CHING* E4 .... 402 E3
 CVI SS8 .... 461 G8
Morningtons *HLWW/ROY* CM19 .. 321 K1
Morrells *VGE* SS16 .... 17 D6
Morrin's Cha *SBN/FI* SS3 .... 467 J2
Morrins Cl *SBN/FI* SS3 .... 467 J2
Morris Av *BCAYE* CM11 .... 414 E4
 COS CO15 .... 290 A7
Morris Ct *CHING* E4 .... 402 C6
 LAIN SS15 .... 436 C6
 WAB EN9 .... 348 B8
Morris Harp *SAFWN* CB10 .... 71 F2
Morris Rd *CHLM/GWD* CM2 .... 15 E3
 HARH RM3 .... 430 C2
Morrow La *RCOLE* CO7 .... 157 K7
Mors End *RCOLE* CO7 .... 121 G3
Morses La *RCOLE* CO7 .... 255 K5
Morston Hall Rd *FX* IP11 .... 93 K4
Morten Rd *COL* CO1 .... 8 A3
Mortimer Ga *BAR* EN8 .... 347 F1
Mortimer Pl *SUD* CO10 .... 31 F4
Mortimer Rd *RAYL* SS6 .... 419 J8
 RCHLM CM3 .... 308 A1
Morton Rd *MAL* CM9 .... 310 C1
Morton Wy *HSTD* CO9 .... 148 B2
Mosbach Gdns *RBRW/HUT* CM13 .. 412 A5
Moseley St *SOSN* SS2 .... 5 G4
Moss Bank *GRAYS* RM17 .... 483 J3
Moss Cl *VGE* SS16 .... 458 B2
Moss Dr *VGE* SS16 .... 458 B2
Mossfield Cl *COLW* CO3 .... 186 D7
Moss La *NHMKT* IP6 .... 37 H1
 ROM RM1 .... 430 A8
Moss Rd *COLW* CO3 .... 217 K1
 SOCK/AV RM15 .... 470 A5
 WIT CM8 .... 277 H2
Moss Wy *RCOLW* CO6 .... 185 K2
Motehill *VGE* SS16 .... 16 A6
Motherwell Wy *WTHK* RM20 ...... 482 D4
Mottram Cl *RIPW* IP8 .... 61 J3
Motts Cl *BRTR* CM7 .... 209 H1
Mott's La *RCOLW* CO6 .... 215 G1
 WIT CM8 .... 277 G1
Mott St *CHING* E4 .... 376 A5
Motts Yd *GTDUN* CM6 .... 173 K8
Moulsham Cha *CHLM/GWD* CM2 .. 15 D5
Moulsham Dr *CHLM/GWD* CM2 .. 14 C6
Moulsham Hall La *RCHLM* CM3 .. 241 G2
Moulsham Thrift *CHLM/GWD* CM2 .. 332 C3
Moultrie Wy *UPMR* RM14 .... 452 B1
Mountain Ash Cl *COLN* CO4 .... 9 E1
 SBF/HAD SS7 .... 442 C7
Mountain's Farm Rd *GTDUN* CM6 .. 237 G3
Mountains Rd *MAL* CM9 .... 278 D7
Mount Av *CHING* E4 .... 402 B6
 HARH RM3 .... 431 K1
 HOC/HUL SS5 .... 420 E7
 RAYL SS6 .... 441 H2
 RBRW/HUT CM13 .... 412 A3
 WOS/PRIT SS0 .... 463 H5
Mountbatten Cl *SUD* CO10 .... 58 C3
Mountbatten Ct *BKHH* IG9 .... 404 A5
Mountbatten Dr *COLS* CO2 .... 219 J2
 SBN/FI SS3 .... 466 D4
Mountbatten Rd *BRTR* CM7 .... 210 A1
Mountbatten Wy *CHLM/WR* CM1 .. 305 F6
Mount Bovers La *HOC/HUL* SS5 .. 443 F2
Mount Cl *RAYL* SS6 .... 441 H3
 WICKE SS11 .... 417 H5
Mount Crs *BRW* CM14 .... 411 G2
 HOC/HUL SS5 .... 421 F7
 SBF/HAD SS7 .... 460 D1
Mountdale Gdns *LOS* SS9 .... 463 C1
Mount Dr *IPSE* IP3 .... 64 D4
 STSD CM24 .... 167 K8
Mount Echo Av *CHING* E4 .... 402 C4
Mount Echo Dr *CHING* E4 .... 402 C4
Mountfield Cl *SLH/COR* SS17 ...... 474 A2
Mountfields *PIT* SS13 .... 458 E1
Mountfitchet Rd *STSD* CM24 ...... 167 K8
Mount Hl *HSTD* CO9 .... 147 J4
Mounthill Av *CHLM/GWD* CM2 ... 15 E2
Mount Lodge Cha *MAL* CM9 .... 279 F7
Mountnessing *SBF/HAD* SS7 ...... 461 J3
Mountnessing La *BRWN* CM15 ... 384 C4
Mountnessing Rd *BCAYW* CM12 .. 386 D6
 BRWN CM15 .... 384 E2
Mountney Cl *INC* CM4 .... 385 K4
Mount Pleasant *HSTD* CO9 .... 147 K4
 MAL CM9 .... 338 B3
Mount Pleasant Av
 RBRW/HUT CM13 .... 412 D2
Mount Pleasant Est *MAL* CM9 .... 279 C8
Mount Pleasant Rd *CHIG* IG7 ...... 405 G7

RCHLM CM3 .... 392 D6
SAFWS CB11 .... 70 E5
Mount Ri HSTD CO9 .... 147 J4 🔢
Mount Rd BRTR CM7 .... 209 K2
EPP CM16 .... 351 J6
HVHL CB9 .... 27 H6
RCOLW CO6 .... 213 J3
SBF/HAD SS7 .... 460 E1
WICKE SS11 .... 417 H5
The Mount BCAYE CM11 .... 415 F2
BRW CM14 .... 411 F6 🔢
COLW CO3 .... 186 A7
HARH RM3 .... 408 D6
MAL CM9 .... 314 D4
SLH/COR SS17 .... 474 B2
Mount Vw BCAYE CM11 .... 415 F3
Mountview Cl VGE SS16 .... 458 B2
Mountview Crs BOC CM6 .... 342 C4
Mount View Rd CHING E4 .... 11 D2
Mountview Rd COS CO15 .... 417 H5
Mount Wy WICKE SS12 .... 417 H5
Mowerons La RCOLE CO7 .... 255 F3
Mowbray Rd HLW CM20 .... 13 F1
Mowbrey Gdns LOU IG10 .... 378 A5 🔢
Mowlands RIPS/CAP IP9 .... 87 G4
Moxom Av BAR EN8 .... 346 E4
Moy Rd COLS CO2 .... 219 H4
Muckingford Rd TIL RM18 .... 486 A3
Mucking Hall Rd SBN/FI SS3 .... 446 B5
Mucking Wharf Rd SLH/COR SS17 ..... 473 J6
Muirway SBF/HAD SS7 .... 440 A6
Mulberry Av COLS CO2 .... 219 H1
Mulberry Cl BROX EN10 .... 319 F6
CHING E4 .... 402 B5
GPK RM2 .... 430 C6
Mulberry Ct BSF CM23 .... 199 F8
Mulberry Dr PUR RM19 .... 481 G3
Mulberry Gdns WIT CM8 .... 277 H3 🔢
Mulberry Gn HLWE CM17 .... 295 H1
Mulberry Hi BRWN CM15 .... 411 J3
Mulberry Rd CVI SS8 .... 477 C2
Mulberry Wy CHLM/WR CM1 .... 204 C1
Mullberry Gdns VGE SS16 .... 436 C8 🔢
Mullein Ct GRAYS RM17 .... 484 C5
Mullins Cl BRTR CM7 .... 177 J7
The Mullions CHLM/GWD CM2 .... 414 A2
Multon Lea CHLM/WR CM1 .... 305 J4
Mumford Cl RCOLW CO6 .... 185 J1
Mumford Rd IP IP1 .... 36 A5
RCOLW CO6 .... 185 J2
Mumfords La FOS CO13 .... 227 K6
Mundells EBAR EN7 .... 346 A1
Mundon Rd BRTR CM7 .... 210 C5
MAL CM9 .... 338 C4
Mungo Park Rd RAIN RM13 .... 450 C8 🔢
Munnings Cl HVHL CB9 .... 26 D4
IPSE IP3 .... 63 K5 🔢
Munnings Dr RCOS CO16 .... 10 A1
Munnings Rd COLW CO3 .... 186 B8
Munnings Wy MGTR CO11 .... 123 C8
Munro Rd WIT CM8 .... 245 F8
Munro Rd WICKW SS12 .... 417 H8 🔢
Munsons Aly BOC CM0 .... 398 D1
Munsterburg Rd CVI SS8 .... 461 J8
Murchison Cl CHLM/WR CM1 .... 304 A8
Murfitt Wy UPMR RM14 .... 451 H5 🔢
Murray Cl BRTR CM7 .... 177 H7
Murray Rd IPSE IP3 .... 63 J2
Murrell Lock CHLM/GWD CM2 .... 333 J1
Murrels Rd HOC/HUL SS5 .... 420 B6
Murrills Rd IPSE IP3 .... 64 D4
Murthering La ABR/ST RM4 .... 381 D4
Murton Slade CHLM/WR CM1 .... 27 G5 🔢
Muscade Cl K/T/MI CO5 .... 248 B7 🔢
Museum St COL CO1 .... 8 B4 🔢
IP IP1 .... 3 D5 🔢
SAFWN CB10 .... 70 E5 🔢
Musgrave Cl HAR CO12 .... 164 E4 🔢
Muskalls Cl EBAR EN7 .... 346 A1 🔢
Musk Cl COLW CO3 .... 185 J6
Musket Cv LOS SS9 .... 442 C6
Muskham Rd HLW CM20 .... 294 E2
Mutlow Hill London Rd
SAFWS CB11 .... 70 A8
Mutton Rw CHONG CM5 .... 353 J4
Mychett Cl RCOS CO16 .... 258 D7 🔢
Myland Hall Cha COLN CO4 .... 187 K2
Mylne Cl BAR EN8 .... 346 C1
Myln Meadow ING CM4 .... 388 B3
Mynchens LAIN SS15 .... 16 C4
Myneer Pk RCOLW CO6 .... 213 J8
Myrtle Gv COLS CO2 .... 9 D6
SOCK/AV RM15 .... 481 K1
Myrtle Rd BRW CM14 .... 411 F7
HARH RM3 .... 430 D1
IPSE IP3 .... 3 F5

N

Nabbott Rd CHLM/WR CM1 .... 332 A3
Nacton Crs IPSE IP3 .... 63 K3

Nacton Rd FX IP11 .... 5 E6
IPSE IP3 .... 63 H1 🔢
KIR/NAC IP10 .... 64 C6
Naffenton Rd LOU IG10 .... 404 A1 🔢
Nag's Head La UPMR RM14 .... 431 K3
Nags Head Rd PEND EN3 .... 374 C8
Nails La BSF CM23 .... 198 E6 🔢
Nalla Gdns CHLM/WR CM1 .... 304 C7
Namur Rd CVI SS8 .... 461 H8
Nancy Smith Cl COLS CO2 .... 8 B6
Nansen Av RCFD SS4 .... 422 A7
Nansen Rd COS CO15 .... 260 B7
IPSE IP3 .... 63 J3
Napier Av COS CO15 .... 289 K7
SOS SS1 .... 18 C4
Napier Cl HCH RM12 .... 450 C2 🔢
Napier Crs WICKW SS12 .... 417 H8
Napier Gdns SBF/HAD SS7 .... 441 H7
Napier Rd COLS CO2 .... 8 B5
GVW DA11 .... 488 D3
RAYL SS6 .... 442 A2
Narboro Ct ROM RM1 .... 430 B8 🔢
Nare Rd SOCK/AV RM15 .... 470 D8
Narvik Cl MAL CM9 .... 338 A5
Nash Cl COLW CO3 .... 186 C8
MGTR CO11 .... 123 C8
Nash Dr CHLM/WR CM1 .... 304 C2
Nassau Rd RCOS CO16 .... 289 H1
Nathan Cl UPMR RM14 .... 452 B2
Nathan Ct COLS CO2 .... 219 J5
Nathan's La CHLM/WR CM1 .... 330 D8
Nation Wy CHING E4 .... 402 D4 🔢
Nats La SAFWS CB11 .... 69 K7
Naunton Wy HCH RM12 .... 450 E4 🔢
Navestock Cl CHING E4 .... 402 D6 🔢
RAYL SS6 .... 441 F2 🔢
Navestock Gdns SOS SS1 .... 465 J4
Navestock Side BRW CM14 .... 382 E6
Navigation Rd CHLM/GWD CM2 .... 15 D3
Nayland Cl WICKW SS12 .... 417 H6 🔢
Nayland Dr RCOS CO16 .... 290 D1
Nayland Rd BURES CO8 .... 115 J3
COLN CO4 .... 154 E8
FX IP11 .... 4 C4
HVHL CB9 .... 26 E7
RCOLW CO6 .... 118 A6
RCOLW CO6 .... 153 J7
Nayling Rd BRTR CM7 .... 209 F3
Nazeingbury Cl WAB EN9 .... 319 K4 🔢
Nazeing Common WAB EN9 .... 320 E5
The Nazeing BSDN SS14 .... 438 B7
Naze Park Rd WOTN CO14 .... 229 J3
Neale Cl HSTD CO9 .... 147 K4
Neasden Av COS CO15 .... 10 A2
Neath Dr CHTY IP2 .... 62 C4
Neave Crs HARH RM3 .... 430 D3
Neil Armstrong Wy LOS SS9 .... 443 H6
Nelmes Cl EMPK RM11 .... 431 K1
Nelmes Crs EMPK RM11 .... 431 K1
Nelmes Rd EMPK RM11 .... 451 F1
Nelmes Wy EMPK RM11 .... 431 F6
Nelson Av CHLM/WR CM1 .... 14 A2
Nelson Cl BRW CM14 .... 411 G8
RAYL SS6 .... 442 A1
Nelson Crs MAL CM9 .... 338 D5 🔢
Nelson Dr LOS SS9 .... 463 G4
Nelson Gdns BRTR CM7 .... 210 B1
RAYL SS6 .... 442 A1
Nelson Gv CHLM/WR CM1 .... 14 A2
Nelson Ms SOS SS1 .... 19 D5
Nelson Pl RCHLM CM3 .... 392 B4
Nelson Rd BSDN SS14 .... 438 A7
BSF CM23 .... 199 F8
CDH/CHF RM16 .... 472 D6
COLW CO3 .... 185 K6
COS CO15 .... 10 B6
GVW DA11 .... 488 E7
HAR CO12 .... 7 D4
IPNE IP4 .... 37 J6
RAYL SS6 .... 442 A1
RCFD SS4 .... 422 A7
SOCK/AV RM15 .... 470 A1
SUD CO10 .... 58 D4
WOS/PRIT SS0 .... 463 H3
Nelson St RCOLE CO7 .... 255 J8
SOS SS1 .... 19 D5
Nelwyn Av EMPK RM11 .... 431 C7
Ness Cl RIPS/CAP IP9 .... 127 K4
SBN/FI SS3 .... 466 D8
Ness Wk WIT CM8 .... 276 D5
Nestuda Wy WOS/PRIT SS0 .... 443 J7
Nethan Dr SOCK/AV RM15 .... 468 E7
Nether Ct HSTD CO9 .... 148 B4
Netherfield SBF/HAD SS7 .... 461 F1
Nethergate St SUD CO10 .... 31 F7
Netherhall Rd HLWW/ROY CM19 ...... 292 B7
Nether Hl HSTD CO9 .... 81 J7
Nether Mayne VGE SS16 .... 17 E5
Netherpark Dr GPK RM2 .... 430 A4
Nether Priors BSDN SS14 .... 17 F4
Nether Rd SUD CO10 .... 32 C5
Netley Cl CHTY IP2 .... 62 B5
Netteswellbury Farm
HLWS CM18 .... 13 F4 🔢
Netteswell Orch HLW CM20 .... 13 D2
Netteswell Rd HLW CM20 .... 13 E1

Nevada Rd CVI SS8 .... 461 H8
Nevell Rd CDH/CHF RM16 .... 485 G2 🔢
Nevendon Ms PIT SS13 .... 438 D3 🔢
Nevendon Rd PIT SS13 .... 438 D3
WICKK SS12 .... 417 F7
Nevern Cl RAYL SS6 .... 442 A5
Nevern Rd RAYL SS6 .... 441 K5
Neville Rd SAFWN CB10 .... 71 F3
Neville Shaw BSDN SS14 .... 17 F3
Nevill Wy LOU IG10 .... 402 C4
Nevin Dr CHING E4 .... 402 B2
Newark Cl CHTY IP2 .... 62 B4
New Av VGE SS16 .... 456 B1
New Barn La RBSF CM22 .... 232 C4
Newbarn Rd RCOLW CO6 .... 182 E4
New Barns Wy CHIG IG7 .... 404 E6 🔢
Newbery Rd ERITH DA8 .... 480 A7
Newbiggen St GTDUN CM6 .... 139 J7
Newbourne Gdns FX IP11 .... 5 D4
New Bowers Wy CHLM/WR CM1 .... 305 D7
Newbridge Hl RCOLW CO6 .... 185 J3
Newbridge Rd K/T/MI CO5 .... 248 D8
Newbury Av PEND EN3 .... 375 F3
Newbury Cl BSF CM23 .... 198 D5
HARH RM3 .... 430 D1
Newbury Gdns HARH RM3 .... 430 E1
UPMR RM14 .... 451 G4
Newbury Rd HARH RM3 .... 408 D8
IPNE IP4 .... 37 K8
Newbury Wk HARH RM3 .... 408 E8 🔢
Newby Dr IPNE IP4 .... 38 D8
New Captains Rd K/T/MI CO5 .... 284 D7
New Cardinal St IP IP1 .... 2 C4
Newcastle Av COLW CO3 .... 217 K1
New Century Rd LAIN SS15 .... 436 C7
New Church Rd RCOLW CO6 .... 185 J1
Newcomen Wy COLN CO4 .... 155 J7
Newcourt Rd CHLM/GWD CM2 .... 15 E2
Newcroft SAFWN CB10 .... 71 F4 🔢
New Cut BURES CO8 .... 115 H5
COLS CO2 .... 218 A8
RCOLE CO7 .... 223 K5 🔢
SUD CO10 .... 33 H2
New Cut West CHTY IP2 .... 3 E5
New Dukes Wy CHLM/GWD CM2 ...... 333 H1
Newell Av SBN/FI SS3 .... 467 F5
New England Cl RCHLM CM3 .... 363 K4 🔢
New England Crs SBN/FI SS3 .... 467 H3 🔢
New Farm Dr ABR/ST RM4 .... 379 G7
New Farm Rd RCOLW CO6 .... 185 J7
New Ford Rd BAR EN8 .... 347 F8
Newgate St CHING E4 .... 403 F6 🔢
WOTN CO14 .... 229 H5 🔢
Newhall RCFD SS4 .... 421 K7
New Hall Dr HARH RM3 .... 431 F3
New Hall La MAL CM9 .... 367 G4
Newhouse Av WICKW SS12 .... 416 C6
New House La CHONG CM5 .... 325 J4
New House La GVW DA11 .... 488 E8 🔢
SAFWN CB10 .... 72 D2
Newhouse Rd RCOLW CO6 .... 181 G1
Newington Av SOSN SS2 .... 465 H3
Newington Cl SOSN SS2 .... 465 J3
Newington Gdns COS CO15 .... 259 H5
New Kiln Rd COLW CO3 .... 186 D6
Newland Av BRTR CM7 .... 142 C4 🔢
Newland Dr EN EN1 .... 374 B5
Newland Pl WIT CM8 .... 277 G4
Newlands Cl BCAYW CM12 .... 414 C1 🔢
RBRW/HUT CM13 .... 412 C3 🔢
Newlands Dr WIT CM8 .... 277 F3
Newlands End LAIN SS15 .... 436 C5
Newlands La RCOLW CO6 .... 118 C4
Newlands Rd BCAYW CM12 .... 414 C1 🔢
CVI SS8 .... 461 J8 🔢
WFD IG8 .... 403 G5
WICKW SS12 .... 439 G1
Newland St WIT CM8 .... 277 G3
New La K/T/MI CO5 .... 214 C8
New Lodge Cha RCHLM CM3 .... 335 F2
New London Rd CHLM/WR CM1 .... 14 C3 🔢
Newman Cl EMPK RM11 .... 431 F7
Newmans Dr RBRW/HUT CM13 .... 412 B3
Newmans La LOU IG10 .... 377 J7
Newman's Rd GVW DA11 .... 488 E7
SUD CO10 .... 58 B5 🔢
Newmarket Rd SAFWN CB10 .... 43 H2
Newmarket Wy HCH RM12 .... 451 F5
New Meadgate Ter
CHLM/GWD CM2 .... 15 E5 🔢
Newmill La MGTR CO11 .... 124 B4
New Moor Cl BOC CM0 .... 398 E1
New Moor Crs BOC CM0 .... 398 E1
New Nabbotts Wy CHLM/WR CM1.... 305 C6
Newnham Cl BRTR CM7 .... 209 H3
LOU IG10 .... 404 A2
Newnham Ct CHTY IP2 .... 62 A4
Newnham Gn MAL CM9 .... 338 A2 🔢
Newnham Pl CDH/CHF RM16 .... 485 F3 🔢
New Pk HSTD CO9 .... 110 E2
New Park Rd HOC/HUL SS5 .... 421 H5
SBF/HAD SS7 .... 440 B8
New Park St COL CO1 .... 9 D5
Newpasture La GTDUN CM6 .... 206 D1
Newpiece LOU IG10 .... 377 K7

New Pier St *WOTN* CO14 .... 229 H5 🔲
New Place Gdns *UPMR* RM14 ...... 452 A3
New Pond La *SAFWN* CB10 .... 70 D3
Newport Av *RCHLM* CM3 .... 366 D8
Newport Cl *CHLM/GWD* CM2 ...... 333 K7
  HAR CO12 .... 165 K4 🔲
  PEND EN3 .... 374 E3 🔲
Newport Dr *COS* CO15 .... 259 J6
Newports *SBW* CM21 .... 263 C4
Newport Wy *FOS* CO13 .... 229 F7
Newpots Cl *K/T/MI* CO5 .... 251 K8
Newpots La *K/T/MI* CO5 .... 252 A8
Newquay Cl *KESC* IP5 .... 38 D7 🔲
New Queens Rd *SUD* CO10 .... 58 B4
New Rd *ABR/ST* RM4 .... 406 C2
  BCAYW CM12 .... 436 B5
  BOC CMO 398 C8
  BROX EN10 .... 319 F1
  BRTR CM7 .... 208 C4
  BRW CM14 .... 411 G3
  CBE/LN CB1 .... 25 F7
  CHING E4 .... 402 C7
  CHLM/GWD CM2 .... 333 J7
  CHLM/WR CM1 .... 304 D4
  CVI SS8 .... 477 J2
  FX IP11 .... 94 D8
  GRAYS RM17 .... 483 A5
  GVW DA11 .... 489 F4 🔲
  HLWE CM17 .... 295 H1
  HSTD CO9 .... 141 D8
  ING CM4 .... 386 C1
  K/T/MI CO5 .... 246 D3
  K/T/MI CO5 .... 248 B8
  LOS SS9 .... 462 E5
  MAL CM9 .... 314 D3
  MGTR CO11 .... 159 J2
  RAIN RM13 .... 468 B7
  RBSF CM22 .... 168 C3
  RCHLM CM3 .... 275 C2
  RCHLM CM3 .... 308 A2
  RCOLW CO6 .... 184 A3
  RIPS/CAP IP9 .... 90 D8
  ROY SG8 .... 66 B1
  SAFWN CB10 .... 20 B7
  SAFWN CB10 .... 71 F4
  SBF/HAD SS7 .... 461 J2
  SBN/FI SS3 .... 467 H2
  SUD CO10 .... 34 D6
Newry Av *FX* IP11 .... 5 F3
Newson St *IP* IP1 .... 2 C2
Newstead Rd *SBN/FI* SS3 .... 467 G1
New St *BRTR* CM7 .... 209 J3 🔲
  CHLM/WR CM1 .... 14 C3
  GTDUN CM6 .... 204 C5
  HSTD CO9 .... 147 J4
  MAL CM9 .... 338 B3 🔲
  RCOLE CO7 .... 255 K8
  SBW CM21 .... 263 J2
  SUD CO10 .... 58 B5
New Street Flds *GTDUN* CM6 ...... 204 C5 🔲
Newsum Gdns *RAYL* SS6 .... 441 F2 🔲
New Swan Gd *GVE* DA12 .... 489 G4 🔳
Newtewell Dr *WAB* EN9 .... 347 K6
New Thorpe Av *RCOS* CO16 .... 226 D3
Newton Abbot Rd *GVW* DA11 ...... 488 E7
Newton Cl *BRTR* CM7 .... 209 J5 🔲
Newton Cft *SUD* CO10 .... 58 D6
Newton Dr *SBW* CM21 .... 263 H4
Newton Gn *GTDUN* CM6 .... 204 A4
Newton Hall Gdns *RCFD* SS4 ...... 422 A7
Newton Park Rd *SBF/HAD* SS7 .... 441 G6
Newton Rd *HAR* CO12 .... 6 B5 🔲
  IPSE IP5 .... 63 J1
  SUD CO10 .... 58 D6
  TIL RM18 .... 485 F8
Newton Wy *RCOS* CO16 .... 257 G8
Newtown Rd *BSF* CM23 .... 198 E7
New Town Rd *COL* CO1 .... 8 C5
  RCOS CO16 .... 226 C3
New Waverley Rd *LAIN* SS15 .... 16 C1
New Wy *CHTY* IP2 .... 2 A3
New Writtle St *CHLM/WR* CM1 .... 14 C4
Niagara Cl *BAR* EN8 .... 346 D3 🔲
Nicholas Cl *CHLM/WR* CM1 .... 331 H5
  SOCK/AV RM15 .... 470 A3
Nicholas Ct *WIT* CM8 .... 277 F3 🔲
Nicholl Rd *EPP* CM16 .... 350 D5
  LAIN SS15 .... 436 C6
Nicholls Fld *HLWS* CM18 .... 295 F6
Nichols Cl *MGTR* CO11 .... 159 G2
Nicholson Ct *SBF/HAD* SS7 .... 461 G2 🔲
Nicholson Gv *WICKW* SS12 .... 417 H8 🔲
Nicholson Pl *RCHLM* CM3 .... 363 F6
Nicholson Rd *SBF/HAD* SS7 .... 461 G2
Nickleby Rd *CHLM/WR* CM1 ...... 303 K6
Nickolsons Gv *COL* CO1 .... 8 C5
Nien-oord *RCOS* CO16 .... 290 C1 🔲
Nightingale Av *CHING* E4 .... 403 F8
  UPMR RM14 .... 452 B2
Nightingale Cl *CHING* E4 .... 403 F7 🔲
  COLN CO4 .... 188 D5 🔲
  COS CO15 .... 10 C2 🔲

HAR CO12 .... 164 E4 🔲
  RAYL SS6 .... 441 G2 🔲
  SOSN SS2 .... 444 B7
  WIT CM8 .... 276 E5 🔲
Nightingale HI *COLN* CO4 .... 120 C7
Nightingale Ms *SAFWN* CB10 ..... 71 G3 🔲
Nightingale PI *COLW* CO3 .... 217 H1 🔲
Nightingale Rd *CVI* SS16 .... 478 C2 🔲
  IPSE IP3 .... 63 J5
Nightingales *VGE* SS16 .... 436 A8
Nightingale Sq *IPSE* IP3 .... 63 J5 🔲
Nightingale Wy *COS* CO15 .... 10 C2
Nineacres *BRTR* CM7 .... 209 K4 🔲
  ING CM4 .... 356 A3
Nine Ashes Rd *BRWN* CM15 ...... 355 K7
Nine Elms Gv *GVW* DA11 .... 489 F5
Ninefields *WAB* EN9 .... 348 B7
Nipsells Cha *RCHLM* CM3 .... 368 D3
Nita Rd *BRW* CM14 .... 411 F8
Niven Cl *WICKW* SS12 .... 417 H8
Noakes Av *CHLM/GWD* CM2 ...... 333 G8
Noak Hill Cl *BCAYW* CM12 .... 436 D2
Noak Hill Rd *BCAYW* CM12 .... 414 C8
  HARH RM3 .... 408 E6
Nobel Sq *PIT* SS13 .... 439 F3
Nobles Green Cl *LOS* SS9 .... 443 F6
Nobles Green Rd *LOS* SS9 .... 443 F6
The Nobles *BSF* CM23 .... 198 D5 🔲
Nonsuch Meadow *SUD* CO10 ..... 58 B7
The Nook *RCOLE* CO7 .... 221 F4
Norbury Cl *RCOLW* CO6 .... 215 J1
Norbury Rd *CHING* E4 .... 402 B8
  IPNE IP4 .... 37 K6
Nordland Rd *CVI* SS8 .... 478 D1
Nordmann PI *SOCK/AV* RM15 ..... 470 B4
Noredale *SBN/FI* SS3 .... 466 C7
Nore Rd *LOS* SS9 .... 442 D5
Norfolk Av *COS* CO15 .... 260 D7
  K/T/MI CO5 .... 285 F6
  LOS SS9 .... 463 G2
Norfolk Cl *CVI* SS8 .... 461 F8 🔲
  LAIN SS15 .... 436 B7
  MAL CM9 .... 338 A4
Norfolk Crs *COLN* CO4 .... 9 D2
Norfolk Dr *CHLM/WR* CM1 .... 304 C6
Norfolk Gdns *BRTR* CM7 .... 210 A3 🔲
  IPNE IP4 .... 3 E3
  MAL CM9 .... 338 A4
  UPMR RM14 .... 451 H4
Norfolk Rd *GVE* DA12 .... 489 J4
Norfolk Wy *BSF* CM23 .... 198 E8
  CVI SS8 .... 460 E8
Norman Av *BSF* CM23 .... 198 C7
Norman Cl *RCOLW* CO6 .... 215 H2
  RCOS CO16 .... 289 G1
  WAB EN9 .... 347 K7
Norman Crs *IPSE* IP3 .... 63 J5
  RAYL SS6 .... 419 K8 🔲
  RBRW/HUT CM13 .... 411 K6 🔲
Normandie Wy *BURES* CO8 .... 115 H5
Normandy Av *BOC* CMO 398 C8
  COLS CO2 .... 219 H2
Norman HI *RCHLM* CM3 .... 275 F3
Normanhurst *RBRW/HUT* CM13 ... 412 B2 🔲
Norman Rd *COS* CO15 .... 260 B7
  MGTR CO11 .... 159 J1
Normans Cl *GVW* DA11 .... 489 F5
Normansfield *GTDUN* CM6 .... 204 D6
Normanshire Dr *CHING* E4 .... 402 B7
Normanton Pk *CHING* E4 .... 403 F6
Norman Wy *COLW* CO3 .... 186 C8
  RCHLM CM3 .... 287 K2
Norris Cl *BRTR* CM7 .... 178 B8 🔲
  BSF CM23 .... 199 H6
Norris Gv *BROX* EN10 .... 318 C2
Norsey Cl *BCAYE* CM11 .... 414 C2
Norsey Dr *BCAYE* CM11 .... 414 D2
Norsey Rd *BCAYE* CM11 .... 414 C2
Norsey View Dr *BCAYW* CM12 .... 387 H7
Northallerton Wy *HARH* RM3 .... 408 D7
Northampton Meadow
  BRTR CM7 .... 142 B3
Northampton Rd *PEND* EN3 ...... 374 E8 🔲
North Av *CHLM/WR* CM1 .... 304 B8
  CVI SS8 .... 477 K1
  HVHL CB9 .... 26 E5
  SOSN SS2 .... 19 E3
North Barn *BROX* EN10 .... 319 H4
North Benfleet Hall Rd
  WICKW SS12 .... 439 J4
Northbrooks *HLWW/ROY* CM19 ... 12 B4
North Cl *CHIG* IG7 .... 405 K8
  IPNE IP4 .... 3 F1
North Colne *VGE* SS16 .... 458 A1
Northcote Rd *GVW* DA11 .... 488 E6
North Crs *HVHL* CB9 .... 50 C5
  SOSN SS2 .... 443 K8
  WICKW SS12 .... 417 G6
North Crockerford *VGE* SS16 .... 438 A8
Northcroft *SUD* CO10 .... 58 B6 🔲
North Dell *CHLM/WR* CM1 .... 305 F6

Northdene *CHIG* IG7 .... 405 G8
Northdown Rd *EMPK* RM11 .... 450 C1
North Dr *CHLM/GWD* CM2 .... 333 H6
  GPK RM2 .... 430 D5
  RBRW/HUT CM13 .... 413 G2
  RCHLM CM3 .... 368 D3
North End *BKHH* IG9 .... 403 K3
  BOC CMO 370 D8
Northend *RBRW/HUT* CM13 ...... 411 F8
Northend Rd *ERITH* DA8 .... 480 A7
North End Rd *HSTD* CO9 .... 80 D2
  SAFWN CB10 .... 20 B5
Northern Av *SBF/HAD* SS7 .... 440 B8
Northern Rd *SUD* CO10 .... 58 E6
Northfalls Rd *CVI* SS8 .... 479 F2
North Farm *LOU* IG10 .... 403 K2
Northfield *BRTR* CM7 .... 142 C2
Northfield Cl *BCAYE* CM11 .... 414 D3 🔳
Northfield Crs *SBN/FI* SS3 .... 467 F1
Northfield Gdns *COLN* CO4 ...... 187 H1
Northfield Rd *BAR* EN8 .... 346 E6
  SAFWS CB11 .... 71 F5 🔲
  SBW CM21 .... 263 J1
Northfields *GRAYS* RM17 .... 484 B3
North Ga *HLW* CM20 .... 12 C2 🔲
Northgate End *BSF* CM23 .... 198 E5
Northgate St *COL* CO1 .... 8 B4
North Gv *HLWS* CM18 .... 294 E6
North Gunnels *BSDN* SS14 .... 17 F4
North Hall Rd *RBSF* CM22 .... 136 C6
  SAFWS CB11 .... 136 B3
North HI *COL* CO1 .... 8 A3
  RCHLM CM3 .... 307 H7
  SLH/COR SS17 .... 473 F1
North Hill Dr *HARH* RM3 .... 408 E7
North Hill Gdns *IPNE* IP4 .... 3 F3 🔲
North Hill Rd *IPNE* IP4 .... 3 F3
North Kent Av *GVW* DA11 .... 488 B4
North Kent Aveune *GVW* DA11 .. 488 B4
Northlands Ap *VGE* SS16 .... 456 D4
Northlands Cl *SLH/COR* SS17 .... 457 F8
Northlands Farm Cha
  SLH/COR SS17 .... 457 F6
North La *RCOLW* CO6 .... 216 A1
North Lawn *IPNE* IP4 .... 37 K5
Northolme Cl *CDH/CHF* RM16 .... 484 B2 🔲
Northolt Av *BSF* CM23 .... 199 G4
Northolt Wy *HCH* RM12 .... 450 D6
North PI *HLW* CM20 .... 262 E8
  WAB EN9 .... 347 H7 🔲
Northridge Rd *GVE* DA12 .... 489 H8
North Ri *SUD* CO10 .... 58 D7
North Rd *BRW* CM14 .... 411 F4
North Service Rd *BRW* CM14 .... 411 F5
North Shoebury Rd *SBN/FI* SS3 .. 466 C4
North Station Rd *COL* CO1 ...... 8 A3
North St *BOC* CMO 344 A8
  BOC CMO 398 D1
  BSF CM23 .... 198 E5
  EMPK RM11 .... 450 E1
  GTDUN CM6 .... 204 C4
  GVE DA12 .... 489 G5 🔲
  LOS SS9 .... 463 F5
  MAL CM9 .... 281 H8
  MAL CM9 .... 338 D3
  MGTR CO11 .... 159 J1 🔲
  RCFD SS4 .... 444 C3
  SBN/FI SS3 .... 467 G1
  SUD CO10 .... 58 B5
  WAB EN9 .... 320 A4
  WOTN CO14 .... 229 H4 🔲
  WOTN CO14 .... 229 H5 🔳
North Ter *BSF* CM23 .... 198 E5
Northumberland Av *EMPK* RM11 .. 430 D7
  EN EN1 .... 374 B4
  LAIN SS15 .... 16 A5 🔲
  SOS SS1 .... 19 F5
Northumberland Cl *BRTR* CM7 ... 210 A1 🔲
Northumberland Ct
  CHLM/GWD CM2 .... 333 H1 🔲
Northumberland Crs *SOS* SS1 .... 465 G6
Northumberland Rd
  SLH/COR SS17 .... 486 A1
North View Av *TIL* RM18 .... 485 F7
Northview Dr *WOS/PRIT* SS0 .... 18 A2
Northville Dr *WOS/PRIT* SS0 .... 463 K1
North Wall *RCOS* CO16 .... 287 K2
North Weald Cl *WICKE* SS11 .... 418 A7 🔲
Northwick Rd *CVI* SS8 .... 476 E1
Northwood Cl *CDH/CHF* RM16 ... 485 G1 🔲
Northwood Av *HCH* RM12 .... 450 B5

Norton Av *CVI* SS8 .... 478 E2
Norton Rd *CHING* E4 .... 402 B8
  SLH/COR SS17 .... 474 B1
Norton Heath Rd *CHONG* CM5 .... 328 B5
Norton La *CHONG* CM5 .... 327 J7
Norton Rd *CHLM/WR* CM1 .... 14 B2
  HVHL CB9 .... 26 E7 🔢
  ING CM4 .... 386 B1
Norway Crs *HAR* CO12 .... 6 A5
Norwich Av *SOSN* SS2 .... 19 F1
Norwich Cl *COL* CO15 .... 8 C3 🔢
  RCOS CO16 .... 10 A1
  SOSN SS2 .... 19 F2 🔢
Norwich Crs *RAYL* SS6 .... 419 H8
Norwich Rd *IP* IP1 .... 2 B2
Norwood Av *COS* CO15 .... 11 E2
Norwood Dr *SBF/HAD* SS7 .... 460 D4
Norwood End *BSDN* SS16 .... 438 A6
  CHONG CM5 .... 298 E6
Norwood Rd *BAR* EN8 .... 346 E4
Norwood Wy *WOTN* CO14 .... 229 F6
Notcutts *RCOLE* CO7 .... 122 D4
Notley Dr *HVHL* CB9 .... 26 B4
Notley Cl *ON BRTR* CM7 .... 208 E8
Notley La *ON BRTR* CM7 .... A5
Notley Rd *BRTR* CM7 .... 208 C1
Nottage *ON* La *SLH/COR* SS17 ... 474 B1 🔢
Nottidge Rd *IPNE* IP4 .... 3 F5
Nottingham Cl *COS* CO15 .... 260 C7
Nottingham Wy *VGE* SS16 .... 436 A8
Nounsley Rd *RCHLM* CM3 .... 308 B4
Nunnery La *HSTD* CO9 .... 110 C1
Nunns Cl *RCOLW* CO6 .... 213 H3
Nunn's Rd *COL* CO1 .... 8 A4
Nunns Wy *GRAYS* RM17 .... 484 C3
Nunsbury Dr *BROX* EN10 .... 318 C7 🔢
Nun's Meadow *HSTD* CO9 .... 146 D5
Nuns Wk *HSTD* CO9 .... 79 J4
Nunty's La *BRTR* CM7 .... 180 A5
Nursery Cl *COLW* CO3 .... 185 H8
  PEND EN3 .... 374 D5
  RAYL SS6 .... 440 A3
  SOCK/AV RM15 .... 470 A4
  WFD IG8 .... 403 J8
Nursery Dr *BRTR* CM7 .... 177 K8
Nursery Flds *SBW* CM23 .... 263 H5
Nursery Gdns *LAIN* SS15 .... 16 A2
  BRWN CM15 .... 356 A8
  BSF CM23 .... 198 E7
  CHLM/GWD CM2 .... 14 C5
  LOU IG10 .... 377 F8
  SLH/COR SS17 .... 473 K2
  SUD CO10 .... 58 E8
  WAB EN9 .... 319 K4
The Nursery *ERITH* DA8 .... 480 A6
Nursery Wk *FX* IP11 .... 5 F3
Nutberry Av *CDH/CHF* RM16 .... 483 K1 🔢
Nutberry Cl *CDH/CHF* RM16 .... 483 K1 🔢
Nutcombe Crs *RCFD* SS4 .... 444 A1
Nuthatch Cl *BCAYE* CM11 .... 414 D5
Nyth Cl *UPMR* RM14 .... 432 A8

Oakapple Cl *COLS* CO2 .... 218 E4
Oak Av *BCAYE* CM11 .... 437 K1
  COS CO15 .... 290 C3
  UPMR RM14 .... 451 J4
  WICKE SS11 .... 418 B6
Oakbank *RBRW/HUT* CM13 .... 412 D1
Oak Bungalows *BRTR* CM7 .... 209 H2 🔢
Oak Cha *WICKW* SS12 .... 416 D6
Oak Cl *FX* IP11 .... 5 E3
  MAL CM9 .... 338 D5
  RCOLW CO6 .... 185 K2
  RCOS CO16 .... 226 D4
  WAB EN9 .... 347 K8
Oakdale Gdns *CHING* E4 .... 402 D8
Oakdene *BAR* EN8 .... 346 E4
  KIR/NAC IP10 .... 94 C2
Oak Dene Cl *ROM* RM1 .... 430 C8 🔢
Oakdene Dr *PIT* SS13 .... 438 E5
Oak Dr *SBW* CM21 .... 263 H6
Oak End *HLWS* CM18 .... 13 F5 🔢
Oaken Grange Dr *SOSN* SS2 .... 444 B8
Oak Fall *WIT* CM8 .... 245 G8 🔢
Oak Farm Rd *MAL* CM9 .... 336 D3
Oakfield *CHING* E4 .... 402 C8 🔢
Oakfield Cl *SBF/HAD* SS7 .... 460 B2
Oakfield La *RCHLM* CM3 .... 274 C3
Oakfield Rd *HOC/HUL* SS5 .... 421 H5
  RIPW IP8 .... 61 F7
  SBF/HAD SS7 .... 460 B2
Oak Gld *EPP* CM16 .... 351 H3
Oak Gln *EMPK* RM11 .... 431 F5
Oakham Cl *VGE* SS16 .... 436 A8 🔢
Oak Hl *BRTR* CM7 .... 144 D5
Oak Hill La *CHTY* IP2 .... 2 C6

Oak Hill Rd *ABR/ST* RM4 .... 407 J3
Oakhill Rd *PUR* RM19 .... 481 J4
Oak Holm *COLS* CO2 .... 219 H2
Oakhurst Cl *WICKS* SS12 .... 417 H8
Oakhurst Dr *WICKW* SS12 .... 416 E7
Oakhurst Gdns *CHING* E4 .... 403 G4
Oakhurst Rd *PEND* EN3 .... 374 D2
  RAYL SS6 .... 442 A5
  SOSN SS2 .... 19 D2
Oakland Gdns *RBRW/HUT* CM13 .. 412 B1 🔢
Oakland Pl *BKHH* IG9 .... 403 H5
Oakland Rd *HAR* CO12 .... 7 D5
Oaklands Av *COLW* CO3 .... 185 K8
Oaklands Cl *BRTR* CM7 .... 209 G5
  BSF CM23 .... 199 G3
Oaklands Crs *CHLM/GWD* CM2 .... 14 C5
Oaklands Dr *BSF* CM23 .... 199 G4
  HLWE CM17 .... 295 G6
  SOCK/AV RM15 .... 470 A5
Oaklands Gv *BROX* EN10 .... 318 E6
Oaklands Ms *RCFD* SS4 .... 443 K1 🔢
Oaklands Pk *BSF* CM23 .... 199 G3
Oaklands Wy *RCHLM* CM3 .... 335 J3
Oak La *BCAYE* CM11 .... 437 K2
  WFD IG8 .... 403 J7
Oaklea *CHLM/GWD* CM2 .... 15 F1
Oakleigh Av *HOC/HUL* SS5 .... 419 K3
  SOS SS1 .... 465 G5
Oakleigh Park Dr *LOS* SS9 .... 463 F4
Oakleigh Rd *COS* CO15 .... 259 H5
Oakleighs *SBF/HAD* SS7 .... 460 B1
Oakley Av *RAYL* SS6 .... 440 E2
Oakley Cl *CHING* E4 .... 402 D6 🔢
  WTHK RM20 .... 483 F5
Oakley Dr *BCAYW* CM12 .... 387 F8 🔢
  HARH RM3 .... 409 H8
Oakley Rd *BRTR* CM7 .... 177 J6
  HAR CO12 .... 6 C4
  MGTR CO11 .... 162 C8
Oak Lodge Av *CHIG* IG7 .... 405 G8
Oak Lodge Tye *CHLM/WR* CM1 ... 305 J7
Oakmead Rd *RCOS* CO16 .... 288 A2
Oakmoor Wy *CHIG* IG7 .... 405 H8
Oak Piece *EPP* CM16 .... 324 C7
Oak Rdg *HAR* CO12 .... 164 A6
Oak Ri *BKHH* IG9 .... 404 A6
Oak Rd *BCAYE* CM11 .... 389 F8
  BCAYE CM11 .... 437 K1
  CVI SS8 .... 478 C2
  EPP CM16 .... 350 D4
  ERITH DA8 .... 480 B7
  GRAYS RM17 .... 484 B5
  GVE DA12 .... 489 G8
  HARH RM3 .... 431 G3
  HSTD CO9 .... 112 B5
  HSTD CO9 .... 113 C4
  HSTD CO9 .... 147 J5
  K/T/MI CO5 .... 248 A6
  MAL CM9 .... 310 D7
  RCFD SS4 .... 444 A3
  RCOLW CO6 .... 182 E3
  SUD CO10 .... 58 E7
  WIT CM8 .... 245 J6
Oak Rd North *SBF/HAD* SS7 .... 461 K3
Oak Rd South *SBF/HAD* SS7 .... 461 K3
Oakroyd Av *GTDUN* CM6 .... 204 D5
Oaks Dr *COLW* CO3 .... 186 E6
Oaks Gv *CHING* E4 .... 403 F5
Oaksmere Gdns *CHTY* IP2 .... 62 C3
Oaks Pl *COLN* CO4 .... 187 F2
Oakstead Cl *IPNE* IP4 .... 37 H7
The Oaks *BCAYE* CM11 .... 414 B3
  FOS CO13 .... 228 E7
  KESG IP5 .... 39 K7
Oak St *BSF* CM23 .... 198 E7
Oaktree Cl *BSF* CM23 .... 198 E6
Oak Tree Cl *LOU* IG10 .... 378 A5
Oaktree Rd *RBRW/HUT* CM13 ...... 411 J8
Oak Tree Rd *RCOLE* CO7 .... 222 A5
Oakview *HAR* CO12 .... 164 E4
Oakview Cl *EBAR* EN4 .... 346 B1
Oak Wk *HOC/HUL* SS5 .... 421 F6
  HSTD CO9 .... 110 C3 🔢
  SBF/HAD SS7 .... 440 A5
Oakway *CDH/CHF* RM16 .... 471 F8
Oakwood Av *COS* CO15 .... 260 C7
  K/T/MI CO5 .... 285 F6
  LOS SS9 .... 463 F1
  RBRW/HUT CM13 .... 412 D2
Oakwood Cha *EMPK* RM11 .... 451 G1
Oakwood Cl *FOS* CO13 .... 228 D7 🔢
  SBF/HAD SS7 .... 440 A8 🔢
Oakwood Ct *RCHLM* CM3 .... 396 E2
Oakwood Dr *BCAYW* CM12 .... 387 J8
  K/T/MI CO5 .... 285 F6
Oakwood Gdns *K/T/MI* CO5 .... 285 F6 🔢
Oakwood Gv *PIT* SS13 .... 438 E7
Oakwood Hl *LOU* IG10 .... 404 D2
Oakwood Hill Industrial Est
  LOU IG10 .... 404 E1
Oakwood Rd *RAYL* SS6 .... 441 H1
  SLH/COR SS17 .... 474 D1
Oakwood St *SAFWN* CB10 .... 70 E4
Oast Wy *RCFD* SS4 .... 444 C3
Oates Rd *CRW* RM5 .... 407 G8

Oatfield Cl *COLW* CO3 .... 185 J7
Oatlands *RCOLE* CO7 .... 189 J7 🔢
Oatlands Rd *PEND* EN3 .... 374 C5
Oban Ct *WICKE* SS11 .... 418 A8
Oban Rd *SOSN* SS2 .... 19 F3
Oban St *IP* IP1 .... 2 C2
Oberon Cl *COLN* CO4 .... 188 C6
Obrey Wy *BSF* CM23 .... 231 J2
Observer Wy *K/T/MI* CO5 .... 246 D1
Ockelford Av *CHLM/WR* CM1 .... 304 E8
Ockendon Rd *UPMR* RM14 .... 452 A7
Ockendon Wy *WOTN* CO14 .... 229 F5 🔢
Octavia Dr *WIT* CM8 .... 276 E5 🔢
Oddcroft *RCOLW* CO6 .... 149 G4
Odessa Rd *CVI* SS8 .... 478 C2
Office La *MAL* CM9 .... 279 J8
Ogilvie Ct *WICKW* SS12 .... 417 H8 🔢
Okehampton Sq *HARH* RM3 .... 430 D1 🔢
Old Barn La *RCHLM* CM3 .... 390 D4
Old Barn Rd *BURES* CO8 .... 115 J7
Old Barns La *ING* CM4 .... 329 F7
Old Bell Cl *STSD* CM24 .... 167 J7
Old Bell La *RCHLM* CM3 .... 391 F4
Oldbury Av *CHLM/GWD* CM2 .... 333 H6
Old Burylodge La *STSD* CM24 ..... 200 B1
Oldbury Rd *EN* EN1 .... 374 A6
Old Church Hl *VGE* SS16 .... 456 A4
Old Church La *RBRW/HUT* CM13 .. 385 J8
  SUD CO10 .... 83 G2 🔢
Old Church Rd *CHING* E4 .... 402 B6
  PIT SS13 .... 439 J8
  RBRW/HUT CM13 .... 385 K6
  RCHLM CM3 .... 363 F8
Old Coach Rd *COL* CO1 .... 9 D4 🔢
Old Ct *CHLM/WR* CM1 .... 15 E2
Old Crown La *BRW* CM14 .... 383 F6
Oldfield Rd *RIPW* IP8 .... 61 H4
Old Forge Rd *COLS* CO2 .... 218 A8
  RCHLM CM3 .... 306 C5
Old Foundry Rd *IPNE* IP4 .... 3 E5 🔢
Old Hall La *MAL* CM9 .... 314 C1
  RIPS/CAP IP9 .... 88 A2
  WOTN CO14 .... 229 K1
Old Hall Ri *HLWE* CM17 .... 295 J5
Oldhall Rd *RIPS/CAP* IP9 .... 128 E1
Old Haverhill Rd *HVHL* CB9 .... 27 K1
Old Heath Rd *BOC* CM0 .... 398 A3
  COLS CO2 .... 219 K1
Old Hill Av *VGE* SS16 .... 456 C5
Oldhouse Cft *HLW* CM20 .... 13 E1
Old House La *COLN* CO4 .... 155 G3
  HLWW/ROY CM19 .... 293 F8
Old House Rd *RCOLE* CO7 .... 154 A5
Old Ipswich Rd *COLN* CO4 .... 156 B6
Old Jenkins Cl *SLH/COR* SS17 .... 473 H4 🔢
Old Kirton Rd *FX* IP11 .... 94 B5
Old Leigh Rd *LOS* SS9 .... 463 H4
Old London Rd *MAL* CM9 .... 336 D5
  RIPS/CAP IP9 .... 86 E6
  WICKE SS11 .... 418 C7
The Old Maltings *BSF* CM23 .... 199 F6 🔢
Old Md *LOS* SS9 .... 443 H6
Old Mead Rd *RBSF* CM22 .... 168 D1
Old Mill La *K/T/MI* CO5 .... 214 A6
  RBSF CM22 .... 232 B7
Old Mill Rd *COLN* CO4 .... 119 K8
  SAFWS CB11 .... 71 F5
Old Nazeing Rd *BROX* EN10 .... 319 G3
  WAB EN9 .... 319 J4
Old Oaks *WAB* EN9 .... 348 A6 🔢
Old Orch *HLWS* CM18 .... 13 D5
Old Parsonage Wy *FOS* CO13 ...... 228 E8
Old Perry St *GVW* DA11 .... 488 D7
Old Pier St *WOTN* CO14 .... 229 H5
Old Rectory Rd *CHONG* CM5 .... 353 H7
Old River La *BSF* CM23 .... 198 E6 🔢
Old Rd *ABR/ST* RM4 .... 381 K6
  BRTR CM7 .... 179 K8
  COS CO15 .... 10 B4
  FOS CO13 .... 261 K1
  HLWE CM17 .... 263 G7
  HSTD CO9 .... 82 E8 🔢
  PEND EN3 .... 374 C5
  RCOLW CO6 .... 214 A3
Old Rd East *GVE* DA12 .... 489 J6
Old Rd West *GVW* DA11 .... 488 E6
Old Rope Wk *HVHL* CB9 .... 26 E6
Old Rose Gdns *COLN* CO4 .... 186 E1 🔢
Old School Cl *RCOS* CO16 .... 289 G1
Old School Ct *RCHLM* CM3 .... 308 B2 🔢
Old School Fld *CHLM/WR* CM1 ... 14 A1
Old School La *RCOLE* CO7 .... 189 K7
Old School Meadow *SBN/FI* SS3 .. 466 D1
Old Ship La *RCFD* SS4 .... 444 C3 🔢
Old Shire La *WAB* EN9 .... 348 C8
Old Southend Rd
  CHLM/GWD CM2 .... 362 A4
  SOS SS1 .... 19 E5
Old Station Rd *LOU* IG10 .... 404 B1
Old Street Hl *RBSF* CM22 .... 233 J8
The Old St *RIPS/CAP* IP9 .... 87 G4
Old Vicarage Cl *CHLM/WR* CM1 .. 269 G3
Old Vicarage Rd *HAR* CO12 .... 6 C5
Old Wy *FOS* CO13 .... 261 K1
Old Wickford Rd *RCHLM* CM3 ..... 392 B5

Oldwyk VGE SS16 .... 458 B1
Olive Av LOS SS9 .... 462 B3
Olive Gv COLS CO2 .... 218 E3
Oliver Cl WITHK RM20 .... 482 C6
Oliver Pl WIT CM8 .... 277 H3
Oliver Rd BRWN CM15 .... 411 K1
  WTHK RM20 .... 482 C7
Olivers Cl COS CO15 .... 10 B3
  SUD CO10 .... 35 F6
Olivers Crs SBN/FI SS3 .... 467 F1
Olivers Dr WIT CM8 .... 277 G6
Olivers La COLS CO2 .... 218 A6
Olivers Rd COS CO15 .... 10 B3
Oliver Wy CHLM/WR CM1 .... 304 B6
Oliveswood Rd GTDUN CM6 .... 204 C6
Olivia Dr LOS SS9 .... 463 G3
Ollard's Gv LOU IG10 .... 377 F8
Onehouse La IP IP1 .... 36 D4
One Tree Hl SLH/COR SS17 .... 457 G4
Ongar Cl RCOS CO16 .... 290 D1
Ongark Rd CHLM/WR CM1 .... 331 H4
Ongar Pl BRW CM14 .... 411 G5
Ongar Rd CHLM/WR CM1 .... 304 C7
  BRWN CM15 .... 354 D7
  CHLM/WR CM1 .... 329 K6
  CHONG CM5 .... 326 D6
  GTDUN CM6 .... 204 C7
  GTDUN CM6 .... 300 B3
Onslow Cl CHING E4 .... 402 E5
Onslow Crs COLS CO2 .... 219 H4
Onslow Gdns CHONG CM5 .... 354 C1
Ophir Rd RCOLE CO7 .... 255 K8
Orange Rd CVI SS8 .... 478 D5
Orange St GTDUN CM6 .... 139 K3
Orange Tree Cl CHLM/GWD CM2 .... 332 E2
Orange Tree Hl ROM RM1 .... 407 J8
Orchard Av BCAYE CM11 .... 416 A3
  BCAYW CM12 .... 387 J8
  HOC/HUL SS5 .... 421 F6
  HSTD CO9 .... 147 J4
  RAYL SS6 .... 441 F6
  RBRW/HUT CM13 .... 411 J6
Orchard Cl CHING E4 .... 402 B6
  CHLM/GWD CM2 .... 332 E2
  CHLM/WR CM1 .... 331 H3
  GTDUN CM6 .... 139 K2
  HAR CO12 .... 163 K2
  HAR CO12 .... 195 F2
  HOC/HUL SS5 .... 421 G6
  HSTD CO9 .... 52 E7
  HVHL CB9 .... 27 F6
  MAL CM9 .... 314 E4
  MAL CM9 .... 338 B3
  RBSF CM22 .... 264 C5
  RCHLM CM3 .... 308 A1
  RCOLE CO7 .... 189 K7
  RCOLW CO6 .... 216 C3
  RCOS CO16 .... 258 E8
  SAFWS CB11 .... 70 E6
  SAFWS CB11 .... 100 A5
  SBN/FI SS3 .... 467 F1
  SOCK/AV RM15 .... 470 A4
Orchard Cft HLW CM20 .... 294 E3
Orchard Dr BRTR CM7 .... 209 K4
  EPP CM16 .... 378 C2
  FOS CO13 .... 260 E1
  GRAYS RM17 .... 483 K1
  RCHLM CM3 .... 368 E4
Orchard Gdns WAB EN9 .... 347 H8
Orchard Gn KESC IP5 .... 38 E6
  LOS SS9 .... 443 G7
Orchard La BRWN CM15 .... 410 C1
  WFD IG8 .... 403 K7
Orchardleigh Av PEND EN3 .... 374 C6
Orchard Md LOS SS9 .... 443 F8
Orchard Piece CM4 .... 356 D5
Orchard Pightle CBE/LIN CB1 .... 22 D6
Orchard Rd BOC CM0 .... 398 D7
  BOC CM0 .... 425 H1
  BSF CM23 .... 199 G4
  COL CO1 .... 8 A3
  GVW DA11 .... 488 D7
  K/T/MI CO5 .... 246 E2
  MAL CM9 .... 338 B3
  RCOLE CO7 .... 222 A5
  SBF/HAD SS7 .... 440 A7
  SOCK/AV RM15 .... 470 A5
Orchards WIT CM8 .... 277 F4
Orchard Side LOS SS9 .... 443 G7
Orchard Sq BROX EN10 .... 319 F6
Orchard Pightle ...
The Orchard EPP CM16 .... 350 E6
  SBW CM21 .... 263 J3
Orchard St CHLM/GWD CM2 .... 14 C4
The Orchard GTDUN CM6 .... 206 D8
  WICKW SS12 .... 416 E6
Orchard Wy CHIG IG7 .... 405 K6
  SUD CO10 .... 33 H2
Orchid Av WIT CM8 .... 276 E1
Orchid Cl CHTY IP7 .... 62 A1
Orchid Pl RCHLM CM3 .... 392 D5
Orchill Dr SBF/HAD SS7 .... 461 K1
Orchis Gv GRAYS RM17 .... 483 J3
Orchis Wy HARH RM3 .... 431 G1
Ordnance Rd GVE DA12 .... 489 H4
  PEND EN3 .... 374 D3

Oregon Rd KESC IP5 .... 38 E7
Orford Crs CHLM/WR CM1 .... 304 E8
Orford Rd FX IP11 .... 5 E6
  HVHL CB9 .... 27 F7
Orford St IP IP1 .... 2 C2
Oriel Cl SUD CO10 .... 58 E7
Oriole Wy BSF CM23 .... 198 B7
Orion Wy BRTR CM7 .... 210 A1
Orkney Cl HVHL CB9 .... 27 K6
Orkney Rd IPNE IP4 .... 37 J4
Orlando Cl WOTN CO14 .... 229 H5
Orlando Dr PIT SS13 .... 439 F4
Ormesby Chine RCHLM CM3 .... 392 D8
Ormonde Av RCSS S4 .... 444 B2
  SBF/HAD SS7 .... 462 B3
Ormonde Cl RCOLW CO6 .... 185 K1
Ormonde Gdns LOS SS9 .... 462 B3
Ormonde Ri BKHH IG9 .... 403 K4
Ormonds Crs RCHLM CM3 .... 392 B1
Ormsby Rd CVI SS8 .... 477 H3
Orpen Cl RCOLW CO6 .... 185 J1
Orpen's Hl COLS CO2 .... 217 F2
Orrmo Rd CVI SS8 .... 479 F2
Orsett Av LOS SS9 .... 442 D8
Orsett End BSDN SS14 .... 437 K6
Orsett Heath Crs CDH/CHF RM16 .... 485 F2
Orsett Rd CDH/CHF RM16 .... 472 D4
  GRAYS RM17 .... 484 A4
Orton Cl ING CM4 .... 359 G5
Orvis La RCOLE CO7 .... 122 D4
Orwell Cl COLN CO4 .... 188 B4
Orwell Ct WICKE SS11 .... 418 A8
Orwell Pl RIPS/CAP IP9 .... 91 J5
Orwell Rd COS CO15 .... 10 C5
  FX IP11 .... 5 F4
  HAR CO12 .... 7 E4
  IPSE IP3 .... 63 J1
Orwell View Rd RIPS/CAP IP9 .... 128 C2
Orwell Wy RCOS CO16 .... 258 E8
Osbert Rd WIT CM8 .... 276 E5
Osborne Cl COS CO15 .... 259 J6
Osborne Rd BAR EN8 .... 346 E2
  BKHH IG9 .... 403 J4
  BROX EN10 .... 319 G1
  BRWN CM15 .... 410 E2
  EMPK RM11 .... 430 C8
  IPSE IP3 .... 63 J1
  K/T/MI CO5 .... 285 G7
  PEND EN3 .... 374 E6
  PIT SS13 .... 439 H5
  VGE SS16 .... 437 K8
  WOS/PRIT SS0 .... 18 B3
Osborne St COL CO1 .... 8 B5
Osbourne Av HOC/HUL SS5 .... 420 D7
Osea Rd MAL CM9 .... 339 K2
Osea Wy CHLM/WR CM1 .... 305 H8
Osprey Cl SBN/FI SS3 .... 466 D7
Osprey Rd HVHL CB9 .... 27 J6
  WAB EN9 .... 348 C8
Ospreys COS CO15 .... 10 C1
Osprey Wy CHLM/GWD CM2 .... 332 E8
Osterley Dr VGE SS16 .... 436 A8
Osterley Pl RCHLM CM3 .... 392 D8
Ostler Cl BSF CM23 .... 231 G1
Othello Cl RCOLN CO4 .... 188 C5
Otley Ct FX IP11 .... 5 D2
Ottawa Rd TIL RM18 .... 485 F8
Otten Rd SUD CO10 .... 55 G4
Otterbourne Rd CHING E4 .... 402 E6
Ottershaw Wy RCOS CO16 .... 258 D7
Ouida Rd CVI SS8 .... 478 D2
Oulton Cl HAR CO12 .... 6 A5
Oulton Rd IPSE IP3 .... 63 G3
Ousden Cl BAR EN8 .... 346 E4
Ousden Dr BAR EN8 .... 346 E4
Ouse Cha WIT CM8 .... 276 D3
Outing Cl SOS SS1 .... 19 F5
Outing's La BRWN CM15 .... 383 K2
Outpart Eastward HAR CO12 .... 7 F2
Outwood Common Rd BCAYE CM11 .... 414 D6
Outwood Farm Cl BCAYE CM11 .... 415 F3
Outwood Farm Rd BCAYE CM11 .... 415 F3
Oval Gdns GRAYS RM17 .... 484 B2
The Oval BROX EN10 .... 318 E5
Overcliffe GVW DA11 .... 489 F4
Overcliff Rd GRAYS RM17 .... 484 C4
Overhall Hl RCOLW CO6 .... 149 K3
Over Hall La SAFWN CB10 .... 47 G3
Overlord Cl BROX EN10 .... 318 E2
Overmead Dr RCHLM CM3 .... 392 E5
Overshot Br RCHLM CM3 .... 363 J1
Overton Cl SBF/HAD SS7 .... 440 B7
Overton Dr SBF/HAD SS7 .... 440 B7
Overton Rd SBF/HAD SS7 .... 440 A6
Overton Wy SBF/HAD SS7 .... 440 A7
Ovington Gdns BCAYW CM12 .... 387 G8
Owen Ward Cl COLS CO2 .... 218 B2
Owl's Hl RCHLM CM3 .... 275 F2
Owlets Hall Cl HARH RM3 .... 431 G5
Owls Retreat COLN CO4 .... 188 C5
Oxborrow Cl FOS CO13 .... 227 K7
Oxcroft BSF CM23 .... 231 K2

Oxenford Cl HAR CO12 .... 164 E4
Oxford Av CDH/CHF RM16 .... 485 F3
  EMPK RM11 .... 431 H6
Oxford Cl BAR EN8 .... 346 C3
  SUD CO10 .... 58 D7
  VGE SS16 .... 436 A8
Oxford Ct BRW CM14 .... 411 G2
  CHLM/GWD CM2 .... 15 F1
  RCOLW CO6 .... 149 J7
Oxford Crs COS CO15 .... 10 B3
Oxford La HSTD CO9 .... 110 B3
Oxford Meadow HSTD CO9 .... 110 C3
Oxford Rd COLW CO3 .... 186 E7
  COS CO15 .... 10 C3
  CVI SS8 .... 478 C1
  FOS CO13 .... 229 F8
  HARH RM3 .... 431 C1
  HSTD CO9 .... 147 J4
  IPNE IP4 .... 3 F4
  KESC IP5 .... 38 E6
  MGTR CO11 .... 159 J1
  RCFD SS4 .... 444 B1
  SLH/COR SS17 .... 472 E1
  SLH/COR SS17 .... 473 H5
  WFD IG8 .... 404 A8
Oxley Cl GPK RM2 .... 430 D4
Oxley Gdns SLH/COR SS17 .... 473 K1
Oxley Hl K/T/MI CO5 .... 252 B1
  MAL CM9 .... 280 E4
Oxleys Rd WAB EN9 .... 348 C7
The Oxleys HLWE CM17 .... 295 H1
Oxlip Rd WIT CM8 .... 276 E1
Oxney Md CHLM/WR CM1 .... 331 F5
Oxney Vls GTDUN CM6 .... 206 E6
Oxwich Cl SLH/COR SS17 .... 474 C1
Oysterbed Rd FX IP11 .... 130 A3
Oyster Pl CHLM/GWD CM2 .... 333 H1
Oyster Tank Rd RCOLE CO7 .... 155 J8
Ozier Ct SAFWS CB11 .... 71 F6
Oziers RBSF CM22 .... 168 D3
Ozonia Av WICKW SS12 .... 417 F8
Ozonia Cl WICKW SS12 .... 416 E8
Ozonia Wy WICKW SS12 .... 417 F8

P

Paarl Rd CVI SS8 .... 478 A1
Packard Av IPSE IP3 .... 63 K3
Packards La RCOLW CO6 .... 152 D3
Packe Cl K/T/MI CO5 .... 247 F1
Packham Gv GVW DA11 .... 488 E8
Paddock Cl BCAYE CM11 .... 414 D6
  CDH/CHF RM16 .... 472 B5
  HAR CO12 .... 7 D4
  LOS SS9 .... 443 F6
Paddock Dr CHLM/WR CM1 .... 305 G6
Paddock Md HLWS CM18 .... 322 A2
The Paddocks ABR/ST RM4 .... 408 A2
  BURES CO8 .... 115 H5
  CDH/CHF RM16 .... 472 B5
  GTDUN CM6 .... 236 C6
  ING CM4 .... 386 B2
  MAL CM9 .... 310 C1
  RAYL SS6 .... 442 A3
  RCOLE CO7 .... 224 A8
  WIT CM8 .... 277 G3
The Paddock BROX EN10 .... 319 G2
  BSF CM23 .... 231 H2
  ING CM4 .... 588 A3
Paddock Wy RCOLE CO7 .... 221 F2
Padgetts Wy HOC/HUL SS5 .... 419 J2
Padham's Green Rd ING CM4 .... 386 C5
Padstow Rd KESC IP5 .... 38 E7
Pageant Cl TIL RM18 .... 485 H7
Page Crs ERITH DA8 .... 480 A6
Page Gdns KESC IP5 .... 39 J5
Page Rd COS CO15 .... 10 B4
  PIT SS13 .... 439 J6
Pages Cl BSF CM23 .... 198 E8
Pages La MAL CM9 .... 313 K5
Paget Ct RBSF CM22 .... 168 D4
Paget Dr BCAYW CM12 .... 387 G8
Paget Rd IP IP1 .... 2 C2
  K/T/MI CO5 .... 220 C6
  RCOLE CO7 .... 221 F5
Pagette Wy GRAYS RM17 .... 483 K4
Paglesfield RBRW/HUT CM13 .... 412 B2
Paglesham Rd RCFD SS4 .... 423 J7
Paignton Av CHLM/WR CM1 .... 305 F8
Paignton Cl RAYL SS6 .... 419 J8
Paines Brook Wy HARH RM3 .... 431 G1
Painswick Av SLH/COR SS17 .... 457 G8
Painters Ash La GVW DA11 .... 488 C8
Painters La PEND EN3 .... 374 E1
Pakes Wy EPP CM16 .... 378 C3
Palace Gdns BKHH IG9 .... 404 A4
  BSF CM23 .... 198 D8
Palace Gv LAIN SS15 .... 16 C2
Palace View Rd CHING E4 .... 402 C8
Palatine Pk LAIN SS15 .... 436 A7
Paley Gdns LOU IG10 .... 377 K7

Palins Wy *CDH/CHF* RM16 ..... 470 E8
Pallister Rd *COS* CO15..... 10 C1
Pall MI *LOS* SS9..... 332 E7
Palm CI *CHLM/GWD* CM2 ..... 245 G8 🔲
Palmcroft CI *IP* IP1 ..... 36 C2
WIT CM8..... 36 C2
Palmeira Av *WOS/PRIT* SS0 ..... 18 A5
Palmer CI *LAIN* SS15..... 16 B4 🔲
Palmers *SLH/COR* SS17..... 474 B2 🔲
Palmers CI *CBE/LIN* CB1..... 22 D3
Palmers Cft *CHLM/GWD* CM2 ..... 333 J3 🔲
Palmers Gv *GRAYS* RM17..... 484 B3
Palmers Gv *WAB* EN9..... 320 B4
Palmers HI *EPP* CM16..... 350 E3
Palmers La *PEND* EN3..... 374 C5
ROY SG8..... 67 F1
Palmerston Gdns *WTHK* RM20..... 483 G4
Palmerston Ldg *CHLM/GWD* CM2 ..... 333 H6
Palmerston Rd *BKHH* IG9..... 403 K5
IPNE IP4..... 3 F5
RCOS CO16..... 226 D3
WOS/PRIT SS0..... 18 A5
WTHK RM20..... 483 G4
Palmers Wy *BAR* EN8..... 346 E3
Palmerswent CI *SUD* CO10..... 35 F5
Palm Ms *LAIN* SS15..... 16 B1
Pamela Gdns *BSF* CM23..... 231 K2
Pampas CI *COLN* CO4..... 187 H1
Panadown *LAIN* SS15..... 17 D4
Pancroft Rd *RM4* RM4..... 379 F7
Panfield La *BRTR* CM7..... 177 H8
Panfields *LAIN* SS15..... 436 B7
Pan La *RCHLM* CM3..... 362 E8
Pannells CI *SUD* CO10..... 33 H1
Pantile Av *SOSN* SS2..... 19 F1
Pantile CI *WIT* CM8..... 277 G6
Pantile HI *BOC* CM0..... 398 C1
Pantlings La *K/T/MI* CO5..... 213 H8
Panton Crs *COLN* CO4..... 188 D6
Panton Ms *BRTR* CM7..... 209 K5 🔲
Papenburg Rd *CVI* SS8..... 461 F7
Paper Mill Br *RCHLM* CM3..... 307 H7
Papillon Rd *COLW* CO3..... 186 E5 🔲
Paprills *VGE* SS16..... 16 C5
Parade Rd *IPNE* IP4..... 37 H6
The Parade *WOTN* CO14..... 229 J5 🔲
Paradise CI *EBAR* EN4..... 346 B2
Paradise Rd *CHLM/WR* CM1..... 331 H5
WAB EN9..... 347 J8 🔲
Pardoe PI *IPNE* IP4..... 38 C2
Pargat Dr *LOS* SS9..... 442 D6
Pargetters Hyam *HOC/HUL* SS5 .. 421 G7 🔲
Paringdon Rd *HLWW/ROY* CM19 ... 321 K1
Parish CI *HCH* RM12..... 450 E4
Parish Wy *LAIN* SS15..... 16 A3
Parkanaur Av *SOS* SS1..... 466 A7
Park Av *BSF* CM23..... 231 K2
FX IP11..... 131 J2
GVE DA12..... 489 H6
GVW DA11..... 489 G2
HLWE CM17..... 443 F8
LOS SS9..... 443 G1
RBRW/HUT CM13..... 412 B4
UPMR RM14..... 452 B1
WFD IG8..... 403 J4
WTHK RM20..... 482 D5
Park Bvd *COS* CO15..... 260 C7
GPK RM2..... 430 A3
Park Cha *RCOS* CO16..... 257 J8
SBF/HAD SS7..... 461 K3
Park CI *EPP* CM16..... 352 A1
SUD CO10..... 58 D5
WICKW SS12..... 417 F7 🔲
Park Ct *HLW* CM20..... 13 D1
Park Crs *EMPK* RM11..... 450 B1
WOS/PRIT SS0..... 18 C4
Parkdale *RCHLM* CM3..... 335 G6
Park Dr *BRTR* CM7..... 209 K5
HSTD CO9..... 386 C1
ING CM4..... 338 D4
MAL CM9..... 265 H3
RBSF CM22..... 255 J8
RCOLE CO7..... 189 J1
UPMR RM14..... 451 K5
WICKW SS12..... 417 G7
Parker Av *FX* IP11..... 4 B4
TIL RM18..... 485 H7
Parker Rd *CHLM/GWD* CM2..... 15 D4
GRAYS RM17..... 483 J4
Parker's Farm Rd *UPMR* RM14..... 454 E8
Parker's Wy *RCOLW* CO6..... 118 B4
Parker Wy *HSTD* CO9..... 147 K5
Parkes Rd *CHIG* IG7..... 405 J8
Parkeston Rd *FX* IP11..... 5 D3
HAR CO12..... 6 A3
Park Farm Rd *UPMR* RM14..... 451 G6
Park Fids *HLWW/ROY* CM19..... 292 C5
Parkfields *HSTD* CO9..... 110 C8
SBF/HAD SS7..... 461 H1
Parkfield St *K/T/MI* CO5..... 220 C6
Park Gdns *HOC/HUL* SS5..... 421 G8
Park Gate Rd *SLH/COR* SS17..... 457 H5

WIT CM8..... 245 G2
Parkhall Rd *BRTR* CM7..... 145 G6
Park HI *CBE/LIN* CB1..... 25 H3
HLWE CM17..... 295 F2
LOU IG10..... 404 A1
Parkhill CI *HCH* RM12..... 450 D3
Parkhill Rd *CHING* E4..... 402 D3
Parkhurst Dr *RAYL* SS6..... 419 H7
Parkhurst Rd *PIT* SS13..... 438 E8
Parkland Av *UPMR* RM14..... 451 J6
Parklands *BCAYE* CM11..... 414 C2 🔲
BRTR CM7..... 209 K5
CHIG IG7..... 405 F6
CVI SS8..... 461 F8 🔲
RCFD SS4..... 444 A1
RCOLW CO6..... 213 H3
WAB EN9..... 348 A6
Parklands Av *RAYL* SS6..... 441 H5
Parklands Dr *CHLM/WR* CM1..... 15 E2 🔲
Parkland Wy *CHONG* CM5..... 354 B4 🔲
Park La *BAR* EN8..... 346 D7
BCAYE CM11..... 415 K1
BROX EN10..... 318 E1
BSF CM23..... 231 K1
CBE/LIN CB1..... 48 D2
COLN CO4..... 156 B2
CVI SS8..... 479 F2
EBAR EN7..... 346 A1
EMPK RM11..... 450 B1
HLW CM20..... 13 D1
HSTD CO9..... 78 E6
HSTD CO9..... 146 E6
MAL CM9..... 281 F2
RAIN RM13..... 450 D2
RBRW/HUT CM13..... 434 C2
RCHLM CM3..... 271 F1
RCOLW CO6..... 149 J7
SAFWN CB10..... 96 D3
SAFWS CB11..... 469 H8
SOCK/AV RM15..... 19 F4
SOS SS1..... 83 C3
SUD CO10..... 18 C5
WOS/PRIT SS0..... 18 C5
Park Lane CI *RCOLW* CO6..... 149 J7
Park Lane Paradise *BREN* EN10..... 318 A6
Park Md *HLW* CM20..... 12 B2
Parkmead *LOU* IG10..... 404 D1
Park Meadow *BRWN* CM15..... 384 B4
Parkmill CI *SLH/COR* SS17..... 474 C1
Park North *IP* IP1..... 3 E1
Park PI *GVE* DA12..... 489 H4
Park Rd *BAR* EN8..... 346 D7
BOC CM0..... 425 C1
BRW CM14..... 410 E4
CHLM/GWD CM2..... 14 C3
COLN CO4..... 220 D1
COLW CO3..... 188 D2
COS CO15..... 10 A5
CVI SS8..... 479 F3
GTDUN CM6..... 489 C3
HAR CO12..... 7 E1
HVHL CB9..... 26 D4
IP IP1..... 3 D1
LOS SS9..... 462 C4
MAL CM9..... 338 B4
PEND EN3..... 374 E2
RBSF CM22..... 168 E3
RCOLE CO7..... 123 G3
SBF/HAD SS7..... 440 C6
SLH/COR SS17..... 473 H4
SLH/COR SS17..... 474 C2
STSD CM24..... 167 F7
UPMR RM14..... 245 G2
WIT CM8..... 245 G2
WOS/PRIT SS0..... 18 C5
Park Side *BCAYE* CM11..... 414 D3 🔲
BKHH IG9..... 403 J5
GTDUN CM6..... 173 J5
PIT SS13..... 438 D6
WOS/PRIT SS0..... 463 H4
Parkside *BAR* EN8..... 346 E8
CDH/CHF RM16..... 484 C2
Parkside Av *TIL* RM18..... 485 G8
Park Sq East *COS* CO15..... 290 B5
Park Sq West *COS* CO15..... 290 B4
Parkstone Av *EMPK* RM11..... 431 F8
SBF/HAD SS7..... 461 G1
WICKW SS12..... 416 C5
Parkstone Dr *SOSN* SS2..... 18 B1
Park St *GTDUN* CM6..... 139 K4
WOS/PRIT SS0..... 18 C4
Park Ter *WOS/PRIT* SS0..... 18 C4
Park Vale CI *HSTD* CO9..... 110 D1
Park Vw *SOCK/AV* RM15..... 469 F8
Park View Crs *CHLM/GWD* CM2 ..... 333 H8
Park View Dr *LOS* SS9..... 442 B2
Park View Gdns *GRAYS* RM17 ..... 484 A4 🔲
Park View Rd *IP* IP1..... 36 C4

Park Wallis *GVW* DA11..... 488 A3
Park Wy *BRWN* CM15..... 411 J4
COS CO15..... 10 A6
Parkway *CBE/LIN* CB1..... 25 G7
CDH/CHF RM16..... 472 A5
CHLM/WR CM1..... 14 B2
GPK RM2..... 430 A4
HLWW/ROY CM19..... 293 G5
RAYL SS6..... 441 K5
SBW CM21..... 265 J4
SLH/COR SS17..... 457 K8
WFD IG8..... 403 K8 🔲
Parkway CI *LOS* SS9..... 443 G6
The Parkway *CVI* SS8..... 478 B3
Parkwood Av *RCOLE* CO7..... 220 E4
Parkwood CI *HOD* EN11..... 318 E1
Parkwood Dr *SUD* CO10..... 58 B3
Park Wood La *MAL* CM9..... 311 J2
Parliament Rd *IPNE* IP4..... 37 K8
Parmenter Dr *SUD* CO10..... 59 F8
Parnall Rd *HLWS* CM18..... 322 B1
Parndon Mill La *HLW* CM20..... 293 K2
Parndon Wood Rd
HLWW/ROY CM19..... 322 A2
Parnell CI *COLS* CO2..... 219 H4
IP IP1..... 36 B2
Parnell Rd *IP* IP1..... 36 B2
Parnham PI *IPNE* IP4..... 38 D8
Parr CI *BRTR* CM7..... 210 C1
Parr Dr *COLW* CO3..... 217 K1
Parrington Wy *MGTR* CO11..... 159 F2
Parrock Av *GVE* DA12..... 489 H6
Parrock Rd *GVE* DA12..... 489 H5
Parrock St *GVE* DA12..... 489 G4 🔲
Parry CI *SLH/COR* SS17..... 473 K2
Parry Dr *RCOS* CO16..... 258 E8
Parsloe Rd *EPP* CM16..... 321 J3
Parsonage Cha *MAL* CM9..... 367 F5
Parsonage CI *CHLM/WR* CM1..... 304 C4 🔲
FX IP11..... 5 D3 🔲
Parsonage Farm La *SAFWN* CB10... 105 G1
Parsonage Fld *BRWN* CM15..... 384 B3
Parsonage Gv *BURES* CO8..... 115 H5 🔲
Parsonage La *BSF* CM23..... 199 G5
GTDUN CM6..... 238 D2
ING CM4..... 359 G6
LAIN SS15..... 16 A4
RCHLM CM3..... 272 C3 🔲
RCHLM CM3..... 335 H3
RCOS CO16..... 192 E5
SAFWS CB11..... 134 A2
STSD CM24..... 200 A1
Parsonage Leys *HLW* CM20..... 13 F3
Parsonage Rd *RBSF* CM22..... 201 J5
WTHK RM20..... 483 F5
Parsonage St *HSTD* CO9..... 148 A4
Parsonage Wy *CBE/LIN* CB1..... 25 F3
Parson's Fld *RCOLE* CO7..... 121 K7
Parson's Heath *COLN* CO4..... 188 B3
Parson's HI *COLW* CO3..... 186 B7
Parsons La *COLC* CO1..... 9 E5
Parsons Lawn *SBN/FI* SS3..... 466 E4
Parsons Rd *SBF/HAD* SS7..... 440 C6
Parsons Yd *MGTR* CO11..... 159 J1 🔲
Partridge Av *CHLM/WR* CM1..... 304 B7
Partridge CI *HAR* CO12..... 195 C1
Partridge Ct *HLWS* CM18..... 13 E5
Partridge Dr *RCOLW* CO6..... 152 C8
Partridge Rd *CHTY* IP2..... 61 K2
HLWS CM18..... 13 D5
Parvills *WAB* EN9..... 347 K6
Paschal Wy *CHLM/GWD* CM2 ..... 15 F5
Pasfield *WAB* EN9..... 347 K7 🔲
Paske Av *HVHL* CB9..... 27 F6
Paslowes *VGE* SS16..... 458 C1
Passingham Av *BCAYE* CM11..... 414 D7
Passingham CI *BCAYE* CM11..... 414 D6 🔲
Pasteur Dr *HARH* RM3..... 430 E4
Paston CI *RCHLM* CM3..... 392 E4
Pasture High *RCHLM* CM3..... 335 H2
Pasture Loates *STSD* CM24..... 167 J5
The Pastures *IPNE* IP4..... 38 D6
Paternoster Av *WAB* EN9..... 348 B7
Paternoster HI *WAB* EN9..... 348 B6
Paternoster Rw *ABR/ST* RM4..... 408 D4
WOTN CO14..... 229 H5 🔲
Pathfields Rd *COS* CO15..... 10 A3
The Path *RCOLE* CO7..... 223 J5
Pathways *BSDN* SS14..... 438 B8 🔲
Patmore CI *BSF* CM23..... 198 B5
Patmore Fids *RBSF* CM22..... 135 F2
Patmore Rd *COLN* CO4..... 9 F5
WAB EN9..... 348 A8 🔲
Patmore Wy *CRW* RM5..... 407 G8
Patricia Dr *EMPK* RM11..... 451 F2
SLH/COR SS17..... 457 K7
Patricia Gdns *BCAYE* CM11..... 414 E6 🔲
BSF CM23..... 198 D8
Patten CI *RCOLW* CO6..... 215 H2
Patterdale *SBF/HAD* SS7..... 440 A6
Pattern Bush CI *MGTR* CO11..... 123 J5
Patteson Rd *IPSE* IP3..... 3 F5
Pattison CI *WIT* CM8..... 277 C5
Pattiswick Cnr *BSDN* SS14..... 438 B6 🔲
Pattiswick Sq *BSDN* SS14..... 438 B6

Pattocks *BSDN* SS14 ...... 438 A7
Pattocks La *RCOLW* CO6 ...... 183 F3
Pattrick's La *HAR* CO12 ...... 7 D4
Pauline Cl *COS* CO15 ...... 11 E1
Pauline Gdns *BCAYW* CM12 414 A1
Pauline St *CHTY* IP2 ...... 3 D6
Pauls Crs *RCOLE* CO7 ...... 189 J7
Paul Spendlove Ct *COLN* CO4 ...... 188 B4
  LAIN SS15 ...... 16 A2
Pavilion Cl *SOSN* SS2 ...... 465 H4
Pavilion Dr *LOS* SS9 ...... 463 G3
The Pavilions *EPP* CM16 ...... 324 C7
Pavillon Pl *BCAYW* CM12 ...... 414 A1
Pawle Cl *CHLM/GWD* CM2 ...... 360 E3
Paxfords *LAIN* SS15 ...... 436 A7
Paxman Av *COLS* CO2 ...... 218 B2
Paxton Rd *COS* CO15 ...... 259 K5
Paycocke Cl *BSDN* SS14 ...... 438 C3
Paycocke Rd *BSDN* SS14 ...... 438 B3
Paycocke Wy *RCOLW* CO6 ...... 213 H2
Paycock Rd *HLWE/ROY* CM19 ...... 12 A5
Payne Pl *RCHLM* CM3 ...... 363 F7
Payne's La *RCOLE* CO7 ...... 191 H2
  WAB EN9 ...... 319 J6
Paynters Md *VGE* SS16 ...... 458 B2
Peace Cl *COLW* CO3 ...... 185 J6
Peach Av *HOC/HUL* SS5 ...... 421 F6
Peach Cft *GVW* DA11 ...... 488 D8
Peacock Cl *BRTR* CM7 ...... 209 J4
  EMPK RM11 ...... 431 F6
Peacocks *HLWE/ROY* CM19 ...... 293 H7
Peacocks Cl *SUD* CO10 ...... 32 C3
Peacocks Rd *SUD* CO10 ...... 32 C3
Peacock St *GVE* DA12 ...... 489 H5
Peake Av *FOS* CO15 ...... 227 K7
Peakes Cl *K/T/MI* CO5 ...... 279 K1
Pea La *UPMR* RM14 ...... 452 D7
Peal Rd *SAFWS* CB11 ...... 71 G6
Pearce Mnr *CHLM/GWD* CM2 ...... 14 A5
Pearce Rd *IPSE* IP3 ...... 37 J8
Pearcroft Rd *IP* IP1 ...... 36 D2
Peareswood Rd *ERITH* DA8 ...... 480 A7
Pearmain Cl *WICKE* SS11 ...... 417 C4
Pearmain Wy *COLW* CO3 ...... 217 H1
Pearse Wy *IPSE* IP3 ...... 64 C4
Pearson Rd *IPNE* IP4 ...... 38 A8
Pearsons *SLH/COR* SS17 ...... 474 B2
Pearsons Av *RAYL* SS6 ...... 441 G1
Pearsons Wy *RIPW* IP8 ...... 61 F4
Peartree Cl *BRTR* CM7 ...... 209 K4
  BRWN CM15 ...... 384 B4
  MAL CM9 ...... 312 C7
  SOCK/AV RM15 ...... 470 A2
  SOSN SS2 ...... 19 F1
Peartree Hl *BURES* CO8 ...... 151 K1
Peartree La *BRWN* CM15 ...... 384 A3
  RCHLM CM3 ...... 363 K2
  UPMR RM14 ...... 454 E4
Pear Tree Md *HLWS* CM18 ...... 294 E7
Peartree Rd *COLW* CO3 ...... 217 J1
Peartrees *RBRW/HUT* CM13 ...... 434 B3
Peartree Wy *RCOS* CO16 ...... 258 E3
Pease Cl *HCH* RM12 ...... 450 D8
Pease Rd *RCHLM* CM3 ...... 363 F7
Peaslands Rd *SAFWS* CB11 ...... 71 F5
Pebmarsh Cl *COLS* CO2 ...... 219 H5
Pebmarsh Dr *WICKW* SS12 ...... 417 H7
Pebmarsh Rd *BURES* CO8 ...... 114 B4
  RCOLW CO6 ...... 149 G3
Peck's Hl *WAB* EN9 ...... 320 A3
Pecockes Cl *SUD* CO10 ...... 59 F8
Pedder's Cl *COLW* CO3 ...... 218 A2
Pedlars Cl *RCHLM* CM3 ...... 336 A7
Pedlars End *CHONG* CM5 ...... 325 H3
Pedlars Pth *RCHLM* CM3 ...... 336 A7
Peel Av *SBN/FI* SS3 ...... 467 F6
Peel Cl *CHING* E4 ...... 402 C5
Peel Crs *BRTR* CM7 ...... 209 H2
Peel Rd *CHLM/GWD* CM2 ...... 15 F1
Peel Wy *HARH* RM3 ...... 431 G4
Peerage Wy *EMPK* RM11 ...... 451 F1
Peerswood Rd *COLS* CO2 ...... 218 E3
Peewit Hl *FX* IP11 ...... 5 D5
Peewit Rd *CHTY* IP2 ...... 61 J2
Pegasus Cl *GVE* DA12 ...... 489 H8
Pegasus Wy *BRTR* CM7 ...... 177 H8
  COLN CO4 ...... 9 E2
Pegelm Gdns *EMPK* RM11 ...... 451 G1
Peggotty Cl *CHLM/WR* CM1 ...... 304 B7
Peggy's Wk *SAFWS* CB11 ...... 69 K2
Peg Millar's La *RCHLM* CM3 ...... 243 G7
Pegrams Rd *HLWS* CM18 ...... 12 C6
Peldon Gdns *BSDN* SS14 ...... 438 A5
Peldon Rd *HLWW/ROY* CM19 ...... 12 A5
  K/T/MI CO5 ...... 252 C5
Pelham Cl *HAR* CO12 ...... 6 A6
Pelham Pl *SLH/COR* SS17 ...... 474 A1
Pelham Rd *GVW* DA11 ...... 488 C5
  SAFWS CB11 ...... 134 A1
  SOSN SS2 ...... 465 H4
Pelham Rd South *GVW* DA11 ...... 488 E6
Pelican Cl *CHTY* IP2 ...... 62 A2

Pelly Av *WIT* CM8 ...... 277 G5
Pelly Ct *EPP* CM16 ...... 350 D5
Pemberton Av *GPK* RM2 ...... 430 C5
  ING CM4 ...... 386 B1
Pemberton Fld *RCFD* SS4 ...... 421 J1
Pembrey Wy *HCH* RM12 ...... 450 D7
Pembroke Av *EN* EN1 ...... 374 B5
  MAL CM9 ...... 338 B4
  SLH/COR SS17 ...... 474 C1
Pembroke Cl *BCAYW* CM12 ...... 387 G8
  BROX EN10 ...... 318 E6
  CHTY IP2 ...... 2 A4
  COLS CO2 ...... 219 K2
  EMPK RM11 ...... 431 H6
Pembroke Gdns *COS* CO15 ...... 260 C7
Pembroke La *CBE/LIN* CB1 ...... 23 C3
Pembroke Ms *PIT* SS13 ...... 439 F5
Pembroke Pl *CHLM/WR* CM1 ...... 304 C6
  SUD CO10 ...... 58 A3
Penbury Rd *WOS/PRIT* SS0 ...... 463 K6
Pendle Cl *BSDN* SS14 ...... 438 D4
Pendle Dr *BSDN* SS14 ...... 438 C4
Pendlestone *SBF/HAD* SS7 ...... 461 H1
Pendleton Rd *CHTY* IP2 ...... 61 K4
Pendower *RAYL* SS6 ...... 441 G5
Penfold Rd *COS* CO15 ...... 10 B5
  FX IP11 ...... 131 H5
Pengelly Cl *EBAR* EN7 ...... 346 B4
Penhurst Av *SOSN* SS2 ...... 18 C2
Penhurst Dr *RCHLM* CM3 ...... 392 D8
Penlan Hall La *RCOLW* CO6 ...... 152 A7
Penlow Rd *HLWS* CM18 ...... 12 C6
Penn Cl *CDH/CHF* RM16 ...... 472 B4
  RIPS/CAP IP9 ...... 87 G3
Pennial Rd *CVI* SS8 ...... 478 A1
Pennine Rd *CHLM/WR* CM1 ...... 303 K7
Pennine Wy *GVW* DA11 ...... 488 D8
Pennington La *STSD* CM24 ...... 167 J5
Penningtons *BSF* CM23 ...... 198 B8
Penn Ms *BRTR* CM7 ...... 209 K5
Pennsylvania La *K/T/MI* CO5 ...... 247 K8
Penny Flds *BRW* CM14 ...... 411 F7
Penny La *IPSE* IP3 ...... 64 D4
Pennymead *HLW* CM20 ...... 294 E5
Penny Meadow *RIPS/CAP* IP9 ...... 87 F4
Pennyroyal Crs *WIT* CM8 ...... 276 E1
Pennyroyal Gdns *CHTY* IP2 ...... 62 A1
Penny Royal Rd *RCHLM* CM3 ...... 335 H7
Penny's La *ING* CM4 ...... 359 F5
Pennystone Rd *SAFWS* CB11 ...... 71 F5
Penrice Cl *COLN* CO4 ...... 188 B7
Penrith Crs *RAIN* RM13 ...... 450 B6
Penrith Rd *HARH* RM3 ...... 431 H1
Penrose Md *CHLM/WR* CM1 ...... 331 H5
Penryn Rd *KESG* IP5 ...... 38 C6
Penshurst *HLWE* CM17 ...... 295 F2
Penshurst Pl *BRTR* CM7 ...... 208 E7
Penshurst Rd *IPSE* IP3 ...... 64 B1
Penson's La *CHONG* CM5 ...... 353 C2
Pentichton Rd *BRTR* CM7 ...... 209 G3
Pentire Ct *UPMR* RM14 ...... 432 B8
Pentland Av *CHLM/WR* CM1 ...... 304 C7
  SBN/FI SS3 ...... 466 D3
Pentlow Dr *SUD* CO10 ...... 32 E4
Pentlow Hawke Cl *HVHL* CB9 ...... 27 H6
Pentlow Hl *SUD* CO10 ...... 33 G5
Pentlow Wy *BKHH* IG9 ...... 404 B3
Pentney Rd *CHING* E4 ...... 402 E4
Penton Dr *BAR* EN8 ...... 346 D3
Pentrich Av *EN* EN1 ...... 374 A4
Penzance Cl *CHLM/WR* CM1 ...... 305 G8
  COS CO15 ...... 290 E5
Penzance Gdns *HARH* RM3 ...... 431 H1
Penzance Rd *HARH* RM3 ...... 431 H1
  KESG IP5 ...... 38 E7
Peppercorn Cl *COLN* CO4 ...... 8 B1
Peppercorn Wy *CHTY* IP2 ...... 3 D6
Pepper Hl *GVW* DA11 ...... 488 B8
Pepper's Rd *RCOLW* CO6 ...... 155 F4
Pepples La *SAFWN* CB10 ...... 102 A3
Pepys Cl *GVW* DA11 ...... 488 C8
Pepys St *HAR* CO12 ...... 485 H2
Percival Rd *EMPK* RM11 ...... 430 D8
  FOS CO13 ...... 228 C4
  WOTN CO14 ...... 229 J3
Percy Cottis Rd *RCFD* SS4 ...... 444 B2
Percy Rd *LOS* SS9 ...... 462 E3
Percy St *GRAYS* RM17 ...... 484 B5
Peregrine Cl *BSF* CM23 ...... 198 C7
  COS CO15 ...... 10 C1
  SBN/FI SS3 ...... 466 C4
  VGE SS16 ...... 17 F6
Peregrine Dr *CHLM/GWD* CM2 ...... 332 C8
  SBF/HAD SS7 ...... 460 B3
Peregrine Gdns *RAYL* SS6 ...... 441 G2
Peregrine Rd *BARK/HLT* IG6 ...... 406 A8
Peregrin Rd *WAB* EN9 ...... 348 C8
Perham Cl *BROX* EN10 ...... 318 E8
Perriclose *CHLM/WR* CM1 ...... 305 F6
Perrins Cl *EBAR* EN7 ...... 346 A1
Perryfield *HLWE* CM17 ...... 297 J3
Perry Gn *BSDN* SS14 ...... 17 F2

Perry Hl *CHLM/WR* CM1 ...... 15 E2
  WAB EN9 ...... 320 B5
Perry La *COLN* CO4 ...... 156 C1
Perry Rd *HLWS* CM18 ...... 12 C6
  K/T/MI CO5 ...... 247 K8
  SBF/HAD SS7 ...... 460 A2
  WIT CM8 ...... 277 H4
Perrysfield Rd *BAR* EN8 ...... 346 E1
Perry Spring *HLWE* CM17 ...... 295 G7
Perry St *BCAYW* CM12 ...... 414 D1
  GVW DA11 ...... 488 D6
Perry Wy *SOCK/AV* RM15 ...... 468 E7
  WIT CM8 ...... 277 H4
Persardi Ct *COLS* CO2 ...... 219 H6
Pershore End *COLW* CO3 ...... 185 K8
Perth Cl *COLS* CO2 ...... 219 H4
Pertwee Cl *RCOLE* CO7 ...... 255 J5
Pertwee Dr *CHLM/GWD* CM2 ...... 333 H7
  RCHLM CM3 ...... 392 C6
Pertwee Wy *K/T/MI* CO5 ...... 252 D3
Peterborough Av *UPMR* RM14 ...... 452 B2
Peterborough Wy *BSDN* SS14 ...... 438 C5
Peter Bruff Av *RCOS* CO16 ...... 258 E8
Peterfield's La *HSTD* CO9 ...... 146 D8
Peterhouse Cl *CHTY* IP2 ...... 62 A3
Petersfield *CHLM/WR* CM1 ...... 304 D7
Petersfield Av *HARH* RM3 ...... 431 F1
Petersfield Cl *HARH* RM3 ...... 431 H1
Peter's Gv *RIPS/CAP* IP9 ...... 87 F4
Peter St *ING* CM4 ...... 388 B4
Peterswood *HLWS* CM18 ...... 322 B1
Peto Av *COS* CO15 ...... 8 B1
Petrebrook *CHLM/GWD* CM2 ...... 333 J2
Petre Cl *ING* CM4 ...... 386 A3
  RBRW/HUT CM13 ...... 434 B8
Petrel Wy *CHLM/GWD* CM2 ...... 332 E7
Petresfield Wy *RBRW/HUT* CM13 ...... 434 B8
Petrolea Cl *COL* CO1 ...... 8 A2
Pett Cl *HCH* RM12 ...... 450 C3
Pettit La *BRTR* CM7 ...... 244 A1
Pettits La *BRWN* CM15 ...... 384 C3
Petts La *SAFWN* CB10 ...... 45 F4
Pettys Cl *BAR* EN8 ...... 346 D3
Petunia Crs *CHLM/WR* CM1 ...... 305 H7
Petworth Ct *BRTR* CM7 ...... 208 E6
  RCOLE CO7 ...... 221 F5
Petworth Gdns *SOSN* SS2 ...... 465 J3
Petworth Wy *HCH* RM12 ...... 450 A5
Pevensey Dr *COS* CO15 ...... 290 E5
Pevensey Gdns *HOC/HUL* SS5 ...... 420 A5
Pevensey Wy *PIT* SS13 ...... 438 E7
Peverel Av *RCHLM* CM3 ...... 308 C4
Pewsey Cl *CHING* E4 ...... 402 B8
Pewterers Av *BSF* CM23 ...... 231 G1
Pharos La *K/T/MI* CO5 ...... 284 E7
Pheasant Ri *RIPW* IP8 ...... 61 F5
Pheasant Rd *CHTY* IP2 ...... 62 A2
Phelips Rd *EPP* CM16 ...... 321 J2
Philbrick Crs West *RAYL* SS6 ...... 441 G2
Philip Av *FX* IP11 ...... 5 D4
Philip Cl *BRWN* CM15 ...... 410 E2
  WOTN CO14 ...... 229 F5
Philip Rd *CHTY* IP2 ...... 3 D5
  WIT CM8 ...... 276 E5
Philips Cl *BRTR* CM7 ...... 208 C3
Philips Rd *BRTR* CM7 ...... 208 C3
Phillida Rd *HARH* RM3 ...... 431 H4
Phillip Rd *RCOLE* CO7 ...... 220 E5
Phillips Cha *BRTR* CM7 ...... 177 K8
Phillips Field Rd *SUD* CO10 ...... 58 D8
Philmead Rd *SBF/HAD* SS7 ...... 460 A3
Philpot End La *GTDUN* CM6 ...... 237 F2
Philpott Av *SOSN* SS2 ...... 465 G3
Phoenix Rd *IPNE* IP4 ...... 37 J6
Phoenix Wy *SBF/HAD* SS7 ...... 441 H6
Picasso Wy *SBN/FI* SS3 ...... 467 F4
Piccotts La *BRTR* CM7 ...... 175 H5
Pickers Wy *COS* CO15 ...... 260 C6
Picketts *CVI* SS8 ...... 477 H1
Picketts Av *LOS* SS9 ...... 463 F1
Picketts Cl *LOS* SS9 ...... 463 F1
Picketts Rd *FX* IP11 ...... 131 K2
Pick Hl *WAB* EN9 ...... 348 D6
Pickpocket La *BRTR* CM7 ...... 209 G7
Pickwick Av *CHLM/WR* CM1 ...... 303 K7
Pickwick Cl *LAIN* SS15 ...... 16 B3
Pickwick Gdns *CHLM/WR* CM1 ...... 488 C8
Pickwick Rd *CHTY* IP2 ...... 36 A7
Picton Av *IP* IP1 ...... 37 F4
Picton Cl *RAYL* SS6 ...... 441 K4
Picton Gdns *RAYL* SS6 ...... 441 J4
Pier Ap *WOTN* CO14 ...... 229 H6
Pier Av *COS* CO15 ...... 10 B4
Pierce Gld *K/T/MI* CO5 ...... 248 A8
Piercing Hl *EPP* CM16 ...... 378 B1
Piercys *PIT* SS13 ...... 438 D8
Pier Gap *COS* CO15 ...... 10 C5
Pier Hl *SOS* SS1 ...... 19 G5
Pierrefitte Wy *BRTR* CM7 ...... 209 H2
Pier Rd *GVW* DA11 ...... 488 E4
Pigeon's La *RIPW* IP8 ...... 60 D3
Piggotts Wy *BSF* CM23 ...... 198 D4
The Pightle *BRTR* CM7 ...... 106 E7
  HVHL CB9 ...... 27 G5

RIPS/CAP IP9 .... 87 G3
Pightle Wy FOS CO13 .... 229 F6
Pig La BRTR CM7 .... 232 A2
Pigstye Green Rd CHONG CM5 .... 328 D5
Pike La UPMR RM14 .... 452 C6
Pike Wy EPP CM16 .... 352 A1
Pilborough Wy COLW CO13 .... 217 K2
Pilcox Hall La RCOS CO16 .... 192 D6
Pilgrim Cl BRTR CM7 .... 177 J8 ☒
Pilgrims La BRWN CM15 .... 414 C3 ☒
    BRWN CM15 .... 410 C1
    SAFWN CB10 .... 43 J3
    SOS SS1 .... 465 H4
Pilgrim's La BRWN CM14 .... 383 G8
    CDH/CHF RM16 .... 470 A8
Pilgrims Wy SBF/HAD SS7 .... 462 A2 ☒
Pilkingtons HLWE CM17 .... 295 H5
Pilots Pl GVE DA12 .... 489 H4
Pimblett Rw RBSF CM22 .... 137 G8 ☒
Pimpernel La CHTY IP2 .... 2 A6
Pinceybrook Rd HLWS CM18 .... 322 A1
Pincey Rd STSD CM24 .... 201 C2
Pinchpools Rd BSF CM23 .... 167 F2
Pine Av GTDUN CM6 .... 204 A4
    GVE DA12 .... 489 J6
    IP IP1 .... 36 C3
Pine Bank KESG IP5 .... 39 K7
Pine Cl BAR EN8 .... 346 C2
    CVI SS8 .... 477 J2
    LOS SS9 .... 442 C8
    MGTR CO11 .... 123 J5
    RCOLE CO7 .... 224 A5
Pine Ct UPMR RM14 .... 451 H5
Pine Crs RBRW/HUT CM13 .... 412 C1
Pinecroft GPK RM2 .... 430 D6
    RBRW/HUT CM13 .... 412 A3
Pinecroft Gdns COLN CO4 .... 187 J2
Pinecroft Ri SUD CO10 .... 57 K8
Pinecroft Rd IP IP1 .... 36 C5
Pine Dr ING CM4 .... 386 C1
Pine Gv BSF CM23 .... 199 G7
    K/T/MI CO5 .... 284 D6
    WIT CM8 .... 245 G8 ☒
Pinelands BSF CM23 .... 198 E4
Pine Rd SBF/HAD SS7 .... 461 J3
Pines Av EN EN1 .... 374 C2
Pines HI STSD CM24 .... 167 J8
Pines Rd CHLM/WR CM1 .... 303 K8
The Pines CDH/CHF RM16 .... 471 F8 ☒
    LAIN SS15 .... 16 A1
    RCHLM CM3 .... 271 C1
    WFD IG8 .... 403 G6
Pinetree Cl KESG IP5 .... 38 D6 ☒
Pinetrees SBF/HAD SS7 .... 461 H2
Pine View Av IP IP1 .... 2 B1
Pinewood Av LOS SS9 .... 442 E8
Pinewood Cl COS CO15 .... 259 G6
    FOS CO13 .... 228 C7 ☒
    HLWE CM17 .... 295 G7
    HOC/HUL SS5 .... 419 K3
    TIL RM18 .... 486 C2 ☒
Pinewood Rd ABR/ST RM4 .... 407 H7
Pinewood Wy RBRW/HUT CM13 .... 412 C1
Pinkeneys ROY SG8 .... 41 G8
Pinkham Dr WIT CM8 .... 277 F5
Pink La WIT CM8 .... 243 H6
Pinkney Cl SAFWN CB10 .... 102 B3
Pinkuah La SUD CO10 .... 33 F7
Pin Mill Cl RIPW IP8 .... 61 J4
Pinmill Rd RIPS/CAP IP9 .... 91 J5
Pinnacles WAB EN9 .... 348 A8
Pinners Ct BOC CM0 .... 397 K6
Pinnock's Av CVW DA11 .... 489 G6
Pintail Cl CHTY IP2 .... 62 A3
Pintail Crs BRTR CM7 .... 209 F7
Pintoils RCHLM CM3 .... 392 D7
Pipchin Rd CHLM/WR CM1 .... 304 A7
Piper Rd COLW CO3 .... 186 C6
Pipers Cl HVHL CB9 .... 27 J1
Piper's Tye CHLM/GWD CM2 .... 361 F2
Pippins Cl BOC CM0 .... 398 C7
The Pippins HSTD CO9 .... 147 J3 ☒
    SUD CO10 .... 33 J1
Pipps Hill La BSDN SS14 .... 17 F1
Pipps Hill Rd North BCAYE CM11 .... 437 J2
Pipps Hill Rd South BSDN SS14 .... 17 F2
Pirie Rd RCOLW CO6 .... 185 K1
Pishiobury Dr SBW CM21 .... 263 H5
Pitcairn Rd IP IP1 .... 36 A5
Pitfield Wy PEND EN3 .... 374 C5 ☒
Pit La K/T/MI CO5 .... 248 A7 ☒
Pitmans Cl SOS SS1 .... 19 D4 ☒
Pitmire La BURES CO8 .... 84 E7
Pitsea Hall La VGE SS16 .... 458 E4
Pitsea Rd PIT SS13 .... 438 D7
Pitsea View Rd BCAYE CM11 .... 438 A1
Pitseaville Gv VGE SS16 .... 438 B8
Pitt Av WIT CM8 .... 277 G8
Pitt Cha CHLM/GWD CM2 .... 333 G8
Pittfields VGE SS16 .... 436 B8
Pittman Cl RBRW/HUT CM13 .... 412 B8
Pittman's Fld HLW CM20 .... 13 F2
Pitts End RCOLE CO7 .... 122 C2
Place Farm La BRWN CM15 .... 383 J3

Plains Farm Cl RCOLE CO7 .... 156 A7
Plains Fld BRTR CM7 .... 210 C4
Plains Rd MAL CM9 .... 279 H7
The Plain EPP CM16 .... 351 F5
Plaistow Cl SLH/COR SS17 .... 473 K3
Plaistow Green La HSTD CO9 .... 147 H8
Plaistow Wy ROY SG8 .... 66 B3 ☒
Plane Av CVW DA11 .... 488 C5
Plane Tree Cl BOC CM0 .... 398 B7
    CHLM/GWD CM2 .... 332 D7
Plane View Cl COS CO15 .... 290 D3
Plantaganet Pl WAB EN9 .... 347 H7 ☒
Plantation Cl SAFWS CB11 .... 71 F7 ☒
Plantation Rd ERITH DA8 .... 480 B7
    RCHLM CM3 .... 306 D4
Planton Wy RCOLE CO7 .... 255 H6
Plashet Gdns RBRW/HUT CM13 .... 411 K7
Plashets RBSF CM22 .... 264 C4
Plas Newydd SOS SS1 .... 465 H7
Platford Gn EMPK RM11 .... 431 F6
Platters Cl IPSE IP3 .... 63 J6
Platters Rd FX IP11 .... 5 E5
Platts Rd PEND EN3 .... 374 C5
Plaw Hatch Cl BSF CM23 .... 199 G5
Players Ct GTDUN CM6 .... 206 D7
Playfield Rd RIPS/CAP IP9 .... 58 C4
Playford La KESG IP5 .... 40 A7
Playford Rd IPNE IP4 .... 38 B6 ☒
Playhouse Sq HLW CM20 .... 12 C5 ☒
Playle Cha MAL CM9 .... 310 C1
Pleasant Dr BCAYW CM12 .... 413 K1
Pleasant Ms SOS SS1 .... 19 E5 ☒
Pleasant Rd BSF CM23 .... 198 D5
    SOS SS1 .... 19 E5
Pleasant Va SAFWS CB11 .... 70 E6
Pleshey Cl SOS SS1 .... 465 J5
    WICKW SS12 .... 417 H7 ☒
Pleshey Rd RCHLM CM3 .... 271 C1
Plough Dr COLW CO3 .... 186 B8
Plough La SUD CO10 .... 58 A6
Ploughmans Cl BSF CM23 .... 198 B8
Ploughmans Headland
    COLW CO3 .... 185 K8 ☒
Plough Ri UPMR RM14 .... 452 B1
Plough Rd RCOLE CO7 .... 223 K5
    RIPS/CAP IP9 .... 86 E4
Plough St IPSE IP3 .... 228 D7
Plover Cl FOS CO15 .... 228 C7 ☒
Plover Gdns UPMR RM14 .... 452 C2 ☒
Plover Md CHTY IP2 .... 62 A3
Plover Rd CHTY IP2 .... 62 A3
Plovers Md BRWN CM15 .... 384 B2
The Plovers BOC CM0 .... 342 D6
Plowmans RAYL SS6 .... 441 K8
Plowmans Headland RAYL SS6 .... 441 K8
Ploymen St HLWW/ROY CM19 .... 322 A1
Plumberow Av HOC/HUL SS5 .... 421 F5
Plumberow Mount Av
    HOC/HUL SS5 .... 421 F5
Plume Av COLW CO3 .... 218 B1
    MAL CM9 .... 338 B4
Plumleys PIT SS13 .... 438 E6
Plummers Cl BSF CM23 .... 199 G7
Plumpton Av HCH RM12 .... 451 G4
Plump Tree La RCHLM CM3 .... 335 H8
Plumptre La RCHLM CM3 .... 335 H8
Plums La BRTR CM7 .... 175 F1
Plumtree Av CHLM/GWD CM2 .... 305 G8
Plymouth Rd CHLM/WR CM1 .... 305 G8
    FX IP11 .... 5 F1
Plymtree SOS SS1 .... 466 B4
Pochard Wy BRTR CM7 .... 209 F8
Pocklington Cl CHLM/GWD CM2 .... 333 J1 ☒
Pod's Brook Rd BRTR CM7 .... 209 G4
Pods La BRTR CM7 .... 208 A3
Point Clear Rd RCOS CO16 .... 288 D3
Point Cl CVI SS8 .... 479 F2
Point Rd CVI SS8 .... 478 C2
Pointwell La RCOLW CO6 .... 213 H6
Pole Barn La FOS CO13 .... 228 E8
Polecat Rd BRTR CM7 .... 210 E8
Pole Hill Rd CHING E4 .... 402 D3
Pole La WIT CM8 .... 243 G2
Poley Rd SLH/COR SS17 .... 473 J4
Pollard Cl BRTR CM7 .... 405 K8
Pollard Hatch HLWW/ROY CM19 .... 12 B6 ☒
Pollards Cl LOU IG10 .... 403 K1
    RCFD SS4 .... 444 B3
Pollard's Gn CHLM/GWD CM2 .... 333 H5
Pollard Wy RCOS CO16 .... 258 E8
Polley Cl FOS CO15 .... 228 D6 ☒
Polstead Cl RAYL SS6 .... 441 F2
Polsteads VGE SS16 .... 458 B2
Polstead Wy RCOS CO16 .... 290 D1
Pomfret Md BSDN SS14 .... 17 E4
Pompadour Cl BRW CM14 .... 411 F8 ☒
Pond Cha COLW CO3 .... 218 B1
Pond Cl FX IP11 .... 5 D2
Pond Cross Farm SAFWS CB11 .... 100 B5
Pond Cross Wy SAFWS CB11 .... 100 B5 ☒
Ponders Rd RCOLW CO6 .... 184 B2
Pondfield La RBRW/HUT CM13 .... 411 K7
Pondfield Rd COLN CO4 .... 9 F2
Pondholton Dr WIT CM8 .... 277 F6
Pond La RBSF CM22 .... 265 G2
Ponds Rd CHLM/GWD CM2 .... 360 D3
Pond Wk UPMR RM14 .... 452 B3 ☒

Poney Cha WIT CM8 .... 278 B8
Poole Cl IPSE IP3 .... 64 B2
Poole Rd EMPK RM11 .... 451 G1
Pooles La HOC/HUL SS5 .... 419 K2
Poole St HSTD CO9 .... 79 K6
    SUD CO10 .... 32 C4
Pool's La CHLM/WR CM1 .... 357 K1
Poore St SAFWS CB11 .... 98 E5
Poors La HAR CO12 .... 461 K1
Poors La North SBF/HAD SS7 .... 442 D8
Poperinghe Rd COLS CO2 .... 219 G1
Popes Ct HVHL CB9 .... 28 A8
Popes Crs PIT SS13 .... 438 D8
Pope's La COLW CO3 .... 8 A4
Pope's Rd RCOLW CO6 .... 183 F1
Popes Wk RAYL SS6 .... 442 A3
Poplar Av COS CO15 .... 290 C3
Poplar Cl CHLM/GWD CM2 .... 332 E7
    COS CO15 .... 290 D3
    HSTD CO9 .... 148 A5
    HVHL CB9 .... 26 D4
    ING CM4 .... 356 C5
    ING CM4 .... 386 A3
    RCHLM CM3 .... 392 C5
    SOCK/AV RM15 .... 470 B4
    WIT CM8 .... 245 G8
Poplar Dr RBRW/HUT CM13 .... 412 B2
Poplar Gv BOC CM0 .... 398 A8
Poplar Grove Cha MAL CM9 .... 310 D6
Poplar La RIPW IP8 .... 61 G2
Poplar Rd CVI SS8 .... 478 C2
    RAYL SS6 .... 442 A5
    SUD CO10 .... 58 E6
Poplar Rw EPP CM16 .... 378 C3
Poplars Av HOC/HUL SS5 .... 443 F1
Poplars Cl RCOLE CO7 .... 222 A6
Poplar Shaw WAB EN9 .... 348 B7 ☒
The Poplars ABR/ST RM4 .... 379 F7
    GTDUN CM6 .... 204 B3 ☒
    MGTR CO11 .... 13 J3
Poplar Wy FOS CO13 .... 228 C7
Poppy Cl CHTY IP2 .... 2 A4
Poppyfield Cl LOS SS9 .... 442 E7
Poppy Gdns COLS CO2 .... 219 K2
Porchester Cl EMPK RM11 .... 431 F6
Porchester Rd BCAYW CM12 .... 387 C8
Porchfield Cl GVE DA12 .... 489 H7
Pork La FOS CO13 .... 227 H7
Porlock Av WOS/PRIT SS0 .... 463 H1
Porter Cl WTHK RM20 .... 483 F5
Porter La IPSE IP3 .... 64 D4 ☒
Porters PIT SS13 .... 439 F5
Porters Brook Wk COLN CO4 .... 9 E1
Porters Cl BRW CM14 .... 410 D4
    COLW CO3 .... 184 E2
Porter's La COLW CO3 .... 184 E2
Porters Pk RCHLM CM3 .... 306 E2
Porter Wy RCOS CO16 .... 290 D7
Portland Av GVE DA12 .... 489 G7
    HAR CO12 .... 7 D5
    SOS SS1 .... 19 E5
Portland Cl BRTR CM7 .... 210 A2 ☒
Portland Crs HAR CO12 .... 7 D5 ☒
Portland Dr EBAR EN7 .... 346 A3
Portland Pl BSF CM23 .... 198 E6 ☒
Portland Rd BSF CM23 .... 198 E6
    COLS CO2 .... 8 B5 ☒
    CVW DA11 .... 488 C5
Port La COL CO1 .... 9 D5
    RBSF CM22 .... 232 B3
Portlight Cl MGTR CO11 .... 160 B1
Portman Dr BCAYW CM12 .... 387 H6
Portman Rd IP IP1 .... 2 C4
Portman's Wk IP IP1 .... 2 B4
Portmore Gdns CRW RM5 .... 407 F9
Portobello Rd WOTN CO14 .... 229 H6
Portreath Pl CHLM/WR CM1 .... 304 C6
Portsea Rd TIL RM18 .... 485 H1
Portsmouth Rd COS CO15 .... 290 E5
Portway CHLM/GWD CM2 .... 333 K1 ☒
Portway Ct HSTD CO9 .... 148 C4
Posford Cl COLN CO4 .... 155 G6
Postman's La RCHLM CM3 .... 335 J2
Post Meadow BCAYE CM11 .... 414 E2
Post Mill Cl IPNE IP4 .... 37 H2
Post Office La MAL CM9 .... 311 K1
Post Office Rd CHLM/WR CM1 .... 304 D5
    HLW CM20 .... 12 C2
    ING CM4 .... 386 B2
    MAL CM9 .... 336 E8
Potash La RIPS/CAP IP9 .... 87 K5
Potash Rd BCAYE CM11 .... 387 K2 ☒
    HLWE CM17 .... 297 K5
Pot Kiln Cha HSTD CO9 .... 82 A7
Pot Kiln Rd SUD CO10 .... 58 E2
The Pot Kilns SUD CO10 .... 59 F7
Potters Cl LOU IG10 .... 377 G3
    RCHLM CM3 .... 336 A3
Potters Fld HLWE CM17 .... 295 H1
Potters La RCHLM CM3 .... 391 H1
Potter St BSF CM23 .... 198 E6 ☒
    HLWE CM17 .... 295 G4
    HSTD CO9 .... 110 D6
Pottery La WY SOSN SS2 .... 444 C5
Pottery La CHLM/WR CM1 .... 304 C6

HSTD CO9 ... 110 E2
Pouch MI FX IP11 ... 94 C7
Poulk Hall La RCHLM CM3 ... 241 J7
Poulteney Rd STSD CM24 ... 167 K5
Poulton Cl MAL CM9 ... 338 C5
Pound Cl WAB EN9 ... 320 A5
Pound Farm Dr HAR CO12 ... 6 A5
Poundfield Rd LOU IG10 ... 404 D7
Pound Flds CHLM/WR CM1 ... 331 H5
Pound Ga GTDUN CM6 ... 173 J7
Pound La CDH/CHF RM16 ... 472 A4
  LAIN SS15 ... 16 B2
  PIT SS13 ... 439 J2
  RIPS/CAP IP9 ... 86 E5
  RIPW IP8 ... 61 G6
  WICKW SS12 ... 439 J4
Pound Lane Central LAIN SS15 ... 16 B1
Pound La North LAIN SS15 ... 436 E3
Pound Wk SAFWN CB10 ... 70 E3
Powdermill La WAB EN9 ... 347 H7
Powdermill Ms WAB EN9 ... 347 H7
Powdermill Wy WAB EN9 ... 347 H6
Powell Rd BKHH IG9 ... 403 K3
  LAIN SS15 ... 436 C6
Powers Hall End WIT CM8 ... 276 C2
Powling Rd IPSE IP3 ... 63 J3
Pownall Crs COLS CO2 ... 219 C1
Poynder Rd TIL RM18 ... 485 G7
Poynings Wy HARH RM3 ... 431 F3
Poyntens RAYL SS6 ... 441 H4
Poynter Pl FOS CO13 ... 228 D6
Poynters La SBN/FI SS3 ... 466 C3
Pratts Farm La RCHLM CM3 ... 304 E1
Pratt's La RIPS/CAP IP9 ... 90 D3
Premier Av CDH/CHF RM16 ... 484 B1
Prentice Cl RCFD SS4 ... 444 C3
Prentice Hall La MAL CM9 ... 314 A5
Prescott VGE SS16 ... 456 D2
Prescott Cl HCH RM12 ... 450 C2
Prescott Gn LOU IG10 ... 378 A7
Prescott Rd BAR EN8 ... 346 C4
President Rd COLW CO3 ... 185 K3
Preston Dr IP IP1 ... 36 B3
Preston Gdns PEND EN3 ... 374 E3
  RAYL SS6 ... 441 J1
Preston Rd COS CO15 ... 260 B8
  GVW DA11 ... 488 D6
  HARH RM3 ... 408 E7
  WOS/PRIT SS0 ... 18 A4
Prestwick Av FX IP11 ... 131 K1
Prestwick Dr BSF CM23 ... 199 C4
Prestwood Cl SBF/HAD SS7 ... 440 E7
Prestwood Dr CRW RM5 ... 407 H8
  SBF/HAD SS7 ... 441 F6
Pretoria Cl LAIN SS15 ... 17 D1
Pretoria Crs CHING E4 ... 402 D4
Pretoria Rd CHING E4 ... 402 D4
  HSTD CO9 ... 148 A3
Prettygate Rd COLW CO3 ... 186 B8
Pretyman Rd FX IP11 ... 5 E6
  IPSE IP3 ... 63 K2
Priests Fld RBRW/HUT CM13 ... 412 B8
Priest's La BRWN CM15 ... 411 H5
Primley La RBSF CM22 ... 264 C3
Primrose Cl BSF CM23 ... 198 B7
  CVI SS8 ... 461 F7
  VGE SS16 ... 456 C1
Primrose Fld HLWS CM18 ... 13 F6
Primrose Gln EMPK RM11 ... 431 F6
Primrose HI BRW CM14 ... 411 F6
  CHLM/WR CM1 ... 14 A2
  CHTY IP2 ... 2 A5
  HVHL CB9 ... 27 F6
  RIPS/CAP IP9 ... 126 A1
Primrose La K/T/MI CO5 ... 248 A7
  MGTR CO11 ... 162 D4
Primrose Pth EBAR EN7 ... 346 A5
Primrose Pl WIT CM8 ... 276 E1
Primrose Rd COS CO15 ... 260 C7
Primrose Wk BOC CM0 ... 398 C4
Primula Wy CHLM/WR CM1 ... 305 H7
Prince Albert Rd K/T/MI CO5 ... 285 F7
Prince Av WOS/PRIT SS0 ... 443 C8
Prince Charles Av CDH/CHF RM16 ... 472 B4
Prince Charles Cl COS CO15 ... 290 F2
  SUD CO10 ... 58 C5
Prince Charles Rd COLS CO2 ... 219 C4
Prince Cl WOS/PRIT SS0 ... 443 K8
Princedale Cl IP IP1 ... 36 C4
Prince Edward Rd BCAYE CM11 ... 414 D3
Princel La RCOLE CO7 ... 121 J6
Prince of Wales Dr IP IP2 ... 62 C3
Prince of Wales Rd WIT CM8 ... 310 C1
Prince Philip Av CDH/CHF RM16 ... 471 F7
  COS CO15 ... 290 E4
Prince Philip Rd COLS CO2 ... 219 G4
Princes Av BOC CM0 ... 398 D1
  PEND EN3 ... 374 E2
  RCHLM CM3 ... 368 E5
  SBF/HAD SS7 ... 440 E7
  SLH/COR SS17 ... 474 C2
  WFD IG8 ... 403 J7
Princes Cl BCAYW CM12 ... 387 J7
  EPP CM16 ... 324 C7
  LAIN SS15 ... 16 C2

Princes Ct BCAYW CM12 ... 387 J7
  BSF CM23 ... 198 B6
Prince's Esp WOTN CO14 ... 229 J5
Princesfield Rd WAB EN9 ... 348 D7
Princes Gdns FX IP11 ... 5 F3
Princes Ga BSF CM23 ... 198 B6
Princes Ms BCAYW CM12 ... 387 J7
Princes Pk RAIN RM13 ... 450 B8
  BOC CM0 ... 398 B7
  BRW CM14 ... 382 C6
  CHLM/GWD CM2 ... 14 B6
  COS CO15 ... 260 B8
  CVI SS8 ... 477 K2
  FX IP11 ... 131 H4
  HAR CO12 ... 6 C5
  MAL CM9 ... 338 C3
  ROM RM1 ... 430 B7
Princess Anne Cl COS CO15 ... 290 E4
Princess Av TIL RM18 ... 486 D5
Princess Gdns RCFD SS4 ... 421 K8
Princess Margaret Rd TIL RM18 ... 486 C5
Princess Rd RAYL SS6 ... 442 A2
Princess St CVW DA11 ... 489 G4
  IP IP1 ... 2 C5
  WOS/PRIT SS0 ... 18 C4
Princess Wy HVHL CB9 ... 26 E5
Prince St SUD CO10 ... 58 B5
Princes Wy BKHH IG9 ... 403 K5
  RBRW/HUT CM13 ... 411 K5
Princethorpe Rd IPSE IP3 ... 64 A1
Princeton Ms COLN CO4 ... 187 J1
Prince William Av CVI SS8 ... 460 E7
Printers Wy HLW CM20 ... 262 E8
Prior Cha GRAYS RM17 ... 483 J3
Prior Cl HSTD CO9 ... 147 J5
The Priories HOC/HUL SS5 ... 419 J4
Priors Cl BSDN SS14 ... 437 K7
Priors East BSDN SS14 ... 437 K7
Priors Pk HCH RM12 ... 450 D4
Prior's Wy BOC CM0 ... 398 E1
  RCOLW CO6 ... 213 H2
Prior's Wood Rd RBSF CM22 ... 201 K6
Prior Wy COLN CO4 ... 186 E5
Priory Av CHING E4 ... 402 A6
  HLWE CM17 ... 263 F8
  HVHL CB9 ... 27 F6
  SOSN SS2 ... 18 C1
Priory Cl BROX EN10 ... 318 E6
  BRWN CM15 ... 410 D1
  CHING E4 ... 402 A6
  CHLM/WR CM1 ... 332 A3
  RCHLM CM3 ... 308 B4
  RCOS CO16 ... 289 C7
  SAFWN CB10 ... 43 F2
Priory Ct BSF CM23 ... 198 D6
  HLWS CM18 ... 295 F8
Priory Crs SOSN SS2 ... 464 B1
Priory Dr STSD CM24 ... 157 K8
Priory Farm Rd RCHLM CM3 ... 308 B3
Priory Ga BAR EN8 ... 347 F1
Priory Gn HARH RM3 ... 409 F7
Priory La RCHLM CM3 ... 363 K4
Priory Md BRWN CM15 ... 384 A2
Priory Ms HCH RM12 ... 450 C2
Priory Pth HARH RM3 ... 409 F6
Priory Rd COS CO15 ... 10 B4
  HARH RM3 ... 409 F6
  LOU IG10 ... 377 G8
  RCHLM CM3 ... 363 J4
  RCOLW CO6 ... 182 C7
  SLH/COR SS17 ... 474 A2
  SUD CO10 ... 58 A4
  WIT CM8 ... 279 H2
Priory St COL CO1 ... 8 C4
  RCOLW CO6 ... 149 J6
The Priory BCAYW CM12 ... 387 J7
  CHLM/WR CM1 ... 331 H5
Priory View Rd LOS SS9 ... 443 F8
Priory Wk SUD CO10 ... 58 B7
Priory Wd HSTD CO9 ... 110 D1
Priory Wood Crs LOS SS9 ... 443 F8
Priory Wood Rd RBSF CM22 ... 200 B5
Prittle Cl SBF/HAD SS7 ... 441 H8
Prittlewell Cha WOS/PRIT SS0 ... 463 K2
Prittlewell Cl CHTY IP2 ... 62 B4
Prittlewell Sq SOS SS1 ... 18 C5
Prittlewell St SOSN SS2 ... 19 D3
Proctor Cl K/T/MI CO5 ... 252 D3
Proctors Wy BSF CM23 ... 232 A4
Proctor Wy RCOLW CO6 ... 215 H2
Progress Ct BRTR CM7 ... 209 H2
Progress Rd LOS SS9 ... 442 D7
Progress Wy RCOS CO16 ... 258 D7
Promenade COS CO15 ... 289 K7
  HAR CO12 ... 7 D6
  RCHLM CM3 ... 368 D3
Promenade Wy RCOLE CO7 ... 255 H8
Prospect Av SLH/COR SS17 ... 473 H4
Prospect Cl RCHLM CM3 ... 308 A2
  SOS SS1 ... 19 F5
Prospect Gv DA12 ... 489 J5
Prospect HI SUD CO10 ... 85 G2
Prospect Pl GRAYS RM17 ... 484 A5

GVE DA12 ... 489 J5
SAFWS CB11 ... 71 G4
Prospect Rd BAR EN8 ... 346 C3
  EMPK RM11 ... 431 C5
  IP IP1 ... 2 B3
  WFD IG8 ... 403 K8
Prospect Wy RBRW/HUT CM13 ... 385 H8
Prospero Cl COLN CO4 ... 188 C6
Protea Wy CVI SS8 ... 478 B1
Provence Cl COLW CO3 ... 185 H6
Providence BOC CM0 ... 425 H1
Providence La IP IP1 ... 2 B2
Provident Sq CHLM/GWD CM2 ... 15 D3
Prower Cl BCAYE CM11 ... 414 C4
Prunus Ct COLS CO2 ... 219 H6
Prykes Dr CHLM/WR CM1 ... 14 A3
Pryor Cl WIT CM8 ... 277 G4
Pryors Cl BSF CM23 ... 199 F7
Puckleside VGE SS16 ... 16 A6
Pudding La CHIG IG7 ... 405 H2
  COLS CO2 ... 250 B2
The Pudgell ROY SG8 ... 66 B5
Pudsey Hall La RCFD SS4 ... 422 D3
Puffin Pl SBN/FI SS3 ... 466 D4
Puffinsdale COS CO15 ... 10 C2
Pugh Pl SLH/COR SS17 ... 473 K1
Pulham Av BROX EN10 ... 318 E2
Pulpitfield Cl FOS CO13 ... 229 F5
Pulpits Cl HOC/HUL SS5 ... 421 G6
Pump HI BUNT SG9 ... 132 D3
  CHLM/GWD CM2 ... 333 H7
  LOU IG10 ... 377 H6
  RCOS CO16 ... 289 J1
Pump La EPP CM16 ... 321 K6
  RCHLM CM3 ... 270 E4
  RCHLM CM3 ... 365 K4
Pump Mead Cl BOC CM0 ... 398 D1
Pump St SLH/COR SS17 ... 473 G3
Punchard Wy FX IP11 ... 94 D7
Purbeck Rd EMPK RM11 ... 450 B1
Purcell Cl CHLM/WR CM1 ... 331 G4
  COLN CO4 ... 188 B7
  LAIN SS15 ... 16 B2
  SLH/COR SS17 ... 473 J2
Purdeys Wy RCFD SS4 ... 444 D5
Purdis Av IPSE IP3 ... 64 D4
Purdis Farm La IPSE IP3 ... 64 D3
  KIR/NAC IP10 ... 65 G3
Purdis Rd KIR/NAC IP10 ... 65 H3
Purfleet By-pass PUR RM19 ... 481 K4
Purfleet Rd SOCK/AV RM15 ... 468 D8
Purford Gn HLWS CM18 ... 294 E6
Purleigh Cl PIT SS13 ... 439 F4
Purleigh Gv RCHLM CM3 ... 366 D8
Purleigh Rd RAYL SS6 ... 441 G2
Purleigh St RCHLM CM3 ... 366 B4
Purley Wy RCOS CO16 ... 258 D7
  WOS/PRIT SS0 ... 443 K8
Purlieu Wy EPP CM16 ... 378 C1
Purplett St CHTY IP2 ... 3 E5
Purvis Wy COLN CO4 ... 155 J8
Putney Rd PEND EN3 ... 374 D2
Putticks La RCOLE CO7 ... 122 D2
Pyefleet Cl K/T/MI CO5 ... 221 F7
  RCOLE CO7 ... 255 J6
Pyefleet Vw K/T/MI CO5 ... 252 D2
Pyesand FOS CO13 ... 228 B5
Pygot Pl BRTR CM7 ... 209 H1
Pym Pl GRAYS RM17 ... 483 K3
Pyms Rd CHLM/GWD CM2 ... 360 D2
Pynchbek BSF CM23 ... 231 J2
Pynchon Paddocks RBSF CM22 ... 232 D6
Pyne Ga CHLM/GWD CM2 ... 360 D4
Pynest Green La WAB EN9 ... 376 C3
Pyrles Gn LOU IG10 ... 377 K5
Pyrles La LOU IG10 ... 377 K6
Pytt Fld HLWE CM17 ... 295 F6

Q

Quadling St IP IP1 ... 2 C4
The Quadrant PUR RM19 ... 481 K3
Quaker La WAB EN9 ... 347 J8
Quaker's La HVHL CB9 ... 27 G6
Quale Rd CHLM/GWD CM2 ... 333 K1
Quantock Cl KESG IP5 ... 38 D6
Quarry HI GRAYS RM17 ... 483 K4
Quarry Ms PUR RM19 ... 481 H3
Quarry Springs HLW CM20 ... 294 E5
Quarry Wy WTHK RM20 ... 482 C5
Quarter Ga RCHLM CM3 ... 392 E8
Quay La FOS CO13 ... 228 C4
  RCOS CO16 ... 226 E1
  SUD CO10 ... 58 B7
Quay St MGTR CO11 ... 159 J1
  RCOLE CO7 ... 220 E6
The Quay BOC CM0 ... 425 H1
  HAR CO12 ... 7 E2
Quebec Av SOS SS1 ... 19 D4
Quebec Cl SOS SS1 ... 19 E4
Quebec Dr KESG IP5 ... 39 F5

Quebec Rd *TIL* RM18 .... 485 F8
Queech La *RIPS/CAP* IP9 ...... 124 C5
The Queech *RIPS/CAP* IP9 ...... 87 C3 ⊡
Queen Anne Dr *K/T/MI* CO5 ...... 285 F7
Queen Anne Gdns *K/T/MI* CO5 .. 285 F7 ⊡
Queen Anne Rd *K/T/MI* CO5 ...... 285 F7
Queen Anne's Dr *WOS/PRIT* SSO .. 463 K1
Queen Anns Av *HOC/HUL* SS5 .... 419 J5
Queenborough La *BRTR* CM7 .... 208 D4
Queenborough Rd *BOC* CM0 ...... 398 D1
Queenbury Cl *K/T/MI* CO5 .... 285 G7 ⊡
Queen Edith Dr *HVHL* CB9 .... 50 C7
Queen Elizabeth Av *COS* CO15 .. 290 E4
.... *TIL* RM18 ...... 486 D3 ⊡
Queen Elizabeth Cha *RCFD* SS4 .. 444 C6
Queen Elizabeth Dr
.... *SLH/COR* SS17 ...... 457 G8
Queen Elizabeth li Br *WTHK* RM20 .. 482 B8
Queen Elizabeth Wy *COLS* CO15 .. 219 H4
Queen Mary Av *TIL* RM18 .... 486 D3 ⊡
Queen Mary Cl *ROM* RM1 .... 430 A8
Queen's Av *LOS* SS9 .... 463 F4
.... *MAL* CM9 .... 538 C4
.... *WFD* IG8 .... 403 J8
Queensberry Rd *IPSE* IP3 .... 63 J4 ⊡
Queensbury Av *RCOLW* CO6 ...... 184 C3
Queenscliffe Rd *CHTY* IP2 .... 2 B6
Queen's Cl *SBW* CM21 .... 263 K1
.... *STSD* CM24 ...... 167 K5
.... *SUD* CO10 .... 58 B5 ⊡
Queens Crs *BSF* CM23 .... 198 D8
Queensdale Cl *IP* IP1 .... 36 D4
Queen's Dr *BAR* EN8 .... 347 G8
Queen's Gdns *BRTR* CM7 .... 176 D6
.... *UPMR* RM14 .... 432 C8
Queensgate Dr *IPNE* IP4 .... 37 H5
Queen's Gate Ms *BCAYW* CM12 .. 387 J8 ⊡
Queen's Grove Rd *CHING* E4 ...... 402 E4
Queen's Head Rd *COS* CO15 ...... 154 E3
Queensland Av *RCFD* SS4 .... 290 E4
Queensland Crs *CHLM/WR* CM1 .. 303 K8
Queensland Dr *COLS* CO2 .... 219 H4
Queensmere *SBF/HAD* SS7 .... 441 G8
Queens Park Av *BCAYW* CM12 .... 387 G8
Queens Park Rd *HARH* RM5 .... 431 G3
Queen's Rd *BAR* EN8 .... 346 E8
.... *BCAYE* CM11 ...... 437 J1
.... *BKHH* IG9 .... 403 J3
.... *BOC* CM0 .... 398 B8
.... *BRTR* CM7 .... 177 J8
.... *BRW* CM14 .... 411 F6
.... *CHLM/GWD* CM2 .. 15 E3
.... *COLW* CO3 .... 186 D7
.... *COS* CO15 .... 290 E4
.... *EPP* CM16 .... 324 C7
.... *FOS* CO13 .... 261 K1
.... *FX* IP11 .... 131 H3
.... *GVE* DA12 .... 489 H8
.... *HAR* CO12 .... 16 A1
.... *LAIN* SS15 .... 16 A1
.... *LOS* SS9 .... 463 F5
.... *LOU* IG10 .... 377 J2
.... *RAYL* SS6 .... 441 J4
Queen's Sq *IPSE* IP3 .... 63 K3
Queens St *HVHL* CB9 .... 26 C1
.... *HVHL* CB9 .... 27 G5
Queen St *BOC* CM0 .... 398 B1 ⊡
.... *BRW* CM14 .... 411 F8
.... *CHLM/GWD* CM2 .. 14 B4
.... *CHONG* CM5 .... 327 C3
.... *COL* CO1 .... 8 B4
.... *FX* IP11 .... 131 H3
.... *GVE* DA12 .... 489 G4
.... *HSTD* CO9 .... 110 D2
.... *HSTD* CO9 .... 110 E6
.... *MAL* CM9 .... 538 C5
.... *RCOLE* CO7 .... 255 K7
.... *RCOLW* CO6 .... 213 H3
Queens Wk *CHING* E4 .... 402 E4 ⊡
Queens Wy *BAR* EN8 .... 347 F8 ⊡
.... *IPSE* IP3 .... 63 K3
Queensway *CHONG* CM5 .... 326 B8
.... *COS* CO15 .... 260 B8
.... *HVHL* CB9 .... 26 E5
.... *K/T/MI* CO5 .... 248 A7
.... *MGTR* CO11 .... 159 H1
.... *PEND* EN3 .... 374 C8
.... *SOS* SS1 .... 19 E5
.... *SUD* CO10 .... 58 B8
Queenswood Av
.... *RBRW/HUT* CM13 .... 412 C1
Queen Victoria Dr *RIPS/CAP* IP9 .. 129 G5
Quendon Dr *WAB* EN9 .... 347 K7
Quendon Rd *BSDN* SS14 .... 438 B5
Quendon Wy *FOS* CO13 .... 229 F7
Quennell Wy *RBRW/HUT* CM13 .. 412 B3
Quentin Cl *IP* IP1 .... 36 A5
Quickset Rd *SAFWS* CB11 .... 42 A8

Quilp Dr *CHLM/WR* CM1 .... 304 B6
Quilter Dr *RIPW* IP8 .... 61 J4
Quilter Rd *FX* IP11 .... 131 J3
Quilters Cl *BSDN* SS14 .... 438 A5 ⊡
.... *COS* CO15 .... 260 D7 ⊡
Quilters Dr *BCAYW* CM12 .... 414 B5
Quilters Straight *BSDN* SS14 .... 438 A5
Quince Cl *MGTR* CO11 .... 123 J4 ⊡
Quince Tree Cl *SOCK/AV* RM15 .. 470 A4 ⊡
Quinion Cl *CHLM/WR* CM1 .... 303 K6
Quinton's La *FX* IP11 .... 131 K2
Quintons Rd *RCOLE* CO7 .... 122 B2
Quinton Wy *WAB* EN9 .... 375 J1
Quorn Gdns *LOS* SS9 .... 462 B4
The Quorn *INC* CM4 .... 386 A3

R

Rachael Clarke Cl
.... *SLH/COR* SS17 ...... 474 A1 ⊡
Rachael Gdns *WIT* CM8 .... 244 E1 ⊡
Rackenford Dr *BSDN* SS14 .... 466 C5 ⊡
Radburn Cl *HLWS* CM18 .... 322 E1
Radcliffe Dr *CHTY* IP2 .... 61 K3
Radford Ct *BCAYW* CM12 .... 414 C2 ⊡
Radford Crs *BCAYW* CM12 .... 414 B2
Radford Rd *BCAYW* CM12 .... 414 B2
Radiator Rd *SUD* CO10 .... 58 D8
Radley Green Rd *INC* CM4 .... 329 G7
Radleys La *RCOLW* CO6 .... 117 H1
Radstocks *BCAYW* CM12 .... 414 C2
Radwinter Av *WICKW* SS12 ...... 417 G8
Radwinter Rd *SAFWN* CB10 ...... 46 E5
.... *SAFWS* CB11 .... 71 G4
Raeburn Cl *FOS* CO13 .... 228 E6 ⊡
Raeburn Rd *IPSE* IP3 .... 63 H4
Raeburn Rd South *IPSE* IP3 ...... 63 G4
Raglan Av *BAR* EN8 .... 346 D8
Raglan Ms *COS* CO15 .... 290 E2 ⊡
Raglan Rd *FOS* CO13 .... 228 E8
Rahn Rd *EPP* CM16 .... 350 E5
Raile Wk *SUD* CO10 .... 35 F5
Railey Rd *SAFWS* CB11 .... 71 F6
Railway *FX* IP11 .... 131 H2 ⊡
.... *LAIN* SS15 .... 436 B7
Railway Pl *GVE* DA12 .... 489 G4 ⊡
Railway Rd *BAR* EN8 .... 347 F7
Railway Sq *BRTR* CM7 .... 209 K2
.... *CHLM/WR* CM1 ...... 14 B2
.... *MGTR* CO11 .... 159 J1
Railway Ter *SOSN* SS2 .... 19 D1
Rainbow Av *CVI* SS8 .... 478 C1 ⊡
Rainbow La *SLH/COR* SS17 ...... 474 B4
Rainbow Md *RCHLM* CM3 .... 275 K8
Rainbow Rd *CDH/CHF* RM16 .... 485 F3
.... *CVI* SS8 .... 478 A3
.... *HLWE* CM17 .... 296 E2
.... *K/T/MI* CO5 .... 285 F7
Rainbow Wy *RCOLW* CO6 .... 149 G4
Raine Av *HVHL* CB9 .... 26 D5
Rainer Cl *BAR* EN8 .... 346 D3
Rainham Av *RAIN* RM13 .... 450 A8
Rainham Rd *FOS* CO13 .... 229 C7
Rainsford Av *CHLM/WR* CM1 .... 14 A2
Rainsford Cl *CHLM/WR* CM1 .... 14 A2
.... *STSD* CM24 .... 167 J5
Rainsford Wy *HCH* RM12 .... 450 A8
Raleigh Cl *ERITH* DA8 .... 480 A5
.... *SUD* CO10 .... 58 D3
Raleigh Rd *SUD* CO10 .... 58 D3
Raliegh Dr *LAIN* SS15 .... 16 B5
Rambler Cl *COLW* CO3 .... 185 J6
Rambley Wy *BOC* CM0 .... 425 J1
Ram Gorse *HLW* CM20 .... 12 B1
Ramney Dr *PEND* EN3 .... 374 E2
Ramparts Cl *RCOLW* CO6 .... 154 C6
The Ramparts *RAYL* SS6 .... 441 K6
Rampart Rd *SBN* FI SS3 .... 466 E7
Rampart Ter *SBN/FI SS3 .... 467 F7
Ramplings Av *COS* CO15 .... 10 B2
Rampton Cl *CHING* E4 .... 402 B6 ⊡
Ramsay Dr *VGE* SS16 .... 458 B2
Ramsay Gdns *GPK* RM2 .... 430 C3
Ramsden Cl *COS* CO15 .... 11 D2
Ramsden Park Rd *BCAYE* CM11 .. 415 K4
Ramsden View Rd *WICKW* SS12 .. 416 E7
Ramsey Cha *RCHLM* CM3 .... 367 J7
.... *WICKW* SS12 .... 417 J8
Ramsey Cl *CHTY* IP2 .... 62 C4
.... *MAL* CM9 .... 539 F1
Ramsey Rd *HAR* CO12 .... 164 C3
.... *HSTD* CO9 .... 147 J5
Ramsgate Dr *IPSE* IP3 .... 63 K2
Ramshaw Dr *CHLM/GWD* CM2 .. 333 H2
Ramuz Dr *WOS/PRIT* SSO 18 A2
Rana Ct *BRTR* CM7 .... 209 J1
Rana Dr *BRTR* CM7 .... 209 J1

Randall Cl *GTDUN* CM6 .... 204 C4
.... *KESG* IP5 .... 39 J6 ⊡
Randall Dr *HCH* RM12 .... 450 D5
Randalls Dr *RBRW/HUT* CM13 .... 412 D2
Randolph Cl *LOS* SS9 .... 463 F2
.... *MAL* CM9 .... 538 B5 ⊡
Rands Rd *GTDUN* CM6 .... 236 D5
Rands Wy *IPSE* IP3 .... 63 K4
Randway *RAYL* SS6 .... 441 J4 ⊡
Randwell Cl *IPNE* IP4 .... 37 K8
Ranelagh Gdns *GVW* DA11 ...... 488 E5
Ranelagh Rd *CHTY* IP2 .... 2 A4 ⊡
.... *FX* IP11 .... 131 H4
Range Rd *GVE* DA12 .... 489 J5
Ranger Wk *COLS* CO2 .... 219 J2
Rangoon Cl *COLS* CO2 .... 218 C4
Ransome Crs *IPSE* IP3 .... 63 K3
Ransome Rd *IPSE* IP3 .... 63 K3
Ransomes Wy *CHLM/WR* CM1 .. 14 C1
.... *IPSE* IP3 .... 64 B5
Ransom Rd *K/T/MI* CO5 .... 248 A8
Rantree Fold *VGE* SS16 .... 17 D6 ⊡
Ranulf Cl *HLWE* CM17 .... 263 G7
Ranulph Wy *RCHLM* CM3 .... 308 B2
Raphael Av *ROM* RM1 .... 430 A5
.... *TIL* RM18 .... 485 F7
Raphael Dr *CHLM/WR* CM1 ...... 305 H6
.... *SBN/FI SS3 .... 467 F5
Raphael Rd *GVE* DA12 .... 489 J5
Raphaels *LAIN* SS15 .... 16 C5
Rapier Cl *PUR* RM19 .... 481 G3
Ratcliffe Ct *K/T/MI* CO5 .... 246 D3 ⊡
Ratcliffe Rd *COLW* CO3 .... 185 K8
Rat HI *RIPS/CAP* IP9 .... 127 J4
Rathmore Rd *GVW* DA11 .... 441 H5
Rat La *SBF/HAD* SS7 .... 441 H5
Rattington Cha *BOC* CM0 .... 398 C3
Rat's La *LOU* IG10 .... 376 D4
Rattwick Dr *CVI* SS8 .... 479 F2
Ravel Gdns *SOCK/AV* RM15 .... 468 E6
Ravel Rd *SOCK/AV* RM15 .... 469 F6
Raven Cl *BCAYW* CM12 .... 414 A1
Raven Crs *BCAYW* CM12 .... 414 A1
Ravencroft *CDH/CHF* RM16 ...... 485 G1 ⊡
Ravendale Wy *SBN/FI SS3 .... 466 C3
Raven Dr *SBF/HAD* SS7 .... 460 A3
Raven La *BCAYW* CM12 .... 414 A1
Ravenoak Wy *CHIG* IG7 .... 405 H8
Ravens Av *HSTD* CO9 .... 148 A5
Ravensbourne Crs *HARH* RM3 .. 431 G5
Ravensbourne Dr *CHLM/WR* CM1 .. 332 A3
Ravenscourt Cl *HCH* RM12 ...... 451 F4 ⊡
Ravenscourt Dr *HCH* RM12 ...... 451 F4
.... *VGE* SS16 .... 438 B8
Ravenscourt Gv *HCH* RM12 ...... 451 F5
Ravens Crs *GTDUN* CM6 .... 207 F6
Ravensdale *COS* CO15 .... 10 C1
.... *VGE* SS16 .... 17 F6
Ravensfield *BSDN* SS14 .... 438 C7
Ravensfield Rd *IP* IP1 .... 36 A3
Ravensmere *EPP* CM16 .... 350 E4
Ravenswood Cha *RCFD* SS4 .... 444 C6
Ravenswood Cl *CRW* RM5 .... 407 G8
Raven Wy *COLN* CO4 .... 187 F1
Rawden Cl *HAR* CO12 .... 6 C4
Rawlings Crs *COLN* CO4 .... 155 J8
Rawreth La *RAYL* SS6 .... 419 H7
.... *WICKE* SS11 .... 419 F6
Rawstorn Rd *COLW* CO3 .... 8 A4 ⊡
Ray Av *HAR* CO12 .... 6 B4
Rayburn Rd *EMPK* RM11 .... 451 H1
Raycliff Av *RCOS* CO16 .... 259 G6
Ray Cl *CVI* SS8 .... 478 A3
.... *LOS* SS9 .... 462 C4
Raydon Wy *SUD* CO10 .... 59 F7
Rayfield *EPP* CM16 .... 350 D4
Rayfield Cl *GTDUN* CM6 .... 238 A1
Rayhaven *HAR* CO12 .... 164 B3
Ray Lamb Wy *ERITH* DA8 .... 480 C5
Ray La *HAR* CO12 .... 128 D8
Rayleigh Av *LOS* SS9 .... 442 C5
.... *WOS/PRIT* SSO 18 B3
Rayleigh Cl *BRTR* CM7 .... 210 B1
.... *COLN* CO4 .... 9 D2
.... *RBRW/HUT* CM13 .. 412 B3
Rayleigh Downs Rd *RAYL* SS6 .. 442 B6
Rayleigh Dr *LOS* SS9 .... 462 C2
Rayleigh Rd *IP* IP1 .... 36 A4
.... *LOS* SS9 .... 442 D6
.... *RBRW/HUT* CM13 .. 412 B2
.... *SBF/HAD* SS7 ...... 441 C6
.... *SLH/COR* SS17 ...... 473 H4
Rayley La *EPP* CM16 .... 324 A6
Ray Md *RCHLM* CM3 .... 272 B6
Rayment Av *CVI* SS8 .... 478 D2
Rayment Drift *KESG* IP5 .... 39 G6 ⊡
Raymond Gdns *CHIG* IG7 .... 406 A6
Raymonds Cl *RCHLM* CM3 ...... 392 C6 ⊡
Raymonds Dr *SBF/HAD* SS7 .... 440 E7
Rayne Rd *BRTR* CM7 .... 208 D3
Rayner Rd *COLS* CO2 .... 218 C1
Rayner Wy *HSTD* CO9 .... 147 K4
Raynham Cl *BSF* CM23 .... 199 H6
Raynham Rd *BSF* CM23 .... 199 G5
Raynton Rd *PEND* EN3 .... 374 D3

Ray Rd *CRW* RM5...................... 407 G8
Rayside *BSDN* SS14.................. 437 K8
The Ray *CHLM/WR* CM1........... 305 G8
Ray Wk *LOS* SS9...................... 462 C4
Read Cl *HOC/HUL* SS5.............. 443 H1
Read Ct *WAB* EN9..................... 348 C7
Reade Rd *RIPS/CAP* IP9............ 90 A7
Reading Cl *VGE* SS16............... 436 A8 🖫
Reading Rd *IPNE* IP4................. 37 K6
The Readings *HLWS* CM18......... 13 F6
Reaper Rd *COLW* CO5............... 218 B1
Rebecca Gdns *WIT* CM8....... 244 E1 🖫
Rebecca Meade *GTDUN* CM6..... 171 J5
Rebels La *SBN/FI* SS3............... 465 J1
Rebow Rd *HAR* CO12................... 6 B6
.... *RCOLE* CO7.......... 220 E5 🖫
Reckitts Cl *COS* CO15................. 11 E3
Recreation Av *HARH* RM3.......... 431 G4
.... *LOS* SS9............. 463 G3
.... *SLH/COR* SS17..... 457 J8
Recreation Cl *FX* IP11................ 5 F1 🖫
Recreation Gnd *STSD* CM24....... 167 J7
Recreation La *FX* IP11............... 5 F1
Recreation Rd *COL* CO1.............. 9 D6
.... *COS* CO15........... 10 C4
.... *HSTD* CO9........... 110 C5
.... *HVHL* CB9............ 27 F6
Recreation Wk *BCAYE* CM11... 388 E8 🖫
.... *SUD* CO10............ 58 E8
Recreation Wy *IPSE* IP3........... 63 K3
Rectory *RCFD* SS4................... 255 H6 🖫
Rectory Cha *BRWN* CM15...... 384 A3
Rectory Cl *CHING* E4............... 402 B6
.... *COLN* CO4............. 8 A1
.... *ING* CM4............ 386 B1 🖫
.... *RCHLM* CM3....... 272 C7
.... *SAFWS* CB10...... 70 A1 🖫
.... *SBF/HAD* SS7..... 461 K2
Rectory Fld *HLWW/ROY* CM19... 12 B5
.... *RIPS/CAP* IP9...... 91 H6
Rectory Gdns *PIT* SS13........... 439 F8 🖫
.... *UPMR* RM14........ 452 A3
Rectory Garth *RAYL* SS6.......... 441 J2
Rectory Gv *LOS* SS9................ 462 E5
.... *WICKE* SS11........ 417 J6
Rectory Hl *RCOLE* CO7............ 122 B4
.... *RCOLE* CO7.......... 221 F4
Rectory La *BSF* CM23............. 166 B7
.... *CHLM/WR* CM1..... 14 C1
.... *HAR* CO12........... 163 K4
.... *HLWW/ROY* CM19.. 12 B5
.... *HSTD* CO9............ 82 D7
.... *K/T/MI* CO5......... 252 E2
.... *KIR/NAC* IP10....... 94 C1
.... *LOU* IG10........... 377 J6
.... *MAL* CM9............ 337 F7
.... *MGTR* CO11......... 123 K4
.... *RBRW/HUT* CM13... 434 D2 🖫
.... *RCHLM* CM3......... 241 F6
.... *RCHLM* CM3......... 395 K1
.... *SAFWB* CB10........ 46 D4
.... *WIT* CM8............ 245 G7
Rectory Meadow *BRTR* CM7..... 211 H3
Rectory Park Dr *PIT* SS13........ 438 E8
Rectory Rd *BCAYW* CM12........ 436 A8
.... *BRTR* CM7........... 179 G6
.... *CDH/CHF* RM16..... 472 B5
.... *CHLM/WR* CM1...... 331 H5
.... *CHTY* IP2............. 3 D6
.... *COLN* CO4............ 120 C7
.... *FOS* CO13............ 260 E2
.... *GRAYS* RM17........ 484 C2
.... *HAR* CO12........... 163 J4
.... *HOC/HUL* SS5....... 443 H2
.... *HSTD* CO9............ 110 C4
.... *HVHL* CB9............ 28 D3
.... *K/T/MI* CO5......... 220 B6
.... *K/T/MI* CO5......... 248 A8
.... *MAL* CM9............ 281 G4
.... *MAL* CM9............ 336 D2
.... *MGTR* CO11......... 162 D2
.... *PIT* SS13............ 439 F6
.... *RCHLM* CM3......... 394 C5
.... *RCOLE* CO7......... 191 K5
.... *RCOLE* CO7......... 221 F3
.... *RCOLE* CO7......... 222 D4
.... *RCOLW* CO6......... 183 J5
.... *RCOLW* CO6......... 216 B4
.... *RCOS* CO16......... 225 H8
.... *RCOS* CO16......... 258 E2
.... *RIPS/CAP* IP9...... 127 F2
.... *SBF/HAD* SS7....... 461 K2
.... *SLH/COR* SS17...... 473 J4
.... *SUD* CO10............ 59 K1
.... *SUD* CO10............ 84 B1
.... *TIL* RM18............ 485 J3
Rectory Wd *HLW* CM20............. 12 C2
Redan St *IP* IP1...................... 2 C1 🖫
Red Barn La *HAR* CO12........... 194 E3
Red Barn Rd *RCOLE* CO7......... 255 K5

Redbridge Rd *COS* CO15.......... 259 H5
Redcar Rd *HARH* RM3.............. 409 G8
Redcliff Dr *LOS* SS9................ 463 G5
Redcliffe Rd *CHLM/WR* CM2.... 14 B4 🖫
Redden Court Rd *HARH* RM3.... 431 H5
Reddings Cl *SAFWS* CB11......... 71 F6 🖫
Reddings La *BOC* CM0............ 371 J2
Reddy Rd *ERITH* DA8.............. 480 A5
Rede Wy *SUD* CO10................. 59 F7
Redfern Gdns *GPK* RM2............ 430 E4
Redgate Cl *WICKE* SS11.......... 417 K5
Redgate La *RIPS/CAP* IP9........ 62 E8
Redgates La *SAFWN* CB10....... 72 A1
Redgates Pl *CHLM/WR* CM1..... 15 F1 🖫
Redgrave Rd *VGE* SS16............ 458 B1
Redhills Rd *RCHLM* CM3.......... 392 E5
Red House Cl *FX* IP11............. 94 B5
Redhouse La *RCOLW* CO6........ 154 E3
.... *SUD* CO10............ 58 B6
Red House La *SUD* CO10.......... 84 D1
Red House Wk *KIR/NAC* IP10.... 92 D1
The Redinge *BCAYE* CM11....... 414 E6
Redlands Rd *PEND* EN3............ 374 C5
Red La *RIPS/CAP* IP9.............. 87 F5
Redlie Cl *SLH/COR* SS17......... 473 K1
Red Lion Crs *HLWE* CM17........ 295 G7
Red Lion La *HLWE* CM17......... 295 G7
Redmayne Dr *CHLM/WR* CM2... 14 A6
Redmill *COLW* CO5................. 218 B2
Redricks La *HLW* CM20........... 262 D7
Red Rd *BRW* CM14................. 410 E2
Redrose La *ING* CM4............... 356 C4
Redruth Cl *CHLM/WR* CM1....... 305 G8
Redruth Rd *HARH* RM3............ 409 G8
Redshank Cl *HVHL* CB9........... 27 J6
Redshank Crs *RCHLM* CM3...... 392 D4 🖫
Redshank Dr *MAL* CM9........... 310 E8
Red Sleeve *RIPS/CAP* IP9........ 86 E4
Redstock Rd *SOSN* SS2........... 19 D2
Redvers Cl *BRW* CM14............ 410 E2
Red White And Blue Rd *BSF* CM23... 199 G3
Red Willow *HLWW/ROY* CM19.. 293 H8
Redwing Cl *CHTY* IP2.............. 61 K2
Redwing Dr *BCAYE* CM11........ 414 D5
Redwood Cha *SOCK/AV* RM15... 470 B4 🖫
Redwood Cl *COLN* CO4............ 188 B5
.... *WIT* CM8............ 245 G8 🖫
Redwood Dr *CHLM/WR* CM1..... 331 F4
.... *LAIN* SS15........... 16 B1
Redwood Gdns *CHING* E4......... 402 C2 🖫
The Redwoods *CVI* SS8............ 477 J2 🖫
Reed Cl *RCOS* CO16................ 258 E8
Reed Hall Av *COLS* CO2........... 218 E2
Readings Wy *SBW* CM21......... 263 K1
Reedland Wy *FX* IP11............... 5 D2
Reed Pond Wk *GPK* RM2.......... 430 A4
.... *VGE* SS16............ 456 C1 🖫
Reeds La *HVHL* CB9................. 27 G5
Reeds Wy *WICKW* SS12........... 417 F5
Reeve Gdns *KESG* IP5.............. 39 G6
Reeves Cl *BRWN* CM15............ 355 K8
.... *VGE* SS16............ 456 A1 🖫
Reeves Pightle *ROY* SG8.......... 66 C3
Reeves Wy *RCHLM* CM3.......... 392 E6
Refinery Rd *HAR* CO12............ 128 C8
Regal Cl *CHLM/GWD* CM2........ 15 E5
Regan Cl *SLH/COR* SS17.......... 474 A1
Regarder Rd *CHIG* IG7............. 406 A8
Regency Cl *BSF* CM23............. 198 D6
.... *CHIG* IG7........... 405 F8 🖫
.... *CHLM/GWD* CM2.. 15 E2 🖫
.... *RCFD* SS4........... 444 B3
.... *WICKE* SS11........ 417 G3
Regency Ct *BRW* CM14............ 411 F5 🖫
.... *HLWS* CM18......... 294 E8
.... *MAL* CM9............ 310 C8
Regency Gdns *EMPK* RM11...... 450 D1
Regency Gn *COLW* CO5............ 218 A1
.... *SOSN* SS2........... 18 C2
Regent Cl *CDH/CHF* RM16....... 484 E1
.... *RAYL* SS6............ 441 G1
.... *RCOLE* CO7......... 255 G1
Regent Rd *EPP* CM16............... 350 D4
.... *RCOLE* CO7......... 255 K6
Regents Cl *BCMO* CM0............ 398 D1 🖫
.... *COLN* CO4............ 155 K8
Regents Pl *LOU* IG10............... 404 A3
Regent St *K/T/MI* CO5............. 220 C5
.... *MGTR* CO11......... 159 J1 🖫
Regina Cl *IPNE* IP4................. 37 K8
Reginald Rd *HARH* RM3........... 431 H3
Regina Rd *CHLM/WR* CM1........ 15 D2
Reigate Av *RCOS* CO16............ 10 A1
Reigate Cl *IPSE* IP3................. 63 K2 🖫
Rembrandt Cl *CVI* SS8............. 478 A2
.... *SBN/FI* SS3.......... 467 F5
Rembrandt Dr *GVW* DA11........ 488 C3
Rembrandt La *CHLM/WR* CM1... 305 G7
Rembrow Rd *RIPS/CAP* IP9...... 87 F4
Remembrance Av *BOC* CM0...... 425 C1
.... *RCHLM* CM3......... 308 A2
Remercie Rd *MGTR* CO11........ 160 B2
Renacres *VGE* SS16................ 17 D6

Rendlesham Rd *FX* IP11........... 5 D2 🖫
Renfrew Rd *IPNE* IP4............... 38 A4 🖫
Rennie Pl *CHLM/GWD* CM2....... 333 K2
Rennie Rd *CHLM/GWD* CM2..... 15 E4
Renoir Pl *CHLM/WR* CM1......... 305 H6
Repton Av *GPK* RM2............... 430 B5
Repton Cl *PIT* SS13................ 438 D4
Repton Dr *GPK* RM2............... 430 B6
Repton Gdns *GPK* RM2............ 430 B5
Repton Gv *LOS* SS9................ 443 H6
Retford Cl *HARH* RM3.............. 431 H1
Retford Pth *HARH* RM3............ 431 H1
Retford Rd *HARH* RM3............. 431 H2
Retingham Wy *CHING* E4......... 402 C5 🖫
Retreat Rd *HOC/HUL* SS5........ 421 F7
.... *WOS/PRIT* SS0...... 18 B5
The Retreat *BRW* CM14........... 410 E4
.... *GRAYS* RM17........ 484 A5 🖫
.... *RBRW/HUT* CM13... 412 A2
.... *RCOLW* CO6......... 185 K2
.... *WIT* CM8............ 277 G4
Retreat Wy *CHIG* IG7.............. 400 A6
Rettendon Cl *RAYL* SS6........... 441 F2 🖫
Rettendon Gdns *WICKE* SS11.... 417 H4
Rettendon Vw *WICKE* SS11...... 417 J5
Reubens Rd *RBRW/HUT* CM13.. 412 A2
Reymead Cl *CHLM/WR* CM1.... 284 E6
Reynard Copse *BSF* CM23....... 198 E4
Reynards Cl *FOS* CO13............ 228 C7
Reynards Copse *COLN* CO4...... 187 H2
Reynolds Av *COLW* CO3........... 186 C8
.... *IPSE* IP3............. 63 J5
Reynold's Cl *HVHL* CB9........... 26 D4 🖫
Reynolds Ga *RCHLM* CM3........ 392 E7 🖫
Reynolds Rd *IPSE* IP3............. 63 J5
Rhoda Rd *SBF/HAD* SS7.......... 460 C1
Rhoda Rd North *SBF/HAD* SS7.. 440 D8
Rhodes Av *BSF* CM23.............. 198 E8
Rhugarve Gdns *CBE/LIN* CB1... 23 F3 🖫
Riby Rd *FX* IP11...................... 5 F4
Richard Av *RCOLE* CO7............ 221 F2
Richard Burn Wy *SUD* CO10..... 58 B3
Richardson Pl *CHLM/WR* CM1... 14 A2
Richardson Rd *RCOLE* CO7...... 122 C2
Richardsons La *RIPS/CAP* IP9... 91 C6
Richardson Wk *COLW* CO3....... 186 A8
Richards Wk *RCOS* CO16......... 10 B1 🖫
Rich Cl *RCHLM* CM3............... 241 H6 🖫
Riche Cl *GTDUN* CM6.............. 206 C8
Richmond Av *CHING* E4........... 402 C8
.... *SBF/HAD* SS7........ 460 B3
.... *SBN/FI* SS3.......... 466 C7
.... *WOS/PRIT* SS0...... 18 B4 🖫
Richmond Cl *BSF* CM23........... 198 B6 🖫
Richmond Ct *BROX* EN10......... 319 F2 🖫
Richmond Crs *CHING* E4.......... 402 B8
.... *HAR* CO12............ 6 C6
Richmond Dr *COS* CO15........... 290 C4
.... *RAYL* SS6............ 441 J5
.... *WOS/PRIT* SS0...... 463 K1
Richmond Rd *CHING* E4........... 402 E4 🖫
.... *CHLM/GWD* CM2... 333 J1
.... *GRAYS* RM17........ 484 B4
.... *IP* IP1................. 2 A2
.... *K/T/MI* CO5......... 285 F7 🖫
.... *ROM* RM1............ 430 A8 🖫
.... *WICKE* SS11........ 417 F3
Richmond St *SOSN* SS2........... 465 G4
Ricketts Dr *BCAYW* CM12........ 414 A2
Rickling Cl *RCOS* CO16............ 258 C7
Rickling *VGE* SS16.................. 458 C1
Rickling Green Rd *SAFWS* CB11. 135 K4
Rickling Rd *SAFWS* CB11......... 99 G7
Rickstones Rd *WIT* CM8........... 245 G1
Riddiford Dr *CHLM/WR* CM1..... 14 A1
Riddings La *HLWS* CM18......... 322 E1
Riddles Dr *COLN* CO4.............. 8 B1
The Ride *PEND* EN3................. 374 C7
Ridgemount *SBF/HAD* SS7....... 460 D1 🖫
The Ridge *RCHLM* CM3........... 335 J5
.... *WOTN* CO14......... 229 G5 🖫
Ridgeway *BCAYW* CM12.......... 414 B5
.... *GRAYS* RM17........ 484 D3
.... *ING* CM4............ 386 A4
.... *MAL* CM9............ 333 C5 🖫
.... *RAYL* SS6............ 441 H4
.... *RBRW/HUT* CM13... 412 A4
.... *WFD* IG8.............. 403 K7
Ridgeway Av *GVE* DA12........... 489 G8
Ridgeway Gdns *WOS/PRIT* SS0.. 463 J5 🖫
Ridgeways *HLWE* CM17........... 295 J5
The Ridgeway *BRTR* CM7........ 209 K4
.... *CBE/LIN* CB1........ 23 G3
.... *CHING* E4........... 402 D4
.... *GPK* RM2............ 430 D6
.... *HAR* CO12............ 6 B5
.... *HARH* RM3........... 431 F3
.... *LOS* SS9............. 463 H5
.... *WOS/PRIT* SS0...... 463 J5
Ridgeway Valley Vw *COLN* CO4. 187 H1 🖫
Ridgewll Av *CHLM/WR* CM1...... 14 A1
Ridgewell Rd *HSTD* CO9.......... 52 B3
.... *SUD* CO10........... 53 F4
Ridgewell Wy *COLS* CO2.......... 219 G4
Ridgwell Av *CDH/CHF* RM16..... 472 A4

The Ridings BSF CM23 .... 231 H1
  CHLM/GWD CM2 .... 15 E6
  CVI SS8 .... 461 F8 ▣
  RCFD SS4 .... 444 D4
Ridlands CI BRTR CM7 .... 210 D7 ▣
Ridley CI HARH RM3 .... 430 C3
Ridley Gdns RBSF CM22 .... 168 D3
Ridley Rd CHLM/WR CM1 .... 304 D5
  PIT SS13 .... 439 F4
Riffams Ct PIT SS13 .... 439 F5 ▣
Riffams Dr PIT SS13 .... 439 F5
Riffams RBRW/HUT CM13 ...... 412 A6
Riffams Dr CHLM/GWD CM2 ... 333 H6
Riffams La RCHLM CM3 .... 335 G5
Rifle HI BRTR CM7 .... 209 J4
Rigby Av MGTR CO11 .... 160 B2
Rigby Gdns CDH/CHF RM16 ... 485 G3
Rignals La CHLM/GWD CM2 .... 361 F2
Riley Av COS CO15 .... 290 A7
Riley Rd PEND EN3 .... 374 C4
Rimini CI COLS CO2 .... 218 D3
Ringham Rd IPNE IP4 .... 37 J7
Ringwood Av RCHLM CM3 ...... 392 C7
Ringwood Dr LOS SS9 .... 442 C6
Ripley CI RCOS CO16 .... 258 D7
Ripley Vw LOU IG10 .... 377 K4
Ripley Wy EBAR EN7 .... 346 B4
Rippleside BSDN SS14 .... 438 C8
Ripple Wy COLN CO4 .... 9 D2
Risby CI IPNE IP4 .... 37 K7
  RCOS CO16 .... 290 C1
Risdens HLWS CM18 .... 12 C6 ▣
Risebridge Cha ROM RM1 ...... 430 A2
Risebridge Rd GPK RM2 .... 430 A3
Rise Pk LAIN SS15 .... 17 D4
Rise Park Bvd GPK RM2 .... 430 A3
The Rise BKHH IG9 .... 404 A4 ▣
  COLW CO3 .... 185 F5
Riseway BRWN CM15 .... 411 H6
The Rising BCAYE CM11 .... 414 D4
Ritabrook Rd CHTY IP2 .... 62 A4
Rivendell V RCHLM CM3 .... 392 C7
Rivenhall SBF/HAD SS7 .... 441 G5
  WICKE SS11 .... 417 K7
Riverbank CI SUD CO10 .... 31 G6 ▣
River CI BAR EN8 .... 347 G8
  HSTD CO9 .... 148 A4
Riverdale LOS SS9 .... 442 E6
River Dr UPMR RM14 .... 431 K8
Riverfield La SBW CM21 .... 263 J2 ▣
River HI RCHLM CM3 .... 275 F2
Rivermill HLW CM20 .... 6 A3
River Rd BKHH IG9 .... 404 B4
  BRW CM14 .... 410 B7
Riversdale GVW DA11 .... 488 D7
Riverside BRTR CM7 .... 211 J2
  BSF CM23 .... 198 E6
  GTDUN CM6 .... 204 D4
Riverside Av BROX EN10 .... 319 C4
Riverside Av East MGTR CO11 . 123 H5
Riverside Av West MGTR CO11 . 123 H5
Riverside Ct CHING E4 .... 402 C2 ▣
  HLW CM20 .... 263 G7
  IP IP1 .... 2 A2
Riverside Wk WICKW SS12 .... 416 E5 ▣
Riverside Wy K/T/MI CO5 ...... 246 E4
Rivers St IPNE IP4 .... 37 H6 ▣
Riverton Dr BOC CMO 342 B4
Rivertons VGE SS16 .... 458 C1
River Vw WOS/PRIT SS0 .... 188 B4
River Vw WIT CM8 .... 277 C5
Riverview VGE SS16 .... 458 D1
Riverview Gdns HOC/HUL SS5 . 419 H2
River View Rd RIPS/CAP IP9 ... 126 E3
  SBF/HAD SS7 .... 460 C3
River View Ter RCHLM CM3 ... 396 C3
River Wy HLW CM20 .... 262 E8
  LOU IG10 .... 404 D2
Rivey CI CBE/LIN CB1 .... 23 F2
Rivey Wy CBE/LIN CB1 .... 23 F3
Riviera Dr SOS SS1 .... 19 F4
Rivish La SUD CO10 .... 34 E6
Roach Av RAYL SS6 .... 441 H4
Roach V COLN CO4 .... 168 B4
  LOS SS9 .... 443 G6
Roach Valley Wy HOC/HUL SS5 . 443 H5
  RCFD SS4 .... 443 J6
  RCFD SS4 .... 446 B1
Robeck Rd IPSE IP3 .... 63 G4
Robert CI BCAYW CM12 .... 414 A3
  CHIG IG7 .... 405 J8
  CHLM/GWD CM2 .... 333 H1
Roberts CI BAR EN8 .... 346 E4 ▣
  HARH RM3 .... 430 C3
Robert's HI BURES CO8 .... 151 J2
Robertson CI BROX EN10 ...... 318 E8 ▣
Robertson Dr WICKW SS12 .... 417 H8 ▣
Roberts Rd COLS CO2 .... 8 B6 ▣
  LAIN SS15 .... 436 C6 ▣
  RCHLM CM3 .... 394 C6
Robert Wallace CI BSF CM23 . 198 E4
Robin CI BCAYW CM12 .... 387 J7

RCOLE CO7 .... 223 J5
Robin V BRTR CM7 .... 217 H1
Robin Crs COLW CO3 .... 61 K2
Robin Dr CHTY IP2 .... 410 E3
Robin Hood Rd BRWN CM15 .. 168 D4
  RBSF CM22 .... 168 D4
Robinia Av GVW DA11 .... 488 C5
Robinia CI LAIN SS15 .... 16 B1
Robinsbridge Rd RCOLW CO6 . 213 G3
Robinsdale COS CO15 .... 10 C1
Robinson CI BSF CM23 .... 198 E8
  HCH RM12 .... 450 C8 ▣
Robinson Rd CDH/CHF RM16 . 472 D1
  RCOLE CO7 .... 256 A6
The Robins BRWN CM15 .... 384 B1
Robin Wy CHLM/GWD CM2 .... 332 D8
  SUD CO10 .... 57 K8
Robjohns Rd CHLM/WR CM1 . 332 A5
Robletts Wy RCOLW CO6 .... 152 D1
Robsons Ct BAR EN8 .... 346 C3 ▣
Robyns Cft GVW DA11 .... 488 D8
Rochdale Wy COLN CO4 .... 188 B7 ▣
Roche Av RCFD SS4 .... 444 B3
Rochefort Dr RCFD SS4 .... 444 E5
Rochehall Wy RCFD SS4 .... 444 C5
Rochelle CI GTDUN CM6 .... 139 K2
Rochester CI BRTR CM7 .... 210 C1
Rochester Dr WOS/PRIT SS0 .. 463 K1
Rochester Ms WOS/PRIT SS0 .. 463 K1
Rocheway RCFD SS4 .... 444 D3
Rochford Av BRWN CM15 ...... 411 K1
  WAB EN9 .... 347 K8
  WOS/PRIT SS0 .... 18 B3
Rochford CI BROX EN10 .... 318 C2
  HCH RM12 .... 450 C7 ▣
  WICKE SS11 .... 417 J7 ▣
Rochford Garden Wy RCFD SS4 . 444 A2
Rochford Gn LOU IG10 .... 378 A7
Rochford Hall CI RCFD SS4 .... 444 C4
Rochford Rd BSF CM23 .... 199 G4
  CHLM/GWD CM2 .... 15 D4 ▣
  CVI SS8 .... 478 D2
  RCOS CO16 .... 289 G4
  SOSN SS2 .... 464 A1
Rochford Wy FOS CO13 .... 229 F6 ▣
Rockall SOSN SS2 .... 445 H6
Rockall CI HVHL CB9 .... 27 K6
Rockchase Gdns EMPK RM11 . 431 F8 ▣
Rockingham Av EMPK RM11 ... 430 C8
Rockingham CI COLN CO4 ...... 188 A2 ▣
Rockleigh Av LOS SS9 .... 463 H4
Rockleigh Ct BRWN CM15 ...... 411 K3
Rockwood Gdns LOU IG10 ..... 378 A7
Rodbridge Dr SOS SS1 .... 465 J5
Rodbridge HI SUD CO10 .... 57 J1
Roddam CI COLW CO3 .... 186 D7
Roden CI HLWE CM17 .... 295 K1
Rodeo CI ERITH DA8 .... 480 C7
Roding CI CHONG CM5 .... 327 F5 ▣
  SBN/FI SS3 .... 467 C1 ▣
Roding Dr BRWN CM15 .... 383 H5
Roding Gdns LOU IG10 .... 404 B2
Roding La BKHH IG9 .... 404 B4
  CHIG IG7 .... 404 B4
Roding Leigh RCHLM CM3 ..... 392 E6 ▣
Roding Rd LOU IG10 .... 404 C1
Rodings Av SLH/COR SS17 .... 473 K1
The Rodings LOS SS9 .... 442 E6
  UPMR RM14 .... 432 A8
Roding Vw BKHH IG9 .... 404 A4
  CHONG CM5 .... 327 F5
Roding Wy WICKW SS12 .... 417 H6
Rodney Gdns BRTR CM7 .... 210 B1 ▣
Rodney Rd CHONG CM5 .... 354 B3
Rodney Wy CHLM/WR CM1 .... 332 A6
Roebuck La BKHH IG9 .... 403 K4
Roedean Av PEND EN3 .... 374 C5
Roedean CI PEND EN3 .... 374 C5
  SOSN SS2 .... 465 J4
Roedean Gdns SOSN SS2 ...... 465 J3
Roehampton CI GVE DA12 ..... 489 K5
Rogation CI COLW CO3 .... 185 J8
Rogers CI FX IP11 .... 5 F1 ▣
Rogers Rd GRAYS RM17 .... 484 B3
Roggel Rd CVI SS8 .... 478 D3
Rokells BSDN SS14 .... 17 E3
Rokell Wy FOS CO13 .... 228 E7
Rokescroft PIT SS13 .... 438 D8
Roland La CVI SS8 .... 478 B2 ▣
Rollestons CHLM/WR CM1 ..... 331 F4
Rolley La K/T/MI CO5 .... 246 E3
Rolls Park Rd CHING E4 .... 402 C2 ▣
Rolph CI RCOS CO16 .... 226 D3
Romagne CI SLH/COR SS17 ... 473 F2
Romainville Wy CVI SS8 .... 477 G2
Roman CI BRWN CM15 .... 385 J5
  MAL CM9 .... 338 B1 ▣
Roman Ct BRTR CM7 .... 210 B4 ▣
Roman Ri SBW CM21 .... 263 H3
Roman Rd BRWN CM15 .... 385 K4
  COL CO1 .... 8 C3
  GVW DA11 .... 488 E6
  ING CM4 .... 358 E7
  RCHLM CM3 .... 272 D7
Romans PI CHLM/WR CM1 ..... 331 H4 ▣

Romans Wy CHLM/WR CM1 ... 331 H4
Roman V HLWE CM17 .... 263 C8
Roman Wy BCAYW CM12 .... 414 B5
  BOC CMO 398 B6
  HVHL CB9 .... 27 K7
  RCOS CO16 .... 288 A2
  SUD CO10 .... 34 E7
Romeland WAB EN9 .... 347 J7
Romford CI COLN CO4 .... 9 D2
Romford Rd CHIG IG7 .... 406 A7
  CHONG CM5 .... 354 A7
  SOCK/AV RM15 .... 468 E3
Romney Cha EMPK RM11 ...... 431 H8 ▣
Romney CI BRTR CM7 .... 177 H7
  FOS CO13 .... 228 D6 ▣
  RCOLE CO7 .... 255 J4
  RCOS CO16 .... 10 A1
Romney Rd BCAYW CM12 ...... 414 A4
  GVW DA11 .... 488 D8
  IPSE IP3 .... 63 J5
Romsey CI HOC/HUL SS5 ...... 420 E7
  SLH/COR SS17 .... 473 H4 ▣
Romsey Crs SBF/HAD SS7 ..... 440 A8
Romsey Rd SBF/HAD SS7 ...... 439 K8
Romsey Rd SBF/HAD SS7 ...... 439 K8
Romsey Wy SBF/HAD SS7 ..... 440 A8
Romulus CI COLN CO4 .... 155 G8
Ronald Dr RAYL SS6 .... 441 F1
Ronald Hill Gv LOS SS9 .... 462 E4
Ronald Park Av WOS/PRIT SS0 . 463 K4
Ronald Rd HARH RM3 .... 431 H3
  HSTD CO9 .... 147 K5
Roneo Cnr ROMW/RG RM7 ... 450 A2
Roneo Link HCH RM12 .... 450 A2 ▣
Roodegate BSDN SS14 .... 17 E4
Rook End La SAFWS CB11 ..... 110 J1
The Rookeries RCOLW CO6 .... 216 A1 ▣
Rookery Cha RCOLE CO7 .... 157 H3
Rookery CI RAYL SS6 .... 441 H3
  RCHLM CM3 .... 276 A8 ▣
  SAFWN CB10 .... 43 J2
  SLH/COR SS17 .... 473 H4
Rookery HI SLH/COR SS17 .... 474 E2
Rookery La K/T/MI CO5 .... 248 A6
  MAL CM9 .... 279 G6
  RCHLM CM3 .... 394 A4
  SAFWS CB11 .... 99 K1
Rookery Rd RCHLM CM3 .... 392 D5 ▣
Rookery Rd ING CM4 .... 356 A3
The Rookery MGTR CO11 ...... 159 H1 ▣
  STSD CM24 .... 167 K5 ▣
  WTHK RM20 .... 482 D5
Rookery Vw GRAYS RM17 ..... 484 C5 ▣
Rookes SAFWN CB10 .... 70 E1
Rookwood Av LOU IG10 .... 378 A7
Rookwood CI GRAYS RM17 .... 484 A3
  RCOS CO16 .... 259 F6
Rookwood Gdns CHING E4 .... 403 C5 ▣
Rookwood Wy HVHL CB9 .... 27 G7
Rookyards VGE SS16 .... 438 B8 ▣
Roosevel Av CVI SS8 .... 478 A1
Roosevelt Rd LAIN SS15 .... 436 B7 ▣
Roosevelt Wy COLS CO2 .... 219 J1
Roos Hill Debden Rd SAFWS CB11 . 71 F8 ▣
Roots Hall Av SOSN SS2 .... 18 C2
Roots Hall Dr SOSN SS2 .... 18 B2
Roots La WIT CM8 .... 310 A1
Ropers Av CHING E4 .... 402 D8
Ropers La SUD CO10 .... 57 J1
Ropes Dr KESG IP5 .... 39 H5
Rope Wk IPNE IP4 .... 3 E4
  MAL CM9 .... 338 C4
Rosabelle Av RCOLE CO7 .... 220 E4
Rosalind CI COLN CO4 .... 188 C6
Rosary Gdns WOS/PRIT SS0 .. 463 J1
Rosbach Rd CVI SS8 .... 478 D2
Rosberg Rd CVI SS8 .... 478 E2 ▣
Roscommon Wy CVI SS8 .... 477 C1
Rose Acre BSDN SS14 .... 438 C7
Roseacre CI EMPK RM11 .... 451 G2
  RCOS CO16 .... 201 K6
Roseacres RBSF CM22 .... 201 K6
  SBW CM21 .... 263 H2
Rose Av COLW CO3 .... 217 H1
  GVE DA12 .... 489 K6
Rose Bank BRW CM14 .... 411 G6
Rosebank HAR CO12 .... 117 H5
  WAB EN9 .... 348 A8
Rosebank Av HCH RM12 .... 450 D6
Rosebank Gdns GVW DA11 .... 488 D6
Rosebank Rd K/T/MI CO5 .... 284 C7
Rosebay Av BCAYW CM12 ..... 387 F8
Rosebay CI WIT CM8 .... 288 D2
Roseberry Av SBF/HAD SS7 ... 440 B7
  VGE SS16 .... 456 C1
Roseberry CI UPMR RM14 ..... 432 C8
Roseberry Gdns UPMR RM14 . 452 C1
Rosebery Av COL CO1 .... 8 C4
Rosebery Ct GVW DA11 .... 488 E6
Rosebery Rd CHLM/GWD CM2 . 14 C5
  FX IP11 .... 131 J3
  GRAYS RM17 .... 483 H5
  IPNE IP4 .... 37 H8
Rose CI WICKW SS12 .... 417 H8 ▣
Rose Ct EBAR EN7 .... 346 A1

RIPS/CAP IP9 .... 128 E2
Rose Crs *COLN* C04 .... 186 E5
Rosecroft Cl *COS* C015 .... 10 B1
  VGE SS16 .... 456 B1
Rosecroft Rd *IP* IP1 .... 36 C3
Rosedale Rd *GRAYS* RM17 .... 484 C4
Rosedale Wy *EBAR* EN7 .... 346 A3
Rose Dr *BOC* CM0 .... 398 D2
Rosefinch Cl *HVHL* CB9 .... 27 J6
Rose Gdns *BRTR* CM7 .... 209 K3
  RCOS C016 .... 289 H7
Rose Gln *CHLM/GWD* CM2 .... 15 D6
Rose Hl *BRTR* CM7 .... 209 K3
Rosehill Crs *IPSE* IP3 .... 63 H1
Rosehill Rd *IPSE* IP3 .... 63 H1
Roselaine *BSDN* SS14 .... 17 F3
Rose La *BCAYW* CM12 .... 414 B3
  IPNE IP4 .... 3 D4
  MAL CM9 .... 282 B5
  RCOLE C07 .... 220 E6
  SAFWN CB10 .... 43 K3
Rosemary Av *BRTR* CM7 .... 209 J1
  FX IP11 .... 131 J1
  ROM RM1 .... 430 A5
Rosemary Av *GTDUN* CM6 .... 204 B4
  K/T/MI C05 .... 248 A8
  SOCK/AV RM15 .... 470 A3
Rosemary Crs *COS* C015 .... 10 C5
  GTDUN CM6 .... 204 B4
  K/T/MI C05 .... 248 A8
Rosemary Cresecent
  GTDUN CM6 .... 204 B4
Rosemary Gdns *SUD* C010 .... 58 C3
Rosemary La *GTDUN* CM6 .... 173 H6
  GTDUN CM6 .... 204 B3
  HSTD C09 .... 80 E8
  HSTD C09 .... 147 K3
  RCOLE C07 .... 223 G8
Rosemary Rd *COS* C015 .... 10 C5
Rosemary Rd West *COS* C015 ...... 10 B5
Rosemead *SBF/HAD* SS7 .... 440 B6
Rosemead Gdns *RBRW/HUT* CM13 .. 385 H8
Rosemount *HLWW/ROY* CM19 .... 12 B6
Roserna Rd *CVI* SS8 .... 478 D2
Rose Rd *CVI* SS8 .... 478 A2
Rose St *GVW* DA11 .... 488 E3
Rose Va *BRW* CM14 .... 411 F6
Rose Valley Crs *SLH/COR* SS17 .... 473 K1
Rose Wy *RCFD* SS4 .... 444 D5
Rosewood Av *RCH* RM12 .... 450 B6
Rosewood Cl *COLN* C04 .... 187 H1
  SOCK/AV RM15 .... 470 C3
Rosewood Rd *SBN/FI* SS3 .... 466 E7
Rosherville Wy *GVW* DA11 .... 488 D5
Rosilian Dr *HOC/HUL* SS5 .... 420 D4
Roslings Cl *CHLM* CM1 .... 303 K7
  HARH RM3 .... 431 F4
Roslyn Cl *BROX* EN10 .... 318 E3
Roslyn Cl *HOC/HUL* SS5 .... 421 F6
Roslyn Gdns *BCAYW* CM12 .... 414 A3
  HOC/HUL SS5 .... 421 F7
Ross Rd *IPNE* IP4 .... 37 K4
Ross Wy *VGE* SS16 .... 456 C2
Roswell Cl *BAR* EN8 .... 346 E4
Rothbury Rd *CHLM/WR* CM1 .... 331 K4
Roth Dr *RBRW/HUT* CM13 .... 412 A5
Rotherfield Rd *PEND* EN3 .... 374 D3
Rothesay Av *CHLM/GWD* CM2 ...... 14 B5
Rothmans Av *CHLM/GWD* CM2 ...... 333 G7
Rothwell Cl *LOS* SS9 .... 442 C4
Rotten Rw *SUD* C010 .... 59 K8
Rouge La *GVE* DA12 .... 489 G4
Roughtallys *EPP* CM16 .... 351 K1
Roughtons *CHLM/GWD* CM2 .... 360 C2
Roundacre *HSTD* C09 .... 147 K5
  LAIN SS15 .... 17 E5
Roundbush Rd *K/T/MI* C05 .... 249 H4
  MAL CM9 .... 366 C5
Round Cl *COLW* C03 .... 186 C6
Round Coppice Rd *RBSF* CM22 ..... 200 B5
Round Hill Rd *SBF/HAD* SS7 .... 461 F5
Roundhills *WAB* EN9 .... 348 A8
Roundmead Av *LOU* IG10 .... 377 J6
Roundmead Cl *LOU* IG10 .... 377 J6
Roundmoor Dr *BAR* EN8 .... 346 E3
Roundridge Rd *RIPS/CAP* IP9 ...... 87 G3
Roundwood Av *RBRW/HUT* CM13 .. 411 K4
Roundwood Gv *RBRW/HUT* CM13 .. 412 A3
Roundwood Rd *IPNE* IP4 .... 37 J6
Rounton Rd *WAB* EN9 .... 348 A7
Rous Cha *CHLM/GWD* CM2 .... 360 C2
Rous Rd *BKHH* IG9 .... 404 B4

Routh Av *IPSE* IP3 .... 64 D4
Rover Av *COS* C015 .... 290 A6
Rowallan Cl *COLW* C03 .... 218 B2
Rowan Cl *COLW* C03 .... 217 J1
  COS C015 .... 290 E2
  HAR C012 .... 6 C5
  RAYL SS6 .... 419 D2
  RCOLE C07 .... 224 A5
Rowan Dr *BROX* EN10 .... 319 F6
  MAL CM9 .... 310 E8
Rowan Gn East
  RBRW/HUT CM13 .... 411 J6
Rowan Gn West
  RBRW/HUT CM13 .... 411 J6
Rowan Gv *SOCK/AV* RM15 .... 468 E7
Rowanhayes Cl *CHTY* IP2 .... 2 C6
The Rowans *BCAYE* CM11 .... 414 E5
  BROX EN10 .... 318 E1
  SOCK/AV RM15 .... 468 E8
Rowans Wy *LOU* IG10 .... 377 H8
  WICKE SS11 .... 417 H5
Rowan Wk *EMPK* RM11 .... 430 E6
  LOS SS9 .... 442 E7
  SBW CM21 .... 263 J3
Rowan Wy *RCFD* SS4 .... 423 H4
  RCHLM CM3 .... 308 A2
  SOCK/AV RM15 .... 470 B4
  WIT CM8 .... 245 C4
Rowarth Av *KESC* IP5 .... 39 G6
Rowcroft Cl *HVHL* CB9 .... 27 G3
Rowenhall *LAIN* SS15 .... 436 A7
Rowhedge Cl *RBRW/HUT* CM13 .... 411 K6
Rowhedge Cl *PIT* SS13 .... 439 G3
Rowhedge Ferry Rd *RCOLE* C07 .... 220 D5
Rowhedge Rd *COLS* C02 .... 220 A3
Rowherns La *RCOLE* C07 .... 224 A1
Rowland Crs *CHIG* IC7 .... 405 H7
Rowlands Cl *BAR* EN8 .... 346 D4
The Rowlands *SBF/HAD* SS7 .... 460 D1
Rowland's Yd *HAR* C012 .... 164 D3
Rowley Cl *MGTR* C011 .... 123 J5
Rowley Ct *HVHL* CB9 .... 28 A8
Rowley Hl *HVHL* CB9 .... 27 K8
Rowley Md *EPP* CM16 .... 323 G7
Rowmarsh Cl *GVW* DA11 .... 488 C3
Rowney Av *SAFWN* CB10 .... 102 B3
Rowney Gdns *SBW* CM21 .... 263 G5
Rowney Wd *SBW* CM21 .... 263 G5
Rowntree Wy *SAFWS* CB11 .... 70 E6
The Row *RCOLE* C07 .... 121 F3
Roxburgh Av *UPMR* RM14 .... 451 K4
Roxburghe Rd *RCOS* C016 .... 225 G7
Roxburgh Rd *IPNE* IP4 .... 37 K4
Roxwell Av *CHLM/WR* CM1 .... 331 K2
Roxwell Gdns *RBRW/HUT* CM13 .. 412 B1
Roxwell Rd *CHLM/WR* CM1 .... 305 H7
Royal Artillery Wy *SOSN* SS2 ...... 465 H2
Royal Av *BAR* EN8 .... 346 E7
Royal Cl *RCFD* SS4 .... 422 A8
Royal Ct *COLN* C04 .... 188 A4
  MAL CM9 .... 338 C4
Royal Ms *SOS* SS1 .... 19 D5
Royal Oak Dr *WICKE* SS11 .... 417 K5
Royal Oak Gdns *BSF* CM23 .... 198 D7
Royal Pier Rd *GVE* DA12 .... 489 G4
Royal Ter *SOS* SS1 .... 19 D5
Roy Av *IPNE* IP4 .... 37 K8
Royce Cl *BROX* EN10 .... 319 F3
Roy Cl *KESC* IP5 .... 39 F6
Roydon Br *BSDN* SS14 .... 438 A5
Roydon Cl *LOU* IG10 .... 404 B3
Roydon Rd *HLWW/ROY* CM19 ...... 293 G4
Royer Cl *HOC/HUL* SS5 .... 443 H1
Royle Cl *EPP* RM2 .... 430 C7
Royston Av *CHING* E4 .... 402 B8
  LAIN SS15 .... 16 B1
  SOSN SS2 .... 19 E1
Royston Dr *CHTY* IP2 .... 61 K3
Royston La *SAFWN* CB10 .... 41 K5
Royston Rd *HARH* RM3 .... 431 H2
  SAFWS CB11 .... 69 H8
Ruaton Dr *COS* C015 .... 290 E1
Rubens Cl *SBN/FI* SS3 .... 467 F5
Rubens Gn *CHLM/WR* CM1 .... 305 H6
Rubens Rd *IPSE* IP3 .... 63 J4
Rubicon Av *WICKE* SS11 .... 417 J5
Rudkin Rd *COLN* C04 .... 155 G8
Rudlands *RIPW* IP8 .... 61 J4
Rudsdale Wy *COLW* C03 .... 186 B1
Rue De St Lawrence *WAB* EN9 .... 347 J8
Rue's La *FX* IP11 .... 95 K7
Ruffels Fld *GTDUN* CM6 .... 205 K1
Ruffles Cl *RAYL* SS6 .... 441 K2
Rugby Rd *SUD* C010 .... 84 E1
Rugosa Cl *COLW* C03 .... 185 H6
Rumbullion Dr *BCAYW* CM12 ...... 414 A2
Rumsey Flds *RCHLM* CM3 .... 335 K6
Rumsley *EBAR* EN7 .... 346 A1
Rundells *HLWS* CM18 .... 322 E1
Rundells Wk *BSDN* SS14 .... 438 B6
The Rundels *SBF/HAD* SS7 .... 441 F8
Runnacles St *WIT* CM8 .... 211 H8
Runnacles Wy *FX* IP11 .... 5 D2

Running Mare La
  CHLM/GWD CM2 .... 360 C2
Running Waters
  RBRW/HUT CM13 .... 411 K7
Runnymede Cha *SBF/HAD* SS7 .... 461 F1
Runnymede Rd *CVI* SS8 .... 478 B2
  SLH/COR SS17 .... 473 J4
Runsell Cl *RCHLM* CM3 .... 335 K6
Runsell La *RCHLM* CM3 .... 335 K5
Runsell Vw *RCHLM* CM3 .... 335 K5
Runwell Gdns *WICKE* SS11 .... 417 G3
Runwell Rd *WICKE* SS11 .... 417 G5
Runwell Ter *SOS* SS1 .... 18 C5
Rupert Rd *BOC* CM0 .... 398 C1
Rural Cl *HCH* RM12 .... 450 C2
Rural V *GVW* DA11 .... 488 D5
Rurik Cl *MAL* CM9 .... 338 A5
Rushbottom La *SBF/HAD* SS7 ...... 440 A7
  WICKW SS12 .... 440 A5
Rushbury Cl *IPNE* IP4 .... 37 K5
Rush Cl *SBF/HAD* SS7 .... 440 A7
Rushdene Rd *BCAYW* CM12 .... 414 A5
  BRWN CM15 .... 411 F3
Rushdon Cl *CDH/CHF* RM16 .... 483 K2
  ROM RM1 .... 430 B7
Rushes La *BOC* CM0 .... 371 G4
Rushes Md *HLWS* CM18 .... 13 E5
Rushfield *SBW* CM21 .... 263 J3
Rush Green Rd *RCOS* C016 .... 290 D2
Rush La *RBSF* CM22 .... 168 D5
Rushleigh Av *BAR* EN8 .... 346 D4
Rushleigh Gn *BSF* CM23 .... 231 H2
Rushley *PIT* SS13 .... 439 G5
Rushley Cl *CDH/CHF* RM16 .... 471 H8
  SBN/FI SS3 .... 467 F1
Rushleydale *CHLM/WR* CM1 .... 305 G8
Rushmere Av *UPMR* RM14 .... 451 K4
Rushmere Cl *K/T/MI* C05 .... 284 E7
Rushmere Rd *IPNE* IP4 .... 37 J6
Rushmere St *KESC* IP5 .... 38 B4
Rushton Gv *HLWE* CM17 .... 295 H5
Ruskin Av *SOSN* SS2 .... 19 D2
  UPMR RM14 .... 451 K1
  WAB EN9 .... 348 A8
Ruskin Cl *FOS* C013 .... 228 D6
  HVHL CB9 .... 26 D4
Ruskin Dene *BCAYW* CM12 .... 414 B2
Ruskin Gdns *HARH* RM3 .... 430 C3
Ruskin Rd *CDH/CHF* RM16 .... 485 F3
  CHLM/GWD CM2 .... 15 F3
  IPNE IP4 .... 37 H8
  SLH/COR SS17 .... 473 J4
The Ruskins *BRTR* CM7 .... 208 C4
Ruskoi Rd *CVI* SS8 .... 460 E8
Russell Cl *BRWN* CM15 .... 410 E3
  LAIN SS15 .... 436 C7
Russell Gdns *CHLM/GWD* CM2 ..... 360 C1
  WICKE SS11 .... 417 H6
Russell Gv *RCFD* SS4 .... 444 D3
Russell Rd *BKHH* IG9 .... 403 K4
  CHING E4 .... 402 A7
  COS C015 .... 11 D4
  FX IP11 .... 5 F5
  GVE DA12 .... 489 J4
  IP IP1 .... 2 C4
  RCHLM CM3 .... 394 D4
  TIL RM18 .... 484 D7
Russell's Dr *BAR* EN8 .... 346 E5
Russell's Ride *BAR* EN8 .... 346 D5
Russell's Rd *HSTD* C09 .... 147 H5
Russel Rd *GRAYS* RM17 .... 483 K3
Russet Cl *BRTR* CM7 .... 209 K4
  SLH/COR SS17 .... 473 K2
Russets *EMPK* RM11 .... 431 F6
Russets Cl *CHING* E4 .... 402 E6
The Russets *RCFD* SS4 .... 422 A8
Russetts *VGE* SS16 .... 436 B8
Russet Wy *BOC* CM0 .... 398 C7
  HOC/HUL SS5 .... 421 F5
Rustic Cl *UPMR* RM14 .... 452 B7
Rutherford Cl *CHLM/WR* CM12 ... 387 C8
  LOS SS9 .... 442 D7
Rutherfords *CHLM/WR* CM1 .... 304 D4
Ruthven Av *BAR* EN8 .... 346 D7
Ruthven Cl *WICKW* SS12 .... 417 G7
Rutland Ap *EMPK* RM11 .... 431 H7
Rutland Av *COLS* C02 .... 218 C2
  SOS SS1 .... 465 H5
Rutland Cl *LAIN* SS15 .... 436 B7
Rutland Dr *EMPK* RM11 .... 431 H7
  RAYL SS6 .... 419 G6
Rutland Gdns *BRTR* CM7 .... 209 K1
  RCFD SS4 .... 421 K8
Rutland Rd *CHLM/WR* CM1 .... 304 C7
  RCHLM CM3 .... 394 C6
Rydal Cl *HOC/HUL* SS5 .... 419 J3
  RAYL SS6 .... 441 K3
Rydal Wk *IPSE* IP3 .... 64 A3
Rydal Wy *BRTR* CM7 .... 209 F7
Ryde Av *COS* C015 .... 259 J6
Ryde Cl *LOS* SS9 .... 442 C8
Ryde Dr *SLH/COR* SS17 .... 473 J5
Ryder Gdns *RAIN* RM13 .... 450 A7
Ryder Wy *PIT* SS13 .... 439 G3
The Ryde *LOS* SS9 .... 442 C8

Rye Cl COLW CO3 .... 185 J8
  HCH RM12 .... 450 D6 ⊡
  IPSE IP3 .... 64 B1
  RCHLM CM3 .... 308 A2
  RCOLE CO7 .... 255 J4
Ryecroft HLWW/ROY CM19 .... 12 B3
Ryedene VGE SS16 .... 458 B3
Ryedene Cl VGE SS16 .... 458 B2 ⊡
Ryedene Pl VGE SS16 .... 458 B2 ⊡
The Rye Fld RCHLM CM3 .... 335 H2
Rye Hill Rd HLWS CM18 .... 322 B2
Rye Hills HSTD CO9 .... 148 A5
Rye La COLS CO2 .... 251 G1
Rye Mill La K/T/MI CO5 .... 247 F1
Ryes La RBSF CM22 .... 233 H6
  SUD CO10 .... 83 H3
Rye St BSF CM23 .... 198 E4
Rye Wk ING CM4 .... 386 A3
Rygate Rd COL CO1 .... 8 B3
Rykhill CDH/CHF RM16 .... 485 G2
Rylands RIPS/CAP IP9 .... 91 H6
Rylands Rd SOSN SS2 .... 19 F2
The Ryle CHLM/WR CM1 .... 331 G5
Rylstone Wy SAFWS CB11 .... 71 G5
Rysley RCHLM CM3 .... 335 H1

S

Sabina Rd CDH/CHF RM16 .... 485 H3
Sabines Rd ABR/ST RM4 .... 382 B7
Sackville Cl CHLM/WR CM1 .... 332 A2
Sackville Crs HARH RM3 .... 431 F3
Sackville Rd SOSN SS2 .... 465 H4
Sacombs Ash La SBW CM21 .... 230 C6
Saddington St GVE DA12 .... 489 G5
Saddle Ri CHLM/WR CM1 .... 305 G5 ⊡
Saddleworth Sq HARH RM3 .... 430 D1 ⊡
Sadler Cl COLS CO2 .... 219 J1
Sadlers SBF/HAD SS7 .... 440 A6
Sadlers La BCAYE CM11 .... 387 K8
  FOS CO13 .... 228 B7
Sadlers Md HLWS CM18 .... 294 E6
Saffory Cl LOS SS9 .... 442 D6
Saffron Cl BRTR CM7 .... 143 K2 ⊡
  RBRW/HUT CM13 .... 434 C8
  SLH/COR SS17 .... 473 G2
Saffron Ct SAFWS CB11 .... 70 E4
  SLH/COR SS17 .... 473 F4
Saffron Gdns BRTR CM7 .... 143 J2
  SLH/COR SS17 .... 473 F4
Saffron Rd CDH/CHF RM16 .... 483 F3
Saffron Wk K/T/MI CO5 .... 280 A1
  BRTR CM7 .... 143 J2
Sage Rd GVE DA12 .... 489 K8
Sages RBSF CM22 .... 137 G8
Sages End Rd HVHL CB9 .... 49 F5
St Agnes Ct CVI SS8 .... 477 H1
St Agnes Rd BCAYW CM12 .... 436 D2
St Agnes Wy KESG IP5 .... 38 D7
St Aidan's Wy GVE DA12 .... 489 K8
St Albans Av UPMR RM14 .... 452 B2
St Alban's Cl GVE DA12 .... 489 J8
St Alban's Gdns GVE DA12 .... 489 J8
St Alban's Rd COLW CO3 .... 186 E6
  COS CO15 .... 11 D4
  EPP CM16 .... 351 H3
St Andrews Av HCH RM12 .... 450 A6
St Andrew's Av
(Colchester By-pass Rd)
  COLN CO4 .... 9 E4
  EPP CM16 .... 324 C6
  IPNE IP4 .... 38 B8 ⊡
  RCOLE CO7 .... 222 A6
St Andrew's Dr RIPS/CAP IP9 .... 91 H6
St Andrews Gdns COLN CO4 .... 9 D5
St Andrews La LAIN SS15 .... 16 A3
St Andrews Pl BRWN CM15 .... 411 J5
  RCOLE CO7 .... 255 J4
St Andrew's Ri SUD CO10 .... 57 F8
St Andrew's Rd COS CO15 .... 10 B4
  FX IP11 .... 131 H2
  GVE DA12 .... 489 G5 ⊡
  HSTD CO9 .... 147 K3
  RCFD SS4 .... 444 B3
  RCHLM CM3 .... 306 D4
  RCHLM CM3 .... 308 A1
  RCOS CO16 .... 225 G4
  SBN/FI SS3 .... 466 B7
  SUD CO10 .... 58 D7
  TIL RM18 .... 484 D8
St Annes Cl CDH/CHF RM16 .... 471 F8 ⊡
  EBAR EN7 .... 346 A2 ⊡
  RCOLW CO6 .... 213 J5
St Anne's Dr BROX EN10 .... 319 G2
St Anne's Rd BRWN CM15 .... 385 G5
  COLN CO4 .... 9 D3 ⊡
  CVI SS8 .... 478 D2
St Anns Rd COS CO15 .... 10 B3
  SOSN SS2 .... 19 D3

St Anthony's Dr CHLM/GWD CM2 ... 15 D6
St Aubyns Rd IPNE IP4 .... 37 J8
St Augustine Rd CDH/CHF RM16 ... 485 G3
  IPSE IP3 .... 64 B1
St Augustine's Av SOS SS1 .... 466 A7
St Augustines Cl BROX EN10 .... 319 F2 ⊡
St Augustines Dr BROX EN10 .... 319 F2
St Augustine's Gdn IPSE IP3 .... 64 A2
St Austell Cl KESG IP5 .... 38 E7
St Austell Rd COLN CO4 .... 188 A2
St Austin's La HAR CO12 .... 7 F2 ⊡
St Barbara's Rd COLS CO2 .... 218 E1
St Bartholomew Cl COLN CO4 ...... 187 K2 ⊡
St Bartholomews La SUD CO10 ...... 58 A4
St Benedict's Av GVE DA12 .... 489 K8
St Benet's Rd SOSN SS2 .... 18 C1
St Bernard Rd COLN CO4 .... 188 A2
St Botolph Rd GVW DA11 .... 488 C8
St Botolph's St COL CO1 .... 8 B5 ⊡
St Botolph's Ter WOTN CO14 ... 229 H5 ⊡
St Botolph's Wy HVHL CB9 .... 27 F5
St Bride Cl COLN CO4 .... 9 F1
St Catharine's Rd BROX EN10 .... 319 G1
St Catherines Cl COLS CO2 .... 218 E4
  WICKE SS11 .... 417 J5 ⊡
St Catherine's Ct CHTY IP2 .... 64 A4
St Catherines Rd CHING E4 .... 402 B5
  CHLM/WR CM1 .... 332 A3
  SUD CO10 .... 34 E6
St Cecilia Rd CDH/CHF RM16 .... 485 G3
St Chads Cl LAIN SS15 .... 16 A3 ⊡
St Chad's Dr GVE DA12 .... 489 K8
St Chad's Rd TIL RM18 .... 485 F7
St Charles Dr WICKE SS11 .... 417 H6
St Charles Rd BRW CM14 .... 410 E5
St Christopher Rd COLN CO4. .... 9 F1
St Christophers Cl CVI SS8 .... 477 H1
St Christophers Wy COS CO15 ...... 290 B6
St Clair Cl COS CO15 .... 259 H5
St Clair's Dr RCOS CO16 .... 257 H8
St Clair's Rd RCOS CO16 .... 257 H8
St Clare Dr COLW CO3 .... 186 B6
St Clement Rd COLN CO4 .... 9 F1
St Clements GTDUN CM6 .... 139 K3
St Clement's Av LOS SS9 .... 463 F3
  WTHK RM20 .... 482 D5
St Clements Ct PUR RM19 .... 481 H5 ⊡
  HOC/HUL SS5 .... 443 H1
  SBF/HAD SS7 .... 440 B8 ⊡
St Clement's Crs SBF/HAD SS7 ...... 440 C8
St Clement's Dr LOS SS9 .... 463 F2
St Clement's Rd SBF/HAD SS7 ...... 440 B8
  WTHK RM20 .... 483 F6
St Cleres Crs WICKE SS11 .... 417 J6
St Cleres Hall La RCOS CO16 .... 289 H3
St Cleres Wy RCHLM CM3. .... 335 H7
St Columba's Cl GVE DA12 .... 489 K8
St Columb Ct COLN CO4 .... 9 E1
St Cross Ct HOD EN11 .... 319 G1 ⊡
St Cyrus Rd COLN CO4 .... 9 F1
St Davids Cl COLN CO4 .... 9 E4
St David's Dr BROX EN10 .... 319 F1
  SBF/HAD SS7 .... 462 B2
St David's Rd IPSE IP3 .... 63 K2
  VGE SS16 .... 456 C1
St Davids Ter LOS SS9 .... 462 B2
St David's Wy WICKE SS11 .... 417 J6 ⊡
St Denis Cl HAR CO12 .... 165 F4
St Dominic Rd COLN CO4 .... 9 F1
St Dunstan's Dr GVE DA12 .... 489 K8
St Edith's Cl BCAYW CM12 .... 414 B4 ⊡
St Ediths La BCAYW CM12 .... 414 B4 ⊡
St Edmunds Cl HAR CO12 .... 165 F4 ⊡
  SOSN SS2 .... 19 F1 ⊡
St Edmund's Ct COLN CO4 .... 9 E5 ⊡
St Edmunds Flds GTDUN CM6 .... 204 D5
St Edmund's HI SUD CO10 .... 85 G7
St Edmunds La BURES CO8 .... 204 D3
St Edmund's PI IP IP1 .... 3 D1
St Edmund's Rd FX IP11 .... 5 E5
  IP IP1 .... 2 C1
St Edmund's Wy HLWE CM17 .... 295 G1 ⊡
St Edmund Wy BURES CO8 .... 115 K4
  RCOLE CO7 .... 122 C6
  SUD CO10 .... 35 G2
St Egberts Wy CHING E4 .... 402 D4
St Fabian's Dr CHLM/WR CM1. .... 332 A1
St Faith Rd COLN CO4 .... 9 F1
St Fillan Rd COLN CO4 .... 9 F2
St Francis Wy CDH/CHF RM16 .... 485 H1
St Gabriels La PIT SS13 .... 438 E8 ⊡
St George's Av EMPK RM11 .... 451 G1
  GRAYS RM17 .... 484 B3
  HAR CO12 .... 7 D6 ⊡
St Georges Cl BRWN CM15. .... 383 K1
  RCOLE CO7 .... 100 D4
St George's Dr WOS/PRIT SS0 .... 18 B1
St George's La SBN/FI SS3 .... 466 E7
St George's Park Av
  WOS/PRIT SS0 .... 463 J3
St George's Rd FX IP11 .... 131 K1

St George's St IP IP1 .... 3 D3 ⊡
St Georges Wk SBF/HAD SS7 .... 440 A7 ⊡
St Giles Cl CDH/CHF RM16 .... 472 A5 ⊡
  HSTD CO9 .... 111 J3
  MAL CM9 .... 338 A3
St Giles Crs MAL CM9 .... 338 A3
St Gregory's Ct SUD CO10 .... 58 B5 ⊡
St Gregory's Crs GVE DA12 .... 489 K7
St Guiberts Rd CVI SS8 .... 460 D8
St Helena Ms COLW CO3 .... 186 E8
St Helena Rd COLW CO3 .... 186 E8
St Helens Av COS CO15 .... 259 J6
St Helen's Gn HAR CO12 .... 7 F2
St Helen's La COL CO1 .... 8 B4 ⊡
St Helen's Rd WOS/PRIT SS0 .... 18 B4
St Helen's St IPNE IP4 .... 3 F5
St Helens Wk BCAYW CM12 .... 414 A1 ⊡
St Hilda's Wy GVE DA12 .... 489 K8
St Isidores KESG IP5 .... 39 H6
St Ives Cl HARH RM3 .... 431 G2 ⊡
  KESG IP5 .... 38 E7
  RCOS CO16 .... 290 D2
St Ives Rd K/T/MI CO5 .... 252 A7
St Ivians Dr GPK RM2 .... 430 B5
St James' Av CHONG CM5 .... 354 B4
  SOS SS1 .... 466 A7
St James Av East SLH/COR SS17 .... 474 A2
St James Av West SLH/COR SS17 ... 474 A2
St James Cl CVI SS8 .... 477 H1 ⊡
  WOS/PRIT SS0 .... 463 H2
St James Gdns WOS/PRIT SS0 .... 463 H2
St James Ms BCAYW CM12 .... 414 B3 ⊡
St James Pk CHLM/WR CM1 .... 331 K1
St James Rd BRTR CM7 .... 177 J8
  VGE SS16 .... 438 B8
St James's Av GVW DA11 .... 489 F5
St James's Rd BRW CM14 .... 411 F6
  GVW DA11 .... 489 F5
St James's Wk GVW DA11 .... 489 F4 ⊡
  HSTD CO9 .... 110 E1
St James's Wk HOC/HUL SS5 .... 420 D7 ⊡
St James Wy BSF CM23 .... 198 A8
  BSF CM23 .... 231 J3
St Johns Av BRTR CM7 .... 201 G7
  BRW CM14 .... 411 G7
  CHLM/GWD CM2 .... 14 C5
  COL CO1 .... 8 B5 ⊡
  HLWE CM17 .... 295 G1
St John's Cl COLN CO4 .... 187 K1
  LAIN SS15 .... 16 A3 ⊡
  RAIN RM13 .... 450 B8 ⊡
  RCOLE CO7 .... 188 A1
  SAFWS CB11 .... 70 E6
St John's Ct BKHH IG9. .... 405 J4
  MAL CM9 .... 314 C0
St Johns Crs CVI SS8 .... 477 H1
  STSD CM24 .... 167 K6
St Johns Dr RAYL SS6 .... 440 E7
St John's Gn CHLM/WR CM1 .... 331 H4 ⊡
St John's La STSD CM24 .... 167 K6 ⊡
St Johns Ms SLH/COR SS17 .... 474 B1 ⊡
St John's Rd BCAYE CM11 .... 414 C2
  CDH/CHF RM16 .... 485 G4
  CHING E4 .... 402 C6
  CHLM/GWD CM2 .... 14 C4
  CHLM/WR CM1 .... 331 H4
  COLN CO4 .... 188 A2
  COS CO15 .... 10 B2
  CRW RM5 .... 407 H8
  EPP CM16 .... 350 D6
  GVE DA12 .... 489 J5
  IPNE IP4 .... 37 H7
  LOU IG10 .... 377 H6
  RCOLE CO7 .... 221 F6 ⊡
  RCOS CO16 .... 258 D8 ⊡
  SBF/HAD SS7 .... 461 H2
  SBN/FI SS3 .... 467 G2
  STSD CM24 .... 167 K6
  WOS/PRIT SS0 .... 18 B4
St John's St COL CO1 .... 8 A5
  MAL CM9 .... 314 C0
St Johns Wk HLWE CM17 .... 295 G1 ⊡
St John's Wy SLH/COR SS17 .... 474 B1
St Joseph Rd COLN CO4 .... 187 K2
St Jude Gdns COLN CO4 .... 9 F1
St Judes Cl COLN CO4 .... 9 F1
St Kilda's Rd BRWN CM15 .... 410 E3
St Laurence Dr BROX EN10 .... 318 E5
St Laurence Rd BOC CM0 .... 342 B5
St Lawrence Gdns ING CM4 .... 356 C5 ⊡
  LOS SS9 .... 443 F7
St Lawrence HI BOC CM0 .... 342 E8
St Lawrence Rd BOC CM0 .... 343 H8
  COLN CO4 .... 9 F1
  UPMR RM14 .... 451 K3
St Lawrence Wy KESG IP5 .... 39 F5
St Leonards Cl SAFWS CB11 .... 100 B3 ⊡
St Leonard's Rd COL CO1 .... 9 E5
  IPSE IP3 .... 63 K2
  SOS SS1 .... 19 H5
  WAB EN9 .... 319 K6
St Leonards Wy HCH RM12 .... 450 C7
St Luke's Cha K/T/MI CO5 .... 280 B1 ⊡
St Luke's Cl COLN CO4 .... 9 F1
  CVI SS8 .... 477 H1 ⊡

St Luke's Rd *SOSN* SS2 .... 19 F1
St Margaret's Av *SLH/COR* SS17 .... 473 J5
St Margaret's Crs *GVE* DA12 .... 489 K8
St Margaret's Rd *CHLM/GWD* CM2.... 15 F2
St Mark Dr *COLN* CO4 .... 9 F1
St Mark's Av *GVW* DA11 .... 488 D5
St Mark's Fld *RCFD* SS4 .... 444 C3
St Marks Rd *COS* CO15 .... 10 B3
   CVI SS8 .... 477 H1
   SBF/HAD SS7 .... 461 H2
St Martins Cl *COS* CO15 .... 10 B3
   EN EN1 .... 374 B5
   GTDUN CM6 .... 266 E6
   RAYL SS6 .... 441 H5
   SBF/HAD SS7 .... 440 A6
St Martins Ct *KESG* IP5 .... 39 J6 🔲
St Martins Gn *FX* IP11 .... 94 B5
St Mary's Av *BCAYW* CM12 .... 414 A4
   BRWN CM15 .... 411 K1
St Mary's Cl *BRTR* CM7 .... 176 E6
   CHLM/GWD CM2 .... 333 H7 🔲
   FX IP11 .... 94 C7 🔲
   GRAYS RM17 .... 484 C5 🔲
   GVE DA12 .... 489 H7
   SBF/HAD SS7 .... 460 C4
   SBN/FI SS3 .... 466 C4
   SUD CO10 .... 58 E3
St Mary's Crs *FX* IP11 .... 5 E1
   PIT SS13 .... 439 F6
St Mary's Dr *SBF/HAD* SS7 .... 460 D4
   STSD CM24 .... 168 A7
St Mary's La *MAL* CM9 .... 338 D3
   UPMR RM14 .... 451 H3
St Marys Md *CHLM/WR* CM1 .... 304 C4 🔲
St Mary's Pl *GTDUN* CM6 .... 205 J6
St Mary's Rd *BAR* EN8 .... 346 C5
   BOC CM0 .... 398 B7
   BRTR CM7 .... 210 A2
   CDH/CHF CM16 .... 485 C3
   COS CO15 .... 10 B3
   FOS CO13 .... 229 F8
   K/T/MI CO5 .... 246 E3
   RCOLE CO7 .... 224 A8 🔲
   SBF/HAD SS7 .... 460 C5
   SOSN SS1 .... 18 C2
   WICKW SS12 .... 416 E8
   WIT CM8 .... 245 H6
St Marys Vw *SAFWN* CB10 .... 71 F1
St Mary's Wk *HVHL* CB9 .... 50 C7
St Marys Wy *CHIC* IG7 .... 404 D8 🔲
   NHMKT IP6 .... 37 H1
St Matthew's Cl *RAIN* RM13 .... 450 B8 🔲
St Michaels Av *PIT* SS13 .... 458 E1
St Michael's Cha *RCOLW* CO6 .... 216 C3
St Michael's Cl *HLW* CM20 .... 13 E2
   KESG IP5 .... 38 E7 🔲
   RCHLM CM3 .... 367 J8
   SOCK/AV RM15 .... 468 E7
St Michael's Dr *CHLM/WR* CM1 ...... 302 A8 🔲
St Michael's La *BRTR* CM7 .... 209 J3
St Michael's Rd *BROX* EN10 .... 319 F2
   BRTR CM7 .... 209 J3
   CDH/CHF CM16 .... 485 C4
   COLS CO2 .... 218 D4
   CVI SS8 .... 477 H1
   HAR CO12 .... 6 C6
   RCOS CO16 .... 226 C3
   SBF/HAD SS7 .... 442 A7
St Mildreds Rd *CHLM/GWD* CM2 ...... 14 C5
St Monance Wy *COLN* CO4 .... 9 F1
St Nazaire Rd *CHLM/WR* CM1 .... 304 A7
St Neots Cl *COLN* CO4 .... 9 F1
St Neot's Av *HARH* RM3 .... 431 G2
St Nicholas Av *HCH* RM12 .... 450 B4
St Nicholas Cl *WIT* CM8 .... 277 F1
St Nicholas Fld *BSF* CM23 .... 134 A5
St Nicholas Gv *RBRW/HUT* CM13 ... 412 B8
St Nicholas La *LAIN* SS15 .... 16 B3
St Nicholas Rd *BOC* CM0 .... 372 A1
   WIT CM8 .... 277 F1
St Nicholas St *COL* CO1 .... 8 B4 🔲
St Nicholas Wy *RCOLW* CO6 .... 213 H2
St Olaves Rd *KESG* IP5 .... 39 G5
St Omar Cl *WICKW* SS12 .... 417 G7 🔲
St Osyth Cl *CHTY* IP2 .... 62 B5
St Osyth Cl *COS* CO15 .... 290 E2
   RCOS CO16 .... 258 D5
St Osyth Rd East *RCOS* CO16 .... 258 E4
St Osyth Rd West *RCOS* CO16 .... 258 D4
St Patrick's Pl *CDH/CHF* RM16 .... 485 C3
St Paul's Cl *SOCK/AV* RM15 .... 468 E7 🔲
St Pauls Gdns *BCAYW* CM12 .... 414 B1 🔲
St Paul's Pl *SOCK/AV* RM15 .... 468 E7 🔲
St Paul's Rd *COL* CO1 .... 8 A2
   COS CO15 .... 11 D4
   CVI SS8 .... 477 H1
St Pauls Wy *WAB* EN9 .... 347 K7 🔲
St Peter's Av *CHONG* CM5 .... 326 B8
   MAL CM9 .... 338 B3
St Peter's Cl *BRTR* CM7 .... 209 J1 🔲
St Peters Fld *BOC* CM0 .... 398 A6
St Peter's-in-the-fields *BRTR* CM7.. 209 J1
St Peter's Pavement
   BSDN SS14 .... 438 C4 🔲

St Peter's Rd *BRTR* CM7 .... 209 J1
   BRW CM14 .... 410 E7 🔲
   CDH/CHF RM16 .... 485 G3
   CHLM/WR CM1 .... 332 A3
   CVI SS8 .... 477 H1 🔲
   HOC/HUL SS5 .... 420 C6
   K/T/MI CO5 .... 284 D7
   RCOLW CO6 .... 213 J2
St Peter's St *COL* CO1 .... 8 A3
   IP IP1 .... 3 D4 🔲
St Peter's Ter *WICKW* SS12 .... 417 F6
St Peters Vw *HSTD* CO9 .... 110 C4 🔲
St Peters Wk *BCAYW* CM12 .... 414 A1
   BRTR CM7 .... 209 J2 🔲
St Runwald St *COL* CO1 .... 8 B4 🔲
St Saviour Cl *COLN* CO4 .... 9 F1 🔲
St Stephens Crs *RBRW/HUT* CM13.. 411 K7
St Stephen's Rd *PEND* EN3 .... 374 D5
   RCHLM CM3 .... 394 B1
Saint's Wk *CDH/CHF* RM16 .... 485 H3
St Teresa Wk *CDH/CHF* RM16 .... 485 G3
St Thomas Cl *COLN* CO4 .... 188 B3 🔲
St Thomas Rd *GVW* DA11 .... 488 D6 🔲
   RCFD SS4 .... 421 H1
St Thomas's Av *GVW* DA11 .... 489 G7
St Thomas's Cl *WAB* EN9 .... 348 D7
St Thomas's Pl *GRAYS* RM17 .... 484 B5 🔲
St Valery *RBSF* CM22 .... 201 K6
St Vincent Cha *BRTR* CM7 .... 178 A8 🔲
St Vincent Rd *COS* CO15 .... 10 A6
St Vincents Rd *CHLM/GWD* CM2 .... 14 C5 🔲
   WOS/PRIT SS0 .... 18 B5
St Winifred's Cl *CHIC* IG7 .... 405 F8
Sainty Cl *RCOLE* CO7 .... 221 F5 🔲
Sairard Cl *LOS* SS9 .... 442 E6
Sairard Gdns *LOS* SS9 .... 442 E6
Sakins Cft *HLWS* CM18 .... 13 F6
Saladin Dr *PUR* RM19 .... 481 H3
Salary Cl *COLN* CO4 .... 188 B4
Salcombe Rd *BRTR* CM7 .... 210 B4 🔲
Salcott Crs *WICKW* SS12 .... 417 H6
Salcott St *MAL* CM9 .... 282 B5
Salehurst Rd *IPSE* IP3 .... 64 C2 🔲
Salem Pl *GVW* DA11 .... 488 C5 🔲
Salerno Crs *COLS* CO2 .... 218 D3
Salerno Wy *CHLM/WR* CM1 .... 304 A7
Salesbury Dr *BCAYE* CM11 .... 414 E3
Salfcoral Cl *RCHLM* CM3 .... 391 F4
Saling Gn *LAIN* SS15 .... 437 G3 🔲
Salisbury Av *COLW* CO3 .... 186 C7
   RAYL SS6 .... 475 K4 🔲
   SLH/COR SS17 .... 473 K4 🔲
   WOS/PRIT SS0 .... 18 B3
Salisbury Cl *BSF* CM23 .... 198 E8
Salisbury Crs *BAR* EN8 .... 346 D6
Salisbury Rd *CHING* E4 .... 402 B6
   COS CO15 .... 260 C8 🔲
   GPK RM2 .... 430 C7
   GRAYS RM17 .... 484 B5
   GVW DA11 .... 488 C5
   IPSE IP3 .... 63 J2
   LOS SS9 .... 462 D4
   PEND EN3 .... 375 F3
Salix Rd *GRAYS* RM17 .... 484 C5
Sallows Cl *IP* IP1 .... 2 A2 🔲
Salmon Cl *COLN* CO4 .... 218 A1
Salmon's Gv *RBRW/HUT* CM13 ...... 412 B8
Salmon's La *RCOLW* CO6 .... 214 D1
Saltcoats *RCHLM* CM3 .... 392 D5
Saltcote Maltings *MAL* CM9 .... 339 G1 🔲
Salter Pl *CHLM/GWD* CM2 .... 333 H3 🔲
Salters *BSF* CM23 .... 231 G1
Salter's Meadow *MAL* CM9 .... 313 H1
The Saltings *SBF/HAD* SS7 .... 461 J2
Salt's Gn *CHLM/WR* CM1 .... 301 H3
Salvia Cl *COS* CO15 .... 290 E1
Salwey Crs *BROX* EN10 .... 319 F2
Samford Cl *RIPS/CAP* IP9 .... 90 A6
Samphire Cl *WIT* CM8 .... 276 D2
Samphire Dr *GRAYS* RM17 .... 484 D5
Sampson Dr *SUD* CO10 .... 35 F5
Sampson's La *K/T/MI* CO5 .... 284 A1
Samsons Cl *RCOLE* CO7 .... 255 J5
Samson's Rd *RCOLE* CO7 .... 255 J4
Samuel Ct *IPNE* IP4 .... 3 E3
Samuel Mnr *CHLM/GWD* CM2 .... 333 J3 🔲
Samuel Rd *VGE* SS16 .... 456 C1
Samuels Dr *SOS* SS1 .... 466 A5
Sanctuary Gdn *SLH/COR* SS17 ...... 474 A3 🔲
Sanctuary Rd *LOS* SS9 .... 462 B2
Sandbanks *SBF/HAD* SS7 .... 461 J3
Sanderling Gdns *MAL* CM9 .... 310 E8 🔲
Sanderlings *SBF/HAD* SS7 .... 460 B3 🔲
Sanders Dr *COLW* CO3 .... 186 C6
Sanderson Cl *RBRW/HUT* CM13 .... 434 B8 🔲
Sanderson Ms *K/T/MI* CO5 .... 220 C5
Sanders Rd *CVI* SS8 .... 461 F7
Sandford Av *LOIG* IG10 .... 378 A7
Sandford Cl *RCOLE* CO7 .... 221 F5
Sandford Mill Rd *CHLM/GWD* CM2.. 333 J3
Sandford Rd *CHLM/GWD* CM2 .... 15 E2
Sandhill Rd *LOS* SS9 .... 442 C5
Sandhurst *CVI* SS8 .... 477 G2
Sandhurst Av *IPSE* IP3 .... 63 H1 🔲
Sandhurst Cl *LOS* SS9 .... 463 G1
Sandhurst Crs *LOS* SS9 .... 463 G1

Sandhurst Rd *TIL* RM18 .... 485 H8
Sandleigh Rd *LOS* SS9 .... 463 H4
Sandle Rd *BSF* CM23 .... 199 F6
Sandling Crs *IPNE* IP4 .... 38 C8
Sandon Br *CHLM/GWD* CM2 .... 334 D6
Sandon Cl *BSDN* SS14 .... 438 C8
   RCFD SS4 .... 444 A2 🔲
   RCOLW CO6 .... 154 D6
Sandon Ct *BSDN* SS14 .... 438 C8 🔲
Sandon Hall Bridleway
   CHLM/GWD CM2 .... 362 B2
Sandon Hl *RCHLM* CM3 .... 239 G6
Sandon Pl *CHONG* CM5 .... 354 C4
Sandon Rd *BAR* EN8 .... 346 C4
   BSDN SS14 .... 438 C8
Sandown Av *HCH* RM12 .... 450 E3
   WOS/PRIT SS0 .... 463 J3
Sandown Cl *COS* CO15 .... 259 J5
   WICKE SS11 .... 417 K6 🔲
Sandown Rd *CDH/CHF* RM16 .... 472 E5
   IP IP1 .... 36 C2
   SBF/HAD SS7 .... 441 G6
   WICKE SS11 .... 417 K6
Sandpiper Cl *COLN* CO4 .... 188 D6
   HVHL CB9 .... 50 C7
   SBN/FI SS3 .... 466 D5
Sandpiper Dr *ERITH* DA8 .... 480 C6
Sandpiper Rd *CHTY* IP2 .... 62 A3
The Sandpipers *GVE* DA12 .... 489 J7
Sandpit Cl *IPNE* IP4 .... 38 D8
Sandpit La *BOC* CM0 .... 398 C8
   BRW CM14 .... 410 C2
Sandpit Rd *SBN/FI* SS3 .... 467 G5
Sandringham Av
   HLWW/ROY CM19 .... 293 G5
   HOC/HUL SS5 .... 420 D7 🔲
Sandringham Cl *CHTY* IP2 .... 62 B3
   SLH/COR SS17 .... 474 A2
Sandringham Dr *COLS* CO2 .... 219 H3
Sandringham Pl
   CHLM/GWD CM2 .... 15 D3 🔲
Sandringham Rd *BRWN* CM15 .... 410 E1
   LAIN SS15 .... 16 C2
   SOS SS1 .... 465 C5
Sandringham Wy *BAR* EN8 .... 346 C8
Sandwich Cl *BRTR* CM7 .... 177 H7 🔲
Sandwich Rd *COS* CO15 .... 291 F5 🔲
   RCOLE CO7 .... 255 K5
Sandy Bank Rd *GVE* DA12 .... 489 G6
Sandy Cl *FX* IP11 .... 94 C5
Sandy Hl *RCOLW* CO6 .... 152 C1
Sandyhill La *IPSE* IP3 .... 63 G4
Sandy La *CDH/CHF* RM16 .... 485 G5
   FRAM/WMKT IP13 .... 39 H1
   SOCK/AV RM15 .... 468 C7
   SUD CO10 .... 57 G8
   WTHK RM20 .... 482 E5
San Remo Pde *WOS/PRIT* SS0 .... 18 B5
San Remo Rd *CVI* SS8 .... 478 D2
Sapphire Pl *IPNE* IP4 .... 38 C8 🔲
Sapling Pl *IPNE* IP4 .... 38 C8 🔲
Sappers Cl *SBW* CM21 .... 263 K3
Saran Ct *RCOLE* CO7 .... 220 D3 🔲
Sarcel *BRTR* CM7 .... 179 H7
Sargeant Cl *COLS* CO2 .... 219 J2 🔲
Sarre Av *HCH* RM12 .... 450 D7 🔲
Sarre Wy *RCOLE* CO7 .... 255 J5
Sassoon Wy *MAL* CM9 .... 338 C4 🔲
Satanita Rd *WOS/PRIT* SS0 .... 463 K5
Saul's Av *WIT* CM8 .... 277 G5
Sauls Bridge Cl *WIT* CM8 .... 277 G5
Saunders Av *BRTR* CM7 .... 209 G1
Saunders Cl *BAR* EN8 .... 346 C2
   GVW DA11 .... 488 D7
   RBSF CM22 .... 168 D4 🔲
Saunton Rd *HCH* RM12 .... 450 B3
Savernake Rd *CHLM/WR* CM1 .... 332 A4
Saville Cl *SAFWS* CB11 .... 134 A1
Saville St *WOTN* CO14 .... 229 H4
Savill Rd *COLS* CO2 .... 219 K3
Savoy Cl *VGE* SS16 .... 436 B8
Savoy Wd *EPP* CM16 .... 321 K3 🔲
Sawbridgeworth Rd *RBSF* CM22 .... 232 C6
   SBW CM21 .... 264 C2
Sawells *BROX* EN10 .... 319 F3
Sawkins Av *CHLM/GWD* CM2 .... 333 F7
Sawkins Cl *CHLM/GWD* CM2 .... 333 F7
Sawkins Gdns *CHLM/GWD* CM2 .... 333 F7
Sawmill La *KIR/NAC* IP10 .... 65 F7
Sawney Brook *CHLM/WR* CM1 .... 331 G4
Sawpit La *BSF* CM23 .... 134 C6
Sawston Cl *CHTY* IP2 .... 62 C3 🔲
Sawyers Cl *RIPS/CAP* IP9 .... 87 F4
Sawyer's Hall La *BRWN* CM15 .... 411 F3
Sawyer's Rd *MAL* CM9 .... 312 A1
Saxlingham Rd *CHING* E4 .... 402 E6 🔲
Saxmundham Wy *RCOS* CO16 .... 290 C2
Saxon Bank *BRTR* CM7 .... 210 A3 🔲
Saxon Cl *COLW* CO3 .... 218 A1
   GVW DA11 .... 488 B8
   HARH RM3 .... 431 G4
   HSTD CO9 .... 148 A3 🔲
   RAYL SS6 .... 419 K8
   RBRW/HUT CM13 .... 411 K6
   WICKE SS11 .... 417 H4
Saxon Dr *WIT* CM8 .... 276 E2

Saxon Gdns *SBN/FI* SS3	466	B6
Saxon La *RIPW* IP8	60	D5
Saxon Shore Wy *GVE* DA12	489	H4
Saxonville *SBF/HAD* SS7	460	A1
Saxon Wy *CHLM/WR* CM1	304	D6
COS CO15	260	D7
MAL CM9	338	D4
SAFWN CB10	70	D4
SBF/HAD SS7	460	B3
Sayers *SBF/HAD* SS7	441	F7
Sayesbury Av *SBW* CM21	263	H2
Sayesbury Rd *SBW* CM21	263	J3
Sayes Gdns *SBW* CM21	263	K3
Sarwell Brook *CHLM/GWD* CM2	333	J3
Scalby Rd *BOC* CM0	398	A3
Scaldhurst *PIT* SS13	439	F5
Scarborough Rd *BOC* CM0	398	A3
LOS SS9	463	F3
Scarfe Wy *COLN* CO4	188	B7
Scarletts *BSDN* SS14	437	K5
Scarletts Cl *WIT* CM8	277	C6
Scarletts Rd *COL* CO1	9	E6
Sceptre Cl *MAL* CM9	314	D3
Schneider Cl *FX* IP11	130	E7
Scholars *CHING* E4	402	D4
School Cha *HSTD* CO9	147	K5
School Cl *CDH/CHF* RM16	405	J7
CHIG IG7		
CHLM/WR CM1	269	F2
CHONG CM5	296	D7
CHONG CM5	299	C2
COLS CO2	250	A2
GTDUN CM6	170	A7
HLW CM20	13	E1
HVHL CB9	26	D5
ING CM4	387	K3
K/T/MI CO5	282	E1
MGTR CO11	141	J5
MGTR CO11	159	F3
MGTR CO11	160	A1
RBRW/HUT CM13	434	B1
RBSF CM22	137	G8
RCHLM CM3	241	G5
RCOLE CO7	121	G3
RCOLE CO7	121	J6
RCOLE CO7	122	A2
RCOLE CO7	223	F5
RCOLW CO6	117	J8
RCOLW CO6	154	B3
RCOLW CO6	185	K1
SAFWS CB11	67	K6
SAFWS CB11	100	A4
SBF/HAD SS7	460	C5
SUD CO10	34	E4
WICKW SS12	439	K3
School Rd *BCAYE* CM11	389	H8
BCAYE CM12	414	C5
BRTR CM7	208	B6
BRWN CM15	383	C3
CHLM/WR CM1	269	G8
CHONG CM5	353	F4
COLN CO4	156	B1
COLS CO2	219	H3
FOS CO13	228	D8
GVE DA12	489	H8
HAR CO12	195	F2
HSTD CO9	80	C2
HSTD CO9	82	C8
HSTD CO9	110	C5
HSTD CO9	112	C5
HVHL CB9	28	C5
K/T/MI CO5	248	A4
MAL CM9	310	D2
MAL CM9	311	K3
RCOLE CO7	189	K8
RCOLW CO6	117	J8
RCOLW CO6	216	C3
RCOS CO16	193	F8
RIPS/CAP IP9	88	E3
RIPS/CAP IP9	129	G5
SUD CO10	32	E7
WIT CM8	244	E2
WIT CM8	278	B8
School St *SAFWN* CB10	43	J3
SUD CO10	33	K7
SUD CO10	33	B6
School View Rd *CHLM/WR* CM1	14	A2
School Wk *BRTR* CM7	209	J2
School Wy *LOS* SS9	463	G2
Schreiber Rd *IPNE* IP4	37	K6
Scimitar Pk *PIT* SS13	439	G3
Scofield Ct *SUD* CO10	58	D7
Scopes La *KESG* IP5	39	G5
Scotland Green Rd North		
PEND EN3	374	D8
Scotland Rd *BKHH* IG9	403	K4
Scott Av *BRTR* CM7	107	K8
Scott Cl *BRTR* CM7	209	K5
Scott Crs *ERITH* DA8	480	A7
Scott Dr *COLW* CO3	186	A7

WICKW SS12	417	G8
Scott Rd *BSF* CM23	198	D7
CDH/CHF RM16	485	F3
IPSE IP3		
Scotts Cl *HCH* RM12	450	D6
Scotts Hall Rd *RCFD* SS4	423	G5
Scraley Rd *MAL* CM9	310	E7
Scratton Rd *SLH/COR* SS17	473	K3
SOS SS1	18	C5
Scrip's Rd *RCOLW* CO6	213	H6
Scrivener Dr *RIPW* IP8	61	H3
Scrub La *SBF/HAD* SS7	461	K2
Scrub Ri *BCAYW* CM12	414	A5
Scurvy Hall La *RCHLM* CM3	272	D4
Scylla Cl *MAL* CM9	310	E7
Scythe Wy *COLW* CO3	218	A1
Seaborough Rd *CDH/CHF* RM16	485	H2
Seabrook Gdns *RCHLM* CM3	306	D4
Seabrook Rd *CHLM/GWD* CM2	333	J7
Sea Cornflower Wy *COS* CO15	290	C6
Sea Crs *COS* CO15	290	B7
Seafield Av *MGTR* CO11	160	C1
Seafield Rd *HAR* CO12	6	C1
Seafields Gdns *COS* CO15	11	F2
Seafields Rd *COS* CO15	11	F2
Sea Flowers Wy *COS* CO15	290	C6
Seaforth Dr *SOSN* SS2	19	F2
Seaforth Dr *BAR* EN8	346	D8
Seaforth Gdns *WFD* IG8	403	K8
Seaforth Gv *SOSN* SS2	465	G3
Seaforth Rd *WOS/PRIT* SS0	18	A5
Seagers *MAL* CM9	310	D1
Sea Glebe Wy *COS* CO15	290	C6
Sea Holly Wy *COS* CO15	290	C7
Sea King Crs *COLN* CO4	187	J1
Sea Lavender Wy *COS* CO15	290	C6
Seamans La *ING* CM4	388	D3
Seamer Rd *BOC* CM0	398	A3
Seamore Av *SBF/HAD* SS7	440	B7
Seamore Cl *SBF/HAD* SS7	440	A7
Sea Pink Wy *COS* CO15	290	C7
Sea Reach *LOS* SS9	463	F5
Searle Wy *COLW* CO3	185	G4
Sea Rd *FX* IP11	5	F5
Sea Rosemary Wy *COS* CO15	290	C6
Sea Shell Wy *COS* CO15	290	C7
Sea Thistle Wy *COS* CO15	290	C6
Seaton Cl *MGTR* CO11	159	G2
Seaton Rd *FX* IP11	5	E2
Seaview Av *HAR* CO12	164	B6
K/T/MI CO5	285	C6
VGE SS16	458	A2
Seaview Dr *SBN/FI* SS3	467	H3
Seaview Hts *WOTN* CO14	229	H6
Sea View Pde *BOC* CM0	342	C4
RCHLM CM3	222	C4
Sea View Prom *BOC* CM0	342	B4
Seaview Rd *CVI* SS8	478	E3
LOS SS9	463	F5
RCOLE CO7	255	K6
SBN/FI SS3	466	C7
Seaview Ter *RCOS* CO16	288	A2
SBF/HAD SS7	461	J4
Sea Wy *COS* CO15	290	B6
Seaway *BOC* CM0	342	C5
CVI SS8	478	B3
SOS SS1	19	E5
Seawick Rd *RCOS* CO16	289	H7
Seax Ct *LAIN* SS15	436	A6
Seax Wy *LAIN* SS15	436	A6
Sebastian Av *BRWN* CM15	411	K2
Sebastian Cl *COLN* CO4	188	B6
Sebert Cl *BCAYE* CM11	414	C5
Seckford Cl *IPNE* IP4	38	D3
Second Av *BCAYW* CM12	413	K6
BRWN CM15	356	A8
CHLM/WR CM1	304	C8
COS CO15	11	E3
CVI SS8	477	H1
FOS CO13	261	J1
FX IP11	94	C3
HAR CO12	7	D5
HLWS CM18	13	F3
HOC/HUL SS5	420	A5
HSTD CO9	14	A4
RCOS CO16	225	G5
RCOS CO16	289	J7
SLH/COR SS17	473	K2
SUD CO10	58	C4
WICKE SS11	417	K2
WOS/PRIT SS0	463	J6
WOTN CO14	229	K2
WTHK RM20	482	D5
Seddons Wk *HOC/HUL* SS5	421	F7
Sedgefield Cl *HARH* RM3	409	G7
Sedgefield Crs *HARH* RM3	409	G8
Sedgefield Wy *BRTR* CM7	210	A4
Sedge Gn *HLWW/ROY* CM19	320	B1
WAB EN9	320	A2
Sedgemoor *SBN/FI* SS3	466	C4
Sedley La *LOU* IG10	377	H6
Sedop Cl *SAFWS* CB11	70	E6
Seeleys Rd *HLWE* CM17	295	C1
Selbourne Rd *HOC/HUL* SS5	421	F7
SBF/HAD SS7	440	C8

SOSN SS2	19	F2
Selby Cl *COLS* CO2	218	E4
Seldon Cl *WOS/PRIT* SS0	463	J2
Seldon Rd *K/T/MI* CO5	248	B8
Selkirk Rd *IPNE* IP4	38	A5
Selsey Av *COS* CO15	290	E5
Selvale Wy *FX* IP11	5	E3
Selwood Rd *BRW* CM14	410	C6
Selworthy Cl *BCAYE* CM11	414	D6
Selwyn Cl *CHTY* IP2	3	D5
Selwyn Rd *SOSN* SS2	19	F2
TIL RM18	484	E8
Semper Rd *CDH/CHF* RM16	485	H1
Semples *SLH/COR* SS17	474	B3
Serpentine Rd *IPSE* IP3	63	K3
Serpentine Wk *COL* CO1	8	A3
Settle Rd *HARH* RM3	409	H7
Seven Acres *WICKE* SS11	417	H5
Seven Arches Rd *BRW* CM14	411	H6
Seven Ash Gn *CHLM/WR* CM1	304	E8
Seven Cottages La *KESG* IP5	38	A4
Seven Devils La *SAFWS* CB11	70	E7
Sevenoaks Cl *HARH* RM3	408	D7
Seventh Av *CHLM/WR* CM1	304	D7
CVI SS8	477	J1
Severalls La *COLN* CO4	155	H6
Severn Rd *TIL* RM18	486	C2
Severn Av *GPK* RM2	430	C5
Severn Dr *EN* EN1	374	A4
UPMR RM14	432	A8
Severn Rd *COS* CO15	10	C2
IPSE IP3	63	H2
SOCK/AV RM15	468	E6
Severns Fld *EPP* CM16	350	E3
Sewards End *WICKW* SS12	417	H7
Sewardstone Rd *CHING* E4	375	H3
WAB EN9	347	J8
Sewardstone St *WAB* EN9	347	J8
Sewardstone Wy *WAB* EN9	375	J2
Sewell Harris Cl *HLW* CM20	13	F2
Sewell's La *SUD* CO10	55	F4
Sewell Wontner Cl *KESG* IP5	39	G5
Sexton Cl *COLS* CO2	219	J5
Sexton Rd *TIL* RM18	484	E7
Sextons La *WIT* CM8	278	D3
Seymour Rd *CDH/CHF* RM16	483	F2
CHING E4	402	C4
CHTY IP2	3	D5
COS CO15	290	A4
GVW DA11	488	E6
SBF/HAD SS7	462	A2
TIL RM18	484	E7
WOS/PRIT SS0	463	K4
Seymours *HLWW/ROY* CM19	12	A6
Seymour St *CHLM/GWD* CM2	14	B3
Shackleton Cl *HAR* CO12	164	E4
Shackleton Rd *IPSE* IP3	63	K2
Shadowbush Cl *HVHL* CB9	27	F4
Shaftesbury *LOU* IG10	377	F7
Shaftesbury Av *HAR* CO12	6	C4
PEND EN3	374	D6
Shaftesbury Rd *CHING* E4	402	E4
EPP CM16	350	D3
ROM RM1	430	A8
Shafto Rd *IP* IP1	36	A5
Shair La *RCOLE* CO7	224	C3
Shakespeare Av *BCAYE* CM11	414	D5
RAYL SS6	442	A3
TIL RM18	485	G8
VGE SS16	436	B8
WOS/PRIT SS0	18	A2
Shakespeare Cl *BRTR* CM7	209	K6
Shakespeare Dr *MAL* CM9	338	C5
WOS/PRIT SS0	18	B2
Shakespeare Rd *COLW* CO3	186	A7
IP IP1	36	A1
ROM RM1	430	A8
Shakeston Cl *CHLM/WR* CM1	331	H5
Shakletons *CHONG* CM5	354	C2
Shalcross Dr *BAR* EN8	347	F4
Shalford Rd *BCAYE* CM11	414	B3
BRTR CM7	208	C2
Shamrock Av *CHTY* IP2	62	A1
Shamrock Cl *MAL* CM9	314	D3
Shamrock Rd *GVE* DA12	489	K5
Shangani Rd *BSF* CM23	198	B8
Shanklin Av *BCAYW* CM12	414	B3
Shanklin Cl *COS* CO15	259	J5
Shanklin Dr *WOS/PRIT* SS0	463	H3
Shannon Av *RAYL* SS6	441	H4
Shannon Cl *HVHL* CB9	27	K6
LOS SS9	463	F1
Shannon Rd *IPSE* IP3	63	J5
Shannon Wy *CVI* SS8	477	H2
SOCK/AV RM15	468	E6
Shardlow Cl *HVHL* CB9	26	C4
Sharland Rd *GVE* DA12	489	H7
Sharlands Cl *WICKE* SS11	417	J5
Sharnbrook *SBF/HAD* SS7	466	C3
Sharon Rd *PEND* EN3	374	E6
Sharpecroft *HLWW/ROY* CM19	12	C3
Sharpington Cl *CHLM/GWD* CM2	360	E2
Shatters Rd *COLS* CO2	250	A4
Shawbridge *HLWW/ROY* CM19	12	C6
Shaw Cl *BAR* EN8	346	C3

FOS CO13 .... 228 E6 ▣
HCH RM12 .... 450 C2 ▣
WICKW SS12 .... 417 G8
Shaw Crs RBRW/HUT CM13 .... 412 C1
TIL RM18 .... 485 H1
Shaw Dr BRTR CM7 .... 107 K7
SUD CO10 .... 35 F5
WIT CM8 .... 245 F8
The Shaw RBSF CM22 .... 265 G2
The Shearers BSF CM23 .... 231 F1
Shearers Wy RCHLM CM3 .... 306 D4 ▣
Shears Crs K/T/MI CO5 .... 285 F8
Sheds La SAFWN CB10 .... 71 F3
Sheepcoates La MAL CM9 .... 311 H3
Sheepcote La BSF CM23 .... 166 D2
RCHLM CM3 .... 272 E6
WIT CM8 .... 211 K8
Sheepcot Rd HSTD CO9 .... 110 C2
Sheepen Pl COLW CO3 .... 8 A3
Sheepen Rd COLW CO3 .... 186 A3
Sheepgate La KIR/NAC IP10 ..... 95 C3
Sheepshead HI SUD CO10 .... 59 F7
Sheering Ct RAYL SS6 .... 441 F2 ▣▣
Sheering Dr HLWE CM17 .... 295 H3
Sheering Lower Rd SBW CM21 .. 263 K5
Sheering Mill La SBW CM21 ..... 263 K5
Sheering Rd HLWE CM17 .... 263 K8
Sheering Wk COLS CO2 .... 219 G3
Sheerwater Cl BOC CM0 .... 398 B8 ▣
The Sheelings EMPK RM11 ...... 431 C7
Shelborn Br BRTR CM7 .... 211 H1
Shelbourne Cl KESG IP5 .... 39 H6 ▣
Sheldon Cl HLWE CM17 .... 295 J5
SLH/COR SS17 .... 457 J8
Sheldon Rd CVI SS8 .... 478 E2
Sheldrake Dr CHTY IP2 .... 62 A3
Shellbeach Rd CVI SS8 .... 478 C3
Shellcroft RCOLW CO6 .... 149 G4
Shellduck Crs BRTR CM7 .... 209 H6
Shelley Av HCH RM12 .... 450 A3 ▣
SUD CO10 .... 58 E7
Shelley Cl CHONG CM5 .... 328 C5 ▣
MAL CM9 .... 338 C5 ▣
Shelley Gv LOU IG10 .... 377 H8
Shelley La RCOS CO16 .... 259 H3
Shelley Pl RAYL SS6 .... 441 F2
TIL RM18 .... 485 H1
Shelley Rd CHLM/GWD CM2 .... 15 E3
COLW CO3 .... 186 A7
RBRW/HUT CM13 .... 412 C3
Shelley Sq SOSN SS2 .... 19 E2
Shellow Rd CHONG CM5 .... 328 B1
Shelly Av CVI SS8 .... 456 B8 ▣
Shelsley Ct HLWS CM18 .... 12 C6 ▣
Shenfield Crs BRWN CM15 ...... 411 H5
Shenfield Gdns RBRW/HUT CM13 .. 412 A2
Shenfield Pl BRWN CM15 .... 411 H5
Shenfield Pl BRWN CM15 .... 411 H5
Shenfield Rd BRWN CM15 .... 411 H5
Shenley Rd IPSE IP3 .... 63 K4
Shenstone Dr IP IP1 .... 36 C4
Shenstone Gdns HARH RM3 ..... 430 D3
Shepard Cl LOS SS9 .... 443 H7
Shepeshall LAIN SS15 .... 16 C4
Shepherd Dr RIPW IP8 .... 61 J3
Shepherds Cl BSF CM23 .... 231 C1 ▣
SBF/HAD SS7 .... 461 K1
Shepherds Cft COLW CO3 .... 185 J8
Shepherds HI HARH RM3 .... 431 H4
Shepherd St GVW DA11 .... 488 C5
Shepherds Wk SBF/HAD SS7 ... 461 K1
Shepherds Wy SAFWN CB10 .... 71 C3
Shepley Cl HCH RM12 .... 450 E6 ▣
Shepley Ms PEND EN3 .... 375 G4
Sheppard Cl EN EN1 .... 374 B4
RCOS CO16 .... 10 A1
Sheppard Dr CHLM/GWD CM2 .. 333 J1
Sheppards HLWW/ROY CM19 ... 293 H8
Sheppards Wy KESG IP5 .... 39 H6
Sheppey Cl ERITH DA8 .... 480 C6
Sheppy Pl GVE DA12 .... 489 C5
Sherborne Av IPNE IP4 .... 37 J3
PEND EN3 .... 374 C6
Sherborne Rd CHLM/WR CM1 .. 305 F8
Sherbourne Cl FOS CO13 .... 228 E6 ▣
SOSN SS2 .... 444 B7 ▣
Sherbourne Dr PIT SS13 .... 438 C4
Sherbourne Gdns SOSN SS2 .... 444 C7
Sherbourne Rd COLN CO4 .... 188 C6
Sheredan Rd CHING E4 .... 402 E8
Sheredes Dr HOD EN11 .... 519 F1
Sherfield Rd GRAYS RM17 ...... 484 A5
Sheridan Av SBF/HAD SS7 ...... 461 G2
Sheridan Cl HARH RM3 .... 430 C2
RAYL SS6 .... 442 A3
Sheriden Wk BROX EN10 .... 318 E2
Sheriffs Wy RCOS CO16 .... 259 C6
Sheringham Cl SLH/COR SS17 .. 474 A2
Sheriton Sq RAYL SS6 .... 441 J1
Shernbroke Rd WAB EN9 .... 348 B8

Sherrington Rd IP IP1 .... 2 B1
Sherry Wy SBF/HAD SS7 .... 441 K7
VGE SS16 .... 456 B1 ▣
Sherwood Crs SBF/HAD SS7 .... 461 K1
Sherwood Dr CHLM/WR CM1 ... 331 K4
COS CO15 .... 10 D1
Sherwood Flds KESG IP5 .... 39 G6 ▣
Sherwood Wy K/T/MI CO5 .... 247 F1
SOSN SS2 .... 465 H3
Shetland Cl IPNE IP4 .... 37 J5
Shetland Rd HVHL CB9 .... 27 K5
Shevon Wy BRW CM14 .... 410 C7
Shillibeer Wk CHIG IG7 .... 405 J6
Shillingstone SBN/FI SS3 .... 466 C4
Shillito Cl COLW CO3 .... 218 A1
Shingle Ct WAB EN9 .... 348 C7
Ship La MGTR CO11 .... 161 F2
SOCK/AV RM15 .... 482 A1
Ship Launch Rd IPSE IP3 .... 3 F6
Ship Rd BOC CM0 .... 425 H1
CHLM/GWD CM2 .... 360 D8
Shipwrights Cl SBF/HAD SS7 ... 461 C3
Shipwrights Dr SBF/HAD SS7 ... 461 C3
Shirebourn V RCHLM CM3 .... 392 D7
Shire Cl BCAYE CM11 .... 414 E1
BROX EN10 .... 319 F8 ▣
CHLM/WR CM1 .... 305 H6
Shire HI SAFWS CB11 .... 71 G4
Shire Hill La SAFWN CB10 .... 71 H5
Shirley Cl BAR EN8 .... 348 C7
BROX EN10 .... 319 F6 ▣
IP IP1 .... 36 C2
Shirley Gdns HCH RM12 .... 450 D3
PIT SS13 .... 439 F5
Shirley Rd LOS SS9 .... 443 F8
Shoebridge's HI RCOLE CO7 ..... 121 H7
Shoebury Av SBN/FI SS3 .... 466 E6
Shoebury Common Rd
SBN/FI SS3 .... 466 B8
Shoebury Rd SBN/FI SS3 .... 467 G2
SOS SS1 .... 465 K4
Shonks Mill Rd ABR/ST RM4 .... 381 K1
Shooters Dr WAB EN9 .... 320 A4
Shopland Hall Rd RCFD SS4 ..... 445 J1
Shopland Rd RCFD SS4 .... 445 F6
Shop La K/T/MI CO5 .... 286 D2
Shop Rd MGTR CO11 .... 159 G2
Shorefield SBF/HAD SS7 .... 460 A2
Shorefield Gdns WOS/PRIT SS0 . 18 B5 ▣
Shorefield Rd WOS/PRIT SS0 ... 18 A5
Shoreham Rd COS CO15 .... 290 E5
Shore La KIR/NAC IP10 .... 92 A2
RIPS/CAP IP9 .... 126 D3
Shore Rd BOC CM0 .... 425 H1 ▣
The Shore GVW DA11 .... 488 B3
Shortacre BSDN SS14 .... 437 K7
Short Cft BRWN CM15 .... 383 H3 ▣
Shortcroft BSF CM23 .... 199 J5
Short Cut Rd COL CO1 .... 8 A4 ▣
Shorter Av BRWN CM15 .... 411 J2
Shortlands CHTY IP2 .... 61 K4
Shortlands PI BSF CM23 .... 198 E5 ▣
Short La BCAYE CM11 .... 415 K2
Shortmead Dr BAR EN8 .... 346 E5
Shortridge Ct WIT CM8 .... 276 E5 ▣
Short Rd CVI SS8 .... 478 B1
SBF/HAD SS7 .... 461 J3
Short St SOSN SS2 .... 19 D3
Short Wyre St COL CO1 .... 8 B4 ▣▣
Shotley Cl FX IP11 .... 5 D3
RIPW IP8 .... 61 J3
Shotley Wk RIPS/CAP IP9 .... 92 D8 ▣
Shrewsbury Cl VGE SS16 .... 436 A8 ▣▣
Shrewsbury Dr SBF/HAD SS7 ... 440 C6 ▣
Shropshire Cl CHLM/GWD CM2 . 333 H8 ▣
CHLM/GWD CM2 .... 333 J8 ▣
The Shrubberies CHIG IG7 .... 405 F8
CHLM/WR CM1 .... 331 F5 ▣
Shrubbery Cl LAIN SS15 .... 16 B2 ▣
Shrubbery Rd GVE DA12 .... 489 G6
The Shrubbery UPMR RM14 ..... 451 K4
Shrub End Rd COLW CO3 .... 218 D2
Shrubland Av IP IP1 .... 36 A4
Shrubland Cl COS CO15 .... 11 C2
Shrubland Dr IPNE IP4 .... 38 D8
Shrubland Rd COLS CO2 .... 8 B5 ▣
MGTR CO11 .... 160 A2
Shrublands SAFWN CB10 .... 71 F2
Shrublands Cl CHLM/GWD CM2 . 15 D3
Shums La FOS CO13 .... 228 B5
Sian Pl SUD CO10 .... 58 B6
Sidegate Av IPNE IP4 .... 37 J5
Sidegate La IPNE IP4 .... 37 J5
Sidegate La West IPNE IP4 ...... 37 H4
The Sidings BROX EN10 .... 319 F4 ▣
Sidmouth Av WOS/PRIT SS0 .... 444 A8
Sidmouth Rd CHLM/WR CM1 ... 305 C7 ▣
Sidney Rd EPP CM16 .... 378 B2
Sidney Ter BSF CM23 .... 198 E2
Sidwell Av SBF/HAD SS7 .... 460 D4
Sidwell Cha SBF/HAD SS7 .... 460 D4

Sidwell La SBF/HAD SS7 .... 460 D4
Sidwell Pk SBF/HAD SS7 .... 460 D4
Siena Ms COLS CO2 .... 219 J1
Siggin's La CBE/LIN CB1 .... 23 F7
Silcock Cl COLN CO4 .... 9 E1
Silcott St RCOLE CO7 .... 255 J7
Silent St IPNE IP4 .... 3 D4 ▣
Silks Wy BRTR CM7 .... 209 J3
Sillett Cl RCOS CO16 .... 10 A1
Silva Island Wy WICKW SS12 ... 417 J8 ▣
Silvanus Cl COLW CO3 .... 186 E7 ▣
Silver Birch Av CHING E4 .... 402 A8
EPP CM16 .... 351 J1
Silver Birches RBRW/HUT CM13 . 411 K4
Silverdale RAYL SS6 .... 441 K5
SBF/HAD SS7 .... 440 E6
SLH/COR SS17 .... 473 K1
Silverdale Av WOS/PRIT SS0 ... 18 B2
Silverdale Cl IP IP1 .... 36 C4
Silverdale Dr HCH RM12 .... 450 C6
Silverdale East SLH/COR SS17 .. 473 K1
Silverfield BROX EN10 .... 319 F4
Silver HI RIPW IP8 .... 60 A2
Silver La CHONG CM5 .... 328 E3
Silver Leys RIPS/CAP IP9 .... 87 K7
Silverlocke Rd GRAYS RM17 .... 484 C5
Silvermere VGE SS16 .... 436 B8 ▣
Silverpoint Marine CVI SS8 ..... 479 G2
Silver Rd BOC CM0 .... 425 H1
GVE DA12 .... 489 K7
Silversea Dr WOS/PRIT SS0 ..... 463 H5
Silver St ABR/ST RM4 .... 379 F7
BRTR CM7 .... 143 J2
HVHL CB9 .... 26 A1
HVHL CB9 .... 49 A5
MAL CM9 .... 338 B2 ▣
STSD CM24 .... 167 J7
WAB EN9 .... 347 J8 ▣
WIT CM8 .... 244 D1
Silverthorn Cl RCFD SS4 .... 444 A1
Silverthorne CVI SS8 .... 477 K2
Silverthorne Cl COLS CO2 .... 219 H2 ▣
Silverthorn Gdns CHING E4 ..... 402 B5
Silvertown Av SLH/COR SS17 ... 473 K3
Silvertree Cl HOC/HUL SS5 ..... 420 C7 ▣
Silver Wy WICKE SS11 .... 417 F5
Silverwood Cl CDH/CHF RM16 . 470 E7 ▣
CVI SS8 .... 477 J2
Simmonds La MAL CM9 .... 366 C4
Simmonds Wy RCHLM CM3 ..... 335 K5
Simmons La CHING E4 .... 402 E5
Simmons PI CDH/CHF RM16 .... 470 E8 ▣
Simons La COL CO1 .... 9 D5
Simpson Rd RAIN RM13 .... 450 A7
Simpsons La K/T/MI CO5 .... 279 J2
Sims Cl RCOLW CO6 .... 149 J6
ROM RM1 .... 430 A6
Sim's La HVHL CB9 .... 29 F4
Sinclair Cl COLN CO4 .... 8 B1
Sinclair Dr CHTY IP2 .... 3 D6
Sinclair Rd CHING E4 .... 402 A8
Sinclair Wk WICKW SS12 .... 417 G8
Singer Av COS CO15 .... 290 A6
Singleton Cl HCH RM12 .... 450 A5 ▣
Singleton Ct SUD CO10 .... 58 D8 ▣
Singlewell Rd GVW DA11 .... 489 G8
Sinnington End COLN CO4 ...... 187 K1
Sioux Cl COLN CO4 .... 187 K1
Sirdar Rd IP IP1 .... 2 B3
RAYL SS6 .... 441 J5
Sir Francis Wy BRW CM14 ...... 410 E5
Sir Isaac's Wk COL CO1 .... 8 B4 ▣▣
Sir Walter Raleigh Dr RAYL SS6 . 441 H1
Siskin Cl COLN CO4 .... 188 C5
Sittang Cl COLS CO2 .... 218 D4
Sitwell Cl MGTR CO11 .... 159 G1
Siward Rd WIT CM8 .... 276 D5
Six Bells Ct BRTR CM7 .... 177 J8 ▣
Sixth Av CHLM/WR CM1 .... 304 D7
CVI SS8 .... 477 J1
STSD CM24 .... 200 D2
Skarnings Ct WAB EN9 .... 348 C7
Skate's HI SUD CO10 .... 33 H3
Skeins Wy SAFWS CB11 .... 134 D1
Skelmersdale Rd COS CO15 ..... 10 C4
Skelton Cl MGTR CO11 .... 159 H1
Skerry Ri CHLM/WR CM1 .... 304 D6
Skiddaw Cl BRTR CM7 .... 209 G6
Skinner's La CHLM/GWD CM2 .. 360 D2
Skinners St BSF CM23 .... 231 G1
Skipper Ct BRTR CM7 .... 209 H3
Skitts HI BRTR CM7 .... 209 K3 ▣
Skreens Ct CHLM/WR CM1 ..... 331 K1 ▣
Sky Hall HI COLN CO4 .... 119 K6
Skylark Cl BCAYE CM11 .... 414 D4
Skylark La RIPW IP8 .... 61 J3
Skyrmans Fee FOS CO13 .... 228 D7
Sladburys La COS CO15 .... 260 B6
Slade End EPP CM16 .... 378 C2
Slade Gdns ERITH DA8 .... 480 A7
Slade Green Rd ERITH DA8 ..... 480 A7
Slade Rd COS CO15 .... 11 F1
Slade's La CHLM/GWD CM2 .... 360 C2
The Slades VGE SS16 .... 458 B5
Slade St IPNE IP4 .... 3 E4
The Slade SAFWN CB10 .... 45 G6

Slate HSTD CO9 .... 148 A4
Slaters Cl FOS CO13 .... 228 E7
Sleaford Cl CHTY IP2 .... 2 C6
Sleepers Farm Rd CDH/CHF RM16 .. 485 C01
Slewins Cl EMPK RM11 .... 430 D7
Slewins La EMPK RM11 .... 430 D7
Slipe La BROX EN10 .... 319 F6
Sloe Hl HSTD CO9 .... 147 H3
Slough Farm Rd HSTD CO9 .... 147 J3
Slough House Cl BRTR CM7 .... 210 C4
Slough La RCOLE CO7 .... 157 H8
　RCOLE CO7 .... 188 E7
Slough Rd CHLM/WR CM1 .... 269 F3
　MGTR CO11 .... 123 H3
　RCHLM CM3 .... 364 C3
Slushy La RIPS/CAP IP9 .... 126 E2
Smaley La SUD CO10 .... 34 E5
Smallbridge Entry BURES CO8 .... 116 C5
Smallgains Av CVI SS8 .... 478 D1
Small Gains La CM4 .... 387 K5
Smallgains La ING CM4 .... 388 A5
Smallwood Rd COLS CO2 .... 218 C2
Smart Cl RCOS CO16 .... 258 E7 [3]
Smart's La LOU IG10 .... 377 G8
Smarts Rd GVE DA12 .... 489 C03
Smartt Av CVI SS8 .... 478 A1 [1]
Smeaton Cl COLN CO4 .... 155 K8
　WAB EN9 .... 348 A6 [1]
Smeaton Rd WAB EN9 .... 375 G4
　WFD IG8 .... 404 C8
Smeetham Hall La SUD CO10 .... 57 F7
Smither's Cha SOSN SS2 .... 444 E8
Smithers Cl RIPS/CAP IP9 .... 87 F4
Smithers Dr CHLM/GWD CM2 .... 333 J7
Smiths Av RCHLM CM3 .... 368 E5
Smiths Fld BRTR CM7 .... 208 C3
　COL CO1 .... 9 E6
Smiths Pl KESG IP5 .... 39 H6 [6]
Smith St SBN/FI SS3 .... 466 E7
Smyatts Cl BOC CM0 .... 398 D2
Smythe Cl MAL CM9 .... 313 H1
Smythe Rd RCOS CO16 .... 258 E7 [3]
Smythies Av COL CO1 .... 8 C4
Snakes Hl BRW CM14 .... 382 E7
Snakes La RBSF CM22 .... 168 B3
　SOSN SS2 .... 443 H8
Snape Cl RCOS CO16 .... 290 C1
Snape Wy RCOS CO15 .... 228 E6 [7]
Snaresbrook Dr BSDN SS14 .... 420 E8
Sneating Hall La FOS CO13 .... 227 H5
Snelling Av GVW DA11 .... 488 E7
Snelling Gv CHLM/GWD CM2 .... 333 H7
Snipe Cl ERITH DA8 .... 480 C6
Snivellers La K/T/MI CO5 .... 225 K2
Snoreham Gdns RCHLM CM3 .... 367 J8
Snowberry Cl BRTR CM7 .... 210 C1 [3]
Snowberry Gv COLS CO2 .... 219 H2 [3]
Snowcroft RIPS/CAP IP9 .... 87 F4
Snowdonia Cl PIT SS13 .... 439 F5
Snowdon Rd CHTY IP2 .... 62 D3 [2]
Snowdrop Cl BSF CM23 .... 198 B7
　CHLM/WR CM1 .... 305 G6 [3]
　WIT CM8 .... 276 E1 [3]
Snow Hl SUD CO10 .... 31 F4
Soames Md BRW CM15 .... 355 J7
Soane St PIT SS13 .... 438 E5
Soft Rd SUD CO10 .... 56 A6
Softwater La SBF/HAD SS7 .... 461 J2
Soham Rd PEND EN3 .... 163 H8
The Soils HAR CO12 .... 163 H8
Solid La BRWN CM15 .... 383 H5
Solway TIL RM18 .... 486 D2
Somerby La BROX EN10 .... 319 G3
Somerset Av RCFD SS4 .... 444 B2
Somerset Cl COLS CO2 .... 218 C2 [3]
Somerset Cl WOS/PRIT SS0 .... 463 J1
Somerset Gdns EMPK RM11 .... 451 J2
　PIT SS13 .... 438 E7 [5]
Somerset Pl CHLM/WR CM1 .... 304 C5
Somers Rd COLW CO3 .... 218 B1
Somerton Av WOS/PRIT SS0 .... 463 H1
Somerville Gdns LOS SS9 .... 465 G5
Somme Rd COLS CO2 .... 218 E1
Somnes Av CVI SS8 .... 460 D7
Sonell Ct RCOLE CO7 .... 220 C3 [3]
Sonning Wy SBN/FI SS3 .... 466 C4
Sonters Down RCHLM CM3 .... 391 C08
Soper Cl CHING E4 .... 402 A3
Soper Ms PEND EN3 .... 375 G4 [3]
Sorrel Cl CHTY IP2 .... 2 A6
　COLN CO4 .... 186 D3
Sorrell Cl MAL CM9 .... 312 C6
　RCHLM CM3 .... 272 D7
The Sorrells SLH/COR SS17 .... 474 B3
The Sorrels SBF/HAD SS7 .... 440 C6
Sorrel Wk ROM RM1 .... 430 A5
Southall Wy BRW CM14 .... 410 C7
South Av CHING E4 .... 402 C3
　HOC/HUL SS5 .... 419 K4
　SOSN SS2 .... 19 E3

VGE SS16 .... 456 C6
South Beech Av WICKE SS11 .... 417 C6 [1]
Southborough Dr WOS/PRIT SS0 ...... 463 J3
Southborough Rd CHLM/GWD CM2.. 14 B5
Southbourne Gdns WOS/PRIT SS0 .. 463 J1
Southbourne Gv HOC/HUL SS5 .... 421 C07
　WICKW SS12 .... 416 D5
　WOS/PRIT SS0 .... 463 J2
Southbrook SBW CM21 .... 263 J4
Southbrook Dr BAR EN8 .... 346 D2 [6]
Southbury Av EN EN1 .... 374 A8
Southbury Rd HCH RM12 .... 450 E6 [3]
Southbury Rd EN EN1 .... 374 B8
Southchurch Av SBN/FI SS3 .... 467 F6 [1]
　SOS SS1 .... 19 J5
Southchurch Bvd SOS SS1 .... 465 H4
Southchurch Hall Cl SOS SS1 .... 19 H4
Southchurch Rd SOS SS1 .... 19 D4
Southcliff SBF/HAD SS7 .... 460 B1
　WOTN CO14 .... 229 H6 [3]
Southcliff Pk COS CO15 .... 229 H6
Southcliff Prom WOTN CO14 .... 229 H6
South Cl HSTD CO9 .... 147 K5
South Colne VGE SS16 .... 458 A1
Southcote Crs BSDN SS14 .... 438 B5
Southcote Rd WIT CM8 .... 277 F1 [3]
Southcote Row BSDN SS14 .... 438 C5
South Crs WOS/PRIT SS0 .... 444 A8
South Crockerford VGE SS16 .... 458 B1
Southcroft Cl FOS CO13 .... 228 B7
Southdown Rd EMPK RM11 .... 450 C1
South Dr BRW CM14 .... 411 G8
　GPK RM2 .... 430 D5
Southend Arterial Rd BSDN SS14 .... 437 J3
　EMPK RM11 .... 431 F5
　LAIN SS15 .... 16 B1
　RAYL SS6 .... 441 F5
　RBRW/HUT CM13 .... 432 E7 [7]
　SBF/HAD SS7 .... 441 H5
Southend La WAB EN9 .... 348 D8
Southend Rd BCAYE CM11 .... 414 C4
　BCAYE CM12 .... 414 C4 [3]
　GRAYS RM17 .... 484 B3
　MAL CM9 .... 336 C8
　RCFD SS4 .... 444 C6
　SBN/FI SS3 .... 466 B2
　SLH/COR SS17 .... 457 H7
　WICKE SS11 .... 417 K6

Southend Road Main Rd
　HOC/HUL SS5 .... 420 E8
Souther Cross Rd CHLM/GWD CM1 .. 269 H8
Southern Dr LOU IG10 .... 404 C2
　RCHLM CM3 .... 392 C6
Southernhay BSDN SS14 .... 17 F4 [3]
　LOS SS9 .... 442 E8
　LOU IG10 .... 404 A1 [3]
Southern Wy HLWE CM17 .... 295 G7
　HLWS CM18 .... 13 D6
　HLWW/ROY CM19 .... 12 B6
Southey Cl MAL CM9 .... 338 E1 [5]
Southey Wk TIL RM18 .... 485 C7
Southfalls Rd CVI SS8 .... 479 F7
Southfield SAFWN CB10 .... 43 F2
Southfield Cha CHLM/GWD CM2 ...... 435 K4
Southfield Cl SBF/HAD SS7 .... 441 K8
Southfield Dr SBF/HAD SS7 .... 441 K8
Southfield Rd BAR EN8 .... 346 E6
Southfields RCOLE CO7 .... 121 J7
Southfield Wy BOC CM0 .... 398 C1
Southfleet Rd GVW DA11 .... 488 E6 [3]
South Ga CHLM CM20 .... 13 D3 [3]
　PUR RM19 .... 481 K3
Southgate Cl K/T/MI CO5 .... 248 C8
Southgate Gdns SUD CO10 .... 34 E7
Southgate St SUD CO10 .... 34 E7
South Green Rd K/T/MI CO5 .... 253 H2
South Hanningfield Rd
　RCHLM CM3 .... 390 A5
South Hanningfield Wy
　WICKE SS11 .... 417 C02
South Heath Rd RCOLE CO7 .... 257 F2
South Hl FX IP11 .... 5 F4
　SLH/COR SS17 .... 456 B6
South Hill Crs SLH/COR SS17 .... 473 C2
South Hill Rd GVE DA12 .... 489 C08
South House Cha MAL CM9 .... 338 D6
South Kent Av GVW DA11 .... 488 B4
Southlands Cha CHLM/GWD CM2... 362 C03
Southlands Rd BCAYE CM11 .... 416 A7
South Mayne PIT SS13 .... 438 D7
Southmead Crs BAR EN8 .... 346 E4
Southmill Rd BSF CM23 .... 199 F7
Southminster Rd BOC CM0 .... 371 F2
Southminster Road Button's Hl
　RCHLM CM3 .... 396 E1
Southminster Road Scotts Hl
　BOC CM0 .... 398 A1
South Ordnance Rd PEND EN3 .... 375 C03
South Pde CVI SS8 .... 478 E3
South Pl HLW CM20 .... 294 E2
South Primrose Hl CHLM/WR CM1.. 14 A2
South Rdg BCAYE CM11 .... 414 D4
South Riding BSDN SS14 .... 438 B7

South Rd BCAYE CM11 .... 416 A8
　BSF CM23 .... 199 F8
　CBE/LIN CB1 .... 21 F2
　ERITH DA8 .... 480 A5
　HLW CM20 .... 294 E3
　RBSF CM22 .... 201 K5
　SAFWS CB11 .... 71 F4
　SOCK/AV RM15 .... 470 A3
Southsea Av LOS SS9 .... 462 E3
South Strd MGTR CO11 .... 123 H8
South St BOC CM0 .... 344 C3
　BOC CM0 .... 372 A2
　BRTR CM7 .... 209 K3
　BRW CM14 .... 411 F5
　BSF CM23 .... 198 E7
　COLS CO2 .... 489 C5
　GVE DA12 .... 489 C05
　IP IP1 .... 2 C2
　MAL CM9 .... 313 H1
　MGTR CO11 .... 159 J1
　RCFD SS4 .... 444 C4
　RCHLM CM3 .... 272 A6
　SAFWN CB10 .... 43 J3
South Vw CDH/CHF RM16 .... 472 B5
　GTDUN CM6 .... 204 B5
South View Av TIL RM18 .... 485 F7
South View Cl RAYL SS6 .... 442 A5
Southview Cl RCHLM CM3 .... 392 D5
South View Dr UPMR RM14 .... 451 H4
Southview Dr COS CO15 .... 260 D7 [2]
　WOS/PRIT SS0 .... 463 K3
　WOTN CO14 .... 229 H6
South View Gn RIPS/CAP IP9 .... 87 K7
South View Rd HOC/HUL SS5 .... 421 C6
　RCHLM CM3 .... 335 H7
　VGE SS16 .... 438 A8
Southwalters CVI SS8 .... 477 K1
South Wash Rd LAIN SS15 .... 437 F3
South Wy PUR RM19 .... 482 B2
　WAB EN9 .... 375 H3
Southway COLW CO3 .... 186 A2
　VGE SS16 .... 456 E3
South Weald Dr WAB EN9 .... 347 K3
South Weald Rd BRW CM14 .... 410 D6
Southwell Rd SBF/HAD SS7 .... 460 D1
South Wharf Rd GRAYS RM17 .... 483 J5
Southwick Gdns CVI SS8 .... 477 K2
Southwick Rd CVI SS8 .... 477 K2
Southwold Crs SBF/HAD SS7 .... 440 B8
Southwold Wy RCOS CO16 .... 258 C8
Southwood Cha RCHLM CM3 .... 364 A1
Southwood Gdns RAYL SS6 .... 442 C5
Sovereign Cl BRTR CM7 .... 210 C1
　RCFD SS4 .... 444 B3 [1]
Sowerberry Cl CHLM/WR CM1 .... 304 B6
Sowrey Av RAIN RM13 .... 450 A7
Spa Cl HOC/HUL SS5 .... 421 F7
Spa Dr BOC CM0 .... 342 B4 [1]
Spains Hall Pl VGE SS16 .... 437 K8
Spains Hall Rd CHONG CM5 .... 328 E3
Spalding Av CHLM/WR CM1 .... 304 A8
Spalding Cl BRTR CM7 .... 209 H1
Spalding Wy CHLM/GWD CM2 .... 333 H5
Spalt Cl RBRW/HUT CM13 .... 411 K5
Spanbeek Rd CVI SS8 .... 461 C8 [3]
Spanbies Rd RCOLE CO7 .... 121 C4 [1]
Spareleaze Hl LOU IG10 .... 377 H8
Sparepenny La North
　SAFWN CB10 .... 105 F1
Sparepenny La South
　SAFWN CB10 .... 105 C1
Sparkbridge LAIN SS15 .... 436 B7 [10]
Sparkey Cl WIT CM8 .... 277 C6 [1]
Sparks La HSTD CO9 .... 52 D7
Spar La RCHLM CM3 .... 365 J2
Sparling Cl COLS CO2 .... 218 C3
The Sparlings FOS CO13 .... 228 B5
Spa Rd HOC/HUL SS5 .... 420 E7
　K/T/MI CO5 .... 247 C1
　WIT CM8 .... 276 E2
Sparrow Cl HSTD CO9 .... 110 C5
Sparrow Rd SUD CO10 .... 58 E7
Sparrows La ING CM4 .... 330 A8
Sparrowsend Hl SAFWS CB11 .... 70 B8
Sparrows Herne COS CO15 .... 10 C1 [3]
　VGE SS16 .... 457 H2
Sparrow's La HLWE CM17 .... 266 A3
　RBSF CM22 .... 266 A6
Speckled Wood Ct BRTR CM7 .... 209 H5
Speedwell Cl WIT CM8 .... 276 D2
Speedwell Rd CHTY IP2 .... 2 A5
　COLS CO2 .... 220 A3
Spellbrook Cl WICKW SS12 .... 417 J7
Spellbrook La East BSF CM23 .... 231 K5
Spellbrook La West SBW CM21 .... 198 D1
Spencer Cl BOC CM0 .... 398 D1
Spencer Cl MAL CM9 .... 338 C5 [3]
　RBSF CM22 .... 168 D2 [1]
　STSD CM24 .... 167 K7 [3]
　WFD IG8 .... 403 K8
Spencer Ct RCHLM CM3 .... 392 E6

Spencer Gdns *RCFD* SS4 .... 422 A8
Spencer Rd *RCOS* CO16 .... 226 D3
　SAFWN CB10 .... 43 J2
　SBF/HAD SS7 .... 440 C2
Spencers Cft *HLWS* CM18 .... 294 E7
Spencer St *GVW* DA11 .... 489 F5
Spenders Cl *BSDM* SS14 .... 229 K3 🔲
Spenlow Dr *CHLM/WR* CM1 ...... 305 K6
The Spennells *RCOS* CO16 .... 226 D5
Spenser Rd *IP* IP1 .... 36 A2
Spenser Wy *COS* CO15 .... 290 B4
Spicersfield *EBAR* EN7 .... 346 A1
Spicers La *SUD* CO10 .... 34 E5
Spillbutters *BRWN* CM15 .... 383 K2
Spilsby Rd *HARH* RM3 .... 431 F2
Spindle Beams *RCFD* SS4 .... 444 C4
Spindle Rd *HVHL* CB9 .... 26 D5
Spindles *TIL* RM18 .... 485 F6
Spindle Wd *COLN* CO4 .... 187 H1
Spingate Rd *HARH* RM12 .... 450 E6 🔲
Spinks La *WIT* CM8 .... 276 E4
Spinnaker Cl *COS* CO15 .... 291 F5 🔲
Spinnaker Dr *MAL* CM9 .... 339 G2 🔲
The Spinnakers *SBF/HAD* SS7 ... 440 A8
The Spinnaker *RCHLM* CM3 ...... 392 E8
Spinnel's Hl *MCTR* CO11 .... 161 J4
Spinnel's La *MCTR* CO11 .... 161 K7
Spinney Cl *WICKE* SS11 .... 417 J6
Spinneyfields *K/T/MI* CO5 .... 248 B7
The Spinneys *HOC/HUL* SS5 ..... 420 E8
　LOS SS9 .... 443 G6
　RAYL SS6 .... 442 B4
The Spinney *BCAYW* CM12 .... 414 C1
　BROX EN10 .... 319 F1 🔲
　BRTR CM7 .... 210 B4 🔲
　CDH/CHF RM16 .... 472 A4 🔲
　CHONG CM5 .... 354 B4
　IPNE IP4 .... 64 D1
　RBRW/HUT CM13 .... 412 B2
　SAFWS CB11 .... 100 B6
　STSD CM24 .... 167 K8
Spinning Wheel Md *HLWS* CM18.. 294 E8
Spire Cl *GVE* DA12 .... 489 G6 🔲
Spire Rd *LAIN* SS15 .... 16 A3
The Spires *CHLM/GWD* CM2 ..... 333 H7
Spital La *BRW* CM14 .... 410 C6
Spital Rd *MAL* CM9 .... 337 K6
Sporehams La *CHLM/GWD* CM2 .. 362 D1
Sporhams *VGE* SS16 .... 17 D6
Sportsmans La *RCHLM* CM3 ..... 308 A3
Sportsway *COL* CO1 .... 8 B3
Spout La *ING* CM4 .... 356 D2
Spratts La *MCTR* CO11 .... 191 F1
Spriggs La *ING* CM4 .... 356 D2
Springbank Av *HCH* RM12 .... 450 D6 🔲
　MCTR CO11 .... 159 G2
Spring Cha *RCOLE* CO7 .... 220 E3
　RCOLE CO7 .... 255 J6
Spring Cl *COLN* CO4 .... 187 K2 🔲
　RCHLM CM3 .... 307 H8
　RCOS CO16 .... 258 D3
Spring Elms La *RCHLM* CM3 ..... 335 K2
Springett's Hl *BURES* CO8 .... 115 G3
Springfield *EPP* CM16 .... 350 D6
　SBF/HAD SS7 .... 461 J1
Springfield Av *FX* IP11 .... 131 H1
　RBRW/HUT CM13 .... 412 D3
Springfield Cl *CHONG* CM5 .... 326 B8
Springfield Dr *WOS/PRIT* SS0 ... 18 A1
Springfield Gdns *UPMR* RM14... 451 K4
Springfield Gn *CHLM/WR* CM1 .. 15 F1
Springfield La *IP* IP1 .... 2 A1
Springfield Lyons Ap
　CHLM/GWD CM2 .... 305 J8 🔲
Springfield Park Av
　CHLM/GWD CM2 .... 15 E3
Springfield Park La
　CHLM/GWD CM2 .... 15 F2
Springfield Park Pde
　CHLM/GWD CM2 .... 15 E3 🔲
Springfield Park Rd
　CHLM/GWD CM2 .... 15 E3
Springfield Pl *CHLM/WR* CM1 ... 305 F8 🔲
Springfield Rd *BAR* EN8 .... 346 E6
　BCAYW CM12 .... 387 H8
　BOC CM0 .... 398 A7
　CDH/CHF RM16 .... 484 D1
　CHING E4 .... 403 F4
　CHLM/GWD CM2 .... 15 D3 🔲
　CVI SS8 .... 479 F2
　SUD CO10 .... 58 B4
　WICKE SS11 .... 417 J5
Springfields *BROX* EN10 .... 319 F1
　BRTR CM7 .... 209 F3
　GTDUN CM6 .... 204 B5
　RCOLE CO7 .... 255 K7
　VGE SS16 .... 458 C2
Spring Gdns *HCH* RM12 .... 450 C5
　RAYL SS6 .... 441 H3
Spring Gardens Rd *RCOLW* CO6 .. 151 G6
Spring Gv *GVE* DA12 .... 489 G6
　LOU IG10 .... 404 A2

Springhall La *SBW* CM21 .... 263 J4
Springhall Rd *SBW* CM21 .... 263 J3
Springhead Rd *ERITH* DA8 .... 480 A5
　GVW DA11 .... 488 B5
Spring Hl *SAFWS* CB11 .... 70 B4
Springhill Cl *RCOLE* CO7 .... 190 D4
Springhill Rd *SAFWS* CB11 ...... 70 E5
Spring Hills *HLW* CM20 .... 12 A2
Springhouse La *SLH/COR* SS17 . 474 C2
Springhouse Rd *SLH/COR* SS17 . 474 A1
Springhurst Cl *IPNE* IP4 .... 37 H7
Springland Cl *IPNE* IP4 .... 37 J7
Spring La *COLW* CO3 .... 185 F5
　COLW CO3 .... 186 B6
　MAL CM9 .... 339 D1
　MAL CM9 .... 309 F3
　RCHLM CM3 .... 307 G3
　RCOLE CO7 .... 220 E3
　RCOLW CO6 .... 185 K1
　WIT CM8 .... 277 G6
Springmead *BRTR* CM7 .... 209 C6 🔲
Spring Meadow *NHMKT* IP6 ..... 39 F1
Spring Pond Cl *CHLM/GWD* CM2 . 15 F5
Spring Pond Meadow
　BRWN CM15 .... 356 A8
Spring Rd *IPNE* IP4 .... 3 F3
　K/T/MI CO5 .... 280 A1
　RCOLE CO7 .... 255 K6
　RCOS CO16 .... 289 C1
　RIPW IP8 .... 60 D3
Spring Sedge Cl *COLW* CO3 ..... 185 H6
The Springs *BROX* EN10 .... 318 E7
Springvalley La *RCOLE* CO7 ..... 189 F2
Spring Wk *BROX* EN10 .... 318 C3
Springwater Cl *LOS* SS9 .... 442 D6
Springwater Gv *LOS* SS9 .... 442 D6
Springwater Rd *LOS* SS9 .... 442 C5
Spring Wy *HSTD* CO9 .... 110 D4
Springwell Rd *SAFWN* CB10 ..... 44 B8
Springwood Dr *BRTR* CM7 .... 209 F1
Springwood Wy *ROM* RM1 .... 430 B7 🔲
Sprites End *FX* IP11 .... 94 E8
Spriteshall La *FX* IP11 .... 94 E8
Sprites La *CHTY* IP2 .... 61 J3
　RIPW IP8 .... 61 J4
Spruce Cl *K/T/MI* CO5 .... 284 D6
　LAIN SS15 .... 16 A1
　WIT CM8 .... 277 G1
Spruce Hl *HLWS* CM18 .... 322 C2
Sprundel Av *CVI* SS8 .... 478 D3
Spur Cl *ABR/ST* RM4 .... 379 F7
Spurgate *RBRW/HUT* CM13 ..... 411 K5
Surgeon Cl *HSTD* CO9 .... 110 D4 🔲
Spurgeon St *COL* CO1 .... 9 E5 🔲
The Spur *BAR* EN8 .... 346 D2 🔲
Squadrons Ap *HCH* RM12 .... 450 D7
The Square *BOC* CM0 .... 372 A1
　BROX EN10 .... 319 F1
　ING CM4 .... 388 A3
　SBW CM21 .... 263 J3 🔲
　WFD IG8 .... 403 H8
Squires Cl *BSF* CM23 .... 198 B5
Squire St *RCHLM* CM3 .... 392 E6
Squirrels Ct *CHLM/WR* CM1 ..... 304 B8 🔲
Squirrels *VGE* SS16 .... 456 C2
Squirrel's Cha *CDH/CHF* RM16 .. 485 F1 🔲
Squirrels Cl *BSF* CM23 .... 198 E5 🔲
Squirrels Fld *COLN* CO4 .... 155 G8
Squirrel's Heath Av *GPK* RM2 .. 430 C5
Squirrels Heath La *EMPK* RM11 . 430 D6
Squirrels Heath Rd *HARH* RM3 . 431 F4
The Squirrels *RIPS/CAP* IP9 ..... 87 F3
Stable Cl *COLW* CO3 .... 185 J7
　K/T/MI CO5 .... 285 G6
Stablecroft *CHLM/WR* CM1 ...... 305 G5
Stablefield Rd *FOS* CO13 .... 305 G5
Stable Ms *K/T/MI* CO5 .... 285 G5
Stacey Dr *VGE* SS16 .... 456 D3
Stacey's Mt *BCAYE* CM11 .... 415 K8
Stackfield *HLW* CM20 .... 295 F2
The Stackyard *SAFWN* CB10 .... 43 F2
Staddles *RBSF* CM22 .... 232 B4
Stadium Rd *SOSN* SS2 .... 19 D2
Stadium Wy *HLWW/ROY* CM19 . 293 H4
　SBF/HAD SS7 .... 441 H6
Staffa St *WICKW* SS12 .... 417 J8
Stafford Av *EMPK* RM11 .... 430 E5
Stafford Cl *BAR* EN8 .... 346 B3
　CDH/CHF RM16 .... 483 F5
　FOS CO13 .... 228 D7
　LOS SS9 .... 443 H7
　SLH/COR SS17 .... 486 B2
Stafford Crs *BRTR* CM7 .... 210 C1
Stafford Dr *BROX* EN10 .... 319 G2 🔲
Stafford Gn *VGE* SS16 .... 456 A1
Staffords *HLWE* CM17 .... 295 J1
Stagden Cross *BSDN* SS14 .... 228 D7
Stag La *BKHH* IG9 .... 403 J5
Stainers *BSF* CM23 .... 198 B8
Stains Cl *BAR* EN8 .... 346 E2
Stainton Rd *PEND* EN3 .... 374 C5
Stairs Rd *SBN/FI* SS3 .... 467 J1
Stalin Rd *COLS* CO2 .... 219 J1
Stallards Crs *FOS* CO13 .... 228 D7
Stambourne Rd *HSTD* CO9 .... 52 C8

Stambridge Rd *COS* CO15 .... 290 E1
　RCFD SS4 .... 423 H8
Stamford Cl *CHTY* IP2 .... 62 B5
Stammers Pl *KESC* IP5 .... 39 J5 🔲
Stammers Rd *COLN* CO4 .... 187 G1
Stanbrook Rd *GVW* DA11 .... 488 E6
Standard Av *COS* CO15 .... 289 K6
Standard Rd *COL* CO1 .... 9 E5 🔲
　PEND EN3 .... 374 E4
Standen Av *HCH* RM12 .... 450 E4
Standingford *EPP* CM16 .... 321 K2 🔲
Standley Rd *WOTN* CO14 .... 229 J4
Stane Cl *BSF* CM23 .... 198 E5
Stane Fld *RCOLW* CO6 .... 215 H2
Stanes Rd *BRTR* CM7 .... 177 J7 🔲
Staneway *VGE* SS16 .... 456 E2
Stanfield Cl *COS* CO15 .... 217 K2
Stanfield Rd *SOSN* SS2 .... 19 D2
Stanford Cl *WFD* IG8 .... 404 B8
Stanford Ct *WAB* EN9 .... 348 C7 🔲
Stanford Gdns *SOCK/AV* RM15 . 469 G8
Stanford-le-Hope By-pass
　CDH/CHF RM16 .... 472 C6
　SLH/COR SS17 .... 457 H5
Stanford Rivers Rd *CHONG* CM5 . 354 C5
Stanford Rd *CDH/CHF* RM16 .... 471 K7
　CVI SS8 .... 478 A3
　SLH/COR SS17 .... 473 H4
Stanhope Rd *BAR* EN8 .... 346 E7
Stanier Cl *SOS* SS1 .... 19 F4 🔲
Stanley Av *GPK* RM2 .... 430 B6
　IPSE IP3 .... 63 J1
　RCOLE CO7 .... 256 A6
Stanley Cl *GPK* RM2 .... 430 B6
　HCH RM12 .... 450 D3
Stanley Pi *CHONG* CM5 .... 354 C3
Stanley Ri *CHLM/GWD* CM2 ..... 333 H2 🔲
Stanley Rd *CHING* E4 .... 402 E4
　COS CO15 .... 290 E3
　CVI SS8 .... 478 C1
　FX IP11 .... 131 H4 🔲
　GRAYS RM17 .... 484 A4
　HCH RM12 .... 450 D3
　HSTD CO9 .... 147 J3
　RCFD SS4 .... 421 K6
　RCOLE CO7 .... 221 F4
　SAFWN CB10 .... 43 K2
　SBF/HAD SS7 .... 440 C8
　SOS SS1 .... 19 E5
　SUD CO10 .... 58 B5
　UPMR RM14 .... 454 E5
Stanleys Farm Rd *SAFWS* CB11 . 71 G5 🔲
Stanley Ter *BCAYW* CM12 .... 414 B4
Stanley Wood Av *SUD* CO10 .... 58 C4
Stanley Wooster Wy *COLN* CO4 . 188 B6
Stanmore Cl *COS* CO15 .... 10 A2
Stanmore Rd *WICKE* SS11 .... 418 A7 🔲
Stanmore Wy *LOU* IG10 .... 377 J3
　RCOS CO16 .... 289 H1
Stannard Wy *SUD* CO10 .... 58 D7
Stannetts *LAIN* SS15 .... 456 C5 🔲
Stansfield Rd *SBF/HAD* SS7 ..... 440 A6
Stansgate Rd *BOC* CM0 .... 341 K8
Stanstead Rd *HSTD* CO9 .... 148 A5
Stansted Cl *BCAYE* CM11 .... 414 E3 🔲
　CHLM/WR CM1 .... 332 A4
　HCH RM12 .... 450 D7 🔲
Stansted Rd *BSF* CM23 .... 199 F5
　COLS CO2 .... 219 H2 🔲
　RBSF CM22 .... 168 D4
Stansted Wy *FOS* CO13 .... 229 F7
Stanstrete Fld *BRTR* CM7 .... 208 E8 🔲
Stanton Hughes Wy *MCTR* CO11 . 159 G1
Stanway Cl *CHIG* IG7 .... 405 H8
Stanway Rd *SBF/HAD* SS7 .... 440 B8
　WAB EN9 .... 348 C7
Stanwell St *COL* CO1 .... 8 B5 🔲
Stanwyck Gdns *HARH* RM3 ...... 408 C8
Stanwyn Av *COS* CO15 .... 10 B4
Stapleford Cl *CHING* E4 .... 402 D6 🔲
　CHLM/GWD CM2 .... 15 F5
Stapleford End *WICKE* SS11 ..... 418 A8 🔲
Stapleford Rd *ABR/ST* RM4 ...... 380 B8
Staplegrove *SBN/FI* SS3 .... 466 B5
Staplers Cl *MAL* CM9 .... 310 D1 🔲
Staplers Heath *MAL* CM9 .... 310 D1
Staplers Wk *MAL* CM9 .... 278 D8
Staples Rd *LOU* IG10 .... 377 G7
Stapleton Crs *RAIN* RM13 .... 450 B7
Starfield Cl *IPNE* IP4 .... 37 K7
Star La *EPP* CM16 .... 350 E4
　GTDUN CM6 .... 205 G3
　ING CM4 .... 386 C1 🔲
　IPNE IP4 .... 3 D4
　SBN/FI SS3 .... 466 D2
Starling Cl *BKHH* IG9 .... 403 H4
Star Md *GTDUN* CM6 .... 139 K3
Starr Rd *RBSF* CM22 .... 137 G8
Station Ap *BAR* EN8 .... 346 E6 🔲
　BOC CM0 .... 398 B8
　BRTR CM7 .... 209 K5
　CVI SS8 .... 460 E7
　FOS CO13 .... 228 E8

HOC/HUL SS5 .... **421** F7 🔳
LAIN SS15 .... **16** A5
RCHLM CM3 .... **392** C5
RCHLM CM3 .... **394** D3
SOS SS1 .... **19** D4 🔳
SOSN SS2 .... **18** C2
VGE SS16 .... **458** E1
WICKE SS11 .... **417** C3
Station Approach Rd *TIL* RM18.. **489** F2
Station Av *RAYL* SS6 .... **441** H2
SOSN SS2 .... **19** D1
WICKE SS11 .... **417** F4
Station Crs *RAYL* SS6 .... **441** J2
RCHLM CM3 .... **366** B8
Station HI *BURES* CO8.............. **115** H5
Station La *HAR* CO12 .... **7** D4
HCH RM12 .... **451** F3
ING CM4 .... **386** B2
PIT SS13 .... **439** F8
Station Pde *HCH* RM12 .... **450** C5 🔳
Station Rd *BAR* EN8 .... **347** G8
BCAYW CM12......................... **414** A3
BOC CM0 .... **398** D1
BOC CM0 .... **425** G1
BROX EN10 .... **319** F2
BRTR CM7 .... **208** C6
BSF CM23 .... **198** E6
BSF CM23 .... **199** F7 🔳
CBE/LIN CB1 .... **22** D3
CHIG IG7 .... **404** E6
CHING E4 .... **402** E4
COS CO15 .... **10** C4
CVI SS8 .... **478** E3
EPP CM16 .... **350** E5
EPP CM16 .... **352** B1
FOS CO13 .... **228** A7
FX IP11 .... **94** D8
GPK RM2 .... **430** C6
GTDUN CM6............................ **204** D5
GTDUN CM6............................ **206** A6
GVW DA11 .... **488** A4
HAR CO12 .... **6** A3
HAR CO12 .... **7** E4
HAR CO12 .... **7** F3 🔳
HARH RM3 .... **431** G3 🔳
HLWE CM17 .... **295** C1
HOC/HUL SS5 .... **421** F7
HSTD CO9 .... **110** C3
HSTD CO9 .... **110** C3
HVHL CB9 .... **27** C5
K/T/MI CO5 .... **246** E2
K/T/MI CO5 .... **280** A1
LOS SS9 .... **463** F2
LOU IG10 .... **404** B1
MAL CM9 .... **281** J8
MAL CM9 .... **314** D3
MAL CM9 .... **338** C2
MGTR CO11 .... **123** G8
MGTR CO11 .... **161** F3
MGTR CO11 .... **163** J8
RAYL SS6 .... **441** H2
RBRW/HUT CM13 .... **168** D3
RBSF CM22 .... **168** D1
RBSF CM22 .... **201** K6
RCHLM CM3 .... **275** K8
RCHLM CM3 .... **366** C8
RCHLM CM3 .... **396** D4
RCOLE CO7 .... **220** E5
RCOLE CO7 .... **221** K5
RCOLE CO7 .... **222** E7
RCOLE CO7 .... **223** F5
RCOLE CO7 .... **223** K6
RCOLE CO7 .... **255** J7
RCOLW CO6 .... **149** G4
RCOLW CO6 .... **149** H6
RCOLW CO6 .... **150** B6
RCOLW CO6 .... **151** C7
RCOLW CO6 .... **215** K1
RCOS CO16 .... **226** C5
RIPS/CAP IP9 .... **87** J7
SAFWS CB11 .... **69** K8
SAFWS CB11 .... **70** E5
SAFWS CB11 .... **100** B5
SBF/HAD SS7 .... **460** C5
SBW CM21 .... **263** K2
SOS SS1 .... **466** A5
STSD CM24 .... **167** K7 🔳
SUD CO10 .... **31** G6
SUD CO10 .... **54** E8
SUD CO10 .... **58** B6
TIL RM18 .... **486** C6
UPMR RM14 .... **451** K3
WAB EN9 .... **348** A1
WICKE SS11 .... **417** F3
Station St *CHTY* IP2 .... **3** D6
SAFWS CB11 .... **70** E4
WOTN CO14 .... **229** H6
Station Wy *BKHH* IG9 .... **404** A4
VGE SS16 .... **17** E5
Staverton Rd *EMPK* RM11 .... **430** E8 🔳
Stays La *CHONG* CM5 .... **328** E2
Steam Mill Rd *MGTR* CO11 ...... **160** D5

Stebbing Rd *GTDUN* CM6........ **206** C6
Stebbings *VGE* SS16 .... **16** A6
Steed CI *HCH* RM12 .... **450** C3 🔳
Steeds Meadow *SUD* CO10 ...... **34** E5 🔳
Steeds Wy *LOU* IG10 .... **377** G7
Steele CI *RCOLW* CO6 .... **215** J2 🔳
Steen CI *ING* CM4 .... **386** B1
Steeple Bumpstead Rd *HVHL* CB9 ... **49** J5
Steeple CI *MAL* CM9 .... **339** F1
RCFD SS4 .... **444** A2
Steeplefield *LOS* SS9 .... **443** F7
Steeplehall *PIT* SS13 .... **438** D8
Steeple Hts *SBF/HAD* SS7 .... **440** A7 🔳
Steeple Mdw *BOC* CM0 .... **398** B1
Steeple Rd *BOC* CM0 .... **370** B7
RCHLM CM3 .... **367** K7
Steeple Vw *BSF* CM23 .... **198** E5
Steeple Wy *BRWN* CM15 .... **383** K3 🔳
Steerforth CI *CHLM/WR* CM1 .. **303** K6 🔳
Stell Av *CVI* SS8 .... **460** E8
Stella Maris CI *CVI* SS8 .... **479** F2
Stennetts CI *FX* IP11 .... **94** C7
Stenning Av *TIL* RM18 .... **277** H3
Stepfield *WIT* CM8 .... **450** B7
Stephen Av *RAIN* RM13 .... **27** F5 🔳
Stephen CI *HVHL* CB9 .... **34** D8
SUD CO10 .... **34** D8
Stephen Cranfield CI
K/T/MI CO5 .... **220** D6 🔳
Stephen Marshall Av *BRTR* CM7 .. **106** D7
Stephen Rd *KESG* IP5 .... **39** J5
Stephens CI *HARH* RM3 .... **408** D8
Stephen's Ct *IPNE* IP4 .... **37** K7 🔳
Stephens Crs *SLH/COR* SS17 ... **475** F2 🔳
Stephenson Av *TIL* RM18 .... **485** F7
COLN CO4 .... **156** A7
COS CO15 .... **259** K5
LOS SS9 .... **442** D7
RCHLM CM3 .... **394** C5
Stephenson Rd West *COS* CO15 .. **259** J4
Sterling Av *BAR* EN8 .... **346** D8
Sterling CI *COLW* CO3 .... **185** K8
Sterling Rd *COLW* CO3 .... **478** D1
Stevens CI *CVI* SS8 .... **207** C7
Stevens La *GTDUN* CM6 .... **207** C7
Stevenson CI *ERITH* DA8 .... **480** C6 🔳
Stevenson Rd *IP* IP1 .... **2** C3
Stevenson Wy *WICKW* SS12 .. **417** F8
Stevens Rd *WIT* CM8 .... **276** E4
Steward CI *BAR* EN8 .... **346** E4
Stewards CI *EPP* CM16 .... **350** E7
FOS CO13 .... **228** A7
Stewards Elm Farm La *RCFD* SS4.. **445** G1
Stewards Green Rd *EPP* CM16 .. **351** F6
Stewart Av *UPMR* RM14 .... **451** J4
Stewart PI *WICKW* SS12 .... **417** J8 🔳
The Stewarts *BSF* CM23 .... **198** D6
Stewarts Wy *BSF* CM23 .... **166** C3
Stewart Young Gv *KESG* IP5 .... **39** H6 🔳
Steyning Av *SOSN* SS2 .... **465** H5
Stifford Clays Rd *CDH/CHF* RM16.. **470** D8
CDH/CHF RM16 .... **470** C7 🔳
Stifford HI *CDH/CHF* RM16..... **470** B8
SOCK/AV RM15 .... **470** A7
Stifford Rd *SOCK/AV* RM15 ... **470** A7 🔳
Stile Cft *HLWS* CM18 .... **294** E7
Stile La *RAYL* SS6 .... **441** J3
Stilemans *WICKE* SS11 .... **417** G5 🔳
Stilemans Wd *BRTR* CM7 .... **210** C5
The Stiles *MAL* CM9 .... **339** G2
Stirling Av *LOS* SS9 .... **462** C5
Stirling CI *RAYL* SS6 .... **419** G8
Stirling Dr *HVHL* CB9 .... **26** E5
Stirling PI *PIT* SS13 .... **438** E5
Stirrup CI *CHLM/WR* CM1 ...... **305** G6
Stivvy's Rd *MAL* CM9 .... **336** C2
Stock Cha *MAL* CM9 .... **310** D8
Stock CI *SOSN* SS2 .... **464** C1
Stockhouse CI *MAL* CM9 .... **280** C5
Stockhouse Rd *K/T/MI* CO5.... **249** F6
Stockingswater La *PEND* EN3 .. **374** E7
Stock La *ING* CM4 .... **386** C1
Stockley CI *HVHL* CB9 .... **27** J6 🔳
Stockmers End *RIPS/CAP* IP9 ... **87** F4
Stock Rd *BCAYE* CM11 .... **414** C1
BCAYW CM12......................... **414** C3
CHLM/GWD CM2 .... **360** C2
ING CM4 .... **388** B2
SOSN SS2 .... **464** C1
Stocksfield *BRWN* CM15 .... **383** H3
Stocks La *BRWN* CM15 .... **383** H3
Stockwell *COL* CO1 .... **8** B4
Stockwell CI *BCAYE* CM11 ..... **414** C7 🔳
EBAR EN7 .... **346** A2
Stockwood *SBF/HAD* SS7 ...... **441** F6
Stoke Br *CHTY* IP2 .... **3** D5
Stokeash CI *RCOS* CO16 .... **290** C2
Stoke Hall Rd *CHTY* IP2 .... **3** D5
Stoke Park Dr *CHTY* IP2 .... **62** A5
Stoke Rd *RCOLW* CO6 .... **118** C4
SUD CO10 .... **30** E7
The Stokes *WOTN* CO14 .... **229** G4
Stoke St *CHTY* IP2 .... **3** D5

Stollery CI *KESG* IP5 .... **39** G6
Stonards HI *EPP* CM16 .... **351** G5
LOU IG10 .... **404** C2
Stondon Rd *CHONG* CM5 .... **354** D4
Stonebridge HI *RCOLW* CO6 .. **148** E6
Stonechat Rd *BCAYW* CM12 .. **414** D5
CHTY IP2 .... **61** J2
Stonecrop *COLN* CO4 .... **186** D3
Stonegrove Rd *FX* IP11 .... **5** D6
Stonehall Dr *RCOS* CO16 .... **259** F4
Stonehall La *RCOS* CO16 .... **193** J4
Stoneham Av *RCOS* CO16 ...... **258** C8
Stoneham St *RCOLW* CO6 ...... **213** G3
Stonehill CI *LOS* SS9 .... **463** C1
Stonehill Rd *CHLM/WR* CM1 .. **329** K1
LOS SS9 .... **463** F1
Stonehill Wy *K/T/MI* CO5 ...... **284** C6
Stonehouse La *PUR* RM19 ...... **482** B4
Stone La *K/T/MI* CO5 .... **279** H3
MGTR CO11 .... **162** C1
Stoneleigh *SBW* CM21 .... **263** H2 🔳
Stoneleigh Av *EN* EN1 .... **374** B3
Stoneleigh CI *BAR* EN8 .... **346** D7 🔳
Stoneleigh Pk *COLW* CO3 ...... **218** A2
Stoneleighs *SBF/HAD* SS7 ..... **440** E7
Stone Lodge La *CHTY* IP2 .... **2** B6
Stone Lodge La West *CHTY* IP2 . **2** A6
Stone Lodge Wk *CHTY* IP2 .... **2** C6
Stoneness Rd *WTHK* RM20...... **482** E5
Stone Path Dr *RCHLM* CM3 .... **307** K1
Stone Rd *RCOLE* CO7 .... **191** G4
Stones Green Rd *HAR* CO12 .... **194** A3
HAR CO12 .... **194** D5
Stone St *GVE* DA12 .... **489** C4
Stoney Common *STSD* CM24 .. **167** K8
Stoney Common Rd *STSD* CM24 .. **167** J8
Stoneyfield Dr *STSD* CM24...... **167** K8
Stoney Hills *BCAYE* CM11 ...... **388** D8
BOC CM0 .... **398** C5
Stoney La *RCOLE* CO7 .... **256** A5
Stonycroft CI *PEND* EN3 .... **374** E6
Stony La *CHONG* CM5 .... **325** H5
GTDUN CM6............................ **139** K3 🔳
Stony Pth *LOU* IG10 .... **377** H5
Stonyshotts *WAB* EN9 .... **348** A8
Stony Wd *HLWS* CM18 .... **13** D4
Stopford Ct *IP* IP1 .... **2** B1
Stores Rd *K/T/MI* CO5 .... **248** A7
Stormonts Wy *VGE* SS16 .... **456** E3
Stornoway Rd *SOSN* SS2 .... **19** F3
Storr Gdns *RBRW/HUT* CM13.. **412** C1
Stortford Hall Pk *BSF* CM23 ... **199** G5
Stortford Hall Rd *BSF* CM23 .. **199** G5
Stortford Rd *GTDUN* CM6 .... **202** E6
GTDUN CM6............................ **204** A5
GTDUN CM6............................ **262** J7
RBSF CM22 .... **264** E1
SAFWS CB11 .... **134** B1
Stort Ldg *BSF* CM23 .... **198** C3 🔳
Stort MI *HLW* CM20 .... **263** F7
Stort Rd *BSF* CM23 .... **198** E7 🔳
Stort Valley Wy *HLW* CM20 ... **263** H6
HLWE CM17 .... **296** E3
HLWW/ROY CM19 .... **292** B5
SBW CM21 .... **264** C3
Stour Av *FX* IP11 .... **5** E4
Stour CI *HAR* CO12 .... **164** C3
SBN/FI SS3 .... **466** D7 🔳
SUD CO10 .... **33** J3
Stourdale CI *MGTR* CO11 .... **159** F2
Stour Gdns *SUD* CO10 .... **84** D1
Stourmead CI *HVHL* CB9 .... **28** C3
Stour Rd *CDH/CHF* RM16 .... **485** F4
HAR CO12 .... **7** E3 🔳
Stourside *RIPS/CAP* IP9 .... **129** F5
Stour St *MGTR* CO11 .... **159** J1
SUD CO10 .... **32** C5
SUD CO10 .... **58** A6
Stourton Rd *WIT* CM8 .... **276** E2 🔳
Stour V *HSTD* CO9 .... **52** A2
Stour Valley Pth *BURES* CO8 .. **115** H3
HVHL CB9 .... **28** C1
RCOLW CO6 .... **117** G3
RCOLW CO6 .... **120** A2
SUD CO10 .... **53** H1
Stour Valley Rd *HVHL* CB9 ...... **27** H6
Stour Valley Wk *SUD* CO10 ..... **32** C3
SUD CO10 .... **58** A7
Stourview Av *MGTR* CO11 ..... **160** B1
Stourview CI *MGTR* CO11 ...... **160** C1
Stour Wy *UPMR* RM14 .... **432** B8
Stowe's La *BOC* CM0 .... **371** J1
Stow Rd *RCHLM* CM3 .... **393** K1
The Stow *HLW* CM20 .... **13** F1
St Peter's Wy *BOC* CM0 .... **344** C8
CHLM/GWD CM2 .... **361** J8
CHONG CM5 .... **355** G3
ING CM4 .... **356** C5
ING CM4 .... **387** J1
RCHLM CM3 .... **364** E4
RCHLM CM3 .... **368** E1
Stradbroke Gv *BKHH* IG9 .... **404** A4
Stradbroke Rd *IPNE* IP4........... **37** J6
Straight Rd *COLN* CO4 .... **155** H1
COLW CO3 .... **185** K7

HARH RM3 .... **408** C8
KIR/NAC IP10 .... **65** G5
MGTR CO11 .... **160** D4
RCOLE CO7 .... **257** G2
Straight Wy COLS CO2 .... **250** A3
The Straits WAB EN9 .... **347** H6
The Strand CHTY IP2 .... **62** E5
Strangman Av SBF/HAD SS7 .... **461** G1
Strasbourg Rd CVI SS8 .... **461** J8
Stratfield Dr BROX EN10 .... **318** E1
Stratford Gdns SLH/COR SS17 .... **473** K3
Stratford PI WOTN CO14 .... **229** J5 ⬚
Stratford Rd COS CO15 .... **260** B7
  IP IP1 .... **36** B3
  RCOLE CO7 .... **121** F6
Strathmore TIL RM18 .... **486** D5 ⬚
Strathmore Gdns HCH RM12 .... **450** A2
Strathmore Rd RCHLM CM3 .... **394** D5
Strattonhall Drift RIP/CAP IP10 .... **92** E3
Stratton Rd HARH RM3 .... **409** H8
Stratton Wk HARH RM3 .... **409** H8 ⬚
Strawberry Cl BRTR CM7 .... **209** K4
Strawberry Flds HVHL CB9 .... **26** D6
Strawberry La K/T/MI CO5 .... **280** C2
Strawbrook HI RCHLM CM3 .... **273** C1
Straw La SUD CO10 .... **58** B6 ⬚
The Street BOC CM0 .... **369** J3
  BRTR CM7 .... **179** J3
  BRTR CM7 .... **208** B4
  BRTR CM7 .... **211** F7
  BRTR CM7 .... **211** J3
  BSF CM23 .... **134** A6
  BSF CM23 .... **166** E3
  CHLM/GWD CM2 .... **360** D3
  CHLM/WR CM1 .... **302** A7
  CHONG CM5 .... **328** B2
  CHONG CM5 .... **355** F1
  FOS CO13 .... **228** B4
  FRAM/WMKT IP13 .... **39** H1
  GTDUN CM6 .... **205** J5
  GTDUN CM6 .... **236** C6
  HAR CO12 .... **163** K4
  HSTD CO9 .... **51** J7
  HSTD CO9 .... **78** E6
  HSTD CO9 .... **113** H6
  HSTD CO9 .... **146** D5
  K/T/MI CO5 .... **214** B8
  K/T/MI CO5 .... **248** D3
  KIR/NAC IP10 .... **65** G8
  MAL CM9 .... **279** K8
  MAL CM9 .... **282** A5
  MAL CM9 .... **336** D3
  MGTR CO11 .... **124** B4
  MGTR CO11 .... **161** F4
  RBSF CM22 .... **200** B8
  RBSF CM22 .... **264** D5
  RCHLM CM3 .... **270** A3
  RCHLM CM3 .... **272** D7
  RCHLM CM3 .... **275** C2
  RCHLM CM3 .... **307** K1
  RCHLM CM3 .... **367** H8
  RCHLM CM3 .... **392** B1
  RCHLM CM3 .... **393** J1
  RCOLE CO7 .... **121** F5
  RCOLE CO7 .... **122** A3
  RCOLE CO7 .... **157** H5
  RCOLW CO6 .... **151** F8
  RCOLW CO6 .... **182** K5
  RCOS CO16 .... **193** F8
  RCOS CO16 .... **225** G4
  RCOS CO16 .... **258** C1
  RIPS/CAP IP9 .... **62** C7
  RIPS/CAP IP9 .... **86** E4
  RIPS/CAP IP9 .... **90** A7
  RIPS/CAP IP9 .... **126** E3
  RIPS/CAP IP9 .... **128** A3
  RIPS/CAP IP9 .... **128** C2
  RIPW IP8 .... **61** F5
  RIPW IP8 .... **61** J7
  SUD CO10 .... **33** G5
  SUD CO10 .... **33** J7
  SUD CO10 .... **52** E2
  SUD CO10 .... **53** D2
  SUD CO10 .... **55** H5
  SUD CO10 .... **57** F8
  SUD CO10 .... **59** K1
  SUD CO10 .... **84** B3
  WIT CM8 .... **243** J4
  WIT CM8 .... **278** A8
Stretford Ct WIT CM8 .... **244** D2 ⬚
Strethall Rd SAFWS CB11 .... **43** F8
Strickmere RCOLE CO7 .... **121** F3
Stromburg Rd CVI SS8 .... **460** D8
Stromness PI WOTN SS2 .... **19** F4
Stromness Rd SOSN SS2 .... **19** F5
Strood Cl K/T/MI CO5 .... **284** D6
The Strood K/T/MI CO5 .... **284** D1
Struan Av SLH/COR SS17 .... **457** F8
Strudwick Cl BRTR CM7 .... **209** J3 ⬚
Strutt Cl RCHLM CM3 .... **308** A1 ⬚
Struttons Av GVW DA11 .... **488** C3
Stuart Cl BRWN CM15 .... **410** E1
  CHLM/GWD CM2 .... **333** K7
  CVI SS8 .... **478** B1

IPNE IP4 .... **37** H6
SBN/FI SS3 .... **466** E1
Stuart Rd GRAYS RM17 .... **484** A4 ⬚
  GVW DA11 .... **489** F4
  SOSN SS2 .... **19** D2
Stuart St SOSN SS2 .... **19** D1 ⬚
Stuarts Wy BRTR CM7 .... **210** A3 ⬚
Stuart Wy BCAYE CM11 .... **415** F4 ⬚
  EBAR EN7 .... **346** B5
Stubbers La UPMR RM14 .... **452** B7
Stubbs Cl FOS CO13 .... **228** D6
  HVHL CB9 .... **26** D4 ⬚
  IPSE IP3 .... **63** J4
  MGTR CO11 .... **159** G1 ⬚
Stubbs La BRTR CM7 .... **210** B3
Stublands BSDN SS14 .... **438** C7
Studd's La COLN CO4 .... **186** E1
Studland Av WICKW SS12 .... **416** C5
Stump La CHLM/WR CM1 .... **115** E1
Sturdee Av IPSE IP3 .... **63** K2
Sturlas Wy BAR EN8 .... **346** D7
Sturmer Rd HVHL CB9 .... **27** J7
Sturrick La RCOLE CO7 .... **223** J4
Sturrocks VGE SS16 .... **458** B7
Stutton Cl RIPS/CAP IP9 .... **125** H3
Stutton Gn RIPS/CAP IP9 .... **125** H4
Stutton La RIPS/CAP IP9 .... **88** D8
Stutton Rd MGTR CO11 .... **124** D1
Styles BRTR CM7 .... **141** J3
Sudbourne Av RCOS CO16 .... **290** C1
Sudbourne Rd FX IP11 .... **5** D2 ⬚⬚
Sudbrook La WICKW SS12 .... **417** G7 ⬚
Sudbury Cl HOC/HUL SS5 .... **443** G5
Sudbury Rd BCAYE CM11 .... **389** J8
  BURES CO8 .... **115** J4
  FX IP11 .... **4** C3 ⬚
  HSTD CO9 .... **148** A2
  SUD CO10 .... **59** K6
Sudburys Farm Rd BCAYW CM12 .... **413** G7
Sudeley Gdns HOC/HUL SS5 .... **420** E7
Sudicamps St WAB EN9 .... **348** C7
Suez Rd PEND EN3 .... **374** E8
Suffield Rd CHING E4 .... **402** E8
Suffolk Av K/T/MI CO5 .... **285** F6
  LOS SS9 .... **463** G2
Suffolk Cl COLN CO4 .... **9** D2
  COS CO15 .... **260** C6
Suffolk Coast & Heaths Pth
  FX IP11 .... **131** J4
  IPSE IP3 .... **63** J7
  KIR/NAC IP10 .... **64** B6
  RIPS/CAP IP9 .... **91** H4
  RIPS/CAP IP9 .... **125** K3
  RIPS/CAP IP9 .... **127** J6
Suffolk Crs MAL CM9 .... **338** A4
Suffolk Dr LAIN SS15 .... **436** C7
Suffolk Rd GVE DA12 .... **489** J4
  IPNE IP4 .... **3** E2
  MAL CM9 .... **338** A4
  SUD CO10 .... **58** B5
Suffolk St WOTN CO14 .... **229** H5 ⬚⬚
  EMPK RM11 .... **431** H6 ⬚
Suffolk Wy CVI SS8 .... **477** J1
Sugar La HSTD CO9 .... **109** C8
Sugden Av WICKW SS12 .... **416** D6
Sullivan Cl COLN CO4 .... **188** B7 ⬚
Sullivan Rd TIL RM18 .... **485** F7
Sullivan Wy VGE SS16 .... **436** B8
Summercourt Rd WOS/PRIT SS0 .... **18** B4 ⬚
Summerdale BCAYW CM12 .... **414** B3
  RCHLM CM3 .... **396** E2 ⬚
Summerfield Cl IPNE IP4 .... **38** B5
Summerfield Rd LOU IG10 .... **404** A2
Summerfields HSTD CO9 .... **110** D4
  ING CM4 .... **386** C2 ⬚
Summer Hill Rd SAFWS CB11 .... **70** E5
Summerwood Cl SBF/HAD SS7 .... **461** H2 ⬚
The Summit LOU IG10 .... **377** H5
Sumners Farm Cl EPP CM16 .... **321** J2 ⬚
Sumpters Wy SOSN SS2 .... **444** C7
Sunbank GTDUN CM6 .... **204** D5
Sunbeam Av COS CO15 .... **290** A4
Sunbury Ct SBN/FI SS3 .... **466** D3
Sunbury Wy MAL CM9 .... **338** B5
Sun Ct ERITH DA8 .... **480** A8
Sundale Cl COS CO15 .... **260** D7 ⬚
Sunderland Av FX IP11 .... **130** E7
Sunfield Cl IPNE IP4 .... **37** K7
Sunflower Wy HARH RM3 .... **430** E3
Sun La GVE DA12 .... **489** H7
Sun Lido Square Gdns BRTR CM7 .... **209** F5
Sunnedon VGE SS16 .... **438** A8
Sunningdale BSF CM23 .... **198** D7
  CVI SS8 .... **478** C1 ⬚
Sunningdale Av IPNE IP4 .... **38** B8
  LOS SS9 .... **463** H4
Sunningdale Dr FX IP11 .... **131** J1
Sunningdale Fall RCHLM CM3 .... **308** B1 ⬚
Sunningdale Rd CHLM/WR CM1 .... **332** A1
  RAIN RM13 .... **450** B8
  RCHLM CM3 .... **308** B1 ⬚
Sunningdale Wy FOS CO13 .... **228** D6
Sunninghill GVW DA11 .... **488** D7 ⬚
Sunnings La UPMR RM14 .... **452** A7
Sunnybank Cl LOS SS9 .... **443** G7

Sunny Cft HLWS CM18 .... **13** F6 ⬚
Sunnycroft Gdns UPMR RM14 .... **452** C1
Sunnydene Av CHING E4 .... **402** E8
Sunnydene Cl HARH RM3 .... **431** G2
Sunnyfield Gdns HOC/HUL SS5 .... **420** C7
Sunnyfields Rd BRTR CM7 .... **178** C3
Sunnymede CHIC IG7 .... **406** A6
Sunnymede Cl SBF/HAD SS7 .... **441** F7
Sunny Point WOTN CO14 .... **229** K2
Sunny Rd HOC/HUL SS5 .... **421** F8
The Sunny Rd PEND EN3 .... **374** D5
Sunnyside BRTR CM7 .... **209** H2
  STSD CM24 .... **167** K7
  VGE SS16 .... **456** A1 ⬚
  WAB EN9 .... **320** B4
Sunnyside Dr CHING E4 .... **402** D3
Sunnyside Gdns UPMR RM14 .... **451** K4
Sunnyside Rd EPP CM16 .... **350** D6
  RCOLW CO6 .... **152** C8
Sunnyside Wy RCOS CO16 .... **258** E4
Sunny Vw BOC CM0 .... **342** C5
Sunray Av FX IP11 .... **131** J1
Sun Ray Av RBRW/HUT CM13 .... **412** D2
Sunrise Av CHLM/WR CM1 .... **304** C8
  HCH RM12 .... **450** D4 ⬚
Sunset Av CHING E4 .... **402** C4
  WFD IG8 .... **403** H8
Sunset Cl ERITH DA8 .... **480** C8 ⬚
Sun St BCAYW CM12 .... **414** B4
  SBW CM21 .... **263** K4
  WAB EN9 .... **347** J7
Surbiton Av SOS SS1 .... **465** G5
Surbiton Rd IP IP1 .... **2** A2
  SOSN SS2 .... **465** G4
Surig Rd CVI SS8 .... **478** A1
Surman Crs RBRW/HUT CM13 .... **412** B3
Surrey Av LOS SS9 .... **463** G2
Surrey Dr EMPK RM11 .... **431** H7
Surrey La K/T/MI CO5 .... **280** A1
Surrey Wy FX IP11 .... **5** F3
  IP IP1 .... **2** B3
Surrey Wy LAIN SS15 .... **436** B7
Sussex Av HARH RM3 .... **431** G2
Sussex Cl CVI SS8 .... **461** F8
  LAIN SS15 .... **436** C7
  RCHLM CM3 .... **306** D5
Sussex Gdns COS CO15 .... **260** C7
Sussex Rd BRW CM14 .... **410** E7
  COLW CO3 .... **186** D6
Sussex Wy BCAYW CM12 .... **387** H7
  CVI SS8 .... **461** F8 ⬚
Sutcliffe Cl WICKW SS12 .... **417** G7
Sutherland Bvd LOS SS9 .... **462** C3
Sutherland PI WICKW SS12 .... **417** G8
Sutton Acres RBSF CM22 .... **232** D6
Sutton Cl BROX EN10 .... **318** E2
  LOU IG10 .... **404** B3
Sutton Court Dr RCFD SS4 .... **444** C6
Sutton Md CHLM/GWD CM2 .... **333** J7 ⬚
Sutton Park Av COLW CO3 .... **218** B2
Sutton Rd RCFD SS4 .... **444** D5
  SOSN SS2 .... **19** D2
Suttons Av HCH RM12 .... **450** D4
Suttons Gdns HCH RM12 .... **450** D4
Suttons La HCH RM12 .... **450** E6
Suttons Rd SBN/FI SS3 .... **467** G5
Swale Cl SOCK/AV RM15 .... **468** E6 ⬚
Swale Rd SBF/HAD SS7 .... **441** G8
Swallowcliffe SBN/FI SS3 .... **466** C4
Swallow Cl CDH/CHF RM16 .... **483** F3
  COLS CO2 .... **218** B8
  FX IP11 .... **95** K8
  RAYL SS6 .... **441** G2 ⬚
Swallowdale COLS CO2 .... **219** K2 ⬚
  COS CO15 .... **10** C1
Swallow Dl VGE SS16 .... **17** F6
Swallow Dr SBF/HAD SS7 .... **460** A3
Swallow Fld RCOLW CO6 .... **149** J7
Swallow Rd CHTY IP2 .... **61** J2
  WICKE SS11 .... **417** F3
Swallows HLWE CM17 .... **295** G1
Swallow's Rw RCOLE CO7 .... **224** C4
The Swallows BCAYE CM11 .... **414** D5
Swallow Wk HSTD CO9 .... **148** A2 ⬚
Swanage Rd SOSN SS2 .... **19** E3
Swan And Pike Rd PEND EN3 .... **375** G4
Swan Av UPMR RM14 .... **452** C2
Swanbourne Dr HCH RM12 .... **450** E5
Swan Cha HSTD CO9 .... **110** D5
Swan Cl COLN CO4 .... **188** B7
  LAIN SS15 .... **16** C4 ⬚
  RCHLM CM3 .... **307** K1
Swan Ct BSF CM23 .... **198** E7 ⬚
  MAL CM9 .... **338** D1 ⬚
  MGTR CO11 .... **160** D2 ⬚
Swan Dl COS CO15 .... **10** C1
Swanfield SUD CO10 .... **34** E6
Swanfield Rd BAR EN8 .... **346** E7
Swan Gv RCOLW CO6 .... **151** F8
Swan HI RIPW IP8 .... **61** G3
Swan La BRWN CM15 .... **383** G3
  HVHL CB9 .... **27** G5
  ING CM4 .... **387** K2
  LOU IG10 .... **403** K3
  NHMKT IP6 .... **37** G1

SUD CO10 .... **34** E6
WICKE SS11 .... **417** G4
Swan Md *VGE* SS16 .... **458** A1
Swan Pas *COL* CO1 .... **8** B4
Swan Rd *RCOS* CO06 .... **194** A8
Swanscomb Rd *RCOLW* CO6 .... **150** C8
Swansea Av *CHTY* IP2 .... **62** D4
Swansea Rd *PEND* EN3 .... **374** C8
Swans Green Cl *SBF/HAD* SS7 .... **441** F7
Swanshope *LOU* IG10 .... **377** K6
Swan Side *BRTR* CM7 .... **209** J2
Swans Rd *BAR* EN8 .... **346** D8
Swanstead *VGE* SS16 .... **458** B1
Swan St *HSTD* CO9 .... **110** D4
K/T/MI CO5 .... **247** F2
RCOLW CO6 .... **185** F2
Swan Wy *PEND* EN3 .... **374** D6
Swan Yd *RCOLW* CO6 .... **213** H3
Swatchway Cl *IPSE* IP3 .... **63** K5
Swaynes *RCOLE* CO7 .... **121** F3
Sweden Cl *HAR* CO12 .... **6** A4
Sweet Briar *BSF* CM23 .... **198** A7
Sweet Briar Av *SBF/HAD* SS7 .... **460** C3
Sweet Briar Dr *LAIN* SS15 .... **16** B1
Sweet Briar Rd *COLW* CO3 .... **185** H6
Sweet Md *SAFWN* CB10 .... **71** F2
Sweyne *HLWE* CM17 .... **295** C8
Sweyne Av *HOC/HUL* SS5 .... **443** H1
WOS/PRIT SS0 .... **18** C5
Sweyne Cl *RAYL* SS6 .... **441** G1
Swift Av *COS* CO15 .... **290** B7
Swift Cl *BRTR* CM7 .... **209** K5
UPMR RM14 .... **452** B2
Swiftsure Rd *CDH/CHF* RM16 .... **483** F3
Swinborne Ct *PIT* SS13 .... **438** E3
Swinborne Rd *PIT* SS13 .... **439** F4
Swinburne Gdns *TIL* RM18 .... **485** G8
Swinburne Rd *IP* IP1 .... **36** A2
Swindon Gdns *HARH* RM3 .... **409** G8
Swindon Rd *HARH* RM3 .... **409** G8
Swinton Cl *CHTY* IP2 .... **61** K4
Swiss Av *CHLM/WR* CM1 .... **14** A1
Sworders Yd *BSF* CM23 .... **198** E6
Sycamore Av *UPMR* RM14 .... **451** H4
Sycamore Cl *CVI* SS8 .... **477** K2
GVE DA12 .... **489** J5
RAYL SS6 .... **419** G7
RBSF CM22 .... **201** K6
RIPW IP8 .... **61** J3
TIL RM18 .... **484** E7
WIT CM8 .... **245** G8
Sycamore Dr *BRW* CM14 .... **411** F4
Sycamore Fld *HLWW/ROY* CM19 .... **321** J1
Sycamore Gv *BRTR* CM7 .... **209** G3
SOSN SS2 .... **19** E2
Sycamore Pl *RCOLE* CO7 .... **223** K5
Sycamore Rd *COLN* CO4 .... **9** F5
MAL CM9 .... **310** C7
SUD CO10 .... **58** E7
The Sycamores *BSF* CM23 .... **199** G7
Sycamore Wy *CHLM/GWD* CM2 .... **332** S7
COS CO15 .... **290** E2
FOS CO13 .... **228** C7
MGTR CO11 .... **123** J5
RCFD SS4 .... **423** G4
SOCK/AV RM15 .... **470** B4
Sydenham Cl *ROM* RM1 .... **430** A6
Sydervelt Rd *CVI* SS8 .... **478** A1
Sydner Ct *CHLM/GWD* CM2 .... **333** J8
Sydney Rd *LOS* SS9 .... **462** C3
SBF/HAD SS7 .... **460** B1
TIL RM18 .... **485** F8
Sydney St *COLS* CO2 .... **219** J4
RCOLE CO7 .... **255** K8
Sykes Md *RAYL* SS6 .... **441** J4
Sylvan Av *EMPK* RM11 .... **431** G8
Sylvan Cl *CDH/CHF* RM16 .... **483** H7
CHLM/GWD CM2 .... **332** D7
CVI SS8 .... **478** B3
LAIN SS15 .... **436** C7
Sylvan Tryst *BCAYW* CM12 .... **414** C1
Sylvan Wy *CHIG* IG7 .... **406** A6
LAIN SS15 .... **436** A6
LOS SS9 .... **462** B1
Sylvesters *HLWW/ROY* CM19 .... **293** H7
Sylvia Av *RBRW/HUT* CM13 .... **412** B5
Symmons Ct *BRTR* CM7 .... **208** C4
Symonds Ct *BAR* EN8 .... **346** D2
Symonds La *CBE/LIN* CB1 .... **22** D2
Symons Av *LOS* SS9 .... **443** F6

T

Tabora Av *CVI* SS8 .... **460** E8
Tabor Av *BRTR* CM7 .... **209** H2
Tabor Ct *RCOLE* CO7 .... **255** J5
Tabor Rd *COLN* CO4 .... **9** E4
Tabors Av *CHLM/GWD* CM2 .... **333** H6
Tabrum's La *RCHLM* CM3 .... **392** B6
The Tabrums *RCHLM* CM3 .... **392** C4
Tabrums Wy *UPMR* RM14 .... **452** B1

Tacket St *IPNE* IP4 .... **3** D4
Tacon Rd *FX* IP11 .... **5** E6
Tadlows Cl *UPMR* RM14 .... **451** J6
Tadworth Pde *HCH* RM12 .... **450** C5
Taffrail Gdns *RCHLM* CM3 .... **392** E6
Tailors Ct *SOSN* SS2 .... **444** C8
Tailors Wy *SOSN* SS2 .... **444** C8
Taits *SLH/COR* SS17 .... **474** B3
Takeley Cl *WAB* EN9 .... **347** K7
Takeley End *VGE* SS16 .... **17** E5
Takely Ride *VGE* SS16 .... **17** E5
Talbot Av *COS* CO15 .... **290** B7
RAYL SS6 .... **441** H2
Talbot Rd *RCOS* CO16 .... **258** C1
SUD CO10 .... **58** C4
Talbot St *HAR* CO12 .... **7** E4
Talbrook *BRW* CM14 .... **410** C6
Talcott Rd *COLS* CO2 .... **219** H3
Talisman Cl *K/T/MI* CO5 .... **248** B7
Tallboys Cl *KESG* IP5 .... **39** G5
Tallis Cl *SLH/COR* SS17 .... **473** J2
Tallis Rd *LAIN* SS15 .... **16** B2
Tallon Rd *RBRW/HUT* CM13 .... **412** D1
Tallow Ga *RCHLM* CM3 .... **392** E6
Tall Trees *COLN* CO4 .... **187** F2
Tall Trees Cl *EMPK* RM11 .... **430** E8
Tally Ho *COLN* CO4 .... **187** J1
Tallyho Cnr *RCOLE* CO7 .... **121** F2
Tally-ho Dr *RBRW/HUT* CM13 .... **413** G4
Talus Ct *PUR* RM19 .... **482** A3
Talza Wy *SOSN* SS2 .... **444** C8
Tamar Cl *UPMR* RM14 .... **432** B8
Tamar Dr *SOCK/AV* RM15 .... **468** E6
Tamarisk *SBF/HAD* SS7 .... **460** B1
Tamarisk Rd *SOCK/AV* RM15 .... **470** A4
SOCK/AV RM15 .... **470** A2
SOCK/AV RM15 .... **470** A3
Tamarisk Wy *COLN* CO4 .... **188** B6
COS CO15 .... **290** B7
Tamar Ri *CHLM/WR* CM1 .... **304** C3
Tambour Cl *RCOLW* CO6 .... **183** F5
Tamworth Cha *COLS* CO2 .... **219** H3
Tanfield Cl *EBAR* EN7 .... **346** A1
Tanfield Dr *BCAYW* CM12 .... **414** B3
Tangent Link *HARH* RM3 .... **430** E3
Tangent Rd *HARH* RM3 .... **430** E3
Tangerine Cl *COLN* CO4 .... **9** F5
Tangham Wk *BSDN* SS14 .... **17** F3
Tangmere Cl *WICKE* SS11 .... **418** A7
Tangmere Crs *HCH* RM12 .... **450** C7
Tan House La *BRW* CM14 .... **382** C7
Tankerville Dr *LOS* SS9 .... **462** E2
Tank Hill Rd *PUR* RM19 .... **481** H3
Tank La *PUR* RM19 .... **481** H3
Tan La *RCOS* CO16 .... **226** B8
Tanner Cl *RCOS* CO16 .... **290** D2
Tanners Meadow *BRTR* CM7 .... **210** B3
Tanners Wy *RCHLM* CM3 .... **392** C5
SAFWN CB10 .... **71** F4
Tanswell Av *PIT* SS13 .... **438** E6
Tanswell Cl *PIT* SS13 .... **438** E7
Tansy Cl *HARH* RM3 .... **431** F1
The Tanyard *GTDUN* CM6 .... **139** L3
Tany's Dell *HLW* CM20 .... **294** E2
Tapley Rd *CHLM/WR* CM1 .... **304** B7
Tapsworth Cl *COS* CO15 .... **10** A2
Tapwoods *COLW* CO3 .... **186** B6
Tara Cl *COLN* CO4 .... **9** F2
Taranto Cl *CVI* SS8 .... **478** D2
Tarnworth Rd *HARH* RM3 .... **409** H8
Tarpan Wy *BROX* EN10 .... **319** F8
Tarragona Av *COLS* CO2 .... **219** J1
Tarragon Cl *K/T/MI* CO5 .... **248** A8
Tasker Rd *CDH/CHF* RM16 .... **485** C2
Tasman Cl *SLH/COR* SS17 .... **474** B1
Tasmania Av *IPNE* IP4 .... **38** B7
Tasman Rd *HVHL* CB9 .... **27** J6
Tatsfield Av *WAB* EN9 .... **319** K5
Tattenham Rd *LAIN* SS15 .... **436** C6
Tattersall Gdns *LOS* SS9 .... **462** B4
Tattersalls Cha *BOC* CM0 .... **398** E1
Taunton Cl *IP* IP1 .... **36** D1
Taunton Dr *WOS/PRIT* SS0 .... **463** J1
Taunton Rd *CHLM/WR* CM1 .... **305** G8
FX IP11 .... **5** F2
HARH RM3 .... **408** D7
Taunton V *GVE* DA12 .... **489** J8
Taveners Green Cl *WICKW* SS12 .... **417** H7
Taverners Cl *WIT* CM8 .... **277** F1
Taverners Wy *CHING* E4 .... **403** F4
Tavistock Av *HARH* RM3 .... **430** E3
Tavistock Dr *BCAYW* CM12 .... **387** F8
Tavistock Rd *CHLM/WR* CM1 .... **305** F2
LAIN SS15 .... **16** A2
LAIN SS15 .... **16** A3
Tawell Ms *K/T/MI* CO5 .... **248** B8
Tawney Cl *RIPS/CAP* IP9 .... **87** F4
Tawney Common *EPP* CM16 .... **352** A6
Tawney La *ABR/ST* RM4 .... **380** C2
EPP CM16 .... **352** C6
Tawneys Ride *BURES* CO8 .... **115** K4
Tawneys Rd *HLWS* CM18 .... **13** F5
Tawny Av *UPMR* RM14 .... **451** J6
Taylifers *HLWW/ROY* CM19 .... **321** J2
Taylor Av *CHLM/WR* CM1 .... **304** A8

Taylor Ct *COL* CO1 .... **8** B4
Taylor Dr *MGTR* CO11 .... **159** H1
Taylors End Rd *STSD* CM24 .... **201** F4
Taylor's Rd *K/T/MI* CO5 .... **220** C5
Tay Wy *ROM* RM1 .... **430** A3
Teagles *LAIN* SS15 .... **16** C4
Teal Av *RCHLM* CM3 .... **368** E5
Teal Cl *BRTR* CM7 .... **208** E8
CHTY IP2 .... **61** K2
RCOLE CO7 .... **188** D5
Teal Wy *K/T/MI* CO5 .... **247** F3
Tedder Cl *COLS* CO2 .... **219** H1
Tees Cl *UPMR* RM14 .... **452** B1
Tees Dr *HARH* RM3 .... **408** E6
Tees Rd *CHLM/WR* CM1 .... **304** E7
Teign Dr *WIT* CM8 .... **276** D3
Teignmouth Dr *RAYL* SS6 .... **466** C5
Teignrace *SBN/FI* SS3 .... **419** J8
Telford Rd *BRTR* CM7 .... **209** K4
COS CO15 .... **259** K5
Telford Wy *COLN* CO4 .... **156** A7
Tempest Wy *RAIN* RM13 .... **450** B7
Templar Rd *BRTR* CM7 .... **210** C3
Templars *WIT* CM8 .... **277** F1
Temple Bank *HLW* CM20 .... **263** F8
Temple Cl *EBAR* EN7 .... **229** F7
FOS CO13 .... **16** A3
LAIN SS15 .... **462** A2
SBF/HAD SS7 .... **9** F1
Temple Ct *COLN* CO4 .... **244** C2
Temple La *BRTR* CM7 .... **292** D5
Temple Md *HLWW/ROY* CM19 .... **277** F2
Templemead *WIT* CM8 .... **123** H6
Temple Pattle *MGTR* CO11 .... **485** F5
Templer Av *CDH/CHF* RM16 .... **218** D3
Temple Rd *COLS* CO2 .... **66** A1
IPSE IP5 .... **402** B7
Templeton Av *CHING* E4 .... **310** B8
Temple Wy *MAL* CM9 .... **188** B4
Templewood Ct *SBF/HAD* SS7 .... **461** J2
Templewood Rd *COLN* CO4 .... **438** E7
PIT SS13 .... **461** J2
SBF/HAD SS7 .... **478** E2
Tempitn Av *CVI* SS8 .... **62** D4
Ten Acre Ap *MAL* CM9 .... **310** B8
Tenby Rd *CHTY* IP2 .... **374** D7
PEND EN3 .... **441** F2
Tendring Av *RAYL* SS6 .... **12** C5
Tendring Rd *HLWS* CM18 .... **192** B5
RCOLE CO7 .... **193** G3
RCOS CO16 .... **484** E2
Tennyson Av *GRAYS* RM17 .... **19** E2
SOSN SS2 .... **348** A8
WAB EN9 .... **462** B5
Tennyson Cl *BRTR* CM7 .... **209** J5
LOS SS9 .... **430** D2
Tennyson Dr *PIT* SS13 .... **458** E1
Tennyson Rd *CHLM/WR* CM1 .... **304** D2
HARH RM3 .... **37** H8
IPNE IP4 .... **338** C4
MAL CM9 .... **412** B3
RBRW/HUT CM13 .... **488** C3
Tennyson Wk *GVW* DA11 .... **485** G8
Tennyson Wy *HCH* RM12 .... **450** A2
Tenpenny Hl *RCOLE* CO7 .... **222** D7
Tensing Av *GVW* DA11 .... **488** D3
Tensing Gdns *BCAYW* CM12 .... **414** A4
Tenterfield *GTDUN* CM6 .... **204** D4
Tenter Fld *RCOLE* CO7 .... **121** G4
Tenterfield Rd *MAL* CM9 .... **338** C3
Tenterfields *PIT* SS13 .... **439** F5
SAFWS CB11 .... **100** A4
Teramo Rd *CVI* SS8 .... **478** D2
Tercel Pth *CHIG* IG7 .... **406** A7
Terence Webster Rd *WICKW* SS12 .... **417** G7
Teresa Gdns *BAR* EN8 .... **346** C8
Terling *VGE* SS16 .... **17** F5
Terling Cl *COLS* CO2 .... **219** H4
Terling Hall Rd *RCHLM* CM3 .... **274** D4
Terling Rd *RCHLM* CM3 .... **275** K7
WIT CM8 .... **276** A3
The Terlings *BRW* CM14 .... **410** D6
Terminal Cl *SBN/FI* SS3 .... **466** E6
Terminus Cl *VGE* SS16 .... **458** E1
Terminus St *HLW* CM20 .... **13** D2
Termitts Cha *RCHLM* CM3 .... **275** K6
WIT CM8 .... **276** C6
Terms Av *CVI* SS8 .... **461** F8
Tern Cl *HVHL* CB9 .... **27** J6
K/T/MI CO5 .... **247** F2
RCHLM CM3 .... **368** E5
Terndale *COS* CO15 .... **10** C1
Tern Gdns *UPMR* RM14 .... **452** B2
Terni Rd *CVI* SS8 .... **478** D2
Tern Rd *CHTY* IP2 .... **62** B3
Tern Wy *BRW* CM14 .... **410** B7
Terrace Hall Cha *RCOLW* CO6 .... **154** D7
Terrace St *GVE* DA12 .... **489** G4
The Terrace *GVE* DA12 .... **489** G4
SBN/FI SS3 .... **466** E7
Teviot Av *SOCK/AV* RM15 .... **468** E6
Tew Cl *K/T/MI* CO5 .... **248** B7
Tewkesbury Rd *COS* CO15 .... **10** B3
Tewkes Rd *CVI* SS8 .... **461** J8

Tey Rd *RCOLW* CO6 .... 150 A7
  RCOLW CO6 .... 183 K5
  RCOLW CO6 .... 213 K5
Tey Road Cl *RCOLW* CO6 .... 149 K7
Thackeray Av *TIL* RM18 .... 485 G7
Thackeray Ct *BRTR* CM7 .... 209 K5
Thackeray Rd *IP* IP1 .... 36 A2
Thackerey Rw *WICKW* SS12 .... 417 G8
Thal Massing Cl *RBRW/HUT* CM13 .. 412 A5
Thames Cl *BRTR* CM7 .... 210 C4
  LOS SS9 .... 462 B4
  RAYL SS6 .... 441 H4
  SLH/COR SS17 .... 474 C2
Thames Crs *SLH/COR* SS17 ...... 457 J8
Thames Dr *CDH/CHF* RM16 ...... 485 F4
  LOS SS9 .... 462 B4
Thames Haven Rd *SLH/COR* SS17 .. 474 C2
Thameside Crs *CVI* SS8 .... 477 K2
Thames Av *CVI* SS8 .... 477 K3
  GRAYS RM17 .... 484 A6
Thames Vw *BOC* CM0 .... 398 A7
  GVW DA11 .... 488 D5
Thamley *PUR* RM19 .... 481 H3
Thanet Rd *IPNE* IP4 .... 37 K7
Thatchers Cl *LOU* IG10 .... 378 A6
Thatchers Cft *RCHLM* CM3 ..... 367 G7
Thatchers Dr *RCOLE* CO7 .... 189 J7
The Thatchers *BSF* CM23 .... 198 B8
Thaxted Gn *RBRW/HUT* CM13 .. 412 B1
Thaxted Rd *BKHH* IG9 .... 404 B3
  SAFWS CB11 .... 71 G6
Thaxted Wk *COLS* CO2 .... 219 H5
Thaxted Wy *WAB* EN9 .... 347 K7
Thear Cl *WOS/PRIT* SS0 .... 463 K1
Theberton Rd *IPSE* IP3 .... 63 K4
Thelma Av *CVI* SS8 .... 478 A1
Theobalds Av *GRAYS* RM17 .... 484 B4
Theobald's Gv *BAR* EN8 .... 346 D6
Theobald's La *BAR* EN8 .... 346 B6
Theobalds Rd *LOS* SS9 .... 462 B4
Thetford *PLAIN* SS15 .... 16 B1
Thetford Rd *IP* IP1 .... 2 A2
Theydon Cl *WAB* EN9 .... 348 D7
Theydon Crs *BSDN* SS14 .... 438 C3
Theydon Gdns *RAIN* RM13 ..... 450 A8
Theydon Ga *EPP* CM16 .... 378 C2
Theydon Gv *EPP* CM16 .... 350 E4
Theydon Park Rd *EPP* CM16 ... 378 C5
Theydon Pl *EPP* CM16 .... 350 D5
Theydon Rd *EPP* CM16 .... 350 B8
Thielen Rd *CVI* SS8 .... 461 F8
Thieves Cnr *CHLM/WR* CM1 .... 331 F1
Third Av *CHLM/WR* CM1 .... 304 D8
  CO SS15 .... 11 E3
  CVI SS8 .... 477 J1
  FOS CO13 .... 261 J1
  HAR CO12 .... 7 D5
  HLWS CM18 .... 13 D3
  HLWW/ROY CM19 .... 12 B4
  HSTD CO9 .... 148 C4
  RCOS CO16 .... 289 H6
  SLH/COR SS17 .... 474 A1
  WICKE SS11 .... 417 K7
  WOTN CO16 .... 229 K2
  WTHK RM20 .... 482 D5
Thirlmere Cl *BRTR* CM7 .... 209 G6
Thirlmere Rd *SBF/HAD* SS7 .... 440 D6
Thirslet Dr *MAL* CM9 .... 338 E1
Thirtieth St *STSD* CM24 .... 201 G2
Thirtle Cl *RCOS* CO16 .... 10 A1
Thissell Rd *CVI* SS8 .... 461 F8
Thistle Cl *CHTY* IP2 .... 2 A5
  LAIN SS15 .... 17 D1
Thistledene Av *CRW* RM5 .... 407 G1
Thistledown *BRTR* CM7 .... 176 D6
  BSDN SS14 .... 437 K7
  COLN CO4 .... 187 J2
Thistle Md *LOU* IG10 .... 377 J7
Thistle Rd *GVE* DA12 .... 489 K5
Thistley Cl *LOS* SS9 .... 463 G1
  MAL CM9 .... 312 C7
Thistley Crs *SAFWS* CB11 ...... 135 K4
Thistley Green Rd *BRTR* CM7 .. 178 A6
Thoby La *BRWN* CM15 .... 384 E3
Thomas Av *FX* IP11 .... 94 D7
Thomas Bata Av *TIL* RM18 ..... 486 C5
Thomas Bell Rd *RCOLW* CO6 .. 149 H7
Thomas Cl *BRWN* CM15 .... 411 H5
  CHLM/GWD CM2 .... 333 H3
Thomas Dr *CVI* SS8 .... 460 D8
  GVE DA12 .... 489 J7
Thomasin Rd *PIT* SS13 .... 439 F4
Thomas Rd *COS* CO15 .... 10 A3
  PIT SS13 .... 439 H6
Thomas Rochford Wy *BAR* 347 F1
Thomas St *RCOLE* CO7 .... 255 K7
Thomas Wakley Cl *COLN* CO4 .. 155 G8
Thomas Wk *SAFWS* CB11 .... 68 E4
Thompson Av *COLW* CO3 .... 186 A7
  CVI SS8 .... 479 F2
Thompson Rd *IP* IP1 .... 2 A1
Thorington Av *SBF/HAD* SS7 .. 441 J7

Thorington Rd *RAYL* SS6 .... 442 B4
Thorin's Ga *RCHLM* CM3 .... 392 C7
Thorley Hl *BSF* CM23 .... 198 E8
Thorley La *BSF* CM23 .... 198 A8
Thorley Park Rd *BSF* CM23 ..... 231 K1
Thorley Rd *CDH/CHF* RM16 .... 470 E8
Thornbera Cl *BSF* CM23 .... 231 K1
Thornbera Gdns *BSF* CM23 .... 231 J1
Thornbera Rd *BSF* CM23 .... 231 K1
Thornberry Av *RCOS* CO16 .... 225 G5
Thornborough Av *RCHLM* CM3 .. 392 E6
Thornbury Rd *COS* CO15 .... 10 C3
Thornbush *LAIN* SS15 .... 16 C4
Thorncroft *EMPK* RM11 .... 430 C8
  SAFWN CB10 .... 71 G5
Thorndale *SBF/HAD* SS7 .... 441 C6
Thorndales *BRW* CM14 .... 411 C7
Thorndon Ap *RBRW/HUT* CM13 .. 434 C2
Thorndon Av *RBRW/HUT* CM13 .. 434 B7
Thorndon Ga *RCOS* CO16 ...... 290 C1
Thorndon Ga *RBRW/HUT* CM13 .. 412 B8
Thorndon Park Cl *LOS* SS9 ..... 442 C8
Thorndon Park Crs *LOS* SS9 ... 442 C8
Thorndon Park Dr *LOS* SS9 .... 442 C8
Thorne Rd *K/T/MI* CO5 .... 246 D3
Thorney Bay Rd *CVI* SS8 .... 477 K3
Thorney Rd *RIPS/CAP* IP9 ...... 87 F3
Thornfield Rd *BSF* CM23 .... 198 D5
Thornford Gdns *SOSN* SS2 ..... 444 C8
Thorn Gv *BSF* CM23 .... 199 G7
Thornhams Wy *CHTY* IP2 .... 2 B6
Thornhill *EPP* CM16 .... 324 C8
  LOS SS9 .... 463 F1
  RCHLM CM3 .... 365 K4
Thornhill Cl *FOS* CO13 .... 228 E6
Thornley Dr *IPNE* IP4 .... 38 A5
Thornley Rd *FX* IP11 .... 131 K3
Thornridge *BRW* CM14 .... 410 E4
Thorns Wy *WOTN* CO14 .... 229 F6
Thornton Dr *COLN* CO4 .... 8 B1
Thornton Pl *ING* CM4 .... 388 B3
Thornton Rd *RBSF* CM22 .... 202 C5
Thornton Wy *LAIN* SS15 .... 436 B8
Thorn Wy *FX* IP11 .... 5 E3
Thornwood *COLN* CO4 .... 187 G1
Thornwood Cl *K/T/MI* CO5 .... 285 F7
Thornwood Rd *EPP* CM16 ...... 351 F2
Thorolds *VGE* SS16 .... 458 B2
Thoroughgood Rd *COS* CO15 .. 10 C4
Thorpe Bay Gdns *SOS* SS1 ..... 465 K1
Thorpe Cl *HOC/HUL* SS5 .... 443 G1
Thorpedene Av *HOC/HUL* SS5 .. 419 K3
Thorpedene Gdns *SBN/FI* SS3 .. 466 C5
Thorpe Esp *SOS* SS1 .... 465 K7
Thorpe Hall Av *SOS* SS1 .... 465 K5
Thorpe Hall Cl *SOS* SS1 .... 465 K5
Thorpe La *FX* IP11 .... 94 A5
Thorpe Park La *RCOS* CO16 ... 226 D6
Thorpe Rd *COS* CO15 .... 259 H6
  FOS CO13 .... 227 J6
  HOC/HUL SS5 .... 443 G1
  RCOS CO16 .... 193 H8
  RCOS CO16 .... 259 H3
Thorpe's Hl *RIPW* IP8 .... 60 C2
Thorp Leas *CVI* SS8 .... 478 B3
Thorrington Rd *RCOLE* CO7 .... 223 H5
  RCOS CO16 .... 258 E1
Thors Oak *SLH/COR* SS17 ...... 474 A3
Thracian Cl *RCOLE* CO7 .... 218 B3
Threadneedle St *RCOLE* CO7 .. 121 J6
Three Acres *RCOS* CO16 .... 289 C1
Three Crowns Rd *COLN* CO4 .. 8 A1
Three Forests Wy *ABR/ST* RM4 .. 380 D3
  CHONG CM5 .... 299 F5
Three forests Wy *CHONG* CM5 .. 327 F1
Three Forests Wy *GTDUN* CM6 .. 267 F5
  HLWW/ROY CM19 .... 292 B5
  LOU IG10 .... 377 F5
  SBW CM21 .... 263 J4
  WAB EN9 .... 321 F3
  WAB EN9 .... 376 E2
Three Forest Wy *RBSF* CM22 .. 200 C8
Three Gates Rd *HSTD* CO9 ..... 147 J5
Three Horseshoes Rd
  HLWW/ROY CM19 .... 12 B4
Tremhall Av *RBSF* CM22 .... 201 G4
Threshelford *VGE* SS16 .... 17 D6
Thresher Cl *BSF* CM23 .... 198 B8
Threshers End *COLW* CO3 ...... 185 J8
Thrifts Md *EPP* CM16 .... 378 C3
Thrift Wd *RCHLM* CM3 .... 363 J4
Through Jollys *KESG* IP5 .... 39 H5
Throwley Ct *PIT* SS13 .... 439 F8
Thrushdale *COS* CO15 .... 10 C1
Thundersley Church Rd
  SBF/HAD SS7 .... 440 C8
Thundersley Gv *SBF/HAD* SS7 .. 440 E8
Thundersley Park Rd
  SBF/HAD SS7 .... 440 D8
Thurlby Cl *WFD* IG8 .... 404 C8
Thurloe Wk *GRAYS* RM17 ...... 483 K2
Thurlow Dr *SOS* SS1 .... 465 J4
Thurston Cl *COLN* CO4 .... 9 F2
Thurlstone *SBF/HAD* SS7 .... 441 H8
Thurmans La *FX* IP11 .... 94 C7

Thurrock Park Wy *GRAYS* RM17 .. 484 C6
Thurso Cl *HARH* RM3 .... 431 J1
Thurstable Cl *MAL* CM9 .... 314 E3
Thurstable Rd *MAL* CM9 .... 314 D3
Thurstable Wy *MAL* CM9 .... 314 E3
Thurstans *HLWW/ROY* CM19 .. 321 K2
Thurston Av *SOSN* SS2 .... 465 H4
Thurston Ct *FX* IP11 .... 4 C4
Thyme Rd *K/T/MI* CO5 .... 248 B8
Thynne Rd *BCAYE* CM11 .... 414 D3
Tiberius Cl *HVHL* CB9 .... 27 K6
Tiberius Gdns *WIT* CM8 .... 276 E5
Tickenhall Dr *HLWE* CM17 ...... 295 H5
Tickfield Av *SOSN* SS2 .... 18 C2
Tideswell Cl *BRTR* CM7 .... 210 C1
Tideway *MAL* CM9 .... 338 D5
Tidings *HSTD* CO9 .... 147 K5
Tidworth Av *WICKE* SS11 ...... 417 H5
Tidy's La *EPP* CM16 .... 350 C8
Tiffin Dr *K/T/MI* CO5 .... 248 C8
Tighfield Wk *RCHLM* CM3 ...... 392 C8
Tilburg Rd *CVI* SS8 .... 478 A1
Tilbury Gdns *TIL* RM18 .... 489 F2
Tilbury Md *HLWS* CM18 .... 294 E7
Tilbury Rd *HSTD* CO9 .... 53 F6
  RBRW/HUT CM13 .... 434 D6
Tile Barn La *MGTR* CO11 .... 158 B3
Tilegate Rd *CHONG* CM5 .... 324 C1
  HLWS CM18 .... 13 F5
Tile House Rd *RCOLW* CO6 ..... 154 C5
Tilkey Rd *RCOLW* CO6 .... 213 G1
Tillingham Ct *WAB* EN9 .... 348 C7
Tillingham Gn *LAIN* SS15 .... 436 B7
Tillingham Rd *BOC* CM0 .... 371 F8
Tillingham Wy *RAYL* SS6 .... 441 F2
Tillwicks Rd *HLWS* CM18 .... 13 F4
Tilney Turn *VGE* SS16 .... 458 C1
Timber Hl *COL* CO1 .... 9 E5
Timberlog Cl *BSDN* SS14 .... 438 B7
Timberlog La *BSDN* SS14 .... 438 B8
Timbermans Vw *VGE* SS16 ..... 458 C2
Timbers Cl *BRTR* CM7 .... 208 E6
Timsons La *CHLM/GWD* CM2 .. 15 F1
Tinabrook Cl *CHTY* IP2 .... 62 A4
Tindall Cl *HARH* RM3 .... 431 G4
Tindal St *CHLM/WR* CM1 .... 14 C3
Tindon End Rd *SAFWN* CB10 .. 104 C3
Tine Rd *CHIG* IG7 .... 405 H8
Tinker Av *BRTR* CM7 .... 107 K7
Tinker's La *RCFD* SS4 .... 444 C4
Tinker St *HAR* CO12 .... 163 J4
Tinnocks La *BOC* CM0 .... 342 B4
Tintagel Wy *MAL* CM9 .... 338 A5
Tintern Av *WOS/PRIT* SS0 ...... 463 K3
Tintern Cl *CHTY* IP2 .... 62 C3
Tiplers Br *BCAYE* CM11 .... 388 D8
Tippersfield *SBF/HAD* SS7 ..... 460 D1
Tippett Cl *COLN* CO4 .... 188 B7
Tipps Cross La *BRWN* CM15 .. 355 K8
Tips Cross Md *BRWN* CM15 ... 385 K1
Tiptree Cl *CHING* E4 .... 402 D6
  EMPK RM11 .... 451 H2
  LOS SS9 .... 463 C1
Tiptree Ct *RBRW/HUT* CM13 .. 412 C1
Tiptree Gv *WICKW* SS12 .... 417 G6
Tiptree Hall La *K/T/MI* CO5 .... 279 K2
Tiptree Rd *WIT* CM8 .... 278 E4
Tiree Cha *WICKW* SS11 .... 417 J8
Titania Cl *COLN* CO4 .... 188 C6
Titan Rd *GRAYS* RM17 .... 483 K4
Titchfield Rd *PEND* EN3 .... 374 E3
Tithe Cl *WIT* CM8 .... 276 E2
Tithelands *HLWW/ROY* CM19 .. 293 H8
The Tithe *WICKW* SS12 .... 416 E2
Titley Cl *CHING* E4 .... 402 B8
Titus Wy *COLN* CO4 .... 155 J7
Tiverton Dr *HARH* RM3 .... 409 H8
Tobruk Rd *CHLM/WR* CM1 ..... 304 B7
  COLS CO2 .... 218 E2
Toddbrook *HLWW/ROY* CM19 .. 12 B4
Toft Av *GRAYS* RM17 .... 484 C3
Tofts Cha *RCHLM* CM3 .... 307 J8
Tofts Wk *BRTR* CM7 .... 209 J2
Toga Cl *COLS* CO2 .... 218 B3
Tog La *RCOLW* CO6 .... 154 B2
Tokely Rd *RCOLE* CO7 .... 223 F2
Toledo Cl *SOS* SS1 .... 19 E4
Toledo Rd *SOS* SS1 .... 19 E4
Toller Rd *IPSE* IP3 .... 3 F6
Tollesbury Cl *WICKW* SS12 .... 417 H7
Tollesbury Rd *MAL* CM9 .... 313 J1
Tolleshunt D'arcy Rd *MAL* CM9 .. 312 D2
Tollgate *SBF/HAD* SS7 .... 441 H7
Tollgate Dr *COLW* CO3 .... 185 G7
Tollgate East *COLW* CO3 .... 185 H7
Tollgate Rd *BAR* EN8 .... 374 D1
  COLW CO3 .... 185 H7
Toll Gate Rd *RIPS/CAP* IP9 .... 87 F4
Tollgate West *COLW* CO3 ...... 185 H6
Tolliday Cl *RCOLE* CO7 .... 220 D3
Tolworth Rd *IPNE* IP4 .... 37 J7
Tomkins Cl *SLH/COR* SS17 ..... 473 J3
Tomkyns La *UPMR* RM14 ...... 432 A5
Tomline Rd *FX* IP11 .... 131 H5
  IPSE IP3 .... 37 J8

Tomlyns Cl RBRW/HUT CM13 .... 412 D2
Tom's La BRTR CM7 .... 106 B7
Tom Tit La MAL CM9 .... 336 E5
Tonbridge Rd HARH RM3 .... 430 E2
  HOC/HUL SS5 .... 421 G6
Tongres Rd CVI SS8 .... 478 A1
Tony Webb Av COLN CO4 .... 187 J1
Took Dr RCHLM CM3 .... 392 C7
Tooley St GVW DA11 .... 488 C5
Toot Hill Rd CHONG CM5 .... 353 F3
Top House Ri CHING E4 .... 402 E3
Toplands Av SOCK/AV RM15 .... 468 D8
Toppesfield Av WICKW SS12 .... 417 F8
Toppesfield Rd HSTD CO9 .... 79 J5
Top Rd MAL CM9 .... 280 C5
  MAL CM9 .... 336 D3
  SAFWX CB10 .... 73 K8
Tor Bryan ING CM4 .... 386 B5
Torney Cl VGE SS16 .... 456 A1
Toronto Rd TIL RM18 .... 419 J8
Torquay Cl RAYL SS6 .... 463 F4
Torquay Rd LOS SS9 .... 463 F4
Torquay Rd CHLM/WR CM1 .... 305 F8
Torrance Cl HCH RM12 .... 450 D2
Torrington SBN/FI SS3 .... 466 C5
Torrington Cl CHLM/WR CM1 .... 305 G8
Torrington Dr LOU IG10 .... 378 A4
Torrington Gdns LOU IG10 .... 378 A8
Torsi Rd CVI SS8 .... 478 D2
Tortoiseshell Wy BRTR CM7 .... 209 H4
Tortosa Cl COLS CO2 .... 219 J1
Torver Cl BRTR CM7 .... 209 F7
Totham Hill Gn MAL CM9 .... 279 G2
Totlands Dr COS CO15 .... 259 H6
Tot La BSF CM23 .... 199 J2
Totman Crs RAYL SS6 .... 441 J5
Totman Crs RAYL SS6 .... 441 H5
Totnes Wk CHLM/WR CM1 .... 305 G7
Totteridge Cl RCOS CO16 .... 10 A2
Totteridge Rd PEND EN3 .... 374 D3
Toucan Cl SBN/FI SS3 .... 466 D4
Toucan Wy COS CO15 .... 10 C1
  VGE SS16 .... 457 H2
Toulmin Rd RCHLM CM3 .... 308 A1
Tovell's Rd IPNE IP4 .... 37 H7
Tovey Cl WAB EN9 .... 320 A5
Tower Av CHLM/WR CM1 .... 14 A2
  LAIN SS15 .... 16 A3
Tower Cl EPP CM16 .... 324 D6
Tower Ct BRW CM14 .... 410 E5
Tower Court Ms WOS/PRIT SS0 .... 18 B5
Tower Cut RCOLE CO7 .... 255 K7
Towerfield Cl SBN/FI SS3 .... 466 D6
Towerfield Rd SBN/FI SS3 .... 466 C6
Tower Hl BRW CM14 .... 411 F5
Tower Mill Rd IP IP1 .... 2 A1
Tower Rd CHLM/WR CM1 .... 331 F4
  COS CO15 .... 10 B6
  EPP CM16 .... 350 C4
  FX IP11 .... 220 E3
  RCOLE CO7 .... 255 K7
Towers Rd GRAYS RM17 .... 484 B4
  MAL CM9 .... 310 E8
Tower St RCOLE CO7 .... 255 K8
Tower Vw CBE/LIN LB3 .... 23 F2
Town End Rd WIT CM8 .... 276 E5
Townfield Cnr GVE DA12 .... 489 H6
Townfield Rd BAR EN8 .... 444 C4
Townfield St CHLM/WR CM1 .... 14 B2
Townfield Wk SBN/FI SS3 .... 466 D1
Towngate BSDN SS14 .... 17 E4
Town Mead Rd WAB EN9 .... 347 J8
Townsend Rd K/T/MI CO5 .... 248 A7
Town St GTDUN CM6 .... 139 K3
Towse Rd RCOS CO16 .... 258 E8
Tracyes Rd HLWS CM18 .... 295 F7
Traddles Ct CHLM/WR CM1 .... 304 B7
Trafalgar Av BROX EN10 .... 319 F3
Trafalgar Cl IPNE IP4 .... 37 H7
Trafalgar Rd COLW CO3 .... 185 K7
  COS CO15 .... 10 B6
  GVW DA11 .... 489 F5
  SBN/FI SS3 .... 466 C6
  SUD CO10 .... 58 D4
Trafalgar Wy BCAYW CM12 .... 387 H8
  BRTR CM7 .... 210 A1
Trajan Cl COLN CO4 .... 155 J7
Tranmere Gv IP IP1 .... 36 B3
Trap's Hill LOU IG10 .... 377 H8
Travers Wy PIT SS13 .... 438 D7
Treebeard Copse RCHLM CM3 .... 392 B7
Tree Cl COS CO15 .... 259 H6
Treecot Dr LOS SS9 .... 463 H1
Treelawn Dr LOS SS9 .... 463 G1
Treelawn Gdns LOS SS9 .... 463 G1
Tree Tops BRWN CM15 .... 411 F4
Treetops FX IP11 .... 95 F8
Trefoil Cl CHTY IP2 .... 2 A5
Trenchard Crs CHLM/WR CM1 .... 305 F6
Trenders Av RAYL SS6 .... 419 G7
Trenham Av PIT SS13 .... 438 C5
Trent TIL RM18 .... 486 D5
Trent Av UPMR RM14 .... 432 A8
Trent Cl BOC CM0 .... 398 A7

WICKW SS12 .... 417 G7
Trent Rd BKHH IG9 .... 403 J4
  CHLM/WR CM1 .... 303 J8
  IPSE IP3 .... 63 H3
  WIT CM8 .... 276 E3
Trescoe Gdns CRW RM5 .... 407 H8
Tresco Wy WICKW SS12 .... 417 J8
Trevor Cl CHLM/WR CM12 .... 414 A6
Trews Gdns K/T/MI CO5 .... 246 E2
Trimble Cl ING CM4 .... 386 B1
Trimley Pl BSDN SS14 .... 437 K6
  RCOS CO16 .... 290 D1
Trimley Rd KIR/NAC IP10 .... 94 C2
Trindehay LAIN SS15 .... 16 C5
Trinder Wy WICKW SS12 .... 416 D7
Tring Cl HARH RM3 .... 409 G7
Tring Gdns HARH RM3 .... 409 F7
Trinity Av FX IP11 .... 4 B4
  WOS/PRIT SS0 .... 18 B5
Trinity Cl BCAYE CM11 .... 414 D7
  BSF CM23 .... 198 E7
  K/T/MI CO5 .... 284 E6
  KESG IP5 .... 38 D6
  LAIN SS15 .... 16 A4
  MGTR CO11 .... 159 J2
  RAYL SS6 .... 441 K4
  RCOLE CO7 .... 221 F5
Trinity La BAR EN8 .... 346 E6
Trinity Link HLWE CB9 .... 27 G4
Trinity Ms K/T/MI CO5 .... 284 E6
Trinity Rd BCAYE CM11 .... 414 D7
  CHLM/GWD CM2 .... 15 E3
  GVE DA12 .... 489 H5
  HSTD CO9 .... 147 J4
  MGTR CO11 .... 159 J2
  RAYL SS6 .... 441 K4
  SOSN SS2 .... 19 F3
Trinity St BSF CM23 .... 198 E7
  COL CO1 .... 8 B4
  HSTD CO9 .... 147 J4
Trinity Wy BSF CM23 .... 198 E7
Trinity Wood Rd HOC/HUL SS5 .... 421 H5
Tripat Ct SLH/COR SS17 .... 458 A8
Tripton Rd HLWS CM18 .... 13 E4
Triton Wy SBF/HAD SS7 .... 441 J5
Triumph Av COS CO15 .... 290 A6
Triumph Cl CDH/CHF RM16 .... 483 F3
Troon Gdns IPNE IP4 .... 37 K5
Troopers Dr HARH RM3 .... 408 C7
Trosley Av GVW DA11 .... 489 C7
Trotters Fld BRTR CM7 .... 210 A2
Trotter's Gap WARE SG12 .... 292 A1
Trotters Rd HLWS CM18 .... 294 E8
Trotwood CHIG IG7 .... 405 G8
Trotwood Cl CHLM/WR CM1 .... 304 A6
Troubridge Cl RCHLM CM3 .... 393 F6
Trowbridge Rd HARH RM3 .... 430 E1
Troys Cha RCHLM CM3 .... 385 J3
Truelove's La ING CM4 .... 436 B7
Truman Cl LAIN SS15 .... 16 A4
Trunette Rd COS CO15 .... 290 E2
The Trunnions RCFD SS4 .... 444 C4
Truro Crs KESG IP5 .... 38 E7
  RAYL SS6 .... 419 H8
Truro Rd GVE DA12 .... 489 J8
Trusses Rd BOC CM0 .... 344 B2
Trustons Gdns EMPK RM11 .... 450 B1
Trust Rd BAR EN8 .... 346 E8
Tucker Dr WIT CM8 .... 277 F5
Tucker's Rw BSF CM23 .... 198 D2
Tuck Rd RAIN RM13 .... 450 B7
Tuddenham Av IPNE IP4 .... 3 F2
Tuddenham La KESG IP5 .... 37 K3
Tuddenham St IPNE IP4 .... 3 E2
Tudor Av EBAR EN7 .... 346 B5
  GPK RM2 .... 430 B5
  SLH/COR SS17 .... 411 J2
Tudor Cl BRWN CM15 .... 404 D7
  CHIG IG7 .... 290 C4
  EBAR EN7 .... 346 B5
  GVW DA11 .... 488 D6
  ING CM4 .... 386 A3
  LOS SS9 .... 442 D6
  RAYL SS6 .... 442 A3
  RCOLE CO7 .... 255 J5
  RIPS/CAP IP9 .... 129 F4
  SBF/HAD SS7 .... 440 E8
  SUD CO10 .... 58 B4
  WFD IG8 .... 403 J8
  WIT CM8 .... 277 F5
  WOTN CO14 .... 229 J3
Tudor Ct LAIN SS15 .... 457 G3
Tudor Dr GPK RM2 .... 430 B6
Tudor Gdns GPK RM2 .... 430 B6
  LOS SS9 .... 462 E2
  SBN/FI SS3 .... 466 C7
  UPMR RM14 .... 451 K3
Tudor Gn COS CO15 .... 290 B4
  SUD CO10 .... 58 B5
Tudor Rd BROX EN10 .... 318 E3
Tudor Rd CVI SS8 .... 477 H2
  LOS SS9 .... 442 D6
  SUD CO10 .... 58 B4
  WOS/PRIT SS0 .... 18 B2

Tudor Rose Cl COLW CO3 .... 185 H6
Tudor Wy HOC/HUL SS5 .... 443 G1
  WAB EN9 .... 347 K7
  WICKW SS12 .... 416 D6
Tudwick Rd K/T/MI CO5 .... 280 C2
  MAL CM9 .... 280 C8
Tufnell Wy COLN CO4 .... 186 D3
Tufted Cl BRTR CM7 .... 209 F8
Tufter Rd CHIG IG7 .... 405 J8
Tufton Rd CHING E4 .... 402 B7
Tugby Pl CHLM/WR CM1 .... 304 A7
Tukes Wy SAFWS CB11 .... 71 G5
Tulip Cl BRWN CM15 .... 410 E1
  CHLM/WR CM1 .... 305 G6
  HARH RM3 .... 430 D1
Tumbler Rd HLWS CM18 .... 294 E6
Tumulus Wy COLS CO2 .... 218 A3
Tunbridge Rd SOSN SS2 .... 18 C2
Tunnmeade HLW CM20 .... 294 E4
Tunstall Cl PIT SS13 .... 439 F8
  RCOS CO16 .... 257 H8
Turin St CHTY IP2 .... 3 D5
Turkentine Cl SUD CO10 .... 59 G8
Turkey Cock La COLW CO3 .... 184 D7
  RCOLW CO6 .... 184 E5
Turkey Oaks CHLM/WR CM1 .... 15 E2
Turkey St EN EN1 .... 374 B3
Turner Av MGTR CO11 .... 123 G8
Turner Cl HVHL CB9 .... 26 D4
  RCOLE CO7 .... 221 F4
  SBN/FI SS3 .... 466 C5
Turner Gv MGTR CO11 .... 39 H5
Turner Rd IPSE IP5 .... 63 J5
Turners Cl CHONG CM5 .... 354 B3
Turners Crs BSF CM23 .... 231 C1
Turner's Hl BAR EN8 .... 346 D4
Turnors HLWW/ROY CM19 .... 12 C3
Turnpike Cl COLN CO4 .... 156 B5
Turnpike Hl COLN CO4 .... 156 B5
Turnpike Hl HVHL CB9 .... 26 C1
Turnpike La CDH/CHF RM16 .... 485 J4
Turnstone End COLN CO4 .... 188 C5
The Turnstones GVE DA12 .... 489 J7
Turold Rd SLH/COR SS17 .... 474 A1
Turp Av CDH/CHF RM16 .... 484 B1
Turpin La ERITH DA8 .... 480 B5
Turpins Av COS CO15 .... 11 F2
Turpins Cl COS CO15 .... 11 F2
Turpins La FOS CO13 .... 228 D6
  WFD IG8 .... 404 C2
The Turpins BSDN SS14 .... 437 K6
Turret La IPNE IP4 .... 3 D4
Turstan Rd WIT CM8 .... 276 E5
Tusser Cl WIT CM8 .... 245 H6
Tusser Ms COLW CO3 .... 185 K6
Tutors Wy CHLM CM3 .... 392 E6
Tweed TIL RM18 .... 486 D3
Tweed Cl HSTD CO9 .... 147 J6
Twelve Acre Ap KESG IP5 .... 39 F6
Twelve Acres BRTR CM7 .... 210 C2
Twentyfirst St STSD CM24 .... 201 G3
Twentyman Cl WFD IG8 .... 403 H8
Twining Rd COLW CO3 .... 217 K1
Twin Oaks CHLM/GWD CM2 .... 333 J1
Twinstead WICKW SS12 .... 417 H7
Twitten La CHLM/GWD CM2 .... 360 D3
Twitty Fee RCHLM CM3 .... 336 A4
Twizzlefoot Br BOC CM0 .... 399 H6
Two Acres RIPS/CAP IP9 .... 87 G3
Twyford Av SBN/FI SS3 .... 467 F1
Twyford Bury La BSF CM23 .... 232 A1
Twyford Cl BSF CM23 .... 199 F8
Twyford Gdns BSF CM23 .... 231 K1
Twyford Rd BSF CM23 .... 199 F8
Twyzel Rd CVI SS8 .... 461 H8
Tyberry Rd EN EN1 .... 374 B7
Tyburn Hl RCOLW CO6 .... 150 D7
The Tyburns RBRW/HUT CM13 .... 412 B5
Tycehurst Hl LOU IG10 .... 377 H8
Tydeman Cl COLW CO3 .... 217 H1
Tye Common Rd BCAYW CM12 .... 413 K8
Tyefields PIT SS13 .... 439 F6
Tye Green Rd RBSF CM22 .... 168 D6
Tye Green Village HLWS CM18 .... 13 F6
Yehurst Crs COLN CO4 .... 9 E1
Tyelands BCAYW CM12 .... 414 A5
Tye La RCOLE CO7 .... 221 H2
Tye Rd RCOLE CO7 .... 189 H6
The Tye Rd RCOLE CO7 .... 224 C5
The Tye RCHLM CM3 .... 363 H6
Tyfield Cl BAR EN8 .... 346 C4
Tyle Gn EMPK RM11 .... 431 F7
Tyler Av LAIN SS15 .... 16 A4
  RCOS CO16 .... 290 D2
Tylers Av BCAYW CM12 .... 387 H8
  SOS SS1 .... 19 D5
Tylers Cl CHLM/GWD CM2 .... 332 D7
Tylers Crs HCH RM12 .... 450 D6
Tylers Gn FX IP11 .... 94 D8
Tylers Ride RCHLM CM3 .... 392 E6
Tylers Rd HLWW/ROY CM19 .... 321 F2
Tyler St HAR CO12 .... 6 A3
Tyler Wy BRW CM14 .... 410 E4
Tylewood SBF/HAD SS7 .... 461 H3
Tylney Av RCFD SS4 .... 444 B2
Tylney Cft HLWW/ROY CM19 .... 12 B5

Tylneys Rd *HSTD* CO9 .... 148 B2
Tyms Wy *RAYL* SS6 .... 441 K1 🔲
Tyndale CI *HOC/HUL* SS5 .... 419 J2
Tyndale Dr *COS* CO15 .... 290 C2
Tyndales La *RCHLM* CM3 .... 336 B8
Tyne CI *UPMR* RM14 .... 432 A8
Tynedale Sq *COLN* CO4 .... 187 J1
Tyne Gdns *SOCK/AV* RM15 .... 468 E7 🔲
Tynemouth Dr *EN* EN1 .... 374 A4
Tyrel Dr *SOS* SS1 .... 19 E4
Tyrells *HOC/HUL* SS5 .... 442 E1
Tyrells CI *CHLM/WR* CM1 .... 15 F1
UPMR RM14 .... 451 J3 🔲
Tyrone CI *BRTR* CM7 .... 414 D7
Tyrone Rd *BCAYE* CM11 .... 414 D7
SOS SS1 .... 465 K7
Tyrrell Rd *SBF/HAD* SS7 .... 460 A4
Tyrrells Hall CI *GRAYS* RM17 .... 484 C5
Tyrrells Rd *BCAYE* CM11 .... 414 E7
Tysea CI *HLWS* CM18 .... 13 F6
Tysea HI *ABR/ST* RM4 .... 408 A4
Tysea Rd *HLWS* CM18 .... 13 F6
Tysoe Av *PEND* EN3 .... 375 F2
Tyssen Md *RCHLM* CM3 .... 306 C3
Tyssen PI *SOCK/AV* RM15 .... 470 A3 🔲
Tythe Barn Wy *RCHLM* CM3 .... 392 C5 🔲
Tythe CI *CHLM/WR* CM1 .... 305 D7
The Tythings *HSTD* CO9 .... 147 J5 🔲

U

Uckfield Rd *PEND* EN3 .... 374 D3
Ullswater CI *BRTR* CM7 .... 209 F7
Ullswater Rd *SBF/HAD* SS7 .... 440 D6
Ullswater Wy *HCH* RM12 .... 450 B6
Ulster Av *SBN/FI* SS3 .... 466 B7
Ulting Hall Rd *MAL* CM9 .... 308 E6
Ulting La *MAL* CM9 .... 308 D7
Ulting Rd *RCHLM* CM3 .... 308 C4
Ulting Wy *WICKE* SS11 .... 417 K5
Una Rd *HAR* CO12 .... 164 D1
PIT SS13 .... 439 J7
Undercliff Rd East *FX* IP11 .... 131 K3
Undercliff Rd West *FX* IP11 .... 5 F4
Underhill Rd *SBF/HAD* SS7 .... 460 A1
Underwood Rd *CHING* E4 .... 402 C8
Underwood Sq *LOS* SS9 .... 462 B1
Union La *RCFD* SS4 .... 444 B3
Union Rd *COS* CO15 .... 290 C5
Unity CI *COLS* CO2 .... 219 J1
Unity Rd *PEND* EN3 .... 374 C3
Unity St *IPSE* IP3 .... 3 F5
Upland CI *BCAYW* CM12 .... 414 A1 🔟
Upland Court Rd *HARH* RM3 .... 431 C4
Upland Crs *K/T/MI* CO5 .... 284 E5
Upland Dr *BCAYW* CM12 .... 414 A1
COLN CO4 .... 9 F4
Upland Rd *BCAYW* CM12 .... 414 A1
EPP CM16 .... 322 E8
IPNE IP4 .... 37 J7
K/T/MI CO5 .... 284 E6
LOS SS9 .... 463 H5 🔲
The Uplands *LOU* IG10 .... 377 H7
Upminster Rd *HCH* RM12 .... 451 C3
Upminster Rd North *RAIN* RM13 .... 468 A3
Upney CI *HCH* RM12 .... 450 E6 🔟
Upper Acres *WIT* CM8 .... 245 H2
Upper Av *PIT* SS13 .... 439 H5
Upper Branston Rd *COS* CO15 .... 10 A3
Upper Brentwood Rd *GPK* RM2 .... 430 D6
Upper Bridge Rd *CHLM/GWD* CM2 .... 14 B5
Upper Chapel St *HSTD* CO9 .... 147 K3 🔲
Upper Cha *CHLM/GWD* CM2 .... 14 B5
RCHLM CM3 .... 396 D3
Upper Cornsland *BRW* CM14 .... 411 C6
Upper East St *SUD* CO10 .... 58 C5
Upper Farm Rd *SUD* CO10 .... 53 C5
Upper Fenn Rd *HSTD* CO9 .... 148 B3
Upperfield Dr *PIT* SS11 .... 131 J1
Upper Fourth Av *FOS* CO13 .... 228 E8
Upper Holt St *RCOLW* CO6 .... 149 K7
Upper Hook *HLWS* CM18 .... 13 F5
Upper Lambricks *RAYL* SS6 .... 441 H1
Upper Market Rd *WICKW* SS12 .... 417 F5 🔟
WICKW SS12 .... 417 G5 🔲
Upper Mayne *LAIN* SS15 .... 17 D3
Upper Mealines *HLWS* CM18 .... 294 E8
Upper Mill Fld *GTDUN* CM6 .... 204 D6
Upper Moors *RCHLM* CM3 .... 272 B6
Upper Orwell St *IPNE* IP4 .... 3 E4
Upper Pk *HLW* CM20 .... 12 B2

LOU IG10 .... 404 A1
RCOLE CO7 .... 255 J6
WICKW SS12 .... 439 G1
Upper Rainham Rd *HCH* RM12 .... 450 A5
Upper Rd *BCAYE* CM11 .... 416 A8
SUD CO10 .... 85 J5
Upper Roman Rd *CHLM/GWD* CM2 .. 14 C4
Upper Ryle *BRW* CM14 .... 410 E3
Upper Second Av *FOS* CO13 .... 228 D8
Upper Stonyfield
HLWW/ROY CM19 .... 12 B3
Upper St *RCOLE* CO7 .... 121 F4
Upper Swaines *EPP* CM16 .... 350 D4
Upper Third Av *FOS* CO13 .... 228 D8
Upper Trinity Rd *HSTD* CO9 .... 147 K4 🔲
Upshers *BCAYE* CM11 .... 71 G5
Upshire Rd *WAB* EN9 .... 348 B6
Upsons Wy *KESG* IP5 .... 39 J5 🔲
Upton CI *IPNE* IP4 .... 3 F3
RCOLW CO6 .... 185 J1
SLH/COR SS17 .... 473 K3
Upway *RAYL* SS6 .... 441 J2
The Upway *BSDN* SS14 .... 17 F3
Urban Av *HCH* RM12 .... 450 D4
Urban Rd *BSF* CM23 .... 199 G5
Urmond Rd *CVI* SS8 .... 478 A1
Usk Rd *SOCK/AV* RM15 .... 468 E6
Usterdale Rd *SAFWN* CB10 .... 71 F2
Uttons Av *LOS* SS9 .... 462 C5
Uxbridge CI *WICKE* SS11 .... 417 J7
Uxbridge Crs *IPSE* IP3 .... 64 A4 🔲

V

Vaagen Rd *CVI* SS8 .... 478 B1
Vadsoe Rd *CVI* SS8 .... 461 C8 🔲
Valance Av *CHING* E4 .... 403 C4
Valance Rd *SAFWS* CB11 .... 97 K6
Vale Av *SOSN* SS2 .... 19 D2
Vale CI *BRWN* CM15 .... 410 C1
COLN CO4 .... 188 B3
Vale End *CHLM/GWD* CM2 .... 360 E2
Vale La *RIPS/CAP* IP9 .... 124 C1
Valence Dr *EBAR* EN7 .... 346 A2
Valence Wy *VGE* SS16 .... 16 A6
Valentines *ING* CM4 .... 388 B5
Valentines Dr *COLN* CO4 .... 9 D2
Valentine Wy *WIT* CM8 .... 244 D1
Vale Rd *GVW* DA11 .... 488 D6
The Vale *BRW* CM14 .... 411 F4
ING CM4 .... 387 K6
VGE SS16 .... 458 A2
Valfreda Wy *BRTR* CM7 .... 106 E7
Valkyrie CI *MAL* CM9 .... 314 D3
Valkyrie Rd *WOS/PRIT* SS0 .... 18 A4
Vallance CI *SOSN* SS2 .... 465 H2
Valletta CI *CHLM/WR* CM1 .... 14 B2
Valley Br *CHLM/WR* CM1 .... 304 D7
Valleybridge Rd *COS* CO15 .... 11 D5
Valley CI *COLW* CO3 .... 217 K2
IP IP1 .... 36 E4
LOU IG10 .... 404 C2
MCTR CO11 .... 123 J4
WAB EN9 .... 347 J6
Valley Crs *RCOLW* CO6 .... 185 K2
Valley Dr *GVE* DA12 .... 489 J8
Valley HI *LOU* IG10 .... 404 B3 🔲
Valley La *RIPS/CAP* IP9 .... 89 G1
Valley Rd *BCAYE* CM11 .... 414 C3
BRTR CM7 .... 209 K1
COS CO15 .... 11 D2
HAR CO12 .... 164 C3
IPNE IP4 .... 37 F4
RCOLE CO7 .... 221 F5
SUD CO10 .... 59 H4
Valley Side *CHING* E4 .... 402 B4
Valley Vw *BRTR* CM7 .... 106 E7
RCOLW CO6 .... 185 K2
Valley View Dr *IPNE* IP4 .... 187 H1
Valleyview Dr *IPNE* IP4 .... 64 D1
Valley Wk *FX* IP11 .... 5 F3
Valmar Av *SLH/COR* SS17 .... 473 H4
Vandenburg Cir *BRTR* CM7 .... 108 A7 🔲
Vanderbilt Av *RAYL* SS6 .... 419 H5
Vanderwalt Av *CVI* SS8 .... 477 J1
Van Dieman's La
CHLM/GWD CM2 .... 15 D5 🔲
Van Diemens Pass *CVI* SS8 .... 479 F2
Van Dyck Rd *COLW* CO3 .... 186 B8
Vandyck Rd *IPSE* IP3 .... 63 J5 🔲
Vane La *RCOLW* CO6 .... 213 H3
Vanessa Dr *RCOLE* CO7 .... 220 E4
Vange Corner Dr *SLH/COR* SS17 .... 457 J4
Vange Hill Dr *VGE* SS16 .... 438 A4
Vange Park Rd *SLH/COR* SS17 .... 457 J4
The Vanguards *SBN/FI* SS3 .... 466 E6
Vanguard Wy *BRTR* CM7 .... 210 A1 🔲
SBN/FI SS3 .... 466 E5
Vanners Rd *HVHL* CB9 .... 27 G6
Vansittart St *HAR* CO12 .... 7 E3

Vantorts CI *SBW* CM21 .... 263 J3
Vantorts Rd *SBW* CM21 .... 263 J4
Varden CI *CHLM/WR* CM1 .... 304 B7
Vardon Dr *LOS* SS9 .... 462 C2
Varney CI *EBAR* EN7 .... 346 A1
Vaughan Av *HCH* RM12 .... 450 E5
Vaughan CI *BRTR* CM7 .... 208 C3
RCFD SS4 .... 422 B8
Vaughan St *CHTY* IP2 .... 3 D5
Vaughan Williams Rd *LAIN* SS15 ... 16 A2 🔲
Vaulx Rd *CVI* SS8 .... 478 B1
Vaux Av *HAR* CO12 .... 164 E4
Vauxhall Av *COS* CO15 .... 290 A7
Vauxhall CI *GVW* DA11 .... 488 C5
Vauxhall Dr *BRTR* CM7 .... 209 G3
Velizy Av *HLW* CM20 .... 13 D2
Vellacotts *CHLM/WR* CM1 .... 304 D6
Venables CI *CVI* SS8 .... 478 C2
Venlo Rd *CVI* SS8 .... 461 C8 🔲
Venmore Dr *GTDUN* CM6 .... 204 D5
Ventnor Dr *COS* CO15 .... 259 J5
Veny Crs *HCH* RM12 .... 450 E6
Vera Rd *BCAYE* CM11 .... 416 D3
Verbena CI *SOCK/AV* RM15 .... 470 A6 🔲
Verderers Rd *CHIG* IG7 .... 405 K8
Vere Gdns *IP* IP1 .... 36 E3
Vere Rd *LOU* IG10 .... 378 A8
Vermeer Crs *SBN/FI* SS3 .... 467 F5
Vermeer Ride *CHLM/WR* CM1 .... 305 H6 🔲
Vermont CI *COS* CO15 .... 11 D3
PIT SS13 .... 439 F5
Vermont Crs *IPNE* IP4 .... 3 E2
Vermont Rd *IPNE* IP4 .... 3 E2
Vernon Av *PEND* EN3 .... 374 E2
RAYL SS6 .... 441 G1
Vernon Cnr *ING* CM4 .... 387 K3
Vernon Crs *RBRW/HUT* CM13 .... 411 K6
Vernon Rd *CRW* RM5 .... 407 H8
LOS SS9 .... 462 D4
RCHLM CM3 .... 394 C4
Vernon's CI *RBSF* CM22 .... 137 G8
Vernons Rd *RCOLW* CO6 .... 151 H8
Vernon St *CHTY* IP2 .... 3 D5
Vernon Wy *BRTR* CM7 .... 178 B8
Veronica CI *HARH* RM3 .... 430 D2
Veronica Wk *COLN* CO4 .... 9 F4
Vesta CI *RCOLW* CO6 .... 213 G3
Vestry CI *LAIN* SS15 .... 16 A3
Vexil CI *PUR* RM19 .... 482 E3
Veyses End *RCOLE* CO7 .... 121 G3
Viaduct Rd *CHLM/WR* CM1 .... 14 B3 🔲
Vian Av *PEND* EN3 .... 374 E1
Viborg Gdns *MAL* CM9 .... 338 A5 🔲
Vicarage Av *WIT* CM8 .... 243 K4
Vicarage CI *BRTR* CM7 .... 175 H5
BRW CM14 .... 410 B7
CVI SS8 .... 477 H2
LAIN SS15 .... 16 A3 🔲
MAL CM9 .... 313 H1 🔲
Vicarage Crs *RCHLM* CM3 .... 308 B1
Vicarage Dr *GVW* DA11 .... 488 B4 🔲
Vicarage Fld *SUD* CO10 .... 58 E8
Vicarage Gdns *COS* CO15 .... 10 A5
Vicarage HI *SBF/HAD* SS7 .... 460 E3
Vicarage La *BOC* CM0 .... 372 A1
BSF CM23 .... 134 A5
CHIG IG7 .... 405 G6
CHLM/GWD CM2 .... 361 H2
EPP CM16 .... 324 B6
GTDUN CM6 .... 139 K2
MAL CM9 .... 367 G2
RBSF CM22 .... 136 A8
RCOS CO16 .... 226 C3
RIPS/CAP IP9 .... 62 D8
SUD CO10 .... 58 E1
WOTN CO14 .... 229 H5 🔲
Vicarage Meadow *BOC* CM0 .... 398 D2
HSTD CO9 .... 147 K4
Vicarage Rd *BRTR* CM7 .... 106 E7
CHLM/GWD CM2 .... 14 B5
CHLM/WR CM1 .... 302 C8
EPP CM16 .... 351 G3
FX IP11 .... 5 D3
HCH RM12 .... 450 B2
RCHLM CM3 .... 270 E3
SUD CO10 .... 55 F4
Vicarage Sq *GRAYS* RM17 .... 483 K5 🔲
Vicarage Wd *HLW* CM20 .... 13 F2
Vicars Orch *SUD* CO10 .... 57 F8
Vicerons PI *BSF* CM23 .... 231 H1
Viceroy St *COLS* CO2 .... 219 J2
Vickers Rd *SOSN* SS2 .... 444 A7
Victor Ap *HCH* RM12 .... 450 E2
Victor Av *PIT* SS13 .... 439 G7
Victor CI *HCH* RM12 .... 450 E2
Victor Dr *LOS* SS9 .... 463 G5
Victor Gdns *HCH* RM12 .... 450 E2
HOC/HUL SS5 .... 421 G8
Victoria Av *CDH/CHF* RM16 .... 484 B1
FOS CO13 .... 228 C5
RAYL SS6 .... 419 G8
SAFWS CB11 .... 71 F5
VGE SS16 .... 456 D2 🔲
WICKW SS12 .... 416 E5
Victoria Cha *COLW* CO3 .... 8 A3

Victoria Cl *CDH/CHF* RM16 .... 484 B1
  LAIN SS15 .... 436 C6 🖫
  RCOLE CO7 .... 220 E3
Victoria Crs *CHLM/WR* CM1 .... 14 C2
  LAIN SS15 .... 16 A2 🖫
  MGTR CO11 .... 159 H1
  RBRW/HUT CM13 .... 412 A5
  WICKW SS12 .... 416 E6
Victoria Dr *LOS* SS9 .... 463 F4
  SBN/FI SS3 .... 467 H3
Victoria Esp *K/T/MI* CO5 .... 285 F8
Victoria Gdns *COLN* CO4 .... 187 J2
  SAFWN CB11 .... 71 F4 🖫
Victoria Pl *COL* CO1 .... 9 D5
  RCOLE CO7 .... 255 K7
Victoria Rd *BKHH* IG9 .... 404 A5
  BRW CM14 .... 411 F7
  CHING E4 .... 403 F4
  CHLM/WR CM1 .... 14 C2
  COLW CO3 .... 186 D8
  COS CO15 .... 11 D3
  FX IP11 .... 5 F4
  GVW DA11 .... 488 E6
  HVHL CB9 .... 26 D6
  LAIN SS15 .... 436 C6 🖫
  LOS SS9 .... 463 F5
  MAL CM9 .... 338 C3
  RAYL SS6 .... 441 K2
  RCHLM CM3 .... 366 B7
  RCHLM CM3 .... 392 D7
  RCOS CO16 .... 225 J8
  ROM RM1 .... 430 A7
  SLH/COR SS17 .... 473 J3
  SOS SS1 .... 19 F4
  UPMR RM14 .... 454 E5
  VGE SS16 .... 458 A3
  WAB EN9 .... 347 J8
  WOTN CO14 .... 229 H5
Victoria St *BRTR* CM7 .... 209 J3
  FX IP11 .... 131 H5
  HAR CO12 .... 7 E4
  IP IP1 .... 2 B3
Victor Mew *CI WICKW* SS12 .... 417 C8
Victor Rd *COL* CO1 .... 9 D5
Victor's Crs *RBRW/HUT* CM13 .... 412 A5
Victory Rd *COS* CO15 .... 10 A4
  IPNE IP4 .... 37 J6
  K/T/MI CO5 .... 284 C7
Vienna Cl *HAR* CO12 .... 165 F4
View Cl *CHIG* IG7 .... 405 G8
View Point Rd *FX* IP11 .... 130 E8
Vigerons Wy *CDH/CHF* RM16 .... 485 G3
Viking Cl *GVW* DA11 .... 488 B8
  MAL CM9 .... 338 A5
Vikings Wy *CVI* SS8 .... 477 H2
Viking Wy *BRWN* CM15 .... 410 E2
  COS CO15 .... 260 D7
  WICKE SS11 .... 417 G3
Village Cl *CHING* E4 .... 402 D6
  FOS CO13 .... 228 C6
Village Dr *CVI* SS8 .... 477 J2
Village Ga *CHLM/GWD* CM2 .... 333 J2
Village Hall Cl *CVI* SS8 .... 477 H2 🖫
Village Wy *FOS* CO13 .... 228 C7
Villa Rd *COLW* CO3 .... 185 F5
  SBF/HAD SS7 .... 460 B1
Villiers Pl *RCHLM* CM3 .... 306 C4
Villiers-sur-marne *Av BSF* CM23 .... 198 C3
Villiers Wy *SBF/HAD* SS7 .... 440 E8
Vince Cl *K/T/MI* CO5 .... 284 E7
Vincent Cl *BAR* EN8 .... 346 E2
  IP IP1 .... 36 A5
  SBN/FI SS3 .... 466 E3
  SLH/COR SS17 .... 474 D2
Vincent Wy *BCAYW* CM12 .... 387 F8
Vine Dr *RCOLE* CO7 .... 221 F2
Vine Farm Rd *RCOLE* CO7 .... 221 F2
Vine Gv *HLW* CM20 .... 262 B8
Vine Rd *K/T/MI* CO5 .... 247 K7
Vinesse Rd *RCOLW* CO6 .... 153 J4
Vine St *BRTR* CM7 .... 142 C3 🖫
Vineway *BRW* CM14 .... 411 F4
The Vineway *HAR* CO12 .... 6 B4
Vineyard Ga *COL* CO1 .... 8 B5 🖫
  COL CO1 .... 8 B4 🖫
Vineyard St *COL* CO1 .... 8 B5 🖫
Vint Crs *COLW* CO3 .... 186 D7
The Vintners *SOS* SS2 .... 444 C8
Viola Cl *SOCK/AV* RM15 .... 470 A3
Violet Cl *CHLM/WR* CM1 .... 305 G6
  CHTY IP2 .... 2 A5
Virgil Rd *BROX* EN10 .... 319 F5 🖫
Virgil Rd *WIT* CM8 .... 245 F8
Virginia Cl *COS* CO15 .... 290 C4
  SBF/HAD SS7 .... 440 A6
Virley Cl *MAL* CM9 .... 339 F1
Viscount Dr *COLN* CO4 .... 155 K8
Vista Av *FOS* CO13 .... 228 C4
  PEND EN3 .... 374 C6
Vista Rd *COS* CO15 .... 11 D4
  WICKE SS11 .... 417 J6
Vitilus Cl *COLN* CO4 .... 155 J7 🖫
Vivian Ct *WOTN* CO14 .... 229 H5

Volwycke Av *MAL* CM9 .... 338 B5
Voorburg Rd *CVI* SS8 .... 478 D1 🖫
Vowler Rd *VGE* SS16 .... 456 C1
Voysey Gdns *PIT* SS13 .... 438 E4

W

Waalwyk Dr *CVI* SS8 .... 478 A1
Waarden Rd *CVI* SS8 .... 478 A1
Waarem Av *CVI* SS8 .... 478 A1
Wacketts *EBAR* EN7 .... 346 A1 🖫
Waddeson Rd *HAR* CO12 .... 7 E4
Wade Reach *WOTN* CO14 .... 229 F5
Wade Rd *COS* CO15 .... 259 K5
Wade's La *RIPS/CAP* IP9 .... 92 C7
Wadgate Rd *FX* IP11 .... 5 E3
Wadham Cl *ING* CM4 .... 386 B1
Wadham Park Av *HOC/HUL* SS5 .... 420 B5
Wadhurst Rd *IPSE* IP5 .... 64 B2
Wagon Md *RBSF* CM22 .... 265 C2
Wagtail Dr *MAL* CM9 .... 310 E8
Wainwright Av *RBRW/HUT* CM13 .... 412 C3
Wainwright Wy *KESG* IP5 .... 39 H5
Wakefield *SAFWN* CB10 .... 43 J2 🖫
Wakefield Av *BCAYW* CM12 .... 414 B3
Wakefield Cl *COL* CO1 .... 8 C3
Wakelin Cha *ING* CM4 .... 386 A2
Wakelin Wy *WIT* CM8 .... 277 H3 🖫
Wakerfield Cl *EMPK* RM11 .... 431 G6 🖫
Wakering Av *SBN/FI* SS3 .... 466 E6
Wakering Rd *SBN/FI* SS3 .... 465 K3
Wakescolne *WICKE* SS11 .... 417 K7
Wakeshall La *SUD* CO10 .... 54 B6
Wakes St *RCOLW* CO6 .... 150 E7
Walcot Rd *PEND* EN3 .... 375 H4
Waldegrave Cl *MGTR* CO11 .... 159 C2
Waldegrave Gdns *UPMR* RM14 .... 451 J3
Waldegrave Rd *MGTR* CO11 .... 159 H2
Waldegraves La *K/T/MI* CO5 .... 285 J6
The Waldegraves *BURES* CO8 .... 115 J5
Waldegrave Wy *MGTR* CO11 .... 159 G2
Walden Av *SAFWN* CB10 .... 102 B3
Walden Cl *MAL* CM9 .... 310 C1
Walden House Rd *WIT* CM8 .... 278 C1
Walden Rd *CBE/LIN* CB1 .... 22 D7
  EMPK RM11 .... 430 E8
  GTDUN CM6 .... 103 J8
  SAFWN CB10 .... 43 K2
  SAFWS CB11 .... 70 A7
Walden Wy *EMPK* RM11 .... 430 E8
  FOS CO13 .... 229 F7
Waldgrooms *GTDUN* CM6 .... 204 B4
Waldingfield Rd *SUD* CO10 .... 58 C5
Waldon Rd *TIL* RM18 .... 486 C3
Waldringfield *BSDN* SS14 .... 17 F3
Walford Pl *CHLM/GWD* CM2 .... 333 H3
Walfords Cl *HLWE* CM17 .... 295 C2
Walford Wy *RCOLW* CO6 .... 213 H3
Walker Av *CHONG* CM5 .... 327 F5
Walker Cl *IPNE* IP4 .... 38 A4
Walker Dr *LOS* SS9 .... 462 B3
Walkers Cl *CHLM/WR* CM1 .... 305 F6
Walkers Sq *SLH/COR* SS17 .... 473 K4
Walkey Wy *SBN/FI* SS3 .... 467 C5
The Walk *COLW* CO3 .... 185 F5
  EMPK RM11 .... 451 C3
  HOC/HUL SS5 .... 419 J5
  KESG IP5 .... 39 F5
Wallace Binder Cl *MAL* CM9 .... 338 B4
Wallace Cl *HCH* RM12 .... 419 J2
Wallace Crs *CHLM/GWD* CM2 .... 15 D5
Wallace Dr *WICKW* SS12 .... 417 H8
Wallace La *RCHLM* CM3 .... 239 H6
Wallace Rd *GRAYS* RM17 .... 483 K3
  IP IP1 .... 36 A5
Wallace's La *RCHLM* CM3 .... 306 D1
Wallasea Gdns *CHLM/WR* CM1 .... 305 H8 🖫
Wallbutton Rd *ERITH* DA8 .... 480 D6
Wallenger Av *GPK* RM2 .... 430 C5
Waller's Cl *ROY* SG8 .... 66 C4
The Walls *MGTR* CO11 .... 159 K1
Wall St *RCOS* CO16 .... 288 C7
Walnut Cl *HOC/HUL* SS5 .... 421 F6 🖫
Walnut Ct *BSF* CM23 .... 231 H2
  WIT CM8 .... 277 C1
Walnut Gv *BRTR* CM7 .... 209 H3
Walnut Tree Av *SBW* CM21 .... 263 J1
Walnut Tree Crs *SBW* CM21 .... 263 J2 🖫

Walnut Tree La *RIPS/CAP* IP9 .... 126 E3
  SUD CO10 .... 58 A6
Walnut Tree Wy *COLS* CO2 .... 218 C2
  K/T/MI CO5 .... 248 A6
Walnut Wy *BKHH* IG9 .... 404 A6
  COS CO15 .... 290 E2
  RCOLE CO7 .... 255 J6
Walpole Cl *GRAYS* RM17 .... 484 B3 🖫
Walsingham Cl *LAIN* SS15 .... 16 A3 🖫
  SUD CO10 .... 59 F8
Walsingham Rd *COLS* CO2 .... 8 B5
  SOSN SS2 .... 19 E1
Walsingham Wy *BCAYW* CM12 .... 387 F8
Walter Radcliffe Wy *RCOLE* CO7 .... 221 F6
Walters Cl *CHLM/GWD* CM2 .... 360 E2
  LOS SS9 .... 443 F7
Walter Wy *WIT* CM8 .... 211 H8
Waltham Cl *CHTY* IP2 .... 62 C3
  RBRW/HUT CM13 .... 412 B2 🖫
Waltham Crs *SOSN* SS2 .... 19 E1
Waltham Gdns *PEND* EN3 .... 374 C5 🖫
Waltham Ga *BAR* EN8 .... 318 E8
Waltham Gln *CHLM/GWD* CM2 .... 15 D6
Waltham Rd *RAYL* SS6 .... 441 C2
  RCHLM CM3 .... 274 D4
  WAB EN9 .... 320 A8
Walthams *PIT* SS13 .... 438 E6
Walthams Pl *PIT* SS13 .... 438 E6
Waltham Wy *CHING* E4 .... 402 B5
  FOS CO13 .... 229 F8
Walton Av *FX* IP11 .... 4 C4
Walton Cl *LAIN* SS15 .... 16 A2 🖫
Walton Gdns *RBRW/HUT* CM13 .... 412 B1
  WAB EN9 .... 347 H7
Walton Rd *COS* CO15 .... 10 C4
  FOS CO13 .... 227 H3
  RCOS CO16 .... 226 E2
  SOS SS1 .... 465 J7
Walton's Hall Rd *SLH/COR* SS17 .... 473 H8
Wambrook *SBN/FI* SS3 .... 466 C4
Wambrook Cl *RBRW/HUT* CM13 .... 412 B5
Wamburg Rd *CVI* SS8 .... 478 D1
Wansfell Gdns *SOS* SS1 .... 465 J4
Wansford Cl *BRW* CM14 .... 410 C6
Wantz Cha *MAL* CM9 .... 338 C3
Wantz Hvn Rd *MAL* CM9 .... 338 C3 🖫
Wantz Rd *ING* CM4 .... 359 F4
  MAL CM9 .... 338 C3
Wapping La *RCOLE* CO7 .... 255 F3
Warboys Crs *CHING* E4 .... 402 D8
Warburton Av *HSTD* CO9 .... 110 C5 🖫
Warburtons *SLH/COR* SS17 .... 474 B2
Ward Av *GRAYS* RM17 .... 484 A3
Ward Cl *EBAR* EN7 .... 346 A1 🖫
Ward Crs *BSF* CM23 .... 198 D7
Warde Cha *WOTN* CO14 .... 229 G3
Warden Av *CRW* RM5 .... 407 H8
Wardle Wy *CHLM/WR* CM1 .... 304 A6 🖫
Wardley Cl *CHTY* IP2 .... 61 K4
Ward Pth *CHLM/GWD* CM2 .... 333 K1
Ward Rd *RIPW* IP8 .... 61 H3
Wards Cft *SAFWS* CB11 .... 70 E6
Wareham Av *IPSE* IP3 .... 64 B2
Warehouse Rd *GTDUN* CM6 .... 174 A8
Warescot Cl *BRWN* CM15 .... 410 E3
Warescot Rd *BRWN* CM15 .... 410 E3
Wares Rd *CHLM/WR* CM1 .... 269 K8
Wargrave Rd *COS* CO15 .... 10 A3
Warham Rd *HAR* CO12 .... 164 D4
Warley Cl *BRTR* CM7 .... 210 B2
Warley Gap *RBRW/HUT* CM13 .... 432 E2
Warley Hl *RBRW/HUT* CM13 .... 411 F8
Warley Mt *BRW* CM14 .... 411 F7
Warley Rd *RBRW/HUT* CM13 .... 432 B4
  St UPMR RM14 .... 453 G1
Warley Wy *FOS* CO13 .... 229 G7
Warner Cl *BCAYE* CM11 .... 414 E4 🖫
  BRTR CM7 .... 208 C4
Warners *GTDUN* CM6 .... 204 C5 🖫
Warners Av *HOD* EN11 .... 319 F1
Warners Bridge Cha *RCFD* SS4 .... 444 C7
Warners Gdns *SOSN* SS2 .... 444 B7
Warner Wy *SUD* CO10 .... 58 D5
Warnham Cl *RCOS* CO16 .... 258 D7 🖫
Warren Cha *KESG* IP5 .... 39 J6 🖫
  SBF/HAD SS7 .... 461 F1
Warren Cl *CHLM/WR* CM1 .... 304 D2 🖫
  RAYL SS6 .... 441 H5
  RBSF CM22 .... 202 A6
Warren Ct *CHIG* IG7 .... 405 G7
Warren Dr *HCH* RM12 .... 450 B4
  WICKE SS11 .... 417 K5
Warren La *SLH/COR* SS17 .... 473 K4
Warren Fld *EPP* CM16 .... 350 E6
Warrenfield Cl *EBAR* EN7 .... 346 A1 🖫
Warren Heath Av *IPSE* IP3 .... 64 B3
Warren Heath Rd *IPSE* IP3 .... 64 B3
Warren Hl *LOU* IG10 .... 403 K1
Warren La *BRWN* CM15 .... 383 C5
  CDH/CHF RM16 .... 483 C3
  COLW CO3 .... 217 C4
  RIPS/CAP IP9 .... 128 B7
Warren Pond Rd *CHING* E4 .... 403 G3
Warren Rd *BRTR* CM7 .... 210 B3

CHING E4 .... 402 D5
HSTD CO9 .... 147 J4 🔲
LOS SS9 .... 462 B2
RCHLM CM3 .... 389 K7
The Warrens FOS CO13 .... 228 D7
WIT CM8 .... 278 A8
The Warren BCAYW CM12 .... 413 K1
Warrington Gdns EMPK RM11 ...... 430 D8
Warrington Rd IP IP1 .... 2 C2
Warrington Sq BCAYW CM12 .... 414 A2 🔲
Warrior Av HCH RM12 .... 450 E3
Warrior Sq SOS SS1 .... 19 D4
Warrior Sq East SOS SS1 .... 19 D4 🔲
Warrior Sq North SOS SS1 .... 19 D4
Warrior Square Rd SBN/FI SS3 ...... 466 E8
Warwick Bailey Cl COLN CO4 .... 186 E3 🔲
Warwick Cl BRTR CM7 .... 209 K1
CVI SS8 .... 461 F8
MAL CM9 .... 338 C9
RAYL SS6 .... 442 A4
SBF/HAD SS7 .... 440 C6
Warwick Crs COS CO15 .... 10 B3
MAL CM9 .... 338 C4
Warwick Dr BAR EN8 .... 346 D2
MAL CM9 .... 338 B4
RCFD SS4 .... 444 C6
Warwick Gdns GPK RM2 .... 430 D5
RAYL SS6 .... 442 A4
Warwick Gn RAYL SS6 .... 442 B4
Warwick La RAIN RM13 .... 468 B2
Warwick Pl BRW CM14 .... 382 E8
GVW DA11 .... 488 A3
VGE SS16 .... 456 A1
Warwick Rd BSF CM23 .... 199 G7
CHING E4 .... 402 B8
COS CO15 .... 10 A4
IPNE IP4 .... 3 F5
PEND EN3 .... 375 F3
RAYL SS6 .... 442 A4
RBSF CM22 .... 202 B5
SOS SS1 .... 465 J7
Warwick Sq CHLM/WR CM1 .... 14 A1
Washford Gdns COS CO15 .... 10 A5
Washington Av LAIN SS15 .... 436 B7
Washington Cl MAL CM9 .... 338 A4 🔲
Washington Rd HAR CO12 .... 6 B6 🔲
MAL CM9 .... 338 B4
Wash La COS CO15 .... 10 A6
MAL CM9 .... 311 K4
Wash Rd LAIN SS15 .... 16 A1
RBRW/HUT CM13 .... 412 D1
The Wash BUNT SG9 .... 133 G8
Watchfield La RAYL SS6 .... 441 H4
Watch House Rd GTDUN CM6 .... 173 K8
Watchouse Rd CHLM/GWD CM2 ... 360 D3
Waterdales GVW DA11 .... 488 A3
Waterdene CVI SS8 .... 460 D8
The Waterfalls VGE SS16 .... 456 C2 🔲
Waterford Rd SBN/FI SS3 .... 466 E4
Waterfront Wk BSDN SS14 .... 17 F1
Waterhale SOS SS1 .... 465 K4
Waterhall Av CHING E4 .... 403 F7 🔲
Water Hall La BRTR CM7 .... 144 C7
Waterhouse Moor HLWS CM18 ...... 13 E4
Waterhouse La CHLM/WR CM1 ..... 332 A4
Waterhouse St CHLM/WR CM1 ..... 14 A5
Water La BRTR CM7 .... 176 C2
BRTR CM7 .... 211 H1
BSF CM23 .... 198 E5
BURES CO8 .... 115 H4
COLW CO3 .... 186 D5
GTDUN CM6 .... 171 F6
HLWW/ROY CM19 .... 321 F5
HSTD CO9 .... 113 H6
HVHL CB9 .... 28 B8
HVHL CB9 .... 49 H6
HVHL CB9 .... 56 B7
PUR RM19 .... 481 H3
RCOLW CO6 .... 118 A5
SAFWN CB10 .... 73 H5
SAFWS CB11 .... 100 B4
SAFWS CB11 .... 101 J4
STSD CM24 .... 167 K7
SUD CO10 .... 32 D3
Waterloo Cl CHLM/WR CM1 .... 14 C3
Waterloo Rd BRW CM14 .... 411 F4
IP IP1 .... 2 B2
SBN/FI SS3 .... 466 C6
Waterloo St GVE DA12 .... 489 H5 🔲
Watermans Wy EPP CM16 .... 352 A1
Watermeadow Cl ERITH DA8 .... 480 C7 🔲
Watermill Rd K/T/MI CO5 .... 247 G1
Waterside CROLE CO7 .... 255 J8
STSD CM24 .... 167 K7 🔲
Waterside Cl HARH RM3 .... 431 H2
Waterside Rd BOC CM0 .... 344 B2
RCFD SS4 .... 425 F8
Watersmeet HLW/ROY CM19 .... 321 K1
Waterson Rd CDH/CHF RM16 .... 485 G3
Waterson V CHLM/GWD CM2 ...... 15 D3
Waterton Av GVE DA12 .... 489 K3
Waterville Dr VGE SS16 .... 458 D1
Waterville Ms COLS CO2 .... 219 J2 🔲
Waterwick Hl SAFWS CB11 .... 96 E3

Waterworks Cl COLS CO2 .... 250 E1
Waterworks Dr RCOS CO16 .... 258 D8
Waterworks La SLH/COR SS17 ...... 457 K7
Watery La BSF CM23 .... 166 B4
CHONG CM5 .... 297 K5
GTDUN CM6 .... 236 E3
RCOLW CO6 .... 212 B4
WICKE SS11 .... 419 H4
Wates Wy BRWN CM15................ 411 G4
Watkins Cl PIT SS13 .... 439 G4
Watkins Wy SBN/FI SS3 .... 466 E4
Watling La GTDUN CM6 .... 139 J1
Watling St GTDUN CM6 .... 139 J2
MEO DA13 .... 488 A8
Watlington Rd HLWE CM17 .... 295 H1
SBF/HAD SS7 .... 460 A3
Watson Cl SBN/FI SS3 .... 466 C6
WTHK RM20 .... 482 D7
Watson Rd COS CO15 .... 10 A4
Watts Cl GTDUN CM6 .... 238 B1
Watts Crs PUR RM19 .... 481 K3
Watts Rd COLS CO2 .... 218 C3
Wavell Av COLS CO2 .... 218 D1
Wavell Cl BAR EN8 .... 346 E1
CHLM/WR CM1 .... 305 F5 🔲
Waveney Dr CHLM/WR CM1 .... 304 E7
Waveney Rd FX IP11 .... 5 E4
IP IP1 .... 36 A5
Waveney Ter HVHL CB9 .... 27 G6 🔲
Waverley Av CHING E4 .... 402 A7
Waverley Crs HARH RM3 .... 430 D1
WICKE SS11 .... 417 F2
Waverley Gdns CDH/CHF RM16 .... 485 K1
Waverley Rd LAIN SS15 .... 16 C1 🔲
SBF/HAD SS7 .... 440 B8
Wavertree Rd SBF/HAD SS7 .... 460 A1
Wanring Av FOS CO15 .... 228 D6
Waxwell Rd CHLM/WR CM1 .... 305 F7
The Wayback SAFWN CB10 .... 71 F5
Way Bank La HSTD CO9 .... 29 G7
Waycross Rd UPMR RM14 .... 432 B8
Wayfarer Gdns BOC CM0 .... 398 A8 🔲
Wayfaring Gn GRAYS RM17 .... 483 J4 🔲
Wayletts LAIN SS15 .... 436 B6
LOS SS9 .... 442 C7
Wayre St HLWE CM17 .... 295 C1
Wayside RCHLM CM3 .... 335 J5
Wayside Av HCH RM12 .... 450 E3
Wayside Cl ROM RM1 .... 430 A5
Waytemore Rd BSF CM23 .... 198 D8
Weald Br EPP CM16 .... 324 E4
Weald Bridge Rd EPP CM16 .... 324 E4
Weald Cl BRW CM14 .... 410 D6
Weald Hall La EPP CM16 .... 323 C7
Weald Park Wy BRW CM14 .... 410 D6
Weald Rd BRW CM14 .... 409 H4
The Weald CVI SS8 .... 477 J1
Weale Rd CHING E4 .... 402 E6
Wear Dr CHLM/WR CM1 .... 305 F7
Weare Gifford SBN/FI SS3 .... 466 B5
Weaverdale SBN/FI SS3 .... 466 D4 🔲
Weaverhead Cl GTDUN CM6 .... 139 J2
Weaverhead La GTDUN CM6 .... 139 K2
Weavers VGE SS16 .... 458 C1
Weavers Cl BCAYE CM11 .... 414 C3 🔲
COLW CO3 .... 186 A8
GVW DA11 .... 489 F6 🔲
Weavers Dr SUD CO10 .... 33 H1
Weaversfield WIT CM8 .... 211 H8
Weavers Gn RCOLW CO6 .... 152 C7
Weavers La COLS CO2 .... 58 B6
Weavers Rw HSTD CO9 .... 148 A4
Weaver St BSF CM23 .... 231 G1
Webber Cl ERITH DA8 .... 480 C6 🔲
Webbs Ct KESG IP5 .... 39 G6 🔲
Webster Cl HCH RM12 .... 450 E3
HSTD CO9 .... 110 C5 🔲
WAB EN9 .... 348 C7 🔲
Webster Pl ING CM4 .... 388 A3 🔲
Webster Rd SLH/COR SS17 .... 474 A3
Websters Wy RAYL SS6 .... 441 J5
Weddell Rd HVHL CB9 .... 27 J7
Wedds Wy SBN/FI SS3 .... 467 G1
Wedgewood Cl EPP CM16 .... 350 E4
Wedgewood Dr COLN CO4 .... 8 A1 🔲
HLWE CM17 .... 295 H6
Wedgwood Wy HLWW/ROY CM19 .. 12 C3
Wedhey HLWW/ROY CM19 .... 12 C3
Wedlake Cl EMPK RM11 .... 451 J2 🔲
Wednesbury Gdns HARH RM3 .... 431 G2
Wednesbury Rd HARH RM3 .... 431 G3
Wednesbury Rd HARH RM3 .... 431 G2
Wedow Rd GTDUN CM6 .... 139 K2
Weeley By-pass Rd RCOS CO16 .... 225 F4
Weeley Rd RCOLE CO7 .... 224 A8
RCOS CO16 .... 258 C1
Weelkes Cl SLH/COR SS17 .... 473 J2
Weel Rd CVI SS8 .... 478 D3
Weggs Willow COLN CO4 .... 9 E4
Weight Rd CHLM/GWD CM2 .... 15 D3
Weir Farm Rd RAYL SS6 .... 441 H5
Weir Gdns RAYL SS6 .... 441 H5
Weir La COLS CO2 .... 219 J6
K/T/MI CO5 .... 220 B5
Weir Pl KIR/NAC IP10 .... 94 C1

Weir Pond Rd RCFD SS4 .... 444 C3
Weir Wynd BCAYW CM12 .... 414 B4
Welbeck Cl FX IP11 .... 94 E8 🔲
HOC/HUL SS5 .... 443 G1
Welbeck Dr VGE SS16 .... 456 B1
Welbeck Ri VGE SS16 .... 456 B1 🔲
Welbeck Rd CVI SS8 .... 478 A3
Welch Cl SOSN SS2 .... 465 H2
Welland Av CHLM/WR CM1 .... 303 J8
Welland Rd BOC CM0 .... 398 A7
Wellands WIT CM8 .... 278 A8
Wellands Cl WIT CM8 .... 277 K8
Weller Gv CHLM/WR CM1 .... 304 A6
Wellers Gv EBAR EN7 .... 346 A2 🔲
Wellesley Rd BRW CM14 .... 411 F4
COLW CO3 .... 8 A5
COS CO15 .... 10 B4
IPNE IP4 .... 37 H8
Well Fld CHLM/WR CM1 .... 331 G4
HSTD CO9 .... 148 A5
Wellfield LOU IG10 .... 377 J4
Wellfield Wy FOS CO13 .... 228 C6
Well-green Cl SAFWS CB11 .... 71 F6 🔲
Wellingbury SBF/HAD SS7 .... 440 B8 🔲
Wellington Av CHING E4 .... 402 B5
HOC/HUL SS5 .... 419 J4
WOS/PRIT SS0 .... 463 H4
Wellington Cl BRTR CM7 .... 210 B1
CHLM/WR CM1 .... 303 K8
Wellington Hl LOU IG10 .... 376 D9
Wellingtonia Av ABR/ST RM4 .... 407 K6
Wellington Ms BCAYW CM12 .... 387 F8 🔲
Wellington Pl BRW CM14 .... 411 F8
Wellington Rd EPP CM16 .... 352 A1
HAR CO12 .... 7 F2
MAL CM9 .... 338 B3
RAYL SS6 .... 442 A2
TIL RM18 .... 489 F1
The Wellingtons BOC CM0 .... 398 D2 🔲
Wellington St COLS CO2 .... 8 A5 🔲
GVE DA12 .... 489 H5
IP IP1 .... 2 B2
RCOLE CO7 .... 255 K7 🔲
Well La BRWN CM15 .... 385 H7
CDH/CHF RM16 .... 470 C8
CHLM/GWD CM2 .... 360 D3
HLW CM20 .... 12 A3
HLWW/ROY CM19 .... 12 A2
ING CM4 .... 388 A4
K/T/MI CO5 .... 215 K7
RCHLM CM3 .... 335 G7
SUD CO10 .... 31 F6
Well Md BCAYW CM12 .... 414 D6 🔲
Wells Av SOSN SS2 .... 444 A7
Wells Ct CHLM/WR CM1 .... 305 F8 🔲
GTDUN CM6 .... 204 B4 🔲
Wellsfield RAYL SS6 .... 441 H4
Wells Gdns RAIN RM13 .... 450 A7
Wells Hall Rd SUD CO10 .... 85 F1
Well Side RCOLW CO6 .... 215 H2
Wells Rd COL CO1 .... 8 C3
Well's St CHLM/WR CM1 .... 14 B2 🔲
Wellstead Gdns WOS/PRIT SS0 ..... 463 J2
Well St RCOLE CO7 .... 255 J6
Wellstye Gn BSDN SS14 .... 438 B5
Welshwood Park Rd COLN CO4 ..... 188 B3
Welsummer Wy BAR EN8 .... 346 D1
Wembley Av RCHLM CM3 .... 368 D5
Wendene VGE SS16 .... 458 C1
Wendon Cl RCFD SS4 .... 443 K1 🔲
Wendover Gdns RBRW/HUT CM13 .. 412 C1
Wendover Wy HCH RM12 .... 450 D6 🔲
Wendy Cl RIPS/CAP IP9 .... 91 J6
Wenham Dr WOS/PRIT SS0 .... 18 B2
Wenham La RCOLE CO7 .... 86 B5
Wenham Rd RIPW IP8 .... 60 D6
Wenlock Rd RCOS CO16 .... 225 G7
Wenlocks La ING CM4 .... 356 C7
Wennington Gn RAIN RM13 .... 468 A7
Wensley Cl CRW RM5 .... 407 F8
Wensley Rd SBF/HAD SS7 .... 461 G1
Wentford Vw SUD CO10 .... 31 F4
Wentworth Cl RCHLM CM3 .... 308 B1
Wentworth Crs BRTR CM7 .... 177 J8
Wentworth Dr BSF CM23 .... 198 C2
FX IP11 .... 131 K1
RIPW IP8 .... 61 J3
Wentworth Mdw MAL CM9 .... 338 B3
Wentworth Pl CDH/CHF RM16 ...... 484 C2 🔲
Wentworth Rd SOSN SS2 .... 19 D1
Wesel Av FX IP11 .... 5 D4
Wesley Av COLN CO4 .... 9 E5
Wesley End Rd HSTD CO9 .... 78 A2
Wesley Gdns BCAYW CM12 .... 387 F8 🔲🔲
Wesley Rd SOS SS1 .... 19 E5
Wessem Rd CVI SS8 .... 461 G8 🔲
Westall Rd LOU IG10 .... 377 K7
West Av CHLM/WR CM1 .... 304 B8
COS CO15 .... 10 B5
HOC/HUL SS5 .... 419 H2
RCHLM CM3 .... 368 C4
VGE SS16 .... 455 K1

West Beech Av WICKE SS11 .... 417 G6
West Beech Cl WICKE SS11 .... 417 H6
West Belvedere RCHLM CM3 .... 335 K6
Westborough Rd WOS/PRIT SS0 .... 463 J3
Westbourne Cl HOC/HUL SS5 .... 421 H6 🔟
  SBF/HAD SS7 .... 441 H8
Westbourne Dr BRW CM14 .... 410 C2
Westbourne Gdns
  BCAYW CM12 .... 387 H8 🔟
Westbourne Gv CHLM/GWD CM2 ...... 15 E6
  WOS/PRIT SS0 .... 463 J1
Westbourne Rd IP IP1 .... 36 B4
West Bowers Rd MAL CM9 .... 336 C1
Westbury BAR EN8 .... 346 D4 🔟
  RCFD SS4 .... 443 K1
Westbury Cl RCOLW CO6 .... 184 C8
Westcliff Dr LOS SS9 .... 462 E4
Westbury La BKHH IG9 .... 403 K5
Westbury Ri HLWE CM17 .... 295 H6
Westbury Rd BKHH IG9 .... 403 K4
  BRW CM14 .... 411 F5
  FOS CO13 .... 227 K8
  IPNE IP4 .... 37 K5
  SOSN SS2 .... 19 F2
Westbury Ter UPMR CM14 .... 388 B2
West Cha MAL CM9 .... 338 B2
  MAL CM9 .... 367 C4
Westcliff Av WOS/PRIT SS0 .... 18 B5
Westcliff Dr LOS SS9 .... 462 E4
Westcliff Gdns CVI SS8 .... 478 E2
Westcliff Pde WOS/PRIT SS0 .... 18 B5
Westcliff Park Dr WOS/PRIT SS0 ...... 18 A2
West Cloister BCAYE CM11 .... 414 C3 🔟
Westcott Av GVW DA11 .... 489 F4
Westcott Cl RCOS CO16 .... 10 A1
West Crs CVI SS8 .... 477 K1
West Crescent Rd GVE DA12 .... 489 G4
Westcroft Cl PEND EN3 .... 374 C4 🔟
Westcroft Ct BROX EN10 .... 319 G1 🔟
West Dene Dr HARH RM3 .... 408 E8
West Dr BRTR CM7 .... 143 J2
West End La HAR CO12 .... 165 G4
Westend La HVHL CB9 .... 28 D3
West End Rd IP IP1 .... 279 H2
  K/T/MI CO5 .... 305 F6
Westerdale CHLM/WR CM1 .... 3 E1
Westerfield Rd IP IP1 .... 279 H2
Westergreen Meadow BRTR CM7 ..... 209 H4
Westerings RCHLM CM3 .... 363 K3
The Westerings CHLM/GWD CM2 ..... 333 H8
  HOC/HUL SS5 .... 421 F8
  RCOLW CO6 .... 118 A3
Westerland Av CVI SS8 .... 478 B3
The Westerlings BRTR CM7 .... 210 D7
Western Approaches LOS SS9 .... 443 H6
Western Av BRW CM14 .... 411 F4
  EPP CM16 .... 350 D6
  GPK RM2 .... 430 D4
  HVHL CB9 .... 26 E4
Western Cl IPNE IP4 .... 64 D1
  WIT CM8 .... 244 E2
Western Esp CVI SS8 .... 478 B3
  SOS SS1 .... 18 C5
  WOS/PRIT SS0 .... 18 A5
Western La WIT CM8 .... 244 E2
Western Ms BCAYW CM12 .... 414 B3
Western Prom RCOLE CO7 .... 255 H8
Western Rd BCAYW CM12 .... 414 B3 🔟
  BOC CM0 .... 425 G1
  BRW CM14 .... 411 F5
  LOS SS9 .... 462 B4
  RAYL SS6 .... 441 G4
  RCOLE CO7 .... 255 J7
  ROM RM1 .... 430 A7
  SBF/HAD SS7 .... 441 K7
  WAB EN9 .... 320 A4
  WIT CM8 .... 245 F2
Western's End MGTR CO11 .... 123 J5
Westfield HLWS CM18 .... 13 E4
  LAIN SS15 .... 436 B5
  SUD CO10 .... 30 E7
Westfield Av CHLM/WR CM1 .... 14 B1
Westfield Cl BAR EN8 .... 347 F5
  BSF CM23 .... 198 D5
  PEND EN3 .... 374 E7
  RAYL SS6 .... 441 F4
  WICKE SS11 .... 417 J5
Westfield Dr RCOLW CO6 .... 213 G2
Westfield Rd BSF CM23 .... 198 D5
West Flds SAFWS CB11 .... 71 F5
Westgate BSDN SS14 .... 17 E4
West Ga HLW CM20 .... 21 H2
Westgate St IP IP1 .... 3 D3 🔟
  SUD CO10 .... 34 E3
West Gn SBF/HAD SS7 .... 440 A8
West Hanningfield Rd
  CHLM/GWD CM2 .... 361 F7
West Hayes RBSF CM22 .... 265 G2
Westhill Cl GVE DA12 .... 489 G6
Westholme Rd IP IP1 .... 36 C4
West Hook VGE SS16 .... 456 A2
West House Est BOC CM0 .... 398 C1
West Kent Av GVW DA11 .... 488 B4

Weymarks LAIN SS15 .... 16 B3
Weymouth Cl COS CO15 .... 291 F5
Weymouth Rd CHLM/WR CM1 .... 305 G7
  IPNE IP4 .... 37 H7
Whadden Cha ING CM4 .... 386 A2
Whalebone Cnr COLN CO4 .... 120 C6
Whaley Rd COL CO1 .... 9 E4
Wharf Cl SLH/COR SS17 .... 473 K4 🔟
Wharfedale Rd IP IP1 .... 36 C4
Wharf La BURES CO8 .... 115 J5
Wharf Rd BROX EN10 .... 319 F6
  BRW CM14 .... 411 F6
  BSF CM23 .... 198 E7
  CHLM/GWD CM2 .... 15 D3
  GRAYS RM17 .... 483 J5
  GVE DA12 .... 489 K4
  MAL CM9 .... 339 H1
  SLH/COR SS17 .... 474 A6
Wharley Hook HLWS CM18 .... 13 F6
Wheat Cft BSF CM23 .... 231 J1 🔟
  CBE/LIN CB1 .... 23 F2
Wheatear Pl BCAYE CM11 .... 414 D4 🔟
Wheatfield Rd COLW CO3 .... 185 J7
Wheatfields HLWE CM17 .... 263 H7 🔟
  PEND EN3 .... 374 E5
  RCFD SS4 .... 445 C1
Wheatfield Wy CHLM/WR CM1 .... 14 A2
  VGE SS16 .... 456 B1
Wheatlands RCOLE CO7 .... 189 J7
Wheatley Av BRTR CM7 .... 210 B2
Wheatley Cl EMPK RM11 .... 430 E7
  RCFD SS4 .... 444 A1
  SBW CM21 .... 263 G4
Wheatley Rd SLH/COR SS17 .... 457 J8
Wheatley Terrace Rd ERITH DA8 ...... 480 A5
Wheaton Rd WIT CM8 .... 277 H3
Wheatsheaf Cl RCOLW CO11 .... 162 A2
Wheatsheaf La MGTR CO11 .... 162 A2
Wheatsheaf Rd ROM RM1 .... 430 A8 🔟
Wheatsheaf Wy CBE/LIN CB1 .... 23 F2
Wheeler Cl COLN CO4 .... 188 B7
Wheelers EPP CM16 .... 350 E3 🔟
Wheelers Farm Gdns EPP CM16 ...... 324 B8 🔟
Wheeler's HI RCHLM CM3 .... 272 E7
Wheelers La BRW CM14 .... 382 C8
  SLH/COR SS17 .... 458 A8
Wheelwrights Cl BSF CM23 .... 231 C1 🔟
The Wheelwrights FX IP11 .... 94 D7 🔟
  SOSN SS2 .... 444 D8
Whernside Av CVI SS8 .... 461 H8
Wherstead Rd CHTY IP2 .... 3 D6
Whinchat Cl CHTY IP2 .... 61 K2
Whinfield Av HAR CO12 .... 164 E4
Whinhams Wy BCAYW CM12 .... 414 A2
The Whinneys KESG IP5 .... 39 H5
Whist Av WICKE SS11 .... 417 J4
Whistler Ri SBN/FI SS3 .... 467 F5
Whitakers Wy LOU IG10 .... 377 H5
Whitbreads Farm La RCHLM CM3 .... 273 F1
Whitby Av RBRW/HUT CM13 .... 434 C1
Whitby Rd BOC CM0 .... 398 B3
  IPNE IP4 .... 37 H5
Whitchurch Cl HARH RM3 .... 409 F7 🔟
Whitcroft VGE SS16 .... 456 D2
White Av GVW DA11 .... 488 E8
White Barns RCHLM CM3 .... 239 H7
Whitebarns La BUNT SG9 .... 132 D6
Whitebeam Cl CHLM/GWD CM2 ...... 14 A6 🔟
Whitebeam Dr SOCK/AV RM15 .... 470 A3
White Bear STSD CM24 .... 167 K5 🔟
Whiteditch La SAFWS CB11 .... 100 A3
White Elm Rd RCHLM CM3 .... 364 A3
White Elm St IPSE IP3 .... 3 F5
Whitefields Rd BAR EN8 .... 346 C2
Whitefriars Crs WOS/PRIT SS0 .... 463 K6
Whitefriars Wy COLW CO3 .... 186 B8
Whitegate Rd RCOLE CO7 .... 256 A7
  SOS SS1 .... 19 D4
White Gates HCH RM12 .... 450 D3 🔟
Whitehall Cl CHIG IG7 .... 405 K6 🔟
  COLS CO2 .... 219 K1
White Hall Cl SLID CO10 .... 59 H2
Whitehall Ct WAB EN9 .... 320 H3 🔟
Whitehall Ct WIT CM8 .... 277 G3
Whitehall Gdns CHING E4 .... 402 E4
Whitehall La BKHH IG9 .... 403 H5
  BSF CM23 .... 198 E4
  ERITH DA8 .... 480 A8
  GRAYS RM17 .... 484 B5
  RCOS CO16 .... 225 K2
  SLH/COR SS17 .... 457 K6
Whitehall Rd BSF CM23 .... 198 D4
  CHING E4 .... 403 F5
  COLS CO2 .... 219 K2
  GRAYS RM17 .... 484 B5
White Hall Rd SBN/FI SS3 .... 467 C1
White Hart La HOC/HUL SS5 .... 421 F8 🔟
  RCOLW CO6 .... 153 K8
Whitehill Cl GVE DA12 .... 489 J8
Whitehill Pde GVE DA12 .... 489 H8 🔟
Whitehill Rd GVE DA12 .... 489 H7
Whitehills Rd LOU IG10 .... 377 J7
White Horse Av HSTD CO9 .... 147 J5
White Horse Cl FX IP11 .... 131 K1 🔟

White Horse HI *RIPS/CAP* IP9 .... 88 E4
White Horse La *MAL* CM9 .... 338 B3
  SAFWS CB11 .... 100 B4
  WIT CM8 .... 277 F2
White Horse Rd *HVHL* CB9. .... 28 C3
  RCOLE CO7 .... 122 C4
  RIPS/CAP IP9. .... 87 G4
White House Cha *RAYL* SS6 .... 441 K5
White House Crs *CHLM/GWD* CM2. .... 15 E5
Whitehouse HI *MAL* CM9 .... 282 A6
Whitehouse La *RCOLW* CO6. .... 185 J2
  SUD CO10 .... 55 G4
Whitehouse Mdw *LOS* SS9 .... 443 H7
Whitehouse Rd *GTDUN* CM6 .... 174 A8
White House Rd *LOS* SS9 .... 443 G7
Whitehouse Rd *CHLM* CM3 .... 392 D5
Whitelands *BRWN* CM15 .... 384 B1
Whitelands Cl *WICKE* SS11 .... 417 H4
Whitelands Rd *HARH* RM3 .... 430 E3
White Lodge Crs *RCOS* CO16 .... 227 F4
White Lyons Rd *BRW* CM14 .... 411 F6
White Md *CHLM/WR* CM1 .... 304 C3
White Post Fld *SBW* CM21 .... 263 H5
Whitesbridge La *ING* CM4 .... 359 F4
Whites Fld *RCOLE* CO7 .... 122 A2
White's HI *ING* CM4 .... 388 B3
Whiteshott Wy *SAFWN* CB10 .... 71 G3
Whites La *RCHLM* CM3 .... 241 G7
Whitesmith Rd *BCAYW* CM12. .... 413 K2
White St *GTDUN* CM6 .... 204 C5
Whitethorn Gdns *CHLM/GWD* CM2 .... 15 D6
  EMPK RM11 .... 430 D8
Whitethorn Rd *IPSE* IP3 .... 64 D4
White Tree Ct *CHLM* CM3 .... 392 B7
Whitewaits *HLW* CM20 .... 13 E2
Whiteways *BCAYE* CM11 .... 414 E3
  CVI SS8 .... 478 D3
  LOS SS9 .... 443 G7
Whiteways Ct *WIT* CM8 .... 276 E2
Whitewell Rd *COLS* CO2 .... 8 B5
Whitfields *SLH/COR* SS17 .... 474 B3
Whit Hern Ct *BAR* EN8 .... 346 C4
Whitland Cl *CHTY* IP2 .... 62 C5
Whitlock Dr *HSTD* CO9 .... 79 J4
Whitmore Av *CDH/CHF* RM16 .... 471 F7
  HARH RM3 .... 431 F4
Whitmore Cl *CDH/CHF* RM16. .... 472 E6
Whitmore Rd *BSDN* SS14 .... 438 B4
Whitmore Crs *CHLM/GWD* CM2 .... 333 K2
Whitmore Rd *BSDN* SS14 .... 17 F3
  BSDN SS14 .... 438 A6
Whittaker Wy *K/T/MI* CO5. .... 284 D6
Whittingham Av *SOSN* SS2 .... 465 H3
Whittington Rd *RBRW/HUT* CM13 .... 412 C2
Whittington Wy *BSF* CM23 .... 231 J2
Whittle Rd *CHTY* IP2 .... 2 A3
Whitton Church La *IP* IP1 .... 36 A1
Whitworth Ct *CHTY* IP2 .... 61 K3
Whybrews *SLH/COR* SS17 .... 564 B4
Whytewaters *VGE* SS16 .... 458 C2
Whyverne Cl *CHLM/WR* CM1. .... 305 G7
Wick Beech Av *WICKE* SS11 .... 417 H6
Wick Cha *SOSN* SS2 .... 465 H4
Wick Crs *WICKW* SS12 .... 417 H8
Wick Dr *WICKW* SS12 .... 417 G6
Wicken Rd *SAFWS* CB11 .... 98 E4
Wick Farm Rd *BOC* CM0 .... 342 C5
Wickfield Ash *CHLM/WR* CM1. .... 303 K7
Wickford Av *PIT* SS13 .... 438 C1
Wickford Dr *HARH* RM3 .... 409 G8
Wickford Rd *CHLM* CM3 .... 392 A5
  WOS/PRIT SS0 .... 18 B5
Wick Gln *BCAYW* CM12 .... 414 A1
Wickham Bishop Rd *CHLM* CM3.. .... 308 D1
Wickhambrook Ct *FX* IP11 .... 4 C3
Wickham Cl *EN* EN1 .... 334 B7
Wickham Crs *CHLM/WR* CM1 .... 304 B7
Wickham Hall La *WIT* CM8 .... 509 J2
Wickham Pl *VGE* SS16 .... 437 K8
Wickham Rd *CDH/CHF* RM16.. .... 485 K1
  COLW CO3 .... 186 E8
  WIT CM8 .... 277 H8
Wickham's Cha *CHLM* CM3 .... 364 C3
Wickhay *LAIN* SS15 .... 17 D5
Wick La *HAR* CO12 .... 165 G4
  K/T/MI CO5 .... 254 B2
  RCOLE CO7 .... 156 E5
  RCOS CO16 .... 257 J2
  WICKE SS11 .... 417 H6
Wicklow Av *CHLM/WR* CM1.. .... 303 K7
Wicklow Wk *SBN/FI* SS3. .... 466 B6
Wickmead Cl *SOSN* SS2 .... 465 H3
Wick Rd *BOC* CM0 .... 425 J1
  COLN CO4 .... 119 K3
  COLS CO2 .... 220 A3
  RCOLE CO7 .... 224 C8
Widbrook *BRWN* CM15 .... 584 A2
Wid Cl *RBRW/HUT* CM13 .... 412 C1
Widecombe Cl *HARH* RM3 .... 430 E3
Widford Cha *CHLM/GWD* CM2 .... 14 A6
Widford Cl *CHLM/GWD* CM2 .... 14 A6
Widford Gv *CHLM/GWD* CM2.. .... 14 A6
Widford Park Pl
  CHLM/GWD CM2 .... 14 A6

Widford Rd *CHLM/GWD* CM2 .... 14 A6
Widgeon Cl *CHTY* IP2 .... 2 A6
Widgeon Pl *K/T/MI* CO5 .... 246 E3
Widgeon Rd *ERITH* DA8 .... 480 C6
Widgeons *PIT* SS13 .... 439 F7
Widleybrook La *BRTR* CM7 .... 144 C2
Widworthy Hayes
  RBRW/HUT CM13 .... 412 A4
Wigborough Rd *COLS* CO2.. .... 250 E3
  K/T/MI CO5 .... 283 J1
Wigboro Wick La *RCOS* CO16 .... 288 E3
Wigeon Cl *BRTR* CM7 .... 209 F8
Wiggin's La *BCAYW* CM12.. .... 413 K6
  BCAYW CM12. .... 413 K7
Wigley Bush La *BRW* CM14 .... 410 B5
Wigmore Cl *CHTY* IP2 .... 62 B4
Wignall St *MCTR* CO11 .... 158 E2
Wigton Rd *HARH* RM3 .... 409 F7
Wigton Wy *HARH* RM3 .... 409 F7
Wilberforce St *IP* IP1 .... 2 B3
Wilbye Cl *COLS* CO2 .... 218 C1
Wilde Cl *TIL* RM18 .... 485 C8
Wilding Dr *KESG* IP5 .... 39 H6
Wilding Rd *RIPW* IP8 .... 61 J4
Wilfred St *GVE* DA12 .... 489 G4
Wilkes Rd *RBRW/HUT* CM13 .... 412 C1
Wilkin Cl *COLW* CO3 .... 218 B1
Wilkin Dr *K/T/MI* CO5 .... 248 B5
Wilkinsons Md *CHLM/GWD* CM2 .. 333 J1
Willett Rd *COLS* CO2 .... 218 C2
Willetts Fld *SAFWN* CB10 .... 105 F2
William Booth Wy *FX* IP11 .... 5 D2
William Boys Cl *COLN* CO4 .... 9 F3
William Cl *RCOLE* CO7 .... 221 F1
William Dr *COS* CO15. .... 290 E3
William Groom Av *HAR* CO12 .... 6 B6
William Rd *PIT* SS13 .... 439 H7
Williamsons Wy *SLH/COR* SS17 .... 457 G8
Williams Rd *CHLM/WR* CM1 .... 304 D4
  GVE DA12 .... 489 G5
William's Wk *COL* CO1 .... 8 B4
Willingale Av *RAYL* SS6 .... 441 F2
Willingale Cl *RBRW/HUT* CM13 .... 412 D2
Willingale Rd *BRTR* CM7.. .... 210 C1
  CHONG CM5 .... 327 J2
  LOU IG10 .... 378 A5
The Willingales *LAIN* SS15 .... 436 B7
Willingale Wy *SOS* SS1 .... 465 K4
Willinghall Cl *WAB* EN9 .... 347 K6
Willingham Wy *COLN* CO4 .... 188 B6
Willmott Rd *SOSN* SS2 .... 444 A7
Willoughby Av *K/T/MI* CO5.. .... 285 F7
Willoughby Cl *BROX* EN10 .... 318 E3
Willoughby Dr *CHLM/GWD* CM2 .. 333 H3
Willoughby Rd *CHTY* IP2 .... 2 C5
Willoughby's La *BRTR* CM7 .... 178 B5
Willow Av *FOS* CO15 .... 228 C7
  RCOS CO16 .... 289 H7
Willowbank *CHLM/GWD* CM2 .... 360 D2
Willow Cl *BKHH* IG9 .... 004 A6
  BOC CM0 .... 398 B7
  BRWN CM15 .... 384 B4
  BSF CM23 .... 198 C5
  CHLM/WR CM1 .... 304 D4
  CVI SS8 .... 477 K2
  HCH RM12 .... 450 C4
  HOC/HUL SS5 .... 421 G7
  HVHL CB9 .... 26 D4
  LOS SS9 .... 443 F7
  RBRW/HUT CM13 .... 412 A2
  RCOLE CO7 .... 156 A7
  RCOLE CO7 .... 255 H7
Willow Crs *RCHLM* CM3 .... 308 A2
Willowcroft Rd *IP* IP1 .... 36 C3
Willowdene *BAR* EN8 .... 346 E1
  BRWN CM15 .... 410 C1
  HSTD CO9 .... 110 C3
Willowdene Ct *BRW* CM14.. .... 411 F7
Willow Dr *RAYL* SS6 .... 441 H1
Willowfield *HLWS* CM18 .... 13 D4
Willowfields *LAIN* SS15 .... 16 A2
Willow Gn *ING* CM4 .... 386 B1
Willow Gv *RCHLM* CM3 .... 392 A4
  RCOLW CO6 .... 118 A3
Willow Hall La *MCTR* CO11.. .... 162 A5
Willowhill *SLH/COR* SS17 .... 457 F8
Willowmead *BCAYE* CM11 .... 388 E3
  CHIG IG7 .... 405 K6
Willow Md *SBW* CM21 .... 263 J4
Willow Mdw *HSTD* CO9 .... 110 D5
Willow Pk *RCOLW* CO6 .... 184 D8
Willow Pl *HLWE* CM17 .... 323 K1
Willow Ri *WIT* CM8 .... 245 G8
Willow Rd *ERITH* DA8 .... 480 B7
Willow Springs *BSF* CM23 .... 198 C5
The Willows *BCAYE* CM11 .... 414 E8
  COLS CO2 .... 219 H2
  GRAYS RM17 .... 484 C5
  RCHLM CM3 .... 306 C5
  SAFWN CB10 .... 43 J2
  SBF/HAD SS7 .... 460 A1
  SOS SS1 .... 465 K4
Willow St *CHING* E4 .... 402 C5
Willow Tree Wy *RCOLW* CO6 .... 149 J7

Willow Wk *HOC/HUL* SS5 .... 421 G7
  K/T/MI CO5 .... 248 A6
  RCFD SS4 .... 423 G4
  SBF/HAD SS7 .... 461 J2
  UPMR RM14 .... 452 B2
Willow Wy *COS* CO15 .... 290 C6
  HAR CO12 .... 6 A6
  HARH RM3 .... 431 J1
  HSTD CO9 .... 147 J4
Will's Ayley La *SAFWN* CB10.. .... 72 B3
Wills HI *SLH/COR* SS17. .... 473 K2
Wilmington Rd *COLN* CO4 .... 9 E1
Wilmot Gn *RBRW/HUT* CM13 .... 433 F7
Wilmslow Dr *RIPW* IP8 .... 61 J3
Wilmslowe *CVI* SS8 .... 461 J8
Wilrich Av *CVI* SS8 .... 478 D2
Wilshire Av *CHLM/GWD* CM2. .... 333 H2
Wilsman Rd *SOCK/AV* RM15.. .... 470 A2
Wilsner *PIT* SS13 .... 439 F6
Wilson Cl *BSF* CM23. .... 198 E8
  RCOLE CO7 .... 220 D5
  SLH/COR SS17 .... 473 J5
Wilson Marriage Rd *COLN* CO4 .... 9 E2
Wilson Rd *RIPW* IP8 .... 61 H4
  WOS/PRIT SS0.. .... 18 C5
Wilson's La *RCOLW* CO6 .... 215 H2
Wilton Cl *BSF* CM23.. .... 199 G6
Wiltshire Av *EMPK* RM11 .... 431 G6
Wimarc Crs *RAYL* SS6 .... 441 G1
Wimbish End *PIT* SS13 .... 438 E7
Wimbish Wk *SAFWN* CB10 .... 102 B3
Wimborne Av *IPSE* IP3 .... 64 B1
Wimborne Cl *BKHH* IG9 .... 403 K5
  SBW CM21 .... 263 H3
Wimborne Rd *SOSN* SS2.. .... 19 E3
Wimbourne *LAIN* SS15 .... 436 B6
Wimbourne Gdns *FOS* CO13 .... 228 E6
Wimhurst Cl *HOC/HUL* SS5 .... 421 F6
Wimpole Cl *KESG* IP5 .... 38 D7
Wimpole Rd *COL* CO1 .... 9 D5
Winbrook Cl *RAYL* SS6 .... 441 K5
Winbrook Rd *RAYL* SS6. .... 441 K5
Wincanton Cl *IPNE* IP4 .... 37 J4
Wincanton Rd *HARH* RM3 .... 408 E6
Wincelow Hall Rd *SAFWN* CB10 .... 74 C4
Winchcombe Cl *LOS* SS9 .... 463 F2
Winchelsea Dr *CHLM/GWD* CM2 .... 15 E6
Winchelsea Pl *RCOLE* CO7 .... 255 K5
Winchester Av *UPMR* RM14 .... 452 C2
Winchester Cl *BSF* CM23.. .... 231 H1
  LOS SS9 .... 443 G6
Winchester Crs *GVE* DA12 .... 489 J8
Winchester Gdns *LAIN* SS15 .... 16 A1
Winchester Rd *COLS* CO2. .... 8 C6
  FOS CO13 .... 229 F8
Winchester Wy *CHTY* IP2 .... 62 B5
Winch Vw *EPP* CM16 .... 351 F3
Winckford Cl *RCHLM* CM3 .... 272 D7
Wincoat Cl *SBF/HAD* SS7 .... 460 B2
Wincoat Dr *SBF/HAD* SS7 .... 460 A2
Windermere Av *HCH* RM12 .... 450 B6
  HOC/HUL SS5 .... 419 J3
Windermere Cl *IPSE* IP3 .... 63 K5
Windermere Dr *BRTR* CM7 .... 209 F7
Windermere Rd *BRTR* CM7 .... 209 F6
  COS CO15 .... 11 F1
  SBF/HAD SS7 .... 440 D6
  SOS SS1 .... 19 E4
  SUD CO10 .... 58 C5
Windham Rd *SUD* CO10 .... 58 B5
Windhill *BSF* CM23 .... 198 D7
Wind HI *CHONG* CM5 .... 325 G1
Windhill Old Rd *BSF* CM23 .... 198 D6
Winding Piece *RIPS/CAP* IP9 .... 87 F4
Windmill Cl *COLN* CO4. .... 155 G1
  GTDUN CM6 .... 204 D4
  HAR CO12 .... 163 J4
  UPMR RM14 .... 451 H3
  WAB EN9 .... 348 A8
Windmill Ct *RCOLW* CO6 .... 216 C1
Windmill Flds *HLWE* CM17 .... 295 K1
  RCOLW CO6 .... 113 C2
Windmill Gdns *BRTR* CM7 .... 177 K5
Windmill Hts *BCAYW* CM12 .... 414 C5
Windmill HI *RIPS/CAP* IP9 .... 86 D4
  SAFWN CB10 .... 70 C2
  SUD CO10 .... 34 D3
Windmill La *BAR* EN8 .... 346 E4
Windmill Mdw *GTDUN* CM6 .... 268 A2
Windmill Pk *COS* CO15 .... 10 C2
Windmill HI *HSTD* CO9 .... 147 J4
  MCTR CO11 .... 160 D4
Windmills *RCOLW* CO6 .... 183 F5
The Windmills *CHLM/WR* CM1 .... 304 C2
Windmill St *GVE* DA12. .... 489 G5
Windmill Vw *K/T/MI* CO5 .... 248 A7
Windmill Wy *BRWN* CM15 .... 383 G3
Windrush Dr *CHLM/WR* CM1 .... 304 E7
Windrush Rd *KESG* IP5 .... 39 G5
Windsor Av *CDH/CHF* RM16. .... 484 A1
  COS CO15.. .... 10 A4
  SLH/COR SS17 .... 457 H8
Windsor Cl *COLS* CO2 .... 219 H3
  CVI SS8 .... 478 B2
  EBAR EN7 .... 346 A4

Windsor Ct *RCOLE* CO7 ..... 255 K7 ▣
Windsor Gdns *BRTR* CM7 ..... 210 A1 ▣
 BSF CM23 ..... 198 B6
 HOC/HUL SS5 ..... 443 J1
 SBF/HAD SS7 ..... 461 H1
 WICKE SS11 ..... 417 G4
Windsor Rd *BCAYE* CM11 ..... 389 F8
 RRWN CM15 ..... 410 E2
 CHING E4 ..... 402 C7
 COS CO15 ..... 10 A5
 EMPK RM11 ..... 450 D1
 FX IP11 ..... 5 E4 ▣
 IP IP1 ..... 2 A2
 K/T/MI CO5 ..... 285 F6
 PEND EN3 ..... 374 D2
 PIT SS13 ..... 439 H5
 WOS/PRIT SS0 ..... 18 B3
The Windsors *BKHH* IG9 ..... 404 B5
Windsor Wy *RAYL* SS6 ..... 441 K4
Windsor Wd *WAB* EN9 ..... 348 A7 ▣
Windward CI *PEND* EN3 ..... 374 D1
Windward Wy *RCHLM* CM3 ..... 393 F7
Windy HI *RBRW/HUT* CM13 ..... 412 B4
Winfields *PIT* SS13 ..... 439 F5
Winford Dr *BROX* EN10 ..... 319 F4
Winfrith Rd *IPSE* IP3 ..... 64 B1
Wingate CI *BRTR* CM7 ..... 209 H1 ▣
Wingfield *GRAYS* RM17 ..... 483 J4
Wingfield CI *RBRW/HUT* CM13 ..... 411 K6 ▣
Wingfield Gdns *UPMR* RM14 ..... 432 C8 ▣
Wingfield Rd *GVW* DA11 ..... 489 C5
Wingfield St *IPNE* IP4 ..... 3 D4
Wingletye La *EMPK* RM11 ..... 451 G2
Wingrave Crs *BRW* CM14 ..... 410 B7 ▣
Wingway *BRWN* CM15 ..... 411 H4 ▣
Winifred Av *HCH* RM12 ..... 450 E5
Winifred Rd *PIT* SS13 ..... 438 E7
Winnington Rd *PEND* EN3 ..... 374 C4
Winnock Rd *COL* CO1 ..... 8 C5
Winsey Cha *BRTR* CM7 ..... 106 D7
Winsford Gdns *WOS/PRIT* SS0 ..... 463 H1
Winsford Wy *CHLM/GWD* CM2 ..... 335 K7
Winsley Rd *COL* CO1 ..... 8 C5
Winslow Gv *CHING* E4 ..... 403 F5
Winstanley Rd *SAFWS* CB11 ..... 71 G6
Winston Av *COLW* CO3 ..... 218 C1
 IPNE IP3 ..... 38 A5
 K/T/MI CO5 ..... 248 C8
Winston Churchill Wy *BAR* EN8 ..... 346 C7
Winston CI *BRTR* CM7 ..... 177 H7 ▣
 FX IP11 ..... 5 D2
Winston Wy *HSTD* CO9 ..... 148 B2
Winstree *PIT* SS13 ..... 438 E5
Winstree Rd *BOC* CM0 ..... 398 B8
 COLW CO3 ..... 185 J7 ▣
Winstreet CI *COLS* CO2 ..... 218 A8
Winterbournes *WOTN* CO14 ..... 229 F6
Winter Folly *LAIN* SS15 ..... 16 C5 ▣
Winter Gardens Pth *CVI* SS8 ..... 460 D6
Winter's Rd *K/T/MI* CO5 ..... 249 H4
Winters Wy *WAB* EN9 ..... 348 C7
Winterswyk Av *CVI* SS8 ..... 478 E2
Winton Av *WICKE* SS12 ..... 416 D5
 WOS/PRIT SS0 ..... 18 B5
Winton Dr *BAR* EN8 ..... 346 E3
Wiscombe HI *VGE* SS16 ..... 456 D2
Wisdoms Gn *RCOLW* CO6 ..... 263 G4
Wisemans Gdns *SBW* CM21 ..... 128 C1 ▣
Wistaria CI *BRWN* CM15 ..... 410 E1
Wistaria Pl *COS* CO15 ..... 258 E8
Wiston Rd *RCOLW* CO6 ..... 117 K4
Witchards *VGE* SS16 ..... 17 F5
Witch Elm *HAR* CO12 ..... 6 A6
Witch La *RCOLW* CO6 ..... 181 J5
Witchtree La *SAFWN* CB10 ..... 74 E2
Witham CI *LOU* IG10 ..... 404 B2
Witham Gdns *RBRW/HUT* CM13 ..... 434 C8 ▣
Witham Ldg *WIT* CM8 ..... 276 D5
Witham Rd *BRTR* CM7 ..... 209 K7
 GPK RM2 ..... 430 C2
 MAL CM9 ..... 280 A8
 RCHLM CM3 ..... 275 J4
 WIT CM8 ..... 243 G1
The Witherings *EMPK* RM11 ..... 431 F7
Withersfield Rd *HVHL* CB9 ..... 26 E4
Withipoll St *IP* IP1 ..... 3 F3
Withrick Wk *RCOS* CO16 ..... 257 G8
Withy Md *CHING* E4 ..... 403 F5
The Withywindle *RCHLM* CM3 ..... 392 C7
Witney Rd *BOC* CM0 ..... 425 H1
Wittem Rd *CVI* SS8 ..... 461 G8
Wittenham Av *CHING* E4 ..... 402 C6
The Witterings *CVI* SS8 ..... 461 F8
Witting Rd *RCOS* CO16 ..... 10 A2
Witton Wood Rd *FOS* CO13 ..... 228 D3
Wivenhoe Rd *RCOLE* CO7 ..... 189 F4
Wix By-pass *MGTR* CO11 ..... 161 J8
Wix Rd *HAR* CO12 ..... 163 J4
 MGTR CO11 ..... 161 C5
 RCOS CO16 ..... 194 A5
Woburn Av *BSF* CM23 ..... 198 B6
 EPP CM16 ..... 378 C3
 FOS CO13 ..... 228 C6
 HCH RM12 ..... 450 B5

Woburn Pl *BCAYW* CM12 ..... 387 F8 🔟
Wokindon Crs *CDH/CHF* RM16 ..... 485 C2
Wollaston Crs *PIT* SS13 ..... 439 G3
Wollaston Wy *PIT* SS13 ..... 439 F4 ▣
Wolmers Hey *RCHLM* CM3 ..... 272 B6
Wolseley Av *COS* CO15 ..... 290 B7
Wolseley Rd *CHLM/GWD* CM2 ..... 14 B3
Wolsey Gdns *FX* IP11 ..... 131 H4
Wolsey Rd *EN* EN1 ..... 374 B6
Wolsey St *IP* IP1 ..... 3 D4
Wolton Rd *COLS* CO2 ..... 218 C2
 KESC IP5 ..... 39 G6
Wolves Hall La *RCOS* CO16 ..... 193 F4
Wombwell Gdns *GVW* DA11 ..... 488 C7
Wonston Rd *BOC* CM0 ..... 398 C1
Wood Av *HOC/HUL* SS5 ..... 421 F5
 PUR RM19 ..... 481 K3
Wood Barn La *MGTR* CO11 ..... 158 C4
Woodberry CI *CVI* SS8 ..... 461 F7 ▣
 LOS SS9 ..... 442 D8
Woodberry Down *EPP* CM16 ..... 350 E3
Woodberry Rd *WICKE* SS11 ..... 417 K7 ▣
Woodberry Wy *CHING* E4 ..... 402 D3
 FOS CO13 ..... 229 G6
Woodbine CI *HLWW/ROY* CM19 ..... 12 C5
Woodbridge CI *HARH* RM3 ..... 408 E7 ▣
Woodbridge Gv *RCOS* CO16 ..... 290 C1
Woodbridge La *HARH* RM3 ..... 408 E6
Woodbridge Rd *IPNE* IP3 ..... 38 B6
 KESC IP5 ..... 38 D5
Woodbridge Rd East *IPNE* IP3 ..... 38 A6
Woodbrooke Wy *SLH/COR* SS17 ..... 457 J8
Woodbrook Gdns *WAB* EN9 ..... 348 A7
Woodburn CI *SBF/HAD* SS7 ..... 461 G1
Woodbury HI *LOU* IG10 ..... 377 G6
Woodcock La *COLN* CO4 ..... 188 B7
 HVHL CB9 ..... 27 J6
Woodcock Rd *CHTY* IP2 ..... 62 A3
Woodcote Ap *SBF/HAD* SS7 ..... 440 A6 ▣
Woodcote Av *HCH* RM12 ..... 450 B5
Woodcote CI *BAR* EN8 ..... 346 C4
Woodcote Crs *PIT* SS13 ..... 439 G7
Woodcote Ms *LOU* IG10 ..... 404 A3
Woodcote Rd *LOS* SS9 ..... 463 H3
Woodcotes *SBN/FI* SS3 ..... 466 D4
Woodcote Wy *SBF/HAD* SS7 ..... 440 A6
Woodcroft *HLWS* CM18 ..... 12 C5
Woodcroft CI *SBF/HAD* SS7 ..... 461 H3 ▣
Woodcutters Av
 CDH/CHF RM16 ..... 484 B1 ▣
 LOS SS9 ..... 442 D8
Wood CI *CHLM/GWD* CM2 ..... 333 G7
Woodedge CI *CHING* E4 ..... 403 G4
Wood End Av *HOC/HUL* SS5 ..... 420 E8
Woodend CI *SBF/HAD* SS7 ..... 461 H1 ▣
Wood Farm CI *LOS* SS9 ..... 462 E1
Woodfield Av *GVW* DA11 ..... 489 G4
Woodfield CI *FOS* CO13 ..... 229 F6
 STSD CM24 ..... 167 K7 ▣
Woodfield Dr *GPK* RM2 ..... 430 B6
 K/T/MI CO5 ..... 284 D6
Wood Field End *COLS* CO2 ..... 218 B8
Woodfield Gdns *LOS* SS9 ..... 463 G5
Woodfield La *RIPS/CAP* IP9 ..... 125 F3
Woodfield Park Dr *LOS* SS9 ..... 463 H4
Woodfield Rd *BRTR* CM7 ..... 209 J2
 LOS SS9 ..... 463 H4
 SBF/HAD SS7 ..... 462 B2 ▣
Woodfields *STSD* CM24 ..... 167 K7
Woodfield Ter *STSD* CM24 ..... 167 K8 ▣
Woodfield Wy *HCH* RM12 ..... 450 E2 ▣
 RCHLM CM3 ..... 308 A1
The Woodfines *EMPK* RM11 ..... 430 E8
Woodford CI *COS* CO15 ..... 259 H5
Woodford St *WAB* EN9 ..... 348 C7
Woodgates Rd *RCOLE* CO7 ..... 86 C8
Woodgrange CI *SOS* SS1 ..... 465 H5 ▣
Woodgrange Dr *SOS* SS1 ..... 19 F5
Wood Gn *PIT* SS13 ..... 438 E4
Woodgreen Rd *WAB* EN9 ..... 348 E7
Woodhall CI *SUD* CO10 ..... 58 B4
Woodhall Crs *EMPK* RM11 ..... 451 G1
Woodhall Gv *SBF/HAD* SS7 ..... 198 C7
Woodhall HI *CHLM/WR* CM1 ..... 303 H2
Woodhall Rd *CHLM/WR* CM1 ..... 304 C6
 SUD CO10 ..... 58 B4
Woodhill *HLWS* CM18 ..... 13 G6
Woodhill Common Rd
 RCHLM CM3 ..... 335 F8
Woodhill Rd *CHLM/GWD* CM2 ..... 334 A7
Woodhouse La *CHLM/WR* CM1 ..... 304 C1
 KIR/NAC IP10 ..... 65 C3
Woodhurst Rd *CVI* SS8 ..... 477 J2
Wooding Gv *HLWW/ROY* CM19 ..... 12 B3
Woodland Av *RBRW/HUT* CM13 ..... 412 B1
Woodland Cha *COLW* CO3 ..... 184 B4
Woodland CI *RBRW/HUT* CM13 ..... 412 B1
 RCHLM CM3 ..... 276 A8

 SBF/HAD SS7 ..... 462 A2
 WFD IG8 ..... 403 J6
Woodland Dr *COLW* CO3 ..... 186 A8
Woodland Park Cha *RCHLM* CM3 ..... 368 E6
Woodland Rd *CHING* E4 ..... 402 D4
 CHLM/WR CM1 ..... 14 B1
 LOU IG10 ..... 377 G7 ▣
Woodlands *BRTR* CM7 ..... 210 A2
 BSF CM23 ..... 199 H5
 COLN CO4 ..... 188 C4
 COS CO15 ..... 290 C4
 HAR CO12 ..... 194 E3
 RCHLM CM3 ..... 396 E2
 RIPS/CAP IP9 ..... 91 H6
Woodlands Av *EMPK* RM11 ..... 430 E7
 RAYL SS6 ..... 441 J5
Woodlands CI *CDH/CHF* RM16 ..... 484 D2
 COS CO15 ..... 259 J5
 HOC/HUL SS5 ..... 420 E8
 ING CM4 ..... 386 C1
 RAYL SS6 ..... 441 J5
 VGE SS16 ..... 458 C1
Woodlands Dr *HOD* EN11 ..... 319 G1
 SLH/COR SS17 ..... 457 K4
Woodlands Pk *LOS* SS9 ..... 462 B2
Woodlands Park Dr *GTDUN* CM6 ..... 204 A4
Woodlands Ri *RCOS* CO16 ..... 225 G4 ▣
Woodlands Rd *HARH* RM3 ..... 431 H3
 HOC/HUL SS5 ..... 420 E8
 RIPS/CAP IP9 ..... 89 K6
 ROM RM1 ..... 430 A5
 WICKW SS12 ..... 417 G6
The Woodlands *CBE/LIN* CB1 ..... 22 D2
 RCOLE CO7 ..... 255 J5 ▣
 SBN/FI SS3 ..... 466 E5
Woodland Wy *CHONG* CM5 ..... 354 B4
 EPP CM16 ..... 378 C1
 HSTD CO9 ..... 146 D5 ▣
 RCOLE CO7 ..... 220 E4
 WFD IG8 ..... 403 J6
Wood La *BSF* CM23 ..... 199 K3
 BUNT SG9 ..... 96 D7
 CHONG CM5 ..... 328 B2
 GTDUN CM6 ..... 268 B4
 HCH RM12 ..... 450 B6
 MAL CM9 ..... 310 C8
 MAL CM9 ..... 367 C4
 RCOLW CO6 ..... 184 E4
 WFD IG8 ..... 403 G8
Woodleigh Av *LOS* SS9 ..... 462 E2
Woodley Wk *SBN/FI* SS3 ..... 466 D3 ▣
Woodlow *SBF/HAD* SS7 ..... 441 G7
Woodmanhurst Rd
 SLH/COR SS17 ..... 457 G8 ▣
Woodman La *CHING* E4 ..... 402 E1
Woodman Pth *BARK/HLT* IG6 ..... 405 H8
Woodman Rd *BRW* CM14 ..... 411 F8
Wood Meads *EPP* CM16 ..... 350 E3
Woodpecker CI *BSF* CM23 ..... 198 B7 ▣
 COLN CO4 ..... 188 C5 ▣
Woodpecker Rd *CHTY* IP2 ..... 61 K2
Woodpond Av *HOC/HUL* SS5 ..... 420 E8
Woodredon
 HLWW/ROY CM19 ..... 292 D6 ▣
Woodridden HI *WAB* EN9 ..... 377 F1
Wood Rd *MAL* CM9 ..... 310 D7
Woodroffe CI *CHLM/GWD* CM2 ..... 333 J2
Woodrolfe Farm La *MAL* CM9 ..... 314 F4
Woodrolfe Pk *MAL* CM9 ..... 315 F3
Woodrolfe Rd *MAL* CM9 ..... 314 E4
Woodrows La *RCOS* CO16 ..... 258 D8
Woodrow Wy *COLN* CO4 ..... 188 B6
Woodrush End *COLW* CO3 ..... 185 G7 ▣
Woodrush Rd *IPSE* IP3 ..... 64 B3
Woodside *BKHH* IG9 ..... 403 K5
 BSF CM23 ..... 199 J5
 EBAR EN7 ..... 346 A5
 EPP CM16 ..... 351 H1
 FOS CO13 ..... 229 G7
 LOS SS9 ..... 442 C8
 MAL CM9 ..... 310 D2
 RCHLM CM3 ..... 335 J4
Woodside Av *SBF/HAD* SS7 ..... 440 A5
Woodside Cha *HOC/HUL* SS5 ..... 443 F1
Woodside CI *COLN* CO4 ..... 188 B4 ▣
 RBRW/HUT CM13 ..... 412 C1 ▣
 SBF/HAD SS7 ..... 442 B7
Woodside Gdns *CHING* E4 ..... 402 C8
Woodside Rd *HOC/HUL* SS5 ..... 420 C8
 WFD IG8 ..... 403 H7
Woodside Vw *SBF/HAD* SS7 ..... 440 B5
Woodside Wy *GTDUN* CM6 ..... 203 K4
Woodspring CI *CHTY* IP2 ..... 62 C3 ▣
Woods Rd *RCHLM* CM3 ..... 239 H7
The Woods *SBF/HAD* SS7 ..... 462 A2
Woodstock *K/T/MI* CO5 ..... 284 E6
 LAIN SS15 ..... 436 A7 ▣
Woodstock Av *HARH* RM3 ..... 409 J8
Woodstock Crs *HOC/HUL* SS5 ..... 420 E7 ▣
 LAIN SS15 ..... 436 A7
Woodstock Rd *BROX* EN10 ..... 318 E1
Woodstone Av *IP* IP1 ..... 36 E4
Wood St *CHLM/GWD* CM2 ..... 14 A6
 GRAYS RM17 ..... 484 D5
Wood Vw *GRAYS* RM17 ..... 484 D3

Woodview VGE SS16 .... 455 K1 🔲
Woodview Av CHING E4 .... 402 D7 🔲
Woodview Cl RCOLE CO7 .... 188 A1
Woodview Dr RCHLM CM3 .... 241 J6
Woodville Cl RCFD SS4 .... 444 A1
Woodville Rd CVI SS8 .... 478 D2
  IPNE IP4 .... 37 H8
Woodward Cl GRAYS RM17 .... 484 A3
Woodward Hts GRAYS RM17 .... 484 A3
Woodwards HLWW/ROY CM19 ...... 12 C5
Woodway BRTR CM7 .... 208 E7
Woodway BFRW/HUT CM13 .... 411 K4
Woodyards BOC CM0 .... 344 B2
Woolards Wy RCHLM CM3 .... 392 D6
Woolhampton Wy CHIG IG7 .... 406 A6 🔲
Woolifers Av SLH/COR SS17 .... 474 D1
Woollards Cl IP IP1 .... 2 B3
Woollards Gdns SUD CO10 .... 34 E5
Woollard St WAB EN9 .... 347 J8
Woollard Wy ING CM4 .... 356 C4
Woolmans Cl BROX EN10 .... 319 F4
Woolmergreen LAIN SS15 .... 16 C3
Woolmers Md RCHLM CM3 .... 270 E3
Woolmonger's La ING CM4 .... 355 J5
Woolner Rd RCOS CO16 .... 10 A1
Woolnough Cl HVHL CB9 .... 50 C7
The Woolnoughs KESG IP5 .... 39 H6 🔲
Woolpack La BRTR CM7 .... 177 K8 🔲
Woolpit's Rd BRTR CM7 .... 175 F4
Woolshotts Rd WICKW SS12 .... 416 C6
Woolverstone Cl CHTY IP2 .... 61 K4
Woolwich Rd RCOS CO16 .... 258 E8 🔲
Wootton Cl EMPK RM11 .... 430 E7
Worcester Av UPMR RM14 .... 452 C2
Worcester Cl BRTR CM7 .... 209 K4
  RCHLM CM3 .... 368 E4
  SLH/COR SS17 .... 473 K2 🔲
  VGE SS16 .... 436 A8 🔲🔲
Worcester Crs CHLM/GWD CM2 .... 333 J8 🔲
Worcester Dr RCOLE CO7 .... 222 A5
  WFD IG8 .... 403 J8
Worcester Dr RAYL SS6 .... 442 A4
Worcester Rd BOC CM0 .... 398 C7
  COL CO1 .... 8 C3
  IPSE IP3 .... 63 J5
Worcesters Av EN EN1 .... 374 A4
Wordsworth Av MAL CM9 .... 338 D5
  SOSN SS2 .... 19 E2 🔲
  TIL RM18 .... 485 H8 🔲
Wordsworth Cl HARH RM3 .... 430 D3 🔲
Wordsworth Crs IP IP1 .... 36 A2 🔲
Wordsworth Rd BRTR CM7 .... 177 J6 🔲
  COLW CO3 .... 186 A7
Workhouse Hl COLN CO4 .... 155 F1
Workhouse La RCHLM CM3 .... 392 A3
Workhouse Rd RCOLW CO6 .... 153 H2
Workshop La KIR/NAC IP10 .... 65 F8
Worlds End La K/T/MI CO5 .... 247 F2
Wormley Ct WAB EN9 .... 348 C7 🔲
Wormley Lodge Cl BROX EN10 .... 319 F5 🔲
Wormyngford Ct WAB EN9 .... 348 C7 🔲
Worrin Cl BRWN CM15 .... 411 J4
Worrin Rd BRWN CM15 .... 411 J5
Worsdell Wy COLN CO4 .... 8 B1
Worsley Cl CHTY IP2 .... 61 K3
Wortham Pl HVHL CB9 .... 27 G5
Worthing Ms COS CO15 .... 290 E5 🔲
Worthing Rd LAIN SS15 .... 436 B7
Worthington Wy COLW CO3 .... 218 A1
Wouldham Rd WTHK RM20 .... 483 H5
Wrabness Rd HAR CO12 .... 163 H2
The Wraglins BSF CM23 .... 199 G8
Wrangley Ct WAB EN9 .... 348 C7 🔲
Wratting Rd HVHL CB9 .... 27 G5
Wray Cl EMPK RM11 .... 450 E1
Wraysbury Dr LAIN SS15 .... 16 B1 🔲
Wren Av CHTY IP2 .... 61 K2

LOS SS9 .... 442 D6
Wrenbrook Rd BSF CM23 .... 198 E8
Wren Cl BCAYE CM11 .... 414 D4 🔲
  LOS SS9 .... 442 F6
  RCOLE CO7 .... 223 J4 🔲
  SBF/HAD SS7 .... 440 A7
Wrendale COS CO15 .... 10 C1
Wren Dr WAB EN9 .... 348 C8
Wren Gdns HCH RM12 .... 450 A2
Wren Pl BRW CM14 .... 411 C6
The Wrens HLWW/ROY CM19 .... 12 B3 🔲
Wren Ter LOU IG10 .... 377 K5
Wren Wk TIL RM18 .... 485 G6
Wrexham Rd HARH RM3 .... 408 E7
  LAIN SS15 .... 436 C8
Wright La KESG IP5 .... 39 H5
Wright Rd IPSE IP3 .... 64 A3
Wright's Av BRTR CM7 .... 210 D6
Wrightsbridge Rd BRW CM14 .... 409 G4
Wright's Green La BSF CM22 ...... 232 C6
Wrights La BRWN CM15 .... 384 B2
Wright's Piece RBSF CM22 .... 137 H7
Writtle Cl RCOS CO16 .... 290 D1
Writtle Rd CHLM/GWD CM2 .... 14 B5
  CHLM/WR CM1 .... 332 A4
  ING CM4 .... 359 F2
Wrotham Rd GVW DA11 .... 489 F8
Wroths Pth LOU IG10 .... 377 H5
Wroxham Cl COLW CO3 .... 186 C7
  SBF/HAD SS7 .... 442 C7
Wryneck Cl COLN CO4 .... 187 G2
Wyatts Dr SOS SS1 .... 465 J6
Wyatts Green La BRWN CM15 ..... 384 B2
Wyatt's Green Rd BRWN CM15 ... 384 B2
Wyatts La SUD CO10 .... 85 G5
Wyburn Rd SBF/HAD SS7 .... 441 J7
Wyburns Av RAYL SS6 .... 441 K5
Wyburns Av East RAYL SS6 ...... 441 K5
Wych Elm HLW CM20 .... 12 C2
Wych Elm Cl EMPK RM11 .... 431 H8 🔲
Wych Elm Rd EMPK RM11 .... 431 H8
Wychford Dr SBW CM21 .... 263 G4
Wycke Hl MAL CM9 .... 337 K5
Wycke La MAL CM9 .... 314 E5
Wycliffe Gv COL CO1 .... 8 A2 🔲
Wycliffe Rw GVW DA11 .... 488 E6
Wycombe Av SBF/HAD SS7 .... 439 K7 🔲
Wyemead Crs CHING E4 .... 403 F5
Wye Rd GVE DA12 .... 489 J7
  IPSE IP3 .... 63 J2
Wykeham Av EMPK RM11 .... 430 E8
Wykeham Rd CHLM/WR CM1 ..... 331 H4
Wykes Gn BSDN SS14 .... 437 K6
Wyldwood Cl HLWE CM17 .... 263 G7
Wyncolls Rd COLN CO4 .... 155 K8
Wyndham Crs COS CO15 .... 11 D2
Wynters VGE SS16 .... 17 F6
Wynterton Cl IPSE IP3 .... 63 K4
Wynyard Rd SAFWN CB10 .... 71 F2
Wyse's Rd ING CM4 .... 329 K7
Wythefield PIT SS13 .... 438 D7

Yarwood Rd CHLM/GWD CM2 .... 15 F3
Yeldham Lock CHLM/GWD CM2 .. 333 J3 🔲
Yeldham Pl HVHL CB9 .... 27 G5
Yeldham Rd HSTD CO9 .... 110 B1
Yellowpine Wy CHIG IG7 .... 406 A7
Yelverton Cl HARH RM3 .... 430 D3
Yeoman Rd FX IP11 .... 9 D4
Yeomans Cl BSF CM23 .... 198 C6
Yeomans Wy EN EN1 .... 374 B6 🔲
Yeovil Cha WOS/PRIT SS0 .... 463 J1
Yerril Gdn HVHL CB9 .... 26 E6 🔲
Yevele Wy EMPK RM11 .... 451 F1
Yew Cl BKHH IG9 .... 404 A5 🔲
  LAIN SS15 .... 16 A1
  WIT CM8 .... 245 H8
Yew Ct CHTY IP2 .... 2 B6
Yewlands SBW CM21 .... 263 J4 🔲
Yews Av EN EN1 .... 374 B2
The Yews GVE DA12 .... 489 J7
Yew Tree Cl COLN CO4 .... 188 B6
  RBRW/HUT CM13 .... 412 A2
  RCHLM CM3 .... 276 A8
Yew Tree Gdns CHLM/GWD CM2 .. 332 E7 🔲
Yewtree Gv KESG IP5 .... 38 D6
Yew Tree Pl BSF CM23 .... 198 E5
Yewtree Ri RIPW IP8 .... 61 J4
Yew Wy COS CO15 .... 290 B7
Yorick Av K/T/MI CO5 .... 284 E7
Yorick Rd K/T/MI CO5 .... 284 E7
York Av SLH/COR SS17 .... 457 H8
York Cl BRWN CM15 .... 411 J3
  RAYL SS6 .... 442 B5
  SUD CO10 .... 58 B4
York Crs LOU IG10 .... 377 G7
Yorkes HLWS CM18 .... 13 F5
York Gdns BRTR CM7 .... 210 A1
York Hl LOU IG10 .... 377 G7
York Pl COL CO1 .... 8 C3 🔲
  GRAYS RM17 .... 483 K5 🔲
York Ri RAYL SS6 .... 442 B5
York Rd BAR EN8 .... 346 E8
  BCAYW CM12 .... 387 G8
  BOC CM0 .... 425 H1
  BRWN CM15 .... 411 J3
  CHING E4 .... 402 B8
  CHLM/GWD CM2 .... 14 B5
  COS CO15 .... 260 B8
  EPP CM16 .... 352 A1
  FX IP11 .... 131 H5
  GVE DA12 .... 489 H8
  GVW DA11 .... 488 C5
  HVHL CB9 .... 26 E6
  IPSE IP3 .... 63 J1
  RAYL SS6 .... 442 B5
  RCFD SS4 .... 421 K6
  RCOLE CO7 .... 255 J7
  RCOLW CO6 .... 149 J7
  SLH/COR SS17 .... 473 F1
  SOS SS1 .... 19 D5
  SUD CO10 .... 58 B5
York St MGTR CO11 .... 159 J1
Young Cl LOS SS9 .... 443 H7
  RCOS CO16 .... 258 E8
Ypres Rd COLS CO2 .... 219 F2

Zambesi Rd BSF CM23 .... 198 E8 🔲
Zandi Rd CVI SS8 .... 478 D3 🔲
Zealand Dr CVI SS8 .... 478 E2
Zelham Dr CVI SS8 .... 479 F2
Zider Pass CVI SS8 .... 479 F2
Zion Pl GVE DA12 .... 489 G5 🔲

Y

Yale Ms COLN CO4 .... 187 J1
Yale Wy HCH RM12 .... 450 B5
Yamburg Rd CVI SS8 .... 478 D2 🔲
Yardley Cl CHING E4 .... 402 C1 🔲
Yardley Hall La GTDUN CM6 ..... 103 G7
Yardley La CHING E4 .... 402 C1
Yare Av WIT CM8 .... 276 D2
Yarmouth Cl COS CO15 .... 10 B1 🔲
Yarmouth Rd IP IP1 .... 2 A3
Yarnacott SBN/FI SS3 .... 466 B5

Z

Zambesi Rd BSF CM23 .... 198 E8 🔲
Zandi Rd CVI SS8 .... 478 D3 🔲
Zealand Dr CVI SS8 .... 478 E2
Zelham Dr CVI SS8 .... 479 F2
Zider Pass CVI SS8 .... 479 F2
Zion Pl GVE DA12 .... 489 G5 🔲

Index - featured places

Aaron House Clinic
of Physiotherapy
  WOS/PRIT SS0 .... 463 J2
Abbey Mead Industrial Park
  WAB EN9 .... 347 H8
Abbey Road Surgery
  BAR EN8 .... 346 E8
Abbotsweld Primary School
  HLWS CM18 .... 13 D5
Abbotts Hall Infant School
  SLH/COR SS17 .... 474 A2
A B C Cinema
  GVE DA12 .... 489 G4
Acorn Trading Centre
  WTHK RM20 .... 483 G5
Acton Place Industrial Estate
  SUD CO10 .... 35 K5

Adams Business Centre
  BSDN SS14 .... 438 C4
Adult Community College
  COL CO1 .... 8 C4
Adult Community College
Chelmsford
  CHLM/WR CM1 .... 332 A3
Ainslie Wood Primary School
  CHING E4 .... 402 C8
Airborne Industrial Estate
  LOS SS9 .... 443 F8
Airport Business Park
  SOSN SS2 .... 444 B7
Albany School Grant
Maintained
  PEND EN3 .... 374 D4

The Albany School
  HCH RM12 .... 450 C3
Alderman Blaxill School
  COLS CO2 .... 218 C2
Alderton County Junior
& Infant School
  LOU IG10 .... 404 D1
The Alec Hunter High School
  BRTR CM7 .... 210 B4
Alleyn Court & Eton
House School
  SBN/FI SS3 .... 465 K2
Alleyn Court Preparatory School
  WOS/PRIT SS0 .... 463 K4
All Saints Church
of England Primary School
  HAR CO12 .... 194 E2

The Boswells School
CHLM/WR CM1 .... 305 F7
Bournemouth Park Junior
& Infants School
SOSN SS2 .... 19 D2
Bournes Green Junior School
SOS SS1 .... 466 A5
The Box Gallery
RIPS/CAP IP9 .... 88 E6
Boxted C of E Primary School
COLN CO4 .... 119 G6
Boyd School
UPMR RM14 .... 452 B3
The Brackenbury Sports Centre
FX IP11 .... 131 K2
Bradfield Primary School
MGTR CO11 .... 161 F4
Bradwell Quay Yacht Club
BOC CM0 .... 344 A1
Braintree & Bocking
Urban District Council
BRTR CM7 .... 177 J6
Braintree College
BRTR CM7 .... 177 K8
Braintree District Council
BRTR CM7 .... 209 J2
Braintree District Council
BRTR CM7 .... 210 A2
Braintree District Council
WIT CM8 .... 277 G3
Braintree & District
Golf Club Ltd
BRTR CM7 .... 179 F7
Braintree Rugby Club
BRTR CM7 .... 210 C3
Braintree Town Football Club
BRTR CM7 .... 210 B3
Bramston Sports Centre
WIT CM8 .... 277 F4
Brandler Galleries
BRW CM14 .... 411 G5
Brandy Hole Yacht Club
HOC/HUL SS5 .... 420 B1
Branfil Junior & Infant School
UPMR RM14 .... 451 H5
Brantham Athletic & Social Club
MGTR CO11 .... 123 H6
Brays Grove Comprehensive
School
HLWS CM18 .... 295 F7
Brentwood Borough Council
BRW CM14 .... 411 F5
Brentwood Borough Council
RBRW/HUT CM13 .... 433 G1
Brentwood Chiropody Surgery
BRW CM14 .... 411 F5
The Brentwood Clinic
BRW CM14 .... 411 G4
Brentwood Community
Hospital
BRWN CM15 .... 411 H4
Brentwood County
High School
BRW CM14 .... 411 G6
Brentwood Preparatory
School
BRWN CM15 .... 411 H4
Brentwood Rugby
Football Club
BRW CM14 .... 411 H7
Brentwood School
BRWN CM15 .... 411 G5
Brentwood Sports Ground
BRWN CM15 .... 411 G4
Brentwood Ursuline
High School
BRW CM14 .... 411 G6
Briarswood Clinic
CVI SS8 .... 460 E8
Brickfield Surgery
RCHLM CM3 .... 392 E6
Bridge Hospital
WIT CM8 .... 277 F5
Bridge View Industrial Estate
WTHK RM20 .... 482 D5
Brightlingsea Infant School
RCOLE CO7 .... 255 J7
Brightlingsea Junior School
RCOLE CO7 .... 255 J7
Brightlingsea United
Football Club
RCOLE CO7 .... 255 K6
Brightside County Junior
& Infant School
BCAYW CM12 .... 386 E8

Brimsdown Junior
& Infant School
PEND EN3 .... 374 D7
Brinkley Grove GM
Primary School
COLN CO4 .... 155 J8
Brisco County Junior
& Infant School
IPNE IP4 .... 38 C8
Britannia Business Centre
BAR EN8 .... 347 F8
Britannia Primary School
IPNE IP4 .... 37 K8
Brittania Business Park
BAR EN8 .... 347 F8
Brittons School
RAIN RM13 .... 450 A8
Broadfield School
HLW CM20 .... 13 E2
Broadford Primary School
HARH RM3 .... 430 E1
Brocks Business Park
WICKE SS11 .... 417 J7
Broke Hall CP School
IPNE IP4 .... 38 C8
Bromfords School
WICKW SS12 .... 416 E7
Bromfords Sports Centre
WICKW SS12 .... 416 E8
Brooke Trading Estate
ROM RM1 .... 450 A1
Brook Farm Industrial Estate
ABR/ST RM4 .... 407 J3
Brook Gallery
CHIG IG7 .... 404 E6
Brookhouse Business Park
CHTY IP2 .... 2 A3
Brookland Junior
& Infant School
BAR EN8 .... 346 E2
Brooklands School
MGTR CO11 .... 123 J5
Brook Natural Health Centre
CVI SS8 .... 477 J2
Brook Road Industrial Estate
RAYL SS6 .... 441 J5
Brookside Business Centre
RBSF CM22 .... 231 K4
Brookside Junior & Infant School
HARH RM3 .... 409 F8
Brook Strret Business Centre
COL CO1 .... 9 D5
Brookweald Cricket Club
BRW CM14 .... 410 B4
Broomfield County
Primary School
CHLM/WR CM1 .... 304 D4
Broomfield Football Club
CHLM/WR CM1 .... 304 D5
Broomfield Hospital
CHLM/WR CM1 .... 304 C2
Broomgrove County Infant
& Junior School
RCOLE CO7 .... 220 E2
Broomhills Industrial Estate
BRTR CM7 .... 209 G3
Broom Hill Swimming Pool
IP IP1 .... 2 B1
Broxbourne Borough Council
BAR EN8 .... 318 D8
Broxbourne Business Centre
BAR EN8 .... 318 D8
Broxbourne C of E Jmi School
BROX EN10 .... 319 F3
Broxbourne Sailing Club
HOD EN11 .... 319 K2
The Broxbourne School
BROX EN10 .... 318 E4
Broxbourne Sports Club
BROX EN10 .... 319 F3
Brunel Court Industrial Centre
COLN CO4 .... 155 K8
Buckhurst Hill CP School
BKHH IG9 .... 404 B5
Buckhurst Hill Football Club
BKHH IG9 .... 404 B4
Buckhurst Hill Reform
Synagogue
LOU IG10 .... 404 A1
Bull Hill Industrial Estate
COS CO15 .... 10 C2
Bull Lane Industrial Estate
SUD CO10 .... 35 J5
Bulmer Road Industrial Estate
SUD CO10 .... 57 K6

Bulmer Road Industrial Estate
SUD CO10 .... 57 K7
Bulphan Primary School
UPMR RM14 .... 454 E4
Bures C of E Vc Primary School
BURES CO8 .... 115 J5
Burleigh Primary School
BAR EN8 .... 346 D4
Burlington Road Surgery
IP IP1 .... 2 C3
Burnham Business Park
BOC CM0 .... 397 K7
Burnham Clinic
BOC CM0 .... 398 C8
Burnham Museum
BOC CM0 .... 425 G1
Burnham-on-Crouch CP School
BOC CM0 .... 398 D8
Burnham-on-Crouch
Golf Club Ltd
BOC CM0 .... 397 J7
Burnham Road Clinic
LOS SS9 .... 462 D4
The Burnham Surgery
BOC CM0 .... 398 B8
Burnside Industrial Estate
BARK/HLT IG6 .... 406 A8
Burnt Mill
Comprehensive School
HLW CM20 .... 13 E1
Burntmill Industrial Estate
HLW CM20 .... 294 A2
Burrsville County Junior
& Infant School
COS CO15 .... 11 D1
Burton End CP School
HVHL CB9 .... 26 D6
Bus Depot
IP IP1 .... 2 B4
Business Centre
LOU IG10 .... 378 B8
The Business Centre
HARH RM3 .... 430 E2
Butter Market Shopping Centre
IP IP1 .... 3 D4
Buttsbury County Infant School
BCAYW CM12 .... 387 H8
Buttsbury Junior Gm School
BCAYW CM12 .... 387 H8
The Campion School
EMPK RM11 .... 431 G6
Canal Industrial Park
GVE DA12 .... 489 J4
Canewdon Endowed
Primary School
RCFD SS4 .... 423 H4
Canfield Cricket Club
GTDUN CM6 .... 235 J4
Cann Hall Primary School
RCOS CO16 .... 258 E7
Canons Brook Golf Club
HLW CM20 .... 12 A2
Canvey County Junior
& Infant School
CVI SS8 .... 477 K2
Canvey Island Football Club
CVI SS8 .... 479 F3
Canvey Village Surgery
CVI SS8 .... 477 J2
Capel Manor Primary School
EN EN1. .... 374 A1
Capel St Mary School
RIPS/CAP IP9 .... 87 F4
Capitol Industrial Centre
WICKE SS11 .... 417 K8
Cardinal Park
IP IP1 .... 3 D4
Car Ferry Terminal
HAR CO12 .... 128 D8
Carnarvon Medical Centre
SOSN SS2 .... 18 C2
The Carpet Gallery
CVI SS8 .... 478 C1
The Carpet Gallery
HCH RM12 .... 450 C2
Carterhatch School
EN EN1. .... 374 B5
Castle Camps Primary School
CBE/LIN CB1 .... 48 D2
Castledon School
WICKW SS12 .... 416 E8
Castle Garden Medical Centre
COL CO1 .... 8 C4
Castle Hill Junior & Infant School
IP IP1 .... 36 C2

Castle Manor Upper School
HVHL CB9 .... **26** E5
Castle Middle School
HVHL CB9 .... **26** D5
The Castle Museum
COL CO1 .... **8** B4
Castle Point Borough Council
SBF/HAD SS7 .... **441** F8
Castlepoint Museum
CVI SS8 .... **479** F2
Castle Street Surgery
SAFWN CB10 .... **70** E3
Castle View School
CVI SS8 .... **461** G7
Castle Walk Clinic
STSD CM24 .... **168** A7
Cater Business Park
BCAYW CM12 .... **414** C3
Cathedral of St Mary & St Helen
BRWN CM15 .... **411** G5
The Cathedral Primary School
CHLM/WR CM1 .... **15** D2
The Causeway Business Centre
BSF CM23 .... **198** E6
Causeway Industrial Estate
MGTR CO11 .... **123** G8
Causton County Junior School
FX IP11 .... **5** D1
Cavendish Primary School
SUD CO10 .... **32** C3
Cecil Avenue Surgery
EMPK RM11 .... **431** F5
Cecil Jones High School
SOSN SS2 .... **465** G2
Cecil Road County
Primary School
GVW DA11 .... **488** E6
Cedar Hall School
SBF/HAD SS7 .... **441** G7
Central Health Clinic
CHLM/GWD CM2 .... **14** C3
Central Park Swimming Pool
HARH RM3 .... **409** F8
Central Surgery
FX IP11 .... **131** H2
Central Surgery
SBW CM21 .... **263** J3
Chadwell St Mary Primary School
CDH/CHF RM16 .... **485** F3
The Chafford Hundred
Medical Centre
CDH/CHF RM16 .... **483** H2
Chalkstone Middle School
HVHL CB9 .... **27** G5
Chalkwell Hall Junior School
LOS SS9 .... **463** H4
Chalvedon School
PIT SS13 .... **438** E7
Channels Golf Club
RCHLM CM3 .... **305** G2
Chantry Clinic
CHTY IP2 .... **62** A2
Chantry Gallery
SUD CO10 .... **34** E5
Chantry High School
CHTY IP2 .... **2** A6
Chantry Junior & Infant School
CHTY IP2 .... **62** A1
Chapel Hill County
Primary School
BRTR CM7 .... **210** A3
Chappel C of E
(Controlled) Primary School
RCOLW CO6 .... **151** F8
Charfleet Industrial Estate
CVI SS8 .... **477** G2
Charterhouse Trading Estate
HVHL CB9 .... **27** J7
Chartwell Gallery
SOSN SS2 .... **19** D4
Chase Lane Infant School
CHING E4 .... **402** A7
Chase Lane Primary School
HAR CO12 .... **164** D3
Chelmer Valley High School
CHLM/WR CM1 .... **304** C3
Chelmer Village Retail Park
CHLM/GWD CM2 .... **15** F3
Chelmondiston CP School
RIPS/CAP IP9 .... **91** H6
Chelmsford Athletics Club
CHLM/WR CM1 .... **304** A7
Chelmsford Cathedral
CHLM/WR CM1 .... **14** C2

Chelmsford College
CHLM/GWD CM2 .... **14** B5
Chelmsford County High School
CHLM/WR CM1 .... **14** B1
Chelmsford District Council
CHLM/GWD CM2 .... **360** C3
Chelmsford & Essex Museum
CHLM/GWD CM2 .... **14** B5
Chelmsford Golf Club Ltd
CHLM/GWD CM2 .... **332** B7
Chelmsford Lawford
Mead County Junior School
CHLM/WR CM1 .... **303** K8
Chelmsford Road
Industrial Estate
GTDUN CM6 .... **204** E6
Chelmsford Rugby
Football Club
CHLM/WR CM1 .... **15** F1
Chelmsford Squash Club
CHLM/GWD CM2 .... **14** C6
Cherry Tree School
COLS CO2 .... **219** H5
Cherry Tree Surgery
FOS CO13 .... **261** K1
Cheshunt Community Hospital
BAR EN8 .... **346** C8
Cheshunt Football Club
BAR EN8 .... **346** C6
Cheshunt School
BAR EN8 .... **346** C4
Cheshunt & Waltham Cross
Council
BAR EN8 .... **346** E8
Chesterfield Junior
& Infant School
PEND EN3 .... **374** E3
Chetwood CP School
RCHLM CM3 .... **392** D7
Chief Clerk County Court
COLW CO3 .... **8** A5
Chigwell County Primary School
CHIG IG7 .... **405** F5
Chigwell & Hainault Synagogue
CHIG IG7 .... **405** F8
Chigwell Row County
First School
CHIG IG7 .... **406** B5
Chigwell School
CHIG IG7 .... **405** F5
Childerditch Industrial Park
RBRW/HUT CM13 .... **433** J5
Chilton Industrial Estate
SUD CO10 .... **58** E4
Chilton Industrial Estate
SUD CO10 .... **58** D4
Chinese Herbal Medical Centre
WOS/PRIT SS0 .... **18** A4
Chinese Medical Centre
CHLM/WR CM1 .... **14** B2
Chinese Medical Centre
COL CO1 .... **8** A4
Chinese Medical Centre
HCH RM12 .... **451** F4
Chinese Medical Centre
IP IP1 .... **3** D3
Chinese Medical Centre
WOS/PRIT SS0 .... **18** C4
Chingford C of E Infant School
CHING E4 .... **402** E4
Chingford C of E Junior School
CHING E4 .... **402** E4
Chingford Health Centre
CHING E4 .... **402** A7
Chingford Rugby Football Club
CHING E4 .... **402** B4
Chingford School
CHING E4 .... **402** C4
Chipping Hill County
Infant School
WIT CM8 .... **277** F2
Chipping Ongar Primary School
CHONG CM5 .... **354** B4
Christchurch Mansion
IP IP1 .... **3** D3
Christchurch Park Hospital
IP IP1 .... **3** D2
Christmas Maltings Surgery
HVHL CB9 .... **27** F5
Churchgate C of E
Primary School
HLWE CM17 .... **295** K2
Church Lane School
UPMR RM14 .... **452** E6

Church Langley Primary School
HLWE CM17 .... **295** G5
Church of England Primary School
SAFWN CB10 .... **43** J3
Church Trading Estate
ERITH DA8 .... **480** B6
Church View Surgery
RAYL SS6 .... **441** J3
Civic Centre
CHLM/WR CM1 .... **14** B2
Civic Centre
GVW DA11 .... **489** G5
Civic Centre
IP IP1 .... **2** C3
Civic Halls
CVI SS8 .... **478** B2
Civic Industrial Estate
HVHL CB9 .... **27** F8
Civic Theatre
CHLM/WR CM1 .... **14** B2
Civil Service Sports Club
KIR/NAC IP10 .... **65** G4
Clacton County High School
COS CO15 .... **11** D3
Clacton Covered Market
COS CO15 .... **10** C5
Clacton & District Hospital
COS CO15 .... **10** B6
Clacton Leisure Centre
COS CO15 .... **11** D3
Clacton on Sea Golf Club
COS CO15 .... **290** E5
Clacton Police Station
COS CO15 .... **10** B5
Clacton Rugby Club
COS CO15 .... **11** D2
Clair Gallery
BRWN CM15 .... **411** K2
Clare Middle School
SUD CO10 .... **31** H5
Clare Primary School
SUD CO10 .... **31** F5
Clarklands Industrial Estate
SBW CM21 .... **231** J8
Clavering Primary School
SAFWS CB11 .... **134** B1
Clements CP School
HVHL CB9 .... **26** E6
Clements Hall Leisure Centre
HOC/HUL SS5 .... **443** H1
Clements House Surgery
RCHLM CM3 .... **392** E6
Cliff Lane Primary School
IPSE IP3 .... **3** F6
Clifford Road Primary School
IPNE IP4 .... **37** H7
Clinic
HOC/HUL SS5 .... **419** K3
The Clinic
GVE DA12 .... **489** H8
The Clinic
SBF/HAD SS7 .... **460** C2
Coastal Business Centre
COS CO15 .... **10** A4
Cockridden Farm
Industrial Estate
RBRW/HUT CM13 .... **434** E4
C of E Primary School
SUD CO10 .... **55** F4
Coggeshall Surgery
RCOLW CO6 .... **213** G3
Coggeshall Town Football Club
RCOLW CO6 .... **212** E4
Colbayns High School
COS CO15 .... **10** A3
Colchester Business Park
COLN CO4 .... **155** K7
Colchester County Court
COLS CO2 .... **8** A5
Colchester County
High School for Girls
COLW CO3 .... **186** C7
Colchester District
General Hospital
COLN CO4 .... **187** F2
Colchester Golf Club
COLN CO4 .... **186** D2
Colchester Institute
COLW CO3 .... **186** E5
Colchester Jamiah Mosque
COL CO1 .... **8** C4
Colchester Mercury Theatre Ltd
COLW CO3 .... **8** A4
Colchester Museums
COL CO1 .... **8** B4

Colchester Royal
Grammar School
COLW CO3 .... 186 E7
Colchester Rugby Football Club
COLN CO4 .... 155 H7
Colchester Sixth Form School
COLW CO3 .... 8 A4
Colchester United Football Club
COLS CO2 .... 218 D1
Colchester Zoo
COLS CO2 .... 217 H4
The Colin Dove Practice
ROM RM1 .... 430 A7
College Annexe
IPNE IP4 .... 3 E4
College of Teachers
EPP CM16 .... 378 B2
College St Pierre
LOS SS9 .... 463 H4
Collingwood Primary School
RCHLM CM3 .... 392 E7
The Colne Community School
RCOLE CO7 .... 255 J5
Colne Engaine C of E School
RCOLW CO6 .... 149 H3
Colneis County Junior School
FX IP11 .... 131 J1
Colne Medical Centre
RCOLE CO7 .... 255 J7
Colne View Retail Park
COL CO1 .... 8 C2
Colne Yacht Club
RCOLE CO7 .... 255 K8
Commonside School
HLWS CM18 .... 322 D1
Community Care
& Health Centre
COS CO15 .... 290 C5
Community Clinic
HLWS CM18 .... 13 F6
Community Health Centre
COL CO1 .... 8 B5
Coopersale Hall School
EPP CM16 .... 351 F7
Coopersale & Theydon
Garnon C of E Primary School
EPP CM16 .... 351 H3
Co-ordinated Industrial Estate
SBF/HAD SS7 .... 441 J6
Copdock CP School
RIPW IP8 .... 61 F5
Copdock Cricket Club
RIPW IP8 .... 61 F6
Copford C of E Primary School
RCOLW CO6 .... 216 B3
Copleston High School
IPNE IP4 .... 38 A8
Coppice Primary School
CHIG IG7 .... 405 K8
Coppins Green CP School
COS CO15 .... 10 A2
Corbets Tey School
UPMR RM14 .... 451 J6
Cornard Surgery
SUD CO10 .... 58 E7
Cornelius Vermuyden School
CVI SS8 .... 460 D8
Cornell Estate
CHLM/GWD CM2 .... 15 D3
Corn Exchange
and Film Theatre
IP IP1 .... 3 D3
Cornwallis Business Centre
BSDN SS14 .... 17 E2
Corringham County
Primary School
SLH/COR SS17 .... 474 E1
Corringham Health Centre
SLH/COR SS17 .... 474 D2
The Cottage Museum
BRTR CM7 .... 142 B4
Council Offices
COLW CO3 .... 186 D7
County Hall
CHLM/WR CM1 .... 14 C3
County Hall
IPNE IP4 .... 3 E3
County Junior & Infant School
BRWN CM15 .... 410 D2
County Junior School
CHLM/WR CM1 .... 331 G5
County Primary School
CHLM/WR CM1 .... 358 A1
County Primary School
FX IP11 .... 5 E5
County Primary School
FX IP11 .... 94 D8
County Primary School
RCHLM CM3 .... 366 B8
County Primary School
RCHLM CM3 .... 391 G8
County Primary School
RCOLE CO7 .... 121 F4
Coupals CP School
HVHL CB9 .... 27 K6
Coward Industrial Estate
CDH/CHF RM16 .... 485 G4
Cramphorn Theatre
CHLM/WR CM1 .... 14 B3
Cranes Industrial Centre
BSDN SS14 .... 438 C3
Cranham Health Centre
UPMR RM14 .... 452 B1
Craylands Clinic
BSDN SS14 .... 438 B6
Crays Hill County
Primary School
BCAYE CM11 .... 416 A7
Creffield Road Surgery
COLW CO3 .... 186 E7
Cressing County
Primary School
BRTR CM7 .... 210 D7
Cricket Club
EPP CM16 .... 378 C3
Cricketers Retail Park
PIT SS13 .... 438 D2
Cricketers Retail Park
WICKW SS12 .... 439 G2
Cricket Squash Tennis
& Hockey Club
BSF CM23 .... 198 B5
Crishall C of E Primary School
ROY SG8 .... 67 F2
Criton Industrial Estate
CDH/CHF RM16 .... 472 E6
Crouch Yacht Club
BOC CM0 .... 425 G1
Crown College
WOS/PRIT SS0 .... 18 B3
Crown & County Court
BSDN SS14 .... 17 E4
Crown Hall
RAYL SS6 .... 441 H3
Crown Pools
IP IP1 .... 3 D3
Crowstone Preparatory School
RCFD SS4 .... 444 E5
Crowstone Preparatory School
WOS/PRIT SS0 .... 463 J5
Crusader Business Park
COS CO15 .... 259 J5
Cygnet Leisure Centre
GVW DA11 .... 488 D7
Dabchicks Sailing Club
K/T/MI CO5 .... 284 C6
Dacre Industrial Estate
BAR EN8 .... 346 E3
Dale Hall Primary School
IP IP1 .... 36 D3
Dame Johane Bradbury School
SAFWN CB10 .... 71 G3
Dame Tipping School
ABR/ST RM4 .... 407 J6
Danbury Clinic
RCHLM CM3 .... 335 K6
Danbury Park School
RCHLM CM3 .... 335 G6
D'arcy Gallery
IPNE IP4 .... 3 D4
Darlinghurst School
LOS SS9 .... 463 G3
Davenant Foundation School
LOU IG10 .... 378 A4
Deanes Secondary School
SBF/HAD SS7 .... 441 H7
Debden Sports Club
LOU IG10 .... 405 F1
Deben High School
FX IP11 .... 5 F3
Dedham C of E
(Controlled) School
RCOLE CO7 .... 121 K7
Dedham Sports Club
RCOLE CO7 .... 121 J7
De La Salle RC School
BSDN SS14 .... 17 F2
Deneholm CP School
CDH/CHF RM16 .... 484 B1
De Vere CP School
HSTD CO9 .... 110 D1
Dewhurst St Mary Junior
Middle & Infant School
EBAR EN7 .... 346 B3
Dickens Place Surgery
CHLM/WR CM1 .... 303 K7
Dilkes CP School
SOCK/AV RM15 .... 469 H6
Dipple Medical Centre
PIT SS13 .... 438 E8
District Council Offices
RAYL SS6 .... 441 J3
Doctor Child's Surgery
HAR CO12 .... 163 H8
Doddinghurst C of E
Junior School
BRWN CM15 .... 383 K3
Doddinghurst County
Infant School
BRWN CM15 .... 383 K3
Doggetts CP School
RCFD SS4 .... 444 C2
Dominoes Health Centre
GRAYS RM17 .... 483 K5
Doucecroft School
K/T/MI CO5 .... 246 E2
Dovercourt Swimming Pool
HAR CO12 .... 165 G4
Dover Road Primary School
GVW DA11 .... 488 D6
Downfield School
BAR EN8 .... 346 E5
Downhall Primary School
RAYL SS6 .... 419 J8
Downham C of E
Primary School
BCAYE CM11 .... 415 K1
Downing Primary School
CHTY IP2 .... 62 B3
The Downs CP School
HLW CM20 .... 13 D3
Drakes Lane Industrial Estate
RCHLM CM3 .... 273 K6
Drapers Sports Club
MAL CM9 .... 311 F8
Dr Guile Surgery
COS CO15 .... 259 J5
Dr Mirza Practice
COS CO15 .... 10 B4
Dry Ski Slope
RBRW/HUT CM13 .... 433 F2
Dukes Park Industrial Estate
CHLM/GWD CM2 .... 333 H1
The Dukes Priory Hospital
CHLM/WR CM1 .... 15 E1
Dunmow C of E Junior School
GTDUN CM6 .... 204 B5
Dunmow County Infants School
GTDUN CM6 .... 204 C4
Dunmow Sports Centre
GTDUN CM6 .... 204 B2
Dunningford Primary School
HCH RM12 .... 450 A6
Durants School
EN EN1 .... 374 C5
Dycorts School
HARH RM3 .... 409 H7
Eagle House Surgery
PEND EN3 .... 374 C8
Earls Colne CP School
RCOLW CO6 .... 149 J7
Earls Hall Infant School
WOS/PRIT SS0 .... 464 A1
Earthworks Gallery
HCH RM12 .... 451 F2
East Anglian Railway Museum
RCOLW CO6 .... 151 G7
East Bergholt High School
RCOLE CO7 .... 122 C1
East Bergholt Primary School
RCOLE CO7 .... 122 A2
Eastern Angles Theatre Co
IP IP1 .... 2 A2
East Essex Adult
Community College
MAL CM9 .... 338 B3
East Essex Aviation Society
& Museum
RCOS CO16 .... 287 J1
Eastfield Primary & Infant School
PEND EN3 .... 374 D4
Eastgate Business Centre
BSDN SS14 .... 17 F4

Eastgate Shopping Centre
IPNE IP4 .... **3** E3

East Hanningfield
C of E Primary School
RCHLM CM3 .... **363** F6

East Herts District Council
BSF CM23 .... **198** E5

East Herts District Council
SBW CM21 .... **263** J3

East Thurrock Football Club
SLH/COR SS17 .... **474** D2

East Tilbury Surgery
TIL RM18 .... **486** C3

Eastwood Gm Infant School
LOS SS9 .... **443** G8

Eastwood Gm Junior School
LOS SS9 .... **443** G7

Eastwood High School
LOS SS9 .... **443** G8

Eastwood Industrial Estate
LOS SS9 .... **442** D7

Edith Borthwick School
BRTR CM7 .... **177** J5

Edward Francis
Community Junior School
RAYL SS6 .... **441** K2

Edwards Hall Junior
& Infant School
LOS SS9 .... **442** D6

Edwin Lambert Schooll
EMPK RM11 .... **430** B8

Eight Ash Green C of E
Primary School
RCOLW CO6 .... **184** E4

Eldon Way Industrial Estate
HOC/HUL SS5 .... **421** F7

Eleanor Estate
BAR EN8 .... **347** F8

Elm Green School
RCHLM CM3 .... **335** H2

Elm Hall County Primary School
WIT CM8 .... **245** F7

Elms Business Park
WICKW SS12 .... **439** H1

Elmstead Market Surgery
RCOLE CO7 .... **189** K8

The Elmwood CP School
RCHLM CM3 .... **392** D6

Elton Park Business Centre
CHTY IP2 .... **36** A7

Elton Park Industrial Estate
CHTY IP2 .... **36** A7

Elwyn House Felsted School
GTDUN CM6 .... **206** D7

Emerson Park School
EMPK RM11 .... **451** J1

Endeavour School
BRWN CM15 .... **411** J6

Enfield Business Centre
PEND EN3 .... **374** C6

Enfield College
PEND EN3 .... **374** C7

Enfield Football Club Ltd
EN EN1 .... **374** A7

Engaines Primary School
RCOS CO16 .... **259** F3

Engayne Junior School
UPMR RM14 .... **432** B8

Enterprise Trading Estate
BRTR CM7 .... **208** C4

Epping County Infant School
EPP CM16 .... **350** C3

Epping County Junior School
EPP CM16 .... **350** D4

Epping Forest District Council
CHIG IG7 .... **405** G8

Epping Forest District Council
EPP CM16 .... **350** D4

Epping Forest District Council
EPP CM16 .... **350** E4

Epping Forest District Council
LOU IG10 .... **378** A8

Epping Forest District Council
LOU IG10 .... **405** F1

Epping & Ongar Rural
District Council
EPP CM16 .... **351** H7

Theydon Bois Golf Club
EPP CM16 .... **350** D5

Theydon Bois Golf Club
EPP CM16 .... **350** B8

Epping Town Council
EPP CM16 .... **350** D5

Epping Upland Cofe
Primary School
EPP CM16 .... **321** K7

Erith Small Business Centre
ERITH DA8 .... **480** A5

Erith Theatre Guild
ERITH DA8 .... **480** A4

Essex County Council
BKHH IG9 .... **404** A6

Essex County Council
BRW CM14 .... **410** A4

Essex County Council
BRW CM14 .... **411** G5

Essex County Council
BSDN SS14 .... **438** B6

Essex County Council
CHIG IG7 .... **405** F4

Essex County Council
CHONG CM5 .... **326** C8

Essex County Council
CVI SS8 .... **477** J1

Essex County Council
EPP CM16 .... **350** D4

Essex County Council
GRAYS RM17 .... **484** A4

Essex County Council
LOU IG10 .... **377** K7

Essex County Council
LOU IG10 .... **377** J6

Essex County Council
PIT SS13 .... **439** F3

Essex County Council
RAYL SS6 .... **441** J4

Essex County Council
RAYL SS6 .... **441** J3

Essex County Council
RBRW/HUT CM13 .... **432** E1

Essex County Council
RCFD SS4 .... **444** B3

Essex County Council
SBF/HAD SS7 .... **460** E1

Essex County Council
SOSN SS2 .... **444** D8

Essex County Council
TIL RM18 .... **485** F8

Essex County Council
WAB EN9 .... **347** J7

Essex County Cricket Club
CHLM/GWD CM2 .... **14** B3

Essex County Hospital
COLW CO3 .... **186** E7

The Essex Nuffield Hospital
BRWN CM15 .... **411** H4

Europa Trading Estate
WTHK RM20 .... **483** G4

Everest Sports Club
BAR EN8 .... **346** B3

Everik Business Centre
RBRW/HUT CM13 .... **412** D1

Eversley College
SBW CM21 .... **263** H3

Eversley CP School
PIT SS13 .... **439** F7

The Eye Clinic
LOS SS9 .... **462** B3

The Eye Clinic
SBN/FI SS3 .... **466** C7

Fairfield Clinic
BKHH IG9 .... **403** J4

Fairfield Infant School
FX IP11 .... **131** H2

Fairfields Junior Middle
& Infant School
EBAR EN7 .... **346** A1

Fairhouse Junior
& Infant School
BSDN SS14 .... **438** A7

Fairways Primary School
LOS SS9 .... **462** D1

The Fairways
BAR EN8 .... **318** D8

Farnham School
BSF CM23 .... **166** C7

Fawbert & Barnards
(UNDL) Primary School
HLWE CM17 .... **295** G2

Feering Primary School
K/T/MI CO5 .... **247** G1

Felixstowe General Hospital
FX IP11 .... **131** H3

Felixstowe International College
FX IP11 .... **131** K2

Felixstowe Port & Town
Football Club
FX IP11 .... **5** D6

Felixstowe Rugby Club
FX IP11 .... **5** E4

Felmore County Infant School
PIT SS13 .... **438** E5

Felsted CP School
GTDUN CM6 .... **206** E6

Felsted Preparatory School
GTDUN CM6 .... **206** C8

Felsted School
GTDUN CM6 .... **206** C7

Felsted School
GTDUN CM6 .... **206** D7

Fern House Surgery
WIT CM8 .... **277** F4

Finchingfield C of E
Primary School
BRTR CM7 .... **106** E7

Fingringhoe C of E School
K/T/MI CO5 .... **220** C8

Fire Station
IP IP1 .... **2** C4

The Firs Junior School
BSF CM23 .... **198** D7

Fitzwimarc Secondary School
RAYL SS6 .... **441** K2

Flamstead End Junior School
EBAR EN7 .... **346** A1

Fledgelings Pre-school
CHLM/GWD CM2 .... **332** C8

Fleetway Sports Club
GVE DA12 .... **489** H6

Flitch Industrial Estate
GTDUN CM6 .... **204** C6

Florance Nightingale
Health Centre
HLWE CM17 .... **295** G5

Follyfield Felsted School
GTDUN CM6 .... **206** D8

Fondu Sports Club
PUR RM19 .... **481** K3

Football Stadium
IPNE IP4 .... **38** E8

Ford End C of E Primary School
RCHLM CM3 .... **239** H7

Fordham C of E Primary School
RCOLW CO6 .... **184** C1

Forest Medical Centre
LOU IG10 .... **404** B1

Forrester Park Golf
& Tennis Club
MAL CM9 .... **278** E8

Forty Hill C of E School
EN EN1 .... **374** A3

Four Hands Gallery
ING CM4 .... **386** C1

The Four Swanns Jmi School
BAR EN8 .... **346** E7

Foxearth Primary School
SUD CO10 .... **33** J7

The Foxhall Hospital
KIR/NAC IP10 .... **65** F1

Frances Bardsley School for Girls
ROM RM1 .... **430** B8

Franklin Way Practice
RCHLM CM3 .... **390** D8

Franklin Way Practice
WICKE SS11 .... **417** H5

Freshwell Health Centre
BRTR CM7 .... **106** E7

Friars Clinic
SUD CO10 .... **58** B6

Friars County Junior School
SBN/FI SS3 .... **466** E5

Friars Grove Junior
& Infant School
COLN CO4 .... **9** E1

Friends School
SAFWS CB11 .... **71** F5

Frinton Golf Club
FOS CO13 .... **261** J3

Frinton on Sea CP School
FOS CO13 .... **228** D8

Frinton on Sea Lawn
Tennis Club
FOS CO13 .... **261** J2

Frinton Road Medical Centre
COS CO15 .... **260** B7

Frinton Summer Theatre
FOS CO13 .... **228** E8

The Frinton & Walton
Heritage Museum
WOTN CO14 .... **229** K4

Frinton & Walton
Swimming Pool
WOTN CO14 .... **229** J4

Frobisher Primary School
COS CO15............................. 290   B4
Fronks Road Family Surgery
HAR CO12.............................. 7   D5
Frost Business Centre
BRTR CM7.............................. 211   H2
The Fryerns Medical Centre
BSDN SS14............................ 438   B5
Fyfield Dr Walkers C of E
Primary School
CHONG CM5........................... 327   F3
Gable Hall Gm School
SLH/COR SS17....................... 457   G8
Gainsborough Clinic
IPSE IP3................................. 63   J4
The Gallery at Lakeside
WTHK RM20............................ 482   E3
The Gallery
BOC CM0................................ 425   H1
The Gallery
CHLM/GWD CM2...................... 14   C4
The Gallery
COLW CO3.............................. 217   K1
The Gallery
IPNE IP4................................. 3   E4
The Gallery
SBF/HAD SS7......................... 460   C4
The Gallery
SUD CO10.............................. 31   F6
Galleywood County
Infant School
CHLM/GWD CM2...................... 360   D3
Ganges Museum
RIPS/CAP IP9......................... 129   H5
Garfield Gallery
RAYL SS6............................... 441   J3
Gateway
BSDN SS14............................ 17   F4
Gaynes School
UPMR RM14............................ 451   K6
Gepps House Felsted School
GTDUN CM6............................ 206   C7
Ghyllgrove County
Junior School
BSDN SS14............................ 17   E3
Gidea Park College
GPK RM2................................ 430   B5
Gidea Park Primary School
GPK RM2................................ 430   A6
Gidea Park Sports Ground
GPK RM2................................ 430   D4
Giffards County Junior
& Infant School
SLH/COR SS17....................... 474   B1
Gilberd School
COLN CO4.............................. 155   J8
The Glade Business Centre
WTHK RM20............................ 482   C4
Glebe Infant School & U H I
RAYL SS6............................... 441   H2
Glenwood School
WICKW SS12........................... 439   K6
Globe Industrial Estate
GRAYS RM17........................... 484   B5
Globe Works Industrial Estate
GRAYS RM17........................... 484   C4
Goffs School
EBAR EN7............................... 346   A3
Goldings Hill Clinic
LOU IG10............................... 377   J6
Golds Nurseries Business Park
RBSF CM22............................ 168   C2
Gorseland Primary School
KESC IP5................................ 39   K5
Gorse Lane Industrial Estate
COS CO15.............................. 259   K5
Gosbecks Junior
& Infant School
COLS CO2.............................. 218   B2
Gosfield Lake Golf Club
HSTD CO9.............................. 146   B5
Gosfield Primary School
HSTD CO9.............................. 146   D5
Gosfield School
HSTD CO9.............................. 147   F3
The Gowan Gallery
SBW CM21............................. 263   J3
Grange Paddock
Swimming Pool
BSF CM23.............................. 198   E4
Grange Park Industrial Estate
COLS CO2.............................. 220   A2
Grange Primary School
WICKW SS12........................... 416   E7

Grange Road Primary School
FX IP11................................. 5   D3
Grange Way Business Park
COLS CO2.............................. 220   A2
Gravesend County Court
GVE DA12............................... 489   G4
Gravesend Cricket Club
GVW DA11.............................. 489   F5
Gravesend Grammar
School for Boys
GVE DA12............................... 489   J5
Gravesend Grammar
School for Girls
GVW DA11.............................. 489   F6
Gravesend Museum
GVW DA11.............................. 489   G4
Gravesend & Northfleet
Football Club Ltd
GVW DA11.............................. 488   B4
Gravesend & North
Kent Hospital
GVW DA11.............................. 489   F4
Gravesend Rowing Club
GVE DA12............................... 489   H4
Gravesend Yacht Club
GVE DA12............................... 489   J4
Gravesham Borough Council
GVW DA11.............................. 488   B6
Gravesham Borough Council
GVW DA11.............................. 489   C5
Grays Athletic Football Club
GRAYS RM17........................... 484   A5
Grays Business Centre
GRAYS RM17........................... 484   B2
Grays Convent High School
GRAYS RM17........................... 484   A3
Grays County Court
GRAYS RM17........................... 483   K5
The Grays Gm School
GRAYS RM17........................... 484   A2
Grays Health Centre
GRAYS RM17........................... 483   K4
Great Baddow High School
CHLM/GWD CM2...................... 333   F7
Great Bardfield County School
BRTR CM7.............................. 142   C3
Great Bentley CP School
RCOLE CO7............................. 223   J6
Great Berry CP School
VGE SS16.............................. 456   A1
Great Bradfords County
Infant School
BRTR CM7.............................. 210   A1
The Great Clacton Surgery
COS CO15.............................. 10   C1
Great Cornard Middle School
SUD CO10.............................. 85   F1
Great Cornard Upper School
SUD CO10.............................. 84   E1
Great Dunmow Town Council
GTDUN CM6............................ 204   B5
Great Leighs CP School
RCHLM CM3............................ 241   J6
Great Oaks Clinic
BSDN SS14............................ 17   E4
Great Sampford County
Primary School
SAFWN CB10.......................... 105   F2
Great Stony School
CHONG CM5........................... 354   C1
Great Tey Primary School
RCOLN CO6............................. 183   F4
Great Totham County
Primary School
MAL CM9................................ 278   C8
The Great Wakering
Health Centre
SBN/FI SS3............................ 466   E1
Great Wakering
Primary School
SBN/FI SS3............................ 467   F2
Great Wakering Sports Centre
SBN/FI SS3............................ 466   E1
Great Waldingford VC
Primary School
SUD CO10.............................. 59   J2
Great Waltham C of E School
RCHLM CM3............................ 272   A6
Greenstead Clinic
COLN CO4.............................. 188   B5
Greensted County Infant School
BSDN SS14............................ 438   B7
Greensward College
HOC/HUL SS5......................... 421   F6

Greensward Surgery
HOC/HUL SS5......................... 421   G6
Greenwich Business Park
IPSE IP3................................. 63   G3
Greenwood School
HSTD CO9.............................. 148   A2
Greenwood Surgery
RCHLM CM3............................ 392   E6
The Group Surgery
COLW CO3.............................. 186   E7
Grove Junior & Infant School
RAYL SS6............................... 442   B4
Grove Lodge Surgery
COS CO15.............................. 260   B8
Grove Tennis Club
CHLM/GWD CM2...................... 14   C6
Grundy Park Leisure Centre
BAR EN8................................ 346   E4
Guardian Business Centre
HARH RM3.............................. 430   E2
Guildhall & Museum
BRTR CM7.............................. 106   E7
Guildhall Surgery
SUD CO10.............................. 31   F6
Gulpher Business Park
FX IP11................................. 95   G7
Guru Gobind Singh
Khalsa College
CHIG IG7................................ 404   C4
Guru Nanak Sports Club
GVE DA12............................... 489   H5
Gusford Primary School
CHTY IP2............................... 61   K4
GX
CHLM/WR CM1......................... 332   A6
GX Superbowl
CHLM/WR CM1......................... 332   A6
Hacton Infant School
HCH RM12.............................. 451   F5
Hadleigh Business Centre
SBF/HAD SS7......................... 461   K3
Hadleigh Castle
SBF/HAD SS7......................... 461   K4
Hadleigh Clinic
SBF/HAD SS7......................... 461   H2
Hadleigh Junior School
SBF/HAD SS7......................... 461   K2
Hainault Forest High School
CHIG IG7................................ 405   K8
Hainault Industrial Estate
BARK/HLT IG6......................... 406   B8
Halifax Primary School
CHTY IP2............................... 62   D3
Hallmark Industrial Estate
BOC CM0................................ 398   E1
Hall Mead School
UPMR RM14............................ 452   A1
Hall Road Industrial Estate
BOC CM0................................ 398   E2
Hallsford Bridge
Industrial Estate
CHONG CM5........................... 354   E5
Hallsford Business Centre
CHONG CM5........................... 354   E5
The Hall
SAFWS CB11.......................... 137   F1
Halstead Business Centre
HSTD CO9.............................. 147   K4
Halstead Hospital
HSTD CO9.............................. 147   K2
Halstead Primary School
HSTD CO9.............................. 148   A4
Halstead Town Football Club
HSTD CO9.............................. 147   K3
Hamford CP School
FOS CO13.............................. 228   E6
Hamilton School
COLW CO3.............................. 186   E8
Hamstel Primary School
SOSN SS2.............................. 465   G3
Handford Hall Primary School
IP IP1................................... 2   B3
Hare Street County Junior
& Infant School
HLWW/ROY CM19..................... 12   C3
Harlowbury School
HLWE CM17............................ 295   H1
Harlow Business Park
HLWW/ROY CM19..................... 293   G5
Harlow College
HLW CM20.............................. 12   C3
Harlow College
HLW CM20.............................. 13   E2
Harlow Museum
HLWS CM18............................ 12   C4

Harlow Rugby Football Club
  HLW CM20 .... **12** B1
Harlow Sailing Club
  RCHLM CM3 .... **368** D3
Harlow Sports Centre
  HLW CM20 .... **12** C1
Harlow Sports Centre
  HLW CM20 .... **13** D1
Harlow Urban District
  Swimming Pool
  HLW CM20 .... **13** E1
Harold Court School
  HARH RM3 .... **431** H2
Harold Wood Clinic
  HARH RM3 .... **431** G4
Harold Wood Jmi School
  HARH RM3 .... **431** H5
The Hartswood Clinic
  RBRW/HUT CM13 .... **432** E1
Harvey Centre
  HLW CM20 .... **12** C3
Harwich County Primary School
  HAR CO12 .... **7** F3
Harwich County Primary School
  HAR CO12 .... **7** F3
Harwich & District Hospital
  HAR CO12 .... **6** B5
Harwich Golf Club
  HAR CO12 .... **6** A4
Harwich Industrial Estate
  HAR CO12 .... **6** A3
Harwich & Parkeston
  Football Club
  HAR CO12 .... **7** D5
The Harwich School
  HAR CO12 .... **6** B6
Harwich Sports Centre
  HAR CO12 .... **6** B6
Harwich Town Sailing Club
  HAR CO12 .... **7** F2
Haselmere Industrial Estate
  BSF CM23 .... **232** A1
Haslemere Business Centre
  EN EN1 .... **374** B8
Haslemere Industrial Estate
  HLWW/ROY CM19 .... **12** A4
Hassenbrook School
  SLH/COR SS17 .... **474** A3
Hassengate Medical Centre
  SLH/COR SS17 .... **473** J2
Hatfield Heath CP School
  RBSF CM22 .... **265** G2
Hatfield Peverel County
  Infant School
  RCHLM CM3 .... **308** B2
Haven Health Surgery
  FX IP11 .... **5** D3
Haverhill Golf Club Ltd
  HVHL CB9 .... **28** A7
Haverhill Rovers Football Club
  HVHL CB9 .... **27** G7
Haverhill Sports Centre
  HVHL CB9 .... **27** H6
Havering College of Further
  & Higher Education
  EMPK RM11 .... **431** F6
Havering College of Further
  & Higher Education
  EMPK RM11 .... **450** C1
Havering College of Further
  & Higher Education
  HARH RM3 .... **409** G7
Havering Court Nursing Home
  ROM RM1 .... **407** K8
Havering Cricket Club
  ABR/ST RM4 .... **381** F7
Havering Hospitals N H S Trust
  HARH RM3 .... **431** F3
Havering Sixth Form College
  EMPK RM11 .... **451** G2
Havers Infant School
  BSF CM23 .... **198** D8
Hawkesbury Road
  Doctors Surgery
  CVI SS8 .... **477** J2
Hawkswood School & Centre
  CHING E4 .... **402** D1
Hawthorn Surgery
  COLN CO4 .... **9** F4
The Hayward School
  CHLM/WR CM1 .... **14** B1
Hazelmere Junior School
  COLN CO4 .... **188** B5
The Health Centre
  HARH RM3 .... **409** F8

Health Service Clinic
  COLS CO2 .... **219** H4
Heathcote School
  CHING E4 .... **403** F5
The Heathcote School
  RCHLM CM3 .... **335** J6
Heath CP School
  KESG IP5 .... **39** F6
Heathlands Primary School
  RCOLW CO6 .... **153** K8
Heath School
  COLW CO3 .... **185** J8
Heathside Special School
  IPNE IP4 .... **38** A7
Heavitrees Surgery
  CHLM/GWD CM2 .... **14** B5
Heddington Castle
  HSTD CO9 .... **110** E1
Hedgerows Business Park
  CHLM/WR CM1 .... **305** J7
Hedingham County
  Secondary School
  HSTD CO9 .... **110** C2
Hedley Walter High School
  BRWN CM15 .... **411** F3
Helena Romanes School
  GTDUN CM6 .... **204** B3
Helsinki Health Centre
  IPSE IP3 .... **64** B2
Henham & Ugley CP School
  RBSF CM22 .... **137** G8
The Hereward County School
  LOU IG10 .... **378** B5
Herington House
  Preparatory School
  BRWN CM15 .... **411** K2
Herons Gate Trading Estate
  BSDN SS14 .... **438** D3
Herringham County
  Infant School
  CDH/CHF RM16 .... **485** G3
Hertfordshire & Essex General
  Hospital
  BSF CM23 .... **199** H7
Hertfordshire & Essex
  High School
  BSF CM23 .... **199** G6
Heybridge CP School
  MAL CM9 .... **310** E8
Heybridge House
  Industrial Estate
  MAL CM9 .... **338** D1
Heybridge Swifts Football Club
  MAL CM9 .... **311** F7
Heydon Grange Golf Club
  ROY SG8 .... **40** A4
High Beech C of E Primary
  School
  LOU IG10 .... **376** C5
Highfields County Primary
  School
  MGTR CO11 .... **159** H1
Highlands Surgery
  LOS SS9 .... **462** C3
High Ongar CP School
  CHONG CM5 .... **354** E1
High Street Surgery
  & Medical Centre
  EPP CM16 .... **350** E4
Highwood Hospital
  BRWN CM15 .... **410** E4
Highwoods County
  Primary School
  COLN CO4 .... **187** J1
Highwoods Surgery
  COLN CO4 .... **187** J1
Hilldene Junior School
  HARH RM3 .... **430** D1
Hillgrove Business Park
  WAB EN9 .... **319** J4
Hillmead JMI School
  BSF CM23 .... **199** H4
Hillside Primary School
  CHTY IP2 .... **3** D6
Hillside Special School
  SUD CO10 .... **58** C4
Hilltop Junior & Infant School
  WICKE SS11 .... **417** K5
Hilton Nurse Surgery
  HSTD CO9 .... **110** D5
Hinguar Primary School
  SBN/FI SS3 .... **466** E6
Hintlesham & Chattisham
  VC Primary School
  RIPW IP8 .... **60** A2

Hm Customs and Excise
  IPNE IP4 .... **3** D4
Hoblongs Industrial Estate
  GTDUN CM6 .... **204** D7
Hockerill Anglo European
  GM School
  BSF CM23 .... **199** G6
Hockerill Sports Club
  BSF CM23 .... **199** G8
Hockley Primary School
  HOC/HUL SS5 .... **420** D7
Hogarth Primary School
  BRWN CM15 .... **411** J6
Holbrook CP School
  RIPS/CAP IP9 .... **90** A7
Holbrook High School
  RIPS/CAP IP9 .... **90** A7
Holdbrook Junior Middle
  & Infant School
  BAR EN8 .... **347** F8
Holland Haven Primary School
  COS CO15 .... **260** C7
Holland Park Primary School
  COS CO15 .... **11** E2
Holly House Private Hospital
  BKHH IG9 .... **403** J5
The Holly Trees County
  Infant School
  BRW CM14 .... **410** E7
Hollytrees Junior School
  BRW CM14 .... **410** E7
Hollywood Bowl
  BSDN SS14 .... **17** F1
Holmwood House School
  COLW CO3 .... **185** J5
Holt Farm Infant School
  RCFD SS4 .... **444** A2
Holy Cross RC Primary School
  HLWS CM18 .... **294** E7
Holy Cross RC School
  SOCK/AV RM15 .... **469** K7
Holy Family RC Primary School
  WIT CM8 .... **277** F5
Holy Family School
  SBF/HAD SS7 .... **460** C1
Holy Trinity C of E
  Primary School
  BAR EN8 .... **346** D6
Holy Trinity C of E
  Primary School
  HSTD CO9 .... **147** J3
Holy Trinity C of E School
  GVE CA12 .... **489** H5
Holywells High School
  IPSE IP3 .... **64** A4
Home Farm CP School
  COLW CO3 .... **185** K7
Homestead School
  COLN CO4 .... **156** B1
The Honeywood School
  RCOLW CO6 .... **213** H2
Honilands Junior
  & Infant School
  EN EN1 .... **374** B2
Hornchurch Clinic
  EMPK RM11 .... **451** F2
Hornchurch Sports Centre
  HCH RM12 .... **450** D3
Horndon Industrial Park
  RBRW/HUT CM13 .... **434** B8
Horndon-on-the-Hill C
  of E Primary School
  SLH/COR SS17 .... **473** F1
Howard Business Park
  WAB EN9 .... **347** K8
Howbridge Infants School
  WIT CM8 .... **277** F5
Howbridge Juniors School
  WIT CM8 .... **277** F5
Howe Green House School
  RBSF CM22 .... **232** D3
Hullbridge Clinic
  HOC/HUL SS5 .... **419** J3
Hullbridge Parochial
  Church Council
  HOC/HUL SS5 .... **419** J3
Hullbridge Sports Club
  HOC/HUL SS5 .... **419** K4
Hurst Drive JMI School
  BAR EN8 .... **346** D8
Hutton All Saints C of E
  Primary School
  RBRW/HUT CM13 .... **412** C2
Hutton Clinic
  RBRW/HUT CM13 .... **412** C2

Hyland House & Park
CHLM/WR CM1 .... 331 J8
Hylands School
CHLM/WR CM1 .... 331 K4
Ilford Trading Estate
BSDN SS14 .... 438 B3
Imperial Retail Park
GVW DA11 .... 489 F4
Industrial Centre
IPSE IP3 .... 3 E5
Industrial Estate
EPP CM16 .... 323 G7
Industrial Estate
RCHLM CM3 .... 363 F7
Industrial Estate
RCHLM CM3 .... 369 F5
Industrial Park
BAR EN8 .... 347 G8
Ingatestone County
Infant School
ING CM4 .... 386 A1
Ingatestone & Fryerning
C of E Primary School
ING CM4 .... 386 A1
Ingrave Johnstone
C of E School
RBRW/HUT CM13 .... 434 B1
Ingrebourne CP School
HARH RM3 .... 408 D7
International Business Centre
CVI SS8 .... 477 H2
International Business Park
CVI SS8 .... 477 G2
Ipswich Bc Crown Court
IP IP1 .... 2 C3
Ipswich Civic College
IP IP1 .... 3 D2
Ipswich Golf Club
IPSE IP3 .... 64 D3
Ipswich High School for Girls
RIPS/CAP IP9 .... 91 F3
Ipswich Hospital N H S Trust
IPNE IP4 .... 38 A7
Ipswich Museums & Art Gallery
IP IP1 .... 2 C3
Ipswich Regent Theatre
IPNE IP4 .... 3 E3
Ipswich Rugby Union
Football Club
IPNE IP4 .... 37 K3
Ipswich School
IP IP1 .... 2 C1
Ipswich School
IP IP1 .... 3 D2
Ipswich Sports Club
IP IP1 .... 36 E4
Ipswich Town Football Club
IP IP1 .... 2 C4
Ipswich Transport Museum
IPSE IP3 .... 64 A3
Island Golf
CVI SS8 .... 460 E7
Island Surgery
CVI SS8 .... 478 C3
Ivry Street Medical Practice
IP IP1 .... 2 C2
Ivy Chimneys Primary School
EPP CM16 .... 350 D6
Jacques Hall School
MGTR CO11 .... 161 H2
Janet Duke County
Infant School
LAIN SS15 .... 16 B4
Jerounds Junior
& Infant School
HLWW/ROY CM19 .... 12 B6
The John Bramston School
WIT CM8 .... 277 F4
John Bunyan Junior
& Infant School
BRTR CM7 .... 209 H1
John Cotgrove Gallery
LOS SS9 .... 463 F5
John Ray CP School
BRTR CM7 .... 209 J5
John Russell Gallery
IPSE IP3 .... 3 E4
The Jones Family Practice
HOC/HUL SS5 .... 420 E8
Jotmans Hall Primary School
SBF/HAD SS7 .... 460 A1
Joyce Green Hospital
DART DA1 .... 481 G8
Jubilee Sports Ground
CHING E4 .... 402 E7

Katherine Semar Junior School
SAFWS CB11 .... 71 F7
Katherines Primary School
HLWW/ROY CM19 .... 293 H7
Kedington Primary School
HVHL CB9 .... 28 C3
Kelrose Swimming Pool Centre
RBRW/HUT CM13 .... 433 H7
Kelvedon Hatch CP School
BRWN CM15 .... 383 G2
Kelvedon St Marys C of E
Primary School
K/T/MI CO5 .... 246 E3
Kendall Primary School
COL CO1 .... 219 K1
Kenneth Mark Practice
SAFWN CB10 .... 70 E3
Kenningtons Primary School
SOCK/AV RM15 .... 468 E6
Kent County Council
GVW DA11 .... 488 D8
Kent County Council
GVW DA11 .... 489 F4
Kent County Council
GVW DA11 .... 489 F5
Kents Hill Junior School
SBF/HAD SS7 .... 460 C1
Kents Hill Road Surgery
SBF/HAD SS7 .... 440 C8
Kesgrave High School
KESG IP5 .... 39 H4
King Edmunds School
RCFD SS4 .... 422 B8
King Edward Grammer
Sports Ground
CHLM/WR CM1 .... 304 B1
King Edward Vi
Grammar School
CHLM/WR CM1 .... 14 B2
King Harold Comprehensive
School
WAB EN9 .... 348 A7
The King John School
SBF/HAD SS7 .... 461 G2
Kingsdale Industrial Estate
CHLM/WR CM1 .... 14 C2
Kingsdown School
LOS SS9 .... 443 H7
Kings Estate
HCH RM12 .... 450 B5
Kingsfleet Primary School
FX IP11 .... 131 K1
Kingsford County Junior
& Infant School
COLS CO2 .... 218 D2
Kingsmead School
EN EN1 .... 374 A8
Kingsmoor Junior
& Infant School
HLWW/ROY CM19 .... 322 A1
Kingsmoor Recreation Centre
HLWW/ROY CM19 .... 321 K1
Kings Road Junior School
CHLM/WR CM1 .... 14 A4
Kingston CP School
SBF/HAD SS7 .... 440 D7
Kingsway Hall Art and Theatre
HAR CO12 .... 7 E4
Kingswode Hoe Special School
COLW CO3 .... 186 D6
Kingswood County Junior
& Infant School
VGE SS16 .... 17 F5
Kingswood Medical Centre
VGE SS16 .... 17 F6
Kings Wood School
HARH RM3 .... 409 H7
Kingswood Surgery
VGE SS16 .... 17 F5
Kirby Le Soken Primary School
FOS CO13 .... 228 A6
Knightsmead School
SOCK/AV RM15 .... 469 J7
Lady of Lourdes RC School
LOS SS9 .... 463 H3
Laindon Health Centre
LAIN SS15 .... 436 C7
Laindon Park CP School
LAIN SS15 .... 16 C2
Laindon Road Clinic
BCAYW CM12 .... 414 B5
The Laindon School
LAIN SS15 .... 436 C5
Lakeside Shopping Centre
WTHK RM20 .... 482 E2

Lambourne CP School
ABR/ST RM4 .... 379 F8
Landseer Business Park
IPSE IP3 .... 3 E6
Langenhoe CP School
K/T/MI CO5 .... 252 C3
Langer Park Industrial Estate
FX IP11 .... 5 E5
Langham Primary School
COLN CO4 .... 156 C1
Langtons Junior
& Infant School
EMPK RM11 .... 451 F2
Lansdowne County
Primary School
TIL RM18 .... 484 E8
Larkswood Junior
& Infant School
CHING E4 .... 402 C7
Laser Clinic
EBAR EN7 .... 346 B4
Latchingdon C of E
Primary School
RCHLM CM3 .... 367 K7
Latton Bush Business Centre
HLWS CM18 .... 13 F6
Latton Bush Recreation Centre
HLWS CM18 .... 13 E6
The Laurels Surgery
RCHLM CM3 .... 306 D5
Laurence Industrial Estate
SOSN SS2 .... 443 J7
Lawford C of E Gm
Primary School
MGTR CO11 .... 159 F3
Lawn CP School
GVW DA11 .... 488 B4
Leas School
COS CO15 .... 10 A5
Lea Valley High School
PEND EN3 .... 374 C1
Lee Chapel CP School
VGE SS16 .... 17 D6
Leigh Beck Primary School
CVI SS8 .... 478 E2
Leigh Junior & Infant School
LOS SS9 .... 463 F5
Leigh Parish Council
LOS SS9 .... 463 F4
The Leventhorpe School
SBW CM21 .... 263 J1
Lexden CP School
COLW CO3 .... 185 K7
Lexden Springs School
COLW CO3 .... 185 K6
Lexden Squash Club
COLW CO3 .... 185 J6
Ley Park CP School
BROX EN10 .... 319 F4
Lime Grove Estate
HVHL CB9 .... 27 J8
The Limes Medical Centre
EPP CM16 .... 324 B8
The Limes Medical Centre
EPP CM16 .... 351 F3
Lincewood County Junior
& Infant School
VGE SS16 .... 456 C2
Lingwood Clinic
SLH/COR SS17 .... 473 J4
Links Business Centre
BSF CM23 .... 199 H6
Linton C of E (Aided)
Infant School
CBE/LIN CB1 .... 22 E3
Linton Health Centre
CBE/LIN CB1 .... 22 E3
Linton Heights Junior School
CBE/LIN CB1 .... 23 F3
Linton Village College
CBE/LIN CB1 .... 22 D3
Linton Zoological Gardens
CBE/LIN CB1 .... 22 D4
Lionmede Bowling Club
& Tennis Courts
CHLM/GWD CM2 .... 15 E2
Lister Medical Centre
HLWS CM18 .... 12 C6
Little Bealings CP School
FRAM/WMKT IP13 .... 39 H1
Littlegarth School
RCOLW CO6 .... 118 C6
Little Hallingbury
C of E Primary School
RBSF CM22 .... 232 C5

Little Margraves
  Industrial Estate
  UPMR RM14 .... 456 A4
Little Oakley C of E School
  HAR CO12 .... 164 A6
Little Thurrock County
  Primary School
  GRAYS RM17 .... 484 C2
Little Waltham C of E
  Primary School
  RCHLM CM3 .... 272 D6
Llewelyn Surgery
  WAB EN9 .... 347 J7
London Road Surgery
  RAYL SS6 .... 441 G2
London Road Surgery
  WICKW SS12 .... 417 F6
London Stansted Airport
  RBSF SS8 .... 201 H2
Longfield Medical Centre
  MAL CM9 .... 310 D8
Longfield Medical Centre
  MAL CM9 .... 338 C3
Long Gallery
  BSDN SS14 .... 17 F5
Longlands Junior Middle
  & Infant School
  BROX EN10 .... 318 E7
The Long Melford Practice
  SUD CO10 .... 34 E5
Long Melford Primary School
  SUD CO10 .... 34 E6
Long Ridings Junior
  & Infant School
  RBRW/HUT CM13 .... 412 A1
Long Surgery
  CVI SS8 .... 477 J2
Longshaw Primary School
  CHING E4 .... 402 E6
Lord Butler Leisure Centre
  SAFWS CB11 .... 71 G5
Loughton Cricket Club
  LOU IG10 .... 377 H7
Loughton Hall Clinic
  LOU IG10 .... 377 K7
Loughton Health Centre
  LOU IG10 .... 377 G7
Loughton Mental
  Health Centre
  LOU IG10 .... 404 B1
Loyola Preparatory School
  BKHH IG9 .... 403 K4
Lubbins Park Primary School
  CVI SS8 .... 478 C3
Lychgate Industrial Estate
  SBF/HAD SS7 .... 440 D4
Lynn Tait Gallery
  LOS SS9 .... 462 E5
Lyons Hall County
  Primary School
  BRTR CM7 .... 210 C1
Magistrates' Court
  IP IP1 .... 2 C4
Magnet Estate
  WTHK RM20 .... 483 F4
Maidenhall Sports Centre
  CHTY IP2 .... 62 E3
Maidstone County Infant School
  FX IP11 .... 5 E2
Malden All Saints C of E
  Primary School
  MAL CM9 .... 338 A3
Maldon Agricultural Museum
  MAL CM9 .... 312 C6
Maldon Court School
  MAL CM9 .... 338 B2
Maldon District Council
  MAL CM9 .... 338 C3
Maldon Museum
  MAL CM9 .... 338 D3
Maldon Primary School
  MAL CM9 .... 338 C3
Maldon Town Council
  MAL CM9 .... 338 C2
Mallard House Business Centre
  FRAM/WMKT IP13 .... 39 H2
The Maltings Industrial Estate
  BOC CM0 .... 398 E1
The Maltings Industrial Estate
  SBW CM21 .... 263 K3
Manford Industrial Estate
  ERITH DA8 .... 480 C5
Mangapps Farm
  Railway Museum
  BOC CM0 .... 398 A5

Manifest Theatre
  MGTR CO11 .... 159 J1
The Manningtree Gallery
  MGTR CO11 .... 159 J1
Manningtree High School
  MGTR CO11 .... 159 H2
Manningtree Sports Centre
  MGTR CO11 .... 159 H1
Manor County Junior
  & Infant School
  BSDN SS14 .... 437 K5
Manor Fields Jmi School
  BSF CM23 .... 198 C8
Manor Gallery
  GVE DA12 .... 489 G5
The Manor of Groves
  SBW CM21 .... 262 D3
The Manor Primary School
  ROM RM1 .... 430 A7
Manor Trading Estate
  SBF/HAD SS7 .... 440 C7
Manor Trading Estate
  SBF/HAD SS7 .... 440 C6
Manor Way Industrial Estate
  GRAYS RM17 .... 484 B6
Manuden CP School
  BSF CM23 .... 167 F3
Maple River Industrial Estate
  HLW CM20 .... 263 F7
Mardyke Surgery
  PUR RM19 .... 481 H3
Margaretting C of E
  Primary School
  ING CM4 .... 358 E5
Marillac Hospital
  RBRW/HUT CM13 .... 433 G1
Market Field School
  RCOLE CO7 .... 189 K8
Market (Open Air)
  IP IP1 .... 2 C3
Mark Hall Comprehensive
  School
  HLWE CM17 .... 295 G2
Mark Hall Cycle Museum
  HLW CM20 .... 295 F2
Markhams Chase Leisure Centre
  LAIN SS15 .... 16 B4
Marks Hall Arboretum
  RCOLW CO6 .... 181 F6
Martells Industrial Estate
  RCOLE CO7 .... 157 H7
Martells Industrial Estate
  RCOLE CO7 .... 157 G8
Matching Green C of E
  Primary School
  HLWE CM17 .... 297 K3
Matching Green Surgery
  BSDN SS14 .... 438 A5
Maunds Wood CP School
  HLWS CM18 .... 322 B1
May Avenue Industrial Estate
  GVW DA11 .... 488 E6
Mayfair Industrial Estate
  RCHLM CM3 .... 367 H7
Mayfield County Infant School
  BAR EN8 .... 346 E1
Mayflower Comprehensive
  School
  BCAYW CM12 .... 387 J8
Mayflower County
  Primary School
  HAR CO12 .... 6 C4
Mayflower Retail Park
  BSDN SS14 .... 438 A3
Mayland Branch Surgery
  RCHLM CM3 .... 368 D4
Maylandsea CP School
  RCHLM CM3 .... 368 D5
Maylandsea Medical Centre
  RCHLM CM3 .... 368 C4
Maylands Golf Club
  HARH RM3 .... 409 J8
Meadgate CP School
  CHLM/GWD CM2 .... 15 F5
Mead Industrial Park
  HLW CM20 .... 294 D1
Mead Infant School
  HARH RM3 .... 431 G1
The Mead School
  HLWS CM18 .... 13 E5
The Medical Centre
  K/T/MI CO5 .... 248 B8
Medical Surgery
  GTDUN CM6 .... 204 C5

Melbourne House Surgery
  CHLM/WR CM1 .... 304 A8
Merrylands Junior School
  LAIN SS15 .... 436 B7
Mersea Community
  & Sports Centre
  K/T/MI CO5 .... 284 E7
Mersea Island Gm School
  K/T/MI CO5 .... 284 E7
The Mersea Road Surgery
  COLS CO2 .... 219 H3
Messing CP School
  K/T/MI CO5 .... 248 A3
Mid Essex Adult
  Community College
  RBRW/HUT CM13 .... 412 A2
Mid Essex Magistrates Courts
  CHLM/WR CM1 .... 14 C3
Mildmay Industrial Estate
  BOC CM0 .... 398 B8
Milehams Industrial Estate
  PUR RM19 .... 481 H2
Millbrook Junior Middle
  & Infant School
  BAR EN8 .... 346 E3
Milldene School
  K/T/MI CO5 .... 248 B7
Millfields (GM) Primary School
  RCOLE CO7 .... 221 G4
Millhouse County Junior
  & Infant School
  LAIN SS15 .... 16 A2
Mill Road Surgery
  COLN CO4 .... 187 F1
Millwards CP School
  HLWW/ROY CM19 .... 321 K1
Milton Hall Junior School
  WOS/PRIT SS0 .... 18 B4
Milton Road Business Park
  GVE DA12 .... 489 H5
Mistley Norman C of E
  Primary School
  MGTR CO11 .... 160 B1
Mitchell Junior School
  HCH RM12 .... 450 C7
Monkwick Primary
  & Infant School
  COLS CO2 .... 219 G3
Monkwick Sports Centre
  COLS CO2 .... 219 G3
Monro Industrial Estate
  BAR EN8 .... 346 E8
Montessori School
  RBSF CM22 .... 201 J2
Montgomerie Infant School
  SBF/HAD SS7 .... 440 A6
Montgomery County
  Infant School
  COLS CO2 .... 218 D3
Moonhall Business Park
  HVHL CB9 .... 27 G8
Moreton Bay Industrial Estate
  GPK RM2 .... 430 E4
Moreton C of E Primary School
  CHONG CM5 .... 325 J2
Morland Primary School
  IPSE IP3 .... 63 J5
Mosque
  WOS/PRIT SS0 .... 18 B4
Moulsham High School
  CHLM/GWD CM2 .... 14 C6
Moulsham Infant School
  CHLM/GWD CM2 .... 14 C6
Moulsham Lodge Clinic
  CHLM/GWD CM2 .... 332 D7
The Mountfitchet School
  STSD CM24 .... 200 A1
Mountnessing C of E
  Primary School
  BRWN CM15 .... 385 H5
Mrs Lipmans School
  GTDUN CM6 .... 206 C8
M S F Whitehall College
  BSF CM23 .... 198 D4
Murrayfield Primary School
  IPSE IP3 .... 63 J2
Museum
  WAB EN9 .... 347 J8
The Museum
  SAFWN CB10 .... 70 E3
Myland CP School
  COLN CO4 .... 187 F1
Nabbotts County Junior School
  CHLM/WR CM1 .... 305 G6

Prince Avenue Primary School
WOS/PRIT SS0............... **444** A8

Prince of Wales Junior
& Infant School
PEND EN3 .... **375** F4

Princess Alexandra Hospital
HLW CM20 .... **12** B2

Priory Heath Infant School
IPSE IP3 .... **64** A4

Priory Park Industrial Estate
SOSN SS2 .... **464** D1

Priory School
WOS/PRIT SS0 .... **18** B1

Prittlewell C of E School
SOSN SS2 .... **18** C2

Prospect Business Park
LOU IG10 .... **378** B8

Prout Industrial Estate
CVI SS8 .... **479** F2

Public Baths
IPNE IP4........................... **3** E4

Purdeys Industrial Estate
RCFD SS4 .... **444** D5

Purdeys Industrial Estate
RCFD SS4 .... **444** D4

Purfleet Primary School
PUR RM19 .... **481** H3

Purford Green School
HLWS CM18 .... **294** E7

Purleigh CP School
RCHLM CM3 .... **365** K4

Quarry Hill County
Junior School
GRAYS RM17 .... **484** A4

The Quay Theatre
SUD CO10 .... **58** B7

Queen Elizabeth Museum
CHING E4 .... **403** F3

Queens Theatre
EMPK RM11 .... **450** E1

Queen Street Dental
Health Centre
COL CO1 .... **8** B4

Queensway Business Centre
PEND EN3 .... **374** C8

Quest End Industrial Estate
RAYL SS6 .... **419** H7

Quilters Junior & Infant School
BCAYW CM12...................... **414** B4

R A Butler Infant
Grammar School
SAFWS CB11 .... **71** F4

Radford Business Centre
BCAYW CM12...................... **414** A2

Radwinter C of E Aided
Primary School
SAFWN CB10 .... **73** J6

Raeburn Infant School
IPSE IP3 .... **63** H4

Rainsford High School
CHLM/WR CM1 .... **332** A1

Ramsden Hall School
BCAYE CM11 .... **415** G2

Ramsey County Primary School
HAR CO12 .... **163** J4

Ramsey School
HSTD CO9 .... **148** B3

Ranelagh Primary School
CHTY IP2 .... **2** A4

Ransomes Industrial
Estate Post Office
IPSE IP3 .... **64** C5

Ranworth Surgery
COS CO15......................... **10** B5

Raphael School
EMPK RM11 .... **430** B8

Ravensbourne School
HARH RM3........................ **430** E3

Ravenscroft School
RCOS CO16 .... **290** D1

Rawreth Industrial Estate
RAYL SS6 .... **419** G8

Rayleigh Lanes Indoor Market
RAYL SS6 .... **441** J3

Rayleigh Primary School
RAYL SS6 .... **441** H3

Rayne CP School
BRTR CM7 .... **208** B3

Raynham Road
Industrial Estate
BSF CM23 .... **199** G5

Redden Court School
HARH RM3........................ **431** G5

Regency Art Gallery
COLS CO2 .... **8** C5

Regent Leisure Centre
SLH/COR SS17 .... **473** K4

Regional Sports Centre
TIL RM18 .... **485** G8

Register Office
IPNE IP4........................... **3** E4

Rhodes Museum
& Commonwealth Centre
BSF CM23 .... **199** F8

Rice Bridge Industrial Estate
RCOS CO16 .... **226** D6

Richard Tudor Gallery
CHING E4 .... **403** F3

Richard Whittington
Jmi School
BSF CM23 .... **231** J1

Richmond Avenue
Junior School
SBN/FI SS3........................ **466** C6

Rickling C of E Primary School
SAFWS CB11 .... **135** K5

Rickstones School
WIT CM8 .... **245** F7

Ridgewell C of E (Aided)
Primary School
HSTD CO9 .... **52** E6

Rivenhall C of E Primary School
WIT CM8 .... **245** H5

Rivenhall Oaks Golf Club
WIT CM8 .... **277** H1

The Rivermead Gate
Medical Centre
CHLM/WR CM1 .... **14** C1

River Road Practice
BKHH IG9.......................... **404** B4

Riverside Business Park
STSD CM24 .... **167** J7

Riverside Clinic
IPSE IP3 .... **3** F6

Riverside Health Centre
MGTR CO11 .... **159** H1

Riverside Ice & Leisure Centre
CHLM/WR CM1 .... **15** D3

Riverside Industrial Estate
MAL CM9 .... **338** B1

Riverside Industrial Estate
RCFD SS4 .... **444** C4

Riverside Industrial Park
CHTY IP2 .... **3** E6

Riverside Junior School
HOC/HUL SS5 .... **419** K2

Riverside Retail Park
CHLM/WR CM1 .... **15** D2

Roach Vale Primary School
COLN CO4 .... **188** B4

Robert Drake Primary School
SBF/HAD SS7 .... **440** C6

The Robert Frew
Medical Centre
WICKW SS12 .... **417** J8

Rochford Adult
Community College
RCFD SS4 .... **444** D3

Rochford District Council
RCFD SS4 .... **444** C3

Rochford Parish Council
RCFD SS4 .... **444** B3

Rochford Primary School
RCFD SS4 .... **444** B3

Rochford Swimming
Pool Services
RCFD SS4 .... **444** D3

Rodings Central Primary School
GTDUN CM6....................... **268** A5

Roding Valley High School
LOU IG10 .... **377** K8

Roding Valley High School
LOU IG10 .... **404** B1

Rolph C of E Primary School
RCOS CO16 .... **226** C4

Romford Clinic
ROM RM1.......................... **430** A6

Romford County Court
ROM RM1.......................... **430** A6

Rosedale Clinic
EBAR EN7 .... **346** A1

Rose Hill Primary School
IPSE IP3 .... **63** J1

Rose Villa Surgery
PIT SS13 .... **438** E8

Rosewood Medical Centre
HCH RM12 .... **450** C6

Rosherville C of E School
GVW DA11 .... **488** D4

Rosshill Industrial Park
SOSN SS2 .... **464** E1

Rowhedge Surgery
K/T/MI CO5 .... **220** C5

Roxwell C of E Primary School
CHLM/WR CM1 .... **302** A7

Royal Burnham Yacht Club
BOC CM0 .... **425** H1

Royal Corinthian Yacht Club
BOC CM0 .... **425** H2

Royal Hospital School
RIPS/CAP IP9 .... **126** A2

Royal Liberty School
GPK RM2 .... **430** D5

Royal London Sports Centre
COLN CO4 .... **155** J7

Royal Mail Sorting Office
IP IP1 .... **2** C5

Royal Navy
CHLM/WR CM1 .... **14** C2

The Royals Shopping Centre
SOS SS1 .... **19** D5

Roydonbury Industrial Estate
HLWW/ROY CM19.............. **293** H5

Roydon CP School
HLWW/ROY CM19.............. **292** D5

Roydon Leisure Park
HLWW/ROY CM19.............. **292** C4

Rugby Club
BSF CM23 .... **198** C4

Runwell CP School
WICKE SS11 .... **417** G3

Runwell Parish Council
WICKE SS11 .... **417** H3

Rush Green Sports Centre
RCOS CO16 .... **290** D2

Rushmere Golf Club
IPNE IP4........................... **38** B7

Rushmere Hall CP School
IPNE IP4........................... **37** K4

Rushmere Sports Club
KESG IP5 .... **38** C4

Russet House School
EN EN1 .... **374** B5

Ryedene County
Primary School
VGE SS16 .... **458** C2

The Sacred Heart
of Mary RC School
UPMR RM14 .... **451** J3

Sacred Heart RC School
SOS SS1 .... **19** F4

Saffron Business Centre
SAFWN CB10 .... **71** H3

Saffron Walden County
High School
SAFWS CB11 .... **70** D5

Saffron Walden Golf Club
SAFWN CB10 .... **70** D3

Saffron Walden Hospital
SAFWS CB11 .... **71** H3

Saffron Walden Town
Football Club
SAFWN CB10 .... **70** E3

Sailing Club
RCOLE CO7 .... **255** J8

St Albans RC Church
& Presbytery
HCH RM12 .... **450** B6

St Albans RC High School
IPNE IP4........................... **38** B6

St Albans RC Primary School
HLW CM20 .... **13** F1

St Albans RC School
RAIN RM13........................ **450** C8

St Andrews Church
of England Primary School
RCOS CO16 .... **225** F5

St Andrews C of E (GM)
Primary School
EPP CM16 .... **324** C6

St Andrews C of E
Primary School
RCOLW CO6 .... **215** H2

St Andrews County
Junior School
COLN CO4 .... **188** B6

St Andrews Junior School
RCHLM CM3 .... **308** B2

St Andrews School
SUD CO10 .... **83** G2

St Anne Line Junior School
LAIN SS15......................... **17** D4

St Anne Line RC Infant School
LAIN SS15......................... **17** D4

St Annes CP School
COLN CO4 .... 9 E2
St Annes Preparatory School
CHLM/GWD CM2 .... 14 B4
St Antonys RC Primary School
WFD IG8 .... 403 H7
St Benedicts College
COLW CO3 .... 186 C7
St Bernards High School
WOS/PRIT SS0 .... 18 B4
St Botolphs C of E
Primary School
GVW DA11 .... 488 C5
St Cedds Primary School
BOC CM0 .... 344 D3
St Chads School
TIL RM18 .... 485 F7
St Christopher School
LOS SS9 .... 463 G1
St Clares Roman
Catholic School
RCOS CO16 .... 290 D1
St Clements Hospital
IPSE IP3 .... 63 K1
St Clements Hospital Lodge
IPSE IP3 .... 38 A8
St Clements Mixed
Junior School
BAR EN8 .... 346 E1
St Cleres School
SLH/COR SS17 .... 473 J5
St Cross RC Primary School
HOD EN11 .... 319 G1
St Felix RC Primary School
HVHL CB9 .... 26 D6
St Francis RC Primary School
BRTR CM7 .... 209 J1
St Francis RC Primary School
MAL CM9 .... 338 B2
St George's C of E
Primary School
RCOLE CO7 .... 190 D4
St Georges C of E School
GVW DA11 .... 489 F7
St Georges Hospital
HCH RM12 .... 451 F5
St Georges Infant School
COLS CO2 .... 8 C6
St Georges Primary School
COLS CO2 .... 8 C6
St Georges RC School
SBN/FI SS3 .... 466 D5
St Giles C of E Primary School
HSTD CO9 .... 111 J3
St Gregory V CP School
SUD CO10 .... 58 A6
St Helena School
COLW CO3 .... 186 E5
St Helens Junior School
BRWN CM15 .... 411 G3
St Helens Primary School
IPNE IP4 .... 3 F3
St Helens RC Infant School
BRW CM14 .... 411 G5
St Hildas School
WOS/PRIT SS0 .... 463 K4
St Ignatius College
EN EN1 .... 374 A3
St James Church School
HLWS CM18 .... 322 B1
St James C of E Primary School
PEND EN3 .... 374 C6
St James School
COL CO1 .... 9 D4
St James Surgery
COS CO15 .... 10 A5
St John Fisher RC Junior School
LOU IG10 .... 378 A6
St John Payne RC
Comprehensive School
CHLM/WR CM1 .... 304 C7
St John Payne RC School
CHLM/WR CM1 .... 304 B7
St Johns C of E
Controlled Primary School
COLN CO4 .... 188 A1
St Johns C of E Primary School
BKHH IG9 .... 403 J4
St Johns C of E Primary School
IPNE IP4 .... 37 J6
St Johns C of E Primary School
RCHLM CM3 .... 335 K6
St Johns C of E School
EPP CM16 .... 350 C4

St Johns Green County
Primary School
COLS CO2 .... 8 B5
St John's Hospital
CHLM/GWD CM2 .... 332 B7
St Johns Industrial Estate
RBSF CM22 .... 202 B6
St Johns RC Comprehensive
School
GVE DA12 .... 489 J6
St Johns RC Primary School
GVE DA12 .... 489 J6
St Johns School
BCAYW CM12 .... 414 C2
St Johns Special School
WFD IG8 .... 404 D8
St John the Baptist
Primary School
HSTD CO9 .... 113 J5
St Josephs College
CHTY IP2 .... 2 B6
St Josephs Preparatory School
GVE DA12 .... 489 H7
St Josephs RC Jmi School
BAR EN8 .... 346 E7
St Josephs RC Junior Middle
& Infant School
BSF CM23 .... 198 C7
St Josephs RC Primary School
HAR CO12 .... 6 C6
St Josephs RC Primary School
SLH/COR SS17 .... 473 K3
St Josephs RC School
CVI SS8 .... 478 B1
St Josephs RC School
GVW DA11 .... 488 C5
St Josephs RC Va Primary School
SUD CO10 .... 58 A5
St Josephs School
UPMR RM14 .... 451 J3
St Joseph the Worker
RC Primary School
RBRW/HUT CM13 .... 412 B2
St Katherine School
CVI SS8 .... 461 F8
St Lawrence C of E
Primary School
K/T/MI CO5 .... 220 C5
St Lawrence C of E School
WAB EN9 .... 348 B7
St Leonards C of E Va
Junior School
BOC CM0 .... 398 D1
St Leonards Hospital
SUD CO10 .... 58 C6
St Lukes C of E Primary School
K/T/MI CO5 .... 248 B8
St Lukes RC Primary School
HLWW/ROY CM19 .... 12 C5
St Lukes Special School
LOU IG10 .... 377 J8
St Margarets Hospital
EPP CM16 .... 351 F3
St Margarets Preparatory School
HSTD CO9 .... 146 C5
St Margarets Primary School
HSTD CO9 .... 79 F6
St Margarets School
PIT SS13 .... 439 H8
St Marks C of E
Comprehensive School
HLWS CM18 .... 13 E4
St Marks RC Primary School
CHTY IP2 .... 2 A6
St Martins School
RBRW/HUT CM13 .... 412 B4
St Mary's Business Centre
COLW CO3 .... 186 E6
St Marys Catholic School
BSF CM23 .... 198 D6
St Marys C of E Aided
Primary School
RCHLM CM3 .... 392 B1
St Marys C of E Primary School
BRWN CM15 .... 411 J2
St Marys C of E Primary School
RBSF CM22 .... 234 B7
St Marys C of E Primary School
RCOLE CO7 .... 157 G5
St Marys C of E Primary School
STSD CM24 .... 167 K6
St Marys Hare Park School
GPK RM2 .... 430 D5

St Marys High School
EBAR EN7 .... 346 B4
St Marys Primary School
IPNE IP4 .... 37 H7
St Marys Primary School
SAFWN CB10 .... 70 E3
St Marys RC Church & School
HCH RM12 .... 450 B2
St Marys RC County
Primary School
TIL RM18 .... 484 E8
St Marys RC Primary School
CHING E4 .... 402 E4
St Marys RC Primary School
PEND EN3 .... 374 D8
St Marys School
COLW CO3 .... 186 D6
St Marys School C of E
Primary School
BOC CM0 .... 398 C7
St Marys School for Girls
COLW CO3 .... 184 E8
St Matthews C of E School
IP IP1 .... 2 C3
St Michaels C of E Junior School
CHLM/GWD CM2 .... 360 E3
St Michaels Hospital
BRTR CM7 .... 209 H2
St Michaels Preparatory School
LOS SS9 .... 462 D4
St Michaels Primary School
BSF CM23 .... 198 D6
St Michaels School
BRTR CM7 .... 209 G3
St Nicholas C of E
Primary School
WICKE SS11 .... 418 D6
St Nicholas School
HLWE CM17 .... 295 K2
St Nicholas School
SOSN SS2 .... 465 H3
St Osyth C of E Primary School
RCOS CO16 .... 289 H1
St Pancras RC Primary School
IP IP1 .... 36 B3
St Pauls C of E Primary School
BRW CM14 .... 383 F7
St Pauls Roman Catholic
Jmi School
EBAR EN7 .... 346 B1
St Peters C of E Primary School
BRW CM14 .... 410 B5
St Peters C of E Primary School
HSTD CO9 .... 110 C5
St Peters C of E Primary School
RCOLW CO6 .... 213 H3
St Peters C of E School
CHLM/GWD CM2 .... 389 H1
St Peters High School
BOC CM0 .... 398 B7
St Peters Hospital
MAL CM9 .... 338 B3
St Peters RC Primary School
BCAYE CM11 .... 415 F7
St Philomenas Convent
Day School
FOS CO13 .... 228 E8
St Pius RC Primary School
CHLM/WR CM1 .... 304 B7
St Teresa RC School
RCFD SS4 .... 444 A2
St Theresas RC Primary School
COLW CO3 .... 185 K8
St Thomas Moore RC
Primary School
SAFWS CB11 .... 71 F5
St Thomas More High
School for Boys
WOS/PRIT SS0 .... 463 H2
St Thomas More RC School
COL CO1 .... 8 C4
St Thomas of Canterbury
Junior & Infant School
BRWN CM15 .... 411 G3
St Thomas RC Primary School
GRAYS RM17 .... 484 A3
St Ursulas Junior School
HARH RM3 .... 430 C1
Salvation Army
IPNE IP4 .... 3 E4
Samuel Ward Upper School
HVHL CB9 .... 27 H4
Sanatorium Felixstowe College
FX IP11 .... 131 K3

The Sanders Draper
Secondary School
HCH RM12 .... **450** D5
Sandon School
CHLM/GWD CM2 ...... **333** K7
Saracen House Business Centre
IPNE IP4 .... **3** E3
Saracens House Business Centre
IP IP1 .... **3** D3
Sarbir Industrial Park
HLW CM20 .... **263** G8
Sawbridge Health Clinic
SBW CM21 .... **263** J3
Schoolhouse
ABR/ST RM4 .... **408** E5
School House Aveley School
SOCK/AV RM15 .... **469** G8
Schooling Licensed
Conveyancers
GRAYS RM17 .... **484** A4
School Street Surgery
SAFWN CB10 .... **43** J3
Scimitar Park Industrial Estate
PIT SS13 .... **439** G3
Scott Park Surgery
LOS SS9 .... **443** G6
Scotts Primary School
HCH RM12 .... **450** D6
Seedbed Business Centre
SBN/FI SS3 .... **466** E6
Severall Hospital
COLN CO4 .... **155** F8
Severalls Park Industrial Estate
COLN CO4 .... **156** A7
Sharon Crickitt Complementary
Health Centre
RCOLE CO7 .... **220** E5
Shaw County Junior
& Infant School
SOCK/AV RM15 .... **469** K6
Shears Green CP School
GVW DA11 .... **488** E8
Shears Green Infant School
GVW DA11 .... **488** E8
Sheepen Road Retail Park
COLW CO3 .... **186** E7
Sheering C of E Primary School
RBSF CM22 .... **264** D4
Shelley County Primary School
CHONG CM5 .... **326** A8
Shenfield Cricket Club
BRWN CM15 .... **411** J2
Shenfield High School
BRWN CM15 .... **411** K1
Shenfield Sports Centre
BRWN CM15 .... **411** K1
Shenval Industrial Estate
HLW CM20 .... **294** E1
Shoeburyness High School
SBN/FI SS3 .... **466** C6
Shotley Primary School
RIPS/CAP IP9 .... **128** E2
Shotley Sailing Club
RIPS/CAP IP9 .... **129** G5
Shrub End Clinic
COLS CO2 .... **218** C2
Shrub End Surgery
COLW CO3 .... **218** B1
Siam Surgery
SUD CO10 .... **58** B6
Sidegate Primary School
IPNE IP4 .... **37** J5
Sikh Temple
GVE DA12 .... **489** G6
Sikh Temple
IP IP1 .... **2** B3
Silver End County
Primary School
WIT CM8 .... **244** E2
The Silver Tree Craft Gallery
MGTR CO11 .... **159** J1
Sir Charles Lucas School
COLN CO4 .... **188** B5
Sir Charles Lucas School
COLN CO4 .... **188** C6
Skillion Business Centre
BSDN SS14 .... **17** E2
Slade Green Football Club
ERITH DA8 .... **480** C7
Slade Green Infant School
ERITH DA8 .... **480** B6
Smilers Industrial Estate
PIT SS13 .... **439** J5
Snap Theatre
BSF CM23 .... **199** F6

Social History Museum
COL CO1 .... **8** B4
Somers Heath School
SOCK/AV RM15 .... **469** J7
Sooriakumaran Surgery
SOSN SS2 .... **464** B1
Sopwith Crescent
WICKE SS11 .... **418** A8
South Benfleet Gm
Primary School
SBF/HAD SS7 .... **460** B3
Southbourne Grove Surgery
WOS/PRIT SS0 .... **463** J1
Southbury Primary
& Infant School
PEND EN3 .... **374** C8
Southbury Primary School
PEND EN3 .... **374** B8
South East Essex College
SOSN SS2 .... **18** C3
South East Essex
Sixth Form College
SBF/HAD SS7 .... **441** F8
Southend Adult
Community College
SOS SS1 .... **19** F4
Southend Borough Council
SOSN SS2 .... **18** C3
Southend Borough
Football Club
WOS/PRIT SS0 .... **443** J7
Southend County Court
SOS SS1 .... **19** D4
Southend High School for Boys
SOSN SS2 .... **18** B1
Southend Hospital N H S Trust
WOS/PRIT SS0 .... **463** K2
Southend Rugby Football Club
SOSN SS2 .... **444** C7
Southend United Football Club
SOS SS1 .... **18** B2
South Essex Clinical Trials Centre
LOS SS9 .... **462** C3
South Essex Health Authority
RAYL SS6 .... **441** H4
South Essex Health Authority
RBRW/HUT CM13 ..... **411** F8
Southfields Industrial Park
LAIN SS15 .... **436** A6
South Green County
Infant & Junior School
BCAYW CM12 .... **414** C6
South Green Surgery
BCAYE CM11 .... **414** D6
Southminster Infant School
BOC CM0 .... **398** D2
Southminster Medical Centre
BOC CM0 .... **398** D1
South Street Surgery
BSF CM23 .... **198** E7
South Suffolk Business Centre
SUD CO10 .... **58** D6
Southview Park Surgery
VGE SS16 .... **458** A2
Southview School
WIT CM8 .... **245** F7
South West Essex
Magistrates Court
BSDN SS14 .... **17** E4
South Woodham Ferrers
Leisure Centre
RCHLM CM3 .... **392** E6
Sovereign Business Centre
PEND EN3 .... **375** F7
Spa Pavillion Theatre
FX IP11 .... **131** J4
Spellbrook Jmi School
BSF CM23 .... **231** K6
The Spinney Junior School
HLW CM20 .... **294** E4
Springfield County
Primary School
IP IP1 .... **36** A5
Springfield Cricket Club
CHLM/GWD CM2 ...... **15** F1
Springfield Industrial Estate
BOC CM0 .... **397** K8
Springfield Junior School
IP IP1 .... **2** A1
Springfield Medical Centre
CHLM/WR CM1 .... **305** F7
Springfield Surgery
CHONG CM5 .... **354** E4
Spring Meadow Primary School
HAR CO12 .... **6** A5

Sprites Junior & Infant School
CHTY IP2 .... **61** J3
Squirrels Heath Junior School
GPK RM2 .... **430** C7
Squirrels Heath Junior School
ROM RM1 .... **430** B7
Stadium Trading Estate
SBF/HAD SS7 .... **441** H6
Stafford Industrial Estate
EMPK RM11 .... **430** E5
Stambridge Primary School
RCFD SS4 .... **445** G3
Stanford Industrial Estate
SLH/COR SS17 .... **473** J4
Stansted Clinic
STSD CM24 .... **167** K6
Stanway CP School
COLW CO3 .... **185** H7
Stanway Fiveways CP School
COLW CO3 .... **185** J8
The Stanway School
COLW CO3 .... **185** J8
Stanway Surgery
COLW CO3 .... **185** H7
Stanway Swimming Centre
COLW CO3 .... **184** E8
Stapleford Abbotts
County Primary School
ABR/ST RM4 .... **407** G1
Staples Road Junior
& Infant School
LOU IG10 .... **377** G7
Staple Tye Shopping Centre
HLWS CM18 .... **13** D6
Star Lane Industrial Estate
SBN/FI SS3 .... **466** E2
Station Yard Industrial Park
GTDUN CM6 .... **204** D6
Steeple Bumpstead CP School
HVHL CB9 .... **50** C7
Stewards Comprehensive
School
HLWS CM18 .... **322** A1
Stifford Clays County
Junior School
CDH/CHF RM16 .... **471** F8
Stifford Clays Health Centre
CDH/CHF RM16 .... **471** F8
Stifford County
Primary School
GRAYS RM17 .... **483** H4
Stock C of E Primary
ING CM4 .... **387** K2
Stock Industrial Park
SOSN SS2 .... **464** D1
Stockwell Lodge
Medical Centre
EBAR EN7 .... **346** A2
Stoke College
SUD CO10 .... **53** F2
Stoke High School
CHTY IP2 .... **62** E3
Stonehall Surgery
SUD CO10 .... **31** F6
Stortford Hall Industrial Park
BSF CM23 .... **199** G6
Stort Valley Industrial Estate
BSF CM23 .... **199** G3
Stour Sailing Club
MGTR CO11 .... **159** J1
Strand Gallery
SOSN SS2 .... **465** G4
The Street Industrial Estate
MAL CM9 .... **310** D8
Strumer End Industrial Estate
HVHL CB9 .... **27** H7
Stuarts Industrial Estate
CHLM/GWD CM2 ...... **15** E4
Stutton Primary School
RIPS/CAP IP9 .... **125** H3
Sudbury Bowl
SUD CO10 .... **58** D4
Sudbury Business Centre
SUD CO10 .... **58** B6
Sudbury Health Centre
SUD CO10 .... **58** C5
Sudbury Rugby Union
Football Club
SUD CO10 .... **84** E1
Sudbury Town Football Club
SUD CO10 .... **58** A7
Sudbury Tudor
Voluntary Controlled School
SUD CO10 .... **58** C4

Sudbury Uplands Middle School
SUD CO10 .... 58 C4
Sudbury Upper School
SUD CO10 .... 58 C4
Sue Ryder Foundation
SUD CO10 .... 32 D4
Suffolk County Council Offices
IPNE IP4 .... 3 F4
Suffolks Junior & Infant School
EN EN1 .... 374 B6
Summercroft Junior
& Infant School
BSF CM23 .... 199 H5
Sumners Community Recreation Centre
HLWW/ROY CM19 .... 321 J1
Sunnymede County Junior School
BCAYE CM11 .... 414 E4
Sutherland Lodge Surgery
CHLM/GWD CM2 .... 15 E5
Suttons JMI School
HCH RM12 .... 450 E5
Suttons Manor Clinic
ABR/ST RM4 .... 380 E4
Swaines Industrial Estate
RCFD SS4 .... 444 B2
Swan Mead Junior School
VGE SS16 .... 438 A8
The Sweyne Park School
RAYL SS6 .... 441 H1
Swimming Pool
SLH/COR SS17 .... 474 B1
Swimming Pool Centre
BCAYE CM11 .... 415 K1
Tabor High Upper School
BRTR CM7 .... 209 G1
Tabor Middle School
BRTR CM7 .... 209 H2
Takeley Business Centre
RBSF CM22 .... 201 K6
Takeley Gm Primary School
RBSF CM22 .... 201 K5
Tanys Dell Junior School
HLW CM20 .... 294 E2
Tattingstone C of E V CP School
RIPS/CAP IP9 .... 88 E6
Templars County Infant School
WIT CM8 .... 245 F8
Templars County Junior School
WIT CM8 .... 245 F8
Temple Sutton Primary
& Infant School
SOSN SS2 .... 19 F1
Tendring Adult
Community College
COS CO15 .... 10 B4
Tendring CP School
RCOS CO16 .... 193 F7
Tendring Sixth Form College
FOS CO13 .... 229 F6
Tendring Technology College
& Sixth Form College
RCOS CO16 .... 226 C3
Tennyson House Surgery
CHLM/WR CM1 .... 304 B7
Terling C of E Primary School
RCHLM CM3 .... 275 G2
Thameside Community
Health Care
VGE SS16 .... 438 A8
Thameside Community
Healthcare N H S Trust
BCAYW CM12 .... 414 C2
Thameside County
Infant School
GRAYS RM17 .... 484 B5
Thameside Theatre
GRAYS RM17 .... 483 K4
Thaxted Primary School
GTDUN CM6 .... 139 K3
Theydon Bois CP School
EPP CM16 .... 378 C2
Theydon Gallery
EPP CM16 .... 378 B3
Thomas Lord Audley School
COLS CO2 .... 219 G3
Thomas Rivers Medical Centre
HLW CM20 .... 263 G6
The Thomas Rivers
Medical Centre
SBW CM21 .... 263 G4
Thomas Tallis School
WAB EN9 .... 348 B7
The Thomas Willingale
Gm School
LOU IG10 .... 378 A7

Thomas Wolsey School
IP IP1 .... 36 A2
Thorley Hill Jmi School
BSF CM23 .... 231 K1
Thorn Grove Primary School
BSF CM23 .... 199 G7
Thorpe Bay School
SOS SS1 .... 465 J4
Thorpe Bay Surgery
SOS SS1 .... 465 K6
Thorpedene Gm Junior School
SBN/FI SS3 .... 466 B6
Thorpe Hall School
SBN/FI SS3 .... 465 K3
Three Rivers Golf Club
RCHLM CM3 .... 366 A8
Threshelfords Business Park
K/T/MI CO5 .... 247 G2
Thriftwood School
CHLM/GWD CM2 .... 360 C2
Thundersley Junior
& Infant School
SBF/HAD SS7 .... 441 F7
Thurleston High School
IP IP1 .... 36 C1
Thurrock Borough Council
GRAYS RM17 .... 484 A5
Thurrock Borough Council
SOCK/AV RM15 .... 469 J6
Thurrock Business Centre
WTHK RM20 .... 482 C5
Thurrock College
CDH/CHF RM16 .... 484 E3
Thurrock Council
PUR RM19 .... 481 G3
Thurrock Council
for Voluntary Services
GRAYS RM17 .... 484 A4
Thurrock Council Office
GRAYS RM17 .... 484 A4
Thurstable School
K/T/MI CO5 .... 248 B7
Tilbury Fort
TIL RM18 .... 489 H2
Tilbury Manor Infant School
TIL RM18 .... 485 G6
Tilbury Surgery
TIL RM18 .... 485 F8
The Tile Gallery
LOS SS9 .... 463 H4
Tile House Surgery
BRWN CM15 .... 411 G4
Tillingham Medical Centre
BOC CM0 .... 372 A2
Tillingham St Nicholas
C of E Primary School
BOC CM0 .... 371 K1
Tiptree Heath CP School
K/T/MI CO5 .... 279 K2
Tiptree Sports Centre
K/T/MI CO5 .... 248 B6
Titan Industrial Estate
GRAYS RM17 .... 483 K3
Tollesbury CP School
MAL CM9 .... 314 D4
Tollesbury Sailing Club
MAL CM9 .... 315 F3
Tolleshunt Darcy C of E
Primary School
MAL CM9 .... 313 H1
Tooley's & Smarts Almshouses
IPNE IP4 .... 3 E4
Toot Hill Golf Club
CHONG CM5 .... 353 F5
Torells County Secondary
School for Girls
CDH/CHF RM16 .... 484 E1
Tower Business Park
K/T/MI CO5 .... 247 K6
Tower Ramparts
Shopping Centre
IP IP1 .... 3 D3
Towers Infant School
EMPK RM11 .... 450 D1
Towers Junior School
EMPK RM11 .... 450 D1
Trading Estate
WTHK RM20 .... 482 D4
Trafalgar Trading Estate
PEND EN3 .... 375 F8
Treetops School
GRAYS RM17 .... 484 A3
Tricor Business Park
BAR EN8 .... 346 E8

Tricor Trading Estate
BAR EN8 .... 346 E8
Trimley St Martins
County Primary School
FX IP11 .... 94 C3
Trinity Catholic Lower
High School
WFD IG8 .... 403 H7
Trinity Catholic Upper
High School
WFD IG8 .... 403 H7
Trinity Road Primary School
CHLM/GWD CM2 .... 15 E2
Tudor Court CP School
CDH/CHF RM16 .... 483 J1
Tunnel Industrial Estate
WTHK RM20 .... 482 C3
Tunnel Industrial Estate
WTHK RM20 .... 482 C5
Turnford School
BAR EN8 .... 346 E2
Twyford Business Centre
BSF CM23 .... 199 F8
Twyford Business Centre
BSF CM23 .... 232 A1
The Tyrrells CP School
CHLM/WR CM1 .... 305 G8
U C I Cinema
BSDN SS14 .... 17 F1
U C I Cinema
WTHK RM20 .... 482 C3
Uniterian Meeting House
IP IP1 .... 3 D4
Unity Health Centre
SUD CO10 .... 58 B6
University College Suffolk
IPNE IP4 .... 3 F4
University College
Suffolk Annexe
IPNE IP4 .... 3 E3
University of Essex
COLN CO4 .... 188 C7
University of Essex
COLN CO4 .... 220 C1
University of London
ENC/FH EN2 .... 374 A2
University Yacht Club
RCOLE CO7 .... 255 K8
Upminster Infant School
UPMR RM14 .... 451 J4
Upminster Primary School
UPMR RM14 .... 451 K4
Upper Clapton Rugby
Football Club
EPP CM16 .... 323 F6
Upshire CP School
WAB EN9 .... 348 D6
Uttlesford District Council
GTDUN CM6 .... 204 C5
Van & Car Surgery
PEND EN3 .... 374 D8
Vineyard Gallery
COL CO1 .... 8 B5
Virgin Cinema
IP IP1 .... 2 C4
Virgin Cinemas
HLW CM20 .... 294 D1
Walnut Tree Hospital
SUD CO10 .... 58 A6
Waltham Abbey
Swimming Pool
WAB EN9 .... 375 K1
Waltham Holy Cross Council
WAB EN9 .... 347 H7
Waltham Holy Cross
Junior School
WAB EN9 .... 347 K7
Walton & Frinton Yacht Club
WOTN CO14 .... 229 H4
Walton Gm Primary School
WOTN CO14 .... 229 H4
Walton Surgery
FX IP11 .... 5 E1
Wansfell College
EPP CM16 .... 378 B1
Warden Lodge Surgery
BAR EN8 .... 346 D5
Wardmaster Infirmary
RIPS/CAP IP9 .... 126 A2
Warley County Junior School
BRW CM14 .... 411 F8
Warley Hill Business Park
RBRW/HUT CM13 .... 433 F1
Warley Hospital
BRW CM14 .... 410 E8

Page 13

F4
1 Nettesbullury Farm

Page 15

E3
1 Hill Crs
2 Morris Rd
3 Springfield Park Pde

E4
1 New Meadgate Ter

Page 16

A2
1 Arne Ct
2 Arne Ms
3 Bramley Gdns
4 Tavistock Rd
5 Vaughan Williams Rd
6 Victoria Crs
7 Walton Ct

Page 27

H6
1 Elmhurst Cl
2 Pentlow Hawke Cl

Page 36

E7
1 Black Horse La
2 Butter Market
3 Elm St
4 High St
5 Museum St
6 St George's St
7 Westgate St

E8
1 Curriers' La
2 Cutler St
3 Lower Brook St
4 St Peter's St
5 Silent St
6 Turret La

Page 39

H6
1 Banyard Cl
2 Browns Cv
3 Dickinson Ter
4 Godbold Cl
5 Shelbourne Cl
6 Smiths Pl
7 Stewart Young Gv
8 The Woolnoughs

Page 58

B6
1 Cheyne St
2 Church Wk
3 Edgworth Rd
4 Francis Rd
5 Grammar School Pl
6 Meadow La
7 Northcroft
8 Straw La

C6
1 Burroughs Piece Rd
2 Cavendish Wy
3 Chelsea Ct
4 Chelsea Rd

Page 129

K7
1 Angelgate Esp
2 Castlegate St
3 Golden Lion La
4 Kings Quay St
5 Market St
6 Outpart Eastward
7 St Austin's La

Page 130

E2
1 Brackley Cl
2 Bredfield Cl
3 Childers Fld
4 Feathers Fld
5 Generals Ms
6 Kiln Fld
7 Larkhill Wy
8 Mickfield Ms
9 Otley Ct
10 Rendlesham Rd
11 Sudbourne Rd
12 William Booth Wy

Page 187

F6
1 Balkerne Gdns
2 Church St
3 Church Wk
4 Crowhurst Rd
5 Rawstorn Rd
6 Short Cut Rd

F7
1 Alexandra Ter
2 Chapel St North
3 Wellington St

G3
1 Coeur De Lion
2 Peppercorn Cl

Page 13

G6
1 Culver St East
2 East Stockwell St
3 George St
4 Long Wyre St
5 Maidenburgh St
6 Museum St
7 St Helen's La
8 St Nicholas St
9 St Runwald St
10 Short Wyre St
11 Sir Isaac's Wk
12 Swan Pas
13 Vineyard Ga
14 William's Wk

C7
1 Arthur St
2 Osborne St
3 Portland Rd
4 St Botolph's St
5 St John's Av
6 Shrubland Rd
7 Stanwell St
8 Vineyard Ga
9 Vineyard St

G8
1 Roberts Rd

H5
1 Hereford Rd
2 Inverness Cl
3 Lichfield Cl
4 Norwich Cl
5 York Pl

J1
1 Grassmere
2 Princeton Ms
3 Tally Ho

J5
1 St Anne's Rd

K5
1 Arnstones Cl
2 Dinsdale Cl
3 Fairfield Gdns
4 Fairhead Rd South
5 Frank Clater Cl
6 St Edmund's Ct

Page 188

C6
1 Finham Cl
2 Imogen Cl
3 Jessica Cl
4 Learn Cl

Page 198

E6
1 Barrett La
2 Devolls La
3 Market St
4 Nails La
5 Old River La
6 Portland Rd
7 Sworders Yd

Page 209

H1
1 Wingate Cl

H5
1 Brimstone Ct
2 Clouded Yellow Cl

J2
1 Blyth's Meadow
2 Drury La
3 Great Sq
4 Market Pl
5 St Peter's Wk
6 Swan Side
7 Tofts Wk

J4
1 Darwin Cl
2 Edison Cl
3 Fleming Cl
4 Gatekeeper Cl
5 Jenner Cl

K4
1 Bramley Cl
2 Harrison Dr
3 The Lindens
4 Longacres
5 Nineacres
6 Russet Ct

K5
1 Austen Cl
2 Bennett Cl
3 Betjeman Cl
4 Bronte Cl
5 Buchan Cl
6 Conan Doyle Cl
7 Cowper Ms
8 Dickens Cl
9 Hardy Cl
10 Haskell Ms
11 Panton Ms
12 Penn Ms
13 Swift Cl

Page 210

A1
1 Cumberland Cl
2 Essex Rd
3 Norfolk Gdns
4 Northumberland Cl
5 Orion Wy
6 Vanguard Wy
7 Westminster Gdns
8 Windsor Gdns

Page 228

D6
1 Bloomfield Av
2 Brightside
3 Hogarth End
4 Larkway
5 The Larneys
6 Polley Cl
7 Poynter Pl
8 Romney Cl
9 Ruskin Cl

E6
1 Chaplins
2 Grasmere Gdns
3 Haslemere Gdns
4 Raeburn Cl
5 Shaw Cl
6 Sherbourne Cl
7 Snape Wy
8 Thornhill
9 Wimbourne Gdns

Page 229

H5
1 Agar Road Ap
2 Alfred Ter
3 Church Rd
4 Crescent Rd
5 Newgate St
6 New Pier St
7 North St
8 Orlando Ct
9 Paternoster Rw
10 St Botolph's Ter
11 Suffolk St
12 Vicarage La

Page 245

G8
1 Ash Fall
2 Cherrytree Ri
3 Larch Gv
4 Magnolia Cl
5 Maple Dr
6 Oak Fall
7 Palm Cl
8 Pine Gv
9 Redwood Cl
10 Sycamore Cl

Page 263

J3
1 Church Rd
2 Duckling La
3 Linwood
4 The Orchards
5 Rushfield
6 The Square

Page 276

E5
1 Brock Cl
2 Constantine Rd
3 Edmund Rd
4 Hadrians Cl
5 Nightingale La
6 Octavia Dr
7 Philip Rd
8 Shortridge Ct
9 Tiberius Gdns

Page 277

H3
1 Armiger Wy
2 Bevington Ms
3 Charlotte Wy
4 Kynaston Pl
5 Oliver Pl
6 Wakelin Wy

Page 294

D8
1 Sunny Cft
2 Tye Green Village

E2
1 The Chantry

Page 332

C2
1 Cedar Av West
2 Coval La
3 Well's St

C4
1 Belle Vue
2 Haig Ct
3 Redcliffe Rd
4 Stapleford Cl

E4
1 Golday Rd
2 Rochford Rd

Page 333

F5
1 New Meadgate Ter

H3
1 Cartwright Wk
2 Caswell Ms
3 Hurst Wy
4 Mitton V
5 Salter Pl
6 Thomas Cl
7 Willoughby Dr

Page 338

A5
1 Brompton Gdns
2 Crayford Cl
3 Hemmings Ct
4 Linford Ms
5 Viborg Gdns

C6
1 Memory Cl

D1
1 Coates Cl
2 Swan Cl

Page 346

A2
1 Betjeman Cl
2 St Anne's Cl
3 Wellers Gv

B5
1 Ermine Cl
2 Greenwood Cl
3 Hargreaves Cl
4 Lilac Cl

D2
1 Campine Cl
2 The Colonnade
3 Drakes Cl
4 Faverolle Gn
5 Hamburgh Ct
6 Southbrook Dr
7 The Spur
8 Symonds Ct

D7
1 Lambton Av
2 Leven Cl
3 Monarch's Wy
4 Park Rd
5 Ston-leigh Cl

E2
1 Bromleigh Cl
2 Cordell Cl
3 Fraser Rd
4 Goodwin Ct
5 Lensbury Cl

E4
1 Foster Cl
2 Guinevere Gdns
3 Roberts Cl
4 Roswell Cl

E5
1 Acton Cl
2 Garland Cl
3 Holme Cl
4 Russell's Dr

E8
1 Abbey Rd
2 Lodge Crs
3 Station Ap
4 Trust Rd

Page 348

C7
1 Bromefield Ct
2 Stanford Ct
3 Sudicamps Ct
4 Tillingham Ct
5 Webster Ct
6 Wormley Ct
7 Wormyngford Ct
8 Wrangley Ct

Page 374

C6
1 Archers Dr
2 Ashdown Ct
3 Ashley Rd
4 Burncroft Av
5 Carterhatch La
6 Edington Rd
7 Hertford Ct

C8
1 Glyn Rd
2 Hertford Road High St
3 Swansea Rd

D1
1 Abridge Cl
2 Dewgrass Gv
3 The Greenway
4 Hawksmead Cl
5 Kingsfield Wy

D5
1 Addis Cl
2 Dison Cl
3 Logan Cl

D6
1 Burncroft Av
2 Lindhill Cl
3 Shaftesbury Av

E3
1 Coldham Gv
2 Cornhill Dr
3 The Generals Wk
4 Johnby Cl
5 Newport Cl

E8
1 Fairfield Cl
2 Northampton Cl

Page 387

F8
1 Beresford Ct
2 Colville Ms
3 Dolphin Gdns
4 Edward Cl
5 Granville Cl
6 Lorrimore Ct
7 Oakley Dr
8 Queen's Gate Ms
9 Tavistock Dr
10 Wesley Gdns
11 Woburn Pl

G8
1 Berkeley Cl
2 Boleyn Ct
3 Brompton Cl
4 Dorchester Rd
5 Eccleston Gdns
6 Farriers Dr
7 Montpelier Cl
8 Pembroke Cl
9 Rutherford Cl

Page 392

D8
1 Drywoods
2 Penhurst Dr

E7
1 Reynolds Ga

Page 402

B5
1 Belle Staines Pleasaunce
2 Dove House Gdns

B8
1 Burley Cl
2 Garden Cl
3 The Lawns
4 Pewsey Cl

D6
1 Ashingdon Cl
2 Daphne Gdns
3 Navestock Cl
4 Oakley Cl
5 Stapleford Cl

E4
1 Cambridge Rd
2 Carbis Cl
3 Cranworth Crs
4 Glendower Rd
5 The Green Wk
6 Pentney Rd
7 Queens Wk
8 Richmond Rd
9 Shaftesbury Rd

E8
1 Belmont Cl
2 Greenwood Dr

Page 403

G4
1 Littleton Av

H8
1 Butterworth Gdns
2 Colwall Gdns
3 Elrington Rd
4 Gardenia Wy
5 High Elms
6 Johnston Rd
7 Twentyman Cl

K8
1 Ewanrigg Ter
2 Frankland Cl
3 Hillside Cl
4 Meadow
5 Parkway

Page 414

A1
1 Buckwyns Ct
2 Celandine Cl
3 Crescent Cl
4 Crescent Gdns
5 The Foxgloves
6 Hallam Cl
7 Pauline Gdns
8 Pavillion Pl
9 St Helens Wk
10 Upland Cl

C3
1 High Cloister
2 Hurlock Rd
3 Lower Cloister
4 Mayflower Rd
5 Pilgrims Cl
6 Saffron Wk
7 Weavers Cl
8 West Cloister

D3
1 Abbots Ride
2 The Chase
3 Copford Rd
4 David's Wk
5 Felsted Rd
6 Heather Bank
7 High Meadow
8 Jacksons Ms
9 Kelvedon Rd
10 Northfield Cl
11 Park Side
12 Shakespeare Av

Page 417

F5
1 Upper Market Rd

G5
1 Beccles Ct
2 Station Ap
3 Stilemans
4 Upper Market Rd

G7
1 Champion Cl
2 Donald Thorn Cl
3 St Omar Cl
4 Sudbrook Cl

H4
1 Whitelands Cl

H7
1 Bannister Gn
2 Beazley End
3 Erskine Pl
4 Horkesley Wy
5 Ingrave Cl
6 Mackenzie Cl
7 Pleshey Cl
8 Sewards End
9 Taveners Green Cl
10 Tollesbury Cl

H8
1 Balfour Cl
2 Buchanan Gdns
3 Caladonia La
4 Chatton Cl
5 Chisholm Ct
6 Drummond Pl
7 Grant Cl
8 Lamont Cl
9 Madaren Wy
10 Munro Ct
11 Nicholson Gv
12 Ogilvie Ct
13 Robertson Dr
14 Rose Cl

J8
1 Boyd Ct
2 Brodie Wk
3 Duncan Cl
4 Irvine Pl
5 Knox Ct
6 Silva Island Wy
7 Stewart Pl

Page 430

E3
1 Buttercup Cl
2 Copperfields Wy
3 Hatherleigh Wy
4 Widecombe Cl

G4
1 Chadwick Rd
2 Fleming Gdns
3 Messant Cl

Page 431

F2
1 Melksham Gn

F6
1 Banyards
2 Macdonald Wy
3 Peacock Cl
4 Russets

H6
1 Cornwall Cl
2 Hampshire Rd
3 Pembroke Cl
4 Suffolk Wy

Page 436

A8
1 Alnwick Cl
2 Amersham Av
3 Cambridge Cl
4 Flint Cl
5 Ipswich Ms
6 Lancaster Dr
7 Maple Tree La
8 Monmouth Ms
9 Oakham Cl
10 Osterley Dr
11 Oxford Cl
12 Reading Cl
13 Shrewsbury Cl
14 Worcester Cl

Page 437

F5
1 Buckingham Rd
2 Palace Gv

Page 438

C4
1 St Peter's Pavement

E7
1 Carisbrooke Cl
2 Pevensey Wy
3 Somerset Gdns

Page 441

F2
1 Bromley Av
2 Broomfield Av
3 Denham V
4 Goldhanger Cl
5 Gosfield Cl
6 Hanningfield Cl
7 Kelvedon Cl
8 Langham Dr
9 Latchingdon Cl
10 Navestock Cl
11 Newsum Gdns
12 Rettendon Cl
13 Sheering Cl
14 Wethersfield Cl

Page 450

A8
1 Theydon Gdns

B7
1 Adnams Wk
2 Beaumont Crs
3 Freeborne Gdns
4 Tempest Wy

C4
1 Landseer Cl
2 Napier Cl
3 Prescott Cl
4 Priory Ms
5 Shaw Cl

C4
1 Beech Cl
2 Hazel Cl
3 Maple Cl
4 Willow Cl

C6
1 Derwent Wy

C8
1 Dawson Dr
2 Esmond Cl
3 Heron Flight Av
4 Hesselyn Dr
5 Kestrel Cl
6 Leathart Cl
7 Mungo Park Rd
8 Pease Cl
9 Robinson Cl

D5
1 Canberra Cl
2 Chestnut Cl
3 Lawford Cl

D6
1 Carvers Wd
2 Foys Wk
3 Ganels Cl
4 Hammonds La
5 Hickstars La
6 Paddock Cl
7 Passingham Cl
8 Well Mead

G8
1 Gascoigne Wy
2 Hatfield Dr
3 Henham Cl
4 Holbrook Cl
5 Shalford Rd
6 Stansted Cl

E7
1 Anthony Cl
2 Copperfield
3 Homefield Cl
4 Lorraine Cl
5 Stockwell Cl

B7
1 Becketts
2 Brampstead
3 Braxteds
4 The Chignalls
5 Cumberland Dr
6 Easton End
7 Eisenhower Rd
8 Marden Ash
9 Roosevelt Rd
10 Sparkbridge
11 Truman Cl
12 The Willingales

B8
1 The Lindens
2 Macaulay Rd
3 Shelly Av
4 Silvermere

C7
1 Byron Ct
2 Ferndale Cl
3 Sylvan Ct

D5
1 Arne Ct
2 Arne Ms
3 Bramley Gdns
4 Tavistock Rd
5 Vaughan Williams Rd
6 Victoria Crs
7 Walton Ct

D6
1 Altar Pl
2 Chantry Dr
3 Copperfields
4 St Chads Cl
5 St Johns Cl
6 Tavistock Rd
7 Temple Cl
8 Walsingham Cl

D8
1 Little Oxcroft
2 Northumberland Av

E4
1 Box Cl
2 Doves Ms
3 Sweet Briar Dr
4 Wraysbury Dr

E6
1 Markhams Cha
2 Pickwick Cl

Notes